SELF-DETERMINATION THEORY

Also Available

Handbook of Mindfulness:
Theory, Research, and Practice

*Edited by Kirk Warren Brown, J. David Creswell,
and Richard M. Ryan*

Self-Determination Theory

Basic Psychological Needs in Motivation, Development, and Wellness

Richard M. Ryan
Edward L. Deci

THE GUILFORD PRESS
New York   London

Copyright © 2017 The Guilford Press
A Division of Guilford Publications, Inc.
370 Seventh Avenue, Suite 1200, New York, NY 10001
www.guilford.com

Printed in the United States of America

This book is printed on acid-free paper.

Last digit is print number: 9   8   7   6   5   4   3   2   1

Library of Congress Cataloging-in-Publication Data is available from
the publisher.

ISBN 978-1-4625-2876-9

About the Authors

Richard M. Ryan, PhD, is a clinical psychologist, Research Professor at the Institute for Positive Psychology and Education at Australian Catholic University, and Professor of Clinical and Social Sciences in Psychology at the University of Rochester. Dr. Ryan is a Fellow of the American Psychological Association, the Association for Psychological Science, the American Educational Research Association, and the Society for Personality and Social Psychology. He received distinguished career awards from the International Society for Self and Identity and the International Network on Personal Meaning, as well as a Shavelson Distinguished Researcher Award, presented by the International Global SELF Research Centre, among other honors. An honorary member of the German Psychological Society and the recipient of an honorary doctorate from the University of Thessaly in Greece, he is also a recipient of a James McKeen Cattell Fund Fellowship and a Leverhulme Fellowship. Dr. Ryan has also been a visiting professor at the National Institute of Education in Singapore, the University of Bath in England, and the Max Planck Institute in Berlin, Germany.

Edward L. Deci, PhD, is the Helen F. and Fred H. Gowen Professor in the Social Sciences at the University of Rochester, with secondary appointments at the University College of Southeast Norway and Australian Catholic University. Dr. Deci is a Fellow of the Association for Psychological Science, the American Psychological Association, and the Society for Personality and Social Psychology, among other associations. His numerous honors include a distinguished scholar award from the Society for Personality and Social Psychology, a lifetime achievement award from the International Society for Self and Identity, and a distinguished scientific contribution award from the Positive Psychology Network. He was named honorary president of the Canadian Psychological Association and is a recipient of a James McKeen Cattell Fund Fellowship.

Preface

When we began the project of developing self-determination theory (SDT), it was with a particular paradigmatic concern in mind. Both as researchers and clinicians, we felt there was a need for a Copernican turn in empirical approaches to human motivation and behavior change, finding the dominant approaches to these topics focused not on understanding how organisms naturally learn, develop, and self-organize actions, but on how they could be controlled to behave or change using external contingencies and cognitive manipulations. To us, this was a science pointing in the wrong direction. Our interest was not in how motivation can be controlled from without, but instead in how human motivation is functionally designed and experienced from within, as well as what forces facilitate, divert, or undermine that natural energy and direction.

The publication of this volume represents for us, if not the culmination of this effort, at least a further touchstone in providing a general paradigm for researchers and practitioners who are interested in active human functioning and wellness. Herein we hope to have provided a comprehensive statement of self-determination theorizing and the most up-to-date review of research since our initial volume together in 1985.

Having said that, from our personal viewpoint, this book remains unfinished. That is not because we didn't try. We have been writing and revising each year, synthesizing the experimental and field research, the intervention results, and new theoretical extensions emerging around the globe. But each year there has been an enormous amount of new material to consider, with ever more studies appearing and additional phenomena being addressed. Finally, we simply had to surrender to the idea that this book must be published, however incomplete. The SDT community of researchers has been too active, too diverse, and too generative, reducing any attempt to review the theory as a whole to merely a snapshot of where the research and theory are at this particular moment.

There are many people who can be held responsible for this incessant growth of research in SDT, which has continually outpaced our ability to summarize it. But most generally we lay the blame upon the large and still growing community of SDT scholars who share information, methods, and practices through the Center for Self-Determination

Theory (CSDT) website (*www.selfdeteminationtheory.org*) and at our triennial SDT International Conferences, held thus far in Rochester, New York (twice); Ottawa, Toronto, and Victoria, Canada; and Ghent, Belgium. This network of international scholars from more than 40 nations has been challenging, refining, and extending SDT's propositions in ways we had not imagined when we began this theoretical endeavor.

First, from early on in the formulation of SDT research, Canadian scholars have played an especially prominent role. Robert Vallerand, Luc Pelletier, and Richard Koestner enriched SDT through both basic and applied research. They are today joined by creative researchers across Canada, including, in random order, Fred Grouzet, Philip Wilson, Marc Blais, Frederick Guay, Genevieve Mageau, Mireille Joussemet, Isabelle Green-Demers, Celene Blanchard, Kim Noels, Michelle Fortier, Natalie Houlfort, Claude Fernet, Caroline Senécal, Gaëtan Losier, Cameron Wild, Jacques Forest, Lisa Legault, Marina Milavskaya, and the many others who have made Canada a major center for SDT. Three of our six SDT conferences have been held in Canada, attesting to the fact that it continues to be a strong center of SDT research.

In the European community, SDT is similarly thriving. In Ghent and Leuven, Maarten Vansteenkiste, Bart Soenens, and their many colleagues, including Bart Duriez, Bart Neyrinck, Wim Beyers, Anja Van den Broeck, Luc Goossens, Beiwen Chen, Stijn Van Petegem, and the late Willy Lens, have stimulated an enormous amount of new research on developmental and clinical processes associated with need-supportive and need-thwarting environments. Their highly original work is often longitudinal or experimental and has contributed greatly to the theory. Nearby in the United Kingdom, scholars such as Martyn Standage, Ian Taylor, David Markland, Helga Dittmar, Joan Duda, Kou Murayama, Simon Sebire, and Kimberly Bartholomew have explored SDT formulations in varied spheres. In Norway, Hallgeir and Anne Halvari and their collaborators, such as Anja Olafsen, have extended SDT findings in organizations, sport, and medicine. Indeed, all around Europe are colleagues who have embraced SDT, including scholars such as Andreas Krapp, Bruno Frey, Nicola Baumann, Athanasios Papaioannou, Symeon Vlachopoulos, Nicholas Gillet, Rashmi Kusurkar, Martin Olesen, Mia Reinholt, Leen Haerens, Pedro Teixeira, Marlene Silva, Frank Martela, Stefan Tomas Güntert, Margit Osterloh, Isabel Balaguer, Philippe Sarrazin, Phillipe Carre, Alexios Arvanitis, Krzystof Szadejko, and Juan Alanso.

In Israel, especially centered at Ben-Gurion University, Avi Assor, Guy Roth, Haya Kaplan, Idit Katz, Yaniv Kanat-Maymon, Moti Benita, and others have built yet another major SDT research hub. They have opened up new territory in areas of parenting and education and have made theoretical breakthroughs in basic SDT ideas about internalization and regulation in development, emotion regulation, and relationships.

In Asia, scholarship on SDT has been robust and increasingly active. In Singapore, the Motivation in Education Research Lab (MERL) includes scholars such as Woon Chia Liu, John Wang, Bee Leng Chua, Youyan Nie, Caroline Koh, Mingming Zhou, Coral Lim, and Masato Kawabata, who have applied SDT to multiple domains, but especially to education and sport. In Korea, Hyungshim Jang, Johnmarshall Reeve, Woogul Lee, Ayoung Kim, and other scholars have been advancing SDT in terms of its analysis of teaching and learning processes and interventions, as well as exploring the neurological underpinnings of autonomous versus controlled motivations. In Japan, Shigeo Sakurai, Tadashi Hirai, Nobuo Sayanagi, Takuma Nishimura, Ayumi Tanaka, and Quint Olga-Baldwin; and in China, Shui-fong Lam, Jian Zhang, Ye Lan, Liang Meng, Wilbert Law, Qingguo Ma, Qin-Xue Liu, and Junlin Zhao are just a few of many Asian colleagues applying SDT to important problems, from language learning to Internet use.

The University of Rochester has been a long-time base from which we launched the Motivation Research Group, and we have many people to thank in Rochester for friendship and support over the years. Perhaps a large part of the problem of SDT's growth should be laid at the doorsteps of our former doctoral students, visiting scholars, and postdocs at Rochester, who have stimulated the various advancements of SDT by asking driving questions and mastering the best methodologies over our multidecade, Friday-afternoon, free-ranging discussions. Again, we have too many former Rochester-based scholars to recognize, but the following are just some of the inspiring people who have worked directly with us in what, we hope, was experienced as an autonomy-supportive research atmosphere: Wendy Grolnick, Tim Kasser, Ken Sheldon, Kirk Brown, Arlen Moller, Geof Williams, Chantal Levesque-Bristol, Christina Frederick-Recascino, Holley Hodgins, Virginia Grow Kasser, Jessica Solky-Butzel, Chip Knee, Nikki Legate, Jennifer La Guardia, Valery Chirkov, Jaine Strauss, Jesse Bernstein, Heather Patrick, Robert Plant, Netta Weinstein, Andrew Przybylski, Veronika Huta, and Youngmee Kim. Paul Adachi, Cody DeHann, Patricia Schultz, Thuy-vy Nguyen, Behzad Behzadnia, Özge Kantas, and Myunghee Lee are among those currently working with us in Rochester. We have also grown through our collaborative work with Rochester faculty past and present, including Jim Connell, Chris Niemiec, Harry Reis, Ron Rogge, Ellen Skinner, Martin Lynch, Laura Wray-Lake, Diane Morse, and Randall Curren.

In reflecting on our Rochester associates, we also must acknowledge the loss of fellow Rochester scholars Cynthia Powelson, Cristine Chandler, Michael Kernis, Allan Schwartz, Jack Davey, Louise Sheinman, and Allan Zeldman, each of whom contributed to our thinking and our spirits, and who remain alive in our hearts.

The Australian Catholic University has more recently become a new home for our studies. Within the Institute for Positive Psychology and Education (IPPE) at ACU, we are forming new discussions of the organismic processes on which mindfulness and autonomy must be based. Herbert Marsh and Rhonda Craven were especially instrumental in bringing us to Sydney. Australia more generally has become a particularly vibrant continent for SDT research. Scholars on the east coast include Chris Lonsdale, Stefano Di Domenico, Rafael Calvo, Dorian Peters, Paul Evans, Gordon Spence, Gary McPherson, Anne Poulsen, Jenny Ziviani, and David Wadley. On Australia's west coast, Nikos Ntoumanis, David Webb, Marylène Gagné, Martin Hagger, Nikos Chatzisarantis, Eleanor Quested, and Cecilie Thogersen-Ntoumani, among others, are creating a new and vital concentration of SDT scholarship in Perth.

Outside these centers of SDT research, scholars in the United States and many other countries have contributed to research on the basic principles, utility, and generalizability of SDT. Often working alone or in small groups are scholars such as Lennia Matos in Peru; Cicilia Chettiar in India; Athanasios Mouratidis, Omar Simsek, Ahmet Uysal, and Zumra Atalay in Turkey; and Ken Hodge and Maree Roche in New Zealand, as well as U.S. researchers such as Patricia Hawley, Todd Little, Michael Wehmeyer, Sam Hardy, Erika Patall, Dan Stone, and Benjamin Hadden, all doing work that is extending SDT.

There are also many, many others, and we apologize sincerely to all, wherever your places of study, if your names are not included in this acknowledgment. We do very much appreciate your work. Because SDT is focused on basic human needs and the diversity of ways they are expressed and satisfied, the hope is to continue to test its applicability and utility across economic contexts and cultures, and the kind of broad international and multidisciplinary involvement SDT has received is critical to this mission.

As SDT is becoming ever more global, its center of gravity remains at the CSDT, under the care of Shannon Robertson Hoefen Cerasoli. Shannon has enthusiastically and skillfully facilitated the SDT project for over a decade. Her invaluable service to SDT warrants our highest gratitude, as well as our deepest affection. We also thank Stephanie Green, who assisted Shannon in the final stages of editing this book. We have additionally benefited from the initiating sponsorship of Immersyve Inc. in helping to establish and maintain the center and our website (*www.selfdeterminationtheory.org*). Immersyve CEO Scott Rigby is not only a supporter but also a leading scholar of SDT in his own right.

We also are extremely grateful to several granting agencies and foundations that have supported our research, writing, and collaborations with close colleagues. Four institutes within the National Institutes of Health, the National Science Foundation, the Institute of Education Sciences, the James McKeen Cattell Foundation, the United States–Israel Binational Science Foundation, the Bill and Melinda Gates Foundation, the Australian Research Council, and the Leverhulme Trust have been among them.

Finally, we have our own families and friendship communities to thank. Rich especially thanks the most loving children a father could wish for—William and Alexandra—and the most supportive partner a man could so happily grow up, and old, with—Miriam Gale. Rich also thanks all his close nonacademic friends in both Rochester and Sydney, who keep him grounded and vital. Ed is grateful for his "D-bury" family, and for all who are involved in his "other" life of art and community on Monhegan Island. And, finally, each of us thanks the other for the extraordinary collaboration and close friendship we have had for nearly 40 years. It has been an intrinsically rewarding journey for us thus far, and one that we hope will continue for the SDT community long after our voices have silenced.

RICHARD M. RYAN
EDWARD L. DECI

Contents

PART I

Introduction

CHAPTER 1

Self-Determination Theory

An Introduction and Overview

Self-determination theory (SDT) is an empirically based, organismic theory of human behavior and personality development. SDT's analysis is focused primarily at the psychological level, and it differentiates types of motivation along a continuum from controlled to autonomous. The theory is particularly concerned with how social-contextual factors support or thwart people's thriving through the satisfaction of their basic psychological needs for competence, relatedness, and autonomy. Although the theory is psychological, research has also given attention to biological underpinnings of these psychological processes and places them in an evolutionary perspective. In this chapter we provide an overview of what appears in the chapters that follow, including a layout of SDT's six mini-theories; a discussion of a range of phenomena related to human development; an argument for the theory's applicability to real-life domains such as education, health care, work, psychotherapy, sport, and virtual worlds; and a consideration of social, political, and cultural factors that influence motivations and basic need satisfactions.

Self-determination theory (SDT), as reflected in both the scientific research and the applied practices stemming from it, is centrally concerned with the social conditions that facilitate or hinder human flourishing. The theory examines how biological, social, and cultural conditions either enhance or undermine the inherent human capacities for psychological growth, engagement, and wellness, both in general and in specific domains and endeavors. SDT research thus critically inquires into factors, both intrinsic to individual development and within social contexts, that facilitate vitality, motivation, social integration and well-being, and, alternatively, those that contribute to depletion, fragmentation, antisocial behaviors, and unhappiness.

This focus on wellness and flourishing and the conditions that support (or thwart) them is of obvious importance, because the outcomes of human development vary so widely. Clearly, it is in our "natures" (i.e., our evolved capacities and acquired propensities) to attain greater or lesser degrees of healthy psychological, social, and behavioral functioning and to more or less realize our human capacities and talents. We can also see natural experiments everywhere in which promising human potentials are diminished by impoverished or oppressive social conditions. SDT thus uses both experimental studies and field observations of such natural experiments toward understanding what humans really need from their psychological and social environments to be fully functioning and to thrive.

Investigation of factors that optimize development and functional integrity in living entities has long been an important topic of research within the biological and psychological sciences (e.g., Harlow, 1953b; Mayr, 1982; Raff et al., 1993). Whether studying plants, single-cell entities, or multicellular animals, establishing an organism's needs for particular nutrients and supports has been, in fact, a traditionally Baconian endeavor. It entails observation or manipulation of variations in deprivation or provision of presumed nutrients and assessing their observable effects on growth and functioning. Such studies are common in fields from agriculture to comparative biology. SDT brings this same functional viewpoint to the study of *psychological* growth and development and, in doing so, investigates some of the basic features and mechanisms underlying social behavior, its development, and its pathology.

Besides its value for basic science, this functional approach of SDT also turns out to be both *practical* and *critical*. SDT is *practical* insofar as it points to how features of contexts more or less facilitate or undermine the motivations and satisfactions underlying effective self-regulation and wellness. By identifying (and measuring) varied types of motivational regulation and the conditions that foster them, SDT can be thoughtfully and systematically applied within varied social contexts, including families, classrooms, sports teams, health clinics, interactive media, and workplaces. At the same time, SDT is inherently *critical* insofar as it examines and compares social contexts in terms of their adequacy in supporting versus impairing human thriving. This critical approach applies to proximal social contexts, such as parent–child, classroom, and workplace relationships, as well as to analyses of more pervasive cultural, political, and economic conditions as they affect basic human need satisfactions and the developmental and social assets they foster. In this sense SDT is not a relativistic framework; it hits bedrock in its conception of certain universals in the social and cultural nutrients required to support healthy psychological and behavioral functioning.

An Organismic, Empirical Approach

SDT is an *organismic perspective*, approaching psychological growth, integrity, and wellness as a life science. SDT specifically assumes that humans have evolved to be inherently curious, physically active, and deeply social beings. Individual human development is characterized by proactive engagement, assimilating information and behavioral regulations, and finding integration within social groups. From infancy on (when in need supportive environments), people manifest intrinsic tendencies to take interest in, deeply learn about, and gain mastery with respect to both their inner and outer worlds. These inclinations include the inherent propensities to explore, manipulate, and understand associated with *intrinsic motivation* (discussed in Chapters 5–7) and the propensity to assimilate social norms and regulations through active *internalization and integration* (discussed in Chapter 8). SDT focuses on the circumstances under which these two deeply ingrained developmental processes optimally proceed, as well as how contexts can interfere with or compromise them.

Important within SDT is the idea that these active propensities for intrinsic motivation, internalization, and social integration are accompanied by, and indeed grounded in, specific phenomenal satisfactions. SDT posits that inherent in such pursuits are satisfactions in feeling competence, autonomy, and relatedness. These proximal satisfactions reflect, in the deepest sense, the essence of human thriving, and they predict any number of indicators of wellness and vitality. Moreover, SDT research documents that in social contexts in which there is psychological support for these satisfactions, people's curiosity, creativity, productivity, and compassion are most robustly expressed.

As humanistic as these formulations might sound, these active tendencies of intrinsic motivation and integration in development are by no means uniquely human. The early experiments on intrinsic motivation, for example, were done with primates (Harlow, 1950), and one can observe both intrinsic motivation and dependence on psychological needs in primates and other mammalian species (de Waal, 2009; Waller, 1998). Primates have built-in intrinsic motivations upon which their development substantially depends. In fact, mammalian psychological development reflects a more general principle that in theoretical biology is called *organization*—the tendency of living entities, under supportive conditions, to progress toward increased differentiation and integration (Jacob, 1973; Kauffmann, 2000; Maturana & Varela, 1992; Mayr, 1982). Simply stated, individual organisms are endowed with, and energized by, propensities to expand and elaborate themselves in the direction of organized complexity and integrated functioning.

In human development, organizational propensities are evident from the earliest stages of psychosocial development in infants' exploratory urges and their social interest and responsiveness. These propensities are continuously active across development, as children and adults, when healthy, strive to assimilate and integrate events and experiences and remain connected to and integral within their social groups. Through transformations in foci and integrative span, self-organization remains central to healthy functioning over the life course (Cicchetti, 2006; Ryan, Kuhl & Deci, 1997; Vansteenkiste & Ryan, 2013). SDT examines the perceptions, attributions, affective experiences, patterns of behavior, and mechanistic underpinnings that characterize healthy self-organization. In terms of the social-psychological aspect of the theory, SDT's interest is then focused on understanding the contextual factors that facilitate or thwart these "central-to-life" synthetic functions.

This principle of self-organization in psychological development and functioning is not new and has been recognized within many historically important and varied theories. These include cognitive-developmental perspectives (e.g., Werner, 1948; Piaget, 1971), humanistic psychology (e.g., Goldstein, 1939; Rogers, 1963), and psychodynamic approaches (e.g., Freud, 1923; Loevinger, 1976; White, 1963; Winnicott, 1965), among others (e.g., Assagioli, 1965; Hermans, 2002). In fact, the application of the organization framework to human psychological development and wellness has many precedents and has been supported by the observations of some of history's most renowned clinicians and theorists (discussed in Chapter 2).

SDT shares an organismic view of psychological development with these prior theories, yet unlike a number of them, SDT is deliberate in its embracing of empirical methods, placing emphasis on explicit hypotheses, operational definitions, observational methods, and statistical inferences, as central and meaningful to its epistemological strategy. Although we accept, and indeed draw upon, past theoretical approaches and clinical observations, SDT's theoretical propositions have been primarily formulated, sustained, and refined using empirical evidence as a core resource and focus. In doing such research, we have asserted that it is possible and appropriate to employ both descriptive and experimental methods to study the active, synthetic nature of human beings. Indeed, SDT-based research has on occasion documented phenomena that had previously only been matters of speculation, as well as uncovered new insights on topics from the controlling aspects of rewards to the relations of benevolence to enhanced vitality. SDT's empirical approach also facilitates the development of evidence-supported interventions. At the same time, embracing an empirical approach acts as a strong constraint on SDT, setting limits on what the theory can meaningfully describe, predict, or prescribe.

A Psychological Theory

The fundamental norm for science is to advance descriptions and explanations that are organized by theories that, in turn, are validated by the demonstration of their capacities for prediction and control, especially in novel circumstances. Theories, as true "bodies" of knowledge with authentic, organic connections, have advantages over mere collections of facts because they afford generalizations that can address new events, as well as illuminate past ones. They also provide a common language for investigators, allowing them to better anticipate events, and observe, refine, compare, and extend understanding and prediction. Theories thereby help us select what information is important and prospectively provide useful principles for practice. In contrast, facts without theoretical extension or organization have little to no prescriptive value. As Loevinger (1957) long ago reasoned, they are merely *ad hoc*.

Theories not only organize facts but also connect with larger systematic philosophies or meta-theories. Disconnected, unsystematic collections of facts not only have limited applicability or predictive value but also often lack logical coherence and connectivity within larger frames of thought. Consider that many approaches in psychology today consist of "models" composed of hypothesized relations between several measured variables or constructs. These models fall short of being theories, however, often being either isolated from even neighboring models that are not similarly framed or assessed or ambiguous with respect to their implications across varied levels of analysis. Many are also poorly grounded in, or even inconsistent with, the foundational theories and philosophies from which they derive.

A good theory also *explains*—it makes sense of phenomena and allows an understanding of mediating processes that prove to be critical within experiments and systematic interventions. Insofar as SDT investigates how developmental propensities and social conditions interact to facilitate or undermine various forms of human motivation and wellness across domains, it thus identifies principles that can directly inform effective social practice. This relates to another characteristic of good theory: It can reliably guide action and intervention. One goal of science is to turn discovered knowledge into practice and, in an evidence-supported manner, apply what can enhance human functioning in real-world settings. Thus our approach has, in an ongoing way, iterated between systematically testing hypotheses in experimental contexts and then retesting them in field studies and controlled interventions that might further demonstrate the utility and generalizability of hypotheses and theory.

With regard to utility, we believe that the most practical of extant theories of human behavior are *psychological* in focus. As a psychological theory, SDT is concerned with behavior as a function of the conscious or nonconscious reasons or motives that organize it. These motives and reasons, frequently taking the form of desires, fears, reflective values, and goals, are sometimes salient in awareness and sometimes denied or defended against. They can often be assessed using subjective reports, but they can also be assessed using other means, such as implicit measures, behavioral observations, or physiological indicators. Yet however assessed, values and motives are potent variables. Insofar as the causes of intentional (rather than reflexive) behaviors lie in the necessary events that initiate and sustain them, it is the forces that "move" people, as conceptualized within the scope of motivational psychology, that frequently supply the most relevant and practical predictive models and the most meaningful explanations of behavior. In other words, it is the perceived satisfactions, rewards, and values (and the imagined costs, drawbacks, and frustrations) that drive action, and therefore understanding the lawful dynamics underlying these psychological phenomena is what most practically informs behavior change.

In this regard we consider psychological constructs, whether conscious or nonconscious, to comprise the *regnant causes* of most intentional behaviors. It is at the level of motives and intentions, and the experiences of external and internal forces that instigate and affect them, where the most relevant determinants of behaviors are taking place (Ryan & Deci, 2004a). In stating explicitly the importance of psychological variables in the determination of behavior, we of course are merely echoing the views of Heider (1958). He famously argued that it is *naïve psychology*—people's perceptions of their social environments—that guides their subsequent behaviors and actions. SDT concurs, and, as we shall review in Chapter 3, it is partly derived from Heider's seminal work.

Psychological mediators reign. It is, for example, the perception of being controlled that undermines a worker's initiative; the felt rejection implied by an insult that gives rise to withdrawal or aggression; the experience of mastery that gratifies and sustains an effort. Although such psychological phenomena can be described at various levels of analysis from micro-mechanisms to molar behaviors, it is at the psychological level that change can often be most readily leveraged. A boss, a parent, a teacher, or a clinician is not likely to influence behavior by directly manipulating another's genes, brain tissue, or motor functioning. Instead, behavioral outcomes are most easily changed by appealing to the person's motives, goals, and expectations or by altering the proximal features of social environments that give rise to them. Thus the level of analysis that is most needed for the scientific understanding of motivation and behavior change is the level encompassing the psychological processes operating within the individual and the variables and influences within social contexts that activate or diminish those processes.

In stating this point, we in no way suggest that psychological theories are distinct from biological or reductive accounts with which they must ultimately be fully coordinated and through which they can be refined (Ryan & Di Domenico, 2016). Autonomous actions, for example, are biologically distinct from controlled behaviors, but both are dependent on specific mechanisms (Ryan, Kuhl, Deci, 1997). Moreover, pervasive psychological experiences impact the brain, predisposing certain motivational orientations and regulatory capabilities (e.g., Bindman, Pomerantz, & Roisman, 2015; Vansteenkiste & Ryan, 2013). SDT is thus being meaningfully extended through the exploration of the mechanistic underpinnings of its core psychological processes (e.g., Di Domenico, Fournier, Ayaz, & Ruocco, 2013; Di Domenico, Le, Liu, Ayaz, & Fournier, 2016; Lee, Reeve, Xue, & Xiong, 2012). Yet too often we lose sight of how important, and lawful, psychological events are in their own right: Not only are they often the phenomenally proximal causes of behavior, but they also represent, again, typically the most practical level at which we can intervene in human behavioral affairs.

Similarly, SDT's models of motivation and need satisfaction also link well with emerging theories within evolutionary psychology concerning more ultimate foundations of our nature. First, SDT as a psychological theory identifies the necessary and sufficient proximal satisfactions associated with behavioral phenomena such as curiosity, internalization, and prosocial actions, in turn suggesting that these proximal satisfactions support multiple forms of adaptive functioning. Proximal psychological need satisfactions, that is, are seen as having been essential to procuring and expanding both individual and social resources important in group settings, thereby potentially playing a critical role in both individual and group selection processes (e.g., Ryan & Hawley, 2016).

SDT thus specifies social conditions and psychological processes through which growth, self-regulation, and social integrity are optimized and aspires to place these findings and principles within the larger frame of reference of integrated science. Our stance, applied throughout this work, is that SDT represents an empirically based psychological theory, fully oriented toward consilience. Its specification of motivational and psychological principles must not only fit within, but also be informed and constrained by, what we know about evolution, psychophysiology, and neuroscience on the reductive side and by economics and sociocultural theory, and the influences they specify, on a higher order level. Such is the fate of a nested science such as ours.

Supporting and Impairing Human Development

Being primarily a psychological theory, SDT is concerned with the nature, structure, and functioning of a person in action, including the person's inherent proactive capacities to selectively engage, interpret, and act on external environments. Contained within the conception of proactive, self-regulated engagement and functioning, and at the very heart of self-determination, is a specific view of *self* that is theoretically detailed throughout this book.

Extending the attribution traditions of Heider (1958) and de Charms (1968), SDT defines the self, first and foremost, phenomenologically. SDT is thus focused on the experiences underlying autonomous actions, those involving a sense of volition and self-endorsement, rather than on people's self-concept, identities, or self-evaluations and appraisals. In turn, acting with a sense of autonomy requires integration, as experiences of full volition are characterized by lack of inner conflict and willing engagement.

The development of capacities for self-regulation and volition, as expressed in persons who can openly experience events and reflectively and congruently choose and regulate behavior, is nonetheless highly dependent on supportive social conditions (Deci & Ryan, 1985b, 1987). These self-regulatory capacities are vulnerable to need-thwarting social contexts, which can foster more controlled and defensive functioning and hinder capacities for autonomy and integration.

Persons do not begin tabula rasa, but instead with what might be called a nascent self, a set of rudimentary processes and characteristics that represent the starting point for ongoing psychological development. Infants are intrinsically active, manifesting the inherent tendency to engage the environment and to act volitionally. Thus within each individual we observe a natural tendency toward growth and development, which represents an ongoing tendency toward organismic integration. Yet this integrative propensity, while natural, is also conditional; it requires social and environmental support for persons to satisfy basic psychological needs—the needs for autonomy, competence, and relatedness. These three needs describe, in fact, critical psychological satisfactions necessary for the healthy development of self as the individual engages the world within and around him- or herself. Finally, SDT recognizes and researches the role of an inherent human capacity for developing awareness and self-reflection, including being aware of one's needs, values, and goals, and experiencing the difference between being autonomous and being controlled. This capacity for awareness plays a direct role in healthy self-regulation.

Growth and Defense

SDT's assumptions of intrinsic activity and organismic integration seem well supported by observations of early development and of people taking interest, seeking challenges, and striving for voice and connection across the lifespan, even in the face of countervailing social forces. Nonetheless, with equal readiness one can observe the human capacities to be apathetic and alienated, to disconnect from and dehumanize others, and to behave in ways that imply fragmentation and inner division rather than integration. These seemingly contradictory human natures, with capacities for activity *and* passivity, integrity *and* fragmentation, caring *and* cruelty, can be theoretically approached in different ways. As briefly mentioned, one approach, taken by the more behavioristic schools of thought, has assumed that organisms can be conditioned, programmed, or trained to be more "positive" in functioning, or they can be programmed, conditioned, or trained to be more "negative." In other words, the contradiction is resolved within such theories by assuming a relatively empty or highly plastic organism that is shaped to be either more positive or more negative, with little need to consider the constraints or contents of human nature.

The SDT alternative is to begin with the assumption that there is a human nature, which is deeply designed to be active and social and which, when afforded a "good enough" (i.e., a basic-need-supportive) environment, will move toward thriving, wellness, and integrity. Yet some of the very features of this adaptive nature also make people vulnerable to being derailed or fragmented when environments are deficient in basic need supports. Social contexts can be basic need-thwarting, with various developmental costs, including certain defensive or compensatory strategies. When individuals experience need-thwarting environments, such as contexts that are overly controlling, rejecting, critical, and negative or that otherwise frustrate autonomy, relatedness, and competence needs, individuals are more likely to become self-focused, defensive, amotivated, aggressive, and antisocial. Indeed, the presence of these more negative human capacities is typically indicative of social contexts that are thwarting of fundamental or basic psychological needs. According to SDT, therefore, our manifest human nature is, to a large degree, *experience dependent*—its forms of expression are contingent on the conditions of support versus thwarting and satisfaction versus frustration of these basic needs. SDT places human beings, with their active, integrative tendencies, in dialectical relation with ambient social contexts that can either support or thwart those tendencies.

More specifically, SDT's approach revolves around the proposition that the processes of active development and organization require specific nutrients from the social environment. As such, the nexus in the theory is a set of *basic psychological needs* that may be either satisfied or frustrated, conducive either to the relative prominence of healthy psychological growth or to psychological stagnation and psychopathology. Need-supportive environments facilitate the development of integrated self-regulation, including capacities to manage the multiple drives, impulses, emotions, and motives that arise within every individual (e.g., Bindman, et al. 2015; Di Domenico et al., 2013). If basic needs are thwarted, there is alternatively fragmentation and defense rather than integration (Ryan, Legate, Niemiec, & Deci, 2012; Ryan, Deci & Vansteenkiste, 2016). Thus the interpersonal vulnerabilities, emotion dysregulation, and compromised behavioral functioning that people manifest are understood within SDT to frequently be the result of the active thwarting of these fundamental human needs during development. In short, the support versus neglect of basic needs is critical in influencing the flourishing or diminishment of people's inherent capacities to fully function.

Human Needs

Within the history of empirical psychology, various theories have considered the concept of *human needs* (see Chapter 4). Some have focused on needs that are based in physiological processes that underlie drive states (Hull, 1943), whereas others have focused on needs that are conceptualized in terms of psychological processes (Baumeister & Leary, 1995; McClelland, Atkinson, Clark, & Lowell, 1953; Murray, 1938). SDT falls within the second category in that we conceptualize needs at the psychological level. Yet our approach differs from most other approaches that theorize about psychological needs because we posit a core set of psychological needs that, like physiological needs, are universally essential for optimal human functioning, regardless of developmental epoch or cultural setting. That is, we use the term *need* in a manner that is both specific (as there can be relatively few universal needs) and functional. It is also a usage of the concept of need that has considerable support from philosophical analyses, which have provided ample arguments for the viability of human needs, including psychological needs, as constructs within both scientific theories and practical knowledge (e.g., Braybrooke, 1987; Deci & Ryan, 2000; Dover, 2016; Doyal & Gough, 1991; May, 2010).

Within SDT, needs are specifically defined as *nutrients that are essential for growth, integrity, and well-being*. Accordingly, *basic physiological needs* pertain to nutrients required for bodily health and safety, and include such requirements as oxygen, clean water, adequate nutrition, and freedom from physical harms. Alongside such physical needs, SDT posits that there are also *basic psychological needs* that must be satisfied for psychological interest, development, and wellness to be sustained.

As mentioned, SDT's three basic psychological needs are those for *autonomy, competence,* and *relatedness*. Like physical needs, these needs are said to be *objective* phenomena in that their deprivation or satisfaction has clear and measurable functional effects, effects that obtain regardless of one's subjective goals or values. Insofar as they are needs, thwarting or deprivation of any of them will lead to observable decrements in growth, integrity, and wellness, irrespective of whether they are valued by the individuals or their cultures. Thus, although the desire, goal, or value for any of these nutrients may have an impact upon the likelihood of their being satisfied, value alone is not determinative of their functional effects (e.g., Chen, Vansteenkiste, et al., 2015). This assertion is analogous to the idea that whether or not one subjectively values, desires, or prefers vitamin C, extended deprivation of it will still lead to scurvy.

The first of the basic needs specified within SDT is *autonomy,* or the need to self-regulate one's experiences and actions. Autonomy is a form of functioning associated with feeling volitional, congruent, and integrated (de Charms, 1968; Friedman, 2003; Ryan, 1993; Shapiro, 1981). Autonomy considered as this sense of voluntariness is, therefore, not the same as independence (or self-reliance), as people can be either autonomously or heteronomously dependent, independent, or interdependent depending on the context and behaviors entailed (Ryan & Lynch, 1989). The hallmark of autonomy is instead that one's behaviors are self-endorsed, or congruent with one's authentic interests and values (see Chapter 3). When acting with autonomy, behaviors are engaged wholeheartedly, whereas one experiences incongruence and conflict when doing what is contrary to one's volition. In SDT's view only some intentional actions are truly self-regulated or autonomous—others are regulated by external forces or by relatively nonintegrated aspects of one's personality. As such, a person may behave without a sense of volition or self-endorsement of her or his actions. Self is, in this sense, *not* synonymous with person. Indeed, we shall show much of people's behavior and expression of values can be initiated and/or regulated by internal or external pressures that either overrule or bypass true self-regulation.

Competence is one of the most researched issues in psychology and is widely seen as a core element in motivated actions (Bandura, 1989; Deci, 1975; Harter, 2012; White, 1959). In SDT, competence refers to our basic need to feel effectance and mastery. People need to feel able to operate effectively within their important life contexts. The need for competence is evident as an inherent striving, manifested in curiosity, manipulation, and a wide range of epistemic motives (Deci & Moller, 2005). It energizes myriad behaviors, from people in leisure moments playing mobile video games to scientists discovering the laws of the universe. Competence is, however, readily thwarted. It wanes in contexts in which challenges are too difficult, negative feedback is pervasive, or feelings of mastery and effectiveness are diminished or undermined by interpersonal factors such as person-focused criticism and social comparisons.

Relatedness (Bowlby, 1979; Baumeister & Leary, 1995; Ryan, 1995) concerns feeling socially connected. People feel relatedness most typically when they feel cared for by others. Yet relatedness is also about belonging and feeling significant among others. Thus equally important to relatedness is experiencing oneself as giving or contributing to others (Deci & Ryan, 2014a). Relatedness pertains, moreover, to a sense of being integral to social organizations beyond oneself, or what Angyal (1941) so aptly described in his construct of *homonomy*. That is, both by feeling connected to close others and by being a significant member of social groups, people experience relatedness and belonging, for example through contributing to the group or showing benevolence (see especially Chapters 12 and 24).

These three basic needs of autonomy, competence, and relatedness were initially identified functionally because they served well to integrate the results of behavioral experiments concerning the effects of environmental events and interpersonal contexts on intrinsic motivation (see Chapters 6 and 7) and the internalization of extrinsic regulations (see Chapter 8). Subsequent investigations confirmed that these needs, unlike a variety of other human desires or gratifications that motivate behavior, are essential not only for optimal motivation but also for well-being (see Chapter 10). Need satisfaction is strongly linked with vitality, whereas need-frustration predicts motivational depletion (Ryan & Deci, 2008a). Further work has shown that, when basic needs are thwarted, people will predictably react, albeit in complicated and dynamic ways. Some will fall into passive or fragmented modes of functioning, often characterized as psychopathology (see Chapter 16). Others attempt to compensate for what is missing, as manifested in motives of greed, power, addictive distractions, or aggression that follow from need-frustrating contexts (see Chapters 11 and 24). In fact, throughout this book, we detail many "dark sides" to human nature resulting from threatened or thwarted basic psychological needs in social development.

Our postulate of the essentialness and universality of certain basic psychological needs sets the stage for a *dynamic* theory of motivation. We can analyze behavior in terms of its relation to the three psychological needs, even when the surface content of a behavior may not appear to be directly related. For example, we argue in Chapter 16 that many forms of psychopathology have their etiology in developmental deprivations of basic psychological needs for autonomy, competence, or relatedness (Ryan, Deci,

Grolnick, & La Guardia, 2006; Vansteenkiste & Ryan, 2013). Perfectionism, for example, can be a battle for love via competence, yet accompanied by a loss of autonomy. Antisocial behavior can reflect the impairment of internalization in contexts that have been controlling and cold.

In fact, many behaviors are driven by substitute and compensatory motives resulting from the frustration of basic psychological needs. SDT's analysis of materialism and status seeking (Chapter 11) indeed suggests that these motives often result from insecurities fostered by non-nurturing, rejecting, or controlling psychological conditions in earlier development (e.g., Kasser, Ryan, Zax, & Sameroff, 1995; Williams, Hedberg, Cox, & Deci, 2000) and that they can be activated by more proximal threats and frustrations (Kasser, 2002a). Still other analyses, reviewed in Chapter 13, indicate that parents' use of conditional regard creates a conflict between the needs for autonomy and relatedness, resulting in a variety of psychological disturbances (e.g., Assor, Roth & Deci, 2004). SDT is also able to address the split between nonconscious and conscious motives as a result of controlling forces and the deleterious impact of the resulting inner lack of integration (e.g., Weinstein, W. S. Ryan, DeHaan, et al., 2012). These selective examples suggest how positing basic needs implicates a deep structure of the psyche, around which secondary motivations, desires, and defenses are built, that results in dynamically patterned behavioral outcomes.

The Importance of Social Contexts

Specifying fundamental human needs serves a variety of purposes. It gives content to human nature by describing inherent tendencies and inclinations readily manifested under conditions of environmental supports. It also provides a basis for understanding the development of individual differences in integration versus fragmentation or defense. In addition, it represents a framework for making a priori predictions about which aspects of a given social context will enhance versus undermine high-quality motivation, healthy development, and well-being. Simply stated, aspects of a social context that are likely to support satisfaction of the fundamental psychological needs are predicted to promote effective functioning and integrated development, whereas features of a social context that are likely to thwart need satisfaction are predicted to diminish effective functioning and to support nonoptimal developmental trajectories (e.g., Joussemet et al., 2008).

We thus characterize social environments in terms of the extent to which they are: (1) *autonomy supportive* (versus demanding and controlling); (2) *effectance supporting* (versus overly challenging, inconsistent, or otherwise discouraging); and (3) *relationally supportive* (versus impersonal or rejecting). Autonomy support includes affordances of choice and encouragement of self-regulation, competence supports include provisions of structure and positive informational feedback, and relatedness supports include the caring involvement of others. Predictions about the effects of specific contextual factors (e.g., positive feedback, presence of contingent rewards, provision of choice) on people's engagement, performance, and experience are based on a consideration of the expected relations of these factors to satisfaction of the basic psychological needs.

Our conceptualization of the effects of social contexts is pertinent to both motivation and behavior in immediate situations and to development and wellness over time. In other words, supports for autonomy, competence, and relatedness not only are theorized to facilitate more self-determined and high-quality functioning in the immediate situation, but they are also understood to promote the development of more effective self-functioning, resilience, and enduring psychological health for the long term. Indeed, as we shall see in various chapters, the dynamics of psychological need satisfaction predict cultural, organizational, and personal functioning and vitality and their fluctuations over time.

Motivation and Self-Determination

Our analysis of the relation of self-determination to development, behavior, performance, and well-being is based, first and foremost, in motivational processes. In other words, we employ motivational concepts to address these important human issues and use empirical methods for hypothesis testing and theory building. To show the relation of our theoretical constructs to those of other empirically based motivation approaches, we turn to a brief discussion of the concept of motivation as it has been treated within empirical psychology.

Motivation, etymologically, concerns what "moves" people to action. Theories of motivation more specifically focus on both what *energizes* and *gives direction* to behavior. Throughout the history of experimental psychology various theories of motivation have thus attempted to predict learning, performance, and behavior change. Within these theories, the concept of motivation has generally been treated as a unitary entity, which is to say that it has been studied in terms of amount or strength but has not typically been differentiated with respect to types, qualities, or orientations. As early as 1908, Yerkes and Dodson related the amount of motivation to performance, proposing an inverted-U relation in which small amounts of motivation yield poor performance, moderate amounts yield maximal performance, and large amounts again yield poor performance, presumably because being "too aroused" interferes with one's effectiveness. Later in the 20th century, when drive theories (Hull, 1943) dominated the field of motivation and learning, the central motivational concept was drive state. Different types of physiological disequilibria—hunger, thirst, and sexual appetite, for example—combined to yield the total amount of drive state (i.e., of motivation). Together with associative bonds, which developed through past instances of drive reduction, the amount of motivation was used to predict learning and performance.

The advent of cognitive theories brought many changes to empirical psychology, but cognitive theories of motivation still for the most part clung to a unitary view of motivation. Specifically, the cognitive theories that replaced drive theories as the leading approach to conceptualizing motivation and behavior change within the experimental tradition (Bandura, 1996; Lewin, 1951; Tolman, 1959; Vroom, 1964) were of two types: expectancy–valence theories and cognitive-behavioral or social learning theories. Expectancy–valence theories (e.g., Feather, 1990; Vroom, 1964) predict behaviors and attitudes from the amount of motivation, which is said to result from the valence or psychological value of outcomes multiplied by the probability of being able to attain those outcomes. Similarly, cognitive-behavioral theories predict motivation from the strength of one's beliefs about being able to achieve outcomes (Rotter, 1954; Seligman, 1975) or, in a somewhat more differentiated formulation, one's contingency and efficacy expectations (Bandura, 1977, 1996). Cognitive theories contrast this undifferentiated or unitary concept of motivation with the lack of motivation (i.e., with being unmotivated). For example, in Bandura's (1996) theory, the concept of self-efficacy is said to be the central mechanism underlying all motivated behaviors, and being unmotivated is what results from lack of self-efficacy. Thus, across cognitive theories, the focus has been on the level of motivation, considered as a unitary concept.

The Differentiation of Motivation

Where SDT is especially different from other approaches to motivation is in its emphasis on the different types and sources of motivation that impact the quality and dynamics of behavior. Rather than simply seeing motivation as a unitary phenomenon, SDT suggests that some forms of motivation are entirely volitional, reflecting one's interests or values, whereas others can be wholly external, as when one is coerced or pressured into doing something he or she does not find of value. Clearly, sources of motivations differ, as do the effects of being energized by these different motives. Put simply, different motives are not just different in magnitude; they vary in the phenomenal sources that initiate them, the affects and experiences that therefore accompany them, and their behavioral consequences, including the quality of persistence, performance, and health benefits (or costs) they yield. SDT therefore explicitly differentiates the concept of motivation in order to consider the varied effects of different types of motivation on such relevant outcomes.

A central dimension used within SDT to differentiate types of motivation is the *autonomy–control continuum*. Varied types of motivation can be characterized in terms of the extent to which they represent *autonomous* versus *controlled* regulations. As we mentioned, behaviors are autonomously motivated to the extent that the person experiences volition—to the extent that he or she assents to, concurs with, and is wholly willing to engage in the behaviors. When autonomous, behaviors are experienced as emanating from, and an expression of, one's *self*. In contrast, behaviors characterized within SDT as controlled are those in which a person feels externally or internally pressured or compelled to act. For example, a person is controlled when his or her motivations to act are based in feeling coerced by external persons or forces to act in ways that are incongruent or alien with respect to the person's sense of self.

Our initial window into the distinction between autonomous and controlled motivation stemmed from early empirical research on *intrinsic motivation* (Deci, 1975; Deci & Ryan, 1980a; see also Chapters 5 and 6 in this volume). Intrinsically motivated behaviors are those that are performed out of interest and for which the primary "reward" is the spontaneous feelings of effectance and enjoyment that accompany the behaviors. Intrinsic motivation contrasts with *extrinsic motivation,* represented by behaviors that are instrumental for some separable consequence such as an external reward or social approval, avoidance of punishment, or the attainment of a valued outcome (Ryan & Deci, 2000a). Intrinsically motivated behaviors are, by definition, autonomous; they are experienced as being volitional and emanating from one's self, a point made early on by de Charms (1968). In contrast, extrinsically motivated behaviors can vary widely in the degree to which they are controlled versus autonomous (Ryan & Connell, 1989). One can be extrinsically motivated because of externally imposed reward or punishment contingencies, in which case one's behavioral regulation is likely to be characterized as relatively controlled; but one can also be extrinsically motivated insofar as the behavior yields outcomes that are personally valued or important, in which case the behavior is likely to be experienced as relatively autonomous.

More specifically, SDT proposes that extrinsic motivation may be more or less *internalized* to or congruent with one's self, so the degree of internalization reflects the degree to which the behavioral regulation is relatively autonomous versus controlled. Behaviors can be *externally regulated,* meaning they are directly controlled by external and self-alien forces; or they can be controlled through *introjection,* in which case the person has taken in but not fully accepted external controls. In introjection the person is motivated by guilt, shame, contingent self-esteem, and fear of disapproval, or by their "approach" counterparts, namely a sense of self and other approval, self-aggrandizement, and ego enhancement. Introjected behaviors are thus experienced as "internally controlling" (Ryan, 1982), whereas external regulations are phenomenally controlled by external entities or persons. Although both external and introjected types of regulation represent controlled motives, it is important to note that they differ in both the nature of the phenomenal drivers and the qualities of behavior that follow from them. For example, whereas external regulation tends to be highly dependent on the ambient contingencies of rewards and punishments, introjected motivation, being internally driven, can drive behaviors even when external contingencies are absent. Instead, introjected regulations are typically associated with internal pressure, tension, and conflict.

Extrinsically motivated behaviors can also be more autonomously motivated through one's *identification* with and acceptance of the value of the extrinsic behavior. Extrinsic motivation can be even more autonomous when such identifications have been *integrated* with one's other values and beliefs. These more autonomous forms of regulation are experienced as more volitional, and quality of persistence and performance is higher than with controlled motives for acting.

Thus each of the varied forms of extrinsic motivation specified within SDT (i.e., external, introjected, identified, or integrated) has its own dynamic causes, supports, and character, and yet they are phenomenally "ordered" in their degrees of autonomy (Ryan & Connell, 1989). The more autonomous the motivational form, generally the more the individual has access to organismic supports for acting, which in part explains the energetic, affective, and cognitive advantages of autonomy as a characteristic of action. Chapter 8 details SDT's conceptualization of internalization and the causes and consequences of the varied forms of motivation depicted within it.

Autonomous and controlled types of motivation are, of course, hypothetical concepts, reflecting psychological processes within individuals that are not typically directly observable by researchers. Still, individuals reliably experience the differences between these varied volitional and controlled behaviors, and the differential results that follow from these experiences are observable. In fact, explicit and implicit measures of psychological processes both represent windows through which researchers can gain access to the regulatory processes underlying behavior. This is especially so when both between- and within-person variations in experience are considered (Brown & Ryan, 2004). Moreover, the neurological processes that subserve autonomous versus controlled motives are increasingly being distinguished (e.g., Lee et al., 2012; Leotti & Delgado, 2011; Murayama, Matsumoto, Izuma, & Matsumoto, 2010; Murayama, Matsumoto, et al., 2015).

Researchers can also directly examine the functional impact of conditions that vary in their support for autonomy on people's quality of experience, performance, and subsequent behavior. For instance, one can stimulate external regulation by using controlling reward contingencies (see Deci, Koestner & Ryan, 1999); stimulate introjection by fostering ego involvement and contingent self-esteem (e.g., Roth, 2008; Ryan, 1982); promote identification by providing convincing rationales for acting (e.g., Reeve, Jang, Hardre, & Omura, 2002); facilitate integrated regulation with a combination of acknowledging feelings, providing a rationale, and highlighting choice instead of control (Deci, Eghrari, Patrick, & Leone, 1994); or incite intrinsic motivation by affording people interesting and optimally challenging tasks (e.g., Danner & Lonky, 1981; Grolnick & Ryan, 1987). That is, particular types of regulation can be reliably instigated through exposure to different social environments.

Phenomenally based reports and experimental investigations thus both provide important inroads to the understanding of the varied types of motivational regulation underlying human behavior. They are complemented within SDT by domain-specific field studies that focus on naturally occurring variations in contextual supports for psychological needs as they relate to variations in the quality of human functioning.

In sum, within SDT human motivation is considered in a differentiated way. People are not only more or less motivated, as most motivation theories have suggested, but they can be motivated by intrinsic and by varied types of extrinsic motivations, often simultaneously. SDT research details the functional differences in both the quality of behavior and psychological health and well-being that follow from behaviors that are to different degrees underpinned by external, introjected, identified, integrated, and intrinsic forms of motivation.

Amotivation

Intrinsic and the varied types of extrinsic motivation all represent *intentional* or *personally caused* actions (de Charms, 1968; Ryan & Deci, 2000a). Differentiation of these intentional behaviors constitutes a critical point of divergence between the traditional cognitive theories of motivation and SDT. In fact, much of the research reported in this book focuses on the importance of distinguishing between various autonomous and controlled forms of intentional behavior, because they are accompanied by different experiences and are differentially associated with quality of action and degree of well-being.

Increasingly, just as SDT research compelled us to differentiate motivation into different types, recent research and theory suggests varied types of *amotivation*. We use the concept of amotivation to describe people's lack of intentionality and motivation—that is, to describe the extent to which they are passive, ineffective, or without purpose with respect to any given set of potential actions. Yet, within SDT, amotivation can take several forms (e.g., Pelletier, Dion, Tuson & Green-Demers, 1999; Vansteenkiste, Lens, De Witte, & Feather, 2005). In the first form, people do not act because they feel they are not able to effectively attain outcomes. This type of amotivation occurs either as the result of a person's perception that people cannot, through any action, control outcomes (universal helplessness) or because the person perceives that he or she personally cannot effectively perform the required actions. In either case, this first form of amotivation is based in a felt lack of competence. A second form of amotivation stems not from competence or control concerns but, rather, from a lack of interest, relevance, or value. People remain amotivated when behaviors have no meaning or interest for them, especially when it fails to connect with the fulfillment of needs. This second type of amotivation may be present even when the individual has the efficacy or competence to act. A third type of amotivation concerns defiance or resistance to influence (e.g., Van Petegem, Soenens, Vansteenkiste & Beyers, 2015). Here, what appears to be amotivation for a specific act is really a motivated nonaction or oppositional behavior to defy demands that are thwarting a basic need for autonomy or relatedness. Each of these types of amotivation may have different duration and impact, and each has a unique set of determinants and dynamic implications.

Motivation in Social Contexts

The concepts of autonomous motivation, controlled motivation, and amotivation are theorized to mediate between social contexts and outcomes such as effective performance and well-being. For example, social contexts that support satisfaction of all three psychological needs also facilitate more autonomous functioning, which in turn yields more effective performance and greater wellness, whereas social contexts that fail to support and/or actively thwart these basic psychological needs tend to promote controlled motivation or amotivation, which in turn yields poorer performance and ill-being.

Research on social contexts began with experiments exploring the effects of various contextual factors on intrinsic motivation. As the results accumulated, it became clear that intrinsic motivation could be facilitated by supports for competence and autonomy and undermined by conditions hostile to those needs (Deci & Ryan, 1980a; 2000). Factors as diverse as rewards, evaluations, deadlines, surveillance, and negative feedback were all explored in experimental and field studies. Repeatedly it was found that factors that engender perceptions of being externally regulated and/or incompetent undermine intrinsic motivation, whereas those—such as opportunities for choice, positive feedback, and acknowledgment of people's internal frame of reference—that support perceptions of autonomy and feelings of competence maintain or enhance intrinsic motivation. Additional research, particularly with children, showed that feelings of relational security are also necessary for curiosity and intrinsic exploration to be robust.

Subsequent research determined that the same contextual supports that maintained and enhanced intrinsic motivation also play a critical role in promoting the internalization and integration of extrinsic motivations. Whereas perceived autonomy and competence were the main proximal psychological factors implicated in intrinsic motivation (see Deci & Ryan, 2000), relational supports played an invariant and far more salient role in the internalization of extrinsic motivation. Indeed, the internalization of socially transmitted regulations, goals, and values is largely based in the desire to connect with relevant groups (e.g., family, peer groups, or society). That is, people "naturally" tend to internalize the values and goals of those with whom they are or wish to be connected or affiliated. For example, teenagers who are alienated from parents may reject the parents' values and goals, but they may readily adopt the standards and ideals of peers they admire (e.g., Ryan & Lynch, 1989). Similarly, persons readily learn and adapt to cultures with which they identify but do not easily adopt or fully internalize the norms of groups to which they have less desire to belong. Yet, although internalization is based in actual or desired relatedness to others, the individuals will not become securely connected to those others and the internalizations will not become fully integrated and volitionally persistent without supports for autonomy and competence (e.g., La Guardia, Ryan, Couchman, & Deci, 2000). Thus the dynamics of autonomy, competence, and relatedness are crucial for understanding human agency and volition with respect to the internalization and transformation of extrinsically motivated activities into self-regulations (Ryan, 1993; Deci & Ryan, 2000).

SDT Applied to Life's Domains

Considerable research to be reviewed in this book supports the contention that contextual supports for the three needs facilitate internalization and integration of behavioral regulations and also the idea that more self-determined functioning is associated with greater creativity, superior learning, better performance, enhanced well-being, and higher quality relationships. A few examples of the work from later chapters will suggest how the basic research models of SDT speak to issues of applied significance.

Schools and Learning

Much SDT work in educational contexts has shown how teacher and parent approaches to motivation can be either controlling or autonomy-supportive (Niemiec & Ryan, 2009; Ryan & Deci, 2000b, 2013, 2016). More controlling motivational climates for learning foster external regulation, and the result is more superficial and less transferable learning. In fact, controlled motivation has been shown to predict not only more impoverished learning but also greater behavioral problems and risk of disengagement or dropout. By contrast school climates that support autonomy foster more self-motivation, persistence, and quality of learning. Structure, as a scaffolding and support for competence, is shown in many SDT studies to complement autonomy support. In fact, classroom climates supporting autonomy, providing high structure, and conveying relatedness and inclusion foster personal well-being and feelings of connection to one's school and community (e.g., Assor, Kaplan, Feinberg & Tal, 2009). The implications of SDT educational research for parenting (Grolnick, 2002; Grolnick & Seal, 2008), classroom teaching behaviors (Reeve & Halusic 2009), and school policies and reforms (Deci & Ryan, 2016) are manifold and cut across age and cultural lines (e.g., Jang, Reeve, Ryan, & Kim, 2009). We review many of these in Chapters 13 and 14.

Workplace Motivation

Just as the issues of support for autonomy, competence, and relatedness affect learning and achievement, they also affect worker motivation and productivity. SDT research investigates managerial styles and why some engender alienation and apathy whereas others lead to committed and energized employees (e.g., Deci, Olafsen, & Ryan, 2017; Van den Broeck, Vansteenkiste, De Witte, Soenens, & Lens, 2010). In addition, specific experimental work in SDT on rewards, evaluations, and directives speaks to why some incentives and feedback systems work and others backfire (Gagné, Deci, & Ryan, 2017). We review the research on SDT and organizational psychology in Chapter 21.

Sport and Exercise

The intrinsic inclinations of humans to play, compete, challenge themselves, and exercise inherent potentials are nowhere better manifested than in sport and exercise. However, because sport for most people depends largely upon their intrinsic motivation (Frederick & Ryan, 1995), coaching climates can heavily impact athletes' enjoyment, persistence, and performance (e.g., Gagné, Ryan, & Bargmann, 2003; Hagger & Chatzisarantis, 2007). Moreover, exercise and sport persistence and engagement is strongly affected by the type of motivation most salient to people at that time, and SDT predicts differential outcomes that result from differences in what energizes people to engage in physical activities—from ego-involvement to interest, and from the goals of attractiveness to health enhancement (e.g., Owen, Smith, Lubans, Ng, & Lonsdale, 2014; Standage & Ryan, 2012). We further explicate these ideas concerning sport and exercise motivation in Chapter 19.

Health Care and Psychotherapy

As a theory of motivation and persistence, SDT has much to say about the conditions that lead not just to short-term behavior change but to change that becomes internalized or assimilated into the person's ongoing way of being (Ryan & Deci, 2008b). Studies in SDT investigate both how patient motivations and practitioner methods of promoting change interact to predict adherence to mental-health-related therapies for both children (e.g., Ziviani & Poulsen, 2015) and adults (e.g., Zuroff, Koestner, Moskowitz, McBride, & Bagby, 2012). Moreover, specific treatment approaches based on SDT are being used in clinical trials to promote healthier behavior and treatment adherence (Ryan, Patrick, Deci, & Williams, 2008) and better training of health practitioners toward support for autonomy (e.g., Williams & Deci, 1996). These ideas concerning motivation in psychotherapy and in health interventions are described further in Chapters 17 and 18, respectively.

Cultural and Religious Socialization

SDT predicts that people within different religions and cultures internalize ambient norms, rules, and values to varied degrees. Some religious practices (e.g., Ryan, Rigby, & King, 1993) and cultural norms (e.g., Chirkov, Ryan, Kim, & Kaplan, 2003) are externally regulated and/or introjected; others are more fully internalized and integrated. SDT shows the positive effects of greater integration on health and well-being and on cultural (Chirkov, Sheldon, & Ryan, 2011) and religious (Neyrinck, Vansteenkiste, Lens, Duriez, & Hutsebaut, 2006) identification, as well as pointing to techniques of socialization that are less or more effective in engaging a culture's constituents. As religious practices are central examples of cultural internalizations, we discuss them in Chapter 8.

Virtual Worlds

Although SDT is a real-world theory in the sense of having applications to everyday life, it is also applicable to media and virtual worlds and people's participation in them (Rigby & Ryan, 2011). SDT explains how factors within media and game worlds enhance or detract from intrinsic motivation to watch or play (e.g., Ryan, Rigby & Przybylski, 2006) and how the role of elements such as violence can be related to the dynamics of psychological need satisfaction (Przybylski, Rigby, & Ryan, 2010; Przybylski, Ryan, & Rigby, 2009). Virtual worlds are increasingly a part of people's experiential lives in our technological age, and thus we discuss in depth the example of motivation in video games as illustrative of the issues involved in this emerging domain of studies (Chapter 20).

These and other topics, including parenting, sustainability, psychopathology, politics, and aging, have all been analyzed using SDT motivational concepts showing further how a basic science concerning the issues of human needs and motivational types bears on practical endeavors across people's life domains. Because motivation is a central issue in every domain, SDT has far-reaching practical implications and applications.

Fields of Psychology and SDT's Mini-Theories

The implications of SDT cut across traditional fields of psychology. The different phenomena to which the theory extends belong to social, personality, developmental, and clinical psychologies and, more recently, to neuropsychology and behavioral economics. It informs applied fields such as educational, sport, and organizational psychologies. Although psychological in focus, the theory further relates to evolutionary and biological factors on the one hand and to cultural and economic factors on the other. Accordingly, the mini-theories within SDT do not correspond directly to traditional subdisciplines of psychology but rather to different aspects of motivation and psychological integration. Each mini-theory is in turn informed by every level of analysis, from the mechanistic to the sociological.

As already noted, early research leading to self-determination theory began with social-psychological experiments (e.g., Deci, 1971) exploring the effects of events such as the offer of rewards, the provision of feedback, or the opportunity for choice on intrinsic motivation. The interest was in how external inputs affected the natural and spontaneous propensities of people to seek challenges, and assimilate new information, as well as to play and be creative with what they already know. As this work progressed, *cognitive evaluation theory* (CET) was formulated (see Deci & Ryan, 1980a). CET is a minitheory that describes the processes through which social environments influence (i.e., facilitate or undermine) intrinsic motivation and, in turn, high-quality performance and well-being. It was the first of our formal proposition sets (see Deci & Ryan, 1985b), and it has effectively organized research on intrinsic motivation since that time (e.g., Deci et al., 1999). It is described in Chapters 6 and 7.

Organismic integration theory (OIT; Ryan, Connell & Deci, 1985) is a second minitheory within SDT, which concerns the development of extrinsic motivation through the process of integration, thus describing the means through which extrinsically motivated behaviors become autonomous. OIT deals with both the inherent tendencies to internalize and integrate social and cultural regulations and the factors in social contexts that promote or inhibit internalization and integration (Ryan & Connell, 1989). It is thus at the interface of developmental and social psychology. Furthermore, because the dynamic between socialization and internalization is at work in all contexts across the globe, OIT is also the cornerstone of SDT's cross-cultural models (e.g., Chirkov et al., 2003; Miller, Das, & Chakravarthy, 2011; Roth, Assor, Kanat-Maymon, & Kaplan, 2006). We review the tenets of OIT in Chapter 8.

The personality aspects of self-determination theory have been researched in part with individual-difference concepts outlined in a third mini-theory called *causality orientations theory* (COT). For us, individual differences represent a developmental outcome of the person interacting with the social environment over time. Assessing these relatively enduring characteristics of the person allows for prediction of various meaningful outcomes.

Although a number of individual-difference concepts have been of interest to SDT researchers, those concerning *causality orientations* (Deci & Ryan, 1985b) have been the most extensively researched individual differences. There are three general causality orientations—the autonomy orientation, the controlled orientation, and the impersonal orientation—which parallel at a more global level the concepts of autonomous motivation, controlled motivation, and amotivation. The autonomy orientation refers to propensities to organize behavior by orienting toward interests, values, and supports for them in the interpersonal context. It also encompasses the capacity to act with autonomy even when the environment contains salient controlling elements. The control orientation refers to propensities to organize and regulate behavior by orienting toward social controls and reward contingencies and either complying with or defying them. As well, it can lead people to experience a context as quite controlling, even if it might, in fact, afford autonomy. The impersonal orientation concerns tendencies to orient toward aspects of the interpersonal context that signify lack of control over outcomes and incompetence and that promote amotivation.

An instrument to assess general causality orientations (Deci & Ryan, 1985a) has provided a personality (i.e., individual-difference) approach to studying the issues associated with the different styles people have in orienting to the regulation of behavior. In addition, COT has been used to understand the nature and impact of *motivational primes*—that is, nonconsciously processed cues that can activate these various orientations within a person and thus affect both the quality of behavior and its consequences (e.g., Weinstein, Hodgins, & Ryan, 2010). Both the causality orientations and the idea of potentiating them via priming methods are addressed in Chapter 9.

As SDT progressed, it became increasingly clear that the three basic need satisfactions that we had identified as facilitating intrinsic and well-internalized motivations also affected psychological health and well-being. Accordingly we developed a fourth mini-theory, namely, *basic psychological needs theory* (BPNT), to detail how the dynamics of basic needs affect well-being and vitality. Especially interesting in BPNT is how need support promotes and need thwarting undermines healthy functioning at all levels of human development and across cultural backdrops and settings. More deeply, the dynamics of need thwarting explain the development of many forms of psychopathology and even negative physical health outcomes (Ryan, Deci, et al., 2006). BPNT has been especially advanced by the advent of multilevel modeling, which has allowed researchers to address not only how between-person differences in need satisfaction affect wellness but also how within-person fluctuations in need dynamics result in changes in mood, mental health states, and even physical symptoms (e.g., Reis, Sheldon, Gable, Roscoe, & Ryan, 2000; Ryan, Bernstein, & Brown, 2010). We also see how need satisfaction impacts human energy, or vitality, as a central marker of wellness (Martela, DeHaan, & Ryan, 2016). Finally, we have researched how awareness supports need satisfaction and therefore full, healthy functioning. BPNT research is reviewed in Chapter 10.

A fifth mini-theory derived through SDT concerns people's goals and their relations to basic need satisfactions and wellness, namely *goal contents theory* (GCT), which we review in Chapter 11. People hold a range of abiding life goals, which, empirically as well as theoretically, fall into two general categories that have been labeled *intrinsic* AND *extrinsic aspirations* (Kasser & Ryan, 1996). Intrinsic aspirations are those goals that are rewarding in their own right, providing relatively direct satisfaction of the fundamental psychological needs for autonomy, competence, and relatedness. Examples are personal growth, meaningful relationships, and community contributions. Extrinsic aspirations, in contrast, are those built around contingent satisfactions—they make a priority of goals that are not in themselves satisfying but that may be seen as instrumental to getting unmet needs fulfilled. They include such goals as attaining wealth and material goods, acquiring fame and power, and maintaining one's attractiveness and outer image. Research relating intrinsic versus extrinsic life aspirations to behavior and well-being has shown that goal contents differ in their relations to basic need satisfaction, and in turn to mental health, a result which has stood up to cross-cultural analyses. Moreover, Vansteenkiste and his colleagues, among others, have shown that behavioral goals can be framed in either intrinsic or extrinsic terms and thus yield differential outcomes through specifiable microprocesses (e.g., Vansteenkiste, Lens & Deci, 2006). These studies have focused on learning and performance, in addition to well-being, as their outcomes.

The most recent mini-theory within SDT, *relationship motivation theory* (RMT), both frames and summarizes what research has increasingly shown—that high-quality interpersonal relationships, both between individuals and within groups, depend upon the individuals' ability to experience not only positivity or regard but also respect for autonomy. This is true from early infant attachment through old age. RMT recognizes that relatedness, a core psychological need in its own right, not only fuels internalization of social practices but is itself also reciprocally facilitated or undermined by them. RMT also more specifically addresses the intertwined nature of relatedness and autonomy needs and their synergism in truly responsive, mutually satisfying relationships. We discuss these relationship issues in Chapter 12.

To summarize, the core of our basic empirical work can be characterized as falling within the purviews of social, personality, and developmental psychologies. The various programs of research can be grouped so far into six mini-theories that together constitute the formal propositions of self-determination theory.

Yet, because SDT is also a theory of motivation and behavior change, it is also a *clinical* theory (Ryan & Deci, 2008b). Indeed, as clinicians ourselves, it has been our ongoing interest to find methods by which to tap the wellspring of energies that are intrinsic to human nature and to avoid the pitfalls of fostering motivation for change through external control. Throughout this book we illustrate this practice, especially in the relevant applied chapters on psychotherapy and health care. Recently, an increasing number of controlled clinical trials and experiments have demonstrated the power of autonomy-supportive interactions in inspiring behavior change in the direction of health, in contrast to approaches that either attempt to control or regulate the person from without (see, e.g., Ryan, Lynch, Vansteenkiste, & Deci, 2011; Ryan, Patrick, et al., 2008).

Our clinical interests also led us to apply SDT toward the understanding of the development of psychopathology and its functional consequences (Ryan, Deci, & Vansteenkiste, 2016). Autonomy disturbances are central to various forms of mental illness and maladjustment. These include those in which controlling external or internal forces are a central element (e.g., obsessive–compulsive personality, introjective depression), and those in which lack of internalization and impoverished self-regulation are defining elements (e.g., conduct disorders, antisocial personality). In addition, we have considered the central role of need thwarting in severe disorders of self, such as borderline and dissociative disorders (e.g., Ryan, 2005). In Chapter 16 we review these and a wide range of clinical issues in terms of the role of basic need frustrations in childhood and their cascading effects on subsequent development.

Between Biology and Culture

A theory of self, particularly an empirically based one, goes against many modern intellectual strains. Certainly numerous contemporary scientists and philosophers have tried to sell us the idea that our sense of self is just an illusion, a fiction, or an epiphenomenon (e.g., Dennett, 1991; Hood, 2012; Wegner, 2002). This idea that the self has no reality or meaning, so implausible to laypeople and so dysfunctional if truly acted upon, comes indeed from many diverse quarters. It comes out occasionally from reductionist neuroscientists, who by no means represent neuroscientists in general. Reductionists consider theories of self to be merely "fanciful homunculi." For example, they explain that the seemingly coherent and volitional functioning that one typically attributes to the self is simply the outcome of "non-conscious bits of organic machinery, as utterly lacking in point of view or inner life as a kidney or a kneecap" (Hofstadter & Dennett, 1981, p. 12). Another related perspective comes from cognitive scientists in the artificial intelligence domain, who conceive of behavior in terms of computational mechanisms—and sometimes of people as machines that think (see Dietrich & Markman, 2000; Turkle, 1995). Using such metaphors, there is no need for postulating or investing in first-person or experiential explanations, which, even if fitting, would be merely epiphenomenal.

Of course, there also remain a few radical behaviorists, who insist that organisms are entirely controlled by their environments, thus making self-determination by definition a nonsensical idea (e.g., Cameron & Pierce, 1994; Reiss, 2013). Skinner (1953, 1971) long ago claimed that any sense of autonomy or agency was simply an ignorance of the actual causes of behavior, which by (his) definition lie in the contingencies of reinforcement in the "external" world. Initiative, choice, and the values that support them are, in this framework, vacuous phenomena, a view still espoused by modern followers. Even most new-look, cognitive-behaviorist schools, while tipping a hat to concepts such as activity and agency, maintain an underlying metapsychology of associationism—the self being so many templates or schema that are activated by environmental cues (e.g., Mischel & Shoda, 1995).

Finally, many postmodernists and cultural relativists have denigrated the self, portraying self and autonomy as simply Western intellectual preoccupations rather than universal concerns. Gergen (1991) portrays the metaphor of a core self that strives for integration to be a Western, postromantic perspective. He suggests instead that the contemporary postmodern self is in reality without a core or unity but rather is fragmented, saturated, and diversely populated by imputed and largely compartmentalized identities. Cultural relativists, as we discuss in Chapter 22, similarly assert that concepts of self, or inherent tendencies toward autonomy and integrity, are merely Western ideals without relevance outside a few individualistic nations, arguing instead that personality is basically imprinted by one's ambient culture (e.g., Cross, Gore, & Morris, 2003; Markus & Kitayama, 2003).

These are just samplings from a somewhat cacophonous intellectual chorus that would have us abandon the idea of self-organization once and for all. Yet what would they leave us with? The idea that we have no self—that we are simply upheavals of bits of machinery or passively programmed by cultural transmissions—seems not only nihilistic but also implausible as a general psychology. In everyday existence people have, regarding at least some experiences and actions, a very clear sense of "my-ness" attached to them. Most all of us can distinguish actions that we "own," endorse, and feel responsible for, from those that seem forced, alien, or imposed. Indeed, it is often a matter of great clinical import when patients report that their thoughts or actions do not "come from themselves" or were not "under their control." Inner conflict, alienation, heteronomy, and "divided selves" are the everyday grist in the mill of clinical practitioners, an issue that few of these negative views on self meaningfully address.

Moreover, most of us also feel we *can* make coherent decisions about what is most important, relevant, meaningful, and in the best interests of ourselves or others for whom we care. Yet to do so we must synthetically process and evaluate events and make choices—weighty responsibilities that no mature human escapes. The role of the self in the organization and mobilization of our capacities to act is perhaps the most practical and functional concern in human life. In the view espoused in this book, the phenomenal senses of self and of autonomy have a direct relationship to the organization of behavior and are emergent properties of the activities of reflective processing and regulation. There is therefore a correspondence between self-organized actions and particular types of brain processes (e.g., Lee & Reeve, 2013; Legault & Inzlicht, 2013; Ryan & Di Domenico, 2016) and, more importantly, psychological experiences. The degree of autonomy entailed in behavioral regulation has, in turn, enormous ramifications for performance, persistence, and well-being. That human actions can be autonomous and self-regulated is therefore not a fiction—it is a functional attribute that can be more or less robust.

Accordingly, we plan in this book to explicate a psychological theory of self and its development that is phenomenologically grounded, has functional implications, and yet can be coordinated with what we know about the diversities of cultural backdrops, on the one hand, and the workings of the brain and its evolved and acquired propensities on the other. Accepting that humans are characterized by intrinsic activity and organismic integration tendencies precludes a uniformly reductionist analysis. Because humans have a quasi-unique self-reflective capacity that allows them to experience the difference between acting volitionally and being controlled, it becomes mandatory to consider the "downward" causal influence that reflective human experience has on behavior and on the biology that underlies it (Ryan & Deci, 2006). Provocative ideas such as autonomy and responsibility are central concerns within SDT. Still, self-reflective capacities do not grant humans a transcendent status, for it is clear that human regulatory processes operate in lawful, specifiable, and predictable ways and are themselves embedded in, and influenced by, one's social and cultural contexts. The results of our analysis will in fact make very clear that the capacities for autonomy and integration in personality only fully develop with multilevel supports from biological systems, proximal interpersonal relationships, and more pervasive institutional and cultural contexts.

It is sometimes said that the purpose of science is to create knowledge and that knowledge is its own justification. Although that may, in some senses, be a worthy ideal, we believe that if knowledge cannot foster change in support of human life and wellness—if it cannot help better the human condition—its value is relatively minimal, particularly given the monumental problems faced in this world related to aggression, pathology, acquisitiveness, and dominance of various sorts. We thus believe in the importance of designing research and interpreting results in ways that have practical import for facilitating the realization of human potentials. In turn, intervention research often reverberates back to basic principles and generates yet greater knowledge.

The fact that SDT does have applied value, and indeed has spawned numerous interventions, clinical trials, and organizational changes, derives in part from our belief that putting theories into practice and evaluating the results is the ultimate test of a theory. It is with that in mind that we have applied SDT to issues of child care, education, work, health care, sport, and virtual worlds, and it is our intention to continue SDT's extension into applied domains.

About This Book

Our last formal theoretical statement of SDT in book form—*Intrinsic Motivation and Self-Determination in Human Behavior* (Deci & Ryan, 1985b)—was published more than three decades before this one. In those intervening years, SDT has been substantially elaborated and refined based on results from now thousands of laboratory and field studies by hundreds of researchers. We have continually been amazed by the utility of the concepts for interpreting research results and for providing a new way to think about a broad array of human concerns and processes. We have also been inspired by the contributions of scholars around the globe who have engaged SDT's theoretical propositions and empirical methods. In this book, we review only a portion of that research, extend the theory in several new directions, and discuss SDT's relevance to manifold macro and micro societal issues.

In essence, SDT attempts to articulate the basic, vital nature of human beings—of how that nature expresses itself, what is required to sustain energy and motivation, and how that vital energy is depleted. To begin that story, however, we must start with certain root issues—such as the nature of organization as a feature of living things, what it means to be a self in connection with others, and the history and conceptualizations of psychological needs and intrinsic motivation. Thus, although our primary intention in this book is to review empirical research and to organize the findings within a coherent theoretical perspective, our discussion begins with meta-theoretical and historical considerations that highlight the intellectual traditions with which SDT is aligned.

Reflecting this, in Part II of this volume (Chapters 2–5), we review the philosophical and historical themes that led to the emergence of SDT and that provided its conceptual foundations. These meta-theoretical and historical considerations highlight the past intellectual traditions that have either inspired or informed SDT's core constructs. In addition in these chapters we discuss some commonalities and contrasts of SDT with other paradigmatic approaches to human motivation and self-regulation.

Those readers who might be impatient to get right to SDT research itself can simply pass over this section and move on to Part III (Chapters 6–12) in which we articulate SDT's formal theoretical propositions and review some of the empirical findings supporting these propositions. We have organized Part III in terms of the presentation of CET, OIT, COT, BPNT, GCT, and RMT—the six mini-theories comprising SDT. From this foundation we then turn in Part IV (Chapters 13–16) to various extensions and considerations that are based in a developmental perspective and stem from the formal mini-theories to address the concepts of parenting, education, the acquisition of self-concepts and identities, and finally how need thwarting in development contributes to various forms of psychopathology.

Part V (Chapters 17–21) presents applied work based on SDT covering domains of psychotherapy, health care, virtual worlds, sport, and work. For us this is a crucial section of the book because, again, we see the value of psychological science as based not only in its explanatory power but also in its capacity to inform social practice.

Finally, we conclude in Part VI with three chapters on the pervasive influences of cultural, political, and economic forms on human motivation and well-being and the brighter and darker manifestations of human nature and the evolutionary and social conditions that catalyze them. These final chapters hopefully place this work in the larger context of evolving societies and their formidable impact on individuals' thriving, wellness, and positive humanity.

PART II

Philosophical and Historical Considerations

CHAPTER 2

Organismic Principles

Historical Perspectives on Development and Integration in Living Entities

Central to SDT is the assumption of an inherent developmental process, which we term *organismic integration.* This assumption is consistent with many classic theories in biology, philosophy, and psychology and is also an important premise in various approaches to psychotherapy and education. In this chapter we trace the emergence of concepts of active integrative tendencies in biological thought and their applications within varied theories of psychology. In cognitive-developmental theory, we focus on Piaget's views of organization as expressed in propensities toward assimilation. Within the psychoanalytic tradition, we emphasize Freud's conception of the synthetic function of the ego and White's assertion of an inherent independent ego energy manifested in intrinsically motivated activities. Regarding object relations theory, we consider the proposal of the primacy of relatedness needs. Finally, we review humanistic concepts of an actualizing tendency and its support through unconditional positive regard. We conclude with a reflection on these broad themes as related to SDT's assumptions of inherent growth tendencies supported by basic psychological needs for autonomy, competence, and relatedness.

In the classical view of human development, individuals are thought to possess an inherent, active tendency toward the extension, progressive transformation, and integration of structures, functions, and experiences. By continuously stretching their capacities, expressing their propensities, and integrating new skills and knowledge into existing structures, people develop in the direction of greater effectiveness, organization, and relative unity in functioning. Regulation of action based on a synthesis of experiences and values provides the basis for a coherent and vital sense of self and integrity. In Western thought, this classic view has been expressed in various forms, from Aristotle through various philosophical dialecticians and constructivists to modern organismic theories in biology and philosophy of science. In Eastern thought, similar ideas concerning an inherent tendency toward growth and unity in being and functioning are apparent in early Taoism and Confucianism and continue in various contemporary philosophical and healing approaches.

Within the more historically delimited field of Western psychology, this view of development has been at the core of both psychodynamic (Freud, 1923; Janet, 1937; Meissner, 1981; Loevinger, 1976) and humanistic (Angyal, 1965; Ford, 1992; Rogers, 1963) theories of personality. Many theories of cognitive and social development (Piaget, 1971; Werner, 1948; Greenspan, 1979; McAdams, 2001; Nuttin, 1984; Rutter & Sroufe, 2000) have also emphasized the integrative tendency as an endogenous feature of mind (see Ryan, 1995).

This assumption of inherent integrative tendencies in human development has also had a tremendous impact within applied psychologies. Many psychotherapists understand their role as that of facilitating growth-related and integrative processes assumed to reside within the client, leading to lower conflict and greater well-being (e.g., Busch, 1995; Miller & Rollnick, 2002; Rogers, 1961; van der Hart, Nijenhuis, & Steele, 2006). Frank (1961) even defined the process of psychotherapy (as opposed to mere behavior change) as that of mobilizing these healing powers that already exist within the individual. Similarly, in education, learner-centered (Montessori, 1967; Rogers, 1969), progressive (Dewey, 1938), and constructivist (Phillips, 1995) traditions all assume an inherent curiosity and interest, a natural orientation to actively explore, create, learn, and connect. Each also embraces the value of this inherent flourishing process for enhancing the diversity and the richness of the human community (see Ryan & Lynch, 2003).

What integrity? Despite its intuitive appeal, there are strong reasons to be skeptical concerning any assumed tendencies toward progressive transformation and integration in development and personality functioning. Within psychology, the most vocal skeptics concerning propensities toward growth or integrity have been behaviorists, who assume that any direction to development is dictated by stimulus–response associations acquired through reinforcement and activated by environmental cues (Schwartz & Lacey, 1982). Skinner (1953) specifically argued that any appearance of an inner organization to behavior or personality is indicative not of an integrative tendency within humans but, rather, of organized or systematic reinforcement contingencies within their environments. Based on these assumptions, contemporary behaviorists continue to eschew development-oriented processes such as intrinsic motivation and internalization (e.g., Cameron & Pierce, 1994).

In a similar vein, some contemporary *social-cognitive* approaches portray personality not as a self-unifying system but, rather, as a collection of selves or self-schemas that are activated by environmental cues. Personality is viewed as a storehouse or "handbag" of identity-related schemata (Ryan, 1995), each of which can be cued by social contexts (e.g., Bargh, 2008; Markus & Nurius, 1986; Mischel & Shoda, 1995). Unlike their operant predecessors, most social-cognitive theorists do not explicitly deny the idea of synthetic tendencies in development but rather ignore or marginalize them, often applying them only within a small set of schema, if at all. Moreover, the natural operation of integrative or organizational tendencies is explicit in none of these approaches. Although this is the typical trend in cognitive theories, it should also be noted that some cognitive theorists have nonetheless provided "nonmotivational" accounts of cognitive consistency, or intolerance of dissonance, which recognize the trend toward a rational order among attitudes, beliefs, and motives (e.g., Abelson et al., 1968).

Some, though by no means all, evolutionary and neuropsychological approaches also oppose ideas concerning integrative processes (see Chapter 24). For example, some modularist neuropsychologists view organismic functioning primarily in terms of specific activations among accumulated mini-systems and adaptations, which become activated or dominant depending on contextual cues (Fodor, 1983; Sperber, 1994). The fact that there are localized or encapsulated functions and structures is clear, yet for some thinkers this architectural feature of the brain precludes capacities for integrative connectivity or more centralized organization. Such modularist views are often linked with an accretive model of both evolutionary adaptations and behavioral functioning. Thus in some, though again not all, modularist views (e.g., see Barrett & Kurzban, 2006; Ellis, 2009), content-independent or domain-general functions such as intrinsic motivation or integrative self-regulation would appear to be ruled out (see Hood, 2012; Pinker, 2002; Tooby & Cosmides, 1992).

Still other psychological theorists have questioned the robustness, if not the reality, of organizational tendencies in development and functioning on quite different grounds. Notions such as an integrative tendency, a centered subjectivity, or an autonomous, responsible self find no friendly home within many postmodern and cultural relativist perspectives (Ryan & Niemiec, 2009). For example, Gergen (1991) rejected the metaphor of a core self, replacing it with a postmodern view of the self as fragmented, saturated, and diversely populated by imputed and largely compartmentalized identities. Cultural relativists have similarly denied any inherent tendencies toward an integrated self, casting such models as merely cultural ideals specific to a Western individualistic outlook and accompanied by ideas such as autonomy, independence, and individuation (Markus, Kitayama, & Heiman, 1996). In the relativist view, identities are more or less imprinted by ambient cultures (Cross, Gore, & Morris, 2003; Iyengar & DeVoe, 2003).

To summarize, it appears that the field of psychology is quite divided on the issue of inherent psychological growth tendencies and the possibility of integrity in behavior. Whereas some theorists see humans as having a self-organizing and growth- and coherence-oriented nature, others see people as wholly lacking such an endowment and instead as being an amalgam of conditioned reactions. Each position seems to have some prima facie evidence in its favor: the apparent active striving toward competence, connectedness, and harmony of the self within social contexts, on the one hand, and the apparent automaticity, fragmentation, inconsistency, and malleability of human behavior and cognition on the other.

The importance of understanding the problem of integration in functioning thus cannot be overstated. As the research we review in this book makes abundantly clear, the ramifications of assuming inherent growth-related, integrative tendencies and capacities for self-organization are pervasive in domains as diverse as psychotherapy, education, work, health care, and culture. Insofar as a leader or practitioner (e.g., manager, coach, teacher, therapist) believes humans have a *natural* tendency toward understanding their world, actualizing their human potentials, and gaining integrity, then he or she will orient toward supporting and nourishing that endogenous tendency. He or she will attempt to provide the environmental and social conditions that will facilitate the natural integrative processes to function optimally. By contrast, if an authority or practitioner assumes that there exists no such inherent tendency toward self-organization and actualization in the direction of integrity, then his or her interventions will more likely focus on exogenous means of propelling and shaping behavior. He or she will train, control, reward, and direct behavior toward the goals he or she deems of value. A supportive approach only makes sense when there is an assumed inner process to support.

In this chapter, we review the history of philosophical and psychological work related to this core assumption of organizational tendencies in animate nature and their expression in the development of human personality and behavioral functioning. We begin by considering in greater depth the concept of organization in the very definition of life within biological theories. We then consider these organismic ideas of inherent or intrinsic tendencies as conceptualized within traditional theories of human cognitive development, especially Piaget's approach, and within perspectives on personality development, such as psychoanalysis and humanistic psychology. Our intent is to highlight some of the intellectual issues associated with past discussions of inherent propensities and needs and some of the deeper conceptual concerns with which a modern empirically based organismic theory, such as SDT, must grapple.

Origins of the Organismic Paradigm

The essential feature of the organismic paradigm is its emphasis on the ideas of *development* and *functional unity* (Ryan, 1993). The latter characteristic is reflected in the very definition of an *organism* as a complex structure of interdependent elements whose relations are largely determined by their function in the whole. The most fundamental attribute of all organisms, as long as they are alive and vital, is their inherent tendency to both maintain and enhance their complexity while preserving an overall integrity (Ruiz-Mirazo, Etxeberria, Moreno, & Ibáñez, 2000). They actively work to preserve or expand their structures and functions and, at the same time, to maintain autonomy and relative unity in functioning (Santelices, 1999).

The concept of *development* thus conveys much more than mere change or growth, for these latter terms can refer to virtually any type of addition or expansion (Rutter & Sroufe, 2000). An adult's waistline may change or grow, but this is hardly development. Development, instead, pertains exclusively to the subset of changes reflecting the organism's elaboration of existing structures in the direction of greater differentiation and integration (Bertalanffy, 1968; Loevinger & Blasi, 1976; Deci & Ryan, 1985b). Thus development is never simply accretive, even among simple biological forms (Medawar, 1961; Maturana & Varela, 1992), but instead implies movement in the direction of greater organization. The organismic paradigm combines both rational and empirical efforts toward the creation of coherent and practical scientific models of this ongoing process of integrated growth and self-maintenance—a process thus far appearing to be unique to animate beings.

Although many theoretical biologists and philosophers of science have acknowledged that organismic principles provide the most general and central framework for the study of living entities (e.g., Jacob, 1973; Mayr, 1982; Rosenberg, 1985; Pepper & Herron, 2008), from an historical viewpoint the organismic paradigm is a relatively recent invention, emerging as a precipitate of debates on the nature of life that occupied scientists in the latter half of the nineteenth century (Hall, 1969; Weiss, 1969). We briefly recall these debates because they take us back to the root of the problem of what differentiates life from nonlife and, more importantly, because these debates ultimately laid a foundation for the metapsychology we employ in SDT.

Reductionists versus Vitalists

At the center of the arguments that ultimately spawned the organismic perspective were two opposing groups of thinkers, typically referred to as reductionists and vitalists. *Reductionists* such as Helmholtz (1873) and Loeb (1906) argued that living entities could be fully understood in terms of material causation using explanations that are not fundamentally different from explanations for inanimate aspects of nature. Analysis of organisms into basic physicochemical processes and their efficient and material causal determinants was, in fact, the essence of the reductionistic program (Helmholtz, 1873), a program that continues to be a robust scientific orientation to this day. In contrast, *vitalists* (e.g., Bergson, 1911; Bichat, 1822; Driesch, 1908) proposed that living things could not be understood exclusively through principles appropriate to mere physical entities and that, indeed, living entities were presumed to possess certain unique and irreducible properties. Driesch (1908), for example, was an embryologist who ascribed to organisms a nonphysical principle he labeled *entelechy,* which guided the ordering and realization of organismic nature, a concept which has much in common with humanistic and psychodynamic concepts such as *actualization* (Rogers, 1963) and *individuation* (Jung, 1959). Similarly, Bergson (1911) viewed organisms as being enlivened by an *elan vital,* an energetic force through which evolution and development blossomed.

The course of these debates took the form of the reductionists making ever more detailed attempts to specify mechanisms and elements that "cause" or enable life and the vitalists responding through renewed attempts to articulate those processes and manifestations of life for which such causal analyses appeared inept. In a sense, then, the vitalists had positioned themselves in an unenviable position of ever-backward retreat, whereas reductionists could, in principle, continually refine or extend their analysis. Nonetheless, as Nobel laureate Jacob (1973) described it, even the reductionists had much to concede. As he put it: "To consider an organism, with its unity, coordination, and regulation, as composed of living elements, it had to be admitted that these elements were not merely stuck together, but integrated" (p. 116). Gould (2002) similarly argued that the "failure of reductionism doesn't mark the failure of science, but only the replacement of an ultimately unworkable set of assumptions by more appropriate styles of explanation that study complexity at its own level" (p. 227). Thus, although neither reductionists nor vitalists ever accomplished their full aims, it was out of the tension created by these arguments that a more appropriate description of living entities was to emerge—that is, a more precise characterization of those processes that needed explanation and a greater appreciation for explanations at multiple levels of analysis.

Among the most basic characteristics differentiating living organisms from inanimate entities were those concerning the concept of *entropy* (Augros & Stanciu, 1987; Schrödinger, 1944). It was observed that the general tendency of inanimate matter is toward entropy; anything that is inorganic tends to deteriorate. By contrast, animate "things," insofar as they are alive and vital, appear to be *negentropic*. They actively maintain and elaborate themselves. That is, it seems to be the very essence of organisms, while alive, to work to preserve and extend their structure and complexity, rather than to move toward entropy (Bartley, 1987; Mayr, 1982; Schrödinger, 1944). Although there has been much misunderstanding concerning the meaning of entropy and its relations to organisms (Laszlo, 1987; Prigogine & Stengers, 1984; Kauffmann, 2000), the conceptual focus on entropy has led to a heightened appreciation of the central feature of animate entities, namely, their tendency toward both greater complexity and integration, a process referred to as *organization* (Mayr, 1982). Notably, it is from this concept of organization that the term *organismic,* which we use throughout this book, is derived.

Theoretical biologists have characterized this negentropic organizational tendency in several ways. Among them is the idea that organisms are first and foremost complex *systems*. In a system "the whole is more than the sum of its parts" (Simon, 1971). In living systems this means not only that the parts cannot be defined without reference to the whole but also that, removed from the whole, they cease to function. Structures, that is, are maintained through their active interconnections with (and dependency upon) other structures.

Second, in organisms, structures within the system are conceptualized as being *hierarchically organized.* Pattee (1973) and Laszlo (1987), for example, have argued that all problems unique to biology concern the notion of hierarchical organization—how elements of lower units combine into new (larger) units that have coherent, unitary functions and properties. These functions or properties are often labeled *emergent* (Jacob, 1973; Kauffmann, 2000), implying that, with the constitution of these more complex coordinated units, properties appear that were not manifested by lower units. However, hierarchical structures are also compatible with a neural Darwinist view, in which selective processes account for the formation of higher order regulations and functions (e.g., Edelman, 1992).

Within the hierarchical view, one "emergent" property that has been widely discussed is that of *downward causation* (Bedau, 2002; Ellis, 2009; Kauffmann, 2000; Lawson, 2013; Sperry, 1976). In downward causation, a higher order unit of organization may not only be driven by lower order elements that comprise it but also may in turn function to entrain or redirect those elements. A similar conception has been advanced by Gottlieb (1992), who argued that development is characterized by increasing complexity of organization at all levels of analysis, from molecular to cellular to organismic. Some influences are within level, which he labeled *horizontal coactions*; others are between systems at different levels in this hierarchy. Gottlieb argued that *vertical coactions* are those representing either lower-to-higher or higher-to-lower influences. Such bidirectional causation, he argued, is essential to understanding individual epigenesis and developmental regulation. By whatever name, these possibilities of bidirectional causation will be especially important when we consider the issue of self-direction and the function of a person's goals and purposes in the regulation of behaviors. Yet for the time being it is critical to see only that downward or vertical causation can be deduced from the concept of organic coordination, because coordination entails organization and redirection of elements.

Biological organizations are also often defined as *open systems* (Bedau, 2002; Bertalanffy, 1968; Kauffmann, 2000; Weiss, 1969), a term that conveys that organizations are in active interaction and exchange with an environment in a manner that preserves and extends the organizations' integrity. The more organized the system, the more it can respond to perturbations or environmental changes by adaptively reconfiguring its elements in order to optimally preserve its integrity. Some theorists refer to this property as *autoregulation*. Maturana and Varela (1992), for example, used the term *autopoietic* ("self-creating") to describe this characteristic renewal, repair, and reproduction inherent in organic systems.

Parenthetically, introduction of the organismic conceptualization in modern biology neither resolved the debates between vitalists and reductionists nor stood in logical contradiction to either position. There is no specific incompatibility between the view that an organism is "merely" a material system and the idea that it possesses special integrative properties that are elaborated through its evolutionary and developmental history. Indeed, even emergentism can be presented as a thoroughly materialistic philosophy (Ellis, 2009; Mayr, 1982; Kauffmann, 2000) or in terms of a vitalism (Flanagan, 2002). In fact, the adoption of organization as a fundamental biological principle allowed these early debates between reductionists and vitalists to be largely transcended (or made increasingly irrelevant) by providing a description of life that is not derived solely by reference to either vitalistic or reductionistic tenets. In this sense, the organization paradigm is itself an emergent concept (Polanyi, 1958), affording a distinct interpretative and descriptive framework within which the facts can be discussed (Jacob, 1973). Further, it has been argued that, with the adoption of organismic principles, biology as a field was supplied with a *raison d'être*, as the task of biology became that of studying living organisms as its basic phenomena. Thus, with the concept of organization, biology had acquired a unique and widely applicable philosophy (Mayr, 1982). We think this fundamental philosophy applies to psychology just as well, given its position as a life science.

To briefly summarize, the concept of organization is rooted in biological thinking and can be linked historically to the problem of defining animate entities. The concept acknowledges (1) the active, open nature of organisms; (2) the structural character of living entities in terms of hierarchical systems; and (3) the need to focus on the unique qualities associated with the properties of active, integrative organization. Introduction of the concept of organization allowed biology to transcend an infinitely regressive debate between reductionists and vitalists, and, more importantly, it supplied the field with a general paradigm that has gained wide acceptance and supplied biology and the life sciences with an independent status within the system of the sciences.

Although the *organismic perspective* emerged from debates about the nature of animate versus inanimate entities, its introduction did not *define* life. Instead, it set the stage for characterizing and modeling the phenomena entailed in the adaptive processes and developmental trajectories manifested by living systems. In fact, as Mayr (1982) argued compellingly, defining life would be an exercise in reification, since life has no (known) existence apart from an organism. We "know" life and distinguish it from nonlife not because of any unique material constituents but because of spontaneous ordering principles that are manifested in its activity (Augros & Stanciu, 1988; Kauffmann, 2000; Polanyi, 1958). As Maturana and Varela (1992) put it, "the central feature in the organization of an organism lies in its manner of being a unity" (p. 198).

The Evolved Deep Structure of Self as an Integrative Process

As we have suggested, the fundamental basis by which one living being is distinguished from another, and from its inanimate environment, is the organized functioning attributed to it. In other words, organisms are not identified, conceptually or ontologically, merely on the basis of their physical–chemical constituents, but instead on the basis of observed organizational tendencies through which they relate in an ordered way to their surroundings and initiate and actively maintain health and integrity. This criterion of organization reflects a belief in what Polanyi (1958) labeled "primordial centres of individuality," which is a foundational concept in biological thought.

Interestingly, this attribution of lifelike qualities as a function of ordered patterns of behavior has been experimentally demonstrated in work by such seminal thinkers as Michotte (1950) and Heider and Simmel (1944). Indeed, our recognition of such ordering processes is, as Polanyi (1958) argued, a *convivial passion,* in which we appreciate patterned operations and attribute them to an active center. At all levels of life organisms are engaged in "biotic performances" that convey an inner organization, and, in this, we humans share a kinship.

Organisms do of course vary in complexity. At some point in the evolution of biotic forms, for example, consciousness was greatly elaborated (Edelman, 1992), probably in concert with the development of perceptual systems that extended and centralized the control of the organism with respect to its environment. It was also at this point that, as Polanyi (1958) argued, there emerged the polarity of subject and object, with its fateful obligations to form expectations and to learn from experience. With this emergence, "the first faint thrills of intellectual joy appeared in the emotional life of the animal" (p. 388). In terms of awareness of that regulation, the study of evolutionary forms indicates that there has indeed been a successive intensification of consciousness. Merker (2007), drawing from Indian discussions of sentience, describes this succession of forms of awareness as looking something like: (1) "This"; (2) "This is so"; (3) "I am affected by this which is so"; and (4) "So this is I who am affected by this which is so." These forms of consciousness each depend upon an increasingly sophisticated architecture of the brain, allowing in turn for new organizational capacities (and challenges) of mind.

It is of course true too that, unlike other species, humans' awareness of themselves as individual centers of perception, thought, and action, and their appreciation of others as similar subjective centers, emerges early in development (see Mitchell, 2003). Yet these unique capacities for reflection and self-awareness are tools or instruments of the organismic center; they do not create that center (Merker, 2007). Human consciousness, with the corresponding sense of personhood, the invention of language, and the appreciation of others as centers of thought, extends the organism's mental outreach and enormously enhances the "intellectual joys" of living action of which Polanyi more eloquently spoke. Nonetheless, even the concept of self, which is central to our theorizing within SDT, must be recognized as not referring to something handed down discontinuously from nature but to an attribute that has manifestations across manifold forms of life. It has its origins or deep structure in the principle that many animate forms entail an organizing center or integrative regulatory functionality (Panksepp, Moskal, Panksepp, & Kroes, 2002).

Evolutionary thinking provides many accounts of why self-organization matters, and has become elaborated and related to the variety of adaptive outcomes yielded by increasingly flexible and yet coordinated behavior (see Chapter 24). Clearly, an organism that fails at the tasks of coordination of its parts and functions is in serious trouble in most contexts. Animals whose motives are divided or in conflict or that fail to hierarchically coordinate their goals will simply be less likely to survive, as, for example, when an animal fails to stop feeding as a predator approaches or lets grooming take precedence over sleep. Furthermore, organisms (particularly mammalian species) that do not explore, assimilate new information, and manipulate novel objects may find themselves less flexible in the face of changes in their niche (Waller, 1998). Intrinsic motivations for exploration and play, both common across mammals (Wilson, 1982), thus directly prepare animals for adaptive challenges.

As noted, for humans, we refer to this regulatory center, with its intrinsically motivated curiosity and capacity for internalization, as the *self,* and we have argued that it too is an evolved process. The situation for evolutionary psychology, then, is strikingly parallel to the early history of motivation theory itself, which, as we will see in greater detail in Chapter 5, spent several decades trying to explain self-initiated behaviors by reference to basic drives such as sex, hunger, and pain avoidance (e.g., Fenichel, 1945; Hull, 1943), before being forced to recognize that these motives occur within the context of overarching integrative and regulatory processes (Deci & Ryan, 1985b; White, 1963). Similarly, when evolutionary theory took hold in psychology in the 1990s, it was focused almost exclusively on the drive-related behaviors—particularly sex, dominance, and aggression—while neglecting the evolution of the central organizing processes that serve to regulate such drive-related behaviors. There was, in fact, great caution toward consideration of any of those general organizational features of life so central to theoretical biologists (Tooby & Cosmides, 1992). Thus, by not placing the idea of organization at its center, one comes to think of evolution as a process through which we have become mere aggregates of adaptations, what we have called the "pile of stones" approach to evolution (see Deci & Ryan, 2000). Yet perhaps the most general and obvious bestowal of the history of life has been the existence within us of the regulatory functions (Polanyi, 1958; Maturana & Varela, 1992; Panksepp & Northoff, 2009), functions that work to coordinate not only these drives, but also other needs, goals, and wants.

In sum, placing the idea of self in a biological perspective acknowledges the continuity of our active phenomenal core with the coordinated and active nature of other biological entities who share with us the condition of *life*. Although other animals may lack humans' highly developed awareness of their individuality, they nonetheless manifest active organizational centers of varying sophistication. It is this center of organization that, in evolutionary perspective, represents the deep structure upon which the phenomenological sense of self and autonomy is likely built.

Organization and Psychological Paradigms

If the concept of organization is, as we have argued, tied to the overall problem of the animate, then to what extent is psychology a life science? And to what extent is the scientific study of psychological processes informed by the idea of organization that serves as the underpinning for biological sciences more generally? These issues particularly concern the fields of personality, motivation, and development, wherein the issues of hierarchical organization and hierarchical causation are critically implicated. In fact, several of the most important macro-theories in the history of psychology have addressed the tie between life and psychological phenomena directly, explicitly embracing the language of an organismic paradigm. Because we draw to varying extents upon these conceptual frameworks, we now turn to a consideration of the organization principle as represented within these well-known approaches.

Organization in Cognitive-Developmental Theory

Theories of cognitive development have typically placed heavy emphasis on the tendency toward organization (Cicchetti, 2006; Deci & Ryan, 2012; Overton, 1991). Heinz Werner (1948) brought this tradition saliently into the field of developmental psychology, arguing that human psychological development is best understood as an instance of organic development. Werner's *orthogenetic principle* specified that psychological development "is expressed in increasing differentiation of parts and an increasing subordination or hierarchization" (p. 41). Werner applied this general model to mental functions such as perception and motility (Gibson, 1969), and, in a more limited way, to personality functions. Thus his formulation of the tendency toward hierarchical integration offers a structural description of the organization function at work, one drawn directly from biological models.

Piagetian Theory

The most renowned developmental theorist to explicitly apply the organismic paradigm was Jean Piaget. Piaget (1971) argued that cognitive functions represent a specialized organ for regulating exchanges with the external world and that both the nature of these exchanges and their organization are drawn from the general forms of living organization—that is, from a biological foundation. For him, cognitive functions were an extension of the organic organization of life, an extension that expands one's functional mastery of the environment.

Piaget described psychological organization in primarily structural terms. That is, the central focus of his work was the description of an invariant progression or sequence of structures or stages in cognitive and affective development that result from life's "tendency to extend itself" (1971, p. 204). Each stage was viewed as building upon and encompassing those prior to it, and each involved an internal coherence or equilibrium of its own. As Piaget (1952) stated it, "there is above all a total organization; that is to say coordination among the various schemata or assimilations" (p. 142).

This "total organization" is accomplished through the function of *reciprocal assimilation,* a natural tendency of the psyche, through which the whole is conserved in "relational totality." Piaget argued that such ongoing reciprocal assimilation is a *functional invariant*—a continuous process throughout successive transformations and covariations of structure. In acting as a whole, the totality in turn reciprocally coordinates all its elements, lending it increased cohesion and equilibrium.

Although Piaget fully embraced the organismic paradigm, it should be noted that he did so in a manner that was steadfastly consistent with structuralism. He explicitly rejected all forms of vitalism, and he also argued against the concept of emergence. For him, to call a structure "emergent" was only to locate a problem, whereas a structural approach would seek to understand the specific transformations and reorganizations entailed (Piaget, 1971). Finally, Piaget's structuralism was not at all focused on the self or agent per se as the constructor of knowledge but, rather, on the coming into being of structures—that is, on constructive processes themselves. Further, although his work deals with increasing self-regulation, Piaget does not typically depict people as knowing or being in command of the mechanisms or functions through which this regulation is achieved (Dean & Youniss, 1991).

Piaget's organizational approach has spawned two major forms of critique, both of which are relevant to SDT's application of organizational principles. The first concerns the generality of developmental progress. Recall that Piaget's organizational framework predicts an internal coherence within each stage of development that results from reciprocal assimilation. These stages, in turn, describe the generalized framework through which people interpret and act within their social and physical environments (Griffin, 1995; Loevinger & Blasi, 1991). Critics have pointed out that this presumed coherence is at best a matter of degree. There are gaps and inconsistencies in stage-related organization, which Piaget described as *decalage,* and these compartmentalized skills and schemata are sometimes quite salient (Chandler & Chapman, 1991). For example, Fischer, Knight, and Van Parys (1993) highlighted how enhanced exposure or opportunities to practice specific skills can lead to advanced cognitive capacities within specific domains relative to others. Moreover, contextual and cultural supports can amplify individual differences in developmental sequences (Deci & Ryan, 1985b; Lewis, 1994). Finally, because there appear to be distinct domains of functioning within cognition, generality of progress is both specific and constrained (e.g., Demetriou, Efklides, & Platsidou, 1993). Piagetians have retorted, however, that there is also evidence of considerable age-level consistencies across a broad array of developmental tasks, especially during middle childhood, even if such generality is somewhat constrained by the distinctiveness of particular domains of cognition (e.g., Case & Okamoto, 1996; Griffin, 1995).

One can question whether the fact of decalage or domain specificity calls into question an overarching organizational view of cognitive development or, instead, simply suggests that the ways in which organizational processes develop and the likelihood that they will be situationally expressed are themselves a function of both pervasive and proximal affordances and supports. This latter view is consistent with our own perspective; the motivation to engage and regulate activity is heightened in particular domains, and forestalled or conflicted in others, as a function of social contextual supports and hindrances, and this in turn influences both cognitive development and sustained interest within any given domain. Similarly, environments supply differential affordances (e.g., stimulating materials, optimal challenges) that amplify or diminish interest, assimilation, and skill development, again domain specifically or, in other cases, with some generality. We thus specifically consider within-person variations in regulatory functioning and developmental outcomes both in terms of opportunities to develop and as a function of the supports for the needs that energize motivation and engagement. We contend that a motivational analysis of developmental processes has much to contribute to the understanding of why the degree of coordination—cognitive, affective, or regulatory—may differ not only from individual to individual but also within person from domain to domain (Deci & Ryan, 2013a).

This leads us, however, to a second, and for us more important, type of critique that has been leveled at Piaget's organizational assumptions. This concerns Piaget's treatment of the *motivation* that underlies cognitive development (Deci & Ryan, 1985b; Ryan & Deci, 2013). As previously suggested, the activity of organization was said by Piaget to be "natural" or "automatic," and thus its motivation or energization received little specific attention. As Wolff (1960) noted, the only explicit motive in Piaget's theory is a "need to function" inherent in the nature of structures. Flavell (1977) similarly stated that Piaget's position was "simply that there is an intrinsic need in cognitive organs or structures, once generated by functioning, to perpetuate themselves by more functioning" (p. 78).

Although not very specific, Piaget's notion that cognitive structures have an "inherent tendency to function" is, as we understand it, consistent with the concept of intrinsic motivation and its determinants as specified in *cognitive evaluation theory* (CET; see Chapters 6 and 7). First, it highlights that one does not need to look outside the system to find the motivation for exercising structures or for developing coordination among structures. In fact, Piagetian apologists (e.g., Flavell, Miller, & Miller, 2002) have argued that in cognitive development at all levels, new assimilatory activities (especially those requiring accommodation) are *typically* intrinsically motivated, whereas one typically uses existing skills and applies already developed schema only for extrinsic reasons (see also Elkind, 1971). Flavell et al. (2002) pointed out, in fact, that Piaget himself observed that children are most receptive to new learning when the main reason to act is something *interesting* in the environment. Moreover, *what* interests them are stimuli that the children can almost, but not quite, understand—those that are "novel, complex, surprising, or puzzling"—and a child will be "motivated to continue to act toward the event until she has somehow made sense of it" (p. 67). As we specify in CET, novelty and optimal challenge are catalyzers of intrinsic motivation, and their motivational "pull" is based in the basic psychological need for competence.

Piaget's (1981) analysis of the affective aspects of assimilation also lends support to the connections between cognitive development and SDT's construct of intrinsic motivation. Although in Piaget's view affect and cognition are functionally inseparable properties of assimilation, he nonetheless argued that the relations between affect and cognition can be further analyzed. Specifically, he stated that "the affective aspect of assimilation is *interest*, defined by Dewey as assimilation to the self" (1981, p. 4). Consider, for example, a child's organization of certain play materials. The cognitive aspects of this action would be contained in the logico-mathematical description of the schema applied by the child, while the corresponding affective aspect would be the child's interest in the task.

We, of course, see *interest* as a central affective marker of intrinsic motivation (Deci, 1992; Krapp, 2002; Reeve, Deci, & Ryan, 2004). According to CET (Chapters 6 and 7), interest is manifested in the child's spontaneous engagement with such play materials, and such interest will be enhanced if these materials are novel and optimally challenging and other extrinsic pressures are not salient (e.g., Danner & Lonky, 1981; Kashdan, Rose, & Fincham, 2004). The implications of this, in turn, are that the conditions that facilitate and undermine intrinsic motivation and interest, which we shall further specify in CET, may have an impact upon cognitive-developmental processes and outcomes within and across domains. Here, motivational perspectives can add a dynamic piece to understanding some of the gaps and desynchronizations identified by cognitive psychologists, in which motivational influences may amplify the domain specificity of cognitive and knowledge structures.

Returning to Piaget's view, he argued that the primary tendency of structures to function (which we describe as intrinsic motivation) is a stage-independent characteristic or, in his terms, a *functional invariant*. At all levels of development, he saw the organism endeavoring to organize the world, to incorporate the external into its own organization, to discover more complex aspects of the world, and to organize all this into a coherent unity. This, too, mirrors a fundamental tenet behind SDT (Deci & Ryan, 1985b, 2012). It is our assumption that there is an intrinsic and natural psychological tendency toward synthesis, which at the same time can be either hindered or fostered by specific social-contextual conditions that either thwart or support satisfaction of the basic psychological needs.

To the extent that Piaget neglected the issue of the motivation behind organizational or developmental change, he did so largely because he ascribed the operation of organization to simply the "nature of life" (see Piaget, 1971; Witherington, 2014), a position that removed motivation from closer scrutiny within his theorizing. In contrast, we believe that viewing assimilation as *a motivated process* that can be undermined or supported provides a meaningful basis for exploring and interpreting the effects of various social factors on this natural tendency toward organization. In turn, this can shed light upon both between-person differences in development and within-person variability, including some (but not all) of the issues associated with decalage and domain-specific advances and delays. In essence, explicitly studying motivational elements allows for a *social psychology* of cognitive development (Ryan & Deci, 2013), something that has been "notoriously lacking" in the Piagetian framework (Schröder & Edelstein, 1991). Thus, insofar as assimilation is intrinsically motivated (Flavell et al., 2002), one can draw explicit hypotheses from the experimental work on intrinsic motivation about the interpersonal and informational conditions that facilitate versus obstruct progress along varied developmental pathways. Such a social psychology attends not only to general facilitating environments, such as novelty and complexity, but also to irregularities and individual differences that are, in part, due to enriched and impoverished social contexts. The implications are particularly strong for the field of developmental psychopathology, in which interest in the impact of perturbations and nutrients on integrated development is a central issue (Cicchetti & Toth, 2009). As a social-developmental view, need-supportive versus need-thwarting conditions (e.g., as specified in CET) would be understood as modifying, rather than creating, the "natural bent" of our psyches, namely that organizational tendency that Piaget described as "the very nature of life."

Organization in Personality Development

The biological concept of self-organization has been applied not only to cognitive development but also to personality development and to virtually every theory in which a role is given to a self or ego system in the regulation of behavior. Because these matters are implicated within our work in SDT, we turn now to a consideration of how the organization principle has been historically applied within macro-theories of personality development. We begin with the seminal example of psychoanalysis and its transition to ego psychology, and after that we turn to humanistic and existential traditions.

The Psychoanalytic Tradition

The self-organization principle plays a central, though often unrecognized, role in psychoanalytic theorizing. Although early in Freud's work this emphasis on organization was largely implicit, by the latter half of his career, he was explicitly placing importance on the organizational tendency, particularly through his postulate of the ego's *synthetic function*. Moreover, throughout his career, Freud viewed psychological integration and unity as a key indicator of mental health.

Interestingly, Freud's early scientific training as a physiologist involved a highly reductionistic worldview (Sulloway, 1979) in which he enthusiastically embraced the philosophies of Helmholtz and his contemporaries. Yet as Freud turned his attention to psychological phenomena, it is apparent that the relative integration of the psyche quickly took center stage. In his very first psychoanalytic work, namely his collaboratively developed theory of hysteria (Breuer & Freud, 1893–1895/1955), hysterics were characterized as people who suffer from "reminiscences" that are not integrated with the rest of their psychic makeup. As Freud (1900/1953) subsequently argued, "an idea becomes pathogenic when its content is in opposition to the predominant trend of the patient's mental life" or is dissociated because it is incompatible with the "dominant mass of ideas" (p. 109). This formulation implies a relative unity or connectedness within the dominant mass as a healthy characteristic of the psyche and the inability to integrate experiences within this relative unity as indicative of pathology. Accordingly, Freud's early approaches to treatment entailed bringing these disconnected ideas to consciousness (along with the emotional charge accompanying them) and thereby connecting them with the totality or dominant mass of ideas already available to consciousness. That is, even this very early psychodynamic model reveals Freud's assumption that in a healthy personality there is coherence and integration (Eagle, 1991; Lettieri, 2005).

Freud took great interest in, and indeed spent the middle of his long career focused on, what kinds of experiences tend to be split off or not integrated into consciousness. He found in the largely female patients he worked with that it was particularly sexual and aggressive experiences and motives that were unintegrated. We have no reason to doubt, given the nature of Victorian culture and its restrictive societal norms (especially for women), that he was indeed in touch with a major focus of repression and controlled forms of self-regulation. As SDT might formulate it, people experienced or anticipated various negative contingencies for too explicitly expressing sexuality, and the controlling culture for women led to introjections that supported sexual repression and associated symptoms of ill-being. That is, the regulation of sexual desires would not be integrated for most of Freud's patients, lest patients experience a loss of connections to and positive regard from parents, living or dead. For us, then, it is not sex per se that leads to nonintegration but the controlling social attitudes that led people to feel the pressure to repress it (e.g., see Weinstein, W. S. Ryan, et al., 2012, with respect to homosexuality in contemporary cultures).

Freud's full embrace of an explicit concept of organization appeared only in 1923 with the advent of his structural model, in which the ego is posited as a central structure of personality. Freud defined the *ego* as the primary organ of adaptation, mediating between the demands of the innate biological drives and the constraints and prohibitions of reality (primarily, the family). Although Freud characterized the ego (*das Ich,* or "I") as merely a "poor creature owing service to three masters" (the id, the environment, and the superego), he at the same time proposed that it culls its own *independent energy* out of what were originally erotic drives. Specifically, Freud hypothesized that the ego has at its disposal a "desexualized" or neutralized energy, stemming from a narcissistic store of libido.

We turn shortly to Freud's model of how the ego acquires this neutralized energy, but for now we note that in his view these now neutralized energies continue to express the original aim of life—unity and assimilation (*Eros*). Once appropriated by the ego, this energy retains its inherent tendency toward integration or cohesion. Freud (1923) thus noted that the ego's energy has as its main purpose "that of uniting and binding—insofar as it helps toward establishing the unity, or tendency to unity, which is particularly characteristic of the ego" (p. 35). This *synthetic function of the ego,* as Freud referred to it, represents a foundational concept upon which much of subsequent psychoanalytic developmental psychology would be built.

We note that, etymologically, *synthesis* means "to bring together," and thus the ego's energy is oriented toward bringing together alien and contradictory elements within the psyche. The ego's synthetic function, in short, leads people toward exploring, understanding, and making sense of their inner and outer worlds and toward resolving whatever anomalies and contradictions one locates in experience at both boundaries.

Freud highlighted that the ego's pervasive tendency toward unification and synthesis is evident in myriad ways. For example, clinicians often experience the ego's attempts to produce harmony among psychic structures and strivings—in its intolerance of contradiction. Fellow psychoanalysts such as Nunberg (1931) elaborated on the importance of the synthetic function in the human tendency toward causal thinking and organization of reality and in such creative activities as science and art. Nunberg also suggested that symptom formation in neuroses is frequently a manifestation of the ego's attempts to minimize conflict, that is, to do the best it can to attain relative unity under difficult circumstances. Thus, for example, elements that cannot be unified will be dissociated— blocked or compartmentalized by rigid structures—and will be expressed as pathology, a dynamic we especially explore in Chapters 8 and 24. As Freud would put it, symptoms are often *compromise formations,* filling in or compensating where synthesis cannot easily occur.

A central theme for Freud as a practicing clinician was that the existence of a synthetic tendency hardly made psychological unity automatic. Indeed, in the psychoanalytic model, synthesis is an achievement, the outcome of a struggle that can never reach complete fruition. Freud saw the ego, the "I" of each one of us, as ever struggling to maintain some ascendancy over the chaotic, emotional, and destructive aspects within us (Bettelheim, 1982). Thus, in Freud's view, the yardstick of mental health is the relative degree of unity the ego, or "I," attains. That is, unlike Piaget, who focused on the structural regularities that result as the organization process naturally proceeds within cognitive development, Freud saw that the synthetic function of the ego or self, which has to grapple with self and social development, could be readily derailed by both biological and societal forces. This was especially apparent with respect to particular contents, such as sexual identity and relations with family and authority.

Subsequently, Hartmann (1958) placed the synthetic function of the ego in a superordinate role in his model of development. He suggested that the ego, as the specific organ of adaptation, performs the dual functions of differentiation and synthesis in the coordination and hierarchization of other functions. Insofar as the ego is effective, the result will be stability, autonomy, and equilibrium, characterizing the mentally healthy person. The synthetic function is applied to both the "outer" and "inner" worlds across development, leading to improved mastery of the physical and social environment *and* the regulation and expression of drives and affects (Shapiro, 1965). Thus both personality adaptation and coherence are the intertwined outcomes of the synthetic function.

Another prominent ego psychologist, French (1958), similarly viewed the process of synthesis or integration as the core problem of developmental and clinical theory. He argued that the role of the ego or the "I" is not primarily to defend against drives or unconscious material but rather to learn how to *satisfy the needs of the organism.* The process of synthesis concerns the degree to which needs and behavioral consequences are capable of being "taken into account" in the determination of behavior. In French's analysis, both successful development and psychotherapy move in the direction of increasing people's *integrative span*—that is, their ability to accept and satisfy needs in a purposive and practical manner, rather than to interrupt, stifle, or deny them. Further, he suggests that the failure to deal effectively with organismic needs—that is, to integrate them into the determinants of behavior—is the source of much neurotic conflict and pathology.

The notion of personality development as the product of the ego developing through its synthetic function has been perhaps most explicitly argued in the work of Jane Loevinger (e.g., Loevinger, 1976; Loevinger & Blasi, 1991). Loevinger, both a psychodynamic theorist and an empirically focused researcher, adopted a structural view of personality akin to Piaget's theory of intelligence. She considered the organization of personality to be the result of development and ego development to be the progressive structuralization of drives, affects, and cognitions into a stable unity. This unity differs at different stages of development, stages that progressively widen in their scope, understanding, and integrative span. Yet, whereas within Piaget's theory most people progress through each stage in a way that is reasonably age invariant, within Loevinger's many people fail to reach the more mature stages of ego development.

Still, as with Piaget's work, it is not Loevinger's stages of structural development that concern us but rather the stage-independent aspects of her theory. Notably, Loevinger viewed the ego most centrally as a process of synthesis. She stated this clearly: "From my view, the organization of the synthetic function is not just another thing the ego does, it is what the ego is" (1976, p. 5), and "the striving to master, to integrate, and make sense of experience is the essence of the ego itself" (p. 59). Thus in her approach the ego *is* the activity of organization, the result of which can be progressive structure.

Looking across these theoretical and clinical contributions, we see a general trend in psychoanalysis, and particularly in psychoanalytic ego psychology, toward considering how personality development occurs through organizational, integrative activity. The resulting synthesis helps define both the individual's adaptive capacities (his or her competencies) and the coherence and integrity of the regulation of behaviors.

MOTIVATION AND SYNTHESIS: INDEPENDENT EGO ENERGY

Recall that, in setting forth his concept of the ego's synthetic function, Freud modified his theory to include neutralized ego energy (i.e., desexualized Eros), the energy used for the ego's integrative tasks. *Eros,* the original life drive, strives for contact and unity. In its primordial forms, Eros is sexual in the general sense that it aims toward bonding or unifying with others. Yet, even after the ego appropriates this energy for its own purposes (by desexualizing and channeling it), the energy retains its characteristic tendency toward unity and synthesis.

Hartmann (1958) played a pivotal role in the emergence of modern psychoanalysis by reformulating and clarifying the ego's synthetic functions in development. He stressed the role of the ego in adaptation and suggested that the ego derives *conflict-free pleasure* through the exercise of its functions and capacities, a process that results in the growth of competence. We might consider this conflict-free, mastery-oriented energy akin to our concept of intrinsic motivation. Thus, for Hartmann, the infant's curious exploration and the adult's search for insight are both expressions of adaptive, conflict-free ego energy at work. Hartmann, however, retained Freud's idea that these ego energies were products of neutralization, which means that they are ultimately derivative of deeper erotic strivings rather than being primary organismic propensities in their own right. This afforded Hartmann a concept of quasi-independent, or non-drive-dependent, motives for adaptation, without placing him in conflict with the orthodox Freudian postulates concerning the primacy of sexual drives.

It thus remained for White (1963) to take psychoanalytic thinking a final, and historically crucial, step further by providing a theory-based place for an *intrinsic ego energy* that serves to organize personality. White agreed with Hartmann concerning the theoretical need for independent ego energy, especially in reference to adaptive activities such as play, curiosity, exploration, and understanding. Yet White noted that the supposed process of "neutralization" of libido lacks specificity and at times leads to circuitous explanations. Citing evidence from studies of both child development and animal learning, White hypothesized that the ego is not simply a derivative of conflict but rather has intrinsic energy of its own, such that people derive natural satisfactions and pleasure from the exercise of their capacities and functions. He referred to this energy as *effectance*, and the corresponding affect as the *feeling of efficacy*. As White stated: "Effectance thus refers to the active tendency to put forth effort to influence the environment, while the feeling of efficacy refers to the satisfaction that comes with producing effects" (p. 185). For White, *competence* was the accumulated result of one's interactions with the environment.

White's (1959) seminal work was not only the forerunner of current theories of intrinsic motivation (Deci, 1975; Deci & Ryan, 1985b) but also influenced the field of developmental psychology by specifying effectance motivation as the central force behind children "playing" their way toward a knowledge of the external world. White considered his central premise compatible with the Piagetian view that structures have an inherent propensity to function, and he also subscribed to a natural continuity hypothesis by explicitly citing examples of effectance motivation in a variety of species. He once commented, "squirrels too have a 'push from within' that governs their actions" (R. White, personal communication, June 1990).

In SDT we draw on these dynamic formulations in our understanding of the self in self-determination. In line with Loevinger (1976; Loevinger & Blasi, 1991) and Eagle (1991), we view the self as, in essence, a synthetic function, reflecting the psyche's inherent tendency toward organization and integration. At the same time, we agree with the point that psychoanalysts have long recognized—namely, that not all aspects of the person are well synthesized and that some are internalized in merely an introjected fashion, whereas others remain quite external or alien to the self (e.g., Schafer, 1968; Meissner, 1981). As also recognized within ego psychology, we suggest that, to the degree that people operate from well-integrated as opposed to less integrated regulations, they will exhibit more vitality, coherence, and well-being. This thinking is reflected in many of our postulates in OIT (Chapter 8).

At the same time, there are fundamental differences between our views and those of psychoanalysis, especially more orthodox psychoanalytic schools. Primary among these is our understanding that human beings have fundamental psychological needs and that these basic needs energize and guide much human motivation and behavior. In our view, of course, the most basic *psychological* needs are those for competence, relatedness, and autonomy, and it is the struggle to experience satisfaction of these needs that we use to explain the dynamics of most human behaviors, as we shall elaborate. Although drives such as sex, aggression, and hunger have import in human affairs, it is primarily because they interact with the basic psychological needs that they become highly salient. Thus, when Freud's Victorian patients failed to integrate their sexual natures, leading to repression and dysfunction, this was, in our view, not a reflection of the primacy of sex per se. Rather, it reflected the fact that, in that cultural context, being sexual and more generally having voice and empowerment in their relationships (especially for the middle-class women Freud treated) was socially suppressed and thus was incompatible with relatedness and could not be "owned" as part of their identity. The struggles and introjects observed by Freud, although palpable, are explicable to us in terms of the dynamics of a social world that was oppressively pressuring and controlling concerning sexual contents, resulting in what we will observe as internally controlling states.

Similarly, a central dynamic in Freud's work concerns the Oedipal complex and, more generally, a series of psychosexual stages that are presumed to shape later personality. With Freud we share a belief in the importance of early experience in the family. Yet, where he saw repression of anality, we focus on the impact of excessive parental control versus autonomy support in the developing toddler; where he focused on castration fears, we focus on the problem of internalization and the dynamics of autonomy and relatedness in early to middle childhood; and where he (and followers such as Blos, 1979) focused on a reemergence of Oedipal issues in adolescence, we focus on the dynamics of autonomy and relatedness in a period of widening social influences and attachments (e.g., Ryan & Lynch, 1989).

In short, social norms differ with history and culture, and in many modern cultures sex per se is less dynamically implicated in the etiology of mental illness. Nonetheless, Freud and his followers, although they did not formulate it in this way, had an acute sense of the way in which persons, if excessively controlled, rejected, or hampered in self-organization (i.e., if needs for autonomy, relatedness, and competence were thwarted), would react in defensive, compensatory, or need-substituting fashions (e.g., A. Freud, 1937). As clinicians, we continue to marvel at his dynamic approach and insights, while using more contemporary dynamic thinking based on a model of fundamental psychological needs that differs from his early drive-based psychology. As regards the issues of underlying motivations, SDT has more in common with modern ego psychology (and its focus on autonomy and competence) and object relations theories (with their focus on relatedness) than with classical psychoanalytic theory. It is to these more recent perspectives that we briefly turn.

INTERPERSONAL SYNTHESIS: OBJECT RELATIONS AND ATTACHMENT

It is of special interest for our discussion of psychological organization that cognitive-developmental and ego-psychological theories focused primarily on the coordination and cohesion of cognitive and intrapsychic processes, while placing relatively less emphasis on the organizational issues that concern cohesion and coordination within the interpersonal and social realms. Yet dyads, groups, and societies are also organizational structures made up of individuals who strive to achieve or maintain cohesion and unity within their relationships and groups (Laszlo, 1987).

The importance of interpersonal factors was apparent in early psychoanalysis, which, although explicitly intrapsychically focused, considered the tendency toward unity of the self to be only secondary to the aim of unity with others. Freud was, in essence, arguing that the drive toward union with others is a psychological force that grows out of organic nature and plays a principal role in organizing mind and behavior. Subsequently, as ego psychology evolved, with its focus on the ego's independent energy and synthetic tendencies, another strand of psychoanalytic thought was evolving with a focus on this basic and innate striving for connection and union with others. Its most notable proponents are referred to as *object relations* theorists, who moved psychodynamic thinking increasingly toward the importance of relationships in personality development and functioning (Mitchell & Black, 1995).

Object relations theorists largely rejected the orthodox view that the motivation to sustain relationships is derivative of the sexual drive and instead proposed that psychic energy (libido) is principally relationship seeking (e.g., Fairbairn, 1952). Eros seeks not to discharge sexual energy but rather to build and maintain connections with others, and it is this basic assertion that is the starting point for the analysis of personality development.

This assumption is key. First, it suggests a fundamental need for relatedness that people's natural energies are prone to satisfy (Slavin & Kriegman, 1992). Second, object relations theorists argue that the quality of care and nurturance afforded to the developing individual affects that person's ongoing capacity to integrate conceptions of self and other and to regulate behavior. Indeed, as Winnicott (1965) highlighted, the development and functioning of a "true self" and the capacity for autonomy are themselves dependent upon having a sensitive and responsive caregiving environment.

Another interpersonally oriented theory also born from this matrix of psychoanalytic thinking is Bowlby's (1969, 1973) attachment theory. Like the object relations theorists, Bowlby maintained that there is a primary human striving—indeed, a *need*—to form and maintain a secure sense of belonging and connectedness with others. Bowlby emphasized that this striving is not unique to humans and pointed out the continuity of human attachment processes with those of other primates and mammalian species.

As with Winnicott, within attachment theory, a key to the formation of secure attachments is, interestingly, a sensitive and responsive caregiving environment. Sensitivity and responsiveness, in turn, concern support for the child's basic needs. As Bretherton (1987, p. 1075) stated: "In the framework of attachment theory, maternal respect for the child's autonomy is an aspect of sensitivity to the infant's signals." Sroufe (1990) similarly described support for autonomy and competence efforts, against a backdrop of warmth and caring, as essential to the development of secure attachment. Even in the dynamics of adult attachments, supports for all three needs are essential to security with specific social partners (La Guardia, Ryan, Couchman, & Deci, 2000). Thus relatedness, an essential psychological need, is inexorably intertwined with people's feelings that their other two basic psychological needs are also supported in the context of a relationship.

Later in this book (especially Chapters 12, 13, and 16) we take up the issue of how the SDT's basic need for *relatedness* relates to modern research derived from attachment theory. As we have argued, relatedness can be viewed as an intrinsic psychological need, essential to well-being and development, that fuels processes linking the individual to the social group and motivates the processes of identification and internalization and many spontaneous interests. For now, within this historical review, we merely lay out the possibility that relatedness represents a synthetic process between and among individuals that Angyal (1965) referred to as *homonomy* and that complements the synthetic process within individuals that he referred to as *autonomy* and that is emphasized by ego psychologists.

Organization as Actualization: The Humanistic Approach

Growth, assimilation, and synthesis are thus seen as intrinsic properties of psychological organization in psychoanalytic and cognitive-developmental thought. A related core concept that pervades humanistic psychologies is that of *actualization,* a construct whose modern roots can be traced to Kurt Goldstein. Goldstein's (1939) pioneering work was an attempt to place the study of personality squarely within the scope of the life sciences. He stated that the organism's "tendency to actualize its nature, to actualize 'itself,' is the basic drive, the only drive by which the life of the organism is determined" (p. 196). Goldstein was convinced that organisms have specific potentials, along with a need to actualize them.

For Goldstein, actualization was thus the basic nature of animate life. It pertained equally to biology and anthropology, and the development of personality was for him simply an extension of this characteristic of life. This need to actualize one's potentials, that is, was considered to be operative across the strata of animate nature and to be fully applicable to the psychological life of humans. Goldstein saw in the principle of actualization a basis for understanding the creative power of people, and he understood psychopathology as a disruption of this tendency.

THE PERSON-CENTERED APPROACH

Carl Rogers, perhaps the most influential of humanistic theorists, made extensive use of Goldstein's idea of actualization and, like Goldstein, explicitly connected the tendency for actualization in personality to its biological roots. In a memorable passage, he wrote:

> Whether we are speaking of this sea plant or an oak tree, of an earthworm or a great night-flying moth, of an ape or a man, we will do well, I believe, to recognize that life is an active process, not a passive one. Whether the stimulus arises from within or without, whether the environment is favorable or unfavorable, the behaviors of an organism can be counted on to be in the direction of maintaining, enhancing and reproducing itself. This is the very nature of the process we call life. (Rogers, 1963, p. 3)

Rogers considered the actualizing tendency to be operative at all times in all organisms and to be the basic motivational tendency underlying behavior. In fact, for Rogers the actualizing tendency was the only motive required for explaining organismic activity, as all behavior, at some level, reflects the propensity of the organism to act toward its own maintenance and enhancement.

Notably, however, in Rogers's view, the actualization tendency can often be obscured or diverted in the human personality because of people's capacity to internalize social teachings, not all of which are congruent with the basic organismic actualization tendency. According to Rogers, feeling strongly connected to and loved by others is a necessary condition for individuals to maintain and enhance their sense of self. Yet, if the love or positive regard of significant others is made contingent upon individuals' feeling or behaving in certain ways, they may internalize the requisite prescriptions, values, and opinions and then act "as if" those prescriptions were a part of themselves. Insofar as what is internalized is incongruent with people's organismic conditions, neurosis is the likely outcome. In fact, like SDT and psychoanalysis, Rogers sometimes used the concept of introjection to refer to the process of internalizing prescriptions that are incongruent with people's organismic and psychological needs and then using them as a basis for pressured regulation. Rogers argued, and SDT research has further shown, that introjection is most likely to occur in social circumstances that are controlling, including those characterized by conditional regard (e.g., see Roth, Assor, Niemiec, Ryan, & Deci, 2009).

In Rogers's theorizing, the need to be related to, or positively regarded by, others is a central aspect of actualization: A sense of relatedness serves the maintenance and enhancement of the self and organism. Further, Rogers also explicitly theorized that authenticity and autonomy are also necessary for actualization. Thus the dual motives of relatedness and autonomy are organismically complementary, and the social conditions that support both motives provide the greatest opportunity for integration and the development of a "fully functioning" person. Yet these dual motives are often made incompatible within specific social conditions, most notably when positive regard is used as a vehicle of control by being made contingent upon compliance. Rogers's approach to psychotherapy is based on this synthetic view and involves the provision of noncontingent positive regard as a means of allowing the client "to be the self that one truly is" (Rogers, 1961). SDT has similarly viewed contingent regard as a basis for introjected regulation and as undermining wellness (e.g., Assor, Roth & Deci, 2004) and has similarly specified the importance of autonomy-supportive conditions in psychotherapy as an opportunity for renewing thriving and integrity (Ryan & Deci, 2008b).

There is much more to Rogers's construct of actualization and its relations to the organism and the self than we review here. Our intent is simply to highlight several foundational points. First, Rogers's concept of actualization was understood by him to be an expression of the basic organizational nature of living things. The concept of actualization, that is, was explicitly rooted in an organismic view, in part derived from Goldstein (1939). Second, the actualization tendency applies not only to organismic processes in living things but also to the maintenance and enhancement of the self that humans possess. Yet nonaccepting and contingently regarding social environments may result in introjections, or poorly integrated aspects of personality, that cause tension and maladjustment. Finally, for Rogers the resolution of psychological difficulties involves catalyzing the actualizing tendency in a supportive, warm, noncontrolling relationship. Indeed, as a number of commentators have pointed out, although the theories differ in details, specific foci, and the methods through which the theories were formulated, there is much convergence in the views of person-centered approaches and SDT (see, e.g., Patterson & Joseph, 2007).

Illustratively, a neo-Rogerian perspective on therapy, namely, Miller and Rollnick's (2002) *motivational interviewing* (MI) approach, at least originally, emphasized the importance for lasting behavior change of engaging a person's "intrinsic" (we would say, more exactly, "autonomous") motivation. As argued by Markland, Ryan, Tobin, and Rollnick (2005), it is the inherent tendency found within the person that must be mobilized if persistent change in behavior is to occur, and both MI and SDT assume that that tendency can be located and supported in clinical contexts. MI's specific techniques of reflection, encouragement of self-exploration, rolling with resistances, and noncontrolling interventions are all consistent with the motivational principles we espouse in the SDT autonomy-supportive approach to therapy (see Chapter 17).

ANGYAL'S HUMANISTIC FRAMEWORK

Less well known today than Rogers's person-centered approach is the theorizing of Andreas Angyal, whose writings synthesize conceptions of actualization in a particularly comprehensive manner. Angyal's (1941, 1965) views, like Rogers's, were explicitly based on the organization metaphor, and, although decades old, his thinking shares some general themes with SDT.

Angyal argued that humans, like all living entities, exhibit a basic organismic propensity toward the maintenance and elaboration of structures and functions—a propensity toward organization. Yet, as noted earlier, he specified that this process of self-expansion is manifested in two general trends: *autonomy* and *homonomy*. The first refers to the tendency of organisms to gain mastery and to become self-regulating with respect to both their drives and their environment; the second refers to the tendency of organisms to strive for synthesis or unification with a larger, superordinate whole. This latter function is primarily apparent in the need for interpersonal relatedness, but also shows itself in various religious, aesthetic, and political endeavors.

The trends toward autonomy and homonomy are the double orientations of organismic nature, and the interplay of these trends accounts, in Angyal's theory, for both normal and pathological development. With regard to the latter, he argued that psychological problems arise primarily from persistent trauma, in which trauma "represents an interference not with something minor but with some condition necessary for the unfolding of the basic pattern of life—the exercise of self-determination and the achievement of belonging" (1965, p. 118). Angyal viewed therapy as a process through which these trends toward autonomy and homonomy were facilitated and hopefully brought into harmony. He saw these trends, in fact, not as irreconcilable opposites but rather as "part aspects" of one overall organismic propensity. As he put it: "The human being is both a unifier, an organizer of his immediate personal world, and a participant in what he conceives to be the superordinate whole to which he belongs. His striving for mastery is embedded in his longing for participation" (1965, p. 29).

The Path Ahead

Our review of these prior theoretical perspectives is intended to make transparent some of the historical foundations upon which our specific organismic view has been constructed. SDT, that is, embraces and builds upon many of the observations and tenets of these and other previous organismic theories. With them, SDT assumes that, when healthy, life ideally develops toward increasing differentiation, assimilation, and unity in functioning and, even further, that within human psychological development, the self-as-process supports and reflects that core tendency. At each phase of development, prior behavioral regulations and the psychological beliefs and practices that support them are either assimilated to the self by means of hierarchic integration or annexed into behavioral controls through introjected or compartmentalized structures. It is through these means that both continuities and fractures in development are carried forward (Cicchetti, 2006; Vansteenkiste & Ryan, 2013). Both the intrinsic integrative tendencies and the defensive structures that emerge when conditions are nonoptimal are deeply evolved (e.g., see Chapters 16 and 24). That is, experiences of autonomy, competence, and relatedness are subserved by adaptations that preserve and protect the processes to which they refer.

Yet there are aspects of these classic organismic views that are worth reconsidering or refining. First, given the assumption of inner growth or developmental tendencies, there has not been enough attention to differences and variations in the robustness of such processes. Individual differences result from both genetic factors and physical perturbations that affect the integrity of biological processes, as well as obstructions and facilitators in one's formative social environments and the transactions of these internal and external factors. The grand theories of the past have not focused sufficiently on the existence and causes of between-person and, more especially, within-person variability in integration and the social-contextual conditions that promote it. Understanding more about enhancers and inhibitors of assimilation and integration, particularly those that are social and psychological, will help account for variability in functioning.

A primary focus of SDT is the intrinsic organizational nature of the psyche, and yet, because this synthetic process is motivated, it can also be energized or depleted (Ryan & Deci, 2008b; Martela, DeHaan, & Ryan, 2016), as well as self-guided or derailed by external controls (Deci & Ryan, 2000). It follows that there are both between- and within-person variations that must be dynamically modeled and that will vary with different contexts and domains of life that entail different constraints and affordances. SDT will focus on context-to-context, and even moment-to-moment, changes in integrative, vital functioning, noting the supports and thwarts that account for such variations.

Second, most of these grand theories in twentieth-century Western psychology have a decidedly individualistic bent, as they focus primarily on the integration of the individual without sufficient attention to the fact that every individual is embedded within interpersonal and social organizations within which they are more or less integrated. For clear historical and cultural reasons, Western theories have put too little emphasis on our inherent homonomous tendencies. In our view, the dual tasks of integration within both intrapersonal and larger social organizations unfolds as a dynamic interplay between autonomy, competence, and relatedness, and that dynamic interplay supplies the main foci of self-determination theory. A central concern in SDT is, therefore, how these universal features of our human nature, specifically our basic needs, are differentially expressed and satisfied across cultures, impacting both individual and social wellness and integrity. Results throughout this volume show that relatedness and connection to others ideally involve autonomy and, moreover, that what is called individualism can be variously motivated and difficult to integrate.

Third, although these rich historical frameworks represent both detailed observations and sophisticated theorizing, they have not always been formulated or pursued in terms of hypotheses that could be readily operationalized, examined, and refined through rigorous empirical methods. SDT is specifically oriented toward creating an empirical framework that embraces much of this rich historical thinking, but in a manner that is open to tests and elaborations based on the findings that emerge. Empirical methods are a central epistemological strategy for SDT, allowing it to be subject to various forms of meaningful critique and elaboration.

Finally, as an organismic theory, SDT views integrative processes as anchored in the biology of the individual, and thus the coordination of neuropsychological, physiological, and psychological data is relevant to understanding all of their sources and promotion. This was, of course, a central aim of both Freud (see Sulloway, 1979) and Piaget (1971), but it has often been a more peripheral concern within other organismic traditions in psychology. Recent work in neuroscience (e.g., Lee, Reeve, Xue, & Xiong, 2012; Merker, 2007; Murayama, Matsumoto, Izuma, & Matsumoto, 2010; Murayama et al., 2015; Panksepp & Northoff, 2009) seems to increasingly dovetail with our views that the intrinsically active and integrative tendencies central to healthy self-functioning have deep roots in the evolution of our species, leading to the specific architecture of human integrative functioning. Understanding both the mechanistic and social underpinnings of these capacities and propensities is thus also essential to our task.

CHAPTER 3

Human Autonomy

*Philosophical Perspectives
and the Phenomenology of Self*

Autonomy and self are two central, and linked, concepts within SDT, and in this chapter we examine relevant philosophical and theoretical views of self and autonomy. Reviewing phenomenological, analytical, and existentialist views, we find agreement that the self is not an entity one can directly perceive or experience as a phenomenal object. Rather, people know the self through autonomy and self-organization: They perceive when (or to what degree) their actions stem from and are supported by volition and willingness versus feeling alien, forced, or compelled. Analytic philosophers similarly argue that autonomy reflects volition and willingness. To be autonomous means acting in accord with one's reflective considerations; thus autonomous actions are those that can be self-endorsed and for which one takes responsibility. We further distinguish autonomy from the ideas of *independence* (or nonreliance) and *freedom* (or lack of constraints). We also review the concepts of authenticity and true self that are widely used in humanist and dynamic literatures as they relate to our view of autonomy. Finally, turning from philosophy to psychology, we trace how the attribution tradition, especially through the work of Heider (1958) and de Charms (1968), allowed phenomenological themes concerning autonomy and self-determination to enter empirical psychology. De Charms specifically differentiated internal versus external perceived locus of causality and linked it with intrinsic motivation. This laid some important foundations for our early work in SDT. We end by juxtaposing our idea of autonomy with some current concepts of free will, self-control, and nonconscious behavior regulation.

Living entities are characterized by organizational propensities (Maturana & Varela, 1992; Mayr, 1982), and, as we reviewed in the previous chapter, this foundational assumption has been reflected in many of psychology's most prominent theories. In the psychoanalytic tradition, this idea is represented in an emphasis on the *synthetic function of the ego* (Nunberg, 1931); in the humanistic tradition, in the centrality of the *actualizing tendency* (Rogers, 1963); and in the cognitive-developmental tradition as the functional invariant of *organization* (Piaget, 1971).

In SDT, we embrace organizational thinking as most fitting for the study of people's inherent propensities toward *intrinsic motivation* and *internalization*. We see human psychological development as dynamically adaptive and entailing tendencies toward cohesive and integrated functioning. Central to this healthy, coherent functioning is the *self,* a construct concerning integrative, albeit fluid, processes with a great deal of functional meaning and scientific import. Within SDT, the self is both the psychological organization that integrates and the structure to which new functions, narratives, values, regulations, and preferences are integrated. To the extent that action is regulated through the integrated (and integrating) self, it is said to be *autonomous.*

In this second historical chapter, we consider the meaning of the concepts of self and autonomy as discussed in both philosophical and past psychological perspectives. We delineate the philosophical traditions that inform our view, and we relate our view to other theories employing similar conceptions of self, pointing out some contrasts. As in the prior chapter, our aim herein is simply to expose some of the historical and analytic underpinnings of SDT, particularly as they relate to autonomy and self as we use these terms. We also want to outline and highlight some of the issues and controversies that have been raised by these past and current conceptualizations of self and autonomy.

Two Views of Self

The term *self* carries quite distinct meanings in different psychological theories, and there is a particularly salient contrast between its meaning within social-cognitive perspectives and in organismic approaches. Most social-cognitive views can be traced to the tradition of the *looking-glass self* (Cooley, 1902; Mead, 1934), in which the term *self* is primarily employed to represent an *object* of one's own perceptions. In this tradition, the self is understood as a constructed concept, image, or representation (viz., self-concept) accompanied by a collection of mechanisms for governing action (viz., self-schemas) that are usually oriented toward verifying, enhancing, or protecting this representation. Thus the self referred to in the constructs of self-concept, self-perception, self-esteem, and many other hyphenated self- terms concern what McAdams (1990) referred to as *self-as-object.* As Harter (2012) recently summarized, most of the attention in empirical psychology has historically been on this self-as-object or "me-self" idea, and it continues to be an active focus of research (e.g., Oyserman, Elmore, & Smith, 2012; Sedikides & Gaertner, 2001). We turn to this me-self, especially as it pertains to identity and self-esteem, in Chapter 15.

By contrast, the self of organismic psychologies has typically (though with some notable exceptions) concerned what McAdams (1990) characterized as the *self-as-subject* and what we refer to as *self-as-process* (Ryan, 1995; Ryan & Rigby, 2015)—that is, the self that is phenomenally experienced as both a center of experience and as the initiator and regulator of volitional behavior. In this chapter, we examine the concept of self-as-process as it has been understood within both varied philosophical and psychological approaches to personality and development and their relations to core constructs within SDT.

Philosophical Views of Self

Self-as-Process

Comprehension of the self as the center of synthesis and initiation has deep roots within constructivist and phenomenological traditions of philosophy. Immanuel Kant, for example, emphasized that experience is produced by the synthetic activity of mind and that one's consciousness of self is essentially one's consciousness of this synthetic activity. Kant (1899) highlighted that, apart from the experience of this synthetic activity, there is no direct apprehension of a *self,* because one's self can never phenomenally appear as a direct object of consciousness. The self is therefore not directly experienced as an object, entity, or thing but rather is sensed as the means through which experience is ordered.

Edmund Husserl, a principal founder of the phenomenological tradition in philosophy, elaborated, critiqued, and refined this Kantian theme that the experienced world is constituted by a perceiver, endowing that world with significance and meaning. Yet Husserl (1980) also noted that any postulated "I," "ego," or "self" that is doing the perceiving of the world cannot become a direct object of that perceiving. One can at best reflectively glance at a past moment of activity. In this sense, the "I" remains transcendent, not available to direct perception. Husserl recognized as well that one knows the world only through one's experienced relation to it.

Heidegger (1962), in an extension and critique of both the Kantian and Husserlian analyses, stressed as they did that the self cannot be conceived of as a substance or a thing, nor does the self-as-subject appear as a phenomenal object in any direct way. Instead, he emphasized that the nature of the self is to be found in its relating to the world, in what he called its *caring* (*sorge*). One is, at any given moment, concerned or caring about something. Heidegger's term *Dasein* expressed this insofar as the "being" of human beings is *there,* in the world. Heidegger argued that, in an everyday sense, the term self, or "I," is used to refer to the world that is "mine" (as opposed to others'). But on an ontological level the "I" is deeply founded in the experience of *authentic caring,* of being-in-the-world in a manner that he characterized as *Stanigkeit des Selbst* (1962, p. 369), as an autonomous manifestation of one's caring. People are burdened, in a sense, with the ontological necessity of finding that their caring and concerns are their own, and this responsibility both defines and describes the meaning of self in its deepest sense (see Frankfurt, 2004, for an analytic version of this theme). The particular foci and scope of concern and caring differs by family of origin, culture, and historical epoch, but each individual feels this sense of self as a locus of responsibility.

For our purposes thus far, our discussion has merely highlighted that from a self-as-process view the self is *not* primarily an object of perception or evaluation but, rather, is phenomenally accessed as the sense of activity in contacting, relating, assimilating, constructing, and caring in the world. This construct called "self" that encompasses an active, agentic being-in-the-world is thus better conceived of as a process than an object. Yet how can one study a self that is primarily a process and not a thing?

Autonomy and Heteronomy in Relation to Self

We suggest that greater understanding of the self-as-process can be more optimally achieved not by attempts to directly apprehend the self per se but, rather, by examining self-functioning. One can examine the difference between behaviors people phenomenally experience to be their own—to be expressions of self—relative to when they experience their behaviors to be controlled by forces alien to the self. In other words, one can contrast self-organized actions with those that are experienced as not self-organized.

The term *autonomy* is particularly germane to this analysis. *Autonomy* literally means "self-governing" and connotes, therefore, regulation by the self. Its opposite, *heteronomy,* refers to regulation by an "other" (*heteron*) and thus, of necessity, by forces experienced as other than, or alien to, the self. By beginning with an understanding of the phenomenal experience of autonomy versus heteronomy, it is possible, we suggest, to develop a fuller understanding of what it means for thoughts, feelings, and behaviors to emanate from, or be an expression of, the self to varying degrees.

The concept of autonomy is central within the aforementioned Kantian tradition. The human capacity for self-consciousness renders us able to transcend our experience and, ultimately, to confer value on objects and aims, including values arrived at through the application of reflection and reason. In this view, it is one's choices that ultimately affirm or disaffirm features of objects that may attract or repel us, allowing for autonomous actions (see, e.g., Korsgaard, 2009). These acts of transcendence and choice allow us to reflect on, organize, and prioritize our inclinations, aversions, and values. This very process is synthetic in the sense that through it action becomes unified, with the associated experience of integrity.

As early as 1908, Pfander (1967) was using phenomenological methods drawn from Brentano (1973) and Husserl (1980) to distinguish between self-determined acts, those that reflect one's *will,* and acts that results from other forms of striving or motivation. According to Pfander, acts of will are experienced "precisely not as an occurrence caused by a different agent but as an initial act of the ego-center itself" (1967, p. 20). In his view, even if one's actions are initiated by strong inner impulses or by external demands, they can still be self-determined insofar as the actions are characterized by an *endorsement* of the behavior by the self, or, in his terms, one's "ego center." In contrast, non-self-determined actions are those perceived to be compelled by forces outside the self with which one does not concur.

Ricoeur (1966) further examined the complexities of will and self-determination, similarly underscoring that the terms *will* and *willing* refer to acts that are fully endorsed by the self. Like Pfander, Ricoeur highlighted that self-endorsement of an action need not imply a literal absence of salient external cues or even strong pressures to be acting. People can at times be volitional and "free" even under such pressures, provided they concur with the behaviors being mandated. Concurring means specifically that they comply because their authentic evaluation of the circumstances engenders in them self-endorsed reasons for acting in accordance with the pressures. People, for instance, do not necessarily lose their sense of will or autonomy when ordered to do something the value of which they support. For example, one can willingly obey a "doctor's orders" insofar as one agrees with or values those inputs. The issue of autonomy thus lies in the true ascent to the authority and the sense of its *legitimacy* (see also Chapter 23). Accordingly, Ricoeur understood that self-determination can apply not only to spontaneous self-initiated choices but also to acts of willfully consenting to, or being truly receptive of, external obligations or legitimate demands and moral responsibilities.

Ricoeur noted, following Kant, that because we can reflect on our possibilities and our own valuing of things, choice is possible. Indeed, he argued that the capacity to evaluate and potentially redirect one's propensities can even allow one to go so far as to try to *oppose aspects of one's nature* (e.g., one's drives and inclinations) or even view them as *alien.* Ricoeur (1966) described this as the "possibility of refusal," a refusal to submerge oneself in one's nature. In refusal, one rejects one's condition, as when one might try to wrench oneself from one's character, temperament, or other natural tendencies. Ricoeur argued that the capacity to refuse is inexorably linked with gaining a sense of one's freedom and one's possibilities.

Although, indeed, such freedom to redirect one's nature may exist, in our view it is limited by what is real and actual. In other words, an authentic freedom is one that is enacted in the context of, and responsive to, one's nature and present needs rather than one that reactively suppresses them. This means that part of the art of being fully human entails selectively assenting to some aspects of nature while redirecting or transforming others. Insofar as human self-consciousness appears to represent a rupture in nature, it can be bridged by coming to grips with the workings of one's inner life—with one's basic needs, physical and psychological, and with the corresponding conditions of necessity within the social context.

Within the framework of SDT, we explicitly recognize that humans have capacities to selectively support some aspects of their natures and to oppose others. Some of these endorsements or inhibitions will be the product of autonomy and others of heteronomy and introjections, suggesting that one should not mistake *willpower* (overpowering one part of the personality by another) as autonomy. It is working in accordance with one's needs, rather than opposing them, that typically represents the more congruent and autonomous forms of living.

In sum, autonomy, self-determination, and will (for the moment used interchangeably) pertain to acts that are experienced as freely done and endorsed by the self. This, of course, applies to behaviors that are easily chosen (e.g., playing tennis if one experiences it as fun and interesting), as well as to more difficult choices (e.g., working on a tedious but valued volunteer task). In the latter case, the self endorses the behavior because it fits with abiding values and personal commitments, so it is experienced as volitional. Difficult moral actions would also fall into this latter category, provided they have the backing of the self. The point is that the self is *phenomenologically* implicated in actions that have the character of volition and/or inner commitment. By contrast, the very definition of *alienated* behavior, what we shall classify as controlled forms of motivation within SDT, is that one's acts lack integrated self-endorsement and are not therefore felt to be autonomous.

From a Different Quarter: Analytical Perspectives

Modern analytical approaches, which are based more on an analysis of the meaning and usage of terms, have arrived at some very similar conclusions to those of phenomenological perspectives regarding the meaning of autonomy. Frankfurt (1971) initiated an especially important chain of thinking on this topic. He began by defining autonomy as an issue of authentic assent—that is, assent that is congruent with one's reflective considerations. He argued that the issue of autonomy concerns not whether or not one's behavior is prompted by outside influences but, rather, whether one decisively favors enacting the behaviors. In more recent writing, Frankfurt (2004) expresses this reflective endorsement in another way: When people are autonomous, not only do they endorse what they are doing, but they also support and accept the desire or reason that moves them to do it. When they endorse both the content and the motive of their actions, Frankfurt argued, they are "as close to the freedom of the will as finite beings, who do not create themselves, can intelligibly hope to come" (p. 20).

Dworkin (1988), building on Frankfurt's early work, similarly argued that autonomy does not simply mean behaving without constraint. Clearly, one can assent to certain constraints and, in doing so, still be autonomous. In one example, people may think of a particular traffic light as constraining, but if they assent to the idea that traffic laws are useful and legitimate for ensuring their own and indeed everyone's safety, they might willingly consent to stopping for the light without losing autonomy.

Dworkin thus spoke of autonomy as entailing endorsement of one's actions at the *highest order of reflection*. When a person reflects on the motives that spontaneously emerge and appraises them to accord with abiding values and interests, that person will be autonomous to that degree. However, this reflective appraisal must be at an appropriately high level. For example, in an impatient moment, one might have the impulse to run a red light and even feel it as a personal desire. Yet there is perhaps a higher order level of reflection at which one would find that the action was, in fact, not volitional—not fully in accord with his or her value system. If, however, at the appropriate level of reflection, one finds a full degree of endorsing an action, the action would be autonomous. This might happen, for example, when sitting at a red light at 3:00 A.M. on a country road when absolutely no traffic is in the area. Here, even reflectively, the value of common laws might not seem to apply.

The issue of an appropriate level of reflection is not as vague as it might seem (Wolf, 1990). First, practically, relatively few levels of reflection and meaningful considerations are possible with respect to most actions. Second, one can learn to experience the difference between a reflection that is free, relaxed, or interested and one that is pressured or insistent (Ryan & Deci, 2008b). The difference between impulse and considered action is, in fact, available to the modal adult (Loevinger & Blasi, 1991). Later, in examining this psychologically, we relate such reflective processing to *mindfulness* (Brown & Ryan, 2003), in which one is open to experiencing what is actually going on and to holistic self-representation (Kazén, Baumann, & Kuhl, 2003) in which options are fully processed with regard to their *self-compatibility*. A third, but important, point is that it is not necessary for a behavior to be consciously reflected upon at that moment in order to be autonomous. It is, however, required that the behavior be informed by one's sensibilities and values such that, were it to be reflected on, it would be authentically and fully endorsed (Ryan & Deci, 2004a).

Marilyn Friedman's work extends this analytic perspective, adding that the act of engaging in self-reflection itself can deepen the sense of self-determination or autonomy, as one evaluates and identifies with particular wants, desires, goals, and opinions. For example, she describes the process as follows:

> To realize autonomy a person must first somehow reflect on her wants, desires and so on and take up an evaluative stance with respect to them. She can endorse or identify with them in some way or be wholeheartedly committed to them, or she can reject or repudiate them or be only halfheartedly committed to them. If she endorses or identifies with her wants and desires, she makes them more truly hers, more genuinely a part of who she is, and thus, more a part of the very identity as a particular distinctive self than are wants and desires that she has not thus self-reflectively reaffirmed. (Friedman, 2003, p. 5)

A critical point to be derived here is that there are *degrees of autonomy* and that the extent of autonomy is often dependent upon the extent to which the individual has mindfully and reflectively identified with and integrated a particular regulation or value. The varied types of internalization that we empirically explore within SDT reflect differences in this depth of integration.

Another critical point to be derived from these philosophical analyses is that autonomy is not equivalent to independence from others or freedom from external inputs (Ryan & Deci, 2004a; Kerr, 2002). This is a distinction relevant to the basic conceptualization of autonomy and to its application in relationships, human development, and cultures. A person can autonomously follow another (e.g., willingly relying on the other's guidance, or volitionally adhering to that person's leadership). More generally, a person can volitionally endorse duty, care, and responsibility to others, as well as dependence on them (see Chapter 22). In contrast, a person can also feel controlled in her or his motivations to follow, depend on, or obey others. Although attempts at coercion or external control need not always undermine a sense of autonomy, Friedman (2003) argues (and SDT's empirical findings support) that they typically do.

The mistaken equating of autonomy with independence and self-reliance has led some thinkers to cast autonomy as antirelational. This is so in some earlier feminist writings (e.g., Code, 1991; Jordan, 1991) in which, quite rightfully, notions of autonomy in terms of "self-made men" and freedom from "the ties that bind" were being rejected. Yet, more recent feminist philosophy has revisited this whole nexus of autonomy and relatedness, considering their relations from the viewpoint of autonomy as self-endorsement (e.g., see Barclay, 2000; Friedman, 2003; Mackenzie & Stoljar, 2000). In these "synthetic" views, it becomes clear both that people can be autonomous within relationships and, moreover, that the idea of a fully "independent person" is largely mythical. Even the capacity for, and content of, the self-reflections that support autonomy emerge in a social context.

In sum, Frankfurt, Dworkin, Friedman, and other analytically oriented philosophers concur with phenomenologists such as Pfander and Ricoeur on the fundamental point that autonomy is concerned with integrated, self-endorsed actions: a willingness to act as one does and an endorsement of the motivation that leads one to do it. Autonomy thus does not entail "being subject to no external influences" (e.g., one's parents, teachers, role models, or leaders). Rather, it concerns whether following external inputs reflects mere obedience or whether it reflects an acceptance and valuing of the direction or guidance that these inputs provide. Indeed, there is no possible world that is absent of external influences, and therefore it is in the degree to which one assents to some and not other influences that the question of autonomy becomes meaningful. Finally, as Dworkin (1988) emphasized, although autonomous actions always entail a self-attribution of responsibility, people can also be held responsible by others when not acting autonomously. People who passively let others choose for them do not escape responsibility; in fact, they are responsible for precisely *that*, for having relinquished choice. Here, analytic accounts, though coming from a distinct epistemic foundation, seem to converge with existentialist thought, to which we now turn.

Existentialism, Authenticity, and the Self

Having examined some phenomenological and analytic accounts of autonomy, we focus now on existential views, about which we have previously written (e.g., Ryan & Deci, 2004a; 2006; Ryan, Legate, Niemiec, & Deci, 2012). Existentially oriented writers have, of course, been very concerned with issues of autonomy, responsibility, and connection. In this tradition the terms *authentic* and *inauthentic* distinguish actions that are volitional and self-determined from those that are not, and these concepts provide our starting point.

It is important to highlight that the term *authentic* has two meanings: First, it means something *proceeding from its reputed source or author*. Second, *authentic* means something that is *genuine*, or *real* (Wild, 1965). Both definitions of authenticity pertain to our analysis. Authentic actions are thus those that one identifies as one's own and for which one willingly takes responsibility (authorship) *and* those that are not mere fantasy or whimsical but are actually grounded in and fitting with what is actually occurring. In contrast, a person's actions, even intentional ones, are inauthentic insofar as they are experienced as not truly reflecting or emanating from the self and/or are simply not "in touch" with what is taking place in the person's context (see also Barilan, 2011).

Søren Kierkegaard initiated the modern literature of authenticity, and his view of authenticity is particularly deeply connected to the issue of *self*. For him, as for many other post-Kantian authors we have already cited, the self is the continual activity of synthesis or integration. As he put it, the "self is a relation which relates itself to its own self . . . in short it is a synthesis" (1987, p. 146). Yet Kierkegaard strenuously objected to the idea that this synthesis is an automatic tendency or connotes some *inevitable* progression, an idea he thought was overemphasized in the dominant Hegelian dialectical philosophy of his time (Mullen, 1981; Olafson, 1967). Rather, for Kierkegaard, being a *self* represented a brave and intentional undertaking, requiring ongoing self-assessment and reflection. To achieve a self is to be committed to the struggle of relating the self to the self, of taking responsibility for continually reevaluating what one believes, and then enacting it. When acting authentically, one persistently asks, "What am I to become?"

In Kierkegaard's view, a genuine, authentic human being is "infinitely interested in his existence," and what he or she does is the current best synthesis of all that he or she truly believes, knows, and feels. To the extent that synthesis is complete and one is not duplicitous or self-deceptive, then one will act in accord with one's self and will experience some, always relative, sense of integration. Yet to fail or balk at this task of selfhood is to be inauthentic, which Kierkegaard described as being in *despair*. Such is the case when one's behavior does not emanate from the self—when one is merely being a mindless conformist or when one is self-deceptive. Thus, for Kierkegaard, the degree to which actions are authored by the self was a relevant measure of one's integration and, ultimately, one's humanity.

Kierkergaard's description resonates with Taylor's (1991) understanding of authenticity not as a stable attribute but as the exercise, rather than avoidance, of earnest attempts to reflectively formulate what is most important. As he stated, even our best formulations "are intrinsically open to challenge" and require ongoing reevaluations concerning how to act. Yet in authenticity such reevaluations are taken on with "a stance of attention, as it were, to what these formulae are meant to articulate and with a readiness to receive any Gestalt shift in our view" (p. 222). In other words, synthesis is an ongoing process, as the very nature of our considerations undergo constant change. Yet, as Taylor highlights, because "this self-resolution is something we do, when we do it, we can be called responsible for ourselves" (p. 224). Similar to Kierkegaard, in Taylor's view the exercise of self-resolution is the essence of what it means to be a person.

Martin Heidegger (e.g., 1927/1962) synthesized these existential themes into his phenomenological–hermeneutic perspective, distinguishing authentic from inauthentic being. He suggested that persons are typically not dwelling in the authentic. Instead, they are too often caught up in events and have only a vague awareness of how and why they are relating to the world. In some moments, however, people may engage the world authentically. In such moments, they recognize that the world is theirs, and their responsibility. For Heidegger this means taking ownership—and thus an experience of both "mineness" and togetherness. In the words of Moran (2000), authenticity is a movement toward wholeness: "Being authentic is a kind of potential to be whole: humans have the urge to get their lives together, one wants to make it whole, to unify it. In later works, Heidegger will make the connection between *whole* and *healthy*" (p. 240).

This general belief that persons have capacities for authenticity, in which they take ownership and responsibility and, in doing so, feel more whole and integrated, has informed a variety of organismic and humanistic perspectives in both philosophy and psychology up to the present (e.g., Yalom, 2002). Of note is that these existential views, like those of the analytical and phenomenological authors we previously examined, locate the definitions of self-determination or autonomy in a manner that will tie directly to SDT's psychological theory. They specify that an act is autonomous only to the extent that it is "endorsed" by the self. They also underscore that the self organizes or synthesizes experiences and actions and that there will be a relative unity to one's action if it is autonomous. The phenomenological analyses also convey that autonomy is *not* defined by the presence or absence of external influences but rather, when external influences prompt behaviors, by one's subjective assent to those influences. Moreover, autonomy and self-regulation are not inherently selfish or individualistic. One can autonomously care for, be cared for, or depend on and even follow others. In fact, love and care for others are often autonomously motivated. Finally, because autonomy is based in self-endorsement, it also is supported and deepened by authentic self-reflection and mindfulness.

Theories of the "True Self"

Having reviewed, albeit in only a cursory manner, a number of philosophical perspectives on autonomy, we turn now to several theoretical perspectives within psychology that also fall in the tradition of self-as-process theorizing, namely those that posit a "true," "real," or "core" self. Again, we do this to bring out interconnections, to acknowledge these historical predecessors from whom we have drawn both inspiration and insight, and to draw some contrasts.

A True Self?

The idea of listening to and following one's *true self* is ancient and has been expressed in many forms, both artistic and scholarly. Presumably, the concept of a true self has persisted through the ages because there is a deep phenomenological referent or experiential truth to the idea contained within the concept. Because humans can conceive of themselves, and act, in ways that oppose their own deeply held identifications, values, and convictions (e.g., when controlled by immediate reward contingencies, introjected beliefs, or social pressures), there is the ever-present possibility for them to be false with respect to their own sensibilities and abiding values.

A variety of linguistic expressions convey the ideas centrally linked with the concept of true self. People are said to have *integrity* when their actions appear to express what they truly feel and value, and this quality of integrity, cross-culturally, seems to engender trust and respect. The etymology of the term *integrity* derives from the Latin "integer," meaning that integrity expresses wholeness and entirety. Nor are such expressions limited to Western cultures. Japanese language, for example, contains the word *jibun*, which is sometimes translated as "true self" and conveys a deeper self that must be discovered which facilitates one's health and connections with others (Kumagai, 1988; Johnson, 1993). Similarly, Doi (1973) pointed out the awareness among Japanese of potential discrepancies between inner sensibilities and outward presentation, as illustrated by the existence of complementary terms such as *tatemae/honne*. Chong (2003) similarly highlights related conceptions within Confucian philosophy. Clearly, concern with authenticity or the true self of others is present in varied cultural contexts.

Another word also closely connected with true self is *spontaneity*. People who are spontaneous come out with what they really feel, not censoring their experience but expressing it directly. Spontaneous means, literally, something that emanates from within, rather than from compulsion, constraints, or self-controls. Typically, people who are spontaneous appear to possess a vitality that reflects access to their true self.

Integrity and spontaneity seem, however, to tap different aspects of the meaning of true self. The former connotes more of its serious side (commitment, reflective truth, and value), whereas the latter seems to express its lighter side, replete with energy, directness, and honesty. With some caveats, we will see that spontaneity relates well to intrinsic motivation and integrity to integrated internalizations. Nonetheless, both convey something unmasked, something true to heart, and, as we shall see, both elements are at play in various prominent theories of personality that have featured a concept of the true self. A consideration of their definitions and usage will help to illuminate how this construct relates to organismic thinking and how social-contextual dynamics bear on the construct.

Psychoanalytic Approaches

Theoretical writing about a true self within psychology has primarily resided within psychodynamic traditions (Miller, 1981). Although early Freudian theorizing did not contain such a concept, more contemporary theorizing in traditions such as ego psychology and object relations theory have found the concept useful. We now have a look at some of the theories for which true self is an important component.

WINNICOTT

Among the most well-known psychological theorists concerned with the true self is Donald Winnicott, who argued that much of the psychopathology he encountered as a clinician was the result of an inflation of the false self and a corresponding underdevelopment of a true self. In Winnicott's (1965, 1971) view, people who are in touch with their true self have a sense of feeling real because they have access and sensitivity to their feelings and needs. Although the ideas of "true self" and "feeling real" may seem relative and abstract, Winnicott was working within the clinical sphere, in which such individual experiences have concrete meaning for individuals and are directly relevant to therapeutic change.

For Winnicott, one's capacity to experience and function in accordance with one's self is related, developmentally, to having had a "facilitating environment," which is an interpersonal matrix that provides a secure or stable base and a caretaker who is responsive to and validating of one's spontaneous strivings. Being responsive includes a process Winnicott called *mirroring,* in which the caretaker accurately receives and reflects the child's strivings and accomplishments, along with the conveyance of loving support. This validation of inner experience aids the child's developing capacity to be "in touch" with the self and to develop the resulting confidence and vitality that are intimately related to this capacity. Conversely, an impinging, unresponsive, or overly controlling caretaking environment forces the developing child to distort or ignore inner experience, resulting in a hypertrophy or amplification of a false self and an "as-if" personality. As he stated it, "impersonal management cannot succeed in producing a new autonomous human child" (1971, p. 127). Although the capacity to put forth a false self is also something most people develop as an adaptive tool, a hypertrophied false self represents a pathological form of adaptation to chronically unresponsive, controlling, or neglectful caregiving. The person must pervasively function in a compliant way and hide or repress spontaneous feelings and needs. This may serve to keep alive the necessary dyadic connection but at the cost of the experience and energy of a true self. That is, the enlarged and complex false self attempts to preserve relatedness, and the price of this is the loss of autonomy.

Along with this loss, according to Winnicott, goes the loss of the person's creative nature and ability to freely initiate, to be vital, and to deeply enjoy existence.

HORNEY

Also operating in a psychodynamic tradition, Karen Horney articulated a concept of the *real self,* which she defined as the *"original* force toward individual growth and fulfillment" (1950, p. 158). This real self is not acquired through learning but is an "intrinsic potentiality" or "central inner force, common to all human beings" (p. 17) that is the deep source of development. Although the real self represents an innate developmental tendency, Horney, like Winnicott, emphasized that it requires favorable conditions for growth. She specifically argued that these conditions included an atmosphere of sensitivity, warmth, and support.

The provision of such interpersonal nutrients, Horney suggested, allows the child to experience the inner security and freedom that enable access to and expression of his or her feelings and needs. Conditions that are unresponsive to these needs produce a *basic anxiety* that ultimately prevents the child from relating to others in a spontaneous and authentic manner. In order to allay this anxiety, the child loses touch with his or her real self. Following Kierkegaard, Horney believed that loss of (or failure to find) the real self results in despair at not being conscious of this "alive center," of not being willing to be oneself. In her view, most neurotic phenomena involve being alienated from this vital core of psychic life and thus "abandoning of the reservoir of spontaneous energies" (Horney, 1950, p. 159) provided by the self.

JUNG

Among the most complex of the dynamic psychologies of self is that developed by Carl Jung, who also viewed the self as an organismic endowment. Jung (1951, 1959) referred to the self (to be distinguished from both ego and persona) as the center of the psyche that represents the potential for integration or unity of the whole personality. The self provides the impetus or spirit for realization of potentialities, which ultimately involves the unification and synthesis of the personality as a whole. For Jung, this tendency toward realization and integration, which he described also as *individuation,* was a vital principle so basic that it simply described the very propensities of life (Nagy, 1991).

Jung's phenomenology of self differs considerably from that of many other thinkers. For Jung, although the self exerts an organizing, synthetic influence on the psyche throughout the lifespan, it is rarely directly experienced or felt. In other words, the self operates largely at an unconscious level and receives expression in symbols and dreams, many of which concern the theme of unity or wholeness. For Jung, much of people's subjective experience is a function of the ego. However, to the extent that the ego is open to and in dialogue with the self, growth and unity are catalyzed. The process of integration is especially served, according to Jung, by the *transcendent function* of the self, which is the process that catalyzes symbol formations that help connect conscious and latent, or unconscious, aspects of personality. Despite its differences, Jung's theory of self, like others we have reviewed, entails an inherent and definitional directionality in life toward the integration of differentiated experience and authentic self-realization. The self is both the process of integration and the integrated representation of this inherent life process, reaching back to phylogeny and forward to potentiality (Nagy, 1991).

Elements of a True-Self View

There are a number of other well-known theories in which a construct of true self, or a close equivalent, figures centrally. They include the works of Jourard (1968) in humanistic psychology, Rank (1932) and Fromm (1955) in psychodynamic psychology, and Laing (1960) and Frankl (1959) in existential psychology. The theories differ from each other and from those we reviewed in terms of nuances and specifics, but there are common elements that can be abstracted. First, the true self is typically viewed as a natural endowment, as a potential that is present from birth. The true self is therefore not merely a social construction or cultural implant but rather is a nascent force that is affected in an interactive way by the social conditions surrounding one. Second, the true self is not understood in these theories as merely a cognitive representation or concept but rather as a motivational force or tendency. Theories from Winnicott to Horney to Jung ascribe to the true self an energy that has direction toward what is variously described as the realization of one's potentials, full functioning, or eudaimonia. Third, the true self is integrative in nature; it serves a synthetic function in the organism and represents a centering and health-promoting force in development. Finally, although the true self is innate to all human beings, it is not the only motivational force at work in development. Instead, it is a force that can be dissuaded, disrupted, or diminished in the dialectical interaction between developing persons and their social worlds. As the character Demian decried in the novel of the same name by Hesse (1965), "I only wanted to live in accord with the promptings of my true self. Why was that so difficult?" (p. 99).

That the theories of true self we just reviewed grew out of clinical perspectives is not an accident, insofar as so much of the distress clinicians deal with every day arises from people's experiencing themselves as controlled by alien forces, social pressures, or unintegrated motives (Ryan, Deci, Grolnick, & La Guardia, 2006). A common theme is, further, that psychological ill-health is the all-too-typical product of alienation from one's true self—that is, from an integrative core that develops over time. These theories also argue that controlling and unresponsive social influences can disrupt one's sense of self and subsequent capacities for congruent actions. Such social influences range from lack of responsiveness and overcontrol in early development to contingent regard in adulthood. Such contexts can lead the individual to ignore or distort his or her own inner experiences, and thus they interfere with healthy self-regulation.

When we turn to SDT research, we will see a number of these theoretical notions tested empirically. We suggest that, throughout the lifespan, there are social factors that can compromise self-organization and integrated, autonomous functioning. These include direct control, contingent regard or esteem from self and others, and the pervasive seductions and rewards that subtly and yet pervasively can co-opt integration in the modern age. The dynamics of why the voice of the true self is so difficult to hear and to follow thus present an interesting puzzle for psychological study. A primary agenda in developing SDT is, accordingly, to capture this clinical wisdom by creating an empirical framework that speaks to the fundamental issues of coherent and optimal self-functioning.

Eastern Traditions

Throughout this book, we emphasize the universal significance of autonomy in human functioning, and in Chapter 22 (and elsewhere) we review much empirical evidence for this claim through extensive cross-cultural research. Although thus far we have focused primarily on Western philosophical approaches to autonomy, the concept of self as a center of volition and organizer of experience has a rich history within a variety of Eastern traditions. Paranjpe (1987), for example, provided a review of the importance of the concept of self as both process and agent in Indian thought, dating as far back as the earliest Upanishad texts. Paranjpe argued that the idea that the self is both a silent witness to events and also capable of actively and reflectively evaluating and considering feelings, values, and commitments in such a way as to enhance self-realization is important within multiple Indian traditions. Work by Cheng (2004), Lo (2003), and others has similarly pointed out the important role of self in the analytics of Confucius as it relates to both the regulation of behavior and the developmental process of *self-cultivation*. Confucian traditions place an important role on reflective capacities and our capacities for personal and moral choice that run counter to claims by Iyengar and DeVoe (2003) and others who deny that concepts of self-regulation and autonomy have any grounding in Eastern or other non-Western cultures.

Self, No-Self, and the Buddhist Perspective

One of the perspectives that we have deeply appreciated in our own understanding of self is that of Buddhism, particularly with regard to the role of mindfulness in fostering healthy self-regulation (e.g., Brown & Ryan, 2003; Deci, Ryan, Schultz, & Niemiec, 2015; Ryan & Rigby, 2015). Yet many familiar with Buddhist perspectives will note immediately a seeming contradiction—for fundamental to Buddhist philosophy is a denial of the existence of self and the centrality of the concept of *no-self*, or *anatta*, in Buddhist doctrine (e.g., see Hanh, 1998). Although we use the term *self* to describe the processes through which integrated, holistically endorsed actions occur, we see no contradiction between the concept of no-self as employed within Buddhism and our perspective of self-as-process. Let us briefly consider this issue.

The self that is explicitly "denied" in Buddhist texts is of several types. One is the notion of self as eternal, which is itself inconsistent with the central idea of Buddhism that all is impermanent. Not only, then, is there not some eternal soul identified with a person; neither is there a continuous and stable perceiver or organizer of events. Buddhism also denies the reality of self as a thing—as a place, object, or entity. More importantly, however, Buddhism denies the existence of an essential self that is so often clung to with the notion of identity and self-concept (Khema, 1983). The idea that one is "a good person," "a psychologist," "an athlete," "a patriot," or any number of other self-representations involves an attempt to create an identity or self-definition that is based on both attachments and illusions. There is no more reality to the idea that one "is" a particular role than there is to the idea that one's clenched hand "is" a fist. When the fingers stretch, where is the "fist"? This does not mean that one cannot value acting in accordance with specific roles or practices. Rather, it means that this is not either an essence or a permanence on which one can rely, a theme echoed in many varied existential writings in the West as well (e.g., Kierkegaard). Thus an important truth of Buddhism is that these identities to which people can cling as representations of self have no permanence or fixed reality.

Moreover, in one's attachment to such identities, one has much to lose. If one were to identify as a successful achiever, then setbacks in the person's goals are not just setbacks; they represent a blow to the constructed "self." Such threats to identity are thus all the more painful because of the attachment to the constructed identity as defining of self (Brown, Ryan, Creswell, & Niemiec, 2008). Beyond any concrete setback, there is a blow to one's ego. If one thinks his or her success is "proof" of self-worth, the person is likely to be inflated and swelled by success and buffeted about in self-esteem by failures. We relate this phenomenon to *ego involvement* (Ryan, 1982) when one's esteem and identity are tied up in specific investments and outcomes.

As SDT argues, such "self-esteem," whether it is high or low, is a form of functioning based in introjection (Ryan & Brown, 2003) and is a source of instability and control rather than autonomy and liberation (see also Kernis & Paradise, 2002). These reifications of self are, of course, all connected to the self-as-object, which Buddhism rightly rejects. That is, the self as a thing—as some continuous essence "inside" the person, or as a defining image or "concept" in which one strenuously invests—are all repudiated in Buddhism.

Yet another highly important implication of Buddhism is one we also wish to underscore. Buddhism emphasizes the "groundlessness" of consciousness, the idea that we cannot reasonably image the self as an originating or an initiating cause of anything. Indeed, as emphasized in the work of Heidegger (1962), Merleau-Ponty (1962), and other phenomenologists, when we look closely at experience, we never find a self, we only find a *relation*. When someone smells the flowers, that person's experience is not of an "I" who is smelling flowers but is instead simply "the smell of flowers." When one hammers a nail, contact with the nail is experienced, not an "I" holding a hammer. There is no self to be found in any such relation: Were there no flower, there would be no smelling; without the nail, no hammering. All these events are of interdependent origin.

This Buddhist perspective is echoed in the work of the Gestalt psychology of Fritz Perls and his colleagues (e.g., Perls, Hefferline, & Goodman, 1951). In the Gestalt approach, the self is an emergent, fluid, and changing contact. The origins of contact grow out of what Perls et al. (1951) and cognitive theorists Varela, Thompson, and Rosch (1991) described as "the middle mode," neither from the self (or the physiology of the person) nor from an environment. Rather, there is emergence. Buddhist meditation teaches that, as we watch the ongoing upheavals of consciousness and their fading, self is not well conceived as the original initiator of thoughts or acts. It is, however, in our view within SDT, a capacity through which some of those arising impulses and motives are reflectively valued or felt to be fitting and thus are refined and carried forth, whereas others are "allowed to pass."

Self-regulation then, is not about a belief in a permanent, grounded, or essential self or an identity to which we should attach, but it does concern the process through which we mindfully support some possibilities rather than others (Ryan & Rigby, 2015). Throughout this book we shall see that these Buddhist sensibilities, despite the differences in terminology, aim toward a recognition of the importance of awareness, mindfulness, and integration in action, rather than attachments to and defense of self-concepts or other reifications of self and the ego involvements that derive from them (Ryan & Brown, 2003).

Psychological Attributions: Perceived Locus of Causality and the Self of SDT

The phenomenological and clinical approaches reviewed thus far in this chapter are relatively divorced from the literature of mainstream empirical psychology. Yet, as often happens, important philosophical perspectives enter this empirical arena of psychology through a side door, without much fanfare or explicit acknowledgement. The phenomenological aspects of self-determination and autonomy made just such an entrance, being introduced to mainstream psychology largely through the seminal works of two figures, Fritz Heider and Richard de Charms.

Heider (1958) was concerned with how people perceive themselves and each other in the context of everyday interpersonal events and how those perceptions play a determinative role in behavior. He attempted to articulate the commonsense principles, or *naïve psychology,* by which people make sense of their own or others' actions. He argued that it is this naïve psychology that "we use to build up our picture of the social environment and which guides our reactions to it" (p. 5).

Heider's interest in the phenomenal interpretation of the world underlying human behavior is very clear in his original work, although this phenomenological sensibility has not been carried through by many of the theorists who developed subsequent attributional models. Still, Heider emphasized that subjective variables such as motives, beliefs, and interpretations shape behavior and thus are, in their own right, appropriate objects of scientific inquiry. He stated that "motives and sentiments are psychological entities . . . mentalistic concepts . . . that bring order into behavior" (p. 32). Heider's perspective does not suggest that causal analyses—for example, of the physiological underpinnings of cognitions or motives—are without scientific interest. Rather, he was highlighting that they do not supplant or preclude the importance of a phenomenal analysis in scientific discourse and, further, that the latter is unlikely to be meaningfully reduced to the former. As we suggested in Chapter 1, it is the phenomenal level of analysis that forms the theoretical bedrock of the SDT propositions, many of which have been examined in causal analyses.

Among the most central and important constructs within naïve psychology is that of *perceived locus of causality (PLOC).* Specifically, Heider (1958) argued that action and/or its outcomes could be perceived as either intentional and thus personally caused or nonintentional and thus impersonally caused. The inference of intentionality, which is critical for *personal causation,* depends upon evidence of both *ability* and *effort* toward some end. Heider, therefore, detailed the circumstances that lend support to phenomenal judgments of effort (e.g., apparent exertion, overcoming obstacles, equifinality) and ability (e.g., observed talents or skills). In contrast, *impersonal causation* involves nonintentionality, which is inferred from the absence of ability or initiation and exertion with regard to an action or its outcomes. Thus, believing an outcome to be impersonally caused means that one thinks it was not within the person's control to bring it about (or to prevent it).

Heider argued that it matters greatly in terms of subsequent behavior whether people attribute actions to personal or impersonal causes. To use a simple example, imagine that you have an appointed time to meet an acquaintance, but she appears an hour late. If you come to the phenomenal belief that she could have been timely but did not bother to exert much effort toward that end, you will likely hold her personally responsible for being late, resulting in various possibilities, perhaps even anger and resentment. Yet if you believe her lateness was impersonally caused (e.g., you have evidence that the subway train broke down), you are likely to be more receptive and forgiving, even sympathetic. These distinctions between attributions of personal versus impersonal causality are even used in legal deliberations when assigning responsibility, as for example the differential consequences of a jury's attribution of negligent (impersonally caused) homicide versus first-degree murder (an intentional and thus personally caused action). Such legal judgments are typically made on Heiderian grounds; namely, attributions are made concerning the accused person's motives, effort, and ability to carry out the crime.

De Charms (1968) subsequently extended and applied Heider's work, arguing that intentional (personally caused) action is itself not always freely chosen or self-initiated. In fact, he argued that people often perform intentional actions precisely *because* they feel pressured or coerced to do so by external agents. The bully "makes me" hand over my lunch money, or my boss will reward me only if I take on an extra duty at work. Pulling out my lunch money requires intention but is not done willingly. And although I want the boss's reward, or fear the consequences of not doing the extra work, my doing the work is due to his or her causal pull rather than being self-initiated.

To clarify the differences between freely performed and externally induced intentional actions, de Charms therefore proposed a distinction that he believed applied *within* Heider's category of personally caused behavior. Specifically, he suggested that some intentional acts are accompanied by an *internal perceived locus of causality* (I-PLOC), whereas other intentional acts are characterized by an *external perceived locus of causality* (E-PLOC). Only the former, I-PLOC, category concerns actions that are truly volitional and for which one experiences oneself as an *origin* of action. The latter, E-PLOC, category represents instances in which one feels made to behave, in which one is a *pawn* to external pressures or potent inducements. With behaviors having an E-PLOC, one intends the behaviors and their effects, so they are personally caused, but one experiences the behaviors not as chosen, but rather as compelled or impelled by either external or introjected forces.

The differences between these two types of intentional behavior can be exemplified through manifold everyday occurrences. A woman may intentionally proceed to the workplace each morning to engage in her job only because she feels forced to work by financial need or social pressure. In this case, she largely experiences "having to" rather than "choosing to" work. She thus lacks a full sense of volition, and to that extent she is not self-determined in her work. In fact, she would experience herself as a pawn in de Charms's sense of that term, and her PLOC for her job would be external. In a second case, a woman may "want" to go to work—may feel value and a sense of commitment to her work—even though she, too, needs the money to live comfortably. She would see her work more as an expression of her interests and values, and she would feel more like an origin, rather than pawn, as a worker: more self-determined and willingly engaged. Her PLOC would be internal. In essence, what we have described is the difference between alienated labor and autonomous labor, and we would expect functional outcomes to follow, both in performance and well-being.

The introduction of the PLOC construct by Heider and de Charms was especially important in offering an operational inroad into the issues of agency and self-determination versus heteronomy and control. The PLOC of a particular behavior is something a person experiences and can thus often consciously report, and it is assumed that as the PLOC changes, the underlying motivational dynamics would be changing as well. In other words, it is assumed that by assessing (or experimentally manipulating) PLOC, we have a reflection of motivational dynamics. Thus we have the possibility of tracing contextual conditions to PLOC and in turn to behavior, and presumably in so doing we would be investigating the motivational processes associated with an I-PLOC versus an E-PLOC and their consequences. Conditions that add salience to external forces would be hypothesized to shift the PLOC from internal toward external, and those that make salient one's freedom or choices would be expected to shift the PLOC from external toward internal, thus representing self-determination.

In terms of the regulatory processes of SDT, the concepts of motivation versus amotivation exemplify the distinction Heider made between a personal and an impersonal PLOC, and the concepts of autonomous versus controlled forms of motivation exemplify the distinction de Charms made between an internal and external perceived locus of causality.

De Charms made a further claim that anticipated another of the primary propositions of SDT. He stated that people have a "primary motivational propensity" to be origins of their behavior. This implies not only that people can be the origins of their behavior (i.e., have an I-PLOC) but also that they are "constantly struggling against being confined and constrained by external forces—against being moved about like a pawn into situations not of [their] own choosing" (de Charms, 1968, p. 273). It requires but a small additional step to suggest, as we have done, that people have a psychological *need* to feel like an origin in order to function effectively and to remain healthy. Of course, for de Charms (and for us) the distinction between being an origin and a pawn (having an I-PLOC vs. an E-PLOC) is not an all-or-none affair; it is a continuum in which "a person feels more like an origin under some circumstances and more like a pawn under others" (p. 274).

There is yet another extremely important conceptual point made by de Charms that warrants emphasis. Unlike the behaviorist applications of attribution theory, in which people are said to make inferences about their own internal states postbehaviorally (e.g., Bem, 1967), de Charms held the view (with which we concur) that knowledge of one's volition is typically *not* derived inferentially, that is, by taking oneself as an object of social perception. Rather, it is (or at least can be) directly known, an aspect of *personal knowledge* (Polanyi, 1958). One does not usually need to infer one's motives, for one can feel directly when one has originated or supported an action or has been coerced or pressured into doing it. Thus, whereas a Heiderian analysis is essential for making inferences about others' motives, it is usually secondary for understanding one's own motives.

The process of knowing oneself phenomenally, through direct personal experience, which has been emphasized by de Charms and Polanyi as the basis for perceiving one's own motivation, stands in stark theoretical contrast to the views of symbolic interactionists (Cooley, 1902; Mead, 1934) and social learning theorists (e.g., Bem, 1967; Markus & Nurius, 1986), who emphasize that knowing oneself is primarily a process of seeing oneself *from the outside,* as if through the eyes of others, and internalizing as one's self these reflected external judgments and inferences. Instead, it suggests that one has direct organismic experiences of autonomous regulation, which will of course also be manifested in differential experiential qualities and neurological patterns of activation (e.g., Lee, Reeve, Xue, & Xiong, 2012; Murayama, Matsumoto, Izuma, & Matsumoto, 2010; Ryan, Kuhl, & Deci, 1997).

Perceived Locus of Causality in Relation to Intrinsic and Extrinsic Motivation

De Charms (1968) specifically suggested that one of the significant effects of shifts in PLOC would be changes in *intrinsic motivation*. Building on White (1959), he stated that intrinsic or effectance motivation is evidenced only when one experiences an I-PLOC. In saying this, he argued that the desire to be a causal agent—that is, an origin—is a primary motivational propensity and that feeling like an origin requires perceiving that one's behavior is of one's own choosing. Exploration, curiosity, creativity, and spontaneous interest are all characterized by self-determination, and, in fact, de Charms believed that factors which detract from the perception that action is self-determined will lead to an E-PLOC, which will in turn diminish the occurrence of origin-like behavior.

The theoretical link between intrinsic motivation and an I-PLOC is important in several respects. First, the fact that intrinsic motivation is manifested from the earliest moments of infancy, as evidenced in the spontaneous and active striving for effects and responsiveness in infants' environments, even though not conscious and deliberate, suggests that a nascent core self is also present from birth. In other words, the roots of the self as an active organizer of action and an integrative center of experience are prereflective, as long recognized by dynamic developmental theorists (e.g., Slavin & Kriegman, 1992; Stern, 1985). What becomes identified or understood as the self is the vital aspect of the human organism characterized by interest, curiosity, and organization. The self is thus the psychological manifestation and extension of the inherent activity and organizational properties common to all living things.

Rudimentary forms of personal knowledge, also present from birth, allow the child to know whether actions have their impetus from the self or from sources external to the self. Observers, as well as parents, know well that children have a sense that intrinsically motivated actions, such as age-linked manipulation of objects and exploration, are an expression of their own interests, for the children happily persist at such activities and are displeased when made by external forces to stop. As we review later, even in toddlerhood, children's spontaneous and intrinsic motives can be "undermined" by external rewards (e.g., Warneken & Tomasello, 2008). This phenomenal sense of self-initiation represents a rudimentary form of what is described by the attributional dimension of PLOC, and it represents a conceptual link between the constructs of intrinsic motivation, PLOC, and our deeply structured sense of self.

In fact, de Charms's (1968) hypothesis concerning the relations between PLOC and intrinsic motivation has been widely sustained. Research has shown that when intrinsically motivated, people report experiencing freedom and choice, and when prompted by factors such as rewards, evaluations, and threats, people report less choice and display less intrinsic motivation (e.g., Deci, Koestner, & Ryan, 1999). Thus it seems that de Charms was correct in proposing that an I-PLOC is integral to being intrinsically motivated.

Yet de Charms also argued that in contradistinction to intrinsic motivation, extrinsically motivated behavior is characterized by an E-PLOC. That is, he argued that any instrumental behavior (i.e., any behavior that is done "in order to" achieve a specific goal that is separable from the action itself) is invariantly accompanied by a sense of being a pawn to external forces. In fact, it is perhaps because of this sharp division, in which intrinsically motivated behavior is viewed as self-determined and extrinsically motivated behavior is viewed as other determined, that most early experiments and self-report scales pitted extrinsic motivation against intrinsic motivation as motivational opposites (e.g., de Charms, 1976; Harter, 1981).

However, let us consider this important latter proposition in more detail. It is certainly the case that some extrinsically motivated behaviors are characterized by an E-PLOC—by a sense of being externally controlled—and it is for this reason that they can diminish people's perceived choice and intrinsic motivation. Thus, for example, a boy who does a chore only because he expects a reward from his parents (or only because he expects to avoid a punishment) is engaging in a behavior for a perceived external cause. He himself needs no internal value for initiating the action and would likely not do it unless the contingency were in effect.

One can also imagine, however, a wide variety of extrinsically motivated actions that are more *self*-motivated; actions to which people have assented so that they have an I-PLOC despite the behaviors being instrumental in nature. For example, the same child might on another occasion do a chore to be helpful to his parents, whom he loves and wants to support. Here his behavior would have a more volitional feel. He would experience self-initiation, and, although he does it for extrinsic reasons (to be helpful to his parents), he would value and endorse the actions. Similarly, a woman who works extremely hard on an unpleasant task for a nonprofit organization would clearly be performing nonintrinsically satisfying actions but could easily be doing it for self-determined reasons (Millette & Gagné, 2008; Ryan & Deci, 2000b). If so, her behaviors would have an I-PLOC. Indeed, people can perform duties and responsibilities to others with full volition and autonomy (e.g., Sheldon, Kasser, Houser-Marko, Jones, & Turban, 2005).

Indeed, our research has shown that extrinsically motivated actions can vary in character from very heteronomous or controlled to very autonomous or self-determined—that is, from a fully external PLOC to a highly internal PLOC (Ryan & Connell, 1989). Thus, when one fully endorses the reasons for pursuing an extrinsic goal, or when one engages in extrinsically motivated behavior as an outcome of a well-integrated value, the person can be fully autonomous. Yet to the extent that one engages in an extrinsically motivated activity wholly as a function of external contingencies, or to the extent that the value underlying an activity is not personally embraced, then the person's behavior is, to that degree, characterized by heteronomy and alienation. Between these two extremes lie extrinsically oriented activities that reflect partial internalization of values and goals whose motivational basis is thus only somewhat self-determined. The main point is that extrinsic behavior is best understood as being varied in its relative autonomy, a point we more fully develop in Chapter 8. For the moment, we simply assert that the key to whether a nonintrinsically motivated activity is autonomous is whether its value and regulation have been internalized and integrated to the self. To the degree that integration has occurred, the activity will be performed autonomously and will be supported and endorsed by the self, and, to the degree that it has not, the activity will be controlled.

In our work we use the terms *autonomy, self-determination,* and *I-PLOC* to reflect the same concept, namely, that the regulation of an activity is either intrinsic or well integrated and that the activity is therefore performed freely or volitionally. The attributional terminology of I-PLOC is particularly useful for empirical work because one can operationalize a variety of factors that either facilitate or undermine the experience of an I-PLOC. For example, whereas threatening a person with respect to an activity will likely lead the person to perceive the activity as having its cause or basis in an external factor (viz., the threat), creating a nonpressuring atmosphere and allowing choice should facilitate the experience of self-determination or of an I-PLOC. Thus these predicted effects on PLOC and subsequent motivation can be empirically tested using experimental manipulations, along with behavioral, self-report, and implicit indicators of volition.

Importantly, the referent for the term *internal,* when used in the phrase "internal perceived locus of causality," is not the *person* but rather the *self.* This is a critical conceptual issue, because in the SDT framework there can be intrapsychic (or intrapersonal) pressures that, although internal to the person, can be experienced as self-alien and controlling (Ryan, 1982). Specifically, introjected attitudes or regulations are in some sense internal to the person but external to the self, and as such they would have a relatively external PLOC. They are an instance of non-self-determination. They can even diminish one's intrinsic motivation (e.g., Plant & Ryan, 1985).

It is interesting in this regard to consider Baumeister's (1991) concept of *escaping the self.* In his discussion of "flights from the burden of selfhood," he is referring primarily to the burden of introjects, to the anxiety and despair associated with critical and punitive values that, in spite of the phrasing, do not at all represent the SDT *self.* This is also the case for much of what Leary (2004) discussed as the "curse of the self"—namely, the burdens of self-evaluations, introjected conceptions of worth, and attachments to ego investments that indeed create distress, as our own findings show. We can well understand the urge to escape such alien and painful aspects of one's psychic makeup, but it is conceptually important to recognize that from an organismic perspective these plaguing and depleting aspects might better be referred to as *nonself* than *self.* Surely, in the face of such intrapersonal controlling burdens, one might well feel pressured and depleted and want to escape to *these* experiences.

To summarize, the processes that are related to the experience of being autonomous versus controlled, of being authentic versus inauthentic, of being true versus false to one's self, become more amenable to rigorous empirical investigation once framed in the terminology of PLOC. This is particularly true if one does not lose sight of the phenomenal sense in which Heider portrayed the attribution of causality and thus of the connections between the language of attribution and the theoretical meanings of autonomy and self.

Psychologists and the Rejection of Autonomy

The philosophical and organismic analyses herein discussed concerning autonomy and the emergence of self as a potential organizing force in behavior connect with the central concepts of our theorizing within SDT. Yet it is noteworthy that a number of prominent theories in empirical psychology, often on quite varied grounds, have rejected ideas concerning autonomy and personal causation, or concepts that might seem closely related to them. Thus, in the context of discussing accounts of autonomy, we take a brief opportunity to review some of these perspectives and how they relate to the ideas of self-as-process and the autonomous functioning we have thus far reviewed.

Behaviorism and Neo-Behaviorism

B. F. Skinner, the foremost voice in 20th-century behaviorism, was explicit in his rejection of autonomy. Specifically, Skinner (1971) relegated autonomy to the category of concepts used when one is ignorant of the actual causes of, or factors that control, behavior. In Skinner's operant system of thought, all control over behavior was, by definition, external to the organism and lay in environmental contingencies of reinforcement. Skinner (1971) argued further that "If we do not know why a person acts as he does, we attribute his behavior to him" (p. 53). Because Skinner viewed all recurrent behavior as under the control of external reinforcements, what he thus meant by "not knowing" specifically referred to not yet having identified the external contingencies of reinforcement that he tautologically assumed to be controlling behavior. In taking this stance, Skinner did not see the relevance of considering whether external contingencies, even where they were operative, might be experienced as controlling or, alternatively, as something with which the actor might concur or volitionally choose to follow. Thus Skinner's work represents a prime example of how pitting the idea of autonomy *against* that of external influences can lead to a premature abandonment of this construct that is nonetheless crucial for a practical psychology of human motivation. He and other operant behaviorists have thus ignored volition when implementing reinforcements, which has been a major problem in their effectiveness (Ryan, Lynch, Vansteenkiste, & Deci, 2011).

Using a similar argument, Bandura (1989, 1996), in his social-cognitive theory of agency, wrote off the concept of autonomy by defining autonomy as actions that are "entirely independent" (1989, p. 1175) of the environment. He then reasoned that, because no behaviors are entirely independent of an environment, autonomy does not merit further consideration as an account or element of agency. As with Skinner's view, the relevance of assent, consent, or volition with respect to an environmental influence is not deeply considered in this view, nor is the idea that behaviors or motives may be more or less congruent or integrated with one's core or abiding values. The result is that the self-efficacy approach does not account for issues of alienation, undermining, or reflective commitment, nor does it contrast authentic living with empty, inauthentic success. We live in world where we can observe a lot of people being efficacious and high achieving, many driven by needs for approval or rewards, and at the same time too often lacking guidance by even their own moral centers.

Cultural Relativism

As we have previously discussed, this conceptual demarcation between independence and autonomy is critical not only in regard to the idea of independence from an environment but also in regard to one's social context and interconnections. We reviewed in this chapter a variety of contemporary philosophical analyses that support the viability and importance of this distinction. Yet conflating independence and autonomy has led some theorists to denigrate the universal importance of autonomy and to suggest that it is merely a "Western" (e.g., Iyengar & DeVoe, 2003; Markus, Kitayama, & Heiman, 1996) or male (Gilligan, 1982; Jordan, 1991) preoccupation. As characterizations and critiques of individualism and independence, these arguments may have substantial merit, but they are not meaningful critiques of *autonomy* as employed within SDT or as reflected in the rich philosophical traditions we have been reviewing (Ryan, 1993).

Moreover, to construe autonomy as exclusively a Western, male cultural value is to run the risk of denying the importance and salience of self-determination to all women and all persons in non-Western cultures, which, of course, constitutes a regressive and potentially disempowering stance, both politically (see Mackenzie & Stoljar, 2000) and clinically (see Lerner, 1988; Ryan & Deci, 2008b). Finally, it ignores the growing evidence that across cultures, the extent to which people internalize and integrate their own cultural practices matters greatly for their own mental health and cultural fit (e.g., Chirkov, Ryan, Kim, & Kaplan, 2003; Miller, Das, & Chakravarthy, 2011).

We view autonomy as an evolved potentiality that is characteristic of healthy human functioning, and we see it as relevant to the processes through which cultural contents of any type, whether collectivistic or individualistic, Western or Eastern, capitalist or socialist, become internalized and integrated. This does not mean for us that all cultural contents or values are equally assimilable, however, as some may be more or less congruent with people's basic psychological needs. We address this issue more fully throughout.

Autonomy as Individuation and Separateness

Similar to the cultural relativist position, in some theories of adolescent development and maturation, autonomy is cast in terms of a relinquishing of attachments to significant others (e.g., Blos, 1979). Thus, for example, Steinberg and Silverberg (1986) defined an *emotionally autonomous* adolescent as one who detaches and separates from parents and forgoes his or her reliance on their guidance or advice.

We would not, however, view such separation as necessarily advancing autonomy or self-regulation. Instead, in the SDT framework, detachment (especially from parents) is typically considered counterproductive with regard to the development of autonomy and self-regulation (Ryan & Lynch, 1989), and we detail empirical findings that support that view in Chapter 13. Instead, a capacity to self-reflect is important, and this is probably best cultivated in a network of warm and autonomy-supportive relationships. Yet, for the moment, and appropriate to this chapter, let us again have a philosopher talk. As Friedman (2000) stated:

The human capacity for autonomy develops in the course of socialization. By neglecting to mention the role of socialization in the development of mature autonomy competency, traditional accounts of autonomy ignore one crucial way in which autonomous persons are ultimately dependent after all, and in particular, on women's nurturing. (p. 39)

In short, as we have argued in this chapter and elaborate throughout, there is nothing antithetical about autonomy and relatedness or autonomy and dependence or interdependence. Indeed, the most volitional acts of persons are typically relational, and even the acquisition of autonomy and the values it supports are products of dependency in the deepest sense.

Similarly, Frankfurt (2004) makes a compelling argument for the compatibility of caring and autonomy. When we care for and love others, we identify with their interests, and we can thus endorse supporting them and willingly acting on their behalf (see also Kerr, 2002). Every loving parent knows there is nothing more autonomously endorsed than caring for one's child. Not only are helpfulness, care, and duty to others possibly autonomous, they are regularly so (Martela & Ryan, 2015).

Human beings, out of their inherent and basic need for relatedness, are oriented toward attachments and internalizing the practices and values of those to whom they are attached, just as they begin immediately to express and strive for autonomy. As we argue in SDT, both relatedness and autonomy are fundamental needs, and their dynamic relation to one another is continually explored in studies throughout this book.

Autonomy and the New Reductionism: The Oz Self

As psychology has advanced in its understandings of the neurological substrates of behavior and cognition, some have interpreted such knowledge as undermining ideas of self-determination or autonomy. Consider, for example, this passage from a popular book by Hood (2012, p. 3): "We know the power of visual illusions to trick the mind into perceiving things incorrectly, but the most powerful illusion is the sense that we exist inside our heads as an integrated, coherent individual or self." In Hood's view we are duped into a fake sense of self "because our brains are constructing simulations or stories to make sense of our experiences" (p. 3). He goes on to criticize theories of self as employing a homunculus, even as in his writing "the brain" now linguistically replaces that construct. The "brain" is now the wizard behind the curtain, constructing stories.

Similarly, consider this statement by well-known author Steven Pinker:

Each of us feels that there is a single "I" in control. But that is an illusion that the brain works hard to produce. . . . The brain does have supervisory systems in the prefrontal lobes and anterior cingulate cortex, which can push the buttons of behavior and override habits and urges. But these systems are gadgets with specific quirks and limitations; they are not implementations of the rational free agent traditionally identified with the soul or the self. (2002, p. 43)

Like Hood, Pinker substitutes the "I" with a new intentional agent, "the brain," which pushes the buttons and controls urges. Here, too, the brain, like the Wizard of Oz, is standing behind the curtain working the illusion machine. In such depictions, the sense of self and volition is a postbehavior " illusion," whereas the brain, reified as if it were a nonsubjective but active and manipulative agent, does the acting, deciding, "button pushing," and storytelling to an apparently highly gullible individual. Pinker (2002) contrasts this brain-as-agent account with the myth of a "free rational agent," the latter apparently comprised of some disembodied force. Pinker (2002, p. 183) later argues that society can influence human behavior by "appealing to that inhibitory brain system" (i.e., the prefrontal cortex). Here society becomes the agent, and its audience is not people, or even their reflective capacities, but rather one part of one human organ.

Now, of course, such statements are polemical, and no doubt intended to highlight the mechanisms that support behavior. But the logic here unnecessarily separates, in a quite dualistic way, first-person accounts from biological accounts of action. Hood and Pinker are not alone in employing such logic; it is found all too commonly in contemporary psychology and neuroscience. In this narrative, the self and any sense of volition or self-direction are "merely" illusions created by the brain. For example, Bargh (2007, p. 133) argued: "subjective feelings of free will are one of the positive illusions (Taylor, 1989) we hold dear. Yet he added that this "is irrelevant to the scientific status or truth value . . . it is still an illusion" (p. 133). Wegner (2007) similarly equated any sense of self and volition as akin to "magic," an illusion that dupes us and masks the "real" workings of mind and behavioral causation. Hood (2012) opines that any subjective experience of personal control over one's actions reflects people's "ignorance of the mechanisms" that determine their behavior (p. 124). Indeed, "neuroscience tells us that we are mistaken" when we imagine we can make decisions or assert a choice: "we think we have freedom but, in fact, we do not" (p. 121). The reasoning here appears to be that if the brain is involved in action, it is therefore the ultimate and most relevant cause of behaviors, and therefore any psychological account of causation and will is illusory. Such thinking is so popular, in fact, that the November 1999 issue of *American Psychologist* had as its cover headline "Science Watch: Behavior—It's Involuntary," as if that were a scientific finding rather than a sloppy meta-theoretical viewpoint, and as if there were no meaningful distinctions between volitional and nonvolitional behaviors.

Such interpretations entail a fundamental loss of perspective in terms of the multiple levels of analysis available across the varied disciplines of science. They rest logically on the view that autonomy or will must be some non-brain-related force that intervenes in action, much like Descartes's soul tilted the pineal gland to alter otherwise purely mechanical sequences of action. We know of no such force, and it is no wonder that autonomy, when so defined, would be understood as antiquated and illusory.

Clearly, both autonomous self-regulation and controlled regulatory processes operate within an organism, involve the brain, and have distinct biological supports (Ryan, Legate, Niemiec, & Deci, 2012; Ryan, Kuhl, & Deci, 1997). The distinct regulatory processes associated with autonomous and nonautonomous actions are also clearly linked with distinct contextual influences, as well as different affective and behavioral consequences (e.g., Legault & Inzlicht, 2013; Murayama et al., 2015; Reeve & Lee, 2012; Ryan & Di Domenico, 2016). In short, the antecedents, consequences, and functional underpinnings of autonomous versus nonautonomous behaviors are divergent (Kuhl, Quirin, & Koole, 2015). Grasping these facts at every level of analysis is important for scientific understanding, and this is what defines interdisciplinary consilience. None of this makes the psychological level of analysis merely illusory or irrelevant. Indeed, it is at the psychological level of events where, in most cases, the most practically relevant causal factors can be located (Heider, 1958; Ryan & Deci, 2004a).

Whereas "Oz self" theorists want to denigrate or write off sensibilities concerning self and autonomy as merely illusions, SDT has a deeper agenda—to coordinate what we know about these motivational states and their functional consequences with both social science and neuroscience. As psychologists we don't want to write off psychological experiences; rather, we attempt to understand these phenomena at their level of appearance (Gould, 2002) and map out their consequences, mechanistic underpinnings, and the social-cultural circumstances in which they arise.

All events in the universe can (potentially) be described in material and efficient causal terms and can be described from molecular to molar levels of analysis and parsing of events. At times, we are interested in those most concrete and microscopic sequences of events entailed in actions. Yet at other times, particularly when concerned with the relevant causes of molar behavioral events, our focus is on social forces, personal goals, and subjective interpretations. At still other times, we may be interested in the interaction of multiple levels of causal analysis and the constraints posed by each.

Consider a person who walks to the local food store. One appropriate causal account of this event can be found in the physical events inside the organism's brain that regulated balance, the motor movements of the legs, and the guidance of walking by perceptual systems such as vision. Let us suppose we know these events in total detail, down to the molecular sequence of change. Has the person's behavior thus been "explained"?" Of course, at one level of analysis it has. But we submit that in most contexts an explanation of the sequence from stimulus conditions to brain cells to motor output would be highly unsatisfying, if not irrelevant and distracting. The most meaningful and relevant level of analysis for the cause of this behavior lies instead in the interpretations and construal of events that gave rise to the molar behavior, rather than in the brain processes that sub-served it. It is likely to be more informative to know, for example, what prompted him to go to the store and why (i.e., for what phenomenal reasons) he went. The psychological goal or subjective motivation, in turn, may be more or less volitionally endorsed, helping to further explain whether he is dragging his feet or enthusiastically going. These phenomenal and social facts, that is, will likely be the most critical considerations in explaining whether, how, and why he goes to the store, including what "gadgets" in the brain get activated in the process.

In short, the mere fact that an explanation is offered at a lower level of analysis does not make it better, fuller, or more definitive. Indeed, it can make it more irrelevant. Such causal explanations are not incorrect, but they are often misplaced, as in the case of a quite famous neuropsychologist we know who authoritatively informed an experienced clinician that her warm provision of relatedness and support was "simply" an adjustment of the patient's amygdala. Helpful, indeed.

At times a neurological/physiological explanation is the most relevant and regnant level of explanation for a behavioral event. This is particularly true for behavior that would fall under Heider's (1958) category of *impersonal causation,* such as a motor tic in a patient with Tourette's disorder or an episode of rage after an unexpected face slap. Even here, it is still interesting to also view these events from a psychological point of view. Such behaviors are typically experienced as uncontrolled and nonintentional, as phenomenologists have specifically explicated (e.g., Ricoeur, 1966). When action mechanisms bypass all mediation by the reflective, evaluative capacities of the person, people are quite unlikely to report feeling autonomy. Instead, they typically say, "it happened to me," or "I couldn't help it." Similarly it is clear that psychological trauma can directly increase tendencies toward chronic hyperarousal, posing obstacles for integrative processing and self-regulation (van der Hart, Nijenhuis, & Steele, 2006). Understanding the mechanics of these events is extremely important for behavioral scientists, and at the same time they can shed considerable light on human volition and its absence.

Behavioral events, their biological underpinnings, and their phenomenology are reciprocally informative types of data. As motivational psychologists, we are centrally concerned with social contexts and their subjective meaning to and impact on the actors within them. Social events have a *functional significance* (Deci & Ryan, 2000), influenced both by interpersonal supports and by the controls and contingencies that confront the actor. This functional significance, in turn, shapes the organization of subsequent action. Where autonomy enters the picture is in this realm of meaning. When researchers look into the meanings of events and their predictive relations to what follows, they are not denying material causation or the necessity of a brain that underlies or sometimes moderates these processes. Yet they are also not losing sight of the regnant processes associated with behavior.

Nonconscious Determination versus Autonomy

Another recent concern with autonomy has surfaced with the demonstration that many actions, even ones that are intentional, may be brought about or caused by factors of which people are unaware. Bargh and Ferguson (2000), for example, cited several studies in which people are implicitly or unconsciously primed to enact particular behaviors and then postbehaviorally attribute their actions to will or self-initiation. For them, such experiments call into question whether all acts are nonconsciously determined and whether our attributions of being self-motivated have any veracity.

Bargh's (2007) evidence that feelings of free will are illusory stems primarily from his idea that any action that is not initiated wholly by the individual, without any outside cue, prompt, or inspiration, is not free will. Here he follows Wegner and Wheatley (1999), who specifically stated: "people experience conscious will when they interpret their own thought as the cause of their action" (p. 480). Yet, as we outlined earlier, this is clearly *not* the definition of "will" in modern existential-phenomenological or analytical philosophies (nor is this the SDT definition of autonomy). Further, such a criterion for will—namely, one's conscious thoughts are the initial cause of behavior—seems designed to cast the concept of will into the intellectual wastebasket, where we agree it would belong if so defined. It is a "straw man" conceptualization, quite easily knocked over. It is unlikely by any analysis that thoughts about initiating behaviors, even reflective ones, come from nowhere or are disconnected from underlying brain processes or any prior external events and circumstances. We suggest instead that the exercise of will and autonomy has nothing to do with being an *initial* cause or stimulus to action. It concerns, rather, the capacity to effectively evaluate the meaning and fit of potential actions with one's overarching values, needs, and interests, whatever influences might be initiating the actions.

Autonomy is not based in people's capacity to have a conscious thought be the *causa sui* for their actions, nor must autonomous behavior be detached from any prior influence. The prompts, goals, and initiating cues for most, if not every, action are, in fact, located in and in relation to one's past or current environment or bodily states. In fact, we agree with Wegner (2002) that people are often wrong when they imagine that their own thoughts were the *initial* causes of their impulses or actions. We do not create goals and purposes *ex nihilo,* or, as Friedman (2003) put it, "self-determination does not require humanly impossible self-creation" (p.8). Instead, the issue of people's autonomy lies in the regulatory process through which the behaviors we engage in, even if originally nonconsciously prompted, are governed. When people are (versus are not) open to their experience, when they take interest in an urge or possible action, they can evaluate its worth. This formulation is consistent not only with our earlier analysis of self-reflection but also with experimental findings. For example, Libet (1999) showed in often-cited research that certain volitional actions (ones that we would typically think of as simple rather than the kind that require reflection or endorsement) could be preceded by a readiness potential in the brain before any awareness of intention. Yet Libet further stated that consciousness has its function in approving (or vetoing) the commission of the act. It is the latter aspect that is often not emphasized in those citations.

Wegner (2002), however, raised another important fact: People also suffer illusions of control over outcomes. They sometimes think their actions bring about outcomes that they cannot, as he demonstrated in some clever experiments. We agree with this fact but find it nonetheless noteworthy that many of the best experimental demonstrations he offered of the "illusion" of a connection between one's intentional behavior and outcomes take place in ambiguous and strange situations—people using Ouija boards or dowsing for water. In unfamiliar turf where causal knowledge is lacking, misattributions will be more likely. In addition, the illusions often concern one's actual *control over outcomes* rather than the autonomous or controlled regulation of the acts themselves. As has been detailed elsewhere, there is no isomorphism between perceived locus of *causality* and one's locus of *control* over outcomes (Deci & Ryan, 1985a). Hypothetically, at least, a person might autonomously divine for water, believing it to be a valuable activity, even though the person's capacity to find water may be, in actuality, completely unreliable. As well, someone could heteronomously drill wells for water (i.e., do so because external authorities force or pressure him or her to do this drilling) and yet reliably find water. Here, the person might be neither deluded nor autonomous. In other words, there is no logical connection between having a correct causal analysis in mind and being autonomous or controlled. At one time, some people autonomously tried to make gold through alchemy. They might have been wrong about their physics, but they were not necessarily lacking autonomy in their search.

Despite the issue of terminology, Wegner has provided compelling, and we think important, evidence that people are vulnerable to illusion and self-deception and, in certain circumstances, they can be tricked or fooled. Yet this idea that people can be deluded or delude themselves is not really problematic for a psychology of autonomy. Indeed, self-deception is, according to both philosophical and SDT analyses, an important human vulnerability, as well as a primary way in which people escape from the burdens of freedom and responsibility. What the evidence does *not* show, however, is that people cannot differentiate between autonomous and controlled actions or that they cannot, in nontrivial situations, reflectively evaluate behavioral possibilities and select those that are more congruent with, rather than contradictory to, their values and interests. That is the essence of autonomous self-regulation, and without it we might be nothing but a twitching mass of contradictory impulses, torn in a hundred directions at once.

Can people be deceived about causes or control? The answer is clearly yes. The more ambiguous the context, the less certain the values, or the more salient the social pressures, the more this seems to be so. No one concerned with the dynamics of autonomy has ever argued that self-deception and delusions are not possible or that well-designed experiments might not deceive people as to their choices and needs. But this only shows the importance of mindfulness (Brown & Ryan, 2003), integrated processing (Di Domenico, Le, Liu, Ayaz, & Fournier, 2016), or a well functioning "self-compatibility" checker (Kuhl & Kazén, 1994)—in other words, a capacity for integrative awareness of one's sensibilities, values, and the consequences of possible actions (Deci & Ryan, 2000; Hodgins & Knee, 2002).

Interestingly, after many provocative statements about "will" being merely an illusion, Wegner (2002) argued almost parenthetically that this illusory experience of free will or volition may be of critical importance to humans. He describes an *authorship emotion* that is more or less present for any action and that supplies a useful guide to the selection and regulation of behavior. In other words, at the end of a book in which Wegner's primary point is essentially that self and autonomy are illusory, he acknowledges that our human sensibility concerning the authorship of actions is both informative and functional. Such an authorship emotion is, of course, no doubt an aspect of the sense of volition, or of being an origin versus a pawn, that a long tradition in psychology from de Charms to SDT has kept in focus.

Not only can people be mistaken about control over outcomes, but also they can sometimes be mistaken, or more specifically, actively self-deceptive, about the autonomy of their actions. For example, in the SDT framework, people experience a high degree of autonomy when they identify with and endorse the personal importance of certain activities. Yet it is sometimes the case that, when these identifications are more reflectively considered (as in a good therapy session), one finds them contradictory to other identifications in ways not previously considered. In fact, we specifically suggest that under certain conditions of social control some identifications are *compartmentalized* and remain relatively unintegrated within the person (see Chapters 8 and 24). One "tries not to see" how one value might conflict with another. To the extent that compartmentalization is active, it represents a form of self-deception (e.g., Weinstein, Deci, & Ryan, 2011).

Similarly, it is often the case in clinical work that what appears at first blush to be a volitional undertaking, when actively unpacked turns out to be an introject—a value or goal that was not really assimilated as one's own. A classic example is the student who (tells himself that he) "wants" to be a doctor but who seems in reality to lack enthusiasm for his studies. Upon a reflective analysis, this "identification" turns out to be his parents' aspiration for him, not a reflection of his own interests. To maintain relatedness, he has, in the words of Perls (1973), "swallowed whole" the approved-of identity as if it were his own vocational wish. When such self-deception occurs, it is motivated by and can almost invariably be traced back to a conflict between needs—in this case, between relatedness and autonomy.

Implicit and Explicit Motivational Processes

Another argument against will or volition has been that behavior is often motivated by implicit processes—processes of which the individual may not be consciously or explicitly aware. Within the conceptual framework of SDT, the issue of implicit and explicit motivation needs to be distinguished, however, from the issue of autonomous versus heteronomous motivation, although there are some interesting interfaces (e.g., Deci & Ryan, 1980b; Weinstein, Hodgins, & Ryan, 2010). Notably, in our view, implicit or nonconscious events may prompt either autonomous or controlled behaviors, just as behaviors that are automatic may be regulated by either autonomous or controlled motivations.

Consider, for example, a driver who, while listening to a newscast, automatically shifts her car into fourth gear when the cue of engine noise prompts it. In doing so, she may be acting fully autonomously, even though she was not conscious of the cue or even of the act. Yet were she to reflectively consider that action, she would (provided the correct gear was selected) no doubt wholly endorse it. Conversely, some implicit motives can drive heteronomous behavior. A person who has made a personal commitment to quit smoking may, after exposure to a cigarette ad, find himself mindlessly grasping for a smoke. Were he to reflectively consider it, he might agree that the behavior was inconsistent with his self-endorsed higher order goal to quit. Once committing the act, one marker of his heteronomy would be the guilt or self-recrimination that followed the smoking.

Explicit motives, too, may be heteronomous or autonomous, but this is more obvious. When someone explicitly decides to give in to a coercive demand, he or she may be aware of the decision but still not feel any autonomy. On the other hand, explicit motives can be autonomous, as when someone openly considers an urge that has arisen and assents to its enactment because it "fits" with his or her central values. In short, the issue of automaticity versus conscious deliberateness is not isomorphic with the issue of autonomy versus heteronomy. Some habits and reactions are ones we would experience as autonomous; others seem alien, imposed, or unwanted.

Still, there is an important concern with nonconsciously prompted behaviors and priming of certain actions or attitudes. From the perspective of SDT, emitted behaviors, however instigated, are autonomous to the degree that they accord with one's interests and values, and this is facilitated when the person is mindful or nondefensively aware of both interests and needs, as well as of the urges or intentions that arise (Schultz, Ryan, Niemeic, Legate, & Williams, 2015; Schultz & Ryan, 2015). Thus the more "automatic" one's behavior, the more one is *at risk* for being controlled. This is one reason why mindfulness is associated with greater autonomy (Brown & Ryan, 2003; Levesque & Brown, 2003). Without mindfulness or reflective attention, people's actions will more often be controlled, and often costly, as experiments we subsequently review will demonstrate (e.g., Niemiec, Brown, et al., 2010).

Similarly there is good reason to believe, from a variety of experiments, that, when people are most autonomous—when they are self-determined—in their values and commitments, they show more congruence between their implicit and explicit motives and attitudes. Legault, Green-Demers, Grant, and Chung (2007) have shown this with respect to prejudice. It is also the case that people may show more convergence between implicit and explicit identities when conditions are autonomy-supportive, as shown by Weinstein, W. Ryan, et al. (2012), with regard to sexual attractions. Using different methods to address implicit–explicit incongruence, Schattke, Koestner, and Kehr (2011) suggested such discrepancies are more common in people who suffered autonomy and relatedness-need thwarting in early development, thus potentiating more defensive processing and lower access to internal states. Our point is not then that implicit motivational processes can never compromise autonomy—we just disagree that they *always* do.

Indeed, it was for all these reasons that, even in our earliest work in SDT, we argued for a distinction between automatic and automatized behaviors (Deci & Ryan, 1980b). At that time we defined *automatic* behaviors as those that are nonconsciously pushed by controlled processes and whose occurrence is not consistent with one's reflective commitments and cannot be easily brought into the realm of active choice. In contrast, *automatized* actions are habitual ones that, if reflected upon, would fit with one's values or needs and could be readily changed when they no longer do. Behavior becomes automatized because it is efficient and conserves resources, but it is not necessarily heteronomous (e.g., the shifting of a car gear). Behavior that is automatic, however, may be rigidly unconscious for dynamic reasons (e.g., automatic eating, or acting on prejudice). Such a distinction between these two types of nonconsciously prompted behaviors, even if given a more modern terminology, is still needed.

Summarizing across Critiques

For us, the importance of these recent critiques of freedom and will as illusory lies not in their categorical conclusions but rather in their highlighting yet more sources of human vulnerability to nonautonomous regulation. As SDT has long argued, experiences of being coerced or seduced into actions can undermine people's autonomy for the actions and leave them more rigid and defensive (Deci & Ryan, 2000). In that state, people may, among other things, deceive themselves into thinking they have control over outcomes or autonomy concerning their behavior, and they may adamantly and insistently proclaim as much. Moreover, we can only agree that people often do not know what prompts or gives rise to a desire, impulse, or action tendency. Indeed, as clinicians, we see this every day. We also agree, as Wilson (2003) pointed out, that people do not know how their inner machinery works. All the more reason to have a psychology of autonomy that would prompt people to reflectively consider what they are doing and, from that basis, to regulate subsequent behavior.

Concluding Comments

In this discussion of philosophical, clinical, and psychological thought, we reviewed a number of formulations that serve as a backdrop to our empirical inquiries and theoretical proposals concerning the self and autonomy. First, it is evident that *self-as-process* (the *I* rather than the *me*) is not an object or thing but is fundamentally a set of integrative processes deeply rooted in nature. The self is never directly experienced or apprehended, because, as phenomenological studies reveal, experience is always *of* something. The self is also fluid and emergent. It is not a thing, but a spontaneous process that aids in regulating action and adapting to circumstances. Second, autonomous functioning is based in our capacity to experience activities as self-endorsed versus alienated or, in existential terms, authentic versus inauthentic. Autonomy refers to the experience of an action as fitting with interests and integrated values that one is wholeheartedly behind. Inauthenticity, in contrast, refers to the experience of actions that are based in externally controlled or introjected values or prescriptions and are thus not integrated to the self. The important point concerning authenticity or autonomy, therefore, is not whether or not there are external demands or influences, but whether people have integrated and assented to them or have merely introjected and/or been controlled by them.

We also reviewed clinical perspectives on the true self and relations between this concept and ideas of authenticity, autonomy, and integration. We then traced the origins of the concept of autonomy within SDT from its roots in the work of Heider and de Charms and their concept of perceived locus of causality. We connected this with de Charms's speculations about intrinsic motivation and the relevance of his thinking to SDT.

Finally, we defended the idea of autonomy against a number of attacks and misconceptions within modern psychology. These include accounts of autonomy as independence from all external influence; autonomy as implying separateness and individualism; autonomy as freedom from implicit motives or mistaken attributions of cause; or autonomy as a disembodied or immaterial causal force that does not require a brain. These mischaracterizations of autonomy impede the empirical study of this important behavioral attribute.

We would conclude that the functional importance of autonomy, as a quality of behavioral regulation, has considerable scientific import, as does the subjective experience of autonomy and self. At the same time, autonomy as a functional property of behaving persons is not something that can be assumed; rather, it is variable and vulnerable and, in part, dependent on specific supports in the social environment. It is to these issues that we now turn.

CHAPTER 4

Psychological Needs

Varied Concepts and a Preliminary Description of SDT's Approach

One of psychology's most critical questions concerns the internal or external conditions necessary to support human flourishing and to avoid serious harms. SDT has addressed this issue using the concept of *basic psychological needs,* defined functionally as satisfactions required for healthy development and wellness. We compare SDT's concept of needs with that of other theories. For example, Murray (1938) included psychological desires that may or may not support human flourishing, and Hull (1943) was focused on physiological needs rather than psychological ones. Closer to SDT's approach is that of Doyal and Gough (1991), who emphasized human needs for autonomy and health. We discuss our criteria for basic needs, suggest that some motives (e.g., power) that are called needs in other theories are compensations for basic need frustrations, and argue against some conceptions of need hierarchy. We then provide a preliminary overview each of SDT's three basic psychological needs: competence, relatedness, and autonomy. Finally, and again in only a preliminary way, we specify the primary functional outcomes that result from basic need satisfactions—namely, enhancement of intrinsic motivation, internalization and integration, and individual and social wellness and vitality—and we contrast these outcomes with the developmental harms and well-being costs of basic need frustration.

An organismic approach orients motivational thinking away from questions about what controls behavior toward what supports living functions. Among the fundamental properties distinguishing living beings from inanimate entities is the dependence of the former on exchanges with their environments. Living things must draw from their environments the resources and necessities that allow them to preserve, maintain, and enhance their existence. Stated differently, living things have *needs* that, when fulfilled, sustain and fortify their persistence and thriving.

Insofar as SDT is concerned with both human flourishing and degradation, the issue of basic needs has been very salient within the theory, dating back to its earliest statements (e.g., Deci, 1975; Deci & Ryan, 1980a, 1985b) and continuing thereafter (e.g., Deci & Ryan, 2000; Ryan, 1993; 1995). Our early interest in needs came from the observed effects of autonomy, competence, and relatedness satisfactions and frustrations on people's quality of motivation and vitality. The research pointed to the contextual conditions of support conducive to thriving and what kinds of circumstances undermined it.

Yet the concept of needs—the idea that there are fundamental nutrients or supports that individuals must have to thrive—is both complex and controversial. Moreover, to assert the status of being a *basic* need is to make certain claims about both universality and priority and suggests commonalities in terms of human nature. Conceptualizing needs as basic and essential to wellness also implicates issues of care, social obligations, and fundamental human rights. In fact, the philosophy of needs has been increasingly explored and refined by other authors such as Plant, Lesser, and Taylor-Gooby (1980), Reader (2005), Samuels (1984), Braybrooke (1987), Dover (2016), Doyal and Gough (1991), Wiggins (2005), Gaspar (2007), Hamilton (2003), Thompson (2006), O'Neill (2011), and others.

In Chapter 10 we present the specific propositions and empirical evidence concerning how basic psychological needs relate specifically to people's wellness. These are embedded within an SDT mini-theory called *basic psychological needs theory* (BPNT), which focuses on specifically psychological health versus ill-being. Yet because our use of the construct of basic psychological needs pervades work in SDT, we focus in this preliminary discussion on the general meaning of the term *need* as we use it, especially in juxtaposition to other uses the term has had within the field. We also discuss various concerns with need constructs and their utility within our research frameworks.

The Concept of Needs

The concept of needs is relatively common in the field of biology, a field that focuses primarily on the physical structure of the organism, its survival, and its reproduction (e.g., Ehrlich, 2000; Jacob, 1973). Agreement exists that there are specifiable, physiological requirements, the fulfillment of which is essential to the life of the individual organism and the deprivation of which leads to serious harm and ill health. Indeed, specification of basic needs in endangered species is critical to establishing policy targets (e.g., Svancara, Scott, Groves, Noss, & Pressey, 2005). Some requirements are even common across organisms. For example, all organisms we know of need water, hydration being fundamental to all life. This is why we look only to planets with water as potentially life-bearing. Yet if one were to argue that water is not needed by a particular species, this claim could be readily tested simply by withholding water from those organisms and observing the ensuing changes (e.g., deterioration) in functioning and health.

The concept of needs rests thus most fundamentally on two related ideas: (1) that the deprivation of certain resources or nutrients results in degraded forms of growth and impaired integrity, that is, it leads to serious harms; and (2) that providing certain resources or nutrients reliably facilitates thriving and the fuller expression of the organism's nature and potential. Any candidate need must minimally meet these two criteria, among a number of others.

The concept of needs is therefore unlike some "motivational" concepts with which it is often conflated, such as wants, preferences, or desires, because the concept of needs is fundamentally built around a potentially objective and empirically specifiable criterion. If something is merely a want, its satisfaction may or may not advance the organism's thriving. I might "want" more chocolates after finishing the box, but satisfying that desire might not enhance my health and wellness; indeed, it might even have negative consequences. Having more chocolates is not a need. To be a *basic need,* there must be observable and meaningful positive consequences for health and thriving stemming from its satisfaction and significant harms stemming from its deprivation or frustration, regardless of preferences.

The issue of needs pertains, then, prescriptively, to life. If one wishes to nurture an organism, first one must know what that organism requires to develop and function optimally, and second the needed elements must be supplied or afforded. In turn, the organism must actively assimilate those nutrients. Thus, for example, it is observable and, in principle, testable that we have minimal requirements for dietary nutrition, with their satisfaction contributing to vitality and their lack of satisfaction leading to depletion and ill health. Once these nutritional needs are identified, caring for humans would be redefined as ensuring that they can access the proper nutrition, among other elements.

As mentioned, the concept of *physical needs* has, despite its complexity, been treated as intuitively clear. For several centuries now, scientists have assumed that there are necessary nutrients in food that are required for growth and sustained health, even as there has been ongoing research to refine our understanding of what those nutrients are. In fact, when the U.S. Department of Agriculture (USDA) first published dietary recommendations in 1894, many of the vitamins and minerals considered essential today had not yet been discovered. Yet foods were recommended for their observed effects on health, even as the underlying mechanisms (e.g., mineral deficiencies) were yet to be revealed. Nutritional guidelines continue to change frequently as we understand more and more about optimizing nutrition.

In contrast, the postulation of *psychological needs* has taken several directions and been much more a subject of debate. Psychology, as a branch of the life sciences, deals with the development, integrity, and health of individuals, including the organization of the perceptual, experiential, and regulatory processes essential to wellness and social adaptation. Yet empirically oriented psychologists have been reluctant to address the issue of what fundamentally nurtures and is essential to the growth, development, coordination, and coherence of these processes, beyond the obvious fact that the psyche (housed in an organic brain and its physiological connections) is dependent upon the fulfillment of physical and safety needs. Indeed, few have made attempts to specify psychological essentials.

Basic Psychological Needs

SDT forwards the proposition that there are specifiable psychological and social nutrients which, when satisfied within the interpersonal and cultural contexts of an individual's development, facilitate growth, integrity, and well-being. Conversely, when these psychological need satisfactions are frustrated or thwarted, there are serious psychological harms (Deci & Ryan, 2000; Ryan, 1995). We refer to these necessary satisfactions for personality and cognitive growth as *basic psychological needs*. This construct describes these universal, cross-developmental propensities upon which integrated functioning depends and the support of which, in an ultimate sense, determines both the well-being of individuals and of the communities that comprise them.

SDT is not the first tradition within empirical psychology to employ the concept of *needs* (Pittman & Zeigler, 2007). In fact, there is a history of need-related concepts in the field, including by such luminaries as Allport (1937), Goldstein (1939), Hull (1943), Maslow (1943), Fromm (1955), Murray (1938), McClelland (1985), and others. These past traditions provide, in fact, some interesting points for comparison and contrast with SDT's psychologically focused and yet empirically driven approach to inherent needs.

Murray's Need Theory

Perhaps the most well-known prior use of the concept of psychological needs was by Henry Murray, whose work using the *Thematic Apperception Test* and other methods has had broad influence on the fields of personality and social psychology. Murray (1938) defined a *need* as a construct that stands for "a force which organizes perception, apperception, intellection, conation and action in such a way as to transform in a certain direction an existing, unsatisfying, situation" (p. 124). Based on this expansive definition, Murray postulated a wide variety of needs, both psychological and organic. For him, psychological needs were largely "social reaction systems" (p. 150) whose function was to raise or maintain social status, to enhance affiliations with social institutions, or to avoid disliked or hostile circumstances. Yet so broad was his view that Murray posited more than 20 primary needs, including not only quite general needs, such as that for affiliation, but also quite specific desires, such as the need to dominate others—as well as its opposite, the need to defer and submit. That is, some were universal needs, some idiosyncratic.

Fitting with this, Murray and scholars who have followed him in the *personological tradition* (e.g., McAdams, 1993; McAdams & Pals, 2006) have primarily focused on the assessment of individual differences in the *strength* of these various needs and used them to predict a range of outcomes (Ryan & Manly, 2005). The result has been a rich and productive body of research, as well as of generative theory (e.g., Bauer, McAdams, & Sakaeda, 2005; Koestner & McClelland, 1990; McAdams, 1993; McClelland, 1985) and assessment methods (e.g., Morgan & Murray, 1935; Schultheiss, 2008; Schüler, Brandstätter, & Sheldon, 2013).

Accordingly, our major contention with Murray's concept of needs is less substantive than terminological. Murray's definition of need encompasses virtually *any* motivating force in people. People's desires, motives, wants, and strivings all represent "forces that organize perception and action." Thus Murray's definition of need applies with equal appropriateness to a starving man's utterance that he "needs food" (Murray's hunger need) and a billionaire's remark that he "needs another vacation home" (Murray's acquisitive need). Although both are motivators that may organize and activate behavior and cognition, there is clearly some sense in which only one of these people speaks of a true need. The other articulates merely a personal desire, whose essentialness, even if the desire is strong, is not at all clear (see Kasser, 2002a, 2002b; Ryan, Sheldon, Kasser & Deci, 1996). Murray's conception of need therefore fails to differentiate acquired desires, preferences, motives, and appetites from actual basic needs.

In fact, some of the motives Murray identified in his list of needs, when especially strong, may produce as much damage as good for the organism's psychological health (e.g., the need for aggression, or the need for abasement). In addition, some of Murray's needs are peripheral or idiosyncratic motivational patterns, applying in no way universally to humans (e.g., the exhibition need, or a need for orderliness). This in no way detracts from the importance of the research on individual differences in these motives, especially with respect to motives for achievement, power, intimacy, and others that have both generality and broad impact. Such individual differences may in fact affect people's attention to, and capability of assimilating, the more fundamental psychological nutriments that will be the focus of SDT. Instead our point is only that Murray's was a list of motives with respect to which there are large individual differences rather than a list of basic needs, at least as we define them.

Although both Murray's definition of needs and SDT's definition are focused at the psychological level, the SDT conceptualization is in some senses more similar to the concept of biological needs (e.g., Hull, 1943), for both specify necessities. There are, we suggest, psychological supports and satisfactions that human beings must have in order to thrive and that, when fulfilled, enhance and sustain development. Conversely, frustration of these needs, no matter what might be supplied in their place, leads to deficiencies and degradation in psychological integrity and social development, affecting both wellness and vitality.

There are, however, important differences between the physiological needs at the heart of Hull's drive theory and the psychological needs at the heart of SDT, and among them is the difference between deficit needs and growth needs. A physiological need motivates action primarily when the organism has been deprived of that need satisfaction, so the organism acts to satisfy the deficit need and then, having returned the organism to equilibrium, will not be motivated by that need for some period of time. There are also psychological concerns that operate as deficit needs—for example, needs for safety or security—and they are activated primarily when their satisfaction is threatened (Deci & Ryan, 2000). The basic needs of SDT, in contrast, do not require deficiencies to motivate action.

Distinguishing Basic Needs

Basic psychological needs have considerable developmental importance because, as a mammalian species, we have a protracted period of dependence in which social connection is critical and active cognitive growth is essential. As SDT research will detail, during this early developmental period supports for relatedness, autonomy, and competence are required for infants and young children to be intrinsically motivated, to attach to others and form secure social bonds, and to integrate social regulations into their self-regulatory capacities (discussed in Chapter 13), all processes essential to adaptation and thriving in "cultural animals" such as humans. Yet their importance goes beyond these early developmental issues, to bear on wellness, relationship qualities, experience, and quality of behavior in virtually every domain and at all ages across the lifespan.

Clarifying what is essential to the thriving of an organism, including the exploration of need candidates and consequences, can in fact tell us much about the *nature* of that being. Organisms are, most fundamentally, entities whose basic and fundamental organization concerns the fulfillment of needs, some common and some species specific. In each species, physical, behavioral, emotional, and cognitive adaptations exist that are specialized for fulfilling these needs. This extends to psychological structures, as organisms must be built to orient toward the "right" phenomena and possess sensibilities and experience satisfactions that facilitate adaptions. In humans, given our social natures, any such inherent tendencies and perceptual sensitivities must ultimately have been related to the procurement of individual and group resources. Specification of people's basic psychological needs can thus tell us much about what was entailed in thriving during our species' history, including our propensities toward curiosity, skill building, and social belonging. In fact, the idea that psychological need satisfactions can function as proximal motivators of propensities and behaviors that have yielded advantages at multiple levels of selection is consistent with recent developments in evolutionary psychology (Ryan & Hawley, 2016; see also Chapter 24).

Yet to claim that the satisfaction of certain psychological needs is essential and adaptive does not mean that people will always be aware of their importance, or even that they will consciously place value on these satisfactions over others. In fact, as research that we subsequently review demonstrates, people may or may not want what they need, or may not need what they want. Social controls, seductive reward contingencies, and cultural introjections can all lead to the motivated neglect or frustration of basic psychological need satisfactions.

Basic needs are, however, *objective* rather than merely subjective phenomena (Braybrooke, 1987; Plant et al., 1980). As with physical needs, psychological needs are defined in SDT in terms of functional effects on thriving versus ill-being. To be classified as a need there must be, by definition, functional costs of need frustration or neglect and benefits of flourishing for satisfying them. Thus the validity of SDT's claim that autonomy, competence, and relatedness are basic psychological needs rests on the pervasive demonstration that these propensities are salient themes in human nature and that practices and values that undermine or thwart their expression and satisfaction expectably yield developmental and social dysfunction and ill-being. That is, wherever need satisfactions are neglected or blocked, failures in thriving and compensatory, defensive behaviors should increase. On the opposite side of this ledger, conditions conducive to need satisfaction should foster thriving and the signs of wellness, such as openness, nondefensiveness, and empathy, that are empirically associated with them. Without these patterns of association, claims concerning a status of need cannot be sustained.

There are other conditions for defining a need as such. Psychological needs should be associated with seeking out or preferring certain types of experiences and with feeling good and thriving when those basic experiences are obtained (Deci & Ryan, 2000; Ryan & Hawley, 2016). These two aspects—needs as motivations and needs as requirements—are salient at different stages of an action sequence, motives at the inception of action and experienced enhancement at its conclusion (Sheldon, 2011). Moreover, hundreds of studies to be reviewed in SDT have assessed the conditions, correlates, and consequences of these need satisfactions, revealing that need satisfaction and frustration are salient issues and predictive of an array of positive and negative functional and wellness outcomes. Many intrinsically motivated activities yield need satisfactions, learning, and well-being enhancements, even though phenomenally obtaining such positive outcomes is not necessarily what proximally motivates action (Ryan & Deci, 2013).

Our focus in SDT is on basic or universal needs, and therefore another criterion for any candidate need is demonstration that it is essential across developmental periods and across cultural contexts. That is, frustration of the need should be associated with harm and satisfaction with greater thriving across age and contexts. This does not mean that there may not be specific or idiosyncratic individual or group needs (see Watkins & Kavale, 2014) but that, being specific, they would not meet this criteria for a *basic* human need. A focus on universal needs also highlights common humanity and allows both within- and between-culture comparisons (see Chapter 22).

Baumeister and Leary (1995), in arguing for a basic *need to belong,* reviewed their standards for defining a basic need. They suggested nine standards for identifying a basic need, some of which overlap with our distinctions thus far. First, Baumeister and Leary argued that the satisfaction of the need should produce positive effects readily under all but adverse conditions. Second, its satisfaction should have affective consequences. Third, they suggested, a need should direct cognitive processing. Fourth, thwarting a need should lead to negative effects on health or well-being. Fifth, they proposed that needs should elicit or organize goal-oriented behaviors designed to satisfy them. The four final standards are that a need should be universal; that it not be derivative of other motives; that it have impact across a broad array of behaviors; and that it have implications beyond immediate psychological functioning. All of these standards apply to the basic psychological needs for autonomy, competence, and relatedness that SDT has proposed, and throughout this book we review evidence that the consequences of satisfaction versus frustration of the three SDT needs do meet these standards. Indeed, we add additional standards when we formally explicate *basic psychological need theory* in Chapter 10.

Because of the restrictiveness of our definition of needs as denoting the essential nutrients for wellness and thriving, SDT's list of basic psychological needs is very short. Indeed, a parsimonious list of needs is particularly important to making the concept of needs useful, for the very idea of a need is that it dynamically ties together a wide range of disparate behaviors that are associated with need fulfillment or frustration. Further, because there are such diverse values, mores, and cultural practices across the globe, there are only a few widely applicable essential psychological nutrients or conditions that are universally and cross-developmentally required for human beings to thrive. As we will see in Chapters 10, 22, and throughout the book, our list of just three basic psychological needs not only meets the criteria for needs but also explains an extraordinary range of phenomena.

Autonomy was described in Chapter 3, and it is a topic on which we continue to elaborate in terms of its development, neurological underpinnings, and cross-cultural significance throughout this work. It refers to feeling willingness and volition with respect to one's behaviors (de Charms, 1968; Deci & Ryan, 1985b; Ryan & Connell, 1989). The need for autonomy describes the need of individuals to experience self-endorsement and ownership of their actions—to be self-regulating in the technical sense of that term. The opposite of autonomy is heteronomy, as when one acts out of internal or external pressures that are experienced as controlling. Autonomy does *not,* as we use it, refer to independence. In our view and evidence (e.g., Ryan, La Guardia, Solky-Butzel, Chirkov, & Kim, 2005; Ryan & Lynch, 1989), the phenomena of independence, dependence, and interdependence can each be either autonomously or heteronomously motivated, a point important to understanding developmental (Chapter 13), relationship (Chapter 12), and cultural (Chapter 22) dynamics and outcomes.

Competence refers to feeling effective in one's interactions with the social environment—that is, experiencing opportunities and supports for the exercise, expansion, and expression of one's capacities and talents (Deci & Ryan, 1980a; Deci & Moller, 2005; Ryan & Moller, 2016; White, 1959). Where individuals are prevented from developing skills, understanding, or mastery, the competence need will be unmet.

Relatedness refers to both experiencing others as responsive and sensitive and being able to be responsive and sensitive to them—that is, feeling connected and involved with others and having a sense of belonging (Baumeister & Leary, 1995; Ryan, 1993; Deci & Ryan, 2000). Relatedness is experienced both in being cared about and in caring. The need is satisfied when others show concern toward the individual, as well as when the individual has opportunities to be benevolent toward others, as both directions of caring enhance a sense of connectedness (Deci, La Guardia, Moller, Scheiner, & Ryan, 2006; Deci & Ryan, 2014a; Weinstein & Ryan, 2010).

We theorize that, when any of these three basic psychological needs is frustrated or neglected either in a given domain or in general, the individual will show motivational, cognitive, affective, and other psychological decrements of a specifiable nature, such as lowered vitality, loss of volition, greater fragmentation, and diminished well-being. Thus general need support will predict general vitality and well-being, but we can also look at need support within specific contexts, such as a classroom, a workplace, or an athletic team, expecting that basic need satisfactions versus frustrations will affect context-specific functioning and experience.

By using a restrictive and verifiable definition of basic psychological needs, we avoid what have historically been perhaps the most common criticisms of need theories, including Murray's approach, namely, that there is a potentially infinite list of needs that can be postulated and that needs and preferences cannot be distinguished. In fact, we have seen little evidence for any psychological needs beyond the three we have isolated (see, e.g., Ryan & Deci, 2000a).

Of course, one could take these three general needs and subdivide them, or define these same needs slightly differently, and indeed some such differentiations will follow. Basic psychological needs are, after all, *psychological constructs*—descriptions of broad categories of satisfactions and frustrations that have been identified with motivational and wellness outcomes. The constructed nature of need variables is illustrated by the fact that different thoughtful approaches to the problem of needs can yield different conceptions.

For example, Doyal and Gough, in *A Theory of Human Need* (1991), highlighted two basic human needs, those for *autonomy* and for *physical health*. For them, the latter is the need to sustain one's body, or survive: the need to have "a body which is alive" (p. 52). The health need is, of course, for us something that falls in the category of physical needs. The other of Doyal and Gough's two needs, namely, *autonomy,* is in their view a broad psychological need. They define autonomy as the opportunity "to make informed choices about what should be done and how to go about doing it" (p. 53). For them, autonomy plays a central role in the procurement of other outcomes and resources that allow a person to flourish, and without autonomy a human being cannot pursue a meaningful existence.

In terms of direct comparisons, Doyal and Gough's definition of autonomy includes aspects of what we would subdivide into competence and autonomy. Relatedness, for them, is an "intermediate need" that supports and is supported by autonomy. Although Doyal and Gough's (1991) criteria for autonomy differ in nuanced ways from those we use in SDT, their definition, like ours, presupposes that individuals need to feel agentic and in charge of their lives and recognizes, as does SDT, varied degrees of autonomy. In any case, it is clear that by using a restrictive definition of needs, Gough and Doyal similarly and independently generated only a very short list. In turn, they have applied their concept of needs to social policy and issues of human rights.

Earlier, Braybrooke (1987) advanced a theory of human needs as well. His entailed a two-part list, with the first part pertaining to physical needs and the second part to various psychosocial needs and capabilities, all pointed toward affording personal development. Braybrooke rightly emphasizes that any declaration of needs is a statement about priorities, with implications across a number of disciplines.

SDT's list of needs had its origins in experimental studies and fieldwork concerning what supported intrinsic motivation, volition, and well-being (Deci & Ryan, 1985b, 2000). Needs for autonomy, competence, and relatedness were thus arrived at both deductively, from organismic ideas about healthy organization (see Chapter 2), and inductively, from findings concerning the functional importance of these psychological satisfactions (Ryan, 1995). The inductive aspect is particularly crucial given our functional view of needs, for they must show the objective characteristics of being necessary for thriving.

Each of the basic psychological needs posited by SDT (or other theories) could be broken into smaller components that may be more or less central to the satisfaction and more or less useful to predicting certain kinds of outcome. Associated with the need for relatedness, for example, are experiences of interpersonal connection, trust, recognition, caring, and benevolence, among other facets. Part of the empirical process is to examine how such relational phenomena are interrelated or independent and how each might differentially contribute to general need satisfaction and wellness. They can be further refined, both in terms of their phenomenology and underlying mechanisms and of the conditions associated with their satisfaction. Precisely because needs should both have coherence and be predictive of objective outcomes, research can, over time, separate the wheat from the chaff—the necessary from the merely desirable, in terms of what defines and supports a basic need.

Implications of SDT's Definition of Needs

One important implication of our definition of psychological needs is that they reflect our adaptive human design and are therefore universal. Psychological needs are an invariant aspect of human makeup and thus apply to all humans in all cultures. Thus part of SDT's program of research is testing the functional benefits of need across varied social and cultural contexts. Specifically, SDT sees need satisfactions as facilitating social and personal functioning, especially within social groups, and thus as serving individual wellness. Indeed, we shall revisit this issue of needs as part of our human natures, looking at evidence across cultures (Chapter 22) and in terms of evolutionary foundations (Chapter 24). Moreover, throughout this book we review evidence for the multiple individual and group benefits associated with attaining satisfactions of these very basic psychological needs and of harms associated with their neglect or frustration.

The claim that there are basic needs that are inherent and universal features of the psyche requires, first and foremost, evidence of the generalizability of those needs across individuals and cultures. It does not, however, depend on the claim that all individuals or cultural groups will equally value, satisfy, or recognize needs or that all individuals are equally well equipped to attain need fulfillments. As we intend to show, the vehicles through which psychological needs are expressed and satisfied differ at different ages and in different cultures and societies, and yet across these contextualizing variables their functional necessity is unchanging. This conceptualization has been supported in various ways. For example, recently Chen, Vansteenkiste, et al. (2015) measured basic need satisfactions and need frustrations in multiple cultures, as well as differences in desires for these satisfactions. As expected, they demonstrated that the need variables predict important wellness outcomes across cultures. More relevant here was that they also showed that desires for these need satisfactions did not moderate these relations with wellness; desired or not, need satisfactions mattered.

Although cultures and groups differ—for example, with some espousing the primacy of the group over the individual and others espousing the primacy of the individual over the group—this does not negate the underlying necessities of the needs we articulate. Indeed, it will be a fundamental tenet of SDT that the reason people have a readiness to adopt and internalize such differing ambient cultural values is that by doing so they can better satisfy needs within their groups (Chirkov, Ryan, Kim, & Kaplan, 2003). It is by assimilating the values of one's group that one becomes more connected and related and more competent and effective. Furthermore, the general tendency to make ambient values one's own and to adopt them as central to identity is an expression of the need for autonomy. Put differently, need satisfactions supply the underlying processes that explain how differing cultural contents become an integral part of individual personalities, as well as how some cultural contents become only partially internalized and thus can lead to alienation. These dynamics of basic needs will, in fact, be apparent across historical, cultural, political, and economic contexts.

At the same time, not all cultural or socially supported values or regulations can be readily internalized, because some can be inherently contradictory to or frustrating of basic need satisfactions. For example, we argue that cultural or group values that deny autonomy (e.g., a belief that one has no rights to pursue what one values) or that are injurious to loved ones (e.g., that one must ostracize an offspring) may be internalized (e.g., can be introjected), but we suspect they will rarely if ever be capable of integration or full autonomous endorsement (see Chapters 10, 22, and 24 for examples). That is quite simply because some values and practices directly and profoundly conflict with basic needs for autonomy or relatedness. Cultural relativists may, of course, disagree, and they can often find individuals who will explicitly endorse values or practices that SDT would consider need-thwarting, from denial of human rights (Chapter 23) to female infibulation (Chapter 22) to genocide (see Chapter 24). Yet a *dynamic* theory looks not just to surface statements of endorsement but to what motivates the endorsement and how congruently the practices or values are anchored within the psyches of the individuals who express them.

SDT suggests, in fact, that differing familial, organizational, historical, economic, and cultural contexts can all be analyzed in terms of the degree to which they have been conducive to the fulfillment of basic human psychological needs. In this sense, not all social contexts, value systems, or structures are equally "good" for humans. Thus, just as patriarchal religious cultures can have need-thwarting practices, so too can individualist–consumer cultures and vertical–collectivist ones. In fact, every culture and social environment has features that support and features that thwart the basic need satisfactions of its members, with predicable effects on their thriving.

This point differentiates SDT from the more extreme cultural relativisms that characterize much of modern psychology (e.g., Iyengar & DeVoe, 2003; Shweder & Sullivan, 1993), in which cultures are viewed as the absolute sculptors of human nature and behavior and in which values are simply "constructions" without reference to any natural tendencies or sensibilities. If this malleability were so, no cultural transformation or instability could be explained. A psychology of needs, on the other hand, suggests the limits of familial, organizational, and cultural impositions, and the bases by which people will seek change or, if they do not, suffer compromised functioning and suffering. A focus on needs can inform us, that is, about where social, cultural, or economic arrangements stifle human nature. It helps explain why some practices are experienced as oppressive and functionally hurt those subjected to them, whereas others advance human flourishing. These themes will recur throughout this book.

Needs as Individual Differences

Another implication of our definition is that the concept of individual differences in need strength, so central to the theories of Murray (1938) and McClelland (1985), has a different kind of importance in our theory (Deci & Ryan, 2000). Because needs are essential for everyone and are thus theorized to relate to psychological health, differences in people's reports of the strength or salience of need-related motives is not considered as the most essential, or even reliable, predictor of the critical outcomes of behavioral quality and well-being. Rather than predicting outcomes primarily from need strength, within SDT we predict them primarily from the extent to which a person's needs have been either satisfied or frustrated, or from the extent to which social contexts are or have been either supporting or thwarting of need satisfaction. Individual differences in need-related motives (e.g., strong affiliation motives) may at times influence need satisfaction, but just as often these motives may become salient and gain phenomenological import precisely because of need deficiencies. SDT holds that basic need satisfactions are important regardless of motive strength and, moreover, that they are generally dependent on social contextual conditions, because these support or thwart satisfaction of those basic needs. Typically, need strength will not substantially moderate these main effects (e.g., Chen, Vansteenkiste, et al., 2015).

Furthermore, although many personal motives or strivings can be potent energizers of action and thought, they will not be considered needs unless they satisfy the criteria of being intrinsic and essential to growth, integrity, and wellness. More specifically, we suggest that many acquired strivings or desires do not promote mental health or wellness; indeed, some of them, precisely because they distract from or compete with activities that could fulfill basic psychological needs, hamper growth and well-being, even when they are important to the person and the person is highly efficacious with respect to them (Ryan et al., 1996). Research that we report in Chapter 11 on *goal contents theory* (GCT) strongly supports this postulate by confirming that aspiring for, and even attaining, some culturally sanctioned goals, such as lavish material success, outer image, and fame, are not reliably associated with health and well-being. Thus many motives and goals that organize and activate behavior can be viewed dynamically as peripheral, derivative, compensatory, or substitutive in nature.

Indeed, several of the motives that Murray labeled needs, such as for dominance, acquisitiveness, power, and abasement, are themselves derivative of basic needs, which is to say that they are often either *need substitutes* intended to compensate for a previous lack of fulfillment of basic needs or are acquired motives that serve as indirect and therefore more or less satisfactory avenues to basic need satisfaction. Thus Kasser, Ryan, Zax, and Sameroff (1995) showed that teenagers who become materialistic often come from homes in which caregivers were controlling or cold. Pursuing material goods, or external signs of worth, thus appeared to be a compensation for lacking an inner feeling of worth (see Chapter 12). Even something as widely accepted as the "need for achievement" is typically not simply a pure reflection of the need for competence, even though that is an important source of this motive (see Deci & Moller, 2005; Koestner & McClelland, 1990). Beyond a desire for competence per se, achievement is often valued by individuals who believe that being a high achiever will make them more worthy or lovable; it is an attempt to gain relatedness. This can be manifested in compulsive overachievement or an excessive drive to excel, often connected to conditional parental regard (Roth, Assor, Niemiec, Ryan, & Deci, 2009; Ryan & Moller, 2016). To use another example, the pursuit of social dominance and power may often dynamically represent not a basic need in its own right but a compensation for having previously been deprived of feelings of effectance and autonomy. Lammers, Stoker, Rink, and Galinsky (2016) recently showed, for example, how gaining autonomy quenched the desire for power. As ends in themselves, therefore, such motives are often substitutes for need fulfillment, much like feeding off junk food when one requires nutrition.

SDT findings thus show that efficacious satisfaction of some desires or motives can actually be associated with ill-being rather than well-being (e.g., Kasser & Ryan, 2001; Niemiec, Ryan, & Deci, 2009). This is an extremely important point with regard to basic theories of motivation (Ryan & Deci, 2001). Much of modern empirical psychology touts the importance of efficacy or goal attainment without taking a critical stance concerning efficacy *for what*. Without considering *the nature of the goals* one efficaciously pursues and achieves (e.g., Bandura, 1996; Locke & Latham, 1990), much predictive value is lost.

We do not mean to suggest that some "nonessential" motives, when fulfilled, cannot ever enhance felt happiness. A materialistic person who desires an expensive new suit may, upon acquiring it, be temporarily buoyant and prideful. Modern consumerism depends upon just those reactions, and marketing experts work to create a sense of "needing" certain goods. A person high in desire for dominance may assert control over a passive bystander and briefly feel potent. But attaining such dominance is unlikely to yield any basic need satisfactions and thus is unlikely to foster any durable sense of well-being (see Chapter 11). Many such satisfactions are identified within SDT as *compensatory, derivative,* or *defensive* in nature and often the result of proximal or pervasive need frustrations. They may hold their functional importance primarily as substitutes or symbolic satisfiers of more basic needs that have been thwarted. By contrast, gaining love, gaining new skills, or acting in accord with an abiding value are more likely to fulfill basic needs and thus quite directly enhance wellness. Indeed, the value of a theory of basic needs is that it can help inform us about which motives are derivative, compensatory, or substitutes for what is (or was) really needed by the individual. A theory of needs, therefore, supports a dynamic psychology, which is something deeply missing within most contemporary empirical frameworks.

We also maintain that, unlike drives (e.g., Freud, 1920/1961; Spence, 1958; Zajonc, 1965), basic psychological needs do not operate in a homeostatic manner, and they cannot be sated in the same way as can a drive such as hunger or thirst. People can indeed eat too much, but they cannot have too much autonomy, too much competence, or too much relatedness in the way we define these terms. They can, of course, have too many social interactions but not too much sense of feeling deeply connected. Moreover, psychological needs do not show the homeostatic patterns wherein satisfaction leads to less interest in behaviors that satisfy needs or that deprivation of needs necessarily strengthens motives to gratify them. In contrast, as we subsequently review, there are circumstances under which need deprivations are associated with both of these outcomes, as moderated by other considerations and affordances.

Terror Management Theory and SDT

Another interesting interface of SDT's theory of needs is with *terror management theory* (TMT; Greenberg, Solomon & Pyszczynski, 1997; Pyszczynski, Greenberg, Solomon, Arndt, & Schimel, 2004). We have particularly appreciated TMT as an empirically driven, and yet existentially informed, psychological theory, thus sharing characteristics with SDT (see Ryan & Deci, 2004a). Nonetheless, our view of basic psychological needs and their dynamics differs from those of TMT, resulting in strongly different research emphases (Ryan & Deci, 2000a, 2004b; Ryan, Legate, Niemiec, & Deci, 2012).

The main focus of TMT is on a basic organismic need for self-preservation (which for us represents a basic physical need), as well as the derivative human psychological need that TMT posits to protect against awareness of death and mortality (Pyszczynski, Greenberg, & Solomon, 1997). In fact, avoidance of death awareness, and its resultant anxiety, represents TMT's most fundamental human psychological need. The need to avoid awareness of mortality leads to a secondary need for *self-esteem*, which buffers death anxieties and provides people at least a symbolic immortality. People are said to act to defend or shore up self-esteem whenever mortality becomes salient. TMT thus explains group identifications, as well as outgroup prejudices, as a function of mortality threats, as these protect or enhance self-esteem. In addition, to stave off awareness of mortality, people strive for symbolic continuity, and through this mechanism TMT explains social conformity and concerns with image, along with the need for belonging. In fact, to gain self-esteem people are motivated to connect, create meaning, and contribute to society—again largely to quell mortality awareness rather than because these provide intrinsic satisfactions.

In this sense TMT represents to us a deficit-need theory, since the motivations it has in focus are primarily defensive and reactive in nature. As we have argued (Ryan & Deci, 2004b), however, if the most fundamental human need were that of avoiding anxiety and awareness of death, people would be more prone to hide from stimulation and shrink from exploration and integrative activity rather than to be active and inherently interested in growth and stimulation. In fact, we do not think it is possible to explain well the vital, forward-moving nature of mind and life as motivated by avoidance of the awareness of death (Ryan & Deci, 2004a).

We note, however, that after its early formulations, TMT expanded its perspective to acknowledge, alongside its basic self-protective need, a *self-expansion need* (e.g., Greenberg, Pyszczynski, & Solomon, 1995; Pyszczynski et al., 2004), thus providing a potential growth motivation that speaks to some of the issues SDT directly addresses. Nonetheless, because TMT treats the self-expansion motive as something that exists primarily to allow people to survive until they can procreate and to protect their self-esteem, we still see the overarching view as deficit-oriented. The active nature of human development is more driven by interest and engagement than by anxiety, avoidance, or defense. Perhaps more important, when it comes to the dynamics of everyday human behavior, we see satisfaction and frustration of our three basic psychological needs as more explanatory than those associated with episodic mortality threats.

Therefore, we believe that TMT has highlighted an important human vulnerability, and in doing so brought attention to capacities for defense. TMT research shows that one *can* experimentally produce varied defensive reactions to mortality threats. Yet we think the underlying motivational theory of TMT is less apt at explaining the more general positive trajectories of human development, especially our robust intrinsic motivational and integrative tendencies (see Ryan, Legate, et al., 2012). Even less so does TMT specify the underlying dynamics through which psychological wellness and psychopathology are shaped in family and social environments (Ryan & Deci, 2000a).

Multiple Needs and the Absence of a Need Hierarchy

Another implication of our needs framework is that people cannot psychologically thrive by satisfying one need alone, any more than people can live healthily with water but not food, or plants can thrive on soil without sunlight. Social environments that afford, for example, opportunities to experience competence but fail to nurture relatedness are ones conducive to an impoverished human condition. For example, career development that requires so much time that one is unable to satisfy relational needs (a condition of epidemic proportions in many modern societies) will extract a high cost on well-being, regardless of how effective in and valuing of a career one is. Worse yet are contexts that specifically pit one need against another, thus creating conflicts that inevitably produce ill-being and sometimes maladjustment. For example, parents may require that a child relinquish autonomy to gain relatedness (e.g., when they intrusively control the child with contingent love) and in so doing set the stage for the development of ill-being (e.g., maladaptive perfectionism) or even psychopathology (Ryan, Deci, Grolnick, & La Guardia, 2006).

The necessity of satisfying all three basic needs across the lifespan separates our theory from yet another type of need theory, namely, those that specify a *hierarchy of needs* in which one level of basic needs must be well satisfied before another level energizes as a salient motivating force (e.g., Alderfer, 1972; Maslow, 1954). For Maslow, as for us, there are basic psychological needs whose fulfillment is considered essential to healthy development; but in his view they do not emerge until the physical needs are relatively well sated, and then they are addressed in a more or less serial fashion: first security, then love, then esteem, then self-actualization (Di Domenico & Ryan, in press).

In our contrasting view, if the fulfillment of any of the three basic psychological needs is blocked within a given domain or in a given period of one's life, specifiable experiential and functional costs within that domain or in that life phase are to be expected. For instance, if one must forgo satisfaction of autonomy in order to acquire skills from a controlling, authoritarian instructor, one is predicted to pay a price in wellness. Even if the decision to forgo satisfaction of one need for another is rational or adaptive given the situation, there will be negative functional effects. More importantly, if the thwarted satisfaction persists, not only will there be immediate negative effects but healthy development itself will be diminished (Chen, Van Assche, Vansteenkiste, Soenens, & Beyers, 2015). Reflecting this, the three basic needs of autonomy, competence, and relatedness, even though quite distinct in definition, are typically highly intercorrelated when measured at the general or domain level at any given point in development, bespeaking their interdependence rather than hierarchical nature.

Thus, despite the appearance of Maslow's (1943) pyramid-shaped hierarchy in most every introductory psychology textbook and its intuitive appeal, empirical evidence for his hierarchy of psychological needs is quite thin. Nor does one need to look far to find problematic cases for the hierarchy. People often put their safety at risk to experience actualization (think of any explorer or traveler), and people frequently pursue relatedness and generativity at cost to their personal security. It is also true that issues of actualization are continuously occurring for both youth and adults, alongside issues of self-esteem and issues of personal and relational security. Thus, despite the plausibility of the pyramid model of a needs hierarchy, we submit that it is neither developmentally descriptive nor true in terms of the kind of necessary "prioritization" such a hierarchy would dictate. Nonetheless, the concept of need hierarchies persists in popular and organizational lore, even though it has received relatively little empirical scrutiny or support. Maslow's hierarchy does convey an idea: Many people will feel unable to pursue some "higher" gratifications when externally controlled or economically deprived in terms of basic securities.

In fact, a related notion to Maslow's hierarchy, but one which is more consistent with SDT, is recent work by Welzel (2013), which distinguishes between *surviving* and *thriving* priorities. As Welzel's population-level research indicates, when people are occupied by material deprivation and threats to survival, their inherent propensities toward emancipative values, personal growth, and thriving can be crowded out. They often must focus on what he labels "extrinsic strategies." Yet Welzel (2013) adds: "extrinsic priorities prevail in a population only as long as necessary, whereas intrinsic priorities begin to predominate as soon as possible" (pp. 176–177). In both this view and ours, the more people are under external controlling pressures, either material or social, the less they can direct their resources and energies to the satisfactions of flourishing. Congruent with this, considerable evidence suggests that pursuit and attainment of basic psychological need satisfactions often becomes derailed or even distorted under materially and culturally unsupportive conditions, which we further discuss in Chapters 22 and 23. Yet even under conditions of economic struggle, basic need satisfactions remain critical to wellness (Rasskazova, Ivanova, & Sheldon, 2016). Moreover, we also show that, on an individual level, both material and psychological deprivations in development can lead people to defensive or compensatory functioning that interferes with basic need satisfactions and with their ultimate wellness (Kasser et al., 1995; Ryan, Deci, & Vansteenkiste, 2016).

Needs as Organismic Guidance Systems

Finally, SDT's approach to basic needs implies that individuals, to the extent that they are healthy, will tend to gravitate toward those domains and activities in life that feel sustaining to them—that is, to those areas in which basic psychological needs can be potentially fulfilled (Ryan, 1993; Sheldon & Gunz, 2009). Accordingly, people will tend either to avoid or to engage only under duress those domains and activities that appear less likely to fulfill one or more of the basic needs. Of course, this tendency to gravitate toward need-satisfying situations operates effectively only to the extent to which the individuals are relatively autonomous in their functioning. In other words, acting freely to satisfy basic needs requires having not established controlled behavior patterns that keep one rigidly tied to pursuit of nonhealthy aspirations or desires. In addition, it requires capabilities to pursue that which one deems worthwhile (see Chapter 23).

Throughout this book, we review evidence showing that there are costs in terms of motivation, interest, persistence, performance, and well-being in environments that thwart basic need satisfactions. We also discuss how the dynamics of need fulfillment account for why people migrate toward specific interests, vocations, and relationships and why people function differentially within such areas or relationships as a direct function of how needs are addressed therein. The psychological gravity of specific activities and relationships—their motivational power—we argue is a function of their relation to fulfillment of the three basic needs we have specified.

In sum, to the degree to which a culture, domain of activity, group, or personal relationship affords the three basic psychological need satisfactions, persons within them will show greater vitality, growth, integration, and well-being. Conversely, to the degree to which a domain, group, or relationship blocks the fulfillment of one or more basic psychological need, there will be more signs of impoverished or defensive motivations and lower quality of engagement, productivity, and psychological health. This formulation, which seems so simple and parsimonious, will show itself to have many embedded complexities and to operate differently as a function of differences in both individuals and social contexts. But it is a formulation whose ring will reverberate as a clear and distinct note throughout all of our subsequent discussions.

Three Basic Psychological Needs

Although in this chapter we do not provide a complete description of the three basic psychological needs specified within SDT, we do offer a brief account of their nature and their role in the energization of action and development. A fuller account of each need and their interdependencies is elaborated across subsequent chapters.

The focus of SDT has from the outset been on intrinsic motivational dynamics in human development and behavior. In particular, it has been on the functional impact of contextual influences on such processes as intrinsic motivation, integration of values and regulations, self-congruent behavior, and, ultimately, psychological health. Our task has been to identify the specific factors that facilitate these processes, as well as those that disrupt them. It is from these functional studies that the idea of basic psychological needs emerged, because there appeared to be a few dimensions along which facilitators or forestallers of these phenomena could be parsimoniously classified.

Competence

An obvious and well-researched issue for development is that of competence. We derive our perspective on competence from the work of White (1959), who argued that there exists a nonderivative or primary organismic propensity toward feeling competent and having effects on one's environment, a propensity he labeled *effectance motivation*. In his words, effectance motivation concerns our natural active tendency to influence the environment, from which we derive the feeling of efficacy, that is, "the satisfaction that comes with producing effects" (White, 1963, p. 185). For White, competence was the accumulated result of one's effectance-motivated interactions with the environment.

White's (1959) seminal discussion of competence gave birth to a modern era in motivation research, for he convincingly showed that drive-based theories of behaviorists and of early psychoanalysts failed to provide a satisfactory account of the active nature of childhood learning, of play, of exploration, and of other growth-oriented activities that are typically initiated because of the inherent pleasure of the activities themselves. The importance of White's theorizing was to give the need for competence an independent status, free from both the drives that had been posited by earlier theorists and from the outcomes that might accrue from efficacious activity. That is, White took the position that effectance motivation is not derivative of drives and also that, even apart from the rewards and material benefits that might accrue from competent behavior, there is a strong intrinsic need to experience feelings of efficacy. His position differs from that of others, such as Bandura (1977), for whom competence is a central theoretical construct, because White's focus was on the intrinsic satisfaction associated with effective activity rather than the extrinsic satisfaction associated with the desired outcomes or reinforcements to which effective activity might lead. Thus, for White, effectance motivation reflects an innate, biologically based propensity, evident in a variety of organisms, to exercise and extend their capacities and functioning.

While this active, growth-oriented propensity associated with the need for competence undoubtedly results in the acquisition of skills that have broad adaptive value, even that is not the proximal goal or reason for their occurrence. Instead, the experience of satisfaction and enjoyment of efficacy inherently accompanies the activities. According to White (1959, 1963), the development of various competencies, from walking to manipulating symbols to handling objects dexterously, although surely dependent on maturation, also require learning, and such learning requires motivation. The need for competence supplies the energy for this process of learning. And whereas the biological function (the ultimate goal) of effectance-motivated activity may be adaptation, the *experiential* or proximal aim is often just the spontaneous feeling of competence that comes from producing effects on one's external or internal environment. Children, for example, exercise and stretch their competencies simply for the pleasure or satisfaction that the activity provides. In fact, externally applied rewards and reinforcers, under many circumstances, often stifle rather than facilitate this tendency (e.g., Danner & Lonky, 1981; Grolnick & Ryan, 1987; Warneken & Tomasello, 2008).

As a psychological need, competence is not only functionally important but is also experientially significant to the self. Phenomenally, feelings of effectance nourish people's selves, whereas feelings of ineffectance threaten their feelings of agency and undermine their ability to mobilize and organize action. Thus, to develop a true sense of perceived competence, people's actions must be perceived as self-organized or initiated; in other words, people must feel ownership of the activities at which they succeed (Deci & Ryan, 1985b). Studies have shown, for example, that performing well on a task for which they do not feel a sense of self-initiation and self-regulation does not reliably enhance perceived competence, intrinsic motivation, or vitality (e.g., Nix, Ryan, Manly & Deci, 1999; Ryan, 1982).

Much of modern psychology focuses on competence. It can be found under the names of *efficacy, optimism, achievement motivation, success expectancies,* and many other terms. The important differences between much of this work and ours is not only that we understand the intrinsic importance of competence but also that we make a distinction between competence at activities that originate from the self and those that are governed by introjects or by external demands (Ryan & Moller, 2016). Competent activity that is alienated, that results from controls, does not have the important positive effects that accrue from feeling efficacious at an activity that is autonomously initiated or endorsed.

Relatedness

A second basic psychological need that we examine is the need for *relatedness*. It is an axiom of most current-day theorizing that behavior is determined within social contexts. Yet when we look more deeply into why this is so, the answer goes beyond the fact that people require others' concrete care, help, and provisions in order to survive and adapt. It is not merely the achievement of tangible goods or physical supplies that orients people toward others. Rather, one of the primary goals of behavior is the feeling of belonging and of being significant or mattering in the eyes of others. There is a basic need to feel responded to, respected, and important to others, and, conversely, to avoid rejection, insignificance, and disconnectedness, a fact that applies not just to humans but other primates as well (see de Waal, 2009). Reis (1994) suggested that the core of relatedness across many varied forms of social interactions involves having others respond with sensitivity and care, conveying that one is significant and appreciated.

The meaning and motives of a great deal of human behavior can be linked, either directly or indirectly, to the need for relatedness, from forms of dress and hygiene to the readiness to engage in social rituals to preoccupations with image, status, or achievement. Out of the need for relatedness, people often behave in ways that are intended to bring them acceptance, approval, and group membership (Baumeister & Leary, 1995). The need to relate or belong is especially critical for understanding people's tendencies to internalize values and behaviors from their cultures (Ryan & Deci, 2011). Because of the need to feel connected, people take interest in what others believe and do, what others expect of them, so they are in a position to behave in ways that ensure acceptance and involvement. For better or for worse, they have a readiness to adopt external views as part of their own psychic makeup. The critical issue, from the SDT perspective, concerns the degree to which such internalized goals and values become integrated as opposed to remaining relatively alien to the self in the form of introjects or external regulations.

Another important and closely related issue within SDT concerns the differentiation between behaviors intended to achieve relatedness and those that actually *satisfy* this basic psychological need. People can behave in ways that they think others would like in order to feel connected to those others, but unless the people feel somehow personally acknowledged and affirmed for their actions, the relatedness need will not be fulfilled. People motivated by the need for relatedness may put a life's worth of effort into looking beautiful, being rich, or doing what modern culture convinces them to do without ever feeling loved for themselves, without having the need for relatedness truly satisfied. Among the fundamental dynamic issues we consider are the conditions under which people actually derive a sense of relatedness (e.g., Assor, Roth, & Deci, 2004; Deci & Ryan, 2014a; Ryan, 1993). Thus, like the idea that people's competence must be "owned" to enhance true self-esteem, it is not merely being admired that counts. Rather, people must have the perception that others care for them unconditionally rather than conditionally and that they are accepted for who they are, as we elaborate in relationship motivation theory (RMT; see Chapter 12).

Autonomy

The final basic psychological need in our conceptualization is the need for *autonomy,* no doubt the most controversial and yet central construct in this work. This is the reason it has already received considerable attention in Chapter 3. As noted there, autonomy concerns the regulation of behavior by the self, and, indeed, etymologically it refers to *self-regulation.* Quite simply, the concept of autonomy is deeply linked to the problem of integration and the feelings of vitality and experiences of wholeness in functioning that accompany it.

Because it is through the regulation of behavior that people access and fulfill other basic needs, both physical and psychological, autonomy has a special status as a need. It is a vehicle through which the organization of personality proceeds and through which other psychological needs are actualized. We have already noted that people will internalize a sense of competence, especially when they feel efficacy at an activity they have initiated or willingly undertaken. In other words, the full satisfaction of competence is enhanced when autonomy is collaterally satisfied. Similarly, we have suggested, and will deal with in considerable detail in Chapter 12, that people have the experience of relatedness and intimacy especially when others willingly care for them and/or they are willingly connected and caring for the other. Nonautonomous connections do not satisfy this need for relatedness, except in degraded forms.

In this same regard, one can see the interrelation of internalization (Chapter 8) with satisfaction of all three basic psychological needs. The needs for competence and relatedness would lead one to predict internalization for acting in accord with group norms and values, because such behaviors are a path to effective performance of activities sanctioned by others. As such, this internalization could provide some satisfaction of the needs for competence and relatedness. However, such internalization of regulations could either be merely introjected or could be more integrated. It is through fuller integration that people can experience not only satisfactions of competence and relatedness but also of autonomy, as they now truly concur with, and willingly enact, adopted values and practices.

As detailed in Chapter 3, autonomy can be understood as both a phenomenological and a functional issue. Phenomenally, autonomy concerns the extent to which people experience their behavior as volitional or as fully self-endorsed, rather than being coerced, compelled, or seduced by forces external to the self. Actions that people fully "stand behind," that are experienced as congruent expressions of the self, and that do not involve one part of the personality dominating others, are autonomous actions. By contrast, when people feel that the source for the initiation and regulation of their actions is external to the self—for example, when they merely comply with forces that are pressuring them—then heteronomy or alienation is in evidence.

Autonomy is, however, not simply a phenomenological issue—it is also a functional one. When people act with full volition they bring into the action the whole of their resources, interests, and capacities. Congruent actions—those that are integrated and self-endorsed—are functionally distinguishable from more heteronomous states of motivation because the latter entail less access to the person's cognitive, affective, and physical capacities and thus involve only partial functioning. In the research reported throughout this book, we repeatedly see the functional impact of differences in relative autonomy on cognitive performance, creativity, persistence, and other qualitative aspects of behavior. Autonomous actions more fully engage individuals' talents, abilities, and energies. In contrast, we show empirically how, when people are motivated for controlled reasons, they often produce lower quality outputs.

It is worth noting that Murray also spoke of a *need for autonomy*. Yet, as Koestner and Losier (1996) demonstrated, autonomy as conceptualized by Murray was primarily about reactivity and rebellion against feeling controlled, and not about volition and choice. Murray defined autonomy as a person's desires to defy authority and to be free to act on impulses without constraint. Although no doubt an interesting motive in its own right, it does not overlap, either in definition or empirically, with the positive sense of endorsement and responsibility represented by our use of the term *autonomy*. Koestner and Losier showed, in fact, that the two types of autonomy have distinct correlates and consequences, with autonomy as volition having ones that were much more positive. More recent work by Van Petegem, Soenens, Vansteenkiste, and Beyers (2015) and Van Petegem, Vansteenkiste, Soenens, Beyers, and Aelterman (2015), again to be reviewed later, similarly differentiated reactivity, defiance, and rebellion from volitional autonomy.

The concept of autonomy as volition and self-endorsement had, prior to SDT, been largely ignored within the landscape of mainstream empirical psychology. In fact, as we reviewed in the previous chapter, the concept has been criticized not only by behaviorists but also by some postmodern and relativist theorists (e.g., Markus & Kitayama, 1991a) and some reductionists (e.g., Hood, 2012). In part, these criticisms have really been against the concept of autonomy conflated with other concepts, such as independence, separateness, self-sufficiency, or the perpetual straw man of "free will." We, however, distinguish autonomy from these other concepts. Individuals who are autonomous will also, to a significant degree, be dependent in important relationships and interdependent with relevant groups (e.g., Ryan, et al., 2005). Independence does not imply autonomy but, rather, implies being either separate and/or not reliant on others (Ryan & Lynch, 1989; Soenens et al., 2007). Autonomy as volition is as relevant for females as for males, for Easterners as for Westerners, for collectivists as for individualists. It is a basic human issue.

Manifestations of Optimal Psychological Development, Integrity, and Well-Being

One of the primary aims of SDT is to specify the factors that subserve and reflect optimal human development. We have postulated that, in spite of the variegation apparent in human cultural forms and economic arrangements, there are basic and universal psychological needs that are necessary for optimal development, and we similarly propose that there is a small set of outcomes—of general criteria—by which we can gauge such optimal development.

As we define it, a basic need is essential for growth, wellness, and integrity. Accordingly, optimal development, supported by basic need satisfaction, will be manifested in the motivational processes of (1) intrinsic motivation, a fundamental psychological growth process; (2) the internalization and integration of behavioral regulations and social prescriptions and values, which results in psychological coherence and integrity; and (3) an experience of vitality and wellness. We briefly consider these three central criteria in turn.

Intrinsic Motivation

A major process through which cognitive and personality development proceeds is *intrinsic motivation,* a construct that has a history of more than sixty-five years in empirical psychology, and one that is the focus of the next chapter in this historical section of the book. SDT's empirical framework grew out of studies of this phenomenon, because it represented a prototype of the active organism's propensities toward greater differentiation and integration. Intrinsic motivation is defined as spontaneous activity that is sustained by the satisfactions inherent in the activity itself, and it is contrasted with activity that is functionally dependent for its occurrence or persistence on separable rewards or reinforcements. When not under the pressure of physical need deprivation, people have a primary propensity to seek out novelty and challenges, to explore new environments, and to undertake new adventures, and through these activities to experience interest and gain competence (Deci & Moller, 2005; Ryan & Deci, 2013). Thus one reason we use intrinsic motivation as a criterion for optimal development is that, without intrinsic motivation, developmental processes would be greatly hampered, if not debilitated. In childhood, play, interest, and exploration are intrinsically motivated processes that serve adaptive functions. Yet across the lifespan, intrinsic motivation continues to play a critical role in people's growth, creativity, vitality, and sense of well-being (Ryan & Moller, 2016).

Despite the fact that intrinsic motivation is a natural and important process in development, however, it is also clear that it can be inhibited or blocked, and this is where the issue of basic psychological needs comes into play. The spontaneous satisfactions that support the intrinsic motivational processes include feelings of autonomy or self-determination and feelings of effectance or competence. In presenting *cognitive evaluation theory* (CET; Chapters 6 and 7), we review an abundance of research showing the reduction of intrinsic motivation (as well as the creativity, cognitive growth, and quality of engagement that are associated with it) in contexts that fail to support autonomy and do not afford optimal challenges and competence-enhancing feedback. Studies are also reviewed that indicate that contexts absent of relational security lead to preoccupations that interfere with intrinsically motivated activity. Thus we will see evidence for relations between satisfaction of needs for autonomy, competence, and relatedness and the occurrence of intrinsic motivation.

Internalization and Integration

Although the acquisition of new schemas and competencies is dependent upon intrinsic motivation, another essential process in optimal development is the assimilation and self-regulation of social practices and values. This active process of *internalization* concerns the extent to which people take in practices and regulations from their social groups, transforming them into self-regulations, allowing them to be executed independently and (optimally) volitionally. Whether speaking of values concerning social behavior, work ethics, manners of dress and speech, morality, or other culturally transmitted regulations, internalization is a critical process. Quite simply, it determines not only social adjustment but also personal wellness.

A central argument of SDT states that social contexts supportive of basic psychological need fulfillment facilitate the internalization and integration of social values and practices and thus enhance social effectiveness and connectedness. Autonomy-supportive, relationally supportive, and competence-supportive social environments are those most conducive to internalization and psychological integration. By contrast, social environments that are excessively controlling, overchallenging, or rejecting disrupt the natural human tendency toward social internalization and again produce alienation, interpersonal and intrapersonal conflict, and a less full engagement of human potentials.

The issue of integration concerns two broad problems within the socialization of individuals. One is the problem of accepting and regulating the motivation for doing activities that are not inherently enjoyable and thus not intrinsically motivated. Household chores, work tasks, cultural rituals, obeying laws, and many other types of behavior require internalization and serve as examples of activities that people would likely not do out of intrinsic interest. People will, however, be motivated to do these activities in the service of competence and relatedness—internalizing these practices and values allows people to feel more effective and connected to their social group. Full internalization, however, entails one not only carrying out these activities but doing so volitionally, based in self-valuing of the activity or its outcomes; in such cases, the behaviors, though extrinsically motivated, will be autonomous and better sustained. The other problem at the heart of socializing individuals concerns the development of processes for regulating emotions and impulses. Integrating emotions is, in part, a matter of internalizing the regulations that allow people to manage feelings and impulses and find ways to express and harness them. Emotional regulation is thus also a matter of internalization involving experiences of competence, relatedness, and autonomy.

The importance of internalization is obvious and thus serves as an indicator of optimal development. In Chapter 8 we specifically review a substantial body of research showing that social contexts supportive of basic need satisfaction facilitate internalization and integration of values and regulatory processes and, in turn, effective functioning and psychological health.

Well-Being and Health

Psychological development is thus supported and characterized by intrinsic motivation and active internalization and integration. In addition, it is associated with people's functional and experiential well-being. In the development of SDT, as we saw how basic need satisfactions facilitated greater intrinsic motivation and more integrated internalization and effective self-regulation, we also repeatedly found empirically that these same need satisfactions were associated with both lower psychopathology and ill-being and greater attainment of psychological health and wellness.

In Chapter 10 we discuss our conception of wellness at length. For us, the assessment of wellness is neither simple nor superficial—for example, it is not just about happiness (Ryan, Huta, & Deci, 2008). Although states of happiness are related to well-being, they by no means ensure it, because they do not, in our view, fully define what it means to be fully functioning or flourishing. Although happiness is often a symptom of wellness, SDT instead suggests that true well-being is a state of being able to nondefensively experience events and access one's capabilities and energies to engage in purposive, valued, and coherent living (Ryan, Deci, & Vansteenkiste, 2016). In wellness, one is free of debilitating inner conflicts and able to operate with awareness, vitality, and integrity. The characteristics entailed in well-being are addressed more fully in Chapters 10 and 11.

SDT also finds that individual wellness and the characteristics of larger social systems, groups, and organizations are intertwined (Deci & Ryan, 2012; DeHaan, Hirai, & Ryan, 2015). People are embedded within social structures that provide more or less support for basic need satisfactions and opportunities to pursue that which they value. Reciprocally, for systems or organizations to be stable and to flourish, they require well-integrated members who will enact their values and solve their problems willingly. This occurs, however, only when the members are empowered and enabled to fulfill their basic psychological needs for autonomy, competence, and relatedness through such volitional activity. Controlling or coercive organizations, cultures, and governments often fail to mobilize that kind of human capital. This rather sweeping cultural hypothesis speaks to the question of what group and cultural characteristics are most conducive to individual development and why institutions at times find it necessary to employ ever more repressive tactics in an attempt to gain individual compliance. It also speaks to the issue of why people have sometimes failed to thrive even when they have complied with organizational or cultural mores, and also why at times people have rebelled against various forms of authority or regulation that ultimately do not allow for intrinsic need satisfactions. SDT suggests, in fact, that resistance to control, oppression, and other psychological need deprivations is a function of a natural push from within, something seen in familial, classroom, organizational, political, and cultural contexts alike. The concept of basic need satisfaction thus provides a bridge between psychology, which analyzes individuals, and broader sociological, economic, and historical systems that are rarely examined from the standpoint of empirical psychology, issues we take up especially in the final chapters of this book.

Concluding Comments

In this chapter we have only briefly described a conception of needs as those satisfactions essential to human thriving—to growth, integrity, and wellness. We distinguished physical from psychological needs, and we argued that SDT is primarily focused on the latter. In defining basic psychological needs as essential requirements for psychological growth, integrity, and wellness, we also distinguished our use of the term from other past and present uses, such as the construct of needs as preferences, individual differences, or hierarchically arranged goal structures. Needs are instead defined in SDT by the functional effects of their deprivation and frustration versus affordance and satisfaction on developmental and wellness outcomes. They are thus not neurological or anatomical constructs, even as the mechanisms through which needs are pursued and satisfied and through which their objective functional consequences are produced are the focus of much current investigation. Neither are they merely subjective concerns, as their functional impacts operate whether or not these satisfactions are preferred or valued.

We then defined in a preliminary way the three specific basic psychological needs posited by SDT, namely those for autonomy, competence, and relatedness. Each need is more fully explicated in the context of the empirical work using these constructs, which we review in Chapters 6–14. However, to anticipate that body of evidence, we described how basic need satisfaction leads to fuller functioning that includes more robust tendencies toward intrinsic motivation, the integration of extrinsic regulations where these are fitting (and rejection of those unfitting), and to greater awareness, vitality, and well-being. Finally, we suggested that the affordance of need supports conduces toward social harmony and identification, which in turn is a source of stability within social systems. Each of these global claims is explored in more extensive detail in the chapters to come.

CHAPTER 5

A Brief History of Intrinsic Motivation

By their very nature, human beings actively engage with their environments, rather than passively waiting to be acted upon by them, and they explore, investigate, and assimilate information without external pressure or reward. For more than half a century, this inherent activity has been described with the concept of *intrinsic motivation,* which has been linked to play, exploration, environmental mastery, the emotion of interest, and the novelty and challenges that might prompt interest. A primary reason that the construct of intrinsic motivation emerged in the mid-20th century was that the behaviorist theories of the day were unable to explain such phenomena. Thus, within operant theory, exploratory behaviors and curiosity were not well explained by reinforcements, and intrinsic motivation came to be defined as behaviors in which the reinforcements are inherent. Similarly, within behaviorist drive theories, anomalies arose from observations that animals engaged in behaviors that not only did not reduce drive states but in many cases actually increased them. In a parallel manner, difficulties emerged in the psychoanalytic tradition for accounting for non-drive-based behaviors associated with independent ego energies. We trace these histories and their culmination in a landmark paper by White (1959), which drew together the evidence for an evolved effectance motivation, the forerunner of SDT's concept of intrinsic motivation.

Spontaneous activity is pervasively evident in humans. In their healthiest states, people are inquisitive, curious, playful, active creatures who explore and assimilate their inner and outer worlds (Kashdan, Rose, & Fincham, 2004; Silvia, 2006). The renowned ethologist Lorenz (1950) once described humans as *Neugierwesen,* or "curiosity creatures," reflecting our unquenchable readiness to learn (c.f. Hass, 1970, p. 95). More recently, Brown (2009) discussed the role of play in the development of many species and observed: "Of all the animals, humans are the biggest players of all" (p. 58). Whereas all animals display a tendency to operate on their environments, the more wide-ranging a creature's potential ecological niche and adaptive opportunities are, the more central are curiosity and exploration to its nature. Humans, whose expansive neoteny includes a protracted period of dependency and protected growth, represent the quintessential curious species.

The concept of a natural, spontaneous energy vitalizing the unfolding of development through interest and activity is central to SDT's organismic conception of human nature. Organismic thinking rejects the idea that humans are naturally inert or passive, waiting to be acted upon by external prods or prompts. Neither are they primarily seeking quiescence. Instead, even when free from homeostatic or emotional urges, individuals become actively engaged with the objects, people, events, and ideas of their world. Although some behaviors are emitted as direct responses to external forces and to homeostatic perturbations, the critical point is that organismic activity is not invariantly a function of such antecedents. Indeed, humans are prone to engage in various activities that do not fit with explanations based in external determinants or physiological imbalances. They too often behave to elicit uncertainties, promote imbalances, seek out external challenges, and defy external prods. Mere equilibrium is by no means the central organismic goal.

Yet, despite its fit with functional (e.g., Pellegrini & Smith, 1998) and evolutionary (e.g., Ryan & Hawley, 2016; Waller, 1998) thinking, the concept of an active organism has not always been well assimilated into scientific psychology. Even though some psychologists writing a century ago (e.g., Groos, 1901; Woodworth, 1918) used concepts that were congruent with SDT's ideas about inherent activity and integrative tendencies with adaptive benefits, the more dominant approaches to scientific psychology that followed focused primarily on efficient causal explanations that place causality in forces that *operate on* the organism and are precedent to its behavior rather than being inherent active propensities.

Paradoxically, however, it was behavioristic positions within scientific psychology, most notably Skinner's operant theory and Hull's drive theory, that gave rise to the first empirical studies of intrinsic motivation. Because these approaches were rigorously theoretical, as well as empirically testable, research testing them could expose limitations of these theories for certain types of learning and behavior. In our view, it was, in fact, the theoretical integrity of these behaviorist approaches that set the stage for exploring phenomena that could *not* be satisfactorily explained within their paradigms. As those explorations proceeded, it became clear that much of the problem was in the mechanistic or passive-organism meta-theory upon which these theories were based.

In this chapter, we continue our exploration of SDT's historical and philosophical roots with a historical review of concepts within the behavioral theories of experimental psychology, along with some interesting parallels in psychoanalytic psychology, that lend credence to organismic models and their core assumption of spontaneous activity as integral to human development and health. In presenting the review, we particularly focus on the evolution of the concept of *intrinsic motivation,* beginning with theories that predated behaviorism and ending with a contemporary view of that construct (see also Ryan & Deci, 2000c).

Early Psychological Concepts of Activity

Groos

As early as 1898, Groos had observed that animals of many varieties engage in the spontaneous and unrewarded exercise of their capacities. In his theory, activities such as rough-and-tumble wrestling, solitary vocalizations, curious manipulations of objects, and other forms of play were for the purpose of exercising the capacities and would yield adaptive advantages in development. As he put it, the "animals do not play because they are young, but they have their youth because they must play" (Groos, 1898, p. 67). Yet, Groos also recognized that the future adaptive advantages resulting from play could not exert much of a *motivating* role on a youthful animal, so there must be pleasure in such activities themselves. Play must, that is, involve an inherent experience of pleasure, which he attributed to "the feeling of freedom which is closely connected with the joy in being a cause" (Groos, 1901, p. 82). This idea of a pleasure as an inherent aspect of some forms of activity is reiterated across our writings in SDT (e.g., Deci, 1975; Deci & Ryan, 1985b), and the writings of Csikszentmihalyi and his colleagues, (e.g., Csikszentmihalyi, Abuhamdeh, & Nakamura, 2005), among other modern perspectives.

Woodworth

Robert Woodworth was an early motivation theorist whose work anticipated many themes in modern intrinsic motivation research. Similar to Groos's arguments, Woodworth's *behavior-primacy theory* (1918, 1958) emphasized the importance of spontaneous activity and of behavior that is connected to the "pleasure of being a cause." He stated that "It may at least be said to be part of the native equipment to be active in a motor way, as well, indeed, as in the way of exploration" (Woodworth, 1918, p. 50). He proposed, in fact, that the ongoing stream of behavior was primarily directed toward having effects on one's environment and that drive-oriented motives are better thought of as perturbations to this ongoing activity rather than as drivers of them. In these ideas we see inherent activity as a departure point, along with a preliminary conception of intrinsically motivated behavior.

Woodworth further posited general motives such as curiosity, constructiveness, and self-assertion that energize various activities and are, in one sense, their own ends but that also provide satisfaction of the general motives. In this way, he argued that although extrinsic motives (such as pursuing a reward) may initiate a behavior, "only when it is running on its own drive . . . can (it) run freely and effectively." This notion, later referred to as *functional autonomy* in the work of Allport (1937), suggests that autonomous activities, regardless of the motives into which they might tie, are essential.

In the work of Woodworth, we find several important points that presage central concepts employed within SDT. These include: the concept of inherent activity, which is represented in our theory by the concept of intrinsic motivation; the idea that even activities that are not intrinsically interesting can become functionally autonomous, which we address through the notions of internalization and integration; and the postulate that activities that seem to be their own reward do, in fact, relate to underlying needs. Thus, both Woodworth and we implicitly agree with the point later emphasized by Berlyne (1971) that activities are themselves rewarding only insofar as they create internal conditions that are rewarding for the organism.

Dewey

Perhaps the most seminal thinking on curiosity and interest during the early part of the 20th century was that of philosopher, educator, and psychologist John Dewey. Dewey (1922) employed what he called a *functionalist* perspective on behavior, within which he posited a primary role of *interest* in the development of mind and culture. In his view, interest is spawned by novelty and challenge in relation to that which is already familiar or known. Pragmatically and dynamically, according to Dewey, mind is ever striving to exceed itself, a point that was later echoed by Piaget (1971). Curiosity and interest, Dewey suggested, are energizers of this developmental process, but the energy and the process are relatively vulnerable in the face of strong environmental forces, so they require support and guidance. In Dewey's work, which formed the basis of a progressive approach to education, one finds intrinsic activity, an inherent growth tendency, and the dialectic between active organisms and social forces that can either diminish or nurture the natural activity and growth, all concepts that find correspondences within SDT.

These early viewpoints might well have continued to illuminate the active nature of organismic development had they not been overshadowed by the advent within American psychology of behaviorism (Thorndike, 1913; Watson, 1913), with its emphasis on measurement of observable variables (and eschewing of psychological constructs), and on the control of behavior through the manipulation of independent, external variables.

Behavioral Theories

John Watson, who was schooled in functionalist thinking by Dewey at the University of Chicago, argued in contradiction to Dewey that behavior rather than mind was the true subject matter of scientific psychology. Explanations of behavior, he said, need not implicate consciousness; indeed, he rejected consciousness as an explanatory approach, as well as introspection as a method of studying the causes of behavior (Watson, 1913). Instead, he advocated direct observation of behaviors emitted in response to the experimental manipulation of hypothesized causes. From this starting point, Watson argued that animals—humans and other species alike—adjust to their environments with habit mechanisms through which responses are linked to stimulus demands. This, of course, suggests great malleability of behavior. It also placed relatively little emphasis on the nature of, or needs pertaining to, any specific species, as all were assumed to be shaped by essentially the same processes.

The work of Thorndike (1913) complemented that of Watson by specifying the means through which new habits are acquired and lost. Specifically, Thorndike proposed the *law of effect,* which asserted in essence that if a behavior is followed by a satisfier (later referred to as a *reinforcer*), the likelihood of the behavior's recurring will be increased (i.e., a habit will be strengthened). If, however, the behavior is followed by an "annoyer," its likelihood will decrease.

Both Watson and Thorndike were critical of Dewey's functionalist theory and argued that, in fact, behaviorism, with its focus on stimulus events and observable behaviors, was the only true functionalism, for it clearly specified the functional relation between stimuli and responses. More precisely, the work of Watson and Thorndike, when taken together, asserted that behavior is a direct function of external stimuli and the application of observable reinforcing events. These ideas set the stage for the emergence of operant psychology (Skinner, 1938), which quickly became one of the dominant forces within twentieth-century American psychology and still informs many contemporary cognitive and neuroscience perspectives.

Operant Theory

Operant psychology (e.g., Skinner, 1953) has from its inception been primarily concerned with response rates. It has focused on specific, observable behaviors and more specifically on the number of occurrences of such a behavior in a given amount of time. The issue of central concern has been how the rate of responding changes as a function of the consequences of the behavior.

According to the theory, response rates change as a function of contingencies of *reinforcement*. That is, certain consequences increase the rate of responding, and those consequences are considered reinforcers. When a reinforcing event is terminated and the frequency of behavior decreases, the process is referred to as *extinction*. Reinforcers may be either positive (the addition of a positive event) or negative (the removal of a negative event), but in both cases they increase the rate of responding.

The properties of what reinforces have rarely been the focus of traditional operant work; instead, the emphasis is on their functional properties. Yet certain events seem to reinforce widely, even on first presentation to an organism. Particular foods, for example, can reinforce, especially if the organism has been deprived of nutrients. Other reinforcers seem to acquire their reinforcing value over time. Skinner referred to these latter reinforcers as conditioned reinforcers, suggesting that a stimulus that does not itself reinforce (e.g., the dish on which food is provided) may become a reinforcer (a conditioned reinforcer) if it is present when operant reinforcement is occurring. The process through which this occurs is classical conditioning, and, as a result, the conditioned reinforcer will be able to strengthen behaviors.

Although in Skinner's view the organism is controlled by external events, there was nonetheless an active component in his theory of behavior: the *operant*. As the term suggests, Skinner acknowledged that organisms actively and spontaneously "operate" on the environment. Yet in this framework operants were treated as essentially random rather than systematic events. These random outputs were then essentially "selected" by the contingencies of reinforcement in the environment. Operants, that is, would theoretically not be recurrent unless externally reinforced.

Advocates of the operant viewpoint frequently argue that all operant (i.e., voluntary) behaviors that recur are under the control of reinforcers. More specifically, they are under the control of the organism's past reinforcement history. It is notable, too, that, within the theory, animals do not emit recurring behaviors *in order to* get reinforcement; they emit these behaviors because the behaviors were reinforced in the past and the relevant stimuli are currently present. This is a critical point, because the idea of doing something *in order to* obtain a reinforcement requires that cognitions and goals be given a causal role in the analysis of behavior, a point that distinguishes social cognitive and expectancy theories (e.g., Bandura & Walters, 1963; Rotter, 1954; Vroom, 1964) from operant theory.

Because any operant behaviors that recur were said to be under the control of reinforcement processes, much research focused on the most effective schedules of reinforcement for increasing response rates and maintaining the increases over time. When a schedule of reinforcement has been terminated, the rate of responding is expected to return to baseline, but some schedules greatly slow the time and/or raise the cumulative responses it takes for the response to be extinguished.

Operant Theory and Motivation

Strictly speaking, there are no motivational concepts within operant theory, although in practice they are implicit within the theoretical approach. For example, although reinforcers are defined as events that change the rate of responding, events that are typically selected as reinforcers by behaviorists in laboratory studies (e.g., food, drink, sexual contact) gain their power to reinforce precisely because they tie into conditions within the organism that are more typically referred to with motivational terms. This also extends to reinforcements such as praise and social approval (Rotter, 1954). Quite simply, we suggest, reinforcing events change response rates precisely because they satisfy physiological drives or psychological needs. Skinner, for example, used food to reinforce his pigeons (typically after depriving them), but to our knowledge he never attempted to use a gold star or a dollar bill with this organism. He thus intuitively knew about needs, even though they were not discussed as such.

Similarly, there is no concept of *rewards* within operant theory, because the very idea of a reward carries psychological connotations. Nonetheless, the concept of reinforcers, at least as typically used in applying the theory to practical situations, is indeed very similar to the concept of rewards. At least loosely speaking, it is reasonable to say that the operant viewpoint suggests that all voluntary behaviors are under the control of external reward (or punishment) contingencies. Thus, when it comes to intrinsic motivation, it has often been said by those partial to the operant viewpoint that the concept of intrinsic motivation is obscure and simply refers to those behaviors for which the reinforcement contingencies have not yet been identified (e.g., Carton, 1996; Flora, 1990). In part, this stems from the technical definition of a reinforcement, which is operationally defined as an external event that is separable and distinct from the behavior itself (Skinner, 1953); that is, reinforcements must by definition lie in the environment, precluding a concept of inherent rewards in behavior (Deci & Ryan, 1985b). If one cannot allow any internal satisfactions to be recognized as behavioral supports or rewards, this will certainly lead one to believe that intrinsic motivation is an obscure concept.

The Mystery of the Operant

There is a concept within operant theory which is too seldom mentioned by behavioral theorists but which can be thought of as representing, at least in a muffled form, what we think of as intrinsic motivation. Specifically, as we previously mentioned, Skinner suggested that each behavior has a baseline or operant level. In other words, he recognized that animals engage in many behaviors, such as exploring their cages or manipulating levers, before the behaviors have been reinforced. Animals "operate" on their environment. These baseline levels of responding are not under the control of reinforcements, but reinforcements are what move the response rates for specific actions away from the baseline level.

To us, the fact of spontaneous behavioral propensities to explore novel environments and curiously manipulate new objects implies inherent activity and can be thought of as evidence for intrinsic motivation. It is especially representative of the intrinsic motivation for exploration, the discovery of what is novel, and what objects do. Yet within operant theory, operants have received little motivational significance, and their role in development or self-regulation has not been deeply considered. Rather, as mentioned earlier, they are typically treated as "random" initial response rates that are strengthened or weakened as a function of external conditions. Thus, although in a sense one could say that operants are initially intrinsically motivated, because of operant theory's emphasis on the control of all behaviors through the process of reinforcement, operant theory has difficulty conceptualizing behaviors that involve an inherent energization and organization of action, and that are potentially sustained by internal rewards.

It is worth noting, further, that insofar as one thinks about the operant or baseline level of behavior as being "intrinsically motivated" and about reinforcements as extrinsic rewards, then the theory implies, functionally, that intrinsic and extrinsic motivations are additive. In other words, when reinforcers (i.e., extrinsic motivators) are added to baseline-level responding (i.e., intrinsic motivation), the amount of responding increases, and when the reinforcers are removed, responding is said to return to its operant level, implying that intrinsic motivation is not affected by the extrinsic motivators. It is this point—this extrapolation from operant theory—that has been a major point of contention and controversy concerning the relation of operant theory to SDT. We consider this issue further in Chapter 6.

Drive/Learning Theory

The other dominant reinforcement approach during the middle part of the 20th century was the theory of Clark Hull. Like Skinner, Hull was focused on the strengthening of behaviors through processes of reinforcement. Yet Hullian theory was in many respects very different, for it addressed deeper issues about the "content" of nature—about *why* something is reinforcing. On theoretical, rather than just empirical, grounds, Hull predicted the kinds of events that would be reinforcing.

According to Hull (1943), all behaviors can be reduced, ultimately, to four physiological needs. Specifically, it is within the nature of humans and many other species to need food, water, sex, and freedom from pain. Animals will thus engage in a wide variety of behaviors that have, in the past, provided satisfaction of these physiological needs. These needs are said to be manifest as non-nervous-system-tissue deficits that give rise to drive states and instigate consummatory behaviors. Particular consummatory behaviors are emitted because in the past they have returned the organism to equilibrium—that is, they have satisfied the need and reduced the drive—and in the process have become bonded to the drive stimulus. The three central concepts within the theory are, thus, *drives,* which energize behavior and are based in the physiological needs; *reinforcements,* which are drive reductions that strengthen associations between drive stimuli and the behaviors that led to drive reduction; and those *associative bonds* that regulate or direct behavior and develop through the reinforcement process.

Within the theory, the derivative process of *secondary reinforcement* explains much of the behavior of organisms. Whereas anything that directly reduces one of the four drives is considered a primary reinforcer, an object or event that does not reduce a drive but is paired with a drive reducer can itself take on reinforcing properties, becoming a secondary reinforcer. Yet to retain its reinforcing properties, a secondary reinforcer must periodically be re-paired with primary drive reduction, or its power to reinforce will dissipate.

Drive and Operant Theories

There are both important similarities and important differences between these two behaviorist theories. First, the concept of reinforcement being essential for learning is central to both. However, in operant theory, reinforcement is defined functionally in terms of whether it changes the rate of responding, whereas in drive theory it is defined in terms of drive reduction. Further, both theories allow for initially neutral stimuli to become reinforcers—conditioned reinforcers in Skinnerian thought and secondary reinforcers in Hullian theory—and the pairing of the stimulus with reinforcement is the means through which this occurs. The fundamental difference between the definitions of reinforcement is also evident in the accounts of acquired reinforcers. In operant theory, a conditioned reinforcer is functionally defined—it did not initially affect response rates, but it acquired the characteristic of affecting response rates. In Hullian theory, it is defined in terms of being paired with drive reduction. Even the term *secondary reinforcer* conveys that there are theoretically primary reinforcers (namely, direct drive reducers).

Second, both theories suggest that learning is a process of strengthening stimulus–response associative bonds through the process of reinforcement. Yet, in operant theory, the stimuli that get bonded to responses are typically external contingencies of reinforcement, whereas in drive theory they are often internal drive stimulations, again highlighting the most central difference between the two theories, namely the use by Hull but not by Skinner of the motivational concept of *drive*. Hull was concerned with the inner nature of the organism (although not with experiential states), whereas Skinner was not.

Still, both behavioral theories explained behaviors in terms of external reinforcers—namely, outcomes separable from the behavior itself and that lie outside the organism. Thus, practically, both theories viewed animal and human behavior, in a very real sense, to be a kind of economic transaction—behavior is performed or allocated in exchange for the attainment of rewards or the avoidance of punishments that are controlled by the external environment—although neither theory employs or requires cognitions about such "exchanges."

Perhaps the most important thing to be learned from the substantial research guided by the two behavioral theories is that, under specified circumstances, many behaviors can be brought under the control of external reinforcements. With strong or selectively important enough rewards, animals will tend to act reliably in concert with experimenter mandates. Some exceptions have been identified, such as mandates that run against the grain of instinctual behaviors (Breland & Breland, 1961; Garcia & Koelling, 1966), but generally speaking these instinctual drifts were considered within these approaches to be mere anomalies of neural wiring. Thus the economic model of animals behaving as a function of external rewards and punishments (Schwartz & Lacey, 1982) still possesses considerable explanatory power and the adherence of many followers.

The fact that rewards *can,* in laboratory settings, control the behavior of an organism does not necessarily imply, however, that rewards *do* control the organism's behavior in the real world. This was a central point that McCall (1977) made under the rubric of the "can versus do" problem and that we have recently reiterated as a common conceptual error in experimental social and behavioral psychology (Ryan, Legate, Niemiec, & Deci, 2012). Further, even though rewards actually *do* control behavior in some real-world settings, there is no logically necessity, as is assumed by many behaviorists, that therefore *all* behaviors are controlled by external reinforcements in the real world. It was over these issues, rather than the issue of whether rewards *can* control behavior, that the generality of behavioristic approaches came into question and into some paradigmatic clashes with SDT (e.g. Deci, Koestner & Ryan, 1999; Ryan & Deci, 1996).

Empirical Challenges to These Behaviorist Theories

Observers of animal and human behavior began increasingly to recognize that organisms exhibited a variety of behaviors that were not well explained by reinforcement processes or (to use a purposive description) that were not done in order to get specific rewards or avoid punishments. These observations were more difficult to specify precisely with regard to operant theory than drive theory because of the different definitions of reinforcement in the two theories. In drive theory, a reinforcer is something that reduces a drive, so the proposition that a reinforcer strengthens associative bonds (i.e., behaviors) can be falsified. If a drive reducer did not strengthen a behavior, that would represent negative evidence with respect to the theory. But in operant theory, a reinforcer is an event that strengthens a behavior, so the proposition cannot be falsified. If an event does not strengthen a behavior, it is simply said not to be a reinforcer, but that is not negative evidence with respect to the general proposition.

Accordingly, the observations that raised doubts about the adequacy of operant theory were ones in which there did not appear to be reinforcements associated with particular behaviors. For example, infants (human and mammalian) begin engaging in exploratory types of behavior soon after birth (Stern, 1985). Human adults seemed to engage in a variety of sport, artistic, or intellectual leisure-time activities that do not seem to be associated with identifiable reinforcing conditions. Operant theorists counter with the fact that in such cases the reinforcing external contingencies have simply not yet been identified, some, for example, suggesting that there may be some generalized approval that accrues from and thus controls such activities (see, e.g., Dickinson, 1989).

In spite of these attempts, many psychologists found it increasingly problematic to attribute all behavior to reinforcement processes. Thus the idea of intrinsic motivation (which we suggested was latent within the field since the days of Woodworth), surfaced in reaction to the operant postulate that all behavior was controlled by operationally separable reinforcers. In this movement of reaction, intrinsic motivation became defined negatively as activities that were not dependent on external reinforcements and positively as activities performed by humans (and other animals) for which the *activity itself is inherently rewarding*. The idea of rewards being inherent in the activity contrasted with the orthodox operant idea that all behavior is functionally controlled by operationally separable consequences in the environment. This idea is further discussed later in the chapter.

One of the earliest findings that was anomalous with respect to both drive and operant theories was reported by Nissen (1930). He observed that rats would cross an electrified grid (and thus endure pain) in order to get to a novel maze area on the other side. Because neither the grid crossing nor the novel space had been paired with reinforcements and because the pain was a drive enhancer rather than a reducer, there was no logical explanation for the behavior within Hullian theory. Behaving in a way that elicited a shock was counter to drive-theory predictions, and novelty could not be easily understood in drive terms as a reinforcer.

Subsequently, Butler (1953) showed that rhesus monkeys would learn discrimination problems simply for the opportunity to visually explore the environment, even though no drive-related reinforcement was associated with that exploration. Butler posited an innate drive for visual exploration and suggested that the drive underlies considerable learning in primates. Montgomery (1955) provided rats with a choice between exploring a maze area or returning efficiently to their home nest and found that drive-sated rats showed a preference for exploration, even though it had never been paired with primary reinforcement.

Harlow (1953b) reviewed numerous experiments, including ones that indicated, for example, that rhesus monkeys would solve discrimination tasks for the sole reward of being able to manipulate novel objects and that this "manipulation drive" was remarkably resistant to extinction (e.g., Harlow, Harlow, & Meyer, 1950). He also reviewed an observation by Gately (1950) that monkeys who were reinforced with food for puzzle solving were no more efficient than monkeys who solved the puzzles without food. Further, the food-rewarded monkeys tended to abandon a puzzle once having solved it, whereas unrewarded monkeys were more likely to continue playing with the puzzles for long periods. The seeming interference of rewards with curiosity and exploration is an issue that we take up at length in the next chapter.

Harlow was convinced that the issues of investigatory and curiosity behaviors were inadequately handled not only by drive theory but also by operant theory. These traditional reinforcement theories, he felt, have limitations that caused psychologists to lose sight of common sense. He argued stridently that the focus on reinforcement, whether defined operationally or with respect to physiological needs, was overemphasized to the neglect of other sources of energy and initiation for behavior. In a poignant passage, Harlow (1953a) stated:

> An informal survey of neo-behaviorists who are also fathers (or mothers) reveals that all have observed the intensity and omnipresence of the curiosity-investigatory motive in their own children. None of them seriously believes that the behavior derives from a second-order drive. After describing their children's behavior, often with a surprising enthusiasm and frequently with the support of photographic records, they trudge off to their laboratories to study, under conditions of solitary confinement, the intellectual processes of rodents. (p. 29)

In fairness, the endeavor of operant and drive theorists was obviously not to ignore common sense but rather to account for all behavior by pushing a systematic theoretical account to its limits. The effort was a worthy one in terms of understanding both what could be and what could not be, accounted for either in terms of separable reinforcement contingencies or drive-based stimuli. (We are doing the same with tenets of SDT!). It was the curiosity and exploratory behaviors that eluded systematization within the reinforcement accounts, and it was the consistent application of the basic principles of the reinforcement theories that made this clear.

In fact, Harlow (1950) is the first scientist we know of to have used the term *intrinsic motivation*. It appeared in the title of a report, "Learning and satiation of response in intrinsically motivated complex puzzle performance by monkeys," in the *Journal of Comparative Psychology*, wherein Harlow reported on observations of how exploratory behaviors persisted without reinforcement and did not show the typical properties of drive reduction. However, he did not persist with the term intrinsic motivation, instead focusing on explorative and manipulation drives.

Drive-Theory Accounts

Although some researchers, such as Harlow, suggested that orthodox drive theory could not explain exploratory behaviors, others attempted to provide accounts of such behaviors in ways that required minimal or no change to the basic theory. One account held that novel stimuli are anxiety provoking and that, because anxiety is painful, exploratory behaviors reduce the pain and reinforce the behaviors (Brown, 1961). This account, which required little change to the theory, did have surface plausibility. Certainly, both animals and humans, when placed in certain types of novel environments, show signs of fear and then proceed cautiously to engage the new terrain (e.g., Whiting & Mowrer, 1943). Presumably, the exploration would reduce the fear and reinforce the behavior.

Yet the more obvious response to a novel space, if the novelty were anxiety provoking, would be to avoid rather than explore. In most cases, entering the space would increase rather than decrease the anxiety, and, in fact, fear inductions have typically been found to reduce rather than enhance the tendency to explore (e.g., Montgomery, 1955). Further, researchers such as Harlow (1953b) reported that animals facing novel stimuli typically display excitement rather than fear. Similarly, human infants' and children's exploration is much more robust in conditions of interest and safety rather than of fear or anxiety. Thus it seems that anxiety reduction does not provide a very satisfactory account of exploration, as Woodworth (1958) expressed with clarity when he argued that, without an exploratory tendency that is stronger than anxiety, animals (and people) would be paralyzed and helpless in new circumstances.

Another drive-theory account of exploration used the concept of secondary reinforcement, suggesting that because venturing forth into novel spaces has led to primary drive reduction (e.g., food has been found), exploration itself takes on secondary reinforcing properties. No doubt there are cases in which exploration has resulted in reinforcing outcomes, but this account does not explain the fact that young animals often exhibit very persistent exploratory urges soon after birth, before the exploration has had a reasonable chance to be paired with primary drive reduction. Further, as Butler (1953) demonstrated, exploratory or curiosity behaviors show great resistance to extinction, persisting with no pairing with primary reinforcers. It appeared that exploration functions more like a primary reinforcer in its own right.

A final approach to explaining exploratory-type behavior within a drive-theory format has been dubbed the *drive-naming* approach. We have already mentioned an exploratory drive (Montgomery, 1952), a visual-exploration drive (Butler, 1953), and a manipulation drive (Harlow, 1953b), and there were others, such as a boredom drive (Isaac, 1962). But the problem with this approach, other than its obvious lack of parsimony, was that accepting these as drives would have required a major change in the definition of drive, for these are not based in non-nervous-system-tissue deficits and do not necessarily produce consummatory behaviors that result in drive reduction (recall, for example, that these exploratory tendencies seem to defy extinction, which is to say that, unlike the conventional drives, they persisted and did not seem to be easily sated). Thus the drive-naming approach to explaining what came to be called intrinsically motivated behaviors also turned out to be theoretically unsatisfactory. As the famous neurologist Hebb (1961) concluded, "Emphasis on biological needs seems to limit animal motivation too narrowly" and has "the unfortunate effect of preventing the student who takes the hypothesis seriously from seeing many of the facts of behavior" (p. 179).

An Alternative: White's Effectance Motivation

After a decade of controversial research and discussion of behaviors such as exploration, manipulation, and play, White (1959) contributed a seminal paper that summarized the issues and in some ways cemented a crisis in the dominant paradigms that had been brewing from several quarters. White concluded that accounts of these behaviors based on the physiological needs (or drives) were not compelling, nor were accounts based on functionally defined reinforcements. White suggested instead an approach that has evolved into the central view of intrinsically motivated behavior still held in modern motivational psychology. He proposed that such behaviors could be reconsidered not as drives but as *innate psychological tendencies*. White summarized these tendencies under the concept of *competence*, which he described as a motive to produce effects. Referring to the motive as *effectance motivation*, White suggested that it involves the feeling of satisfaction and pleasure in doing something, in being active, and he believed this to be a basic biological endowment. Of course, something such as play, with functional value that conveys selective advantages, would expectably be attended by such experiences of satisfaction and pleasure, just as sex, consumption of sweets, making social connections, and various other human activities are associated with such experiences. Indeed, we, too, understand the selective advantages in finding inherent satisfactions in activities such as exploration and play (Stump, Ratliff, Wu, & Hawley, 2009; Ryan & Hawley, 2016).

We return to the work of White later in the chapter, but we raise it at this point because White, who had worked with Murray (1938) in his exploration of psychological needs, was positing an approach to interest, curiosity, exploration, and play that pointed in the direction of specifying universal psychological needs that, in complement to the physiological needs (i.e., drives), are critical for understanding human behavior. Although White tended to avoid the concept of "need" because the term had been so closely linked to the physiological needs that created drive states and because his work was essentially contrary to drive-theory accounts, he did, nonetheless, suggest that competence-promoting behavior "satisfies an intrinsic need to deal with the environment" (1959, p. 318). He thus set the stage for an enormous amount of subsequent work that concerned not only competence but also basic psychological needs (e.g., Deci, 1975; Deci & Ryan, 1980a, 1985b; Ryan, 1995).

To summarize, stemming from the two traditions of experimental research (i.e., operant and drive approaches) that led to the "discovery" (or, more properly, rediscovery) of intrinsic motivation, there have been two main types of definitions for the concept of intrinsic motivation. Each derives from the fact that the concept was initially proposed as a critical reaction to these behavioral theories that were dominant in empirical psychology at the time (see Ryan & Deci, 2000c). Specifically, because operant theory (Skinner, 1953) maintained, in essence, that all behaviors are motivated by reinforcements (i.e., by operationally separable consequences), intrinsically motivated activities were said to be ones for which the reinforcement or "reward" was in the activity itself (not external or operationally separable). This led subsequent researchers to investigate the characteristics—for example, optimal challenge (Csikszentmihalyi, 1975; Deci, 1975; Harter, 1978b)—that make an activity or task interesting or inherently rewarding. In contrast, because learning theory (Hull, 1943) asserted that all behaviors are motivated by *physiological* drives and their derivatives, intrinsically motivated activities were said to be ones that provided satisfaction of innate *psychological* needs. This then led researchers to explore quite different questions of what basic psychological needs are satisfied by intrinsically motivated behaviors.

Psychoanalytic Theory: Parallel Developments

Within psychoanalytic ego psychology, a remarkably parallel theoretical struggle was occurring contemporaneous with the upheavals within behavioral drive theory, a struggle which we described in Chapter 2. Because classic psychoanalytic theory had been developed to account for psychopathology, ego psychologists, who were studying normative human development within the confines of psychoanalytic drive theory, found the theory unwieldy. The problem, basically, concerned Freud's (1923) fundamental assumption that all motivational energy for behavior was ultimately derived from sexual or erotic drives. How these libidinal origins of psychic energy could possibly be diverted or converted into non-drive-gratifying activities such as exploration and play, activities that were central to normal development, was unclear. True, some rarified forms of play appear to give expression to sexual aims, and perhaps a larger set of actions might be tangentially associated with aggressive gratification, but the majority of behaviors associated with curiosity and playful interest could be tied to these drives only through quite circuitous explanatory routes. The ego seemed to have a reserve of energy that was expressed in play, learning, and exploration, often quite vigorously, but the question was, from whence came this energy?

As reviewed in Chapter 2, Freud (1923) suggested that the ego might have the capacity to *neutralize* libidinal energies to use for its own purposes, and Hartmann (1958) later proposed that, through neutralization, the ego obtains its own *independent energies* that can be used for normal developmental tasks such as play, exercise of functions, and curious exploration. In a sense, the idea of neutralization within psychoanalytic theory can be seen as the parallel to the secondary reinforcement explanation of exploration and manipulation within the experimental psychological literature, for each represents a process of derivation through which energization by a primary drive is diverted into the motivation for exploration, assimilation, and the exercise of capacities.

There were two other explanations of play behaviors within psychoanalytic theory that, interestingly, paralleled the explanations in experimental psychology. Hendrick (1942), unsatisfied with the neutralization or drive-derivative explanation, posited a new drive, referred to as the *instinct to master,* which he described as "an inborn drive to do and learn how to do" (p. 40). Hendrick believed that there was a *primary pleasure* in effective action and that this gratification underlay the instinct to master. His postulate can be seen as parallel to the drive-naming approach used by Montgomery, Butler, and others who had observed vigorous exploration and competence-directed activity in rats and monkeys.

Fenichel (1945), in a classic psychoanalytic treatise on this issue, proposed that anxiety reduction fueled the mastery behaviors that were central to normal development, again paralleling a similar approach in the Hullian experimental literature on mastery. Yet, as we saw, explaining proactive positive behaviors in terms of an avoidance mechanism such as anxiety reduction did not fit with the observable curious demeanor of organisms during exploratory episodes and, furthermore, did not seem plausible as an account of such behaviors, as avoidance of anxiety would more likely lead to inhibition rather than activity.

White (1963), in discussing effectance motivation, agreed with the viewpoint of Hendrick, Hartmann, and others who suggested that the motivational theory underlying psychoanalysis required revision. Yet White argued not for a new instinct, or for a neutralized libidinal energy, but rather for the recognition of a psychological tendency that operates primarily when drives are relatively quiescent. Thus, in his work, White was attempting to resolve the paradigmatic dilemmas of both behaviorism and psychoanalysis by positing a type of non-drive-derivative tendency and energy for growth that complemented the drives that were the focus of the motivational theories within each tradition.

Independent Ego Energy

Much of White's argument applied similarly to the two theoretical domains of behaviorism and psychoanalysis. He noted that there are positive adaptive consequences to a biological endowment to orient toward, explore, and assimilate one's environment and, through playful activity, to exercise and extend one's capacities. In so behaving, organisms increase their competence, a propensity as germane to the natural psychological development of children as to the exploratory tendencies of rats in a maze or monkeys in a primate compound. But White made the further interesting point that the adaptive consequences of exploration and play are not the *reason* that organisms are active in that way. Rather, they "play and explore because it is fun—because there is something inherently satisfying about it—not because it is going to have value at some future time" (p. 35).

In this postulate, White was echoing points made half a century earlier by Groos (1898), Woodworth (1918), and others but seemingly ignored in the meantime—that being curious about and acting upon one's world is natural and primary and that, although it has important developmental consequences, its phenomenal support is the immediate experience of interest and enjoyment, the pleasure of engagement and proactivity, rather than the long-term advantages it yields. Motivationally, this is an important point, for it emphasizes that organisms can have in their natures a set of motivational processes through which the growth and development are facilitated; namely, activities can have *experientially* rewarding consequences (Ryan & Deci, 2000d). We would add that the very *enjoyability* of certain proactive, assimilative, and relational tendencies can itself yield selective advantages, and thus it has emerged as a pervasive and important psychological feature in many species, just as the preference for sweet taste at one time yielded such advantages (before the advent of junk food). That is, the fact that certain behaviors elicit such satisfactions may itself be an evolved proximal support for such behaviors (see Ryan & Hawley, 2016; Chapter 24, this volume).

Although White was applying the same fundamental concept within the two disparate traditions of psychology, his application of the concept to psychoanalytic theory carried the postulate that the ego has an inherent, independent ego energy. Thus White (1963) was taking the final step in the theoretical developments that began with Freud's (1923) suggestion that the ego had its own adaptive energy derived from the sexual drive and extended through Hartmann's proposal that it was through neutralization that the ego acquired a source of energy that was independent of the id (as discussed in Chapter 2). Specifically, White was suggesting that the ego has an inherent energy that underlies adaptation and growth, that it is indeed independent of the id and not derivative of physiological drives. This natural, *independent ego energy,* White argued, is essential for understanding developmental progress, including the progress inherent in overcoming the conflicts that Freud (1925, 1953/1900) described in psychosexual terms and Erikson (1950) described in psychosocial terms.

White's theory of effectance motivation represents the theoretical forerunner of *intrinsic motivation* and of our psychological needs formulation of intrinsically motivated phenomena. The idea is that there is a class of actions emitted by organisms that are inclined by inherent satisfactions or pleasurable feelings. Being natural inclinations and tendencies, they cannot be explained by a psychology that locates the causes of all behavior in environmental reinforcers, and being proactive rather than reactive, these tendencies cannot be well represented as drives, for they lack many of the defining characteristics associated with drives. Rather, there is an independent energy in the sense that it is inherent and not derived from other sources, and this energy is involved in a wide range of actions.

White's formulation was so far outside the boundaries of the behavioral drive theories that dominated psychology at that time that it was subsequently cited as the death knell of motivation theory. Hilgard (1987), for example, dated the "end of motivation as a field" to White's (1959) landmark paper. However, in our view, White's paper, rather than extinguishing motivation theory, simply refocused it on its proper object—namely, the active, developing organism that is liberally endowed with a propensity to exceed itself and to expand its structures and functions through further activity. It may have marked the end of the dominance of behaviorist drive theories of motivation, but it was the harbinger of a new era in the empirical exploration of the motivation of active organisms. As White once conveyed to the two of us in a casual conversation at his Cambridge home, he felt that "one could not watch a flower grow and still be a behaviorist" (R. White, personal communication, June 1990).

Optimal Stimulation and Discrepancy Theories

Following the publication of White's important work, it was clear that motivational theories, if there were to be any, would have to accept the existence of intrinsic motivation and provide some account of its broad manifestations. During the 1960s, there were two approaches that emerged in response to these problems of behaviorism, one of which can, in a sense, be understood as a neo-Skinnerian approach, and the other as a neo-Hullian approach.

Optimal Incongruity

As noted, at that time there was a shift in the conceptualization of reinforcements from past events to future outcomes and, with that, a focus on cognitive processes. Within that emerging cognitive tradition, discussions of intrinsic motivation revolved around stimuli and the relation of stimulus events to existing cognitive structures. The idea of *optimal incongruity* was proposed, and the central hypothesis was that organisms function most actively and effectively when they encounter optimally discrepant information or events.

Hunt (1965) presented the most lucid discussions of this perspective. Using both open systems (Bertalanffy, 1950) and feedback loop (Miller, Galanter, & Pribram, 1960) models, Hunt suggested that people are attracted toward stimuli that are optimally incongruent with respect to their preexisting cognitive structures. They then operate to reduce that inconsistency, either by expanding the cognitive structures or by changing (either physically or mentally) the stimuli to match their structures. This cognitive approach, like the operant approach it was supplanting, did not postulate needs or proximal satisfactions, nor really a satisfactory conceptualization of the energization of behavior. Further, the idea of a tendency to approach optimally discrepant stimuli was not readily reconciled with a dominant idea of that period, namely that people are motivated to reduce cognitive dissonance (Festinger, 1957) or achieve cognitive balance (Heider, 1960) rather than to seek out discrepancy.

Hunt's formulation had its greatest currency within the circles of Piagetian thought, for at the heart of Hunt's theory is a notion also central in Piaget's structural perspective (as reviewed in Chapter 2): that the nature of cognitive structures is simply to operate, so the assimilation schema is naturally operative and works most effectively with respect to optimally discrepant information. In addition, although not so relevant to intrinsic motivation for play or for prosocial activities, Hunt's work has applicability to exploration and problem solving. Nonetheless, in terms of the further study of motivation, or more particularly of intrinsic motivation, Hunt's perspective has not been persistently researched.

Optimal Arousal

The central tenet of drive theories is that organisms are motivated to reduce internal drive states—that is, to achieve and maintain equilibrium. Drive states are generalized states of arousal caused by the basic physiological needs, which implies that the sought-after state is equilibrium or quiescence.

Hebb (1955) suggested, however, that the optimal state may, in fact, involve a moderate (rather than minimal) amount of physiological arousal. This postulate, and the work that followed from it, can at once be seen to fall within the general drive theory tradition, yet it breaks significantly with the tradition in its position on this issue (Hebb,

1961). According to Hebb's (1955) formulation, behaviors that decrease arousal will be strengthened if the organism is above the optimal level, and behaviors that increase arousal will be strengthened if the organism is below the optimal level. Behaviors that we refer to as intrinsically motivated would be explained in terms of increasing arousal when the organism is below its optimal level. At the psychological level, Hebb suggested that humans find novelty and excitement positively motivating and satisfying, assuming they are not overstimulated, and that underlying this is the process through which the novelty moves one toward a more optimal level of physiological arousal.

Berlyne (1967, 1973) presented a theory that had similarities with both Hebb's and Hunt's. Berlyne viewed humans as information-processing systems in continual interaction with the environment. During times when drives and emotions do not dominate attention, the organism is engaging stimuli and noting their relation to information that is already in memory and, in doing that, is attempting to maintain an optimal level of stimulation. Berlyne addressed the motivating properties of stimuli by referring to *collative stimulus properties* that represent novelty and incongruity and provide stimulation that is intrinsically motivating so long as the organism is below its optimal level.

Each of these theories of optimal incongruity and optimal arousal are more complex and elaborate than the abstracted versions we have presented. We have included them mainly for historical interest and to highlight some of the important ideas with which they struggled. Although some emphasize the features of environments that catalyze interest, and others the state of the organism as an explanation of interest, they converge in their focus on intrinsic motivation directed at the mastery and assimilation of incongruence or novelty.

Early SDT and the Significance of Intrinsic Motivation

Intrinsic motivation refers to activities that are done for their inherent satisfactions. Typical intrinsically motivated actions include play, exploration, sport, games, and avocations—activities done out of interest—although clearly these same activities can at times be extrinsically motivated (i.e., done to achieve consequences that are operationally separable from the behavior per se). Intrinsic motivation, as we have reviewed, has particular theoretical significance because it represents one means through which the active, assimilatory nature of organisms is expressed and because, in humans, it is a prototypical example of autonomous behavior, being willingly and volitionally done.

Intrinsic motivation exists in the relation between individuals and activities. Each individual is intrinsically motivated for some activities and not others, and only in certain social contexts and not others. Therefore, an understanding of intrinsic motivation must consider how the characteristics of an activity and context are experienced and engaged in by the individual in question. An individual will be intrinsically motivated for an activity to the degree that he or she finds it inherently interesting and enjoyable, which is in turn a function of proximal basic need satisfactions. Individuals thus differ in the extent to which they find any particular task interesting, and these differences are influenced by situational, contextual factors and cultural supports.

Individuals and Activities

Because intrinsic motivation exists in the nexus between a person and a task, some authors have leaned toward defining intrinsic motivation in terms of the task having certain characteristics, whereas others have defined it in terms of the satisfactions a person gains from intrinsically motivated task engagement. We have already seen that these differences in definition derive, in part, from the fact that the concept of intrinsic motivation was proposed as a critical reaction to the two behavioral theories that were dominant in empirical psychology from the 1940s to the 1960s and that explained the motivation of behavior quite differently.

Specifically, we suggested that, because operant theory maintained that all behaviors are motivated by operationally separable rewards (or, more properly, by reinforcements), researchers interested in intrinsic motivation argued that intrinsically motivated activities were ones for which the reward is in the activity itself. Although that is in a sense true, the critical point is that the rewarding consequences are within people, so one must also specify how or why individuals are willing to maintain sustained engagement with particular activities in the absence of external rewards. What makes something rewarding? In this regard, and in contrast to the learning theory assertion that all behaviors are motivated by physiological drives (and their derivatives), intrinsically motivated activities were said to be ones that provide satisfaction of basic psychological needs, so researchers, especially within SDT, began to explore what basic needs are satisfied by intrinsically motivated behaviors.

The fact that activities are intrinsically motivating to individuals to different degrees implies that, when a researcher or practitioner classifies an *activity* or a task as being intrinsically motivating, that researcher is simply using a heuristic; he or she is simply saying that, on average, across individuals, this is an activity that tends to be experienced as intrinsically motivating. Yet clearly there are particular properties of tasks and activities that make them more or less likely to be intrinsically motivating (Rigby & Ryan, 2011).

Needs and Affects

Inspired by White's (1959) work, some psychologists have taken interest in the concept of inherent or basic psychological needs and their relation to intrinsic motivation. Although the concept of needs has been defined differently by various researchers, we argued in Chapter 4 that the concept is most meaningfully defined in terms of necessary nutriments for growth and well-being.

Deci and Ryan (1980a) distinguished the needs for competence (i.e., effectance) and autonomy as each being integral to intrinsic motivation. The concept of a need for competence was a short extrapolation from White's assertion that there is an innate tendency toward effectance. The concept of a need for autonomy was a similarly short extrapolation from de Charms's (1968) proposal that humans exhibit a "primary propensity" for being an origin of their behaviors, that is, for having an I-PLOC and experiencing personal causation (as reviewed in Chapter 3). Our positing of these needs was, in part, an acceptance of these theoretical positions expressed by White and de Charms; however, it was also prompted primarily by the results of a program of research that had begun to investigate the effects of various types of external rewards and other external events and conditions on intrinsic motivation. The idea of inherent needs for competence and autonomy that can be either supported or thwarted by aspects of the social context provided a parsimonious and theoretically meaningful way of integrating the results of research that we review in detail in Chapters 6 and 7. With regard to competence, Deci (1975) and later Deci and Ryan (1980a) introduced the concepts of *positive feedback* and *optimal challenges* to describe the match of persons' abilities with task demands in which they gain the feelings of mastery and experience competence satisfactions.

Several other researchers in this time period were, in their studies of intrinsic motivation, focused primarily on *competence* as a central element. For example, Csikszentmihalyi (1975) introduced the concept of *flow,* which is an experience of absorption with the activity and of non-self-conscious enjoyment. He suggested that activities that are autotelic, which is to say that the purpose of the activity is the activity itself, often inspire flow. In his model, people will experience flow when the demands of the task at hand are well matched with the individuals' capacities, that is, when action opportunities afforded by tasks are matched to the action capabilities of the persons. Similarly, Harter (1978a) focused on *perceived competence* as the central element of intrinsically motivated actions. Her focus was on particular domains—cognitive, social, and physical, for example—and she investigated the positive relations between perceived competence and intrinsic motivation within domains (Harter, 1981, 2012). Although neither Csikszentmihalyi nor Harter explicitly postulated a need for competence, their theorizing was compatible with the need-for-competence component of intrinsic motivation within SDT.

The need for competence has been explicitly embraced within modern achievement goal theory. In particular, Elliot, McGregor, and Thrash (2002), building upon the work of White (1959), suggested that the need for competence is an evolved and broad-based appetitive desire to be competent at one's actions, skills, and abilities. Subsequently, we shall examine how this need for competence has been examined within achievement goal theories and how these theories interface with SDT (see also Ryan & Moller, 2016).

Researchers other than those operating within SDT have paid considerably less attention to the need-for-autonomy component than the need-for-competence component. However, using the PLOC formulation discussed in Chapter 3, de Charms was, in essence, considering the issue of autonomy, and his research on being an "origin" and experiencing *personal causation* in the classroom (de Charms, 1976) highlighted the relevance of autonomy for motivation and achievement. His classic 1976 study demonstrated that teachers who supported the voice, choice, and engagement of students while supplying an optimal scaffold of challenges fostered gains in self-motivation and in performance, even within an underprivileged urban school setting. Much subsequent research has supported de Charms's (1968) view that intrinsic motivation is affected by social contextual conditions that support or undermine the individual's sense of being an origin or what in SDT we describe as being autonomous. Consistently, providing choice, minimizing external controls, and acknowledging the actor's perspective, all autonomy-supporting factors, have been found to be important for intrinsic motivation and to facilitate what de Charms (1968) described as an I-PLOC for actions.

Other work on intrinsic motivation, done mainly with infants and young children, had shown that they display curiosity and intrinsic exploration when they feel a sense of security with respect to others, such as a parent or experimenter (e.g., Anderson, Manoogian, & Reznick, 1976; Bernier, Matte-Gagné, Bélanger, & Whipple, 2014; Frodi, Bridges, & Grolnick, 1985). This suggests that the need for relatedness, as well, is involved in intrinsically motivated activity and fits with the idea that a responsive, supportive caregiver can facilitate the active, interested spontaneity of the child (e.g., Winnicott, 1971). Although relatedness does not appear to be necessary, in the proximal sense, for people to be intrinsically motivated on some tasks, it is an important developmental support for children in feeling the security and vitality to explore and play. In contrast, competence and autonomy are invariably proximally implicated in maintaining intrinsic motivation for a particular activity. Put differently, there are some intrinsically motivated activities that a person can pursue in a solitary way (Ryan & Deci, 2000a). However, even these individual moments of being intrinsically motivated are enabled by a background of relational security and the social learning through which such activities are acquired. Moreover, most of the interests individuals adopt are acquired in a context of relatedness and have an underlying social meaning, even for a person acting without others present. Accordingly, our empirical theory of intrinsic motivation, which we turn to in the next two chapters, involves a consideration of the role of three basic psychological needs—those for autonomy, competence, and relatedness.

Concluding Comments

In this chapter we took a brief tour through the history of the construct of *intrinsic motivation,* which is perhaps the most obvious manifestation of the active, organizational tendency in mammalian life and is a tendency with which humans are particularly richly endowed. We began with the early observations of ethologists and behavioral scientists such as Groos, Woodworth, and Dewey, who attempted to describe and explain the nature and adaptive importance of play, curiosity, and interest before the advent of behaviorism. We then reviewed how behaviorists in both the drive-reduction and operant traditions attempted to account for all behavioral processes through reinforcement and the implausibility of these approaches when it came to the spontaneous, active exploratory tendencies of animals. We then turned to the "rediscovery" of intrinsic motivation in the failed attempts within these behavioral paradigms to account for exploratory and curiosity-motivated behaviors, culminating in the seminal work of Robert White. White's (1959, 1963) construct of effectance motivation is argued to represent the theoretical forerunner of modern organismic approaches to intrinsic motivation and the need for competence that underlies it.

The need for competence, however, does not sufficiently account for the necessary conditions for intrinsic motivation because there are many activities for which we have competence but in which we have no interest. De Charms (1968) stressed that, to be intrinsically motivated, the individual had to feel like an origin of action or have an I-PLOC. Early experimental work (e.g. Deci, 1971; Lepper, Greene, & Nisbett, 1973) described in the next chapter verified that, indeed, intrinsic motivation depends upon an I-PLOC (de Charms, 1968), or perceived autonomy, as well as perceived competence, to be sustained.

Together, the dual concept of needs for competence and autonomy, derived in part from the works of White (1959) and de Charms (1968), respectively, were incorporated into SDT as an account of the necessary conditions for supporting intrinsic motivation, and it is this basic model that we used to develop the specific propositions of *cognitive evaluation theory* (CET; Deci & Ryan, 1980a, 1985b), the empirically oriented theory of the determinants of intrinsically motivated actions that is the topic of the next two chapters.

PART III

The Six Mini-Theories
of Self-Determination Theory

CHAPTER 6

Cognitive Evaluation Theory, Part I

The Effects of Rewards, Feedback, and Other External Events on Intrinsic Motivation

Cognitive evaluation theory (CET), the first of SDT's mini-theories, is focused exclusively on *intrinsic motivation*. CET's primary concern is how events in the social environment impact intrinsic motivation. In this chapter, we present the first three formal propositions of CET and review experiments that have tested them. We begin by discussing early experimental work using the *free-choice paradigm,* showing the undermining of intrinsic motivation by extrinsic rewards. Because reward effects on intrinsic motivation are complex, we discuss moderator effects and limiting conditions and review meta-analyses of these effects. We also discuss recent neuroscience work exploring intrinsic motivation and its undermining. We then review the impact of other events on intrinsic motivation, such as evaluations, surveillance, competition, and positive versus negative feedback. CET postulates that events such as rewards, evaluations, or feedback have a particular meaning or *functional significance* that predicts the impact of these events on intrinsic motivation. This meaning largely concerns the implications of such events for one's autonomy or competence.

The phenomenon of intrinsic motivation reflects the primary and spontaneous propensity of some organisms, especially mammals, to develop through activity—to play, explore, and manipulate things and, in doing so, to expand their competencies and capacities. This natural inclination is an especially significant feature of human nature that affects people's cognitive and emotional development, quality of performance, and psychological well-being. It is among the most important of the inner resources that evolution has provided (Deci & Ryan, 2000; Ryan & Hawley, 2016), and because it represents a prototypical manifestation of integrative organismic tendencies, SDT research began with it as a primary focus.

Although intrinsic motivation by no means represents the whole of human motivation, the study of this type of motivation provided a paradigm-shifting area of discovery that has highlighted both the active nature of the healthy organism and its vulnerability to being controlled or stifled. Indeed, even though the human inclination to be intrinsically motivated is both inherent and pervasive, this spontaneous tendency can be readily diminished in many contexts. In classrooms, workplaces, and gymnasiums, participants who otherwise might be active and infused with vitality and interest instead become passive, disengaged, or resistant.

In an attempt to account for this seeming disparity between the active-organism assumption and observations of passivity and amotivation, SDT research has extensively investigated how social-contextual conditions affect intrinsic motivation, guided by the general hypothesis that some social conditions support active engagement, whereas others undermine or thwart it. Hundreds of studies performed over more than four decades are relevant to this theoretical formulation, which states that intrinsic motivation is an inherent human characteristic that may either flourish or wither as a function of ambient social conditions.

Cognitive evaluation theory (CET) represents a formal mini-theory developed within SDT that focuses on factors that facilitate or undermine intrinsic motivation. CET was the first of SDT's mini-theories and was developed primarily during the 1970s and 1980s to organize and integrate the results of emerging experimental studies on how rewards, punishments, evaluations, feedback, and other extrinsic events affect intrinsic motivation. Early on, CET was primarily tested in laboratory experiments, allowing causal interpretations of the factors that influence intrinsic motivation. The assumption of SDT is not that social-contextual events "cause" intrinsic motivation—on the contrary, intrinsic motivation is understood as an evolved and inherent human propensity. The ultimate causes of intrinsic motivation, that is, lie in the selective advantages this propensity yielded in human prehistory. Yet we began with the belief that this inherent propensity could either be enhanced or diminished by social-contextual factors. Accordingly, CET focuses upon the proximal conditions that facilitate, maintain, and enhance intrinsic motivation or alternatively, diminish and undermine it.

CET was introduced in the 1970s (Deci, 1975) and refined during the early 1980s (e.g., Deci & Ryan, 1980a; Ryan, 1982; Ryan, Mims, & Koestner, 1983), and yet its core elements have remained largely intact and empirically well supported since that time. There have, however, been advances in understanding both the nuances of intrinsic motivation across varied periods of development and different domains of activity and its physiological and neurological supports, which we review in this and various chapters that follow.

CET represents both a *social psychology* of intrinsic motivation (as it specifies how social inputs and contexts affect intrinsic motivation and the processes and outcomes associated with it) and a *personality perspective,* in that it specifies a core aspect of human nature and its unfolding. In its most general form, CET argues that events that negatively affect a person's experience of autonomy or competence will diminish intrinsic motivation, whereas events that support perceptions of autonomy and competence will enhance intrinsic motivation. The theory further argues that *both* competence and autonomy satisfactions are necessary to sustain intrinsic motivation. For example, from a CET perspective, experiences of self-efficacy (Bandura, 1989) and optimal challenge (Csikszentmihalyi, 1975; Deci, 1975), both of which are concerned with competence, contribute to intrinsic motivation, but experiences of autonomy, which are not consistent with Bandura's social-cognitive approach to agency (see Bandura, 1989, 1997) nor formalized within Csikszentmihalyi's (1975) "flow" model, are also critically important in CET. In addition, because intrinsic motivation is most robust in a context of relational security and can be enhanced by a sense of belonging and connection, CET suggests that relatedness also plays a role in conducing intrinsic motivation's occurrence, especially for activities that have a social element.

   In this and the following chapter, we provide but a partial history and review of the large body of literature that has characterized and tested CET. We begin by describing early experiments that established the *free choice behavioral paradigm* that has been widely used in investigations of intrinsic motivation and then turn to the central tenets of CET and their empirical support.

Extrinsic Rewards and Intrinsic Motivation: The Early Experiments

CET was born in the context of a highly controversial area of research, namely studies of the relations between externally administered rewards and intrinsic motivation. This is one of the most important and certainly well-known areas of research in SDT and yet also one of the most widely misunderstood and misinterpreted. Because CET identifies circumstances in which externally rewarding intrinsically motivated behaviors undermines or diminishes subsequent interest and intrinsic motivation, this research has also aroused considerable critical fervor, particularly from traditional behaviorists and economists. So even before we begin reviewing this area, it is important to clarify a few points.

   First of all, the fact that rewards can, under well-specified conditions, yield detrimental effects on intrinsic motivation does not mean that SDT is against all rewards, as some claim. Indeed, we find that rewards can have many positive motivational functions, especially in areas in which behavior is not intrinsically motivating. This chapter is exclusively focused on intrinsically motivated activities, which do not encompass, for example, all work behaviors, all educational achievements, or all healthy behaviors. Secondly, even with regard to intrinsic motivation, we do not cast all rewards as problematic. Externally administered rewards and contingencies can be coercive and controlling, but they can also signal competence or value and can be a form of positive feedback if wisely applied.

   Nonetheless, we maintain and clearly demonstrate that externally administered reward contingencies, when used to control behavior, can alienate people from their values and interests and at times reduce their quality of engagement, their performance and creativity, and sometimes even their moral compasses. Particularly because the controlling use of rewards can disrupt autonomy, these negative effects have implications for behavioral regulation, both intrinsic and extrinsic. So with these caveats in mind, let us turn to the research evidence.

Early Studies of Tangible Rewards

The first published studies of intrinsic motivation with humans were performed by Deci (1971). He began with the question: What would happen to a person's subsequent intrinsic motivation for an interesting activity if the person were given a monetary reward for doing it? Stated differently, the question was whether intrinsic and extrinsic motivations are additive as opposed to being in some way interactive. Investigation of this question represented the first attempt to ascertain whether a specific external event—namely, a monetary reward—would facilitate, diminish, or leave unchanged people's natural propensity toward active engagement.

   As noted in the previous chapter, operant psychology, which still represented the dominant paradigm in psychology at the time of this first study, maintained (using different language) that intrinsic and extrinsic motivation would be additive. Total motivation would increase when salient extrinsic rewards were introduced and would return to prereward baseline after the reward was removed. Expectancy-valence theories of motivation also assumed that intrinsic and extrinsic motivation would be additive (e.g., Porter & Lawler, 1968).

To test this question, Deci developed the *free-choice paradigm,* upon which most subsequent experimental work on intrinsic motivation has been based. In this paradigm, intrinsic motivation is operationalized through observation of the amount of time following an experimental manipulation that participants spend working with the target activity when they are alone, are free to choose what to do, and have no external incentive or evaluative reason to persist. Typically, researchers also supplement this behavioral measure with self-reports such as the *Intrinsic Motivation Inventory* (IMI; Ryan et al. 1983), to assess subjective interest/enjoyment, sense of choice, and other related variables.

Deci (1971) created two groups—a reward group and a control group— both working on interesting puzzles. One group received rewards ($1 for each puzzle solved), whereas the second worked without mention or expectation of a reward. The experimental task was followed by the free-choice period, in which participants were left alone with additional target puzzles, as well as other interesting activities. Results revealed what for many behaviorists was a counterintuitive finding—namely, participants who received extrinsic rewards for solving puzzles showed a *decrease* in their subsequent intrinsic motivation (i.e., free-choice behavioral persistence) relative to those who had not received rewards. Stated with more operant terminology, the finding was that following the introduction and then withdrawal of reinforcement, responding went below baseline rather than returning to baseline. Deci (1971) also reported a field experiment in a college newspaper office in which headline writers, paid over a short period for writing headlines, evidenced a decrease in intrinsic motivation for the task once the reward contingency was withdrawn. These undermining effects were quickly replicated (e.g., Deci, 1972b).

Subsequently, Deci (1972a) examined the effects of monetary rewards that did not require specific engagement with the activity or successful completion of it. Whereas, in the studies mentioned above, participants were given a monetary reward for each task they completed successfully, in this study they were paid simply for showing up for the experiment. In this condition, monetary rewards did not decrease intrinsic motivation. It was an important finding because it indicated that not all monetary rewards undermine intrinsic motivation. The effects of rewards instead depended on how they were administered and experienced, as CET (Deci & Ryan, 1980a) ultimately postulated.

These early monetary-reward experiments caused an outcry from behaviorists, who made varied attempts to attribute the findings to experimental flaws and biases (e.g., Calder & Staw, 1975; Scott, 1976). Yet other investigators began to replicate the findings with different tasks, different rewards, different reward contingencies, and different-age participants. For example, Lepper, Greene, and Nisbett (1973) gave preschool children a drawing task using attractive materials. Some were told that they would receive a "good player award" if they did the drawing; others did the same activity with no mention of an award. In a free-choice period held several days later, children who had received the award spent significantly less time engaged with the art materials than children in the no-reward control group, replicating the undermining effect.

In the Lepper et al. (1973) study, there was also a second group of rewarded children who were given the reward after they finished working on the task without having been told about it beforehand. For these participants, rewards did not have a detrimental effect on intrinsic motivation. Thus an *unexpected* reward did not undermine intrinsic motivation. Similarly, an early study by Ross (1975) demonstrated that a reward had to be salient to have a negative effect on intrinsic motivation. He used marshmallows as the reward for children who played with a drum. For half the children, the marshmallows were in plain sight, and for the other half, they were hidden. Only the children for whom the reward was salient showed the undermining effect. It seemed that for rewards to undermine intrinsic motivation, they had to be introduced before task engagement began, made salient, and made contingent on actually working on the activity. As we shall see, these are conditions associated with the controlling use of rewards, which CET postulates undermines intrinsic motivation.

Perceived Locus of Causality

In Chapter 3, we introduced the concept of *perceived locus of causality* (PLOC; de Charms, 1968; Heider, 1958) as an attributional concept that reflects different levels of human autonomy. Specifically, de Charms suggested that an intentional behavior can be either intrinsically motivated, in which case it would have an *internal perceived locus of causality* (I-PLOC), or extrinsically motivated, in which case it would have an *external perceived locus of causality* (E-PLOC). Behaviors with an I-PLOC are experienced as autonomous, and those with an E-PLOC are experienced as controlled (i.e., nonautonomous).

Deci and Ryan (1980a, 1985b) argued that the introduction of extrinsic rewards for an activity that is intrinsically motivated can prompt a change in PLOC from internal to external. Whereas initially participants had been doing the activity because it was interesting and enjoyable, those in reward conditions came to view the activity as something they did in order to get a reward. In the language of basic psychological needs, the rewards undermined autonomy, even as they provided a positive external incentive for acting.

Extrinsic rewards represent a particularly interesting instance of diminishing autonomy, because the receipt of rewards is an event that people often feel positive about. Yet behaving to get such a positive or desired outcome can nonetheless diminish autonomy and undermine intrinsic motivation. Out of people's desire for rewards, they are prone to experience a rewarded activity as something they do *for the rewards*—that is, they develop an instrumental approach toward the activity, thereby seeing the rewards as controlling their behavior rather than that they are engaging in the activity for its own sake, or its inherent satisfactions. In fact, studies such as that by Houlfort, Koestner, Joussemet, Nantel-Vivier, and Lekes (2002) have shown that contingent rewards can undermine participants' sense of autonomy.

Yet it is not always the case. Sometimes rewards can be constructed so as not to be controlling but rather to convey value for the activity itself. Marinak and Gambrell (2008), for example, were interested in third-grade children's reading motivation. They compared a no-rewards condition with a token-reward condition and found that token rewards for reading diminished intrinsic motivation to read. Yet the reward of a book, which essentially encourages and signifies a value for more reading, did not undermine intrinsic reading motivation. It is such differences in how rewards are experienced that, as we shall soon see, CET was built to address.

It is also important to note that the detrimental and facilitating effects of specific types of rewards that are the focus of CET concern people's *subsequent* motivation. Rewards, when salient and potent, can clearly motivate *immediate* behavior (Ryan & Deci, 2000d). The scientific problem here is specifically their impact on the maintenance of intrinsically motivated behavior over time, and the experiences of enjoyment and interest associated with it, subsequent to the reward being terminated. Of course, if a reward is not expected, not salient, or not given for actually doing the task, a person will not be doing the task in order to get the reward. In these cases, the reward is not likely to be perceived as controlling one's behavior, so it is not likely to foster an E-PLOC, undermine autonomy, or diminish intrinsic motivation.

There is another issue with using rewards to motivate. Rewarding a person for doing an activity also conveys, or can signal, that the activity is not worth doing for its own sake. For example, a study by Lepper, Sagotsky, Dafoe, and Greene (1982) showed that when a contingency was created in which people had to do one interesting activity in order to be allowed to do a second one, the contingency undermined intrinsic motivation for the first activity. In short, doing an interesting activity because any outcome is expected to be contingent upon it runs the risk of decreasing intrinsic motivation, and in an attribution sense, demeans the primary activity.

Early Studies of Positive Feedback: Competence Satisfaction and Intrinsic Motivation

Although tangible rewards such as money or prizes are relatively pervasive, positive feedback and praise, also sometimes called "verbal rewards" in the experimental literature, are fully as pervasive, particularly with children. Verbal rewards can take many forms; for example, they might involve telling people that they did well at the activity, that they are good people for doing the activity, or that they did better than other people at the activity; each has different effects.

In the early Deci (1971; 1972b; Deci, Cascio, & Krusell, 1975) studies, some participants were given positive feedback for working on the activity. For example, if they completed the task, they were told, "You did very well in completing the task; many participants did not complete it." If they did not complete the task, they were told, "This was a very difficult one, and you were progressing very well with it." In these studies, participants who were given positive feedback displayed more free-choice persistence than those who were not given feedback. Such competence-focused feedback appeared to enhance rather than undermine subsequent intrinsic motivation.

In interpreting such results, Deci and Ryan (1980a) suggested that such positive feedback or praise can support or enhance recipients' sense of competence. In addition, because positive feedback is less tangible than a material reward and is typically not expected, people are less likely to perceive that they did the task in order to get the positive feedback. Accordingly, positive feedback is less likely to prompt a shift in PLOC from internal to external. Using the language of basic psychological needs, this would mean that, in general, positive feedback satisfies people's need for competence while being less likely than tangible rewards to thwart their need for autonomy.

Positive Feedback and Evaluations

Although positive feedback, by enhancing a sense of mastery or competence, enhances intrinsic motivation, some forms of praise can be experienced as external evaluations, pressure, or control, prompting a more E-PLOC and thus undermining their intrinsic motivation. Smith (1975) performed the first test of this idea. Three experimental groups were assigned to a learning task involving art history. One group was told that they would receive a written evaluation after they completed the learning activity; the two other groups were not. Of those who were not, some received an unanticipated evaluation, and some received none. All evaluations given to participants in the two evaluation conditions were very positive. Results showed that those who did the interesting activity in the expected evaluation condition, even though they received positive feedback, displayed significantly less intrinsic motivation than those who received either unanticipated positive feedback or those who received no feedback. The issue was not what the evaluations conveyed; it was the fact that the people were being evaluated, which undermined their sense of autonomy for the learning. In Chapter 14, we show that this fact has an impact not only on persistence but also on quality of learning.

Ryan (1982) manipulated autonomy while providing positive feedback to participants in two groups. One group was told that they had done well on the activity, which was intended to support their experiences of competence, but in the other group participants were told that they had done well, "just as they should" or "as was expected." In this second group, the aim was to convey an E-PLOC, along with the positive competence feedback. Results indicated that participants in the second group displayed significantly less intrinsic motivation, highlighting that positive feedback alone is unlikely to enhance intrinsic motivation if the participants do not also experience autonomy.

A more recent study of positive feedback was done in a work organization. The researchers found that, overall, positive feedback was not detrimental to intrinsic motivation, as was the case with the experiments reviewed in this chapter; but if the positive feedback was made very salient, it tended to be experienced as controlling, resulting in decreased intrinsic motivation (Hewett & Conway, 2015).

To summarize this research on positive feedback about task performance, results indicated that, in general, positive feedback enhances intrinsic motivation. Further, however, if the situation within which positive feedback was given led recipients to feel evaluated or controlled, if the feedback was given in a controlling context, or if the feedback was made overly salient, participants' intrinsic motivation was not enhanced and in some cases was diminished. It thus seems clear that the experience of perceiving oneself to be competent at an activity can best occur in a situation in which one's autonomy is not undermined in order for the positive feedback to be truly conducive to intrinsic motivation.

Autonomy, Competence, and CET

These early studies indicated that tangible rewards that were salient, expected, or contingent on doing activities tended to undermine intrinsic motivation and that positive feedback tended to enhance intrinsic motivation. We suggested that when tangible rewards undermined intrinsic motivation it was because they thwarted autonomy and prompted more change toward an E-PLOC. We also suggested that when positive feedback allowed people to feel autonomous rather than evaluated or controlled, enhancement of intrinsic motivation often occurred through an increase in the individuals' perceived competence. These elements came together to form the first two formal propositions of CET.

CET Proposition I: External events relevant to the initiation or regulation of behavior will affect a person's intrinsic motivation to the extent that they influence the perceived locus of causality for the behavior. Events that promote a more external perceived locus of causality or have a functional significance of control will thwart autonomy and undermine intrinsic motivation, whereas those that promote a more internal perceived locus of causality will increase feelings of autonomy and enhance intrinsic motivation.

CET Proposition II: External events will also affect a person's intrinsic motivation for an activity to the extent that the events influence the person's perceived competence at the activity. Events that promote greater perceived competence enhance intrinsic motivation by satisfying the person's need for competence. Events that meaningfully diminish perceived competence undermine intrinsic motivation.

Although, as we shall see, there is excellent empirical support for these two propositions as they stand, these statements nonetheless do not provide a full enough account of cases in which various external events are likely to enhance, diminish, or leave unchanged intrinsic motivation. In accord with the tenets of SDT, events influence motivation by altering the person's *experience* of their situation. Deci and Ryan (1980a, 1985b) thus further suggested that the effects of rewards and other events depend on the meaning or interpretation the recipient gives to them. That is, each event has a particular *functional significance* for the recipient, defined in terms of how the event impacts experiences of autonomy and competence. For example, a reward could be experienced primarily as a way of controlling behavior, in which case it would likely diminish satisfaction of the need for autonomy and undermine intrinsic motivation, or it could be experienced as competence affirmation, in which case it would enhance intrinsic motivation.

CET thus specifies that the functional significance of an event can be *controlling* (which means it is experienced as an external pressure or inducement toward a specific outcome) or it can be *informational* (which means it affirms or promotes autonomy and competence). Some events can also be *amotivating*, which means the person experiences them as diminishing either a sense of competence for acting or sense of autonomy or both. Formally:

CET Proposition III: External events relevant to the initiation and regulation of behavior have three aspects, each with a functional significance. The informational aspect, which conveys information about self-determined competence, facilitates an internal perceived locus of causality and perceived competence, thus supporting intrinsic motivation. The controlling aspect, which pressures people to think, feel, or behave in particular ways, facilitates an external perceived locus of causality, thereby diminishing intrinsic motivation. The amotivating aspect, which signifies incompetence to obtain outcomes and/or a lack of value for them, undermines both intrinsic and extrinsic motivation and promotes amotivation. The relative salience of these three aspects for the person, which can be influenced by factors in the interpersonal context and in the person, determines the functional significance of the event, and thus its impact on intrinsic motivation.

The point here is that the impact of rewards, feedback, sanctions, or other external events on intrinsic motivation will depend on the psychological meaning of the event for the individual perceiver with regard to autonomy and competence. For example, to make predictions about the effects of a particular reward, whether it be tangible or verbal, one would have to consider how the reward or sanction is likely to be interpreted by people on average. If a reward is likely to be seen as an attempt by an external agent to get the person to do something, then the functional significance of the reward is likely to be controlling, and to that extent to have an undermining effect. Yet if the reward is interpreted in a way that is seen as acknowledging a job well done or as conveying appreciation for efforts, then it is more likely to be experienced as informational and thus to sustain or enhance intrinsic motivation.

We suggest that tangible, and especially monetary, rewards are likely to be functionally significant as controlling, because people usually are offered and receive such rewards when others are trying to externally motivate them. In contrast, unexpected rewards or positive feedback that is not contaminated by the provider's evaluative statements are likely to be perceived as informational because they convey competence information without being controlling.

In many cases, particular rewards will have conflicting effects for a person, being experienced to some extent as controlling and to some extent as informational. In these cases, the two processes will work against each other, so additional factors must be taken into account in predicting the likely effect of such rewards. Will the controlling aspect be more salient, or will the informational aspect be? One such factor is the *reward contingency,* or what exactly the reward is being made contingent upon.

Reward Contingencies: For What Are Rewards Being Given?

The way in which rewards or feedback are administered will have predictable effects on their functional significance or meaning to the recipients and thus on the recipients' motivation. As an example, suppose an authority is using a reward to compel a level of performance that has been predetermined; the recipient may well experience it as controlling, whereas the same reward given to acknowledge accomplishments or achievements might feel supportive and enhancing of intrinsic motivation. Rewards can be given to people for simply showing up for work; they could be given for actually doing their work; or they can be given for doing the work especially well. Each will likely have a different average functional significance and thus a different impact on motivation.

To clarify the complexities of rewards and their likely relations to functional significance and thus intrinsic motivation, Ryan et al. (1983) developed the first comprehensive taxonomy of reward types and specified how each might affect intrinsic motivation. They also applied that taxonomy experimentally, using the free-choice behavioral paradigm, to demonstrate how predictions based on these categories could be empirically sustained. Ryan et al.'s taxonomy was later refined by Deci, Koestner, and Ryan (1999), partly in response to various behaviorists' claims about reward effects in the literature, although its central features and predictions remained the same. For reference, Table 6.1 contains a definition of each type of reward structure.

Engagement-Contingent and Completion-Contingent Rewards

Deci (1972a) found that rewards given to participants for just reporting to the experiment rather than for doing a specific task were not undermining of intrinsic motivation because they were not typically experienced as controlling the target behavior. Ryan et al. (1983) referred to this type of reward as *task-noncontingent,* because the reward receipt is not contingent upon doing the task. In contrast, Ryan et al. (1983) used the term *task-contingent* to refer to rewards that do require either working on or completing the task but do not have specific performance standards. Task-contingent rewards were hypothesized and shown by Ryan et al. (1983) to have a more detrimental effect than task-noncontingent rewards on intrinsic motivation, presumably because, under most circumstances, task-contingent rewards are readily interpretable as controllers of people's behaviors, so they conduce toward an E-PLOC.

Deci et al. (1999) subsequently emphasized that there are two variants of task-contingent rewards. In one case, the reward is given for engaging in the activity for a

TABLE 6.1. Contingencies Used for Administering Tangible Rewards That Are Expected and Salient

Type of contingency	Definition
Task-noncontingent	Reward is given simply for being present and does not specifically require actually being engaged with the target activity.
Engagement-contingent	Reward is given for spending time being engaged with the target activity.
Completion-contingent	Reward is given for completing a target activity (sometimes within a time limit).
Task-contingent	Refers to a larger category containing both engagement-contingent and completion-contingent rewards.
Performance-contingent	Reward is given for reaching a specific performance standard, for example, doing better than 80% of other people who have done it.
Competitively contingent	Reward is given to the winner of a competition and the loser gets lesser or no rewards.

certain amount of time but does not require completing it. Deci et al. referred to these as *engagement-contingent* rewards. For example, if you were told you would get a reward if you spent half an hour working on a spatial relations puzzle, the reward would be engagement-contingent. However, if you were told that you would receive a reward for finishing the same spatial relations puzzles within a certain amount of time, as was the case in the Deci (1971, 1972b) studies, the reward would have been *completion-contingent.* Deci and colleagues (1999) made this distinction for the sake of clarity, but they hypothesized and found that both engagement-contingent and completion-contingent rewards could undermine intrinsic motivation. Specifically, with engagement-contingent rewards, because people have to work on the task to get the reward, the reward is likely to be experienced as a controller of their task behavior. Moreover, because the reward carries little or no competence affirmation, it is unlikely to increase perceived competence, so there would be no positive influence on intrinsic motivation. With completion-contingent rewards, people have to complete the task to receive the rewards, so the rewards are likely to be experienced as even more controlling because the individuals not only have to work on the activity but they also have to complete it in order to get the rewards. However, because receipt of completion-contingent rewards also conveys some amount of competence affirmation (particularly if the task requires skill), the implicit affirmation contained within the completion-contingent rewards could offset the additional control, although the controlling aspect will likely be the more salient. Thus completion-contingent rewards are predicted to typically be comparably undermining of intrinsic motivation relative to engagement-contingent rewards.

Performance-Contingent Rewards

Finally, Ryan et al. (1983) discussed *performance-contingent rewards,* which are given specifically for performing well, matching some standard of excellence, or surpassing some specified criterion (e.g., doing very well at the task, or doing better than 80% of the other participants). Performance-contingent rewards have a strong risk of having controlling functional significance insofar as one feels pressured to meet an externally specified standard to get the reward. Yet at the same time, receiving performance-contingent rewards can also convey positive competence information, because being given the reward can convey that one has done well at the task. Insofar as performance-contingent rewards affirm competence, this could therefore offset some of the negative effects of control. In short, there are salient cues in performance-contingent rewards conveying control and other cues conveying competence. On average, the resulting effect is still likely to be an undermining of intrinsic motivation because the rewards are salient and demanding, but given both the controlling and competence-affirming aspects of these rewards, their effects are expected to be somewhat variable and to be influenced by additional considerations, such as how they are applied and the features of the social context, as we shall subsequently elaborate (e.g., Chapter 7; also Houlfort et al., 2002).

When experimentally testing the possible effects of performance-contingent rewards, a question arises about the appropriate comparison group. Because performance-contingent rewards convey specific information (e.g., information that one did better than other participants), one approach involves separating the effects of the actual rewards from the effects of the competence information by using a control group in which participants receive positive feedback comparable to the positive information conveyed by the reward. Kruglanski, Riter, Amitai, Margolin, Shabtai, and Zaksh (1975), Ryan et al. (1983), Vansteenkiste and Deci (2003), and other studies that have taken this approach have found that performance-contingent rewards undermine intrinsic motivation relative to positive-feedback control groups. Other studies compare the overall effect of performance-contingent rewards and the positive information inherent in them to no-reward, no-feedback control conditions. Boggiano and Ruble (1979), Greene and Lepper (1974), and Harackiewicz (1979), for instance, all found that performance-contingent rewards undermined the intrinsic motivation, relative to a no-reward, no-feedback control group. Thus, although participants in the performance-contingent reward condition received positive feedback (implicit in the reward), they still displayed a decrement in intrinsic motivation relative to a no-reward, no-feedback control group. In general, then, both approaches find that performance-contingent rewards undermine intrinsic motivation.

There is, however, another highly important point to consider about how laboratory research on performance-contingent rewards, which is focused on isolating specific effects, relate to the use of such rewards in practical life settings. In almost all laboratory studies of performance-contingent rewards, participants are given the maximum rewards available. In other words, if the rewards were offered for being in the top 20% of students, all participants in the rewards condition would receive the reward. In everyday life, of course, that can't happen, and, in fact, such a reward system would mean that 80% of individuals *would not get a reward* at all. Those individuals would be receiving negative feedback— either a lesser reward or no reward, either of which would signify incompetence. Clearly, then, a real-world comparison should include those who experience both the control inherent in the performance contingency and the negative competence feedback many would receive.

Surprisingly, despite the wide advocacy for performance-contingent rewards by some, (e.g., Hidi & Harackiewicz, 2000), few studies have examined the effects on "losers" (nonrecipients). Yet in studies in which "losers" have been included, the results have been very revealing. Daniel and Esser (1980), Pittman, Cooper, and Smith (1977) and Dollinger and Thelen (1978) all set up the situation so that participants would receive less than the maximum amount of rewards that had been specified. For example, Daniel and Esser's (1980) rewarded participants were told that they could earn up to $2, but, subsequently, they were given $1 (implying that their performances had been less than optimal). Findings revealed a large undermining effect using both free-choice and self-report measures of intrinsic motivation. Pittman et al. (1977) and Dollinger and Thelen (1978) similarly reported large undermining effects. In experiments in which some participants in the rewards group did not get any rewards (Pritchard, Campbell, & Campbell, 1977; Vansteenkiste & Deci, 2003), the undermining effect was also very large for both behavioral and subjective measures. These latter studies used a contingency we call *competitively contingent*, which means that the reward is given to those who outperform others—that is, only the winners gets a reward.

The results of these studies have strong real-world implications for using reward contingencies. When practitioners offer rewards that are performance-contingent, many of the people they are attempting to motivate will not receive rewards. In many settings, from classrooms to workplaces, these may even be the majority of individuals subjected to the contingency. These individuals are likely to experience both low autonomy *and* low competence. Although, as we have indicated, not all rewards and not all reward contingencies have negative effects, it is clear that the use of tangible rewards to motivate behavior can run a risk of undermining intrinsic motivation, both for the winners and (especially) for the losers.

Contingent rewards can, in this regard, play something of a gatekeeping function for various domains or activities. Because only winners will likely sustain motivation under such contingencies, those who perform more poorly for whatever reasons are more likely to drop out. This is, of course, an intended strategy in some contexts (e.g., selecting finalists to make a competitive sport team, talent competitions, competitive science awards). In such circumstances, those selecting the top-tier candidates are not concerned with negative motivational outcomes on those who lose, and, on the other end, not receiving rewards may supply important information to losers that this is not their area of talent. But in situations in which a goal is to enhance everyone's motivation, such as in education, public health interventions, environmental initiatives, and other applied settings, the use of such contingent reward structures can often produce unintended negative effects. Thus a reward contingency that might make sense for professional sport managers might not for the physical education teachers who want all their students to be motivated and engaged. It is because of such effects that a nuanced approach to rewards such as that developed within SDT is critical.

Controversies Concerning Reward Effects

Despite well over one hundred published articles that report experiments examining reward effects, the issue has always remained controversial, with various heated debates and numerous attacks on CET and other positions that have cautioned about the use of rewards. Many of the most strident attacks have been from behaviorist researchers, some of whom have tried to simply and assertively deny existing evidence (e.g., Catania, 2013) and others who instead claim that clearly demonstrated negative effects "are of no great social importance" (Pierce & Cameron, 2002, p. 227). Others have eschewed the concept of intrinsic motivation, arguing that the phenomenon is obscure and that the very study of it impedes scientific progress (e.g., Cameron & Pierce, 1994; Carton, 1996). Still others have said that the so-called undermining effect results from methodological artifacts and confounds (e.g., Eisenberger, Pierce, & Cameron, 1999). Yet with a continued string of new studies every year showing the same phenomenon using varying methodologies, in multiple domains, settings, and cultures, such positions become ever more untenable.

Behaviorists have long suggested that reinforcements can control behavior, and although it is often missed in behaviorist attacks on SDT, we completely agree with that point. Indeed, it is a central premise of CET that rewards can, when salient and large enough, control immediate behavior (Ryan & Deci, 2000d). The point of disagreement is about whether, when rewards are used to prompt or sustain intrinsically motivated behavior, there can be negative consequences for subsequent motivation and behavior. Given clear evidence, even from detractors, that this can be the case, the claim that the undermining effect is merely a myth (e.g., Catania, 2013; Eisenberg & Cameron, 1996) seems somewhat like an ostrich approach. Yet given the controversy, it is worth reviewing the most comprehensive meta-analysis on the matter framed through CET and published by Deci et al. (1999) to ascertain what effects have been substantiated and also highlighting the limiting conditions of those effects.

A Meta-Analysis of Reward Effects

Deci et al. (1999) used a hierarchical approach to do a pair of meta-analyses, first for experiments that used free-choice behavioral measures of intrinsic motivation, which we believe to be the more important one, and then for experiments that used self-reported interest as the primary measure. Each began with a calculation of the effects of all rewards on intrinsic motivation for interesting tasks. If the effects were not homogeneous, the category was separated into nested subcategories that made theoretical and/or empirical sense. The researchers continued within each subcategory to further separate subcategories until the effects in each subcategory were homogeneous. In this way, Deci and colleagues (1999) analyzed separately for verbal rewards and tangible rewards and then continued separating into additional subcategories. The term *verbal rewards* (rather than our preferred language of *positive feedback*) was adopted for the purposes of the meta-analysis because that was the terminology used by behaviorists who were claiming that no meaningful undermining effects existed (e.g., Eisenberg & Cameron, 1996). Tangible rewards were then further analyzed, first as to whether they were expected versus unexpected, and the expected tangible rewards were examined in groups of task-noncontingent, engagement-contingent, completion-contingent, and performance-contingent and then various other nested subcategories. These analyses included 128 laboratory experiments that spanned the period from 1971 to 1996. Figure 6.1 depicts some of these results and supplies a visual representation of the empirical results for various subcategories.

All Rewards

Given CET's differentiated view, we would not expect all rewards to affect intrinsic motivation in a uniform way. For example, CET expects noncontrolling positive feedback to generally enhance intrinsic motivation and contingent tangible rewards to generally undermine intrinsic motivation, with various but predictable moderators and nuances. As such, combining all feedback and reward studies into a single group to examine their overall effects is a dubious endeavor, for its outcome will likely depend primarily on how many studies of each type are included in the analyses. Nonetheless, the results showed a significant undermining effect of rewards for the free-choice measure of intrinsic motivation and a nonsignificant effect on the self-report measure.

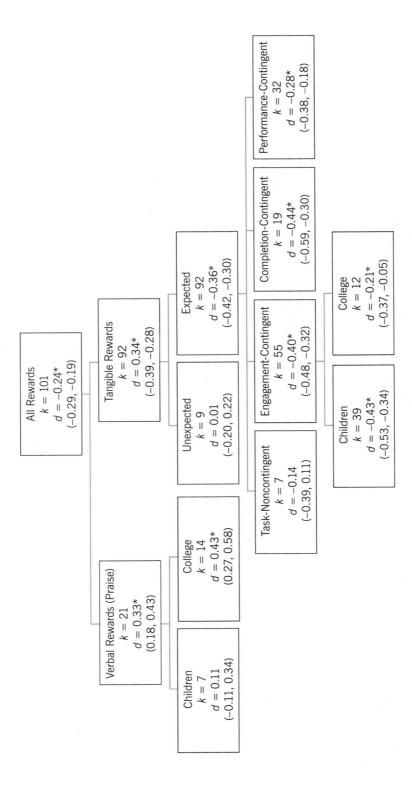

FIGURE 6.1. A summary of the primary findings from the meta-analysis of experiments examining reward effects on intrinsic motivation. The symbol k refers to the number of effect sizes in each composite effect size. The d refers to effect size, and each d entered into the composite effect size was corrected for sample size. An asterisk next to a composite effect size means that it is significantly different from 0.00. The pair of numbers in parentheses is the 95% confidence interval for the composite effect size shown just above it. Adapted from Deci, Koestner, and Ryan (1999). Copyright © 1999 the American Psychological Association. Adapted by permission.

Positive Feedback (Verbal Rewards)

As would be expected from CET, positive verbal feedback significantly enhanced intrinsic motivation as assessed with both the free-choice and self-report measures. According to CET, the informational aspect of positive feedback rather than its controlling aspect is, in general, the more salient to recipients.

However, an additional and interesting finding was revealed from this heterogeneous effect. Some studies were done with college students, whereas others were done with preschool and school-age children, and there was a significant difference between these two groups. For the free-choice behavioral measure, positive feedback significantly enhanced the intrinsic motivation of college students, but not of children. Presumably, whereas college students focused on the informational aspects of the praise, for children praise may often be experienced as a form of control, offsetting any positive effect the competence affirmation might have had. This is an important result because people often "use" praise as a motivational strategy, especially for children, and their controlling intent may affect its functional significance. We consider this more deeply in Chapter 7.

Noteworthy in this regard, a subsequent comprehensive review of praise research by Henderlong and Lepper (2002) concluded that, among other factors, praise that is informational facilitates intrinsic motivation, whereas praise that is saliently evaluative and/or controlling does not. Moreover, praise that enhances perceived competence also enhances intrinsic motivation. In short, the impact of praise on subsequent intrinsic motivation is reliably affected by these need satisfactions, consistent with the CET framework.

Tangible Rewards

In many life situations, tangible rewards are used as a way to try to induce people to do something—that is, to control people's behavior. This is especially true of material rewards such as money and prizes, but it is also true for symbolic rewards, such as trophies or awards. Thus CET suggests that, whatever their power to extrinsically motivate (Chapter 8), they are frequently likely to have a negative effect on intrinsic motivation. In line with this, the meta-analysis indicated, as expected, that when all tangible reward effects were taken together, the overall effect was a significant undermining of intrinsic motivation using both the free-choice and self-report measures. Of course, we have regularly argued that a full understanding of the effects of tangible rewards requires a consideration of additional factors, such as the reward contingency, but these results for all tangible rewards highlight the general risks associated with the unreflective use of tangible rewards.

As noted, the effects of verbal rewards were significantly different for college students and children. Deci and colleagues (1999) compared the effects of tangible rewards used with children to those used with college students. Again, there was indication of a difference, although it was primarily for engagement-contingent rewards. The effects of these tangible rewards were significantly undermining for both age groups, but these effects were significantly more negative for children than for adults on both measures of intrinsic motivation. Again, these results have significant real-world implications in that, when it comes to children, many parents and teachers rely on tangible rewards as a motivational strategy. Rewards may indeed serve effectively to control the children's immediate behavior, but they can have negative consequences in terms of the children's interest, vitality, and ongoing engagement.

To illustrate the potential costs of such reward strategies on children, consider a more recent experiment by Warneken and Tomasello (2008). They examined the effects of rewards on very young children's intrinsic motivation for helping others. After helping another, children received either no reward or a tangible reward. The authors found that the reward condition significantly undermined subsequent helping behavior. The study is important both for demonstrating the undermining effect at an age (20 months) at which cognitive discounting, or the so-called "overjustification" effect, could not be the mediator (Morgan, 1981) and for its implications about promoting and undermining children's natural interests in helping others.

Of course, we can find the same kind of phenomena occurring in adults' volitional giving behaviors. In a classic report, Titmuss (1971) documented that many blood donors stopped giving after rewards for donations were introduced. It seems that, when otherwise wholly volitional behaviors come to be seen as something done for an external reward, the original reason for doing them (in this case, the intrinsic satisfactions of helping) can be "crowded out," as Frey (1997) has described it. Of course, one must be careful to distinguish intrinsically motivated activities from autonomous instrumental behaviors (Chapter 8), but such studies nonetheless demonstrate how rewards can undermine an I-PLOC for acting.

UNEXPECTED REWARDS AND TASK-NONCONTINGENT REWARDS

As already noted, early studies indicated that rewards that were not expected do not affect intrinsic motivation. As CET would predict, if people are not doing a task in order to get a reward, they are not likely to experience their task behavior as being controlled by the reward. Similarly, early studies also indicated that rewards not requiring task engagement were unlikely to have a negative impact on intrinsic motivation for the task. About 20 studies of either unexpected rewards or task-noncontingent rewards were contained in the 1999 meta-analysis, and results revealed no evidence that either reward type significantly affected intrinsic motivation.

ENGAGEMENT-CONTINGENT REWARDS

Within this category, rewards are offered simply for working on the target activity, with no specific performance requirements. When children were told they would get a good-player award for doing an art activity (Lepper et al., 1973), the reward was engagement-contingent. When college students were told they would receive a reward if they engaged in a hidden-figures activity, the reward was engagement-contingent (Ryan et al., 1983). In all, more than 50 experiments in the meta-analysis used this contingency. Results confirmed the CET expectation that engagement-contingent rewards significantly diminished intrinsic motivation, as indexed by both behavioral free-choice and self-report measures. Further, the undermining was stronger for children than for college students.

Engagement-contingent rewards are perhaps the most prevalent type of tangible rewards. In most work situations, for example, people get paid simply to work at their jobs. Although certain contexts do tie pay to performance in very direct ways, as with sales commissions or piece-rate payments, most simply pay people for being at work and doing the tasks associated with the job. The current findings imply, therefore, that most wages, which are of course a necessary aspect of a job, can be antagonistic to people's intrinsic motivation for their work, particularly if the rewards are administered in controlling ways. In Chapter 21, we revisit this issue as we discuss ways to reward and motivate people in the workplace, including strategies to ameliorate or buffer the potentially negative effects that pay can have on employees' intrinsic motivation and interested work engagement.

COMPLETION-CONTINGENT REWARDS

The meta-analyses revealed that completion-contingent rewards undermined intrinsic motivation using both behavioral and self-report dependent measures. The effect sizes were comparable to those obtained for engagement-contingent rewards, especially when using the free-choice measure. Further, analyses indicated that completion-contingent rewards tended to be more detrimental for children than for college students, as was the case with engagement-contingent rewards.

PERFORMANCE-CONTINGENT REWARDS

As previously discussed, performance-contingent rewards are particularly interesting because they tie people's rewards to the quality of their performances (Ryan et al., 1983). However, as we said, most experimental studies of performance-contingent rewards are not ecologically valid in that all participants get rewards indicating they had performed excellently, something not likely to occur in life. Still, the results of such performance-contingent reward studies are informative in isolating reward effects.

First, the meta-analysis indicated that on the free-choice measure, performance-contingent rewards significantly undermined intrinsic motivation, whereas the self-report measure did not show a significant effect. Performance-contingent reward studies were then separated into four categories, two of which we mentioned earlier in the section on performance-contingent rewards when discussing the Ryan et al. (1983) taxonomy. The categories were: (1) effects involving everyone in the experimental group getting the maximum possible rewards and everyone in the control group getting no rewards and no feedback; (2) effects involving experimental-group participants not necessarily getting the maximum possible rewards, with everyone in the control group getting no rewards and no feedback; (3) effects involving everyone in the experimental group getting the maximum possible rewards and everyone in the control group getting no rewards but getting feedback comparable to that implicit in the rewards to the experimental group; and (4) effects involving everyone in the experimental group getting rewards indicating poor performance and everyone in the control group getting negative feedback comparable to that implicit in the low rewards to the experimental group. The first and third are the control groups previously discussed, because in most studies of performance-contingent rewards, participants are told they have succeeded and receive the maximum rewards.

As we expect on the basis of CET propositions, the four different categories of performance-contingent reward experiments showed somewhat differing results. For studies in category 1 with no-reward, no-feedback control groups in which everyone in the experimental group got the maximum possible rewards, there was significant undermining with a modest effect size; for studies in category 2 with no-reward, no-feedback control groups in which experimental-group participants did not all get the maximum possible rewards, there was significant undermining with a very large effect size; for studies in category 3 with control groups getting no rewards but getting comparable feedback and with everyone in the experimental group getting maximum rewards, there was again significant undermining; and for category 4, with control groups getting the same negative feedback that was implicit in the low rewards given to all participants in the experimental groups, there were only three studies, and the results did not show significant undermining.

Two of these four comparisons deserve further comment. First, consider the group in which at least some participants received less than the maximal rewards. We indicated earlier that, in the real world, when performance-contingent rewards are used, this is the situation one would typically find. The meta-analysis confirmed that this type of reward had a considerably larger effect size than any other reward category used in the entire meta-analysis, indicating clearly that rewarding people as a function of their performances runs a very serious risk of negatively affecting their intrinsic motivation (see also Ryan & Brown, 2005).

Second, the results for the studies in which all participants received negative feedback are interesting. As an example, Rosenfield, Folger, and Adelman (1980) gave rewarded participants a small reward for performing in the bottom 15% of all participants; control-group participants were simply told they performed in the bottom 15%. There have been only three studies of this sort, and their results suggested that if people get strong negative feedback and a small reward, the effect was no more negative than it is if they just got the strong negative feedback without the reward (Vansteenkiste & Deci, 2003). Presumably, strong negative feedback leaves people without much intrinsic motivation to be further undermined by the reward. Still, within the meta-analysis, there were only three studies in this category, so the issue deserves further attention.

Summary of Reward Effects

To summarize, the primary findings from the primary meta-analysis framed through CET were strongly supportive of this SDT mini-theory's differentiated predictions. Results showed that tangible rewards and positive feedback (i.e., verbal rewards) function very differently. Verbal rewards were found to enhance intrinsic motivation, and tangible rewards were found to undermine intrinsic motivation. Also as predicted by CET, unexpected tangible rewards and task-noncontingent rewards did not affect intrinsic motivation, but engagement-contingent, completion-contingent, and performance-contingent rewards all decreased intrinsic motivation. Because task-contingent rewards are simply the aggregate of engagement-contingent and completion-contingent rewards, they also undermined intrinsic motivation. Finally, within the performance-contingent category, the type of reward that was the most detrimental of any reward category was the one most ecologically valid, namely, the one in which people's rewards are a direct function of their performance, such that those who perform best get the largest rewards and those who perform less well get smaller rewards.

Longevity of Effects and the Assessment of Intrinsic Motivation

The Deci et al. (1999) meta-analysis also compared the size of tangible-reward effects when the measure of intrinsic motivation was taken immediately following the reward period with the size of effects when the assessment of intrinsic motivation was delayed several days. The issue here is whether the undermining is simply a transitory phenomenon that quickly dissipates. The comparison showed that the effect size for the immediate-assessment group of studies was virtually identical to that for the delayed-assessment group, with both showing a moderate undermining effect.

Another consideration concerns the fact that, although the results of the analyses with the two dependent measures showed parallel results, those for the self-report measure were considerably weaker than those for the free-choice measure. In fact, the two measures tend to only be modestly correlated (e.g., Ryan et al., 1983; Ryan, Koestner, & Deci, 1991), and the different magnitude of effects raises the question of which set of results is likely to better reflect the actual intrinsic motivation effects.

We believe that findings for the free-choice behavioral measure more validly reflect the actual effects of extrinsic rewards on intrinsic motivation. The self-report measure asks participants how interesting and enjoyable they found the activity. Self-report measures differ in their reliability, some based on a single item and others using varied combinations of items. Further, because questions ask participants to indicate how interesting/enjoyable they found the activity, it is possible that, for a rewarded activity, people will confuse their interest in the task and their enjoyment of getting a reward, especially when self-report items are ambiguously targeted. Finally, the free-choice measure is unobtrusive because participants typically believe that the experimenter will not know whether or not they persisted at the activity during the free-choice period. Thus demand characteristics are unlikely to affect it, whereas the self-report measure is transparent, so participants' beliefs about what the experimenter might want them to say could affect their responses.

Nonetheless, a problem with the free-choice measure, as argued by Ryan et al. (1991), is that under some circumstances the extrinsic motivation manipulated during the experimental phase could persist into the free-choice period, leading to some free-choice behavior that is a reflection of extrinsic, rather than intrinsic, motivation. This has been found to occur primarily when the manipulation stimulates *ego involvement* (more fully discussed in Chapter 7) and when feedback about outcomes is ambiguous, such that participants persist during the free-choice period not because they are intrinsically motivated but because they are trying to assuage concerns about performance. In the case of reward studies, however, it is unlikely that ego involvement is being stimulated, so this limitation is not likely to be operative. Further, if it occurred and did affect the results, it would actually be *increasing* the free-choice behavior for the reward groups, which means that this measure would, like the self-report measure, actually be underestimating the undermining effects.

Previous Meta-Analyses

Prior to publication of the Deci et al. (1999) meta-analysis, four other meta-analyses of reward effects had been published, though none as extensive as that of Deci and colleagues (1999). For completeness, we mention them briefly. Rummel and Feinberg (1988) conducted the first meta-analysis to test the CET hypothesis that extrinsic rewards with a salient controlling aspect would undermine intrinsic motivation. They included 45 studies and found strong support for the undermining of intrinsic motivation by controlling rewards. Wiersma (1992) included 16 tangible-reward studies that used the free-choice behavioral measure. Results showed that rewards undermined intrinsic motivation, complementing Rummel and Feinberg's results. Tang and Hall (1995) reviewed 50 studies. Rather than doing aggregate tests, such as whether all rewards, or all tangible rewards, affect intrinsic motivation, they evaluated specific hypotheses. They found that both task-contingent and performance-contingent rewards undermined intrinsic motivation, providing strong support for CET.

The only anomalous meta-analytic findings prior to Deci and colleagues' (1999) came from Cameron and Pierce (1994), whose hierarchical meta-analysis of reward effects was subsequently republished as Eisenberger and Cameron (1996). It presented separate analyses for free-choice behavior and self-reported interest and included several of the same reward and contingency categories as the Deci et al. (1999) meta-analysis. Cameron and Pierce (1994) found enhancement of intrinsic motivation by verbal rewards and undermining by tangible rewards. However, they reported no undermining by either completion-contingent or performance-contingent rewards and concluded that there is no reason not to use reward systems. They also called for "abandoning cognitive evaluation theory" (1994, p. 396). Yet their analyses were fraught with errors, inappropriate comparisons, and invalid interpretations, and these were specifically detailed and tabled in Deci et al. (1999). When their errors and misjudgments were corrected and the studies they had omitted were included in the Deci et al. (1999) meta-analysis reviewed above, the results were consistent with the results of the meta-analyses by Rummel and Feinberg (1988), Wiersma (1992), and Tang and Hall (1995), all of which supported CET's predictions. Eisenberger and Cameron's different conclusions, in short, were accounted for by their inappropriate classifications and documented errors, errors which the authors did not dispute in their invited (Eisenberger et al., 1999) reply. Nonetheless, this flawed report continues to be the empirical support upon which contemporary behaviorist critics still rely (e.g., Catania, 2013).

Further Considerations: The Effects of Outcome-Focused Rewards, Naturally Occurring Rewards, and Small or Insufficient Rewards

The research reviewed in this chapter has shown that externally administered rewards can control behaviors, which both we and behaviorists predict, and yet the very process of externally controlling behavior can undermine intrinsic motivation, which only we predict. Further, as CET describes, for this to occur, the rewards need to be expected, contingent, and salient, as these properties or features of reward structure make the external control more obvious.

Rewarding Outcomes versus Behaviors

In recent years there has been a strong emphasis on the use of rewards to increase performance in so-called *high-stakes* situations (Ryan & Brown, 2005; Ryan & La Guardia, 1999). Typically, this involves individuals, groups, schools, or organizations being rewarded in accordance with the *outcomes* they produce: Get better test scores, receive more rewards; earn higher quarterly profits, reap greater cash and stock benefits. Such approaches are touted as being effective because the rewards presumably control (i.e., strengthen) the behaviors that foster these valued outcomes.

The problem, however, is that it is a very different matter to reward a *behavior* than to reward an *outcome* (Ryan & Brown, 2005; Ryan & Weinstein, 2009). For example, to reward a student for study behaviors with an engagement-contingent reward is to reward a behavior, and it is likely to produce more studying behaviors as long as rewards are continuously applied and large enough to be an incentive. This may enhance outcomes, although it will probably undermine intrinsic motivation for studying. In contrast, to reward a test score or a final grade, as is done within the high-stakes approach, is not to reward a *behavior*; it is to reward an *outcome*. The consequence of rewarding an outcome is that it can reinforce *any* antecedent behaviors that might produce the outcome. Research indicates that when outcomes are rewarded (or when failing to reach them is punished), people tend to take the shortest path to the rewarded outcome—that is, they choose those behaviors that are easiest to do and/or are most likely to yield the requisite outcome.

This shortest path strategy manifests in different ways. First, in experimental settings in which rewards were offered for each solved puzzle and people were given a choice of which puzzles to work on, they chose easy puzzles, whereas when people were allowed to choose from among the same puzzles in the same situations without rewards, they chose more difficult puzzles (Danner & Lonky, 1981; Shapira, 1976). Participants take the shortest path to getting the rewards, thereby precluding themselves from building competencies through choosing more challenging puzzles.

Even more disturbing, when people are focused on the shortest path to achieve a rewarded outcome, they may engage in nonconstructive, even immoral behaviors. Such behaviors are unwittingly *rewarded* under outcome-contingent reward scenarios, as the focus is on the outcome rather than the process. We have sometimes referred to this as the "Enron effect" (e.g., Ryan & Brown, 2005), based on a company whose officers were offered stock options based on promoting higher prices for Enron stock; they cheated and distorted results to obtain the higher stock market prices that made them hugely wealthy while ruining the lives of numerous employees of the company. Similarly, *high-stakes testing* (HST) has led school administrators to famously cheat or misreport outcomes to avoid outcome-contingent sanctions (e.g., see Amrein & Berliner, 2002; Ryan & Weinstein, 2009). Relatedly, Gino and Mogilner (2014) found that implicitly activating "money" enhanced adults' likelihood of cheating when given the opportunity to do so. Vansteenkiste, Sierens, Soenens, Luyckx, and Lens (2009) found controlled motivation for studying to be related to a more approving attitude toward cheating and more self-reported cheating.

We shall return to the issue of how outcome-focused rewards and other high-stakes contingencies in various life domains such as education and business can yield these kinds of negative behaviors and unintended collateral damage, but for now the important point is that, for rewards to reliably control specific behaviors, they must be linked to those behaviors and not to outcomes. As they control behavior, they will also undermine intrinsic motivation for the behavior, but at least (if well constructed and closely monitored) they will often yield the desired behavior while the contingencies are in effect. In contrast, when rewards are instead linked to outcomes, they less reliably control specific behaviors but may instead prompt people to search for the easiest route to the rewards. Unfortunately, the easy routes rarely involve the behaviors that were desired when the outcome contingency was established (Ryan & Moller, 2016).

It is also true that when motivators become outcome-focused rather than process-focused they tend to be more controlling, undermining intrinsic motivation. Gurland and Grolnick (2003), for example, predicted that more controlling parental styles would focus children on the outcomes rather than the processes of learning. Children of controlling parents thus would adopt outcome-focused goals such as getting good grades in school (i.e., performance goals) rather than focusing on increasing their knowledge or skills (i.e., learning goals). Gurland and Grolnick's results supported this formulation, verifying that children of parents who were rated as more controlling during parent–child interactions were more likely to endorse performance goals than parents rated as more autonomy-supportive. Kenney-Benson and Pomerantz (2005) similarly found that more controlling parenting was associated with children having more perfectionistic achievement concerns that are antithetical to intrinsic motivation.

Naturally Occurring Rewards

The rewards we have been considering thus far are those in which an external agent (an experimenter, manager, authority figure) offers or imposes a reward contingency to motivate another person or group. Yet there is another way to characterize rewards that has been seldom discussed in the rewards literature. Some "rewards" are natural occurrences in life, and outcomes of volitional activity in contrast to those that are externally administered or imposed. For example, a person who is exploring a nearby forest finds a berry patch. Discovering this "reward" does not in any way make the exploration feel less autonomous. In fact, even a return trip to retrieve more berries (now a reinforced behavior) may have a strong I-PLOC and feel very volitional and self-organized. Such naturally occurring rewards have been important in our evolutionary history, and they are the basis upon which many ideas about rewards were originally formed, and they are often pursued quite autonomously.

Where heteronomy by rewards comes in is with contingent administration and control by an external agent. Consider a scenario in which a woman plants a garden in her backyard, watering and weeding it during the subsequent weeks. The succulent tomatoes, the beautiful flowers and the tasty basil that she eventually harvests would all be "rewards." Will these rewards leave her feeling controlled? Unlikely. The rewards are natural, rather than arbitrary, consequences of her behavior, and they were not externally imposed by a controlling other to "make" her tend her garden. On the contrary, she would experience them as the endogenous outcomes of the behavior, and they are likely to both affirm her feelings of competence as a gardener and be a source of pleasure.

Now suppose that a wealthy neighbor, seeing her garden, asks her to manage his garden and conveys that he will reward her monetarily in accord with how well the harvest meets his standards. What, then, is likely to be the result? Here the experience of the gardener is likely to be less positive. Her intrinsic motivation to work his garden would likely have been undermined, and she would be likely to tend his plants willingly in the future only with clear external incentives. It would have to be "worth her while."

The point being made, although it is not one that has received much direct empirical attention, is that rewards in the form of naturally occurring consequences are much less likely to be controlling and thus detrimental to intrinsic motivation than rewards that other people (or human organizations) create and administer to externally motivate or control behavior. Naturally occurring rewards (and obstacles) simply don't have the functional significance of being controlling, in large part because they are not being contingently administered by another individual but are instead outcomes of one's initiative and interactions with the world. Again, the practical implications of this distinction are taken up throughout this book.

Small or "Insufficient" Rewards

As mentioned earlier, a cognitive explanation of why rewards undermine intrinsic motivation was the idea of *overjustification* (e.g., Lepper et al., 1973). In that formulation, the undermining effect of rewards was explained in terms of the discounting principle of attribution theory (Kelley, 1967), which suggests that if people receive rewards for doing an interesting activity, they will have more than adequate justification for doing the activity, so they are likely to discount the internal reason, thus attributing less intrinsic motivation to themselves than they would have had before getting the rewards. As we explained earlier in this chapter, research by Morgan (1981) showed that this was not an adequate explanation for the undermining process, because children under about 8 years of age cannot use that principle.

Related to the overjustification effect is the *insufficient justification effect,* which has been explained with both cognitive dissonance theory (Aronson, 1969) and self-perception theory (Bem, 1967, 1972), both of which suggest that if people are doing something for a very small reward, they would not have an adequate reason for doing the activity, so the reward would be less likely to undermine intrinsic motivation. In fact, the insufficient justification hypothesis would suggest that under those conditions individuals might even attribute more intrinsic interest to themselves. In a cognitive account such as self-perception theory, people's motivation is shaped by postbehavioral (defensive) attributions rather than by any internal experience or personal knowledge, as de Charms (1968) had suggested.

SDT has a different explanation of why small rewards are less likely to undermine: They are unlikely to be experienced as controlling, and they may, if used well, signify competence. Typically, a small reward is something given not to exert control over or externally motivate behavior but rather to acknowledge or encourage it. Given that small rewards are not typically powerful enough to externally regulate behavior, SDT suggests that they would thus not typically have a functional significance as controlling and would thus run a lower risk of undermining than do large rewards. In addition, because they can be used to acknowledge effort or performance, they can have informational significance. In fact, as we shall see in Chapter 20, video games are often designed to use small rewards as both acknowledgment and as informational feedback, often without any negative effects on autonomy and with positive effects on perceived competence.

The Undermining Effect: Neuropsychological Support

Recently, researchers have begun to examine the undermining effect of rewards as manifested in neuropsychological processes. Notably, Murayama, Matsumoto, Izuma, and Matsumoto (2010) performed an experiment in which Japanese students worked on an interesting activity that involved a reaction-time game using a virtual stopwatch. Participants all received feedback about whether they succeeded or failed on each trial, with half the participants receiving an expected performance-contingent monetary reward for each successful response and the other half later receiving a comparable unexpected reward simply for participating in the activity. Expected performance-contingent rewards have been shown to undermine intrinsic motivation, whereas unexpected task-noncontingent rewards have been shown not to have an undermining effect. Thus the second group was the control group in the experiment.

The design involved four periods: (1) Session 1, in which participants worked on the activity with functional magnetic resonance imaging (fMRI); (2) a free-choice period during which participants were out of the scanner and had 3 minutes to do more of the target activity or other interesting tasks; (3) Session 2 in the scanner with no rewards; and (4) a second free-choice period out of the scanner. Rewards were given to all participants after the first session and before the first free-choice period. Of interest was, first, whether participants who received performance-contingent rewards would show the undermining effect in the first free-choice period and whether the effect would be maintained in the second free-choice period. Second, and most importantly, was the difference in brain activity for the participants who received performance-contingent rewards and evidenced undermining relative to those who did not receive the rewards.

Results showed that the participants who received the performance-contingent rewards displayed significantly less free-choice activity in both free-choice periods relative to those for whom the rewards were noncontingent, thus conceptually replicating many previous studies as highlighted by the Deci et al. (1999) meta-analysis. Importantly, the results further showed significantly different brain activity for the participants receiving the expected versus unexpected, noncontingent rewards. Of particular interest was striatal activation and midbrain activity, for these represent activation of the affective reward network. First, in both groups participants showed greater bilateral anterior striatum and midbrain activity when participants succeeded relative to failed, thus suggesting that the paradigm was working effectively because the feedback was affecting reward-network activation in expected ways. Further, in the first session, when one group of participants was working to get rewards and one was not, the reward group showed significantly greater bilateral striatum activation and midbrain activity than did the no-reward group, indicating that the reward was working to activate the reward network. Yet notable and important is the fact that both groups showed significant activation, indicating that the task was "rewarding" even for those who were not being externally rewarded. However, in the second session, after the expected rewards were removed, there was significantly *less* reward-network activation in the expected-reward group than in the unexpected-reward group. This indicated that indeed, as predicted, rewards that were expected and contingent resulted in decreased activity in the anterior striatum and midbrain. Parallel results were also reported for the right lateral prefrontal cortex, indicating that the formerly rewarded group was significantly less cognitively engaged after reward than those not receiving expected rewards. As well, levels of activity in the three regions (i.e., anterior striatum, midbrain, and right prefrontal cortex) were correlated with each other, and those who spent less free-choice activity with the target activity were those who showed lower brain activity in these three regions during Session 2. From these results the authors concluded that the corticobasal ganglia valuation system plays a central role in the undermining effect and that value-driven and cognitive processes are involved and are linked to the brain activity, with the strong incentive value of monetary rewards decreasing the intrinsic value of task success.

The focus of the Murayama et al. (2010) study was on the common motivational resources used in both intrinsic and extrinsic motivation, and it showed that these can be undermined by expected, performance-contingent extrinsic rewards. Another recent study also suggested that, when people were intrinsically versus extrinsically motivated, some distinct neurological processes were also at work. Lee and Reeve (2013) did an fMRI study in which participants were asked to make decisions about doing various tasks, such as writing a paper. In one condition, they were deciding to act because the task was autonomously motivated (e.g., writing an enjoyable paper), whereas in another they were deciding to act for controlled reasons (e.g., writing a paper to obtain course credit). In a third, "neutral" condition, no motive was specified (e.g., writing an assigned paper). As predicted by the authors, manipulated intrinsic reasons for acting recruited more anterior insular cortex (AIC) activity, and this AIC activity during autonomous behavior was strongly correlated with intrinsic satisfactions. In contrast, controlled (i.e., extrinsic reward-based) reasons for acting recruited greater posterior cingulate cortex (PCC) activity, which was associated with a low sense of agency. In addition, reaction-time data suggested more deliberative processes were involved in the reward-based condition. In short, intrinsic and extrinsic reward-based motives appear to involve both common and distinct motivational resources and decision processes.

This area of research is relatively new, but studies of the neuropsychological patterns associated with motivational dynamics specified in CET are rapidly emerging (e.g., DePasque & Tricomi, 2015; Izuma, Akula, Murayama, Wu, Lacoboni, & Adolphs, 2015; Legault & Inzlicht, 2013; Leotti & Delgado, 2011; Marsden, Ma, Deci, Ryan, & Chiu, 2015; Ma, Jin, Meng, & Shen, 2014; Murayama, Matsumoto, Izuma, Sugiura, et al., 2015), and such studies are highlighting that the phenomenological distinctions made within SDT have reliable correspondence to expected areas of brain activity. Indeed, this interface holds great promise for deepening our understanding not only of the reward-undermining effect but also of many other phenomena encompassed by SDT.

The Undermining Effects of Other External Events

Studies of reward effects on intrinsic motivation showed that the event of receiving tangible external rewards, whether material (Deci, 1971; Ryan et al., 1983) or symbolic (Lepper et al., 1973), tended to diminish intrinsic motivation for an activity if the reward contingency required performance of the activity. We interpreted this as indicating that the rewards prompted a shift in PLOC from internal to external and thwarted people's need to feel autonomous. If this explanation for reward effects is reasonable, then other specific events that would tend to be experienced as externally controlling ought also to occasion decrements in intrinsic motivation.

Threats of Punishment

One of the most frequently used motivational techniques is threat of punishment, whether it is explicit, as in overt coercion, or more subtly implicit within an organizational structure. If rewards were detrimental to intrinsic motivation, then one would certainly expect punishments to be. Surprisingly, there have been almost no studies of the effects of threatened punishment on intrinsic motivation, perhaps because the prediction seems so obvious or the expected result seems so clear. In fact, Deci and Cascio (1972) did the only experimental study of threat effects on intrinsic motivation of which we are aware. They used an avoidance paradigm in which participants worked on interesting puzzles after being told that if they did not complete each of four puzzles in a specified time, a noxious buzzer would sound. Results suggested that participants who solved the puzzles in the implicitly threatened noise condition displayed less subsequent intrinsic motivation than those who knew nothing of the buzzer.

Using CET to analyze the issue of threatened punishment would maintain that a threat of punishment contingent on engagement or performance would clearly have a controlling functional significance, conducing to an E-PLOC, diminishing the experience of autonomy, and undermining intrinsic motivation.

Evaluations

When rewards or punishments are administered, it is typically under conditions of evaluation. Someone else—an external source—is observing and making judgments about the quality or effectiveness of people's performances. As noted earlier in the chapter, there have been specific studies that examined the effects of people being told that their performances would be evaluated. Studies by Harackiewicz, Abrahams, and Wageman (1987); Maehr and Stallings (1972); Ryan (1982); Smith (1975); and others have indicated that evaluations of people's performances decreased their intrinsic motivation, even when the evaluations were positive.

Grolnick and Ryan (1987) specifically examined this evaluation effect in an experiment done in a school context. They found that telling children they would be tested on material they were about to read diminished their interest in the material relative to students who were not told that they would be tested. Evaluative conditions, relative to nonevaluative conditions that contained comparable feedback, were also found to undermine intrinsic interest in Japanese elementary school children (Kage & Namiki, 1990). These and several other studies thus converge on the result that evaluation tends to have a negative effect on intrinsic motivation, presumably because of its phenomenological significance as a form of external control.

What is remarkable about most of these studies that show the undermining of intrinsic motivation by anticipated evaluation is that the negative effects have occurred under conditions in which people have been quite positively evaluated. In all likelihood, therefore, the degree to which external evaluations compromise intrinsic motivation is *underestimated* by these studies because real-world evaluative structures often convey more negative feedback to the majority of people exposed to them, and these messages could further squelch people's interest. They would likely feel both controlled and low in competence. In most of the extant experiments, however, it would have been only the autonomy component of the undermining effect that was affected.

This in no way means that all evaluation and feedback undermines intrinsic motivation. As we have emphasized, feedback can be informational and enhance intrinsic motivation. Even negative feedback can be given without undermining, provided it is done with support and efficacy promotion in mind, as we subsequently review and describe (e.g., see Carpentier & Mageau, 2013; Mouratidis, Lens, & Vansteenkiste, 2010).

Surveillance

Imagine that when you are happily immersed in an interesting activity, someone such as a parent, teacher, or boss comes up and begins to look over your shoulder. The presence of the other raises the possibility that evaluation will follow. Under such a circumstance, you might well feel controlled and pressured, as even the most benign and supportive of mentors has witnessed so many times.

This need not be uniformly the case, of course, as you might feel supported by surveillance that you invited, as when you ask another to observe and provide informational feedback. Thus surveillance, like rewards, can be a complex phenomenon. Yet to date, the laboratory studies of surveillance have shown largely negative effects, presumably because the surveillance has had a controlling functional significance. For example, studies with young children (Lepper & Greene, 1975), as well as with college students (Plant & Ryan, 1985; Ryan et al., 1991) have found undermining effects stemming from video surveillance. Pittman, Davey, Alafat, Wetherill, and Kramer (1980) found the same results for in-person surveillance. In these studies, participants in one group were asked to work on an activity either with a video camera oriented toward them or an experimenter watching them closely. Their subsequent intrinsic motivation was then compared with that of participants who had not been so observed, and results showed decrements in intrinsic motivation for the observed participants. A study by Amabile (1996) focused on creativity suggested that this surveillance effect may in part be explained by an expectation of being evaluated. She found that the presence of others who either were not evaluating the target individuals or were coactors with them on a task did not have the same negative effects as surveillance by people who might be evaluating them. This again bespeaks the importance of considering the functional significance of events in predicting their effects on intrinsic motivation, a theme we explore much more deeply in Chapter 7. That, of course, is consistent with the idea that, insofar as surveillance undermines intrinsic motivation, it is due to the impact of the event on people's PLOC and sense of autonomy.

Deadlines and Imposed Goals

Another common motivational strategy is to impose a deadline on people's work. The reasoning is simple—a deadline will provide a structure to help keep them on track. Yet, as with the other motivational strategies we have discussed, deadlines can be either controlling or informational, and when controlling they lead to a shift in one's PLOC from internal to external.

Amabile, DeJong, and Lepper (1976) did the first deadline studies and found that giving deadlines to students working on a word game led to less intrinsic motivation, assessed with both the free-choice and self-report measures, compared with either a control group in which there was no mention of time or a group in which participants were asked to work as quickly as they could. Reader and Dollinger (1982) did a similar study in which students performed a clinical judgment task either with or without a time constraint. Results confirmed that the imposed deadlines decreased subsequent intrinsic motivation. Mossholder (1980) specifically used CET to predict that the imposition of goals would be experienced as controlling. Mossholder's approach to studying the question was to have participants work on an interesting assembly task and assign goals to the experimental group but not to the control group. The goals concerned the number of objects to be assembled within stipulated amounts of time. Results indicated that participants who were assigned goals for this task subsequently displayed less task interest, task persistence, and satisfaction with the activity than comparison participants.

Deadlines can be construed or even presented as *goals,* which are generally defined as cognitive representations of some desired future state. The relation of externally set goals to autonomy and intrinsic motivation is an interesting and complex one, and different aspects of that relation are addressed throughout the coming chapters. In essence, the issue revolves around the extent to which a goal has an I-PLOC and is reflectively self-endorsed (Deci & Ryan, 2000). When goals (including deadlines) are set with a clear rationale and in noncontrolling ways, they can be energizing and positively motivating. Yet, when set in controlling ways, often backed by threats or contingent rewards, they can be highly undermining of intrinsic motivation, and sometimes decrease people's quality of engagement. At various points in this book we consider how goals can be created in ways that preserve autonomy and support feelings of competence, as well as how they can be applied in ways that frustrate these psychological needs. The point here is that CET emphasizes that it is the functional significance that attends the use of feedback, goals, and deadlines that will determine their effects.

Competition: Trying to Win

Competition is an integral part of sports, games, and the arts, as well as many other domains. It is a situational element that can add excitement and energy to activities, and thus it is widely used as a motivational strategy to "get the best out of people." Yet, although competition can incite motivation, the question in any context should be, motivation of what kind?

Deci, Betley, Kahle, Abrams, and Porac (1981) did an experiment intended to begin sorting out the nature of the motivational processes involved in attempting to win a competition—that is, to beat opponents. Participants worked on a puzzle in the presence of another "participant" (who was actually an experimental accomplice). Half of the actual participants were told that they should try to beat the other person by solving each puzzle faster than that person; the other half were simply told to solve the puzzles as quickly as they could. The experimental task consisted of working on three puzzles, and in both conditions the accomplice allowed the participant to finish first. Thus, in the competition condition, the participant "won" all three competitive trials, and in the no-competition condition, participants got the same implicit "positive feedback" in that they could see that they finished before the other. Following the experimental period, the actual participant was left alone in the room for a standard free-choice period (while the other participant was presumably being interviewed). Results indicated that those instructed to compete spent significantly less free-choice time engaged with the puzzles than those who were not explicitly competing. In other words, the group that tried to win the competition (and did) showed lower subsequent intrinsic motivation than the group that simply tried to do their best.

Yet within CET the effects of competition are expected to be negative only when there is pressure to win or a controlling context (Deci & Ryan, 1985b; Standage & Ryan, 2012). As Reeve and Deci (1996) argued, competition can also be highly informational. When people are competing, they are often afforded optimal challenges and valuable feedback about performance as they exert effort against effortful opponents. This is indeed what can make competition "fun," especially when there are neither high-stakes rewards nor ego-involving pressures (Standage, Duda, & Pensgaard, 2005; Vansteenkiste, Smeets, Soenens, Lens, Matos, & Deci, 2010). We return to the complex issue of competition in Chapter 19, but for now we simply highlight that whether competition is enhancing or undermining will depend on both the relative autonomy one experiences while engaged and the competence feelings that result.

Summary of Events That Tend to Undermine Autonomy and Intrinsic Motivation

Many experiments have investigated how various specific external events affect intrinsic motivation, with results indicating that, on average, controlling rewards, threats of punishment, evaluations, surveillance, deadlines, and imposed goals all tend to undermine intrinsic motivation. Each of these commonly used motivational techniques represents a salient and powerful external stimulus that, when introduced into a situation in which a person is engaged with an interesting task, can have the functional impact of inducing a shift more toward an E-PLOC and leave the person feeling controlled. That raises the question of whether any specific events could have the opposite effect, namely, enhancing intrinsic motivation by inducing a shift toward a more I-PLOC.

External Events as Supports for Intrinsic Motivation

To feel autonomous—that is, to have an I-PLOC with respect to a particular behavior—means that one experiences a sense of volition and choice. Thus we hypothesize that any event that would leave a person feeling a greater sense of volitional engagement in an activity would enhance intrinsic motivation. For example, if people were allowed to choose what activity to do or how to do it, CET would predict that they would tend to experience a greater sense of autonomy with respect to that behavior—that is, the PLOC would likely become more internal. If the tasks available were interesting or the rationale for them clear, this, too, should lead to enhanced intrinsic motivation.

Research on Choice

Zuckerman, Porac, Lathin, Smith, and Deci (1978) examined the issue of choice versus no choice in a controlled experiment. They gave half their participants a choice about which three out of six puzzles to work on and how to allot their total problem-solving time among the chosen puzzles. The other participants were yoked to those in the first group such that each no-choice participant was given the same puzzles and time allotments selected by the person in the choice group to whom he or she was yoked; this ensured comparability in terms of the puzzles worked on and the times allotted to them. Results indicated that participants who had been given choice were significantly more intrinsically motivated than those who did not have choice.

In a study of students, Patall, Cooper, and Wynn (2010) found that students who were provided with choice within homework tasks were more intrinsically motivated for the homework, had higher perceived competence regarding the homework, and performed better on tests that encompassed the homework than students assigned homework without a choice. There was also some evidence that the students with choice had higher rates of homework completion. Further, analyses showed a relation between perceptions of teacher autonomy support and students' intrinsic motivation for schoolwork, and this relation was accounted for by students' reports of receiving choices from the teachers.

Reeve, Nix, and Hamm (2003) also investigated the issue of choice, making a distinction between *option* and *action* choice. Whereas option choice involves allowing people to choose from an array of diverse options (e.g., which topic will we discuss in today's class?), action choice involves providing ongoing choice during the activity engagement itself. Such action choice can have to do with when, where, how, and with whom activities are carried out. For instance, choice can be given surrounding the order of executing a series of actions and the rhythm of switching between different activities. In three experimental studies, Reeve et al. (2003) found that action choice was the more beneficial for eliciting a sense of volition, an I-PLOC, and intrinsic motivation. Reeve and colleagues concluded that, in order for the provision of choice to positively affect intrinsic motivation, allowing ongoing action choices within activities may be most effective.

Mouratidis, Vansteenkiste, Sideridis, and Lens (2011) examined whether class-to-class variation in the affordance versus denial of action choice during physical education classes would produce class-to-class variation in students' vitality and intrinsic motivation. In one condition, teachers provided choice to the late-elementary-school students regarding the pace of switching to different physical education exercises, as well as the order in which they were carried out, during some classes; in another, the teachers determined these issues. The students' course enjoyment and energy levels at the end of the classes systematically covaried with the presence versus absence of action choice.

The experiments we have just reviewed represent merely a subset of studies of the impact of choice on intrinsic motivation. In fact, a meta-analysis by Patall, Cooper, and Robinson (2008) of 41 such studies examined the effect of choice on intrinsic motivation and related outcomes in both child and adult samples for a variety of behaviors. Results strongly indicated that providing choice enhances intrinsic motivation, as well as related variables such as effort, task performance, and perceived competence, among others. Their comprehensive review of this literature was therefore fully consistent with CET's emphasis on choice as a positive factor for supporting autonomy and intrinsic motivation.

Taken together, the research suggests that it is indeed possible to present tasks in a way that will maintain or even enhance people's intrinsic motivation, specifically by giving them a greater sense of choice over what they do and how they do it. Allowing them to make choices is one way of doing this, although merely making decisions among options will not necessarily enhance intrinsic motivation—for instance, when none of the options has real value to the person or when there are so many options to choose from that the process becomes burdensome (e.g., Iyengar & Lepper, 2000). That is, not all decisions between options feel like meaningful choice.

Just as investigators have begun to examine the neurological underpinnings of the undermining effects of tangible rewards, they have also begun to examine the underpinnings of choice. For example, Murayama and colleagues (2015), using fMRI, examined participants engaged in a game task involving a stopwatch. Their task was to press a button on the watch to stop it within 50 milliseconds of the 5-second point. Half the participants chose the stopwatch they would use from different attractive ones, although the workings of these watches were identical. Participants in the control condition were simply assigned one of the watches. Results indicated that the experience of choice improved performance on the task, even though the choice had no relation to the difficulty of the task, thus replicating the frequently replicated choice phenomenon (Patall et al., 2008). Results for the neuroimaging further indicated that participants in the choice condition were resilient to negative feedback such that there was no drop in ventromedial prefrontal cortex (vmPFC) activity following failure in this group, but there was in the no-choice condition. Further, the vmPFC activity was correlated with performance. Accordingly, the results indicate that the vmPFC activation is a very important underpinning of autonomous motivation, as had been suggested by Ryan, Kuhl, and Deci (1997).

More recent work by Meng and Ma (2015) also showed pathways by which choice enhances intrinsic motivation and performance. They manipulated the opportunity to choose between tasks of equal difficulty while tracking electrophysiological activity. They identified that in conditions of choice there was greater stimulus-preceding negativity (SPN), indicated an enhanced expectation toward a positive outcome, and an enlarged feedback-related negativity (FRN) loss–win difference wave (d-FRN), suggesting intensified intrinsic motivation toward the task. They also reported that choice conditions enhanced subjective enjoyment and intrinsic motivation to accomplish the task.

Perceived Competence: Optimal Challenge and Informational Feedback

Earlier in the chapter we reviewed studies of positive feedback using the rubric of "verbal rewards" in order to fit those studies into the framework of reward effects on intrinsic motivation. We reported that so-called verbal rewards tended to enhance the intrinsic motivation of college students but tended not to affect the intrinsic motivation of children. The term *verbal rewards* is somewhat problematic, however, because the concept of "rewards" is fraught with a sense of external control and because it also fails to convey that "positive feedback" is a *response* to, rather than an *incentive* for, effective performance. Accordingly, we begin our discussion of perceived competence by taking a step back and reminding ourselves of the meaning of intrinsic motivation.

Intrinsic motivation is theorized to occur spontaneously under conditions of *optimal challenge* (Deci, 1975). Succeeding at a task is not enough to maintain vitality and excitement if the task demands nothing of the person. From our perspective, intrinsic motivation is a *growth* function. It is manifested in circumstances in which people have the opportunity to exercise and stretch existing capacities or skills (Flavell, 1977; Ryan, 1993). Situations in which people have well mastered a skill are thus ones that would yield high rates of success but would not typically provide opportunities for growth; they neither stretch nor exercise people's competencies. The most compelling feeling of effectance comes from exercising and enhancing skills or abilities. The positive feelings that come from demonstrating overlearned mastery are not intrinsic satisfactions but are more typically extrinsic pleasures associated with impressing others or receiving the rewards that may attend such displays of competence.

CET also emphasizes that optimal challenge must occur within the context of some degree of perceived autonomy for there to be a positive effect on intrinsic motivation (e.g., Ryan, 1982). Thus feeling coerced into doing an activity that provides a perfect challenge given one's level of ability will be unlikely to yield a sense of interest, involvement, or flow. Thus, unlike Csikszentmihalyi's (1990) formal flow theory, the emphasis within CET is not only on the skill–demand balance but rather on ongoing feelings of competence in the context of some degree of felt autonomy (Ryan & Moller, 2016).

When people are intrinsically motivated, they will tend to select optimal challenges, and the experience of feeling competent when volitionally undertaking such tasks is what sustains intrinsic motivation over time. This means being regularly in a zone of mastery. For instance, Graves, Juel, and Graves (2007) argued that "if children are going to be motivated and engaged in school and learn from their schoolwork, they need to succeed at the vast majority of tasks they undertake" (pp. 56–57). We agree and suggest that this is true not just in school, but in all life domains. Imagine how long a beginning carpenter might persist if her constructions keep falling down, or a skier if he is always placed on slopes he cannot negotiate. Within SDT, then, optimal challenge means facing demands that most often one can master, rather than ones that are continuously at the leading edge of one's capabilities. That type of high difficulty challenge should, however, be an intermittent element, in which case it can enhance and heighten intrinsic motivation.

Danner and Lonky (1981) used CET to formulate a classic experiment on intrinsic motivation, optimal challenge, choice, and reward effects. In it they assessed children's cognitive abilities on a set of classification tasks and then provided each child with the opportunity to select a learning center from among ones whose tasks varied in the level of classification ability that was required to perform them. Results suggested that children spent most free-choice time with and rated as most interesting the learning center with tasks that were one step ahead of their pretest ability levels. In other words, when free to choose the tasks they wanted to work with, children selected those that represented a modest challenge. As already noted, Danner and Lonky (1981) also showed that rewarding children for doing the optimally challenging learning activities fostered an E-PLOC and undermined the children's interest and persistence at optimally challenging tasks. Similarly, Shapira (1976) reported that when college students were free to choose puzzle problems, they chose quite challenging ones unless there was an extrinsic reward dependent on their solving the puzzles, in which case they chose easy tasks. Harter's work (1974, 1978b) further showed that children who were working on optimally challenging tasks, rather than tasks that were very easy or very difficult, displayed greater pleasure as rated by observers. Together, these various results confirm that when individuals are free to select tasks, they select ones that provide optimal challenge, and that intrinsic motivation is most likely to be evident when people work successfully on such optimally challenging tasks (see Deci & Ryan, 2012; Ryan & Deci, 2013).

Feedback Effects

When people are engaged in activities that provide opportunities for mastery and optimal challenge, we expect that positive feedback will typically enhance their intrinsic motivation, as discussed earlier in the chapter. In fact, a large number of studies have provided direct evidence for the explanatory (i.e., mediating) role of the need for competence between positive feedback and intrinsic motivation (e.g., Grouzet, Vallerand, Thill, & Provencher, 2004; Vallerand & Reid, 1984; Vansteenkiste & Deci, 2003). Work also suggests that the beneficial effects of positive feedback radiate to feelings of vitality and energy (Mouratidis, Vansteenkiste, Lens, & Sideridis, 2008) and enhanced concentration during task engagement (Grouzet et al., 2004), among other benefits.

As one of many illustrations in the literature, Hagger, Koch, and Chatzisarantis (2015) recently compared conditions of positive, competence-enhancing feedback to no feedback on an interesting puzzle task. Using a behavioral free-choice measure, they confirmed the positive impact of positive, efficacy-relevant feedback on intrinsic motivation. To elaborate this point, it is necessary to distinguish between two types of positive feedback. The first is spontaneous, *task-inherent feedback* that accompanies the performance of many tasks. As people work on crossword puzzles, they get feedback from the task itself (i.e., the letters fit), and they are likely to feel a sense of joy from making progress at puzzles that challenge them. They are either figuring out the words or they are not; the results are perceptually available and obvious. Similarly, as people climb a mountain, they experience the ongoing results of their efforts in the progress they make (Csikszentmihalyi, Abuhamdeh, & Nakamura, 2005). No external source of feedback is required, and, surely, the task-inherent positive feedback is gratifying and helps sustain interest and persistence.

Nonetheless, there are other activities for which task-inherent feedback is not available, so some type of other-mediated feedback may be necessary to gauge one's competence. Some tasks, because of their complexity or because people do not know the relevant parameters, do not allow the individuals to gain an accurate sense of their effectiveness. To take a simple example, in a hidden-figures task such as the one used in experiments by Harackiewicz (1979), Ryan (1982), and others, participants could not easily tell how well they were doing because they did not know how many figures were hidden in each puzzle, nor what level of performance might be expected from people of their age and education level. To take a more complex example, when people are acquiring the skills of psychotherapy, it may be rather difficult to judge their own effectiveness. Accordingly, an avid psychotherapy trainee seeks feedback from his or her supervisors. Also interesting are tasks or games in which the central criteria are themselves norm-referenced, such as pinball, test taking, and other competitive activities. Here the task-inherent feedback is often less salient than the feedback that comes from external or normative sources.

These two different types of feedback in some ways parallel the distinction we made between naturally occurring tangible rewards, as discussed above with the example of the gardener, and tangible rewards administered by others. Task-inherent or naturally occurring positive feedback is likely to be experienced as informational rather than controlling, whereas positive feedback mediated through others can be either informational or controlling depending on how it is administered. This latter point was made clear in the experiment by Ryan (1982), in which an experimenter provided positive feedback in either an informational or a controlling way and, accordingly, enhanced or undermined intrinsic motivation, respectively.

Experiments that have explicitly evaluated the effects of positive feedback on intrinsic motivation have typically used either verbal or written feedback provided by an experimenter. It is those studies that were reviewed earlier in this chapter and summarized in the rewards meta-analysis. Such studies have important practical significance for parents, teachers, managers, and other authority figures, all of whom frequently find themselves in the position of needing to provide feedback.

As also mentioned previously, there are complexities to the effects of positive feedback on intrinsic motivation. Children may be especially sensitive to the controlling aspects of praise, perhaps as we speculated, because adults so often try to use praise to "motivate" them. Positive feedback has also been found to enhance intrinsic motivation for optimally challenging tasks but not for tasks that were too easy (Danner & Lonky, 1981). Further, individuals' interpretations of the feedback can moderate its effects. For example, Mouratidis et al. (2008) found that when participants were engaged in an easy shuttle run task, the provision of mild positive feedback resulted in a decline in perceived competence, whereas the provision of strong positive feedback left feelings of competence intact. Thus, if one is expecting to do well on an easy task and is given moderately positive feedback, such feedback may even come across as critical and competence-undermining. As well, studies reviewed earlier showed that when positive feedback involved controlling language (e.g., "good, you did just as you *should*"), the effects were negative rather than positive. In other words, when the positive feedback was delivered with a controlling style, the control not only neutralized the potentially positive effect of the competence information but could even undermine intrinsic motivation (e.g., Kast & Connor, 1988; Ryan, 1982). In fact, some evidence indicates that positive feedback enhances intrinsic motivation only if the person experiences an I-PLOC for the behavior and a sense of ownership over the lauded performance (e.g., Fisher, 1978; Ryan et al., 1991). It thus seems clear that whether considering task-inherent or other-mediated positive feedback for activities in which the action demands match one's skill level, the positive effects of competence affirmation on intrinsic motivation accrue only when the recipient of feedback feels at least some degree of personal autonomy with respect to the behavior and its outcome.

The reviewed findings that both perceived autonomy and perceived competence predict intrinsic motivation have been supported by varied methodologies, and for many types of tasks, even though we have thus far emphasized a narrow set of illustrative experiments, especially earlier ones. For example, using survey ratings of perceived autonomy and perceived competence, Li, Harmer, Duncan, Duncan, Acock, and Boles (1998) and Jang, Reeve, Ryan, and Kim (2009) employed structural equation modeling to show that intrinsic motivation was predicted by both perceived autonomy and perceived competence. Koka and Hein (2003) used surveys to relate more positive and constructive forms of feedback to intrinsic interest. Ryan, Rigby and Przybylski (2006) similarly related autonomy and competence ratings in video games to predict players' intrinsic motivation and game preferences. Peng, Lin, Pfeiffer, and Winn (2012) specifically manipulated autonomy (choice) and competence (challenge-related) features of games to demonstrate effects on intrinsic motivation and their mediation by perceived autonomy and competence, as CET would predict. These are just a few of now hundreds of examples from laboratory and field experiments attesting to the utility of CET's formulations regarding the delivery of feedback and its motivational impact.

To summarize, positive feedback mediated by others can have positive effects on people's intrinsic motivation, but if it is administered with a controlling style or in a context of control and evaluation, it may undermine intrinsic motivation. Further, if the praise is hollow, providing no meaningful information about one's competence, it is very possible that the recipients will not perceive it as informational, perhaps instead feeling controlled. In short, for positive feedback to have positive effects on intrinsic motivation, the communicator would generally need to have the intention of informing and acknowledging, rather than "motivating" or controlling.

Negative Feedback

Positive feedback is not always easy to provide in a way that does not diminish intrinsic motivation, and the situation for negative feedback is considerably more difficult. First, research has indicated that negative performance feedback tends to decrease intrinsic motivation relative to both positive feedback and no feedback (e.g., Deci & Cascio, 1972; Karniol & Ross, 1977; Vallerand & Reid, 1984). When people's competence is derogated, either explicitly or implicitly, they tend to lose intrinsic motivation.

Relatively few studies have explored the effects of negative feedback, perhaps because the issue seems so straightforward. But there are, in all likelihood, some interesting complexities concerning the effects of negative feedback on intrinsic motivation (e.g., see Baranes, Oudeyer, & Gottlieb, 2014; Burgers, Eden, Van Engelenburg, & Buningh, 2015), just as there were concerning the effects of positive feedback, because under some circumstances negative feedback is very informational and ultimately competence-supportive (Carpentier & Mageau, 2013) whereas in others it is simply amotivating. First, we have emphasized that intrinsic motivation is facilitated by optimally challenging activities, ones for which people could expect to fail some of the time and succeed some of the time. This implies that a modest amount of negative feedback on an activity that stretches people's abilities may actually serve to challenge and thus motivate, rather than demotivate. Yet to date there is relatively little evidence for anything other than a perceived competence effect—namely, positive feedback that enhances perceived competence enhances intrinsic motivation, and negative feedback that diminishes perceived competence decreases intrinsic motivation.

Second, it seems probable that the style of administering negative feedback would have a substantial effect (Carpentier & Mageau, 2013; Koka & Hein, 2003). When people present negative feedback in a way that pressures and demeans the recipients, for example, by calling their worth into question, the negative feedback may be devastating. But it is also possible for people to provide negative feedback in a more constructive way, a way that approaches poor performance outcomes not as a reason to humiliate the performers but as a problem to be discussed and solved in an open-minded, interactive way. Although there is little research directly addressing this issue, it has immense real-world importance.

Mouratidis and colleagues (2010) attempted to shed light on this issue by examining whether sport coaches' perceived autonomy-supportive versus controlling styles of providing constructive feedback yielded different motivational consequences. Consistent with CET, an autonomy-supportive style related to greater perceived legitimacy of the constructive feedback, which, in turn, related to more intrinsic motivation, well-being, and intentions to engage in their sport in the future. Similarly, Carpentier and Mageau (2013) showed that coaches' attitudes toward change-oriented feedback, when clearly intended to improve and aid athletes, enhanced rather than diminished motivation. Issues related to the intent of motivators in giving feedback are a central theme in Chapter 7, and in other chapters as well.

Finally, it is interesting to consider the effects of negative feedback with respect to extrinsic motivation, as well as intrinsic motivation. Specifically, not only could negative feedback imply that people are not competent at some interesting activity but it could also imply that they do not have control over desired extrinsic outcomes. In other words, negative feedback could decrease their extrinsic motivation, as well as their intrinsic motivation, leaving them with a high level of amotivation. In fact, the idea of negative feedback is contained within the reformulated model of helplessness (Abramson, Seligman, & Teasdale, 1978). Specifically, feedback implying that one is incompetent has been found to produce personal helplessness, which is one type of amotivation.

Concluding Comments

In this chapter, we introduced CET and the first three of its propositions. In brief, they suggest that intrinsic motivation is dependent on experiences of autonomy and competence; factors in the environment that detract from these experiences undermine intrinsic motivation and factors that enhance the experiences augment intrinsic motivation. We also argued that these effects of events are dependent on the meaning or functional significance given to them by the person in context. We then applied CET's formulations to the complex issue of reward effects, including the presentation of a detailed taxonomy of rewards and their likely outcomes. We also reviewed other events that affect the functional significance associated with acting, including negative factors such as evaluations, deadlines, threats, and impositions, and positive ones such as the provision of choice. We also presented a further discussion of the perceived competence-promoting factors that have been studied within CET.

In the next chapter, we continue the discussion of the development of CET, presenting additional formal propositions of the theory. These new propositions include the idea that internal—that is, intrapersonal—events can be informational or controlling, just as external, interpersonal ones can be. Additionally, we consider how the interpersonal climate surrounding behavior can influence the functional significance of events, conducing toward their having informational, controlling, or amotivational salience.

CHAPTER 7

Cognitive Evaluation Theory, Part II

Interpersonal and Intrapersonal Processes
Affecting Intrinsic Motivation

We continue the discussion of CET, beginning with a focus on how the social contexts or interpersonal climate can differentially support or thwart basic psychological need satisfactions and, thus, intrinsic motivation. We review both experimental and field studies specifically comparing the effects of autonomy-supportive versus autonomy-thwarting social contexts on people's intrinsic motivation. Moving from interpersonal influences to *intra*personal influences on people's intrinsic motivation, we review studies of ego involvement and other "internally controlling" states, finding that they undermine intrinsic motivation. Finally, we examine studies showing that, when intrinsically motivated, people tended to learn more deeply, be more creative, and perform better at tasks requiring heuristic or high-quality engagement.

In the previous chapter, we focused on the effects of specific types of external events, such as reward contingencies, positive and negative feedback, threats of punishment, deadlines, and opportunities for choice, on intrinsic motivation. The experimental research revealed that certain kinds of events can, on average, be expected to influence experiences of autonomy and competence and thereby facilitate or undermine intrinsic motivational processes.

Yet it should not be forgotten that, as social and cultural creatures, few such events take place outside of social contexts and interpersonal relationships. When rewards are given, deadlines assigned, or feedback delivered, these are almost always delivered by another person or group of persons whose goals, relations with the target person, and approach shape how these events will be interpreted. The interpersonal styles, attitudes, intentions, and techniques of motivators, be they managers, teachers, parents, or coaches, convey support for or diminish the person's sense of autonomy, competence, and relatedness and therefore affect the functional significance of any event (feedback, reward, etc.) being delivered.

Beyond the influence of external others, each individual experiences his or her own *intrapersonal* context (e.g., self-motivating styles, standards, values, and pressures) that influences her or his intrinsic motivation and persistence. People, that is, can regulate their own behaviors in ways that are self-controlling versus self-supporting, or critical versus benign, affecting the dynamics of motivation, just as external others can do.

In this chapter, we broaden CET to consider both inter- and intrapersonal contexts as they affect the functional significance of events and thus their impact on intrinsic motivational outcomes. Here again we shall focus solely on intrinsic motivation; factors affecting extrinsic motivations and how they are internalized and maintained are addressed in Chapter 8. We begin with the interpersonal issues, in part because it is these social relationships that, over time, often become mirrored within individuals as intrapersonal dynamics.

Interpersonal Contexts and the Functional Significance of Events

One of the foundations of CET is that the effects of events on intrinsic motivation depend upon the interpretations that individuals give to those events. It is not external events or occurrences per se but rather their psychological meaning—what we call their *functional significance*—to individuals that determines their effects on intrinsic motivation. Thus, for example, although experiments show a main-effect undermining of intrinsic motivation by engagement-contingent rewards, this does not occur because such rewards are inherently controlling but, rather, because people tend, on average, to experience them as controlling. This interpretation does not happen in a vacuum. People are usually offered such rewards because others are trying to get them to do something, and thus there is, on average, a salient element of external causality. Yet many factors can temper these "on average" effects, most notably the way in which the *intent* behind the rewards is perceived.

The fact that the most proximal determinant of the effects of an external event on intrinsic motivation is the person's experience of the event should not suggest, however, that people's interpretations of events are whimsical or unsystematic, nor even that they are primarily a function of individual differences (for that issue, see Chapter 9). On the contrary, SDT suggests that, whether in explicit awareness or not, people have an ongoing readiness to interpret and experience specific events or other social-contextual factors in accordance with their basic psychological needs for autonomy, competence, and relatedness. Moreover, there is considerable commonality in the way individuals are likely to construe events, which, of course is the reason that group differences so reliably emerge for events such as surveillance, negative feedback, or unexpected rewards, as we discussed in Chapter 6. As Heider (1958) suggested, there are lawful principles of *naive psychology*, and in this chapter we continue to describe some of the elements that constitute them as they pertain to the issue of intrinsic motivation.

Interpersonal Contexts and External Events

Subtleties in the way an event such as the offer of a reward or the provision of competence feedback is introduced influence whether the controlling or the informational aspect of the event is likely to be more salient to the recipient. In addition, there can be a general ambience or climate to a setting such as a classroom, a home, a clinic, or a work group that will influence or amplify perceptions of support and encouragement or, alternatively, its demanding and critical qualities.

These interpersonal climates are characterized to a significant extent by the orientations, intentions, and behaviors of the people in positions of authority (e.g., teachers, managers, parents). Some teachers and managers relate to their students and employees by understanding their perspectives; they communicate respect and support for autonomy, and they demonstrate caring and connection. Other authorities, in contrast, relate to subordinates via control—by rewarding or pressuring them or by conveying evaluation and conditional regard. Such leaders set the tone or context in which events such as praise or rewards are interpreted and given meaning.

> *CET Proposition IV:* Interpersonal contexts can be characterized in terms of the degree to which the motivational climate tends to be controlling, autonomy supportive, or amotivating. This quality of the overarching interpersonal climate both directly impacts motivation and the likely interpretation or functional significance of specific events, with corresponding effects on intrinsic motivation. Environments that are most facilitating of intrinsic motivation are those that support people's basic psychological needs for autonomy, competence and relatedness.

Relating to proposition IV, we turn now to a review of two areas of research that have examined the effects of interpersonal contexts on intrinsic motivation and closely related variables. First, we review field studies in which the general orientations of teachers, parents, and managers have been used to predict the intrinsic motivation of their students, children, and employees, respectively. Based on CET, we expect that the amount of autonomy support, competence support, and relatedness support conveyed by authority figures will predict the intrinsic motivation of those the authorities are attempting to motivate. Second, we review laboratory experiments in which the interpersonal context is examined for its impact on intrinsic motivation. These experiments were designed to test the general hypothesis that, when external events are administered in an interpersonal context that is informational or supportive of people's initiation and autonomy, the events will have less negative or more positive effects on intrinsic motivation than when the events are administered in interpersonal contexts that are pressuring and controlling. Later chapters in the relevant domains (e.g., schools, work, and parenting) present even more detailed and nuanced research on the real-world significance of these principles.

Orientations toward Autonomy Support versus Control

In an early study, Deci, Schwartz, Sheinman, and Ryan (1981) assessed the motivational orientations of 36 fourth- through sixth-grade public school classroom teachers. This assessment was done during a summer break before the teachers were introduced to the students they would teach in the coming year. The teachers were presented with various "problems in school" regarding students and asked to rate their endorsements of various solutions that ranged from highly controlling to highly autonomy-supportive. If a child were falling behind and failing to turn in assignments, one approach would be to provide external rewards (gold stars) or threats of punishment (stay in from recess) to ensure that the student started performing up to expectations. This type of solution, because it focuses wholly on using external contingencies to control behavior with the aim of ensuring specific outcomes, is considered controlling. By contrast, an autonomy-supportive approach would be exemplified by trying to first understand from the student's perspective, or *internal frame of reference,* the obstacles he or she faces and then working with the child to identify or problem-solve a solution. This assessment was thus intended to tap their general orientations toward being autonomy supportive or controlling.

Subsequently, at less than 2 months and again at approximately 8 months into the school year, students who had been assigned to the classrooms of these teachers completed surveys assessing their own motivation and self-perceptions. As expected, by 2 months into the year, children in classrooms with teachers who had endorsed more controlling strategies and attitudes were already reporting lower levels of intrinsic motivation, perceived cognitive competence, and self-esteem than students in classrooms with more autonomy-supportive teachers. These fairly robust associations at the first assessment remained comparable in magnitude 6 months later. When teachers were more controlling, students reported being less curious about schoolwork, preferring easy rather than challenging assignments, feeling less initiative in their approach to school, and less good about themselves both as students and in general.

The fact that the correlations were already so strong by 2 months into the year led Deci, Schwartz, and colleagues (1981) to do a follow-up study in another school district. In this second study, they preselected teachers who, again prior to meeting their students, endorsed either highly controlling or highly autonomy-supportive motivational strategies. Students' intrinsic motivation and perceived competence were then assessed in the first week of school and then again about 2 months later. During this brief longitudinal assessment, change happened rapidly and systematically. Students in classrooms of autonomy-supportive teachers showed enhancements of intrinsic motivation and perceived competence relative to baseline; students in classrooms of teachers with controlling styles showed diminished intrinsic motivation and perceived competence. This confirmed that teachers' self-endorsed strategies for motivating students, and specifically their orientations toward autonomy support versus control, can have a significant impact on students' motivation within the earliest weeks of a school year.

Expanding on this theme, Ryan and Grolnick (1986) assessed students' perceptions of their *classroom climates*. Drawing from earlier work by de Charms (1976), they assessed whether the atmosphere was one in which students were treated more like *origins* or more like *pawns*. Ryan and Grolnick (1986) found that perceptions along this autonomy-supportive-to-controlling classroom-climate dimension were predictive of students' intrinsic motivation, self-esteem, feelings of personal control, and perceived cognitive competence. Moreover, these effects were apparent at both between- and within-classroom levels of analysis.

As part of this study, students from multiple classrooms were asked to write projective stories in response to a picture depicting a neutral, and quite traditional, classroom scene. Noteworthy was that the stories they produced systematically reflected the motivational climates they were experiencing in their own current classrooms. Children from classrooms that were, on average, perceived as more controlling wrote stories in which student protagonists were either compliant or rebellious, and there were more expressions of aggression and negativity. Children from more autonomy-supportive classrooms described more self-initiating and constructively oriented scenarios. Teachers in the stories were also depicted in manners parallel to children's descriptions of their actual teachers, suggesting internalization of the classroom climate.

Deci, Connell, and Ryan (1989) conducted a field study of managers and their subordinates in a major corporation that paralleled the Deci, Schwartz, et al. (1981) classroom study we described above. Instead of a "Problems at School" assessment, they used a "Problems at Work" survey, again having managers endorse various strategies they might use to deal with problem employees. They also collected questionnaire data from the work group members of each manager. They found that workers whose managers were more controlling expressed more alienation toward the company and lower job satisfaction than those who worked for more autonomy-supportive managers. The employees of more controlling managers also placed greater importance on extrinsic work factors, such as pay and promotions, suggesting lower intrinsic motivation for work. Clearly, these dynamics are not limited to children, as much research will show.

Nor are such findings limited to teachers and managers. Deci, Driver, Hotchkiss, Robbins, and Wilson (1993) studied interactions between mothers and their 6- to 7-year-old children during a play task involving block construction. These mother–child interactions were recorded, and later coders rated the audiotapes and placed each maternal vocalization into a category concerning autonomy support and control. The researchers then calculated an overall score for each mother, placing her along the autonomy-supportive-to-controlling continuum. After the interactive play period, the mothers left the room for about 10 minutes, and the children's intrinsic motivation for the target activity was measured using a "free choice" behavioral paradigm. Specifically, the amount of time the child spent with that activity was assessed during this time when the children were free to do whatever they chose. The children also subsequently rated how interesting they had found the target activity. Analyses revealed that mothers who were rated by observers to be more autonomy supportive in their communication styles had children who showed more free-choice intrinsic motivation and expressed more interest in the target activity than mothers who displayed more controlling communication styles.

These early studies have been replicated and extended in various ways by different research teams, showing how the classroom, organizational, and parenting climates can have an impact on an array of motivational and wellness outcomes. We review many of these studies in the applied chapters to come. For clarification, subsequent work has shown that not only can managers, coaches, clinicians, teachers, and parents be low in their support of autonomy and other basic needs, resulting in less psychological need satisfaction and intrinsic motivation, but they can also sometimes be directly *autonomy-thwarting* and thus actively frustrating the needs of those exposed to them. As we will see, this leads to even worse outcomes.

Perhaps the first study to explicitly address active autonomy-thwarting styles was accomplished by Bartholomew, Ntoumanis, Ryan, Bosch and Thøgersen-Ntoumani (2011). They independently assessed not just need support but also need thwarting in the interpersonal climates created by coaches in various levels of U.K. athletics. Coaches' autonomy-supportive and autonomy-thwarting styles each directly predicted the need satisfaction and need frustration of athletes in expected ways. Perceived autonomy support directly related to need satisfaction, which in turn predicted positive outcomes and well-being; perceived need thwarting was associated with the athletes' need frustration, and accordingly more negative affect and symptoms of burnout. In one study reported by Bartholomew, Ntoumanis, Ryan, and Thogersen-Ntoumani (2011), relatively elite athletes were given a mouth swab prior to scheduled practices, from which an assay for secretory immunoglobulin A (SIgA) was collected. SIgA is a protective secretion in the mucosa that represents a reaction to acute stress. Need-thwarting coaches had more stressed athletes as indicated by this assay.

Since that study, there has been increasing attention in the SDT literature to interpersonal factors that actively thwart versus actively support psychological needs, and with the corresponding outcomes of need frustration and satisfaction (e.g., Chen, Vansteenkiste, et al., 2015). Need thwarting has been shown to result in motivational undermining and decreased wellness, accounting for more variance than previous approaches that only assessed levels of need support (e.g., see De Meyer et al., 2014; Roth & Assor, 2012; Soenens, Sierens, Vansteenkiste, Dochy, & Goossens, 2012), especially with respect to negative outcomes. In fact, it is important to recognize that many contexts have features that are need-supportive alongside features that are need-thwarting, suggesting the need to assess these as potentially independent aspects of social climates (Vansteenkiste & Ryan, 2013).

Interpersonal Style as a Moderator of the Effects of External Events

The studies above are field studies, reflecting principles of CET that have also been tested in the lab. For example, in an experiment by Ryan, Mims, and Koestner (1983), two groups of participants who received performance-contingent rewards were compared with two no-reward groups who were given positive feedback comparable to that conveyed by the performance-contingent rewards. Relevant to the interpersonal climate issue, for half the participants the rewards or feedback were administered in a controlling style; for the other half, they were administered in a noncontrolling, autonomy-supportive manner. Within the controlling conditions, the feedback conveyed to the participant was "you have done well, just as you should." In the informational or autonomy-supportive style, the positive feedback was provided with no mention of how participants "should" have performed. Results revealed two main effects. First, as we reported in the prior chapter, the two reward groups showed diminished intrinsic motivation relative to the two comparable positive-feedback control groups. Relevant here, however, is that participants who received the feedback delivered in the more controlling way, whether they were in the reward or no-reward groups, evidenced lower intrinsic motivation relative to those in the autonomy-supportive groups. This is important with respect to reward effects because it indicates that, although performance-contingent rewards tend to undermine intrinsic motivation (Deci, Koestner, & Ryan, 1999), these reward effects will be less negative if the rewards are administered in an autonomy-supportive way. Indeed, the Ryan et al. (1983) study showed that, although informationally administered performance-contingent rewards undermined intrinsic motivation relative to informationally administered positive feedback, the informationally administered rewards led to a higher level of intrinsic motivation than a no-reward, no-feedback control condition in which the interpersonal context was neutral (i.e., neither autonomy-supportive nor controlling). *How* rewards are delivered thus matters in terms of their functional significance.

Ryan (1982) experimentally examined the effects of positive feedback administered in a controlling versus informational way, with feedback for half the participants being self-administered and for the other half being experimenter-delivered. The self-administered feedback was written on paper that the participants were given before they began the target activity of solving puzzles, so they read a statement to themselves after each puzzle they worked on. Results indicated that when positive feedback was presented controllingly, it decreased intrinsic motivation relative to when it was administered in an autonomy-supportive way, regardless of whether it was self- or other-administered. Although positive feedback would typically enhance intrinsic motivation because of its competence salience, when presented in a controlling way even positive feedback or praise can undermine intrinsic motivation. Research by Kast and Connor (1988) similarly showed that feedback worded in controlling ways undermined intrinsic motivation relative to feedback administered informationally.

Limit Setting

Koestner, Ryan, Bernieri, and Holt (1984) extended this idea that the autonomy-supportive versus controlling style of communication matters, even (or perhaps especially) when setting limits on behavior. The focus on communicating behavioral limits was of interest because limits on behavior can so often be perceived as constraining and inhibiting, and yet as Koestner and colleagues (1984) argued, it should be possible to set limits in a relatively autonomy-supportive way so they are not detrimental to intrinsic motivation. To show this, they did a study in which limits were set on the behavior of second-grade children, who were asked to paint a picture during an individual session with an experimenter. Although the painting activity was interesting, the limit setting concerned keeping the art materials neat while working with them. For example, the children were asked to wash out their brushes before changing colors and not to paint beyond the borders of the paper. The authors argued that being autonomy supportive in such a situation would involve several elements, including: (1) minimizing the use of controlling language, (2) acknowledging the children's feelings of not necessarily wanting to be neat, and (3) providing the children a meaningful rationale for the limits. The researchers found that if these autonomy-supportive features were part of the limit setting, children evidenced higher levels of intrinsic motivation for painting compared with those for whom the limits were more controlling. Indeed, this study highlights an important idea we especially elaborate in the chapters on parenting and education: namely, that one can set limits and provide structure without thwarting children's experiences of autonomy (e.g., Grolnick, Raftery-Helmer, Marbell, Flamm, Cardemil, & Sanchez, 2014).

Perceived Intentions and Motives of the Motivator and Their Functional Effects

The experiments cited thus far pertain to the autonomy-supportive versus controlling communication styles used by the motivators. Results confirm that the ways in which rewards, feedback, and limits are communicated does indeed affect motivation, in part because they convey to the recipient the intent of the motivator. Is the motivator trying to control me to get some specific outcome, or is he or she supporting my autonomy?

If people believe that their bosses, teachers, coaches, or practitioners, for example, are motivated by extrinsic goals or have controlling intentions to get them to behave or perform in preordained ways, then this is likely to color their interpretations of feedback or rewards administered by those motivators and thus their subsequent intrinsic motivation. A number of studies have tried to manipulate the perceived intentions and motives of the motivators to see how these affect recipients' intrinsic motivation.

One of the first experiments in this vein was reported by Wild, Enzle, and Hawkins (1992). They examined music lessons delivered by tutors, who in one condition were said to be volunteers with an interest in teaching others and in the other condition were said to be doing the tutoring for the pay. In fact, however, the actual tutors were naïve to these descriptions and simply proceeded to teach the standardized lesson. Results confirmed that motives attributed to the tutors influenced subsequent attitudes and intrinsic motivation. Specifically, students who believed their tutors were simply volunteers enjoyed the lesson more, expressed more interest in future learning, and evidenced more exploratory behaviors regarding the subject matter during a free-choice period than students who believed their tutors were receiving payments. Attributing more volitional, or less controlled, motivation to authorities can thus potentiate different perceived climates, leading the individuals within them to experience the same events differently, with corresponding changes in intrinsic motivation (see also Wild, Enzle, Nix, & Deci, 1997).

Such attributions are not only functionally important, but they can also impact organizational and educational atmospheres through a mechanism of *social contagion*, as demonstrated by Radel, Sarrazin, Legrain, and Wild (2010). Paralleling the Wild et al. (1992) study, participants in a physical education context were taught by an instructor who was described as either doing it for pay or volunteering. When the participants believed the instructors were doing it for pay, they evidenced lower interest and free-choice behavior than when they believed the instructors were volunteers, again despite the fact that the instructors were naïve to these attributions. Now for the contagion effect: Subsequently, these participants were asked to instruct others. Students of those students who had attributed extrinsic motives to their own instructors also showed lower interest and free-choice persistence. The perceived attitudes of the original instructors were clearly contagious, shaping the overall climate and radiating to a second generation of students within the context.

Further highlighting that it is not always the events but their functional significance that determines a motivational effect, Enzle and Anderson (1993) examined how the effects of surveillance might differ as a function of the perceived controlling versus non-controlling intent of the individuals doing the surveillance. Some participants doing a task were led to believe that an observer was there to be evaluative and enforce rules. In another condition, the observer was said to simply be an interested and curious onlooker. For the former group, the experience of autonomy was lower, as was subsequent intrinsic motivation measured behaviorally. In contrast, when the observer was portrayed as non-controlling, participants' autonomy was higher, as was their intrinsic motivation. Interestingly, in a subsequent experiment, these investigators also showed that an ambiguous surveillance condition fostered distrust, as the intent was assumed by participants to be controlling or evaluative. Thus their intrinsic motivation and autonomy were lower.

Summary of Interpersonal Context Effects

Studies from a variety of field settings, as well as from the psychological laboratory, indicate that interpersonal contexts differ in terms of the degree to which they tend to be controlling versus autonomy-supportive. Illustrative field studies in education, parenting, and management showed that the quality of the interpersonal climate or ambience can be related directly to the intrinsic motivation of people within it: When the climate is informational or autonomy-supportive, people's intrinsic motivation tends to be higher; when the interpersonal climate is controlling, intrinsic motivation tends to be lower. Further, laboratory experiments showed the causal effects of controlling and autonomy-supportive communication styles and perceived intentions on intrinsic motivational processes.

There is, of course, great practical significance to these findings about the effects of interpersonal contexts in intrinsic motivation, as we show later in this book when we discuss areas of application, but there is also important theoretical significance. Specifically, these findings support the theoretical position that external events such as rewards, feedback, deadlines, choice, and surveillance are social events. They are embedded in an interpersonal climate with a functional significance or meaning with respect to basic needs for autonomy, competence, and relatedness. Various interpersonal behaviors, such as the style of communicating structures, can influence what the functional significance is likely to be.

Relatedness and Its Support

So far in this chapter, we have focused on satisfaction versus thwarting of the needs for autonomy and competence and the social contexts that support or thwart them as the pivotal experiences that enhance or diminish intrinsic motivation. Research has shown these experiences to be critical, proximal determinants of intrinsically motivated activities, especially those studied in laboratory tasks. Nonetheless, *relatedness*, as an aspect of the motivational climate, also plays a role in the facilitation versus forestalling of intrinsic motivation, even for individual tasks or activities.

What was likely the first experimental demonstration of this effect was accidental. Anderson, Manoogian, and Reznick (1976) were examining the effects of rewards and feedback on young children's intrinsic motivation for an interesting activity. The children were run individually in a room with an experimenter whom they did not know. In an attempt to create a condition in which there was no praise or positive feedback, the experimenter was instructed to be silent and not to respond to overtures from the children. This condition, which was supposed to be a no-reward, no-feedback control group, turned out to have the lowest level of intrinsic motivation of any group in the study, even though (as a control group) it had been expected to yield a moderately high level of intrinsic motivation. Clearly, the children felt rejected by the adult experimenter, and their intrinsic motivation was decimated. In other words, the thwarting of their need for relatedness had a decidedly negative effect on their intrinsic motivation.

Attachment theory (e.g., Bowlby, 1979) also implies that security of attachment, which occurs when people feel satisfaction of their need for relatedness, is important for intrinsic motivation. Intrinsic motivation in infants takes the form of curiosity and exploratory behaviors, and attachment theorists have found that that exploration is more evident when infants are securely attached to a primary caregiver. Studies of mothers and their infants have shown that maternal autonomy support, as well as the attachment security it fosters (Bretherton, 1987), are both associated with exploratory behaviors (e.g., Frodi, Bridges, & Grolnick, 1985).

Extending this idea to later development, Ryan, Stiller, and Lynch (1994) surveyed a large sample of junior high students concerning their felt security with teachers (as well as with other figures in their lives). Students who experienced more felt security with their teachers also reported more autonomous motivation for school, including greater intrinsic motivation, as well as more school engagement.

Research by Bao and Lam (2008) examined the importance of choice on intrinsic motivation and performance in young Chinese students and added an interesting nuance to the prior findings by considering relatedness to the authorities who make choices for the students. The researchers found that, in general, making their own choices, relative to having the choices made by their mothers or teachers, enhanced the children's intrinsic motivation. Yet there was also an interaction with how close the children felt to the adults. Children who did *not* feel close to their mothers or teachers evidenced significantly less intrinsic motivation when the adults made choices for them than when the children made their own choices, whereas children who felt close to their mothers or teachers showed no difference in intrinsic motivation when the adults made the choices or the children made their own. Presumably, feeling close to the adults raised the children's trust so they willingly endorsed the choices that were made by significant adults on their behalf. Yet for these Chinese children, when parents or teachers to whom the children did not feel close made a choice for them, intrinsic motivation was undermined. Said differently, people do not necessarily lose a sense of volition and autonomy when denied choice if they concur with, or place trust in, the options selected for them (see also Van Petegem, Beyers, Vansteenkiste, & Soenens, 2012). Yet we should also note that results from Bao and Lam (2008) also indicated that, regardless of closeness, when children made their own choices they *performed* better than when others chose for them, even close others. Moreover, in terms of predicting school engagement, both autonomy and relatedness were important. Results such as these by Bao and Lam (and numerous other studies of

Asian children and adults) also cast doubt on the oft-cited claims by Iyengar and Lepper (1999) that true choice, and the autonomy that typically would follow from it, are not important or meaningful to Asians.

Fitting with this discussion, Costa, Ntoumanis, and Bartholomew (2015) explored relatedness need support and relatedness need thwarting as a factor in predicting a sense of autonomy and competence in relationships. An important finding in their work and in work reviewed in Chapter 12 is that a climate of relatedness conduces to more feelings of *both* autonomy and relatedness. Although we have not emphasized this thus far, when people are being autonomy-supportive, they tend to take the other's frame of reference, which is then experienced as caring. Autonomy and relatedness support thus tend to co-occur in any interpersonal climate and to operate synergistically (e.g., Deci, La Guardia, Moller, Scheiner, & Ryan, 2006; La Guardia, Ryan, Couchman, & Deci, 2000).

In many situations people do not appear to need to experience relatedness to be intrinsically motivated for a specific activity. For example, many people are quite intrinsically motivated when engaged in behaviors such as solitary hiking, solving crossword puzzles, and reading, suggesting that direct relational support may not be necessary as a *proximal* factor for maintaining intrinsic motivation. Nonetheless, a secure relational base may well be necessary as a distal support for intrinsic motivation to flourish and function robustly, and, of course, intrinsically motivated events all occur within a cultural context that lends them meaning and significance.

Overall, it appears that need-supportive climates foster greater autonomous motivation, and even leave people prone to interpret specific events as more supportive. More generally, it is clear that apart from specific events, people experience their classrooms, teams, and work groups as having a general ambience or climate, and this affects their overall functioning within them.

Intrapersonal Events: Ego Involvement and Internally Controlling States

Intrinsic motivation is manifested as people's engagement in activities that interest them. It is in evidence when people feel free to follow their interests, and it represents the prototype of autonomous motivation. With full willingness, people undertake activities that challenge, excite, and satisfy them.

Autonomy is another term for self-regulation, and when intrinsically motivated people are self-regulating; they have an internal perceived locus of causality (I-PLOC) and feel self-determined as they act. An important question, however, is whether all forms of internal motivation necessarily have an I-PLOC. In other words, are there some types of internal motivations that do not represent autonomy and for which people experience the locus of causality to be external or self-alien, even though the motivation is within them? SDT has long held that some forms of internal motivation are actually controlling, some even coercive, and thus, like controlling external events, they can have effects such as undermining intrinsic motivation.

This question arose early in our work on intrinsic motivation, as we observed how people could be very self-controlling and self-pressuring, even for activities that might otherwise be inherently enjoyable, such as learning, puzzle solving, or playing sports. Ryan (1982) used the term *internally controlling* to describe the idea that there can be such motivational forces within individuals, and he specifically highlighted the concept of *ego involvement* in this regard. He further argued that if ego involvement is internally controlling, it should be antagonistic to intrinsic motivation, a prototype of autonomous functioning. We thus begin our discussion of internal control by reviewing this idea of ego involvement.

Ego Involvement versus Task Involvement and Intrinsic Motivation

In its most general definition, ego involvement pertains to circumstances in which people feel a pressure to perform in ways that would be valued by a reference group to which they do or would like to belong. As Sherif and Cantril (1947) put it in their classic discussion, ego-based strivings are the "individual's effort to place himself securely in those constellations of human relationships that represent for him desirable values, that will make his status or position secure" (p. 115). The concept of ego involvement had thus been prominent in social psychology for decades before the Ryan (1982) experiment, although it had generally been thought of mainly as a way of heightening motivation and investment rather than as a problematic or controlling form of motivation. For example, in early work on the *Thematic Apperception Test* (TAT), the common instructional set was to induce ego involvement by suggesting that the narrative task was a "test of one's creative aptitudes" (see Ryan & Manly, 2005).

Greenwald (1982) pointed out, however, that the term *ego involvement* had actually been used in three different ways in psychology. The first describes ego involvement as a striving based in threats to esteem by others—one's ego is on the line with respect to evaluation by others. The second, closely related definition suggests that ego involvement is based in threats to self-esteem; in other words, it is a situation in which one's ego is on the line with respect to self-evaluation rather than evaluation by others. The third usage of the term represents a more general or undifferentiated phenomenon in which one is invested in an activity because it has some type of personal importance. This third usage, applied in some studies, does not necessarily imply evaluative pressure (e.g., Sansone, 1986; Gendolla & Richter, 2013). We are primarily concerned here with the first and second of these definitions, in which ego involvement entails a state of needing to prove one's worth to oneself or others.

As we have already reviewed, people who feel that others are evaluating them tend to feel externally controlled and undermined in their intrinsic motivation. Ryan (1982) raised the possibility that ego involvement in which one is self-evaluative is internally controlling and should therefore similarly undermine intrinsic motivation. Ryan (1982) specifically drew from de Charms (1968), who had considered ego involvement as a state in which a person's self-esteem is hinged upon attaining a specified outcome. In the words of de Charms (1968), ego involvements put people "on trial," with themselves as the judge. Later, in a similar vein, Nicholls (1984) would define ego involvement as a self-evaluative state in which people's goals are to maintain self-worth by demonstrating high competence relative to others. De Charms, Ryan, and later Nicholls all contrasted this pressured, self-evaluative state with *task involvement,* in which people's concern is to act, learn, or gain mastery as an end in itself. In essence, task involvement suggests intrinsic motivation, whereas ego involvement is a form of controlling extrinsic motivation.

Ryan (1982) hypothesized that if people became ego involved in performing an interesting activity, the ego involvement would undermine their intrinsic motivation for that activity because it would diminish their feelings of autonomy. This reasoning represented an extension of CET beyond interpersonal to *intrapersonal* events, suggesting that certain forms of "self"-regulation may be inherently self-controlling and nonautonomous.

This undermining effect was expected to occur even when people succeeded and felt competent at the activity.

In Ryan's (1982) initial experiments, some participants were introduced to interesting hidden-figures puzzles in a manner that was designed to induce ego involvement by telling them that the task, which required the breakdown and reorganization of perceptual fields and was actually reflective of creative intelligence. For the others, there was no mention of task performance reflecting intelligence, being told only that it was an experimental puzzle task. All participants then worked on the puzzles, and all received highly positive feedback about their performances (which in a hidden-figures task is always plausible, as people cannot readily tell how many hidden figures they have missed). For participants in the ego-involved condition, the positive feedback would essentially allow them to feel effective and save them from feeling incompetent, but it should nonetheless diminish feelings of autonomy, because it is self-controlling. As predicted, in a subsequent free-choice period, participants who were in the ego-involvement condition displayed significantly less intrinsic motivation than those in the task-involvement condition.

One presumes that the task-involved, as well as the ego-involved, participants in this experiment were desirous of performing well; indeed, the need to feel competent is central to being intrinsically motivated or task-involved (e.g., Deci & Ryan, 1980a; Nicholls, 1984; White, 1959). The point, however, is that when participants' orientations toward a task shift from being interested in performing well to feeling that they *have to* perform well to maintain a sense of self-worth, the nature of the motivation has changed from autonomous to heteronomous. This experiment thus set the stage for further explorations of intrapersonal processes through which people operate nonautonomously (i.e., are controlled) even when they are not under direct, external controls (an issue that is addressed in much greater depth in Chapter 8 with the concept of *introjection*).

Other studies (e.g., Butler, 1987; Koestner, Zuckerman, & Koestner, 1987; Plant & Ryan, 1985) soon replicated this negative effect of ego involvement on intrinsic motivation. An exception was a study by Sansone (1986), although it involved an induction in line with Greenwald's third definition of ego involvement (viz., personal importance), which, as we mentioned, is not inherently controlling and does not implicate contingent self-worth. In fact, personal importance can reflect the valuing of activities, which is typically an indicator of autonomous motivation and which we describe as a type of internalization called *identification* (see Chapter 8).

In sum, ego involvement (or other self-esteem-related pressures to perform well, such as self-critical perfectionism and contingent self-esteem) are in essence internal or intrapersonal events that are experienced as controlling and undermine intrinsic motivation. Indeed, many people are driven by internalized "shoulds" and "have to's" in which they become their own controlling "boss" or tyrannical parent, often taking the joy and interest out of activities. We shall see that ego involvement becomes especially catalyzed for a person in social contexts in which others are *conditionally regarding*, thus also making the person's sense of worth contingent on doing well or living up to specific standards (Deci & Ryan, 1995; Roth, Assor, Niemiec, Ryan, & Deci, 2009).

Research on ego involvement provides the basis for the fifth CET proposition concerning the effects of internal motivational processes that are antagonistic to intrinsic motivation and, in some cases, to both intrinsic and extrinsic motivation.

CET Proposition V: Intrapersonal events that bear on the initiation and regulation of behavior can differ in their functional significance. Accordingly, internally informational events are those that facilitate intrinsic motivation by facilitating an internal perceived locus of causality and perceived competence; internally controlling events are those experienced as pressure toward specific outcomes and facilitate an external perceived locus of causality, thereby undermining intrinsic motivation; and internally amotivating events are those that make salient someone's incompetence and inability to attain desired outcomes, thereby diminishing both intrinsic and extrinsic motivation.

Further Exploration of Internally Controlling States

Plant and Ryan (1985) argued that the state of objective self-awareness (Duval & Wicklund, 1972) or public self-consciousness (Fenigstein, Scheier, & Buss, 1975; Carver & Scheier, 1981), in which people are aware of themselves as if through the eyes of another, often function similarly to ego involvement by putting people into an evaluative stance with respect to themselves, and thus having a controlling functional significance. Rather than simply being engaged in a task, a person objectifies him- or herself and is concerned about how his or her behaviors or performance might appear. This concern is, in fact, often a projection, others may or may not be watching, judging, or evaluating the person's performance. Plant and Ryan (1985), therefore, suggested that such self-objectification would amount to an internally controlling type of motivation, and they hypothesized that being in a state of public self-consciousness while working on an interesting task should decrease people's intrinsic motivation. Plant and Ryan (1985) operationalized this internally controlling motivation by placing participants in front of a camera that appeared to be on or a mirror that reflected their image, whereas in a control condition these elements were absent. They found that focusing participants' attention on themselves in this self-consciousness-inducing way decreased their intrinsic motivation.

A number of further experiments in this area have elaborated on this relation between public self-consciousness and intrinsic motivation. In two experimental studies mentioned earlier in this chapter, Enzle and Anderson (1993) applied CET in their study of the undermining effects of surveillance on intrinsic motivation. They showed, as predicted by CET, that it was the controlling aspects of surveillance that undermined intrinsic motivation, whereas noncontrolling surveillance did not have a negative effect. Furthermore, they showed how unexplained surveillance can be particularly undermining because people are apt to project a controlling intent.

It seems that people can be as dictatorial to themselves as others can be to them. Indeed, astute clinicians, coaches, teachers, leaders, and parents can find manifold instances of people being self-pressuring and self-controlling—people driven to achieve certain standards who are prideful and self-aggrandizing when they succeed and self-shaming and critical when they fail. Pressuring themselves toward goals, or needing to "appear" to themselves and others in certain ways, they may feel stressed and harried, put their health at risk, and develop unhealthy relationships. These intrapersonal processes, we argue, have their derivation in interpersonal processes—that is, they result from the internalization of social controls. Stated differently, people come to use the standards and contingent approval on themselves that others had used on them, all in the pursuit of the feelings of relatedness and self-worth. We return to this issue in Chapter 8.

Ego-Involvement and Negative Feedback

As mentioned, in the Ryan (1982) study, all participants were given positive feedback about their performances so we could rule out competence issues and detect the negative effects of ego involvement on autonomous motivation. Positive feedback would confirm their competence and thus provide the sought-after outcome, yet they would then be unlikely to continue engaging in the task because their intrinsic motivation would have been undermined by the pressure, even as their extrinsic goal would have been achieved.

This raises an interesting question about what might happen if ego-involved participants were not given such confirming feedback. Might they persist at the activity during a free-choice period in a continuing attempt to prove their worth to themselves? Were this to occur, it would create a problem for the standard free-choice paradigm (Deci, 1972a), because participants would be persisting at the activity during the free-choice period because of an internal motivation that was not intrinsic motivation. The persistence would be ego involved; it would be a pressured, internally controlled persistence aimed at restoring feelings of self-worth. This subtle problem reflects the change in the nature of the extrinsic motivations that was being studied. The extrinsic motivators that had been examined in earlier studies were ones that could be terminated by the experimenter. The experimenter simply had to make clear in some way that there would be no more rewards, no more evaluations, and no more surveillance prior to the beginning of the free-choice period, and then there would be no extrinsic reason to persist. Yet an experimenter cannot reliably "turn off" a participant's ego involvement, so if it is not satisfied by positive feedback, it could persist into the free-choice period.

A study by Anderson and Rodin (1989) provided some evidence for our conjecture that nonconfirming feedback in ego-involving situations could lead to internally controlling persistence during a free-choice period. In that study, participants were told that they would be evaluated, so they should do their best. Later, participants in one group were given positive feedback (they were told their performances were at the 95th percentile), while the other group was given nonconfirming feedback (they were told their performances were at the 55th percentile). Results showed greater free-choice persistence for participants who got nonconfirming feedback than positive feedback, but the moods of those who got nonconfirming feedback were more negative than those of the participants who received positive feedback. This suggested that the free-choice persistence following nonconfirming feedback was not intrinsically motivated, for one would expect intrinsically motivated persistence to be accompanied by positive affect.

Another example of free-choice persistence that likely did not reflect intrinsic motivation appeared in a study by Baumeister and Tice (1985). Participants high and low in self-esteem who were working on anagrams were given either positive feedback, negative feedback that allowed face saving, or humiliating negative feedback that did not allow face saving. The highest level of persistence during a subsequent free-choice period was shown by the individuals with low self-esteem who had received the humiliating negative feedback. The authors concluded that that group was the most intrinsically motivated, yet it seems to us very unlikely that these participants were experiencing the interest, enjoyment, and volition that are the phenomenological markers of intrinsic motivation. Instead, their persistence was likely a reflection of a desperate attempt to salvage some feelings of self-worth in the face of the internal pressure and humiliation.

To test these conjectures directly, Ryan, Koestner, and Deci (1991) presented a set of three experiments exploring the effects of positive feedback versus nonconfirming or no feedback on the free-choice persistence of ego-involved versus task-involved participants. They argued that if participants' persistence during a free-choice period were intrinsically motivated, it should be positively correlated with feelings of interest and choice, but if their persistence were not intrinsically motivated, there should not be a correlation between their behavior and these positive feelings—that is, they would be persisting for reasons other than interest in the activity. They also expected that ego-involved participants who received nonconfirming feedback would persist longer than those who received positive feedback (who, as in Ryan's 1982 study, would not persist, as they already had their "reward").

Results of these studies indicated, as predicted, that when participants were task-involved positive feedback led to greater persistence than nonconfirming feedback and that persistence was significantly positively correlated with self-reported interest/enjoyment. Yet when participants were ego involved, nonconfirming feedback led to greater persistence than positive feedback, and that persistence was not correlated with self-reported affect. It does seem, therefore, that when participants are ego involved and fail to get the affirmation they need, they may persist in an attempt to prove themselves worthy. It also appears that examination of the within-cell correlations between behavior and self-reported affect is a useful way of helping to distinguish intrinsically motivated persistence from internally controlled persistence. We would add that when people are either ego involved or task involved and then receive *very* negative feedback, all motivation, both intrinsic and extrinsic, is likely to be undermined, and there would be little persistence.

Burgers, Eden, Van Engelenburg, and Buningh (2015) recently reported an intriguing experiment on a "brain training" game that related to this idea of both intrinsically and nonintrinsically motivated persistence. Their target game was presumably designed to be interesting and engaging. Yet, at the same time, as a "brain training" exercise, ego involvement could readily be potentiated. They created conditions in which the valence of feedback was negative or positive. These conditions were crossed in an analysis of variance design with three types of feedback: descriptive, comparative, and what the researchers described as evaluative (competence praising). Following the game, they assessed participants' experience of autonomy and competence need satisfactions, their motivation, and their intention to play the game again. Even though presumably this interesting game had extrinsic benefits (i.e., brain training), they found that it was intrinsic motivation that was most important in predicting people's choice to play the game again. Second, they found that both perceived autonomy and competence were positively related to intrinsic motivation, increasing the likelihood of future play. However, they also found that those who received negative feedback were more likely to persist in an immediate way. They reasoned that those getting positive feedback did not need, or want, to continue the immediate training. We suspect, in contrast, that many of those told they performed poorly were persisting and ego involved. Finally, the evaluative (positive praise) and descriptive feedback styles better supported choices to continue play than the comparative one, in which participants' normative standings were provided. Such normative feedback can feel truly evaluative in an ego-involving sense. Here we see the general tenets of CET being supported, along with the complexities that come from potentially ego-involving mindsets and motives.

Ego-Involved Winning and Losing

In the Reeve and Deci (1996) study of competition discussed in the previous chapter, the researchers took a different tack on distinguishing between intrinsically motivated persistence and internally controlled persistence in a study of winning versus losing a competition. They suggested that part of the reason that competition can undermine intrinsic motivation is that people get ego involved. Thus, if participants were to lose a competition, they might subsequently feel internally pressured to persist in an attempt to regain some self-esteem.

To distinguish the two types of persistence, Reeve and Deci reasoned that if, during the free-choice period, participants had access both to the puzzle problems they had already done and to new puzzle problems, then returning to problems they had already done would represent a type of perseveration indicative of internally controlled persistence, whereas moving on to new puzzle problems would be more reflective of the interested, exploratory nature of intrinsic motivation. Applying this analysis, Reeve and Deci found that participants who had lost at a competition spent virtually no free-choice time engaging with new problems, but they spent a great deal of time with the problems on which they lost the competition. In contrast, those who had won a competition spent considerable time with new puzzle problems but virtually no time on the puzzle problems they had done during the competition. This difference was not due to actual performance differences; winning versus losing was an outcome manipulated by a well-trained confederate who could easily declare the same level of performance as either a win or a loss. The researchers concluded that losing the competition relative to winning it decreased intrinsic motivation, but it nonetheless prompted internally controlling persistence.

Rawsthorne and Elliot (1999) completed a meta-analysis of the effects of ego involvement versus task involvement on intrinsic motivation and on what Dweck's (1986) terminology distinguishes as learning goals and performance goals (which, prior to the introduction of Elliot's [1999] achievement goal theory distinctions, were directly conflated with task involvement and ego involvement). The meta-analysis of 23 experiments confirmed that ego involvement and performance goal manipulations led to significantly less subsequent intrinsic motivation than task involvement and learning goal manipulations. Yet they also performed follow-up analyses and found that confirming versus nonconfirming feedback moderated the ego involvement versus task-involvement effects. Specifically, as mentioned above, under task-involvement conditions, confirming feedback led to more intrinsically motivated persistence than nonconfirming feedback, whereas under ego involvement conditions, nonconfirming feedback led to greater persistence, reflecting internally controlling persistence rather than intrinsic motivation.

Intrinsic Motivation and Performance: When Interest Matters

CET was formulated to predict and organize the effects of interpersonal and intrapersonal influences on intrinsic motivation. Because intrinsic motivation is a pleasurable state, one might value that state simply for its own sake. In other words, one might argue that being intrinsically motivated is its own justification. Yet, within SDT more broadly, intrinsic motivation is important in part because it is theorized to play a crucial role in enhancing the quality of engagement and, therefore, both performance and learning (Ryan & Deci, 2013). In fact, numerous studies have investigated the question of whether intrinsic motivation is related to more effective functioning, creativity, and performance, many of which have been done within the framework of CET.

Learning Outcomes

Benware and Deci (1984) did an early study of college students' learning to test the hypothesis that students in conditions that facilitate intrinsic motivation would display greater conceptual learning than students in conditions of external control. They reasoned that intrinsically motivated students would be more flexible in their thinking and thus more open to grasping concepts and relations among facts; in other words, intrinsically motivated students would process information more deeply or fully with a genuine sense of interest. The reasoning evolved out of the view of intrinsic motivation as a growth-oriented source of energy that leads people to take on optimal challenges in an attempt to master their environments by stretching their skills and knowledge, whereas extrinsic incentives prompt motivation that is more involved with the exercise of existing skills and knowledge and with a more focused and rigid pursuit of a goal extraneous to the learning itself (Elkind, 1971; Flavell & Wohlwill, 1969).

Participants in this study were asked to spend about 3 hours studying relatively complex material on neuropsychology. Half were told they would have an opportunity to put the material to active use by teaching it to others, whereas the other half were told they should study because they would be tested on their learning. After studying the material, all students were given the same examination, even though the put-the-material-to-use group had not expected the exam. Exam questions were classified as assessing either rote memorization or more conceptual learning. Results revealed that participants who studied in order to use the material to teach others evidenced significantly greater intrinsic motivation and demonstrated significantly better conceptual understanding than participants who learned in order to take an exam. Rote memorization did not, however, differ between the two groups.

Grolnick and Ryan (1987) performed a learning experiment in an elementary school setting. Fifth-grade students were brought individually to a reading laboratory in the school and were asked to read age-appropriate textbook material. Some were told they would be tested and graded on their learning (i.e., a controlling condition), whereas others were told they would be reading in order to answer questions about how interesting and difficult the passage was (i.e., a noncontrolling condition). All children were tested immediately after the learning and then (unexpectedly for both groups) again a week later. Results indicated that the noncontrolling condition led to more interest in the material and greater conceptual understanding than the controlling condition at both testing sessions. Results also indicated that the controlling condition yielded greater rote memorization than the noncontrolling condition immediately after the reading, but the controlled group also evidenced greater deterioration of memorized material over the subsequent week, leaving their rote learning outcomes no greater at the end of the week than that of the noncontrolling group.

Cordova and Lepper (1996) did a study of intrinsic motivation and learning in which they explored the effects both of choice and of making the material more personally relevant. They predicted and found that both factors led to enhanced intrinsic motivation and to enhanced learning performance.

Lewthwaite, Chiviacowsky, Drews, and Wulf (2015) applied SDT tenets to motor learning. Specifically, they investigated whether choice, even over tangential elements in the situation, might support participants' feelings of autonomy during training and thus heighten motivation and increase motor learning and performance. In two experiments, they let participants in one condition simply undergo training at a golf putting task, and in a yoked condition, the training was preceded by opportunities to choose the color of the balls or to make other peripheral choices such as selecting pretasks they might do or a painting that might be hung on the wall. Remarkably, these autonomy-promoting choice elements in the task situation enhanced both intrinsic motivation for the task and performance learning, even assessed after a 24-hour interval.

Gottfried, Marcoulides, Gottfried, and Oliver (2009) reported on the longitudinal effects of parental motivational practices on academic intrinsic motivation in math and science. Task-intrinsic practices by parents, such as encouragement of children's enjoyment and engagement in learning, showed positive effects with regard to children's initial levels of motivation at age 9 and lower declines in motivation through age 17. By contrast, task-extrinsic practices, such as parents' provision of external rewards and consequences contingent on children's task performance, yielded adverse effects on children's motivation both at age 9 and across the 8-year study interval.

Taken together, these and other studies that we review throughout this book (see especially Chapter 14) confirm that learning is indeed typically greater under conditions that foster intrinsic motivation than under those that emphasize extrinsic motivators.

Performance

Although learning and its demonstration through test results represent one type of performance, researchers have also studied other types of performance. For example, McGraw and McCullers (1979) did a study in which some participants were offered financial rewards for solving a series of problems and some did the same problems with no mention of rewards. The structure of the task was such that participants developed a cognitive set while working on the first few problems, but the key to continued success was being able to break that set and approach each new problem flexibly. Results of the study indicated that those participants who were rewarded had a harder time breaking the mental set than did participants who were not offered a reward. We infer from the results that the rewards resulted in a more rigid focus on the reward and a less cognitively flexible approach to the problems.

McGraw (1978) reviewed a number of studies of reward effects on performance and concluded that task-contingent rewards impair performance on interesting, complex, or what he called "heuristic" activities but might even improve performance on dull, uninteresting, or what he called "algorithmic" tasks. A study by Fabes, Moran, and McCullers (1981) confirmed this. In it, college students were given problems from the Wechsler Adult Intelligence Scale (WAIS). Some required algorithmic thinking, and some required heuristic thinking. Some of the participants received monetary rewards, and some did not. Results indicated that rewarded students did significantly poorer on the heuristic problems than the nonrewarded students, but the groups did not differ in their performance on the algorithmic tasks. These results parallel those of Benware and Deci (1984) and Grolnick and Ryan (1987) in their findings concerning conceptual versus rote learning, although, in the Fabes et al. (1981) study, the controlling condition involved receiving monetary rewards, whereas in these other studies it involved being examined. The point, however, is that the use of controls to motivate performance on an interesting or complex activity seems to lead individuals to narrow their focus and take a shortcut to the extrinsic outcome rather than taking interest in and having a fuller engagement with the activity itself.

These findings extend as well to internally controlling states. For example, Ryan, Connell, and Plant (1990) did two experiments in which students were directed to read academic materials and were later tested for comprehension and recall. Those who approached the reading activity with a more ego-involved mental set demonstrated less comprehension and less recall than those more task-involved. Presumably, ego involvement, like other controlling contexts, interferes with deeper processing, and thus learning.

In addition, ego involvement potentiates a number of defensive and possibly performance-debilitating processes. Standage, Treasure, Hooper, and Kuczka (2007) provided one example. These researchers randomly assigned participants to ego- and task-involving conditions prior to an endurance task. Those in the ego-involving context evidenced great self-handicapping prior to performing. Bober and Grolnick (1995) assigned individuals who had previously described their own personality styles to either ego-involving or task-involving experimental conditions. They then gave individuals feedback that was "counter schematic," or discrepant from their own self-assessments. Those who were ego involved subsequently shifted in their self-evaluations, showing less self-consistency. Finally, when we get to the literature of sport, we will see a number of studies showing the relationship of ego involvement to increased aggression, cheating, and other forms of poor sportsmanship (e.g., Donahue, Miquelon, Valois, Goulet, Buist & Vallerand, 2006; Vallerand & Losier, 1994; Vansteenkiste, Mouratidis, & Lens, 2010).

Creativity

Amabile (1983) introduced what she labeled the "intrinsic motivation hypothesis of creativity," arguing that people are more creative under conditions that conduce toward intrinsic motivation than under conditions that tend to diminish intrinsic motivation. She reviewed numerous studies that supported the hypothesis, albeit with various limiting conditions that are expectable when exploring such a complex phenomenon.

Amabile and her colleagues have used a consensual-assessment method to measure the creativity of artistic projects, which means that something such as a poem or collage is considered creative to the extent that a set of judges rate it as creative. Even if the researchers or judges cannot say what makes something creative, it is considered creative if people agree that it is. In one study, college students made collages that they either did or did not expect to have evaluated (Amabile, 1979). Subsequently, the work of all participants was evaluated by artists for creativity, and the results indicated that participants who had worked with the expectation of evaluation produced collages rated as less creative than those made by participants who did not expect to be evaluated. In another study (Amabile, 1982), children made collages, with half the participants being told that the best works would be given prizes, whereas the other half was told nothing about competing for a prize. Results showed that those who engaged in this artistic activity under competitive conditions made less creative collages than those who did not compete. Similarly, studies of both children and college students doing a variety of creative tasks showed that when participants engaged in an activity specifically to get a reward, they were judged less creative than those who had not contracted for a reward (Amabile, Hennessey, & Grossman, 1986). It seems clear, then, that in general people do not produce their most creative works when they work in response to controlling contingencies.

Joussemet and Koestner (1999) engaged gymnasts in a creative task under either a no-reward or a contingent-reward condition. They assessed creativity using both Amabile's consensual technique and an assessment of the rarity of solutions offered. Results indicated that rewards led the young children in the study to generate less appropriate themes (the "easy route to an end" idea discussed in the prior chapter) and led children of all ages to produce less creative products on these target tasks.

In contrast, other studies of creativity have provided insights about how to support someone's creative ventures. For example, in a study that paralleled the study by Zuckerman, Porac, Lathin, Smith, and Deci (1978) of the positive-choice effects on intrinsic motivation, Amabile and Gitomer (1984) found that providing children choice about materials led to artistic products judged to be more creative than those done by children not given choice, even though a yoking procedure was used to ensure that the children in the no-choice condition had the same materials as the children given choice. Koestner et al. (1984) found that minimizing the use of controlling language and acknowledging children's feelings facilitated their creativity on a painting task. Clearly, the use of extrinsic controls in an attempt to promote more creative products is unlikely to produce the desired results, whereas support for autonomy through choice and noncontrolling language can facilitate creative performance.

Utman (1997) reported a meta-analysis of experiments that examined performance effects for conditions known to support intrinsic motivation versus those known to diminish it. In the meta-analysis, he contrasted the quality of performance under conditions of ego involvement, evaluation, or performance goals with performance under conditions of task involvement, nonevaluation, or learning goals. The 24 experiments in this meta-analysis included activities ranging from solving anagram and hidden-figure puzzles to playing basketball and writing poetry, with dependent measures ranging from the quality of learning and the number of puzzles solved to the creativity of artistic endeavors. Results of the meta-analysis strongly supported the prediction that task-involvement and learning-goal conditions, which are associated with intrinsic motivation, would lead to higher quality performance than ego involvement and performance-goal conditions, which are associated with controlled extrinsic motivation. In moderator analyses, it was also found that the advantage of the intrinsic motivation inductions was limited to complex tasks that require open, flexible, or creative engagement.

Collectively, these findings have great significance for creative human endeavors. Intrinsic motivation is involved in some of the most cherished human activities. Activities such as music and the arts, reading and intellectual discovery, sport, performing arts such as dance, and a host of other fulfilling pursuits are often, if not primarily, sustained by the joy of the activity itself. However, it is precisely because the *products* of such activities are valued by others that these endeavors can end up being pursued for reasons other than their intrinsic interest. Although valuing aesthetically meaningful objects or performances is itself laudable, it carries with it the risk that it will work against itself. Paradoxically, insofar as others' valuing of various qualitative aspects of an activity leads them to use extrinsic controls in an attempt to promote it, the quality is likely to suffer. The art of motivation concerns how to value and support creative performances or learning and work endeavors without using controls in an attempt to produce or enhance them, a point to which we return at various points through this book.

Some Summary Notes

CET evolved out of research on the effects of external events on intrinsic motivation. The early findings that tangible rewards tended to undermine intrinsic motivation was controversial and noteworthy because, prior to that time, the negative consequences of rewards had been largely unnoticed and rewards were widely advocated as an effective way to change behavior and socialize children. In part, the failure to notice that rewards may not always be the optimal way to promote learning, healthy development, and effective performance stemmed from the pervasive use of the passive-organism assumption in empirical psychology at that time. It is the active-organism assumption—the belief that there is an inherent growth tendency within individuals that needs to be supported—that leads people to wonder whether externally controlling behavior might sometimes have negative consequences for development and behavior change.

As the rewards research unfolded, new questions continued to emerge. Research explored other external factors, such as deadlines, evaluations, feedback, and other events, as they affected intrinsic motivation. It was found that the functional significance of events, from tangible contingencies to interpersonal communications, accounted for facilitating or undermining effects. CET was also extended to intrapersonal events—to the ways in which individuals support or pressure themselves during activities. We saw substantial evidence that individuals' own styles of self-regulation influence their intrinsic motivation, with internally controlling styles and ego involvement yielding undermining effects.

The previous two chapters have summarized just a small part of the SDT-based research addressing these questions. Later in the book we highlight research that demonstrates the great practical importance of these findings. For instance, we will see how learners' interest varies, even from day to day, with teacher autonomy support (e.g., Tsai, Kunter, Lüdtke, Trautwein, & Ryan, 2008) and how outcomes, from work performance to health, can be influenced by intrinsic motivation and its supports (e.g., Ryan & Deci, 2000c). Yet for now we leave intrinsic motivation and CET to explore a separate, and equally important concept—that of extrinsic motivation.

CHAPTER 8

Organismic Integration Theory

*Internalization and the Differentiation
of Extrinsic Motivation*

Whereas the focus of the previous two chapters was on intrinsic motivation, the current chapter is concerned with various forms of extrinsic motivation and their causes and consequences. In addressing extrinsic motivation, we present the second of SDT's mini-theories: organismic integration theory (OIT). Central to OIT are the concepts of internalization and integration, which can result in four major types of motivational regulation—external, introjected, identified, and integrated—which vary in their degree of autonomy, as well as in their specific antecedents and effects on experience and behavior. SDT hypothesizes that greater relative autonomy is associated with higher quality behavior and greater persistence. We review research supporting that hypothesis and also showing that need support facilitates internalization and integration, whereas need thwarting can inhibit or forestall internalization. We discuss the anomaly of compartmentalized identifications in which a regulation or value is internalized and yet defensively segregated from other values, goals, and needs. We also discuss self-concordance and the application of the internalization continuum to ideographic goals.

Intrinsic motivation is an important phenomenon, as it concerns a quintessential expression of the growth-oriented tendencies of the human psyche. When intrinsically motivated, individuals move autonomously toward new challenges, wider frames of experience, and increased coherence in understanding. They enact behaviors that interest them, seek stimulation, test limits, and openly assimilate what is novel.

Yet socialized life is not all fun and games. As group animals, we engage in many behaviors that may not be intrinsically motivated, including chores, work, duties, rituals, and exercising self-restraint. We often adopt such practices because socializing agents expect, promote, laud, or even compel them.

In this chapter we focus on what motivates individuals to engage in behaviors and practices that are not necessarily intrinsically interesting. In particular, we address what motivates people to engage goals or practices deemed valuable by families, groups, or societies, especially those that are not inherently enjoyable, and to refrain from (potentially enjoyable) behaviors deemed wrong or problematic. The motivation for adopting such behaviors is *extrinsic*; that is, people engage in such behaviors because of the instrumental value of the behaviors. At issue is whether people can become autonomous for such extrinsically motivated behaviors and, if they can, how socializing agents facilitate or undermine such autonomous engagement.

These are the issues addressed by *organismic integration theory* (OIT), the second mini-theory within SDT. OIT describes people's inherent tendencies toward assimilating and integrating social regulations. In addition, just as in CET, which focuses on supports or thwarts for intrinsic motivation, within OIT we examine the factors in social and interpersonal contexts that represent supports or thwarts of this integrative propensity.

The Concept of Internalization

Extrinsic motivation comes in varied types. To differentiate these types within SDT, we apply the concept of *internalization,* defined as the process of taking in values, beliefs, or behavioral regulations from external sources and transforming them into one's own (Ryan, Connell, & Deci, 1985). Internalization is the internal psychological process that corresponds to the externally observable interpersonal and cultural process of *socialization.* Through socialization, a society transmits behavioral regulations, attitudes, and values to its constituent members. Yet socialization is not truly effective if behaviors or regulations are enacted only when others monitor or enforce them. Rather, to be effective, the individuals must both assimilate and carry out the behaviors *on their own,* in the absence of immediate contingencies or surveillance. Indeed, a person who engages in culturally valued acts only when made to do so is, in a very real sense, not well socialized. Thus effective socialization requires that societal teachings be well anchored in the minds, values, and motivations of individuals and that the requisite behaviors occur independently of direct, proximal external prompts and controls. Internalization reflects the processes through which extrinsic behaviors become an established aspect of people's minds and motives.

The acquisition of extrinsic regulations and values through internalization is a critical aspect of the development of personality. Like intrinsic motivation, internalization represents a natural growth process—a process of active learning and self-extension. Indeed, internalization is a manifestation of the inherent tendency toward *integration,* for it concerns both the assimilation by the individual of ambient practices within her or his social context (i.e., homonomy) and the coordination and harmonization of relevant values and behavioral regulations within the individual (i.e., autonomy). Internalization is thus a humanizing process, for it promotes not only individual growth but also the growth and coherence of culture, as well as many of culture's aesthetic and civil expressions.

From an evolutionary standpoint as well, internalization supports the cooperation and the cohesive functioning of groups, enhancing adaptive advantage at both individual and group levels of analysis (Boehm, 2012; Ryan & Hawley, 2016). In these regards we agree with Rogoff (2003), who argued that all individuals develop as participants in cultural communities—although, as we shall further argue, each is more or less well integrated therein as a function of how cultures support that development and the psychological needs that nurture it.

Nonetheless, internalization has its darker sides, for not only can higher forms of social conduct and morality be taken in by individuals but so too can some of the less positive manifestations of our social existence. Just as humans can internalize ethical self-restraint and prosocial values, they can internalize prejudice, malevolence, and hate, although, as we shall propose, not with equal ease or integrity. Internalization can thus lead not only to greater respect and tolerance in the human community but also to more greed and selfishness, even violence (Fiske & Rai, 2015). And although internalization can lead to smoother and more effective functioning, some forms of internalization can lead to self-tyranny and internal conflict, as people attempt to live up to rigidly internalized but poorly integrated standards or values.

Consideration of the promise and perils of internalization, both for the individual and for the social world, is a complex matter, having to do with both process and content. First, there are different forms of internalization, and although some have positive correlates, the desired correlates for others are absent or negative. Furthermore, the *contents* of the regulations and values that are culturally transmitted and internalized make an important difference, with some contents more or less fitting with basic psychological needs and therefore more or less easily integrated. Here we begin by considering the different forms of internalization and their varied concomitants. The contents of the practices and regulations are dealt with especially in Chapters 11 and 24.

Internalization: All or None?

In Chapter 7, we considered the concept of *ego involvement,* depicting it as a form of internal motivation in which people pressure themselves to behave or perform up to certain standards because their feelings of worth have become dependent on their doing so. Early research by Ryan (1982) and by Plant and Ryan (1985) demonstrated that when people become ego-involved concerning their performance on an interesting activity, they tended to lose intrinsic motivation for that activity. This finding highlighted ego involvement as an internal yet *controlled* form of motivation that tends to undermine intrinsic motivation.

Ego involvement illustrates that not all internal motivations are truly volitional or characterized by autonomy. In fact, people enact many values and practices for controlled reasons. Often they are prompted by others—their families, peers, or cultural institutions—and feel pressured by guilt or fears of shame and disapproval if they do not conform or because they seek approval and inclusion. Such motives (e.g., fear of disapproval or pressure to receive positive regard) are internal to the person but are nonetheless controlling. Yet people can also embrace and enact cultural and familial values and practices wholeheartedly. The same practice that one person or cultural group might do from guilt or from pressure may be one that others might perform from a sense of value or meaning (e.g., see Ryan, Rigby, & King, 1993; Miller, Das, & Chakravarthy, 2011). Thus any conceptualization of self-motivation needs to account for this variability in the way internal motivations operate.

Such variation in the quality of endorsement or acceptance of social values is readily illustrated. Consider an adolescent boy whose parents have emphasized the importance of religious beliefs or practices. He may, especially if his parents are controlling, attend religious services compliantly, doing so to avoid feelings of guilt (e.g., Brambilla, Assor, Manzi, & Regalia, 2015). Alternatively, and under conditions of autonomy support, he may more fully accept his religion and its teachings, in which case he would not only attend services with enthusiasm but would also be more likely to actively assimilate the family's religious values and transfer these into his daily social behavior. Similarly, a girl whose parents emphasize the importance of achievement and scholarship might achieve in school mainly to gain their approval or to avoid a loss of regard that would accompany

any failure to meet their standards. Alternatively, she could achieve because she authentically appreciates the value of knowledge and learning (e.g., see Grolnick & Ryan, 1989).

Translating this into attribution terminology, when it comes to extrinsically motivated behaviors, there can be a great range in the perceived locus of causality (PLOC) with which they are undertaken. Thus, as many philosophers have suggested (see Chapter 3), one can fully endorse an activity that a society advocates or even demands of its members. Yet, just as surely, people often perform such activities resentfully or with a resigned sense of compulsion or alienation. Observations both within and between groups, organizations, and cultures reveal tremendous variability in the willingness and volition people exhibit when carrying out commitments or obligations.

It was to address this complex phenomenon of internalization that we developed OIT. The theory specifies that the more fully people internalize regulations of culturally valued extrinsically motivated activities, the more the PLOC will be internal, and the more the people will experience autonomy in carrying out the behaviors. Regulations that are less well internalized will have a more external PLOC, and thus behaviors will be more halfhearted, or dutiful, and there will be more experience of conflict. Variations in the quality of action and experience follow from these differences in relative autonomy.

OIT also proposes that the process of internalization is a natural tendency, reflective of the more general development toward organization and integration. The internalization continuum thus describes the extent to which individuals have taken in a social prescription or proscription and integrated it—that is, adopted and transformed the externally conveyed regulation into true self-regulation. Finally, this integrative process is argued to function optimally only under conditions of support for the individual's basic psychological needs. These ideas form the basis for the first propositions of OIT.

> **OIT Proposition I:** The process of organismic integration inclines humans naturally to internalize extrinsic motivations that are endorsed by significant others. However, the process of internalization can function more versus less effectively, resulting in different degrees of internalization that are the basis for regulations that differ in perceived locus of causality and thus the extent to which they are autonomous.

A Model of Internalization and Integration

We defined internalization as the process of taking in values, beliefs, or behavioral regulations from external sources and transforming them into one's own. Transformation involves actively making the internalized material one's own, which, more precisely, means assimilating the regulation or value and integrating it with the other values, behaviors, attitudes, and emotions that are themselves inherent and/or have been deeply internalized by the individual. Thus, when a regulation that was originally socially transmitted has been fully internalized, it will largely be in harmony or congruence with other aspects of one's values and personality, and enacting it will be experienced as autonomous.

Critical to the SDT view is the idea that internalization is an active process that involves not just taking in values and practices but working to integrate what is internalized. This, of course, means that internalization is not something that merely gets done to people by the social world but, rather, is something people do in relation to the social world. People actively acquire social practices; they do not just comply with them. Still, there remains the question of *why* people assimilate socially prescribed behaviors and what leads individuals to take on (or reject) particular social regulations and values. From a motivational perspective, the most meaningful answer would be formulated in terms of the basic psychological needs that people satisfy by internalizing cultural beliefs or mores. Accordingly, we postulate that internalization allows people to better fulfill their basic psychological needs.

Internalization and Need Satisfaction

Effective internalization is highly relevant to satisfying the *need for competence*. The joy children feel when modeling parents' actions in building or cooking or playing a sport is in part driven by an interest in what they are doing and a sense of challenge to master the observed behaviors and produce similar effects. In this regard, internalization paves the way for assuming roles and positions that allow people to feel efficacious, contributing to their overall sense of personal and social competence. Throughout the lifespan, internalization supports the growth of competence and adaptation. We can also expect people to gravitate toward practices and value systems within which they can feel effectance and competency and to fail to fully internalize those that are beyond their understanding or capacities. This latter point has great relevance to developmental psychology in terms of the pacing of demands and value transmissions in accordance with a child's emerging capacities and to applied practices in parenting, education, therapy, and other domains.

Yet the need for competence does not by itself explain the selective nature of internalization. People also internalize social information because it allows them to feel a sense of connectedness to others—to their families, peer groups, organizations, or society more generally. Indeed, the *need for relatedness* plays a central role in energizing internalization. As individuals internalize familial and cultural practices and values, they experience a sense of participation and belonging that satisfies needs for relatedness. It is also the case that children take interest in and model the behaviors of those to whom they do or would like to feel attached, or whose regard and connectedness they most desire. In this regard, relatedness motives also play a selective role in internalization. As we shall see, when adolescents are securely attached with parents, they are more likely to internalize their guidance and values; but those who feel unrelated and detached from parents will be more oriented toward internalizing the values of peers or extrafamilial subcultures to which they feel (or wish to feel) attached.

Finally, the idea of an internalization continuum, which conveys that a regulation can be more or less fully integrated with one's sense of self, underscores the point that, insofar as people are successful in fully internalizing a regulation, they will experience their behavior as more volitional—that is, they will be more autonomous or self-determined with respect to the associated actions. By more fully internalizing a regulation, the PLOC will shift from external to internal. Accordingly, different forms of internalization will differentially satisfy people's needs for autonomy, and in turn this will explain the maintenance, transfer, and stability of these regulatory structures, as well as the qualities of experience that accompany them.

In sum, internalization is a critically important process through which people are able to satisfy their fundamental psychological needs for relatedness, competence, and autonomy. Although important in child development, internalization is a lifespan process. It broadens as the experiences of individuals expand beyond the family and neighborhood into larger cultural communities and the adult worlds of work and society. Internalization allows them to connect with and experience meaning and coherence in the various organizations and communities within which they are embedded. Thus children more or less internalize the household rules of their parents. The student will internalize, more or less, the rules of the classroom. An employee will internalize, more or less, the values of the leadership in his or her organization. In every social setting, at every age after infancy, internalization is therefore a relevant construct. In their different life contexts, different socializing agents and authorities will supply different supports for and barriers to internalization. These facilitating and undermining effects contribute to both between- and within-person variation in motivational styles and regulations for different behaviors (Grolnick, Deci, & Ryan, 1997; Soenens & Vansteenkiste, 2010). When effective, internalization will ultimately serve both autonomous and homonomous aspects of integration, as well as the ends of both individual and collective integrity.

Types of Internalization and Regulation

To provide a framework distinguishing various types of extrinsic motivation, OIT specifies four general regulatory styles, each representing how regulations and values can be internalized in distinct ways (Deci & Ryan, 1985b; Ryan et al., 1985). These different motivations vary not only in their dynamic characteristics but also in their perceived locus of causality, with some experienced as relatively autonomous and others as more controlled. These regulatory styles can also be coexistent within a behavioral domain, and often several will be operative as motivations even within a single activity.

External Regulation

Undoubtedly the most studied type of extrinsically motivated regulation is *external regulation*. A behavior is externally regulated if it is motivated by and dependent upon external reward or punishment contingencies. The regulation of behavior through externally controlled rewards and punishments has been the principal focus of behavioral psychologists, especially operant theorists, who for decades maintained that all behavior is dependent on such external contingencies for its reliable occurrence. Within that tradition, countless studies detailed that behaviors can be made dependent on rewards (or, more precisely, on reinforcements) and also that some schedules of reinforcement will lead to longer periods of postreinforcement responding before the effect extinguishes. Yet, because of their initial assumptions, behavioral theories do not recognize internalization per se as a means of the behavior becoming independent of the external contingencies that may initially have been responsible for its occurrence.

Within OIT, external regulation is defined by the experience or perception that one is doing the behavior because of an external contingency. Therefore, the dependence of the behavior on a contingency is a function of the fact that, when externally regulated, individuals will perform the behavior only when there is an expectancy (implicit or explicit) that the contingency is in effect. Thus there is behavioral dependence on the reward or punishment contingencies: People perform the behavior because they expect a separable consequence. The problem with external regulation is not primarily ineffectiveness, because powerful rewards and punishments can control behavior, but is rather lack of maintenance, because without the expectancy in place, behavior is typically not sustained over time.

An example of external regulation is an adolescent girl whose parents threaten punishments if she is caught drinking. Although she might at times drink, her external regulation for not drinking would be manifested as her abstention when she believes there is a chance she will be caught. Thus she might drink only when her parents are away; or, if she fears their monitoring is pervasive, she might show ongoing abstention. She waits until she goes away to college. Another example is a student who helps others in his school, but only because he can receive "good citizen" points and cash prizes. When the incentive program is in place, he does good deeds, but only when he thinks he may be observed. When the program is discontinued, the desired behavior also stops, for he no longer "has a reason" to be good. It is the direct dependence of behaviors on contingencies that characterizes external regulation, and because the reason for the behavior is the contingency (or, more precisely, the outcome to which it will lead), this type of regulation is characterized in attribution terms as having an *external perceived locus of causality* (E-PLOC). In other words, the behavior is *controlled*. Even when one finds the receipt of rewards pleasant, the attribution of an E-PLOC can still have a detrimental effect on a person's sense of autonomy.

As our review of research will show, external regulation is a quite common form of motivation. External regulators can, in fact, be powerfully motivating in an immediate sense—they can compel or seduce people into action, and they offer quick tools to mobilize behavior. The issue we shall raise about them is not their potential short-term potency but, rather, the fact that they have not been internalized and that, therefore, the external regulation is often associated with poor maintenance and transfer (Deci & Ryan, 1985b; Ryan & Deci, 2008b). In addition, external regulation tends to lead people to experience these behaviors as merely instrumental (rather than representing a personal value), often leading them to accomplish the behaviors in the least effortful way, with less attention to quality. These relations among internalization, persistence over time, and quality of performance are central to motivation as addressed by OIT and have many applied implications.

Introjected Regulation

Whereas external regulation is a form of extrinsic motivation that depends on specific external contingencies, *introjection* is a process through which, to a significant degree, behavior can be freed from those external contingencies. *Introjection* is a type of internalization that involves taking in or adopting a regulation or value, yet doing so in a way that is only a partial and incomplete transformation or assimilation. Phenomenally speaking, an introject is experienced as a demanding and controlling force, albeit an internal one, acting on the self—a sense that one "should" or "must" do something or face anxiety and self-disparagement. On the positive side, compliance with internal demands, as in introjected perfectionism, can lead to certain forms of self-esteem, self-satisfaction, and feelings of pride about oneself.

If the teenager from a previous example had introjected the regulation for not drinking, she might abstain because she would feel ashamed or self-critical if she drank. She might also feel prideful and morally righteous when judging others who do not abstain. Similarly, if the boy had introjected the regulation for doing good deeds, he might be helpful to others regularly because he feels he must be good to receive general approval, and he might feel guilty or unworthy if he neglected this task.

Introjection is an *intrapersonal* form of regulation and thus has the advantage of being a bit more enduring a form of extrinsic motivation than is external regulation. The reason is that the introjected regulation is based on affective and evaluative contingencies *within* the individual rather than being dependent on the direct presence of external contingencies and monitoring. Introjection is a form of control that people enact on themselves, emphasizing internal judgments and evaluations upon which feelings of worth are conditional. The greater the introjection, the more self-esteem is also likely to be unstable, fluctuating in response to relevant outcomes and evaluations (Kernis & Paradise, 2002; Ryan & Brown, 2006).

Although introjection is based on internal, self-esteem contingencies and their affective consequences (e.g., pride vs. guilt), introjected regulation is also strongly associated with, and in part is based on, *projection*. When regulating through introjection, individuals often project their self-approval or self-disapproval onto others, imaging that these others will approve or disapprove of them conditionally as a function of the target behavior or outcome. Thus fear of shame is salient, as are concerns with approval and standing, and these avoidance and approach forms of introjected regulation are therefore inexorably intertwined and highly correlated. External others may or may not be judging an individual, but when regulating through introjection, the individual may perceive that they are.

Accordingly, the regulation of introjected behavior is powered by the contingent feelings of worth (Deci & Ryan, 1995), whether these be the imagined approval (versus disapproval) of others or the internal sense of ego inflation and pride (versus deflation and self-disparagement). Not surprisingly, as we review in Chapter 13, research shows that introjection is often derived from the actual conditional regard conveyed by significant others during development, which potentiates and solidifies this form of regulation within many individuals (e.g., Roth & Assor, 2012; Roth, Assor, Niemiec, Ryan, & Deci, 2009).

Many situational factors can catalyze introjected regulation, especially those that heighten ego involvement, self-consciousness, and critical self-evaluation. Moreover, introjection and ego involvement seem to commonly attend domains in which competition and interpersonal comparisons are salient (e.g., image, attractiveness, achievement, sports, financial success). In fact, people with harsh introjects will often be highly self-critical for failing at standards even when others would not directly disapprove of their performance, a common dynamic in introjected perfectionism (e.g., see Powers, Koestner, & Zuroff, 2007; Soenens, Luyckx, Vansteenkiste, Luyten, Duriez, & Goossens, 2008; see also Chapter 16, this book).

Introjection is thus not merely a childhood phenomenon or a phase of development; both the process of introjection and the form of controlled regulation that follows from it can persist throughout one's life. Insofar as one's significant others or cultural ingroups convey that the worth of a person depends on the display of possessions, image, achievements, or any other nonintrinsic attribute, they can be contributing to regulation by introjection, playing into people's contingent-esteem vulnerabilities. Some commentators indeed suggest that introjection and the kind of social conformity it involves may be the modal way of living for most people (e.g., Loevinger, 1976). Yet, even when people are successful in living in accordance with introjects, the resulting feelings of worth represent a kind of *false self-esteem*, because they depend on the continual display of certain characteristics or behaviors rather than being anchored in a deeply felt sense of self (Deci & Ryan, 1995). In addition, because introjected regulation is not fully integrated, it is less volitional than is autonomous regulation and requires more energy. As research will show, because one part of the person is controlling other parts, enacting introjects is frequently vitality draining or ego depleting, even when one is efficacious at meeting them (Nix, Ryan, Manly, & Deci, 1999; Ryan & Deci, 2008b).

INTERNAL CONTROL AND THE SELF

Many modern theories distinguish between external control and self-control, with self-control often conceptualized as primarily a positive strength or capacity (e.g., Bandura, 1995, 1997; Mischel & Shoda, 1995). Yet as Fujita (2011) warns: "Self-control is not . . .

necessarily and prescriptively a good thing" (p. 353). This is definitely the case within OIT, as some forms of self-control do not represent autonomy. Specifically, introjected regulations, values, and beliefs represent a form of internal motivation that is not fully self-determined, and yet can underpin effortful self-control. The PLOC is still relatively external to the self, because the person's experience is of feeling compelled to behave. Thus, although introjection is a type of internalization and phenomenally has a somewhat more internal perceived locus of causality than external regulation, it still has a controlling quality, typically related to self-evaluative pressures. Introjection is thus perhaps the most instructive instance of how internalization is by no means an all-or-nothing phenomenon. Introjected regulations are a kind of partial internalization that can results in self-control but yet not represent true self-regulation.

Our conceptualization also relates to a concept used by Kuhl and his colleagues (e.g., Kuhl & Kazén, 1994; Kuhl, 1996), namely *self-infiltration*. In self-infiltration, individuals adopt goals that someone else holds for them "as if" the goals were their own. It involves misidentifying someone else's goals as their own goals. Similarly, through introjection, an individual accepts values or regulations without fully discriminating how they fit with his or her own needs, goals, and values, without doing what Kazén, Baumann, and Kuhl (2003) called *self-compatibility checking*. Thus, when introjected, a value or regulation becomes part of the person but does not become integrated into a person's *holistic self-representation*.

The term *introjection* also appears in the writings of psychoanalytically oriented writers, particularly those within the tradition of modern ego psychology. Ego psychologists, who are focused on the ego's synthetic and integrative tendencies, have long recognized internalization as a process of assimilating outer regulations and models, and indeed there is a long history of different internalization terms, from Freud through modern times (see Wallis & Poulton, 2001). Most notably, the earlier work of ego psychologists Schafer (1968) and Meissner (1981) distinguished between introjection and identification, with the latter involving more integration of regulations to the self or ego. Much of their phenomenological descriptions overlap with ours, recognizing that introjected regulations can have the feel of an independent organization within the psyche that pressures or controls the self. Yet, because SDT traces the development and etiology of introjects to the dynamic interplay between the basic psychological needs for autonomy and relatedness rather than the classical drive-related formulations of ego psychology, we do not equate our technical use of these terms with theirs.

Regulation through Identification

Identification is a type of internalization that falls further along the internalization continuum of relative autonomy, located between introjected and integrated regulation. Identifications are defined by a conscious endorsement of values and regulations. Thus people who have truly identified with the value and importance of a behavior will say they see it as something personally important for themselves. Relative to introjects, therefore, identifications are characterized by the experience of greater autonomy and have a more internal perceived locus of causality (I-PLOC).

To follow through with our examples, if the girl identified with the importance of not drinking, she would abstain willingly, whether or not she was being monitored, and likely see it as of value for her health or safety. If the boy identified with the goal of helping others because he endorsed its importance for a better society, he would then help others regularly and do so willingly because of its perceived value, whether or not there were prizes being given for it. Having understood and personally accepted the value of the acts (whether inhibitions or commissions), individuals are able to feel more volitional in carrying them out.

It is also worth noting again that our theory of internalization is formulated in terms of specific values, behaviors, and regulations. Our use of the concept of identification differs from its use by Kelman (1958), as well as some psychoanalytic usages (e.g., Schafer, 1968). Thus, in outlining the processes of attitude change, Kelman explained how people can change their attitudes by identifying with particular individuals and thereby accepting the attitudes of those people. The dynamic element in Kelman's characterization, therefore, is the person's relation to the crucial other. However, in OIT, the dynamic element is the person's relation to the value and behavior and the congruence of the valued behavior with respect to his or her own needs, goals, and values. Others playing a role in influencing congruence and valuing processes within SDT are among a variety of factors affecting internalization.

Regulation through identification is more autonomous or volitional than external or introjected regulation. In acting out of identified regulations, people are not simply complying with an external or introjected demand but are instead acting out of a belief in the personal importance or perceived value of the activity. Still, identification does not necessarily imply that the person has engaged in a full self-compatibility check (Kazén et al., 2003) or achieved full integration. Through identification, people accept the importance of an action, but they may not have necessarily examined the relation of that action to other aspects of their identity. It is the relation between a new identification and other internalized values and goals that is the crucial issue in moving beyond identification to a fuller internalization. Indeed, as we subsequently discuss, the phenomenon of *compartmentalization* involves particular identifications remaining more or less actively and defensively unintegrated.

Identification, in relation to introjection, involves the experience of greater volition. There is a conscious endorsement of one's acts as worthwhile and therefore a relative lack of conflict and resistance to behaving. Accordingly, regulation through identification has clear functional advantages over introjected regulation in terms of its stability, persistence, energy demands, and affective accompaniments.

Integration and Self-Determination

Integrated regulation represents the fullest type of internalization and is the basis for the most autonomous form of extrinsic motivation. Achieving the integration of an identification or an introject is an active and transformational process and typically requires self-reflection and reciprocal assimilation. Integrated regulation entails that one bring a value or regulation into congruence with the other aspects of one's self—with one's basic psychological needs and with one's other identifications. Thus it may involve modification of the value and/or accommodations of other values or attitudes one has previously held. When achieved, one can experience a more wholehearted endorsement of the behavior or value and an absence of conflict with other abiding identifications. Integrated internalizations are thus experienced as fully authentic (Ryan & Deci, 2004a, 2006).

For integration to occur, an identification will have passed Kazén et al.'s (2003) self-compatibility check, so to speak, and as such will be holistically embraced. In SDT terms the identification will be reflectively and nondefensively endorsed. Any elements that are not compatible, that cannot be brought into congruence with other aspects of one's self, would thus not have been integrated—a point to which we return later. Accordingly, integration is a process through which, often by being mindful and using higher-order reflection, people are able to bring an externally imposed, value-based action into the realm of fully volitional activity. The result of integration is a highly stable and mature form of self-regulation that allows for the flexible guidance of one's action and represents a fully autonomous form of extrinsic motivation.

The more fully integrated a value or goal is, the more the person is effective in self-regulation. This was exemplified in a "dual process" experiment by Legault, Green-Demers, Grant, and Chung (2007), in which they assessed, using the SDT taxonomy of motives, people's relative internalization of the motivation to regulate expressions of prejudice. They then had participants complete both explicit (i.e., self-report) and implicit (i.e., Implicit Association Test [IAT]) measures of prejudice. Results demonstrated that those with more highly autonomous motivation to regulate prejudice exhibited not only lower explicit prejudice but also lower prejudice on implicit assessments. This indicated that greater integration of this extrinsic motivation supported greater congruence in the regulation of action, affecting both explicit and implicit processes.

Although the psychological and behavioral manifestations and effects of more integrated motivation are well documented, the biological underpinnings of more integrative processing are just beginning to be explored. Ryan, Kuhl and Deci (1997) argued early on, for example, that integration depends upon access to self-related information and values and thus, in situations of inner conflict, would likely involve being able to access right medial prefrontal cortical (MPFC) areas, in which such self-knowledge processing occurs (i.e., self-compatibility checking). More recently, Di Domenico, Fournier, Ayaz, and Ruocco (2013), using functional near-infrared spectroscopy (fNIRS), demonstrated that people with higher basic need satisfaction were more likely to show MPFC activation when facing difficult preference decisions. In a subsequent study, Di Domenico, Le, Liu, Ayaz, and Fournier (2016), this time using event-related potential (ERP) measures, found that those with higher need satisfaction also showed larger conflict negativity (CN) amplitudes when making conflict-ridden decisions. They also provided further evidence that this was associated with anterior cingulate cortex (ACC) activation, indicating decisional conflict. It seems that conflict detection in those with high need satisfaction adaptively signals the need for the refinement of existing self-knowledge structures in the service of more efficient, self-congruent decision making. Obviously, integrative decision making entails the assembly and coordination of multiple neural structures and functions, involving access to both self-knowledge and conflict monitoring, and mechanistic studies such as these are suggestive of how greater need supports can result in more integrated behavioral and attitudinal outputs (see also Kuhl, Quirin, & Koole, 2015).

Internalization and Need Satisfaction

We suggested earlier that internalization, as a manifestation of organismic integration, is a natural process that operates in the service of one's basic psychological needs for relatedness, competence, and autonomy. Having now considered the various forms of internalization, one can see that internalization in all its forms allows people to preserve their relatedness to groups and, to a significant extent, become socially competent. Whether introjected or integrated with respect to a group-endorsed value, individuals will typically carry out the actions without external prompting and will thus be more likely to gain the group's acceptance and approval. By acting in accordance with the socially sanctioned rules or values, the individual will likely feel more personally and socially efficacious. Yet it is only through identifying with and then integrating a regulation that people can also attain a state of personal autonomy. It is through the full operation of integration that people can satisfy their needs for both autonomy and relatedness and thus experience the two manifestations of healthy development described by Angyal (1965) as homonomy (integration with their groups) and autonomy (integration within themselves).

We further argue, however, that although people can sometimes experience greater belonging and competence through introjecting a regulation, the relatedness and competence they experience through internalization would be fuller if they identified with or integrated the regulation. With introjection, the conflict and underlying resentment that accompany controlled behavior (e.g., Assor, Roth, & Deci, 2004) will not allow them to relate to others as fully and openly as when they are more integrated, and the anxiety that accompanies introjection can, as we will see, interfere with the person's effectiveness when performing the relevant behaviors.

Amotivation

Outside the confines of the continuum of extrinsic motivation is the separate but important category of of regulation called *amotivation*. Amotivation describes a state in which one either is not motivated to behave, or one behaves in a way that is not mediated by intentionality. According to the cognitive tradition (e.g., Heider, 1958), people are motivated only to the extent that their actions are intended. But when an individual finds no value, rewards, or meaning in an act, he or she will likely have no intention of performing it; he or she will be amotivated.

All types motivation, both extrinsic and intrinsic motivation, involve the intention to behave, even those that are not autonomous motivations. Thus the demarcation between amotivation and motivation lies in the issue of intention. Motivated behaviors are consciously or nonconsciously intentional. This is a distinction that is central to all empirical cognitive theories of motivation, most of which do not go further than to differentiate amotivation from intentional motivation (e.g., Bandura, 1996; Heider, 1958; Vroom, 1964). Heider, for example, used the distinction between impersonal and personal causation to distinguish between nonmotivation and motivation, proposing that intention was the essential ingredient for an action to be personally caused. Bandura (1977), Seligman (1975), and others in the social-cognitive tradition have distinguished between motivation based in perceived control and efficacy from uncontrollability and helplessness. These other theories do not distinguish between SDT's four types of extrinsic motivation, or even between controlled and autonomous motivation, nor do they explicitly or meaningfully recognize the important energizing influence of intrinsic motivation.

Just as motivational types are differentiated within SDT, amotivation is also a differentiated concept because it is seen as potentially resulting from two central sources. The first and most salient form of amotivation is that which results from a lack of perceived competence. This lack of perceived competence in turn can lead to what Rotter (1954) described as an *external locus of control* (not to be confused with our construct of external perceived locus of causality, or E-PLOC). This type of amotivation, with its impersonal causality and an external locus of control, has two forms (Pelletier, Dion, Tuson, & Green-Demers, 1999): a perceived behavior-outcome independence (i.e., believing that acting will not yield a desired outcome) and/or a feeling of incompetence in regard to enacting the requisite behavior (i.e., believing that one cannot perform adequately). These are also the two sources of amotivation recognized within Bandura's (1996) social-cognitive theory. Considerable research has shown that the first type of amotivation, the belief that a behavior will not lead reliably to desired outcomes, will leave people without motivation to behave (e.g., Skinner, 1995). As Abramson, Seligman, and Teasdale (1978) described it, they will learn to be universally helpless. Second, research has also shown that if a behavior and desired outcomes were reliably linked but people felt incompetent to perform the instrumental behavior, they would be unmotivated or personally helpless (Abramson et al., 1978; Bandura, 1996). Here it is a lack of perceived personal competence that undermines motivation.

There is yet a second source of amotivation uniquely noted within SDT that is less about issues of competence than autonomy. It involves people perceiving a lack of value or interest in a behavior. This type of amotivation thus stems not from lack of efficacy or perceived contingency but, rather, from indifference about the activity or its relevant outcomes; one does not care to act. At times, this latter type of amotivation will be autonomous (e.g., Vansteenkiste, Lens, De Witte, De Witte, & Deci, 2004), as when people reflectively have neither intrinsic interest in a behavior nor a desire for the outcomes it might yield, so they choose not to do it (Ryan & Deci, 2006). Yet it can also have other sources, such as nonexposure to the potential value of acting.

Amotivation thus encompasses the state of nonintentionality represented in both of these cases—perceived inability to attain an outcome and absence of interest or utility. Yet these two types of amotivation can have quite different affective consequences, because in the latter case the person can still experience a sense of control and, sometimes even autonomy, in not acting. For example, Vansteenkiste, Lens, et al. (2004) measured both autonomous and controlled reasons for unemployed persons not searching for a job (being amotivated). Results of two studies indicated that autonomous reasons for not searching were (not surprisingly) negatively related to commitment to having a job and to expectations about finding a job. Yet they were positively associated with more pleasant job search experiences and greater life satisfaction. In contrast, although controlled motivation to not search was also negatively related to expecting to find a job, it was not predictive of life satisfaction. Thus understanding people's reasons for being amotivated helps further distinguish the effects of their absence of intentions to act. People's amotivation, that is, is not always a function of helplessness or lack of efficacy, and indeed it can reflect a self-endorsed absence of motivation to act. One can thus be amotivated for a behavior such as whimsically harming others, which rather than being problematic might be indicative of a healthy and integrated set of prosocial values.

The Continuum of Relative Autonomy

As we have characterized these different forms of regulation (which tend to co-occur to different degrees in most complex behaviors), we have also implicitly organized them along a continuum of autonomous experience and integrity. The second formal proposition of OIT makes this assumption explicit (and testable) by specifying degrees of internalization of extrinsic motivation and the different types of regulation associated with this process.

> *OIT Proposition II:* Internalization of extrinsic motivation can be described in terms of a continuum that spans from relatively heteronomous or controlled regulation to relatively autonomous self-regulation. *External regulation* describes extrinsic motivation that remains dependent on external controls; *introjected regulation* describes extrinsic motivation that is based on internal controls involving affective and self-esteem contingencies; *regulation through identification* describes extrinsic

motivation that has been accepted as personally valued and important; and *integrated regulation* describes extrinsic motivation that is fully self-endorsed and has been well assimilated with other identifications, values, and needs. Regulations that lie further along this continuum from external toward integrated are more fully internalized, and the resulting behaviors are more autonomous.

The varied forms of behavioral regulation as they fall along the continuum of relative autonomy are depicted schematically in Figure 8.1. The middle section of the figure presents the major forms of extrinsically motivated behavior. External regulation, which requires no significant internalization, depends on specific external contingencies. The process of introjection, which entails a partial internalization, represents an internally controlling regulation. The process of identification represents yet a fuller type of internalization, and thus results in more autonomous self-regulation. Finally, integration is the most autonomous or self-determined form of extrinsic motivation. Although we specify that these various forms of regulation differ in their relative autonomy, it is important to note that each of these regulatory types nonetheless also has its own specific sources, qualities, and phenomenology; thus each differentially affects experience, performance and well-being.

Assessment of an Autonomy Continuum

The specification of this continuum in Proposition II has many empirical ramifications. Specifically, it suggests that assessments of motives associated with the forms of regulation will fall systematically along a continuum of autonomy, a result that, although phenomenologically clear, is also empirically testable (e.g., see Hagger, Chatzisarantis, Hein, Pihu, Soos, Karsai, 2007; Lonsdale, Hodge, Hargreaves & Ng, 2014; Ryan & Connell, 1989; Vallerand, 1997).

Ryan and Connell (1989) developed an early psychometric approach to assessing regulatory styles and indexing their relative autonomy. The initial instrument assessed elementary school children's external, introjected, and identified regulatory styles for doing schoolwork, as well as their intrinsic motivation. A second one assessed regulations underlying prosocial behaviors. The format of this and subsequent *self-regulation questionnaires* (SRQs) involved asking why individuals do a particular behavior or class of behaviors—for example, "Why do you do your homework?"—and then providing a set of reasons that were preselected to reflect different types of regulation. For example, "Because I want to get a reward from my teacher," or "So my parents won't yell at me" would be considered external regulations; "Because I would feel like a bad person if I didn't," or "So I will feel like others accept me" would be introjected; and "Because it feels personally important to me to make progress in school" or "So I won't fall behind in reaching my personal goals" would be identified reasons. Intrinsic motivation is reflected in reasons such as "Because I find it interesting and fun to study." In this research, integrated regulation was not assessed because it is a mature type of regulation that was not expected to be relevant to the children being studied, nor easily assessed through self-report.

Ryan and Connell (1989) confirmed that the external, introjected, identified, and intrinsic subscales formed a *quasi-simplex* pattern, meaning that those theorized to be closer together along the continuum were more highly correlated than those theorized to be more distant (Guttman, 1954). Table 8.1 presents a hypothetical simplex pattern. Such a pattern is consistent with the idea that the different regulatory styles are systematically

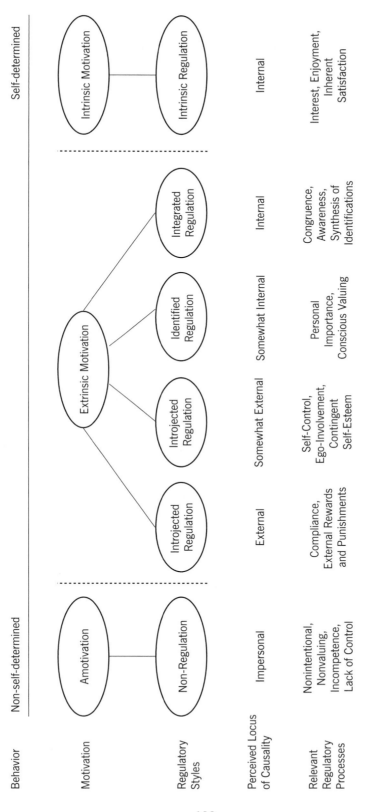

FIGURE 8.1. The Organismic Integration Theory (OIT) taxonomy of regulatory styles. Adapted from Ryan & Deci (2000c). Copyright 2000 by the American Psychological Association. Adapted by permission.

193

TABLE 8.1. Correlations among the Types of Motivations Illustrating a Simplex Pattern

	Intrinsic	Integrated	Identified	Introjected	External
Intrinsic					
Integrated	.46				
Identified	.34	.48			
Introjected	.16	.25	.34		
External	−.06	.01	.11	.40	
Amotivation	−.31	−.17	−.01	.07	.27

ordered along an underlying dimension, which we suggest is the continuum of relative autonomy. These investigators also found a similar pattern of ordered correlations in the prosocial domain. Similarly, in a study with college students using a different set of items that included amotivation and integrated regulation, Vallerand and Bissonnette (1992) found that their six subscales were ordered in accordance with the simplex pattern, thus further confirming that there is an underlying autonomy continuum. Yamauchi and Tanaka (1998) designed items for Japanese elementary students to reflect the variables of external, introjected, identified, and intrinsic motives for schoolwork. They, too, found a quasi-simplex pattern and corresponding validity results. In fact, many dozens of studies that we review have used this approach to assessing motivation in various domains and have found evidence of quasi-simplex or simplex patterns, supporting the idea that these varied forms of regulation differ along an underlying continuum of autonomy.

Other techniques have been used to explore the hypothetical ordering of OIT's taxonomy along a continuum of autonomy. One is *small space analysis,* a derivative of multidimensional scaling (MDS), which has been used to show the underlying continuum of autonomy and the relative placements of external, introjected, identified, and intrinsic regulations along it (e.g., see Roth, Assor, Kanat-Maymon, & Kaplan, 2006). Another article claimed to find evidence against an underlying autonomy continuum (Chemolli & Gagné, 2014). Yet the data they presented actually supported (in our view) the hypothesized simplex pattern of subscale relations. We also suggest that the statistical approach they applied (Rasch modeling) could not appropriately model SDT's assumption that regulatory styles are each distinct types of motivation that at the same time systematically differ in relative autonomy. Subsequent papers have thus further tested the continuum of autonomy idea by utilizing a bifactor-ESEM framework (e.g., Howard, Gagné, Morin, Wang, & Forest, 2016; Litalien, Morin, Gagné, Vallerand, Losier, & Ryan, 2016). These bifactor-ESEM models identify what has been interpreted as a "global self-determination score" on which the various SDT variables cross-load in the theoretically predicted manner, with autonomous forms of motivation loading more highly, and controlled forms more weakly. These loadings are thus consistent with a continuum of autonomy. Bifactor models also yield a set of specific factors presumably reflecting the unique variances of each subscale controlling for global autonomy, with most of the specific variances lying in controlled forms of motivation. The construct validities of these new scores are just beginning to be examined. Finally, researchers using samples from the United States and Russia, and techniques such as multidimensional scaling, factor analyses, and simplex/circumplex modeling, reported robust evidence for the underlying continuum of autonomy (see Sheldon, Osin, Gordeeva, Suchkov, & Sychev, 2016).

Thus, it seems that across methods of analysis, and across most behaviors, periods of development, domains of activity, and cultural contexts, research has shown that the varied types of motivations identified within OIT are ordered along a continuum of autonomy, even as they each have their own unique attributes. These different types of extrinsic motives clearly vary in the attributes of both how autonomous and how controlled they are. Accordingly, differences in their relative strengths will bear on the quality of a person's behavior in any domain or specific activity.

Because SDT expects multiple motives to be typically in play in any given action, these forms of regulation can also be considered in terms of their concurrent influences on the quality and consequences of any given action (Ryan & Connell, 1989). Indeed, the theory suggests that various forms of dynamic scoring and profile analyses are highly relevant to SDT research.

Predictive Indexes and Profiles

Each type of motivation described within OIT has, as we have discussed, different antecedents, distinct qualities, and unique phenomenological features. Thus a first order interest in SDT research is investigating how each regulation predicts outcomes across individuals. In addition, within variable-centered research, regression analyses and structural models help identify the sources of variance influencing outcomes positively and negatively. Yet at an individual level, predicting optimal motivation provides a different challenge. Because people typically have multiple motivations when behaving, in order to predict overall quality of motivation, researchers have often looked to various combinations of subscale scores.

One such approach used in many studies is to calculate the individuals' *relative autonomy index* (RAI) with respect to a target behavior or domain of action (e.g., Grolnick & Ryan, 1987). In reality the RAI should be labeled *a relative autonomy versus control index* because it algebraically combines the subscale scores of the regulatory styles with those reflecting autonomy weighted positively, those reflecting control weighted negatively, and those reflecting more of the quality being given larger weights. For example, applied to Ryan and Connell's (1989) SRQ-A, the external subscale would be weighted −2, the introjected subscale −1, the identified subscale +1, and the intrinsic subscale +2. Researchers have sometimes used different numbers of subscales and/or different weighting procedures depending on the self-regulation measures they used (e.g., Pelletier, Rocchi, Vallerand, Deci, & Ryan, 2013). This way of combining and weighting scores essentially reflects an *hypothesis* about higher quality of motivation as reflecting *both* a greater influence of autonomous motivations and lesser influence of controlled forms of regualtion. This index has accordingly often been very predictive of outcomes, from behavioral persistence (e.g., Pelletier, Fortier, Vallerand, & Brière, 2001) to customer loyalty (e.g., Doshi & McGregor, 2015). Yet despite their predictive value, RAIs raise the psychometric issues associated with weighted contrast scores, and they can also obscure specific profile configurations of importance within a domain or activity.

Another related approach has been to calculate a contrast between autonomous and controlled subscales, based on the findings that the continuum can be modeled by two overarching factors (e.g., see Brunet, Gunnell, Gaudreau, & Sabiston, 2015, for a dichotomous modeling approach). Contrasts between autonomous and controlled subscales, like the RAI, reflect the idea that the highest quality of motivation is most often represented by high autonomous and low controlled forms of regulation. These simpler contrasts have also been very predictive of motivational outcomes.

Sill another approach to OIT research is cluster analysis (e.g., Ntoumanis, 2002), or more recently *latent profile analyses* (LPA). LPA attempts to identify relatively homogeneous subgroups, called latent profiles, which differ from one another in their configuration of motivation types (Morin, Arens, & Marsh, 2016). Illustrating this in OIT research, Wang, Morin, Ryan, and Liu (2016) recently compared LPA solutions using the four motivation types (intrinsic motivation, identification, introjection, and external regulation) versus the two higher-order dimensions (autonomous and controlled motivation) in relation to perception of autonomy-support climate, perceived competence, enjoyment, and intention to be physically active. The results showed that profiling using the four motivation types provides more differentiated and meaningful description of PLOC, compared to profiling using two higher-order factors. The findings also supported the SDT continuum hypothesis of human motivation, in that profiles tended to reflect adjacent forms of motivation consistent with a simplex view. Most important, the derived profiles differed significantly from each other in terms of autonomy-support, perceived competence, enjoyment, and intention to be physically active.

Clearly the OIT taxonomy of motives, and its specification of both the unique qualities of these regulations and their ordered relations along a continuum of autonomy, has provided rich material for modeling motivational dynamics within and across activities and domains. Which modeling approach is used depends on what questions are being asked, and we expect this to be an area for exciting breakthroughs within the next several years, in both variable-centered and person-centered types of research.

Beyond progress in statistical modeling, however, it warrants noting that SDT-based measures of internalization have proliferated in the literature, and despite variability in content and structure, have generally been highly predictive and shown extensive validity. Yet many precede some refinements in SDT (e.g., distinctions between goal contents and regulations; approach and avoidance differentiations; psychometric advances) that would bear on item content. In our view the psychometric infrastructure of SDT, which has been an important bridge between theory and observations in both experimental and field settings, is in some domains in need of a bit of repair. Yet in saying this we suggest that such psychometric repair work is not simply a boring technical pursuit, but rather, as Loevinger (1959) classically emphasized, a bootstrap for psychological theory, entailing ever-refined attempts to represent the constructs at which theory aims and assess the validity of SDT's use of them in a multi-method framework.

Intrinsic Motivation, Extrinsic Motivation, and Autonomy

Infants initially express autonomy through intrinsically motivated engagement and mastery, but gradually, as they develop into toddlerhood, childhood, and adulthood, less of their behavior is intrinsically motivated and more of the autonomy they experience is displayed through internalized regulation of behaviors. Harter (1981) reported, for example, that over the years from third to eighth grades, children exhibit progressively less intrinsic motivation in schools, with decreasing scores on curiosity, preference for challenge, and independent mastery attempts. Since then, a number of studies have similarly pointed to mean-level changes away from intrinsic motivation and toward extrinsic motivation across the school years (e.g., Otis, Grouzet, & Pelletier, 2005). Based on the research reported in Chapters 6 and 7, we can speculate that the loss of intrinsic motivation is due in part to the fact that parents, teachers, and other significant adults use controlling strategies such as rewards, deadlines, and evaluations to motivate school behaviors—even for behaviors that could be intrinsically motivated. Whether or not they do so with the intent to control, these motivators are likely to have a negative effect on the children's intrinsic motivation.

Yet perhaps more importantly, the developmental challenges that children face involve accommodating to the customs, values, and mores of the social world. In undertaking this accommodation, their attention is increasingly shifted away from exploration and play—away from purely intrinsically motivated activity—and oriented toward social demands and expectations. Corresponding to this shift is a change in caregiving. In early development, when play and discovery have a crucial role in development of basic competencies, caregivers typically provide a protective sphere that allows children room to manipulate and explore. Yet as children age, parents and teachers spend more of their time providing structures and prompting children to internalize valued behaviors and practices that are not intrinsically motivated. Examples extend from the earliest hygiene training through prescriptions concerning social amenities and assumption of responsibilities for chores and schoolwork. Indeed, as Chandler and Connell (1987) showed in their cross-sectional research, as children get older they evidence increasingly internalized motivations for many behaviors that are not intrinsically motivated, such as hygiene or chores.

Across the lifespan, internalization continues to represent an important basis of action, and, reciprocally, intrinsically motivated activities grow proportionally less predominant as people age and move across the stages of adulthood. Adulthood brings with it more duties, responsibilities, and social obligations that, although not always fun and enjoyable as activities, are nonetheless increasingly salient and ideally capable of being internalized and integrated. As we shall see, not all socially transmitted responsibilities or values are equally capable of being integrated.

Intrinsic Motivation and Internalized Regulation

In Chapters 5 through 7 we focused on the concept of intrinsic motivation, pointing out that intrinsically motivated behavior is the prototype of autonomous or self-determined activity and invariantly has an I-PLOC. In this chapter, we have outlined the processes through which extrinsic motivation varies in terms of its PLOC and degree of self-determination. Thus, we see that both intrinsic motivation and integrated regulation (i.e., integrated extrinsic motivation) represent highly autonomous or self-determined types of behavior.

It is nonetheless important to recognize that when extrinsic motivation is integrated, it is still *not* typically transformed into intrinsic motivation because it retains its instrumental nature. In other words, integrated regulation involves doing activities because they are *important for* and *congruent with* one's goals or values, whereas intrinsic motivation involves doing activities because the activities themselves are inherently *interesting and enjoyable*. This is an important point theoretically because it highlights the different processes that underlie intrinsic motivation and integrated regulation. At the same time, for purposes of prediction in most settings, two points are salient. First, it is typically the degree to which an action is experienced as autonomous that functionally matters most; and, second, both intrinsic and integrated forms of regulation are facilitated by supports for the three basic psychological needs.

Intrinsic motivation appears at the right end of the relative autonomy continuum in Figure 8.1, indicating that it is a prototypically autonomous type of motivation. However, it is separated from integrated regulation not to convey greater value or greater autonomy but to indicate that it is a different type of motivation. Integrated regulation is still a type of extrinsic motivation, albeit a highly autonomous type; but it does share qualities of flexibility and volition with intrinsic motivation.

Another important difference concerns time perspective. With intrinsically motivated activity, people are experiencing the rewards of interest and satisfaction as they engage in the activity itself. Their aim is the enjoyment inherent in the activity, so the future typically plays little role in their reflection about task engagement. As White (1959) emphasized, although intrinsically motivated activity is crucial for developing competence, competence enhancement is *not* typically the proximal aim of such activity. Rather, the "aim" is the spontaneous satisfaction experienced while doing the activity. Thus the focus is on present experience rather than future goals, and it is a clearly adaptive aspect of human growth tendencies that people find interest and enjoyment in activities and interactions that ultimately promote effectance.

With internalized regulation, however, the focus is more on future goals or outcomes, for a defining element of extrinsic motivation is its instrumental nature, regardless of how autonomous one has become with respect to it. In a sense, then, to feel fully volitional with respect to an activity that is not providing intrinsic satisfaction, the individual must bring the future into the present so that he or she will experience not only the satisfaction of being self-regulating but also the satisfaction of making progress toward an important future goal. Consider, for example, a woman who would enjoy nothing more than tending her garden, but instead spends her time indoors at her computer. In finding the energy to engage in her work at the computer volitionally, she might well focus, even if only in passing, on her reasons for working: its utility for her long-term goals. Being mindful of her purpose provides a rationale that supports her identified regulation of an activity that may not be as inherently interesting to her in that moment as gardening.

Yet another important difference between intrinsic and internalized regulation concerns the fact that intrinsically motivated activities are typically spontaneous, representing what people are interested in doing at that time, whereas extrinsically motivated activities are often initially prompted by external conditions or authorities. This may require a higher-order reflection in which people view their instrumental actions, even those imposed from the outside, in terms of their values, goals, and purposes rather than in terms of the authority or imposition. Through such reflection they can disengage from the power struggle that is implicit in both external and introjected regulation, instead focusing on the meaning of the activity and its value or utility.

Although process research on how reflection conduces to more autonomous regulation is rare, Davis, Kelly, Kim, Tang and Hicks (2016) provided some illustrative and novel research. Coming primarily from a meaning-in-life perspective, they suggested that higher level reflections on a goal should foster more sense of meaning and purpose, as well as more integrated motivation for engaging in goal-relevant behaviors. In two experiments, they manipulated high-level versus low-level construal of an academic goal. Following this construal task, they assessed the perceived meaningfulness and the relative autonomy (self-concordance) of the person's motivation to pursue the goal. High-level construal was found to promote both a greater sense of meaning and goal autonomy, a pattern that was significant in both experiments. These authors suggested that the findings supported the idea that reflecting on "why" one pursues a goal can enhance more congruent, autonomous functioning.

The Internalization Continuum and Psychological Development

Although we have proposed that the forms of extrinsic motivation can be ordered along a continuum of relative autonomy, we do not suggest, or wish to imply, that this is a *developmental* continuum. In other words, it is not necessary for persons to progress through each stage of internalization for each behavior in order for that regulation to become integrated. Indeed, once children have developed the necessary cognitive capacities for self-regulation, they can internalize new behavioral regulations at any point along this continuum, depending upon the interpersonal context within which the regulation is prompted and upon their prior experiences with internalization (Deci & Ryan, 1991; Ryan, 1995). Furthermore, unlike structural stage theories such as psychosexual development (Freud, 1920), moral development (Kohlberg, 1969), cognitive development (Piaget, 1952), or ego development (Loevinger & Blasi, 1991), we are not suggesting that there are particular ages or progressions in which, for example, introjection or identification represent children's general stage of development. Rather, we focus on the degree of internalization of a particular regulation and its underlying value at a particular time, and we assume substantial within-person variation in regulatory styles within and across developmental epochs.

There are, nonetheless, some interesting developmental issues still to be addressed with respect to the different types of internalization. As we noted, Chandler and Connell (1987) found in their study of 5- to 13-year-old children that the regulation of "disliked activities" tended to become increasingly less external and more internalized over that age span. Yet the development of specific capacities that allow for introjection, identification, and integration to occur have not been carefully examined with respect to individual behaviors. There are clearly behaviors that socializing parents, teachers, and other authorities sometimes demand of children that, given their developmental capacities, they may not be ready to identify with or authentically value. Therefore, such demands can at best be introjected. For example, one might prompt a child of 16 months to remain quiet and still during adult conversations. The child may be able to comply with the request but not yet be able to identify with, or comprehend, the value of doing so.

The more general point is that, although some behavioral acquisitions may begin with external regulations and then proceed through introjection toward identification and integration, it is nonetheless possible for people to immediately introject or identify with the importance of new behaviors. For example, when people learn for the first time that wearing safety belts in automobiles is mandatory, some may immediately see the value in the behavior and quickly identify with and even integrate its regulation—they then "buckle up" reliably and volitionally. Others, however, may initially view the law as an infringement on their freedom, so they might reach for the belt only when a police car is closing in on them (external regulation) or when they think someone might see them *sans* belt and be disapproving (introjection). Yet toddlers cannot be expected to either understand the value of the law or to feel volitional about being buckled in. They cannot reflectively identify with the regulation, so parents must take responsibility for their safety and make the decision for them to wear seat belts. Understanding the reasons that would allow one to autonomously internalize this behavioral regulation thus requires a certain level of cognitive maturation.

Further, transitions between styles of regulation for a particular behavior can proceed out of sequence. A man who has recently begun to exercise might move quickly from external regulation (his doctor told him he had to do it) to identification (he grasps its personal importance) as he starts to feel greater vitality after exercising. There can also be *regressive transitions,* as, for example, when a controlling teacher turns a student who had previously developed a relatively strong identification with studying into an externally regulated learner by placing too much emphasis on evaluations, rewards, and performance. In fact, a study of fourth- through sixth-grade students did show that when students entered classrooms of controlling teachers, the students in those classrooms became less autonomous in the regulation of their schoolwork within 2 months (Deci, Schwartz, Sheinman, & Ryan, 1981). Similarly, a patient in psychotherapy may openly explore an introject or an identification, soon find in it little personal value, and thus become amotivated to enact it (Ryan & Deci, 2008b). In short, one's motivation can move up or down the continuum of autonomy as a function of both internal and contextual factors.

Internalization and Compartmentalization

The concept of a relative autonomy continuum was introduced as a basis for differentiating forms of extrinsic motivation and placing them into theoretical relation to each other and to amotivation and intrinsic motivation. A central idea is that the more fully regulations are brought into coherence and congruence with each other and with basic needs, the more autonomous the person will be in executing the corresponding behaviors.

Introjection is typically characterized by regulations that are rigid and fragmented. People hold internal standards and demands, and they act in accordance with those demands. It is not unusual for people to hold inconsistent, even conflicting, introjects and perhaps not even be aware of the inconsistencies. When acting from one introject, they may focus only on its demands and not bring any reflective capacity to bear on the relations of this introject to other introjects or identifications.

When people identify with a behavior and its value, however, the regulation is typically more flexible and is at least consciously endorsed by the self. People act with a sense of volition, and they are more likely to bring reflective capacity to an examination of the relations among different identifications, for that is the basis through which an identification will become more integrated.

A troubling issue, however, one that we have witnessed in many clinical contexts, is that in which a strong identification is *compartmentalized* from other identifications and from other perceptions, attitudes, needs, and values. Although more autonomous regulatory styles are generally more open and flexible relative to more controlled regulations, certain introjects may be very strong—strong enough that they are understood by the actor to be identifications. However, their rigidity betrays an underlying controlled process. Thus, when a person strongly but rigidly identifies with a regulation or value and is defensive concerning it, we refer to this psychological dynamic as a *closed* or *compartmentalized identification.* It involves people identifying with self-alien values and regulations and maintaining the identification by isolating it from other identifications, sensibilities, and perceptions while remaining closed to information or feedback concerning the identification and its relation to others.

Compartmentalized Identifications

The rather subtle distinction between open identifications, which are not defensively held, and closed identifications, which are consciously held and vigorously defended, is important for addressing some anomalies represented by the darker side of human behavior (Ryan & Deci, 2000a; Chapter 24, this volume). Although the evidence for this is still largely theoretical and anecdotal, the concepts and phenomena are compelling and add theoretical complexity to an account of the issues surrounding internalization.

Organismic integration theory in particular, and SDT more generally, are built upon the assumption that humans have an active, growth-oriented nature that is manifested through development toward greater autonomy and homonomy. In other words, our approach assumes that individuals are inclined to develop toward greater organization or integration of their inner values, behaviors, emotions, experiences, and representations (i.e., toward greater autonomy), as well as toward greater connectedness with the true selves of others and with humanity more generally (i.e., toward greater homonomy).

Of course, these dual developmental tendencies can function more or less effectively, as we discuss later in the chapter, but the critical point is that people have an active tendency to integrate unless there is some need-related conflict or thwart. That point is relevant to this discussion because it makes clear that *some identifications may inherently conflict with either intrinsic motives and needs* or with other deeply internalized values and sentiments and thus not easily be integrated. It is precisely those identifications that must therefore be closed—that must be isolated from other aspects of experience to be effective and powerful motivators.

The nature of closed identifications was illustrated in a recent series of studies reported by Weinstein, Ryan, DeHaan, Przybylski, Legate, and Ryan (2012). These investigators reasoned that when individuals grow up with autonomy-thwarting parents, they may be prevented from exploring and integrating certain felt values and potential identities and, as a result, be more prone to wall off or compartmentalize aspects of themselves that are perceived to be unacceptable. Given the stigmatization of homosexuality, these researchers hypothesized that individuals perceiving low autonomy support from parents might be especially motivated to conceal or compartmentalize same-sex sexual attractions, not only from others but even from themselves, leading to defensive processes such as reaction formation. Weinstein and colleagues did four studies testing a model wherein perceived parental autonomy support was associated with lower discrepancies between self-reported sexual identifications and implicitly assessed sexual orientations (measured using a reaction-time task). Results showed, indeed, that the more controlling and homophobic the parental (especially paternal) climate was, the more likely individuals were to evidence discrepancies between the implicit and explicit measures. Thus, for example, although some participants identified explicitly with heterosexuality, this identification was compartmentalized from their underlying (implicit) attraction to same-sex others. Moreover, presumably to protect this compartmentalized identification, they were more likely to act with bias or even advocate more aggression toward gay and lesbian targets, apparently finding these outside targets threatening to their identification. In sum, this study bears out the idea that some identifications may be strongly held yet not well integrated, resulting in various defensive processes. Compartmentalization also helps illuminate the moral desensitization that can accompany ingroup versus outgroup dynamics, as we further discuss in Chapter 24.

In a certain sense, the very notion of integrity suggests openness as well as coherence and internal consistency, as it is our nature to be synthetic and self-organized in our functioning. Yet as with any evolved tendency, compensatory devices can emerge, and their very existence teaches us about our human nature under adverse (non-need-supportive) conditions. As we continue to explore organismic integration, we shall see that the natural tendency toward internalization not only facilitates social integration but, in its complexities, can also spawn defense. Avoidance of certain information, rigidity in the face of challenges, and implicit and explicit discrepancies provide inroads into understanding both the synthetic functioning of people and their vulnerabilities to defense and compartmentalization in the face of controlling social contexts.

Strategies of Socialization and Internalization

Cultures and societies ask much from their members, for without social coordination groups would not be able to function. Fortunately, there is a natural, indeed evolved, readiness on the part of individuals to take on the regulation of activities that are valued by groups to whom they are attached, as doing so is a means through which people satisfy their basic psychological needs. By adopting attitudes and acting in ways that are modeled and endorsed by family, peers, or other significant social groups, individuals can feel a greater relatedness and sense of belonging. By effectively mastering social practices, they can also feel greater competence in navigating their social terrain. Finally, by integrating social mores and regulations into their own system of values and beliefs, they experience greater autonomy and volition as they act. In this way, effective internalization yields all three basic need satisfactions and a greater sense of belonging and wellness.

OIT addresses the issue of how individuals internalize the practices and values that are ambient or normative in family, group, and cultural environments and the consequences of such internalizations. SDT especially argues that in need-supportive contexts people more fully internalize extrinsic regulations and values and thus experience a true sense of willingness and congruence in doing the behaviors.

Research by Knafo and Assor (2007) supported this reasoning. They found that when individuals from both university and community samples perceived their parents to be more autonomy-supportive when transmitting their values, they tended to be more autonomously motivated and less controlled in their motivation to enact them. Furthermore, those who were more autonomously motivated perceived greater congruence between their own values and those of their parents, and they evidenced greater psychological wellness. The data showed, in fact, that autonomous motivation mediated the relations between the parents' autonomy support and their children's well-being, even after controlling for the amount of congruence between the values of the two generations. In contrast, controlled motivation for adopting parents' values was associated with greater feelings of guilt and agitation. Such evidence supports our view that individuals are able to more fully internalize ambient social values under need-supportive conditions and that, when they do so, they evidence both more reliable behavioral regulation and greater well-being.

Need Support and Internalization

Even though we have deeply evolved propensities to internalize and integrate socially salient practices and values, this process requires nutrients and supports. In this regard, understanding that internalization and integration operate in the service of psychological need satisfactions provides a basis for making predictions about how internalization and integration can be facilitated. Generally speaking, factors in the social environment that support people's feelings of relatedness, competence, and autonomy with respect to a relevant behavior or domain will facilitate greater internalization. However, each of these need supports is differentially implicated in each of the forms of regulation within our OIT taxonomy.

Specifically, external regulation can occur under controlled conditions and even when people are socially alienated. However, even external regulation requires some minimal sense of competence to carry out the behavior. A person may not personally value or want to follow traffic laws and thus may only respond to laws for fear of law enforcement. But even to do that, he or she must have competencies to drive and learn to read the road signs and watch for police. Indeed, all forms of intentional behavioral regulation, autonomous or controlled, require at least minimal competencies. In contrast, to introject a behavior, one must not only feel some competence to perform it but also must care about what others think. Introjection requires a sense that performing prescribed behaviors bear on one's worth, and ultimately self-worth is a social concern. Thus introjecting a behavioral regulation requires at least some attachment of the self to others and, therefore, a concern with their approval. In this sense, introjection depends on some basic supports for both competence and, (at least conditional) relatedness. Finally, for a person to identify with or integrate a value or practice, he or she will need to "take ownership" of it—to feel it is something that is personally endorsed and valued. Factors that support autonomy are thus important for promoting identification and integration. Therefore, the most optimal conditions for encouraging internalization and integration of values and regulations are those that allow satisfaction of all three needs for relatedness, competence, and autonomy. When situations allow this triad of satisfactions, individuals in fact become both more autonomous and more homonomous (Angyal, 1965)—that is, both more integrated within themselves and more integrated with the social world around them.

Accordingly, this leads to OIT's Proposition III, which concerns the conditions that facilitate internalization and integration of the values and regulations.

> *OIT Proposition III:* Supports for the basic needs for competence, relatedness, and autonomy facilitate the internalization and integration of non-intrinsically motivated behaviors. To the extent that the context is controlling, and/or relatedness or competence needs are thwarted, internalization, and particularly identification or integrated regulation, will be less likely.

The hypothesis that contextual supports for autonomy, competence, and relatedness will promote more integrated self-regulation is both social psychological and developmental in nature. Contextual supports facilitate self-regulation in the immediate situation in which they are provided. Moreover, the provision of basic need supports over time catalyzes the development of autonomous self-regulation and is the basis for individual differences in longer term capacities for self-determination.

Research on Internalization and the Social Context

Considerable research has supported OIT's Proposition III at both the social-psychological and developmental levels of analysis, and we review much of this in the context of forthcoming developmental and parenting chapters as well as other applied chapters to come. In the current chapter we consider just a few illustrative studies that have tested the general proposition that internalization and integration are facilitated by social contexts that foster a sense of connection, are optimally structured so as to allow feelings of efficacy, and are supportive of self-regulation and autonomy. When interpersonal contexts provide these nourishments, and particularly when they do not pit any one need satisfaction against another, circumstances for socializing individuals to integrate values and regulations are most optimal.

Much of the SDT research has focused specifically on autonomy support because of its critical role in promoting more integrated forms of regulation. Authority figures (parents, teachers, bosses, and doctors, among others) who are autonomy-supportive also typically provide the type of interpersonal context within which people also feel competent and related. Specifically, because autonomy support begins with taking the others' perspective, it opens the door to more responsiveness to needs in general. Furthermore, autonomy support allows the individual to be more proactive in the process of assimilation and transforming external practices into one's identity and style of life.

Ryan and Connell (1989), in their validation of the academic self-regulation questionnaire (SRQ-A), assessed elementary students' perceptions of their teachers' autonomy support and found preliminary support for Proposition III. They reported that children's perceptions of the autonomy supportiveness of their classroom climates related to the students' displaying more internalized, and in particular more identified, academic regulation.

Grolnick and Ryan (1989) soon thereafter performed one of the earliest in-depth studies of how social-contextual variables impact internalization (see also Chapter 14). They did in-home interviews with the mothers and fathers (separately) of upper-elementary-school children, paying particular attention to how parents motivated children to do schoolwork and household chores. Following the interviews, both the interviewer and a trained observer did independent ratings of the degree to which the parents were *involved* with their children (i.e., devoted time and attention to them), provided *structure* (e.g., clear guidelines and expectations), and were *autonomy-supportive* (used autonomy-supportive techniques, expressed value for autonomy, and minimized external control). These ratings were used to predict their children's internalization, adjustment, and achievement, assessed with teacher ratings of classroom competence and adjustment; school records of grades, behavioral reports, and achievement test scores; and children's self-reports of relative autonomy (collected separately in the school context).

Results indicated that parental autonomy support (as rated by the interview team) predicted children's relative autonomy for schoolwork. That is, parents using autonomy-supportive techniques had children who reported more identification and intrinsic motivation. Further, parent autonomy support also predicted teacher-rated classroom adjustment and children's actual academic achievement scores. Interviewer-rated involvement also predicted children's classroom achievement, as well as measures of their understanding of what controls school outcomes, which is an aspect of competence. These findings confirmed that it was the children of more autonomy-supportive and involved parents who displayed greater internalization and the outcomes expected to be associated with it.

It was clear in these interviews that many of the parents who were rated as highly controlling were quite well intentioned. Many were, in fact, concerned with their children's outcomes, and it was out of that concern that they were using controlling techniques in an attempt to ensure that their children would succeed. We shall see in Chapter 13 that these controlling practices often stem from parents' insecurities and concerns about their children's future or their own unfulfilled dreams and aspirations. Yet, paradoxically, this control undermines both the autonomous internalization and intrinsic motivation that typically best sustain engagement and foster achievement (Grolnick & Seal, 2008). In fact, when parents are highly controlling, they may not only fail to foster internalization, but they may even prompt oppositional defiance, especially during adolescence (Vansteenkiste, Soenens, Van Petegem, & Duriez, 2014).

Following up on Grolnick and Ryan's interview research, Grolnick, Ryan, and Deci (1991) examined the relations of children's perceptions of their parents and their internalization outcomes. As expected, children who perceived their mothers and fathers as more involved and autonomy-supportive reported more autonomous motivation and greater perceived competence with regard to doing their schoolwork. These motivation variables, which the authors described as the children's *inner resources* for school, in turn predicted the children's school performance, thus serving as mediators between the home context and children's performance in school.

Illustrating how need support impacts internalization in a later developmental period, Niemiec, Lynch, Vansteenkiste, Bernstein, Deci, and Ryan (2006) examined mothers' and fathers' support for relatedness and autonomy in predicting high school students' internalization of the motivation for going to college. Within this middle-class and generally upwardly mobile sample, perceived parental need support was indeed associated with adolescents' autonomous self-regulation for pursuing further education, which in turn related to measures of both well-being and ill-being. In fact, internalization of motivation for college partially mediated the relations between parental need support and the adolescents' general psychological health.

These factors assessed in field studies can also be observed in controlled laboratory experiments. In one of the earliest of these, Deci, Eghrari, Patrick, and Leone (1994) had participants perform a relatively boring task. It consisted of watching a computer screen for dots of light that flashed randomly around the screen, pressing a key as quickly as possible once they saw the light. The researchers manipulated three factors that were hypothesized to allow participants to experience greater autonomy satisfaction. First, some participants were given a *meaningful rationale* so that they could find value or personal importance in this activity; they were told the task was being examined as a potential attention-training activity. Second, some participants had an experimenter who *acknowledged their feelings,* explicitly recognizing that a vigilance task of this sort could be boring. This second element was meant to convey that the experimenter was concerned with the participant's internal frame of reference. Finally, for some participants, the experimenter's instructions emphasized *choice* and minimized control, whereas for the other half the instructional set was more controlling and directive. These three factors formed a $2 \times 2 \times 2$ factorial design. After the performance period, participants were left alone in the experimental room, where they could either continue the boring task or read magazines. Deci et al. (1994) reasoned that the more time they spent with the boring activity during the free-choice period, the more they must have internalized a value for this non-intrinsically motivating activity. Results revealed that these three facilitating factors—providing a rationale, acknowledging potential negative feelings, and highlighting choice—led to greater internalization, as reflected in more free time spent with the activity. Questionnaire results paralleled those of the behavioral measure, revealing that the facilitating factors also added to people's perceived choice, perceived utility of the activity, and even their enjoyment of the task.

Although there was greater internalization in conditions with more facilitating factors, there was still some persistence even in conditions that were low in opportunities for need satisfaction. Deci et al. (1994) thus analyzed this internalization that occurred in conditions with two or three facilitating factors (i.e., high support) as compared to conditions with no or one facilitating factor (i.e., low support). Specifically, they correlated the amount of free-time persistence (the measure of internalization) with how participants felt (i.e., perceived choice, perceived utility, and enjoyment of the task). The idea was that the more positive the relationship between their behavior and their feelings was, the more they would have integrated the regulation, whereas negative correlations would imply introjection because the participants would be behaving in spite of not feeling choice, utility, or enjoyment (see Ryan, Koestner, & Deci, 1991). Results indeed showed that the internalization that occurred in conditions supportive of self-determination was more integrated, as reflected by more positive correlations or congruence between persistent behavior and perceived choice, utility, and enjoyment. In contrast, the internalization that occurred in the non-need-supportive conditions was likely introjected, as reflected by weak or negative correlations between behavioral and self-report variables.

The findings from this and other studies (e.g., Roth et al., 2006) that internalization that occurs within controlling conditions is likely to be introjected rather than integrated is important in terms of SDT's theory of internalization and behavior change. Use of rewards and other structures that are likely to be experienced as controlling has been advocated within many behavioral and cognitive-behavioral traditions, and there is clear evidence that some internalization does occur. Yet although such conditions may in fact promote some internalization, it will be less congruent or authentic than the internalization that occurs in autonomy-supportive contexts, and the behavior will less likely be maintained over time.

Illustrating the importance of these internalization dynamics, Legault, Gutsell, and Inzlicht (2011) recently reported two studies that demonstrated the causal influence of autonomy-supportive contexts on internalization, in this case, regarding the regulation of expressions of prejudice. In a first experiment, they assigned participants to one of three conditions. In one condition, participants were given a pamphlet containing an autonomy-supportive message concerning the importance of nonprejudice—a message emphasizing the value and social importance of being nonprejudiced, as well as the fact that the reader has choice within this domain. A second, controlling condition involved a pamphlet that was more prescriptive and pressuring, emphasizing nonprejudiced attitudes that participants "should" embrace. A third condition provided no message (control condition). Legault and colleagues (2011) also measured the various reasons why participants might constrain prejudice, using the OIT internalization taxonomy. Ironically, controlling messages *increased* explicit prejudice relative to the control condition. In contrast, autonomy-supportive messages reduced its expression. In a second study to more deeply examine these processes, the experimenters used an implicit prime procedure to either create autonomy-supportive or controlling orientations for constraining prejudice, and they then measured both implicit and explicit indices of prejudice. Remarkably, controlling primes preceding antiprejudice messages increased both implicit and explicit prejudice, whereas autonomy-supportive primes reduced both types. In both studies, the OIT measure of relative autonomy significantly mediated the relations between context and outcomes. These results powerfully show how contexts affect both internalization and the resulting attitudes and behaviors that follow from it.

To summarize, these and numerous other studies on OIT suggest that if the interpersonal context fails to support self-initiation and choice—that is, if significant others are controlling or not accepting—people will be less likely to internalize values, attitudes, and behaviors than if the significant others are autonomy-supportive and positively involved. Furthermore, when the context fails to provide the necessary nutrients, internalization that does occur will likely have the quality of introjection, thus being rigid, conflicted, or marked by negative emotionality.

Autonomy Support and Internalization

Many additional studies have documented the relations between autonomy-supportive contexts and both greater internalization and the more autonomous regulation of behavior that follows from it. We review just a few studies from different domains, recognizing that this is only a small sample of the relevant research available and that we will review additional studies within each of our applied chapters.

In studies of multicultural students, Downie, Chua, Koestner, Barrios, Rip, and M'Birkou (2007) tested how parental autonomy support related to cultural internalization and well-being. In their first study, multicultural students living in Canada were shown to have more fully internalized their host and heritage cultures and to have higher well-being if they experienced their parents to be more autonomy-supportive. In a second study, Chinese-Malaysian sojourners were shown to have more fully internalized their heritage culture and to be experiencing higher well-being when they perceived their parents as autonomy-supportive. Interestingly, in both studies, heritage cultural internalization was also associated with higher wellness.

Williams, Gagné, Ryan, and Deci (2002) did a study in which physicians counseled patients to stop smoking tobacco. Each counseling session was tape-recorded and subsequently rated for the degree to which the physician was autonomy-supportive in the interview. Immediately after the meeting with their doctors, patients completed a version of the SRQ developed to assess their motivation for medical treatment. Results indicated that patients whose doctors had been rated as more autonomy-supportive expressed more autonomous reasons for attempting to stop smoking than patients whose doctors had been rated as more controlling. They had, that is, more fully internalized the value and self-motivation for stopping smoking.

Another series of studies concerning the interactions between health-care providers and their patients investigated the question of whether the perceived autonomy supportiveness of providers related to patients' autonomous motivation for behaving in healthy ways (see Ryan, Williams, Patrick, & Deci, 2009). The studies, which examined a variety of health-relevant behaviors—for example, smoking cessation, improved diet, regular exercise, glucose control among patients with diabetes, and weight loss among morbidly obese patients—focused on physicians as the providers in some studies and teams of providers in others. In one study (Williams, Grow, Freedman, Ryan, & Deci, 1996), morbidly obese patients reported their perceptions of the autonomy supportiveness of the staff in a medically based weight-loss clinic. Part way through the 6-month program, patients' autonomous (i.e., identified and integrated) motivation versus controlled (i.e., external and introjected) motivation was assessed. Results supported a model in which greater perceived autonomy support from the staff predicted higher patient autonomous motivation, which in turn predicted more attendance and weight loss over the 6 months of the program. Even more interesting, however, was that patients' autonomous motivation predicted better maintenance of weight loss at a 2-year follow-up.

The follow-up issue is an extremely important one with respect to internalization, because it is precisely through internalization that *maintenance* over time and *transfer* to new situations succeed (Ryan & Deci, 2008b). SDT expects that careful use of external controls can produce behavior change in the short term. For example, the offer of rewards or approval contingent upon weight loss, if salient enough, may produce weight loss among those who care about the rewards or the approval. But the more important and penetrating issue concerns the persistence of that behavior change (i.e., the weight loss) when the controls were no longer in effect (e.g., when rewards cease), and it is here that the autonomy support and resulting internalization and integration of behavioral regulations are so crucial. Because autonomy support promotes the acceptance of regulations as one's own, reflected in autonomous reasons for actions, there is a meaningful theoretical reason for expecting it to persist after the treatment program is no longer in effect. Indeed, when patients had truly accepted the value of a healthier diet and regular exercise as being personally important, they were more likely to carry through on those important behaviors.

Indeed, there are many studies examining autonomy support and internalization in health care clinics and health-promotion settings, several of which will be discussed in more detail in Chapter 18. For now, it is worth noting that a recent meta-analysis of 184 independent datasets from studies that utilized SDT found that autonomy support strongly predicted autonomous motivation for health-behavior change (Ng et al., 2012).

From these and related studies we conclude that autonomy support contributes greatly to the internalization of social values and the regulation of nonspontaneous behaviors, which in turn influence behavior and affect. More nurturing environments allow satisfaction of the basic psychological needs for relatedness, competence, and autonomy, which is the basis for integration. Unfortunately, such ideal contextual conditions are not widely prevalent, so full integration of regulations is often not attained. In such cases, when socializing agents are relatively controlling or uninvolved, internalization operates nonoptimally, with values and regulations never being fully assimilated.

The Consequences of Internalization

The foregoing discussion on the social-contextual factors that influence the internalization of extrinsically motivated behaviors included some information about the consequences as well as the antecedents of the different regulatory styles that result from different degrees of internalization of extrinsic motivation. Results consistently show that the more fully internalized an extrinsic motivation, the greater the behavioral persistence in the absence of external controls, the higher the quality of performance, and the more positive the psychological experience and affective accompaniments of the behavior. Greater autonomy in regulation is associated with less internal conflict and a greater holistic dedication of self to actions, thus more fully engaging the individual's cognitive, affective, and energetic resources that enhance performance. Moreover, autonomous actions, which reflect organismic integration, are also likely to be more congruent with, and to satisfy, basic psychological needs, thereby enhancing wellness. This reasoning (and early empirical findings) led to the fourth and fifth propositions of OIT, which concern the correlates and consequences of internalizing a value or regulation more or less fully.

> *OIT Proposition IV:* To the degree that people's behavior is regulated through more autonomous or integrated forms of internalization, they will display greater behavioral persistence at activities, a higher quality of behavior, and more effective performance, especially for more difficult or complex actions.

> *OIT Proposition V:* To the degree that people's behavior is regulated through more integrated forms of internalization, they will have more positive experiences and greater psychological health and well-being.

A large number of studies in addition to those already mentioned have explored these hypotheses, most using the general approach to assessing the degree of internalization introduced by Ryan and Connell (1989), although different researchers have developed variants of this scale in different behavioral domains (e.g., Lonsdale et al., 2014; Losier, Perreault, Koestner, & Vallerand, 2001; Pelletier, Tuson, Green-Demers, Noels,

& Beaton, 1998; Vallerand, Pelletier, Blais, Briere, Senecal, & Vallieres, 1993; Wilson, Rodgers, & Fraser, 2002; and several others). The different scales have included different numbers of the six motivational categories within SDT—amotivation; the four extrinsic categories of external, introjected, identified, and integrated regulation; and intrinsic motivation—depending on the behavior, domain, and age of the participants. Also, as previously mentioned, data from the self-regulation scales have been combined in various ways. In some studies, scores for the individual regulatory styles have been used to predict behavioral, experiential, or affective outcomes. In other studies, scores for the autonomous styles (identified, integrated, and intrinsic) have been combined to form an autonomy versus control score, which has been used to predict outcomes, and in still other studies, the RAI has been formed and used to predict outcomes.

Ryan and Connell's (1989) studies looked at the consequences of varied forms of internalization, finding that more identified regulation of school-related activities was positively correlated with positive affect and proactive coping, whereas the less autonomous styles (i.e., external and introjected) were positively correlated with negative affect and maladaptive coping. Introjection, in particular, was highly correlated with anxiety and with anxiety amplification following failure, thus highlighting the inner stress and vulnerability caused by controlling introjects. Using the scale that assessed regulation of prosocial behaviors, Ryan and Connell (1989) found that identified regulation was associated with greater empathy, more mature moral reasoning, and more positive relatedness to others. Investigators have since extended the investigation of regulatory styles to many other domains, including religion (O'Connor & Vallerand, 1990; Neyrinck, Vansteenkiste, Lens, Duriez, & Hutsebaut, 2006), health care (Ryan, Plant, & O'Malley, 1995; Williams et al., 1996), psychotherapy (Pelletier, Tuson, & Haddad, 1997), aging (V. Kasser & Ryan, 1999; Vallerand & O'Connor, 1989), and sport (Biddle, 1999; Chatzisarantis, Biddle, & Meek, 1997), among many others. Although we briefly review a few illustrative studies here, most of the discussion of the functional outcomes of the regulatory styles in these applied areas will be in the relevant applied chapters later in the book, wherein we will be able to consider the nuances and complexities contained within each domain.

Internalization, Behavioral Persistence, and Goal Attainment

New Year's Eve resolutions are notorious for being goals that few people complete. To understand why, Greenstein and Koestner (1996) studied New Years' resolutions among a group of college students. They assessed both the specific goals the students resolved to attain and the strength of the various reasons why they initiated each—that is, the strength of their external, introjected, identified, and intrinsic reasons. The researchers found in a 2-month follow-up assessment that students who had stronger identified and intrinsic reasons were more likely to have maintained their resolutions than students expressing stronger external and introjected reasons.

In a series of studies about people's motivation for behaving in ways that support the environment, Pelletier and colleagues assessed people's reasons for engaging in behaviors such as recycling, reusing packaging materials, purchasing environmentally friendly goods, and conserving energy. In one study, they found that those whose reasons were more autonomous sought out more information about the environment and were more persistent in carrying out behaviors that protected the environment (Séguin, Pelletier, & Hunsley, 1999). In another, Green-Demers, Pelletier, and Menard (1997) found not only that there was a positive relation between self-determined motivation and behaviors protective of the environment but also that the relation got stronger as the behaviors involved became more difficult. Thus, whereas people who were more controlled in their motivation did some environmentally preserving behaviors, as the behaviors got more difficult, it was only those with more internalized, autonomous motivation who persisted at these important behaviors. The Pelletier group also considered why people do not even try to protect the environment, examining people's general sense of amotivation with respect to the environment. They found that the amotivation resulted both from people's believing that the behaviors do not really help protect the environment and/or that they do not feel capable of doing the necessary behaviors (Pelletier et al., 1999), thus implicating both of SDT's major subtypes of amotivation.

Pelletier, Fortier, Vallerand, Tuson, Briere, and Blais, (1995) studied competitive swimmers, assessing the athletes' perceptions of the autonomy support of their coaches, as well as the swimmers' own motivations for engagement. They found that perceived autonomy support of the coaches was associated with greater internalization and autonomous motivation among the swimmers. In a subsequent, three-wave prospective study of athletes, Pelletier et al. (2001) found that identified and intrinsic motivation at Time 1 were strong predictors of persistence at Times 2 and 3; that introjected motivation at Time 1 was a moderate predictor of persistence at Time 2 but not at Time 3; and that external regulation at Time 1 did not predict persistence at Time 2 and was a negative predictor at Time 3. Thus self-determined forms of motivation were found to be positive predictors of persistence over time, whereas controlled forms were weak predictors at Time 2 and got even weaker as time passed. In fact, over time, external regulation became a negative predictor of persistence at the sport.

Münster-Halvari, Halvari, Bjørnebekk, and Deci (2012a) found that patients' perceptions of the degree to which their dental professionals were autonomy-supportive (relative to controlling) positively predicted patients' psychological need satisfaction and autonomous motivation for dental home care, and these variables positively predicted dental health behaviors and oral health.

Evans and Bonneville-Roussy (2015) studied students in university-level schools of music in Australia and New Zealand to examine need satisfaction and relative autonomy for music learning. They found that greater relative autonomy predicted more frequent practice, more frequent high-quality practice, and a higher preference for challenging pieces of music.

Ryan and colleagues (1995) found that patients in an alcohol treatment program who reported more internal (identified and introjected) reasons for participating attended more regularly and were rated by their clinicians as more involved in treatment. Interestingly, in this instance both internalized forms of extrinsic motivation, identified and introjected, were associated with more treatment engagement, reflecting that changing patterns of alcohol abuse were driven by both internalized value and guilt over past behaviors. A similar pattern was uncovered in research by Zeldman, Ryan, and Fiscella (2004) among persons with opiate dependence. Those who indicated internalized motives were more likely to attend treatment and abstain from drug use, as verified through regular urine tests. External motivation for drug dependence treatment yielded no evidence for positive effects, despite the fact that many patients were externally pressured, in some cases even court mandated, to be in treatment. In short, with heavy addictions, autonomous motivation is an important predictor of positive outcomes, but the presence of introjected regulation may supplement autonomy in predicting positive outcomes, a pattern that has not emerged in relation to other kinds of behaviors.

A quite different context was used for assessing the performance dynamics of distinct regulatory styles in a study of voting behavior among Canadians by Koestner, Losier,

Vallerand, and Carducci (1996), who examined the strength of people's introjected versus identified reasons for following political issues. They found that identification was associated with being more active in seeking relevant political information, holding more complex political positions, and actually voting in the relevant elections, whereas introjection was associated with relying on the opinions of important others, experiencing conflicted emotions about political outcomes, and being vulnerable to persuasion.

Koestner, Houlfort, Paquet, and Knight (2001) did a study of environmental attitudes to further investigate the relations of regulatory styles and vulnerability to persuasion. They assessed participants' introjected and identified reasons for engaging in pro-environmental behaviors and then subjected them to arguments against recycling. The arguments were either weak or strong and made by attractive versus unattractive communicators. Results of the study suggested that individuals high on introjected reasons for pro-environmental behaviors were vulnerable to persuasion, especially by attractive sources, whereas those high on identified reasons were resistant to persuasion, even to strong arguments.

In a follow-up study of political behavior, Losier and Koestner (1999) took the interesting approach of comparing the correlates of two types of autonomous motivation with each other rather than comparing autonomous to controlled types of motivation. They assessed participants' identified and intrinsic reasons for following politics before two important elections and then later ascertained whether the individuals had voted, how strongly they held their beliefs, and how they felt about the outcomes. Results indicated that identification was a stronger predictor of actual voting behavior than was intrinsic motivation and also that those high in identification tended to have stronger beliefs and to feel more positive if their side won, relative to those high in intrinsic motivation. In other words, when people follow politics because of having internalized its importance, they are more likely to vote and to feel strongly about issues than people who follow politics simply out of interest. In contrast, those high in intrinsic motivation were indeed interested in the issues and gathered a great deal of information but were less committed to an outcome. It seems, therefore, that in situations in which the actions involved may be less than fun (e.g., actually voting), autonomous motivation that has been internalized may be preferable to intrinsic motivation.

We highlight these specific studies to emphasize two important features of SDT's model of internalization. First, SDT emphasizes multiple and distinct types of motivation, each of which is related differently to antecedents, phenomenological features, and consequences. Second, the model specifies that these different types of motivation most often co-occur in the determination of behavior. Thus there can be different configurations of motives in different domains or for different individuals. This approach, which is, of course, more complex than the unitary view of motivation embraced by many other theories, is, however, appropriate given the actual complexity of motivation in everyday life. OIT affords us the opportunity to look in-depth into the sources, styles, and outcomes of how people are moved to act across highly varied domains, developmental epochs, contexts, and cultures.

Self-Concordance

Sheldon and Elliot (1999) employed the term *self-concordance* to explore the autonomy of people's idiographic goals—that is, the personal goals that they generate for themselves and that are thus assumed to have conscious salience in their lives. Such idiographic goals are sometimes referred to as *personal strivings* (Emmons, 1986). Defining self-concordant personal strivings as those that are deeply congruent and conducive to growth, Sheldon and Elliot (1999) turned to SDT, and OIT in particular, with its conceptualization of internalization and integration. Basically, the measure of self-concordance is directly reflective of relative autonomy.

There were, however, two specific things that differentiated the assessment of self-concordance from the assessments of internalization and integration as outlined in other studies we have reviewed within OIT. First, in most OIT research, the goals or behaviors being examined are ones that researchers (rather than participants) have selected and asked the participants to respond to, rather than being ones the participants had spontaneously generated for themselves. In self-concordance research, people generate their own goals or life strivings. Second, each of four regulatory styles (external, introjected, identified, and intrinsic) in the self-concordance measure are typically assessed with a single item, allowing the multiple simultaneous goals people are typically pursuing to be readily assessed. This brief self-concordance measure thus captures the degree to which ideographic goals are autonomous versus controlled as defined within SDT, rather than focusing on specific subtypes of regulation.

In their initial studies, Sheldon and Elliot (1999) found that when people pursued more self-concordant (or autonomous) goals, they applied more sustained effort, which increased the likelihood of successful goal attainment. Furthermore, self-concordance ratings interacted with attainment outcomes to predict greater basic need satisfactions and thus well-being. In other words, when one is successful at attaining personal goals and those goals are autonomously motivated and congruent, need satisfaction is especially robust.

Using this strategy, a number of studies have shown that the more self-concordant (relatively autonomous) an individual's personal goals and striving are, the higher his or her well-being is (Sheldon, 2014), and these findings have been sustained across diverse cultural contexts (e.g., Sheldon, Elliot, et al., 2004).

Work on self-concordance suggests, as does OIT research more generally, that the more autonomous people's personal goals are, the more they will engage in higher quality goal-related behaviors, and the more the people will experience satisfaction of basic psychological needs and the positive affect associated with this need satisfaction, which in turn leaves them more able to pursue concordant goals. Sheldon and Houser-Marko (2001) specifically referred to this process sequence as the *upward spiral,* in which more concordant, autonomous motivations lead to enhanced personality functioning and adjustment over time (see also Sheldon et al., 2010).

Koestner, Lekes, Powers, and Chicoine (2002) conducted studies in which they examined the importance of self-concordance for personal goal progress. More specifically, they explored the degree to which self-concordance of personal goals and goal implementation intentions related to each other and in predicting successful goal attainment. Implementation intentions are concrete mental plans about when, where, and how to proceed with the pursuit of a goal (Gollwitzer, 1999), and research by Gollwitzer and Brandstätter (1997) had shown that holding such intentions increased the likelihood of making progress in attaining the goal.

A first study by Koestner et al. (2002) showed that both of these factors contributed to making progress in the pursuit of goals, such that having implementation intentions and being self-concordant or autonomous in the goal pursuit were predictive of progress. In a second study, this one of New Year's resolutions, Koestner and colleagues found that self-concordance predicted progress on the resolutions, although implementation intentions did not predict progress. Still, however, self-concordant goals and implementation intentions interacted positively to facilitate resolution progress.

Goal Attainment: Summary Comments

Numerous studies in varied behavioral domains and using various assessment strategies indicate that more autonomous and self-concordant motivation is associated with greater behavioral persistence, as specified in OIT's Proposition IV. Clearly, when people more fully internalize the value and importance of a behavior or domain, they are more likely to maintain relevant behaviors and beliefs than when they engage in such behaviors for more controlled reasons. One result of this is a higher probability of actually achieving the goals people pursue.

Internalization, Relative Autonomy, and Well-Being

The tendency to internalize and integrate values, attitudes, and behavioral regulations, although a natural human tendency, requires the types of contextual supports that allow people to satisfy their basic needs for relatedness, competence, and autonomy while engaging in the relevant behaviors. Because SDT defines these basic needs as nutrients that are essential for well-being, it is an immediate corollary of our view of internalization that fuller internalization of behavioral regulations will be associated with greater well-being, especially for behaviors that are central in a person's life. This is the theoretical basis of Proposition V. Here again, a considerable amount of empirical research provides support for that hypothesis, of which we review just a few examples.

Ryan et al. (1993) examined the degree of internalization of religious values and behaviors in Christian samples, including students in a religious college, churchgoing adults, and evangelical teenagers. Specifically, they considered the degree to which individuals engage in religious behaviors for introjected and identified reasons. Results indicated that identified regulation was positively related to indicators of well-being such as self-actualization, self-esteem, and identity integration, whereas introjected religiosity was negatively related to these indicators. Further, introjected regulation was positively related to indicators of ill-being such as anxiety, depression, and somatization, whereas identified regulation was negatively related to these ill-being indices. Clearly, people's more autonomous reasons for engaging in religious behaviors were associated with better psychological well-being.

Vallerand and O'Connor (1989) studied the motivation of elderly individuals by assessing their reasons for behaving in six different life domains. The reasons included controlled extrinsic motivations (i.e., regulations that had not been well internalized) and autonomous extrinsic motivations (i.e., regulations that had been well internalized). The researchers found that, after controlling for health status, autonomous motivation was positively associated with self-esteem, meaning in life, and being active, whereas nonautonomous motivation was negatively associated with these variables. On the other hand, nonautonomous motivation was positively associated with depression, whereas autonomous motivation was negatively associated with that indicator of ill-being.

Deci, Hodges, Pierson, and Tomassone (1992) found that elementary school children diagnosed with emotional difficulties and attending a special education school who were higher in autonomous motivation displayed more self-esteem and were less likely to use maladaptive coping strategies when they had failed at an activity.

Another important point regarding our model of internalization is that it is neutral with respect to cultural contents. People may more deeply internalize certain practices or behaviors in some cultures compared with others, yet regardless of these differing contents, we expect internalization to matter for wellness (e.g., see Chirkov, Ryan, Kim, &

Kaplan, 2003). An excellent example of this is the issue of conforming to duties or obligations to one's family. In Western contexts, conformity and obligation are often characterized as nonautonomous. Yet, among Indians who embrace Hindu traditions, concepts of duty are often more fully internalized and thus may be accompanied by a greater sense of choice and volition. This was shown in a series of studies by Miller et al. (2011). They found that being expected to help family and friends was positively correlated with identification, as well as a sense of satisfaction and choice among Indians, but not among Americans. This shows how the contents of internalization can differ, yet across cultures, the issue of relative autonomy matters for experience and wellness.

From these and many other studies we will be reviewing in upcoming chapters, there is ample evidence that those who are more autonomously motivated and who experience the greater need satisfaction implicit in more internalized motivation also display better psychological health and adjustment, as specified in Propositions IV and V of OIT. The studies relating the need-supportive aspects of social environments to the degree of internalization of values and regulations have confirmed the central OIT hypothesis that contexts that afford the satisfaction of the basic psychological needs facilitate internalization. The results are also consistent with the supplemental hypothesis that supports for competence and relatedness may promote internalization, but only when there is also support for autonomy will the internalization tend to be integrated and thus provide the basis for self-determined actions.

Concluding Comments

Although in infancy and early childhood intrinsic motivation is a prominent form of regulation, there is a gradual shift in the balance of behavior, from intrinsic motivation being more prevalent to extrinsic motivations being more prevalent, as increasing demands are put on the child to behave in accordance with social and cultural rules and norms. The lifespan trajectory of this balance between intrinsic and extrinsic motivations will differ by cultural contexts (e.g., in some cultures people retire and do what interests them), but in most societies after early childhood extrinsic motivation takes more and more the center stage. How well these extrinsic regulations are internalized then predicts both quality of functioning and wellness.

In this chapter, we focused on the internalization of extrinsic motivations as a manifestation of our natural propensities for organismic integration. The SDT model of internalization differentiates types of extrinsic motivation that differ from each other in their sources, their phenomenology, and their functional consequences. The major categories are external regulation, introjected regulation, identified regulation, and integrated regulation. These categories vary systematically in their relative autonomy, with external regulation being least autonomous and integration being highly autonomous.

Social contexts can facilitate greater internalization of extrinsic motivations by supporting the satisfaction of the individual's basic psychological needs for competence, autonomy, and relatedness. For internalization to occur at all, the need for relatedness is of central importance. People have a natural interest in the practices and attitudes of others, and to the degree to which they have or desire connection with them, they are more likely to internalize what they observe or are taught. Competence is also implicated. People are more ready to internalize behaviors that they can efficaciously enact and the values of which they can comprehend. Yet, when socializing agents demand behaviors for which the individual is developmentally or cognitively unprepared (e.g., not yet competent enough), then disruptions in internalization can occur. In particular, forcing children to acquire values or behaviors prematurely fosters at best introjection and at worst amotivation. For a value and regulation not just to be introjected but to be regulated through identification or integrated regulation, the need for autonomy becomes especially salient. However, in some social contexts, the needs for autonomy and relatedness tend to be turned against each other, requiring people to give up one in an attempt to attain the other, as shown in studies of parental conditional regard (e.g., Roth et al., 2009). In such situations, people tend to introject regulations, which may allow them to gain the approval of others yet still may leave them alienated and lacking in autonomy.

We reviewed just a portion of an ever-growing body of evidence supporting the five formal propositions of OIT. This evidence shows that when people act through more fully internalized motivations, such as identification and integration, they: (1) will more reliably engage in activities and perform them more effectively; and (2) will evidence greater psychological health and well-being. In contrast, more controlled forms of internalization, such as external regulation and introjection, compromise the quality of behavior regulation and people's experience while enacting it. These propositions, therefore, have both developmental and applied significance, and this is explored in the chapters to follow.

CHAPTER 9

Causality Orientations Theory

Individual Differences in,
and Priming of, Motivational Orientations

When discussing CET and OIT, we focused on social-contextual influences on intrinsic motivation and the internalization of extrinsic motivation. In this chapter, we change the focus to individual differences in motivational styles. The primary individual differences studied within SDT are people's autonomous, controlled, and impersonal *causality orientations*. People high in the autonomy orientation tend to give informational functional significances to contexts; they take interest in events and see possibilities for choice and self-determination. Those high in the control orientation tend to focus on the controlling aspects of environments and the presence of external rewards and social pressures. Finally, those high in the impersonal orientation tend to see environments as uncontrollable or amotivating. We review the correlates and consequences of the three orientations, finding the most positive outcomes to be related to the autonomy orientation, less positive related to the control orientation, and the most negative associated with the impersonal orientation. We also review research that has primed autonomous and controlled causality orientations, allowing for causal investigations of their effects. We discuss other individual differences pertinent to motivation and a hierarchical model of motivation that addresses motivation at different levels of generality.

Effective functioning of the organismic integration process, facilitated by social supports for competence, autonomy, and relatedness, is the means through which development is optimized. When people are more successful at satisfying needs, they exhibit more intrinsic motivation, and they more fully internalize and integrate cultural values and regulations, resulting in greater behavioral effectiveness and psychological well-being. Yet to the extent that deprivation or frustration, rather than satisfaction, of basic psychological needs has occurred, there will be diminished autonomous motivation, along with fragmentation, rigidity, and defense, rather than organization, flexibility, and openness. This nonoptimal development will be manifested in various types of ill-being or psychopathology (Ryan, Deci, & Vansteenkiste, 2016).

Although need satisfaction and frustration have proximal effects across individuals, persistent differences in contextual supports versus deprivations can lead over time to significant individual differences in how people orient to their environments. Especially with regard to motivation, people can learn to focus more on certain affordances, rewards, or pressures and less on others. They develop characteristic approaches to regulating their emotions and behaviors and what is psychologically salient in their organization of actions.

Two of the more important individual-difference concepts used in SDT concern variability in the processes and orientations that regulate behavior. The first is *regulatory styles*, which we discussed at length in Chapter 8, presenting the external, introjected, identified, integrated, and intrinsic styles of regulation as they pertain to particular behaviors or domains and how they characterize to relative degrees an individual's autonomous and controlled motivations.

A second individual-difference construct that has been widely researched within SDT is *general causality orientations* (GCO), which is a still broader, more general concept that applies across domains, times, and situations. Causality orientations describe motivational sets or characteristic ways of perceiving and organizing motivationally relevant perceptions and information. They are "characteristic adaptations" (McAdams & Pals, 2006) reflecting people's propensities to orient to different motivationally relevant aspects of situations, especially with respect to whether the individuals will exercise autonomy, attend to controls, or fear noncontingent reactions to their initiations and behaviors. Such motivational orientations can also be "pulled for" or potentiated by contexts, or *primed*, making one or more of these motivational orientations more likely to be evidenced by individuals.

General Causality Orientations

Deci and Ryan (1985a) proposed three GCO: the autonomy orientation, the controlled orientation, and the impersonal orientation. These three individual-difference constructs were intended to describe orientations toward the environment and toward one's own motivations. They were also expected to be theoretically and empirically connected with specific antecedents and consequences. As a result of this early research, we developed *causality orientations theory* (COT) as a third mini-theory within SDT.

The *autonomy orientation* describes the degree to which people orient toward their environments by treating them as sources of relevant information, as they take interest in both external events and the accompanying inner experiences. It also involves their experiencing choice with respect to their actions and reactions and finding or creating opportunities for the engagement and expression of what they find interesting and important. When autonomy-oriented, people are "interest-taking," putting them in a position to be more self-regulating. Thus when people are high in the autonomy orientation, they tend to use the identified and integrated styles of regulation and to have a high level of intrinsic motivation.

The *controlled orientation* describes the degree to which people's attention and concerns tend to be oriented toward external contingencies and controls. Individuals in a controlled orientation experience social contexts in terms of rewards and social pressures that they either comply with or defy, and in so doing they often lose sight of their own values or interests. When people are high in the controlled orientation, they tend to use the external and introjected styles of regulation and to have a low level of intrinsic motivation. Frequently, they are acutely occupied with "what others might think" and/or with what external judgments or contingencies might attend their actions.

Finally, the *impersonal orientation* describes the degree to which people orient toward obstacles to goal attainment, readily experience anxiety and incompetence, and react to their lack of control over outcomes and thus are relatively prone to be amotivated. The term *impersonal* as employed here was drawn historically from Heider's (1958) concept of *impersonal causality*, which seemed fitting insofar as people high in the impersonal orientation tend to lack intentionality, initiative, and a sense of personal causation. When so oriented, people are relatively passive and are easily overwhelmed by environmental forces and by their own internal drives and emotions.

The autonomy orientation is the causality orientation most associated with positive motivation, health, and wellness outcomes. When so oriented, people have the vitality and vigor associated with intrinsic motivation and are more ready to act in accordance with integrated values and interests. A strong autonomy orientation reflects their success in satisfying the three basic psychological needs. As an example, although tangible rewards have been shown many times to undermine intrinsic motivation (see Deci, Koestner, & Ryan, 1999), Hagger and Chatzisarantis (2011) found that people high in autonomy orientation did not show a significant decrement in intrinsic motivation following the externally controlled contingent rewards, suggesting that this individual-difference orientation buffered them against the rewards' effects.

The controlled orientation indexes the degree to which people tend to orient to external or introjected contingencies and to use these to regulate their behavior. People high in the controlled orientation are thus motivated but are also more vulnerable to having their autonomy thwarted. In the Hagger and Chatzisarantis (2011) experiment mentioned above, the intrinsic motivation of people high in the control orientation was more readily undermined by tangible rewards. In addition, the control orientation is not reliably linked to positive wellness outcomes.

The impersonal orientation is the least healthy and effective orientation, for it is salient and operative when people have lost their sense of volition, intentionality, and engagement. They instead experience a sense of being ineffective and unable to attain desired outcomes. This orientation develops as people experience a considerable degree of unpredictable thwarting of their basic psychological needs, leaving them feeling nonautonomous, ineffective, and anxious. Impersonal orientations often foster amotivation or akrasia, leaving the individuals unable to master or take command of themselves or situations.

> *COT Proposition I:* People have three different motivational orientations—called *causality orientations*—that represent global-level individual differences. Causality orientations are propensities to focus on certain aspects of environments and inner capacities that concern motivation and the causes of their behaviors. These are labeled the *autonomy orientation,* the *controlled orientation,* and the *impersonal orientation.* These orientations affect people's situation-specific motivation, as well as their general need satisfaction, behavior, and experience.

COT suggests that people differ in the relative strengths of these three orientations. It does not suggest, however, that persons are exclusively one of these types but, rather, that people have some degree of each of the three orientations. In other words, each person has a readiness to engage with the world to some degree in an autonomy-oriented way, to some degree in a controlled way, and to some degree in an amotivated way. Thus the assessment of causality orientations has typically involved measuring all three orientations, and the *General Causality Orientations Scale* (GCOS; Deci & Ryan, 1985a; Vallerand, Blais, Lacouture, & Deci, 1987) provides people with a score on each orientation. Although these orientations are considered general or cross-domain, any one of a person's orientations may be activated by contextual factors, and thus there can be some variability in which of a person's orientations is more salient in relation to different people with whom he or she might be interacting or in different contexts (e.g., in school, or at a sporting event). Accordingly, the causality orientation concept has been applied within domains of activity, such as physical activity (e.g., see Rose, Markland, & Parfitt, 2001).

Accordingly, in research on causality orientations, the three dimensions are assessed, and all three are used to predict various behaviors or experiences. Furthermore, there are other analytic strategies that are sometimes used to examine particular kinds of questions. For example, if one wanted to test a hypothesis that people high on autonomy would experience a strong correlation between certain attitudes and behaviors, one might decide to select a group of participants for the study who are relatively high (e.g., above the mean) on the autonomy orientation and relatively low on the other two orientations. We return to the issue of research strategies later in the chapter when we discuss GCOS-based research.

In addition, because causality orientations represent motivational sets that guide individuals to focus on particular aspects of a context and potentiate specific types of functional significance, motivational orientations can also be activated by specific cues in the context, often ones of which the individuals are not aware. Thus, we also discuss research in which the autonomy or control orientations can be *primed*, leading to distinct and predictable downstream effects.

Why Study Individual Differences?

From the perspective of SDT, one of the important reasons for specifying individual differences in causality orientations is to provide accounts both of individuals' acting autonomously in contexts that are controlling or amotivating—that is, in contexts that tend to undermine autonomy—and of people being controlled or amotivated in contexts that are autonomy-supportive and informational. Stated differently, although research has confirmed beyond question that the quality of social contexts affects motivation, behavior, development, and wellness, the association of the quality of interpersonal contexts (i.e., the degrees to which they are autonomy-, competence-, and relatedness-supportive) to people's behaviors and experiences (e.g., persistence, vitality) is by no means one-to-one. People in controlling contexts are not always controlled (some are resilient), and people in autonomy-supportive contexts are not always autonomous (some are highly vulnerable). Instead, people actively interpret and give psychological meaning to contexts and then act in accordance with their interpretations rather than with objective characteristics of the context. To a significant extent, these interpretations are affected by people's personalities—including both classic traits and individual differences in causality orientations.

For example, people who have been continually subjected to controlling environments will tend to develop a strong controlled orientation and will, in turn, have a tendency to interpret new environments they encounter as being controlling, even when the contexts are relatively autonomy-supportive. Moreover, people often seek out contexts rather than just respond to the ones in which they find themselves. Thus, for example, people who are high in the autonomy orientation tend to seek out interpersonal contexts that encourage and support their initiative and choice, whereas people who are high in the control orientation may gravitate to contexts in which external directives abound. Further, to some degree, people may not only seek contexts that are consistent with their personalities, but they may also act on the contexts they are in, changing the contexts to make them more consistent with their own orientations. As such, whether they do it intentionally or unintentionally, people influence the quality of the interpersonal contexts that in turn influence them. For example, people with a strong controlled orientation may "pull on" their teachers, coaches, or supervisors to control them—that is, they may behave in ways that increase the chances of those authorities being controlling with them.

All these phenomena—differentially seeking out, interpreting contexts, and influencing social contexts—are described within COT. Thus, despite SDT's strong emphasis on the potent influence of social contexts, individual differences in causality orientations are expected to account for some of the variance in people's motivation, behavior, and well-being at any given time and often to moderate the effects of social events.

Development and Causality Orientations

As implied in the previous paragraph, causality orientations are both an outcome of development—that is, of the organismic integration process—and an input to development. For example, people who are high in the autonomy orientation at a given time will have developed that strong orientation in part from having had their autonomy supported over time. In turn, a strong autonomy orientation will lead them to interpret newly encountered contexts differently—that is, engaging in the situations more congruently and openly, with less defensive responding, and giving them a more informational functional significance (e.g., Koestner & Losier, 1996; Weinstein & Hodgins, 2009). That will then further the development of their autonomy. Parallel dynamics would function for people high in the controlled and impersonal orientations. Thus someone high in the controlled orientation would be more likely to give a social context a controlling functional significance and someone high in the impersonal orientation, an amotivating functional significance.

At any given time, an aggregate of motivational changes will have occurred that affect the individuals' orientations toward causality. For example, a child who grows up with an anxious parent may be more controlled in early development and display less intrinsic motivation and greater introjection. With such a background, he or she may be sensitive to external pressures and evaluations, and thus these elements of situations will be highly salient. Such a child may tend to interpret each new social context as controlling, which may further undermine intrinsic motivation and autonomy, thus eliciting controlling reactions from adults. Over time, through this ongoing bidirectional process, development will affect the strength of each causality orientation within a person, and the person's causality orientations will affect further development.

Each orientation thus represents an individual-difference variable indexing the strength of that motivational orientation, and each can be used to predict other relevant variables. Thus COT does *not* categorize people as types. Rather than being concerned with autonomy-oriented people or impersonally oriented people, for example, the theory views people as having a set of these three related characteristics, each with its own strength that develops through organismic integration being more or less successful and in turn influencing a range of motivational, behavioral, and well-being outcomes.

> *COT Proposition II:* Causality orientations are developmental outcomes that are influenced over time by biological and social-contextual factors that impact satisfaction of the basic psychological needs for autonomy, competence, and relatedness. To the degree that individuals' social environments are substantially and persistently autonomy-supportive, controlling, or amotivating over time, people will, respectively, tend to develop strong autonomy orientations, controlled orientations, and impersonal orientations.

Assessing General Causality Orientations

Deci and Ryan (1985a) described the construction and validation of an initial instrument to assess GCO. The GCOS gives three subscale scores, one for each orientation, that can be used separately or together in making various predictions.

The Autonomy subscale indexes the degree to which a person focuses on interesting or personally important activities and takes interest in and orients toward autonomy-supportive aspects of the social environment; the Controlled subscale measures the degree to which the person orients toward controls and directives concerning how he or she should behave or the rewards and punishments associated with their behaviors; and the Impersonal subscale assesses the degree to which the person focuses on cues that signify incompetence or lack of control over outcomes and on avoiding intentional action. In terms of motivational processes, the three orientations comprise, respectively, the tendencies toward (1) intrinsic motivation and well-internalized extrinsic motivation; (2) external and introjected regulations; and (3) amotivation and lack of intention.

Because they emerge from the relations between persons and contexts and pertain specifically to how environments are construed or interpreted, causality orientations are distinct from personality traits, such as the *five-factor model* (FFM) of individual differences in personality (McCrae & Costa, 2003). In fact, in two studies by Olesen and colleagues (Olesen, Thomsen, Schnieber, & Tønnesvang, 2010; Olesen, 2011), one with a sample of university students and the other with a representative sample of Danish adults, it was confirmed that causality orientations as measured with the GCOS are empirically distinct from the "Big Five" personality factors of the FFM. Autonomy and control were particularly distinct from the FFM traits, although control was correlated (negatively) with agreeableness and autonomy was positively associated with extraversion and openness. The impersonal causality orientation was both distinct and overlapping with neuroticism, as would be theoretically expected. These studies also found that the causality orientations explained additional variance in a range of outcomes over and above that explained by the dimensions of the FFM.

Autonomy Orientation: Empirical Results

Research using the GCOS (Deci & Ryan, 1985a) has shown the autonomy orientation to be positively correlated with self-esteem, ego development, and self-actualization. Koestner and Zuckerman (1994) reported that students high in the autonomy orientation tended to adopt learning rather than performance goals and tended to have high confidence in their academic abilities. Other studies have shown that being high on the autonomy orientation was related to experiencing low levels of boredom (Farmer & Sundberg, 1986), being careful in weighing their interests and abilities in making career decisions (Blustein, 1989), and focusing on interest and challenge at work (Amabile, Hill, Hennessey, & Tighe, 1994).

Soenens, Berzonsky, Vansteenkiste, Beyers, and Goossens (2005) also found the autonomy orientation to be related to the informational style in Berzonsky's (1990) model of adolescent identity styles. This style involves the adolescents' actively constructing an identity through experimenting with and evaluating relevant information, remaining open to change as a function of relevant new information, and being generally flexible in their identity development. They are also cognitively complex, persistent, and problem focused in their coping (Berzonsky, 2004). Further, the autonomy orientation has been related to people's tendency to support the autonomy of others. That is, the more strongly individuals are autonomy-oriented in their own lives, the more likely they are to be autonomy-supportive of others (e.g., Deci & Ryan 1985a).

Other research using the GCOS showed that cardiac patients high on the autonomy orientation viewed their surgery more as a challenge than a threat and reported more positive postoperative attitudes than patients low on the autonomy orientation (King, 1984). Further, morbidly obese patients high on the autonomy orientation who were in a very-low-calorie liquid diet program were more likely to lose weight than were patients low on the autonomy orientation (Williams, Grow, Freedman, Ryan, & Deci, 1996). The higher the patients' scores on the autonomy orientation were and the more they tended to see their health-care providers as autonomy-supportive, the more autonomous were their regulatory styles for following the program guidelines, the more regularly they attended patient group meetings, and the greater was their maintained weight loss over a 2-year period.

In a laboratory study of romantic partners that was designed to emphasize differences in how the partners viewed the relationship, Knee, Patrick, Vietor, Nanayakkara, and Neighbors (2002) found that individuals who were high on the autonomy orientation displayed less negative emotions, more positive behaviors, and more relationship-maintaining coping strategies. Those high in the controlled orientation, in contrast, were more negative and wanted their partners to be more like themselves.

In fact, such results have much to do with the significant role played by autonomy orientations in the processing of threats and negative events. For example, Weinstein and Hodgins (2009) exposed individuals to disturbing films that would engender negative emotions. Although nearly all individuals initially reacted with lower well-being and vitality, those with a high autonomy orientation, especially if given an opportunity to express their experiences, showed better coping in a reexposure session. In processing their experiences, persons high in the autonomy orientation evidenced more ownership of feelings and openness to what had occurred, allowing themselves to better assimilate and cope. In turn, in the second session they showed lower costs in terms of energy and wellness. Priming of autonomy and controlled orientations produced similar results.

In two studies of prosocial behavior, one with college students and one with adults from the community, Gagné (2003) assessed people's autonomous orientations and their prosocial activities. The college students reported on whether they had volunteered time to nonprofit organizations, contributed money to charity, given to a food drive, recycled, or participated in six other behaviors. The primary dependent variable was the students' overall level of participation in these prosocial activities. The adults in the community sample were all individuals who worked as volunteers for an animal shelter. In this study, the primary dependent variable was the number of hours the participants volunteered at the animal shelter. In both studies, the autonomy orientation was a significant predictor of the amount of prosocial behavior in which the individuals participated.

Neighbors and Knee (2003) did a study to examine people's affect following comparisons of their own performances with the performances of others who had done either better or worse than they had. The researchers assessed the participants' autonomy orientation and separated them into those high in autonomy and those low in autonomy. When people high in the autonomy orientation compared themselves with others who had done better than they had, their positive affect was at the same level as when they compared themselves to others who had done worse than they had. However, when people low in autonomy orientation compared themselves with others who had done better than they had, their affect was much less positive than it was when they compared themselves to others who had done worse than they had.

Bridges, Frodi, Grolnick, and Spiegel (1983) assessed the autonomy orientation of the mothers of 1-year-old infants who had been in the Strange Situation paradigm (Ainsworth, Blehar, Waters, & Wall, 1978). Results showed that the mothers of infants who had been classified as having a secure attachment had higher scores on the autonomy orientation than the mothers of infants who had been classified as either avoidant or resistant in their attachments. Mothers of the infants classified as resistant were higher on the controlled orientations than were the other two groups of mothers, and mothers of children classified as avoidant were higher on the impersonal orientation than the other two groups of mothers.

To summarize, the autonomy orientation has been associated with a variety of other variables that represent such outcomes as psychological well-being, persistence, complex and flexible thinking, prosocial involvement, healthy behavior change, and more positive and effective interacting with social partners.

Controlled Orientation: Empirical Results

Deci and Ryan (1985a) reported that the control orientation was positively correlated with public self-consciousness and with the Type-A coronary-prone behavior pattern (using instruments by Jenkins, Rosenman, & Friedman, 1967; Fenigstein, Scheier, & Buss, 1975), indicating that the focus tends to be outward and hard driving, as would be expected. Further, McHoskey (1999) found that people high on the control orientation tended to be more Machiavellian (Christie & Geis, 1970). Lonky and Reihman (1990) discovered that people who were highly controlled tended to cheat more when given the opportunity to do so, suggesting the lack of integration characterizing controlled regulation. Zuckerman, Gioioso, and Tellini (1988) found that highly controlled individuals preferred image-based rather than quality-based approaches to advertising; and Kasser and Ryan (1993) found that people high in the control orientation also tended to place very high value on amassing wealth relative to more intrinsic aspirations.

The control orientation was also found to relate to the normative identity style among adolescents (Soenens, Berzonsky, et al., 2005). This style, from Berzonsky's (1990) theory of identity, refers to adolescents relying on the expectations and prescriptions of others such as parents for dealing with identity-related issues. Those who are high in the normative style are less flexible and more rigid than adolescents high in the informational style. They also are firmly committed to their goals and are high in conscientiousness (Dollinger, 1995). This highlights an interesting point, which is that people high in the normative style, as well as the controlled orientation, behave in some adaptive ways, although, in general, as we see, there are negative well-being concomitants to the controlled orientation because it tends to thwart satisfaction of the need for autonomy.

Koestner and Zuckerman (1994) found that students high in the controlled orientation tended to adopt performance goals rather than learning goals (Dweck & Leggett, 1988), and, in the face of failure feedback, they tended to persist in a rigid ego-involved way. This is consistent with the idea that the controlled orientation prompts motivated action, but it is a nonoptimal form of motivation that is inflexible, accompanied by negative affect and associated with poorer performance, especially on heuristic activities that require cognitive flexibility, deep thinking, conceptual understanding, problem solving, or creativity.

Neighbors and Larimer (2004) found that college students with a strong control orientation gamble more frequently, spend more money gambling, have more negative gambling consequences, and are more likely to meet clinical or subclinical criteria for disordered gambling, even after accounting for other risk factors. In other words, the focus on external contingencies and cues makes people less able to regulate themselves effectively, even when the behavior has serious negative consequences. In a similar vein, Neighbors, Larimer, Geisner, and Knee (2004) found that college students high in the controlled orientation drink more alcohol, have strong motives for drinking (including social, enhancement, coping, and conformity motives), and also have more alcohol-related problems in their lives. Clearly, a strong controlled orientation places people at risk for problem behaviors involving compromised self-regulation, such as gambling and alcohol use.

Connecting with this idea, research has linked the controlled orientation to road rage among drivers. For example, Knee, Neighbors, and Vietor (2001) found that the control orientation of college students was related to feeling more anger about other drivers' actions, more aggressive driving, and more traffic citations. In short, people high in the controlled orientation appear to represent a risk to other drivers on the road. In a follow-up study, Neighbors, Vietor, and Knee (2002) found that drivers high in the controlled orientation experienced more pressure and ego defensiveness while driving, which led to more anger and aggression in their driving. For example, control-oriented drivers, when angered, were more likely to honk, make obscene gestures, and refuse lane access to the other drivers.

Indeed, there seem to be compelling links between the controlled orientation and tendencies to be interpersonally aggressive. For example, Goldstein and Iso-Ahola (2008) hypothesized and found that parents on the sidelines of their children's sporting events who had a higher controlled orientation were more likely to feel anger and hostility when negative events occurred on the field, leading to more subjective aggression and aggressive behaviors. Moller and Deci (2010) showed that persons with greater controlled orientations were more prone toward both interpersonal aggression and endorsements of violence. This was to some extent mediated by their increased tendency to dehumanize others, which is consistent with the view that when controlled persons feel more like objects, they evidence decreased empathic sensibilities.

To summarize, when people are high on the controlled orientation, they tend also to be high in Type-A personality, public self-consciousness, ego involvement, performance goals, and the normative identity style. Further, they are more likely to have problems with gambling and drinking alcohol, and they are more likely to be prone to aggression. Being high in the controlled orientation is associated with being motivated and persistent, but the form of motivation is nonoptimal and is predictive of poorer well-being than is the case with the autonomy orientation.

Impersonal Orientation: Empirical Results

In Deci and Ryan's (1985a) initial research, the impersonal orientation was positively related to social anxiety, public self-consciousness, self-derogation, and depressive symptoms and lower self-esteem. It was also related to lower ego development (Loevinger, 1976). Further, McHoskey (1999) reported that the impersonal orientation was positively related to the powerless and self-estrangement aspect of alienation (Seeman, 1991). Koestner and Zuckerman (1994) reported that students high on the impersonal orientation tended to hold performance (rather than learning) goals, accompanied by low confidence in their ability to do well in their course work. This is the classic helplessness pattern found by Dweck and Leggett (1988), which makes sense because the impersonal orientation involves expectations of not being able to control outcomes and, as mentioned above, is associated with greater depressive symptoms.

More recently, Cooper, Lavaysse and Gard (2015) designed an adapted version of the GCOS for use with clinical populations, especially those experiencing more severe mental illnesses (the GCOS-CP). Applying this measure, they compared individuals with schizophrenia to others without the disorder, finding that those with schizophrenia showed lower autonomy orientations and higher impersonal orientations.

Soenens, Berzonsky, et al. (2005) reported that adolescents high in the impersonal causality orientation tended also to be high in a diffuse–avoidant identity style, which means that they tend to procrastinate, deny internal conflicts, put off decisions and actions, use maladaptive coping styles, and be high in neuroticism (e.g., Duriez, Soenens, & Beyers, 2004). Simply stated, the impersonal causality orientation appears to be the motivational basis of a diffuse–avoidant identity style.

A study by Strauss and Ryan (1987) showed that women who were diagnosed with restrictive anorexia nervosa were significantly higher on the impersonal orientations than a comparison group of women who were matched for relevant demographics. In other words, not being able to control outcomes and feeling an overwhelming sense of ineffectance appears to be integral to anorexia nervosa as theorized by Bruch (1973).

In sum, the impersonal orientation is associated with social anxiety, public self-consciousness, self-derogation, depressive symptoms, lack of motivation, performance goals combined with low confidence, a diffuse–avoidant identity style, an external locus of control, and a more severe clinical issues, such as schizophrenia. Clearly, impersonality is indicative of adaptive issues and compromised functioning.

> *COT Proposition III:* Causality orientations affect people's effectiveness in engaging with their surroundings, as well as their psychological well-being, as mediated by types of domain- or situation-specific motivations and need satisfactions. The autonomy orientation promotes greater integration of personality, which strengthens itself and promotes effective performance and well-being. The controlled orientation promotes introjection and rigidity, which strengthens itself and promotes less effective self-regulation and less positive experience. The impersonal orientation promotes the experience of ineffectance and amotivation, thereby strengthening itself and leading to the least effective performance and lower well-being outcomes.

Locus of Control and Locus of Causality

Research by Deci and Ryan (1985a) also found the impersonal causality orientation to be related to an external locus of control—that is, to the belief that behaviors and outcomes are independent, that one cannot attain one's desired outcomes—which is a basis for amotivation and the lack of intentionality. The concept of *locus of control* (Rotter, 1966) is sometimes confused with that of *perceived locus of causality* (PLOC; de Charms, 1968; Heider, 1958). *Locus of control* refers to believing that one either does or does not have control over reinforcements—that is, that one is or is not able to attain desired outcomes by engaging in requisite behaviors. Believing that one *can* attain outcomes through one's action is a marker of an *internal locus of control,* and believing that one *cannot* is a marker of an *external locus of control*. In contrast, an *internal perceived locus of causality* (I-PLOC) means that one sees oneself as the source of initiation and regulation of behavior and feels a sense of volition and endorsement of the actions; an *external perceived locus of causality* (E-PLOC) means to be controlled by desired outcomes and the contingencies that lead to them, experiencing a sense of pressure and compulsion; and an *impersonal locus of causality* means to feel that one cannot attain desired outcomes, especially ones related to the competence and relatedness needs, and to feel a sense of passivity and amotivation. From this, one can see that the external locus of *control* is conceptually related to the impersonal locus of *causality* because both involve the experience of not being able to attain desired outcomes, and the data have shown that the impersonal causality orientation is strongly related to an external locus of control.

It is worth considering the issue of locus of control and locus of causality a bit further, as they are important but distinct concepts. Locus of control was introduced by Rotter to explain the difference between people being either motivated or unmotivated. People with an internal locus of control were expected to have a high level of motivation, and people with an external locus of control were expected to have a low level of motivation. In SDT, this is equivalent to the distinction between being motivated and being amotivated. Amotivation is a manifestation of the impersonal causality orientation, so it follows logically that the external locus of control would be related to the impersonal causality orientation, as mentioned above. Further, people high in an internal locus of control (which means to be low on external locus of control, because these concepts are two ends of the same continuum) are expected to be highly motivated. However, the locus of *control* concept (unlike the locus of *causality* concept) does not differentiate types of motivation. Thus an internal locus of control (which implies motivation) does not align well will either an internal locus of causality (which is based in autonomous motivation) or an external locus of causality (which is based on controlled motivation). Hence, a person high in internal locus of control could, theoretically, be high in either an internal or an external locus of causality. And therein lies the potential confusion. An external locus of control is aligned with the impersonal (rather than external) locus of causality, and an internal locus of control could be aligned with either an internal or an external locus of causality.

Other Theoretically Important Empirical Results

Research employing the GCOS has also been used to confirm several important theoretical points central to SDT. These include: (1) that autonomy is a reflection of greater integration in personality; (2) that causality orientations relate to need satisfaction, with greater autonomy orientation predicting more basic need satisfaction, independent of variance predicted by the quality of the social context; (3) that causality orientations predict differences in people being open to experience (vs. being defensive) in a variety of situations and in the quality of people's social interactions; and (4) that causality orientations explain variance in regulatory styles, over and above that explained by the quality of social contexts. Consider each in turn.

Autonomy and Integration

Integration, which is theorized to result when the organismic integration process functions effectively, is facilitated by social contexts that support basic psychological need satisfaction. It is characterized by holism, awareness, and congruence, and it is the means through which people develop stronger autonomy orientations. A strong autonomy orientation in turn is displayed in part as coherence or integration among traits, motivations, beliefs, and behaviors. An important set of studies by Koestner, Bernieri, and Zuckerman (1992) tested this reasoning in an exploration of the relation between autonomy and integration in personality. The researchers separated participants into those high in autonomy versus those high in control and examined the degree of integration or consistency exhibited by each group. This set of studies was one instance in which the GCOS has been used to classify people as being primarily of one type or another rather than just using the causality orientation dimensions to predict other variables. Using this approach allowed the researchers to explore the relations among other variables within individuals who fall into either the high-autonomy group or the high-controlled group.

Using college student participants, Koestner et al. (1992) converted scores on the autonomy and controlled orientations from the GCOS into z-scores and formed a group of high-autonomy-oriented individuals and a group of high-control-oriented individuals in accordance with which of their z-scores was higher. The researchers then tested the general hypothesis that autonomy-oriented participants would evidence greater integration or consistency across various aspects of personality than would participants high in the controlled orientation.

Koestner et al. (1992) began with two experiments that examined the correlations between the free-choice *behavioral* measure and the self-reported *interest* measure of intrinsic motivation (described in Chapter 6) as a way of indexing consistency or integration in personality. The idea was that people who were higher in autonomy than in control would show stronger relations between the behavior and internal states than would people who were higher in control than in autonomy. In order to interpret the results of the Koestner et al. studies, it is important to begin by noting that in a meta-analysis, summarized in Chapter 6, of studies examining reward effects on intrinsic motivation (Deci et al., 1999), 17 of the 128 experiments used both the behavioral and self-report measures of intrinsic motivation and reported the correlations between the two measures. The average correlation was .35.

In the Koestner et al. (1992) experiments on consistency, the researchers performed two intrinsic motivation laboratory experiments using the free-choice paradigm, and they examined the correlations between the behavioral and self-report measures of intrinsic motivation. In both experiments, the correlation between the two measures when all participants were taken together was very similar to the .35 average found for the 17 studies in the meta-analysis. However, the researchers then calculated correlations separately for the autonomy-oriented group and the control-oriented group, and the results for these two groups were very revealing. Specifically, the correlation between free-choice behavior and self-reported interest within the autonomy-oriented group was in excess of .6 in both studies, whereas within the control-oriented group the correlation was essentially zero in both studies. Thus the autonomy-oriented participants displayed greater integration between behaviors and attitudes/feelings than did the control-oriented participants.

Whereas the free-choice behavior of the autonomy-oriented individuals was a reflection of their interest in the activity, the free-choice behavior of the control-oriented group was apparently based on controlling thoughts or introjected contingencies rather than on their feelings or interests.

In another study, Koestner et al. (1992) considered the relationship between traits and behaviors. They had participants report to a lab and complete a trait measure of conscientiousness (Costa & McCrae, 1985). Then, as the participants were about to leave, the experimenter gave them a questionnaire and asked them to complete it at home and drop it off at the psychology department office. The researchers then correlated participants' conscientiousness scores, reflecting a personality dimension, with their conscientious behavior of returning the questionnaire as requested. Results indicated that the correlation between trait and behavior for the autonomy-oriented group was significantly greater than for the control-oriented group, thus providing additional evidence of greater integration within individuals highly autonomous relative to those highly controlled.

Finally, the researchers examined the relationship between how people perceive themselves and how they are perceived by others, expecting that people who are more autonomy-oriented would be more authentic, acting in accordance with the way they perceive themselves, so there would be a higher correlation between self and other perceptions for people high in autonomy than for those high in control. The researchers had a same-sex roommate of each participant rate the participant on various traits, including conscientiousness, and the researchers correlated the self-ratings and peer ratings on that trait. The correlation for autonomy-oriented participants was somewhat stronger than for control-oriented participants, also suggesting greater integration, or at least self-awareness, for participants higher in autonomy. Taken together, the Koestner et al. (1992) studies indicated that autonomy is associated with greater congruence between psychological variables and actions, which implies that it is related to greater personality integration. As such, these studies provide an empirical link between the concept of autonomy or self-determination and that of integration, which we have theorized to be the developmental process through which behaviors motivated by extrinsic values and emotions can become self-determined.

A more recent set of five experiments took a quite different approach to examining integration (Weinstein, Deci, & Ryan, 2011). In some of the studies, participants completed the GCOS, from which they got a score representing where they stood on autonomous versus controlled orientations; in the others they were primed with either the autonomous orientation or the controlled orientation. Then, in all studies, participants were asked to think about themselves 3 years earlier, focusing either on positive or negative characteristics of themselves at that earlier age or else on either positive or negative life events from that time. After they took a bit of time to reflect on those prior experiences, they were asked various questions about how much they accepted those prior experiences as part of themselves at the time of the study and how relevant the past experiences were to their current identities.

Interestingly, in all studies, whether motivation was measured with the GCOS or was primed experimentally, people's motivations interacted with positive versus negative prior experiences in predicting whether those experiences were accepted as aspects of who the people were at the time of the study 3 years after the experiences. In short, if participants were high in autonomy or if autonomy had been primed for them, they accepted both positive and negative past characteristics or life events as being very much a part of who they were years later; whereas if they were high in control or if control had been primed for them, they accepted the positive past characteristics or life events as being part of them, but they rejected the negative past experiences, indicating that those negative experiences were not part of who they were at the time of the study.

Stated differently, people who were more autonomous were more integrated, having accepted both positive and negative past aspects of their lives, whereas people who were more controlled accepted only past positive aspects and somehow rejected or compartmentalized the negative aspects, not acknowledging that those experiences were part of themselves.

Causality Orientations and Need Satisfaction

To be self-determined or autonomous in their actions, people must (1) be aware of the needs, processes, feelings, cognitions, and relationships that make up their true or integrated sense of who they are and (2) act in accordance with that integrated sense of self. To a large extent, this involves people allowing their basic needs to emerge and behaving in ways that satisfy those needs. Thus we theorize that when people are more autonomous, they will also experience a greater degree of satisfaction of their three universal psychological needs.

Accordingly, we suggest that the relationship of causality orientations (and the associated regulatory styles) to performance and well-being is a function of the degree to which the different orientations facilitate satisfaction of the basic needs for competence, autonomy, and relatedness. High levels of the autonomous causality orientation are hypothesized to facilitate greater need satisfaction, over and above the contributions to need satisfaction made by autonomy support in the interpersonal context. Accordingly, high levels of autonomy orientation should be associated with positive performance and well-being outcomes. Controlled and impersonal orientations, on the other hand, are hypothesized to be associated with less need satisfaction, generally impaired performance, and poorer well-being.

A study by Baard, Deci, and Ryan (2004), performed in two work organizations, tested this hypothesis. Employees completed several questionnaires, including the GCOS; the Work Climate Questionnaire (WCQ), which assesses employees' perceptions of the degree to which the work climate is autonomy-supportive; a scale measuring employees' experience of satisfaction of each of the three basic psychological needs in the workplace; and three indicators of mental health—namely, vitality and the inverses of anxiety and somatization. In addition, the researchers obtained the employees' performance ratings.

Results of the study indicated first that, as predicted, both performance ratings and well-being were predicted by need satisfaction. Further, both the employees' autonomy orientations from the GCOS and the autonomy supportiveness of the work climate from the WCQ positively predicted independent variance in need satisfaction. Those employees who experienced the work climate as more autonomy-supportive reported greater need satisfaction and, in turn, displayed better performance and adjustment. However, and most importantly for our current discussion, individual differences in the autonomous causality orientation significantly predicted need satisfaction (and, in turn, performance and well-being) over and above the effects on need satisfaction of the social context being autonomy-supportive. Employees who were higher on the autonomy orientation of the GCOS experienced greater need satisfaction, performed better, and displayed higher well-being independent of the social context. This finding was later extended by Lam and Gurland (2008), who found that the employees' autonomy orientation predicted their autonomous work motivation and, in turn, their job satisfaction and commitment to their work.

Causality Orientation, Open Engagement, and Social Experiences

Several studies have used the GCOS in a variety of situations to predict the level of people's open engagement and mindful experiencing versus their guarded and defensive responding. In one experiment, Knee and Zuckerman (1996) found that people high in autonomy and low in control displayed less self-serving bias—that is, had less of a tendency to take undue credit for successes and diminished responsibility for failures—than did people who were high in control and low in autonomy. In another study, Knee and Zuckerman (1998) found that participants high in autonomy and low in control were less likely than other participants to use self-handicapping strategies and avoidant coping during stressful periods—that is, people high in autonomy were less likely to use strategies in which they created barriers to their successes in order to have an excuse for their anticipated failures.

A program of studies conducted by Hodgins and colleagues examined whether individuals who were more autonomy-oriented would display greater openness and interest, rather than defending against experience, in the domain of interpersonal relationships. In the first such study, Hodgins, Koestner, and Duncan (1996) followed the interactions of college students with their parents over a 3-week period. They found that students who were high in autonomy and low in control were more honest and disclosing, reported more pleasant affect, and felt better about themselves in their interactions with parents than were students high in the controlled orientation. In a follow-up study, Hodgins et al. (1996) examined all the interpersonal interactions of another sample of students over a week-long period. Results indicated that, relative to students who were more controlled, those who were more autonomous also were more disclosing and honest with others who reciprocated; reported more positive affect in their interactions; felt better about themselves; and were generally more trusting of others, all of which suggests that autonomy was indeed associated with greater openness and engagement within relationships.

In other studies, Hodgins and colleagues (Hodgins & Liebeskind, 2003; Hodgins, Liebeskind, & Schwartz, 1996) looked at how people responded to conflict or stresses within their relationships, specifically investigating whether people high in autonomy would tend to accept greater responsibility and be less blaming with respect to interpersonal problems. Results of a variety of studies indicated that individuals who were more autonomous relative to those high on the other orientations used fewer lies in explaining wrongdoings and provided more apologies, especially apologies that were more complex, when they had caused harm to others.

These studies by Hodgins and colleagues not only show that individuals who are more autonomous tend to be more open and less defensive, but they also address the relations between autonomy and relatedness in human interactions. Each of the studies just reviewed focused on the quality of relationships of individuals high in autonomy relative to those high in control. The results indicated that people high in autonomy have higher quality interactions with their relational partners. This is an important finding, because various writers (e.g., Gilligan, 1982; Jordan, 1991) have suggested that autonomy and relatedness tend to be antagonistic in relationships, that men tend to be more focused on autonomy and women on relatedness. The Hodgins et al. studies indicate that, rather than being antagonistic, autonomy and relatedness are indeed compatible. People high in autonomy also tend to be more successful in satisfying their relatedness needs.

As mentioned elsewhere in the book, part of the reason for the confusion about autonomy and relatedness is that many past researchers tend to interpret autonomy as meaning independence rather than volition—as being detached from others rather than being engaged with them in an autonomous way. Two studies by Koestner and colleagues speak directly to this issue. Specifically, they showed the different correlates and consequences of two different types of autonomy—one that means volition and one that means independence.

Reflective and Reactive Forms of Autonomy

Koestner and Losier (1996) pointed out that several personality theorists, beginning with Murray (1938) and including Gough and Heilbrun (1983), have also interpreted autonomy to mean independence from others. Koestner and Losier (1996) referred to this as *reactive autonomy*. They contrasted it with the autonomy in SDT, which they referred to as *reflective autonomy* and defined in terms of acting with a sense of choice. In their research, Koestner and Losier used the GCOS to measure reflective autonomy. In contrast, they used the Autonomy/Independence subscale from the Adjective Check List (ACL; Gough & Heilbrun, 1983) to measure reactive autonomy. Reactive autonomy assessed with the ACL had previously been related to a dislike of teamwork on the job (O'Reilly, Chatman, & Caldwell, 1991), being more likely to drop out of college (Heilbrun, 1965), and engaging in criminal behavior (e.g., Platt, 1975), all characteristics and behaviors that are very unlike the correlates of reflective autonomy as assessed with the GCOS.

In the Koestner and Losier (1996) research, reactive autonomy assessed with ACL was not significantly related to reflective autonomy assessed with the GCOS, but reactive autonomy (ACL) was significantly related to the controlled subscale of the GCOS, clearly indicating that the two types of "autonomy" are very different. Further, in a daily diary study, these researchers found reactive autonomy to predict reports of more negative daily events and more negative mood, whereas reflective autonomy was related to reporting of more positive daily events and more positive mood.

In another study in that series, Koestner and Losier (1996) found that reflective autonomy was positively related to reporting pleasant interactions with peers and with sharing more with peers, whereas reactive autonomy was unrelated to these variables. In contrast, reactive autonomy was related to reporting more negative interactions with authority figures, whereas reflective autonomy was not related to the valence of interactions with authorities. Stated differently, being high on reflective autonomy, which means volition, was positively related to positive interactions with peers and was not related to the valence of interactions with authority figures, whereas being high in reactive autonomy was related to negative interactions with authority figures and unrelated to the valence of interactions with peers. It is thus clear that when autonomy is defined as independence (reactive autonomy), it is incompatible with positive relationships, but when it is defined as volition (reflective autonomy), as is the case in SDT, it is quite compatible with positive relationships. In Chapter 12 we return to the issue of autonomy versus independence.

A study by Koestner, Gingras, Abutaa, Losier, DiDio, and Gagné (1999) further examined the relationships of people high in reflective versus reactive autonomy with authority figures. In a betting task during horse races, participants were offered advice from credible experts. They found that reflective autonomy (assessed with the GCOS) was significantly positively related to following the advice of credible experts, whereas reactive autonomy was significantly negatively related to following the advice of these experts. Here again we see that people high in reactive autonomy are reactive or rebellious in relation to authorities, but people high in reflective autonomy appear better adjusted in relation to authorities and are able to use their credible recommendations.

To summarize, numerous studies have shown that people high in autonomy as it is defined in SDT are more open and engaged with others and are less defensive and guarded. They are also more positively involved with their peers and are better adjusted in their relationships with authorities. When autonomy is defined as independence, the picture is very different. People high in independence often have more negative relations with parents or peers and are also often reactive and rebellious in their interactions with authorities (Ryan & Lynch, 1989; Van Petegem, Beyers, Vansteenkiste, & Soenens, 2012).

Causality Orientations and Self-Regulation

As noted earlier, within SDT, causality orientations refer to personality orientations that reflect differences in the extent to which individuals tend, in general, to be self-determined in their ongoing interactions with their social surrounds, whereas self-regulation refers to differences in the reasons for which individuals are doing particular behaviors or classes of behaviors. Thus causality orientations and regulatory styles represent different levels of analysis—different levels of generality—and one would expect that individuals high in general autonomy as assessed with the GCOS would tend to be more autonomous in their regulation of behaviors within specific domains or situations. Various studies have examined this hypothesis.

In one study of medical students taking an interviewing course from one of several instructors, Williams and Deci (1996) assessed (1) the medical students' GCO before they entered the course, (2) the degree to which the interpersonal climate of the course tended to be autonomy-supportive, and (3) the students' autonomous regulation for studying the course material at two points during the course. These were assessed at the beginning and again at the end of the course. Results of the study showed that the autonomy orientation on the GCOS predicted students' autonomous regulation for studying the course material independent of the contribution made by the autonomy supportiveness of the instructors. When the instructors were perceived as more autonomy-supportive, the students became more autonomous in their regulatory styles over the period of the course, but this effect was independent of the effect of the students' autonomous causality orientation, which also predicted the students' autonomous regulation. In sum, the autonomy-supportiveness of a social context does facilitate individuals' becoming more autonomous for particular behaviors, but a relatively enduring aspect of the individuals' personalities—namely, their autonomous causality orientation—also affects the degree to which they are autonomous for those behaviors in that situation, independent of the social context.

A study of obese participants in a 6-month weight-loss program with a 2-year follow-up assessed participants' causality orientations and their perceptions of the autonomy supportiveness of the clinical climate (Williams et al., 1996). Analyses of the data indicated that the autonomous individual difference and the autonomy support from the interpersonal context each predicted substantial independent variance in the participants' autonomous motivation for losing weight, which in turn predicted attendance at weekly clinic meetings and maintained weight loss over the 2 years.

So far, we have reviewed evidence about the correlates and consequences of the three GCO. A multitude of studies has shown that people's autonomy orientation is positively associated with a wide range of performance, persistence, adjustment, and well-being outcomes, including relationship to greater personality integration and to having higher quality relationships with peers and less conflicted relationships with authorities. In contrast, the controlled and impersonal orientations have much less positive and more negative correlates and consequences. We have also seen that people's GCO relate to their motivations for specific domains, in particular situations, or for specified behaviors. Such relations have been organized in a model of intrinsic and extrinsic motivation at various levels of generality (e.g., Vallerand, 1997).

The Hierarchical Model

Noting the difference in level of generality of the motivational concepts contained within causality orientations and regulatory styles, Vallerand (1997; Vallerand & Ratelle, 2002) presented a hierarchical model involving three levels of generality of intrinsic and extrinsic motivation.

The first feature of the model is types of motivation: *autonomous motivation* (i.e., intrinsic motivation and identified/integrated forms of extrinsic motivation), *controlled motivation* (i.e., introjected and external forms of extrinsic motivation), and *amotivation*. As the second feature, each type of motivation exists at three levels of generality. The most general level concerns individual differences in motivational orientations. GCOs represent this global level of generality. A less general level concerns motivational differences within domains. Regulatory styles as typically measured represent this more specific level of generality. For example, a person might be quite intrinsically motivated (i.e., autonomous) in the domain of athletics, more introjected (i.e., controlled) in the domain of academics, and quite amotivated in the domain of interpersonal relations. Finally, the least general level of motivation is situation-specific motivation. For example, in all the experiments on intrinsic motivation reviewed in Chapter 6, the intrinsic motivation that was assessed was people's intrinsic motivation for a particular activity in a particular setting at a particular time. Similarly, one can assess the regulation underlying an action within a domain, such as the reasons for doing a particular work assignment. Predicting performance on that activity at that time and place would typically be most effective if the person's motivation were assessed at that situation-specific level of generality.

A third feature of the hierarchical model concerns the prediction of motivation at a particular level. The model suggests that motivation at a particular level is determined by social-contextual factors at the same level and by motivation at the next higher (i.e., more general) level. Thus, for example, motivation at the domain-specific level is determined by the degree to which the social environment at that same level is autonomy-supportive, controlling, or amotivating and by motivation at the more global level of GCO. In fact, studies reviewed earlier in the chapter provide support for this proposition. For example, the study of medical students learning medical interviewing showed that the students' motivation for learning depended on autonomy support provided by the faculty (i.e., factors in the social context at the same level of generality) and on motivation at the more general level, namely, the students' autonomous causality orientation (Williams & Deci, 1996). The same was true for the weight-loss study just reviewed (Williams et al., 1996).

It is worth noting that, developmentally, influence among levels of motivation can function in a bottom-up fashion as well. For example, as one becomes more autonomous at studying arithmetic (the situation level), that could gradually affect one's level of autonomy for doing schoolwork more generally (i.e., the domain-specific level), which could in time affect one's general level of motivational orientation (i.e., the global or personality level). But the reverse is also true. A generally controlling climate in the workplace can lead to people feeling alienated even for tasks they might otherwise enjoy or find interest in.

A final feature of the model is that consequences of motivation—for example, the quality of performance, positivity of affect, or physical symptoms—also occur at different levels of generality. A man could, for example, be agitated and angry much of the time (the general level), or just when he is at work (the domain-specific level), or when he is with a particular manager or doing a particular task (the situation level). The importance of this is that making predictions about consequences at a particular level of generality is best accomplished by motivation variables when assessed at the same level of generality. Thus, for example, to make predictions about behavior and experience at the domain-specific level (e.g., how people will perform on the job), one will be able to account for the greatest variance in such outcomes if the motivational predictors (i.e., regulatory styles) are assessed within the same domain as the outcomes—that is, if autonomous and controlled styles of regulation with respect to work are used to predict work performance.

Priming Motivational Orientations

Earlier in the chapter, we emphasized that everyone has each of the three general causality orientations to differing degrees. We are each somewhat oriented toward affordances for autonomy, toward extant external controls, and toward the impersonal or uncontrollable aspects of our environments. Orientations are, in this sense, sets or attitudes that are more or less pervasive and salient. Each of these three general orientations can thus be viewed as a kind of "averaging across" various domains, relationships, situations, and circumstances. For example, when a young man is with his father, with whom he has unresolved authority issues, the young man's controlled orientation is likely to be quite salient (likely being manifested as both compliance and defiance) and his autonomous orientation rather low, but, when he is with his grandmother, who was always very supportive of him, his autonomous orientation may be quite salient and his controlled orientation relatively quiescent. Similarly, he might be more autonomous at schoolwork but quite impersonal with respect to public speaking. The point of this is that the three types of motivation (autonomous, controlled, and amotivation) will vary from situation to situation in terms of their salience, even though, when considered as a whole across such situations, domains, and relationships, people have certain overall degrees of readiness or strength for each of their causality orientations. This suggests that various aspects of a situation could potentially stimulate one of the causality orientations, bringing it into the foreground and leading the person to act primarily from the perspective of that orientation in that situation.

> *COT Proposition IV:* All individuals have all three causality orientations to some degree. Subtle cues in the environment may make different orientations more salient at that time and place. Thus, it is possible to prime people's motivational orientations such that their behavior and experience will be significantly affected by the primed motivation even if that orientation is, in general, relatively weak.

As we said earlier in the chapter, this aspect of the general causality orientations sets the stage for a consideration of recent studies that have primed different causality (i.e., motivational) orientations. In fact, we have already reviewed one set of studies by Weinstein and colleagues (2011) in which some of the studies examined motivational orientations by assessing them with the GCOS and other of the studies examined the orientations by priming them, with the results showing parallel outcomes for the two different methods. We now turn to a fuller consideration of priming the causality orientations.

Levesque and Pelletier (2003) did the first studies of this sort. Using the scrambled sentence method (e.g., Bargh, Chen, & Burrows, 1996), Levesque and Pelletier primed the autonomous orientation with words such as *interested, involved, challenge, satisfied,* and *mastering*; they primed the controlled orientation with words such as *obligation, evaluated, constrained, demanded,* and *forced*. They then gave participants in each condition 15 minutes to work on an interesting puzzle task that was presented as part of a different experiment. Intrinsic motivation for this target task was assessed with a self-report questionnaire, and participants' performance on the puzzle task was also assessed. Results suggested that participants primed for the autonomy orientation expressed more intrinsic motivation, interest, and perceived choice than those primed for the controlled orientation. These results suggest that, indeed, autonomous versus controlled orientations can be primed, as reflected in different reports of interest and choice. Importantly, results also showed that participants given the autonomous prime performed better on the puzzle task than those given the controlled prime. Thus the prime served to affect not only people's experiences but also their behavior, with the results for these two primed orientations paralleling those for the orientations when assessed with the GCOS or when manipulated with autonomy-supportive versus controlling contextual conditions.

In a subsequent study, Levesque and Pelletier (2003) reasoned that if participants had a strong chronic motivational orientation—that is, if either their autonomy orientation or their controlled orientation were chronically accessible—the primes would not have as strong an effect as they would if the participants did not have a strong chronic motivational orientation. To test this, the investigators used the same priming procedure and the same self-report measures as in the study described above, but they used a different puzzle task and they used the free-choice behavioral measure of autonomous motivation. Results of this study replicated those of the previous study by showing that participants given the autonomy prime were higher on the self-report measures of intrinsic motivation, interest, and choice, as well as on the free-choice behavioral measure, than were participants given the controlled prime. Further, as predicted, the researchers found an interaction of priming with motivational chronicity. The primes had a stronger effect on participants who did not have a strong chronic orientation than on participants with a strong chronic orientation, whether that chronic orientation was autonomous or controlled. Finally, there was a main effect for motivational chronicity, with the chronically autonomous individuals displaying more self-reported and behavioral autonomous motivation for the target activity than the chronically controlled individuals. Thus the results showed a clear parallel between the main effect for the chronic orientations and the main effect for the primed orientations.

In a series of studies, Hodgins and her colleagues primed motivational orientations and examined their effects on various types of defensiveness, performance, and well-being. In one study, Hodgins, Yacko, and Gottlieb (2006) used the scrambled sentence approach (Bargh et al., 1996) to prime the autonomous, controlled, and impersonal orientations in groups of participants. Following the prime, participants engaged in several unrelated tasks and then completed a questionnaire in which they reported their desire to escape from the current situation, which was interpreted as a measure of defense. Results indicated, as predicted, that participants who had been autonomy primed showed low defense (i.e., the least desire to escape), those who had been control primed showed moderate defense, and those who had been impersonally primed showed high defense. In a second study, these authors used the same priming procedure and then had participants work on an anagram task, for which they received either success or failure feedback. Subsequently, they completed an attributional questionnaire, which was used to calculate participants' self-serving bias in accounting for their performance. A main effect indicated that autonomy-primed individuals were least self-serving when giving accounts of their performances, control-primed individuals were somewhat more self-serving, and impersonally primed individuals were the most self-serving. This study thus showed the same result for primed orientations that Knee and Zuckerman (1996) had found with people whose orientations were explicitly assessed with the GCOS.

Finally, a third study in the Hodgins et al. (2006) paper examined the relation of primed motivational orientations to the defensive process of self-handicapping. In self-handicapping, people who have an important task ahead of them make up excuses for why they might fail at it, perhaps going so far as to behave in ways that increase the chances of failing. For example, students who are afraid of doing badly on a test might stay up late the night before so they will have a way of justifying the feared poor performance. The maladaptive aspect of self-handicapping is that it can actually contribute to the person's doing poorly, but at least it gives the person an excuse. In this Hodgins et al. (2006) study, participants who received the autonomy prime displayed the least self-handicapping; those who received the control prime displayed more self-handicapping; and those who received the impersonal prime displayed the most self-handicapping. Thus these results parallel those found by Knee and Zuckerman (1998), who also examined self-handicapping using the GCOS to measure causality orientations rather than priming them.

In yet another set of experiments, Hodgins, Brown, and Carver (2007) related the priming of autonomy and control orientations to self-esteem, both implicitly and explicitly assessed. Recall that the autonomy orientation is positively associated with self-esteem, but the control orientation is not. In this Hodgins et al. experiment, the primed autonomy orientation led to higher reported self-esteem, whereas the primed control orientation decreased it.

An additional experiment from this lab explored the priming of autonomous and controlled motivational orientations on defensiveness and performance, assessed with verbal, nonverbal, and physiological behaviors during an interviewing task (Hodgins et al., 2010). After being primed for autonomy or control using a scrambled sentence approach, participants were assessed electrophysiologically and videotaped while they were being subjected to a stressful interview in which they were asked threatening questions. Defensiveness was measured with such assessments as coding of videotaped behaviors for low awareness of inner states and high degrees of distortion (Feldman Barrett, Cleveland, Conner, & Williams, 2000), types of words used and length of answers to stressful questions, the ratio of perceived threat to perceived coping ability (Tomaka, Blascovich, Kelsey, & Leitten, 1993), and physiological indicators, including ventricular contractility (Mendes, Blascovich, Hunter, Lickel, & Jost, 2007). To control for chronic motivational orientations and defensiveness, participants completed the GCOS, as well as the Balanced Inventory of Desirable Responding (Paulhus, 2002), which is often used as a measure of defensiveness. Finally, participants were asked to give a brief speech, imagining that they were attempting to convince a prospective student to attend their college. These speeches were assessed for quality of performance. Results indicated that, across the range of indicators, participants given the autonomy primes were less defensive than those given the control primes. As well, those given the autonomy primes performed better in their speech making. Finally, the researchers did analyses showing that the links from the autonomy and control primes to performance on the speech was mediated by the level of defensiveness. That is, participants primed with autonomy (after controlling for chronic motivational orientation and defensiveness) were less defensive and in turn gave better speeches than was the case for participants primed with control.

These priming studies from the Hodgins lab are important because they show a clear parallel between the correlates of causality orientations when assessed as an individual difference and those resulting from the priming of motivational orientations. Further, such priming experiments allow causal interpretations of the relations between autonomy orientations and various performance and well-being outcomes. Specifically, the priming studies imply that being high in the autonomy orientations, so that it is salient more frequently, can lead people to perform better, be less defensive, and be better adjusted. Finally, the studies are important in their demonstration that causality orientations can operate automatically, as well as consciously.

Social environments include various factors that can prime people's overall motivation and affect the interpersonal styles they apply to others. Niemiec (2010) did a set of laboratory experiments to examine whether specific factors in the environment that had previously been found to be either autonomy-supportive or controlling would have a meaningful effect on the development of new relationships when the new partners were engaged in mutual self-disclosure. Specifically, would autonomy-supportive factors in a context lead people to feel more closeness, relationship satisfaction, and desire to spend additional time together? Would controlling factors in an environment lead people in them to feel less closeness, satisfaction, and desire for further interactions?

In each of four experiments, the strategy involved doing a manipulation that had previously been found to be either autonomy-supportive or controlling—namely, being provided choice, a rationale, and an acknowledgment of feelings, which have been found to be autonomy-supportive (Deci, Eghrari, Patrick, & Leone, 1994), and monetary rewards and ego involvement, which have been found to be controlling (e.g., Deci et al., 1999; Ryan, 1982). These experimental manipulations then served as a backdrop as people made new acquaintances in the lab setting. Because these laboratory experiments involved the manipulation of specific autonomy-supportive versus controlling conditions, the studies thus provided a basis for examining how ambient factors might affect developing relationships.

Results indicated that participants who were in the controlling (i.e., monetary payment or ego involvement) conditions were less satisfied with the new relationships, felt less positive affect, experienced less need satisfaction, and displayed less well-being than was the case for comparison-group participants. A further experiment examined the effects of autonomy support, operationalized as providing participants with choice about how they proceeded through the conversation, reflection of their feelings, and a rationale for doing the task relative to a comparison group. Results indicated that these participants, relative to those in the neutral comparison group, reported greater relationship satisfaction, positive affect, emotional reliance, and well-being. Thus a manipulation such as monetary payments that "controlled" the participants decreased their development of closeness and satisfaction, whereas a manipulation such as choice and acknowledgment that supported the participants' autonomy increased their development of closeness in new relationships. Together these studies show how contextual cues regarding autonomy and control can bleed over into relationships occurring within the context, changing their quality as well.

Concluding Comments

GCO's reflect individual differences in general motivational tendencies to be autonomous, controlled, or amotivated. These orientations are aligned in a parallel fashion with regulatory styles: an autonomous orientation is associated with tendencies toward intrinsic, integrated, and identified regulation; controlled orientation is associated with tendencies toward introjected and external regulation; and the impersonal orientation is associated with tendencies to be amotivated or unregulated (at both the external and internal boundaries). As well, they are parallel with three types of social contexts—autonomy-supportive, controlling, and amotivating. These three parallel sets of concepts have been organized in the hierarchical model of motivation (Vallerand, 1997).

The concept of causality orientations helps to explain why different people are differentially healthy, effective, and happy even when they are in the same social context. The arguments and data presented in this chapter make clear that the autonomy orientation is associated with the healthiest development and greatest personality integration; the controlled orientation is associated with more rigid functioning and defensiveness; and the impersonal orientation is associated with amotivation and the poorest well-being. These results have been found both when a psychometric instrument was used—namely, the GCOS—and when the motivational orientations were primed in experimental settings.

CHAPTER 10

Basic Psychological Needs Theory

Satisfaction and Frustration of Autonomy,
Competence, and Relatedness in Relation
to Psychological Wellness and Full Functioning

In previous chapters we documented how conditions that support the satisfaction of basic psychological needs for autonomy, competence, and relatedness facilitate intrinsic motivation, internalization and integration of extrinsic motivation, and more autonomous causality orientations. In this chapter we extend this work, formalizing the propositions of *basic psychological needs theory* (BPNT), the fourth of SDT's mini-theories. BPNT concerns the relations of basic psychological need satisfactions and frustrations to well-being and ill-being. We review a small sample of research from the large body of studies concerning these relations. Along the way we revisit our definition of basic needs as essential elements for wellness and flourishing and discuss why our list of needs has thus far been restricted to three. We also discuss the influence of basic need satisfactions and frustrations on vitality versus depletion and other factors associated with vital human functioning, including the impact of natural environments. Finally, we consider the concept of awareness, primarily using research on mindfulness, as a critical aspect of the processes underlying need satisfaction and eudaimonia.

On Wellness

In this chapter and the next, we explore the basic psychological needs and the life goals that conduce to wellness. Before doing so, it behooves us to first consider our criteria for wellness because, in fact, what constitutes well-being is a matter of considerable debate. For example, some psychologists have equated the idea of well-being with *happiness* (Kahneman, Krueger, Schkade, Schwarz, & Stone, 2006). According to this *hedonic* approach, well-being is primarily defined as the presence of positive affect and the absence of negative affect (e.g., Kahneman, Diener, & Schwarz, 1999). Diener (2000) also added to this combination of affects a cognitive or evaluative element of life satisfaction; when combined, these elements are described as *subjective well-being* (SWB). As Kashdan, Biswas-Diener, and King (2008) highlighted, focusing on SWB allows researchers to determine empirically the good life, because it will be defined not by a priori or "elitist" notions but rather by what people say makes them happy and satisfied. This hedonic approach also allows for systematic and evidence-based comparisons of how life conditions affect people's happiness (e.g., Diener, Inglehart, & Tay, 2012).

Yet, despite these measurement conveniences, many philosophers, religious masters, and psychologists have argued that subjective happiness and satisfaction alone do not constitute a full or appropriate definition of well-being (Delle Fave, 2009; Ryan & Huta, 2009). Aristotle (1869), for example, considered hedonic happiness as a life goal to be a "vulgar" ideal, making humans slavish followers of desires. He posited instead that "true happiness" is to be found in the expression of human excellence and virtue—that is, in the doing well of what is *worth* doing (Ryan, Curren, & Deci, 2013). Aristotle characterized such a life of pursuing aims that are inherently worthy and admirable as *eudaimonia*. Indeed, he opens his *Nicomachean Ethics* by asserting that eudaimonia is a basic human goal, and in this formulation he clearly has in mind a life that is *both* happy (i.e., subjectively pleasant) *and* expressive of what is truly worthy. The word *flourishing* is a common translation for eudaimonia, as it captures Aristotle's idea that the actualization of our best human potentials is also likely to be experienced as pleasant and satisfying (Curren, 2013; Huppert & So, 2013).

As we have frequently argued (e.g., Ryan et al., 2013), this eudaimonic view is empirically testable rather than simply a set of assertions; it suggests that cultivating and expressing the best within us represents a reliable path to happiness. What is also interesting about the Aristotelian position is that it is inherently *critical*: Living well, or eudaimonia, entails actions of a specific character, so it is prescriptive (Ryan & Huta, 2009). It suggests that certain types of purposes, projects, and aspirations represent a thriving, vital life, whereas others, even if they may yield hedonic satisfactions, will represent less than fully realized and fulfilling human lives (Ryan, Huta, & Deci, 2008). Indeed, as discussed by Fromm (1976), this Aristotelian conception of well-being requires distinguishing between subjectively felt desires whose satisfaction may simply yield pleasure and basic human needs whose realization conduces toward growth and well-being. Thus he was making the critical distinction between (merely) subjectively felt desires and objectively valid needs, suggesting that the former could sometimes be harmful to human growth, whereas the latter, being in accordance with the requirements of human nature, would promote human growth and wellness. In this, Fromm was explicitly embracing a eudaimonic rather than hedonic view (Deci & Ryan, 2008; Ryan & Deci, 2001).

In SDT our view similarly asserts that wellness is more than merely a subjective issue. In contrast, *happiness* (e.g., assessed by the presence of positive affect and absence of negative affect) *is* a subjective issue, and one that can be meaningfully assessed with self-reports (Kashdan et al., 2008). It is not that happiness is unrelated to wellness, nor should happiness be ignored. Instead, as we have previously described, within SDT we see happiness as a *symptom* of wellness (Ryan & Huta, 2009), because it typically accompanies or follows from eudaimonic living and is associated with basic need satisfaction and growth.

Happiness cannot fully define well-being, nor can its absence define psychopathology (Ryan, Huta, & Deci, 2008). For example, in clinical settings one often sees patients who may feel satisfied or happy but who are not necessarily well. Consider, for example, a patient with bipolar disorder who is in the early stages of a manic upswing in mood. Here the elation being felt is a symptom of illness rather than health. Similarly, consider a drug addict who has money in her pocket, is well connected, and currently high. She may feel considerable pleasure in this state, but this should not be understood as any manifestation of wellness. Finally, consider an antisocial member of the corporate elite who impoverishes and intimidates all those around him while inflating his own resources and ego. Happy in moments perhaps, but by what criteria would this represent human wellness? Conversely, we also see people who are appropriately bereft of happiness but who are nonetheless quite well. For example, consider a man who is very sad following the death of a loved one. We would deem him to be well (although unhappy) precisely because he is emotionally in touch with the loss and has the capacity to fully grieve and express such feelings. Or imagine a woman who is saddened in witnessing another person's oppression. She is similarly, by virtue of having capacities for perception, empathy, and compassion, psychologically well, whereas a cold, unfeeling observer may be less saddened or less distressed, yet, we think, less fully human.

As these examples illustrate, critical to understanding well-being is *considering the functions and processes through which subjective states accrue* (Niemiec & Ryan, 2013; Ryan, Legate, Niemiec, & Deci, 2012). In the SDT view, wellness is better described in terms of *thriving* or being *fully functioning* rather than merely by the presence of positive and absence of negative feelings. Thriving is characterized by vitality, awareness, access to, and exercise of one's human capacities and true self-regulation. Fully functioning individuals enjoy a free interplay of their faculties in contacting both their inner needs and states, nondefensively perceiving the circumstances in which they find others and themselves. They can be spontaneous and not constrained or holding back their interests or powers of orientation. They are not compartmentalized in their experience. This type of essential functioning reflects what Perls, Hefferline, and Goodman (1951) described as *creative adjustment*—an ability to be open, welcoming of novelty, and reflective—able to integrate inner and outer inputs into coherent actions.

In line with Aristotle, we have hypothesized that, on average, when people are functioning in a healthy way, they will also tend to report more happiness or SWB, as well as other signs of wellness, such as lower symptoms of anxiety or depression, greater energy and vitality, more sense of coherence and meaning, less defensiveness, and fewer somatic symptoms. Because they are fully functioning, they will have deeper relationships, greater clarity of purpose, and a sense of, and concern with, meaning (Ryff, 1989). Thus, for us, wellness is best captured by looking at multiple existential, social, and clinical indicators of full functioning, of which happiness is certainly one.

Our focus in SDT is particularly on the health of the self—of the integrated set of processes, structures, and representations that are the basis of autonomous functioning rather than the attainments of recognition, status, esteem, or rewards upon which some types of identity so often precariously ride. As we discuss at length in Chapter 15, the self disassembles and reassembles identities throughout development and across contexts, but it is self-functioning—the orienting, assimilating, and creative contact with the world and one's values that is the focus of SDT's definition of wellness. It is when the organism is integrated, therefore fully self-organized, vital, and coherent, that wellness is in evidence.

The capacity to be fully functioning is multiply determined (Ryan, Deci, & Vansteenkiste, 2016). Each individual faces unique affordances and obstacles in development, including biological (e.g., temperament, physical disabilities, intellectual capacities), social (parental values and socialization styles), and political and economic (e.g., educational opportunities, poverty) factors. Each of these issues can have an impact on wellness. For instance, as we review in Chapter 23, socioeconomic factors clearly affect well-being and health outcomes. Yet a good deal of the variance in that relationship between socioeconomic circumstances and wellness is mediated by basic psychological needs (e.g., see DeHaan, Hirai, & Ryan, 2015; Di Domenico & Fournier, 2014; González, Swanson,

Lynch, & Williams, 2016). Similarly, challenges due to physical social oppression and stigma compromise wellness, even as these are buffered by supportive proximal relationships (e.g., W. Ryan, Legate, & Weinstein, 2015). Again we look at how these biological, social, and cultural-economic obstacles and affordances affect basic psychological need satisfactions and frustrations, which to a large degree mediate wellness, vitality, and the motivational status of the individual.

Basic Psychological Need Satisfaction and Wellness

As discussed in Chapter 4, many theories have used the concept of psychological needs as explanatory concepts. Some have viewed them in terms of individual differences that are acquired or learned as a function of socializing processes (e.g., McClelland, 1985; Murray, 1938). Depending on factors such as parenting styles, people develop different degrees of the various needs, such as the need for achievement or affiliation. Accordingly, these theories use *need strength* as their central individual-difference concept. The relative strength of needs for achievement or for control, affiliation, or uncertainty reduction has thus been used to predict relevant outcomes.

In contrast, SDT views all people as affected by the satisfaction of the basic psychological needs for competence, relatedness, and autonomy. It is differences in the degree of satisfaction and frustration of these basic needs, rather than differences in the strength or value of the needs, that is primarily used for making predictions within this approach (Chen et al., 2015). People may differ in terms of how subjectively salient these needs are or how centrally the needs are represented in their personal goals and lifestyles, and these individual differences might affect need satisfaction. Nonetheless, central to the SDT approach is the assumption that greater basic need satisfaction will result in enhanced wellness and greater need frustration diminish wellness, regardless of these conditional factors.

> *BPNT Proposition Ia:* There are three basic psychological needs, the satisfaction of which is essential to optimal development, integrity, and well-being. These are the needs for autonomy, competence, and relatedness. Failure to satisfy any of these needs will be manifested in diminished growth, integrity, and wellness. In addition, need frustration, typically due to the thwarting of these basic needs, is associated with greater ill-being and more impoverished functioning.

Psychological need satisfaction is posited as a *necessary condition* for human thriving or flourishing, and need frustration is injurious to well-being. It is important to note that needs are a functional construct. They identify those psychological factors upon which full functioning is dependent. Research studies, of which we review only a small portion in this chapter, have strongly supported this view, showing that variations in need satisfaction and need frustration lead to a variety of important well-being consequences.

The studies directly linking satisfaction of the autonomy, competence, and relatedness needs to wellness have been of two general types. The first type considers need satisfactions as a *between-person* variable. In these studies, individual differences in general need satisfaction have been used to predict overall well-being and life satisfaction (e.g., Chen et al., 2015; DeHaan et al., 2015). Narrowing that focus, other between-person research has been conducted within *domains*, examining the degree to which basic need satisfaction within a domain or life setting such as work, sports, or school is related to positive functioning and health within the corresponding setting and in general.

Perhaps more tellingly, insofar as needs are deemed essential to optimal functioning and wellness, BPNT further suggests that at a *within-person* level of analysis, variations in need satisfaction and need frustration over time or situations will predict variations in optimal functioning and wellness versus ill-being. Thus some research has examined within-person variations in need satisfactions within different relationships (e.g., with mother, father, partner, friends), using relationship-specific outcomes as dependent variables (e.g., La Guardia, Ryan, Couchman, & Deci, 2000). Still others have examined variations in need satisfaction over time, focusing, for example, on day-to-day fluctuations in need satisfaction as they relate to fluctuations in well-being or ill-being (e.g., Ryan, Bernstein, & Brown, 2010). Within-person research suggests the following proposition that complements Proposition I-a:

> **BPNT Proposition Ib:** Psychological need satisfactions and frustrations vary within persons over time, contexts, and social interactions. Any factor or event that produces variations in need satisfaction or need frustration will also produce variations in wellness, and this principle extends from highly aggregated levels of analysis down to moment-to-moment or situation-to- situation variations in functioning.

As noted, well-being is not simply a subjective experience of positive versus negative affect but represents a fullness and vitality of organismic functioning in which people are aware, psychologically flexible, and integrated rather than depleted, defensive, rigid, or compartmentalized (Deci & Ryan, 2008; Ryan, Deci, Grolnick, & La Guardia, 2006). They are *also* typically happier and more satisfied with their lives. BPNT predicts that variability in need satisfaction will directly predict variability in these capacities to be fully functioning.

Between-Person Studies of Need Satisfaction

At the most general level, greater satisfactions of the three basic psychological needs are so integral to a sense of wellness that they correlate very highly with most central outcomes. For example, in cross-cultural research, robust relations between basic need satisfaction and wellness outcomes such as subjective well-being and lower symptoms of psychopathology have been identified across diverse cultures (e.g., Chen, et al., 2015; Church, Katigbak, Locke, et al., 2013; Sheldon, Abad & Omoile, 2009; Sheldon, Elliot, et al., 2004). Such general levels of analysis ask individuals to subjectively aggregate across time and domains of life, supporting the centrality of the general relations between basic need satisfactions and wellness outcomes across varied cultures. Yet moving to more specific relations of needs within domains brings us closer to the causal connections of needs to wellness.

Some of the earliest studies attempting to assess more domain-specific outcomes associated with need satisfaction did so within work settings. Need satisfactions experienced *on the job* were used to predict both work-related and personal wellness outcomes. For example, Ilardi, Leone, Kasser, and Ryan (1993) examined the need satisfaction of employees working in a shoe factory in the United States. In general, participants in this manufacturing setting received relatively low pay for arduous work. Nonetheless, the degree to which employees experienced satisfaction of competence, relatedness, and autonomy needs directly predicted not only satisfaction with their jobs but also their well-being, as indexed by measures of self-esteem and general mental health. In another early BPNT study, employees in both Bulgarian state-owned industries and a U.S. data processing company who experienced greater satisfaction of the three basic needs displayed greater work engagement and higher well-being on the job (Deci, Ryan, Gagné, Leone, Usunov, & Kornazheva, 2001). Further multicountry research showed that satisfaction of the three needs promoted well-being even in situations in which the participants were relatively unsafe (Chen, Van Assche, Vansteenkiste, Soenens, & Beyers, 2015).

Subsequently, a study of employees of two investment banking firms who reported higher levels of satisfaction of their autonomy, competence, and relatedness needs in the workplace evidenced enhanced vitality and lower anxiety and somatization (Baard, Deci, & Ryan, 2004). Work within other central life domains, such as education (e.g., Jang, Reeve, Ryan, & Kim, 2009; Sheldon, Abad, & Omoile, 2009) and sports training (e.g., Hodge, Lonsdale, & Jackson, 2009), has similarly shown the positive impact of need satisfaction on wellness. Moreover, the more important the life domain is to the individual, the more important the impact of need satisfaction within the domain is to overall wellness.

In fact, it was in considering need-related dynamics among athletes in a domain of great importance to them that SDT researchers became acutely aware of the need to independently examine both need satisfaction as a predictor of well-being and need frustration as a source of ill-being. Bartholomew, Ntoumanis, Ryan, Bosch, and Thøgersen-Ntoumani (2011) assessed both the support and the thwarting of psychological needs and how these, in turn, affected indicators of both well-being and ill-being. In two cross-sectional studies, structural latent factor models showed first that need satisfaction was predicted by perceived autonomy support, whereas need frustration was predicted by controlling coach behaviors. In turn, need satisfaction predicted positive outcomes (e.g., vitality and positive affect), whereas need thwarting more consistently predicted maladaptive outcomes (e.g., disordered eating, burnout, depression, negative affect, and physical symptoms). In addition, athletes' psychological need frustrations prior to training sessions were shown to predict elevated levels of secretory immunoglobulin A (SIgA), a biomarker of stress.

Similar findings concerning the differential relations of need satisfaction and need thwarting on well-being and ill-being, respectively, were found in other studies by Bartholomew, Ntoumanis, Ryan, and Thøgersen-Ntoumani (2011). These studies underscored not only the essential role of need satisfaction in enhancing wellness but also the central role of need frustrations in fostering negative outcomes, a result that has been born out in subsequent research. As just one example, Cordeiro, Paixão, Lens, Lacante, and Sheldon (2016) assessed Portuguese high school students, finding that, whereas greater basic need satisfaction contributed to vitality and life satisfaction overall, need frustration was more predictive of harm-related outcomes, such as symptoms of anxiety, depression, or somatization.

Recent studies further show that the life experiences persons accumulate are each differentially characterized by need satisfaction versus frustration; indeed, need satisfaction represents a critical part of the structure of personal memories. For example, Philippe, Koestner, Beaulieu-Pelletier, Lecours, and Lekes (2012) presented four studies in which they had participants describe a memory for an event, along with other memories related to it. They showed first how episodic memories that differed in need satisfaction and need frustration predicted the individual's wellness, assessed using either self or peer ratings. Further, they showed that priming or activating memories that were differentially characterized by need satisfaction could affect the individual's well-being both in the present and over time. Such evidence suggests first how need satisfaction is "built in" to how we process experiences and, further, how past and present experiences influence people's capacities for full functioning.

Within-Person Variation in Need Satisfaction

Basic psychological need satisfactions, as necessary aspects of optimal functioning, are clearly not only individual difference variables but are also dynamic variables, affected in the moment by both historical and contextual variations and factors. A growing number of studies concern this proposition, linking need satisfaction and well-being over time or contexts within individuals.

In one of the first such studies, Sheldon, Ryan, and Reis (1996) focused on the needs for competence and autonomy, examining daily variations in experiences associated with satisfaction of those two needs. Participants were university students who completed diary-type questionnaires each evening. Multilevel modeling allowed examination of both between-person and within-person relations of perceived need satisfaction to well-being indicators. At the individual-difference level, trait measures of autonomy and competence were significantly related to indices of well-being and ill-being—including positive affect and vitality for well-being and negative affect and the presence of physical stress symptoms for ill-being—aggregated over the 2-week period. Yet independent of this person-level variance, analyses showed that daily fluctuations in the satisfaction of the autonomy and competence needs predicted within-person fluctuations in daily well-being. That is, these students had better days relative to their own averages when their needs for autonomy and competence were being fulfilled and bad days (days with lower well-being than typical) when autonomy and competence needs were less fulfilled.

In a subsequent study, Reis, Sheldon, Gable, Roscoe, and Ryan (2000) examined all three basic psychological needs, expecting each to play a role in daily well-being. They found first that individual-difference measures of autonomy, competence, and relatedness, as well as aggregates of the daily measures of autonomy, competence, and relatedness satisfactions, were all associated with aggregated indicators of well-being, confirming between-person predictions for all three needs. Yet, as in the earlier work, multilevel modeling confirmed that daily fluctuations in satisfaction of each of the three needs predicted unique variance in daily well-being. On days when people experienced satisfaction of their basic needs, this time including relatedness needs, they felt healthier and happier. Taken together, these two studies demonstrated a clear linkage between need satisfaction and well-being at both between-person and within-person levels of analysis, with each need satisfied making independent contributions to overall and daily well-being.

Ryan, Bernstein, and Brown (2010) extended this work to adult working populations and included people working in varied occupations. In addition, they sampled the experiences of these workers three times per day so they could look at patterns within the day, as well as across working and nonworking days. This allowed them to more closely understand daily and weekly cyclic patterns, especially those suggesting a "work effect" and a "weekend effect." Ryan, Bernstein, and Brown (2010) hypothesized that weekends and other nonworking times would be associated with enhanced well-being and that these relations would be mediated by greater satisfaction of autonomy and relatedness needs. Put differently, it was expected that people would experience greater wellness on weekends because they would experience more volition and because they would have more time with others to whom they feel closely connected. Results strongly supported these hypotheses, showing that weekend and nonwork activities were associated with multiple indicators of psychological wellness, including high positive affect and vitality and low negative affect and physical symptoms of stress. Moreover, these relations were partially or fully mediated by basic psychological need satisfactions. Although it is obvious that working people often look forward to the weekends, this study showed more deeply how need satisfactions or deprivations, particularly in the workplace, have an impact on wellness, leading to this desire for satisfying nonwork time. In fact, evidence suggests that via *leisure crafting,* individuals satisfy their basic psychological needs and thereby enhance their wellness, a process that becomes especially important the more work environments are need thwarting (e.g., Petrou & Bakker, 2016).

These are only examples from numerous studies of within-person fluctuations in need dynamics over time as they relate to well-being outcomes. Yet, as mentioned, studies over time are only one way of looking at the dynamic nature of need satisfaction and thwarting as it affects individuals in specific contexts and relationships. Some studies have focused on within-person variations across interpersonal contexts that individuals encounter (e.g., La Guardia et al., 2000; Lynch, La Guardia, & Ryan, 2009). Still others have assessed the balance of within-person variations across the life domains of school, work, home, and leisure settings (e.g., Milyavskaya et al., 2009). Collectively, within-person studies bring into relief the critical roles played by psychological need satisfactions in enhancing personal thriving within domains, situations, and relationships and, conversely, how need thwarting in such contexts can impair an individual's mood and functioning.

Need Satisfaction and Top-Down versus Bottom-Up Effects

The fact that need satisfaction influences wellness at both within-person and between-person levels of analysis also suggests that aggregations of need satisfaction at various levels of analysis are relevant to people's flourishing versus ill-being. In fact, there is evidence that need satisfaction at a general level may affect how people experience immediate situations, and reciprocally need satisfaction in a situation can exert an "upward" influence on domain level and general wellness. For example, Milyavskaya, Philippe, and Koestner (2013) looked at the empirical relations between situational assessments of need satisfaction, domain-level need satisfaction, and general need satisfaction. They found evidence for both top-down and bottom-up effects. Results were particularly strong for bottom-up effects, which suggested that people's general perceptions of need satisfaction are heavily derived from domain and situational experiences. Yet general levels of satisfaction may nonetheless "color" more proximal experiences. These between-level influences in no way detract, however, from our point in Chapter 9 that the best predictions of well-being will be those in which outcomes and predictors are assessed at the same level of analysis, as predicted within the hierarchical model of motivation (Vallerand, 1997). Instead, they further attest to the dynamic nature of basic psychological needs.

Autonomy Support and Need Satisfaction

An important aspect of several of the studies we reviewed above was an assessment of the climate that supported need satisfaction. For example, in the Baard et al. (2004) study, the prediction was that managerial autonomy support would be associated with greater satisfaction not just of the need for autonomy but also for competence and relatedness. Similarly, the studies by Bartholomew and colleagues (Bartholomew, Ntoumanis, Ryan, Bosch, et al., 2011; Bartholomew, Ntoumanis, Ryan, & Thøgersen-Ntoumani, 2011) showed that coaches' autonomy support enhanced need satisfaction, whereas their controlling styles were need thwarting, with the former enhancing well-being and the latter fostering symptoms of ill-being, including physiological indicators of stress. The reasoning within SDT is that when managers, coaches, parents, teachers, and others are autonomy-supportive, they are responsive to the perspectives and important issues faced by the individuals they lead, guide, or care for, and that this will in turn facilitate satisfaction of multiple needs. This role of autonomy support in facilitating need satisfaction is captured in BPNT's second proposition:

> **BPNT Proposition II:** Satisfaction of each of the three psychological needs is facilitated by autonomy support, whereas controlling contexts and events can disrupt not only autonomy satisfactions, but relatedness and competence need fulfillments as well.

The reason for focusing on autonomy support as a predictor of all three basic needs is not that the need for autonomy is in any way more important than the needs for relatedness or competence in relation to wellness. All three are hypothesized to be essential to wellness and to contribute as predictors of outcomes. In fact, in different settings, any one of the three needs will emerge to "take the lead" in terms of its association with wellness outcomes, even as the other two remain important. Yet in most settings having support for autonomy as a contextual factor plays a critical role in allowing individuals to actively satisfy all of their needs—to gravitate toward, make relevant choices in relation to, and employ optimizing strategies for satisfying each basic need.

Support for Proposition II has been found in multiple studies beyond those already described. For example, Gagné (2003) studied volunteer workers at an animal shelter. She found that autonomy support was associated with stronger engagement and lower turnover in the volunteer setting and that these relations were mediated by basic psychological need satisfaction. Sheldon and Krieger (2007), in a 3-year study at two different law schools, found that students at both schools decreased in both psychological need satisfaction and well-being over the 3-year span of the study. Yet law students who perceived greater autonomy support from faculty showed less serious declines in need satisfaction, which in turn was associated with better well-being and better performance, as indexed by both their grades and their bar exam results. Institution-level analyses further showed that, although students at both of these law schools suffered lower need satisfaction over time, one school was perceived as significantly more controlling than the other, which in turn predicted greater difficulties for its students.

A study by V. Kasser and Ryan (1999) examined the well-being of residents in an elderly care facility. The elderly participants were asked to report on the level of autonomy and relational support they experienced from friends and relatives, as well as the nursing home staff. On another day, the participants also answered questions assessing their psychological and physical well-being. It was found that satisfactions of the needs for autonomy and relatedness in the daily lives of these elderly residents were positively related to their vitality and perceived health. It seems that humans never cease being affected by the degree to which others care for them and respect their autonomy in the context of relationships, bespeaking the idea that there are, indeed, basic and enduring psychological needs for autonomy and relatedness (Ryan, 1993).

In summary, autonomy support is seen as a critical aspect of need-supportive environments, an issue we elaborate upon in each of our applied chapters later in the book. When there is support for autonomy, people are also more able to seek out and find satisfactions for both competence and relatedness, as well. This is true at both pervasive (see, e.g., Chapter 23) and proximal levels of social analysis.

Needs and Values: Not Always Congruent

Needs are defined functionally, based upon their *objective* effects on outcomes. Accordingly, even though needs have a subjective aspect, their satisfaction versus thwarting is expected to affect wellness outcomes independently or regardless of people's values or expectations. This sets BPNT apart from the most common mainstream idea about wellness—namely *expectancy* and *expectancy-value theories* (e.g., Bandura, 1996; Vroom, 1964). From those perspectives, it is often assumed that if a person obtains valued outcomes, he or she will experience wellness irrespective of the content of the values. For us, however, some valued outcomes are consistent with basic need satisfaction and some are not. It is only those valued outcomes that are consistent with basic need satisfaction that will yield the functional outcomes of vitality and wellness

Furthermore, it is not necessary for people to explicitly value the satisfaction of basic needs for effects or their support versus thwarting to obtain. Indeed, the fundamental hypothesis of BPNT is that *all* individuals have basic needs for competence, relatedness, and autonomy. This means that basic need satisfactions apply across developmental epochs and cultural contexts, as well as other characteristics, such as gender, socioeconomic status, and beliefs about the importance or value of the needs for themselves.

> *BPNT Proposition III:* Because basic psychological need satisfactions are functional requirements for full functioning and wellness, the effects of satisfaction versus frustration of these needs will be evidenced regardless of whether or not people explicitly desire or value the needs, and regardless of their sociocultural context.

Work across varied developmental epochs and highly diverse cultures provides ample evidence that supports Proposition III. However, one recent study speaks directly to the idea that people's desires to attain or their valuing of a specific need satisfaction does not strongly moderate the effects of satisfaction or frustration of that need. Specifically, Chen and colleagues (2015) examined both need satisfaction and frustration in individuals from Belgium, China, the United States, and Peru. In addition, these individuals rated the strength or importance they placed on each of these three needs. Results indicated that across the four cultures, satisfaction of each of these needs predicted unique variance in well-being outcomes, and of each of the needs predicted unique variance in ill-being outcomes. Further, not only were the magnitude of these effects fairly equivalent across cultures, but more importantly, neither the participants' self-reported need strengths nor their desires for getting the needs satisfied moderated the relations of satisfaction to wellness or need frustration to illness.

Need Satisfactions: Typically Interrelated and Often Balanced

One of the most interesting aspects of SDT's formulations about psychological needs is that satisfaction of all three needs are deemed essential for a person to be fully functioning. Each is independently important, and deprivation of any is seen as problematic. Thus, for persons who have high wellness and mental health, all three needs will tend to be generally satisfied.

In addition, SDT sees these three basic needs as interdependent. Each need facilitates the satisfaction of the others under most conditions. For instance, it is hard to derive competence satisfaction from a domain in which one is not autonomous or volitional, and, reciprocally, a person who feels little competence at an activity will not likely have a great deal of interest or willingness to engage in it. Similarly, in relationships that are controlling or non-autonomy-supportive, a person is not likely to experience a lot of closeness and intimacy. Reciprocally, within interactions or in groups in which one does not feel close or cared for, it is not likely that one will feel a great deal of volition or interest. In short, although on a moment-to-moment basis needs may vary independently (e.g., one feels incompetent while performing a valued activity), SDT expects that the three needs will tend to be highly intercorrelated, especially in measurements that aggregate satisfaction or frustration experiences in a domain or over time.

> **BPNT Proposition IV:** Basic need satisfactions of autonomy, competence, and relatedness will tend to positively relate to one another, especially at an aggregated level of analysis (i.e., across domains, situations, or time).

This intuitively plausible idea might seem obvious, but again one must remember how many psychologists have actively, and sometimes heatedly, disputed this claim. In particular, some cultural relativists (e.g., Markus, Kitayama, & Heiman, 1996; Iyengar & DeVoe, 2003) have often claimed that autonomy and relatedness are in some way in opposition to each other, which would suggest weak or even negative correlations. Similarly, some, especially early, feminist perspectives have seen autonomy and relatedness as opposing developmental and personality tendencies (e.g. Gilligan, 1982; Jordan, 1991). This can often be reduced to the tendency of these theories to conflate independence and separateness with the need for autonomy, which SDT research and theory clearly distinguish from each other, both in definitions and functional effects (e.g., Ryan & Lynch, 1989; Van Petegem, Vansteenkiste, & Beyers, 2013).

Studies, in fact, support high correlations for the three pairs of basic need satisfactions, so much so that factor analysis of basic needs satisfactions scales often identify total need satisfaction as a higher order factor, with the separate needs forming lower order factors (e.g., see Chen et al., 2015). This consideration becomes especially important as well when psychometric measures of needs are developed. Some researchers have tried to "force" the three needs to be psychometrically independent of each other, insisting on a procrustean bed of orthogonality, instead of first listening, as Loevinger (1959) would advocate, to what the data tell us—namely, that these three basic needs, in the natural scheme of wellness, operate convergently. This is, after all, why all three are considered basic.

Because SDT suggests that all three basic needs must be satisfied for healthy functioning to obtain, the question is raised of whether the needs must be equally satisfied. Or might it be the case that having a high degree of satisfaction of one need can compensate for deficits in another, without negative costs to well-being? This is possible, though typically unlikely at an aggregate level, precisely because, as we suggested above, need fulfillments are often interdependent and because social contexts that support satisfaction of one need also will typically support satisfaction of the others. Thus balance among the need satisfactions is normatively expectable.

Yet what if satisfactions are out of balance? Sheldon and Niemiec (2006) directly examined this issue, proposing that *balance* in the satisfaction of the three basic psychological needs is also important to wellness and adjustment. Across four studies, they showed that individuals who experienced more balanced need satisfaction reported higher well-being than those with the same summary score of need satisfaction but who reported greater variability between the three needs in levels of need satisfaction. This finding emerged for multiple measures of needs and adjustment and was independent of factors such as neuroticism. Moreover, these results were obtained consistently across concurrent, prospective, within-person diary and observer-report-based methods. Their findings also controlled for curvilinear effects of satisfaction, suggesting that balance is important for those at both the bottom and top levels of need satisfaction, rather than becoming important only beyond some initial threshold of need satisfaction.

Milyavskaya and colleagues (2009) examined a different kind of balance concerning need satisfaction, namely *balance across life domains*. They argued that when one looks at important life domains, persons can be relatively balanced in need satisfaction across them or highly divergent. In addition to the cumulative effects from each domain, they wondered whether variability itself could be problematic. Using adolescent samples from four countries, they hypothesized and found that imbalanced need satisfaction across important life domains had an additional negative effect on wellness-relevant outcomes beyond the cumulative issue of need satisfaction. This second kind of balance effect was evident above and beyond the balance between needs per se, suggesting that any uneven experience in important domains in terms of need satisfaction produces distress.

Although it is also true that the preponderance of variance is explained by the main effect of satisfaction of the needs, with a much smaller increment in variance being due to balance, Proposition IV is important in understanding need dynamics. It highlights that people cannot meaningfully thrive through the satisfaction of one need alone or in one life domain alone. For example, the achievement-oriented person who thrives on competence satisfactions at the expense of relatedness is likely to be worse off than someone who manages to attend to both areas of life.

In addition, the balance effect, when it does obtain, may frequently reflect a particular role of autonomy within the system of needs. In many circumstances needs for relatedness and competence are dependent for their fulfillment on the person's capacity and freedom to self-organize actions. With empowerment and opportunity, along with a sense of direction, people can obtain the satisfaction of other needs. Autonomy, that is, is essential to the initiation and regulation of behavior through which other needs are better realized. It allows persons to pursue what they deem most valuable, and this will typically include maintaining their important relationships and developing their skills (Alkire, 2007). Moreover, fulfillments outside of autonomy do not have the same resonant impact on the self. For instance, in a study of Nigerian and Indian students, Sheldon, Abad, and Omoile (2009) reported that need balance was most evident when autonomy satisfactions were low.

In sum, Proposition IV suggests that, in full functioning, all three needs are mutually implicated and tend to be very highly correlated. Put metaphorically, well-being is like a three-legged stool; pull out any one of these supports and the stool will fall.

Are There Other Basic Psychological Needs?

From the start, when proposing basic needs, we have recognized that creating a list of basic needs can be a slippery slope to traverse. Without stringent criteria for inclusion, the list can soon become long and cumbersome and thus lose its explanatory power. As we saw in Chapter 5, that happened in the 1950s when researchers extended Hull's (1943) list of four basic physiological needs in their attempt to grapple with phenomena such as exploration, curiosity, and manipulation. It was also an issue with Murray's (1938) list (see Chapter 4), which was so inclusive that it obscured differences between needs, motives, and desires.

Still, we have, throughout the development of SDT, been open to the possibility that there are other essential nutrients of the human psyche. Various candidates have been suggested, yet we have not yet found a truly compelling case for any additional basic needs (e.g., see Ryan & Deci, 2000a, concerning needs for meaning and security; Ryan & Brown, 2003, for self-esteem; and Martela & Ryan, 2015, for a benevolence need). From our perspective, it is first and foremost necessary that the satisfaction of a new candidate need be strongly positively associated with psychological integrity, health, and well-being *and* that its frustration be negatively associated with these outcomes, over and above the variance accounted for by the existing needs. The need must show effects both ways—satisfaction showing enhancement effects and deprivation showing negative effects on wellness. We have, for example, been empirically examining benevolence satisfactions as a potential need (Martela & Ryan, 2015) but thus far have not shown that deprivation of benevolence opportunities hurts (rather than simply fails to enhance) wellness. This important issue, however, is not enough, as there are several additional criteria that must be met.

A second criterion for a need is that it must specify content—that is, the specific experiences and behaviors that will lead to well-being. The competence, autonomy, and relatedness needs, for example, make clear what people need to do in order to be healthy—for example, do important activities well, endorse their actions, and connect with others. In contrast, a concept such as self-actualization (Maslow, 1971) provides little specificity about the contents that would satisfy it. In fact, we would see self-actualization not as a basic need but as a description of the overarching growth and integrative process functioning effectively. This is also true of open concepts such as meaning, which again may be an outcome rather than a specified nutrient (e.g., see Weinstein, Ryan, & Deci, 2012; Martela, Steger, & Ryan, 2016).

A third criterion is that the postulate of a need must be essential to explain or interpret empirical phenomena. Need is a functional concept, with objective criteria, and thus there must be clear and empirically supported costs and benefits from deprivation to satisfaction, respectively. Numerous studies throughout this book have confirmed that satisfaction of the basic needs mediates various empirical relations, such as the relations between supportive work environments and important work outcomes (see Chapter 21), the relations between security of attachment and well-being (see Chapter 13), and between economic equality and advantage and well-being (Chapter 23). Any "new need" must serve as a significant and consistent additional mediator of such relations.

A fourth criterion is that the candidate need be consistent with the idea of a growth need rather than a deficit need. Stated differently, there are two types of psychological needs that could be basic: growth needs that facilitate healthy development and are active on an ongoing basis and deficit needs that operate only when the organism has been threatened or thwarted. Biological needs—the so-called drives—are deficit needs that energize behavior primarily when the organism has failed to experience their satisfaction, and some psychological processes operate similarly. Security is such a need, in that a need for security becomes especially salient primarily when the individual does not have it (e.g., see Rasskazova, Ivanova, & Sheldon, 2016). To be considered a basic psychological need, a candidate must not be operable only when there is a deficit or thwarting of growth-related needs. In addition, if a candidate deficit need becomes operative when the needs for competence, autonomy, and/or relatedness are thwarted, it could be viewed as derivative (i.e., a need substitute) rather than a fundamental need.

A fifth criterion is that, logically, a need be in the appropriate category of variables. More specifically, needs are variables that, when satisfied, lead to positive outcomes, such as wellness, and that, when thwarted, lead to negative outcomes, such as illness. Thus, for example, it would not make sense to speak of a need for psychological or mental health because psychological health falls in the category of outcome variables that are increased or decreased as a function of whether basic needs are satisfied. Thus, for example, vitality would not be considered a need because it is an indicator of well-being, and it is the satisfaction of basic psychological needs that yield high vitality.

A final criterion that a candidate variable must satisfy in order to be considered a fundamental or basic psychological need is that it operate universally—that is, for all people at all ages in all cultures. This issue we briefly address later in this chapter and then in more detail in Chapter 22. Corresponding to this, there must be a reasonable fit between specified needs and evolutionary considerations—the need must convey adaptive advantages that would have resulted in its universality (see Chapters 4 and 24).

In Chapter 4 we discussed basic needs in relation to a set of nine standards that Baumeister and Leary (1995) proposed for a construct to be considered a need. We argued there that our three basic psychological needs fully satisfy those standards, an argument that has been supported by a plethora of research reviewed throughout the book. In this chapter we have listed criteria that overlap considerably with Baumeister and Leary's standards but that were intended to specify the qualities that characterize an SDT-type need. We now use those criteria to show why various candidate needs are actually not SDT needs.

Variables That Have Been Suggested as Candidate Needs

The three variables that people have most frequently argued should be considered basic psychological needs are meaning, self-esteem, and security. We consider each in turn.

Meaning

The desire for one's life to have meaning is most certainly a part of human experience, and many philosophers and writers have grappled with this concept (Wong, 2012). Frankl (e.g., 1978) is perhaps the best known of these scholars, with his most prominent book (Frankl, 1959) being an account of his own struggle to maintain meaning during his internment in a World War II death camp.

Meaning is also an important concept within SDT (Martela, Steger, & Ryan, 2016; Weinstein, Ryan, & Deci, 2012). Before going into the SDT view of meaning, however, it is important to note that there are two quite different definitions of the term *meaning* within the literature. The more intuitive and commonly used definition concerns the degree to which, when people reflect on their lives, they feel a sense that they are and have been living in a truly fulfilling and satisfying way. That is, if people were at the end of their lives, could they look back upon their lives and feel that they had lived in a fully meaningful way? The other definition, which appears in some empirical work and is also sometimes used in a casual way, concerns whether or not people have purpose in their lives. That is, do they have a central and significant agenda they are attempting to accomplish—for example, giving their children the nutrients and experiences that support their healthy development, or working to conserve wild animals in a world that has been infringing on their habitats?

The SDT perspective of meaning suggests that the concepts of intrinsic motivation and organismic integration can be viewed as processes through which people create meaning, whichever way defined, from their ongoing experiences. Intrinsic motivation is an organismic process that leads people into novel and interesting experiences that promote growth and often provide meaning. Organismic integration is a process in which people work to give meaning to their experiences as they assimilate them into a coherent and integrated sense of self. Thus, within SDT, meaning is viewed as an *outcome* of the natural, inherent growth processes of intrinsic motivation and organismic integration, such that the effective operation of these processes, in social contexts that allow satisfaction of the basic psychological needs, will allow people to reflect upon their lives with a sense that their lives have been well lived and deeply meaningful (Szadejko, 2007).

The SDT view, more specifically, has three primary postulates. The first is that, just as need satisfaction is the basis for psychological health and well-being, it is also the basis for a meaningful life. In other words, people will experience meaning in their lives to the extent that their basic psychological needs are satisfied on an ongoing basis. Meaning theorists have not typically related need satisfaction to meaning, but Weinstein, Ryan, and Deci (2012) argued that a careful examination of the work of numerous writers implicitly links need satisfaction to meaning. For example, Frankl (1978) argued for the importance of autonomy in having meaning when he emphasized that people will experience meaning to the extent that the behaviors they choose to enact are ones that reflect their personal values. Little (1998) claimed that the theme of intimacy and connectedness (i.e., relatedness) is central to meaning. And Pines (2004) maintained that a sense of meaning comes from effective or competent engagement in useful activities. Empirical studies also show such a linkage, with basic need satisfactions reliably predicting meaning (e.g., DeHaan et al., 2015). In fact, recent research suggests that one's sense of meaning in life is largely accounted for by SDT's basic psychological needs, along with the feeling of benevolence, which itself is need-satisfying (Martela, Steger, & Ryan, 2016).

The second postulate of the SDT view of meaning is that life purposes or goals are not necessarily experienced as meaningful and do not promote well-being unless they satisfy basic psychological needs. In fact, basic need satisfaction is predicted to both mediate and moderate the relation between having a purpose or aspiration and the outcomes of meaning and well-being. This view stands in sharp contrast to the view that any life purpose provides meaning (e.g., Heine, Proulx, & Vohs, 2006), because it specifies that only some purposes satisfy needs and thus lead to meaning and well-being. A study by Deci, Weinstein, and Ryan (2006) tested this postulate. They found that pursuing some purposes in life did tend to be associated with greater need satisfaction and higher well-being. Further, and importantly, need satisfaction mediated the relation between pursuing purposes and psychological well-being. Deci, Weinstein, and Ryan (2006) then examined the moderation issue. As we will see in Chapter 11, strong intrinsic aspirations or purposes tend to be associated with well-being, whereas strong extrinsic aspirations tend to be associated with ill-being. Deci, Weinstein, and Ryan (2006) used a measure of meaning with three factorial subscales: (1) wanting meaning, (2) searching for meaning, and (3) having meaning (Steger, Frazier, Oishi, & Kaler, 2006), and they found that, whereas pursuing intrinsic aspirations was associated with wanting, searching for, and, notably, *having* meaning in life, pursuing extrinsic aspirations was associated with wanting and searching for meaning, but it was not associated with *having* meaning in life. Further, pursuing and attaining intrinsic aspirations, which involve greater need satisfaction, have been shown to be associated with well-being, whereas pursuing and attaining extrinsic purposes tend to be associated with ill-being (Niemiec, Ryan, & Deci, 2009). In short, life purposes that allow greater psychological need satisfaction lead to meaning and well-being in life, whereas life purposes that do not promote need satisfaction tend not to lead to meaning and well-being in one's life.

The third SDT postulate concerning meaning is that, although some writers have proposed meaning as a basic psychological need (e.g., Andersen, S. Chen, & Carter, 2000), meaning is better viewed as an outcome of basic need satisfaction than as a basic need in its own right (Ryan & Deci, 2000a). Meaning is associated with well-being, but it does not specify content—that is, it does not make clear what people need to do to achieve meaning.

Deficit Needs: Self-Esteem and Safety

Autonomy, competence, and relatedness are the satisfactions of a thriving person, but there are other needs that can become very salient and that represent adaptations to threat and need-thwarting. These are the deficit needs, and within SDT we have considered two: safety and self-esteem. Safety concerns the protection of individuals and those with whom they are connected. It becomes salient when people feel threatened or insecure regarding self-maintenance. Self-esteem is a safety need of the self—a need to feel worthwhile. Although a healthy person *has* self-esteem (i.e., feelings of worth), needing self-esteem becomes salient when needs are thwarted and the person is without satisfactions.

The Security Need

The concept of security appears in many psychological theories. For example, within attachment theory, when the attachment process does not function effectively, people become insecurely attached (Ainsworth, Blehar, Waters, & Wall, 1978), and within emotion security theory, the experience of emotional security is an important precursor of mental health (Davies & Sturge-Apple, 2007). We agree that the experience of security versus insecurity is an important psychological state with substantial motivating power. Still, we argue that security is not a need in its own right, for people are primarily concerned with security only when they have been threatened or thwarted in a way that makes them insecure (Carroll, Arkin, Seidel & Morris, 2009; Rasskazova et al., 2016; Welzel, 2013). Further, people can often ameliorate a deficit need through defensive or compensatory functions, without enhancing growth or integration.

Self-Esteem as a Need

There are two ways to consider self-esteem. One is as an outcome of optimal functioning. The second is as a need that is salient to some individuals. We consider each of these approaches to the concept, beginning with its treatment as a need.

Some consider self-esteem to be a fundamental human need. For example, in *terror management theory* (TMT; Pyszczynski, Greenberg, Solomon, Arndt, & Schimel, 2004), self-esteem is considered to be a basic human need, as we discussed in some detail in Chapter 4. Yet, as we pointed out, it is largely a defensive need, as, according to TMT, people seek self-esteem in order to defend against the otherwise debilitating awareness of their mortality. The primary means for feeling self-esteem (and thus managing awareness of one's ultimate demise) is to defend one's beliefs and worldviews, including the derogation of anyone who might oppose them, which helps maintain a sense of affiliation and belongingness with enduring groups. In this formulation, self-esteem is thus clearly a defensive or compensatory need that must be satisfied before people can turn their attention to growth motivation, which TMT also acknowledges as a potent, existential force (e.g., see Greenberg, Pyszczynski & Solomon, 1995).

Beyond TMT's focus on mortality, there is also no doubt that people devote considerable effort to bolstering their sense of self-esteem and approval especially where they perceive others' approval is contingent upon behaving in particular ways—for example, achieving at a high level, looking attractive, or adopting the prevalent worldview. Such *contingent self-esteem* is, within SDT, not a basic need but rather a result of conditional regard (e.g., Roth, Assor, Niemiec, Ryan, & Deci, 2009). When parents or important others positively regard the person only if they live up to certain standards, people may introject this conditional regard, only being self-loving or esteeming when they meet these (originally external) criteria. The result is often unstable self-worth, as we shall elaborate in Chapter 15. In any case, such strivings for contingent self-esteem, even when successful, are thus not indicators or requirements for health but rather indicative of ill-being (Deci & Ryan, 1995; Kernis & Paradise, 2002).

This does not mean that having self-esteem is always problematic. On the contrary, the SDT perspective is that self-esteem, measured as a basic sense of confidence, love worthiness, and self-acceptance (as opposed to one's comparative value or status), is an outcome that results when the basic needs for competence, relatedness, and autonomy are authentically satisfied (Deci & Ryan, 1995; Moller, Friedman, & Deci, 2006; Ryan & Deci, 2004a, 2004b). In fact, we often use self-esteem as an outcome variable in research studies on wellness and adjustment. Yet when people feel a deep and true sense of self-esteem, then self-esteem is neither salient nor motivating for them. In fact, the healthier they are, the less self-esteem is an issue—they are not focused on esteeming themselves or on getting approval and esteem from others (Ryan & Brown, 2003).

In short, both safety/security and self-esteem are issues that become most salient to people when they are under threat or in question. Consideration of these dynamics thus contributes to another hypothesis of BPNT.

> **BPNT Proposition V:** Deficit needs (such as needs for security and self-esteem) become salient under circumstances of threat, distress, or thwarting of growth needs such as autonomy, competence, and relatedness. Satisfaction of deficit needs can stave off aspects of ill-being but do not typically contribute to enhanced wellness or flourishing. That is, deficit needs emerge as most salient under adverse conditions (threat, deprivation, exclusion, etc.), but they are not aspects of ongoing thriving, and their satisfactions may set the stage for, but do not necessarily promote, optimal human functioning.

The Universality of the Basic Psychological Needs

SDT in general, and basic psychological needs theory in particular, take a very strong position on the issue of the universality of basic psychological needs. Because needs are defined as inner human conditions that are necessary for optimal psychological development and well-being, the implication is that the needs apply to all individuals. Further, although some individuals may report desiring far less of a particular need than other individuals, our position is that all these individuals will suffer ill effects when any of their needs are thwarted. Thus, for example, even though some people in some cultural or organizational contexts will deny that they need autonomy, BPNT says not satisfying the need will nonetheless have well-being costs.

The typical way of accumulating evidence about the universality of human characteristics such as basic needs is to collect data in different cultures or countries that have substantially different degrees of valuing the characteristics—that is, differing degrees of valuing autonomy, competence, and relatedness. SDT researchers have done numerous cross-cultural studies that are directly pertinent to this issue and that argue for the universality of the basic needs. Because this is an extremely important issue with a considerable amount of relevant research, we have devoted Chapter 22 to reviewing this work.

Vitality, Basic Needs, and Well-Being

Basic psychological need satisfactions supply the foundations of wellness. In defining wellness, we suggested that our considerations go beyond hedonic outcomes; psychological wellness must be conceptualized in terms of *full functioning*. A person who is psychologically well is not just free of psychopathology, nor merely "happy." He or she can mobilize and harness psychological and physical energy to pursue valued activities, particularly activities for which the person feels ownership and motivation. This leads us to the issue of *vitality*, perhaps the most general characteristic of a fully functioning person. Vitality is concerned with the energy for action: not just feelings of arousal but energy available to the *self*.

The field of motivation is often defined as the study of both the energy and direction of behavior. Early motivation researchers such as Hull (1943) focused on the basic physiological needs (often called drives), such as hunger, thirst, and sex, as the source of energy for action and associative bonds as the concept explaining direction. When cognitive approaches replaced such drive theories of motivation, more attention was given to the direction of behavior, as indicated by voluminous research on goals and self-regulation, and the energetic component was often neglected.

From the time we began the research that led to SDT, we have thought of the basic psychological needs for autonomy, competence, and relatedness as a centrally important source of energy for action, both as a correlate of motivation and an indicator of wellness (e.g., Ryan & Frederick, 1997). More recently, SDT work on vitality has interfaced with empirical studies on *ego depletion* (e.g., Martela, DeHaan & Ryan, 2016; Muraven & Baumeister, 2000; Muraven, 2012), a seemingly opposite phenomena to the experience of vitality. Although experiments on ego depletion have been questioned for their reliability (e.g., Carter, Kofler, Forster, & McCullough, 2015), the idea that people can be drained or diminished in their subsequent motivation and experience lower vitality after engaging in certain forms of self-control is a matter of great interest for SDT.

The feeling of having energy is one of the most familiar and salient phenomenal experiences people have and one about which they readily and reliably can report. Vitality varies from person to person as an individual difference and, even more saliently, varies within persons in patterned ways. People's vitality has, of course, clear diurnal cycles, and it corresponds with states of nutrition and with physical illness and health (Ryan & Frederick, 1997). Yet, as we shall also see, vitality is strongly affected by social contexts and their need-supportive or need-thwarting elements. The fact that vitality and energy are not wholly a function of physical conditions is itself a matter of strong interest (e.g., Kazén, Kuhl, & Leicht, 2015).

In part, of course, human energy, including the subjective energy needed for volition and the self-regulation of action, requires physical nutrients. It is also the case, however, that *even with* adequate liquid and caloric nutrients, both body and mind can feel tired and depleted. Conversely, *even without* adequate food intake, individuals can sometimes still feel vital and energized (Ryan & Frederick, 1997). Similarly, when too much energy is expended without rest, exhaustion and depletion set in. Thus sleep deprivation and sleep quality directly affect energy and vitality. However, sometimes when a person is fatigued, sleep may not rejuvenate; lack of rest may not be the problem. Further complicating this picture, expenditure of physical energy is not invariantly depleting, nor is sleep invariantly vitalizing. Finally, people can often feel even more energized after some effortful activities, for example, after running, outdoor hiking, or playing sports, although these same activities do frequently have the opposite effect. In addition, people are sometimes depleted by factors other than physical activity. In fact, idleness itself can be depleting, as lack of stimulation and boredom drain energy and excitement.

In sum, it is clear that feeling alive, energetic, and vital requires more than such physical nourishments as oxygen, water, and rest; it also requires psychological nutrients (Ryan & Deci, 2008a). People who are depressed, even if well fed and rested, frequently manifest low energy, or experience anergia. Experiences in people's lives, from loss and disappointment to frustration and rejection, can also lead them to feel a loss of spirit, manifested in a lack of enthusiasm and motivation, even for unrelated events. Conversely, a creative inspiration or insight, a gleam of love in another's eyes, or an incredible walk at sunset can flood a person with a sense of aliveness and *joie de vivre*. To understand the dynamics of human energy requires some different ideas concerning how enthusiasm and spirit are derived and depleted.

In beginning our investigations into this area, Ryan and Frederick (1997) used the concept of *subjective vitality* to describe this energy of self, defining it as the experience of feeling alive, vigorous, and energetic. In assessing it, they developed items reflecting these ideas, excluding from the measure characteristics that are merely associated with vitality and energy, such as happiness, extraversion, optimism, mental health, and physical health, so that correlates, antecedents, and consequences of vitality could be empirically determined. The researchers hypothesized that subjective vitality would be readily accessible to people—that is, people can often directly experience how much vitality and aliveness they possess, and that it would reflect both organismic and psychological wellness.

In a series of studies, Ryan and Frederick (1997) documented varied correlates and contributions to energy. For example, they showed that people experienced lower subjective vitality when physically fatigued or ill. They also related vitality to the experience of pain, showing that it was particularly uncontrollable pain that was energy draining. Yet Ryan and Frederick also established that somatic factors did not supply a full account of subjective vitality—psychological factors were also strongly involved. Subjective vitality was not, for example, equivalent to physiological arousal, which is often thought to reflect energy; in fact, subjective vitality was *negatively* related to feelings of anger and hostility, in which arousal is a central component. This is of interest especially because anger and hostility have often been associated with need thwarting, which may account for their negative relations with vitality (e.g., Legate, Ryan, & Weinstein, 2012; Przybylski, Deci, Rigby, & Ryan, 2014).

Subjective vitality was, in fact, particularly related to basic need-related satisfactions of autonomy, competence, and relatedness and to variables that reflect high need satisfaction, such as self-actualization. Ryan and Frederick (1997) also reviewed evidence, available even at that time, showing that subjective vitality was negatively related to investment in extrinsic life goals, such as wealth and fame, relative to intrinsic life goals, such as personal growth and community contributions, that are more closely aligned with satisfaction of the basic psychological needs (e.g., Kasser & Ryan, 1996). This evidence dovetailed with additional findings that fluctuations in subjective vitality were related to fluctuations in psychological need satisfactions (e.g., Ryan, Bernstein, & Brown, 2010; Sheldon et al., 1996). In sum, this early evidence connected subjective vitality directly to the constructs of basic psychological need satisfactions and demonstrated that vitality could represent a robust and holistic index of organismic wellness.

Following up on Ryan and Frederick's (1997) suggestion that activities and lifestyles associated with basic need satisfaction foster greater vitality, Nix, Ryan, Manly, and Deci (1999) demonstrated experimentally that when participants worked successfully on a variety of tasks that were self-directed or autonomously motivated they displayed significantly greater vitality than when successfully working on the tasks while their behavior was other-directed or motivated by controlling forces. In other words, when the situation allowed satisfaction of the autonomy need, people reported greater vitality. Kasser and Ryan's (1999) study of elderly persons in a nursing facility similarly showed that individual differences in psychological vitality were positively associated with perceived physical health and psychological well-being and were negatively associated with depression and anxiety. Further, vitality was predicted by the degree to which these residents experienced autonomy support from the care staff and by the extent to which, in day-to-day activities, they experienced their own actions as self-regulated or autonomous, rather than controlled.

Subsequent research continued to elaborate this body of evidence. Studies such as that by Baard and colleagues (2004) in the domain of work and by Deci, La Guardia, Moller, Scheiner, and Ryan (2006) in the domain of friendship found that both receipt of autonomy support and satisfaction of the basic psychological needs were positively related to subjective vitality. Finally, studies continued to relate intrinsic rather than extrinsic aspirations to greater vitality (e.g., Schmuck, Kasser, & Ryan, 2000).

Ryan and Deci (2008a) summarized this accumulating research on vitality in a review, stressing that energy is not simply a bodily based resource that is depleted by activity and self-controlled action. In fact, because vitality is also a psychological phenomenon, there are activities and experiences that *enhance* vitality through satisfying the needs of the self. Thus the Ryan and Deci formulation suggested that whereas controlled activities deplete subjective vitality, autonomous activities can maintain or enhance it. Moreover, experiences of basic need satisfaction (e.g., falling in love as a relatedness satisfaction, finding a sense of purpose as an autonomy satisfaction, discovering a new skill as a competence satisfaction) can enhance vitality precisely because they invigorate the self. This theorizing also suggested that investment in extrinsic goals, because it yields lower need satisfaction, would over time reduce vitality.

> ***BPNT Proposition VI:*** Subjective vitality is based on more than physical nutrients; it also reflects satisfaction versus thwarting of basic psychological needs for autonomy, competence, and relatedness. Therefore, both externally controlling and self-controlling states are expected to deplete vitality, whereas basic psychological needs satisfactions are expected to enhance it.

Taken together, the empirical findings strongly supported the view that vitality should be understood as *energy that is available to the self*, energy that can be used in volitional activity. It is the energy that allows people to decide how to behave, to hold other appealing behaviors in abeyance, and to maintain a positive attitude toward the activities in which the individuals decide to engage. Nutrients that support the self enhance vitality.

As the early explorations of vitality within SDT were unfolding, Muraven, Baumeister, Vohs, and colleagues (e.g., Muraven, Tice, & Baumeister, 1998; Muraven & Baumeister, 2000; Vohs & Heatherton, 2000) began to elaborate a different model of energy called the *strength model of self-control*. Central to their conception is the postulate that self-regulation is a limited resource—to use it means to deplete it. In the view of that model, self-regulation requires resources and exertion, and thus energy resources become depleted when people engage in self-regulated behaviors. More specifically, this model, also called the *ego-depletion model*, proposed that self-regulation is "like a muscle"—when employed, it is expending energy and thus is drained; when relaxed or calorically nourished, it can rejuvenate. Over time, as with a muscle, the more one engages in self-regulation, the stronger "the muscle" becomes. This model is often referred to as the ego-depletion model because in the short term the exercise of the ego or self is said to deplete energy, as manifested in diminished abilities to persist at or control oneself on subsequent tasks (Baumeister, Bratslavsky, Muraven, & Tice, 1998; Baumeister, Muraven, & Tice, 2000). Indeed, Baumeister et al. (1998) suggested that all acts of self-regulation are effortful and result in ego depletion.

Although it would seem that this "muscle model" and our model of vitality are contradictory, this is only partly true; in certain areas, they have overlapping predictions. However, one area of disagreement occurs because Baumeister et al. (1998) equated the concepts of self-control and self-regulation, treating them as if they were the same thing. In contrast, SDT has long differentiated these concepts (Ryan, 1982; Ryan, Connell, & Deci, 1985), pointing out that self-control typically entails external and introjected regulations. Introjection in particular is an internally controlled form of regulation in which one part of personality overruns another, whereas true self-regulation refers to autonomous regulation consisting of more fully integrated regulation and intrinsic motivation.

The consequences of these modes of regulating oneself are quite different. Thus the self-regulatory strength model and the SDT model of vitality concur on the idea that self-controlling forms of regulation will be vitality-depleting. The SDT-based model uniquely suggests, however, that more autonomous self-regulation will be less depleting and at times even energizing. Put differently, from the perspective of SDT, it is controlling regulation (i.e., self-control) that is especially likely to diminish subjective vitality, and in those situations people will also likely show less subsequent motivation and effort. In contrast, when people are autonomously motivated, they will be satisfying rather than thwarting their need for autonomy and thus potentially enhancing their vitality—that is, the *energy available to the self.*

One place in which the above-mentioned differences in theory became especially apparent was in the proposal by Baumeister et al. (1998) that the process of making any choice would be depleting relative to not making a choice. For SDT, however, if people make a meaningful choice, it should facilitate autonomy and self-regulation and thus not deplete. Baumeister and colleagues reported a study that they interpreted as supporting their hypothesis. These researchers manipulated choice by having participants decide which side of a controversial issue they would like to align themselves with. Participants were told that later they would be taping a persuasive argument in line with the position they chose. Yet, under the guise of ensuring comparable activities, the experimenter then told each person in the "choice" condition that enough participants had already chosen a specified side of the argument and that it would be very helpful if the participant chose the other side, adding, however, that it really was up to him or her to decide which side to take. This was referred to as the "high-choice" condition. In contrast, in the "no-choice" condition, participants were simply assigned to one of the two sides of the issue. In a subsequent phase of the experiment, before any speeches were made, participants were given an unsolvable puzzle task. The time participants persisted at the activity provided the assessment of ego depletion. Results showed that, as they predicted, relative to the no-choice condition, participants in the so-called high-choice condition persisted for a shorter period of time before quitting, suggesting a depletion effect.

That result would seem to be incongruent with our argument that the experience of choice and the self-endorsement of one's actions can be important facilitators of autonomous motivation, which Ryan and Frederick (1997) also found to be associated with positive affect and energy. Further, providing people the opportunity to make a choice among options, if the options were meaningful and there were no pressures to select one of them, has been found to enhance the experience of choice and to promote autonomous motivation (e.g., Zuckerman, Porac, Lathin, Smith, & Deci, 1978). So how are we to make sense of the Baumeister et al. (1998) study?

Our interpretation of the Baumeister et al. (1998) results is that their experimental manipulation had not really given the participants a feeling of choice but instead had controlled them in a subtle way. They were told they had choice, then pressured to pick one of the options, even as they were told that it really was their choice. In fact, a prior experiment by Pittman, Davey, Alafat, Wetherill, and Kramer (1980) had used just such a manipulation as a *controlling condition*. In that study, when participants were similarly told that, although they had a choice, selecting a particular option would be helpful to the experimenter, the participants experienced their behavior as having an E-PLOC, and their intrinsic motivation for the task was diminished. So in our view the so-called "high-choice" manipulation in the Baumeister et al. (1998) experiment really instantiated a circumstance in which participants would have felt controlled—that is, they would *not* have experienced choice or autonomy.

Accordingly, Moller, Deci, and Ryan (2006) did an experiment to test this interpretation. Using methods that paralleled those used by Baumeister et al. (1998, Study 2), Moller and colleagues included three experimental conditions. In one condition, participants were given what the researchers referred to as "true choice" in which participants were told about the two sides of a controversy and asked which side they would prefer to be aligned with so that they could, later in the experiment, make a persuasive speech endorsing that side of the issue. There was no pressure and no suggestion, so they chose the side they preferred. A second condition, which Moller, Deci, and Ryan (2006) referred to as "compelled choice," was essentially identical to the so-called high-choice condition in the original Baumeister et al. (1998) experiment. In it, the participant was yoked to the previous participant in the true-choice condition and was told that picking one side of the controversy was his or her choice but, because enough participants had already selected one side of the issue, it would be very helpful if the participant chose the other side. The third condition was a no-choice condition in which each participant was also yoked to the decision of the most recent true-choice participant, but he or she was simply told which side to argue for without being given the "illusion of choice" about which side to endorse. By using this yoking procedure, the researchers were able to accomplish the aim of having comparability across the three conditions in terms of the numbers of each speech that the participants would make in each condition, while also allowing true choice in the one condition. Results of this study replicated the previous Baumeister et al. results in that the "compelled-choice" participants (referred to as high-choice by Baumeister et al.) again showed greater ego depletion than the no-choice participants. Yet the "true choice" participants were significantly more energized than the "compelled choice" participants. In short, there was no evidence that true choice was ego depleting.

Autonomy, Control, and Depletion

Despite this and other differences in our assumptions about motivation and energy (e.g., Martela, DeHaan, & Ryan, 2016; Ryan & Deci, 2008a), some research on the self-regulatory strength model has directly related SDT's subjective vitality construct to depletion effects. For example, Muraven, Gagné, and Rosman (2008) had experimenters instruct participants to avoid thinking about a white bear, using the autonomy-supportive rationale that they were making an important contribution to the research. Others received the same instruction, but by an experimenter who treated participants like a "cog in the machine." Those performing for the more autonomy-supportive experimenter showed less depletion—that is, less impairment in motivation in subsequent performance. Moreover, Ryan and Frederick's (1997) measure of subjective vitality mediated the link between the experimental conditions and these outcomes. Because people in the autonomy-supportive condition felt more vitality, they exhibited less depletion.

In another relevant set of experiments by Muraven, Rosman, and Gagné (2007), participants were given either performance-contingent rewards or task-noncontingent rewards for doing a self-control task. According to CET (Chapter 6), task-noncontingent rewards are relatively noncontrolling and typically do not undermine autonomy, whereas performance-contingent rewards are more often experienced as controlling and thus more readily undermine autonomy (see Deci, Koestner, & Ryan, 1999; Ryan, Mims, & Koestner, 1983). The results achieved by Muraven et al. (2007) showed that those who received the performance-contingent rewards performed more poorly on the subsequent test of self-control than participants given noncontingent rewards. On the basis of these results Muraven et al. (2007) concluded that: "it appears that even small changes in feelings of autonomy surrounding the activity can affect how depleting the task is" (p. 329).

Extending these findings, Muraven (2008) showed that the relative autonomy of people's reasons for exerting self-control affected depletion outcomes. A plate of cookies was placed in front of participants with the instructions not to eat them unless absolutely necessary. They then completed a questionnaire that measured their relative autonomy for not eating the cookies. Those who refrained for more controlled reasons exhibited more depletion, as assessed by squeezing a handgrip for less time than was the case for those who did not eat the cookies for more autonomous reasons. Here we see the negative effects on subsequent motivation after people have felt controlled within this experimental setting.

These studies by Muraven and colleagues are thus quite consistent with and supplement that of Moller, Deci, and Ryan (2006), showing both that autonomously motivated acts, even those involving resisting temptation, have a less negative effect on subsequent effort and also that these depletion effects are mediated by changes in subjective vitality. Of course, how depleting the regulation of any given behavior would be is a relative issue, because autonomy varies in degree, as does the effort and exertion involved. Yet to the extent that people are autonomous, more energy is evidenced and applied to subsequent tasks, whereas the inhibition, dividedness, and control required when doing something that is not wholeheartedly endorsed is more draining and depleting of vitality within the same setting or context.

Recently, Kazén et al. (2015) applied both SDT and *personality systems interaction* (PSI; Kuhl, 2000) theories to this phenomenon. Like SDT, PSI distinguishes *self-control*, which they conceptualize as a dictatorial form of executive functioning, with *self-regulation*, which is described as a more democratic and self-congruent mode of carrying out intentional actions. Kazén et al. (2015) argued that self-regulated actions might invigorate, whereas self-controlled actions might deplete energy. To test this, they examined glucose allocation and expenditure during effortful tasks. They found that, in a condition of external control, participants showed the depletion effect predicted by Baumeister and Vohs (2007), specifically evidenced by both performance decrements on a subsequent task and by decreased levels of blood glucose. In contrast, in a condition characterized as autonomy-supportive, participants showed a *rise* in blood glucose levels and better performance compared with the controlled group.

Enhancing Vitality and Energy through Need-Satisfying Activity

We have seen that, insofar as activities satisfy the need for autonomy, more energy and vigor are in evidence both for and subsequent to task performance in any given setting. Thus, as noted, the SDT view of energy goes beyond a limited resource model, which has predominated since the time of Freud (1925). Instead, SDT research suggests that energy is derived not just from physical need supports (nourishment and rest) but also from supports for basic psychological needs. Although we have focused thus far on the tendency of self-controlling forms of regulation (i.e., introjected and external regulations) to reduce vitality and of autonomous regulation to maintain or even enhance it, the other basic psychological needs also affect one's available energy.

For example, Vlachopoulos and Karavani (2009) examined predictors of subjective vitality in a sample of nearly 400 Greek exercise participants, with ages varying from 18 to 61. Mainly, they were focused on autonomy support and its relation to vitality outcomes, a main effect that was robust. However, they also looked at whether psychological need satisfaction partially mediated this relationship, and they found that it did. Although all three needs correlated with vitality, the positive relations of autonomy support were most strongly mediated by *competence satisfactions*, which makes sense in this domain of activity in which psychological needs for competence are so salient (see also Quested & Duda, 2009).

Vitality can also be spurred by relatedness, as anyone who has experienced "falling" in love will report. Although in some sense one might think that accepting a new love relationship would require an investment of energy, as the psychoanalytic concept of *cathexis* (Freud's *besetzung*) suggests, in fact people feel more energy and vivacity when they give and receive relatedness with others. Weinstein and Ryan (2010) demonstrated this in a series of experiments on helping in which, when persons helped others for autonomous rather than controlled reasons, they showed enhanced vitality, an effect mediated by the three basic psychological needs, including relatedness. As well, Deci et al. (2006) showed that giving autonomy support to best friends was associated with enhanced vitality for the giver as well as the receiver.

Ryan, Bernstein, and Brown's (2010) study of work life showed that daily vitality among adult U.S. workers was higher when psychological needs were satisfied and that each of the psychological needs had an independent influence on vitality. Vitality was especially high on weekends for most of these workers, a result specifically mediated by enhancements of relatedness and autonomy. When people were engaged in volitional activities and were in contact with persons to whom they felt connected, vitality was significantly higher.

In short, not only can vitality be a source of energy that is depleted through self-controlled activity, as the regulatory strength model suggests, but it can also be enhanced when activities satisfy basic psychological needs. These psychological need satisfactions can *engender* energy and, in interaction with physical influences on the individual, determine the overall energy available to the self.

Research has also shown that vitality is more than just a positive hedonic feeling. Instead, it is increasingly being understood as being robustly associated with a variety of objective outcomes. It has been linked with specific configurations of brain activation and positive response mechanisms (e.g., Barrett, Della-Maggiore, Chouinard, & Paus, 2004; Rozanski, Blumenthal, Davidson, Saab, & Kubzansky, 2005; Selhub & Logan, 2012), as well as with more productive coping with stress and challenge and with greater psychological health (e.g., Penninx, Deeg, Van Eijk, Beekman, & Guralnik, 2000; Ryan & Frederick, 1997; Weinstein & Ryan, 2010). In addition, growing evidence suggests that it is specifically vitality that may render people more resilient to physical and viral stressors and less vulnerable to illness (e.g., Benyamini, Idler, Leventhal, & Leventhal, 2000; Cohen, Alper, Doyle, Treanor, & Turner, 2006; Polk, Cohen, Doyle, Skoner, & Kirschbaum, 2005). These consequences make vitality a continuing and important focus of research.

A final source of vitality is one that falls, at least partially, outside our usual "big three" needs of autonomy, competence, and relatedness. This is the issue of *exposure to nature*. Because of its uniqueness and its interest value within an organismic viewpoint, we turn to that effect with a bit more detail.

Nature and Vitality

Human nature evolved within the rich, complex world of living things we find outside: that is, the world of living nature. Nature is obviously important to people and represents a principal focus of leisure and recreation. People wake up early to watch the sunrise, hike enormous distances to experience vistas and wildlife, or spend hours tending gardens. Others spend fortunes for oceanfront property, fight to preserve green space, or spend vacations in the wilderness. There are costs in energy and resources to each of these nature-involved activities, which indicates that people strongly value them. Even when people cannot be outdoors, they often bring the outdoors in, decorating their homes and offices with indoor plants and scenes of nature.

Despite our attraction to nature, it is evident that consumerism and modern lifestyles can sometimes conduce to people being increasingly divorced from nature. Across nations there is an increase in "screen time," with people sitting indoors before TVs and computers (Bjelland et al., 2015; Rigby & Ryan, 2011). Work hours in the United States and some other nations have also increased over time, leaving many workers indoors for longer periods each day. People spend time shopping and consuming, often for items they don't really need, and natural environments may be destroyed as a result of this activity without their being aware of it. One might wonder whether, with so much indoor, non-nature-filled experience, people are also paying organismic costs of which they are unaware.

For us, this is a critical issue, highly pertinent to well-being and vitality. Nature brings out some of our inherent or intrinsic motivational tendencies, and it plays an important role in human leisure, as well as in human health and wellness. It was thus, especially within our research on vitality using experience-sampling methods and our studies of sports and exercise environments, that we began to wonder about a specific connection between exposure to nature and vitality. The possibility emerged that one impact of nature on well-being is that immersion in nature can provide or catalyze subjective vitality. Some data in the rich literature on *restoration* had already pointed to this possibility (see, e.g., Kaplan & Kaplan, 1989). Greenway (1995) had noted, for example, that 90% of participants in an outdoor experience described "an increased sense of aliveness, well-being, and energy" (p. 128).

To test this more directly, Ryan, Weinstein, Bernstein, Brown, Mistretta, and Gagné (2010) used multiple methods to look for a reliable connection between exposure to nature and subjective vitality. To do so, they employed two different measures of the positive energy that nature experiences might facilitate. In addition to the Subjective Vitality Scale (SVS; Ryan & Frederick, 1997), Thayer (1987, 2003) had developed a two-dimensional circumplex model of mood that he saw as closely associated with general bodily arousal, encompassing the components of energy (versus fatigue) and tension (versus calmness). Thayer's model thus defines mood not only in terms of hedonic (i.e., positive and negative) tone but also in terms of activation level. This model seemed to connect nicely with Ryan and Frederick's (1997) construct of subjective vitality, representing an "activated" positive emotion, distinct from happiness per se (Nix et al., 1999). It is also distinct from arousal per se, as it entails only positive energy that is available to the self, as Ryan and Frederick's research had shown. Tense or nervous energy, for example, is not vitalizing, as it drains energy from the self, a finding common both to Thayer's (1996) and Ryan and Frederick's (1997) research.

Ryan, Weinstein, and colleagues (2010) conducted five studies utilizing survey, experimental, and diary methods that all assessed the effects of being outdoors or around natural elements on subjective vitality. In the first, they used a vignette method in which participants rated how much vitality and energy they would feel in various scenarios in which physical activity, social interactions, and being outdoors versus indoors were randomly varied. Above and beyond physical activity and social interaction, being outdoors was associated with higher ratings of vitality. A second study explored vitality through an experimental design contrasting indoor and outdoor walks. Participants were walked through an outdoor pathway environment or, alternatively, an indoor environment through a university complex. The conditions controlled for the level of physical activity (e.g., speed of walking) and the amount of social interaction with the experimenter. The outdoor walk resulted in a greater pre–post change in vitality. In a third study, participants were exposed to photographic scenes of either natural or built environments and asked to imagine themselves in these scenes. Results showed that only the nature scenes enhanced subjective vitality from pre- to postexposure. Finally, studies 4 and 5 used a diary method to examine within-person variations in subjective energy as a function of being outdoors, again controlling for physical and social interactions. Across these studies and varied methodological strategies, being outdoors or exposed to natural elements was shown to be associated with greater vitality, a relation that was mediated by the presence of natural elements—meaning the more natural the surroundings, the greater the effect.

Specific elements of landscapes may help carry these effects. For example, Shalev (2016) reported two studies, in which she compared visualizing or viewing images of an arid desert scene versus landscapes containing water and living plants. She then assessed people's confidence in their ability to change negative habits. She found that viewing desert versus water scenes had more negative effects on confidence for changing bad habits, and, furthermore, these relations were mediated by subjective vitality. In a third study, she found further support for these findings, suggesting that pictures of arid landscapes were experienced as more devitalizing than landscapes with water and were more strongly associated with stress; however, desert scenes were perceived as more attractive and less stressful than urban scenes.

Another physical factor in nature contexts that may be entailed in enhancing vitality is exposure to daylight. In a multilevel modeling study, Smolders, de Kort, and van den Berg (2013) assessed within-person changes in vitality as a function of the light to which people were exposed. Being in daylight significantly predicted feelings of vitality on an hour-by-hour basis, even controlling for sleep patterns and other person characteristics. Light exposure was, on the other hand, not predictive of feelings of tension or of positive and negative affect, and thus the effect seemed specific to subjective vitality. Light exposure also appeared to be of more benefit to persons who were already in a low vitality state before exposure.

Such varied findings suggest that more research is clearly needed to understand how elements in nature enhance vitality and produce the positive effects of vitality on other variables. But clearly nature can yield enhancing effects on both need satisfactions and energy.

In the city of Rochester, where this book's authors have resided for most of the past few decades, several of our most beautiful public parks were designed by Frederick Law Olmsted, a landscape architect of the 19th century who is perhaps most famous for his design of New York City's Central Park. Olmstead was a strong believer in the vitalizing effects of nature. For example, in 1865, in defending the importance of parkland at Yosemite, he stated:

> If we analyze the operation of scenes of beauty upon the mind, and consider the intimate relation of the mind upon the nervous system and the whole physical economy, the action and reaction which constantly occurs between bodily and mental conditions, the reinvigoration which results from such scenes is readily comprehended. (Olmstead, 1865)

Here Olmstead seemed to have intuitively recognized the total organismic benefits of being in nature. Vitality, a variable that encompasses both body and mind, is clearly affected by our connections with nature.

BPNT Proposition VII: Other factors aside, meaningful exposure to living nature has a positive effect on subjective vitality relative to exposure to non-natural, built environments without living elements, and this relation is mediated in part by basic psychological needs.

Weinstein, Przybylski, and Ryan (2009) further extended the research on how living nature can influence human nature by examining its capacities to enhance people's relational and prosocial attitudes and tendencies. They reasoned that if nature produces vitality through putting people in a more centered autonomous mode of functioning, it might also enhance relational sensibilities. They examined this highly speculative idea in four studies. In the first three, participants were exposed to images of either natural or non-natural environments, and they reported on their intrinsic and extrinsic aspirations both before and after these image presentations. Results showed that participants exposed to nature increased in their valuing of intrinsic goals and decreased their valu-ing of extrinsic goals as a function of this exposure, whereas this was not the case for those exposed to scenes of artificial, built environments. These effects were evident even when controlling for positive affect. Moderation analyses further showed that it was those individuals who were more immersed in these scenes of nature who largely carried this effect. In a fourth study, rather than using nature scenes, Weinstein, Przybylski, and Ryan (2009) had people in a room in which they either were or were not in the presence of indoor living plants while they engaged in a paradigm involving reward distributions. Participants had to decide either to share money made available to them, knowing only that the money would be shared with a second student and that they could potentially lose all the funds, or to keep the money without risk of loss but without benefit to another student. Those in the more natural setting were more generous, even though it carried risk, whereas those immersed in non-natural settings were less likely to give to others.

In the last two studies in this series, Weinstein, Przybylski, and Ryan (2009) exam-ined variables that might mediate these prosocial effects of exposure to nature. They found, interestingly, that feelings of autonomy and a sense of relatedness to nature were higher in the nature scene conditions and that these satisfactions significantly mediated the relations between experimental conditions and participants' willingness to give to others. In other words, the enhanced autonomy and relatedness to nature engendered by natural environments appeared to promote a focus on intrinsic values for social relation-ships and community rather than on personal gain. It is particularly noteworthy that nature conduced toward feelings of autonomy and relatedness, attributes that are also associated with enhanced vitality. In short, it appears that satisfaction of the basic needs does account for at least a part of the reason that nature enhances vitality, although it remains to be determined whether there might also be other direct factors through which nature influences energy available to the self.

Such connections between exposure to nature and relatedness may have important ramifications for how we design human environments and communities. For example, Weinstein, Balmford, DeHaan, Gladwell, Bradbury, and Amano (2015) recently used interviews of people across the United Kingdom to assess the perceived quality of people's access to views of nature and the amount of time they spent in nature while also measur-ing their sense of community cohesion. Their results suggested significant connections between these variables, showing that more access to nature was linked to greater com-munity cohesion, which, in turn, predicted lower crime and also greater well-being.

Awareness as a Foundation of Autonomous Motivation and Basic Need Satisfaction

Considerable research within SDT has focused on the social-contextual factors that affect autonomous functioning and need satisfaction (Ryan & Deci, 2000c). Nonethe-less, acting with autonomy and finding opportunities for need satisfaction are not simply a function of one's external context; they are equally dependent upon one's active use of the organizational tendencies that each person possesses. That is, although supports from the social context are important, people nonetheless have inherent capacities to act in the service of their own self-determination and need satisfaction, sometimes even despite impeding social-contextual conditions within which they might find themselves. Simply stated, we have intrapersonal processes that can support self-regulation even when con-textual forces are not optimal (Ryan, Legate, Niemiec, & Deci, 2012).

The concept of *awareness* is seen within SDT as a foundational element for proactively engaging one's inner and outer worlds, and meeting demands and challenges. Awareness is crucial to eudaimonic living and can facilitate basic need satisfaction and wellness (Deci, Ryan, Schultz, & Niemiec, 2015; Ryan, Huta, & Deci, 2008). The concept of awareness in SDT refers to open, relaxed, and interested attention to oneself and to the ambient social and physical environment. Such receptive attention has long been discussed within dynamic approaches to psychotherapy (e.g., Brooks, 1974; Perls, 1973; Rogers, 1951; Ryan & Deci, 2008b). When people become more aware, they become more likely to experience insight and to regulate themselves more effectively, experiencing more choice, vitality, and volition. Awareness is conducive to congruence, allowing greater contact with one's needs, feelings, interests, and values and with the conditions surrounding them so the person can more effectively select goals and behaviors. When people are less aware of their inner and outer circumstances, the ability to self-organize and autonomously regulate actions is diminished (Deci & Ryan, 2000; Ryan & Deci, 2008b).

Mindfulness

One avenue through which awareness has been explored within SDT is investigations of *mindfulness*, especially as it connects with autonomous self-regulation and need satisfactions. Brown and Ryan (2003) described mindfulness as an open receptive awareness of what is happening both internally and externally in the present moment. It is a quality of consciousness in which humans are openly and nondefensively aware of what is truly taking place (Kabat-Zinn, 2003). It is very much an "allowing" and receptive form of experiencing, such that when people are more mindful, they are more accepting of what they experience without focusing, resisting, or manipulating it.

This is a very simple definition, but one drawn from a deep tradition in Buddhist thinking (Suzuki, 1970). For example, Nyanaponika Thera (1972) called mindfulness "the clear and single-minded awareness of what actually happens to us and in us at the successive moments of perception" (p. 5). Hanh (1976) quite similarly described mindfulness as "keeping one's consciousness alive to the present reality" (p. 11). Defined simply in terms of receptive attention and awareness, mindfulness as so defined differs from conceptualizations and measures of mindful awareness that include additional components, such as active and novel cognitive operations on external stimuli (e.g., Langer, 1989), the holding of particular beliefs or philosophies (e.g., Leary & Tate 2007), or other attributes, such as compassion, kindness, or empathy, that others have included in their definitions of mindfulness. In our view, although many of these attributes accompany or are consequences that follow from mindfulness, they are not essential components of mindfulness itself (see Brown & Ryan, 2003, 2004; Brown, Ryan & Creswell, 2007).

Self-Regulation, Autonomy, and Mindfulness

Autonomy is a function of integration, and for integration to occur, people need to freely process and find the grounds for the endorsement of particular actions. Because mindfulness relates to people's capacity to openly attend to current internal and external experiences, it allows people greater insight and the self-reflection necessary to ensure that their perceptions and values are congruent with their behavior (Goldstein & Kornfield, 1987; Siff, 2014).

Within SDT, we have long posited that people's open awareness is especially valuable in facilitating the selection of and engagement in behaviors that are consistent with the people's values, interests, and basic needs (Deci & Ryan, 1980b). In contrast, we have suggested that automatic or controlled processing often precludes perceptions and considerations of options that would be more congruent with people's needs and interests (Ryan, Kuhl, & Deci, 1997). In this sense, mindfulness would be expected to facilitate both greater autonomy and satisfaction of the basic psychological needs for autonomy, competence, and relatedness (see also Hodgins & Knee, 2002).

Brown and Ryan (2003) explicitly investigated the relations of mindfulness and autonomous functioning. The authors developed and validated the *Mindful Attention Awareness Scale* (MAAS), a measure of mindfulness as a trait or disposition. They also developed a "state" version of the MAAS to assess within-person fluctuations in mindful awareness. The MAAS, as expected, was positively related to constructs such as openness to experience (Costa & McCrae, 1992), which involves receptivity to and interest in new experiences.

To examine the connections between mindfulness and autonomy, Brown and Ryan (2003) conducted an experience sampling study in which participants, after having completed the mindfulness "trait" measure, recorded their state mindfulness and rated the autonomy three times a day on a quasi-random basis over the course of 2 weeks for student participants and 3 weeks for a working adult sample. In both samples, higher levels of dispositional and trait mindfulness predicted more autonomous activity in daily life. Results also showed that individuals with higher dispositional mindfulness also tended to have higher dispositional autonomy and greater need satisfaction more generally (i.e., more relatedness and competence, as well as autonomy). Yet perhaps most important were findings showing that when experiencing state mindfulness, individuals were more likely to be acting autonomously. Interestingly, the effects of trait and state mindfulness on autonomy were both significant and independent, suggesting that even momentary experiences of mindfulness contribute to a more volitional self-regulation and emotional well-being. That is, when individuals, regardless of their dispositional tendencies, were openly aware of and receptive to what was occurring, they showed enhanced self-regulation.

> *BPNT Proposition VIII:* Mindfulness, defined as the open and receptive awareness of what is occurring both within people and within their context, facilitates greater autonomy and more integrated self-regulation, as well as greater basic psychological need satisfaction, which contributes to greater well-being.

Having established a connection between mindfulness and higher quality self-regulation and basic need satisfaction, we might ask how this connection occurs. As argued by Weinstein, Brown, and Ryan (2009) and Brown et al. (2007), there are multiple reasons. In what follows we discuss several of these.

DECREASED "AUTOMATIC" BEHAVIORS

In the 1980s, Deci and Ryan began speculating about the role of mindfulness and present-centered awareness in the regulation of behavior. In that work, they differentiated between *automatized* behaviors, which are volitional behaviors that had become so well integrated they could be done without consciousness, and *automatic* behaviors, which are those that are controlled by forces that lie outside of awareness (Deci, 1980; Deci & Ryan, 1980b, 1985b). Since that time, much research on automatic and implicit processes has shown that a substantial part of our day-to-day cognitive, emotional, and overt behavior does not require conscious awareness and attention (e.g., Bargh, 1997; Ryan & Deci, 2006). Despite the many pragmatic benefits of some types of automated behaviors, including reduced use of cognitive resources and speed in response to situational demands (see Aarts & Custers, 2012), there are also potential costly consequences. When acting nonconsciously, one is more susceptible to engaging in many habitual problematic and self-defeating behaviors, which, if reflected upon, would be incongruent with one's self-endorsed values or goals (Levesque & Brown, 2007; Ryan & Deci, 2004a; Ryan, Legate, Niemiec, & Deci, 2012). That is, although what we referred to as automatized behaviors may be self-congruent, automatic ones often are not. Mindfulness, through relaxed attention, pulls people closer to what is currently taking place without judgmental or evaluative attachments. This state of more heightened observation and awareness of what is occurring, in turn, allows people to take stock of conditioned or automatic responses and allows the individuals to reflect and select or decline actions with greater choice, thus promoting more self-endorsed behavior (Brown et al., 2007; McLeod, 2001).

Mindfulness has been empirically shown to be a protective factor against automatic behavior and a facilitator of more integrated, autonomous self-regulation. For example, Levesque and Brown (2007) investigated the role of mindfulness as a moderator between implicit regulation, as assessed using the Implicit Association Test (e.g., Greenwald, McGhee, & Schwartz, 1998), and explicit regulation of behavior using an experience-sampling strategy. Both implicit and explicit measures assessed the degree to which the participants' regulation was autonomous or controlled. Results showed that people's implicit regulation style predicted day-to-day regulation for those individuals low in dispositional mindfulness, suggesting that their behavior was indeed more controlled by the nonconscious processes. This, therefore, underscored the importance of mindfulness for gaining greater consciousness and enabling more autonomous self-regulation of behaviors that had been automatic.

Brown and Ryan (2003) reported that individuals higher in trait mindfulness showed greater congruence between implicit or nonconscious emotional states (again assessed with the Implicit Association Test) and their explicit self-reported counterparts. These results indicated that individuals more disposed toward mindfulness had greater concordance, with their explicit awareness being more in touch with implicit processes. Complementing these findings, Brown and Ryan (2003) found in a separate sample that mindfulness was associated with the emotional intelligence dimension, reflecting clarity of emotional experience (Salovey, Mayer, Goldman, Turvey, & Palfai, 1995).

The open, nondistortive, explorative attention of mindfulness also fosters autonomous behavior because it frees individuals from external and internal controlling forces that are alien to the authentic self (Brown et al., 2007). The more mindful individuals are, the more they have an observant stance toward experience, which allows more opportunity both to deeply process events and to not be reactive or engage in controlled responses. As Brown, Ryan, Creswell, and Niemiec (2008) put it, mindfulness "entails a shift in the locus of personal subjectivity from conceptual representations of the self and others to awareness itself" (p. 82).

MINDFULNESS AND TERROR MANAGEMENT

Illustrating the importance of mindfulness for more autonomous action and wellness, Niemiec, Brown, et al. (2010) conducted several experiments informed by terror management theory (TMT; Greenberg, Solomon, & Pyszczynski, 1997). TMT posits, and has assembled considerable empirical support for, the idea that humans often respond defensively and automatically to reminders of mortality and death. Specifically, they are said to be prone, in an immediate sense, to suppress thoughts of death, and, if they are distracted from them, these suppressed thoughts will remain accessible at the edge of awareness and thus be threatening. TMT posits that people will then engage in defensive attempts at self-esteem enhancement and cultural worldview affirmation, which would serve to attenuate this threat of mortality. Cultural worldview defense typically entails people acting in ways that are prejudicially diminishing toward outgroup members or persons who hold values different from their own, while enhancing ingroup members.

Niemiec, Brown, et al. (2010) reasoned that these automatic processes of defense are products of a lack of mindful engagement in what is occurring, and as such people who are low in mindfulness would display the TMT defenses when faced with a mortality salience (MS) induction, whereas people high in mindfulness would be less likely to do so. Although such moderation had not been acknowledged in the TMT literature, it makes considerable sense even within the TMT logic. Specifically, the TMT empirical literature has shown that the defenses operate only when people have been distracted from attending to the existential terror such that death thoughts are at the edge of their awareness. In contrast, Cozzolino, Staples, Meyers, and Samboceti (2004) found that, when people were instructed to attend deeply to their own deaths, they did not evidence the standard defenses following an MS manipulation.

In a series of seven laboratory-based experiments, Niemiec, Brown, et al. (2010) tested this reasoning and demonstrated that high trait mindfulness mitigated the types of defensive responses frequently observed in the TMT literature. Indeed, individuals high in mindfulness showed less immediate suppression of death thoughts (indicated by higher death thought accessibility), as they were more fully processing these thoughts immediately after an MS manipulation, and they also showed less accessibility after the distraction period. Those low in mindfulness showed less accessibility immediately following the manipulation but more accessibility following the delay and distraction period. Most importantly, more mindful individuals did not show the classic MS defensive responses predicted by TMT—they did not derogate or act in prejudicial manners toward outgroup members.

These studies by Niemiec, Brown, and colleagues (2010) fit within a growing body of research on topics as diverse as conflicts within romantic relationship (Barnes, Brown, Krusemark, Campbell, & Rogge, 2007), capacities for affective awareness (Creswell, Way, Eisenberger, & Lieberman, 2007), responses to emotional threat (Arch & Craske, 2006), and reactivity to ego threats (Hodgins, 2008), all showing that greater mindfulness promotes fewer defensive reactions and greater capacities for autonomous regulation.

Decreasing Threat Appraisal and Enhancing Coping

In another sequence of studies, Weinstein, Brown, and Ryan (2009) further demonstrated how mindfulness fosters less defensive responding and less distorted and potentially maladaptive thinking patterns. In four studies using varied methods (including experimental, longitudinal, and experience-sampling designs), the authors found that individuals high in mindfulness were less likely to react to challenges with feelings of stress and more likely to show positive coping with the stress they experienced and that their more adaptive stress feelings and responses mediated either fully or partially the positive relations between mindfulness and well-being.

In another related study, Schultz, Ryan, Niemiec, Legate, and Williams (2015) looked at the role of mindfulness in coping with negative conditions in the workplace. They found, as expected, that both managerial autonomy support and mindfulness were directly related to greater employee wellness. But important here is that mindfulness was also key in buffering the effects of controlling management styles on need frustration in the workplace. People higher in mindfulness were less likely to feel need frustration, even in unsupportive managerial environments, which in turn conduced to greater employee adjustment (i.e., lower burnout, fewer turnover intentions).

In sum, it appears that mindfulness conduces to a more objective and realistic observation of internal and external events, which in turn reduces the need for defensiveness, enhances coping, and allows the "space" for reflective, autonomous regulation of actions to occur. This means that behavior is less likely to be a function of automatic reactions to ego threat (see Niemiec, Ryan, & Brown, 2008) and, instead, is more likely to represent self-congruent, integrated, or autonomous regulations.

Mindfulness Summary

Being psychologically present and "awake" allows for a clarity and freshness that can liberate people from automatic responses and foster more self-endorsed behavior. Mindful people are open and receptive to what is occurring in the present moment, allowing them greater access to the information about both outer events and inner reactions and feelings that is required for healthy coping and self-regulation (Fogarty, Lu, Sollers, Krivoschekov, Booth, & Consedine, 2015). Mindfulness or awareness can thus be a critical component of the integrative processes that lead to basic need satisfactions, vitality, and human wellness.

Fortunately from a practical point of view, which we discuss further in Chapter 17 on psychotherapy, mindfulness is an attribute that can be actively cultivated. For example, Brown and Ryan (2003) found that people who practiced Zen meditation showed higher levels of mindfulness than a matched sample, indicating that mindfulness can be nurtured with practices that involve quiet reflecting and meditating. In addition, a study in the Brown and Ryan (2003) series showed that cancer patients who, as a result of training, became more mindful evidenced declines in mood disturbance and stress, even after controlling for changes in physical symptoms. Such studies indicate that an orientation toward greater mindful awareness—that is, greater openness to experience and mindful reflection—can be self-cultivated. People can thus decide to make the effort to become more mindful, more aware, and more autonomous.

CHAPTER 11

Goal Contents Theory

Aspirations, Life Goals, and Their Varied Consequences

Much work in SDT is concerned with people's motives—with the reasons *why* they are engaging in a behavior or pursuing a goal. In this chapter, we address not the why but rather the *what* of people's behaviors—that is, the content of the life goals they are pursuing. Early research indicated that many life goals fall into two broad categories: *extrinsic* (e.g., pursuit of wealth, fame, and image) and *intrinsic* (e.g., pursuit of personal growth, relationships, and contributing to community) and that these different categories of goals relate differently to well-being. This research led to the formulation of *goal contents theory* (GCT), which posits, in line with eudaimonic theorizing, that a relatively strong focus on extrinsic aspirations is related to lower well-being, whereas placing a priority on intrinsic aspirations is related to greater well-being. SDT research shows that this pattern of results is largely due to the greater tendency of extrinsic goals to be controlled rather than autonomous and to be less satisfying of basic psychological needs. Goal contents are examined both as individual differences and as varying within persons across domains and settings, such as work and classrooms.

SDT holds that not all goals are created equal (Ryan, Sheldon, Kasser, & Deci, 1996), for the *content* of people's goals and life pursuits affects their integration and wellness. Wanting and attaining some goals will satisfy basic psychological needs and, in turn, foster wellness and learning, whereas wanting and attaining other goals may leave people devoid of basic need satisfactions and sometimes even less well.

In this chapter, we outline the fifth mini-theory of SDT, *goal contents theory* (GCT), which concerns the goals and aspirations that organize people's lives and the relations of these goals and aspirations to basic need satisfactions, motivation, and wellness. Our discussion begins with SDT-based research concerning the "what" of people's goal-directed behaviors—that is, whether they are pursuing *intrinsic* versus *extrinsic life goals or aspirations* (e.g., Kasser, 2002b; Kasser & Ryan, 1993, 1996) and how these goals and behaviors relate to well-being outcomes. We then turn to some other categories of goals as they relate to wellness outcomes, addressing how a GCT-based analysis would add to our understanding of the differential relations with psychological wellness of pursuing and attaining different types of goals.

Intrinsic versus Extrinsic Aspirations as the Basis for GCT

In the 1990s, SDT researchers began to ask questions concerning the relations of personal goals to basic need satisfactions and the wellness outcomes associated with them. Presumably, people adopt and pursue goals with the expectation of fulfillment and satisfaction, and such expectations contribute to the *value* component of expectancy-value theories. People form or adopt goals they hope will lead, directly or indirectly, to consequences they value.

Yet the definition of value within expectancy-value theories is, from an SDT perspective, ambiguous, because the pursuit of a value could be either autonomous or controlled, and, in addition, the valued goals being pursued could be more or less fulfilling of basic needs. Thus, unlike expectancy-value theories, SDT has a critical perspective on goals and aspirations, arguing that some types of goals will yield satisfaction of the basic needs of the self and some will not. The consequences of this perspective on goals are manifold.

Research on the Relations of Aspirations and Goals to Well-Being

There are many different ideas about the best pathway to "the good life." Some people espouse the idea that the pursuit of human virtues and excellence leads to the greatest well-being. Yet, especially salient in popular media, one can find a different message: Money, image, and fame seem to be the keys to happiness.

The selection of life's priorities is not merely a philosophical question, but rather a choice people in modern societies must make. SDT research on intrinsic and extrinsic goals is in essence an empirical foray into this value-laden territory. In essence it tests the validity of the eudaimonic claim that it is the pursuit of what is intrinsically worthwhile, and thus the satisfying of basic human needs, that most fosters wellness and flourishing.

Research on intrinsic versus extrinsic goal contents began with work by Kasser and Ryan (1993, 1996), who distinguished *intrinsic aspirations* (e.g., goals such as forming close affiliations, experiencing personal growth, and giving to one's community), which were expected to be closely associated with basic need satisfaction, and *extrinsic aspirations* (e.g., gaining wealth, fame, and image), which were expected to be only indirectly related to basic need satisfactions (and in some instances even need-frustrating). Asking individuals to rate the importance of various aspirations or life goals and their beliefs about the likelihood of attaining those goals, Kasser and Ryan derived an aspirations index (AI) representing *relative importance* of each type of life goal.

In their initial studies, Kasser and Ryan (1993) considered three intrinsic aspirations (personal growth, relationships, and community involvement) relative to people's extrinsic aspirations for financial success and wealth. An initial cross-sectional survey study revealed that the AI for each of the three intrinsic aspirations was positively related to wellness indicators, whereas the higher the relative importance of financial success was, the lower was the participant's experience of self-actualization and vitality. Results of a second study replicated and extended these findings, also revealing that intrinsic aspirations for personal growth and meaningful relationships were negatively related to symptoms of depression and anxiety, whereas the relative importance of the extrinsic aspiration for financial success was positively related to these distressing outcomes.

A third study focused on 18-year-olds from mixed socioeconomic status (SES) backgrounds, drawn from a community sample. Two clinical psychologists rated structured interviews with these emerging adults to attain indicators of (1) global social functioning, (2) conduct disorder, and (3) social productivity. Using this different type of sample and clinically derived mental health indicators, results nonetheless paralleled the earlier studies. Whereas the intrinsic aspirations related positively to global social functioning and social productivity and negatively to conduct disorders, the opposite was true for financial success aspirations. The findings of these three studies were the first to show that the contents of people's valued life goals may have a direct relation to well-being.

Kasser and Ryan (1996) subsequently expanded on this earlier work by including the initial four aspirations, as well as two additional extrinsic aspirations, specifically, attractiveness (image) and social recognition (fame). Higher order factor analyses revealed two clear overarching factors, one for the intrinsic subscales of personal growth, relationships, and community contributions and the other for the extrinsic scales of wealth, image, and fame, supporting the theoretically based intrinsic-versus-extrinsic distinction. Assessing both urban adults and college samples, they then related intrinsic and extrinsic aspirations to varied indicators of wellness concerning self-actualization, energy and vitality, depressive symptoms, narcissism, and common physical symptoms. Placing high relative importance on intrinsic aspirations was found to be associated with greater self-actualization and vitality, less depression, and fewer physical symptoms, whereas high relative importance on extrinsic aspirations was associated with lower self-actualization and vitality and more physical symptoms.

A number of other studies followed, expanding both the generalizability of these findings to other cultures and ages and the network of variables affected by intrinsic and extrinsic striving. For example, Ryan, Chirkov, Little, Sheldon, Timoshina, and Deci (1999) showed that greater valuing of intrinsic relative to extrinsic goals was predicative of better wellness outcomes in both U.S. and Russian samples, despite their differing economic circumstances. Schmuck, Kasser, and Ryan (2000) similarly showed these effects in Germany. Martos and Kopp (2014) found that adults in Hungary who more strongly valued intrinsic aspirations evidenced greater meaning in life and well-being, whereas extrinsic aspirations contributed to diminished meaning in life and had little relation to well-being. This study was especially important for its inclusion of a representative sample of adults and also for showing that these results obtained within every socioeconomic level. Researchers in Scandinavia (Utvær, Hammervold, & Haugan, 2014) also found that the predicted pattern of outcomes was found in other nations.

Research on the AI was expanded not only with studies from varied nations but also with varied ages and additional outcomes. For example, Williams, Hedberg, Cox, and Deci (2000) used the AI to examine the life goals of U.S. high school students and found that those who had strong relative extrinsic aspirations were more likely to engage in high-risk behaviors, such as the use of tobacco, alcohol, and marijuana. A study by Kasser and Ryan (2001) of midwestern U.S. college students found that those with strong relative extrinsic aspirations also used more drugs and watched more television. Behaviors such as drug and alcohol use, which were related to investment in extrinsic goals for image and popularity, may be done to gain peer approval but can also have negative health consequences. Alternatively, it may be that the basic need frustrations that are associated with extrinsic pursuits may lead to activities such as drinking alcohol and excessive use of media as compensatory outlets or avoidant forms of coping.

Using a very different methodology that focused on the stories people tell of their lives, Bauer, McAdams, and Sakaeda (2005) found that individuals whose life narratives emphasized intrinsic goals of personal growth, meaningful relationships, and community contributions displayed both greater hedonic and eudaimonic well-being than those whose stories emphasized the extrinsic goals of wealth, status, approval, and physical appearance. They appeared, from narratives and the wellness assessments, to enjoy a greater range of positive outcomes as an aspect of living a self-constructed "good life."

These and other such studies thus supply a sampling of both the early and continuing empirical support that has provided the basis for the first three formal propositions of GCT.

GCT Proposition I: Intrinsic goals are defined as those most directly associated with the pursuit of what is inherently valued, such as close relationships, personal growth, and contributing to one's community. Extrinsic goals, in contrast, are those focused on instrumental outcomes, such as money, fame, power, or outward attractiveness. These goals can therefore be understood as lying along an axis from intrinsic to extrinsic.

GCT Proposition II: The more an individual values or prioritizes extrinsic goals relative to intrinsic goals, the lower will be his or her well-being. The more a person puts relative priority or value on intrinsic goals, the better the person's wellness outcomes.

GCT Proposition III: These relations between intrinsic and extrinsic goals and wellness will largely be a function of (i.e., mediated by) satisfaction and frustration of basic psychological needs. In general, intrinsic goal pursuits are more satisfying of basic psychological needs. In addition, effects may also be a function of the regulatory basis of goal pursuits, as extrinsic goals will, on average, tend to be less autonomously regulated than intrinsic goals.

Research using a variety of methods and sampling a wide variety of cultures has provided considerable support for these three propositions. For example, regarding Proposition I, Grouzet et al. (2005) collected samples from 15 nations around the globe, representing quite diverse cultural groups. They assessed the intrinsic and extrinsic aspirations we have discussed so far, as well as a number of other aspirational values, such as hedonism, conformity, spirituality, and other life goals, to yield a circumplex model. This model was built using two dimensions, one representing the intrinsic and extrinsic aspiration dimension we have been considering in GCT and one representing a self-focus versus self-transcendence axis. The intrinsic–extrinsic axis was reliable across cultures, suggesting the relative universality of this dimension. Moreover, the circumplex modeling reveals the antipodal nature of these goals: The more one tends to be focused on extrinsic goals such as fame and wealth, the less likely one is to place importance on issues such as community and close relationships.

Indeed, the general model—that aspirations for wealth, fame, and image tend to be associated with each other and to be differentiated from aspirations focused on growth, intimacy, and community—has now received widespread support across the 15-country study by Grouzet and colleagues (2005), as well as by studies in many individual countries, such as China (Tang, Kuang, & Yao, 2008) and South Korea (Kim, Kasser, & Lee, 2003). Various studies have also confirmed that satisfaction and frustration of the basic needs play a mediating role in the relations between aspirations and outcomes. For example, Unanue, Dittmar, Vignoles, and Vansteenkiste (2014) found in both a mass-consumer society (the United Kingdom) and a fast-developing new economy (Chile) that the materialistic extrinsic aspiration was negatively associated with well-being and positively associated with ill-being. Across these distinct economic contexts, low satisfaction of the basic psychological needs and high frustration of these needs mediated these relations.

Moreover, an array of positive outcomes has been associated with intrinsic goals and aspirations, from greater well-being (Kasser & Ryan, 1996) to higher quality relationships (Kasser & Ryan, 2001), greater school success (e.g., Fryer, Ginns, & Walker, 2014), and both greater spirituality and less greed (Cozzolino, Staples, Meyers, and Samboceti, 2004). In contrast, there have been many negative associations of extrinsic aspirations with a variety of ill-being outcomes (Kasser, 2002b).

It is also worthy of note that such results have been found with young people as well as adults. For example, research by Easterbrook, Wright, Dittmar, and Banerjee (2014) found that a sample of 8- to 15-year-olds who were materialistic, with a focus on possessions and outward indicators of worth, had a low level of well-being, and Ku, Dittmar, and Banerjee (2014) found, in a study of Chinese and British children, that children with a strong emphasis on materialistic aspirations also displayed extrinsic motivation for learning, which led to poorer learning outcomes. In short, Propositions I and II have strong and quite universal empirical support in a continuously growing and evolving literature.

Aspirations: Espousing Them or Enacting Them?

Researchers have examined not only the aspirations that participants espoused but also the behaviors they engaged in that were consistent with those aspirations. Sheldon and Krieger (2014b) found that people were more likely to espouse their aspirations than to act in accordance with them, especially in regard to the intrinsic goals of personal growth, affiliation, and community. Further, participants who were more autonomous and had higher meaning in life showed higher correlations between their aspirations and behaviors than did those who were more controlled and had less meaning. Further, and importantly, the amount of behavior people displayed that was consistent with intrinsic aspirations was more predictive of well-being than were the intrinsic aspirations themselves, and the amount of behaviors they displayed that was consistent with extrinsic aspirations was more predictive of ill-being than were the extrinsic aspirations themselves. Simply stated, actually living one's intrinsic aspirations may be critical to experiencing greater need satisfaction and well-being.

Changes in Aspirations

In people's lives there are likely to be many factors that affect their relative intrinsic and extrinsic aspirations over time. Research has indicated that as people's aspirations change, their well-being changes accordingly. For example, three longitudinal studies, one over a 12-year period, examined changes in people's aspirations and the corresponding changes in well-being. The results indicated that when people became more intrinsically oriented over time, their well-being increased, whereas when they became more extrinsically oriented, their well-being decreased (Kasser et al., 2014). Further, as would be expected from SDT and GCT Proposition III, these changes were mediated by satisfaction of the basic psychological needs. These researchers also reported an experiment in which highly extrinsically oriented, materialistic adolescents were given an intervention to decrease their materialism. Results indicated that those in the intervention showed increased self-esteem relative to that of the control group participants.

Research by Twenge, Campbell, and Freeman (2012) examined life goals, concern for others, and civic orientations among Americans in late adolescence across three post-World War II generations. Results indicated that the adolescents of each generation became less concerned with others, less concerned with community, and less mindful of the environment. The researchers concluded that these changes toward concern with themselves and away from the external world over the half century resulted from the adolescents' focusing increasingly on goals related to extrinsic aspirations (wealth, fame, and image) rather than those related to intrinsic aspirations (self-development, affiliation, and community). These cohort effects suggest that historical forces also impact aspirations, making it ever more important for parents, educational institutions, and societies as a whole to focus on more actively endorsing, modeling, and living in accordance with intrinsic aspirations.

Intrinsic and Extrinsic Goal Attainment

It might be argued that the differential outcomes associated with different life goals concerns not their content but their *attainment*. What happens if people are able to attain their intrinsic or extrinsic aspirations? Whereas the expectancy-value approach asserts that the attainment of any valued goal will lead to greater satisfaction and happiness, the GCT position is that even attaining some valued goals may have negative rather than happiness consequences.

In an early short-term longitudinal study, Sheldon and Kasser (1998) found that well-being was enhanced by the actual attainment of intrinsic goals, whereas success at extrinsic goals provided little well-being enhancement. These results suggested that even when individuals are highly efficacious and end up attaining desired outcomes, they may experience less than optimal well-being if the goals have contents that are more extrinsic than intrinsic.

In a subsequent cross-cultural study of aspirations, Ryan et al. (1999) asked Russian and U.S. participants to rate the extent to which they had attained each of their aspirations and life goals. While attainments in both categories were positively correlated with well-being outcomes, their intrinsic goals were more strongly so. Because the two types of goals shared some variance in well-being, intrinsic and extrinsic goal attainments were allowed to compete in predicting the wellness outcomes. Results showed that extrinsic attainments accounted for no incremental variance in wellness beyond that accounted for by intrinsic goals, but attainment of intrinsic goals was significant even when controlling for extrinsic attainments. Similarly, Kasser and Ryan (2001) found that rated current attainment of intrinsic aspirations was positively associated with well-being, but rated current attainment of extrinsic aspirations was not.

In each of these studies, results revealed a differential yield for success at extrinsic relative to intrinsic goals. Whereas *valuing* intrinsic goals was positively associated with wellness and valuing extrinsic goals was negatively related to wellness, these new results indicated that *attaining* intrinsic goals was associated with enhanced wellness, whereas attaining extrinsic goals was yielding no gains or at best marginal gains. In interpreting these results, we assume that attaining intrinsic goals was more directly associated with basic need satisfactions and was thus more enhancing of well-being. In contrast, attaining extrinsic goals may yield competence satisfactions, but little else. We also assumed that the process of pursuing extrinsic goals has costs in terms of psychological need satisfactions, especially autonomy and relatedness, a point upon which we later elaborate.

A longitudinal study by Niemiec, Ryan, and Deci (2009) used a postcollege sample to examine the effects of intrinsic versus extrinsic goals on both attainments and wellness, while controlling for important potential confounds. They collected data from individuals who had been 1 year out of college and followed them for the subsequent year. At the beginning and end of the 1-year period, participants reported on the importance and attainment of each aspiration and provided indicators of well-being and ill-being, as well as satisfaction of the basic psychological needs. Results indicated that placing importance on either intrinsic or extrinsic aspirations led to greater attainment of the corresponding goals, as would be predicted by various theories, including expectancy-value theories. Yet, whereas attainment of hoped-for intrinsic aspirations led to greater well-being and less ill-being, attainment of hoped-for extrinsic aspirations did not relate to well-being but did predict greater ill-being. Further, and importantly in terms of the preceding theoretical discussion, the strong relation between attainment of intrinsic aspirations and psychological health was mediated by satisfaction of basic psychological needs for autonomy, competence, and relatedness.

Whereas Niemiec, Ryan, and Deci (2009) were looking at importance and attainment in early adulthood and their relations to wellness, other studies have found that the aspirations of both working people and elderly adults can affect how they experience their jobs and their lives more generally. In studies of workers, results indicated that their aspirations can have a major impact on their experiences of their jobs. For example, Montasem, Brown, and Harris (2013) studied the aspiration profiles of working dentists and found that their reports of the importance and likelihood of attaining intrinsic aspirations was associated with subjective well-being, job satisfaction and their satisfaction with their lives.

Van Hiel and Vansteenkiste (2009) investigated aspirations of individuals later in the adult developmental spectrum. In two studies, they asked older adults to reflect on and rate their intrinsic and extrinsic goal attainments, using these to predict their levels of ego integrity, psychological well-being, and death attitudes. In their initial study, adults with a mean age of 68 years showed that, after controlling for extrinsic goal attainment, intrinsic goal attainment contributed positively to subjective well-being and ego integrity and negatively to despair, whereas extrinsic goal attainment was unrelated to psychological health and contributed positively to despair. In the second study, adults with a mean age of 75 years indicated that intrinsic goal attainment contributed to lower ill-being, greater acceptance of their own deaths, and less death anxiety, whereas extrinsic goal attainment was negatively associated with death acceptance. Thus it appears that, in this more summative assessment of life's attainments, adults' wellness is more associated with having been successful at intrinsic rather than extrinsic goals.

In an interesting, real-world examination of life-goal attainment, Sheldon and Krieger (2014a) identified more than one thousand private-firm lawyers who had high-paying jobs within money-focused firms (e.g., doing securities-related work) and a similar number of public-service lawyers who had jobs focused on serving the public good (e.g., doing sustainability-related work for nonprofit organizations). As one would expect, those lawyers in the money-focused jobs had much larger annual incomes than those in the service-focused jobs, and yet those high-paid lawyers nonetheless reported more negative affect, lower well-being, and more alcohol consumption. Again, we see that a focus on and attainment of extrinsic goals, especially for great wealth, does not give people more happiness and wellness. In fact, it may interfere with those very outcomes.

Across these studies of life-goal attainment, results are consistent with our third GCT proposition:

> **GCT Proposition IV:** Progress and success at attaining extrinsic goals will tend to be associated with less enhanced wellness relative to progress and attainment of intrinsic goals. Progress and attainment of intrinsic goals is predicted to yield especially enhanced wellness. These effects are largely mediated by basic psychological need satisfaction.

Proposition IV reflects the idea that attaining intrinsic goals is more likely to promote basic need satisfactions, which have been shown in many studies to promote a wide range of wellness and effective performance outcomes (e.g., Howell, Chenot, Hill, & Howell, 2011), whereas basic need satisfaction is less likely to follow when extrinsic goals are attained (e.g., Sheldon, Ryan, Deci, & Kasser, 2004). Moreover, this proposition reflects findings that the *process* of extrinsic goal attainment may often involve compromises to autonomy, competence, or relatedness that have direct negative consequences.

Nonetheless, the consequences of succeeding at either type of goal may depend on (be moderated by) the individuals' intended use of the goal attainments or outcomes. For example, when people intend to use their monetary attainments to support charities or educate their children, their attainment may satisfy basic needs and enhance wellness.

On the Independence of Goal Contents and Autonomous Regulation

The research on aspirations discussed so far has concerned the specific content of people's goals—for example, the degree to which they aspire to amass surplus wealth or to nurture relationships. As noted earlier, we have often referred to this as the "what" of goal-directed behavior (Deci & Ryan, 2000), and within SDT the concept of intrinsic versus extrinsic goals is the key concept with respect to "what." This is different from the "why" of behavior, which, as also noted, refers to the motives or reasons people have for pursuing those goals. In SDT, the "why" is addressed with the concept of autonomous versus controlled regulatory styles, which we have discussed at length in Chapter 8 and elsewhere.

We expect that, on average, intrinsic goals will be more autonomously regulated than extrinsic goals, as has been shown by Kasser and Ryan (1993), Sheldon and Kasser (1995), and others. The reason is that, because intrinsic goals are directly satisfying of basic needs for autonomy, competence, and relatedness, they are more easily integrated and volitionally undertaken. Further, being autonomously motivated, like having intrinsic aspirations, is satisfying of the basic psychological needs. In contrast, we also believe that experiences of need thwarting during development may lead people to focus less on intrinsic aspirations and more on substitute and compensatory extrinsic aspirations. That is, extrinsic goals are often more controlled, in part because they are precipitated by need thwarting and are often attempts to obtain the (contingent) regard of others. However, although autonomy and intrinsic goals are correlated, we believe that there are nonetheless independent effects for the *why* and the *what* components of goal pursuits.

In the first study that addressed both the what and why of behavior using an SDT perspective, Sheldon and Kasser (1995) studied the relatively short-term strivings (Emmons, 1986) of undergraduates, assessing their reasons for pursuing each striving (Ryan & Connell, 1989) and the helpfulness of each striving for attaining the longer term intrinsic versus extrinsic aspirations (Kasser & Ryan, 1996). Analyses of their data indicated, first, that the degree to which the regulation of striving pursuits was autonomous (versus controlled) predicted a variety of well-being outcomes and, second, that the extent to which the students believed that the strivings would lead to the attainment of long-term intrinsic (versus extrinsic) aspirations was also positively related to well-being. In other words, both the autonomous regulatory processes motivating people's goal pursuits and the intrinsic outcomes they expected, eventually, to attain were positive predictors of their eudaimonic well-being.

Within the SDT framework, we have proposed that both the what and the why of goal pursuits would affect well-being outcomes because both the content of goal pursuits and the reasons why they are being pursued are theorized to affect the degree of satisfaction of the basic psychological needs (Ryan et al., 1996). Still, there is a much longer history of support for the hypothesis that the types of motivation would be differentially associated with well-being than there is for the hypothesis that the types of aspirations would be differentially associated with well-being. Some critics have even suggested that the reason that the two types of aspirations have different relations to well-being outcomes is that strongly pursued intrinsic aspirations are likely to be autonomously motivated, whereas strong extrinsic aspirations are likely to be pursued for controlled reasons. Put differently, from that perspective, it is the autonomous and controlled regulation rather than the intrinsic and extrinsic content of the goals that accounts for the effects of pursuing the aspirations (e.g., Carver & Baird, 1998; Srivastava, Locke, & Bartol, 2001).

In light of this controversy about whether goal contents predict well-being after removing the variance attributable to motives, Sheldon, Ryan, et al. (2004) presented a series of studies that examined whether goal contents and goal motives contributed significant independent variance to the prediction of well-being. Acknowledging that goal contents and motives tended to be correlated, they examined whether each predicted well-being independently, over and above the contribution of the shared variance. The studies used both between-person and within-person designs, took both cross-sectional and longitudinal approaches, and examined participants' attributions about their own well-being in hypothetical situations and reports of their own well-being at a particular time and over a year-long period when they were actually pursuing extrinsic versus intrinsic goals. In all cases, extrinsic versus intrinsic goal contents made an independent contribution to the prediction of well-being outcomes, over and above the contributions made by controlled versus autonomous motives. Specifically, in light of the controversy with Carver and Baird (1998) and Srivastava et al. (2001), analyses confirmed that, after removing the effects of controlled reasons, the three extrinsic aspirations (wealth, fame, and image), taken together, or the aspiration for wealth, taken alone, significantly negatively predicted well-being. In fact, in the longitudinal study, the aspirations reported by college seniors shortly before graduating predicted their change in well-being over the subsequent year. That is, the goals people pursued in the year following graduation from college led to either increases or decreases in their well-being, presumably because some of the goals provided greater satisfaction of the basic psychological needs and others either provided less satisfaction or more frustration of the basic needs.

The Match of Personal Goals and Contextual Values

Although the negative relations between holding strong extrinsic (relative to intrinsic) life goals and well-being seem to be relatively strong, one might wonder whether these effects would be moderated by the types of values that are prevalent in one's social environment. For example, would business students whose environment places high value on wealth accumulation demonstrate the same negative relations between extrinsic aspirations and well-being that have been found with other students? In fact, it is often argued that there is benefit to holding goals consistent with those endorsed by the larger social context. This suggestion is referred to as a *match hypothesis*, which is often advocated in social psychology (Sagiv & Schwartz, 2000), organizational studies (Meglino, Ravlin, & Adkins, 1989), and educational psychology (Harackiewicz & Elliot, 1998).

To address this issue, Kasser and Ahuvia (2002) did a study examining the relation between the relative strengths of business school students' monetary goals and their well-being. The authors found the same negative relations between extrinsic (relative to intrinsic) aspirations and well-being that had been found in numerous other samples of students and adults. Further, Vansteenkiste, Duriez, Simons, and Soenens (2006), comparing business and educational students, similarly turned up no evidence for the match hypothesis. As they predicted, their business student sample rated extrinsic aspirations as more important and intrinsic aspirations as less important than was the case for education students, but the strength of extrinsic aspirations was nonetheless negatively related to well-being for the business students just as it was for their matched sample of education students. More extrinsically focused business students evidenced lower psychological well-being, showed more signs of internal distress, and engaged in more substance use than those who were less focused on extrinsic goals. Thus it appears that the negative association between extrinsic (relative to intrinsic) life goals and psychological well-being applies to students pursuing both business and nonbusiness life courses.

Interestingly, however, there is some evidence that in cases in which the social context is very circumscribed and intense, the relations of various aspirations to well-being might be influenced by the values in the context. For example, Kasser (1996) examined this issue among residents in a high-security prison, where the intrinsic aspiration for physical fitness is strongly supported but the intrinsic aspirations for self-acceptance and close relationships are not supported. He found a positive relation between the residents' levels of the physical fitness aspiration and psychological well-being, whereas their levels of self-acceptance and affiliation were negatively related to well-being, perhaps indicative of the frustration of holding such goals in environments in which they cannot be satisfied. This issue clearly deserves more empirical attention, as around the world there are many cultures and proximal environments that compromise people's opportunities to realize their intrinsic aspirations.

What If Extrinsic Goals Are Put to Virtuous Use?

Focusing only on the aspiration for money, Landry and colleagues (2016) took a different approach to examining why people pursue that extrinsic aspiration and whether the different reasons might relate differently to well-being and ill-being. Landry and colleagues argued that there are three categories of reasons for pursuing money—financial stability reasons (e.g., to use for family support), integrated reasons (e.g., to use for charity and leisure), and nonintegrated reasons (e.g., to use to look better than others and to overcome self-doubt). The researchers found that, controlling for financial stability reasons, (1) integrated reasons predicted greater well-being and lesser ill-being by relating positively to satisfaction of the basic psychological needs and negatively to frustration of the needs, and (2) nonintegrated reasons predicted lesser well-being and greater ill-being by relating negatively with need satisfaction and positively with need frustration. In sum, it appears that, in general, placing strong value on pursuing money is likely to lead to poor psychological wellness, but if the pursuit is being done for more admirable reasons, such as family support, charitable contributions, and experiencing personal freedom, the pursuit may have positive rather than negative consequences.

A cross-cultural study by Frost and Frost (2000) reflected these nuances in how some extrinsic goals can have different meanings. They found that Romanians and Americans both showed positive correlations between psychological well-being and the intrinsic goal of contributing to one's community. Yet the extrinsic goal of financial success was negatively associated with psychological well-being only in the U.S. sample. Their further analyses revealed that this was likely moderated by the different significance given to financial success in the two cultures, especially at that point in time: For the U.S. participants, financial success goals were related to "power" and "security," whereas in the Romanian sample they were more related to "self- direction."

Such research highlights the importance of uncovering the meaning of people's goals and identifying that toward which they are really aiming. It is clear that when an extrinsic goal, such as making money, is being pursued for the sake of a larger intrinsic goal, such as giving to community, it is the latter, hierarchically primary goal that will carry the predictive weight. Conversely, one can find "philanthropists" who contribute to their community only to enhance their fame or image. In such cases, GCT predicts they will not experience the basic need satisfactions and wellness benefits of persons who give to others for its own sake.

Beyond Wellness:
Intrinsic and Extrinsic Goals in Relationships and Society

A number of studies growing out of this literature on goal-content effects have also shown that extrinsic and intrinsic goal pursuits are associated with a number of positive or negative social and societal consequences. For example, Kasser and Ryan (2001) demonstrated that individuals with high extrinsic aspirations experienced their intimate or close relationships as more conflicted and as less satisfying and trusting. This may stem directly from the fact that people who are more extrinsically oriented place less importance on affiliation and caring for others. Also, individuals who are strongly extrinsically oriented reported being less empathic (Sheldon & Kasser, 1995) and are more likely to see relationships as instrumental to their own goals. For instance, they are more likely to report using their friends to get ahead in life (Khanna & Kasser, 1999), and they score higher on scales assessing Machiavellianism (Christie & Geis, 1970)—that is, being willing to use power to manipulate others (McHoskey, 1999).

A more recent study examined the consistency of people's ideal standards for close relationships with their corresponding perceptions of their actual relationships (Rodriguez, Hadden, & Knee, 2015). It has been often suggested that greater consistency between the ideal and the actual lead to high positive evaluations of relationships. However, Rodriguez and colleagues (2015) hypothesized that the types of ideals—namely, whether they are aligned with extrinsic aspirations or intrinsic aspirations—would make a difference. They found that consistency between intrinsic ideals and perceptions of one's partners as matching one's intrinsic ideals strongly predicted high-quality relationship functioning. Yet the same was not true for extrinsic ideal–actual consistency. Further, intrinsic ideal–actual consistency also buffered the relevance of extrinsic ideals for outcomes.

At a broader level, people who are focused on extrinsic goals are more costly to us all. For example, Sheldon and McGregor (2000) did a "tragedy of the commons" experiment in which people were allowed to harvest resources in a game in which they were scarce, People with more extrinsic life goals were more likely to harvest available resources more quickly in this simulation, but *groups* with more extrinsically oriented players performed worse than those with players high in intrinsic values, because they overharvested too quickly. It does not require much imagination to see how this study is a metaphor for our current societal consumption trends. Sheldon and McGregor (2000) further cited *acquisitiveness* as a strong motive in the extrinsic group that led to this more rapid depletion of collective resources. Brown and Kasser (2005) found an extrinsic goal pursuit to negatively predict pro-environmental engagement and to foster a larger environmental footprint. Further, Sheldon, Sheldon, and Osbaldiston (2000) found that people with stronger extrinsic aspirations were more prone to compete rather than cooperate when common resources were scarce. Finally, Duriez, Vansteenkiste, Soenens, and De Witte (2007) found that extrinsic relative to intrinsic goal pursuits were associated with more racial and ethnic prejudices and a greater tendency toward social dominance.

Together, these findings suggest that individuals who are highly extrinsically oriented are more likely to objectify others and to use them as efficiently as possible to attain their own extrinsic ambitions (e.g., Kasser, 2002a), with clear costs to collective wellness. Conversely, as individuals high in the intrinsic orientation are concerned with both their personal growth and the welfare of others, they are more likely to take the perspective of others and to develop more mutually respectful and beneficial relationships.

Extrinsic Aspirations and Materialism in Our Society

Although the research on extrinsic aspirations makes clear that there are a variety of negative consequences to placing strong value on these goals, the Anglo-American capitalist ethos, which has fast been spreading across the globe, holds the extrinsic aspirations—wealth, fame, and image—as central societal values (see Kasser, Kanner, Cohn, & Ryan, 2007). Indeed, the so-called *American dream* involves attaining these very aspirations. Furthermore, the advertising industry is paid many billions of dollars each year to promote the values of consumption. Their job is to make us believe that we will be happier, healthier, more vital, and satisfied with our lives if we purchase more and more material goods. In short, we live in a materialistic society that places strong import on the newest gadgets and products that might make us look more attractive or attain greater social recognition.

In the past few decades, issues related to what we call extrinsic aspirations have been studied as *materialism* (e.g., Dittmar, 2008; Kasser & Kanner, 2004; Kasser & Ryan, 1993; Inglehart, 1981; Richins & Dawson, 1992), which has to do with pursuing and strongly desiring to attain material goods. Materialism quite simply concerns living with the belief that success and happiness are a function of money and the things that money can buy. A recent meta-analysis of studies that examined the associations between materialism, assessed with commonly used multifaceted measures, and well-being, assessed with a variety of different wellness indicators, included 753 effect sizes taken from 259 independent samples (Dittmar, Bond, Hurst, & Kasser, 2014). This vigorous research area, when analyzed as a whole, yielded an effect size of −0.24, indicating that greater materialism was indeed related to lower well-being, including more risky health behaviors and negative self-appraisals. Further, and wholly in line with SDT, these relations were mediated by low levels of satisfaction of the basic psychological needs.

Another meta-analysis of variables associated with materialism examined its relations to pro-environmental attitudes and behaviors (Hurst, Dittmar, Bond, & Kasser,

2013). The analyses, which included more than 3,000 participants from 17 studies, showed that there was a moderately strong negative relation between materialistic values and pro-environmental behaviors and attitudes. The more the participants were guided by extrinsic aspirations, as captured by the concept of materialism, the less their attitudes and behaviors were consistent with the intrinsic aspiration of community contribution.

Unanue, Vignoles, Dittmar, and Vansteenkiste (2016) more recently used both concurrent and prospective data to examine the connections between intrinsic and extrinsic life goals and environmental attitudes and behaviors in two diverse cultures, namely the United Kingdom and Chile. They found that intrinsic versus extrinsic life goals predicted environmentally responsible behavior over a 2-year period, whereas pro-environmental attitudes and identification with the environment by themselves did not. This shows the generalizability of this connection over both an established capitalist economy and a fast-growing but still developing consumer society.

Pieters (2013) performed an interesting 5-year longitudinal study in the Netherlands that examined relations between materialism and loneliness among an online consumer panel. Results indicated that loneliness (i.e., lack of relatedness need satisfaction) was a strong predictor of materialism, suggesting that when people are unable to satisfy one or more of the basic psychological needs—for example, through attaining an intrinsic aspiration such as meaningful relationships—they are more likely to focus on pursuit of extrinsic aspirations. Further, there was some indication that people who were materialistic in their orientations tended to become more lonely, which would tend to create a vicious cycle between these two psychological experiences.

Another clue to this dynamic nature of aspirations was unveiled in a study by Otero-López and Villardefrancos (2015). They examined people's failures to attain intrinsic aspirations and reported that those who said they were unable to attain intrinsic aspirations were more likely to become compulsive buyers. The authors suggested that these individuals may have come to value extrinsic aspirations *as a response* to feeling unable to attain intrinsic goals and presumably to the blow to basic need satisfactions this entailed, and, as a result, they engaged in these less edifying, and perhaps compensatory, behaviors.

Material and Experiential Purchases

Some research has shown that not all purchases and expenditures of significant amounts of money will necessarily have the negative consequences that were highlighted in the Dittmar et al. (2014) meta-analysis. For example, Howell and Hill (2009) found that materialist values were negatively related to well-being and that there was little relation between income and well-being once people's basic psychological needs were satisfied. Beyond that, they further found that the type of purchases people made yielded a difference in wellness. Specifically, they found that experiential purchases (e.g., taking a trip or attending a concert) tended to be positively associated with wellness, whereas materialistic purchases (e.g., getting a bigger television or a new dress) did not contribute to wellness. The relations between experiential purchases and well-being were mediated by enhanced satisfaction of the basic need for relatedness and diminishment of the control-oriented social comparison.

Other research examining experiential versus materialistic purchases found that people interpreted their experiential purchases as being more closely related to their own sense of true self than was the case with materialistic purchases (Carter & Gilovich, 2012). As well, observers reported that they believed they knew more about people's true selves if they had information about the people's experiential purchases than if they had information about the people's material purchases. The positive connection between experiential purchases, basic psychological need satisfaction, and perceptions of true self, as well as an implicit negative connection between experiential purchases and extrinsic aspirations, all make good sense within SDT because experiential purchases so often reflect one's authentic interests or values, resulting in both autonomy and basic need satisfaction.

The Development of Extrinsic Aspirations

SDT has been concerned about the dynamic developmental foundations of extrinsic versus intrinsic aspirations. Because extrinsic aspirations focus on the external trappings of worth and positions of power and status, we have hypothesized that when individuals are unable to satisfy their fundamental psychological needs, or when the needs are thwarted, especially during their childhood and adolescent years, young people will develop insecurities that leave them vulnerable to a focus on extrinsic signs of power or worth. Put differently, extrinsic orientations are often compensatory motives when people's basic psychological needs have been frustrated rather than satisfied, in part because social contexts have thwarted their attempts to satisfy their needs.

> *GCT Proposition V:* Individuals whose basic psychological needs have been neglected or frustrated in development are more prone to adopt need substitutes, such as extrinsic life goals, as being personally important. To the extent that they do so, their well-being will be compromised.

Kasser, Ryan, Zax, and Sameroff (1995) tested this proposition by investigating the developmental antecedents of teenagers' placing high importance on wealth relative to the three intrinsic aspirations of growth, relatedness, and community. The teenagers completed a questionnaire indicating the degree to which their mothers were democratic, noncontrolling, and warm in their parenting styles, and the mothers also provided self-report data on the same variables. It was reasoned that mothers who were authoritarian, controlling, and cold would thwart the basic need satisfaction of their children, leading to a stronger extrinsic aspiration for wealth and greater ill-being. In contrast, if mothers were democratic, noncontrolling, and warm, they would be supportive of the basic needs, leading to more intrinsic aspirations and greater well-being. As expected, the data showed that when mothers were low on democracy and warmth and high on control, either according to their self-reports or to their children's perceptions, the children placed relatively higher importance on the extrinsic aspiration of accumulating wealth, whereas greater need support led to stronger intrinsic aspirations. The results thus suggest that parenting environments that thwart children's need satisfaction facilitate the development of extrinsic aspirations such as wealth that are visible indicators of "worth" and may represent substitutes for basic need satisfaction, which, however, would not be truly satisfying of the needs.

Further, Kasser et al. (1995) examined data that had been collected from these same mothers over a decade earlier, when the children were 4 years old. Trained observers had rated the mothers' coldness in interacting with their 4-year-old children and the rigidity of their parenting beliefs, and an index of these variables was related significantly to the strength of their children's relative extrinsic aspirations for money, assessed more than 10 years after the mothers' ratings had been made. These analyses provide important support for our speculations about the etiology of extrinsic aspirations as substitutes for the lack of basic need satisfaction.

A study by Williams, Cox, Kouides, and Deci (1999) examined high school students' perceptions of the degree to which their parents were autonomy-supportive, and the data indicated that teenagers who experienced their parents as low in autonomy support had significantly stronger relative extrinsic aspirations than those who perceived their parents as high in autonomy support. Further, the analyses indicated that the teenagers' strong extrinsic aspirations mediated between their parents' being controlling and the teens' early engagement in health-compromising behaviors, such as using tobacco, alcohol, and marijuana. It seems that social environments that interfere with need satisfaction do turn individuals toward goals that serve to compensate for the lack of need satisfaction and that the costs to the individuals are considerable, including involvement in behaviors that continue to thwart need satisfaction and are serious risks for both physical and psychological health.

As mentioned, the converse of the idea that need thwarting leads to extrinsic aspirations and poorer well-being is the idea that more supportive, basic need nurturing environments would facilitate the development of intrinsic goals and aspirations, as was found to be the case in the Kasser et al. (1995) study. In part, nurturing conditions supply relatedness and autonomy supports in the form of empathy and caring, which in turn should facilitate a prosocial, connecting orientation in the child. In addition, because we postulate that there is a natural proneness toward both autonomy and relatedness, there should be a tendency for people to be moved toward more intrinsic values over development, other factors aside. This hypothesis has underpinned a number of studies suggestive of this positive human trend (e.g., Sheldon, 2005; Sheldon, Arndt, & Houser-Marko, 2003).

Furthermore, there is evidence that factors in familial, friendship, and cultural settings can influence the aspirations that people hold, in part by affecting basic need satisfaction. For example, concerning relatedness, SDT proposes that the values and goals of others to whom target individuals are most closely affiliated or want to be closely affiliated are likely to be internalized by the target individuals. There are also cultural factors. For example, extrinsic values and materialism can be heightened in cultures in which there is constant exposure to advertising and persuasive messages. For example, it is well documented that children who have greater exposure to television tend to adopt more extrinsic values (Kasser, 2002a), most likely through the pervasive celebrity role models they see in the media who tend to be focused on wealth, fame, and image. Emulating most celebrities would likely conduce to a set of extrinsic aspirations.

Influencing People's Aspirations

Given the linkage from holding relatively stronger intrinsic than extrinsic aspirations to a range of positive outcomes, it is heartening that some research has shown that people's surroundings can promote stronger intrinsic value systems and aspirations in those people. An example of how people's value systems and aspirations can be shaped by their surroundings can be found in parental influences. In a longitudinal study, Wouters, Duriez, Luyckx, Colpin, Bijttebier, and Verschueren (2014) showed that when parents promoted more intrinsic goals in their children, the children had higher levels of self-esteem, and this relation was mediated by basic psychological need satisfaction. Further, intrinsic goal promotion led to less contingent self-esteem, which, as we have seen, is a control-oriented type of motivation that results from introjection. In contrast, when parents promoted extrinsic goals, need satisfaction and high self-esteem failed to follow, but extrinsic goals did relate to contingent self-esteem, which has also been associated with introjected regulation.

As we have already argued, parents who are autonomy-supportive are more likely to have children who develop more intrinsic aspirations, whereas more controlling parents will foster more extrinsically focused children (e.g., Roth, 2008). It thus follows that, when parents are autonomy-supportive and hold intrinsic aspirations, their children will likely emulate them, particularly if there is positive attachment. For example, Roth and Assor (1999) reported that when Israeli students perceived their parents as valuing prosocial behaviors, they were likely to report more autonomy and volition for such prosocial actions.

Yu, Assor, and Liu (2015) introduced the idea of *inherent value demonstration* (IVD), defined as parents' tendency to congruently behave in accordance with values they endorse. The researchers found that, when parents not only transmitted or endorsed intrinsic values but also appeared to authentically engage in the value-consistent behaviors, their offspring were more likely to internalize the value and perform the behaviors autonomously. In fact, their results showed that both parental autonomy support *and* the degree to which parents were perceived as displaying IVD led their children to show more self-congruence, as well as subjective well-being.

Finally, a longitudinal experiment found that, when students were encouraged to write about and then reflect upon intrinsic aspirations (e.g., having close friends) rather than extrinsic aspirations (e.g., being popular) over a 4-week period, they evidenced greater well-being (Lekes, Hope, Gouveia, Koestner, & Philippe, 2012). Further, at the end of the month-long period, those in the intrinsic reflection group also gave greater priority to the intrinsic aspirations.

The Framing of People's Goals

All of the studies of goal contents or aspirations reviewed thus far have focused on individuals' expressed aspirations and attainments. A different line of research includes experiments in which participants' goal contents are manipulated. Specifically, when people are given an activity, the activity can be introduced, justified, or *framed* in terms of the goals to which it might lead. For example, the rationale can either emphasize intrinsic goal attainments that might follow or extrinsic ones. The hypothesis has been that the consequences of these different goal frames would be appreciably different.

> *GCT Proposition VI:* Motivators can frame goals in more extrinsic versus intrinsic terms. The latter will be more likely to produce sustained engagement and, ultimately, wellness.

Studies by Vansteenkiste, Soenens, and colleagues have systematically targeted this differential impact of framing goals. In the first such set of studies, Vansteenkiste, Simons, Lens, Sheldon, and Deci (2004) manipulated goal content (intrinsic versus extrinsic), as well as the social context (autonomy-supportive versus controlling), using a factorial design. In each experiment, Belgian college students were asked to learn about topics as part of their normal classes. Some were students preparing to become preschool teachers who learned about recycling, some were business students preparing to go into marketing who learned about effective communications, and some were physical education students learning to do the activity tae-bo. In each case, when the task was introduced, some students were given a rationale for learning that was intrinsic, and the others were given one that was extrinsic. For example, business students learning about communications were told either that it could help them be more effective in making money (an extrinsic goal) or that it could help them learn more about themselves (an intrinsic goal); the physical education students learning taiboo were told either that it could help them become more attractive (an extrinsic goal) or become more physically fit (an intrinsic goal). Further, in each experiment, half the participants with each goal manipulation were introduced to the task within a controlling learning climate, and the other half were introduced to the task within an autonomy-supportive climate.

Using an analysis of variance format, results of all three studies showed main effects for both intrinsic and extrinsic goals and for autonomy-supportive versus controlling climates on a range of learning-related outcomes. Specifically, those for whom the task was said to be instrumental for intrinsic aspirations were more engaged in the learning, were more likely to get involved in additional, extracurricular learning about the topic, and performed better when tested conceptually about the topic of the learning. Furthermore, in each study, there was an additional interaction between the two manipulated independent variables, such that students in the condition involving intrinsic goals and autonomy-supportive contexts were higher on the learning-related outcomes than would be expected from two main effects. Thus this set of studies was important not only because it was the first to manipulate intrinsic versus extrinsic goal contents experimentally but also because it was the first to go beyond the study of the relations of goal content to well-being outcomes in order to examine the effects of intrinsic versus extrinsic goals on achievement-related outcomes.

Vansteenkiste and colleagues have done several other studies to extend the result of experimentally manipulating intrinsic versus extrinsic goal orientations. For example, Vansteenkiste, Simons, Lens, Soenens, Matos, and Lacante (2004) did a learning experiment in the exercise domain with three goal-content conditions, namely, an intrinsic goal condition, an extrinsic goal condition, and a condition that presented both the intrinsic and the extrinsic goal framing rationale. The expectancy-value position would predict optimal learning in the condition with both intrinsic and extrinsic goal prompts, because that is the condition in which there is greatest overall (presumably additive) value for learning; however, the GCT position argues that the intrinsic goal alone should prompt optimal learning. Results of the study indicated that intrinsic goal framing did lead to better performance and persistence than did either the extrinsic goal framing condition or the two-goal framing condition.

In a second study published in the same paper, Vansteenkiste, Simons, Lens, Soenens, et al. (2004) compared the impact of intrinsic goal framing, extrinsic goal framing, and no-goal framing. Although expectancy-value theory would predict that extrinsic goal framing should yield better learning than the no-goal framing condition, GCT would predict poorer learning in the extrinsic condition than in the no-goal framing condition. Results indicated, as predicted by GCT, that intrinsic goal framing, relative to no-goal framing, led to higher autonomous motivation and better test performance, and it also resulted in greater persistence in both the short and long term. In contrast, extrinsic goal framing, relative to no-goal framing, undermined participants' autonomous motivation, performance, and long-term persistence, although it resulted in better short-term persistence. The latter result makes sense because extrinsic goals can be powerful motivators, especially of rote learning, but the persistence is expected to be of inferior quality and not to be maintained over the long term.

To test this interpretation, the researchers took each condition separately and correlated the participants' persistence with their reports of autonomous motivation. Results indicated that in the intrinsic goal condition, students' persistence was positively correlated with autonomous motivation, whereas in the extrinsic goal condition, participants' persistence was uncorrelated with autonomous motivation. In short, students' persistence in the intrinsic goal condition resulted from their intrinsic valuing and enjoyment of the learning activity, but in the extrinsic goal condition the students persisted for other reasons that were less stable and apparently focused on the anticipated extrinsic outcomes.

All Goals Are Not Created Equal: Applying GCT to Any Goals

The large and continuously growing literature on GCT has allowed SDT to detail how more intrinsic overarching life goals promote the well-being of individuals. It is through consideration of the basic needs—of the essential nutrients for growth and health—that we are able to predict and explain which goal contents and which regulatory processes lead to more effective learning and performance and to more optimal psychological development. All of these studies support a more extended hypothesis, namely, that goals less directly linked to basic psychological need satisfaction will be associated with poorer well-being. From this research follows another GCT proposition:

> *GCT Proposition VII:* Because all goals can be more or less linked to need satisfaction, the relation of personal goals of any type to wellness-related outcomes is a function of (or is mediated by) need satisfactions.

In essence, GCT suggests that the impact and quality of goal pursuits differs as a function of content, with goals that are more extrinsic being less beneficial and those that are intrinsic being more so, and that this difference in goal qualities is a function of their relation to need satisfaction. Kasser and Ryan (1996) began by examining a particular set of goals because the researchers thought, a priori, that the goals were different in kind and might fit into two categories—intrinsic and extrinsic—thus allowing them to test their thinking about different types of goals having different consequences. There were other goals they omitted that remain to be explored. Goals for power and dominance over others, for example, would likely be extrinsic, reflecting perhaps compensation for insecurities and/or loss of control earlier in life. Goals for generativity, similar to the community contribution goals, might be intrinsic, supporting relatedness and autonomy.

Results pertaining to where any particular goal falls along this intrinsic–extrinsic axis will have multiple determinants. These include the wording of the goals and thus the specific meanings and intents behind them. For example, a life goal "to own a home for my family" might appear to be about accumulation of wealth (hence extrinsic), but it may in fact be more closely related to relationships (hence intrinsic) because of the family focus. Moreover, it is important when applying GCT to remember that goals may themselves be instrumental to yet higher order goals (see Ryan, Huta, & Deci, 2008), and these are often unanalyzed or unclear in some goal statements. For example, a medical resident who strongly endorses the striving statement "I want to completely master the skills taught on this rotation" may really be focused on the life goal of growth and competence (intrinsic) but also might be focused on a life goal of outcompeting everyone with whom he or she works (extrinsic). In addition, the same surface goal content may have different meanings or connotations in different cultures. A very good example is the goal of fulfilling one's duty, which in some cultures is a valued relational pursuit and in others suggests an extrinsic burden (Miller, Das, & Chakravarthy, 2011). Nonetheless, the evidence suggests that, once understood, the placement of any goal along this continuum will have functional consequences.

Psychologists study many goals and categories of goals that were not represented in Kasser and Ryan's (1996) study and which on the surface do not seem linearly connected with the intrinsic-versus-extrinsic axis at the center of GCT. Yet other goal categorizations do seem to have some systematic relations. For example, Dweck (2000) and Elliot and McGregor (2001) distinguished between learning (i.e., mastery) goals and performance goals, with considerable evidence showing that, relatively speaking, performance goals have more risks and fewer benefits in most comparisons. A performance focus, which is concerned with how one performs relative to others, is likely to be about attractiveness, fame, and wealth goals, which of course are extrinsic, instrumental, and socially comparative in nature. This does not mean that all normative information is problematic (Elliot, 2005) but rather that when one is focused on shining over others (rather than doing well), the satisfactions are likely to be more extrinsic in nature. In addition, whereas mastery goals are likely to be autonomous, performance goals are often controlled. Similarly, Nicholls (1984) proposed a distinction between *ego* and *task goals*—which are also readily placed within the framework of CET and GCT and their considerations. Ego involvement is classically controlled, and task involvement is more likely autonomous. Crocker (2008) introduced a distinction between *eco-centric* and *ego-centric* goals that resembles SDT's intrinsic–extrinsic distinction. Ego-centric goals tend be focused on goals such as appearance, achievement, or wealth; to be pursuits associated with contingent self-worth and ego involvement; and to often be regulated through controlling motivations, introjections, and ego involvements. In contrast eco-centric goals are often intrinsic goals, and are closely related to basic psychological needs and are better integrated. We thus believe that these disparate goal categories can all be linked through both the extrinsic versus intrinsic goal contents they entail and the controlled versus autonomous regulations underpinning them. Application of GCT (and SDT's need theory more generally) to various goal contents may thus bring out the commonalities and general principles across findings from varied theoretical approaches, linking them with their common roots in human nature.

Mindfulness, Goal Pursuits, and Aspirations

Yet another pathway through which intrinsic goals and the need satisfaction and wellness they facilitate function is through the enhancement of *mindfulness*. In fact, an increasing number of research studies have suggested that mindfulness is associated with a greater focus on intrinsic aspirations and a reduced emphasis on extrinsic aspirations, resulting in greater well-being, as well as collective sustainability.

> *GCT Proposition VIII:* Mindfulness, in promoting more integrated functioning, also conduces to a greater focus on intrinsic goal contents relative to extrinsic goal contents.

For example, Brown and Kasser (2005) used a demographically diverse national sample of adults differing in lifestyles to compare intrinsic and extrinsic life-goal orientations, mindfulness, and multiple indicators of both subjective well-being and ecologically responsible behaviors. Results indicated that higher levels of mindfulness were related to greater intrinsic goal orientations and that both variables were associated with subjective well-being and ecologically responsible behaviors. The authors suggested that mindfulness may foster people's more reflective consideration of their consumption and market choices and the ecological impacts of those choices. In turn, as was noted, environmental and prosocial behaviors supply intrinsic satisfactions that enhance personal well-being (De Young, 1996, 2000; Vansteenkiste, Simons, Lens, Sheldon, & Deci, 2004).

In another relevant project, Brown, Kasser, Ryan, Linley, and Orzech (2009) conducted a series of studies on the relations among mindfulness, financial desire discrepancy (the difference between what one has and what one desires), and subjective well-being. The first study was conducted on British undergraduates. Results revealed that mindfulness was associated with smaller financial desire discrepancy, which partially mediated the positive relations between mindfulness and well-being. Two subsequent studies with working adults replicated these findings, showing that the results still held independent of economic status and other demographic variables. A final, quasi-experimental investigation was conducted to elucidate causal pathways, which remained unclear due to the cross-sectional design of the three previous studies. Participants were attendees at residential mindfulness meditation training centers who participated in a 4-week training program. Findings suggested that increases in mindfulness were related to declines in financial desire discrepancy, thus indicating greater satisfaction with their current financial states and increases in subjective well-being. Further, these relations were not accounted for by financial status or recent financial status changes. Although these studies highlight the relations among mindfulness, intrinsic values, and well-being, other research within SDT has shown that these salutary effects largely stem from the promotion of healthy self-regulation (Brown & Ryan, 2003, 2004; Deci & Ryan, 2000; Kasser & Ryan, 1996).

Mindfulness has also been associated with greater empathy and compassion for others (Brown, Ryan, & Creswell, 2007; Beitel, Ferrer, & Cecero, 2005). Barnes, Brown, Krusemark, Campbell, and Rogge (2007) also found that mindfulness can enhance healthy romantic relationship functioning due to its association with more other-centeredness and a greater disposition to be truly present with the partner, even in challenging situations.

Well-Being: Living an Authentic, Mindful Life

Throughout this and the preceding few chapters, we have reported numerous studies that have used a variety of well-being outcomes when investigating the consequences of intrinsic aspirations, basic psychological need satisfactions, autonomous self-regulation, and mindfulness. In many of these studies the outcomes have focused on subjective well-being, which involves being low in negative affect, high in positive affect, and high in life satisfaction. In the previous chapter, we stated that this concept is often aligned with the hedonic view of well-being and is often referred to as happiness.

As it turns out empirically, when people are functioning eudaimonically, autonomously pursuing and attaining intrinsic aspirations, this way of living tends to make them happy, even though this is not the direct or proximal *aim* of such living (Ryan, Curren, & Deci, 2013). Volitionally pursuing what is intrinsically worthwhile, and doing that which is giving and relational rather than selfish, is thus an evidence-supported way of experiencing wellness and happiness, while also contributing more meaningfully to our collective existence. The dynamic findings in both BPNT and GCT strongly support this idea.

The findings also show that people's selection of motives and aspirations is significantly influenced by experiences of need support or thwarting in their development, and nonetheless their current choices matter, because clearly when it comes to well-being not all goals are created equal. Cultivating mindfulness, and more generally open and interested awareness, can help individuals make more informed and integrated choices, which in turn contributes to flourishing.

CHAPTER 12

Relationships Motivation Theory
The Self in Close Relationships

Whoever says You does not have something for his object.
—Martin Buber (1970, p. 55)

Within SDT, relatedness is one of three basic psychological needs. In this chapter, we out-line *relationships motivation theory* (RMT), a sixth SDT mini-theory concerning the qualities of close relationships and their consequences. RMT proposes that the relatedness need is intrinsic and inclines people to be volitionally engaged in close relationships. Factors that undermine an internal perceived locus of causality for social interactions detract from a sense of relatedness, as do any factors that convey that the other lacks autonomy for connecting. Satisfaction of all three basic needs within relationships is associated with more secure attach-ment, authenticity, and emotional reliance, as well as higher relationship-specific vitality and wellness. In fact, RMT suggests that need satisfaction versus frustration largely mediates the relations between social supports and psychological wellness outcomes. *Receiving* autonomy support from a relational partner facilitates the receiver's need satisfaction, along with authen-ticity, emotional reliance, transparency, and nondefensiveness. RMT further posits that *giv-ing* autonomy support to close others is also satisfying of the giver's basic needs, enhancing the giver's well-being over and above the enhancement that comes from receiving support. Accordingly, *mutuality* of autonomy support especially facilitates satisfaction of basic psycho-logical needs in both partners and more positive relationship dynamics over time. Finally, SDT research shows that when needs for relatedness and autonomy are turned against each other, as in instances of conditional regard or objectification, poorer quality relationships and well-ness outcomes result, with ill effects that often generalize to other relationships.

It is a fundamental tenet of SDT that autonomy and relatedness satisfactions are *not* antithetical but, rather, are intricately connected with one another. Indeed, the fulfill-ment of each need is intertwined with the fulfillment of the other. Relating to another human being as an object or a means to an end, whatever its positive tone or practical yield, does not foster a sense of relatedness in either party. In contrast, respecting the other's perspective in an interaction not only supports the other's sense of autonomy but will often also lead to a sense of closeness and relatedness for each partner. Similarly, caring for the other will also leave the other feeling cared for and related to. Yet the other's gratitude and relatedness would be undermined if he or she sensed that the helper was not autonomously motivated (e.g., was helping for rewards or complying with pressures). The reason is that it is volitional giving or helping that shows that the individual really cares. In fact, the very concept of *love* implies a kind of caring that is both unselfish and yet fully self-endorsed. In short, there is an intriguing set of connections between autonomy and relatedness satisfactions (and frustrations) that is the subject matter of *relationships motivation theory* (RMT), which is SDT's sixth mini-theory.

Although many theories in psychology emphasize the instrumental value of relationships, or focus on an exchange view of human interactions (e.g., Hatfield & Rapson, 2011; Kelley & Thibaut, 1978), RMT posits that, beyond these extrinsic benefits, feeling relatedness with others is *an intrinsic and basic psychological need*—something proximately valued *for its own sake*. Because close relationships have so consistently yielded significant adaptive benefits to individuals, we have evolved to be intrinsically motivated to seek out and maintain close, open, trusting relationships with others. Supporting this behavioral propensity, connecting with and caring for others is directly satisfying of basic psychological needs (Ryan & Hawley, 2016).

In arguing that relatedness is a basic psychological need, SDT distinguishes *ultimate causes* (which lie in selective advantages) from proximal causes and the phenomenal reasons (motives, satisfactions) for acting in close relationships associated with them. These proximal intrinsic motivations for connecting with others are not, from a phenomenal perspective, directed at the adaptive benefits relationships have yielded; instead, they can be enacted for other reasons or sentiments, such as love or caring, and when they are, they are especially satisfying of basic psychological needs (Weinstein & Ryan, 2010). This issue is addressed in greater detail in Chapter 24.

As a basic psychological need, relatedness is subject to both facilitation (support of satisfaction) and undermining (thwarting of satisfaction) by various aspects of the social environment and by attributions concerning others' motivations. For example, at a proximate level, people are oriented to especially value signs that others' caring for them is volitional, or even "selfless" in the sense of not for personal gain. That is, there is a functional significance to others' autonomous caring, as it conveys a true relational bond. Similarly, individuals experience more satisfaction when their own caring for others is done autonomously, rather than for external rewards or due to pressures. Relatedness satisfaction thus depends upon both perceiving the other to be autonomously and willingly engaged and on being autonomous oneself (i.e., having an internal perceived locus of causality [I-PLOC]). Factors in communications or contexts that detract from these perceptions of either autonomy or caring in the other, or in oneself, undermine need satisfaction.

RMT is thus unique among relationship theories in accounting for the importance of multiple basic psychological needs and volitional motivation in close adult relationships. Although in this chapter we focus primarily on adult-to-adult relationships such as friendships and romantic relationships, in the following chapter we discuss parent–child relationships and attachments, both as a foundation for the development of self and as an influence upon subsequent close relationships. Later in the book we turn to yet other types of interpersonal relationships—including teacher–student, manager–employee, coach–athlete, and physician–patient relationships, among others—that are characterized in part by authority differentials, concerns with competence and performance, and other issues that comprise their unique dynamics. But in RMT we set out some principles concerning the conditions supporting authentic and intimate connections between persons and the relations of these connections with wellness and full functioning.

The Importance of Relationships and Relatedness

There is no full functioning without relationships, and on this point there is remarkable convergence among social scientists. In our view, the work of Harry Harlow, albeit controversial to many, brought the importance of relatedness, independent of the resources relationships can provide, into particularly clear relief. In multiple experiments with primates, Harlow (e.g., 1958) and colleagues showed how deprivation of social contact and warmth yielded failure to thrive, manifested as global deficits in social and motivational development. Although some have rightly viewed Harlow's need-deprivation experiments as cruel, it is important to remember that they occurred in a historical context in which behavioral scientists such as Watson (1913) had viewed warmth and relatedness not as a basic need but as a secondary reinforcement that could be withheld and applied contingently to control behavior. Harlow's graphic research made an important point, namely, that above and beyond basic physiological requirements, primate infants *need* relatedness in order to flourish. Although his work was done with mothers and offspring, it nonetheless set the stage for the view embraced within SDT that relatedness among people of all ages is indeed an organismic necessity—that is, a basic psychological need.

Around the same time that Harlow was doing his primate studies, British object relations theorists emerged within the psychoanalytic tradition, also giving voice to the primacy of relationships in healthy human development. Echoing Harlow's experiments, Spitz (1965) described the failure to thrive exhibited by human infants who, although fed and sheltered, were deprived of human contact, thus underscoring that there is no healthy psychological development without relatedness. Clinicians such as Winnicott (1965), Fairbairn (1952), and Bowlby (1969) similarly emphasized an inherent and basic human propensity to relate or "attach" to others.

More recently, social psychologists Baumeister and Leary (1995) have argued that there is a basic *need for belongingness*—that is, a need to maintain a psychological sense of being connected to and accepted by others. They represent a long tradition of adult research in social psychology showing the predisposition to form bonds and loyalties with others (e.g., Sherif, Harvey, White, Hood, & Sherif, 1961), making the need for relatedness or belongingness an important, albeit typically implicit, concept in the field (Fiske, 2004; Shaver & Mikulincer, 2011; Taylor, 2002). These ideas also fit with a vast literature on social support that has similarly suggested that people's experiencing others as providing supportive relationships, independent of any instrumental resources they may provide, directly contributes to wellness (e.g., Clark & Mills, 2011; Lieberman, 2013; Reis & Shaver, 1988; Ryan & Solky, 1996).

Not All Social Interactions Convey Relatedness

Despite the importance of relationships to people, not all social contacts yield a sense of relatedness or satisfy people's basic psychological needs. Consideration of everyday social interactions makes it readily apparent that some are merely impersonal transactions, whereas others are meaningful encounters that are relationally satisfying. For example, exchanges with ticket agents, store clerks, or parking attendants, because of their role-bound and transactional nature, often have little interpersonal or emotional salience. Their value and utility are extrinsic. In contrast, people's contacts with their romantic partners and close friends are often experienced as intrinsically satisfying. In their most satisfying interactions, people want to be present for, and connected with, the others. In fact, Downie, Mageau, and Koestner (2008), in an event sampling study of everyday interactions, found that people were more likely to report both relatedness and autonomy when interacting with family members and friends compared with coworkers and acquaintances.

Yet there are exceptions to these generalities. Encounters with strangers, especially dyadic encounters, such as with someone seated beside you on a train, can sometimes resonate deeply and represent a meaningful connection, even if you never see each other again. Conversely, interactions with family and close friends can sometimes be experienced as impersonal, agenda ridden, or superficial, in which case they will not be experienced as satisfying relatedness. Even in friendships and romantic relationships, one can at times be taken for granted or objectified.

Thus it is not simply by virtue of their "dosage" or status that human interactions yield satisfaction of the relatedness need and associated psychological benefits. Rather, it is specific elements in *how* people relate to each other that afford more or less need satisfaction. Interactions can represent support and enhance feelings of self and wellness, but they can also convey a disconnection or absence of relatedness and thus undermine energy and wellness.

Across and within both transient and enduring human relationships, then, a sense of relatedness is not just a function of contact or positive affect but instead is intertwined with factors such as perceived autonomous and authentic caring between self and other. RMT suggests, in fact, that in the highest-quality personal relationships, there is a concomitant satisfaction of both relatedness and autonomy need satisfactions. It is the experiences that involve *acceptance and support of the self* that people find most truly relational. Relationships in which the others' interest is perceived as unconditional and authentic are the ones that are most satisfying. In contrast, other forms of connection and positive regard (e.g., objectifying admiration, conditional love), because they thwart autonomy and promote inauthenticity, concealment, and defense, represent degradations of the relatedness experience and the benefits it typically yields.

Close Relationships and RMT

The fundamental need for relatedness and its interactions with other basic needs is especially evident in the realm of close personal relationships, which is the focus of RMT. Relationships such as friendships and romantic partnerships, unlike kinship bonds, are "elective" (within cultural limits) and therefore require personal motivation to be maintained. Yet there is also high variability in the quality and endurance of friendships and romantic partnerships. Some friendships are characterized by openness, transparency and trust, others are more transactional and superficial. Some last and some rapidly expire, but people cannot live well without them.

Evidence from both comparative psychology (e.g., Majolo, Ames, Garratt, Hall, & Wilson, 2006) and human relationship sciences (e.g. Karlamangla, Singer, McEwen, Rowe, & Seeman, 2002) has amply established that close personal relationships yield a host of adaptive benefits. Adaptive benefits to having close friends include access to information or resources, having an ally, and reduced stress, among others (Seyfarth & Cheney, 2012). Yet, although people will sometimes befriend others for such instrumental reasons, most of us hope our friends' and partners' attachments to us are about more than such extrinsic benefits. Indeed, as we shall see, if you perceive people to be befriending you *because* of your instrumental value to them (e.g., they want you for status, looks, access to resources, or material gain), SDT suggests that you will feel less rather than more relatedness to those others. In contrast, it is when someone's friendship or love is experienced as *unconditional* that it is most deeply satisfying. Thus, even as there are everyday extrinsic benefits in having close relationships, the real satisfaction of *relatedness* will come from both persons being motivated not by extrinsic contingencies but by an intrinsic caring for each other.

In fact, within RMT we posit that relatedness is the intrinsically satisfying experience of being connected and mattering to another person or group. Quite independent of the concrete resources relationships tend to provide, the experience of relatedness supplies a proximate, basic psychological need satisfaction critical to wellness.

> **RMT Proposition I:** People have a basic psychological need for relatedness, the satisfaction of which is essential to growth, integrity, and wellness, and the frustration of which can play a causal role in ill-being.

Proposition I speaks to the centrality of relatedness satisfaction as a basic psychological need, positing that when people feel relatedness to others they will evidence greater well-being. Strong support for this idea has come from a variety of SDT studies using multilevel modeling and related techniques to assess within-person variation in relatedness satisfaction and its impact on wellness-relevant outcomes (La Guardia & Patrick, 2008). Importantly, these studies (several of which we reviewed with regard to BPNT in Chapter 10) show that satisfaction of the relatedness need is a direct and independent predictor of psychological wellness, even controlling for other basic need satisfactions.

Reis, Sheldon, Gable, Roscoe, and Ryan (2000) used a diary method to follow students' experiences of satisfaction of the competence, autonomy, and relatedness needs over a 2-week period. Because previous experience sampling studies in SDT (e.g., Sheldon, Ryan, & Reis, 1996) had not examined relatedness satisfactions, a central aim was to examine whether satisfaction of the relatedness need, which correlates highly with satisfaction of the autonomy and competence needs, contributes independent variance to prediction of psychological wellness. Using multilevel modeling, the researchers found, at both the between-person and within-person levels of analysis, that satisfaction of the need for relatedness was an independent positive predictor of well-being for both males and females, confirming that satisfaction of the relatedness need does indeed make its own contribution to psychological wellness.

Ryan, Bernstein, and Brown (2010) also used an experience sampling approach, but with working adults. They, too, found that satisfaction of the relatedness need was an independent predictor of wellness at a within-person level of analysis, alongside autonomy and competence. In addition, they showed that relatedness satisfaction fluctuated as a function of day of the week. On average, these working adults felt greater vitality and positive affect on weekends, precisely when they could be with those persons with whom relatedness needs were most highly satisfied.

Gagné, Ryan, and Bargmann (2003) studied female gymnasts over a 4-week period in which they collected data 4 days a week. At the beginning and end of their practice sessions, participants reported their positive affect, vitality, and self-esteem. At the end of each session, the researchers also measured the degree to which the participants had experienced satisfaction of the three basic psychological needs during that practice. Most relevant to this discussion, gymnasts' reports of experiencing relatedness need satisfaction during a workout session predicted increases in positive affect, vitality, and self-esteem from before to after the session. Thus, as relatedness need satisfaction fluctuated from session to session, change in well-being fluctuated accordingly.

In contrast, the thwarting of relatedness is directly and nearly universally related to psychological distress and ill-being, For example, it has been argued that being ostracized or excluded triggers "social pain" involving some of the same neural activation patterns as physical pain (Eisenberger, Lieberman, & Williams, 2003). The distress associated with exclusion has, in fact, been well established in experimental studies, in part thanks to the development of the "cyberball" paradigm (Williams, 2009). In this widely studied laboratory game, players direct an avatar to play catch with two other "players" (presumably in other rooms). Participants can feel ostracized when the other two "player" avatars exclude them by throwing the ball only to each other. Many studies using cyberball have shown that even this relatively tame virtual exclusion led to negative affect and distress (see Williams, 2009). Applying this paradigm, Legate, DeHaan, Weinstein, and Ryan (2013) replicated the finding not only that ostracized participants felt internal distress but also that the relations between the exclusion condition and this negative affect was mediated by lower satisfaction of the need for relatedness.

From such studies we can conclude that satisfaction of the relatedness need facilitates psychological well-being, typically even when considering satisfaction of the needs for autonomy and competence. Conversely, relatedness need frustration can directly lead to distress. Close adult relationships clearly differ in the degree to which they satisfy this relatedness need, and within every relationship there are moments of greater or lesser satisfaction of this need. What qualities characterize interactions that satisfy our need for relatedness?

Being Autonomously Motivated within Close Personal Relationships

From the perspective of RMT, one of the conditions under which people experience satisfaction of psychological needs within relationships is that they are autonomously motivated to enter into the relationships and engage with the close other. When autonomous, people tend to be wholly willing and volitional while interacting with their partners, feeling a sense of choice and endorsement of the interacting. Thus RMT predicts that a person being autonomously motivated for the relationship itself will facilitate a higher quality relationship, among other positive consequences. This leads to the second proposition of RMT.

> **RMT Proposition II:** High-quality relationships are facilitated not only by having close and enduring social contact with a partner but also by experiencing autonomous motivation within and for that contact. Autonomous motivation—that is, the individual's authentic willingness to participate in the relationship—contributes to high satisfaction and greater psychological wellness in both parties within that dyad.

In the first major study employing SDT concepts to examine romantic relationships, Blais, Sabourin, Boucher, and Vallerand (1990) assessed the relative autonomy that married or cohabiting heterosexual couples experienced for engaging in and maintaining their relationships. Blais and colleagues found, as expected, that the greater was the relative autonomy that each partner experienced, the greater was the dyadic adjustment and general relationship satisfaction that each partner reported. Greater autonomy within the relationships was also associated with viewing relationship problems as challenges rather than annoyances, with experiencing less distress, and with being more inclined to work through problems. It seems that adults' feeling self-determined for their involvement in marital or cohabiting romantic relationships is a marker of the relationships' quality. Blais et al. (1990) further tested a structural model in which (1) each partner's autonomous motivation was expected to predict his or her positive relational behaviors, (2) the levels of the two partners' relational behaviors were expected to predict each partner's beliefs about the adaptive nature of the relationship, and (3) these beliefs in turn were expected to predict personal happiness in the relationship. Results confirmed all of these hypotheses.

Four studies by Knee, Lonsbary, Canevello, and Patrick (2005) considerably extended these points made by the early Blais et al. research. The first was a diary study conducted for 10 days in which participants completed short surveys after each *disagreement* with their romantic partners. Results showed that relational autonomy (i.e., being autonomously motivated in the relationship) predicted individuals' experiencing more satisfaction after disagreements. Their second study found that relational autonomy predicted greater understanding of one's partner and less defensiveness in conflicts.

In the third study by Knee and colleagues (2005), both members of romantic relationships participated. For convenience, we call the dyad members in these studies the "person" and the "partner." Both person and partner completed questionnaires concerning their relational autonomy, their understanding and defensiveness during conflicts, and their relational satisfaction. As expected, the person's relational autonomy predicted less defensiveness and more understanding of the partner and, in turn, greater relationship satisfaction. In addition, however, the partner's relational autonomy also contributed significant variance to the person's being more understanding, less defensive, and more satisfied.

Knee et al.'s fourth study involved romantic couples coming into the lab and having discussions about sensitive topics. Prior to the discussions, each completed the relational autonomy questionnaire and agreed to their discussion being videotaped. Subsequently, naïve raters coded each participant's behavior for signs of understanding and defensiveness. Analyses showed that the greater a person's relational autonomy, the more his or her behavior was likely to be coded as understanding and open (i.e., nondefensive) toward the partner. Further, the partner's relational autonomy was also related to the person's being more understanding and less defensive.

Patrick (2007) subsequently took an interesting approach to studying autonomous motivation in romantic relationships by focusing on people engaging in pro-relationship behaviors, such as making sacrifices for their partners. Specifically, she assessed not only how much individuals engaged in such other-supportive behaviors but also the degree to which they did so for autonomous versus controlled reasons. Results indicated that the more people were autonomous in their pro-relationship behaviors, the more they were committed to the relationships, the more relationship satisfaction they experienced and the closer they felt to their partners. In a subsequent daily diary study, Patrick (2007) further found that being autonomous in pro-relational behaviors also left people feeling greater vitality and higher self-esteem.

In a cross-cultural study with American and Japanese participants, Gore, Cross, and Kanagawa (2009) differentiated personal autonomy from relational autonomy. They defined personal autonomy as one's autonomy for being in a relationship with the other, whereas what Gore et al. called *relational autonomy* involves a person being autonomous in supporting the close other's interests or needs. Stated differently, it means a person will engage in an activity volitionally simply *because* it is important to the close other. Gore and colleagues (2009) found that relational autonomy explained variance in positive outcomes over and above the variance explained by personal autonomy. This is a very interesting result, for it suggests to us that relational autonomy reflects one's having integrated the interests and desires of another in such a way that one can act "for the other" in a fully willing and volitional way. Every good parent, best friend, and romantic partner experiences this kind of identification with and care for the other. These results also reiterate a fundamental tenet of SDT, namely that to act autonomously does not necessitate acting independently or selfishly, and in fact that caring acts for others are frequently highly autonomous.

In complementary work, Gaine and La Guardia (2009) developed a *Motivations for Relational Activities Scale* by which they assessed the degree of autonomy for specific behaviors within a close relationship. They found that being autonomous for specific relational activities explained additional variance in variables such as commitment and intimacy value beyond that explained by the level of personal autonomy for being in the relationship. The Gaine and La Guardia study, along with that by Gore et al. (2009), suggest that there is something special about being in close personal relationships that allows people to act in a truly volitional manner simply because it is what their partners need or desire. It is important to a person's relatedness not only that the other acts for the person's welfare but also that the other does so willingly.

What is really at the core of RMT is the idea that people can quite autonomously care for others. Indeed, caring is one of the most important expressions of our autonomy and our values. As analytic philosopher Frankfurt noted, "when a person cares about something . . . he is willingly committed to his desire. The desire does not move him either against his will or without his endorsement" (2004, p. 16). When we care about others, especially when we love others, doing for them is a fully self-endorsed, autonomous activity. And when others care for us autonomously, this is when it is most easy to feel loved.

When one autonomously cares for the other, there is both greater basic need satisfaction and likely a higher quality of caring as well. For example, Kindt and colleagues (2015) studied partners of patients suffering from intense pain. Results confirmed that autonomous, relative to controlled, motives for helping related to less exhaustion and more relationship-based need satisfaction for the helping partner. Furthermore, when the partners' helping motivation was more autonomous, there was higher patient-reported relationship quality and lower distress.

Hadden, Rodriguez, Knee, and Porter (2015) extended this idea that autonomous motivation results in higher quality caring and support. Using both a cross-sectional and a 14-day diary study, they showed that a person's autonomous motivation for a relationship was associated with more availability and responsiveness to the partner and yet less intrusiveness. A third dyadic study expanded upon these findings by utilizing partners' reports of the support they received. Findings revealed that participants who were more autonomously motivated to be in the relationship had partners who felt their basic psychological needs were more supported. These associations were similar for both women and men—that is, there was no interaction effect.

Autonomous Causality Orientations in Relationships

Because people with higher autonomy causality orientations (Deci & Ryan, 1985a) should, on average, take interest in their relationships and also be more volitional in engaging in them, we would expect them to have higher quality relationships than those who are more oriented toward control or amotivation. Hodgins, Koestner, and Duncan (1996) specifically tested this hypothesis that a higher autonomy orientation would be a positive influence on the development of satisfying relationships. They found in two studies, for both men and women, that those who were higher on the autonomy orientation reported more positive and honest relationships in their ongoing lives. A higher autonomy orientation was specifically associated with more self-disclosure and more flexible interaction patterns with partners.

A study of heterosexual romantic relationships by Knee, Patrick, Vietor, Nanayak-kara, and Neighbors (2002) also assessed participants' causality orientations, relating them to behaviors in times of conflict. They found that partners high in autonomy orientation expressed less negative emotion, more relationship-maintaining coping strategies, and more positive relationship-oriented behaviors during the conflicts than did people low in autonomy. Further, those higher in the control orientation engaged in fewer of these positive behaviors.

Priming the Autonomy Orientation in Close Relationships

As discussed in Chapter 9, motivational orientations can be primed by cues in the environment. Studies have accordingly examined the effects of priming autonomy in relationship contexts. In an unpublished, follow-up experiment to a set of studies by Niemiec (2010), two individuals who did not know each other were primed with autonomy, control, or neutral orientations using a scrambled sentence task and were then asked to engage in a structured self-disclosure activity that became increasingly intimate over the study period. Subsequently, self-report and behavioral measures of closeness to the new partner and satisfaction in the newly developed relationship were assessed. Using multilevel modeling, with individuals nested within dyads, results indicated that participants in dyads in which each partner had been primed with autonomy orientations, relative to those primed with control or neutral orientations, felt more satisfaction with the new relationship, more positive affect, more relatedness need satisfaction, and greater well-being. In addition, those primed with autonomy displayed greater closeness using a behavioral measure in which the participants freely set up their chairs closer to each other when asked to prepare for a subsequent task, and they also indicated a greater desire to spend time together in the future.

Weinstein, Hodgins, and Ryan (2010) also examined the effects of priming autonomy or control orientations in the context of dyadic interactions. They focused on interaction quality and performance on creative tasks in pairs of participants who were also meeting for the first time. In this paradigm, dyad members were videotaped as they jointly performed a remote associates task and a game of charades, both tasks requiring creative thinking and cooperative interacting. Ratings of the videotapes of the interactions showed that dyads primed with autonomy were more emotionally and cognitively attuned to one another and more empathic and encouraging of each other, indicating more openness and less defensiveness. Further, the dyads primed with autonomy were more engaged with the tasks, performed the tasks more effectively, and reported more closeness. Because in this study motivational orientations were experimentally manipulated using a priming procedure, results support the idea that more autonomy can exert a causal influence on the quality of communication and closeness of interpersonal relationships.

Perceiving the Other as Being Autonomous

Although we have emphasized that being autonomously motivated in a relationship contributes to need satisfaction and relationship functioning, it is also important for one's own feelings of relatedness that the other person is experienced as acting autonomously. People are sensitive to evidence concerning whether others' interests in them are volitional, and attributions concerning PLOC can impact feelings of gratitude and closeness. For example, in three experiments, Weinstein, DeHaan, and Ryan (2010) had participants read and respond to scenarios depicting various helping events. Embedded in these scenarios were cues suggesting that helpers had either autonomous or controlled (i.e., introjected) motivations for helping. The findings revealed that recipients experienced more gratitude toward autonomous helpers than those helping for controlled reasons. If the helping were seen as autonomous, there were also more positive attitudes toward helpers and more felt closeness. In a third study, these researchers confirmed that attributions of autonomous motivation independently predicted gratitude and other positive reactions to receiving help, even controlling for other factors such as perceived helper empathy, cost to the helper, the perceived value of the help, and perceived similarity with the helper. In other words, knowing that the actor willingly helped stands up as a robust element in predicting the relation of helping to relatedness satisfaction.

Basic Need Satisfactions, High-Quality Relationships, and Well-Being

Research reviewed above confirms that the more autonomy a person experiences within a relationship, because of individual differences, domain- or behavior-specific motivations, or even nonconscious primes, the greater will be the person's likelihood of feeling more closeness and less defensiveness, experiencing greater relationship satisfaction and psychological need satisfaction, and evidencing enhanced positive affect and wellness. RMT nonetheless maintains that satisfaction of the other two basic psychological needs is also important within close relationships, both for their maintenance over time and for the well-being of the partners.

It, of course, makes sense within the SDT framework that the three needs would be correlated and would each contribute to healthy relationships and well-being within them. These three needs, while to some degree independent, are nonetheless mutually supportive of each other. When people experience competence, they tend to feel that they have the skills and ability necessary to get their other needs satisfied; when they experience autonomy, they tend to feel authentic, to more openly communicate with others, and to explore ways of getting their other needs satisfied; and when they experience deep relatedness with others, they tend to feel at least the distal, if not also the proximal, security that is necessary for them to venture out into the world in pursuit of greater confidence and agency.

In relationships, however, these interdependencies between need satisfactions can be magnified by the dynamics of support. An autonomy-supportive partner will also tend to support one's needs for competence and relatedness. He or she will be prone to take the partner's internal frame of reference and thus be more likely to be aware of and responsive to all three needs in the friend or partner. Equally, when a person truly cares for another relationally, he or she wants to understand the other's perspective and support his or her pursuit of interests and valued goals.

> *RMT Proposition IIIa:* Within relationships the satisfactions of all three basic psychological needs for relatedness, autonomy, and competence contribute to, and in fact define, higher quality relationships and facilitate greater relationship satisfaction, attachment security, and well-being.

A set of studies by Patrick, Knee, Canevello, and Lonsbary (2007) examined the role of satisfaction of all three basic psychological needs on relationship quality, conflict management in relationships, and well-being. Results showed that, in general, satisfaction of each need contributed significant variance to personal well-being (i.e., self-esteem, more positive and less negative affect, and vitality), relationship well-being (i.e., commitment to the relationship), and effective management of conflict. Satisfaction of the relatedness need tended to be the strongest predictor of these outcomes, which makes sense given that the study was of personal relationships, but the other two needs also contributed significantly over and above the contribution of the relatedness need.

In a subsequent study presented in that same paper, Patrick and her colleagues (2007) extended this by showing that the need satisfaction of a target individual's romantic partner also contributed to the target individual's relational well-being. In other words, it appears that when a person's partner is getting his or her basic psychological needs satisfied, the person himself or herself will experience greater engagement and likely even support from the partner, which will help the person feel better about the relationship. In all likelihood the partner whose needs are being satisfied will similarly feel better about the relationship. Finally, an additional study in this series indicated that satisfaction of the basic needs within a relationship predicted more successful resolution of relationship conflicts.

Need Satisfaction and Attachment Security

The relations of basic need satisfaction to quality of relatedness are also revealed by studies of security of attachment in adults. Attachment theory originated within the object relations perspective (Bowlby, 1969) and was moved into the empirical realm by Ainsworth and colleagues (e.g., Ainsworth, Blehar, Waters, & Wall, 1978). The theory postulates that when a child's primary caretakers are sensitive and responsive to him or her, especially in times of distress, the child will feel securely attached to the caregivers and will develop an inner working model of having secure relationships to significant others, which will be carried forward into later life (Bretherton & Munholland, 1999). Security of attachment, based on supportive early experiences with caretakers, is thus expected to facilitate the development of individual (i.e., between-person) differences in the level of being securely attached in subsequent relationships such as best friends and romantic partners. This continuity has been researched in studies of adult attachments, wherein adults are expected to have close adult relationships that are to some degree similar in security to the relationships they had with primary caregivers (e.g., Mikulincer & Shaver, 2007).

The concept of secure attachment is quite general, but it clearly overlaps with the concept of relatedness, for both are concerned with being connected with and mattering to another person. However, SDT would expect significant variations in adult security of attachment as a function of differential need supports for autonomy and competence within those relationships over time. Investigating this expectation, La Guardia, Ryan, Couchman, and Deci (2000) argued that even though an individual's attachment security with primary caregivers may lead to between-person differences in attachment security that is manifested across relationships, within any given adult relationship the partners' supports for autonomy, competence, and relatedness will lead to different levels of security with that partner. Thus security of attachment was hypothesized by La Guardia et al. to be a function both of between-person factors (i.e., individual differences), as attachment theory has always maintained, but also of within-person factors (i.e., the need satisfaction provided by different specific partners). In fact, this was one of the first major studies to systematically explore the idea that a substantial degree of the variance in relationship security in adulthood would be due to *relationship-specific* supports for the basic psychological needs.

In three studies, La Guardia and colleagues (2000) examined the security of attachment that college students had with their mothers, fathers, romantic partners, and best friends, as well as the level of satisfaction of the needs for autonomy, competence, and relatedness these students experienced in each of those relationships. Further, the researchers assessed several mental health indices. Using multilevel modeling in all three studies, the results indicated that there was a significant amount of variance in attachment security at the between-person level in each study, thus confirming, as attachment theory suggests, that felt security is a significant individual difference, presumably represented as a working model. On average about 35% of the variance in attachment security was explained at the between-person level, which is substantial. On the other hand, considerably more than half the variance in attachment security remained to be explained, suggesting that people's security of attachment differed appreciably from partner to partner. This within-person variability in attachment security was systematically explained by need satisfaction. In each study, need satisfaction with a relational partner accounted for significant variance in attachment security with that partner. Subsequently, the researchers examined satisfaction of each need separately. As one would expect, satisfaction of the relatedness need within each relationship was the strongest predictor of attachment security with that partner. Importantly, however, the researchers found that satisfaction of the autonomy need within each relationship was also a very significant predictor of attachment security and that competence need satisfaction was a weaker though still meaningful predictor of felt attachment in that relationship. In other words, the degree to which a person experienced satisfaction of each of the three basic psychological needs with an attachment partner affected the degree to which the person was securely attached to that partner.

Relatedness need satisfaction being the strongest predictor of within-relationship attachment security is certainly expectable, and, in a sense, it is nearly tautological. So the researchers reran the multilevel models, leaving relatedness satisfaction out of the analyses, using just the autonomy and competence needs as the primary independent variables. Results indicated again that significant variance in the attachment security within each relationship was significantly predicted by satisfaction of the autonomy and competence needs. Finally, analyses showed that at the between-person level both need satisfaction and attachment security predicted psychological well-being, and, at the within-person level, both need satisfaction and attachment security predicted relationship satisfaction and willingness to rely on the relational partner in emotionally intense times.

Ducat and Zimmer-Gembeck (2007) examined attachment styles, basic psychological need satisfactions, and well-being in young adults. They found significant and expectable relations between individuals' adult attachment styles and both their well-being and relationship quality with their romantic partners. Further, these researchers found that satisfaction of the basic psychological needs within the relationship mediated these relations between attachment security and the relationship outcomes. Similarly, Wei, Shaffer, Young, and Zakalik (2005) found that insecure attachment was related to the outcomes of loneliness, depression, and shame. Furthermore, they found that these relations were mediated by frustration of the basic psychological needs. In other words, need satisfaction was responsible for the relations between level of security of attachment and the outcomes of well-being and ill-being.

In a somewhat related study of adult romantic relationships, Leak and Cooney (2001) found that individuals who were high in secure attachment with their romantic partners were also more autonomous in their relationship engagement, whereas those who were high in the insecure attachment styles were low in autonomous motivation for interacting with their partners. As in many studies in the literature, people who were more securely attached to their partners evidenced strong mental health; however, in the Leak and Cooney study, autonomous motivation for relationship engagement mediated the relations between secure attachment and well-being. Thus it would seem from these studies that the association between security of attachment between romantic partners and well-being was a function of the individuals' experiencing greater satisfaction of autonomy, relatedness, and competence within the relationships.

Together, data on both relationship satisfaction and security of attachment point in the same direction. Relationships that are highly satisfying and secure are those in which the person experiences not only connection but also autonomy and competence. When these three needs are all satisfied within a relationship, they contribute to greater individual wellness.

Yet in highlighting these nutrients, we have failed to address a different, darker side to relationships: need thwarting. In line with discussions in Chapter 10, beyond considering only supports for satisfactions of the needs and their absence, elements within relationships can also thwart satisfaction of the basic psychological needs, leading to need frustration and ill-being.

> **RMT Proposition IIIb:** Within relationships the frustrations of psychological needs for relatedness, autonomy, and competence contribute to relationship dysfunction and defense and greater relationship dissatisfaction, insecurity, and ill-being.

Emphasized in this proposition is the idea that relationships may not only fail to satisfy a person's basic needs but also may actively thwart them. In fact, as discussed within the framework of BPNT, considering need thwarting in relationships is important for predicting the function of people's "darker sides." Need thwarting in close relationships can take many forms, including dominance and control (thwarting autonomy), coldness or distancing (thwarting relatedness), or criticalness and derogation (thwarting competence). In everyday social interactions, it can take the form of stigmatization, prejudice, and exclusion. Clearly, to the extent that basic needs are thwarted within relationships, both satisfaction and wellness are compromised. For example, Costa, Ntoumanis, and Bartholomew (2015) recently showed how need frustration within relationships was uniquely associated with rejection sensitivity, whereas need satisfaction better predicted interpersonal competence.

Autonomy-Supportive Partners:
Facilitating Interdependence and Full Functioning

Much of the research on contextual supports for high-quality relationships has examined the concept of *autonomy support*. This concept grows directly from the meaning of autonomy itself. Autonomy refers to self-regulation or self-governance, to being volitional and fully willing, to being *authentic* in the exacting senses of that term—that is, being both real and owning one's actions (Wild, 1965). In attributional language, autonomy involves an *internal perceived locus of causality* (I-PLOC); it emanates from the *self* of the actor (de Charms, 1968). It therefore follows that autonomy support within relationships will foster more authentic self-expression and leave the person with less of a sense of being contingently valued, controlled, or pressured to think, feel, or behave in particular ways.

Autonomy support speaks, in fact, to a central aspect of contact and encouragement within relationships (Deci & Ryan, 2014a; Ryan, 1993). Autonomy support from a person to a partner allows the partner to feel understood. An autonomy-supportive person is able to take the partner's *internal frame of reference*, conveying a sense of empathy and respect for the partner, and it thus facilitates self-initiated expressions and actions. In supporting a partner's autonomy, the person cares for and supports *the self* of the partner by empathically sharing in his or her feelings and desires; provides informational, rather than controlling, feedback if feedback is desired; and facilitates the partner's self-organization and self-regulation of subsequent behaviors. Further, because autonomy support involves a person's taking the partner's frame of reference and acknowledging the partner's feelings and desires, the recipient partner will also experience more satisfaction of the need for relatedness. Finally, because autonomy-supportive partners encourage each other's initiative, each is implicitly conveying a sense that the partner is competent to carry out the self-chosen behaviors. Accordingly, we suggest that autonomy-supportive relational contexts will tend to foster satisfaction of all three basic needs for people who act within those contexts.

Various studies in other domains (e.g., in work contexts; Baard, Deci, and Ryan, 2004) have shown that autonomy support does facilitate a person's experience of satisfaction across the needs for autonomy, relatedness, and competence. Of course, there are contextual elements other than autonomy support that may support the need for competence or relatedness—for example, structure and feedback promote competence (Jang, Reeve, & Deci, 2010), and devotion of personal resources to a person promotes relatedness (Grolnick & Ryan, 1989)—but autonomy support particularly accounts for significant variance in support of all three basic psychological needs, especially in close adult relationships.

> *RMT Proposition IVa:* Individuals who experience autonomy support from their partners within a close relationship will be more willing to emotionally rely on those partners and to turn to the partners for support.

Unique to SDT is a strong distinction between independence and autonomy. We have argued that a person can be autonomously dependent on another, and moreover this is often a very positive element within close relationships. We have specifically studied *emotional reliance*, or people's willingness to turn to or rely on relational partners at times of heightened emotions, whether the emotions are negative or positive. When people experience negative emotions, others can serve as social supports, helping them cope with the feelings, and when people experience positive emotions, sharing them with others can be a source of joy and delight. But to which others do people most willingly turn?

In a series of studies, Ryan, La Guardia, Solky-Butzel, Chirkov, and Kim (2005) addressed emotional reliance both as an individual difference and as an experience that can vary among a person's relationships, depending on characteristics of that particular relationship. These researchers found, first, that participants of varied ages and cultural backgrounds showed a common main effect: Those who were more willing to turn to others for emotional support had greater wellness. Thus, in contrast to the negative views often put forward about dependence (e.g., Hirschfeld, Klerman, Gough, Barrett, Korchin, & Chodoff, 1977; Steinberg & Silverberg, 1986), volitional or willing reliance on others reflects a healthy individual-difference attribute.

More importantly, the studies looked at what facilitates emotional reliance within particular relationships. For instance, one study looked at within-person preferences for emotional reliance on fathers and mothers. Although, in general, mothers were more likely targets for emotional reliance, the data showed a clear pattern: Willingness to rely on a given parent was strongly associated with that parent's degree of autonomy support. In other words, when a parent was supportive of his or her child's autonomy, the child was more likely to willingly turn to that parent when experiencing strong affect or conflicted experiences.

A subsequent study examined relationships with romantic partners and best friends. Again, at the individual-difference level of analysis, people's emotionally relying on close partners predicted well-being. Data further confirmed that basic need satisfaction mediated the positive relationship between emotional reliance and mental health, suggesting that when people relied volitionally on others, they experienced more basic need satisfaction, resulting in greater psychological wellness. Finally, the study showed that, at the within-person level of analysis, the more an individual experienced a relational partner as providing autonomy support, the greater was the individual's willingness to rely on that partner when emotionally salient events occurred.

A third study in this same paper examined emotional reliance in Russia, Turkey, and South Korea, as well as the United States. Emotional reliance predicted well-being across the four cultures, and the relations between emotional reliance and psychological wellness were again mediated by need satisfaction, suggesting that people do in fact need close satisfying relationships in order to experience a high level of wellness.

Research by La Guardia (2006) found that when people felt greater need satisfaction in relationships, they also reported more contact with their inner emotions, more willingness to examine those emotions, and more self-disclosure of their emotional experiences. These factors contributed to a greater sense of intimacy, as well as more vitality and aliveness when with the other person. It seems that when people make contact with and allow the experience of their own emotions, they are setting the stage for relating more deeply to others, and when they are then supported in authentically sharing their emotions, more intimacy is the common result.

This literature was extended in a study by Lynch, La Guardia, and Ryan (2009). The researchers replicated the results found by Ryan, La Guardia, Solky-Butzel, et al. (2005), in samples of young adults in both Russia and China, showing specifically that volitional reliance—that is, willingly turning to others for emotional support—was predicted by the perceived autonomy supportiveness of the others. Moreover, those who were more willing to rely on relational partners at emotionally charged times evidenced greater psychological well-being.

In sum, when people turn to others in times of emotional arousal, they experience greater wellness. People are, however, selective concerning to whom they turn, preferring those whom they perceive to be more autonomy-supportive.

> *RMT Proposition IVb:* Individuals who experience autonomy support within a close relationship will be more able to "be themselves"—that is, to be authentic and transparent and to function closer to their own ideals.

Relationships most fulfilling of the need for relatedness are those that are authentic, in both senses of the word we discussed earlier—namely, that the person-in-relation is being real rather than fake and is being autonomous rather than scripted or controlled. In an inauthentic relationship, the person is not transparent or open but rather conceals important aspects of him- or herself.

Within SDT there has been a growing amount of research on disclosure and concealment within both everyday life and close adult relationships. Across the findings, it seems clear that concealment or a lack of transparency with close others is potentiated by thwarting rather than supporting their autonomy. When people are inauthentic or feel the necessity to conceal, it negatively impacts relationship satisfaction and commitment.

Concealment

In two early studies in this area, Uysal, Lin, and Knee (2010) found that self-concealment in close relationships predicted thwarting of the basic needs for autonomy, competence, and relatedness, as well as a variety of associated negative outcomes. In addition to correlational findings, they reported a diary study of self-concealment, need satisfaction, and well-being over 16 days that supported these associations between daily self-concealment, daily need frustration, and daily ill-being. They interpreted these findings as evidence that concealing personal information within close relationships diminishes the satisfaction of basic psychological needs and has a variety of negative consequences.

Subsequently, Uysal, Lin, Knee, and Bush (2012) studied self-concealment in individuals who were in romantic relationships. They found that an individual's self-concealment (hiding information from one's romantic partner) was associated with lower relationship satisfaction and commitment. Relevant here, we further note that these associations between concealment and lower satisfaction and commitment were mediated by low levels of satisfaction of the autonomy and relatedness needs. Concealing is associated with lower autonomy and less relatedness, both of which are essential to overall relationship satisfaction. In a second study, these researchers had romantic couples complete daily records over a 2-week span. Analyses indicated that daily self-concealment from one's partner was negatively associated with daily relationship satisfaction and commitment and positively with conflict. Further, cross-lagged analyses showed that a person's concealing from a partner on one day predicted lower relationship well-being the following day. Moreover, results again supported that frustrated basic needs mediated these relations. Finally, additional analyses indicated that the partner's self-concealment also contributed to the diminishment of relational satisfaction and commitment.

Being Oneself in Relationships

Presumably in a high-quality close relationship one is able to be oneself—that is, to be the person one authentically wants to be. Previous SDT research has in fact shown that in both friendships and romantic relationships, authenticity is associated with greater relationship satisfaction and lower strain (Sheldon, Ryan, Rawsthorne, & Ilardi, 1997), and autonomy is associated with less use of self-presentation strategies (Lewis & Neighbors, 2005).

Cross-cultural research by Lynch et al. (2009) examined how autonomy support in personal relationships affects within-person variability in the traits people express, particularly the extent to which people can be closer to their own ideals of personality. Using more than 600 participants drawn from Russia, the United States, and China, the researchers had participants rate how they are typically and how they are "ideally" (i.e., when they are at their best), using the "Big Five" items—that is, the items from the *five-factor model* (FFM; McCrae & Costa, 2003). The Big Five assesses the degree to which people are extraverted, conscientious, open to experience, agreeable; and emotionally stable (versus neurotic). Separately, participants also rated their expression of these Big Five traits within each of six common relationships—namely, when each was with his or her mother, father, roommate, best friend, romantic partner, and a special teacher. Lynch et al. then calculated the discrepancies between participants' ideal views of self and their views of self when they were relating to each of these figures. The researchers also assessed satisfaction and vitality within each relationship and general wellness. The participants further provided information on the extent to which each of their six social partners was autonomy-supportive. Finally, as an additional cross-cultural aspect of this study, participants were also assessed for their cultural orientations, specifically whether they were prone toward a more independent or interdependent self-construal, using the well-known measure developed by Singelis (1994). This is of interest because some theorists have claimed that autonomy and its support have little or no importance to those with an interdependent orientation (e.g., Markus & Kitayama, 2003), a hypothesis Lynch et al. would put to the test.

Results showed that across these different cultural backgrounds and orientations, individuals were likely to be closer to their ideal trait profile when they were with autonomy-supportive partners. Conversely, when people felt less autonomy support, they moved further from their ideals. This generally took the form of being less extroverted, open, and agreeable and more neurotic when they were with less autonomy-supportive others. It was also found (again across cultures) that people felt more relationship satisfaction and vitality in more autonomy-supportive relationships, again a finding supported across these cultures and differences on self-construal.

Mutuality of Autonomy and Autonomy Support in Relationships

We have seen from various studies that being autonomous in general orientation and within a specific relationship is important for a person to experience a high level of satisfaction in the relationship. Further, research showed that when a target person's partner is autonomy-supportive, the person experiences more autonomy and satisfaction in the relationship. Based on the implications of this past research, RMT further proposes that *mutuality of autonomy support* is an important element in close relationships and that each partner benefits from the mutuality, as well as from his or her own autonomous motivation or his or her receipt of autonomy support. When both partners share a sense of autonomy and autonomy support in the relationship, they will experience a true sense of mutuality that will build interactively and give each a deep sense of satisfaction.

RMT Proposition V: Autonomy-supportive partners in close relationships tend to experience a sense of mutuality—that is, when one partner experiences autonomy or autonomy support, the other is more likely to experience it as well—and the greater the degree of mutuality in autonomy or autonomy support within a relationship, the greater is the relationship satisfaction, attachment security, and well-being of both partners.

Two studies by Deci, La Guardia, Moller, Scheiner, and Ryan (2006) on close friendships examined Proposition V. In the first of these studies, close friend dyads reported on the degree to which they received autonomy support from their best-friend relational partners. They also reported on the quality of their relationships, including need satisfaction in the relationship, security of attachment, emotional reliance, dyadic adjustment, and the experience of the friend being included in the self. The researchers expected that the degree to which individuals perceived their partners to be autonomy-supportive would be positively related to their experiences of relationship quality. Yet because the data were collected from both partners, data from the two partners were not independent, so methods appropriate to such dyadic data were employed (Griffin & Gonzalez, 1995). There were three steps to the analyses. First, results at the individual level of analysis showed that each partner's perceptions of the amount of autonomy support he or she *received* from the close friend significantly contributed to higher need satisfaction in the relationship, greater security of attachment, more emotional reliance on the partner, greater dyadic adjustment, and more inclusion of the friend in the self. The second step involved determining the level of mutuality that actually existed within the relationships. The analysis revealed, as proposed in Proposition V, that there was indeed a significant degree of mutuality in the amount of autonomy support provided by each partner: When one person was more autonomy-supportive, his or her partner also tended to be more autonomy-supportive. A third set of analyses indicated that the level of mutuality in perceptions of autonomy support was significantly related to the amount of mutuality in need satisfaction, attachment security, emotional reliance, and inclusion of other in the self.

In their second study on close friend dyads, Deci, La Guardia, et al. (2006) assessed all of the same variables used in the first study and added several others. The first was a measure of each partner's perception of the amount of autonomy support he or she *gives* to the partner, so each partner would report not only on the amount of autonomy support he or she receives but also the amount he or she provides. Also added were (1) a set of psychological well-being measures that were combined to form a well-being composite, (2) the amount of positive and of negative emotions experienced in the relationship, and (3) whether the participants felt willing to express positive and negative emotions with their best-friend partners. At the individual level of analysis, all of the findings from the first study were replicated. Further, perceptions of receiving autonomy support from one's partner positively predicted both well-being and positive emotions in the friendship and negatively predicted negative emotions. Results also confirmed that perceived autonomy support also related positively to feeling able and willing to express positive and negative feelings in the relationship. Thus, even though one has fewer negative feelings in an autonomy-supportive relationship, those that occur are more easily discussed. Finally, at the dyad level of analysis, results indicated that the degree of autonomy support the partners received related significantly to the amount of autonomy support given, as well as to security of attachment, emotional reliance, and dyadic adjustment. Finally, results indicated that *giving* autonomy support had a positive relation to every variable in the study except for expression of negative affect. In fact, a person's giving autonomy support to a friend was related to the person's own experience of relationship quality and well-being, even when controlling for the contribution of *receiving* autonomy support from that friend. Indeed, with respect to well-being, when giving autonomy support and receiving autonomy support competed for variance, it was a person's giving of autonomy support rather than receiving it that had the stronger relation to the person's well-being. In this regard, at least, giving does appear to be better than receiving.

To explicitly examine whether mutuality of autonomy was a gendered issue, Deci, La Guardia, et al. (2006) separated the data from the "best-friend study" into one group of dyads made up of two men and one group made up of two women. The researchers then analyzed the data of the two groups separately. For both female–female partners and male–male partners, perceived autonomy support from friends significantly predicted the indicators of relationship quality.

To summarize, the SDT perspective suggests, and data have supported, that the concepts of autonomy and relatedness are not antagonistic or mutually exclusive. To experience relationship satisfaction and psychological well-being, people need to experience both autonomy and relatedness with respect to their relational partners, and the partners facilitate that by being autonomy supportive.

Conditional Regard: Turning Basic Psychological Needs against Each Other

We have reviewed considerable research confirming that the basic psychological needs for relatedness and autonomy are positively synergistic, that they complement each other in promoting high-quality close relationships. Yet social contexts can be (and often are) structured in ways that turn these two needs against each other. In other words, some situations require, whether implicitly or explicitly, that people must relinquish the satisfaction of one of these needs in order to get satisfaction of the other. According to RMT, this would invariably lead to negative psychological consequences, because it is ensuring deprivation of at least one of the three basic psychological needs.

> *RMT Proposition VI:* Although, inherently, satisfactions of the basic psychological needs are complementary and positive, if the social environment turns any two against each other—for example, if an individual's relational partner requires the individual to relinquish satisfaction of one need (e.g., autonomy) in order to get satisfaction of another (e.g., relatedness)—the individual will experience a poorer relationship quality with that partner and a lower level of wellness.

Conditional Regard in Close Relationships

An example of turning needs against each other is the practice of *conditional regard*—that is, of making the love, attention, and affection an individual receives from a relational partner contingent upon the individual doing what the partner demands. Conditional regard is a common socializing practice that parents use to prompt their children to behave in socially desirable ways. When children do as the parents require, the parents give them more attention and affection; when the children fail to do what is wanted, the parents withdraw affection or expressions of love. As such, the technique is quite controlling, because the children must perform a specified behavior in order to get their parents' love—that is, they must give up autonomy to get relatedness. Research on *parental conditional regard* (PCR) is more extensively addressed in Chapter 13, but we briefly review it here to set the stage for discussing its impacts in close relationships.

Assor, Roth, and Deci (2004) examined college students who reported on the degree to which their parents had been conditionally regarding of them while they were growing up. To the extent the student saw their parents as conditionally regarding, they also reported higher internal pressure to do the behaviors upon which the parents' regard had been contingent. However, pressuring themselves to do the target behaviors had substantial well-being costs, including showing more fragile self-esteem, short-lived satisfaction after successfully enacting the behaviors, shame and guilt when they failed at the behaviors, and poorer coping strategies.

Further, and more relevant here, parents' use of conditional regard had a negative influence on the *parent–child* relationships. Children whose parents had used more conditional regard felt more rejected by their parents because they had not been accepted for *themselves*, and they also reported currently feeling more anger and resentment toward their parents. It seems that the conditional regard that parents conveyed to their children thwarted satisfaction of their need not only for autonomy but also for relatedness.

PCR and Peer Relationships

Moller, Roth, Niemiec, Kanat-Maymon, and Deci (2016) reported a series of studies that examined the association between parent's conditional regard and their children's later experiences in their close relationships. In the first study, results indicated, first, that students' perceptions of conditional regard from both mothers and fathers contributed to less secure attachments with each parent. Further, when mothers and fathers were conditionally regarding, their children experienced less psychological need satisfaction, not only in their relationships with those parents but also with their best friends and romantic partners. Furthermore, at the within-person level of analysis, the amount of need satisfaction that an individual experienced with a particular peer partner also predicted security of attachment with that partner. So, it appears that the more parents are conditionally regarding with their children, the less need satisfaction and attachment security the children will likely experience in their later adult relationships.

Studies of romantic partners by Kanat-Maymon, Roth, Assor, and Raizer (2016) separated *conditional positive regard* from *conditional negative regard* and found that experiencing conditional positive regard predicted poorer quality romantic relationships even after controlling for perceived negative regard and partners' warmth. Important for RMT, these links were mediated by need satisfaction. Thus conditionality of regard contributed to poorer basic psychological need satisfaction, and thus poorer quality relationships, regardless of whether it involved the conditional giving of attention and affection or the conditional withdrawal of attention and affection.

Interestingly, the Moller et al. (2016) studies found that the more the target individuals (i.e., the college students) perceived their parents as giving them conditional regard, the more these students also perceived their peer partners as giving them conditional regard. This finding raises an interesting and important set of questions about (1) whether those students projected their representations of their parents' conditional regard onto their peer partners regardless of whether the partners were actually conditionally regarding, (2) whether those students actually selected friends and romantic partners who were similar to their parents in terms of being conditionally regarding, or (3) whether there was a mix of projection and selection that accounted for the relations.

To begin examining this question, one of the studies in the Moller et al. (2016) series collected data not only from the target college students but also from their peer partners about how they (the partners) treated the target students. Again, the targets' reports of their parents being conditionally regarding were correlated with their reports of their peer partners being conditionally regarding. More importantly, however, it turned out that the partners' reports of being conditionally regarding toward the target individuals were positively related to the targets' perceptions of their parents being conditionally regarding. Stated differently, it appears that if individuals' parents were high in the provision of conditional regard, those individuals also tend to have peer partners who were, by their own accounts, conditionally regarding of the target individuals. This conditional regard from the peers was, of course, negatively associated with the target individuals' reports of secure attachments with their peer partners. In sum, these results are consistent with the idea that to some degree the student participants had selected close peers who were like their parents in terms of conditional regard.

There is a possibility that this relation between PCR and the targets' partners being conditionally regarding could have resulted in some way from the targets "training" their partners to be conditionally regarding, rather than selecting partners who already were. If this were the case, however, it would seem that the longer the target and partner had been together, the stronger would be the correlation between PCR and the partners' self-reported conditional regard. However, that correlation was not significant, suggesting that the "training" interpretation was not veridical, whereas the selection process was.

To examine whether student participants project their perceptions of their parents' conditional regard onto their peers, a different study in the Moller et al. (2016) series set up a situation in the lab with two people who did not know each other—namely, a naïve participant (i.e., the target individual) and an experimental accomplice who acted as a second participant. The two interacted with the aim of getting to know each other. Initially, the target participant reported on the degree to which his or her parents were conditionally regarding. After a somewhat structured interaction designed to facilitate intimacy between the two, the target participant completed several short measures, the most important of which involved rating the experimental accomplice (whom the participant still believed to be another participant) in terms of how conditionally regarding that person had been during their interaction. The data showed that if participants had rated their parents high on conditional regard, they were more likely to rate the confederate high on conditional regard. In this case, of course, the partner (i.e., accomplice) had been trained to relate the same way to all participants, suggesting that these ratings were likely projections. Thus these last two studies highlight that young adults who had experienced their parents as conditionally regarding were more likely to view their close relationship partners as conditionally regarding, as a result of the two processes: an individual's being more likely to have selected partners who behave in conditionally regarding ways and the individual's defensively projecting conditional regard onto his or her close partners.

Relationship-Contingent Self-Esteem

Assor et al. (2004) highlighted that when parents offer affection, attention, and esteem to their children contingent upon specific attributes and behaviors, children can develop contingent self-esteem (Deci & Ryan, 1995)—that is, the children tend to esteem themselves conditionally depending upon their displaying the attributes and behaviors that garnered their parents' esteem. Research by Knee, Canavello, Bush, and Cook (2008) examined the derivative phenomena of relationship-contingent self-esteem in adults—that is, the extent to which participants' self-esteem was contingent upon their romantic relationships. These studies indicated, as would be expected, that relationship-contingent self-esteem tends to be a negative factor in relationships. For example, if both partners were high in relationship-contingent self-esteem, they were often highly committed to the relationship, but their commitment did not lead to feelings of closeness and satisfaction in the relationship. Further, if one partner were high and the other low in relationship-contingent self-esteem, the partner who was low also had very low commitment to the relationship. In short, it appears that relationship-contingent self-esteem makes people very "needy" in the relationship and thus committed to it, but it does not yield closeness, satisfaction, and other positive relationship outcomes.

Relating to Selves, Relating to Objects

Throughout this chapter, we have spoken about high-quality relationships and have used relationship satisfaction, security of attachment, emotional reliance, and disclosure as some of the indicators of such relationships. Underlying these and other such indicators is the idea that a high-quality relationship is, at its core, one in which two people are interacting openly with each other, each from his or her own authentic sense of self. In high-quality relating, each person is empathic and accepting of the other for who the other really is, and each person is as congruent as possible in sharing him- or herself. There are existential risks on both sides of such relationships, but, as we have reviewed, the payoffs for such mutuality are high.

We introduced this chapter with a quote from Buber (1970) suggesting that in a true relationship, one does not have *something for his object*. That is, in a high-quality encounter, one does not treat or relate to the other simply as an object or as something to use (Ryan, 1989). Yet in many relationships people often do just that—they objectify, use, or otherwise fail to respect the self of the other. They relate to the partner not for who he or she really is but rather for what he or she possesses or yields. For example, a person might value a partner for her or his wealth, looks, or status, in which case the connection with the partner is a means to extrinsic interests, rather than being an end in itself. Similarly, as Roberts and Waters (2012) have highlighted, within our society (and others) women are often objectified—that is, viewed and related to in terms of their bodies—and contingently valued on the basis of appearance, crowding out any relating to the women's true selves. Often this is internalized as *self-objectification*, in which one takes an external view of oneself, which as Plant and Ryan (1985) suggested, involves relinquishing a sense of autonomy. Objectification therefore represents an instrumental rather than an intrinsic connection between persons and often precipitates a self-objectifying stance toward herself (or himself) on the part of the individual who had been objectified.

> *RMT Proposition VII:* To the degree that an individual in a relationship relates to the partner more as an object, stereotype, or thing, rather than as a person intrinsically worthy of respect, the partner will accordingly experience thwarting of the basic psychological needs, resulting in a lower quality relationship and poorer well-being.

In Chapter 11 we discussed work by Kasser and Ryan (1996) that characterized goals or values as being relatively intrinsic versus extrinsic. Personal development, meaningful relationships, and community involvement are examples of intrinsic goals and values, whereas having wealth, fame, and image are examples of extrinsic goals and values. Intrinsic goals have been found to be more directly supportive of people's basic psychological needs and to be associated with greater well-being, whereas extrinsic goals, which seek external indicators of worth, do not satisfy the basic needs and have been found to be associated with less wellness.

People who are high on extrinsic life goals or aspirations are hypothesized to view romantic relationships and friendships as opportunities to attain their extrinsic aspirations. In other words, such individuals may select partners because the partners are wealthy, popular, and attractive, in which case the individuals will likely relate not to the true selves of these partners but instead to the partners' external indicators of worth. As such, the partners become objects rather than beings; they become *means* for the individuals to attain what they want, so the partners are not ends in their own right—they are not selves being related to. Clearly, such relationships will be superficial and not deeply satisfying. In fact, research has shown both that holding strong extrinsic goals and values was associated with poorer quality romantic relationships and less satisfying friendships and also that having made more progress in attaining extrinsic goals was associated with having less satisfying romantic relationships and close friendships than was the case for holding and attaining intrinsic goals (Kasser & Ryan, 2001). Other research has shown that developing stronger extrinsic goals resulted from experiencing greater need deprivation developmentally (Kasser, Ryan, Zax, & Sameroff, 1995; Williams, Hedberg, Cox, & Deci, 2000) and that holding and attaining those extrinsic goals in turn led to lower quality romantic relationships and less satisfying friendships.

Other investigators have also examined the relations of what we would call intrinsic versus extrinsic goals and values to relationship quality, although not within the SDT framework. For example, Rempel, Holmes, and Zanna (1985) studied dating or married couples and assessed whether the goals they had for being in their relationships and the goals they perceived their partners to have for being in the relationship were external or extrinsic (e.g., others' approval or personal gain) versus internal or intrinsic (e.g., mutual satisfaction or empathic concern). The researchers reported that the more people's own motives in the relationship were intrinsic, the more they reported love for their partners and the more faith they had that the relationship would endure. Further, the more they perceived their partners as being in the relationship for intrinsic reasons, the more trust they experienced in the relationship. Thus it seems to be important for people both to be more concerned with intrinsic than extrinsic values in a romantic relationship and to perceive their partners as having stronger intrinsic than extrinsic values in order to have trusting, loving, and enduring relationships.

A longitudinal study of college student dating couples (Kurdek & Schnopp-Wyatt, 1997) considered intrinsic relationship values of intimacy and self-enhancement relative to extrinsic relationship values such as dominance, attractiveness, and social approval. In this study, both partners provided information about their values at one point in time; then, 6 months later, they reported whether they were still in that romantic relationship. Results indicated that the strength of the male partner's intrinsic values interacted with the female partner's intrinsic values to predict whether the relationship would be stable over the 6-month period. In short, mutuality in holding intrinsic values for intimacy and self-development within the relationship was an important precursor for the romantic relationship's enduring over time.

In sum, various strands of evidence suggest that when one partner treats another as an object and does not respect the autonomy of the other, there will be various negative ramifications for the relationship. This results both from the frustration of our basic human need for relatedness and autonomy and from the loss of quality in care and responsiveness that results when people are not truly present for each other.

Concluding Comments

RMT proposes that (1) the basic psychological need for relatedness underpins people's intrinsic motivation to engage with other people in high-quality relationships; (2) being autonomously motivated for the relationship is essential for high-quality, securely attached relationships; (3) satisfactions of all three psychological needs within the context of a close relationship promote psychological and relational well-being at both the within-person and between-person levels of analysis; (4) having partners who are autonomy-supportive facilitates more satisfying relationships for the recipient; (5) mutuality of autonomy and autonomy support are key characteristics of high-quality relationships; (6) when the environment turns satisfaction of two needs against each other, people's relationships suffer, and the individuals evidence lower well-being; and (7) when people relate to others as objects rather than persons, the relationships are low in quality and the participants tend to display low wellness.

In support of these propositions, considerable evidence indicates that people experience more high-quality and satisfying relationships when their motivation for being in the relationships is more autonomous and when they are able to satisfy their own basic psychological needs for autonomy, competence, and relatedness within the relationships. Individuals report feeling more securely attached to, and more emotionally reliant on, partners who are supportive of their autonomy and other need satisfactions, and when the autonomy support is mutual, the results are most positive for relationships. Although it is often said that autonomy and relatedness are antagonistic, evidence firmly indicates that, in fact, the two are inherently complementary, although various social processes, such as providing conditional regard, can turn satisfaction of these two needs against each other, and treating others as objects or stereotypes can deprive them of both autonomy and relatedness. As a result, relationships are of lower quality, and both partners can pay considerable costs in terms of wellness.

PART IV

Motivation and Human Development in Families, Schools, and Societies

CHAPTER 13

Parenting and the Facilitation of Autonomy and Well-Being in Development

SDT's approach to development begins with the assumption of inherent growth processes, including intrinsic motivation, relatedness, internalization, and integration. Parents facilitate or hinder these natural processes through their responsiveness to children's basic psychological needs. SDT specifies three critical dimensions of parenting—autonomy support, structure, and involvement—each of which influences internalization and basic need satisfaction. We consider first the issue of attachment, and we contrast Bowlby's (1988) focus on security and anxiety reduction with SDT's emphasis on autonomy support and sensitivity as bases for secure relatedness. Research strongly suggests that autonomy support is critical to the promotion of attachment security, as well as to growth and curiosity, a finding supported across diverse cultures. We also compare SDT's three parenting dimensions with Baumrind's (1967) authoritative–authoritarian–permissive distinctions, as well as the constructs of psychological and behavioral control (e.g., Barber, 1996). Parental psychological control is also discussed in relation to SDT research on parental conditional regard (PCR). Essential to SDT's developmental approach is a clear distinction between autonomy and independence. Autonomy is associated positively and reliably with developmental outcomes, another finding true across cultures, whereas independence or nonreliance on parents can have both positive and negative sources, timing, and consequences. We conclude by summarizing in everyday language what the research tells us about optimal parenting.

Across cultures, parents represent the most significant influence on children's development, not only because they are typically the most critical figures in resource provision but also because they play the most central role in creating the social and emotional contexts children encounter within their formative years (Grolnick, 2009; Pomerantz, Ng, & Wang, 2008). Accordingly, much research within SDT has focused on parents and their pervasive impact on children's psychological development and wellness. A defining feature of SDT is its emphasis on the internal propensities toward growth that require psychological need supports across developmental epochs and domains of life to properly unfold. Nowhere does this emphasis come more to the fore than in discussions of parenting.

Parenting and the Facilitating Environment

Particularly crucial for the healthy development of children is parental provision of *autonomy support,* which represents the active nurturing of the children's capacities to be self-regulating. Autonomy support includes actively taking children's perspectives, as well as providing support and encouragement for self-expression, initiation, and self-endorsed activities (Ryan, Deci, Grolnick, & La Guardia, 2006). When autonomy-supportive parents must be directive, they provide or convey a rationale that, from the child's perspective, helps bring value to the required behavior. Autonomy support nurtures self-development and therefore is critical during the early stages of life, when children are finding their psychological footing, developing rudimentary capacities for becoming aware of emotions and need-relevant internal states, organizing actions, and becoming more attuned to others' feelings and reactions. Yet the importance of autonomy support continues beyond these early years of childhood into adolescence and early adulthood, when offspring can ideally retain a healthy dependence on their parents (or primary caregivers) for caring support and guidance (Ryan & Lynch, 1989).

Clearly there are developmental benefits to autonomy-supportive parenting. Supporting this, a recent meta-analysis of 36 parenting studies showed that when parents are more autonomy-supportive, their children are more autonomously motivated and positively engaged in school, perform better in their academic work, and evidence greater psychological health and well-being. When both parents are autonomy-supportive, the consequences for their children are even more positive than when support is strong from only one (Vasquez, Patall, Fong, Corrigan, & Pine, 2015).

In addition to autonomy support, SDT specifies two additional *nutritive parenting dimensions* (Grolnick & Ryan, 1989; Grolnick, 2009)—namely, the provision of both structure and involvement, dimensions that we more elaborately discuss later in the chapter. In brief, *structure* entails the transmission of information and direction that provides the scaffolding to support and enhance the child's competence development. Structure, that is, facilitates the children's capacities to safely and confidently gain mastery with respect to both their internal and external worlds. *Involvement* concerns the parents' dedication of resources to the children, including attention and engaged caring, provisions that allow the children to feel both relationally connected and emotionally supported as they face the challenges of development. Together, parental autonomy support, structure, and involvement, as shown in Table 13.1, supply the core nutrients for the basic psychological need satisfactions that energize healthy self-development.

In this chapter, we discuss the SDT model of parental nurturance in detail, comparing it with other perspectives on parenting, addressing constructs such as behavioral control, independence promotion, and the use of conditional positive regard, all of which have been considered in some other perspectives as positive approaches to parenting, but each of which we find problematic in specific ways.

Attachment, Trust, and Autonomy Support in Parenting

SDT is relatively unique among current empirically driven theories in its strong emphasis on nutrients and facilitation. Many theories focus on managing children's behaviors (e.g., Baumrind, 1971) or on reinforcing achievement and performance (e.g., Bandura, 1996), but few are so centrally focused on the facilitation of children's self-development through their intrinsic growth tendencies, such as intrinsic motivation and organismic integration, and the need satisfactions that underpin feelings of confidence, vitality, and belonging.

TABLE 13.1. SDT's Three Critical Dimensions of Parenting

Parenting Dimension	Key Elements
Autonomy support	• Take the child's perspective. • Offer meaningful choices. • Encourage and support initiative and voice. • Minimize controlling language. • Provide meaningful rationales for required or requested behaviors.
Structure	• Organize the child's environment to support competence (scaffolding). • Focus on mastery rather than performance goals. • Provide guidelines and effectance-relevant information. • Provide rich feedback that is informational rather than evaluative or controlling. • Explain contingencies and sources of control. • Set limits in noncontrolling way.
Involvement	• Devote time. • Invest attention and resources. • Be caring and supportive. • Show warmth and concern.

Facilitating Environments: Bowlby versus Winnicott?

Perhaps the most influential work on nurturing children is derived from Bowlby's (e.g., 1969, 1973) seminal thinking on the *attachment system* and its central concept of *felt security*. For Bowlby, attachment was first and foremost about safety and protection rather than growth. As Kobak, Cassidy, and Ziv (2004) stated, Bowlby viewed attachment as a "behavioral system activated by appraisals of danger and accompanying signals of fear" (p. 388). Adult attachment theorists agree. As Mikulincer and Shaver (2007) stated: "the goal of the system is a sense of protection and security" (p. 14).

Without doubting the importance of protection and the value of reducing anxiety in moments of danger, we have nonetheless questioned whether this is the proper foundation for an organismic theory of relatedness, let alone for the nurturance of the self (see Ryan, Brown, & Creswell, 2007). Although moments of "dangers and strangers" can be salient, they are typically episodic, and the comfort that follows them does not provide an adequate basis for self-development or closeness in relationships. Security, that is, is merely a necessary, but not sufficient, condition for healthy self-development.

Among the object relations theorists in Bowlby's time, Winnicott (1965) stands out to us as being more attuned to the issue of ongoing positive supports for the nascent self. He specifically highlighted the importance of being warmly held, of receiving empathy, and of having one's spontaneous initiations and expressions of need responded to and amplified through mirroring and responsive care in fostering self-development, rather than focusing on avoiding or being sheltered from threat.

Like Winnicott, SDT posits that supportive, nurturing relationships in infancy and beyond must be conceived of as having a broader base than just security and protection. Indeed, although acting to reduce insecurity in moments of fear is one important type of responsive involvement, parents' or caregivers' responsive involvement is critical in other moments as well. A parent's expression of joy mirroring the infant's smile, a hand that holds out the object for which the child is reaching, and eyes that follow the child's search gaze are also crucially important. These sensitive acts in moments of exploration and growth reflect an active and contingent responsiveness to the infant's initiations and activity, and within SDT we see this loving responsiveness to the child's behavior as being primary in facilitating growth. It is the facilitation of the child's spontaneous activity, rather than mere protection and soothing after moments of anxiety, that actively helps to build the resources of self. Equally important is a trust in the child's development that allows for nonintrusiveness and an absence of controlling and pressuring inputs that might otherwise force the child away from his or her primary tasks of play and growth.

This emphasis on facilitation has, of course, had expression within some attachment theory discussions. As we stated in Chapter 2, authors such as Bretherton (1987) have highlighted that a secure attachment is a relationship that "from the very beginning permits optimal autonomy in the context of emotional support" (p. 1075). She viewed maternal respect for autonomy as a defining characteristic of *sensitivity*. Sroufe and Waters (1977) suggested that sensitive responsiveness to a child's activity will support his or her effectance and self-confidence, a description that is essentially identical to White's (1959) definition of competence. Our point is simply that sensitivity, empathy, and responsiveness to the infant's signals and basic needs are *at the core* of a nurturing environment. A healthy self needs more than security; one needs, as well, ongoing supports for autonomy and competence, as well as relatedness, to be active, confident, and secure. Indeed, studies within the attachment tradition have found that caregiver sensitivity is linked to children's curiosity, competence, and ego resiliency (Arend, Gove, & Sroufe, 1979; Waters, Wippman, & Sroufe, 1979), as well as their self-initiation (Stevenson & Lamb, 1981; Watson, 1966) and resourcefulness (Brody, 1956).

SDT Research on Parental Autonomy Support and Its Effects on Development

Grolnick, Frodi, and Bridges (1984) accomplished an early SDT study reflecting the central importance of parental autonomy support in infancy. They found that the 1-year-olds of mothers who were rated as more autonomy-supportive displayed more exploration and persisted longer at an independent play task than the infants of mothers who were rated as more controlling. Extending this, a study by Frodi, Bridges, and Grolnick (1985) found similar results for the persistence and competence of children at 20 months of age. In this study, indices of sensitivity derived from traditional attachment procedures were highly correlated with the coding system for maternal autonomy support derived from SDT.

Grolnick, Kurowski, McMenamy, Rivkin, and Bridges (1998) subsequently reported that mothers who encouraged their toddlers' self-regulation of emotions and distress, rather than taking responsibility for such regulation, had children who showed less distress in a situation in which the child had to regulate negative emotions independently. These studies suggest that even in the earliest stages of development, parental attunement and support for autonomy are enhancing the child's inner resources for self-regulation.

A longitudinal study by Bernier, Carlson, and Whipple (2010) examined the autonomy support of mothers using the Grolnick, Frodi, and Bridges (1984) coding method when observing mother–infant interactions while they worked on a problem-solving task. The children were between 12 and 15 months old at the time. The researchers also assessed the children's executive functioning (i.e., working memory, impulse control, and set shifting) when the children were 18 and 26 months old. Autonomy support was found to be a very strong predictor of the children's executive function at each point in time, and this relation was stronger than the relation between mother's sensitivity (using the Pederson & Moran, 1995, method) and children's executive functioning.

Landry et al. (2008) took a different approach to applying SDT to infancy by exploring the idea of *organismic trust*. Across four studies, they showed that parents who believed that development is a natural (i.e., organismic) process that unfolds under nurturing conditions were more oriented toward nonpressuring encouragement and autonomy support. In other words, they were more responsive to the children's initiations rather than trying to get the children to behave in specific ways. In their first study, the researchers in fact showed that, among mothers of 1-year-olds, organismic trust was associated with more relaxed parental expectations regarding milestones and fewer social comparisons. In addition, organismic trust was negatively associated with permissive parenting, suggesting that relaxed expectations do not preclude active parental involvement.

In a second study, Landry et al. (2008) observed mothers and their 12- to 13-month-old infants in a problem-solving play situation. The investigators rated maternal autonomy support and competence support (structure) in terms of taking the child's perspective, following the child's pace, and structuring the situation to be optimal given the child's skills. They also assessed autonomy thwarting by rating empathic failures, not following the child's pace, and intervening too quickly, among other indicators. Their analyses revealed that trust in organismic development, even when controlling for parental income, education, child temperament, and the child's level of development, was significantly associated with greater autonomy support as opposed to autonomy thwarting. The investigators followed up on these mother–infant pairs 1 year later to determine whether parental trust in organismic development predicted both mother and child adaptation over time. The results of this third prospective study revealed that parental trust at Time 1 predicted maternal adjustment at Time 2, even when controlling for the initial levels of maternal adjustment and child temperament. More important for our discussion of nurturing environments, parental trust at Time 1, which had predicted a more autonomy-supportive style, also predicted fewer behavior problems in the child at follow-up, controlling for the child's temperament at Time 1. Results also suggested that increases in levels of trust in the natural developmental process over the course of the study were associated with increases in the mothers' satisfaction with role balance and feelings of competence and with the children's having fewer behavior problems.

Finally, results of a fourth study suggested that a mother's capacity to trust in development (and thus support autonomy) does not occur in a social vacuum. In fact, the mother is herself aided in her tasks of trusting in and supporting development by both her partner and her society. Thus a comparison of Norwegian and Canadian mothers found that Norwegian mothers experienced greater tangible support and greater need satisfaction from society than did Canadian mothers, and in turn the Norwegians had higher levels of organismic trust. In addition, across both nations, mothers with more need support from partners were more likely to manifest this facilitating attitude and style.

The importance of trusting the organismic developmental process and thus being supportive of children's autonomy is not limited to infancy but can be found across the childhood years. For example, Deci, Driver, Hotchkiss, Robbins, and Wilson (1993) examined interactions between mothers and their 5- and 6-year-old children. The dyads were videotaped in a free-play situation with "building block" toys. Each comment made by the mother was coded as being autonomy-supportive, neutral, or controlling. Children's intrinsic motivation for the tasks was then surreptitiously assessed with the free-choice behavioral measure during a solitary play period that took place after the mothers had left the room. Analyses indicated that children of mothers who were coded as more autonomy-supportive during the initial play period were more intrinsically motivated during the subsequent free-choice period than were children of mothers whose verbalizations were coded as more controlling.

Joussemet, Koestner, Lekes, and Landry (2005) examined the impact of mothers' autonomy support, first rated when their children were 5 years old, on subsequent adjustment. Their results showed that children with more autonomy-supportive mothers displayed better adjustment 3 years later. In research elaborating on this theme, Joussemet, Vitaro, et al. (2008) presented a 6-year longitudinal study focused on childhood aggression. In it, they showed that mothers who reported a strong belief that children should be controlled (which is the opposite of autonomy support) had children who, ironically, were more likely to show a greater trajectory toward physical aggression during the years sampled (from 6 to 12 years of age). That is, beliefs in controlling children were associated with maintaining or increasing tendencies toward aggression rather than diminishing them, which suggests that the mothers' beliefs in controlling their children thwarted the children's basic psychological needs. Autonomy-supportive social environments thus affect not only the natural human process of intrinsically motivated development but also the internalization of values and regulations for behaviors that are not inherently interesting or intrinsically motivated.

Illustrating this further was a study by Piotrowski, Lapierre, and Linebarger (2013). They conducted a large sample telephone survey primarily with mothers (although some were other caregiving relatives) of children who were between 2 and 8 years of age. The adults were asked questions about their children's abilities to regulate their behaviors and cognitions and about the degree to which they tended to be autonomy-supportive, controlling, or permissive with their children. Results of the study indicated that parents' being supportive of their children's autonomy was associated with the children being more effective at self-regulation, but the parents being either controlling or permissive was linked to substantial self-regulatory deficits. These results dovetail with other research on adolescents showing that parents' being controlling not only impaired internalization but could also prompt oppositional defiance (e.g., Vansteenkiste, Soenens, Van Petegem, & Duriez, 2014).

Parental autonomy support has also been found to be important for children's internalizing a value for learning in schools and applying themselves to achievement in classroom settings. As discussed in Chapter 8, Grolnick and Ryan (1989) conducted separate in-home interviews with the mothers and fathers of elementary school children (grades 3–6). These in-depth interviews focused on the degree to which the parents were autonomy-supportive versus controlling with respect to their children's schoolwork and chores around the house. In addition to the in-home interviews, the researchers obtained in-school assessments of the students' self-reported motivations for doing their schoolwork, as well as teacher ratings of the students' behavior and competence. Finally, the researchers collected the students' school grades and standardized achievement test performances. Results demonstrated that parents who had been rated by the interviewers as more autonomy-supportive had children who had more fully internalized the regulation for schoolwork and who reported themselves as being more autonomous in the school domain. These students were also rated by their classroom teachers as showing better adjustment in school and as having greater mastery and competence in that sphere. Finally, parental autonomy support was associated with the children having higher grades and standardized test scores.

These interviews with parents were revealing in many ways. Sadly, many parents who were rated as controlling were clearly both involved in their children's lives and often well-intended in their attempts at control. Their controlling behaviors in many instances appeared to stem not from malevolence or lack of care but, rather, from their investment in their children's attaining good grades and having success in school. Yet, in their zeal to produce these specific outcomes, they had often failed to promote their children's ownership of these goals and sense of investment and value in achieving. By employing motivational tactics of pressure and external rewards, they often unwittingly undermined their children's personal responsibility and volition for these life tasks, creating instead a reliance on external contingencies rather than self-regulation. As we shall see in the next chapter, this same tactical error is often evident in school environments, wherein policy makers and educators sometimes attempt to foster student achievement and learning through evaluative pressures, sanctions, and rewards (Ryan & Brown, 2005) for both students and teachers, which ironically tend to diminish the students' love of learning, as well as the teachers' creativity and motivation (Hout & Elliott, 2011).

Findings from an important study by Bindman, Pomerantz, and Roisman (2015) highlighted the cognitive-developmental benefits of parental autonomy support. They found that parents who were high in autonomy support, rather than control, during the first 3 years of their children's lives had children who displayed stronger *executive function*—including better sustained attention, longer delay of gratification, and more effective inhibition—a year or two later. As well, the very early autonomy support predicted achievement in the children when they were in elementary and high school, and executive functioning mediated this relation between early parental autonomy support and later school achievement.

Beyond school achievement, controlling and pressured parenting seems to undermine engagement even in an "elective" domain such as sports. For example, O'Rourke, Smith, Smoll, and Cumming (2014) found that young athletes' motivational autonomy in relation to sports participation was significantly related to the motivational climate created by their parents. Parents who were focused on mastery motivation and who were low on ego involvement fostered high levels of autonomy and intrinsic motivation in their children. Moreover, a prospective analysis revealed that these facilitative and nonpressuring parents had children who showed increased autonomy for playing their sport during the course of the season. It is fostering this autonomous motivation that likely leads to continued engagement (Pelletier et al., 2001).

Research by Marbell and Grolnick (2013) showed that autonomy support is important not only in Western, individualist cultures but also in collectivist cultures. They studied sixth-grade children from the collectivist West African country of Ghana, examining the children's perceptions of their parents as autonomy-supportive or controlling. They found that the more the parents were experienced as autonomy-supportive, the more the students were autonomously motivated for and engaged with their schoolwork, and the less they showed symptoms of depression. Further, parental autonomy support also related to their children's more strongly endorsing the collectivist cultural values. Controlling parents, in contrast, had children who were more controlled in their motivation and less engaged in school.

Parental autonomy support is clearly relevant to developmental outcomes in all the significant domains of a child's life. Across various studies of 1- to 12-year-old children, results indicated that autonomy support from socializing agents has a positive influence on maintained intrinsic motivation, enhanced internalization, and greater psychological adjustment and well-being, whereas the agents' control of the children has a negative effect on these important outcomes, leaving the children feeling less engaged, being viewed by teachers as less competent, and becoming more physically aggressive over time. And these general results held in young people from both individualistic and collectivist cultures.

Given its importance as a parenting skill, it is heartening that autonomy-supportive approaches can also be acquired and taught. For example, Joussemet, Mageau, and Koestner (2014) implemented a program called *How to Talk So Children Will Listen* that focused on teaching autonomy-supportive methods to parents. Participants' children were between 8 and 12 years old. Parents reported that their provision of structure, affiliation, and autonomy support increased after the program, compared with baseline. Along with this increasing parental support for autonomy, both internalizing and externalizing problems in the children decreased significantly. Child reports similarly indicated that parental autonomy support increased, and their reports, like those of parents, suggested improved well-being. As we echo in the chapters on education and psychotherapy, the fact that autonomy support can be enhanced with training makes the study of this nurturing variable all the more important.

Parents' provision of autonomy support not only meets the child's basic psychological needs, thus enhancing his or her wellness, but it also leads to the internalization by the child of more supportive relational styles. For example, Kaap-Deeder, Vansteenkiste, Soenens, Loeys, Mabbe, and Gargurevich (2015) showed, in line with BPNT, that children who perceived more maternal autonomy support experienced greater overall satisfaction of their basic psychological needs. Interestingly, maternal autonomy support also predicted the levels of autonomy support experienced between siblings. When siblings felt more autonomy support from their mother, they were, in turn, more respectful of each others' autonomy. In fact, children's need satisfaction mediated the relations between autonomy support from mothers and their children's autonomy support of each other. This might suggest a side benefit to being an autonomy-supportive parent: One's children may get along better!

Three Important Dimensions of Parental Nurturance

Most of the discussion thus far in the chapter has been on organismic trust and autonomy-supportive parenting versus pressuring and controlling parenting, in part because research in the SDT tradition has so consistently found parental autonomy support to be crucial for development and wellness. Nonetheless, we indicated earlier that SDT parenting research has identified three parenting dimensions as being both directly and interactively important for internalization and adjustment (Grolnick & Ryan, 1989). Specifically, they are *autonomy support* (versus control), *structure* (versus a lack of structure and guidance), and *involvement* (versus a lack of attention or dedication of resources; also see Grolnick, Kurowski, & Gurland, 1999).

Provision of Structure

Structure concerns the degree to which socializing agents such as parents organize their children's environments to promote mastery and effectiveness (Grolnick & Pomerantz, 2009; Reeve, 2002). Parents' provision of structure entails their conveying clear and consistent guidelines and rules, providing knowledge about the contingencies between behaviors and outcomes, and offering meaningful dialogue and feedback as their children actively engage in the various domains of life. Structure includes the scaffolding of demands and responsibilities to fit with the child's growing capacities and understandings. When parenting environments are low in structure, and thus unpredictable or chaotic, children will not feel in control of outcomes and are likely to feel ineffective.

Provision of structure by parents is therefore critical to helping children develop a sense of control understanding and perceived competence, which become the basis for effective functioning (Grolnick & Ryan, 1989; Soenens & Vansteenkiste, 2010).

A number of studies have confirmed the advantages of parental structure, especially when combined with autonomy support. For example, Grolnick and Wellborn (1988) assessed parental provision of structure using a questionnaire for children that tapped clarity of parental expectations and predictability of consequences for violating rules and expectations. Higher structure was associated with lower levels of maladaptive control beliefs (e.g., believing that luck determines success) and greater perceived competence. Later, Farkas and Grolnick (2010) developed a structured interview for parents to uncover the components of structure. Their composite variable for structure predicted children's academic perceived control, perceived competence, school engagement, and grades above and beyond the effects of other parenting dimensions. Moreover, findings confirm that outcomes differ depending on whether parents' provision of structure is combined with autonomy support or with control, with more beneficial outcomes occurring under autonomy-supportive, high-structure circumstances (Grolnick, Raftery-Helmer, Marbell, Flamm, Cardemil & Sanchez, 2014; Sierens, Vansteenkiste, Goossens, Soenens, & Dochy, 2009).

Parental Involvement

Parental involvement is the degree to which parents show interest in, have information about, and are actively engaged in their children's lives (Grolnick & Ryan, 1989). Parental involvement has long been found in developmental studies to have positive effects on such outcomes as children's behavioral regulation and emotional adjustment (e.g., Baldwin, Kalhorn, & Breese, 1945; Hatfield, Ferguson, & Alpert, 1967; Patterson, 1976). In Grolnick and Ryan's (1989) interview study, involvement was indexed by the amount of time each parent typically spent with their child, their knowledge of the child's day-to-day life, and their enjoyment of interactions with the child. Involvement positively predicted the child's understanding of who or what controls important outcomes in their lives and their achievement and grades in school, and it negatively predicted the child's acting-out behaviors and learning problems. Grolnick, Ryan, and Deci (1991) similarly found that parental involvement, along with parental autonomy support, predicted children having greater inner resources for school motivation and performance, especially showing greater feelings of autonomy and competence.

Although much SDT research has supported the view that involvement (especially when autonomy-supportive) contributes to many developmental outcomes, Grolnick (2015) recently examined a further question: What is motivating the parent's involvement? Grolnick assessed mothers of fourth- through sixth-grade children regarding their motivation for involvement (measured on a continuum of autonomy). She also measured their level of involvement and their emotions when involved with the child. The more autonomous the mother's motivation for involvement with her child was, the greater was her level of involvement, and the more positive was her affect when involved with her child. Furthermore, both the mother's level of involvement and her identification with that activity was positively related to children's perceived competence for school, their reading grades, and their self-reported self-worth.

In short, there is significant indication that SDT's three parenting dimensions of autonomy support, structure, and involvement are important predictors of children's moving toward increasingly more effective negotiations with their environments and toward greater adjustment and well-being. Grolnick and Ryan (1989), Grolnick and Pomerantz (2009), and Soenens and Vansteenkiste (2010) have suggested that these socializing dimensions are important because each one plays a meaningful role in satisfaction of the children's basic psychological needs. Autonomy support facilitates satisfaction of the children's need for autonomy, and it also enhances relatedness, as specified within *relationships motivation theory* (RMT; see Chapter 12). Structure helps the children satisfy their need for competence. Parent involvement is linked to children's feeling satisfaction of both relatedness and competence needs. Presumably, when parents are more involved with their children, they know them better and understand better how to support their skill development.

Our view of the centrality of these parenting dimensions was also supported, albeit indirectly, in findings by Skinner, Johnson, and Snyder (2005), who set out to identify core features of parenting. Collecting self-report data from more than 1,200 mothers and fathers and from more than 3,500 adolescents, they identified six core aspects of parenting styles, namely: autonomy support, coercion, structure, chaos, warmth, and rejection. Although they favored assessing each of these as a unipolar dimension (rather than as three bipolar dimensions), they also suggested that the dimensions could be aggregated in several ways. It seems clear that these are closely related to our dimensions of autonomy support versus control, structure versus lack of structure (i.e., chaos and permissiveness), and involvement versus lack of involvement. Indeed, their derived dimensions seem quite directly linked to SDT's basic psychological needs for autonomy, competence, and relatedness, and the evidence they reviewed linked being high on autonomy support, structure, and warmth to a range of positive outcomes.

Relations of SDT's Three Parenting Dimensions with Other Perspectives on Parenting

Baumrind's Parenting Styles

Much of the past empirical work on parenting has used concepts of parental styles or patterns, with Baumrind (1967, 1971) having done the pioneering work using this approach. She distinguished among three primary parenting styles: permissive, authoritarian, and authoritative. In her depictions, *permissive parents* may be overindulgent or relatively detached, but in any case they are not actively communicating important guidelines, rules, and limits to their children. For us, permissiveness clearly conveys a lack of structure and guidance. Further, it frequently also implies a lack of constructive involvement, although some permissive parents are very involved with their children, giving them everything they want and requiring very little from them by way of behaving constructively. Finally, permissive parents tend not to make requests and provide meaningful rationales in ways that relate to the children's internal frames of reference, so they would not support the children's autonomous, volitional engagement. In contrast to permissiveness, Baumrind's *authoritarian* parenting, through which parents who value compliance work to condition their children to meet the parents' standards, involves being demanding, controlling, and pressuring of their children, along with providing a high level of structure. Authoritarian parenting thus lacks autonomy support, but it could involve either a quite high level of involvement or, alternatively, hardly any.

From the perspective of SDT, the most interesting pattern of parenting in Baumrind's model is the *authoritative* approach. In this pattern, parents are said to encourage children to be "independent," and yet, at the same time, they firmly require that the children adhere to the parents' rules and guidelines that have been provided for them (Baumrind, 1967, 1971). When we attempt to translate this approach using SDT's nutritive dimensions, we find it to be a somewhat mixed construct. Authoritative parenting as so described could potentially represent the mix of structure and autonomy support, depending on how the parents "require adherence." That is, adherence could be promoted by presenting structure in an autonomy-supportive way. However, although Baumrind rightfully objected to "arbitrary restrictive directives," which she categorized as authoritarian (and we would interpret as highly controlling), she has also advocated that authoritative parents engage in the use "of extrinsic motivators and externally imposed rules and structure" (Baumrind, 1996, p. 405), which have also often been found to be controlling. Thus we have not been surprised to observe that the results of studies on the outcomes associated with authoritative parenting have not always been robust (e.g., see Baumrind, 1971). Further, when she and colleagues extended the requiring of adherence to include corporal punishment (Baumrind, Larzelere, & Cowan, 2002), the SDT view became quite divergent from theirs, because this version of authoritative parenting would clearly be highly controlling. The SDT view is that it is more effective for parents to supply structure in an autonomy-supportive manner, and we have seen no meaningful evidence supporting a socializing advantage to the use of external impositions or extrinsic motivators (e.g., Deci, Koestner, & Ryan, 1999). Even more strongly, we would suggest that coercion and corporal punishment in all its forms are counterproductive for fostering healthy internalization; at best they conduce to external and introjected forms of regulation.

In short, the primary way that the SDT approach to parenting differs from Baumrind's is that it examines the three dimensions of autonomy support versus control, structure versus lack of structure, and high versus low involvement separately, examining how each dimension independently and interactively contributes to desirable socialization outcomes. In contrast we argued using the classic categories, such as authoritative or permissive parenting, masks important information about the effective ingredients in socialization strategies. By using the dimensions and considering the associated needs, a more refined analysis of specific parenting styles and strategies that promote healthy development is made available. The multidimensional approach is also more conducive to profile research (e.g., Morin, Arens, & Marsh, 2016), through which ecologically valid styles of parenting can be assessed in their complexity and related to varied outcomes. In addition we see each of these dimensions as having considerable day-to-day variability across parent–child interactions. Each can be differentially evident in varied situations, whereas parental typographies cannot.

The discussion of parental styles brings to the foreground another issue in the parenting literature of central concern within SDT—namely the concept of *parental control*. Many researchers, including Baumrind, have expressed concerns about permissive and neglectful parenting and have rightly conveyed the importance for children of guidance and monitoring by caregivers. Yet in our view, there has not been an exacting specification of the alternative pole to permissiveness and lack of guidance. From an SDT perspective, it would need to be high structure with low control, but distinctions between control and structure have at times been conflated within the parenting literature, as well as within the construct of authoritative parenting. Accordingly, we now turn to a more specific consideration of how the construct of parental control or controlling parenting has been considered in the general parenting literature, as well as in SDT's literature on parenting.

Parental Control in Developmental Psychology

Within the socialization literature, the concept of parental control has had a long history, with hundreds of articles being devoted to the topic (see Soenens & Vansteenkiste, 2010, for a review). From a socialization perspective, control can be oriented toward the encouragement of sustained behavioral engagement over time. Yet it can also refer to pressuring the child to behave, or to think or feel, certain ways, which from an SDT point of view is inherently controlling or lacking in autonomy support. Thus, control, when representing parents being pressuring rather than encouraging, has been referred to with such descriptive terms as *authoritarian, power assertive, intrusive, demanding, restrictive,* and *domineering,* among others (e.g., Grusec & Goodnow, 1994; Rollins & Thomas, 1979).

Accordingly, during the early years when parental control was being studied (e.g., Baldwin, 1955), the concept of control was viewed primarily as a negative influence on children's development. There was, however, a lack of agreement about what constituted the other end of the control continuum and about whether it would be appropriately characterized as positive. Thus, although early discussions of control, which focused on power assertion, pressure, and dominance, typically considered control to be a negative factor for children's healthy development, writers of that era also pointed out that developing youth still need guidance from parents in terms of how to behave (Baldwin, 1955). For example, if permissiveness anchored the other end of this construct of control, it would not be positive, either.

Schaefer's Dimensional Approach to Parent Styles

Subsequently, Schaefer (1965) distinguished between different types of control, one being primarily negative and a second having potentially positive consequences. The first, called *psychological control,* was defined in terms of aggression, dominance, and capricious use of discipline. Standing in contrast to psychological control was simply the absence of aggressive, dominant, and cold parenting, which Schaefer considered promoting "autonomy," thus making the dimension "psychological control versus autonomy." Because Schaefer considered psychological control to promote a dependence orientation in children, it would mean he was using the term *autonomy* to mean independence. However, this is very different from the SDT concept of autonomy, which means volition and willingness. As such, Schaefer's conceptualization of autonomy promotion does not contain what SDT emphasizes as being essential for optimal, noncontrolling parenting, but his construct of psychological control does fall clearly within the SDT concept of controlling parenting (or need-thwarting parenting). It entails pressuring children toward specific outcomes through external regulations, conditional regard, and the fostering of introjects.

The second type of control, called *behavioral control,* was defined simply as management of behavior, with the relevant dimension being from "firm to lax control." From an SDT perspective, both poles are somewhat problematic. Lax control tends toward permissiveness, for it involves the lack of guidelines or rules. Lax control would thus not be advocated by SDT as a way of promoting volitional regulation or mastery of behaviors, for it lacks structure and other sources of support. Yet neither would "firm control" be advocated, because firm control often conveys being pressuring and demanding, although behavioral control could mean a less demanding type of managing behavior, in which case it would be more akin to what is referred to as "structure" within SDT. In short, there is no concept within Schaefer's theory that would readily be considered optimal from SDT's point of view, which would involve providing a relatively high level of both autonomy support and structure (as well as involvement).

Barber's Revision and Psychological versus Behavioral Control

Barber (1996), building on Schaefer's scheme, attempted to refine the concept of parental control, by bringing the distinction between psychological control and behavioral control to the foreground. Similar to Schaefer, he described *psychological control* as intrusive parenting that manipulates the children's emotions, thoughts, and attachments and thus negatively influences the psychological development of the children. In particular, he highlighted love withdrawal, ignoring the children's perspectives, inducing anxiety and guilt, and shaming the children as features of psychological control. In contrast, Barber defined *behavioral control* as communicating rules and guidelines, and then monitoring and regulating the children's behavior. This, he argued, would be expected to facilitate achievement and decrease externalizing problems. Barber, Olsen, and Shagle (1994) reported that psychological control was, as they predicted, associated with greater internalizing problems, but that behavioral control was associated with fewer externalizing problems, and similar results have appeared in subsequent studies (e.g., Barber, Stolz, & Olsen, 2005).

SDT concurs with Barber and his colleagues concerning the negative effects of psychological control as they define it, a point upon which we shall elaborate. In fact, we would add that the negative impact of being controlling with children is not limited to these psychological manipulation strategies—externally controlling techniques can also hinder development (see also Soenens & Vansteenkiste, 2010). Indeed, what Barber and colleagues described as *behavioral control,* while likely better than permissiveness and lack of involvement, can itself be done in either autonomy-supportive or controlling ways, and we expect this would strongly moderate its impact on children's well-being. Thus, like Schaefer's (1965) earlier construct of firm control, there is no specification that behavioral control should be done in what we would describe as a "noncontrolling" or autonomy-supportive way. In fact, because psychological control is inherently controlling and behavioral control could be (and no doubt often is) done in ways that SDT would consider controlling, the distinction between them in practice may not always be clear-cut (Wang, Pomerantz, & Chen, 2007). Finally, the positive parts of autonomy support—such as taking children's internal frames of reference, communicating rationales for behavioral requests, minimizing use of external inducements, and providing for alternative satisfactions—are not explicitly associated with behavioral control.

The Critical Distinction between Control and Structure

Grolnick and Pomerantz (2009) have argued that use of the term *control* to describe the provision of guidelines and rules for behavior adds more confusion to a field that already has plenty of confusion about the meaning of control and its opposite. While agreeing with the importance of parents communicating guidelines and rules about appropriate behavior, they pointed out that it is possible to present those guidelines and rules in ways that are pressuring and controlling, but it is also possible to present such guides for appropriately negotiating the environment in ways that are quite supportive and promoting of internalization. The former case would constitute attempts to control children's behavior, but the latter case would, quite to the contrary, constitute effective parenting that supports the development of self-regulation without being controlling.

Grolnick and Pomerantz (2009) suggested that the term *structure*, which Grolnick and Ryan (1989) and Grolnick et al. (1999) discussed in terms of organizing children's environments to promote competent functioning, conveys more clearly what is intended with the term *behavioral control*. When parents provide structure, they clearly and consistently communicate rules for behavior, point out the consequences of behaving in these versus alternative ways, acknowledge effective behaviors, and provide constructive feedback following inappropriate behavior. Because behavioral control is not necessarily controlling—that is, it does not necessarily convey *pressuring* children to behave in particular ways—referring to it as *control* adds confusion to discussions of optimal parenting. The term *structure* is descriptively clearer, and it allows for the important distinction between providing controlling structure and providing autonomy-supportive structure, which have been shown to yield different consequences (Grolnick et al., 2014; Skinner, Zimmer-Gembeck, Connell, Eccles, & Wellborn, 1998).

The differential impact of providing structure in autonomy-supportive versus controlling ways was demonstrated early on within the SDT tradition, in an experimental study by Koestner, Ryan, Bernieri, and Holt (1984). The experimenters set up an art classroom within the school, to which individual first- or second-grade children were brought for a session. At the outset of the activities, the experimenter explained that the child would be doing a painting project and then set limits on the behaviors, advocating neatness (staying within the borders on the painting surface) and organization (e.g., rinsing brush before changing colors). These limits were set in either controlling or autonomy-supportive ways in the different conditions. The researchers found that setting controlling limits undermined intrinsic motivation and creativity, whereas setting autonomy-supportive limits concerning the same behaviors did not undermine the children's intrinsic motivation, even compared with a "no-limits" condition.

Similarly, Soenens, Vansteenkiste, and Niemiec (2009) found that when parents were controlling in setting limits on their children's peer relationships, the children were actually more likely to affiliate with deviant peers, but when the parents were autonomy-supportive in setting those limits, the children were less likely to have the deviant affiliations. Further, as noted earlier, Grolnick and Ryan (1989) found that parents who provided structure for their children concerning academic homework and chores around the home facilitated the children's understanding of how to regulate themselves in relation to these behavioral guides. Later, in Chapter 14 on education, we review work by Jang, Reeve, and Deci (2010) that similarly showed the importance of distinguishing between structure and controlling environments, as they show how high structure and high autonomy support independently contributed to positive outcomes within school environments.

Environments that do not provide structure typically present a nonoptimal challenge for children's abilities to cope and organize goals and activities (e.g., Skinner et al., 2005). In many contexts children will struggle without structure to identify appropriate and adaptive patterns of action and to anticipate responses from parents, peers, and other adults in their lives. They would have a more difficult time developing a sense of control and mastery of the environment and experiencing feelings of competence that are essential for adjustment and well-being.

Structure is in no way antithetical to support for autonomy, but this distinction can be lost when structure is described as or conflated with the concept of control. The opposite of being controlling (including being psychologically controlling) is being autonomy-supportive, and this parenting dimension is tied to children's underlying need for autonomy. The opposite of the concept of structure is chaos, which has a direct impact on children's sense of competence. By distinguishing the two concepts, one can assess the meaningful interactions between them, with expectations that controlling structure will have negative effects on development, whereas autonomy-supportive structure will have more positive ones.

As a further issue, SDT also suggests that the autonomy-supportive provision of structure is not enough to facilitate optimal development. Involvement, especially caring, responsive, involvement, is also influential. Parents' heightened involvement in their children's lives is predicted within SDT to enhance children's engagement and mastery. For example, Grolnick and Ryan (1989) found that involvement was associated with greater achievement and classroom adjustment. More recently, Cheung and Pomerantz (2011) found that in both U.S. and Chinese samples, involvement predicted engagement and achievement in schools. Moreover, in both nations, when such involvement was accompanied by autonomy support, children also had greater perceptions of competence and more positive emotional functioning.

The joint effects of autonomy support, structure, and involvement in fostering developmental outcomes is best understood by considering the relations of each of these operationally separable nutrients to basic psychological need satisfactions. Structure is clearly an aid to competence, helping the child to focus on the most salient and important social domains and providing feedback and information to make challenges more optimal. However, without autonomy support, structure is not likely to be internalized to a degree that yields identified or integrated motivation. Finally, because a lack of involvement thwarts children's needs for competence and relatedness, it, too, is expected to have negative effects on motivation and well-being. By clarifying the differences between autonomy support, control, involvement, and structure, all of which have often been conflated in the literature, there is a much greater possibility for understanding the effects of parenting on the socialization and well-being of children.

Psychological Control and Ill-Being Outcomes

Although we think the concept of behavioral control is ambiguous, decades of research on the effects of psychological control has shown its strong negative impact on children's healthy development. These effects have been found with various methods and across cultures (see, e.g., Barber et al., 2005; Stolz, Barber, & Olsen, 2005). For example, Soenens, Vansteenkiste, Goossens, Duriez, and Niemiec (2008) reported that parents' psychological control was related to their children being more physically aggressive and having poorer quality peer relationships. This finding complemented that of Joussemet et al. (2008), which showed that mothers who expressed controlling attitudes about child rearing had children who became more physically aggressive during their elementary school years. Another study found that women in late adolescence who had been hospitalized for eating disorders had fathers who were more psychologically controlling than those of a matched sample of women without the disorder. These women with eating disorders were also higher on maladaptive perfectionism, reflecting their internalization of this controlling parental climate (Soenens, Vansteenkiste, Vandereycken, Luyten, Sierens, & Goossens, 2008). Soenens, Vansteenkiste, and Luyten (2010) subsequently showed that when parents used psychological control to make children more dependent on them, the children indeed showed higher dependence, which, in turn, predicted greater depressive symptoms. Parental psychological control in the academic domain similarly led to greater self-derogation (presumably because their children did not feel that they did well enough to please their parents), and this, too, predicted depressive symptoms. Further, in a study of Belgian and South Korean adolescents, Soenens, Park, Vansteenkiste, and Mouratidis (2012) found that in both cultures parental psychological control related to the adolescents' display of depressive symptoms. As well, Ahmad, Vansteenkiste, and Soenens (2013) found that, in Jordan, which is a vertically collectivist society, there was a negative relation between mothers being perceived to be psychologically controlling and their adolescent children being rated as well-adjusted by their teachers. Importantly, this relation was mediated by the adolescents' basic psychological need satisfaction.

In sum, considerable research has shown that parents' psychological control is associated with negative psychological consequences for children's and adolescents' internalization and well-being, findings highly congruent with SDT. Because of the definition of psychological control, which includes erratic outbursts and personal attacks, as well as guilt-inducing pressure and withdrawal of love, some of the negative outcomes associated with parents' use of psychological control are ones typically associated with controlling parenting—for example, introjected regulation, negative affective experiences and symptoms, and behavioral enactment (e.g., Assor, Roth, & Deci, 2004; Roth, Assor, Niemiec, Ryan, & Deci, 2009)—whereas other of the negative outcomes are ones typically associated with amotivation and impersonal causation, such as depressive symptoms, eating disorders, and maladaptive perfectionism.

Parental Conditional Regard and Internally Controlling Parenting

Soenens and Vansteenkiste (2010) argued that controlling socialization can be organized into the two categories of externally controlling methods and internally controlling methods. *Externally controlling* methods involve reward and/or punishment contingencies, whether the contingencies are explicitly stated or are simply implicit in the nature of the communications, as would be the case when parents imply but do not specify that they will reward the children for doing what is being requested. Discussions of external methods have tended to focus on coercion and threats of punishment, but seduction by external reward contingencies has also been shown to have negative consequences, albeit less detrimental ones. There are thus both "approach" and "avoidance" forms of externally controlling parenting, and both have negative effects on internalization. Children and adolescents whose parents use strong and consistent external controls are likely to be primarily externally regulated, which often takes the form of compliance but can as well be manifested as defiance.

The second category of controlling socialization practices referred to by Soenens and Vansteenkiste (2010) is *internally controlling* practices. This form of socializing has some overlap with psychological control as discussed by scholars such as Schaefer (1965), Barber (1996), and Steinberg (1990, 2005). One type of internally controlling parenting that has been extensively studied within the SDT tradition involves the use of *parental conditional regard* (PCR), in which parents provide more attention and affection when their children act or are as the parents desire and provide less attention and affection when the children do not act or are not as they desire (Assor et al., 2004).

PCR is a concept that describes parents using their attention, affection, and love to control their children's behavior (Assor et al., 2004). As a socializing method, it has been advocated not only by some psychologists (e.g., Aronfreed, 1968; Gewirtz & Pelaez-Nogueras, 1991), but also in the popular literature and media. Yet from the SDT perspective, it is theorized to be controlling and is predicted to promote introjected regulation and various negative consequences. Because PCR involves parents making their affection and esteem contingent upon their children doing as the parents demand, the children can easily introject the contingencies so they will regard and esteem themselves only to the extent that they do as their parents originally demanded and, now, what they demand of themselves. In short, SDT predicts that PCR will reliably lead to contingent self-esteem (Deci & Ryan, 1995) as an internally controlling form of regulation.

One implication of the SDT perspective is that PRC would likely lead children to enact the behaviors desired by parents, as Sears, Maccoby, and Levin's (1957) early work had suggested would be the case. Sears and colleagues spoke of internalization being the basis of the subsequent behavior they had observed. However, because their work pre-dated the differentiated conceptualization of internalization developed within OIT, they did not have the theoretical basis for predicting that the form of internalization would be introjection and therefore would be accompanied by negative affective and cognitive con-sequences. Without this analytic basis, people concerned with promoting behavior would be content with advocating PCR as an effective socializing strategy. Yet SDT research now shows that there are consistent negative effects of PCR on children's adjustment and well-being, just as there are negative effects of introjected regulation.

For example, Assor et al. (2004) surveyed college students concerning their parents' practices, and particularly their use of conditional regard, to motivate them when they were growing up. The researchers focused on the four domains of academics, sports, prosocial behavior, and regulation of emotions, and the students rated the degree to which parents gave them more attention and affection than usual after complying with or succeeding at what their parents demanded and less than usual after noncompliance or failure.

Analyses revealed that perceptions of PCR, assessed separately for mothers and fathers, predicted relevant behaviors within each of these domains. Yet they further posi-tively predicted introjection, assessed as feeling inner compulsion to do the target activi-ties, and negatively predicted identification, assessed as feeling a sense of choice about the activities. Thus, as predicted within OIT, PCR can promote desired behaviors, but it does so through the process of introjection rather than a fuller, more autonomous inter-nalization such as that represented by identification. In this Assor et al. (2004) study, sev-eral well-being and interpersonal variables were also assessed. Results showed that PCR was associated positively with contingent self-esteem, shame and guilt after failure, and short-lived satisfaction after success—all variables that would be expected to be associ-ated with introjection. In addition, the researchers assessed the participants' feelings of rejection by and anger toward their parents. Results showed that college students who had experienced more conditional regard from their parents reported a lingering sense of rejection by and anger toward their parents.

In a second study, Assor et al. (2004) focused on a set of middle-aged women and their college-age daughters. The mothers reported their perceptions of their own moth-ers and fathers (i.e., the students' grandparents) being conditionally regarding, as well as their own well-being and attitudes about parenting. The college student daughters then reported on the degree to which their mothers had been conditionally regarding, thus providing an opportunity to examine the process of *intergenerational transmission*. Results showed first that the mothers who had experienced the grandparents as being more conditionally regarding displayed lower self-esteem and poorer coping skills. They also expressed more positive attitudes toward controlling parenting methods (of which conditional regard is an example). Furthermore, mothers who viewed their parents as using more conditional regard were in turn more likely to be rated by their daughters as being high in conditional regard. In short, PCR, which was found to promote the process of introjection, was also found to be associated with several negative well-being and relationship consequences. Unfortunately, it also tended to be transmitted intergenerationally.

Other research using the same measure of PCR has revealed that when older adolescents experienced their parents to have used more conditional regard, they also reported less secure attachments with their parents, and more conditional regard and less secure attachments with their romantic partners and best friends (Moller, Roth, Niemiec, Kanat-Maymon, & Deci, 2016). The experience of being conditionally regarded seems, then, to generalize from experiences of parents to experiences with peers and partners.

Conditional Positive and Negative Regard

PCR, which is a form of internally controlling parenting, can operate through reward contingencies (i.e., getting attention and affection) for behaving as the parents desire or through punishment contingencies (i.e., losing attention and affection) for not doing what the parents desire. Accordingly, Roth and colleagues (2009) made a further distinction within PCR between *parental conditional positive regard* (providing more attention and affection than usual) and *parental conditional negative regard* (providing less attention and affection than usual). This is an important distinction, because one could argue that it is really the potential loss of attention and love (i.e., negative conditional regard) rather than the receiving of the attention and affection (i.e., positive conditional regard) that has the negative affective and well-being consequences. Thus the researchers tested the utility of the distinction in two studies.

In their first study, Roth et al. (2009) assessed adolescents in grade 9 with regard to two domains: regulating negative emotions (anger and fear) and motivation for school and academics. With regard to the domain of regulating negative emotions, negative PCR (i.e., using withdrawal of love and attention), the strongest significant relations were with emotional dysregulation (i.e., the children not being able to regulate their emotions) and feeling resentment toward their parents. Positive PCR (giving more attention and love) was most strongly related to internal compulsion to comply (i.e., introjection), which was manifested in the form of suppressing the negative emotions. In other words, when children experienced positive PCR for regulating their negative emotions, they tried to force themselves not to acknowledge and express their emotions, and they were somewhat successful at doing so. Interestingly, however, the internal compulsion to comply also had a positive relation to emotional dysregulation, suggesting that the internal compulsion (introjection) adolescents develop for regulating negative emotions seems to put them in a state of inner conflict in which they are trying to comply by suppressing the negative emotions; but they also sometimes defy the parents, as the emotions tend to "leak" out. These emotion regulation results can be seen graphically in Figure 13.1.

In a parallel fashion, with respect to the academic domain, negative PCR was related negatively to engagement and positively to resentment of parents. Positive PCR was associated with internal compulsion to do schoolwork, which was indexed by teachers' reports of the adolescents' engagement being focused on grades rather than learning and the adolescents' reporting that they felt resentment toward their parents.

In a related study, Assor and Tal (2012) found among high school students that their perceptions of their parents being positively conditionally regarding concerning schoolwork led to a pressured overinvestment in school, which showed up as self-aggrandizement after success and critical self-evaluation and poor coping following failure. And these results were significant even when controlling for psychological control

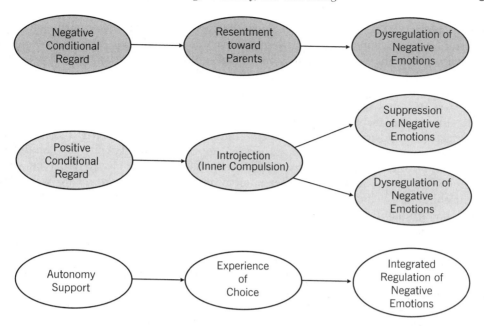

FIGURE 13.1. Parenting approaches and children's regulation of negative emotions. Adapted from Roth, Assor, Niemiec, Ryan, & Deci (2009). Copyright 2009 by the American Psychological Association. Adapted by permission.

(e.g., Barber, 1996), confirming that the finding was not just covariation between positive PCR and another recognized negative approach to parenting.

In a moral reasoning study, Helwig, To, Wang, Liu, and Yang (2014) found that children were critical of negative PCR. More specifically, Chinese and Canadian children from 7 to 14 years old evaluated negative parental conditional regard (i.e., love withdrawal) very negatively and suggested that the children for whom it had been used would suffer negative psychological consequences as a result. The older children in the samples evaluated the approach more negatively than the younger ones.

Thus, across the domains of both emotion regulation and academics, the use of negative PCR (i.e., withdrawal of attention and affection) tended not to achieve the parents' aims, for their adolescents failed to regulate their emotions, were not engaged in school, felt resentment toward the parents, and viewed the approach critically. Yet even with positive PCR, although it seems to achieve some of the parents' aims, the type of compliance regarding both emotion regulation and academics is diminished in quality. The regulation of emotions is accomplished through suppression, which sometimes fails, leading to dysregulation; and the engagement in academics takes the form of being focused on grades, rather than on learning and understanding, and of the development of an internal compulsive pressuring that leads to self-aggrandizement after success and self-criticism following failure.

The second study in the Roth et al. (2009) research sought to compare positive PCR with autonomy support as socializing methods in the emotion regulation and academic domains. This study was prompted by the fact that positive conditional regard is widely endorsed because it can prompt the desired behaviors and provides positive responses from the parents. The question, then, was whether there is an approach to managing socialization that is more effective than positive conditional regard for both outcomes and the processes that yield the outcomes. In this study, autonomy support was assessed with items related to adolescents' perceptions of their parents taking the adolescents' perspectives, providing meaningful rationales, and taking interest in the domains under consideration.

Results of this second study showed that both mothers' and fathers' positive conditional regard was positively related to their children feeling internal compulsion to follow the demands, whereas both parents' autonomy support was unrelated to felt compulsion. In contrast, both parents' *autonomy support* was related to their children's feeling choice about how they responded, but neither parents' positive *conditional regard* was related to their children's feeling choice. These findings provide further indication that parents' positive conditional regard is aligned with introjected regulation, whereas autonomy support is aligned with more autonomous (identified/integrated) types of regulation.

Second, the research showed, in line with the results of the first Roth et al. (2009) study, that both mothers' and fathers' positive conditional regard predicted both suppressive regulation and dysregulation of negative emotions and that both relations were mediated by the adolescents' experiencing internal compulsion. Thus the introjected regulation of negative emotions that is promoted by positive conditional regard created a strong attempt to suppress the emotions but often resulted in the adolescents' being unsuccessful in doing that. In contrast, both mothers' and fathers' autonomy support led to *integrative regulation* of the negative emotions, in which the adolescents took interest in the emotions and decided whether and how to express them. The results also showed that the link from perceived parental autonomy support to more autonomous regulation of emotions was mediated either partially or fully by the experience of choice.

The results for the academic domain in the second Roth et al. (2009) study paralleled those for the emotion regulation domain. First, positive conditional regard from each parent related positively to grade-focused engagement, as it had in the first study, and it also related negatively to interest-focused engagement, indicating that the controlled regulation resulting from positive conditional regard not only facilitated a focus on grades but also inhibited interest in the material being learned. Further, these relations were mediated by the experience of internal compulsion (i.e., introjection), as had been theorized. Second, autonomy support from each parent positively predicted interest-focused engagement, and these relations were mediated by choice.

To summarize, this set of studies showed first that the correlates and consequences of negative PCR and positive PCR were quite different. Negative PCR predicted resentment toward parents and failed to promote the desired behavioral manifestations. Positive conditional regard from parents induced internal compulsion to behave as parents required, which did often prompt the desired behavioral manifestations, although it sometimes failed to do so, and was associated with negative affect.

It thus turns out that contingent withdrawal of love (i.e., negative PCR) does not promote internalization, as Sears et al. (1957) had predicted it would. Rather, what no doubt happened in their research is that the parents who used love withdrawal also used positive conditional regard, and it was the positive PCR that led to the results they reported. This reasoning is consistent with the results of the research by Assor et al. (2004), which showed that overall parental conditional regard (i.e., not separated into negative and positive) did predict behavioral enactment, although of course it had negative affective accompaniments. The Roth et al. (2009) studies further showed that although positive PCR often resulted in the desired behaviors, the quality of those behaviors was impoverished. In short, although positive PCR is advocated as an effective socializing strategy, it is clear that it is only somewhat effective in promoting desired behaviors, and it has a variety of negative psychological and behavioral consequences associated with it.

Alternatively, parents' use of autonomy support in dealing with socializing issues is far more effective than positive conditional regard. With autonomy support, not only are the desired behaviors facilitated, but also the quality of the behaviors and the psychological consequences are far more positive than those stemming from positive conditional regard.

These effects are apparent early in development, although research is only emerging on this. Roth and Assor (2010) performed one study of PCR in 5- to 6-year-old children and their parents. In it, the parents reported the degree to which they used both positive and negative conditional regard with their children to socialize them regarding regulation of sad emotions. This was examined in relation to various assessments of the children's skills in regulating emotions. Results indicated that parents' use of positive and negative conditional regard to regulate sad emotions was related to their children being less aware of their own sad feelings, less able to recognize sad feelings in other children, and less empathic in responding to other children who felt sad. Further, analyses showed that positive PCR accounted for independent variance in these outcomes, even after controlling for the effects of negative PCR. In short, this is the first indication that both forms of PCR (as assessed by parents' reports, not their children's) have clearly negative effects on the development of effective emotion regulation in children as young as 5 or 6 years of age. In contrast, autonomy support fostered more emotional awareness, as well as better self-regulation.

In fact, the most recent research in this area shows not only that conditional regard is controlling but also that unconditional regard is typically associated with highly autonomy-supportive parenting techniques, as well as parental authenticity. Specifically, Roth, Kanat-Maymon, and Assor (2015) presented studies concerning the relationship of parents' unconditional positive regard (UCPR) to parenting practices. In the first study, they hypothesized and found that UCPR predicted rationale-giving and choice-provision practices. Moreover, UCPR moderated the relationship of these autonomy-supportive techniques with adolescents' autonomous motivation—the techniques foster autonomy more effectively when in the context of UCPR. In Study 2, they replicated these associations between UCPR and the parental practices and further demonstrated that mothers' authenticity predicted UCPR, which in turn was related to autonomy-supportive parenting. Thus both studies suggested how UCPR and autonomy support tend to covary and, further, that parents' autonomy-supportive practices can be even more effective when accompanied by UCPR.

Parental Conditional Regard and Need Satisfaction

From the perspective of need satisfaction, the use of PCR is an interesting case of parents structuring the environment so they are essentially pitting the autonomy and relatedness needs against each other. The message from the parent to the child is essentially, "give up your autonomy in order to have my relatedness." Thus, to maintain relatedness, children must comply, irrespective of the fit of the demands with their own interests or with the values they may develop over time. The really interesting thing about this strategy is that, in line with RMT (Chapter 12), research shows that children who experience PCR do not feel accepted even when they do what is required and get the affection. In other words, with positive PCR, in which they are getting "extra" attention and affection, they still feel rejected and resentful because the implicit message is that they are not being accepted for who they are but, instead, for whether they live up to their parents' demands. As such, the use of PCR with children serves to thwart the needs for both relatedness and autonomy (Ahmad et al., 2013).

We hasten to add that the fact of following rules or accepting parents' guidance does not necessarily mean that children will have either their need for autonomy or their need for relatedness thwarted. Indeed, the provision of structure (e.g., limits and guidelines), when done in an autonomy-supportive way, has been found to promote internalization, engagement, and well-being (e.g., Grolnick & Ryan, 1989; Jang et al., 2010; Koestner et al., 1984). Parents who are involved and autonomy-supportive while providing structure allow their children to satisfy their basic psychological needs as they learn and grow. For example, research with high school students has shown that parents' provision of supports for their adolescents' basic needs led to more internalization and autonomous functioning, which in turn was related to greater well-being and less ill-being (Niemiec, Lynch, Vansteenkiste, Bernstein, Deci, & Ryan, 2006).

Why Parents Become Controlling

Although our focus has been primarily on the effects of parents on children, parents themselves are subject to many influences that either support or undermine their capacities to be nurturing and autonomy-supportive with their children. These not only stem from their experiences when they were children but also reflect "upward" influences from their own children, as well as social and economic pressures they face and various interpersonal conditions they experience.

It is well known within the developmental literature that there are reciprocal effects in interpersonal transactions, particularly those between parents and children. For example, a long history of work on child temperament suggests that children with difficult temperaments may make it more difficult for parents both to feel attached to their children and to refrain from more controlling behaviors (e.g., Bell & Chapman, 1986). Such effects have also been identified within the SDT literature. Grolnick, Weiss, McKenzie, and Wrightmen (1996) found that parents of adolescents who perceived their children to be more difficult were more controlling. In addition, it has been found that when children evidence poorer performance or grades in schools, parents often become more controlling (Grolnick, Gurland, Jacob, & DeCourcey, 2002). For example, a study by Pomerantz and Eaton (2001) found that children's low achievement was associated with increased maternal worrying, which was in turn associated with more controlling behavior from the mothers, which then fed back to negatively affect the children's achievements.

Parents' own supports, or lack thereof, can also bear on their capacity to nurture their children. As we pointed out in discussing organismic trust, mothers who experienced greater social and partner supports were more able to trust the developmental process and thus support their children's autonomy. Similarly, Bouchard, Lee, Asgary, and Pelletier (2007) found that fathers' involvement and satisfaction in parenting was related not only to their own perceived competence but also to their perceptions that their partners placed confidence in their parenting abilities. In addition, we pointed out that many parents have been affected by the parenting styles they experienced, thus exhibiting the intergenerational transmission of parenting styles (e.g., Assor et al., 2004). Clearly, there are many factors that affect parents' capacities to provide a nurturing environment, a few of which we now discuss.

Pressures on Parents

More controlling forms of parenting tend to result from a host of pressures that parents may experience from both external and internal sources. For example, external pressures, such as economic strain (Dodge, Pettit, & Bates, 1994), stressful life events (Conger, Patterson, & Ge, 1995; Grolnick et al., 1996), and experimentally induced stress (Grolnick et al., 2002; Zussman, 1980), have all been associated with more controlling parenting behaviors. In a laboratory experiment examining this issue, Deci, Spiegel, Ryan, Koestner, and Kaufmann (1982) had some individuals teach others to solve problems. Those doing the teaching were told that it was their job to make sure the other individuals learned well so they could perform up to high standards. This pressure from the experimenter led to more controlling behavior in the individuals doing the teaching, which led the individuals doing the learning to perform more poorly. In a parallel field study with parents, Gurland and Grolnick (2005) examined mothers' perceptions of environmental threat regarding such issues as economic instability and scarcity and found that the perceptions of threat were positively associated with controlling parental behaviors exhibited during mother–child tasks and, paradoxically, were negatively associated with children's motivation. Moreover, the links from perceived instability and scarcity to children's motivation were mediated by the controlling parental behaviors.

Parents can also experience internal forms of pressure, such as anxieties, ego involvements, and worries—especially worries concerning their children—which have been found to relate to more controlling behaviors toward the children. Often, factors in the parents' social environments stimulated their worries. For example, a group of mothers may be talking together when one mother begins to talk about what a good students her son is and how he gets A's in all his classes. This could easily stimulate ego involvement in another mother, who then needs to see her son do well at his schoolwork in order to feel good about herself, which could lead her to be more demanding and pressuring with her son about schoolwork. In an experimental study examining such a dynamic, Grolnick, Gurland, DeCourcey, and Jacob (2002) put mothers in a high-pressure, ego-involving condition wherein they were led to believe that their children should meet particular standards. Specifically, mothers and their third-grade children worked on a poem task, with mothers in either an ego-involving or a non-ego-involving condition. Mothers in the ego-involving condition exhibited more controlling behaviors during the interactive task. Subsequently, when their children worked on similar tasks themselves, those whose mothers had interacted with them in a more controlling manner wrote less creative poems.

In similar work, Grolnick, Price, Beiswenger, and Sauck (2007) examined the effects of situational pressure and mothers' internal characteristics (viz., contingent self-worth, controlling attitudes) on the mothers' autonomy support versus control in the social domain. Sixty fourth-grade children and their mothers worked on a laboratory task, presumably in preparation for meeting new children. Mothers in an evaluation condition were told that their children would be evaluated by other children and that "based on this, we will determine how much each child was liked and accepted by the peers." In a contrasting no-evaluation condition, mothers received no mention of evaluation. Analyses showed that mothers in the evaluation condition spent more time giving answers to their children, and this was especially true for mothers with more controlling parenting attitudes who also exhibited more controlling behavior. Further, mothers with high social-contingent self-worth in the evaluation condition were most controlling. Results highlighted the importance of interactions between external (e.g., situational) and internal (e.g., maternal) characteristics in determining levels of mothers' autonomy support versus control.

Personality factors within parents are also relevant. For example, Soenens, Vansteenkiste, Duriez, and Goossens (2006) investigated the role of parental separation anxiety and parental maladaptive perfectionism in the prediction of controlling parenting. They reasoned that because parents with high separation anxiety may perceive expressions of their children's autonomy as a threat, they might attempt to restrain age-appropriate autonomous behaviors through psychologically controlling techniques such as guilt induction and conditional regard. In addition, because maladaptive perfectionism in parents would likely be related to pressure toward specified outcomes, it was also expected to be associated with more psychologically controlling styles. Indeed, the results from a large sample of children in middle adolescence and their parents supported these hypotheses, showing that both parental separation anxiety and maladaptive perfectionism were positively related to parents' being psychologically controlling. Further, parental use of psychological control mediated between these parental personality characteristics and adolescent well-being. In fact, several studies have found an association between parental psychological control and maladaptive perfectionism (Soenens, Elliot, Goossens, Vansteenkiste, Luyten, & Duriez, 2005; Soenens et al., 2006). Other studies have found that when mothers were high in conditional self-esteem, which may have resulted from their parents being conditionally regarding toward them, as the intergenerational study would suggest (Assor et al., 2004), the mothers were more likely to use positive conditional regard to get their children to control their emotions (e.g., Israeli-Halevi, Assor, & Roth, 2015). In contrast, other research found that when mothers were high on self-reported authenticity, their children perceived them to be more autonomy-supportive (Roth et al., 2015).

Together, such findings underscore that parenting behaviors are themselves influenced by a variety of factors both external and internal—from the socioeconomic pressures on parents that stretch their resources and prompt insecurities to internalized social pressures to "make" their children achieve to other individual differences that may have resulted from their own developmental experiences. Stresses on parents in the form of threats and pressures thus interrupt organismic trust and capacities for nurturance. On the other hand, it is important to highlight that most parents, because of their inherent attachment and love for their children, naturally seek to provide support and guidance and that even controlling behaviors, although often not helpful, are nonetheless sometimes an expression of parental care.

Autonomy versus Independence

Another important distinction relevant to parenting that is provided by SDT is the distinction between autonomy and *independence*. As discussed in various previous chapters and mentioned earlier in this one, independence and autonomy are understood as conceptually orthogonal constructs within SDT, even though other theories often use them interchangeably (e.g., Douvan & Adelson, 1966; Markus, Kitayama, & Heiman, 1996). Nowhere is this distinction more important than in the domain of parenting.

When it comes to parent–child relations, it is clear that there is a high degree of dependence. From the beginning of life, children rely on their parents not only for tangible goods such as food and shelter but also for psychological aids such as comfort, support, and guidance. Strong dependence for young children is the natural state of things. Even with advancing development, in most cultures children remain dependent on parents long into adolescence and beyond. Although children will develop increasing competencies and will evidence decreasing reliance in some spheres of activity and for some behaviors, dependence is still salient.

Indeed, in our view, what characterizes a good parent–child relationship is a high degree of autonomous dependence at the "growing edge" of development. As children or adolescents move to acquire new skills or to advance within a novel domain, they are optimally most able and, more importantly, most willing to turn to their parents. This volitional reliance, in turn, is expected to be due to the perceptions that their parents are supportive of both competence and autonomy, rather than being either unreliable or controlling (Ryan & Lynch, 1989). What changes over time is not the experience of autonomy, nor the fact of continuing dependencies, but rather the specific kinds of goods and guidance needed.

Emotional Autonomy or Detachment

This view stands in contrast to some other views within developmental psychology that equate autonomy with separation and independence. For example, Blos (1979) portrayed development in terms of an increasing relinquishing of both dependency on and attachment to parents. He viewed maturation in terms of detaching from parents and moving away from help and support, processes that he equated with *individuation.* Drawing on Blos's work, Steinberg and Silverberg (1986) developed a measure for adolescents and young adults assessing *emotional autonomy,* which was intended to reflect this increasing movement away from parents.

The conceptualization of healthy maturation as separation rather than as autonomy or integration is problematic from an SDT viewpoint. SDT emphasizes that the concept of *autonomy* is defined by a sense of volition, choice, and self-endorsement of one's actions (Deci & Ryan, 2013a; Ryan & Deci, 2000a; Shapiro, 1981). People are autonomous to the extent that they fully concur with what they are doing. The opposite of autonomy is not dependence but rather heteronomy, which means to be controlled and pressured by external or internal forces. *Independence,* as used in SDT, means being self-reliant and not relying on or depending on another for guidance or support. Finally, the concept of *detachment* suggests not simply independence but rather separation, and it thus conveys a rupture of relatedness. Detachment refers to adolescents' withdrawing from their families and distancing themselves from them (see, e.g., Freud, 1958), which is very different from autonomy and volition as we have defined those constructs in SDT.

Ryan and Lynch (1989), therefore, argued that "emotional autonomy," as defined and operationalized in the Steinberg and Silverberg (1986) framework, was more an index of independence and detachment than autonomy. Scale items made reference to adolescent behaviors such as "not using parents as resources" and "being different when they are not with parents," rather than to functioning with autonomy. Ryan and Lynch (1989) suggested that such detachment from parents is neither a necessary nor ideal way of developing autonomy and that the emotional autonomy construct conflated separateness with self-regulatory capacities. Ryan and Lynch (1989) argued instead that it was likely to be adolescents who do not have positive relationships with their parents who would report higher levels of this emotional autonomy. Further, they predicted that these highly detached teens would be those who do not perceive their parents as need-supportive or accepting, and they would be more likely to suffer negative psychological health consequences.

In an initial study, Ryan and Lynch (1989) found that the adolescents whose attachment style was categorized as avoidant (i.e., low on security of attachment and low on utilization of parents) were also the ones who scored highest on emotional autonomy. In other words, those who were high on Steinberg and Silverberg's (1986) emotional autonomy construct were insecurely attached and were avoiding reliance on parents (rather than positively "individuating"). Ryan and Lynch (1989) also found significant *negative* relations between emotional autonomy and the adolescents' perceptions of their parents' acceptance of them. Finally, the researchers found that emotional autonomy as assessed by Steinberg and Silverberg's measure was *negatively* related to the adolescents' feelings of lovability—a concept that has been positively related to autonomy as defined by SDT.

This research was important within the SDT framework, demonstrating that the development of autonomy does not require or necessitate either detachment or independence. As adolescents move into young adulthood, they do need to gain a sense of themselves as self-regulating individuals with capacities for autonomy, and this requires that parents increasingly support them in taking responsibility for themselves and engaging in reflective choices. What they do not need is separation, detachment, or an absence of reliance on parents. In other words, adolescents and young adults can be both autonomous *and* dependent.

Since the publication of Ryan and Lynch's (1989) critique of the emotional autonomy construct, studies have continued to assess its consequences and the validity of the conceptualization underlying it. Although this literature is too extensive for the current context, there have been counterarguments to our position that individuation and detachment *from* parents is not a positive model of maturation, and some of these counterarguments have attempted to defend the validity of the emotional autonomy scale. Yet we interpret the continued empirical results as having strongly supported the general SDT position (e.g., see Beyers, Goossens, Vansant, & Moors, 2003; McBride-Chang & Chang, 1998; Parra, Oliva, & Sanchez-Queija, 2015).

Autonomy and Behavioral Independence

Silk, Morris, Kanaya, and Steinberg (2003), using the term *autonomy granting,* discussed the continuum along which parents can either promote independence in their adolescents or work to maintain the adolescents' dependence on them (see also Steinberg & Silk, 2002). These researchers further argued that independence is important for the youth's well-being, and, as we acknowledged earlier, increasing independence is important for adolescents. But this view of granting autonomy in a way that equates autonomy with independence stands in strong contrast to the idea of granting autonomy in a way that promotes a sense of volition and choice.

Illustrating the importance of distinguishing these issues are four studies by Soenens, Vansteenkiste, et al. (2007) that examined the promotion of independence versus the promotion of autonomy. The researchers began with items from a measure of *independence promotion* developed by Silk et al. (2003) and items from a measure of *autonomy support* developed by Grolnick et al. (1991), adding further items of their own. Using exploratory and confirmatory factor analyses, they found two separate factors, one that measures promotion of independence (e.g., "My parent pushes me to think independently") and the other that measures promotion of autonomy (e.g., "My parent, whenever possible, allows me to choose what to do"). The two factors were moderately positively correlated with each other ($r = .47$). Then, to show discriminant validity between these scales, the authors calculated the correlation of each scale with psychological control. They specifically predicted that the negative correlation between autonomy support and psychological control would be significantly stronger than the correlation between independence promotion and psychological control, because within SDT autonomy support and control are viewed as in opposition, whereas independence promotion and psychological control are viewed both by Silk et al. and by SDT researchers as at least somewhat orthogonal. The correlation of psychological control and independence promotion was only $-.25$, whereas the correlation of psychological control and autonomy support was −.68. As expected, the two correlations were significantly different. Further, across the four studies of adolescents, results indicated that, whereas zero-order correlations showed that both independence promotion and autonomy support were related to a composite measure of psychosocial functioning, when the two variables competed for variance in predicting this adjustment outcome, only autonomy support was a significant positive predictor. This finding was in evidence for children in both middle and late adolescence. In other words, the positive aspect of parenting was autonomy support rather than the promotion of nonreliance. A final result showed that the degree to which the participants were autonomous or self-determined in their behavior fully mediated the relation between autonomy support and adjustment.

Related studies showed compatible results using different methods (e.g., Van Petegem, Beyers, Vansteenkiste, & Soenens, 2012). In one study, Kins, Beyers, Soenens, and Vansteenkiste (2009) examined whether the living arrangements of individuals who had recently entered adulthood were dependent upon or independent of their parents. Results showed that these young adults' autonomous motivation for their living arrangements (i.e., living with their parents vs. living independently) explained more variance in their well-being than did the living arrangements themselves. Thus it was their volition rather than their independence that significantly predicted their psychological health. Finally, Soenens, Vansteenkiste, and Sierens (2009) used a cluster-analytic approach to highlight the important difference between independence and autonomy (i.e., volition).

These studies indicate that independence promotion and autonomy support are quite different parenting concepts, with autonomy support being the more important predictor of psychological well-being. The results thus support many discussions and studies within the SDT literature that have theoretically and empirically distinguished autonomy from independence (e.g., Grolnick & Pomerantz, 2009; Ryan & Lynch, 1989; Ryan, Deci, et al., 2006; Soenens & Vansteenkiste, 2010). The discussions further emphasize that, for adolescents, having relationships with their parents that are supportive is optimal for their development into young adulthood and that detachment, which is accompanied by the lack of felt support from parents, will be problematic for healthy self-reliance and self-regulation and may well interfere with the consolidation of an autonomous identity and a positive sense of self.

Autonomy, Independence, and Defiance

Recognizing the difference between autonomy (i.e., volition) and independence is also important for understanding the concept of defiance within SDT. *Defiance* is a behavior enacted by a person that is the opposite of the way an authority figure has told him or her to behave and done precisely because of having been told how to behave. Earlier in the book, we suggested that defiance is a form of controlled behavior, just as compliance is, although in the former case the demand and the behavior are negatively correlated, whereas in the latter case the demand and the behavior are positively correlated. We also reported earlier in this chapter that research by Vansteenkiste, Soenens, et al. (2014) found that, whereas parental autonomy support tends to promote internalization, parental control tends to impair internalization and may promote defiance. Research by Van Petegem, Vansteenkiste, Soenens, Beyers, and Aelterman (2015) showed further that the stronger a youngster's oppositional defiance was during early to middle adolescence, the more independent from parents and the less volitional (i.e., autonomous) the child became in the subsequent years. In short, defiance is not autonomy, and the more defiant an adolescent is, the less volitional he or she becomes in the ensuing years.

Autonomy and Relatedness across Cultures

The fact that autonomy can be understood as volition and willingness rather than independence or detachment is important in understanding the relation of culture to parenting. For example, Bao and Lam (2008) studied Chinese children in Hong Kong, examining how self and parental choices influenced intrinsic motivation. In general, the results showed that when children were allowed to make their own choices, rather than having the choices made by their mothers, the children's intrinsic motivation was higher, as was their performance. Yet there was an additional interaction between how close the children felt to their mothers and the impact of maternal choices on intrinsic motivation. Children who did *not* feel close to their mothers evidenced significantly more intrinsic motivation when they made their own choices than when the parents made the choices for them, but children who felt close to their mothers showed little difference in the two choice conditions. When they felt close to these important adults, the children internalized the mother's decisions and enacted them autonomously, just as they had done when they chose for themselves.

In an additional study, Bao and Lam (2008) further measured these Chinese children's feelings of autonomy for schoolwork using the Ryan and Connell (1989) assessment approach. They also assessed the students' feelings of closeness to their teachers. Results indicated that both autonomous motivation and closeness to the teachers contributed to the students' classroom engagement. In this study, there was no interaction between autonomy and closeness, suggesting that the children's autonomous motivation has a positive effect regardless of the level of closeness with parents or teachers.

We discuss these results here because various writers have stated that in collectivist cultures the emphasis is on duty and obligation to the group, suggesting that autonomy is not important for children in such cultures (e.g., Iyengar & DeVoe, 2003; Markus & Kitayama, 1991b). However, we believe their assertion was based on viewing the concept of autonomy as independence rather than as volition. It may be true that children acting independently is not generally endorsed in collectivist cultures, which value interdependence, but when viewed as volition, children can in fact engage in a duty autonomously and thus behave autonomously in accordance with their parents' decisions. In other words, SDT emphasizes that there is nothing antithetical between being guided by parents and experiencing autonomy, especially when children are closely and positively related to their parents. If the parents are autonomy-supportive—indeed, if they are need-supportive more generally—children will likely feel more securely attached to the parents and be more likely to internalize the parents' values and trust in their decisions, knowing the decisions were made in their (the children's) best interests. This means the children will likely be more autonomous in following their parents' or teachers' lead, because they will more likely concur with them (especially if there is a good rationale for the behaviors in question). In contrast, controlling parents are less securely related, promote a poorer quality of internalization, and display lower personal autonomy.

Switching to yet another culture, SDT's view that autonomy and relatedness are mutually supportive of each other rather than antithetical was also recently supported in a study of Italian adolescents and young adults (Inguglia, Ingoglia, Liga, Lo Coco, & Lo Cricchio, 2015). Their findings verified that both autonomy and relatedness satisfactions were positively correlated and that both were associated with parents' support for these needs. Moreover, both autonomy and relatedness predicted less depression and loneliness, as well as other outcomes associated with better adjustment. The authors suggested, as we do, that both autonomy and relatedness are fundamental needs for both teens and emerging adults, albeit with some differential correlates as a function of age, and that they both are enhanced by parental support.

In Chapter 22 we review additional studies from additional cultural contexts showing the positive impact of parental support for autonomy and relatedness and their positive relations with one another. For now we just offer these few illustrations to make the point that what makes autonomy and relatedness needs, and their support by parents, truly "basic" is, in fact, their universal role in enhancing children's, teens', and emerging adults' healthy development and wellness.

Supports for Attachment

In fact, this last point brings us back full circle to the concept of *attachment* with which we began this chapter. As we pointed out, Bowlby (1969) considered a secure attachment to be a central template in the psychology of the child, supplying a "working model" of the loving, trustworthy possibilities in human relationships. We agree with the importance he placed on parents as a foundation for subsequent social interactions. Where we disagree is only with his understanding of what makes their formative influence positive or negative. A loving parent is someone with whom the child seeks to connect not only in distress but also in joy. The parent would have shown ongoing support for the child's "true self," as Winnicott (1965) would have put it, including the child's spontaneous expressions of feelings and his or her playful initiations. Such a parent would have provided these supports even when the initiating young being, with newfound strengths and curiosities, needs to move away from the parent to understand and connect with the world on his or her own.

SDT research on within-person variability in attachment and relational security has shown that people are most securely attached to the figures who support their basic psychological needs (La Guardia, Ryan, Couchman, & Deci, 2000), a fact that holds up across cultures (Lynch, La Guardia, & Ryan, 2009; Ryan, Deci, et al., 2006). These universal foundational supports for attachment are, therefore, to be found in those caregivers (and, later, friends and partners) who support autonomy, provide structure and guidance to aid feelings of competence, and are caringly involved so as to convey relatedness and belongingness, which can act as an ongoing support in moments of both insecurity and growth. Children will not need to detach from such parents, who will be finding joy in the children's onward development.

Theoretical Summary

The SDT approach to parenting examines parenting behaviors and methods as they affect satisfaction versus thwarting of children's needs for autonomy, competence, and relatedness. SDT is primarily focused on nurturing, facilitating environments that support the growth of the self and its powers of regulation over a widening span of behaviors and choices as development proceeds. As originally presented by Grolnick and Ryan (1989), SDT specifies three nourishing dimensions—autonomy support versus control, high versus low structure, and high versus low involvement—and it views all three as important for supporting healthy self-development. In this chapter, we have argued that these parenting dimensions are systematically related to the satisfaction, deprivation, or thwarting of children's basic psychological needs, and they allow greater specification of optimal parenting relative to mixed and less precise constructs such as Baumrind's (1996) authoritative parenting style.

This, in turn, led to fuller consideration of the term *control* as it has been used in the developmental literature, and particularly in the frameworks of Schaefer (1965) and Barber (1996). We argued that these frameworks are laudable in highlighting the hazards of psychological control and some of the benefits of behavioral control, and yet their employment of the concept of control itself leads to ambiguities. We suggested that even behavioral management by parents can be done in either autonomy-supportive or controlling ways, each of which had distinct effects. Instead, we conceptualize the style that Barber called behavioral control to be the intersection of autonomy support *and* structure.

When it comes to psychological control, we specifically focused on conditional regard, in both its positive and negative forms, because conditional regard is such a pervasive tool in the landscape of parenting and is even advocated not only by some parents but also by some developmental specialists. Research within SDT has, however, documented the negative consequences of conditional regard, even when it takes the form of positive conditional regard (i.e., providing more attention and affection than usual when children do what the parents want them to do). In particular, positive conditional regard tends to foster introjected rather than more autonomous forms of self-regulation. To support this, we reviewed research showing that autonomy support has more positive outcomes for quality of behavior, psychological experiences, parent–child relationships, and well-being than does positive conditional regard.

Stressors and pressures on parents can lead them to be more controlling and can detract from positive involvement with their children. When parents' own psychological needs are not being met, they are less able and likely to be responsive to their children's needs (e.g., Kaap-Deeder et al., 2015; Landry et al., 2008). In addition, social pressures can lead parents to be ego involved or perfectionistic with regard to child outcomes, diminishing organismic trust and tendencies to be autonomy-supportive (Grolnick, 2002). More generally, economic threats and lack of social supports place stress on parents and conduce to more controlling practices (Ryan, Deci, & Vansteenkiste, 2016).

Finally, within SDT, we make strong distinctions between autonomy and independence and between autonomy and separation or detachment. We argue that whereas autonomy is a basic need for children, independence is not. In fact, at every stage of development, children optimally depend on parents for support and guidance, even as the focus and content of these dependencies change with maturation and social experience. In healthy parent–child relationships, children and teenagers will turn to parents for support, but this most readily occurs in those relationships characterized by parental autonomy support and involvement. We also do not characterize optimal development in terms of separation or detachment from parents, as some past perspectives have suggested, but rather as a continued closeness between parents and offspring, with the child growing toward an increasingly wider span of competencies and interests in the world while remaining attached and connected with his or her parents.

Speaking Plainly about Parenting

Before leaving this topic, we would like to balance out the somewhat technical and research-based discussion of parenting with some more direct discussion of the topic. As this book is primarily a review of empirical work on motivation, personality development, and wellness, this chapter on parenting may appear to be highly abstract and in some ways divorced from the day-to-day interactions that take place between parents and their children. When relating to a child or teenager, parents are usually not thinking about concepts such as conditional regard, psychological control, emotional autonomy, or the positive alternatives we propose, such as autonomy support, involvement, and structure. Yet these research constructs and dimensions do show up in real interactions, characterized differentially by more commonly used terms such as *love, understanding, care,* and *guidance.*

It is important to remember that a parent's being *autonomy-supportive* involves more than just refraining from using pressures, rewards, and controlling language to ensure behavior. Central to autonomy support is the idea that interactions between parent and child begin with *empathy,* with understanding and respect for the child's points of view (or internal frame of reference) in relation to any important event. Responsive and empathic parents consider their child's experience. Because they understand the child, when limits must be set on behavior there is readily an acknowledgement of potential contrary feelings and a supportive approach.

Moreover, whether setting limits or guiding new behaviors, it is extremely helpful to provide reasons. Rather than simply being demanding, autonomy-supportive parents convey their expectations, values, and guidance for behavior in terms that the child is able to assimilate. Giving a *rationale* facilitates more autonomous internalization. This autonomy-supportive practice merely recognizes that it is hard for any individual, adult or child, to volitionally comply without a good reason to do so. When parents make the effort to express the reasons for requesting or requiring specific behaviors, it typically results (at least in the long term) not only in more cooperation but also in fuller internalization (see, e.g., Green-Demers, Pelletier, Stewart, & Gushue, 1998; Jang, 2008; Koestner et al., 1984).

A rationale is not simply saying that this is "what is expected" or "because I say so." Even citing traditions or "duties" may not be enough. As important as expectations and traditions may be, particularly in some cultures (e.g., Miller, Das, & Chakravarthy, 2011), they should still be backed by both rationale and modeling, or what Roth and Assor (1999) called *intrinsic value demonstrations.* Receiving reasons and witnessing authentic value enactment both support the child's ultimate autonomy and the likelihood that culturally transmitted behaviors will be followed and maintained over time.

It is also practically important to understand why the use of coercive or seductive controls is so ineffective when children fail to behave up to expectations. Parents' use of rewards and punishments may be well meaning, but in trying to pressure or entice children into specific behaviors, parents may fail to grasp or "diagnose" what barriers, frustrations, or problems are actually interfering with the internalization of desired responses or the achievement of desired levels of performance. In contrast, parents who empathically attempt to understand the barriers from the children's or adolescents' internal frame of reference are in a better position to help their children identify, cope with, and overcome the perceived barriers, obstacles, or concerns, as well as to better understand whatever contrary aims and agendas the children may have. This is why both sensitivity and dialogue are so critical to supportive parenting.

Similarly, the idea of relatedness is often read abstractly in terms of connecting with a child, but one could perhaps substitute the more common word *love.* Since the work of Harlow (1958) and Bowlby (1969, 1973), it has been clear that children need a safe, warm, and comforting base to seek out in times of stress. But far beyond this anxiety reduction function, love is a positive force, expressed in the parents' receptiveness to and interest in the children—manifested in smiles as the children come to the door, excitement when there is learning and discovery, and acceptance for all that the children experience—that truly satisfies this basic need. In love, parents positively regard children unconditionally, as Rogers (1961) recommended, even as the parents experience their own feelings about what children do or say.

Turning to parental competence support and provision of structure means providing helpful guidance and direction for the child's development. This, too, requires communicating "at the child's level," especially when it's time to be explicitly instructive. A structuring parent is thus not one who just sets out rules and communicates consequences but who also facilitates the child in successfully enacting them and who is helpful rather than critical when the child is lost and confused. Communicating consequences does not mean setting out arbitrary rewards and punishments but rather means communicating the real promises and perils of behaving in particular ways. Effective parents inform the children about how the world works, rather than simply shaping the children's behavior through wielding power over them. Such parents also model the behaviors they promote, allowing their children to transparently see them in action in ways that are developmentally attuned and appropriate.

Rather than uniformly valuing independence, parents who are loving and supportive not only take delight in attempts at self-reliance but also welcome dependence and even neediness. Particularly in Western cultures there has often been a disparaging attitude toward dependence when, in fact, some degree of dependence is characteristic of all individuals, at all stages of life. The so-called "self-made man or woman," idealized by some, is never that (Friedman, 2000), but instead there is always a background of support and systematic reliance. Acceptance of that is learned in the loving relationships of families. The growing child needs to learn to be able to comfortably rely on others and to turn to them for emotional support and informational guidance, which is a healthy attribute, as Ryan and Lynch (1989) highlighted. SDT research shows that a willingness to turn to parents for support, advice, and even direct help, which we have labeled *volitional reliance,* is a characteristic of children that positively predicts wellness and adjustment and is associated with parents who are supportive of both autonomy and relatedness, a fact evident across varied cultures (Ryan, La Guardia, Solky-Butzel, Chirkov, & Kim, 2005).

The ideal trajectory of parent–child relationships is therefore not "individuation," insofar as that is in any way characterized by necessarily separating from or growing apart from parents, but instead is a continued trusting and close relationship that transforms over time to become more mutual and reciprocal. In the SDT framework, children need not "detach" from loving parents, even as their relationships change and the children becoming increasingly self-regulating and self-sustaining in contexts outside the family. Further, as we review in Chapter 15 on *identity formation,* children who have the privilege of basic need-supportive parents have the best chance of achieving their unique potentials, fulfilling themselves and the inherent and adaptive human thrust toward diversity.

In many social contexts around the globe, reliance between children and parents will ultimately go both ways. In one of life's many existential ironies, as parents age, it is they who may become more dependent, often on the children they once nurtured. When that occurs, it is likely that those offspring who themselves have experienced basic need supports will be those most fully capable of providing the empathy, support for autonomy, and relational nutrients needed by parents as they face the dependencies of later development. In short, need-satisfying parenting teaches us all how to be volitional and competent, as well as interdependent and caring.

CHAPTER 14

Schools as Contexts for Learning and Social Development

Although SDT suggests that children are intrinsically motivated to learn and to assimilate developmentally meaningful information, many schools fail to capitalize on students' intrinsic motivation and instead emphasize extrinsic motivators. Grades, awards, and social comparisons are commonplace, as are external pressures, controls, and punishments. In this chapter we consider educational environments as they promote or inhibit students' intellectual and social-emotional flourishing. We first examine the importance of intrinsic motivation, its significance for student engagement and cognitive growth, and the conditions that support it in classrooms. We then consider autonomous motivation more broadly, including students' internalization of values for learning and academic achievement. Substantial evidence shows that autonomy-supportive versus controlling teaching strategies foster more autonomous forms of motivation in students and the higher quality engagement, performance, and positive experience associated with it. Such results are evident across all levels of education, as well as across diverse cultures. We relate SDT's framework to the literature on achievement goals, arguing that because performance goals tend to be associated with more controlling motivations than mastery goals, they tend to produce more negative outcomes. Evidence supports this, showing that the effects of performance and learning goals are substantially mediated by the autonomous and controlled motives underlying them. Finally, in discussing the conditions that optimize students' thriving, we find that the quality of teacher motivation is critical. When teachers experience administrative support for their autonomy and competence, they in turn tend to create more supportive classroom climates. Yet teacher motivation can become diminished in the absence of administrative support and under the pressure of high-stakes testing. We conclude by suggesting that the aims of education should be broader than academic achievement and should include the intellectual and personal flourishing of students as they move toward adult roles and identities. To achieve these broader aims, it is essential for educational climates to be attentive to the satisfaction of students' basic psychological needs, including supports for their diverse interests and capacities.

Learning in infancy and early childhood is largely an intrinsically motivated process. Following spontaneous interests, infants engage in two overlapping but functionally distinct intrinsic motivational tendencies: they play and explore. Through such activity they figure out how things work, discover their own capabilities and limitations, and master various problems. When secure and thriving, they show a broad curiosity about the world, and especially about whatever the important others around them do. Play often involves imitating and emulating those they observe, and it seems that their learning, including social learning, is an inbuilt and natural inclination, yielding its own inherent satisfactions.

Although most early childhood learning is intrinsically motivated, as we saw in the previous chapter, caregiving environments nonetheless strongly affect these intrinsic propensities to learn. Research showed that caregivers who lack trust in natural development (Landry et al., 2008) or who are controlling rather than autonomy-supportive (e.g., Bernier, Carlson & Whipple, 2010; Grolnick, Frodi, & Bridges, 1984) can undermine or dampen their children's inherent motivations to learn, master, and explore. Moreover, we saw in the previous chapter that parents who are less psychological need-supportive have children who, well after infancy, exhibit lower intrinsic motivation (e.g., Deci, Driver, Hotchkiss, Robbins, & Wilson, 1993), less autonomous internalization of parental values (e.g., Piotrowski, Lapierre & Linebarger, 2013), greater detachment from parents (e.g., Ryan & Lynch, 1989), and more antisocial attitudes and behaviors (e.g., Joussemet et al., 2008) among other negative consequences. This array of outcomes bespeaks how much the integrative energies for learning and social internalization in childhood are dependent on interpersonal supports for basic psychological needs.

In most developed nations, once children move beyond toddlerhood, learning becomes not just a parental responsibility; it is increasingly an institutional matter. Unless blocked by poverty or cultural restraints, most children in most countries go to schools, where they are segmented away from adults and children of other ages and expected to accomplish their primary learning in a formal, and usually teacher-directed, environment. In the same way that the need supports afforded by parents impact early development and learning, SDT posits that the need supports found in schools and classrooms affect childhood, adolescent, and emerging adult development, achievement outcomes, and well-being. These environments also shape the aspirations and hopes of children within the social order.

Development in the Situation of Modern Schooling

Modern schools represent, in evolutionary terms, a relatively new experiment in human learning. In traditional societies, children learned by watching, imitating, playing at, and pretending to be the adults around them, gradually acquiring skills and roles for adult life. Their "teachers" were typically the adults and older children to whom they were related or to whom they were closely attached (Rogoff, 2003; Ryan & Powelson, 1991).

Rather than the nexus of familial relationships and natural interests and rewards that comprised and motivated learning in previous societies, modern schools have come to rely on alternative instructional methods and evaluative strategies. Typically, a professional adult teaches a large group of children, with a focus on preselected materials that are to be transmitted, not in accordance with unfolding interests and abilities, but in step with a prescribed "age-graded" schedule. Because the content of classroom learning is supplied (often mandated) from the outside, the *internal* basis for engaging in school learning is often unclear. School curricula or materials are often not packaged to be intrinsically motivating, nor in any way made to be particularly meaningful or relevant to the students' daily lives or purposes. In addition, especially under various top-down policy pressures, many modern schools have become extremely focused on a *very* narrow set of cognitive goals, often to the neglect of the varied interests, talents, and more holistic psychological and intellectual needs of students.

It is thus not surprising in these circumstances that educators so often feel they must resort to grades, tests, and other *external* pressures in an effort to make learning happen (Ryan & Deci, 2000b). Highly constrained behaviors are demanded, even in younger children, so rewards for performance and punitive consequences for transgressions are nearly universal. Because grading is salient and often relatively public, strong social comparison is also added to the motivational picture, along with its dynamics of ego involvement and avoidance of shame. In some cultural contexts, this pressure is acute and powerful (e.g., see Wuyts, Chen, Vansteenkiste, & Soenens, 2015). In short, rather than seriously harnessing intrinsic motivations to learn, controlling strategies often become the predominant approach to producing learning within formal educational institutions.

In some nations, leaders have amplified the controlling atmosphere of schools by applying high stakes testing. Policy makers, coupled with assessment partners, decide in a top-down fashion what the contents for learning should be, and these contents are those for which teachers and students are held "accountable." Once establishing the target metrics, externally controlling contingencies, such as linking sanctions and rewards for students, teachers, and administrators to examination outcomes (Ryan & Brown, 2005), are applied presumably to promote greater achievement. We note that this approach is based on two implicit motivational assumptions: (1) that such extrinsic, outcome-focused motivators effectively promote learning and academic success and (2) that these narrow intellectual goals that are the focus of assessments are actually the most important products of schooling. An SDT analysis finds both of these premises questionable.

Fortunately these controlling educational climates are not universal. Both between and within nations, there is more or less emphasis on autonomous motivation and engagement in schools. There is also more or less support for the diversity of learners that schools serve. There are successful educational experiments from which to learn and exemplary teachers from whom to learn. Our review points to the benefits that basic need-supportive parents, teachers, schools, and educational policies can yield and the contexts that foster them.

Schools as Contexts for Development

With all the pressures on educators to foster academic achievement, it is too often forgotten that schools are more than learning factories—they are *contexts for child and adolescent development.* Children learn more than "reading, 'riting and 'rithmetic" in schools; they also learn about authority, industry, social relationships, and how they are perceived and valued by others outside the home. Schools shape the *development of the whole child,* affecting intellectual outcomes as well as motivation, self-concept, and the vitality and integrity of self-development.

We should therefore consider that the promise and hope of schools is not only that they enable and enhance cognitive learning and growth in specific subject areas such as science, technology, engineering, and mathematics (STEM), but also that they facilitate the development of high-quality motivation, engagement, participation, citizenship, and social-emotional well-being. The capabilities for engagement and self-regulation will likely be more serviceable in subsequent life than any particular facts learned in the schools. Conversely, because schools are pervasive developmental contexts, they should also not do *developmental harm.* That is, they should not discourage, demotivate, or kill the confidence of the students they serve or leave them feeling alienated, reactive, excluded from society, or more antisocial.

SDT suggests that when the conditions of nurturance for holistic development are optimized in schools, so are learning and educational outcomes. We see the highest quality learning and achievement occurring when students' interest and engagement in learning are supported, rather than when educators rely on extrinsic incentives and controls to pressure students toward a narrow set of preordained outcomes. Thus, in this chapter, we look at schools as contexts that can support (or undermine) *flourishing* in students. By flourishing we mean becoming motivated, vital, resourceful, and fully functioning adults. Flourishing individuals feel both empowered and confident in their learning and problem solving and feel a sense of belonging to their schools and their larger human community.

We will also see that student motivation is linked with teacher motivation and well-being. Insofar as teachers lack professional autonomy and are pressured toward specific outcomes, they apply more controlling motivational strategies with their pupils, reducing both the students' and their own work satisfaction. Teacher motivation can be linked empirically to administrative autonomy support for teachers, but policies and politics in turn play important roles in shaping the motivations of administrators and their focus and priorities. It is of central interest to us that in contexts in which teachers can be empowered and creative, it is much more likely that their students will become engaged.

We, therefore, examine how different types of student motivation are associated with different qualities of engagement and learning and how the climates created by teachers, parents, and administrators affect both motivation and wellness. Because today's schools are everywhere struggling to find definition and focus, where they end up in their struggle will have a deep impact on the motivation, wellness, and future functioning of their students. SDT research is in the middle of these issues, focused on the factors that facilitate both learning and healthy, whole-student development.

Intrinsic Motivation in the Classroom

Intrinsic motivation is clearly a manifestation of our natural human propensities to assimilate and integrate knowledge. Characterized by curiosity and interest, intrinsic motivation represents the prototype of an active and willing acquisition and integration of knowledge. We begin with a discussion of intrinsic motivation in schools, not because it is the only form of autonomous motivation or engagement, but rather because it is paradigmatic for the relations between motivation and educational contexts. Certain classroom climates ignite this powerful fuel for learning, whereas others smother it. In contrast, when there is little intrinsic motivation for learning and no inherent interest and excitement in what is going on in the classroom, then both learning outcomes and student wellness are in jeopardy, as longitudinal data confirm (e.g., see Gottfried, Gottfried, Morris & Cook, 2008). Thus we begin with the issue of intrinsic motivation in the classroom, in part because of its symptomatic importance and in part because this is where our own initial research in schools began.

In Chapters 6 and 7 we described a number of early laboratory studies that detailed the effects of various external events, such as rewards, deadlines, surveillance, and feedback, on intrinsic motivation. Across such experimental studies, it was found that when external factors were used in controlling ways, they tended to undermine intrinsic motivation. Yet when contexts supported autonomy, competence, and relatedness (e.g., by providing choice, positive feedback, and empathy), intrinsic motivation was enhanced. These experimental findings obviously had relevance to real-world settings such as schools and workplaces. Thus much of our early fieldwork was in classrooms and schools, followed by work organizations.

In one of these early field studies (Deci, Schwartz, Sheinman, & Ryan, 1981), our interest was in how autonomy-supportive versus controlling teaching styles might influence the intrinsic motivation of late elementary (grades 4–6) students. Prior to a new school year, we contacted teachers to assess their general strategies for motivating pupils. The teachers were given scenarios of motivational problems in the classroom and asked to indicate what solutions they would endorse. Some teachers exhibited a controlling philosophy—they endorsed the use of rewards, punishments, and controlling language to ensure that the students behaved as expected. Other teachers were oriented toward supporting students' autonomy and self-regulation; they would tend to refrain from using controls, attempt to understand the students' viewpoint, and provide choice and supportive feedback. These teacher self-reports were fully collected before the beginning of the school year, before teachers had encountered their new students.

Both in the first week of school and again 2 months later, we assessed the students' intrinsic motivation, perceived competence, and self-esteem. Within these first few weeks of the school year, we found that students in the classrooms of teachers who were autonomy-supportive tended to be more intrinsically motivated, to perceive themselves as more competent, and to report higher self-esteem. Yet those in classrooms of teachers who were more controlling were lower in intrinsic motivation, perceived competence, and self-worth, effects that previous work had shown lasted throughout the school year (Deci, Nezlek, & Sheinman, 1981).

In a subsequent study of late elementary students, Ryan and Grolnick (1986) collected students' perceptions of their teachers' classroom motivational styles and examined the relations of these styles to the students' intrinsic motivation. Those who experienced their teachers as more autonomy-supportive evidenced substantially greater perceived cognitive competence, intrinsic motivation, and self-worth than those who perceived their classrooms as more controlling. In the context of this study, Ryan and Grolnick (1986) also asked children to do a projective assessment in which they simply wrote a story based on a picture of a "neutral" classroom scene. Coding of these projective stories revealed that students who perceived a more autonomy-supportive climate in their actual classrooms wrote stories that contained more positively motivated protagonists and less aggression compared with the stories of students who experienced their actual classrooms to be more controlling.

Such studies of classroom climates have been widely replicated, and we review others. But it is important to highlight that this early research not only showed the real-world relevance of lab studies on intrinsic motivation but also showed that the manner in which teachers choose to motivate students powerfully affects the students' interest, engagement, self-concept, and well-being in the classroom. Thus we can see initial evidence for our argument that schools are contexts for development in this early SDT research. When children are in a controlling setting, one of their major natural assets for learning—that is, their inherent intrinsic motivation—is being switched off, as are feelings of confidence and worth. When we think about the fact that children spend a good part of their lives in educational contexts, we can then begin to see why school is so critical to healthy psychological development.

It seemed clear to us from even our earliest research and observations that there are many practices in schools that undermine intrinsic motivation. In fact, research has suggested that intrinsic motivation declines over the school years. Evidence shows, for example, that students in third through eighth grades display a steady year-to-year decline in intrinsic motivation (Harter, 1981; Lepper, Corpus, & Iyengar, 2005). Gillet, Vallerand, and Lafreniere (2012), studying students in Quebec, found a decrease in intrinsic motivation from age 9 to 15. The authors also pointed especially to the role of decreasing teacher autonomy support in mediating this age-related decreasing trend. Interestingly, they also found an increase in intrinsic motivation after that point, which the authors attributed to increased choice over school subjects and classes. More recent evidence using growth modeling also suggests declines in intrinsic motivation, this time in Austrian schools. Specifically, Gnambs and Hanfsting (2015) identified a marked decline in intrinsic motivation between ages 11 and 16. Anticipating much of what we discuss throughout this chapter, this decline was substantially accounted for by the fact that their school environments insufficiently satisfied needs for autonomy, competence, and relatedness.

Such trends are especially unfortunate given the learning, developmental, and personal benefits of intrinsically motivated experiences. We know from developmental studies (e.g. Danner & Lonky, 1981) that intrinsic motivation is associated with more active student learning and cognitive growth. This is true for students both young and old. For example, Ryan, Connell, and Plant (1990) showed a relation between intrinsic motivation and learning. They had college students read typical textbook material in a nondirected, "spontaneous" learning situation, where no testing was expected. Students who were more intrinsically motivated for the reading, who found it interesting and enjoyable, subsequently did better on an unexpected test about the material than did those who found the material less intrinsically interesting.

In fact, longitudinal studies have suggested that intrinsic motivation may be a crucial ingredient in a positive trajectory of achievement. Taylor and colleagues (2014) did a series of studies to examine the relations of specific types of motivation to overall academic achievement. They first performed a meta-analysis of cross-sectional studies, the results of which pointed toward a potentially significant role of intrinsic motivation in predicting school achievement. They followed this with three additional empirical studies of high school and college students in both Canada and Sweden. Across these studies, intrinsic motivation was the only type of motivation that was consistently positively associated with academic achievement over a 1-year period, controlling for baseline achievement.

In another important study, Froiland and Worrell (2016) looked at the role of intrinsic motivation in predicting school achievement in an ethnically and racially diverse student sample. Their results showed that intrinsic motivation was robustly predictive of engagement, which, in turn, predicted higher achievement (in grade point average). This result remained when the sample was limited to the African American and Latino students within this sample, confirming that these effects were generalizable across varied populations.

Teachers who are autonomy-supportive effectively facilitate intrinsic motivation, often despite the external demands and pressures on them, and they remain concerned with the points of view, initiative, and choice of students they teach. Even lesson-to-lesson variations in student interest and motivation are (in part) a function of fluctuations in the teacher's support for autonomy. Tsai, Kunter, Lüdtke, Trautwein, and Ryan (2008) demonstrated this in a study of German public school students. They measured the students' perceived autonomy support from teachers, as well as their interest during instructional periods, in several subject areas over a 3-week span. Using a multilevel modeling strategy, they showed that perceived teacher autonomy support during lessons covaried with students' experiences of interest, above and beyond their typical interest levels. Teacher variations in control had the opposite effects. This study provided strong evidence that classroom autonomy support can enhance interest, whereas controlling teacher behavior diminishes it, even from session to session.

Even when schools offer just some opportunities for intrinsic motivation as part of the day, it can have a positive effect on students' motivation and experience more broadly. For example, Skinner, Chi, and the Learning-Gardens Educational Association (2012) reasoned that engaging uninterested middle-school students more fully in learning would be possible if the students were provided with activities that took place out of the classroom and were more active and meaningful. The researchers chose the activity of gardening, and, after developing valid measures based on SDT, they found that the students who felt more competent, autonomous, and intrinsically motivated while working in the garden learned more about gardening. But even more striking, those students achieved better in their regular classroom courses, suggesting that the intrinsic motivation and interest had generalized to the wider school experience.

In another example, when researchers in Spain encountered high school students who were highly disengaged from their schoolwork, frequently disruptive, and dropping out of school at a high rate, they tested whether, if they introduced gardening to their school activities as Skinner and colleagues (2012) had done, it might improve school engagement and learning. Results indicated that students in the garden-based learning program evidenced a substantial decrease in school failure, school dropout, and disruptive behaviors, while also showing an increase in skills and self-confidence (Ruiz-Gallardo, Verde, & Valdés, 2013). In other words, intrinsic motivation seems to have generalized to traditional school classes and to have had many of the positive consequences that have frequently been shown to be associated with intrinsic motivation.

In an unpublished study done in Rochester, New York, Ryan, Weinstein, and Schultz researched a program called *Generation 2*, developed by a local psychologist, Bruce Gilberg. The program brought volunteers, typically older adults, into schools, each to have a weekly child-centered play session with a child assigned to him or her. Many of the children with whom volunteers interacted were from the poorest urban schools. Longitudinal evidence collected across the year showed that students who were afforded the program became more positive in their school-related attitudes and enthusiasm compared to controls, as rated by both themselves and teachers. It seems that even a small dose of adult autonomy support and relatedness can significantly influence the school experience.

Together, these studies indicated that students of varied ages tended to learn better in situations in which the social context was more supportive of their autonomy and competence needs. That is, these and related studies (see, e.g., Reeve, Ryan, Deci, & Jang, 2007, for a review) showed that when learning conditions are supportive of students' basic psychological needs, intrinsic motivation, well-being, and high-quality learning are likely to result.

We will further discuss classroom factors that enhance or undermine students' motivation, from issues of grading and discipline to structure and interest building. Yet before doing so we first must broaden the discussion beyond intrinsic motivation to include the issue of extrinsic motivation and its internalization. Despite the importance of intrinsic motivation, developing a personal value for schoolwork is crucial for long-term school success. Through internalization and integration, students can become autonomously motivated to learn material they do not find inherently interesting and are not intrinsically motivated to learn but in which they find value. We thus turn to research addressing the educational conditions that support internalization and the outcomes associated with more fully autonomous motivation.

Internalization, Learning, and Well-Being

Most of the studies of internalization of motivation for schoolwork, which cross the span from elementary school to medical school, have been done in the field—in schools and homes—and have focused on (1) the relations of teacher and parent need-supportive approaches to internalization of extrinsic motivation and/or (2) the relations of internalization to subsequent learning and well-being. Guiding much of this work are the core hypotheses that more autonomous forms of extrinsic motivation lead to an enhancement of students' engagement, learning, behavior, and adjustment and that autonomy support from both teachers and parents facilitates this internalization. Studies have also examined, in accordance with SDT, how teachers' and parents' provision of structure and involvement (Grolnick & Ryan, 1989) also contribute to students' internalization and engagement. Of these facilitators, it is autonomy support that has received the most empirical attention.

The Positive Effects of Autonomous Extrinsic Motivation

First, we recall evidence reviewed in Chapter 8 on organismic integration theory (OIT) regarding the positive effects of autonomous relative to controlled forms of motivation on both quality of behavior and wellness. Much of this work was specific to motivation in schools. For example, Yamauchi and Tanaka (1998) showed that among Japanese elementary students both identified (i.e., well-internalized) regulation and intrinsic regulation predicted greater school value, deeper approaches to learning, and less work avoidance, whereas external regulation and introjection did not. These results were similar to those of Ryan and Connell (1989), who showed that U.S. elementary students evidenced more positive effort and adjustment with more autonomous motivations. Indeed, there is a large literature spanning several decades showing such differential correlates of autonomous and controlled motivations in the classroom (e.g., see Burton, Lydon, D'Alessandro, & Koestner, 2006; Chatzisarantis, Hagger, Biddle, Smith, & Wang, 2003; Grolnick, Ryan & Deci, 1991; Guay, Ratelle, Roy, & Litalien, 2010; and many others). These studies span cultures, age groups, and measurement instruments, while revealing a relatively consistent pattern of results.

Classroom Autonomy Support and Structure Facilitates Internalization

Studies in elementary and secondary schools (e.g., Jang, Reeve, & Deci, 2010; Ryan & Connell, 1989; Skinner & Belmont, 1993) have indicated that teachers' autonomy support positively predicted more autonomous (i.e., internalized) motivation in students, which in turn predicted a host of important educational outcomes. For example, in rural American high schools, Hardré and Reeve (2003) found that the students' perceptions of teachers' autonomy support predicted students' autonomous motivation and perceived competence, which in turn predicted both their school performance and intention to stay in school. In high school physical education classes in Great Britain, Greece, and Poland (e.g., Hagger, Chatzisarantis, Barkoukis, Wang, & Baranowski, 2005; Hagger, Chatzisarantis, Culverhouse, & Biddle, 2003), autonomy-supportive teaching predicted students' being more autonomously motivated to engage in physical activity, and a study by Standage, Duda, and Ntoumanis (2006) revealed that the relation between autonomy-supportive teaching and autonomous motivation for physical activity was mediated by the students' experiences of basic psychological need satisfaction.

Research by Jang et al. (2010) studied both autonomy support and structure in American public high schools. They showed that teachers' autonomy support rated by trained observers predicted student engagement, assessed with both ratings by observers and student self-reports. Classroom structure rated by the observers was also related to students' behavioral engagement but not to their self-reported engagement. Thus, in this research, autonomy support was a very strong predictor of student engagement, whereas structure was less important, although it did contribute additional variance in predicting behavioral engagement.

Vansteenkiste, Sierens, et al. (2012) examined students' perceptions of teachers' autonomy support and structure in high school classes. Two prominent configurations emerged: (1) high autonomy support and clear structure and (2) low autonomy support and vague structure. The researchers found, further, that the first configuration was associated with high levels of autonomous motivation and with the self-regulated learning strategies of time management, concentration, deep-level learning, and persistence; it was also associated with low levels of anxiety. In contrast, the second configuration was associated with low levels of autonomous motivation and more maladaptive learning strategies. In other studies from this research group, Mouratidis, Vansteenkiste, Michou, and Lens (2013) found that students' perceptions of structure related positively to learning strategies and positive affect and negatively to negative affect. Mouratidis, Vansteenkiste, Lens, and Sideridis (2008) further showed that positive feedback enhanced engagement, vitality, and other positive educational outcomes by supporting satisfaction of the competence need and in turn enhancing autonomous motivation.

These and numerous other studies indicate that teachers' autonomy support and provision of structure positively relate to students' autonomous motivation and learning in the schools, but one might wonder whether autonomous motivation would similarly predict positive outcomes in the activities students pursue when they leave high school. Litalien, Lüdtke, Parker, and Trautwein (2013) examined the relation of well-internalized motivation for goal pursuits to psychological well-being over a 2-year transition period following high school. As students were graduating from high school, they rated the degree to which they were autonomously motivated to pursue the goals they held for themselves, and then 2 years later they completed various indicators of well-being. At the second time point, some had gone on to university study, some to vocational training, and some to noneducational endeavors. The researchers found that the students' level of autonomy for their goal pursuits was significantly related to their psychological wellness 2 years later, regardless of which track the participants pursued.

Additional research has focused primarily on the motivation of post–high school students who are in college. For example, a study of college students in America and Germany (Levesque, Zuehlke, Stanek, & Ryan, 2004) explored students' perceptions of the level of autonomy support, relative to external pressure, in their learning contexts and found that perceptions of high autonomy support were positively related to students' autonomous motivation and perceived competence. In turn, higher autonomous motivation and perceived competence were positive predictors of well-being in both countries.

Reeve, Jang, Hardre, and Omura (2002) examined the provision of autonomy-supportive structure in two experiments with college students studying conversational Chinese. These students either were or were not given an autonomy-supportive rationale for the importance of learning this language, and the researchers found that the autonomy-supportive rationale led students to more fully internalize the regulation of this learning and to put more effort into the learning. This work extended the findings of an experiment by Deci, Eghrari, Patrick, and Leone (1994) with college students that showed the importance of providing a rationale and supporting choice for facilitating internalization.

Black and Deci (2000) examined the relations among autonomy support, internalized self-regulation (i.e., autonomous motivation), learning, and well-being of college students studying organic chemistry. Students from many different sections of the course rated the degree to which their instructors were autonomy-supportive. Further, at both the beginning and end of the semester, they reported on their own autonomous motivation, perceived competence, and anxiety. Their grades for the course were obtained from university records, as were their GPAs and Scholastic Achievement Test (SAT) scores. Results showed that students who found their instructors more autonomy-supportive evidenced increases in autonomous self-regulation for course learning over the semester. As well, they showed increases in perceived competence and decreases in anxiety. Finally, students with higher autonomous motivation for studying organic chemistry received higher grades for the course, assessed with a test given to all sections of the course and not graded by the students' own instructors. These results held up even after controlling for ability, which was done by removing the effects of the students' GPAs and SAT scores, so the test results can be directly attributed to motivation. In short, students who experienced their instructors as autonomy-supportive internalized the value and regulation of their course work more fully so that they were more autonomously motivated and performed better in the course. Because the students' ability was controlled for, it was clear that the course performance was importantly determined by the students' autonomous motivation.

Reeve and Tseng (2011) provided insight into the biological mediators that may have been at work in various of these studies examining autonomy-supportive versus controlling teaching. In their experiment, Reeve and Tseng examined the biological underpinning of undergraduate students' experiences when they were in one of three conditions, in which their teachers were autonomy-supportive, neutral, or controlling. The researchers used salivary cortisol, which is often called the stress hormone, for it is a hormonal product of the reactivity of the limbic–hypothalamic–pituitary–adrenal axis (Stansbury & Gunnar, 1994; Susman, 2006). They found that, as predicted, students exposed to a controlling teacher had higher cortisol levels than those in the neutral condition and those exposed to autonomy-supportive teaching had lower cortisol levels than those in the neutral condition. In short, when teachers were controlling, students showed a higher level of biological stress than when teachers were autonomy-supportive.

Conversely, autonomy-supportive teaching engages the whole student. Streb, Keis, Lau, Hille, Spitzer, and Sisic-Vasic (2015) vividly illustrated this in showing that when children were in learning environments that emphasized social relatedness and autonomy support (e.g., kindergarten vs. schools; voluntary workshops vs. regular lessons), they evidenced higher heart rates and emotional arousal. Moreover, children who reported a sense of competence also showed increased heart rates. These data suggest that need-supportive environments catalyze the natural, vital engagement associated with autonomous learning motivation.

In fact, high-quality schooling need not imply suffering, grit, and unhappiness. Tian, Chen, and Huebner (2014) sampled Chinese adolescent students' basic psychological needs at school and their school-related subjective well-being at two time points 6 weeks apart. Cross-lagged analyses revealed significant bidirectional longitudinal relationships between autonomy, relatedness, and competence needs satisfaction and these Chinese adolescents' reports of school satisfaction. Such findings support the view that a motivating environment can also be a pleasant one.

We often forget, in this regard, that children (like adults) are not just in institutions to accomplish adult-established cognitive goals but also *to live and to be*. School is where our children spend a great deal of their lives. Their having more positive states of experience does not detract from accomplishment in such settings—indeed, it typically enhances it. As students experience need satisfaction in the classroom, they tend to become more engaged and more vital. In becoming more engaged, they also reap greater need satisfaction, in a deepening positive cycle. A study by Reeve and Lee (2014) demonstrated these reciprocal relations among high school students. They found that if the student's engagement changed during the early part of a semester, there were corresponding changes in their basic psychological need satisfactions by the end of the semester.

The importance of need satisfaction in elementary and secondary school settings for well-being and accomplishment also appears to apply in more advanced educational contexts. For example, in a study of second-year medical students, the degree of autonomy support provided by instructors in a course on medical interviewing predicted the degree to which students internalized the values inherent in the interviewing. More importantly, findings showed that this internalization predicted students' being judged more effective at interviewing patients 6 months after they had completed the course (Williams & Deci, 1996). In other words, autonomy support truly fostered the integration of course learning into the students' medical practices. A study by Williams, Saizow, Ross, and Deci (1997) revealed that the level of preceptors' autonomy support in medical students' third-year rotations predicted the areas the students selected for their residencies. For example, if the surgery preceptor had been more autonomy-supportive than the internal medicine preceptor, subsequently students were more likely to select a surgery residency than an internal medicine one.

Investigating the experiences of law school students, Sheldon and Krieger (2007) found that over their 3 years of study, law students reported a decline in basic psychological need satisfaction and well-being. However, if the students had more autonomy-supportive instructors, they displayed less decline in need satisfaction and well-being. Further, those who experienced more autonomy support also received higher grades in their courses, performed better on the bar exam, and showed a higher level of autonomous motivation in their first jobs after graduation. Need support was thus associated not only with wellness but also with better performance on an important professional benchmark.

Parent Effects on Motivation in School

Not surprisingly, the bulk of the research on educational motivation has been done in schools and focused on teacher strategies and styles. However, anyone who has listened to the perspective of teachers has no doubt heard their experience of students coming to classes with substantially varied amounts and types of motivation. Although teachers accept considerable responsibility for students' motivation, they also understand that parents have a strong impact on their children's motivation for school. Accordingly, there has been a significant amount of research examining the relations of parents' beliefs and behaviors on their children's motivation and performance in school, and, indeed, the results indicate that the interpersonal quality of students' homes, as well as their classrooms, has a very important influence on their motivation, engagement, and learning.

To look closely at parents' roles in school motivation, Grolnick and Ryan (1989) used an in-home interview protocol that we briefly described in Chapter 13. To assess parental approaches to motivating children in late elementary grades, both for school and at home, a team of two researchers did a home interview with each parent separately for approximately an hour, with the focus being on each parent's approach to motivating the child's school and homework activities, as well as the child's household chores and family obligations. Data were also separately gathered from the children at school regarding their internalization of the regulation for doing schoolwork and their feelings of competence in school. In addition, the research team collected data from the children's teachers on the students' adjustment and academic competence, and their school records were accessed for grades and achievement test scores. The study's results indicated that parents who were rated by the interviewers as more autonomy-supportive had children who self-reported more identified (i.e., autonomous) regulation for schoolwork and higher perceived competence. Teachers rated these children as being more academically competent and having fewer adjustment problems. The children also achieved better grades.

Subsequently, Grolnick, Ryan, and Deci (1991) did a study that examined third-through sixth-grade students' perceptions of their parents' motivational approaches. The results indicated that students who experienced their parents as having more autonomy-supportive styles showed greater internalization (more autonomy) and felt more competent than did those who experienced their parents as using more controlling methods. Further, students who reported greater autonomy and competence earned higher year-end grades in math and reading and received higher scores on standardized tests. Research by Niemiec, Lynch, Vansteenkiste, Bernstein, Deci, and Ryan (2006) further found that when high school students perceived their parents as more autonomy-supportive, the students were more autonomously motivated for learning, which in turn was associated with greater psychological well-being.

Gottfried, Marcoulides, Gottfried, and Oliver (2009) did a longitudinal study of parental practices on academic intrinsic motivation in the areas of math and science. They found that task-intrinsic practices by parents, such as encouragement of enjoyment and engagement in learning, yielded positive effects on the children's levels of motivation at age 9 and lower declines in motivation through age 17. Quite the opposite, task-extrinsic practices by parents, such as the use of external rewards and administering consequences contingent on children's task performance, resulted in adverse effects on student's motivation across the 8-year study interval.

Additional studies that investigated students' perceptions of their parents found that parental involvement—that is, parents' devoting time, attention, and resources to their children's learning-related activities—as well as the parents being autonomy-supportive contributed to the children's school achievement and psychological adjustment (e.g., Grolnick et al., 1991; Grolnick & Slowiaczek, 1994; Ratelle, Larose, Guay, & Senécal, 2005).

Katz, Kaplan, and Buzukashvily (2009) looked at one area in which parents have perhaps their most direct influence—namely, homework. They surveyed fourth-grade Jewish Israeli children and one parent of each child. The results revealed that parents' behavior that supported their children's basic psychological needs was positively related to the children's autonomous motivation for homework. More need-supportive parenting was further related to the parents' own autonomous motivation for involvement in helping with homework.

One type of parental control, as opposed to being autonomy-supportive, is providing conditional regard to children in relation to their schoolwork. As mentioned in Chapter

13, this approach involves parents' providing more attention and affection when their children do well at their academics (positive conditional regard) and providing less attention and affection when the children do poorly (negative conditional regard). Research by Roth, Assor, Niemiec, Ryan, and Deci (2009) examined positive parental conditional regard (PPCR) and negative parental conditional regard (NPCR) and found that PPCR promoted introjected regulation of schoolwork (accompanied by feelings of pressure and control) and that NPCR resulted in such consequences as negative emotional experiences and amotivation for schoolwork. Further, because PPCR had more positive outcomes than did NPCR, the researchers compared the use of PPCR regarding schoolwork to the parenting approach of autonomy support, also in the academic domain. Results indicated that children who experienced a high degree of PPCT displayed introjected regulation for learning, which in turn predicted grade-focused school engagement, whereas children who experienced a high degree of autonomy support reported greater choice and autonomy, which in turn predicted interest-focused school engagement. These findings indicated that even the use of PPCR as a socializing strategy impairs the internalization process compared with the use of autonomy support, which promotes fuller internalization and more positive engagement with school. This is an interesting finding because PPCR conveys competence and provides some relational need satisfaction, but because it thwarts the need for autonomy, it leads to inferior educational outcomes when compared with autonomy support.

The use of psychological control to "push" students to achieve at high levels was perhaps most famously popularized by Amy Chua (2011) in her best-seller describing her *tiger mom* approach and its effectiveness at producing high-achieving children. The book was interpreted by many as a manifesto for parents to double down on pressure and control in the "best interests" of their children. We can only concur that not just in Asian children, but in households across the world, parents often pressure their children to succeed out of a sense of concern and care for their children's future. But is this really an account of, for example, Asian American student success?

Much recent scholarship casts considerable doubt on that idea. Most salient was an 8-year longitudinal study by Kim, Wang, Orozco-Lapray, Shen, and Murtuza (2013). They found, first, that so-called tiger parenting is not a common parenting profile in Chinese American families. More telling, tiger parenting was not associated with children showing superior academic performance. In fact, the best developmental outcomes were found among children of supportive parents, which is more consistent with the idea that positive development happens through nurturance and support rather than pressure and contingent love and regard.

Teacher and Parent Effects

A few studies have looked at the joint influences of teachers and parents on school outcomes. Chirkov and Ryan (2001) had Russian and American high school students rate the degree of autonomy support provided by both their parents and their teachers. The students also completed measures of academic self-regulation, as well as of mental health indicators such as self-esteem, self-actualization, and life satisfaction. Based on ethnographic descriptions, these investigators hypothesized and found that, on average, students from Russia perceived the practices of their parents and teachers to be more autonomy-supportive than the practices of their American counterparts. But the primary hypothesis of this study was not about these mean-level differences between cultures but, rather, whether the relations of parent and teacher autonomy support to important educational and well-being outcomes would be similar across both cultures. Findings indeed revealed that autonomy support from parents and teachers in both countries promoted students' greater internalization of motivation for schoolwork and better psychological health. Analyses examining the relative contributions of parents and teachers indicated that teachers' autonomy support was the stronger predictor of classroom intrinsic motivation, whereas both teachers' and parents' autonomy support was associated with internalization of school motivation and with overall psychological well-being.

Other studies confirm that both parents and teachers contribute independently to student motivation and well-being. Guay and Vallerand (1997) found autonomy support from parents and teachers to be positively related to students' perceived competence and autonomous motivation, which subsequently predicted their year-end grades. Research by Soenens and Vansteenkiste (2005) showed that both parents' and teachers' autonomy support were important for Belgian high school students in the domains of job searching and friendship.

In a large-scale study of high school dropouts, Vallerand, Fortier, and Guay (1997) had more than 4,000 high school students rate the degree to which they perceived their teachers and parents to be autonomy-supportive, as well as their own levels of motivation for schoolwork. Results indicated that students who perceived their parents and teachers as more autonomy-supportive also perceived themselves to be more competent and autonomously self-regulated for schoolwork than did the children of more controlling parents. One year later, these researchers obtained a list of all the students who were still enrolled in these public schools to determine who had dropped out. The students who had perceived less autonomy support and had been less autonomous at the first assessment were more likely to have dropped out.

Legault, Green-Demers, and Pelletier (2006) took a slightly broader approach to looking at need support and high school success by assessing support from the students' friends, as well as teachers and parents. Results indicated that lack of support for any of the three needs from any of these three significant sources of interpersonal support contributed to amotivation in the students. Amotivation, in turn, contributed to performing poorly in school, having low academic self-esteem, displaying behavior problems in school, and intending to drop out of school. When the amotivation was based primarily in feelings of incompetence, the consequences were most negative, and, when students failed to value the learning activities and thus felt no autonomy in relation to them, there was also a substantial contribution to poor educational outcomes.

A wide-range of educational research in settings ranging from elementary schools to postcollege educational programs has thus indicated that, when teachers and parents are more supportive of students' needs for competence, autonomy, and relatedness by providing autonomy support and structure, students exhibit more autonomous motivation and greater perceived competence for doing schoolwork. These motivational experiences, in turn, predict greater engagement, conceptual understanding, and effective performance, as well as psychological well-being and adjustment.

Students with Special Needs

As reviewed by Wehmeyer (2011) and colleagues (e.g., Shogren & Shaw, 2016; Wehmeyer & Little, 2011), students with special needs, such as cognitive disabilities or emotional disorders, like all students, thrive more fully when there are supports for their basic psychological needs. Unfortunately, many times educators respond to learning problems or emotional or attentional vulnerabilities as if they were motivational deficits and attempt to change outcomes by exerting more external control. In contrast, SDT argues that often what is interpreted as these students needing more control is really a matter of their needing more structure, delivered in an autonomy-supportive way.

In one study, Grolnick and Ryan (1990) assessed the perceived competence and autonomous motivation in the academic domain of elementary school students who either did or did not have learning disabilities. Those who did were found to be lower on both perceived competence and autonomous motivation than those students without disabilities. However, when the students with learning disabilities were compared to the low-achieving students from the group without disabilities, there were no differences in their motivation or perceived competence. In other words, those diagnosed with a learning disability had the same motivational patterns as those who were low achievers without a diagnosis.

Deci, Hodges, Pierson, and Tomassone (1992) studied more than 450 students ages 8 to 21 who attended self-contained special education schools for students with challenges. Motivational dynamics were investigated in the students whose primary classification was either learning disability (LD) or emotional disturbance (ED). The researchers examined the students' perceptions of autonomy support from their teachers and mothers, as well as the students' own perceived competence, autonomous motivation, self-esteem, and style of coping with failure. Analyses revealed that both autonomy support and autonomous motivation were related to perceived competence, self-esteem, and more positive styles of coping with failure. Further, the autonomy variables tended to be more strongly predictive of the level of well-being (i.e., self-esteem and positive coping) of students with ED than those with LD, whereas the competence variables tended to be more strongly predictive of well-being for students with LD than those with ED. Stated differently, ED appears to be a disability with autonomy deficiencies as a primary element, whereas LD appears to be a disability with competence deficiencies as a central element. As well, the results showed that the motivation and well-being of these elementary school students with special needs tended to be more strongly predicted by mother variables than by teacher variables, whereas the motivation and well-being of these junior and senior high school students tended to be more strongly predicted by teacher variables than by mother variables.

A study of adolescent students with high-functioning autism spectrum disorder (ASD) similarly showed that the students who perceived their teachers as being more autonomy-supportive also reported greater autonomous motivation for doing schoolwork and higher perceived scholastic competence (Shea, Millea, & Diehl, 2013). Further analyses showed that autonomous motivation mediated the relation between perceived teacher autonomy support and students' perceived scholastic competence.

SDT argues that students with disabilities have the same basic psychological needs as all other students. Because of this, interventions for learning or behavior change, no matter how well intended, must first and foremost respect students' autonomy. Pressure toward outcomes can be particularly strong in this population, and this, combined with a history of training techniques based on external control, puts these students at risk for exposure to controlling environments that can add to other influences in promoting disengagement. Promoting autonomy and self-determination, rather than focusing on training and management, ultimately yields more adaptive developmental outcomes (see also Wehmeyer, Shogren, Little, & Lopez, 2016).

Gifted Students

The motivation, achievement, and well-being of students considered gifted have been examined in other studies. In one of these, Vallerand, Gagné, Senécal, and Pelletier (1994) gathered data from students in late elementary school grades and found that gifted students perceived themselves to be more competent and were also more intrinsically motivated for school activities than were regular students. In short, perceived competence, autonomous motivation, and achievement were all interrelated for these gifted participants.

Miserandino (1996) focused on elementary school students with high ability for learning. She found that among these talented students those who were higher in perceived competence and autonomous motivation were also more positively engaged in school than those lower on these motivation variables and indicated less boredom, anger, and other negative experiences. Furthermore, both perceived competence and autonomous motivation were significant predictors of their school grades, even after controlling for standardized achievement scores. Thus these high-ability students' engagement and performance were predicted by the same autonomy and competence variables that are reliable predictors of engagement and learning for students more generally.

Reflecting more on the dark side of the "gifted" status, evidence suggests that talented students may often feel controlling pressure from parents and educators. Soenens, Vansteenkiste, and Luyten (2010) reported that many parents engage in *achievement-oriented psychological control* (APC), in which the parents use coercive, manipulative, and/or pressure-filled methods to communicate the need for high academic performance to their children. Garn and Jolly (2015) showed that APC was both common in gifted populations and associated with higher academic amotivation and more academic failure avoidance. Such issues with gifted students again show that having competence is not enough for a high-quality educational experience; autonomy must also be fostered.

Need-Supportive Teaching Behaviors

In some classrooms teachers and students seem to interact easily, enjoying and respecting each other. Students take initiative as they engage in their work, and teachers respond to the students' initiations. The climate of such classrooms conveys acceptance, support, and encouragement, and students respond positively to such a climate. Many factors contribute to the climate of classrooms, but among the more important factors is the teachers' style of engaging with the students. Within SDT we have examined teachers' styles in terms of the degree to which they are autonomy-supportive versus controlling, and in this chapter we have reviewed several studies showing the advantages for learning and well-being when teachers support students' autonomy (or, more broadly, their three basic needs).

Elements of Autonomy Support

From the perspective of SDT, teachers who support students' needs begin by understanding and relating to the students' perspectives. These teachers provide students with opportunities to take initiative in their learning and to seek out information that is relevant to their interests or assignments. They provide students with choices and options where possible and encourage students to take responsibility for directing aspects of their own learning (see, e.g., Deci, Ryan, & Williams, 1996). As well, these teachers provide students with information, with rationales for their requests, and with other structures to be internalized, but they do this in an autonomy-supportive way. In contrast, controlling teachers pressure students to think, feel, or behave in particular ways while relating to the students from their own (the teachers') perspectives rather than from the students' perspectives. Following through with the ideas of Dewey (1938), autonomy-supportive teachers act in accordance with the belief in education as development from within, whereas controlling teachers act in accordance with the belief in education as formation from without.

Reeve and colleagues have used empirical methods to examine what autonomy-supportive teachers do and say. Reeve, Bolt, and Cai (1999) began this work by having teachers complete the Problems in Schools Questionnaire (Deci, Schwartz, et al., 1981) to assess teachers' self-reports of autonomy support versus control. The teachers then taught a short class in which they were videotaped, and researchers rated these teaching sessions. Finally, using their questionnaire responses, the teachers were separated into an autonomy-supportive group and a controlling group, and the behaviors of the two groups were compared. Teachers who had been classified as more autonomy-supportive based on their questionnaire responses were found to listen more, to make fewer directives, to respond more to students' questions, to attend more to students' desires, to resist giving students answers and problem solutions, to be more supportive of the students' initiatives, and to speak in ways that implied taking the students' perspectives.

Reeve and Jang (2006) did a follow-up study in which they began by identifying specific teacher behaviors that were autonomy-supportive and others that were controlling; they then related these various observed behaviors to the autonomous motivation of the students whom they were teaching. The reasoning was that autonomous motivation of students would be positively related to teacher behaviors that were autonomy-supportive and negatively related to teacher behaviors that were controlling, so positive correlations would confirm that specific behaviors were autonomy-supportive, whereas negative correlations would confirm that specific behaviors were controlling. The analyses indicated that eight teacher behaviors that had previously been categorized as autonomy-supportive—namely, listening to students, making time for students' independent work, giving students an opportunity to talk, acknowledging signs of improvement and mastery, encouraging students' effort, offering progress-enabling hints when students seemed stuck, being responsive to students' comments and questions, and acknowledging students' experiences and perspectives—were positively correlated with students' autonomous motivation, thus providing validation that the teacher behaviors are indeed autonomy-supportive (see Table 14.1). Further, six behaviors that had previously been categorized as controlling—namely, monopolizing the learning materials, providing solutions to problems before the students had time to work independently, telling students answers without giving them an opportunity to formulate them, making directives, using controlling words such as "should" and "have to," and using directed questions as a way of controlling the flow of conversation—were all negatively correlated with students' autonomous motivation, thus confirming that these behaviors do have the functional significance of being controlling for students. Further, two of these controlling teacher behaviors (viz., asking controlling questions and making "should" statements) explained independent variance in the students' lower autonomous motivation. A study of Israeli elementary students also showed that these types of specific controlling behaviors from teachers were associated with less student autonomy (Assor, Kaplan, Kanat-Maymon, & Roth, 2005).

TABLE 14.1. Teacher Behaviors Shown Empirically to Be Autonomy-Supportive, and Those Shown to Be Controlling

Teacher behaviors that promote autonomous motivation	Teacher behaviors that promote controlled motivation
• Listening to students • Making time for students' independent work • Giving students an opportunity to talk • Acknowledging signs of improvement and mastery • Encouraging students' effort • Offering progress-enabling hints when students seem stuck • Being responsive to students' comments and questions • Acknowledging students' experiences and perspectives	• Monopolizing the learning materials • Providing students too little time to work independently on solving problems • Telling students answers without giving them an opportunity to formulate them • Making demands and directives • Using controlling words such as *should* and *have to* • Using directed questions as a way of controlling the flow of conversation

Note. Based on Reeve and Jang (2001).

Research by Patall, Dent, Oyer, and Wynn (2012) used a different approach to examine specific teacher behaviors and their relations to high school students' outcomes. The investigators assessed high school students' perceptions of the extent to which their teachers provided choices, understood and acknowledged the perspectives of the students, and considered the students' interests when selecting activities. They then found that when teachers provided more choices, more often took the students' perspectives, and were more likely to take the students' interests into account, the students reported more satisfaction of their autonomy need, which in turn led the students to experience the course as being more valuable. Teachers' making clear to students the importance and usefulness of the course work also added directly to the students' perceiving that the course had greater value.

Haerens, Aelterman, Van den Berghe, De Meyer, Soenens, and Vansteenkiste (2013) extended this prior work by focusing on the behaviors associated with teacher need support. This included the concept of autonomy support but also included support for relatedness and structure, the latter of which represents support for competence. Although this has been less well validated than Reeve and colleagues' work on autonomy support, the Haerens et al. (2013) work included, for example, the behaviors of "being enthusiastic and eager" and of "putting effort and energy into the lesson" as being relatedness-supportive and the behaviors of "giving clear instructions," "offering the student a rationale for tasks," and "provides positive feedback" as examples of supporting the students' competence. This work, which specifies the behaviors involved in supporting autonomy, as well as relatedness and competence, in the classroom has great practical utility for teachers and administrators, as need support has been robustly linked to enhanced student learning, performance, and well-being.

Understanding the centrality of autonomy support in the design and implementation of educational programs is leading to ever-deeper observations concerning technique. Toward that end, Rogat, Witham, and Chinn (2014) videotaped seventh-grade science teachers to provide a "thick" description of the practices real teachers used to support autonomy. Similarly basing observations on videotapes of actual instructional sessions, Wallace, Sung, and Williams (2014) described classroom management styles in middle school. They noted how skilled teachers scaffold students' autonomous self-regulatory capacities in a variety of ways, helping them sustain volitional engagement in classroom activities by supporting choice about strategy use and by transferring responsibility to students for shaping the learning context.

It is worth noting that when teachers are autonomy-supportive, they are typically also supportive of the students' needs for competence and relatedness. This is likely true because when teachers are autonomy-supportive they understand the students' perspectives, which then allows them to understand when students need relational and competence supports. Because of this, many studies have found that the outcomes associated with assessments of autonomy support are very similar to those in which support for all three needs are assessed.

Effects of Grading, Evaluations, and Classroom Goals on Motivation and Learning

We have focused thus far on teacher styles as they affect student motivation. Yet there are also structural factors in classrooms that impact student motivation and learning in ways that are often unintended. Two such factors are the effects of grading and evaluations and a focus on goals for normative performance versus growing mastery. We take each of these in turn.

Grading and Evaluations

Grading is a ubiquitous feature of modern classrooms. Unlike learning in life, in which experiments, failures, and risk are all part of the learning process, schooling takes a different tactic: namely, grading and evaluating most everything, using normative comparisons. Most all grading applied is indeed not criterion-based (i.e., based on how well a student has mastered a skill or assimilated material in an absolute sense) but rather is comparative—focused on how a student does relative to others.

Grading is so pervasive in school settings that it has become basically an unquestioned feature of these institutions. It's often hard to even imagine a school without constant normative evaluations, along with the pressures, tears, triumphs, and ego dynamics associated with them. Amazingly there is little by way of good theory that defends this pervasive atmosphere of social comparison, yet there is much scattered evidence concerning negative effects.

SDT has a clear perspective on grading, derived from experimental analyses of motivation. As we specified in Chapters 6 and 7, feedback about performance can have two types of functional significance. The informational aspect provides inputs that affirm success and are relevant to and enhancing of subsequent competence. Controlling aspects of feedback are those that are experienced as pressure toward specific behaviors or outcomes. The message of controlling feedback is generally "do better!" Informational aspects enhance intrinsic motivation and internalization, whereas controlling aspects diminish them.

Realizing how little work had been done on grading, Grolnick and Ryan (1987) experimentally investigated how evaluation and grading might affect motivation and learning outcomes on an ecologically valid school task. Working within a public elementary school sample, the researchers gave fifth-grade students a grade-appropriate textbook passage to read under one of three conditions. In a *nondirected* (ND) condition, they were asked to read the passage and simply rate it for how interesting they found the material. ND students were not expecting to be tested on it and were not under any pressure to learn or perform. A second, non-controlling-directed (NCD) group was told to read the passage and to expect a test on it. Yet they were also told the reading and testing was being done so that the researchers could find out what children learned from the texts and that the children would not be graded on it. A third group was called the controlling-directed (CD) group. They were told what most children expect: namely, that they should read the text and that they would be tested and graded on their performance. This is the motivational status quo in most schools, where motivation is commonly being controlled through a grade contingency. Grolnick and Ryan expected that students in the two noncontrolling groups (ND and NCD) to be most intrinsically motivated for learning, whereas those in the third group who were focused on being graded were expected to feel most controlled and to have the least interest in the material.

Given these conditions, the students then read the material, and all were tested on it, even those in the ND group who had not expected a test. The results indicated, first, that students in the two noncontrolling groups (ND and NCD) experienced more interest in the reading than those whose learning was "controlled" by the grading (CD). Second, the two noncontrolling groups also scored better on the questions that assessed deep, conceptual learning than did those who learned expecting to be evaluated by the test (CD). Third, although the students who expected to be graded did worse on conceptual learning than the two noncontrolling groups, they were just as good at the rote memorization as the non-controlling-directed group and significantly better than the nondirected group. Importantly, however, a follow-up test 1 week later showed that the CD group had actually forgotten more of the facts they had memorized than did those in the other two groups, so the CD group was not better on recall of the rote material at the second testing. In short, the evidence suggested that less focus on grades facilitated students' intrinsic motivation, and deeper conceptual learning.

Kage and Namiki (1990) also examined the links among intrinsic motivation, learning, and grades in Japanese middle school history classes. In this study, all students were given weekly quizzes and then a final exam at the end of the term. In one group, these weekly quizzes were teacher graded, and the grades counted toward their final course grade. In the other group, students graded their own quizzes, but these grades did not count toward their course grade. The idea was to have students in the second group use the quizzes as *informational feedback* (Ryan, 1982), and this was expected to support their intrinsic motivation. Results indicated that, at the end of the term, students who had graded their own quizzes not only found the course more interesting, but they also did better on the final exam than did the students whose weekly quizzes had been graded and recorded by the teacher.

This effect is also not limited to younger students. In an experiment, Benware and Deci (1984) had college students spend about 3 hours learning material from a neurophysiology text. Half were told that they would be tested on their learning; the other half were told they would have the opportunity to put their learning to active use by teaching it to other students. The first condition was expected to prompt low intrinsic motivation because the students would likely feel controlled by the evaluative pressure to pass a test, whereas the second condition was expected to prompt higher intrinsic motivation because it would have provided an opportunity to feel autonomous and competent in actively using the material. All students had studied the same materials, and they were given a questionnaire asking how interesting and enjoyable they had found it. Then they were given an exam testing both rote memorization and conceptual learning of the material, even though only half of them (viz., those in the exam condition) had expected this exam. Results indicated that students who learned in order to be tested found the material less intrinsically interesting and gave worse answers on the conceptual questions than did those who learned expecting to put the material to active use. The two groups were comparable on rote memorization. Thus the results suggest that having students learn in order to be tested is detrimental to their intrinsic motivation and leads to poorer conceptual understanding than having them learn material in order to put it to active use.

Capitalizing on a rare large "natural experiment," Klapp (2015) provided an investigation of the overall effects of grading on student outcomes in subsequent grades. The study specifically looked at how grading or not grading students in primary school affected their achievement (i.e., course grades) in grades 7, 8, and 9, as well as their ultimate achievement outcomes at grade 12. The data came from more than 8,000 Swedish students, some of whom did not receive grades in primary school and some whose schools used traditional grading schemes. Findings revealed a significant negative main effect of grading on subsequent achievement in grades 7–9. The negative effects of grading were especially apparent for low-ability students who, if graded in primary school, had lower odds of finishing their secondary educations compared with ungraded students of similar ability.

Given how grades seem to have negative influence on subsequent outcomes, especially for at-risk students, we might ask why they are so central to how schools work. From our perspective, it is because educators often unwittingly assume that grades are a motivational strategy. They assume that by grading students they are creating an *incentive* system that mobilizes rather than diminishes effort. The naïve reasoning is that grades are like money—if you work hard, you get more. Thus if you receive less, you will be motivated to work harder. Yet that naïve view could not be more incorrect. Do we really believe that a student who receives a bad grade will typically be more motivated to study?

Functionally, grading in educational contexts has two functions. One is providing *competence-relevant feedback* to students, presumably as an aid to enhancing subsequent performance. Ideally, this should have strong informational significance. A second is *gatekeeping*. Grades can be used to make sure that only students who have mastered material and are thus qualified are eligible for higher training or, in more advanced education settings, for professional entry. However, as research by Butler (1987) and our own work discussed above have shown, *grades by themselves* typically provide little competence-relevant feedback. They merely let students know where they stand relative to others, and that focus can deter them from wanting to learn rather than facilitate greater effort or interest.

There do, indeed, seem to be few empirical or theoretical supports for the motivational or competence-building advantages of classical grading schemes. Yet, in most school settings, grades and evaluations are employed as if they were the key to motivation, when, in fact, especially for those who need competence supports, they are likely to be undermining influences. This is a kind of system that would be most useful if the aim were to exclude individuals from a domain, but schools should have the aim of keeping all students, perhaps especially those with lower abilities, engaged rather than deflated.

Although we believe that the gatekeeping function of educators is an important responsibility, gatekeeping is most useful at the end of a process, not as a constant intrusion into it. When the system determines whether, for example, physicians will be licensed, tests may be appropriate and essential to that task. However, it is important to keep clear about the difference between that gatekeeping function and a motivational function.

Of course, tests are not invariantly detrimental to autonomous motivation and deep learning. They can serve an important informational function, providing feedback to students about how well they are doing and where they need to devote more attention and effort in order to improve their learning. However, for tests to be usefully informational, they must be administered within an autonomy-supportive learning climate, and the feedback needs to be informationally useful and formative for the process of learning, rather than being experienced as pressuring, judgmental, or focused on social comparisons.

Performance and Mastery Goals

Related to the pervasiveness of grading and evaluations in schools are the goals that students form in the context of learning and that have effects on both learning quality and experience. An important distinction here is the extent to which students are focused on developing and learning new skills or on doing well relative to others. Typically, an emphasis on grading makes normative concerns and comparisons with others highly salient.

This issue has been widely researched in terms of students who are pursuing either mastery goals or performance goals. *Mastery goals* concern learning in order to enhance your competence or knowledge, whereas *performance goals* focus on performing or doing well relative to others. Furthermore, both mastery and performance goals have been differentiated into approach and avoidance types (Murayama, Elliot, & Friedman, 2012). Substantial empirical evidence has suggested that performance goals, and particularly avoidance goals, are the most detrimental in educational settings for both performance and well-being. Performance approach goals have, in contrast, sometimes been associated with improved academic performance but not with enhanced wellness outcomes. Mastery goals, on the other hand, are generally associated with greater well-being and sometimes with enhanced performance (Elliot, 2005).

Applying SDT's concepts of autonomous and controlled motives to this literature has allowed a fuller understanding of how achievement goal outcomes yield their effects. For example, Vansteenkiste, Smeets, Soenens, Lens, Matos, and Deci (2010) predicted that although goal concepts such as performance-approach goals have been found to predict positive educational outcomes, the motives people have for pursuing these goals may explain these relations. The researchers assessed both the strength of performance-approach goals and the reasons (i.e., autonomous and controlled motives) individuals had for pursuing the goals in order to predict the variance explained by the goal strength and by the autonomous and controlled motives in outcomes such as self-regulated learning, achievement, and cheating. They found that when autonomous and controlled motives were entered into the analyses, these motives significantly predicted outcomes, but the performance-goal strength did not. This indicates that it is primarily the reasons—that is, the autonomous and controlled motives—underlying people's performance-approach goals that account for the differential educational outcomes.

Benita, Roth, and Deci (2014) examined autonomous versus controlled motivations in relation to mastery goals, while also considering the autonomy-supportive versus controlling nature of the classroom context. They found that when students adopted mastery goals in autonomy-supportive contexts, they had more positive emotional experiences than when mastery goals were adopted in controlling contexts. Further, when mastery goals were autonomously motivated, they led to more interest and engagement than when the motives underlying the goals were controlled.

These studies suggest that people's SDT-related motives for pursuing achievement goals are more critical to understanding the goals' effects than are the goals themselves. When discussing the studies, Vansteenkiste, Lens, Elliot, Soenens, and Mouratidis (2014) argued that it is important to limit the concept of achievement goals to the aims people have and then to further examine the autonomous and controlled motives that may underlie those aims.

Gillet, Lafrenière, Huyghebaert, and Fouquereau (2015) arrived at the same conclusion. In their work, they measured six types of achievement goals from the 2 × 3 model, including approach and avoidance crossed with task, self, and other. They also measured participants' autonomous and controlled motives for pursuing the various goals in two educational settings. Results indicated that the motives underlying the goals were stronger predictors of subjective well-being than the goal endorsements themselves.

Together, these studies suggest that, among teachers, behaviors that conduce to students' autonomy are those entailed in creating mastery-oriented environments. Autonomous motivation is more likely when there are enriched possibilities to get feedback and to experience growth and efficacy without the fear of social comparison and ego involvement. In contrast, performance goals, even in their approach forms, have many risks and hazards, even when students are successful.

We should especially remember that classic grading schemes (0–100%; A–F, etc.), which are the most widely used evaluation tactics in education, are experienced as performance-goal structures. When applied in classrooms, these performance goals impact children, and, unlike in many laboratory experiments, many students will not fare well on the comparative metric. For these students, performance goals may undermine not only their autonomy but also their sense of competence and relatedness. Indeed, Pulfrey, Buchs, and Butera (2011) examined what happened to students when they had expectations of being graded. It resulted in being less autonomously motivated and more likely to adopt performance-avoidance goals.

Influences on Autonomy-Supportive Teaching

As mentioned above, many experiments and field studies have now made clear that autonomy-supportive learning climates, which allow students to satisfy their basic psychological needs, have a positive influence on the students' motivation, learning, and psychological adjustment. Both the general orientations of teachers toward autonomy support versus control and specific teacher autonomy-supportive behaviors and vocalizations already discussed play critical roles in the degree to which the learning climate will foster students' autonomous motivation, initiative, engagement, and adjustment at school.

However, for teachers being autonomy-supportive is not always easy; it is not something that simply happens when teachers believe it is the best approach to use with students. These teachers, like the students they teach, are often facing external pressures and performance goals. They sometimes lack autonomy over significant aspects of their curricula and classroom practices. Yet we assert that for teachers to support students' autonomy requires that they be afforded their own autonomy professionally. It is, in fact, a necessary part of the equipment they need for responsive, engaging, teaching.

In a study by Roth, Assor, Kanat-Maymon, and Kaplan (2006), the results indicated that when teachers were autonomously motivated for teaching, so that they, presumably, experienced greater need satisfaction at work, their students perceived them to be more autonomy-supportive. This was then associated with the students being more autonomously motivated for learning. Having teachers experience need satisfaction and be autonomously motivated to teach and having students experience need satisfaction and be autonomously motivated to learn is the optimal situation in classrooms. However, there are a variety of factors in schools that interfere with teachers' need satisfaction, resulting in the teachers being more controlling and the students being less autonomous. One of them is outcome focused pressure or what is often termed "accountability."

Deci, Spiegel, Ryan, Koestner, and Kauffman (1982) did an experiment to test the effects of contextual accountability pressures on the behavior of individuals who were teaching problem-solving skills to students. There were several puzzle problems available for the teachers and students to work with, and the teachers were given some time to familiarize themselves with the problems they would be using in their teaching. They were also provided with a set of hints they could use with the students if they chose to. Half the participants in the experiment were told that, as teachers, it was their responsibility to be sure their students performed up to high standards of performance. There was no mention of performance standards or tests to the other half of the teachers. The teaching sessions were recorded, and the teacher behaviors were analyzed for indicators of teachers' autonomy support versus control.

Results concerning the effects of pressure on the *process* of teaching were especially instructive. They showed that teachers for whom performance standards were highlighted talked approximately five times as much as the other teachers. Further, the vocalizations of these teachers were much more demanding and controlling—that is, they contained many more directives and many more instances of controlling words such as *should* and *have to*. Stated differently, the emphasis on performance standards and accountability led teachers to be more controlling rather than autonomy-supportive. As we have reviewed in this chapter, teachers' controlling styles have been shown to result in poorer learning and adjustment outcomes. The Deci et al. (1982) study also examined performance, and results revealed that students of the teachers for whom standards had been emphasized completed more problems but personally solved fewer. That is, if an observer were simply to count the number of problems completed by the students in the two groups, those in the group with teachers for whom standards had been emphasized *completed* more problems than did students in the other group. However, a careful examination of the teachers' behaviors during the teaching session indicated that teachers in the high-standards condition had given the students the solutions for nearly every problem they completed rather than allowing them time to work independently, trying to solve them. Because of the pressure experienced by the teachers in the accountability condition, they were impatient and told students the correct solutions rather than allowing students time to find the solutions for themselves. In contrast, students of teachers for whom standards were not mentioned *independently solved* five times as many problems as did students in the condition where performance standards had been emphasized to the teaching participants. Finally, objective observers who were blind to the conditions of the experiment were asked how much they would like to be taught by each of the teachers whose tapes they listened to. Findings showed clearly that they would prefer to be taught by the teachers who had not been pressured with accountability.

A study by Flink, Boggiano, and Barrett (1990) in actual elementary schools paralleled these experimental findings. In this field experiment some classroom teachers were given a curriculum with the framing that it was being implemented to raise achievement scores. Other teachers implemented the same curricula, but for them it was presented as an experimental approach, so there was no high stakes pressure. Results showed that teachers who were pressured became more controlling and directive with students, talking more and emphasizing what should be done. An additional finding in this study was that, although the teachers who were pressured were more controlling with students, they were judged by naïve observers to be "better teachers." Combining these results and those from the Deci et al. (1982) study, we see that when teachers are pressured, for example with performance standards, the following are the results: they become more controlling and observers would prefer not to be taught by them, yet observers seem to think that the controlling teachers were better teachers. Unfortunately, they were impressed by the level of teacher activity, not considering that sometimes the more active the teacher, the less active the student.

In other research, Pelletier, Séguin-Lévesque, and Legault (2002) took a different approach to examining the effects of pressure on teachers. They suggested that teachers experience pressure from above (e.g., from accountability standards) and also from below (e.g., from students who are inattentive and unengaged), so the researchers gathered data with questionnaires completed by teachers. Results indicated that both pressures from above and pressures from below negatively predicted teachers' autonomous motivation for teaching and, in turn, their provision of autonomy support to their students. Related work (Fernet, Guay, Senécal, & Austin, 2012) has shown that, when teachers experienced increases in overload and in student disruptive behaviors, the teachers experienced less autonomous motivation for teaching and less perceived competence, and those experiences in turn led to greater emotional exhaustion and less sense of personal accomplishment. Further, work by Bartholomew, Ntoumanis, Cuevas, and Lonsdale (2014) found that the more teachers experienced job pressures, the more they evidenced burnout, and this relation was mediated by frustration of the basic psychological needs. In sum, this set of studies provides confirmation that teachers do require satisfaction of the basic psychological needs and that when the needs are frustrated by thwarting environmental pressures, whether from "above" or "below," the teachers will tend to be more controlling with their students and will also be more likely to experience burnout.

High-Stakes Tests

In recent years, the United States, like many other countries, has placed substantial emphasis on educational achievement. In America, the federal government has been concerned about the country falling behind other countries in the international educational competitions, as assessed with tests such as the *Programme for International Student Assessment* (PISA) in reading literacy and the *Trends in Mathematics and Science Study* (TIMSS), based on beliefs that such scores will predict a country's future standing in international economic competition, itself a questionable assumption (Tienken, 2008). Through various policies it has demanded greater educational accountability from teachers and students. Both federal and state legislation has applied high-stakes incentives and sanctions to scores on standardized achievement tests. Most notable has been federal legislation that requires states to administer tests, the scores of which are then used as the basis for administering the incentives and sanctions. This approach to school reform is based on the view that pressuring teachers and school administrators with accountability demands based on test scores will motivate them to provide better education for their students. The exams are therefore not just sources of information but are *high-stakes tests* (HST): When students perform well on the tests, the students, teachers, schools, and/or districts may be rewarded, and when the students do not perform well, there may be negative consequences at one or more of these levels.

High-stakes reform efforts have been quite controversial, and this has led the U.S. National Academies to create a task force to examine all available research on the topic of incentives and test-based accountability. The final report (Hout & Elliott, 2011) concluded that the achievement tests do not provide an adequate assessment of students' learning, that incentives encourage teachers to focus narrowly on the material expected to appear on the tests, and that, based on many randomized trials (e.g., Springer et al., 2010), test-based incentive programs have had essentially no positive effects on achievement. In short, the high-stakes approach applied to schools and teachers was judged to have failed to live up to expectations as an approach to school reform. Further, studies of the use of incentives given directly to students or their families based on the students' achievement have also been found on average to have no positive effect (Fryer, 2011), even as they have been lauded in popular media.

Further, as predicted by SDT (see e.g., Ryan & La Guardia, 1999), there have been a variety of unintended negative consequences from HST policies (e.g., Nichols & Berliner, 2007). Student dropout has increased in numerous places in spite of the fact that districts and schools fail to record and report many of the dropouts that do occur. Districts have engaged in highly questionable practices, such as *not* allowing some students to take the high-stakes tests because they are expected to lower the schools' or districts' scores and, even worse, changing students' answers on the tests or reporting false information related to student performance. It has also been found that in some states improved test scores do not generalize to other, more valid standardized tests, such as the National Assessment of Educational Progress (NAEP) exams that were designed to provide information that is wholly independent of high stakes for any of the relevant parties.

As well, the high-stakes system is amotivating for the people who have not performed competently within it. For people to be motivated, they have to believe it is possible for them to successfully negotiate the system, doing well educationally and obtaining satisfactory employment. Focusing on incentive-based accountability for test scores, rather than supporting other, more promising school reform models that are attentive to the psychological needs of teachers and students (e.g., Deci, 2009), would be a much poorer way of reaching and supporting the disadvantaged students (Greene & Winters, 2005; U.S. Department of Education, 2006).

We have long provided clear motivational accounts of why HST reward- and sanction-focused programs have failed (e.g., Ryan & Brown, 2005). An abundance of research reviewed in this and other chapters of the book makes clear that educational policies and practices that facilitate autonomous motivation—both intrinsic motivation and well-internalized extrinsic motivation—are the ones that promote deep learning and psychological adjustment. As such, our criteria for judging policies and practices concern the degree to which they support autonomous motivation and, in turn, improve learning and adjustment. In considering the relation of SDT research to HST, we have seen, first, that a strong emphasis on accountability results in people being more controlling (Deci et al., 1982). In the case of HST programs, school administrators are likely to experience the tests as pressuring, which will lead them to be more controlling with teachers. That, in turn, will lead teachers to be more controlling with students, which tends to undermine rather than enhance students' autonomous motivation and conceptual learning. Research on evaluation (e.g., Harackiewicz, Abrahams, & Wageman, 1987; Smith, 1975) suggested that the evaluations implicit in the HST would also tend to undermine autonomy even when the evaluations lead to positive performance feedback.

Further, HST are associated with rewards and punishment threats, whether directly or indirectly, and many studies have confirmed that working to earn rewards or avoid punishments has negative consequences for autonomous motivation (e.g., Deci, Koestner, & Ryan, 2001). It is also the case that when people work for rewards but fail to receive them, the people are likely to evidence even greater decrements than those who get the rewards they work for. In the case of HST, there are some districts, schools, and classrooms that fail to live up to standards; they do not receive rewards but instead receive negative feedback and possibly sanctions, which have been found to yield negative consequences for motivation, learning, and psychological adjustment.

In Chapter 6 we also reviewed research that suggested that *outcome-focused rewards* lead to a tendency in people to take the shortest path to those rewards. Teaching to the test is one of those shorter routes. It typically requires focusing exclusively on material that will likely be on the test, and on providing specific training for test formats and response styles, crowding out more process-focused, responsive teaching. Outcome-focused, controlling pressures can also lead in extreme cases to cheating or illegal behaviors. Lonky and Reihman (1990) found, for example, that college students who were in a controlling context were more likely to cheat on a verbal reasoning task. Anecdotal evidence has certainly pointed to a relation between HST and cheating as well. For example, the Georgia Bureau of Investigation in 2011 reported that a large number of schools in the Atlanta Public School District had cheated on a 2009 high stakes exam (Flock, 2011). Teachers and administrators alike reportedly corrected answers entered by students to inflate their school's scores. Sadly it is not the first instance of such cheating connected with HST policies (e.g., Hoff, 2000; Johnston, 1999).

Although our comments here focused on HST in the United States, as we mentioned, HST has been an issue around the globe. Chinese education is, for example, dominated by *gaokao,* or the *National Higher Education Entrance Examination,* which is a form of HST focused primarily on the students rather than the teachers or schools. The strong emphasis on this single exam leads, as we have suggested with other HST policies, to teaching to the test, to excessive stress, and to the crowding out of intrinsic motivation within school learning (Sun, Dunne, Hou, & Xu, 2013).

In sum, although HST takes different forms, to the extent that they are formulated so as to extrinsically reward a narrow set of performances they interfere with more holistic and autonomy-supportive approaches to the development of student interests and capabilities and with deeper forms of learning and overall student wellness.

Making Schools Places That Promote Flourishing

Educational reforms that revolve around HST will likely not be successful in promoting engagement, learning, and well-being. The nature of these approaches is control, and control serves to thwart teachers' and students' basic psychological needs, undermining sustained volitional engagement of teachers and students and diminishing deep learning. The research discussed already suggests that a more promising focus of change would be on creating social contexts across all levels of a school system, from students and parents, to staff and administrators, that support autonomous engagement, along with competence and community of all stakeholders. Thus far few school reform efforts have focused on such multi-level context changes. Still fewer have specifically focused on improving basic need supports as the strategy for leveraging better achievement and completion outcomes.

Instructively we participated in the external evaluation of a large-scale school reform project that took place in some of the poorest and most challenged school districts in the

United States (Early et al., 2016). This was a randomized control trial at the level of high schools, in which the intervention involved training and supporting teachers, and the trial compared math and English progress in intervention versus control schools (randomized within district). The intervention, called *Every Classroom Everyday* (ECED), was focused on enhancing classroom process, particularly on increasing the rigor of teaching, the alignment of curricula with educators' goals, and most important—from our SDT perspective—creating more engaging classroom settings. Results of this intervention demonstrated that, even in challenging schools, achievement outcomes could be raised through concerted system-level efforts. Most interesting to us was that the most predictive element in positive change was increased engagement in classes, which appeared to be the most active ingredient in positive achievement trajectories (Early, Rogge, & Deci, 2014).

Professionalization and Training

Given the importance of classroom process, it is noteworthy that two of the most reliable top performers in international achievement comparisons (however questionable those criteria) are Finland and Singapore. Despite massive differences in curricular approaches, they have one important thing in common: They treat and train their teachers as professionals. These nations have invested in higher salaries and in higher-quality training, so as to recruit the best and brightest, and help them internalize and develop effective classroom practices. In turn, the more competent and professional the population of teachers, the more they can be expected to benefit from, and make good use of, professional autonomy.

Great teaching will not derive from pressuring teachers towards narrowly defined test outcomes but rather by orienting educators toward, and making them accountable for, creating and implementing effective, evidence supported classroom *processes*. Rather than aiming at outcomes, training and evaluation would focus on the best educational strategies and materials being put to use, and their effect on the drivers of motivation and accomplishment, namely experiences of autonomy, competence, and relatedness in the classroom.

In addition, the scope of accountability should be broader than mere cognitive goals. We reiterate that schools are *contexts for human development*. Socioemotional growth is impacted by classroom climate and evaluations, and in turn it affects both student achievement and well-being outcomes, as much evidence we reviewed in this chapter attests. Care for students' basic psychological needs thus warrants increased attention in setting educational policies, goals, and training, given its important role in shaping students' aspirations, motivations, and performance.

Several studies have examined whether directly training teachers or supervisors to be more autonomy-supportive is effective in creating greater engagement and learning. For example, Reeve, Jang, Carrell, Barch, and Jeon (2004) trained classroom teachers to incorporate autonomy support into their teaching styles. Subsequently, well-trained observers did three classroom observations in the classes of both the trained teachers and a control group of teachers and rated the degree of teachers' autonomy support and students' engagement in their classes. Results indicated that the trained teachers displayed significantly more autonomy-supportive behaviors than the control-group teachers and, furthermore, that the students in the classes of the trained teachers were more engaged in their learning than were the students in the control-group classes.

A subsequent study by Edmunds, Ntoumanis, and Duda (2008) employed an intervention in which the trainers in some exercise classes used a more autonomy-supportive teaching style, whereas others used more conventional styles in their teaching. The researchers found that the teachers trained in autonomy-supportive teaching had significantly greater increases in structure and interpersonal involvement, as well as competence and relatedness need satisfaction, and positive affect. Additionally, in a study concerning supervisors and their employees, Hardré and Reeve (2009) used a training intervention intended to facilitate greater autonomy support among the supervisors. Five weeks later, they found that the trained supervisors did display a significantly more autonomy-supportive style than those who were untrained and, further, that the individuals supervised by those who had been trained displayed more autonomous motivation and workplace engagement than those who had not received the intervention. Thus these studies indicate that both administrators and teachers can be trained to be more mindful of the needs of their employees and students and that the more autonomy-supportive the supervisors and teachers are, the more positive will be the consequences for their employees and students.

Su and Reeve (2011) identified 19 studies in which authorities had been trained to be autonomy-supportive. The researchers performed a meta-analytic review of these studies to determine whether the autonomy-supportive interventions intended to help teachers and supervisors would be effective toward that end. The results indicated that, indeed, on average across studies, there was a large effect size (0.63) improvement for the intervention groups becoming more autonomy-supportive relative to the control groups, with autonomy support being assessed with either perceptions of the students or employees or ratings by trained observers.

Other researchers have implemented a more extensive SDT-based reform approach that involved training teachers to be more autonomy-supportive, along with other reform elements. This was done in three Israeli elementary schools that were experiencing a high level of violence and were thus concerned about promoting more friendly interactions among their students (Assor, Kaplan, Feinberg, & Tal, 2009; Feinberg, Kaplan, Assor, & Kanat-Maymon, 2007). The reform began with didactic meetings in which the school administrators and teachers were introduced to the basic principles of SDT. The investigators then assessed the degree of need satisfaction among teachers and students in the schools as a first step in laying out the change process. There was considerable discussion about basic psychological needs and the importance of their satisfaction, and each school developed a unique change plan that resulted from discussions of teachers and administrators with the change agents. The final step involved the change agents' supporting the staff members' basic needs during implementation of the plans they had devised. This reform method is very much a bottom-up approach in which the change agents facilitate the teachers' participation in all decisions that influence them and that are pertinent to the school. Thus the approach involves a high degree of staff ownership right from the beginning, and the plans allow staff members to continue making changes as problems arise. As such, the school staff members are really directing the planning and implementation of the reform, based on their understanding of SDT and its applications, so they are likely to be highly autonomously motivated to implement it and to experience satisfaction of their basic psychological needs as they do.

An evaluation project conducted in the intervention and comparison schools over a 3-year period showed significant changes in the intervention schools relative to the control-group schools. Intervention-group teachers reported feeling more empathic toward their students' needs and feeling better about themselves as teachers. They also displayed increased limit setting on violence. Further, there was reduced violence among the students, and there were increases in students' perceptions of the friendliness and caring within their classrooms. In short, by focusing on need satisfaction of the teachers and students, the schools were able to greatly improve the experiences of those who taught and learned within the schools.

The Umbrella Effect

Political and social demands often place educators in a difficult position—pressuring them toward practices that they know are not optimal for the well-being and future learning of their students. Administrators, too, are often under pressures to make demands on teachers that will not improve the quality of their practice. And teachers often feel constrained from best practice in the service of teaching to tests. In fact, in many countries today conversations with educators are far too often about these external influences crowding out optimal teaching and learning practices.

Research has suggested, however, that individuals can make a difference to those around them. At a local level, when superintendents, principals, or teachers acknowledge and consider the perspectives of the people whom they supervise or teach, and they empower them as much as possible in their activities, they have made the first important steps in providing a need-supportive environment. Individuals can change the outcomes of those with whom they work, even in the context of the political storms surrounding education. We call this the "umbrella effect." As professional educators our first job is not to let the elements harm those for whom we are responsible. Thus we need to hold up an umbrella of need supports and create a sheltered, nurturing educational environment.

Central to nurturing educational environments is autonomy support because taking the internal frames of reference of those with whom they are working or learning allows for more understanding and responsiveness to the obstacles, desires, and needs pertinent to motivation. Beyond this, autonomy-supportive leaders encourage self-initiation and exploration, offer opportunities for choice, provide meaningful rationales when asking others to do something, refrain from using controlling language, and provide constructive feedback among other supports. All of these grow out of a learner-centered, indeed, person-centered, approach to constructing and managing the educational environment, which by its nature requires an atmosphere of openness, inquiry, and choice. Policy makers, educators, and parents alike, no matter what pressures they experience from "above" or "below," can thus strive to provide an umbrella of need-support as a personal approach to positive educational change.

Concluding Comments

Application of the principles of SDT to education focuses on facilitating satisfaction of the basic psychological needs of teachers and students in order for the schools to be places in which all parties can be more autonomously motivated and empowered to engage in their activities. The primary focus is student flourishing—that is, not only growing in cognitive skills and knowledge but also developing and strengthening personal and social skills and experiencing psychological health and well-being in the process.

SDT has generated an enormous amount of educational research, in school settings ranging from elementary to postbaccalaureate. Among the more important and frequently replicated findings is that the provision of autonomy support by both teachers and parents helps students maintain intrinsic motivation for learning and develop more fully internalized extrinsic motivation for their schoolwork. In turn, autonomous motivation enhances both learning quality and psychological wellness. This pattern of findings has been relatively consistent across all ages of students and across diverse cultures, including Western cultures that tend to be individualistic and Eastern cultures that tend to be more collectivistic.

We also looked at grading and achievement goals in educational settings. We found that despite the pervasive use of grades as motivators for student learning, they are often more problematic than helpful. We especially distinguished the informational versus controlling elements of grading and suggested that it is largely the controlling aspect that is salient to students, especially because grading is often more comparative than effectance-relevant in its functional significance. We then discussed achievement goals that are connected with such evaluative systems. Although the literature tends to suggest that mastery goals (doing better than previously) are associated with more positive outcomes than performance goals, the effects of all types of achievement goals are heavily accounted for by the autonomous versus controlled motives underpinning them.

Studies have also indicated that when teachers are pressured from above (e.g., with an accountability emphasis) or from below (e.g., from disengaged students), the teachers tend to become less supportive of the students' autonomy and basic needs. This of course has negative, rather than positive, ramifications for the students' motivation and experience. Such findings help to explain why research has indicated that high stakes testing policies have had a broad range of negative effects on teachers and students alike. Finally, we discussed school-reform approaches that have employed the principles of SDT. Educational models and policies that aim to facilitate satisfaction of the basic psychological needs of students and teachers, thus creating positive changes not only in students' and teachers' motivations and experiences, are most likely to optimize both achievement and broader developmental outcomes.

CHAPTER 15

Identity Development, Self-Esteem, and Authenticity

A major developmental task that has become especially complex in postmodern contexts is that of selecting and enacting personal identities. Although many psychologists equate the concepts of *identity* and *self,* SDT maintains that people have multiple identities, each of which may be more or less fully integrated within the self. People's identities represent the *self-as-object* or the "me" self—that is, the concepts that people hold about themselves and that represent their affiliations, vocations, interests, and beliefs. SDT examines the extent to which the adoption of any given identity is autonomous (e.g., integrated) or controlled (e.g., introjected) and the degree to which need satisfaction versus frustration is associated with adopting particular identities. SDT argues that developmental conditions of basic psychological need support help adolescents develop the inner resources to more autonomously explore and ultimately commit to identities, whereas controlled contexts can forestall, constrain, or rigidify the identity formation process and often catalyze defensive processes surrounding identity. Extending these considerations, we argue that the way the individual internalizes self-concepts and identities is directly linked to the dynamics of *self-esteem,* or evaluative self-worth. SDT differentiates *contingent self-esteem* from *true self-esteem,* and research points to *parental conditional regard* as an antecedent of contingent self-esteem. Finally, we discuss *authenticity* as an expression of integrated identity and the pressures that lead people to adopt self-concepts and beliefs that are not well integrated. The *dualistic model of passion* exemplifies these SDT-based distinctions: Harmonious passions and obsessive passions represent identities that are autonomously regulated or controlled, respectively.

Most of the research we have reviewed up to this point has concerned the *self-as-process,* as this synthetic concept of self is among SDT's most central constructs. As we pointed out in Chapter 3, there are two major Western traditions concerning the self, which we characterized as (1) the tradition of *self-as-process,* which concerns the self as a synthetic and integrative function; and (2) the tradition of *self-as-object,* in which the focus is on people's perceptions and beliefs *about* themselves and the factors that shape the self-concepts people acquire. In this chapter, we consider more deeply how our SDT self-as-process focus interacts with the self-as-object, or *me-self.*

The SDT perspective suggests that, like all aspects of social learning, self-representations, self-concepts, and identities are adopted, elaborated, and integrated to varying degrees. People, that is, internalize and integrate social identities and self-evaluative beliefs to a greater or lesser extent. This, in turn, affects the quality of motivation supporting any given identity and the basic psychological satisfactions and conflicts it may yield. Some identities allow the individual to most fully actualize her or his potentials and richly experience basic need satisfactions, whereas others, being less fitting with either the person or her or his culture, result in compromised autonomy and diminished wellness. It is this dynamic we explore.

Self and Identity in the 21st Century

I am a patriot. A heterosexual. A nurse. An introvert. A sports fan. A poor student. A musician. A mother. An orthodox _____ (fill in the blank). These are but a few examples of ways that people might identify themselves, and these would each represent an identity. As Erikson (1959) recognized, asserting an identity expresses both an ownership of some self-characteristic and a commonality with others who share the attribute. Identities are both individuating and enmeshing. They connect people to some institutions and social groups and separate them from others. Identities can also cohere or conflict, both practically and intrapsychically (e.g., it is currently hard to be both gay and Mormon). Maintaining and preserving such identities, even negative ones, can also be a strong motivator of behaviors (Swann, 1983), and identities often orient and guide people's learning, behavior, and friendships (Ryan & Deci, 2012; Vallerand, 2015).

Unlike the self-as-process, which is part of our native equipment, identities are acquired through experience. Newborns are not yet, at least in any internal, psychological sense, defined by their religious identifications, political views, gender or sex roles, core interests, or group affiliations. Yet immediately others will begin to ascribe such categories and characteristics to them, and as development progresses, there will be social pressures on them to accept some identities and steer away from others. Importantly, from our organismic viewpoint, however, these pressures toward or away from particular identities are *not* exclusively external. There are pushes from *within*—that is, spontaneous leanings toward some activities and identities and repulsion toward others. Dispositions within the individual bring his or her own unique (if too often faint and unheard) voice to identity formation. Thus, throughout development, as social identities are modeled, imposed, discovered, and explored, the individual's integrative propensities are always under the influence of both cultural and dispositional factors. The resulting synthesis is the relative acceptance and integration of some identities and the modification or rejection of others, a process labeled *identity formation* (Soenens & Vansteenkiste, 2011).

This interplay of outer and inner pressures is what makes identity formation such an important focus of SDT research. In forming an identity, an individual is negotiating an intersection of autonomy within relatedness. Successfully internalized, identities can support a sense of belonging, as well as provide activities and social roles the person can endorse and from which she or he can derive satisfaction. Yet, if acquired less optimally, a person's identities can fail to provide either authentic meaning or deep connections, and thus they serve as poor vehicles for a flourishing life.

The very idea that identities—nationalisms, political views, religious affiliations, and even gender and sexual roles—can be more or less autonomously accepted by the individual is itself a radical, even postmodern idea. In earlier times, opportunities to make autonomous choices about what identities to take on were limited by both laws and traditions and were highly constrained toward vertical identities—that is, those inherited from parents. With modernity has come increasing legal rights and opportunities of persons to reflectively select and adopt identities, and there has been greater acceptance of individuals' rights to form the varied identities they choose. There is even international pressure on every nation state to guarantee individuals certain rights to decide their own affiliations and identities (Franck, 2001).

For many people, this increased fluidity and opportunity for choice and divergence affords the potential to live in ways better matched with their interests, talents, and sensibilities. People differ, and the opportunity to have a wide range of choices can help each person find roles that are actualizing. Indeed, diversity of dispositions, talents, and interests is, as Appiah (2005) stated, an "anterior fact about human beings, which must be accommodated by a society conducive to their well-being" (p. 142). Increased fluidity and choice support such diversity and its expression (Solomon, 2012).

However, some writers have emphasized the downsides of mobility and choice in identities. Simply having to choose from among the multiple options is, for many, a struggle (S. J. Schwartz et al., 2011). B. Schwartz (2000) even argued that "self-determination," interpreted by him as a wide range of identity choices, represents a "tyranny" because of its presumed psychological burdens (see also B. Schwartz, 2010).

Of course, both of these positions have some prima facie evidence in their favor. The life narratives of many individuals describe a process of discovery in which they identified with new beliefs or vocations that were not prescribed for them and who felt liberated and actualized because of taking a divergent path (Bauer, McAdams, & Sakaeda, 2005). Solomon (2012) described how finding social support for such horizontal identities (e.g., identities that are unrelated to, or not expected by, parents), is often especially edifying and meaningful. Yet it is equally easy to find persons who are anomic, unable to locate themselves meaningfully within existing societal roles, labels, and structures—a situation of disaffection once aptly described by Goodman (1960) as "growing up absurd." In short, there seems to be an ever-expanding set of options and models available for people to accept as identities and fewer identity constraints, posing both promise and perils for development.

Having to choose identities (including acceptance of cultural defaults) is thus among the most formidable developmental challenges that modern people face. Moreover, developmentally, the heavy lifting of identity formation occurs in adolescent and early adult years, as individuals are attempting to form pathways toward careers, affiliations, and relationships that might organize and guide an ongoing and satisfying life (Adams & Marshall, 1996; Berzonsky, 1990; S. J. Schwartz, 2001). Adolescence is also a period when one is particularly vulnerable to external forces (Soenens, Berzonsky, Vansteenkiste, Beyers, & Goossens, 2005). With the emergence of adolescent egocentrism and self-consciousness (Elkind, 1985), teens tend to see themselves in ways they project or imagine others see them, and they also show a greater tendency to conform in order to be accepted by those others (Ryan & Kuczkowski, 1994). Thus, just as they are attempting to formulate a sense of their "own" identities, they are also struggling with real and imagined social pressures from many external sources, including not only peers but also parents, teachers, and various role models.

Adding to this, all people, but perhaps especially adolescents, are today vulnerable to the multiple external influences of corporately driven media with tremendous reach and power, which attempt to orient people toward particular types of identities and values. For example, in our increasingly global market economies, advertisers and social leaders can reach into the lives of individuals around the clock through mass media and well-crafted imaging (Dittmar, 2008; Kasser, 2002a). They encourage people to define themselves in terms of the clothes they wear, the products they purchase, the celebrities they idolize, and other such commodity-based identities that are visible to others.

Although identity issues are highlighted in adolescence, struggles of identity persist across the lifespan. Identity shifts may, in fact, be more common in the adult years in postmodern cultural contexts than ever in history. The options available for people's identities are greater, as is access to like-minded people with whom they can affiliate. Even fringe identities can find community on the Internet. This combines with fewer of the constraints that have historically channeled people into preordained or "vertical" identities and more rapidly shifting cultural, social class, and religious trends that can loosen or disrupt identities based in older values and perspectives (Ryan & Deci, 2012).

Although pervasive and spreading, this postmodern latitude in identity formation is not equally accepted across the globe or available to all. In many places, there is an ongoing struggle between those attempting to conserve traditional cultural roles, sometimes even through oppression and control, and liberalism with its support for diversity (Appiah, 2005; Franck, 2001). For example, in some cultures, a woman would not have the right to become an athlete, no matter how fitting or how well matched that role might be for her, and she may even be explicitly blocked from such pursuits. She would lack supports for her autonomy and competence as she shows interest in sport. Some social environments may even actively oppress identities. A gay person growing up in any one of a dozen countries in the Middle East or Africa today, where homosexuality can receive lashings or the death penalty, will not readily lay claim to that sexual identity. These examples show that the identity struggle for some people is not only one of finding congruent roles and ideals, but also finding ways of suppressing or concealing potentially authentic aspects of themselves because of controlling external circumstances.

An SDT Approach to Identity Formation

From the perspective of SDT, the formation of identity can best be understood in terms of the concepts of basic psychological needs and organismic integration (Ryan, Deci, & Vansteenkiste, 2016). We propose that (1) people develop identities in an attempt to satisfy their needs for relatedness, competence, and autonomy and (2) the degree to which they experience need satisfaction while forming identities has a strong influence on both the content of those identities and the way they are anchored in the people's psyches.

Specifically, because identities are formed under the dual influences of individual diversities and cultural affordances, the form and degree to which they are internalized will vary. These variations are expected to be a function largely of the basic need supports and satisfactions that individuals experience while exploring and enacting new identities. Second, as noted, SDT sees identities as numerous: One has multiple identities that are more versus less integrated within a single self (Ryan & Deci, 2012). Along with this assumption is the view that identities also tend to be dynamic and fluid, especially during these formative years. Although identity is often thought of as an enduring aspect of persons, in the SDT perspective a person's ownership of varied identities is expected to vary among social contexts, precisely because of the varying relations between the person's self-presentations and the experienced supports or thwarts to need satisfaction that pertain in those various contexts. Thus, as we will see later in the chapter, people conceal certain identities and personal characteristics or highlight them as a function of the interpersonal context they happen to be in. Of course, some people will shift more than others, issues that we address in terms of both the contextual supports for individuals' self-expressions and the individuals' resilience to and flexibility in the face of controlling influences.

Identities and Need Satisfaction

Central to the process of accepting identities are people's inherent desires to experience *relatedness* to individuals, groups, or cultures. By accepting the values, mores, missions, attitudes, and behaviors of others, people feel a sense of connectedness rather than aloneness. That is, they feel part of a group, experiencing a sense of relatedness to others (Ryan, 1993) and belongingness within the social order (Baumeister & Leary, 1995; Ryff, 1995). Further, identities can also support the need for *competence*. Often people orient toward identities—perhaps being a painter or physicist, for example—that require skill acquisition, offer optimal challenges, and allow them to feel effective. Finally, the formation of identities can fulfill people's need for *autonomy* if they engage the relevant activities as an expression of their values and interests and experience a sense of choice while doing so. In short, people tend to gravitate toward those identities that allow maximal satisfaction of their basic psychological needs.

However, many social contexts are controlling, rejecting, or stigmatizing of certain identities, values, and roles. As a result, people sometimes end up adopting identities that have a less authentic fit, and that, especially in need-thwarting contexts, have a perhaps darker and more self-destructive nature. Identities and their associated value systems can, that is, serve a defensive function, being pursued simply in order to appear worthy and gain social acceptance from others or to compensate for insecurities or thwarted need satisfactions (e.g., Cozzolino, Staples, Meyers, & Samboceti, 2004; Kasser, Ryan, Zax, & Sameroff, 1995).

Anchoring Identities within the Self

What is clear from these considerations is that identities are differentially anchored within persons. SDT suggests that there are two interrelated means through which identities form and, to differing degrees, become integrated within self-functioning. The first is through the discovery and differentiation of intrinsic interests and talents, and the second is through the internalization of values and roles.

People manifest individual differences in their competencies, interests, and inclinations. Some children seem inclined, for example, toward music, and others perhaps toward physical activity. These inclinations can be a starting point, a seed, for identities, but the forms that such inclinations take in people's lives are in part a function of the people's interactions with the social world concerning activities that relate to the inclinations. For example, someone inclined toward music might become a singer or a trombone player, focusing on classical or pop music, depending in part on opportunities available and the interests of others within their social contexts. Such inclinations increase the likelihood that the activities will become important parts of the individual's identities (Deci & Ryan, 1985b). As people with strong interests gravitate toward others with similar interests, the activities, values, and relationships associated with those interests become central aspects of the people's lives, as their relatedness needs are satisfied. They may also experience greater competence satisfaction as they get affirmation from their peers, further enhancing their interests in the activities. In other words, people are fortunate when they adopt identities that reflect their intrinsic interests (Krapp, 2002; Soenens & Vansteenkiste, 2011; Waterman, 1993).

Still, for identities to develop out of intrinsic inclinations and to become important aspects of the person's self requires both affordances and social supports. That is, the development of an identity depends to some extent on the cultural affordances available to the person (Erikson, 1994). SDT specifically suggests that those affordances include not only exposure, but also autonomy, competence, and relatedness supports. Of course, this is true for identities in every domain, whether it be related to academics, religion, sports, family, or work, especially because the very construct of identity is social in nature.

Yet few identities emerge and are sustained solely out of intrinsic interests. Instead, most are taken on or elaborated through processes of internalization. As we saw in Chapter 8 and elsewhere, internalizations can take multiple forms that differ in the degree to which they are integrated with the self. When an identity is accepted within the context of pressure and control, it is likely to be introjected. The person will take it on as a "should"; something he or she must do. Often in college settings, for example, one finds individuals who identify as "pre-med" because their parents have always expected them to be doctors, irrespective of their actual interests or predilections. In that case, the young persons' feelings of worth may depend on the enactment of this identity. Such identities can be central to people's self-concepts or self-as-object definitions. As such, identities can be powerful motivators of identity-consistent behaviors. Nonetheless, for an identity to become autonomously engaged, the internalization will have to be more complete. To be both authentic and vital in the pursuit of an identity, people have to integrate the particular identity with their other identities, needs, values, beliefs, behaviors, and interests.

Consider, for example, that a majority of Americans identify themselves as Christians. Among them, however, there is considerable variability in the extent to which that identity has been introjected versus more truly integrated (Ryan, Rigby, & King, 1993). It is, in fact, not hard to find Christians for whom the label is merely skin deep and describes little of what they really value or do. Just as readily, one can also find individuals for whom being Christian deeply characterizes their abiding concerns and day-to-day values and lifestyles. As shown by Ryan et al. (1993), those who have more fully internalized and assimilated their religious beliefs tend to have higher participation rates and greater well-being. Other research shows that they also tend to be both more open and less literal in their interpretation of the religion (Neyrinck, Vansteenkiste, Lens, Duriez, & Hutsebaut, 2006). In fact, whatever the identity—be it social activist, tennis club member, New York Giants fan, Democrat, or what have you—the following principle will apply: These identities will vary in the degree to which they are assimilated and integrated to the self of the individual, and there will be consequences for enacting that identity and for well-being as a function of the degree of integration.

Soenens, Berzonsky, Dunkel, Papini, and Vansteenkiste (2011) recently tested this idea using a sample of older adolescents. They assessed each adolescent's identity commitments and the autonomous versus controlled motives that were associated with them. Identity commitments are aspects of the self-as-object, whereas their relative autonomy reflects the dynamics of self-as-process. The findings by Soenens et al. revealed that even when controlling for the *strength* of identity commitments, those that were autonomously motivated were associated with more positive adjustment. In contrast, controlled identity commitments were predictive of poorer adjustment.

As already noted, healthy identities may be based in intrinsic interests or in the internalized regulation of a set of behaviors, commitments, and self-representations that are more or less well integrated. Accordingly, a need-supportive environment is important in the process of identity formation. As outlined by Soenens and Vansteenkiste (2011), although many theories adopt the "standard social science model" of human plasticity (see Tooby & Cosmides, 1992) and thus view identities as entirely constructed, the SDT perspective views identity formation as equally a process of self-discovery and growth—that is, an ongoing attempt to find life roles and self-definitions that are congruent with their predispositions, interests, and integrated values and that will thus afford need satisfaction and support flourishing.

Integrating Identities

Critical to optimizing the process of discovery and pursuit of intrinsic interests as a basis for identity formation is support for satisfactions of the basic psychological needs. Indeed, need satisfactions facilitate self-discovery and, in turn, a healthy process of identity formation facilitates need satisfactions, thus representing a reciprocal and dynamic process. Research by Luyckx, Vansteenkiste, Goossens, and Duriez (2009) illustrated this model in two studies involving high school and college students. Specifically, they focused on *identity dimensions,* representing the extent of exploration, commitment, and ruminative thought concerning the directions these young people would take in life. Results showed that satisfaction of basic psychological needs was in general positively related to more fully committing to particular identities and to enhanced breadth and depth of identity explorations. Those with less consolidated identity commitments and those who were more ruminative showed less basic need satisfaction. Cross-lagged correlation analyses suggested further that these effects were reciprocal: Need satisfaction facilitated more positive identity formation, and more positive identity formation facilitated greater need satisfaction.

Soenens, Berzonsky, et al. (2005) related Berzonsky's (1990) *identity style model* to individual differences in the causality orientations of students between 17 and 25 years of age. The identity styles model describes three routes or strategies for forming identities. An *information style* describes individuals who seek out self-relevant information and critically evaluate the fit of life roles with their own characteristics and interests. A *normative style* typifies adolescents who rely on the expectations and prescriptions of significant others. They are often closed to contrary information and may engage with identity challenges and threats more defensively. Finally, there is a *diffuse/avoidant style,* in which the individuals try to avoid or delay life decisions and commitments, resulting in a fragmented identity formation process and an absence of solid life goals and directions. Relations with causality orientations were clear. Autonomous causality orientations were positively associated with information styles and negatively with diffuse/avoidant styles; controlled orientations were positively associated with the normative identity styles; and impersonal causality orientations were positively correlated with the diffuse/avoidant styles. These predictive patterns underscore both that identity formation is a motivated process and that it matters what quality of motivational orientation is brought to this developmental process.

Educational settings can play a significant role in identity formation. For example, Madjar and Cohen-Malayev (2013) hypothesized and found across two studies that when adolescents perceived their educational contexts as more supportive of autonomy and exploration, they also evidenced more age-appropriate identity development. These findings are consistent with previous developmental research in this area (Luyckx, et al., 2009; Smits, Soenens, Vansteenkiste, Luyckx, & Goossens, 2010). Madjar and Cohen-Malayev further highlighted the importance of informal education contexts, which were generally perceived by teens as more supportive and which also accounted for a larger portion of the variance in identity formation than formal education settings. These researchers suggested that formal educators might be more influential in helping to promote healthy identity formation if they embraced more opportunities for reflection concerning adolescents' future plans, social roles, and self-identities.

Developing an Inner Compass

Assor, Roth, and their colleagues have suggested that both moral development and identity formation involve inner resources within the developing child, resources that will allow the child to seek and regulate in accordance with what is authentic for her or him. They refer to these inner resources as the *inner compass*—an orientation toward and capacity to be authentic in one's choices and behaviors. An inner compass reflects a personal knowing of whether or not a given behavior or value is truly congruent and self-endorsed. It is thus an important part of making behavioral decisions with moral implications, especially when there may be divergent forces operating. The healthy development of an inner compass is expected to be facilitated by *parental autonomy support*—that is, by parents being receptive and empathic, allowing the child to access inner states without losing positive regard and supporting the identification of feelings and needs (Roth, Assor, Niemiec, Ryan, & Deci, 2009). Yet beyond autonomy support, these researchers have suggested that parental modeling of identities and morals—what they call *intrinsic value demonstrations*—are an important influence. It is the child seeing the parents (or other important socializing adult figures) acting congruently to enact what they value that helps the child develop his or her own inner compass and capacity to act with integrity.

In a preliminary study, Roth and Assor (1999) asked Israeli college students to rate the degree to which their parents demonstrated an intrinsic value for prosocial activities. The more parents showed such intrinsic value demonstrations (e.g., parents who volunteered or showed care and concern for others), the more the students were themselves identified with prosocial values, and the more they reported engaging in prosocial activities. Roth et al. (2009), in a subsequent study, assessed Israeli adolescents concerning their parents' approach to activities such as studying and learning. The findings revealed that adolescents' perceptions of their parents as using autonomy-supportive techniques and demonstrating intrinsic valuing of learning and knowledge predicted the adolescents' feeling greater choice with regard to studying and, in turn, teacher ratings of the students' interest-focused engagement in learning.

Providing yet further support for this model, Brambilla, Assor, Manzi, and Regalia (2015) studied Italian Catholic youth groups as they internalized religiosity. The researchers found that intrinsic value demonstrations by parents and autonomy support from parents and youth group leaders all contributed to more autonomous identification with religiosity. Yu, Assor, and Liu (2015) further showed that the self-congruence and subjective well-being of Chinese youths were predicted by the intrinsic value demonstrations of both parents, even when controlling for the effects of autonomy-supportive practices, which also predicted their congruence and subjective well-being, as SDT would predict.

These and other emerging studies of the inner-compass model thus emphasize not only the importance of autonomy-supportive practices but also the role of authentic adult role models in helping youth identify and realize their own authentic, direction-giving life goals and values. Across cultures as diverse as Israel, Italy, and China, parents who showed that they intrinsically value particular behaviors, morals, or identities appeared to be a significant aid to their children's being able to form their own healthy identifications and system of values. The modeling of intrinsic values may be especially critical in postmodern contexts, which, as we discussed above, present a plethora of icons, influences, and value pathways from which young people must select and consolidate authentic ways of living (Assor, 2011).

Repressing versus Integrating Potential Identities

Although there are clear advantages to integrating identities within the self, some identities remain poorly integrated because they are socially stigmatized, because they conflict with other identities or roles that close others want them to embrace, or because they conflict with the individuals' introjects or ego involvements. Indeed, as we previously discussed in Chapter 8, some identifications, rather than being integrated with other identities, needs, and value attachments of the self, may be resisted by people who are ashamed of them or who compartmentalize or isolate them because they feel pressured to conceal them (Ryan & Deci, 2012).

As but one example of such conflicts, let us consider *concealable identities* (those that an individual can attempt to hide) that are frequently stigmatized, such as being gay, lesbian, bisexual, or transgender (LGBT). An invisible identity is one that, unlike race or certain physical disabilities or features, can be hidden from others (Ragins, 2008). Insofar as a person anticipates being stigmatized or ill-treated by others who are prejudiced concerning her or his invisible identity, the person may chose to conceal or deny the identity. This is, in fact, a common dynamic in persons who identity as LGBT (see, e.g., Quinn et al., 2014).

Concealment of LGBT orientations may be functional in some regards, especially in particularly hostile contexts. Nonetheless, we suggest that it has costs for the person who decides, even in the face of pressure, to conceal or suppress such an abiding identification. For instance Legate, Ryan, and Weinstein (2012) investigated why lesbian, gay, and bisexual individuals vary their disclosures of sexual orientation in different social contexts and the experiences that follow from concealment or being "out." They predicted that within-person variation in disclosure would to a significant degree be a function of the autonomy-supportive versus controlling character of those social contexts. Thus they had LGB individuals rate experiences of autonomy support and control when around their families, friends, coworkers, school peers, and religious communities, as well how "out" they were in each setting. The researchers further assessed context-specific self-esteem, depression, and anger. Using multilevel modeling, they found that LGB individuals were less likely to conceal their orientations in autonomy-supportive contexts. In settings that were controlling, they both disclosed less and showed lower well-being. Furthermore, whereas disclosure or being "out" was associated with more positive well-being in autonomy-supportive contexts, in controlling contexts it was not, presumably because of the social-emotional costs of stigma.

In a related study, W. S. Ryan, Legate, and Weinstein (2015) examined the impact of the initial reactions people experienced when revealing a lesbian, gay, or bisexual identification. They reasoned that initial reactions may be particularly important because the revelation is often made to very significant others, who they hope will be accepting; so these experiences may set up expectations about future identity disclosure. People identifying as LGB were assessed regarding the first persons to whom they disclosed, as well as their experiences of coming out to their mothers, fathers, and best friends. The findings indicated that negative reactions to these initial disclosures were predictive of higher depression and lower self-esteem. Satisfaction of the autonomy need mediated the relation from these initial social reactions to disclosure and well-being.

One may recall the study by Weinstein, W. S. Ryan, DeHaan, Przybylski, Legate, and R. M. Ryan (2012), reviewed in Chapter 8, that individuals with same-sex attractions who were raised in controlling homes not only suppressed those perceptions but were also likely to display homophobia or strong negative prejudices toward gay and lesbian people. This homophobia represents the defense of reaction formation, or acting negatively toward what one secretly desires as a way of sustaining introjected control. It also exemplifies what can happen as uncompromising social constraints clash with seemingly natural expressions of human diversity.

These and a host of emerging studies on sexual identities are particularly important in illustrating how identity integration is influenced by societal contexts, and particularly the presence of prejudice and stigma toward certain identities and personal attributes. It becomes much more challenging to develop an integrated identity in contexts that are unaccepting. This is relevant not just to sexual orientations and racial identities, toward which prejudices are particularly salient. They also pertain to more micro-prejudices—from the family that cannot accept their child's vocational interests to the religious communities that cannot tolerate political diversities. Wherever controlling social contexts impede self-expression, we expect to find such dynamics in operation.

Internal Consistency in Identity

Integrative problems can also stem from the sheer incompatibility of identifications. Suppose in his political identifications a man identifies with an ideology or group that is oppressive to certain subgroups or minorities, and yet in his religious identifications he endorses being unconditionally benevolent and compassionate. Both might be values or roles that he deems important, but their inconsistency requires that he keep them isolated or compartmentalized from one another because advocating harm to others might engender guilt or doubt if his religious identity were also salient. Attempting to integrate these two identities might not only be effortful, but it also might require a significant change in one or both identities, and the changes could entail psychological threat or loss of relatedness. Yet the more people integrate identities and regulations, the more autonomous they will be in those domains, making it advantageous for them to do so.

From the SDT perspective, the ease of integrating identities is in part a function of whether people engage the identities with autonomous versus controlled motivation. The more autonomous their motivation, the more easily they will be able to integrate the identities. Research by Weinstein, Deci, and Ryan (2011) tested this proposition. Across five studies, they specifically examined how autonomous versus controlled motivation, operationalized either through individual differences in the autonomous versus controlled general causality orientations or through the semantic priming of the autonomous versus controlled orientations, would either facilitate or inhibit the integration of positive and negative past identities. Results showed that more autonomously motivated participants felt closer to, and were more accepting of, both their positive and negative past characteristics and life events, whereas more control-motivated participants were closer to and more accepting of the positive, but not the negative, identities and events. Interestingly, although controlled motivation interfered with participants' acceptance of their own negative identities, it did not hinder their recognition of other people's negative identities, suggesting that control-motivated individuals' rejection of negative past identities was an attempt to distance themselves from undesirable parts of themselves and not from negative events in general. In fact, those high in controlled motivation tended to enhance the negative characteristics and events of their associates. Weinstein et al. also showed that these defensive processes, reflected for example in the use of nonpersonal pronouns and stronger escape motives, mediated the interaction effects involving negative versus positive identities, indicating that lower defensiveness allowed fuller integration of negative identities. Finally, results from these studies demonstrated that when participants did more fully integrate both positive and negative past identities, they demonstrated greater vitality and reported finding the personal identities and events to be more meaningful.

These findings concerning the integration of identities and self-related characteristics converge with research within the narrative tradition. For example, Bauer and McAdams (2004) examined autobiographical memories for pathways to both greater psychosocial maturity and well-being. The memories of more mature individuals with greater ego development (Loevinger, 1976) emphasized an integrative focus on growth and learning. Further, the memories of persons who had higher happiness emphasized intrinsic as opposed to extrinsic aspirations and goals. Both kinds of growth memories—those with an integrative focus or intrinsic aspirations—correlated strongly with indicators of eudaimonic living and well-being, as well as traditional indicators of subjective well-being. The authors emphasized that the development of a mature and coherent identity is a matter of self-cultivation and of a focus on integrating experiences and intrinsic values (see also Bauer et al., 2005).

In sum, a growing body of research on identify formation within SDT clearly shows that: (1) persons have multiple identities; (2) these identities vary in their relative autonomy and in their integrity and coherence with one another; (3) more autonomous and integrated identities are facilitated by need-supportive social contexts; and (4) the more integrated an identity is, the greater its benefit is for individuals' flourishing.

The Self and Self-Esteem

Not only is self-esteem a widely studied construct, but it is also a very familiar concept to laypersons and to scholars in other disciplines. People who have never studied psychology know what it means and may be concerned about self-esteem in themselves and others, and it is often highly endorsed as an important human satisfaction (e.g., Sedikides & Skowronski, 2000; Sheldon, Elliot, Kim, & Kasser, 2001). Popular psychologists have offered a multitude of suggestions for how to increase self-esteem, and programs have been developed for use in schools and elsewhere to increase the self-esteem of children.

In general, self-esteem is treated as an asset. Certainly, most people consider feeling good about themselves to be experientially preferable to feeling bad about themselves. And there are literally thousands of studies that have used self-esteem as an indicator of psychological health and well-being, including some of our own (e.g., Ryan & Lynch, 1989). Still, psychologists have recognized that having high self-esteem, as assessed by the typical self-report inventories, is not always associated with positive attributes (e.g., Baumeister, Heatherton, & Tice, 1993; Kernis & Paradise, 2002). For example, high scores on self-esteem may be inflated representations of narcissistic or false pride and may have little correlation with a sense of inner peace or even with personal accomplishments (Hodgins & Knee, 2002). Some people who score high on self-esteem might also be defensively aggrandizing of themselves while at the same time being belittling of others, suggesting that they are not really operating with a secure sense of their own worth (Kernis & Goldman, 2003).

It is for these reasons that the concept of self-esteem requires a more differentiated approach. Accordingly, within SDT, self-esteem is not treated simply as a positive phenomenon; it is differentiated as a function of the satisfactions that give rise to it. SDT's considerations of different bases of self-esteem are specifically relevant to the "me-self" tradition we discussed in this chapter. In self-as-object or me-self perspectives, people attempt to meet standards associated with internalized images and identities, and they derive *self-esteem* when they succeed (Harter, 1999; Kernis, 2003). This leads to forms of esteem that are contingent on outcomes as opposed to self-esteem being an abiding inner resource.

Self-Esteem: Contingency and Fragility

SDT considers the quality of self-esteem as well as its quantity by examining the developmental bases and consequences of different types of self-esteem (e.g., Deci & Ryan, 1995; Kernis, 2003). Building off earlier work on introjection and ego involvement and on parental psychological control, we specifically differentiated varied types of self-esteem that result from development under different social-contextual circumstances that are associated with different types of behavioral regulation and that function differently resulting in different consequences. They are contingent self-esteem and true self-esteem (Deci & Ryan, 2000) and the related concepts of secure and fragile self-esteem (Kernis, 2000).

In *contingent self-esteem,* people's feelings of worth are dependent upon continually meeting standards or expectations that have been introjected. Meeting the standards or expectations signifies that they are worthy, whereas failing to meet the standards or expectations signifies that they are not. Contingent self-esteem is, by its very nature, unstable because of its contingent status—it changes as people meet the standards to differing degrees. In addition, contingent self-esteem is most likely to be focused on attaining extrinsic goals (Kasser & Ryan, 1996; see also Chapter 11, this volume) such as an attractive image, popularity, or professional or material success, although in contingent self-esteem these external yardsticks are transformed into internal criteria of worth. These extrinsic outcomes tend to be the focus of self-esteem because they are so often attributes that lead others to conditionally value the individual.

True self-esteem, in contrast, is inherently more stable, for it is a form of feeling worthy that does not depend upon specific achievements or external indicators of worth. Rather, it is derived from an intrinsic sense of worth—it is authentic and unconditional. When experiencing true self-esteem, individuals are not judging or evaluating themselves in terms of worth, even as they evaluate their success or failure at goals. They are not trying to build their self-esteem through public accomplishments, because the feelings of worth and self-acceptance are a solid component of who they are (Ryan & Brown, 2003). True self-esteem is a more basic sense of feeling worthy, and it tends naturally to accompany a higher level of basic psychological need satisfaction.

Somewhat ironically, from a phenomenological view, true self-esteem reflects a relative lack of concern with esteem per se (Ryan & Brown, 2003). To be esteeming or disesteeming of the self-as-object is indicative of an internally controlling self-evaluative processes that, from an SDT perspective, reflects introjected internalizations and typically stems from social contexts that are or have been contingently regarding (e.g., Assor, Roth, & Deci, 2004).

People whose sense of worth is not contingent upon succeeding or failing at attaining some standard will nonetheless have feelings when they succeed or fail. They may well have expectations or goals for themselves, and they will likely feel pleased or disappointed as a function of how well they do. Attaining their goals may be a source of joy, whereas failing to do so may leave them feeling disappointed and possibly discouraged. Still, the important thing is that their general feelings of worth as people will not be at stake and thus will not vary as a function of their successes and failures. Accordingly, as Kernis (2000) argued, those who have noncontingent or true self-esteem as SDT defines it also have more stable self-esteem. They do not show the temporal fluctuations in feelings of worth that people with contingent self-esteem display.

As we mentioned earlier in the chapter, people with high contingent self-esteem often focus on extrinsic aspirations such as wealth, fame, and image, along with social-comparison-based successes in their chosen identities. In contrast, those with true self-esteem will be more likely to strive for the intrinsic aspirations of personal growth, meaningful relationships, and community involvement (Kasser & Ryan, 1996). Paralleling this, and as reviewed in Chapter 11, holding relatively strong extrinsic aspirations tends to be negatively associated with having experienced need-thwarting environments in development, such as controlling or rejecting parenting (e.g., Kasser et al., 1995). This further supports our contention that contingent self-esteem is built upon underlying insecurity and thus represents a less healthy form of self-esteem (Ryan & Brown, 2003).

Seery, Blascovich, Weisbuch, and Vick (2004) provided direct evidence that contingent self-esteem—or unstable self-esteem, to use Kernis's (1993) term—is associated with poorer well-being. Participants were separated into one group with high true self-esteem and one with high contingent self-esteem. The grouping was determined by the amount of variability the participants showed in state self-esteem on eight assessments over a 1-week period. Those with more variability were considered more unstable and therefore more contingent in their self-esteem, whereas those with less variability were considered more stable and therefore truer in theirs (e.g., Deci & Ryan, 1995). Both the high-contingent and the high-true self-esteem groups then experienced failure on a problem-solving task. Subsequently, both groups were told they would be doing more of the same task. Psychophysiological measures of cardiovascular functioning were obtained from all participants, and the results indicated that those participants with high contingent self-esteem showed a less healthy pattern of cardiovascular functioning consistent with viewing the problem-solving task as a threat, whereas participants with true self-esteem showed a more healthy pattern of cardiovascular functioning consistent with viewing the problem-solving task as a challenge.

It is again worth emphasizing that, when we talk of true versus contingent self-esteem, we are not talking about dichotomous concepts. Most people have areas of vulnerability with regard to self-esteem because they have experienced contingent regard from significant others or projected it onto them. Indeed, these are often specifically in domains in which there is a strong public and extrinsic focus—such as achievement, appearance, or material success. Nonetheless, those with more autonomous forms of self-regulation appear less susceptible to unstable or defensive forms of self-esteem. For example, Kernis, Paradise, Whitaker, Wheatman, and Goldman (2000) showed that more autonomous regulation predicted more self-esteem stability. Further, in two experimental studies, Hodgins, Brown, and Carver (2007) primed participants to create either an autonomous or a controlled motivational set. Those primed with autonomy showed both higher implicit self-esteem and lower defensive self-esteem, the latter variable represented by discrepancies between implicit and explicit assessments of self-esteem. Interestingly, males in general showed more defensiveness by the latter indicator.

A study by Guay, Delisle, Fernet, Julien, and Senécal (2008) examined self-esteem that either was or was not contingent upon acceptance by others. They reviewed the *sociometer theory* of self-esteem (Leary & Baumeister, 2000), which has suggested that self-esteem is primarily an evolved gauge of whether people are accepted within their social world. From the perspective of SDT, however, this does not deal with the potential buffering effect that would be associated with more stable and well-integrated bases of self-worth—namely, autonomous motivation and basic psychological need satisfaction—in the varying social contexts. Accordingly, Guay et al. predicted that people who were high in autonomy would have relatively true and stable self-esteem, so their perceived inclusion should not be a primary determinant of their *state* self-esteem. In contrast, the researchers predicted that, for people low in autonomy, moment-to-moment self-esteem would likely be more dependent upon proximal indicators of acceptance versus rejection. The findings of the study supported their reasoning, suggesting that more autonomous functioning entails a more stable and noncontingent sense of self.

Developmental Considerations and Self-Esteem

Within SDT the degree to which a person's self-esteem is true versus contingent is considered a developmental outcome of the organismic dialectic. Ongoing satisfaction of the basic psychological needs, particularly when people are relatively young, will lead them to become relatively secure with themselves so that they will not need to be continually living up to expectations in order to feel worthy. Yet people vary in the extent to which their feelings of worth are contingent upon their performance in one or more domains. These individual differences in the extent to which people's self-esteem is contingent are likely to be important predictors of a range of performance, well-being, and relational outcomes (Kernis, 2003).

Contingent self-esteem, in contrast to true self-esteem, develops as people feel pressured to live up to values that they tend to introject such that their feelings of self-worth become dependent upon the degree to which they have met the standards. Because the foundation for contingent self-esteem is deficiencies in need satisfaction, resulting in introjection of demands and standards, contingent self-esteem is more defensive in nature. People will try to appease their introjects in order to defend against feeling unworthy so they can experience pride rather than guilt or shame. Thus, to the degree that people's self-esteem is contingent, they will feel less secure and will more likely be controlled rather than autonomous in the regulation of their behavior.

Conditional Regard

One socialization practice that SDT associates with the development of contingent self-esteem is *parental conditional regard* (PCR). As discussed at length in Chapter 13, when parents' regard, affection, attention, and love for their children is conveyed primarily at the times that the children do or are what the parents want or value, the children are put in a position of having two basic needs made antagonistic to one another. That is, the children essentially have to give up their autonomy and sense of choice about how to behave in order to gain or retain their parents' love. Hence, the satisfaction of their relatedness need is essentially dependent upon having their need for autonomy thwarted. Furthermore, as specified within relationships motivation theory (RMT; Chapter 12), receiving love conditionally does not provide full satisfaction of the relatedness need, for children are not being loved and accepted for *who they really are*. In fact, research reviewed in Chapter 13 by Assor and colleagues (2004), Roth and colleagues (2009), and Roth and Assor (2010) showed that when parents' regard was made conditional upon certain behavioral accomplishments, their children tended to introject the contingencies, evidence fragile self-esteem, experience short-lived satisfaction following successes, be ashamed and guilty after failures, exhibit poor self-regulation of emotions, and feel rejected by and resentful toward their parents.

To summarize, to the extent that basic psychological needs are well satisfied within the socializing environment, persons tend to establish identities that are founded in self-endorsed values and interests and that support true self-esteem, whereas to the extent that their needs are thwarted, their self-esteem will tend to be contingent upon introjected standards and externally dictated mores, leading to the adoption of less well-integrated identities.

Authenticity, Identity, and Self-Esteem

Contingencies of self-esteem often drive people away from preferred identities and passions toward those they hope will help maintain their lovability. They are thus associated with less congruent and autonomous functioning, whereas true self-esteem is aligned with the concept of more integrated self-functioning and thus with people's experience of *authenticity* (Kernis & Goldman, 2006). Ryan and Deci (2006) defined *authenticity* as involving two aspects: One's behavior is authored or endorsed by the self (i.e., it is autonomous), and it is not self-deceptive but reflects a considered, meaningful, and open grappling with what is actually occurring.

Our analyses of self and of self-esteem suggest that the degree to which people experience need-satisfaction-associated interpersonal supports for autonomy, competence, and relatedness is the critical issue in the extent to which they will be able to act in accordance with their ideals and values, experience a high level of true self-esteem, and interact with others less defensively and more openly. At the same time, at a within-person level of analysis, the relative need supports supplied in social contexts will vary, and thus conduce to either more or less expression of the individual's valued identities, attributes, and values. This bears directly on how authentic people will be in presenting themselves, as well as how close they will be to their ideal ways of being. It also bears on age-old questions within the science of personality concerning how stable personality attributes and traits are and on the nature and impact of variability.

Authenticity across Roles

Sheldon, Ryan, Rawsthorne, and Ilardi (1997) did one of the earliest studies of variability in personality. It concerned how personality traits vary in different life roles. They had undergraduates respond to questions related to the Big Five personality traits (Costa & McCrae, 1992). These five traits—Extraversion, Neuroticism, Agreeableness, Conscientiousness, and Openness to Experience—are often assumed to be highly stable individual differences that guide people's behavior across roles and contexts. Yet Sheldon et al. hypothesized, in accordance with SDT, that there is likely to be considerable variability in these traits when people described themselves in the different roles of student, employee, child, friend, and romantic partner. In particular, they reasoned that people would depart from their typical "trait selves" in roles in which they did not feel authentic—that is, in which they could not reveal their true selves. Thus these researchers had the participants describe the degree to which they felt *authentic* (as defined by the degree to which they felt they were being congruent and autonomous) in each role, and the researchers further assessed how satisfied the participants were in each role, as well as their levels of general well-being.

Analyses were done at both the within-person and the between-person level. Results at the within-person level indicated that authenticity predicted satisfaction in each of the roles but that consistency (i.e., lack of discrepancy from one's general self-description) did not explain additional independent variance, thus indicating that satisfaction within a role was a function of the degree to which a person was authentic in that role. The degree to which his or her within-role trait profile differed from or was consistent with his or her general profile did not matter. At the between-person level, authenticity predicted the general well-being composite. Interestingly, there was plenty of variation in Big Five traits across roles, and this variation was systematic. When feeling authentic, individuals tended toward higher self-reported extraversion, agreeableness, openness, and conscientiousness and toward lower neuroticism. This tells us a lot about the qualities of authentic living—it is more vital and open, as well as more responsible, thus being associated with more relatedness and competence satisfactions, contributing in turn to more well-being.

Subsequently, Ryan, La Guardia, and Rawsthorne (2005) used a different paradigm to predict wellness from authenticity in different facets of life. They reevaluated Linville's (1985, 1987) self-complexity model, which predicts that complexity in personality (having many different interests, roles, and "facets") helps buffer one against blows or failures in any particular domain. Presumably, more complex people don't have "all their eggs in one basket." But Ryan and colleagues predicted that complex selves also represent a burden. They expected to replicate the buffering effect Linville had detected, but they further suggested that having many selves would also engender more stress—especially to the degree they were not well integrated. They thus expected that stress would be strongly negatively related and wellness strongly positively related to the extent to which people's self-aspects were authentic and self-endorsed. That is just what they found empirically. Whereas there were significant, but small, buffering effects of having a complex personality, authenticity as a marker of the autonomy and integration of self-aspects was a strong negative predictor of overall personal stress and a positive predictor of well-being.

Because people vary in how they present and act in different life roles, many investigators have suggested that variability itself is problematic. Indeed, that point was central to work by Donahue and colleagues, (e.g., Roberts & Donahue, 1994), who argued that variability in trait expressions across different life roles represents *self-fragmentation* rather than integration. However, as suggested from the work by Ryan and colleagues (2005) and Sheldon et al. (1997), it seems more likely, as SDT would suggest, that it is not the variability or multiplicity of traits per se but rather the authenticity or autonomy experienced in people's varied life settings that represents integrated functioning. That is, the most important predictor of wellness both within and across roles would be the extent to which a person feels able to act in accordance with his or her own choices and values.

It appears that integration, autonomy, and authenticity, which are all closely related concepts within SDT (see, e.g., Ryan & Deci, 2006), are indeed important for well-being across diverse cultures (see also Lynch, La Guardia, & Ryan, 2009). Although some theorists have disagreed with this perspective (e.g., Markus & Kitayama, 1991a), we have detailed how this disagreement stems from their conflating autonomy with independence, a conceptual melding that has long created confounds within both developmental and cross-cultural research. More importantly, research on within-person variability falls in line with SDT's emphasis on proximal supports for basic psychological needs, as much of the variability in how an individual acts and feels in different contexts is a function of need supports. It is, therefore, not variability itself that is typically problematic but, rather, the fact that variability in the direction of less authenticity can stem from need frustrations associated with a lack of interpersonal need supports.

Dualistic Model of Passion

People often have strong interests or passions in their lives that are important identities and that centrally define them. In formulating a model of passion, Vallerand and colleagues (e.g., Vallerand, 2010, 2015; Vallerand & Houlfort, 2003; Vallerand, Rousseau, Grouzet, Dumais, Grenier, & Blanchard, 2006) began by examining activities (e.g., golf, gambling, video gaming) for which people were highly intrinsically motivated and thus engaged in the activities frequently and came to see them as passions. The researchers believed that different people had different types of relations with their passions, such that, for example, some people just could not stop doing the activity even if it would in some way harm them to continue, whereas others could be frequently engaged yet also able to stop when appropriate. For some people, it seemed like their self-worth required them to keep at their passions, trying to perform well, whereas for the others the activity was more an area of satisfactions than pressures.

All of these passions seemed to involve a mix of intrinsic interests and extrinsically based regulations, especially as people pursued the passions deeply. But, whereas some of the passions appeared to be identities that were well integrated, such that the behaviors involved were highly autonomous and need fulfilling, other of the passions seemed to be identities that came to control the people, rather than the people controlling the passions. In these latter cases, people tended to be driven by introjections and compulsions to pursue these central life passions.

In the *dualistic model of passion,* Vallerand (2015) specified that the passions that involve people being intrinsically motivated for an activity but having its regulation be introjected represent a relatively maladaptive relation to the activity, because they are engaging in it in a controlled and obsessive way. On the other hand, the passions that involve intrinsic motivation for the activity along with integrated regulation of it are much more adaptive because the person is engaging in it more autonomously and harmoniously. Accordingly, Vallerand (2015) specified *obsessive passions* as those that involve high intrinsic interest with their regulations being controlled and *harmonious passions* as those that entail a high degree of intrinsic motivation and interest but that are well integrated with other aspects of the people's lives. Thus obsessive passions originate from and are in part regulated by intra- and interpersonal pressures and self-esteem-related contingencies, so someone experiencing an obsessive passion would likely feel compelled and ego involved to engage in the activity. In contrast, harmonious passions are undergirded by a fuller, less conflicted internalization so the activity is experienced as highly volitional, and, when it is engaged in, there is a sense of choice and vitality (Vallerand, 2015).

Some evidence suggests, in fact, that obsessive passion is often fueled by a compensatory motivation for need thwarting in other domains of life. That is, a person who has need frustrations may turn addictively to an activity in which intrinsic satisfaction can be or has been found. For example, Lalande et al. (2016) investigated psychological need satisfaction in four studies both inside and outside of people's self-identified passions. The samples were varied in both ages and the passions they pursued. Nonetheless, results showed that those with obsessive passions were more likely to evidence low levels of autonomy, competence, and relatedness satisfactions outside the passionate activities, whereas those individuals with more harmonious passions experienced these need satisfactions outside of, as well as inside of, their passions. These results thus supported the view that more controlled regulations of passions and identities can represent a form of compensatory striving for basic need satisfactions that people are not able to get in other domains or activities in their lives.

As such, whereas harmonious passions are flexibly self-regulated, obsessive passions often entail a rigid persistence at the task, often to the detriment of other aspects of the people's lives and relationships. These two types of passions, therefore, represent individual-difference constructs at the level of behaviors or domains and predict a variety of both behavioral and health-related outcomes.

Based on the passion model, a large literature has developed examining antecedents and consequences of the two types of passion (Vallerand, 2015), of which we provide only a small sampling here. Among the major themes, in line with the general tenets of SDT, is that more controlling social contexts during the formation and maintenance phases of passion development conduce toward obsessive passions, whereas more autonomy-supportive contexts facilitate the development of more harmonious passions. In turn, those with more harmonious passions exhibit more flexible and persistent engagement and greater subjective well-being, thereby supporting better interpersonal relationships and healthier lifestyles through greater basic need satisfaction. In contrast, obsessive passions, like other controlled identities, have been associated with greater symptoms of ill-being and with difficulties related to disengagement because of the partly heteronomous nature of the persistence. Obsessive passions have thus been associated with disrupted relationships, crowding out of other important activities and responsibilities, and susceptibility to depression and self-esteem fluctuations when the passionate activity is blocked or frustrated.

Passions are clearly defining identities for people that can organize much of their time and experiences, so the degree to which the passions are internalized is critical to healthy functioning. The dualistic model confirms the importance of considering not only the strength of people's abiding interests and goals—that is, their degree of passion—but also the motivations through which any given passion is regulated. With the mix of intrinsic motivation and introjected regulation, the objects about which people are passionate will be obsessively pursued, will not be well anchored within the self, and will result in a range of negative consequences. In contrast, with the mix of intrinsic motivation and identified or integrated regulation of relevant behaviors, people's passions will be more harmonious and will yield a range of positive outcomes.

Concluding Comments

Identities are self-representations that refer to the significant roles, activities, passions, and self-concepts that people hold and engage with during their lives. These identities can be more or less central to the individuals, and, in fact, every individual has various identities that are more or less in the forefront in different interpersonal settings or life contexts. At work it may be one's professional identity that is most salient, at home it may be one's role as a parent, and in leisure time it may be one's hobbies or affiliations. Thus the individual has multiple identities, all being managed by values and regulations that have been more or less fully integrated into a single, coherent self (Deci & Ryan, 1991; Ryan & Deci, 2012).

SDT maintains that all of these identities and roles tend to be oriented toward satisfying basic psychological needs, although there is variability in the extent to which specific identities actually do so. Some identities are inadvertently attempting to satisfy the people's compensatory need substitutes and/or may not be supported by significant others, thus being associated with need frustration. Further, because identities are internalized to differing degrees, the less well internalized and integrated an identity, the less it will be experienced as authentic and be need satisfying. Finally, identity integration is strongly related to social contextual supports. Developing and optimizing a meaningful and fitting identity requires responsive and supportive parents, educational institutions, and societies.

We also discussed that integration does not necessarily mean to act consistently, because different situations might suggest that different behaviors related to the integrated attribute are appropriate. In fact, consistency may at times be contrary to flexibility in behavioral regulation. The more critical issue is how authentic—or self-authored and self-endorsed—roles and ways of acting are when they occur. Nonetheless, at least in terms of the Big Five personality traits, there seems to be a tendency for people, when they are feeling more authentic, to be more open, extraverted, and agreeable and to be considerably less neurotic.

People also have different levels of self-esteem in different life contexts. As noted, SDT differentiates self-esteem based on variability between true self-esteem and contingent self-esteem. True self-esteem is a deep and secure sense of oneself as worthy, whereas contingent self-esteem, which is more fragile, is conditional upon meeting introjected standards. Contexts that are more controlling tend to differentially value people on the basis of external attributes and outcomes and can activate conditional evaluations, making self-esteem less secure. This also leaves them vulnerable to inauthentic ways of behaving and to lower relationship satisfaction and wellness.

When identities, roles, and passions are better integrated and self-esteem is less contingent, people are more likely to be authentic and autonomous and thereby experience more psychological need satisfaction and enhanced wellness. Thwarts or deprivations to need supports that people experience in different contexts may result in the people moving away from their ideals and sometimes from their abiding values and interests. Lack of support for autonomy also constrains the expression of human diversity and the flourishing of the unique spirits and talents it can yield.

CHAPTER 16

Development, Basic Psychological Needs, and Psychopathology

Social contexts can either support or thwart satisfaction of basic psychological needs and, as a result, differentially buffer or potentiate vulnerabilities for various psychopathologies. We specifically discuss three categories of psychopathology and their relations to basic need satisfaction and frustration in development. The first involves autonomy disturbances that take the form of rigid internal regulations that result from introjection or compartmentalized identifications and includes the obsessive and paranoid disorders, as well as controlled eating disorders and self-critical depression. A second type comprises disorders for which failures to internalize effective regulations are a central feature. This type includes conduct and antisocial disorders. A third type involves serious intrusive and need-thwarting experiences that lead to personality fragmentation and impaired emotional regulation. Borderline personality disorders and dissociative personality disorders are examples. Our review shows that constructs of psychological needs, and the elements within social contexts that support or thwart their satisfaction across development, are critical not only to the understanding of human flourishing but also to the understanding of ill-being and psychopathology.

Within SDT, people are viewed as inherently oriented to develop in the directions of greater autonomy, relatedness, and self-regulation. Yet the optimal functioning of this developmental thrust toward self-organization requires environmental supports and social nutriments, both across development and more proximally in everyday contexts. Over the past few decades, especially with the emergence of the field of *developmental psychopathology* (e.g., Cicchetti, 2016; Cicchetti & Toth, 2009), it has become increasingly clear that when the appropriate social nutrients are not provided, the negative effects on development can be manifold, impacting biological, psychological, and social capacities. SDT specifically looks at the development of psychopathology in terms of the array of interacting factors that can impinge upon or fail to buttress the natural processes that yield healthy development and flourishing.

Today, as new tools are being developed in both behavioral genetics and neuropsychology, the role of biological vulnerabilities in potentiating psychopathology is an important and widely discussed topic (e.g., Beauchaine & Gatzke-Kopp, 2012). SDT stresses how a lack of social supports and experiential nutrients, or, more seriously, the presence of flagrant deprivations and need-thwarting conditions, not only disrupt normal developmental processes but also exacerbate or in other cases catalyze such emotional and biological vulnerabilities (Ryan & Deci, 2000a). In fact, we see social-contextual and experiential factors as salient precipitating causes of many forms of ill-being and psychopathology (Ryan, Deci, & Vansteenkiste, 2016). Across the spectrum of biological vulnerabilities, the onset and maintenance of pathological episodes can be prompted or amplified by social experiences such as rejection, neglect, domination, humiliation, or debasement brought on by cold, chaotic, nonresponsive, controlling, or abusive people or circumstances. These experiences engender compromised functioning and further frustration of basic psychological needs (Ryan, Deci, Grolnick, & La Guardia, 2006).

Conversely, for people whose biology leaves them prone to various behavioral or psychological disorders, need-supportive experiences and conditions of care can promote strengths and increase their resilience (Vansteenkiste & Ryan, 2013; Weinstein & Ryan, 2011). Indeed, social events can be triggers to and/or amplifiers of vulnerabilities, but they can also be buffers and compensatory protective influences against them (Bindman, Pomerantz, & Roisman, 2015; Ryan et al., 2016). Because contextual and experiential factors related to satisfaction versus frustration of the basic psychological needs have been found to be important to the development, management, and amelioration of psychopathology, and because SDT has been formulated as a primarily psychological theory, our emphasis in addressing psychopathology has been primarily on those interpersonal and experiential processes related to basic psychological needs.

Accordingly, in this chapter on the development of psychopathology we focus on the impact of social and psychological influences, especially the thwarting of people's basic psychological needs for competence, relatedness, and autonomy and the individuals' attempts to cope with the deprivations and pains that result from severe need frustration. Importantly, the theory assumes that although psychopathologies are maladaptive, for they themselves interfere with satisfaction of people's basic psychological needs, they often represent the best adaptations the individuals are able to make given the challenges they have encountered. Responses to abusive, invasive, disregarding, or pressuring social environments that disrupt self-development often become transactional influences. The adaptations may lead others to behave in ways that maintain or increase the level of need thwarting directed toward the individual, which in turn reinforces or exacerbates existing maladaptive coping and patterns of psychopathology.

We restrict our focus here to clinical disorders rather than ill-being more generally, as the continuum of well-being to ill-being has been implicated throughout this book. Instead, we here specifically focus on several classically conceived disorders and the role that is played by basic psychological need thwarting in each of several families of related disorders. Paradoxically, basic need frustrations cut across disorders in patterned ways, suggesting, as does much modern clinical thinking, that they are a central part of underlying dimensions of maladjustment that manifest themselves in varied pathologies (see Vansteenkiste & Ryan, 2013).

Autonomy, Need Thwarting, and Psychopathology

Autonomy, defined as self-regulation and integration in acting, is particularly central to adaptive functioning. Many theories have considered a trajectory toward greater autonomy and integration to be a hallmark of healthy development (e.g., Jahoda, 1958;

Loevinger, 1976; Piaget, 1971), a theme that continues in current developmental perspectives (see Sokol, Grouzet, & Müller, 2013). Indeed, because of the critical import of developing capacities for autonomous behavioral regulation, support for autonomy is acknowledged as an essential skill in parenting by many scholars (e.g., Bindman et al., 2015; Grolnick, 2002; Grusec & Goodnow, 1994; Hmel & Pincus, 2002).

Issues of autonomy and integration are highly salient in the literature of psychopathology (e.g., Ryan, Deci, & Vansteenkiste, 2016; Shapiro, 1981; Winnicott, 1965). In many forms of mental illness, the individual's behaviors, emotions, and cognitions are subjectively experienced as compelled, pressured, or controlled or, alternatively, as uncontrollable (Ryan, Deci, et al., 2006). For example, in some addictive and impulsive disorders, people feel unable to regulate specific behaviors. In other psychopathologies, behavior is highly and rigidly regulated, such as in restrictive eating disorders or some forms of obsessive–compulsive disorders. Still other forms of psychopathology, usually entailing a history of significant trauma or abuse, involve behaviors being emitted without the feeling that they are mediated or regulated by the self. For example, in some dissociative disorders, behaviors can occur without the intentions of the self. In still other pathologies, such as severe depression, the motivation for pursuing intentions and goals is weak or absent. In sum, compromised autonomy is implicated in a range of psychological problems, from those involving impoverished behavior regulation to those that are characterized by rigid self-control. Corresponding to this, caregivers' thwarting of children's autonomy has been implicated in the etiology of a broad range of psychopathologies (e.g., Bruch, 1973; Depue & Lenzenweger, 2001; Ryan, 2005).

Psychopathologies, of course, differ greatly in their processes and symptoms—and in the centrality of autonomy disturbances and impairments in competence and relatedness that are associated with them. Our discussion of pathologies, and particularly autonomy disturbances, is thus not intended to be exhaustive. Instead, for illustrative purposes, we have identified three sets of pathologies for which the type of autonomy disturbance is relatively distinct. We discuss the motivational processes that characterize each set of pathologies.

The first set of disorders relates to *internally controlling regulation,* in which strong and rigid introjected regulations, values, and beliefs dominate people's experiences and behaviors. In some instances, these disorders result from socializing practices that were saliently controlling, whereas in others self-regulatory deficits may be implicated. Yet in both cases standards and values that have been only partially internalized (and thus not integrated) exert persistent pressures on the individuals' thoughts, feelings, and behaviors, with anxiety and self-criticism accompanying the rigid demands and regulations. Within this set of disorders, we discuss the obsessive pathologies, paranoid personality, self-critical depression, and eating disorders.

A second type of disorder concerns *failures of internalization,* which are often the interactive outcome of both biological predispositions and an absence in development of clear and consistent structures and need supports provided by parents or guardians. Thus, whereas with the first of disorders our focus is on strong internal demands, in this second category there is a weakness in regulatory structures, so the individual's urges, emotions, and drives are often inconsistently or poorly regulated. These autonomy disturbances include conduct disorders and antisocial personality disorders, each characterized by impulsivity and antisocial or aggressive behaviors.

Finally, we explore a third set of disorders that is characterized by *serious disturbances of self* and that are related to more malevolent intrusions, insults, abuse, and affronts to children's welfare during development. In many cases, these need-thwarting contexts are on the one hand demanding and punitive but on the other hand chaotic and inconsistent, thus fracturing capacities for internalization and integration, especially in vulnerable personalities. Containing elements of both internally controlling regulation and amotivation, the resulting disorders include borderline personality disorder and dissociative identity disorder.

As we reviewed in Chapter 13 on parenting, healthy psychological development is manifested in intrinsic motivation, more integrated internalization, flexible regulatory structures for managing emotions, and secure attachments. In contrast, the development of psychopathology involves frustration of the basic psychological needs, resulting in the undermining of interest and intrinsic enjoyment; the impairment of internalization; impoverished emotion regulation; and the establishment of insecure attachments and unsatisfactory relationships. Each of these outcomes means that people will fail to self-regulate and manage themselves effectively, and this disturbed autonomy is likely to be manifested as behavioral dysfunction or pathology. Often it is the demanding, coercive, insistent, seductive, rejecting, critical, incoherent, or demeaning social environments that thwart autonomy, competence, and relatedness needs, which impairs autonomy development and compromises people's volitional functioning. As such, many psychopathologies are characterized by diminishment of autonomy, although the nature of the autonomy disturbances can differ substantially. We now turn to discussions of various pathologies of which autonomy impairments are central components.

Disorders Involving Internally Controlling Regulation

From the perspective of SDT, the rigid structures and processes that are involved in this class of disorders are primarily based in the process of *introjection,* in which standards, demands, contingencies, values, and regulatory processes are adopted by people but are not well integrated. Through the process of introjecting aspects of their identities, people develop rigid character structures that in turn continually frustrate their basic needs for autonomy and competence. Horney (1950, p. 64) aptly described this process as as the "tyranny of the should." Behavior becomes heteronomous, and they close themselves off from open or creative ways of engaging themselves and their environments.

As with internalizing disorders more generally, introjected internalizations are frequently potentiated by highly controlling parenting practices applied to vulnerable children (e.g., see Muhtadie, Zhou, Eisenberg, & Wang, 2013). In fact, studies show that the links between parental control and the development of internalizing symptoms are mediated by the thwarting of basic needs. For example, Costa, Soenens, Gugliandolo, Cuzzocrea, and Larcan (2015) examined the links between perceived paternal and maternal psychological control and internalizing symptoms in a sample of young Italian women. They found that the satisfaction of basic psychological needs fully mediated the relations between perceived psychological control by parents and the women's internalizing distress. Pressured or coerced to behave in particular ways or lose support and affection, people will often internalize the external controls but fail to assimilate or integrate them into a sense of self, leaving them without the feeling of volition and need satisfaction (e.g., Grolnick, 2002; Deci & Ryan, 1991, 2000). The rigid introjects thus regulate action in part by blocking awareness of people's natural tendencies toward proactivity and growth.

Introjected regulation involves an inner demandingness, such that people feel they have to or must engage in certain behaviors or reach certain standards. To meet such demands often requires a distortion of perceptions, experiences, or feelings so as to reduce conflict or resolve dissonance. Thus self-deception and defensiveness are frequent concomitants of introjection (Hodgins & Knee, 2002; Weinstein, Ryan, DeHaan, Przybylski, Legate, and Ryan, 2012). Within SDT we have also used the terms *ego involvement* (Ryan, 1982) and *contingent self-esteem* (Deci & Ryan, 1995) to describe the dynamics of introjected regulation. In ego involvement the individuals feel that they must behave in certain ways or lose a sense of worth or self-esteem. Similarly, contingent self-esteem expresses the idea that one's lovability is conditional on certain behaviors or ways of being.

Kuhl and his colleagues (e.g., Baumann, Kuhl, & Kazén, 2005; Koole & Kuhl, 2003; Quirin & Kuhl, 2008) refer to introjected demands and contents as *self-infiltrations*. Object relations theorists such as Winnicott (1965) and Miller (1981) used the term *false self* to describe this process of building a façade with cognitions that have lost their grounding in organismic needs, urges, and feelings. When acting in accordance with introjects, people may display "willpower" (Deci, 1980; May, 1969) rather than autonomous volition, as they force themselves to keep away from needs or motivations that are negatively regarded and to enact internally demanded behaviors, which is in turn depleting rather than vitalizing (Martela, DeHaan, & Ryan, 2016). This core dynamic within people between controlling introjects and their perceptions, motives, desires, or needs that are inconsistent with the introjects characterizes both subclinical and formally diagnosed disorders. We review a few of the latter in what follows.

Introjective Depression

Depression is a broad diagnosis that contains many subtypes, characterized by different etiologies and intrapersonal dynamics. For example, *anaclitic depression* involves feelings of dependence upon others and feelings of threat to or actual loss of those relationships. Feelings of helplessness, weakness, and abandonment often predominate.

In contrast, *introjective depression* results when an individual with strongly internalized standards feels that he or she has failed at them. In a psychodynamic view, introjective depression arises from a harshly critical superego that creates feelings of worthlessness and guilt and a sense of failure. Although a lack of satisfying relatedness is implicated in this type of depression, introjective depression specifically reflects rigid self-control and disturbed autonomy (e.g., Blatt, 2004; Ryan, Deci, et al., 2006), for it is based in people's use of controlling ideals as a measure of their worth or lack thereof (Swallow & Kuiper, 1988). Whereas introjected standards for self-evaluation typically guide and pressure people to do what socializing agents initially required, introjective depression often involves standards that are unattainable, engendering harsh and often devastating self-evaluations.

Among the most salient features of introjective forms of depression are dysphoric affect and difficulty in overcoming inertia. With their ubiquitous feelings of incompetence and low self-esteem, people believe not only that they are failures but also that their shortcomings make them unworthy and unlovable. As such, they are unlikely to establish the kinds of relationships that could buffer them from the pain associated with the negative self-evaluations. In other words, their beliefs create self-fulfilling prophecies resulting in thwarting of their basic needs for competence, relatedness, and autonomy.

The dynamics of introjective depression make clear that autonomy is highly compromised for the individuals who experience this type of depressive disorder. First, there are the introjects that pressure and control, leaving people feeling that they should and have to live up to the standards, thus inciting an external perceived locus of causality

(E-PLOC) and behaviors that are experienced as heteronomous. However, at the same time that they feel controlled, they have the belief in or fear of their own incompetence, leading them to experience amotivation and impersonality (Deci & Ryan, 1985b).

The disturbed autonomy and depressive symptomatology that characterize introjective depression have been related to biological vulnerabilities. Yet it is also the case that social factors, particularly in parenting, appear to play a significant role in their emergence (Zuroff, Mongrain, & Santor, 2004). For example, a high level of control from parents when combined with children's feelings of incompetence can be a precipitant of symptoms in childhood and adolescence (Miller, Birnbaum, & Durbin, 1990). Increasing empirical evidence supports these clinical observations. Noom, Deković, and Meeus (1999) studied 12- to 18-year-old adolescents and found a negative relation between levels of autonomy and depressed mood. Van der Giessen, Branje, and Meeus (2014) found, in a longitudinal study, that the lower the level of parents' autonomy support was, the higher was the level of their adolescent children's depressive symptoms. Similarly, Shahar, Henrich, Blatt, Ryan, and Little (2003) found substantial relations between self-criticism, neediness, low autonomy, and depressive symptoms, as well as more negative life events and fewer positive events in a large sample of adolescents.

Barber (1996) has described *parental psychological control* as the capricious use of discipline and manipulation of childrens's emotions and attachments, as a means of pressuring children to control themselves. Research by Soenens, Park, Vansteenkiste, and Mouratidis (2012) provides evidence for the relations of such controlling paretning to introjective depression. Soenens et al. found that when adolescents from both Belgium and South Korea perceived their parents to be psychologically controlling with respect to both keeping them (their children) close and expecting them to have very high achievement standards, the adolescents reported high levels of both dependency on parents and self-criticism (Blatt, Schaffer, Bers, & Quinlan, 1992), and these in turn predicted depressive symptoms. It also seems likely that introjective depression would often have conditional regard as an important component of its etiology. As noted in an earlier chapter, studies by Assor, Roth, and Deci (2004) indicated that this parenting practice is associated with the children feeling a compulsion to do as the parents require and at the same time feeling rejected by them.

This self-critical, introjective depression has also been linked to *maladaptive perfectionism* (e.g., Flett, Hewitt, & Singer, 1995), which is a state in which people experience substantial pressure to live up to introjected goals, and are highly self-critical when they do not. Self-critcism, of course, is a typical experience for them, because it is nearly impossible to be perfect. Studies have linked self-critical perfectionism to controlled motivation and the controlled causality orientation (e.g., Miquelon, Vallerand, Grouzet, & Cardinal, 2005), both of which are closely aligned with introjection, and to increased need frustration over time (Boone, Vansteenkiste, Soenens, Van der Kaap-Deeder, & Verstuyf, 2014). Self-critical perfectionism has been found to stem in part from parenting that was authoritarian (Flett et al., 1995; Kawamura, Frost, & Harmatz, 2002) and harsh (Frost, Novara, & Rhéaume, 2002), and Enns, Cox, and Clara (2002) linked harsh parenting not only to maladaptive perfectionism but also to increased proneness to depression.

Similarly, Soenens, Vansteenkiste, Luyten, Duriez, and Goossens (2005) found that parental controllingness predicted maladaptive perfectionism, depression, and self-esteem deficits. This research had been built upon early work by McCranie and Bass (1984), who found that self-critical depression in women was associated with having parents who maintained strict control, insisted on high achievement, and were both contingent and inconsistent in their conveyance of love. Their children thus yearned for love but were unsure how to get it, even while trying in all ways to live up to the strict controls. Whiffen and Sasseville (1991) reported similar results concerning introjective depression in both males and females.

All of the above results are consistent with our speculations concerning how need-thwarting social contexts, particularly those involving psychological control and conditional regard, contribute to introjection and lay the foundation for maladaptive perfectionism and introjective depression. In this vein, one can view introjective, self-critical depression as a chronic and pervasive state of ego involvement and internally controlling regulation in which one continually fails to live up to demands and is thus punished.

Eating Disorders

The eating disorders of anorexia and bulimia involve an obsessive concern with food and body image. In anorexia, individuals (most typically young women) hold strong and stable introjects about being thin and restricting their eating, whereas with bulimia the introjects are less stable, leading to occasional binge eating followed by self-induced vomiting and abuse of diuretics. The experience of bulimics following the binge is, of course, guilt and self-derision, for although the introjects are not stable enough to control the binge, they nonetheless are more than adequate to make the people feel bad about themselves.

Bruch (1973) provided the classic account of anorexia, in which she described eating disorders as being based in a pervasive sense of ineffectance (i.e., amotivation) that is covered over by a struggle for control. She traced these feelings of ineffectance to a disturbance in autonomy, related to controlling parenting environments. The body of the young person with anorexia is one place she can exert control. Persons with anorexia develop strong internal controls to eat little and/or to strive for a degree of thinness that is never enough. The introjected controls give the individuals the illusion of self-sufficiency and control in their world, although this rigid self-control bears no relation to autonomous self-regulation. Indeed, it is solidly based in a mix of rigid internal control and amotivation.

Early SDT research on this topic by Strauss and Ryan (1987) provided support for Bruch's description of this disorder and the view that autonomy disturbances are at the heart of eating disorders. The researchers found that persons displaying anorexia or bulimia displayed greater self-oppression and self-rejection than members of a matched control group. These control-group participants also displayed more flexible self-management and self-acceptance than did the participants with eating disorders. As well, Strauss and Ryan documented a heightened impersonal causality orientation (Deci & Ryan, 1985a) among persons with restrictive anorexia, which is indicative of an impoverished sense of personal effectiveness. This is combined with the sense of internally controlled regulation for food intake.

Thus internally controlled regulation is central in the dynamics of eating disorders, as it is to other syndromes we have discussed. Indeed, research suggests that prior to the expression of eating disorders, many patients have already displayed obsessive–compulsive traits and behaviors (Anderluh, Tchanturia, Rabe-Hesketh & Treasure, 2003). Patients with either anorexia or bulimia show a high level of public self-consciousness and an inordinate concern for other people's views of them, as others' approval can help to assuage their critical introjects. As Plant and Ryan (1985) argued, public self-consciousness implies an E-PLOC in which people's introjects and their imagined views of others are coordinated in controlling their eating behaviors. In fact, although a focus on weight is generally paramount, individuals with eating disorders are typically self-conscious, demanding, and self-critical with regard to many aspects of their appearances, feelings, and behavior. This, as we have indicated, leads to a high degree of personal control that is dictatorial in nature and built on a shaky foundation of ineffectance.

Vansteenkiste, Soenens, and Vandereycken (2005) used SDT to provide an account of motivational processes in persons with anorexia. They suggested that their focus on thinness is an attempt to gain a sense of security and worth, yet even as they get thinner, the self-confidence and emotional benefits they expect do not accrue. Never thin enough, yet they work with the belief that feelings of satisfaction require more self-control. The paradox is that achieving their extrinsic goal of improved image is somewhat satisfying and serves to reinforce these strivings. Indeed, their experience seems to tell them that losing weight is part of the solution. Thus the self-restrictions and internal demands are strengthened while they are doing harm to the individuals.

Although persons with restrictive anorexia have a high degree of control in resisting eating, people with bulimia often find themselves overwhelmed by the impulse to eat. Their binges are most likely to occur at times of high stress or anxiety or when they have been using alcohol, because those are times when it is more difficult for their introjected regulatory structures to keep the impulse in check. The binge impulse is often a kind of defiant reaction to their introjected standards and self-derogation or to the pressure and criticism from others, so the episode of binging is an attempt to escape from the painful sense of themselves in the face of the introjected and burdensome standards and evaluations (Baumeister, 1991). It is interesting that, as the psychic threat gets greater for people with bulimia, their regulatory capacity becomes weakened, whereas in people with obsessive–compulsive personality and/or restrictive eating pathologies, the regulatory capacity tends to become even more dominant when they are faced with stress. The instability of the regulatory introjects in people with bulimia thus allows for the akratic episodes of eating, but following the failures, their self-evaluative introjects invariably result in self-derogation and feelings of depression for having lost control. It is interesting that the long-term course for many people with restrictive anorexia involves failing to maintain such effortful control of their eating and thus moving toward a bulimic pattern of coping.

As with other disorders, the onset of bulimia has multiple contributors, yet factors within the family of origin, such as critical withdrawal of love, that promote introjects are certainly implicated. Bruch (1978) was vivid in her depiction of parents contributing to the eating disorders of their daughters by depriving them of autonomy—that is, of the right to live their own lives. Other theorists have reported high levels of enmeshment and intrusive control in families of patients with eating disorders (Minuchin, Rosman, & Baker, 1978), and empirical findings from Strober and Humphrey (1987) indicated that persons suffering from anorexia and from bulimia experience their parents as blaming, rejecting, and critical relative to the reports of a control group of participants without eating disorders. Similarly, Strauss and Ryan (1987, 1988) found evidence for less mutuality of autonomy in the object representations of participants with symptoms of these eating disorders, compared with a comparison group, and lower reported expressiveness within their families.

Obsessive–Compulsive Psychopathologies

There are two distinct obsessive–compulsive syndromes that share many characteristics such as internally controlled regulation but are also different in etiology and in responses to treatment. The first, *obsessive–compulsive personality* (OCP), involves people being preoccupied with order, perfectionism, and mental or interpersonal control. These concerns are often rigid and demanding, thus interfering with the openness, flexibility, and adaptability of the individuals' behavior, and they often seem irrationally rule-bound or even stubborn.

SDT sheds some light on the fact that OCP symptoms can be more or less severe and pervasive. At the least problematic end is an introjected or controlled orientation toward organization and order, which, although it is characterized by rigid control and thus has negative psychological consequences, can be useful in people's lives, especially in certain professions and areas of life. In some work settings, for example, a need for order may serve the people well. In other areas introjection may not serve well, as it can create barriers to both creative problem solving and interpersonal relatedness. It is important to note, however, that the satisfaction someone with mild OCP gets from succeeding at keeping order is quite different from the experience of someone whose motivation for being orderly is autonomous. Nix, Ryan, Manley, and Deci (1999) found, for example, that when people who were autonomously motivated succeeded at tasks, they experienced considerable vitality and aliveness, but when people whose motivation was controlled (as is the case in OCP) succeeded at the tasks, they reported a satisfaction that lacked the vitality and excitement. The free energy available to the self that accompanies autonomy allows people to experience joy and aliveness (Ryan & Deci, 2008a; Ryan & Frederick, 1997), whereas the controlled energy—the willpower or self-control—is often depleting (Moller, Deci, & Ryan, 2006).

At the other end of the continuum are more extreme cases of OCP, in which the person's ability to function can be highly compromised. Internal pressures and preoccupations can create problems both in close relationships, in which rigidity can cause conflict, and in the workplace, where flexibility often yields more effective performance. As such, the more severe the OCP, the less people will experience satisfaction of their needs for relatedness and competence, as well as their need for autonomy. The problem is that people with more severe OCP cannot tolerate even modest violations of internalized rules, and the anxiety associated with being in situations they cannot control can become overwhelming and difficult to tolerate. Accordingly, it is clear that it is not so much the behaviors themselves that define the pathology of OCP, but, rather, it is the rigidity of the behavioral regulation—the internally controlling regulation—that makes the behaviors pathological. And the more rigid and insistent the regulation, the more severe will be the pathology.

People with OCP typically also apply their necessity for order, standards, or propriety to their inner worlds, often resulting in choking their emotions and thus, for example, keeping their hurt, fear, and anger in check, in part through suppression and in part by treating it as a personal matter not to be shared with others. In both cases, it is initial external controls, such as parental conditional regard (PCR; Roth et al., 2009), that lead to suppression or an unwillingness to share with others. With this rigid compartmentalization of negative emotions, people lose the ability to make full contact with their positive emotions, and thus, being unable to share themselves with others, they have diminished relationships. In addition, the very dynamics of inner control result in lower flexibility and vitality, so people with OCP often appear to lack emotional warmth and tenderness and seem unwilling to be vulnerable in personal relationships (MacKinnon, Michels, & Buckley, 2015). Of course, in the more severe cases of OCP, the ritualistic behaviors become more separated from adaptive consequences, in which case these anxiety-binding behaviors themselves become dysfunctional.

OCP is interesting because it is a pathology that is to a substantial degree influenced by social and experiential factors that promote introjection and internal control. This has been highlighted by research on PCR showing that this parenting approach is linked to inner compulsion to engage in the behaviors that yielded the desired regard (Assor et al., 2004). More recently, Assor and Tal (2012) examined adolescents' perceptions of their mothers' degrees of positive parental conditional regard (PPCR) and negative parental conditional regard (NPCR) as it related to their own compulsive overinvestment in the required behaviors, which in the study involved doing well at academics. Results of the research showed that children of mothers who were high in PPCR did indeed do the desired behaviors, so this parenting approach did serve to promote the behaviors the parents desired. However, doing well academically was accompanied by feelings of self-aggrandizement, and doing less well yielded self-disparagement, indicating that there were maladaptive emotional consequences associated with PPCR, and these findings held up when controlling for NPCR, which has been found to be associated with even more negative consequences than PPCR (Roth et al., 2009). In short, the children subjected to the PPCR tended to develop an intensely rigid, compulsive investment in doing well at school and thus exerted great effort in an attempt to do well, buttressed by a dynamic of contingent self-esteem.

Othmer and Othmer (2002) reported that people with OCP often display their characteristic drivenness and inflexibility in situations in which authorities are present. This strong tie to authority and control suggests that there is less biological vulnerability involved with this disorder than with many others, and, consistent with that idea, OCP has been found to be relatively nonresponsive to pharmacological treatments (Jenike, 1991). Nonetheless, there is some evidence that temperament may represent a biological vulnerability for OCP (Sperry, 2003), suggesting that the etiology of this disorder, like the others, is in fact an interaction of biological, social, and experiential factors.

It is also interesting that, although people with OCP can appear rigid and determined in doing what they feel compelled to do, there are times when they are quite uncertain, indecisive, and painfully ruminative, being unable to make even trivial decisions. Specifically, because they are dependent on rules and demands, when those structures are not available, people with OCP can become anxious and hesitant. Once they have blocked access to their basic needs and affective underpinnings, they have no internal basis for making decisions or selecting between preferences. This anxiety of indecision highlights how the adaptive behaviors and determination of people with OCP do not reflect autonomy and wellness.

Underlying OCP is, of course, disturbed autonomy. Typically, this takes the form of compliance and overconscientiousness—that is, obedience with the present or introjected authority—but people with OCP may secretly wish for defiance, perhaps occasionally letting it "leak out" in small ways. For example, the research by Roth et al. (2009) that showed PCR being a precursor to inner compulsion that led to obedient suppression of negative emotions also showed that the inner compulsion had a weaker, though significant, link from inner compulsion to dysregulation.

A second obsessive–compulsive pathology is *obsessive–compulsive disorder* (OCD), which has both similarities to and differences from OCP. The clearest similarities are the ritualized and routine behavior patterns and the experience of being controlled or compelled to enact the behaviors. Characteristic of OCD are persistent and obsessive experiences of intrusive thoughts and demands that can be quieted, at least temporarily, by engaging in rigid, ritualistic behaviors. The thoughts are unwelcome, disturbing, and anxiety provoking, and they are experienced as originating outside the self, often even conflicting with conscious values, ideals, and goals.

An example of OCD is a woman who reported persistent, intrusive thoughts about hurting her infant when she saw objects such as scissors. These thoughts conflicted with her strong conscious feelings about her child and her wish to keep the child safe, and thus the intrusive thoughts of harming the child caused enormous anxiety. To deal with her anxiety, she felt great compulsion to always be on the lookout for objects that represented potential weapons in order to be sure they were out of sight and difficult to access. OCD is classified as an anxiety disorder precisely because obsessive, ritualistic behaviors typically have the function of regulating anxiety, although individuals with OCD often still feel anxious even when enacting the rituals.

From the perspective of the individuals whose discordant thoughts are intrusive and unwanted, the *perceived locus of causality* (PLOC) for the thoughts is impersonal, because they are there without intent, and for the ensuing ritualistic behaviors, it is external, because the people feel strongly compelled to engage in the behaviors, often in very rigid ways. The coercive power that pressures them to engage in the compulsive behaviors is the anxiety that follows when they do not. Accordingly, the motivation for these behaviors is internally controlled, just as it is for people with OCP. Further, as reported by Swedo and Rapoport (1990), because children with OCD feel like they have no real control of their symptoms, they have to exert tremendous effort not to engage in their ritualistic behaviors when they are in public settings. An aspect of the internally controlled regulation is that the compulsive behaviors are typically performed under harsh prescriptions and constraints and failures to comply with the demands may result in anxiety, guilt, and self-disparagement. In extreme cases, panic may follow failures to comply.

Unlike OCP, there is substantial evidence that OCD has an important biological component, and there is indication that OCD can be successfully treated with medication. Still, there is some evidence that social factors play a role in OCD. For example, Rasmussen and Tsuang (1986) found evidence of strict, orderly, and inflexible religious styles in the backgrounds of adult OCD patients. Hoover and Insel (1984) reported family entrapment as common among adolescents with OCD but also emphasized the reciprocal nature of adult–child interactions and vulnerabilities that might produce such patterns. In short, although OCD represents a clear instance of a psychopathology with disturbed autonomy, it is the phenomenology (rather than necessarily the etiology) of self-related demands that characterizes it for us as an internally controlling disorder.

Paranoid Personality

This disorder shares with obsessive–compulsive disorders a characteristically rigid or controlling style of behavioral and emotional regulation. However, whereas people with OCP struggle with their own inner pressures and compulsions, people with paranoid personality disorder (PPD) experience themselves to be in an ongoing battle with external authorities and are thus highly suspicious of those authorities, often ones they do not know. They must therefore scrutinize the environment for the forces working against them, even as they approach that activity with a rigid set of beliefs and interpretations. Stated differently, people with PPD project their punitive introjects and critical ideations onto others, often blaming and feeling rage toward those others.

Interestingly, in the process of seeing themselves as victims of powerful others, people with PPD are able to feel like they have power and significance—they see themselves as so important that presidents, kings, and famous others are concerned with them. Nonetheless, underneath their preoccupations with authorities and their beliefs in their own power, individuals with PPD are highly insecure and have self-disparaging thoughts and feelings. The strong desire for a sense of power and control often represents a means of compensating for or avoiding these underlying unpleasant experiences. PPD is thus characterized by a multifaceted disturbance of autonomy heavily based in internal and external control.

Furthermore, various theorists have suggested that the etiology of PPD is significantly based in controlling parenting practices. For example, Benjamin (2002) argued that parents of PPD patients are often critical, humiliating, and even sadistic, and that many people with the disorder have been victims of abuse. Because of such harsh past treatment, people afflicted with this disorder would logically be on the lookout for danger and would find it difficult to acknowledge their own mistakes or shortcomings because such inadequacies may well have brought on the harsh treatment.

As with the obsessive–compulsive pathologies, the autonomy disturbances in PPD also interfere with intimacy and satisfaction of relatedness needs, for here the suspiciousness precludes the possibility of being trusting and vulnerable with others. Thus, PPD leads people to behave in ways that will continue to thwart their basic psychological needs.

Although the disorders with rigid, introjected demands that we have discussed so far (OCP, OCD, and PPD) involve some level of self-critical evaluation and self-disparagement, people with these disorders can also be self-sustaining in the sense that if they live up to their introjected standards they may feel self-aggrandizement and may get affirmation from others who are invested in their outcomes. So, although they may at times experience depressive affect and feelings of worthlessness, those are not defining aspects of the disorders.

There are, however, internal-control-based disorders for which self-disparagement and feelings of hopelessness are defining characteristics. Examples of these are self-critical or introjective depression and anorexia disorders. In these disorders, the introjected standards and requirements are so strict and harsh that it is nearly impossible for people to behave satisfactorily. Thus they are continually experiencing failure and self-derogation. With their feelings of worth being contingent upon meeting the standards, which they never really do, their overwhelming sense is of inadequacy. In these disorders, then, we see the disturbed autonomy involving both the sense of being controlled that is manifested as introjected demands and the sense of amotivation and depressiveness for which incompetence and rejection are central precipitating factors.

Summary Comments

Each disorder we have discussed so far involves rigid, demanding, critical, and controlling internal regulations, pressuring various behaviors and criticizing their inadequacies. These rigid structures take varied forms and are more or less stable and effective in controlling people's actions. In some cases, most notably the obsessive–compulsive personality and restrictive eating disorders, the individuals can feel a strong sense of personal control and self-efficacy from behaving in the demanded ways—for example, individuals with OCP keep their personal affairs in order and those with anorexia restrict their eating and keep thin. These compensatory competence satisfactions cannot, however, ameliorate frustrations of autonomy and relatedness. These and the other disorders we have discussed so far with their salient introjects constitute disturbed autonomy and can terrorize people with threats of guilt, shame, derision, and low self-esteem. These disorders also highlight SDT's distinctions between self-control and autonomy. To control oneself, to force oneself to do something, is not to be autonomous, so even though self-control can yield desired outcomes.

We turn now to disorders characterized not by the prevalence of introjects but rather by their absence and, more importantly, by the absence of integrated regulations. These forms of psychopathology involve the lack of adequate regulatory structures that allow people to function effectively and cohesively in most social contexts.

Disorders Involving Failures of Internalization

Throughout this book, we have focused on the necessity of supports for satisfactions of the basic psychological needs for competence, autonomy, and relatedness in order for internalization and integration to function effectively. These supports facilitate both secure attachments to caregivers and the assimilation of values and regulations that allow the autonomous self-regulation of behaviors. Familial environments that are controlling, cold, hostile, or neglectful prompt insecure attachments, poor internalization, and impoverished emotion regu.altion (Shields, Cicchetti, & Ryan, 1994; Weiss & Grolnick, 1991) and can thus play roles in externalizing disorders, such as antisocial personality and conduct disorders, as well as disorders of the self, such as dissociative identity and borderline personality disorder. With the insecure attachments and poor internalization come impoverished emotion regulation manifested as dysregulation and poorly managed expression of emotions. We turn now to a brief discussion of each.

Antisocial Personality and Conduct Disorders

Persons with an antisocial personality disorder (APD) tend to be aggressive, negligent, manipulative, and immature, showing little care about how their behaviors affect others. They are, as well, prone to lie, steal, embezzle, act irresponsibly, and be neglectful. This disorder is often a continuation of childhood conduct disorder, in which children are emotionally labile, have difficulty exchanging affection, and seem unable to understand what is right and what is wrong. Often such children evidence an unusual interest in violence and sensational phenomena such as fires or accidents (Magid & McKelvey, 1987). Egocentrism and self-aggrandizement, which frequently accompany their lying about accomplishments, highlight their need to be affirmed and esteemed by others. Like adults with ADP, children with conduct disorder tend to have an impaired conscience and lack the normative levels of concern with what is appropriate for them to do.

The etiology of APD has been addressed in varied ways by different theorists but, as pointed out by many authors (see Burnette & Cicchetti, 2012), it certainly includes genetic factors, such as those conducing to poor autonomic reactivity; sociocultural factors, such as neighborhood economics; and social factors, such as parental need thwarting. We consider APD a pathology of failed internalization and emotion dysregulation. Biological factors may have made internalization more difficult, but the internalization failures in children's early development are strongly influenced by deficits in the social factors that have been shown to be necessary for internalization to occur. In short, we argue that people with APD will have failed to internalize societal ideals, behavioral norms, and moral principles, as well as regulatory processes for managing their emotions, to a significant degree because of the absence of need-supportive, facilitating environments.

Parental provision of autonomy support, involvement, and structure, which support satisfaction of the basic psychological needs (Grolnick, Deci, & Ryan, 1997), can be directly connected with the failure of internalization in individuals with APD. In fact, as we saw in Chapter 8, considerable evidence does point to the importance for internalization of these social-contextual factors. As well, there is the general literature on prosocial values that locates development of prosocial values in socialization patterns within the family (Grusec, 2011). Many investigators have started with the belief that the internalization of prosocial values occurs through a process of children having a strong connection to parents within which the parents implant their own values in the children so that the children will then emulate those values and attitudes espoused or enacted by the parents. This viewpoint implicitly assumes that prosocial values must be put into the children's psyches rather than nurtured. An alternative perspective endorsed by SDT agrees with the importance of children having strong and supportive relations with parents, but it assumes that human nature is prosocial and requires conditions that nurture and encourage it rather than implant it (cf., Deci & Ryan, 2000; Ryan & Hawley, 2016). In either case, the empirical evidence confirms that prosocial values are least likely to be evidenced when caregivers have been low in warmth (Maccoby, 1980) and high in either power-assertive discipline (Hoffman, 1960) or the closely related SDT concept of low involvement and autonomy support (Ryan, 1993; Grolnick et al., 1997; Soenens & Vansteenkiste, 2010).

The experience of growing up in a clearly nurturing, caring, responsive, and autonomy-supportive family setting, rather than a cold, chaotic, and power-assertive one, undoubtedly facilitates children's social competence (Shields et al., 1994), but also their prosocial values, for it provides the structure, involvement, and choice that facilitate satisfaction of the basic psychological needs and frees the children to be concerned with others (Grolnick et al., 1997). As well, when the children have observed their parents as models of caring and concern, they will be more inclined to evidence those characteristics themselves. In a study by Ryan and Connell (1989), the researchers found that children who experienced a high level of relatedness to parents were more autonomously motivated in the prosocial domain. Various clinical and empirical perspectives have suggested, conversely, that antisocial personality, with its features of self-service, manipulation, and hedonic gratification, is, in part, based in a cold, controlling, and inconsistent home setting (e.g., Benjamin, 2002; Greenberg, Speltz, & DeKlyen, 1993; McCord & McCord, 1964). A study by Odgers, Caspi, Russell, Sampson, Arseneault, and Moffit (2012) indeed showed that the lack of parental psychological supports predicted antisocial developmental trajectories beyond what was accounted for by neighborhood characteristics. Numerous studies have also shown that common to the development of children's conduct disorder and then APD are such factors as depression and other pathologies in their parents, loss of important others, high family conflict, and impoverished living conditions that are stressful for the family (Coie & Jacobs, 1993). All of these factors potentiate a lack of the basic nutrients upon which internalization depends—namely, parental autonomy support; adequate structure and guidance; and concerned, caring, and warm involvement that fosters a sense of relatedness and autonomy. Without these nutrients, poor internalization will result, and inner urges and emotions will tend to overwhelm the individuals' capacities for either self-control or autonomous self-regulation. They will thus experience an impersonal PLOC.

Although these models of value acquisition speak well to the matter of why children would fail to internalize the regulation of morality, they do not provide a full account of why those children would take on the nonmoral behaviors such as manipulation, cheating, and hypermaterialism that characterize APD. A fuller model of APD requires explaining not only the failure of internalization but also the roots of aggressive and selfish values and behaviors that can provide people with an external and relatively hollow sense of worth.

Recent studies exploring children's defiance have found that when parents are strongly controlling, their children are more likely to behave in problematic ways that are oppositional and defiant and, further, that this relation is mediated by the children's experience of need frustration (Van Petegem, Beyers, Vansteenkiste, & Soenens, 2012). Subsequent work showed that, when parents who were attempting to socialize their children with respect to morality did it in a controlling way, their children tended to be defiant and resistant (Vansteenkiste, Soenens, Van Petegem, & Duriez, 2014).

Research on children's aggressive behavior has found complementary results. Specifically, an important 6-year longitudinal study of students in elementary school examined trajectories of the students' aggressive behaviors over the period from 6 to 12 years of age (Joussemet et al., 2008). In general, they found that during this period students tended to display a lower level of aggressive behaviors, which makes sense because these are important years for socialization with respect to regulating their aggression. However, the researchers also found that the children whose mothers were relatively controlling in their child-rearing practices did not improve in terms of regulating their aggression but rather tended to show trajectories toward more aggressive behaviors, thus indicating that to a significant degree the development of aggression occurs in parenting environments that thwart children's basic needs.

Other research has focused more on people's self-centered, acquisitive goals and behaviors that serve a compensatory function. Ryan, Sheldon, Kasser, and Deci (1996) argued that when people are deprived of the satisfactions that accrue from autonomy-supportive and caring social contexts and thus experience diminishment of the well-being and deep feelings of worth that accompany need satisfaction, they often strive for extrinsic, narcissistically oriented goals that look worthy to others and give them some fragile sense of importance and esteem. In other words, to the extent that people have not secured a solid and stable sense of self, they aspire to outcomes that signify their worth to the public (see Chapter 11). Such extrinsic aspirations include material possessions and accumulated wealth, fame, and social recognition, winning competitions and holding power over others, and having attractive images associated with whatever is in vogue (Kasser, 2002b). To the extent that people are not anchored with a true or integrated self, their behavior is increasingly organized by values and goals that are narcissistically oriented and aligned with a false, or defensive, sense of self. Research by Kasser and Ryan (1993, 1996) has supported this reasoning by showing that college students who placed excessive emphasis on materialistic possessions also evidenced greater maladjustment, including narcissism and conduct disorders. Other investigators (Kasser & Ahuvia, 2002; Vansteenkiste, Duriez, Simons, & Soenens, 2006) found negative psychological consequences for students with strong extrinsic goals, even when the students were in social contexts in which those goals were normative. And among the various negative consequences associated with relatively high extrinsic aspirations were endorsed discrimination and racism (Duriez, Vansteenkiste, Soenens, & De Witte, 2007).

Kasser, Ryan, Zax, and Sameroff (1995) examined the developmental antecedents of a strongly held extrinsic aspiration for wealth and material goods, relative to one for making prosocial contributions, and found that adolescents who were relatively more materialistic came from homes in which both they and their mothers reported that the mothers provided less autonomy support, warmth, and security than the mothers of adolescents who were less materialistic. The researchers also found greater materialism among adolescents living in more impoverished, high-crime neighborhoods, where the parenting environments tended to be more controlling and hostile. In line with Coie and Jacobs (1993) analysis of conduct disorders, Kasser et al.'s (1995) analysis of clinical interviews with adolescent participants in an at-risk population (defined in terms of maternal psychopathology and low SES) revealed that those who placed greater importance on materialistic values were more likely to be clinically diagnosed as having conduct disorder. A conceptual replication indicated that college students who perceived their parents as controlling and cold showed a relatively higher centrality of materialism in their value orientations. Finally, research by Williams, Hedberg, Cox, and Deci (2000) found that when parents were low in autonomy support, their high-school-age children held strong extrinsic values for wealth, fame, and image and also engaged in more high-risk behaviors, including alcohol, tobacco, and marijuana use and early sexual intercourse.

This set of studies on extrinsic values and goals helps to illustrate that insofar as environments fail to meet people's basic psychological needs, and thus provide them with an authentic sense of self-worth, they often then focus on need substitutes that provide at least visible trappings of worth and perhaps draw admiration or respect, leading to a strong focus on extrinsic values (money, image, etc.). These compensatory goals, in turn, often contribute to the motivations of persons with APD who do not, often for genetic and environomental reasons, have the foundation for devloping a more authentic sense of self-worth. An understanding of the role of need substitutes, such as extrinsic goals for wealth, popularity, or power, discussed with respect to both OCP and APD, highlights the continuity of motivational dynamics between nonclinical and clinical populations.

When interpreted with concepts from SDT, the development of conduct disorders and an asocial and selfish extrinsic goal orientation result from inadequate attachment and failed internalization resulting from social environments that are inconsistent, chaotic, externally controlling, and relationally impoverished. To the extent that social values and economic conditions distort, disable, and distract the caregiving environment, children will be more focused on self-oriented goals that give them temporary feelings of worth and importance (Kasser, Ryan, Couchman, & Sheldon, 2004). Furthermore, this model applies not only to the lives of children with conduct disorder but also, increasingly, to American culture more generally (Kasser, Kanner, Cohn, & Ryan, 2007). In other words, the more we create conditions that disrupt the quality and stability of familial relationships and thus internalization, the more narcissistically oriented (Lasch, 1991) and antisocial will be the people within our culture.

Serious Disturbances of the Self

The third set of disorders that we discuss concerns impairments of autonomy and self-regulation typically associated with severe need thwarting or abuse during development. These disorders bring into focus not only the essentiality of need supports for healthy self-development but also the especially high costs of need thwarting, affecting the very capacities of experiential and behavioral coherence and regulation. Harsh control, rejection, maltreatment, and neglect represent forms of basic psychological need thwarting that produce cascading effects on subsequent functioning, evident in each of these disorders.

Dissociative Identity Disorders

Dissociative identity disorders (DID) involve isolated identities within people's personalities among which they shift, often prompted by cues in their environment. People experience these shifts among identities as being out of their intentional control. That is, the causality for the shifts is perceived as impersonal, as something that befalls them, with neither autonomous nor controlled intentionality playing a role. Moreover, DID reflects a fragmented self in which the identities are not experienced as unified or consistent. Depersonalization, which is a loss of feeling of people's own reality and may involve their bodies seeming to act independently of their intentions, is another symptom of DID that also exemplifies a sense of impersonal causality.

The sense of impersonal causality is, of course, a symptom of a serious disruption of autonomy, for the fragmentation of self is the exact opposite of integration, the latter being the true characterization of an autonomous sense of self and well-being. Violations of self by caregivers are frequently the antecedents to DID, traumatic experiences that shattered the integrity of the developing self. Not surprisingly, therefore, the etiological backdrop of DID is characterized by the extreme thwarting of all three basic psychological needs, resulting in the structural and functional obstacles to integrated functioning and intrusive experiences of impersonal locus of causality and lack of volition. People who should have been providing love were hurtful, and aspects of children's lives and bodies over which they should have had control were violated, often chronically, interfering with internalization and the self-coherence that it would optimally bring. Indeed, Steinberg and Schnall (2001) reported extremely high rates of early physical and sexual abuse among patients with DID, which leaves them unable to establish relationships or act with any sense of intentionality or volition.

With the perceived lack of personal causation, people with DID frequently experience despondency, and sometimes people who appear to be depressed are experiencing the despondency associated with DID, while having isolated and suppressed experiences of sexual or physical abuse. So much of the theraputic work with dissociative symptoms is thus integrative in nature—helping to reestablish the personal grounding and synthetic capacites that were disrupted by repeated traumitization (van der Hart, Nijenhuis, & Stele, 2006).

Borderline Personality Disorders

Borderline personality disorders (BPD), which have become increasingly prevalent in clinical settings (Linehan, 1993), are characterized by the lack of a coherent and secure sense of self, deviance from one's culture, considerable distress and malfunctioning, and, generally, comorbidity with symptoms or syndromes that are both externalizing and internalizing, such as drug and alcohol abuse, depression, anxiety, APD, and DID (e.g., Bemporad, Smith, Hanson, & Cicchetti, 1982; Meissner, 1988; Ryan, 2005). BPD also frequently encompasses such characteristics as emotion dysregulation, self-esteem volatility, impulsivity, self-mutilation, and relationship instability (e.g., Gabbard, 2000; Goldman, D'Angelo, & DeMaso, 1993). People with BPD have especially poor regulation of their anger, which results in destructive actions toward others and inner turmoil when the anger is turned on themselves. They also have difficulty understanding the boundary between themselves and others and can be very dependent on others for support and comforting. Being unable to manage their own anxiety effectively, they rely on others to help them contain it.

The lack of any sense of an integrated self, which is central to this disorder, leaves individuals with BPD without a stable sense of who they are and with difficulty in committing to activities or other people. They may, at times, cling to others in an attempt to feel cohesion, but these attachments are generally short-lived and sometimes destructive.

Further, individuals with BPD lack reflective awareness at critical moments when self-reguialtion is needed (Bleiberg, 2004; Fonagy & Target, 1997).

The phenomenology of persons with BPD includes elements that represent both amotivation and control—that is, these individuals experience a mix of impersonal and external causality loci. They frequently feel like they have no sense of personal initiative or responsibility for their own fate (i.e., amotivation and impersonal), while also feeling pressured by their circumstances (i.e., control and external). One older adolescent with BPD reported that he sometimes enters a state of being lost and disconnected in which an intense impulse to cut himself would befall him, thus suggesting an experience of impersonal causality. At the same time, he felt obliged to do the act to obtain relief from dysphoria and self-criticism, which suggests internally controlling regulation with external causality. In no sense did he feel autonomy and volition associated with such acts, for he was driven, compelled, and helpless. It is interesting that these acts typically followed experiences in which he felt rejection or abandonment from a parent who was at times clinging and at times harshly critical.

Associated with individuals with BPD having no sense of an integrated self or autonomous activity is the loss of connection to their interests and feelings. Thus they sometimes feel empty and isolated (Westen, 1991), and they often report feeling bored, which may lead to impulsive acts, such as substance abuse, careless spending, and binge eating, in an attempt to counteract those feelings.

Although there is some evidence of genetic contributions to borderline disorder, in that many people with BPD appear to have exhibited a difficult-child temperamental profile, considerable evidence focuses on the early environment of the children (e.g., Bernheim, Rescorla, & Rocissano, 1999; Depue & Lenzenweger, 2001). Evidence suggests that these environments were likely to have been devoid of autonomy support and involvement from caregivers, thus impairing the organismic integration process that is a necessity for a stable and cohesive sense of self. At the same time that parents provide no autonomy support or unconditional involvement, they (especially mothers) have difficulty allowing their children to individuate and experience self-sufficiency (Sperry, 2003). The parents' lack of autonomy support, with its critical component of taking the children's perspective, makes it hard for the children to develop reflective awareness in themselves. Further, the parents' general thwarting of the children's basic psychological needs undermines the process of developing an integrated sense of self, which is the basis for autonomous regulation and emotional integration.

Masterson (1985) described the caregivers of people with BPD as unavailable, neglectful, and inconsistent, and other writers (Herman, Perry, & van der Kolk, 1989; Westen, Ludolph, Misle, Ruffins, & Block, 1990; Zanarini, 1997) have pointed to physical or emotional abuse, much as abuse has been linked to DID. For example, the study by Herman et al. reported that four-fifths of the participants with BPD had experienced physical or sexual abuse or had witnessed serious domestic violence (see also Perry, Herman, van der Kolk, & Hoke, 1990). Further, Linehan (1987) argued that the parents of individuals with BPD often invalidate their emotional experiences, allowing no room for fears and anxieties and providing no soothing or comforting. Such actions fail to provide the conditions necessary for the children to internalize the capacity to sooth and comfort themselves, thus resulting in the children being ineffective at regulating their emotions and being unable to tolerate such feelings of pain and discomfort that could provide them with useful information if engaged with interest.

Object relations theorists such as Kernberg (1967) view BPD as being derived from mother–child difficulties, particularly during the period of separation/individuation when children push away from their mothers in an attempt to experience themselves as separate agents of action. The mothers of children who develop the borderline syndrome, however, are unable to allow that self-sufficiency, for it would leave them, the mothers, feeling abandoned. They thus make it difficult for the children by withdrawing love and nurturance whenever the children make any attempts at individuation. From the perspective of SDT, children subjected to this love withdrawal must decide between autonomy and relatedness to their mothers and, because of this no-win situation, the children are likely to give up autonomy and the trajectory of a true integrated self. Further, the relationships to mothers are not experienced as truly satisfying, for the mothers have conveyed that the children are being loved not for who they are but for acting as though they were who the mothers want them to be. In fact, the research by Roth et al. (2009) linked withdrawal of love to emotion dysregulation and resentment toward the parents, both features of BPD. Given the children's conflict and resentment, the mothers do not represent what in object relations theory is referred to as a "good" object that can support the psychological needs leading to a cohesive sense of self, so the children's integrative processes are greatly diminished.

The etiology of the patient with BPD illustrates how lack of consistent involvement, empathy, and autonomy support undermine the development of self-regulatory capacities that underlie the autonomous or integrated self (Ryan, 2005), and when these diminished developmental circumstances include emotional, physical, or sexual abuse, the children, when struggling to develop a sense of self, will face even greater challenges. These conditions, which appear with great frequency in the developmental histories of individuals with BPD and bear similarities with the precursors of DID, which is another disorder of the self, make it clear why there is often comorbidity with BPD and dissociative symptoms (MacKinnon et al., 2015).

Concluding Comments

In a more illustrative than comprehensive way, in this chapter we used SDT to examine the motivational dynamics entailed in a variety of psychological disorders. We began by noting that the development of autonomous self-regulation is a critical aspect of psychological health and well-being that is heavily dependent on autonomy support (e.g., Bindman et al., 2015; Bronson, 2000), and we then examined disturbances to the development of self and autonomy as central aspects of psychopathology. We focused especially on social-contextual factors associated with autonomy, competence, and relatedness need thwarting, insofar as these debilitating factors can catalyze or amplify existing vulnerabilities.

By considering the centrality of basic need satisfaction and autonomous functioning in relation to both psychological health and psychological illness, we have been able to see that psychopathologies can vary in severity. The disturbances in autonomy at both the normal and pathological levels can be understood as relating to the concepts of control (especially the internal control of introjects), with its E-PLOC; amotivation, with its impersonal PLOC; or some mix of the two. For example, we saw that internal control, suppressive emotion regulation, and an E-PLOC were central to the internalizing disorders involving rigid internal standards and punitive structures; that failures of internalization, emotion dysregulation, and an impersonal PLOC were important for the externalizing disorders; and that both external and impersonal causality were present in the disorders involving serious disturbances of the self.

Evidence from SDT highlights the etiological role of basic psychological need frustrations, often prompted by need-thwarting environments, in various psychopathologies. Need thwarting is a general risk factor characterized by *multifinality* (Cicchetti & Rogosch, 1996)—that is, it can potentiate a range of disorders as a function of both moderating factors and proximal challenges to the individual. For instance, research shows that suicidal ideation and risk of suicidal behavior is substantially increased in individuals, low in basic psychological need satisfaction (Britton, Van Orden, Hirsch, & Williams, 2014), as is the frequency of nonsuicidal self-injuries (Emery, Heath & Mills, 2015). Yet analysis of specific disorders also reveals specific configurations of types and severity of psychological need thwarting, each with a corresponding phenomenology. Previous articles (e.g., Ryan, 2005; Ryan, Deci, et al., 2006; Ryan, Deci, & Vansteenkiste, 2016; Vansteenkiste & Ryan, 2013) have reviewed the often-cascading effects of need thwarting, as both a general and specific risk factor for specific syndromes, and the collective evidence on the etiological role of environments that thwart basic psychological need satisfactions is in our view compelling.

Even in disorders that may be primarily caused by factors other than need thwarting, the phenomenology of psychopathology often still implicates the issue of need frustration and autonomy disturbances. For example, in persons with schizophrenia, in which genetic influences loom especially large, symptoms will often feel uncontrollable, and behaviors will lack an internal PLOC (Ryan, Deci, et al., 2006). Evidence shows that individuals who have experienced a first episode of psychosis have lower need satisfaction than a comparison group (Breitborde, Kleinlein, & Srihari, 2012), and individuals with schizophrenia show lower autonomy orientations and higher impersonal or amotivational characteristics (Cooper, Lavaysse, & Gard, 2015). In addition, both interpersonal challenges and stigma associated with severe illnesses can impair ongoing need supports and satisfaction.

Finally, whatever the causes of a disorder, need satisfaction is critical to efforts at coping and adjustment. For example, research by Vancampfort and colleagues (2013) found that the autonomous motivation of patients with schizophrenia predicted greater engagement in health-promoting behaviors. As we shall see, the effectiveness of treatment strategies for a wide range of psychopathologies depends in part on how they support basic psychological need satisfactions. We leave these issues for Chapters 17 and 18, in which we specifically take up the SDT perspective on psychotherapy and behavior change.

PART V

The Application and Practice of Self-Determination Theory in Multiple Domains

CHAPTER 17

Psychotherapy and Behavior Change
Creating Facilitating Environments

Motivation plays a central role in psychotherapy and behavior change, but it is differently conceptualized and mobilized within different schools of practice. We consider two broad categories—*outcome-focused* therapies and *process-focused* therapies—and review how varied approaches within each category attempt to foster autonomy and willing participation of clients, both in theory and in practice. We then review findings suggesting that both client autonomy and therapist autonomy support represent modality nonspecific aspects of treatment that significantly influence retention, effectiveness, and maintenance of change. Finally, we turn to a more informal discussion from our viewpoint as clinicians concerning the key elements comprising a facilitating environment—one that fosters internalization and growth through supporting basic psychological needs and awareness.

Although psychotherapy is a relatively modern idea, the term derives from some ancient concepts. *Psyche* means the soul or spirit; therapy (*therapeia*) derives from the idea of healing. Thus psychotherapy is the healing of the spirit. No doubt there have always been souls and spirits in need of healing, and across history many types of healers and systems of healing have come and gone. Today, practitioners from psychology, social work, nursing, occupational therapy, medicine, and life coaching, among other professions, perform what Frank (1988) defined as *psychotherapy*: an activity in which one consults with a professional (i.e., someone guided by theory) to find pathways to healing. Closely related to psychotherapy is *behavior change*, typically a term applied when there is a preordained focus of treatment. Here, too, psychologists and other practitioners work with clients to bring about change, but in this case they attempt to mobilize and guide clients' behavior toward specific outcomes or treatment goals.

Whether engaged in psychotherapy or behavior change, creating sustained change in the direction of wellness or more effective functioning poses unique challenges for both clients and practitioners. Evidence suggests, in fact, that *motivation* is a major concern in most every psychological intervention setting. For instance, many people coming to therapies *want* to be motivated but still may be conflicted or resistant to specific changes. Others sometimes cannot, due to embedded or necessary defenses, even know what they want, but they nonetheless seek solutions to some inner suffering. Many clients don't even show for their first appointments (Sheeran, Aubrey, & Kellett, 2007), suggestive of ambivalence about change or fears concerning the process. Many other clients "fail" to complete treatments (e.g., Hampton-Robb, Qualls, & Compton, 2003; Ogrodniczuk, Joyce, & Piper, 2007), with multiple reasons for disengagement. Thus, when it comes to changing spirits or behaviors, there can be much internal resistance, ambivalence, and sensitivity.

Given the centrality of the issue of motivation, most every approach to psychotherapy and behavior change has developed strategies and positions regarding how to move clients, although some are more explicitly formulated than others. These strategies vary greatly. For example, some approaches simply make motivation and readiness a prerequisite to participation, ruling out those who are ambivalent or unsure. Others place emphasis on interpersonally supporting clients' autonomy throughout the therapeutic process, especially for treatment activities. Still others utilize more controlling and less need-supportive approaches, to the detriment, we believe, of their ultimate effectiveness and the maintenance of change over time.

In this chapter and the one that follows, we use SDT to reflect on current psychotherapeutic and behavioral change approaches. Because SDT is focused on both how motivational processes can be sustained over time and how basic psychological need satisfactions support wellness, it has unique criteria for evaluating the processes by which therapists and change agents attempt to motivate personality or behavior change.

We begin by reviewing varied therapies for the way in which each addresses or supports motivation and engagement. Our findings might surprise many (see also Ryan, Lynch, Vansteenkiste, & Deci, 2011; Scheel, 2011). We shall see that nearly every school of therapy expresses a value for and attempts to (in some manner and with whatever terminology) promote client autonomy. This is so even when there is no explicit place or value for autonomy or self-determination within the theoretical frame or discourse on which the treatment is based. Still, not all techniques used within current approaches are equally likely to support clients' autonomy, and not all therapists or practitioners behave in ways that engage volition. In what follows we thus critically review both outcome-focused and process-oriented types of therapy, regarding their orientations toward and strategies for promoting autonomous motivation for change.

Following this we turn to empirical evidence for the idea that autonomy and autonomy support can enhance the effectiveness of treatments across methods and approaches. We suggest, in fact, that autonomy and autonomy support represent *common treatment factors* affecting outcomes across modalities and treatment concerns. This issue is especially important given that often the same therapies can be delivered in more or less controlling or autonomy-supportive ways (e.g., Williams, Grow, Freedman, Ryan, & Deci, 1996; Zuroff, Koestner, Moskowitz, McBride, Marshall, & Bagby, 2007) and that the relationship skills required to provide therapy in autonomy-supportive, noncontrolling ways are often not specifically addressed in psychotherapy training (Guiffrida, 2014; Sue & Sue, 2008).

Finally, after considering evidence for the efficacy of more autonomy- and relatedness-supportive delivery of all treatments, we discuss some of the many elements characterizing a *facilitating environment* for psychotherapy and for integrating behavior changes. Our description is largely informal and derived from our clinical experience, although empirical support for some elements is discussed. In providing the list, we hope to emphasize the kinds of considerations that SDT sensibilities can bring to the therapeutic process. Specifically, we identify elements involved in therapeutic support for each of SDT's basic psychological needs, as well as some process elements for facilitating greater awareness, self-regulation, and internalization.

Client Motivation in the Major Psychotherapeutic Traditions

Most therapeutic approaches, both historical and contemporary, can be characterized as residing within one of two traditions that directly affect approaches to motivation. The first can be thought of as the *outcome-focused tradition,* and it encompasses treatments for which the goals for behavior change are established ahead of time and for which the client is typically assumed to be motivated or treatment-ready. Many behavioral and cognitive-behavioral approaches are outcome-focused and hold the goal of bringing about specifiable behavior change. The second, *process-focused tradition,* which includes many dynamic and humanistic approaches, begins with therapist and client engaging in a more open-ended exploration, with goals emerging as part of the interpersonal process. Here, motivation is viewed differently, as even low motivation and resistance are treated as issues to be addressed as part of the process of change. Process-oriented practitioners are more likely to use terms such as *psychotherapy, coaching,* or *counseling* to describe their work. Because of their differences in approach, each tradition grapples with autonomy and motivation differently.

Outcome-Focused Approaches

Many outcome-focused behavior-change techniques are derived from behavioral (e.g., Pavlov, 1927; Skinner, 1953) and cognitive-behavioral (e.g., Bandura, 1995) theories, although practitioners of any persuasion can become outcome-focused in their approaches. Therapies that best fit this category (1) were developed using concrete empirical findings related to behavior control; (2) outline particular interventions intended to yield desired behavioral outcomes when clients have specifiable presenting symptoms; and (3) emphasize the importance of empirically evaluating the degree to which interventions yield the intended behavior-change outcomes.

Behavior Therapy

Classical conditioning (through techniques such as systematic desensitization; Wolpe, 1982) and operant conditioning (through various reinforcement-based therapies; e.g., Kazdin, 1977) have both helped establish behavior therapy as an important approach to treatment. We begin with the latter, operant approaches.

As we have discussed in earlier chapters, operant-behavioral principles focus primarily on what in SDT is refers to as *external regulation.* The aim is to strengthen desired, adaptive behaviors through external reinforcement contingencies (either therapist- or self-administered) so the behaviors will be elicited by the reinforcement contingencies to which they have been linked. In practical terms, reinforcements could be tangible, such as the possibility to win monetary prizes (Petry, Alessi, Hanson, & Sierra, 2007) or vouchers exchangeable for desired goods (Higgins, Wong, Badger, Huag-Ogden, & Dantona,

2000). They can also be social in nature, such as therapist approval or praise (Antony & Roemer, 2003). In all these cases, however, the operant approach views behaviors as being controlled by reinforcement processes and suggests that behavior will persist as long as reinforcement contingencies are in effect.

Strictly speaking, behavior therapy does not represent a *motivational* theory, because motivation per se is not a theory-consistent concept (see Deci & Ryan, 1985b; Moore, 2008). Technically, reinforcements do not motivate behavior but rather function to control its occurrence. When systematically applied by therapists, the use of external contingencies represents instead a powerful way to shape and maintain behaviors.

Meta-analyses by Prendergast, Podus, Finney, Greenwell, and Roll (2006) and Lussier, Heil, Mongeon, Badger, and Higgins (2006) suggest that behavior therapies can have considerable short-term effectiveness. Results show that this control depends on effective contingencies; for instance, it is critical that specific rewards are made saliently contingent on, and directly available following, successful engagement in the targeted activity (Lussier et al., 2006). Moreover, as we have long emphasized within SDT, insofar as behavior is controlled by established external contingencies, there is no expectation that the initiated behavior change will be maintained and transferred once contingencies are removed (Deci & Ryan, 1985b). Indeed, within behavioral theory, there is no assumption that what in SDT we call *internalization* will occur.

The inherent issue is that the theory itself states that behaviors become dependent on the reinforcement contingencies, so if the contingencies do not remain operative when treatment ends, the behavior change would be expected to dissipate. Further, because the contingencies that were created in treatment are typically not in operation in other domains of the clients' lives, the behaviors that are strengthened by reinforcement processes in treatment often tend not to generalize or "transfer" to the other domains, even while the therapy is still in effect. That is, behavior change promoted by reinforcement alone may often not transfer well to new situations or be well maintained over time (Goldstein, Lopez, & Greenleaf, 1979; Westen, Novotny, & Thompson-Brenner, 2004).

From the perspective of SDT, maintenance and transfer would be likely to occur only to the extent that regulation of the behavior change has been fully *internalized*. Yet there is no basis within the behavioral theory for this concept. Instead, maintenance and transfer of treatment gains beyond treatment is focused on strategies such as reinforcement fading, booster sessions, or ongoing monitoring of contingencies, which technically does not constitute maintenance and transfer but, rather, continued treatment or a delay of extinction. Alternatively, therapists must build in self-controlling mechanisms such as self-monitoring and self-reinforcement, behaviors that then themselves must be maintained over time, and thus require motivation.

Yet despite the absence of a specific theoretical basis for supporting autonomy, many behavior therapists in many contexts have adherent clientele who do maintain change. We believe this is facilitated by the fact that important, but non-theoretically based, elements of need support are often added to treatments by effective behavioral practitioners. In fact, although behavioral techniques have no formal place for ideas such as autonomy or internalized motivation within theory, in practice, client autonomy is a concern that is addressed through various strategies. For example, Meichenbaum (1986) specifically suggested that the first phase of behavioral treatment involves helping clients understand their problems and enlisting their *active collaboration* in developing a treatment plan. Behavior therapists also advocate being *transparent* about what will follow in therapy and obtaining the client's explicit agreement for proceeding. Presumably, through transparency and obtaining direct consent, client's autonomous and willing participation is gained. Again, this emphasis on clients' volition, voice, and input in the context of therapy does not appear to be derived from operant theory.

With or without theoretical acknowledgment, current behavioral treatments highlight that behavior therapy should be a *collaborative process*, one in which the client fully consents and has repeated opportunities to influence treatment goals and strategies (Antony & Roemer, 2003; 2014). These ideas express a sentiment of autonomy support. More generally, there is increasing focus on the role of relationship qualities. As stated by Antony and Roemer (2003): "The therapeutic relationship has been underemphasized in behavioral writings. . . . [R]esearchers have tended to focus more on examining the efficacy of particular behavioral techniques, with little discussion of the context in which behavior therapy occurs" (pp. 208–209). Yet the importance of fostering a sense of trust, support, and volition clearly has what in SDT we call functional significance, affecting the quality of clients' engagement in treatment.

Operant theorists have long argued that volition, self-determination, and other constructs related to autonomy are "fictional inner causes" or "epiphenomena" and are thus not consistent with a classical behavioral viewpoint (Moore, 2008; Skinner, 1974; Wolpe, 1982). Nonetheless, this emphasis on clients' experience of choice and self-endorsement of treatment goals is emphasized in both behaviorist ethics and practice. We therefore submit that, although basic behavioral theories don't formally conceptualize issues of autonomy and relatedness as critical, most behaviorists in practice take efforts to support them.

Cognitive-Behavioral Therapies

The most commonly taught techniques within clinical psychology training programs are drawn from an extensive and varied set of models that fall under the rubric of *cognitive-behavioral therapies* (CBT). Although these therapeutic models are substantially varied in focus and theory, they share several central defining features. First, they assume that cognitive processes mediate the impact of the environment on people's behaviors, so effective change of behaviors involves changing its cognitive underpinnings. CBT was, in fact, formulated initially from cognitive-behavioral and social-cognitive theories of behavior (e.g., Abramson, Seligman, & Teasdale, 1978; Bandura, 1977; Rotter, 1966) and thus has especially focused on a set of techniques for changing cognitions, such as people's expectations about behavior-outcome contingencies and about their own efficacy and self-motivation for enacting instrumental behaviors. Finally, like the behavior therapies from which it was spawned, CBT emphasizes the importance of empirically supported practices (Hayes, Luoma, Bond, Masuda, & Lillis, 2006).

Within the core theories underlying CBT (e.g., Bandura, 1989), no distinction is typically made between autonomous motivation and controlled motivation. As such, there is no theoretical basis for advocating autonomy-supportive, as opposed to controlling, interventions and techniques within most CBT techniques or perspectives. Nonetheless, concern with motivation and autonomy within the umbrella of CBT approaches has been heightened by concerns about client selectivity (Westen & Morrison, 2001) and the high attrition observed in some CBT treatments (e.g., see Di Pietro, Valoroso, Fichele, Bruno, & Sorge, 2002; Persons, Burns, & Perloff 1988; Steel et al., 2000). In fact, however, attrition rates across CBT techniques would be better described as uneven, rather than consistently high. It is, however, the high rates of attrition in some CBT interventions that have sparked interest in the role that motivation and autonomy play in therapy retention and adherence (Keijsers, Kampman, & Hoogduin, 2001). So how is motivation for treatment addressed within CBT?

Kanfer and Gaelick-Buys (1991), early in the development of CBT, highlighted the importance of clients' accepting responsibility for change, which they described as a "motivational requirement" (p. 306) for treatment. They argued further, however, that this is not just a client issue; the therapist also has a crucial role in creating favorable conditions for that to occur. They thus suggested that early stages of treatment involve the promotion of clients' accepting responsibility for change and of encouraging participation in the setting of treatment goals. We, of course, agree, and yet the fundamental issue is precisely how one "promotes" such ownership and agency. We again see huge variation on this issue throughout CBT, both within and across treatments.

In fact, one can find examples of motivational advice within CBT methods that span from what SDT considers highly autonomy supportive to highly controlling. On the autonomy-supportive side, CBT approaches, much like operant-behavior therapies, typically strongly endorse the idea of transparency and explicitness during the initial meetings, in part to assess clients' motivation for treatment and in part to inform and obtain consent. Transparency is said to allow the clients to better decide whether to make a commitment and also supplies a way to assess and validate their "readiness" for treatment. Indeed, various studies (e.g., Lewis et al., 2009) have found that clients who were "ready" for therapy had greater success in cognitive-behavioral treatments than have those who were not. Of course, such assumptions suggest that readiness is itself a client problem, rather than an issue of treatment environments.

As a contrasting controlling example, Dryden and Branch (2008), writing about rational–emotive behavior therapy, suggested that therapists apply a principle of rewards and penalties. This entails getting clients to reward themselves when treatment tasks are done and to punish themselves for failures. Penalties and rewards are, however, agreed upon in session, with clients formally contracting with the therapist to apply the contingencies outside treatment. Therapists are also encouraged to use persuasion to enhance commitment. From an SDT perspective, this describes a controlling, therapist-led approach to motivation.

DIALECTICAL BEHAVIOR THERAPY

Another excellent example of a mix of very autonomy-supportive and strongly controlling approaches to getting clients to "accept responsibility" can be found in Linehan's (1993) *dialectical behavior therapy* (DBT). In terms of participating in therapy, Linehan emphasizes the DBT view of the *prerequisite* importance of volition and willingness for treatment. In fact, she has argued that the approach requires motivation. As controlling as that sounds, it is also recognition of the importance of motivation and willingness for therapy to be effective, especially with a difficult population and in a treatment that in part involves group interactions.

Beyond the initial agreement to engage in treatment are the varied methods of motivation advocated within the DBT treatment literature. DBT is, first and foremost, intended to be strongly collaborative and transparent. There is ongoing acknowledgment and validation of experiences and clarity of goals and methods. Yet controlling methods are also advocated. These include strategies such as threats of termination for displaying inadequate motivation (1993, p. 98), or, having cultivated a close relationship, using the relationship as a contingent reward to mobilize change. For example, a female client could be told that "if she does not improve she will lose the therapist much more quickly." Linehan admits that, although done for a benign purpose, this represents a bit of a "blackmail therapy" (p. 98), and of course we would see this as a type of controlling, conditional regard (e.g., see Roth, Assor, Niemiec, Ryan, & Deci, 2009).

In focusing on DBT's mixed motivational approaches, we are not critiquing the overall approach, which (having seen it applied) we see as both reasonably flexible and often highly effective. Moreover, DBT is a type of therapy that is especially effective and designed for a difficult, and often resistant, audience. As discussed in Chapter 16, persons with borderline personality disorder (BPD) have often had particular issues with self-regulation, control, and authority, among others (Ryan, 2005). So one cannot be but sympathetic to the necessity of applying DBT in a way that would establish clear limits and agreements. Our interest, instead, is that DBT techniques can be administered in both autonomy-supportive and controlling ways. We further suggest that both treatment adherence and long-term internalization will be more effectively established using autonomy-supportive approaches to motivation and limit setting. In fact, we see autonomy-supportive approaches as more fitting with the predominant spirit of DBT, which is ultimately about fostering self-acceptance, self-regulation, and mindfulness.

MOTIVATIONAL ENHANCEMENTS

Increasingly in recent years, across cognitive-behavioral approaches, a specific approach for dealing with clients who are low in motivation and readiness has been advocated and employed. It involves using an initial period of perhaps three to four meetings in which a *motivational enhancement therapy* (MET) is introduced to clients before they begin the therapy itself (e.g., Miller, Zweben, DiClimente, & Rychtarik, 1995; Treasure & Ward, 1997).

Among the most common of these motivational enhancement programs is *motivational interviewing* (MI; Miller & Rollnick, 2002). As initially formulated, MI was based on client-centered therapy (Rogers, 1951) and assumed an actualizing tendency as a central aspect of its meta-theory—this being an assumption that is inconsistent with the less-organismic meta-theories that underlie cognitive-behavioral approaches. However, in a more recent formulation, Miller and Rose (2009) put substantial emphasis on change talk—that is, on clients expressing cognitions that are concerned with changing key behaviors—and less emphasis on the autonomy and actualizing that were more central in the earlier formulation. With this current emphasis on change talk, MI is thus more consistent with the CBT and outcome-focused approaches and is considered to be a valuable addition to them by mobilizing people toward the preordained target (e.g., Brenman, Walkley, Fraser, Greenway, & Wilks, 2008; Treasure & Ward, 1997). In fact, several studies (e.g., Buckner & Schmidt, 2009; Treasure, Katzman, Schmidt, Troop, Todd, De Silva, 1999) have shown that the use of a motivational-enhancement process such as MI can be effective in increasing clients' motivation and readiness and decreasing clients' dropout, which research has shown to be a significant problem in cognitive-behavioral treatments (e.g., Persons et al., 1988).

Still another approach to behavior change and growth that, like MI, is sometimes used both as a brief MET and sometimes as a treatment approach in its own right is *acceptance and commitment therapy* (ACT; Hayes, et al., 2006). Despite the difference in the meta-theoretical grounds of ACT and SDT, there are elements of ACT that resonate with us. Mainly, there is an emphasis on how people relate to their various thoughts, emotions, and events. Rather than controlling or suppressing feelings and experiences, ACT promotes accepting and both actively and mindfully relating to experiences of both internal and external events (Hayes & Ciarrochi, 2015). In this sense, it has much in common with SDT's organismic–phenomenological view of people's accepting their feelings and experiences and learning from them.

THERAPEUTIC ALLIANCE

Finally, there has been considerable interest across cognitive-behavioral therapies in the motivational impact of what are called *common treatment factors*. Among the most well-known of these is *therapeutic alliance,* a concept that has been variously defined and measured (Elvins & Green, 2008). Therapeutic alliance, as most generally defined in research quarters, concerns the extent to which clients and therapists have a high-quality relationship (e.g., clients feel understood) and are able to collaborate on the tasks and goals of therapy (Bordin, 1979; Meissner, 1996). As Safran and Muran (2006) pointed out, the therapeutic alliance is by no means a static concept, and, as all therapists know, it can fluctuate, even within sessions.

General measures of therapeutic alliance have, in fact, predicted significant variance in CBT outcomes, as shown in past analyses (Goldsmith, Lewis, Dunn & Bentall, 2015; Horvath & Symonds, 1991; Martin, Garske, & Davis, 2000), yet there are many questions about the exact nature of these relations. From the SDT perspective, the elements associated with therapeutic alliance bear similarity to the ideas of basic psychological need supports: taking the client's perspective, being focused on client autonomy in identifying and planning therapy tasks and goals, and supporting relatedness through unconditional positive regard (e.g., see Pinto et al., 2012). Thus we would expect clients who experience more alliance to have more autonomy and to be more effective in their attempts at change. Indeed, as we shall subsequently review, therapeutic alliance and autonomy support are empirically related constructs, each of which contributes to therapeutic outcomes (Zuroff et al., 2007).

Emphasis within CBT discussions on the importance of empathy and building a therapeutic alliance have in most cases resulted from practicing clinicians' finding these elements to be practically important, rather than because these elements were derived from the basic theories that underlie CBT (see Hayes et al., 2006). Yet, despite the theoretical lacunae, as the above discussion reveals, there is every indication that CBT therapists are highly concerned with the issue of volitional motivation, even as there is substantial variability in how CBT's guiding models address the issue. Thus Kanfer and Gaelick-Buys's (1991) early statement that some behavior-change programs view clients as relatively passive, with change coming from external sources, whereas other programs view clients as active participants in the change process who are eager to accept responsibility for change remains true today. This, we think, is a source of the variability in effectiveness of CBT, as therapists both between and within CBT use methods that differ greatly in the degree to which they are controlling versus autonomy-supportive and thus are associated with different functional consequences.

COGNITIVE THERAPY

Cognitive therapy (e.g., Beck, 1972) was initially formulated as a means of treating depression and is often classified as a form of CBT. Yet accounts of the therapy (e.g.,

Beck & Weishaar, 2008) suggest that behavior is a function of multiple systems, including physiological, affective, motivational, and cognitive processes, and Beck and colleagues (e.g., Beck, Freeman, & Davis, 1990; Beck & Weishaar, 2008) have explicitly drawn from psychoanalytic and humanistic schools of psychotherapy. Thus, although the theory of cognitive therapy has not integrated these divergent perspectives, cognitive therapy, much like CBT, has a list of techniques and elements drawn from many sources, some of which are aligned with process-focused as well as outcome-focused approaches.

Cognitive therapy also highlights issues concerning *autonomous motivation* for treatment, although not by that name. Thus Beck and colleagues have maintained that it is important for therapists to empower clients and support them for making choices. In cognitive therapy, the relationship between therapist and client is viewed as one of *collaborative empiricism* (Beck et al., 1990), in which client and therapist work together to identify the clients' maladaptive cognitions and reactions to events, to test them "empirically" (through discourse and experimentation), and to alter those interpretations and try out new cognitive frameworks in daily life. Because Beck explicitly stated that his approach draws from psychodynamic and humanistic approaches, as well as behavioral systems, it is not clear what the specific theoretical justifications underlying this emphasis on collaboration and active involvement are, but it is nonetheless very motivationally relevant. For example, Beck, Rush, Shaw, and Emery (1979) argued that the collaborative approach engenders a spirit of exploration that fosters greater motivation. Similarly, Beck et al. (1990) stated that a therapeutic alliance is a necessary (though not sufficient) condition for positive movement in therapy, and they emphasized that therapists need to demonstrate empathy, warmth, and other characteristics we would describe as relatedness enhancing. Regarding autonomy, Beck et al. (1990) suggested further that when clients are noncompliant it is "rarely productive for the therapist to take an authoritarian role. . . . If the rationale behind the assignment is clear and the clients recognize they are choosing to do it rather than forced to do it, then there is much less chance of noncompliance" (p. 198). This emphasis on empowerment and the salience of choice seems aimed at maintaining a sense of autonomy in the treatment process. This is important because, as Sue and Sue (2008) argued, a frequent difficulty for both cognitive-behavioral therapists and cognitive therapists is insufficient attention to the therapeutic alliance, perhaps due to stronger emphasis in training on techniques than on relationship building and autonomy support.

Yet cognitive therapy, like DBT, is somewhat mixed in its motivational messages. Although Beck emphasizes collaboration and consensus as positive motivators, this need-supportive focus is sometimes combined with strategies that seem more associated with external control or introjected regulation. For example, Beck, Emery, and Greenberg (1985) advocated intervention strategies that included fostering approval-based motivation and even directly controlling the clients through pressure and authority if they failed to comply with homework assignments. Clients might be asked to sign an agreement to adhere and have it notarized. Material rewards could be used as reinforcements for compliance. Beck et al. (1985) also suggested that the therapist might simply tell the client who is not making progress "that he *has* to do the homework if he wants to get better" (p. 269). Yet, even while proposing these controlling solutions to motivation blocks, Beck et al. (1985) also suggested that such techniques are but temporary props, with the idea that success experiences would ultimately make positive changes self-reinforcing. Thus, underlying the wide array of strategies appears to be the belief that experiences of efficacy, however they might be energized, will in the end supply the basis for sustained motivation.

Outcome-Focused Summary

To summarize, outcome-focused therapies are composed of highly varied theoretical models and diverse techniques. They evolved largely from behavioral and social-cognitive theories and emphasize empirically supported treatments with a focus on prespecified outcomes. Motivation per se has not been a strong explicit focus of the theories underlying the outcome-focused therapies, yet in practice outcome-focused approaches have addressed in varied ways the issue of motivation, even if not always overtly, and to a far lesser extent that of autonomy. These include being initially explicit and transparent about what will occur in treatment and, where possible, explicitly gaining the clients' assent. Some approaches prescribe an initial MET such as brief MI or ACT before applying other cognitive-behavioral methods for clients who are perhaps not ready for treatment, which include an emphasis on autonomy support, even if not so termed. Finally, most outcome-focused approaches advocate that therapists be empathetic and affectively supportive when employing the various techniques and methods, again whether or not they have a meaningful theoretical basis for that treatment climate.

Process-Focused Approaches

The other primary tradition in mental and behavioral health promotion is focused much less on specific outcomes than on the processes of exploration, awareness, and insight, with behavior change resulting from them. A sizable number of therapists view themselves as *process-focused,* and most clinicians, even those schooled primarily in CBT, also employ some of the methods and sensibilities encompassed by the predominant process-oriented therapies (Shedler, 2010).

Psychoanalytic Therapies

This approach to therapy, with its underlying personality theory, was initially developed by Freud (1923). The theory focused on the sexual instincts (i.e., drives) as the central energizing force in development and behavior. However, more contemporary approaches that have their roots solidly in psychoanalytic soil—such as ego psychology, self psychology, and object relations theory—have shifted their focus from the libido (i.e., the sexual drive) to basic psychological needs. What we refer to as the relatedness need is apparent within object relations and self-psychologies, and what we refer to as competence and autonomy needs are apparent in ego psychology. These newer approaches practice varied psychotherapies that may be either short term or long term but that are distinct from psychoanalysis per se.

The classic psychoanalytic approach views most psychopathology as developing during the first 6 or 7 years of life, resulting from the individual's having been unsuccessful in fully resolving the characteristic psychosexual conflicts during the oral, anal, and phallic stages of development. These unresolved conflicts exist primarily in the unconscious, and the job of the analyst is to lead the client through a process of reliving these stages of development so as to achieve fuller resolution of the conflicts. This can be viewed in terms of bringing the relevant material into consciousness, experiencing it fully, and integrating it into one's sense of self (e.g., Meissner, 1981). It is interesting that, although the various psychodynamic approaches consider nonconscious processes to be important determinants of behavior, many social-cognitive researchers (e.g., Bargh, 2007) are now vigorously studying nonconscious determinants of behavior. This research, however, simply describes nonconscious determination, whereas psychodynamic psychotherapists work to bring unintegrated elements into awareness so clients can regulate them effectively in accordance with their needs and values.

The processes of healing that are central to most psychodynamic therapies concern transference and the synthetic function of the ego. Transference refers to the process in which clients transfer onto the therapist feelings toward parents (or other significant figures) from earlier experiences that are unresolved. Within the therapeutic relationship, transference is interpreted to help clients gain insight into themselves regarding unresolved internal conflicts and their continuing influence in other relationships (Gill, 1982). Social-psychological research has begun to clarify how transference operates as a nonconscious process that can be easily primed or cued by elements in one's social context (Andersen & Chen, 2002; Berenson & Andersen, 2006). Of interest in the psychology of transference is that clients can readily introject the values and beliefs of their therapists, in part as a reenactment of earlier authority issues. Yet the task of therapists is to skillfully allow clients to transform such introjections into true identifications.

The synthetic function of the ego (Freud, 1923; Nunberg, 1931), as we described in Chapter 2, is a process that bears similarity to SDT's *organismic integration* process. It is this synthetic process through which clients are able to integrate their newly uncovered feelings and motivations into their sense of self and thus to regulate themselves effectively toward adaptation and resolution of conflict. The synthetic function, which is central to all psychodynamic thought, is clearly based in an organismic meta-theory. That is, it is the assumption of an active integrative process residing within the organism that defines psychodynamic approaches as organismic and that ultimately leads them to be process-oriented rather than outcome-oriented.

As part of a process orientation, dynamic therapies assume people will be conflicted as they approach the processes of change and growth and thus will need to be supported in the process. In this regard, there is a central importance placed on the interpersonal atmosphere in treatment, or the *analytic attitude*, which Schafer (1983) described as perhaps Freud's greatest invention. It concerns the creation of a noncontrolling or nonjudgmental atmosphere in which all experiences are allowed expression.

In psychoanalytic and other psychodynamic approaches, exploring the level and nature of the client's motivation to participate in treatment is part of the agenda. Clients who are not motivated may, for example, be enacting resistance, and psychotherapy is intended in part to deal with the resistances and thus to facilitate motivation (e.g., Kaner & Prelinger, 2005). In fact, resistance is expected, even invited. As therapists reflect upon clients' resistances with interest, curiosity, and respect, the clients are gradually more able to take interest in their own resistances.

Modern psychodynamic approaches continue to subscribe to the general ideas of nonconscious processes, the synthetic function, the utility of examining clients' relationships with their therapists, and the importance of facilitating motivation for therapy and of dealing with resistances in a way that recognizes that they have been serving functions for the clients (Kaner & Prelinger, 2005). The ego psychologists (e.g., Gill, 1982; Schafer, 1983); self-psychologists (e.g., Kohut, 1971); and object relations and attachment theorists (e.g., Bowlby, 1988; Fairbairn, 1954; Winnicott, 1965) form the foundations for contemporary psychodynamic and interpersonal therapies.

For object relations and self-psychology practitioners, the interpersonal relationships are of critical importance, so what we refer to as the basic need for relatedness is viewed as a key motivator. Psychopathology is understood primarily in terms of disturbances in people's important early relationships that are being acted out in their current relationships, including with their therapists. Accordingly, the therapeutic alliance (Bordin, 1979) is considered extremely important for facilitating awareness of nonconscious feelings and motivations, for examining elements of transference in their relationships with their therapists, and for promoting change.

In contrast to the explicit transparency offered in most behavioral and CBT approaches, transparency is a somewhat complex issue in the process-focused psychodynamic approaches. In part, the reason is that it is not always clear from the outset where the exploration of issues and focus of treatment might go. It is indeed often the case that problems clients initially present change with deeper discussion. Many times clients present with a problem that provides an easy (e.g., nonembarrassing) calling card to the clinic or with a goal that reflects only one side of their struggles. Determining an outcome focus too early may foreclose exploration of the deeper issues and the most appropriate goals for treatment.

In this regard, Kaner and Prelinger (2005) argued that, although some clients might benefit from an explanation of the therapy process, beyond outlining the basic frame of therapy (e.g., meeting times, payments) during initial contacts, no extensive information or explanations should be provided. They and other dynamic practitioners (e.g., MacKinnon, Michels, & Buckley, 2015) have suggested instead that information should be provided only in response to clients' concerns or inquiries and kept to a minimum. Again, this stands in strong contrast to the view espoused more frequently in outcome-focused approaches, in which transparency and explicit consent to procedures are heavily emphasized. Yet, given the open-ended nature of the process-focused therapies, the same kind of explicitness and transparency used in behavioral therapies does not apply (Gabbard, 2005). At the same time, interpersonal transparency, including openness to concerns, questions, and criticisms of how the process of treatment is proceeding, is accepted as an important part of psychodynamic approaches. These, in fact, are invited and often seen as helpful in exploring pressing concerns, defenses, and resistances to awareness or change.

Interpersonal Therapy

Developed originally by Klerman, Weissman, Rounsaville, and Chevron (1984) as an approach to treating depression, interpersonal therapy (IPT) has become a more widely applied therapy approach. Based in attachment theory (Bowlby, 1988), IPT has also been influenced by the humanistic therapies in that its focus on relationships is not transference-based but is instead concerned with relationships as they occur in the here and now. The therapist's job includes keeping clients oriented toward examining communication patterns as they exist in the clients' network of current relationships. Interpersonal therapy is considered a short-term intervention and has an evidence base focused on attaining specific outcomes.

As such, IPT has adopted various elements that are more common to CBT. For example, Stuart (2004) suggested that IPT therapists must (1) be focused, (2) be supportive, (3) convey hope, and (4) reinforce gains. As laudable as these elements sound, one could readily see that the elements could be carried out in somewhat different ways. Stuart, for example, stated that the therapist can contain or "control the transference reaction to a large degree by assuming the role of a benevolent expert" (p. 130). From the SDT perspective, that is treacherous territory, for reinforcement of change and being the expert are both ideas that could readily be experienced as controlling rather than autonomy-supportive (e.g., Deci, Koestner, & Ryan, 1999; Ryan, 1982). Similarly, the idea of maintaining focus, while at times useful, can very easily spill over into control, particularly if the focus is on obtaining a priori specified outcomes.

Humanistic Psychotherapies

Humanistic psychology developed as an approach to therapy and personal growth and was based on the idea of an actualizing tendency (Maslow, 1943; Rogers, 1951). The person-centered approach (sometimes referred to as the client-centered approach), developed by Rogers, embraces this actualization assumption as its central tenet, but the assumption also informs a broader set of *experiential approaches* (Elliott, Greenberg, & Lietaer, 2004), which include Gestalt, existential, psychodrama, and expressive therapies, among others. Despite some differences, these approaches all adhere to a core belief that human nature is "inherently trustworthy, growth-oriented, and guided by choice" (Elliott et al., 2004, p. 493), a belief that holds important implications for understanding motivation in therapy. As such, all therapies within this category are staunchly process-focused, oriented toward self-exploration, and reliant on the inherent healing process manifested within the actualizing tendency.

CLIENT-CENTERED THERAPY

Rogers's client-centered therapy was the first comprehensive humanistic theory of personality with a corresponding approach to therapy. In it, Rogers specified three key elements that he said were necessary for supporting meaningful therapeutic change—namely, genuineness, empathy, and unconditional positive regard (e.g., Kirschenbaum & Jourdan, 2005). These elements are highly congruent with the concept of autonomy support, which involves "being present" for clients, while acknowledging and respecting their perspectives. Indeed, recent SDT research on parenting has confirmed the importance of unconditional positive regard, whereas conditional regard has been found empirically to be controlling, leading the recipients to feel both rejected and compelled to do the behaviors that are instrumental to the regard (Assor, Roth, & Deci, 2004). In contrast, unconditional positive regard was found to result in more integrated and autonomous functioning (Roth et al. 2009).

It is important to note, however, that unconditional regard does not mean endorsing the clients' behaviors and values; it means accepting the worth of the clients and taking interest in and prizing the clients' experiences. Endorsing the clients' behaviors and values would have two problems. First, some behaviors and values are morally and functionally bankrupt and should not be endorsed for anyone. Second, even if the behaviors and values are appropriate and commendable, to endorse them would create contingencies that would likely have a controlling functional significance and lead the clients to speak or behave in ways they think would get them praise from the therapists.

The idea of motivating people for treatment per se is, in humanistic therapies, approached largely through implicit creation of rapport and a therapeutic alliance. For Rogers, the conditions of unconditional regard, empathy, and genuineness provided by the therapist create an atmosphere in which the clients' inherent actualizing tendencies will be activated. In this sense, again, it is not through up-front transparency but rather though an ongoing supportive process that the client's motivation for change is facilitated.

MOTIVATIONAL INTERVIEWING

Earlier in the chapter we spoke briefly about motivational interviewing (MI; Miller & Rollnick, 2002) as an MET often attached to the front of CBT that focused heavily on change talk as a means of motivating and readying clients for therapy. However, MI actually began as a process-oriented approach to health behavior change whose techniques were very much aligned with Rogerian, person-centered thinking. It was developed to address problems with abuse of alcohol and other substances, although it has also been applied more broadly in the field of health behavior change. MI aims at supporting clients to examine their own goals and obstacles with respect to the change under discussion so they can make a clear choice about whether they want to make the change. The reasoning is that they will be more effective in changing and maintaining change if they make a true choice independent of any pressures from internal or external sources.

Like client-centered therapy, MI begins by providing unconditional positive regard, which has been found by research to promote both autonomy and relatedness satisfactions (e.g., Assor et al., 2004; Kanat-Maymon, Roth, Assor, & Raizer, 2016). As well, it advocates the provision of relevant information, which is critical for clients to feel and be more competent, and it favors the use of nondirective supports, which is accomplished in part through reflecting feelings without interpreting them and not leading the clients in different directions.

In a commentary on MI, Markland, Ryan, Tobin, and Rollnick (2005) made the point that, although MI has been found effective in facilitating health behavior change, it is not a theory-based approach, so the processes by which the change occurs are not made clear. They argued further that SDT can be viewed as a theory that gives a meaningful account of why MI works and of the processes through which it works. For example, the MI description of creating an optimal climate for change is very consistent with being autonomy-supportive, and autonomous motivation represents the most ideal type of internal motivation, which MI argues is important for change. In fact, Foote et al. (1999) found that clients in an MI group reported significantly greater autonomy support than those in a comparison group. Similarly, Carcone et al. (2013) applied MI in the treatment of obese black youth and found that reflective statements, open questions focusing on the youths' experiences, and support for autonomy were key to facilitating greater motivation for weight loss. In short, the interpersonal climates that promote positive outcomes in MI can be understood as doing so by supporting basic need satisfaction and autonomous motivation.

EXISTENTIAL THERAPY

This approach evolved within the humanistic perspective, drawing from existential philosophy (e.g., Heidegger, 1962; Sartre, 1956). As in other humanistic theories, this therapeutic approach assumes that people are inherently inclined to engage in life, so the therapy, which aims toward greater authenticity, is concerned with identifying and removing the obstacles that are preventing the client from behaving in a psychologically freer and more authentic way (May, 1983; Yalom, 1980). From this perspective, a client's authenticity is the goal, for authenticity is said to represent psychological health. Thus concern with client autonomy is ever present in the work.

Existential therapists, unlike the psychodynamic therapists, argue that being as transparent as possible during therapy is also important for the therapeutic process. As Yalom (2002) argued, transparency is consistent with the goal of authenticity, and it also helps to alleviate clients' anxiety when they are beginning therapy. Yalom (1980) put it this way: "The therapist's goal then is engagement. The task is not to create engagement nor to inspirit the client with engagement—these the therapist cannot do. But it is not necessary, for the desire to engage life is always there within the client, and the therapist's clinical activities should be directed toward the removal of obstacles in the client's way" (p. 482). Yalom also argued that this task of helping clients assume responsibility for change can become "the bulk of the therapeutic task" (p. 231).

Van Deurzen-Smith (1997) described her approach to existential counseling as follows. She attempts to be as open and informative as possible about the nature of the counseling work in an initial session, inviting as many questions as possible. The goal of this session, for which she does not charge, is one of transparency and supporting authentic choice. She asks potential clients to take time in deciding before committing to the work and to recontact her if they wish to move forward. This insistence on making a clear choice about whether to engage in therapy helps establish a readiness to embark on the challenges of existential work.

Clearly, the nature of the information that a transparent therapist would be providing in existential therapy would be quite different from that provided in outcome-focused therapies, because the goal of authenticity and the exploratory processes that lead the client toward greater authenticity are more difficult to concretize than are the outcomes and processes involved in CBT and other outcome-focused work. However, in both approaches, there is some sense in which a readiness barrier is recognized and explicit choice is demanded.

Therapeutic Traditions and Autonomy Support: A Reprise

By having a consistent view about autonomous versus controlled motivation and the supports for autonomy, SDT has a unique analytical vantage point on clinical practices. We saw, first of all, wide variations in approaches to motivating clients in therapy, but a concern within all approaches with autonomy. For instance we saw that even in behavioral and CBT frameworks, where theoretical justifications for autonomy support are generally absent, practitioners nonetheless grapple with and find ways to support autonomy. In such outcome-focused methods, transparency is valued and explicit consent is used as a screening device and a motivational pillar. In dynamic approaches, the emphasis is very much on moment-to-moment autonomy support and relatedness. Thus it is striking that, regardless of the school of practice, autonomy is an important implicit or explicit theme that effective therapists grapple with, although, as we saw, some of the techniques advocated in some of the therapies tend to be counter to therapists' attempts to support autonomy. The evidence we are about to review helps to clarify why support for autonomy is critical to effective treatments and why it is such a struggle for many practitioners.

SDT and Effective Psychotherapy

Given that every therapy deals with the problems of motivating clients to engage and persist in therapy (retention) and helping them to maintain changes over time (maintenance) and to learn to apply their changes outside of the therapy setting (transfer), SDT offers some general claims. The first and best validated set of these claims concerns the cross-modality importance of autonomous motivation in treatment. Client autonomy is associated with higher quality engagement, which is helpful to the therapy process. Just as importantly, autonomy is critical to internalization, which in our view is essential for both maintenance and transfer of whatever gains have been made in treatment, be they behavioral, lifestyle, or self-regulatory in nature.

> *Hypothesis 1:* The relative autonomy of client motivation is an important predictor of treatment engagement and intervention outcomes, especially with regard to maintained changes.

Autonomy is an attribute of individuals, describing their experiences of what is motivating their activity. Although assessed as the client's experience, client autonomy is typically the result of interpersonal rather than just merely personal factors. From SDT's perspective, the more therapists support their clients' autonomy and relatedness need satisfaction, the more the clients' engagement in therapy is likely to be autonomous, the more the therapeutic process is likely to proceed effectively, and the more the internalization of positive changes is likely to occur and maintain.

> *Hypothesis 2:* Across modalities of therapy, counseling, and behavior change, client engagement, outcomes, and wellness will be enhanced by practitioners' autonomy support. Autonomy support contributes to wellness by satisfying basic psychological needs, and also, more directly, by supporting clients' autonomous motivation for change and the integrated internalization of regulations that will allow the change to be maintained across time and circumstances.

Within SDT, the concept of autonomy support is crucial with respect to the conditions that promote individuals' autonomous motivation and engagement. As we have detailed throughout, autonomy support involves such elements as one person (viz., the therapist or counselor) taking the other's (viz., the client's) perspective and thus being empathic, encouraging exploration and initiative, supporting the client's making reflective choices, and minimizing pressure and control to think, feel, or behave in particular ways. Indeed, there are many elements to autonomy support, to which we turn shortly, but all grow out of a fundamental commitment to attend to and support the self-regulation of the other.

Among the first empirical examinations of autonomy in psychotherapy using SDT's conceptualization was a study by Pelletier, Tuson, and Haddad (1997). These researchers developed a self-regulation scale using the general organismic integration theory (OIT) framework presented in Chapter 8 to assess clients' relative autonomy for being in therapy. Using it, clients indicated the degree to which they entered therapy for external, introjected, identified, integrated, or intrinsic reasons. Data from adult outpatient clinics showed that clients endorsing more autonomous reasons for participating in therapy also reported (1) placing more importance on therapy, (2) feeling less conflict about being in therapy, (3) having more focus during therapy, (4) finding therapy more satisfying, and (5) intending to persist at the process longer. Regarding outcomes, they reported higher self-esteem, a lower level of depressive symptoms, and more life satisfaction. Controlled motivation was, in contrast, negatively related to placing importance on therapy and intentions to persist. This research provided initial evidence that having autonomous motivation for being in therapy was associated with a range of positive experiences and outcomes.

Since these early results, a number of studies have shown the importance of autonomy for clinical outcomes. We cite a few illustrative ones. Michalak, Klappheck, and

Kosfelder (2004), studying clients in a German outpatient clinic with anxiety or mood disorders, found that the relative autonomy of psychiatric clients' goals was positively related to desired therapeutic outcomes, even when controlling for levels of symptoms and distress. The researchers argued that the more individuals have autonomous goals for therapy, the more they would be able to confront and overcome difficulties and barriers to change. Carter and Kelly (2015) examined treatment motivation in clients being seen for eating disorders. They found that those with more autonomous motivation for treatment also had a greater sense of social support and expressed more self-compassssion. That is, feeling relationally supported and self-accepting were associated with more willing and volitional pursuit of change. The researchers also found that higher baseline autonomous motivation predicted greater decreases in eating pathology over treatment.

Ryan, Plant, and O'Malley (1995) assessed the motivation of 98 clients who entered an outpatient alcohol treatment program. Outcomes were assessed 8 weeks later in the form of attendance records and clinicians' ratings of both clients' involvement in the treatment program and clinical improvement. Results confirmed that clients who were higher on internalized motivation for being in the program attended more regularly, stayed in the program longer, and showed more clinician-rated engagement and improvement than those low on internalized motivation. There was, however, an interesting additional finding. Specifically, clients who were high in both internalized and external regulation had the best outcomes. In contrast, being low in internalized motivation and high in external regulation led to the lowest retention and involvement. Dealing with an addiction to substances such as alcohol is very difficult, and having internalized motivation to be in treatment working on abstinence is an essential contributor to treatment success. However, having external sources (e.g., a spouse or legal authorities) demanding treatment may help, as long as the individual is substantially internally motivated. External pressures without the clients' autonomy, however, will likely lead to a clear lack of success (e.g., see Wild, Cunningham, & Ryan, 2006).

Also supporting our first hypothesis that internalized autonomous motivation is an important antecedent to treatment success, studies in Chapter 18 show that autonomous motivation for treatment predicts a range of positive health-related behaviors, including maintained weight loss among morbidly obese participants (Williams et al., 1996), long-term tobacco abstinence among smokers (Williams, McGregor, Sharp, Lévesque, et al., 2006), and lowered LDL cholesterol among participants at risk for coronary heart disease (Williams, McGregor, Sharp, Kouides, et al., 2006).

Evidence on Autonomy Support in Various Psychotherapy Modalities

The primary prediction of SDT with respect to psychotherapy and behavior change is that there will be substantial advantages for clients if therapists use autonomy-supportive interpersonal climates, regardless of what therapeutic modality they may be using. Support of autonomy is an approach to interacting and communicating that allows and facilitates the clients' engaging in treatment and finding for themselves, both personally and interpersonally, new ways of being. An experiment with teenage clients shows this in a clear and causal way. Savard, Joussemet, Pelletier, and Mageau (2013) reported on an experimental intervention within a social rehabilitation program for female adolescents with severe emotional and behavioral problems. In the program was a difficult workshop focused on social problem solving for the kinds of issues the girls experienced in their own lives. Participants were assigned to one of two groups, both of which received the same clinical workshop. However, participants in one group had an instructor who was trained to use an autonomy-supportive style in implementing the workshop, whereas the participants in the other group had an instructor who implemented the workshop in the standard way and had not been specifically trained to interact in an autonomy-supportive way. Results showed that the participants in the autonomy-support group liked the workshop better, perceived it as having greater value, expressed less negative affect about the program, and perceived their instructor to be more competent. In short, administering the program in an autonomy-supportive way was found to be associated with more positive program experiences and lower resistance.

This experiment by Savard et al. merely illustrated the kinds of effects we have seen throughout this book when people are afforded respect for autonomy and find basic psychological need supports. Autonomy-supportive conditions allow people to feel less threatened and more empowered and engaged. Because supporting autonomy is also a form of care and nurturance, it enhances relatedness satisfaction. In turn, these need satisfactions promote further receptivity and interest and the relaxation of defenses. In such a space, people have more willingness to experiment and to learn and grow.

Zuroff and colleagues have done a series of important studies on autonomy and autonomy support across therapy approaches. In the initial study, Zuroff et al. (2007) assessed both autonomy support and autonomy while researching three distinct approaches to therapy among psychiatric clients suffering from major depression. The primary therapeutic outcome investigated was changes in symptoms of depression, assessed both before and after the 16-week treatment. Clients received one of three types of treatment: cognitive-behavioral therapy (CBT), interpersonal therapy (IPT), or pharmacotherapy with clinical management. During the third treatment session, clients completed assessments of their autonomous versus controlled motivation for treatment, their perceptions of autonomy support from the therapists, and their experience of therapeutic alliance (Gaston & Marmar, 1994). Analyses indicated that symptomatic improvement occurred in all three of the treatment groups. Beyond that, and across approaches, clients' perceptions of autonomy support positively predicted their autonomous motivation for treatment and their ratings of therapeutic alliance. In turn, autonomous motivation and therapeutic alliance both predicted decreases in depression in each of the treatment conditions (viz., CBT, IPT, and pharmacotherapy). In fact, autonomous motivation was a stronger predictor of improvements in depression than was therapeutic alliance, which had been shown in many prior studies to predict treatment gains (Horvath & Symonds, 1991; Martin et al., 2000).

In another study of clients being treated for depressive episodes, Zuroff, Koestner, Moskowitz, McBride, and Bagby (2012) used multilevel modeling and found that at both within- and between-person levels, autonomous motivation for treatment positively predicted decreases in depression, whereas controlled motivation negatively predicted this treatment outcome. Further, perceived autonomy support from the therapist predicted clients' autonomous motivation, but not their controlled motivation. It was clients' self-criticism that predicted controlled motivation for treatment. Thus these two studies from the Zuroff lab added support to both our first hypothesis about autonomous motivation and our second hypothesis about autonomy support leading to positive outcomes in psychotherapy.

In still another study, McBride et al. (2010) focused specifically on IPT. Seventy-four depressed clients in an outpatient mood disorder clinic at a psychiatric hospital each had 16 sessions of IPT. At the third session, data were collected on the clients' autonomous and controlled motivation for therapy and their experience of therapeutic alliance. Results of the study found that both therapeutic alliance and autonomous motivation predicted a greater likelihood of remission from the disorder and that controlled motivation predicted less likelihood of remission.

Kaap-Deeder, Vansteenkiste, Soenens, Verstuyf, Boone, and Smets (2014) examined female clients being treated in an inpatient facility for serious eating disorders. They found that clients who, at the start of treatment, reported greater parental autonomy support were more volitionally oriented toward change. Those with controlling parents were more resistant. Perceived autonomy support from staff and fellow clients was also related to changes in volitional motivation over the course of treatment, results that were explained by change in psychological need satisfaction. Finally, enhancements in volitional motivation were associated with increases in body mass index throughout treatment in the subgroup of clients with anorexia nervosa, for whom increased weight was a major goal of treatment.

Autonomy and autonomy support in groups is also relevant. Dwyer, Hornsey, Smith, Oei, and Dingle (2011) examined the importance of autonomy for improved outcomes within a CBT treatment group for adults with depressive or anxiety disorders. The groups met only twice a week for 4 weeks. Results indicated that participants who experienced greater autonomy need satisfaction within the group context showed a greater decrease in their symptoms of depression and anxiety. Further, these relations were mediated by the corresponding constructs. That is, greater autonomy satisfaction led to a greater decrease in depressive cognitions, which in turn led to a greater decrease in depressive symptoms. Greater autonomy satisfaction also led to a greater decrease in anxiety cognitions, which in turn led to a greater decrease in anxiety symptoms. These mediations were significant and full. A second study by Dwyer and colleagues focused on depressive symptoms of clients who had various mood disorders and most of whom were on medications for their disorders. In this study, change in autonomy satisfaction during treatment predicted change in depressive symptoms from pre- to posttreatment, and this relation was fully mediated by change in depressive cognitions.

Research by Zeldman, Ryan, and Fiscella (2004) in a methadone maintenance program examined the relations among autonomy support, internalized motivation for the treatment program, and treatment outcomes. In this program, participants were required to attend weekly group meetings and individual counseling sessions and to submit to random urinalysis for assessing relapse. They attended the clinic for a daily dose, although those making progress in the program were allowed to take methadone doses home and self-administer these medications. Thus, having take-home doses represents a positive outcome measure, along with attendance at program meetings and negative urinalysis results. All participants in the study were newly admitted to the program and were followed for 6 months.

Results indicated that more autonomous motivation was associated with better attendance, more negative urine samples, and greater progress in take-home doses. External regulation of clients' involvement in the program tended to relate negatively to attendance and positively to the presence of opiates in their urine samples. Further, there was an interaction between internalized motivation and external regulation on attendance and urine-sample outcomes, indicating that clients who fared least well, being the most nonadherent to the treatment regimen, were those high in external regulation and low in internalized motivation. Finally, and most relevant here, in the Zeldman et al. (2004) study, participants reported on autonomy support from their counselors in the program and analyses indicated that perceiving their providers as autonomy-supportive was associated with fewer relapses, better attendance, and more progress toward being able to have take-home doses. Although it is sometimes argued that people addicted to alcohol and opiates need to be controlled and coerced into treatment programs and into compliance, we suggest a somewhat different story—namely, that clients who are autonomously motivated for treatment are the most effective in managing their addictions and that the autonomy-supportiveness of the providers contributes to positive outcomes among these clients.

SDT also recognizes that the use of pharmacotherapy may be an appropriate option for some clients. Past research has shown how practitioners' autonomy support influences clients' adherence to prescription medications in the health domain (e.g., Kennedy, Goggin, & Nollen, 2004; Williams, McGregor, Sharp, Lévesque, et al., 2006; Williams, Rodin, Ryan, Grolnick, & Deci, 1998). In the sphere of psychotherapy, autonomy support for medication adherence may be even more critical. Indeed, one of the three conditions examined in the Zuroff et al. (2007) study was pharmacotherapy with clinical management, and the study showed that therapists' autonomy support was a predictor of clients' autonomous motivation, and clients' autonomous motivation in that group was a strong predictor of treatment success. In short, the use of medications in the psychotherapeutic process may be appropriate in some cases, but the use of psychotherapy, provided in an autonomy-supportive way to accompany that medication use, is important for more optimal outcomes.

To summarize, a growing body of research has confirmed the importance of individuals' autonomy in psychotherapeutic treatments, and it has shown further that, when therapists are autonomy-supportive, clients experience more positive, maintained therapeutic treatment gains. Clearly this is an area in which much more research is needed, both on how these results generalize across client types and treatment modalities and on the specific elements in therapeutic settings and therapist–client interactions that contribute to perceived therapist autonomy support and ultimately to client autonomy.

On Facilitating Environments: Perspectives as SDT Practitioners

As clinicians, we have long been interested in what comprises a need-supportive therapy environment, characterized by interested exploration, vitality, and sustained engagement in self-improvements. We characterize such settings as *facilitating environments*. A facilitating environment promotes authentic reflection, integration, empowerment, competence, and choice.

The creation of a facilitating environment has very much to do with not just the client's readiness for change but also with how the therapist receives the client and what his or her perspective is on how to approach this encounter with the client. We highlight two types of elements: (1) process-oriented aspects, or specifically how the therapist's support for basic psychological need satisfactions enhances clients' engagement and volition; and (2) content-oriented aspects, or how a therapist's attunement to need satisfactions in everyday life, emotional awareness, and people's goals and aspirations also can inform psychotherapy.

This list of ingredients in an SDT-informed approach to therapy is largely derived from our clinical experiences, although some elements are supported by studies of therapy in clinical settings or experimental analogues that have been mentioned in this chapter. Other elements have been examined in related domains such as education (Chapter 14) or health care (Chapter 18). The contribution of other of these elements to autonomy and positive outcomes remains to be empirically tested. The list focuses on adults, although we suggest that excellent resources on the application of SDT to child therapy exist (e.g., see Ziviani, Poulsen, & Cuskelly, 2013). There are also elements we could add to this list, and many that overlap, as implementing one often entails another. Finally, not every element applies in every therapy setting (e.g., some settings have no need for specific goals or self-monitoring). In sum, we offer this list for its potential heuristic value in articulating strategies and attitudes associated with psychological-need-supportive psychotherapy and behavior-change efforts.

Autonomy-Supportive Techniques

Autonomy support is first and foremost an agapic attitude of unconditional regard and a desire for the empowerment and self-actualization of the client. At its most foundational level, autonomy support begins by embracing the perspective of the client. Thus the first "technique" of therapy we offer concerns this foundational activity.

Taking the Internal Frame of Reference

Listening carefully and empathically to the clients' viewpoints and experiences allows a fuller understanding of their situations and the motivations and values underlying their emotions and behaviors. We describe empathic listening in SDT as taking the client's *internal frame of reference* (IFOR). The therapist nonjudgmentally and compassionately enters into the client's world and, in doing so, acknowledges feelings, perceptions, valuations, and potential conflicts. Taking the client's IFOR is especially important regarding areas of possible ambivalence or perceived barriers to change, which need to be articulated and accepted if they are to be addressed. By being open, accepting, interested, and nonjudgmental, the therapist lowers the likelihood of defensiveness and concealment. In listening with interest and compassion, the therapist also validates the client and energizes curiosity and self-focused interest that can be key to developing insight and internal reasons for change.

EMOTION FOCUS

Gaining access to the important experiences that were and continue to be interfering with need satisfaction and autonomous functioning frequently involves focusing on clients' emotions, whether they are being expressed verbally, nonverbally, or implicitly. By attending to feelings, therapists can identify meaningful points of leverage for bringing significant material into the open that will help move the client toward greater autonomy and need satisfaction.

Emotions are understood within SDT as neither good nor bad but, rather, as sources of *information*. This means that attending to them provides important inputs about subjective reactions, threats, and desires. By taking interest in emotions, without judgment or control, therapists can cultivate more disclosure throughout treatment, expanding the areas of shared experience and having better "radar" for potential pitfalls and feelings of resistance to change. Also modeled for clients is the idea that emotions are inputs to be reflectively considered, rather than mandates to act.

Providing a Meaningful Rationale for Therapeutic Strategies and Activities

Therapy can be a daunting and sometimes opaque process for clients. In addition, the therapists are, for many, ready authority figures, whom the clients might easily see as being in command. It is thus especially important in therapy settings that therapists offer clients a rationale that is tailored or personally meaningful for any activities they are to engage in. As we have previously emphasized, it is hard for people to be autonomously motivated unless they have clear and legitimate reasons to act (Deci, Eghrari, Patrick, & Leone, 1994; Jang, Reeve, & Deci, 2010). Even where the specific strategies cannot be directly revealed, the rationale for why to do them can itself be described, so that the clients can endorse the therapists' way of operating. It is important that there is enough transparency that clients can meaningfully consent to what is occurring and have a grounded rationale for why therapy and each of the activities pursued within it are worthwhile.

Finally, there is no reason for clients to feel "in the dark" about what is occurring in treatment. It is important that they be encouraged to ask questions, express doubts, and wonder why certain events occur. Creating an atmosphere in which questions are prized and respected is thus a strong support to feelings of autonomy.

Acknowledging Feelings of Resistance

As an aspect of both listening and providing a rationale, it is important for the therapist to be sensitive in an ongoing way to clients' resistances to either his or her approach or to change more generally. Empathically embracing resistances is thus both autonomy-supportive and strategic in that it often allows the strongest barriers to therapeutic work to become more fully articulated.

Here it is important that therapists themselves can exercise both mindfulness and self-regulation. Ego involvement, often nonconscious, can drive therapists to want to press their viewpoint of reaching certain goals. Yet from the SDT perspective, if the client is balking, the reason is that there is some barrier, be it emotional, interpersonal, or practical that is perceived or felt to be in the way. It is by embracing the client's perspective on it that the practitioner can best grasp its significance and invite a collaborative effort to overcome it.

Providing Choice and Inviting Meaningful Inputs

It is important to recognize, if it is not clear already, that the term *choice,* as used in SDT, does not mean simply to make decisions or to have options about what to do. Many psychologists (e.g., Iyengar & Lepper, 2000) have interpreted the term *choice* to mean simply "making a decision" from available options. SDT interprets the term differently, as meaning that people experience a sense of choice about what they are doing (Moller, Deci, & Ryan, 2006). Awareness is what allows people to make a decision that is a true choice. This implies, of course, that facilitating choice in psychotherapy is not simply about therapists offering options to clients, although therapists might occasionally point out options that are being overlooked; rather, facilitating choice means that therapists provide the support and responsiveness that allows clients to be more aware and make decisions that they experience as true choices.

Choice can also be concretely facilitated. Therapists and clients can collaboratively devise a course of treatment. Together, they can discuss and review options, including supporting initiatives and experimentation. They also openly embrace discussions or decisions not to change (or to delay change). Fostering opportunities for clients to provide meaningful inputs and to actively participate (or not) in establishing and monitoring goals is critical to feeling volitional.

Avoiding the Use of Controlling Pressures or Incentives, Including Therapist Conditional Approval

Considerable evidence we have reviewed throughout this book suggests that using controlling motivational techniques can undermine autonomy and willingness to be engaged. Thus a critical issue is for the therapist to avoid the use of controlling external rewards and incentives to promote behaviors. Any "rewards" that are employed should be minimal and symbolic—that is, focused on being informational and acknowledging progress rather than representing incentives or sanctions.

Similarly, given the interpersonal nature of the therapy process, there are many interpersonal forms of control that need to be avoided. Therapists can watch for statements of contingent approval, as it can have controlling impacts. They can avoid guilt-inducing phrases and social comparisons. Finally, they can use informational, nonjudgmental statements focused on rationales for goals rather than "oughts" or "musts."

Research on *autonomy support* versus *directive support* is illustrative of how goals can be supported from the inside while strengthening relatedness. Koestner, Powers, Carbonneau, Milyavskaya, and Chua (2012) reported three studies looking at how friends or partners help or hinder goal progress through their style of support over 3-month periods. Autonomy support was defined in terms of empathic perspective taking, whereas directive support was defined in terms of the provision of positive guidance. Dyads differed, some being romantic partners and some being friend dyads, yet across these pairs autonomy support was significantly positively related to goal progress. As predicted, this beneficial effect of autonomy support was mediated by enhanced autonomous goal motivation. Across these studies, autonomy support was also significantly associated with improved relationship quality and subjective well-being. In contrast, directive support was marginally associated with goal progress across studies and was unrelated to well-being or relationship quality. Although this was not a therapy study per se, it shows how, when it comes to life goals, what most people want is support as they pursue their strivings rather than an experience of being directed or controlled.

Need-Supportive Limit Setting

There are cases in therapy in which setting limits is essential. At such times, it is important to recognize that limits can be set in either controlling or autonomy-supportive ways. We have articulated the use of a multistep approach to limit setting that entails being clear about the limit, providing a meaningful rationale for its imposition, acknowledging and being empathic about conflicts with or resistance to the limit, and providing options or choices (Koestner, Ryan, Bernieri, & Holt, 1984).

Comments about Autonomy Support and Integration

A climate of autonomy is conducive to more integrative processing, involving more of the client's reflective capacities, emotional awareness, ownership of actions, and depth of processing about meaning and values. There are many intricacies to these capacities and their expression as springboards of change. However, experimental data can provide analog tests of how conditions of autonomy conduce to therapeutic activity and integration.

In a set of five experiments, Weinstein, Deci, and Ryan (2011) examined the importance of clients' autonomy in integrating past negative identities into their current sense of self. Two of the studies separated participants into an autonomous group and a controlled group based on their scores on the General Causality Orientations Scale (GCOS; see Chapter 9), and the other three studies separated participants randomly and then primed the autonomy orientation in some and the controlled orientation in the others. Participants were then asked to recall two past identities—one a personal characteristic and the other a significant life event—from about 3 years earlier, with some participants being asked to recall positive past identities and some, negative ones. Results indicated that those in the *autonomy conditions,* in processing the information about these past identities, were likely to be accepting of the experience, to see these past characteristics as meaningful and relevant, and to be prone to take a first-person perspective on the events, regardless of whether the characteristics and events were positive or negative. In contrast, participants in the *controlled conditions* were accepting of, found meaningful, and took a first-person perspective on only the characteristics and events that were positive. They were more psychologically distanced from negative identities and events under controlling conditions, whether individual differences or primes. Further analyses indicated that those operating with controlled motivation were much more defended against the negative past material and thus were unable to integrate it into their sense of self, though they readily integrated the positive past material. In the final study in the series, levels of integration of both positive and negative past identities were shown to predict greater vitality, meaning in life, and satisfaction in relationships. In sum, beset with a task of processing past negative identities or events, individuals who were in more autonomous conditions were less defensive and more able to integrate the material into their current sense of self. Greater integration was, in turn, related to higher well-being.

Experimental research by Di Domenico, Fournier, Ayaz, and Ruocco (2013) also suggested that when people experience higher need satisfaction, they are better able to process difficult decisions and align choices with abiding values, reflecting integrative processes. Di Domenico and colleagues specifically proposed that basic psychological need fulfillment amplifies people's neurophysiological responsiveness to decisional conflicts that call for the revision of old self-regulatory schemes. They used functional near-infrared spectroscopy (fNIRS) to examine their hypothesis that individual differences in need satisfaction would influence the activity of the medial prefrontal cortex (MPFC) during the regulation of decisional conflicts. Past research suggests that the MPFC plays an important role in the recruitment of self-knowledge schemes during decisional conflicts, and thus it should be active in a task requiring personal evaluations (Nakao et al., 2009; Nakao et al., 2010). Di Domenico et al. (2013) asked participants to decide between careers with decisions varying in their difficulty, with some options involving high and others low conflict between preferences. Higher levels of need fulfillment predicted longer reaction times and elevated levels of MPFC activity during high- relative to low-conflict decision situations. This was consistent with the idea that people with higher levels of need fulfillment more reflectively attended to decisional conflicts and applied their self-knowledge to resolve decisional conflicts. This study has in fact initiated a new avenue for research on the neural bases of integrative processes (e.g., see Di Domenico & Fournier, 2014).

Such experimental findings provide evidence that supplements field research in highlighting the intrapersonal processes and psychological conditions that are associated with autonomous motivation in the therapeutic process. Forthcoming experimental work will no doubt further refine our understanding of the pathways through which autonomy and basic need-supportive conditions foster integrative processing.

Relatedness-Supportive Techniques

As we have shown in multiple spheres, for internalization to proceed optimally, relatedness support is critical. People are more willing to internalize ideas and inputs from people to whom they feel connected, and connectedness provides a sense of security for moving forward that is especially important in the often highly conflicted area of personal change. Of course, most every school of therapy says that rapport, alliance, and connection are important, but many have no theoretical rationale for why they are important or how to foster this relatedness. We thus specify some relatedness-supportive elements in treatment contexts.

Unconditional Positive Regard

Unconditional positive regard (UCPR) is a concept that was originally introduced by Rogers (1957) as one of his necessary and sufficient ingredients in effective counseling. UCPR means that clients are accepted and valued noncontingently; they are positively valued as persons regardless of how they perform or what they experience. A number of studies in SDT on parenting have shown the importance of UCPR for the development of autonomous motivation (e.g., Roth et al., 2009; Roth et al., 2015). Similar patterns apply in psychotherapy, as Rogers long ago highlighted. UCPR facilitates not only autonomy satisfaction (because it is noncontrolling) but also relatedness satisfaction, fostering a sense of caring and connection irrespective of outcomes. In UCPR, one avoids statements or communications that can be perceived as blaming or judgmental, whether personally disapproving or approving; for even approving ones create contingencies that diminish the value of the behaviors.

Taking Interest in the Person

Nothing expresses involvement and care more than taking sincere interest in the person, being curious and engaged in his or her experiences. Relationally oriented therapists show genuine interest in and concern about their clients' thoughts, perceptions, and experiences.

Acknowledging/Accepting Conflict

Because psychotherapy inevitably raises tough issues and can inspire resistance and sensitivity, moments of conflict and defensiveness are inevitable. Rather than either contradicting or downplaying such experiences, need-supportive therapists embrace and welcome their expression. To be responsive to distress and ambivalence, as well as unhappiness with therapy, responding with concern or compassion rather than judgment is truly connecting, as it is in such moments of conflict in the past in which many clients have felt most rejected or unheard. The current acceptance can thus help heal past rejections.

Authenticity and Transparency

Therapist authenticity in the relationship is critical. Authenticity does not mean sharing all feelings with clients. Instead, it means being honest when expressing concern, interest, or openness. Empathy cannot be feigned. Similarly, transparency does not mean blurting out everything one experiences. It means reflectively sharing important and meaningful perceptions and experiences with the client, in a way that owns the experience rather than imposing on the client. In becoming real and human, connection becomes more possible.

It is clear in discussing these relatedness-supportive elements in therapy that they overlap considerably with autonomy support. This, of course, goes back to our theory about relatedness satisfactions: They indeed derive from the sense that another supports the person's self. Thus the other would be supportive of the person's volition and would be accepting of the person for who he or she truly is.

Competence-Supportive Techniques and the Provision of Structure

Whether we speak of psychotherapy, counseling, coaching, or behavior change, entering into such processes can feel like mysterious territory to many clients. Having feedback and guidance, rather than control or directives, can help a person feel more purposive and confident in engaging in potential change. In therapies focused on specific behavioral outcomes, skill building, as well as effectance-relevant information and feedback, are nearly always useful. But presenting feedback can be precarious, as its functional significance—that is, the extent to which recipients experience it as controlling or demeaning rather than supportive—can vary. In process-oriented therapies, in which the challenges are as much emotional as behavioral, feeling confident and competent to move forward is similarly important. Awareness of optimal and nonoptimal challenges and methods to support efforts at perceived competence for change, including exploration of defenses, is required. In sum, across treatment contexts, supports for the competence need are pervasively essential yet must be provided within the context of autonomy support and responsiveness to the clients' initiations and goals. Among facilitators of competence are the following elements.

Identifying Barriers and Obstacles

Help and encourage clients to identify likely barriers to engaging in personal or behavioral changes. Explicitly and empathically acknowledge that it is often the hidden barriers that block change and that voicing these is always welcome. Sometimes the most formidable barriers are ones only vaguely understood by the client, so working to clarify and accept them as they are encountered is important and supportive.

Focusing on Optimal Challenges

Optimal in SDT means challenges that are readily but not easily mastered and that are not overly stressful or demanding. Accordingly, therapists are attuned to the levels of challenge for which a client is ready and able, and they attempt to tailor interventions to the client's current capacities.

For clients lacking confidence, more proximal goals, readily reached through smaller achievable steps, may help build perceived competence. For others, too easy or too proximal a goal set may leave them feeling underestimated or underchallenged, interfering with perceived competence or confidence in the therapy. SDT research by Koestner, Otis, Powers, Pelletier, and Gagnon (2008) has specifically supported the view forwarded by Gollwitzer (1999) that after a client has adequately deliberated about goals and come to an autonomous decision, concrete plans about how to implement the goals are called for. Exploring people's progress at personal goals, Koestner et al. (2008) showed, across three studies, that autonomous motivation was substantially related to goal progress, whereas controlled motivation was not. Additionally, the relation of autonomous motivation to goal progress was shown to involve implementation planning, underscoring the importance of not only having autonomous motivation for change but also developing implementation plans that mobilize action and engender continuing competence satisfactions.

The concept of optimal challenge is pertinent not only to goal setting in therapy but also in relation to the material that clients engage in more dynamic therapies. When the process of therapy involves facilitating the movement of nonconscious material into consciousness so it can be encountered, examined, and ideally integrated, it is important for the therapist to move at a pace with the uncovering of affective experiences so that the client will be able to examine them without being defensive or overwhelmed.

Promoting an Internal Rather Than External Perceived Locus of Evaluation

When clients are engaged in change-oriented activities, they can typically monitor their own progress, skill level, or performance. Being both the doer and the evaluator can be an empowering activity (because one is not being externally judged), and it is also a competence builder, because assessment involves observation and identification of both skill gaps and mastery. Done in an autonomy-supportive way, self-monitoring is not *self-evaluative*—it is instead *self-informative*, a distinction the therapist helps maintain in listening to reactions to feedback and the results of self-monitoring.

Offering Rich, Clear, and Effectance-Relevant Feedback

Offering relevant and informational feedback (e.g., on goal progress) is especially important in therapy in which specific behavior changes are a focus, but expressing confidence in clients' accomplishments and efforts is useful regardless of modality. Competence supports include communication of structure, strategy options, feedback, and clarity of limits (e.g., Jang, Reeve, & Deci, 2010; Sierens, Vansteenkiste, Goossens, Soenens, & Dochy, 2009). When feedback is provided, it is, again, nonevaluative—it's about the behavior and not the person. Feedback is also something that is not imposed but rather offered. Reactions to feedback, which will often engender self-judgments and internal criticism when negative, are invited and handled empathically. Lack of success is treated informationally—revealing barriers and unanticipated obstacles—rather than evaluatively.

Clients often have questions as part of the feedback process and, in responsive treatment settings, no serious question is ignored or discouraged. Instead, all are answered fully, in a way that can be assimilated (emotionally and intellectually) by the client. Therapists also check in to make sure that their feedback or effectance-relevant information is clear and that they have addressed questions or concerns. Therapists look for any "unfinished business" to which they (the therapists) have not yet been responsive. Even if a question is intentionally being left open for the client to explore, the rationale for this, too, can be discussed.

Encouraging Reflective Consideration of Consequences

Therapists would appropriately facilitate the examination of costs and benefits of behaviors and changes that the clients are either engaged in or are considering. This is to encourage them to exercise reflective choices. At the same time, this has to be done in such a way that the clients' views on costs and benefits are not being judged but rather treated with interest and respect.

Other SDT Content and Process Issues

In a general sense, the SDT therapeutic approach is strongly based on the assumption of an inherent developmental propensity that is also the means through which healing and well-being occur. We refer to this as the *organismic integration process* (see Chapter 8), a concept that bears considerable similarity to the actualizing tendency of humanistic therapies and the synthetic function of the ego in psychodynamic therapies. SDT specifies: (1) the interpersonal conditions and intrapersonal processes that support effective functioning of organismic integration, which yields healing and psychological wellness; (2) the client's behaviors and psychological experiences that indicate impaired development and highlight conditions for which interventions would be useful; and (3) means through which the developmental process can be reinvigorated to deal with the developmental failures that have led the client to the therapist's office. Very importantly, SDT research has confirmed ways to promote full internalization of regulations that represent therapeutic change, thus leading to the maintenance of those changes over time.

Beyond these process aspects of therapy, SDT also has a set of assertions concerning how various contexts, lifestyles, and mindsets are conducive to well-being and eudaimonia or, conversely, contribute to ill-being and psychopathology. The theory suggests that there are various goals, values, and behaviors that are associated with greater wellness, supplying a number of guideposts to which therapist and clients might usefully pay attention.

Attending to Basic Psychological Need Satisfactions and Frustrations in Everyday Life

As stated above, therapists take interest in the dynamics of basic psychological need satisfactions, paying attention to sources of both frustration and satisfaction within the process of therapy or treatment. Yet, any assessment of client wellness outside of therapy would focus on where needs are being neglected or thwarted in everyday life, as this becomes an important focus for therapeutic work. Because SDT holds that these needs are essential to wellness, regardless of whether they are salient or important to the client, this puts a special responsibility on therapists to be attuned to these issues and to bring to light considerations of how the client's values, lifestyle, relationships, and behaviors are affecting these basic need satisfactions.

Attending to Intrinsic versus Extrinsic Aspirations and Goals

As with a sensitivity to need satisfactions, the substantive findings of SDT have much to say about the well-being effects of different types of values and their pursuits. Specifically, goal contents theory (GCT; Chapter 11) suggests strongly that people can be caught up in extrinsic goals that are compensatory in nature and do not typically satisfy basic needs (e.g., Kasser, Ryan, Zax, & Sameroff 1995; Vansteenkiste & Ryan, 2013). Thus eliciting and listening to clients' aspirations and strivings can be helpful in understanding the dynamics and efficacy of their attempts at integration and wellness.

Fostering Awareness and Mindfulness

Cultivating mindfulness, interest taking, and integrative processing of events is a central therapeutic tool (Deci, Ryan, Schultz, & Niemiec, 2015; Schultz & Ryan, 2015). There are, of course, many techniques for raising awareness, some of which are basic, such as using paraphrasing summaries or mirroring expressed affect and content to allow for reflective consideration of experiences. Also, open-ended questions allow exploration, whereas closed questions (e.g., yes/no questions) can make the therapist seem like the expert and the active party in control of the process. Techniques such as reflections and open-ended inquiry, combined with receptive, nonjudgmental responses to clients to support active interest taking and awareness, can facilitate a greater presence and interest. Finally, as described by Roth and colleagues (Roth et al., 2014; Roth, Shachar, Benita, Zohar-Shefer, Moed, & Ryan, 2016), therapists can directly encourage *integrative processing* of emotional events, helping clients to bring nonjudgmental, curious attention to these events and their meanings.

From the early beginnings of SDT, we have argued for a strong role for mindfulness and interested awareness in promoting autonomy and healthy self-regulation (Deci & Ryan, 1980b). *Mindfulness* represents an open, receptive awareness of what is occurring (Brown & Ryan, 2003). Mindfulness allows people to contact information from both internal (needs, feelings, and values) and external (social environmental) sources and to use the information in a reflective way to come to a clear focus and gain a sense of what, all things considered, they would find most helpful to do.

Through this awareness, especially of the difficult experiences, people will reflect upon and work toward resolving and integrating the experiences. For example, Brown and Ryan (2003) found that people high in mindfulness showed greater congruence between implicit and explicit emotions, indicating that they were not blocking their emotions. Further, Niemiec et al. (2010) found that people with more mindful awareness responded less defensively to the mortality salience manipulation frequently used in terror management studies.

One SDT aim in psychotherapy is to facilitate clients' becoming more aware and mindful of what is happening, both in therapy and in life, for awareness facilitates integration. This may at times be accomplished through mindfulness training, although it is more often facilitated simply by therapists' being autonomy supportive and facilitating the clients' interest-taking in their own internal processes. Out of that awareness comes the possibility for clients to examine their inner lives in the kind of interested way that will give them greater capacity for regulating themselves effectively, experiencing satisfaction of their basic needs, and feeling a sense of personal satisfaction. This happens in part because people's mindful awareness supports the organismic integration process by fostering a fuller acknowledgement of the varied parts of their personalities, so the parts can be brought into coherence and harmony with one another and with their overall sense of self (Deci & Ryan, 1991). Indeed, Brown and Ryan (2003) found that greater mindfulness was associated with greater internalization, autonomous regulation, and the experience of vitality and energy being available to the self (Ryan & Deci, 2008a). In short, autonomy support facilitates mindful awareness, which is associated with greater interest-taking, promotes integration, and results in greater autonomy.

The importance of promoting more mindful living is reflected in the way people with greater mindfulness deal with stress. In a series of studies Weinstein, Brown, and Ryan (2009) hypothesized that, in part because they would be more autonomously functioning, individuals high in mindfulness would show greater resilience to stress. Specifically, the research showed that persons with greater mindfulness, relative to those with lesser, perceived less stress from similarly demanding events. They were also more likely to employ constructive and nonavoidant coping strategies in response to stressors. The studies further showed that these more benign stress attributions and improved coping were at least in part responsible for (i.e., mediated by) the relations of mindfulness to well-being outcomes. Thus mindfulness was associated with more adaptive stress processing, including more positive cognitive appraisals and more active coping strategies, each considered a key underpinning for mental health and well-being (e.g., Gross & Muñoz, 1995).

Mindfulness training can be a meaningful contributor to most any treatment (e.g., see Miller, Fletcher, & Kabat-Zinn, 1995). Because mindfulness involves clients being present in the moment and allowing their experiences simply to be, they are more receptive to experiencing emotions and taking interest in whatever emerges. Research has, in fact, supported this idea, showing that mindful awareness is associated with greater autonomous motivation and more satisfaction of all the basic psychological needs (Brown et al., 2007; Schultz & Ryan, 2015).

Being Informational, Not Controlling

Therapists are most centrally facilitators of change. At the same time, in some areas, they can also be "experts" who have information relevant to the clients' concerns and issues, as well as to the relative effectiveness of various approaches. Therapists do not withhold information, but they are also cautious and thoughtful in providing it. Critical in this regard is the distinction between the informational and the controlling aspects of any such communication. The true intent of information is not to direct or pressure, but rather to enhance the person's basis for making authentic choices. Expert inputs, that is, are meant to inform rather than to manipulate or lead. At the same time, they can aid competence, helping the client to identify misconceptions about his or her situation or behaviors and to understand available options in an accessible, open-minded manner. Therapies vary in the extent to which they are supportive or growth focused in their goals (Deci & Ryan, 1985b; Ryan & Deci, 2008). Yet even in supportive modes, external guidance and structure can be implemented in the service of preserving wellness while at the same time respecting autonomy to all degrees possible.

Autonomy as an End Goal of Treatment

Prescriptions from SDT that advocate therapists' providing autonomy support, relatedness cultivation, and competence facilitation may sound either obvious or easy. Yet our involvement in psychotherapy, as well as the supervision and training of therapists, has taught us how often therapists fail to be responsive to the clients' basic psychological needs, as well as how difficult it can be to be responsive. To provide unconditional positive regard, for example, requires setting aside personal biases and agendas and, most especially, ego involvements in the outcomes of the therapy.

Maintaining a freedom from controlling agendas and ego involvements is especially problematic within many health care systems in which specific outcomes *for the therapist* are being contingently controlled. The more the settings have high stakes and outcome pressures, the more likely it is that the therapists will become outcome focused and then, all too often although not necessarily, more controlling in tone. Thus therapists have to be aware of and monitor their own goals, being sure they do not bring the "downward pressures" upon them into their relationships with clients. This is surely a tall task.

In SDT, as with medical ethics more generally (see Chapter 18), we see the ultimate clinical goal as the client's autonomy, rather than particular behavioral outcomes. In our SDT viewpoint, the ultimate goal of therapy would never be simply attaining a specific behavioral benchmark, chemical test result, or skilled performance. These will be meaningful and lasting if they represent achievements the client had come to value. Instead, the ultimate goals of therapy are facilitating people's ability to make informed and reflective choices about how to live their lives and then engage the challenges, often unpredictable, that will ensue. Supporting autonomy and competence is supporting the fundamental human capabilities for living a full life.

This is exactly why psychotherapy has so often been seen as a subversive profession. In it, people can reevaluate, without the proximal pressures of the crowd, kin, or culture, their experiences and judgments, including what matters most. Then, when they turn back to their contexts, what they do there is likely to be more integrated, and the doing more authentic and vital. Psychotherapy, done well, is in fact subversive to all parties, in the culture, in the client, and in the therapist, because, in it, all phenomena, both within and without, are treated with equal mindfulness, interest, curiosity, and compassion. More generally, whether a therapy be primarily supportive (and thus protective) or growth-focused (and thus to some extent subversive), its aims are in the service of enhancing the wellness of the individual, which includes enabling their basic need satisfactions and pursuit of what, to them, matters most.

CHAPTER 18

Health Care and Patient Need Satisfaction
Supporting Maintained Health Behavior Change

Health is an intrinsic goal and is instrumental to the attainment of other intrinsic goals. Yet it is often compromised by habits and lifestyles. Behaviors such as using tobacco, eating unhealthy foods, and failing to exercise can greatly enhance morbidity and mortality. In addition, poor adherence to health care interventions and prescriptions also compromises health outcomes. Motivation thus plays a critical role both in healthy living and in enhancing treatment adherence. Herein we review field studies and clinical trials that examine the utility of SDT concepts for facilitating healthier living and more effective health care practices. We review tests of the SDT health care process model, finding support for the importance of autonomous motivation and perceived competence as proximal predictors of effective health behavior change and the role of practitioners in facilitating motivation and lasting change. Studies focus on a variety of issues, including diabetes, weight and dietary management, elevated low-density lipoprotein (LDL) cholesterol, major cardiovascular events, surgeries, breast cancer, dental health, and the well-being of elderly persons, among others. We also consider people's aspirations or life goals as they relate to health and well-being. We then address issues related to health practitioner training, emphasizing the importance of autonomy support for both faculty and students. Finally, we address autonomy from a philosophical perspective, viewing it as both a medical and moral imperative.

Health care is a particularly interesting arena within which to examine autonomy. On the one hand, there are health care professionals who have clear goals or desired outcomes for their patients. Often these professionals are under pressure—and attaining outcomes can have high stakes in terms of funding and reimbursement. On the other hand, it is a fundamental goal of medical care to preserve and respect patient autonomy. Decisions need to be made and behaviors enacted, but the questions of who makes the decisions, how they are made, and whether patients enact the behaviors willingly and effectively are, as it turns out, crucial for health outcomes.

In acute care, decisions about surgery or other invasive procedures sometimes have to be made quickly and can have profound consequences, including immediate life or death. Most chronic care represents a somewhat different story, however, for the decisions frequently involve patients behaving in treatment-adherent and health-promoting ways over long periods of time to achieve optimal outcomes. These decisions concern either stopping health-compromising behaviors, such as smoking cigarettes, abusing alcohol, and overeating unhealthy foods, or starting healthier behaviors, such as exercising regularly, monitoring and controlling one's glucose level, or reliably following a medication regimen. Such behavior change requires patients to be motivated, and SDT proposes that the most effective change requires not just any motivation but, specifically, autonomous motivation.

There is indeed ample evidence that people's behavior plays a huge role in their morbidity and mortality. Individuals' own behaviors—their tobacco use, sedentary lifestyles, alcohol abuse, failure to take medications, and poor diets—are broadly implicated in premature deaths. For example, tobacco use remains a significant cause of such deaths in the United States (Jha et al., 2013) and deaths caused by obesity, with its primary antecedents being poor diet and insufficient exercise, are also high (e.g., see Flegal, Kit, Orpana, & Graubard, 2013). Such findings make it clear that people's own behaviors can be the biggest risk factor they face in the health domain.

Because such behaviors are at least to some degree intentional, motivational psychology can identify the critical points of leverage at both individual and population levels, where health care outcomes involving personal behaviors can be influenced. SDT researchers around the world have accordingly made concerted efforts to understand more fully how to use SDT to facilitate behaviors that are linked to more positive long-term health consequences.

Research on Autonomy Support, Autonomy, and Competence in Health Care

SDT hypothesizes that the psychological states most essential for making meaningful change are: (1) being autonomously motivated for the change and (2) perceiving oneself to be competent to make the change. As well, it is hypothesized that when relevant social contexts are autonomy-supportive, rather than controlling or amotivating, people will be more likely to exhibit the autonomous motivation and perceived competence that are the more proximal predictors of effective change. Numerous studies through the years have tested these hypothesized links in this general model of health behavior change, using a range of behaviors, such as tobacco cessation and abstinence, medication adherence, dietary improvement, and physical activity, as well as such medical conditions as obesity, diabetes, and coronary heart disease, for which health behavior change is critical for improvement. We begin by reviewing a sample of such studies.

Initial Empirical Investigations

Weight Loss

The first of the SDT health-behavior-change studies examined motivation for weight loss in a sample of morbidly obese patients who were participating in a 6-month, medically supervised, very-low-calorie diet program that involved weekly group meetings at the clinic (Williams, Grow, Freedman, Ryan, & Deci, 1996). It was a longitudinal field study not intended to evaluate the program but, rather, to test motivational predictors of success within the program. Patients provided data at four times over 2 years so as to evaluate longer term effects of the program. Results indicated that more autonomous motivation for losing weight (as measured by the Treatment Self-Regulation Questionnaire [TSRQ]; see Levesque et al., 2007) predicted greater attendance at the 6-month program and weight loss at the end of the program. Further, it predicted patients' sustained exercise at the 23-month follow-up, as well as maintained weight loss. Moreover, autonomous motivation assessed at Time 2 was predicted by the patients' autonomy orientation on the General Causality Orientations Scale (GCOS), as well as by their perceptions of the health care climate (assessed with the Health Care Climate Questionnaire [HCCQ]), after controlling for the patients' autonomy orientation. In sum, as hypothesized, both patients' autonomy orientations and their perceptions of the autonomy support in the treatment climate predicted their autonomous motivation for following program guidelines for losing weight, and that, in turn, predicted their attendance at the program, 6-month weight loss, and exercise and maintained weight loss at 23 months. The study thus provided some of the first evidence that SDT could represent a useful framework for understanding and promoting healthy behavior change. It was also encouraging to find that autonomy-related concepts could be useful in promoting increased exercise and weight loss in persons with morbid obesity because of the serious negative health consequences of that condition.

Glucose Control

Another early health care study based in SDT concerned the regulation of glycosylated hemoglobin (HbA1c) among patients with diabetes (Williams, Freedman, & Deci, 1998). Adult outpatients with either Type 1 or Type 2 diabetes were studied for 12 months while they were receiving treatment at a university-affiliated diabetes clinic. Their autonomous motivation and perceived competence for diabetes management were assessed at the beginning and end of the 12-month period, as were their HbA1c levels. Their perceptions of autonomy support from the practitioners were assessed 4 months into the year-long period. Results indicated that patients who perceived their practitioners as being more autonomy-supportive displayed increases in autonomous motivation over the year. That increase was related to enhancement of their perceived competence, which in turn predicted decreases in the patients' hemoglobin levels into a healthier range. In short, having more autonomy support led patients to be more autonomously involved in their care, to feel more competence and confidence in managing their illness, and to display improvement in a critical, biochemically assessed marker of their health.

Subsequent to these two initial studies of very different medical conditions for which improvement requires behavior change in diet and exercise, many other studies have been conducted in the Rochester labs and elsewhere to examine these issues more broadly and deeply.

Promoting Tobacco Cessation and Abstinence

Several studies have applied SDT to the issue of tobacco use. Studies by Curry, Wagner, and Grothaus (1991) and by Ockene et al. (1991) provided indication that SDT variables can be important for understanding smoking cessation. Our Rochester group initially did field studies and experiments intended to understand the conditions and processes that relate to cessation and abstinence. From this early knowledge base we designed a series of clinical trials to test SDT-based interventions.

A Brief Counseling Intervention

In the first study (Williams, Gagné, Ryan, & Deci, 2002), patients received a brief, one-session counseling intervention from 27 physicians who used the National Cancer Institute's 4-A's model (Ask about smoking, Advice to quit, Assist by negotiating a quit date, and Arrange a follow-up visit within 2 weeks after the quit date). The difference between autonomy-supportive and controlling styles of using the 4-A's intervention was explained to the physicians, and patients were then randomly assigned to receive one of the two styles. The counseling sessions were audiotaped, and, subsequently, trained raters judged the degree to which the physicians were autonomy-supportive, with each patient using five items from the HCCQ. Thus, whereas in the previously discussed studies of weight loss (Williams et al., 1996) and glucose control (Williams, Freedman, et al., 1998), patients used the HCCQ to provide their perceptions of the practitioners' autonomy support, in this study of smoking cessation, trained raters provided perceptions of the practitioners' autonomy support. Participants' smoking status was assessed at 6, 18, and 30 months, and the primary dependent measure was whether they had been abstinent for 7 days prior to each measurement point.

Results indicated that the difference in style used during this one brief counseling session was not powerful enough to cause a difference in abstinence over the 30-month period (Williams & Deci, 2001). However, the experimentally manipulated style used in the intervention did affect the degree to which the physicians were rated as autonomy-supportive in the counseling. When the physicians counseled in the autonomy-supportive condition, the raters viewed them as being, on average, more autonomy-supportive. Further, ratings of physicians' autonomy support, in turn, predicted patients' autonomous motivation, which predicted change in their feelings of competence about quitting from before to after the counseling. Further, both patients' autonomous motivation and their perceived competence predicted their continuous abstinence over 30 months (Williams, Gagné, et al., 2002).

This study also provided an initial opportunity to test the general SDT process model of health behavior change, which is represented in Figure 18.1. The model suggests the following pattern of relations: Interventions should influence practitioner autonomy support, which influences patients' autonomous motivation and, in turn, their perceived competence. Both autonomous motivation and perceived competence then proximally contribute to behavior change, in this case continuous abstinence. Structural equation modeling showed that the data fit the process model well. Especially given the brevity of the intervention, these were promising results.

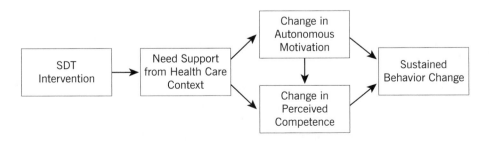

FIGURE 18.1. Core elements of the SDT process model of health-promoting behavior change.

A Brief Intervention for Adolescents

In another brief intervention study, a physician went into high schools to present facts about smoking to the students (Williams, Cox, Kouides, & Deci, 1999). For some, the facts were presented in a way intended to emphasize risks and arouse fear of smoking, which is a common strategy in preventive efforts. For others, the facts were presented with an autonomy-supportive style, emphasizing the students' choice about smoking and encouraging reflective decision making about this behavior. Data were collected at three points in time: a few days before the presentation, when demographics, smoking status, and autonomous motivation for not smoking (TSRQ) were assessed; immediately after the presentation, when autonomous motivation and perceived autonomy support from the presenter were assessed; and 4 months later, when autonomous motivation and smoking status were again assessed. Results indicated that during the 4-month period, participants who experienced the presenter as autonomy-supportive became more autonomous in their motivation for not smoking. Further, both when the students perceived the presenter as being more autonomy supportive and when they themselves were more autonomously motivated not to smoke, they were less likely to be smoking at the end of the 4-month period. Although again promising, the data also suggested that such a brief intervention is also limited in potency for such a difficult-to-change behavior.

Smoking Cessation in a Clinical Trial

With these initial encouraging findings concerning smoking cessation, as well as other findings that were emerging from the examination of SDT variables in the change of other health behaviors, the team of Rochester SDT health-behavior-change researchers designed a more comprehensive randomized clinical trial (see, e.g., Williams, Minicucci, et al., 2002). In this trial, we recruited adult participants into a study of smokers' health. To be eligible, one needed to smoke at least five cigarettes per day and be willing to visit the clinic on four occasions over a 6-month period to discuss their health and tobacco use with health professionals and to complete questionnaires. Wanting to quit smoking was, however, not a requirement. In fact, on their first visit, participants were asked whether they would like to make an attempt to quit within the next 30 days and were accepted whether they answered the question with "yes" or "no." More than half of the 1,000 participants said no, they had no intention to quit. This is noteworthy insofar as many smoking interventions only accept patients deemed ready to change or put up multiple barriers that result in only highly motivated participants actually enrolling. Our goal was the opposite—to have as few barriers to entry as possible and to accept people whether they were motivated or not. Participants also had blood draws, and if they had elevated low-density lipoprotein cholesterol (LDL-C), they were asked to have two additional visits to discuss issues related to their cholesterol.

The design of the study was a stratified randomized trial (Williams, McGregor, Sharp, Lévesque, et al., 2006). Patients whose LDL-C was not elevated were in one stratum and were randomly assigned to either the SDT intervention for tobacco dependence or to a community care condition. Community care patients were encouraged to discuss their tobacco use with their own physicians, were give a list of resources available in the community for dealing with tobacco dependence, and relevant printed materials. Those who had elevated LDL-C were in the other stratum and were randomized to one of three conditions: the SDT intervention for both tobacco and diet; the SDT intervention for tobacco and community care for diet; or community care for both tobacco and diet.

THE INTERVENTION

We trained health counselors to conduct the intervention visits, although patients who at any time said that they were ready to make a quit attempt were also offered a consultation with a prescriber to discuss the use of medications for smoking cessation. During the initial sessions of the intervention, the counselors elicited participants' histories and perspectives regarding smoking in order to understand the patients' internal frames of reference. Further, counselors worked to promote participants' reflections on what smoking provided to them and what harm it might cause them, in part so they had the relevant information with which to make a choice and in part because, if they decided to stop smoking, they would be ready to address alternative means to get the satisfactions provided by tobacco use. For example, if smoking helped them manage their anxiety, they could consider how to manage that without the use of tobacco. Additionally, counselors invited participants to consider how continuing to smoke versus stopping smoking fit with their personal values, needs, and plans for the future.

Throughout treatment, counselors remained neutral with respect to the treatment outcome, endorsing neither continued smoking nor stopping, and not pressuring clients toward cessation. Yet for patients ready to try stopping, discussion then turned to enhancing their perceived competence and techniques for coping with the possible barriers they might encounter. When participants made a change attempt, the focus was on their progress and on any difficulties they had had. If they tried and failed, the attempt was acknowledged, and their feelings about it were elicited. Such attempts were framed not as a failure but as learning opportunities—discovering what works and doesn't. The importance of personal choice regarding smoking was continuously conveyed by the counselors' attitude and behaviors: by not pressuring or criticizing and by accepting the patients' decisions not to try stopping without disapproving either verbally or nonverbally. This intervention, based on the principles of SDT, was also consistent with the Public Health Service's guidelines for treating tobacco dependence (Fiore et al., 2000).

RESULTS

As a clinical trial, the first important question concerns whether the intervention significantly impacted the key outcome, namely smoking cessation. The intention-to-treat analysis, with all participants taken into account (i.e., any participant who dropped out of the study was considered a smoker for these analyses). Analyses revealed that the quit rate in the intervention group was significantly greater than in the community care group, with an odds ratio of 2.9, indicating that nearly three times as many people quit smoking in the SDT group as in community care. The intervention also had an effect on medication taking, with those in the intervention group taking significantly more of the medications that aided cessation. Finally, the intervention also influenced the motivation variables in the directions that would be expected (Williams, McGregor, Sharp, Lévesque, et al., 2006).

As we mentioned, unlike many smoking-cessation trials, which require patients to be motivated to stop smoking in order to participate, there were no such barriers to entry. As a result, more than half the patients in this trial stated that they were not ready to try quitting. Of course, these patients were less likely to be abstinent at the end of the 6-month treatment period than those who had initially been ready to make a quit attempt. Nonetheless, patients in the intervention group who had not been ready to try quitting were significantly more likely to be abstinent at 6 months than were their counterparts in community care. In other words, the SDT intervention facilitated cessation for both precontemplators and those ready to try quitting. Another point of interest about the sample in this trial is that the average income of the patients in the study was considerably below the average income for individuals in the county in which the participants lived. As well, patients in the trial had a much lower education level. This, too, is important for medical care, because it indicates that the SDT intervention is useful for individuals with lower SES.

The 18-month follow-up of this trial (Williams, McGregor, Sharp, Kouides, et al., 2006) indicated that the difference between the SDT-intervention group and the community-care group was still in evidence, with an odds ratio of 2.7, and these differences were still apparent at 24 months posttreatment (Williams, Niemiec, Patrick, Ryan, & Deci, 2009). These effects were partially mediated by changes from baseline to 6 months in both autonomous motivation and perceived competence. Finally, analyses also determined that the intervention was highly cost-effective. Specifically, the analyses found the cost of the SDT intervention for tobacco cessation to be $1,258 per quality adjusted life year saved (QALY), which is extremely cost-effective. By comparison, for example, the cost per QALY for hypertension screening for men between 45 and 54 is $5,200, and the cost per QALY for most surgeries is far, far higher. In short, the SDT intervention for long-term cessation of tobacco use was both effective and cost-effective.

A PROCESS MODEL OF CHANGE

An additional aspect of this tobacco-treatment trial examined the process model through which cessation occurred (Figure 18.1). According to SDT, autonomy support from the treatment context should increase both autonomous motivation and perceived competence for change, which are expected in turn to be proximal antecedents of change. Within this general model, there may be specific additional variables that are affected by the intervention and that affect the health outcome. In the smoking cessation trial, we expected that taking cessation-promoting medications such as nicotine replacement would play such a role in the process model of change.

SDT also maintains that this model of change will be operative in any treatment setting, not only for treatments based on SDT principles. Thus, in the current smoking-cessation trial, we expected the model to significantly predict smoking abstinence for patients in community care, as well as for patients in the SDT intervention. Of course, we expected and found a higher level of change in the SDT-intervention group than in community care, because patients in community care on average perceived their treatment climate to be less autonomy-supportive than those in the SDT intervention group. Accordingly the community care participants were also lower in autonomy, perceived competence, and medication taking than the SDT group.

Multigroup structural equation modeling (SEM) was used to examine whether the data from both groups fit the SDT process model (Byrne, 2001). Results of these analyses supported the view that the SDT process model applied in both treatment situations, although, as we had previously noted, the intervention group experienced their treatment to be more autonomy-supportive, and that led to more positive treatment outcomes.

There is another finding of interest from this clinical trial. Participants also completed measures of depressive symptoms (Radloff, 1977) and vitality (Ryan & Frederick, 1997) at baseline, 6, and 18 months. Analyses of the data by Niemiec, Ryan, Patrick, Deci, and Williams (2010) revealed that participants who were more autonomously motivated to stop smoking experienced greater vitality in their lives and smoked fewer cigarettes. Further, cigarette use at baseline and at 6 months related positively to depressive symptoms at baseline, 6, and 18 months and related negatively to vitality at those three times. In other words, smoking more cigarettes, which is sometimes thought to relieve depression and leave people feeling better, actually seems to do just the opposite, leaving them less vital and more depressed.

A Clinical Trial to Improve Cholesterol

Within the Williams, McGregor, Sharp, Kouides, et al. (2006) smokers' health trial, all patients with elevated LDL-C participated in a "trial within the larger trial." The SDT intervention for cholesterol was very similar to the one for tobacco dependence, except that the former focused on issues of diet and exercise rather than tobacco use. Analyses revealed that participants who received the SDT intervention for cholesterol showed significantly greater improvement in their levels of LDL-C (–8.9 mg/dl) than did those assigned to community care for cholesterol (–4.1 mg/dl).

In sum, the clinical trials for facilitating tobacco cessation and abstinence maintenance for all patients and for lowering LDL-C for those tobacco-using patients with elevated LDL-C were found to be effective for both conditions and were able to improve patients' health status in a very cost-effective manner.

Autonomy Support and the SDT Interventions

Too frequently within medicine, the concept of supporting patients' autonomy is interpreted to mean that practitioners should leave patients alone to make their own decisions relevant to their own health care. This is not, however, a view consistent with SDT, as it represents support for *independence* more than support for *volition*. For patients to make autonomous choices, they need to be supported, informed in language they understand, and encouraged to consider the relevant information carefully. Medical information is often complex and terminology is difficult, so practitioners who are autonomy-supportive need to be concerned with the patients' perspectives, providing information in ways in which it can be understood. Frequently, when patients are visiting a provider, they are anxious, so it becomes even more difficult for providers to be effective in conveying information. The goal in an autonomy-supportive approach is for patients to come to the point of making a true choice after thoughtfully considering the relevant options and information. This requires that providers not pressure patients to choose a particular option but to allow them to consider each. Sometimes, patients fully capable of making their own medical decisions may want their physicians' recommendations as one important piece of information to be considered because physicians are trusted experts. When that is the case, it is appropriate for providers to make a recommendation, but to do it in a way that is informative rather than pressuring. In short, having patients participate autonomously in their health care means neither that the provider will leave patients alone to make decisions nor that the provider will make decisions for them. Rather, it means that provider and patient work together in a partnership to inform and support the patient's autonomous decision (Williams, Deci, & Ryan, 1998).

Medication Adherence

Perhaps half of all medication prescriptions that are written are not followed in ways that would lead to positive outcomes (e.g., Osterberg & Blaschke, 2005). A 2013 report from

National Community Pharmacists estimated that the financial cost to the health care system of nonadherence to prescription medication was $290 billion in the United States alone (National Community Pharmacists Association (2013). Prescriptions are not filled, some are filled but not used, some are filled and used for a short time when long-term use is what is needed, and some are used but at a dose below what is necessary for positive effects (Fischer et al., 2010). Clearly, too, this is a problem for which people's voluntary behavior, and thus their motivation, are integrally involved.

We already mentioned that in the trial by Williams, McGregor, Sharp, Kouides, et al. (2006), patients' autonomous motivation led them to be more adherent in using cessation medication, such as nicotine replacement and bupropion, and that, in turn, led to greater cessation and abstinence. Other SDT-framed studies have also examined medication adherence.

Williams, Rodin, Ryan, Grolnick, and Deci (1998) studied adult outpatients who were on long-term medication regimens for a variety of conditions such as hypertension, menopausal symptoms, and arthritis. In the study, a psychologist conducted a clinical interview about the patients' health and medication prescriptions, and the patients completed assessments of both their autonomy and their prescriber's autonomy support. Assessments of adherence to prescriptions were done both through self-reports and through pill counts. Specifically, patients were called at their homes both 2 days and 2 weeks after the interview and asked to get their pill bottles and count the pills currently in it. The pill count was then compared with what the prescription specified and served as the primary indicator of adherence.

Results of the study indicated that patients' perceptions of the autonomy-supportiveness of their prescribing physicians predicted their autonomous motivation for following their prescriptions, and this in turn predicted their adherence to the medication regimen. Data from the study were found to fit the process model in which autonomy support predicted autonomous motivation, which predicted adherence. Further analyses indicated that autonomous motivation mediated the link between perceived autonomy support and adherence.

In this adherence study, *health locus of control* (Wallston, 1988; Wallston, Wallston, & DeVellis, 1978) was also assessed, in part because internal locus of control is often confused with autonomy (i.e., with an internal perceived locus of causality [I-PLOC]). As we pointed out in Chapter 9, an internal locus of control does not imply autonomy; people can have an internal locus of control and yet be controlled in their motivation. As we expect from SDT, autonomous motivation (i.e., I-PLOC) was highly positively correlated with adherence ($r = .58$), whereas internal locus of control was unrelated to adherence ($r = .00$).

Adherence to HIV Medications

Kennedy, Goggin, and Nollen (2004) employed SDT to examine adherence to antiviral therapy in over 200 HIV-positive patients. The researchers met the patients in the clinic where they went for treatment, conducted a short structured interview, and had the patients complete questionnaires, including measures of autonomy support, autonomous motivation, and perceived competence, each worded to address antiviral medications. They also asked patients to complete the Profile of Mood States (POMS; McNair, Lorr, & Doppleman, 1971) as a measure of psychological distress. All patients provided self-reports of their adherence, and for a subset of them, pharmacy refill logs were obtained to validate the self-reports.

Results of this study confirmed the hypothesis that patients' perceptions of the autonomy-supportiveness of both their practitioners and their families predicted their own autonomous motivation for taking their medications. Autonomous motivation in turn predicted the patients' perceived competence to adhere to the regimen, and that perceived competence predicted adherence, thus mediating the relation between autonomous motivation and adherence. Further, perceived autonomy support was negatively related to psychological distress, and psychological distress was in turn negatively related to adherence.

A study by Williams, Patrick, et al. (2009) examined medication adherence of more than 2,000 patients with diabetes mellitus. They found that perceived autonomy support from practitioners predicted autonomous motivation for medication use, perceived competence for diabetes self-management, higher quality of life, and better medication adherence. Importantly, medication adherence predicted improvements in non-high-density-lipoprotein (HDL) cholesterol, HbA1c, and glucose levels. Thus, this and the two other studies just reviewed indicate that medication adherence contributed significantly to the patients' health and that the SDT motivation variables facilitated the medication adherence.

Glycemic Control among Patients with Diabetes

We have already reviewed the first SDT study of glucose control among patients with diabetes, which examined the autonomy support of practitioners, the autonomous motivation and perceived competence of patients, and the patients' glucose levels (Williams, Freedman, et al., 1998). As well, we just reviewed a study showing the importance of medication adherence for patients with diabetes (Williams, Patrick, et al. 2009). Various other studies in the Rochester labs and elsewhere have examined these and other SDT-related variables in patients with diabetes.

Patients' Active Involvement

In a study of patients with Type 2 diabetes, interactions between the patients and their doctors were tape-recorded, and the degree of patients' active engagement was assessed by trained raters (Williams, McGregor, Zeldman, Freedman, Deci, & Elder, 2005). Regression analyses revealed that patients' active engagement in discussions of their own health and health care predicted improvements in their glucose levels over a 1-year period. Patients' active engagement in their treatment planning and execution is generally expected to be closely related to their autonomous motivation, so the results of this study are consistent with the diabetes studies previously discussed showing a link between autonomous motivation and improved glucose control.

Julien, Senécal, and Guay (2009), in a study of patients with Type 2 diabetes, measured autonomous motivation, active engagement,, and dietary adherence (assessed with the Summary of Diabetes Self-Care Activities questionnaire [SDSCA]; Toobert & Glasgow, 1994) at two times separated by 13 months. Using cross-lagged SEM, it was determined that autonomous motivation and the coping strategy of active engagement and planning were reciprocally related over time, with each variable at the beginning of the period predicting the other at the end of the period, providing further evidence that autonomous motivation is closely linked to active engagement and involvement. Additionally, and most importantly, autonomous motivation at the beginning of the period predicted dietary adherence at the later time point.

Autonomy and Competence in Diabetes Care

In a study of French Canadians with either Type 1 or Type 2 diabetes, Senécal, Nouwen, and White (2000) examined autonomous motivation for carrying out diabetes behavioral regimens and their perceived competence, assessed with a self-efficacy questionnaire. As well, they measured adherence to dietary self-care activities, with the SDSCA, and general life satisfaction (Diener, Emmons, Larsen, & Griffin, 1985). Structural modeling of the data supported the hypotheses that both autonomous motivation and perceived competence would predict both carrying out the diabetes health-related behaviors and more well-being, assessed as satisfaction with life.

Testing a Process Model of Diabetes Self-Management

A 1-year longitudinal study of patients with Type 2 diabetes (Williams, McGregor, Zeldman, Freedman, & Deci, 2004) was designed to test the SDT process model of health behavior change for diabetes. The model for this setting appears in Figure 18.1 (minus the intervention at the left side of the figure) and using hemoglobin A1c as the indicator of health. Correlations confirmed the hypothesized relations between the variables. The best fitting model was the one from the figure, as specified above, except for one variation, namely, that perceived competence mediated the relation between autonomous motivation and HbA1c. That is, both autonomous motivation and perceived competence were related to glucose control, but when all were entered into the model, the direct relation from autonomous motivation to HbA1c was fully mediated through perceived competence.

In this study, patients also provided information about their diabetes self-management. Analyses of these data showed that the behaviors of checking glucose regularly, following a healthy diet, and exercising were all predicted by patients' perceived competence for glucose control, and these behaviors in turn predicted HbA1c. In other words, the link between perceived competence and change in HbA1c was mediated by these three health-promoting behaviors.

Still another study of diabetes care was done by Austin, Senécal, Guay, and Nouwen (2011) with patients with Type 1 diabetes between 11 and 17 years of age. Of interest was how gender of the young patients and the length of time since onset of the disease would affect dietary self-care. Results indicated that girls who had had the disease longer perceived their providers as being less autonomy-supportive. The model showed that perceived autonomy support from both providers and parents facilitated dietary self-care indirectly through the patients' autonomous motivation and perceived competence, and, in addition, perceived autonomy support from parents also contributed to dietary self-care directly. This study contributes to the literature in two ways. First, it shows that the relation of the nonmodifiable factors of gender and disease duration to dietary self-care have their effects by affecting the motivational variables specified by SDT. Second, it provides further support for the general model of health behavior change using adolescent patients for whom their illness was not brought on by their own behaviors. Still, their autonomously motivated behaviors contributed to managing the illness.

A subsequent longitudinal study of adolescents with Type I diabetes confirmed and extended these findings. Specifically, Austin, Guay, Senécal, Fernet, and Nouwen (2013) tested a model that perceived autonomy support from parents and health providers would enhance self-efficacy and autonomous self-regulation in dietary self-care. Longitudinal data were collected from the adolescent patients at two time points, separated by a 2-year interval. Results showed that perceived autonomy support from health care providers indeed predicted self-efficacy and autonomous self-regulation, and self-efficacy and autonomous self-regulation were also associated with better dietary self-care over time, with some reciprocal relations between variables entailed in this positive change process. The authors suggested that autonomy support from health providers can significantly aid adolescents in developing higher quality motivation for adhering to dietary recommendations.

Healthy Eating and Losing Weight

Adopting SDT in a discussion of healthy diets for weight loss and long-term health, Teixeira, Patrick, and Mata (2011) argued that autonomous motivation is critical for adopting and sustaining healthful diets and that health care professionals can create need-supportive environments that are conducive to eliciting patients' autonomous motivation. Interventions that promote people's "owning" their eating behaviors, valuing healthy eating, and experiencing interest in selecting and preparing healthy meals are most likely to succeed in promoting the long-term healthy eating patterns.

Studies of Motivation for Improved Dietary Behavior

Although what constitutes a healthy diet is always a topic for some debate, evidence clearly points to benefits of including fruits and vegetables. Yet for many people, moving diets in a more positive health direction is not something they volitionally do. Research by McSpadden, Patrick, Oh, Yaroch, Dwyer, and Nebeling (2016) shows, however, that autonomous reasons for fruit and vegetable consumption positively predicts their intake, whereas controlled motivations do not.

An interesting and well-controlled experimental study of vegetable consumption tested an important SDT assumption. Dominguez and colleagues (2013) examined how an experience of choice, which is an important component of autonomy support, might affect consumption in children 4 to 6 years of age. Results indicated that those children who were offered choice about their vegetables evidenced significantly more vegetable intake than those offered no choice.

In another eating study—this one with African American adults recruited from their churches—an intervention was developed to be culturally sensitive and to increase participants' motivation for the intake of fruits and vegetables through telephone counseling (Shaikh, Vinokur, Yaroch, Williams, & Resnicow, 2011). Results indicated that the intervention led to increased healthy eating of fruits and vegetables relative to a control group and that the effect was mediated by autonomous motivation, especially for participants initially low in autonomous motivation. In contrast, neither self-efficacy nor social support contributed to the improvement.

Pelletier, Dion, Slovinec-D'Angelo, and Reid (2004) recruited patients from the practices of several primary care physicians to participate in a 6-month study of dietary change. At baseline, participants completed a questionnaire that assessed their global-level individual differences in autonomy orientation, and two measures of baseline eating patterns were taken—a 1-day dietary recall done at that time and a 3-day prospective food record of their eating. One week later participants received extensive dietary counseling from a dietician. After 6 months the measures were repeated. Results showed that participants' global autonomy orientation predicted their specific autonomous motivation for following the dietary regimen. Concerning eating behaviors, weight, and lipid profiles, it is noteworthy that, over the 6-month period, the averages on each variable moved in the positive directions, so participants, on average, showed improvements in eating patterns, cholesterol, and weight loss. However, the important issue for this research was to successfully predict the dietary improvements from the participants' autonomous motivation for healthy eating. Analyses of these issues indicated that participants who had higher scores on autonomous motivation for following the dietary regimen showed greater decreases in both percentage of calories from fat and percentage of calories from saturated fat, indicating that their eating patterns had improved. Further, both of those improvements in eating behaviors predicted significant reduction in body weight. Finally, decrease in percentage of calories from saturated fat also predicted improvements in lipid patterns (i.e., LDL-C, total cholesterol, and triglycerides). Thus this study provided excellent evidence that people's autonomous motivation for improving their diets not only predicts improved eating behaviors but also leads to better physiological health indicators.

Weight Management

In the early weight-loss study of patients with morbid obesity discussed above (Williams et al., 1996), much of the focus of the program was on improved diet and on autonomous motivation for adhering to a prescribed dietary regimen. In a more recent weight-loss study, Powers, Koestner, and Gorin (2008) focused on autonomy support from family and friends as they related to the autonomous motivation and weight loss of college women. The researchers found that the more autonomy support the participants experienced in their close relationships, the more weight they lost, and this was partially mediated by the participants' autonomous motivation, although a significant relation between autonomy support and weight loss still remained after accounting for autonomous motivation. It was also the case, as expected, that controlling strategies from significant others did not facilitate autonomous motivation or weight loss. A subsequent study of weight loss from this group also showed that perceived autonomy support and autonomous motivation of the participants predicted their weight loss at 18 months, whereas directive supports hindered weight loss (Gorin, Powers, Koestner, Wing, & Raynor, 2013).

Similarly, a study by Ng, Ntoumanis, and Thøgersen-Ntoumani (2013) showed that when young adult participants had close others who were supportive rather than controlling they displayed more of the motivation and behaviors that are essential for successful weight management. Longitudinal research by Ng, Ntoumanis, Thøgersen-Ntoumani, Stott, and Hindle (2013) further examined the importance of autonomy support from significant others for need satisfaction, regulation of healthy eating, weight management, and well-being over the longer term. Results indicated that autonomy support from significant others led to increased need satisfaction, whereas controllingness from the others led to more need thwarting. Need satisfaction, in turn, positively predicted the well-being composite, whereas need thwarting negatively predicted well-being and also led to less healthy eating behaviors and poorer weight management.

A RANDOMIZED CLINICAL TRIAL OF WEIGHT LOSS

A significant clinical trial tested a 1-year, 30-session weight-management intervention for obese women based on SDT, compared with a 29-session general health education program dealing with such issues as nutrition and stress management (Silva et al., 2010). The intervention was intended to help participants adopt a healthier diet and increase physical activity in order to better manage their weight. The program administrators provided choice about the participants' diets and physical activity, encouraged them to examine their own motivations and goals as supports for the development of more autonomous motivation for change, and used an autonomy-supportive style while minimizing external rewards and controls.

Participants' physical activity and weight were recorded regularly, and results indicated that, at the end of the 1-year treatment, the intervention group participants perceived the treatment climate to be more autonomy-supportive than did the control group participants, and they reported that they were more autonomously motivated. Further, the intervention group engaged in significantly greater physical activity than the control group and achieved significantly greater weight loss. So the SDT motivation variables were highly effective in predicting change in health behaviors and in the important health outcome of weight loss.

Following the 1-year intervention was a 2-year maintenance period without any intervention, during which physical activity, weight loss, and SDT variables were examined (Silva et al., 2011). Results indicated that the SDT treatment led to more autonomy support at the end of the first year and that the autonomy support predicted greater autonomous motivation at the end of the first and second years, which in turn predicted more vigorous exercise at the end of the first maintenance year (i.e., year 2) and maintained weight loss at the end of the 3-year period.

INCENTIVES TO PROMOTE WEIGHT LOSS

In their efforts to promote weight loss, some health professionals and researchers have called for the use of incentives (generally financial). One study, for example, reported the initiation of notable weight loss when small incentives were used (Volpp, John, Troxel, Norton, Fassbender, & Loewenstein, 2008). The SDT perspective would point out, however, that although change in health behaviors can be promoted by financial incentives, it is the maintenance of the change that is the important issue, and promoting autonomous motivation is essential for maintenance. Indeed, groups receiving meaningful financial incentives would be expected by SDT to yield poorer maintenance than a control group, especially if the rewards are controlling or the recipients have a strong desire for the rewards (Deci, Koestner, & Ryan, 1999; Ryan, Sheldon, Kasser, & Deci, 1996).

Research by Moller and colleagues examined the financial motivation of adult participants in the context of incentives (viz., $175) for improved diet and increased exercise over a 3-week initiation period. Results indicated that, after controlling for general motivation, the participants who were low in financial motivation (i.e., who placed low value on making money for changing their dietary and exercise behaviors) gained in enjoyment of the activities of eating healthier and exercising more during the initial 3 weeks, whereas those who were high in financial motivation did not change in enjoyment during the same 3-week period. Thus, at the end of that period, those participants high in financial motivation enjoyed the activities less than those low in financial motivation (Moller, Buscemi, McFadden, Hedeker, & Spring, 2014). Following the 3-week incentive period was a 4 ½-month maintenance period with only very small incentives for providing data. Analyses of weight-loss maintenance indicated that participants who were high in financial motivation had a steeper slope of regained weight during the maintenance period and that this was especially true of men who were high in financial motivation (Moller, McFadden, Hedeker, & Spring, 2012). This indicates, in accordance with SDT, that people's interpretations of rewards moderates the effects of the rewards on both changes in enjoyment and persistence at incentivized behaviors and thus affects the sustainability or maintenance of weight loss.

Healthy Behaving in Patients with Illnesses

Various studies have examined a range of SDT variables or interventions as facilitators of health-promoting behaviors among patients who were ill or at risk, some of whom had either experienced or would soon experience invasive procedures. An interesting example was a study by Pavey and Sparks (2012) in a medical setting. They examined the importance of autonomy for alcohol use of individuals who were facing the stress of receiving difficult medical information. They used a priming procedure, which is common in social-psychological experiments, and found that those patients who were primed with autonomy, as opposed to having a neutral prime, and who then received unpleasant medical information were more able to manage their alcohol effectively than those who did not receive the autonomy prime.

Lifestyle Change in Patients with Chest Pain

In a 3-year study, Williams, Gagné, Mushlin, and Deci (2005) followed patients who received diagnostic testing after experiencing chest pain suggestive of coronary artery disease (CAD). At baseline (Time 1), patients completed the GCOS, measuring their general autonomy orientation, and also provided information about their diet, exercise, and tobacco use. Their physicians estimated the probability that they had CAD. The patients were then given a series of noninvasive tests for CAD, including a treadmill stress test, and received their results about 2 weeks later at Time 2. Patients completed a measure of their autonomous motivation for lifestyle change at Time 2, and their physicians estimated the probability that the patients had CAD. Then, at the end of 3 years (Time 3), the patients completed measures of their perceptions of their primary care physicians' autonomy support and their autonomous motivation for a second time, as well as another assessment of their dietary, exercise, and tobacco-use behaviors. Finally, their physician indicated whether the patients had CAD at Time 3.

Analyses indicated that patients' scores on the autonomous causality orientation and their perceptions of the degree to which their physicians were autonomy-supportive were both independent, significant positive predictors of change in the patients' autonomous motivation for lifestyle change over the 3-year period. Further, changes in autonomous motivation for lifestyle change led to improvements in the patients' dietary regimens and exercise patterns. It also led to marginally significant decreases in their use of tobacco. In short, then, the central SDT motivation variables all contributed to improvements in patients' healthy lifestyles. In addition, analyses indicated that patients with higher probability of CAD as estimated at Time 2 by their physicians became more autonomous in their motivation and showed greater improvements in their lifestyles than did patients whose probability of CAD was lower.

Motivation for Physical Activity

We've seen already that autonomous motivation and perceived competence are important for facilitating regular exercise and physical activity. For example, in the weight-loss study by Williams et al. (1996), autonomous regulation predicted exercise and maintained weight loss a year and a half after the 6-month program had ended. Further, we saw in the Williams, Gagné, et al. (2005) study of chest-pain patients that autonomous motivation for lifestyle change predicted improved exercise over a 3-year period. And we saw that physical activity was a critical factor of the weight loss in the clinical trial that was still evident 2 years after the treatment ended (Silva et al., 2011). We now review some other studies that have examined the promotion of exercise in medical settings. Still other studies of non-medically based exercise are reviewed in Chapter 19, which deals with physical activity and sports.

D'Angelo, Reid, and Pelletier (2007) studied an exercise program for cardiac rehabilitation patients in which the researchers assessed patients' global orientation toward self-determination, autonomous motivation for exercising, perceived competence for exercising (assessed with a self-efficacy measure), intention to exercise, and specific plans for exercising. It was found that global self-determination predicted autonomous motivation for exercising. Further, autonomous motivation predicted intentions to exercise, with this link being significantly mediated by perceived competence. Finally, intentions to exercise predicted specific exercise planning. Thus the self-determined personality orientation predicted the more specific autonomous motivation for exercise, which predicted perceived competence, exercise intentions, and making concrete plans to exercise.

A study of breast cancer survivors examined the relations of autonomous and controlled motivation to health-relevant outcomes for breast cancer survivors. Researchers found that autonomous motivation was associated with moderate to vigorous physical activity and positive affect, whereas controlled motivation was associated with cancer worry, negative affect, and depressive symptoms (Brunet, Gunnell, Gaudreau, & Sabiston, 2015).

Segatto, Sabiston, Harvey, and Bloom (2013) examined motivation regarding rehabilitation of organ transplant patients and found that those patients who were more autonomously self-regulated engaged in more of the physical activity that was essential for their recovery. In contrast, neither external regulation nor introjected regulation contributed to their health-enhancing physical activity. Similarly, patients who had had major cardiovascular events participated in a study concerning their recovery and the results revealed that those patients with higher levels of autonomous motivation evidenced better physical health and greater life satisfaction over the subsequent year (Guertin, Rocchi, Pelletier, Edmond, & Lalande, 2015).

As many studies reviewed in this chapter have indicated, autonomy support from practitioners and significant others has promoted autonomous motivation, which has resulted in many different positive health outcomes. We have also said that providing choice is one important component of autonomy support. In this regard, Ghane, Huynh, Andrews, Legg, Tabuenca, and Sweeny (2014) found that, when adult patients in a low-income outpatient clinic who were undergoing surgery were given greater choice or decisional control about various aspects of their treatment, they expressed greater satisfaction with their treatment and greater self-reported adherence to their prescribed behaviors regardless of how much decisional control they had initially said they wanted.

A RANDOMIZED TRIAL FOR PHYSICAL ACTIVITY

A large percentage of North Americans engage in less vigorous physical activity than would be optimal for remaining healthy. Fortier, Hogg, et al. (2007) argued that integrating an SDT-trained physical activity counselor into primary care practices could help build patients' autonomous motivation and perceived competence for engaging in regular exercise. Because physicians (or nurse practitioners) do not have time to engage in extensive counseling regarding exercise, supplementing these practitioners' very brief interventions with a more extensive counseling intervention by health educators could be effective for facilitating physical activity. To test this, a randomized clinical trial was conducted with relatively sedentary adult patients from a community-based primary care medical practice.

The trial compared an intervention by physicians or nurse practitioners that lasted 2–4 minutes during which they asked about the patients' exercise, advised them to increase the reported level, and provided a written prescription for the increased physical activity. This intervention represented the control group. The experimental group included the brief practitioner intervention plus a more intensive intervention by counselors that involved six sessions over a 3-month period in which the counselor worked to facilitate basic psychological need satisfaction in the sessions and in the exercise regimens. Further, counselors supported patients' active involvement in the interactions and their initiative and autonomy in planning and executing exercise activities. All physicians and nurse practitioners in the short intervention that was provided for patients in both the control and experimental groups were given training in being autonomy-supportive and patient-centered. Further, the counselors also received extensive SDT-based training.

Fortier, Sweet, O'Sullivan, and Williams (2007), reported that initially the experimental group participants experienced greater autonomy support from providers than did the control group participants. Further, participants in the experimental group reported more autonomous motivation at 6 weeks than did those in the control group and also engaged in significantly more physical activity at 13 weeks than did the control group participants. Finally, analyses indicated that changes in autonomous motivation and perceived competence from baseline to 6 weeks were both significant predictors of 13-week physical activity in the experimental group participants.

Further analyses of this trial examined both patients' quantity of motivation for exercise and the quality of the motivation—that is, whether the motivation was autonomous or controlled. Results indicated that, at the end of the 13-week intervention, the amount of motivation mediated the relation between the intervention and the amount of exercise. However, autonomous motivation moderated that effect. The importance of quantity of motivation for predicting exercise at 13 weeks was significantly stronger when the participants were more autonomously motivated (see Fortier et al., 2011).

Another recent clinical trial was performed with HIV-infected older adults, who face many challenges, both psychological and physical. Often, their lower levels of regular physical activity can further exacerbate their functional decline. Accordingly, Shah et al. (2016) conducted a randomized clinical trial to evaluate whether an SDT-based physical activity intervention could improve the physical functioning and the quality of life in such individuals. Older adults with HIV who were determined to have mild to moderate functional limitations were targeted. Some were randomized to a basic psychological need-supportive counseling condition focused on enhancing physical activity, and others to a "usual care" control group. Both at baseline and at the end of the clinical trial, these patients received a battery of tests measuring their physical functioning, levels of physical activity, depression, and general quality of life, along with assessments of autonomous motivation. Results showed that those who received the SDT-based counseling intervention evidenced greater overall physical performance, gait speed, and measures of endurance and strength and higher levels of physical activity compared with those receiving usual care. In addition, autonomy, especially identified regulation, and measures of depression and quality of life were significantly enhanced in the treatment group relative to the controls. These findings thus showed the potential for a need-supportive physical activity counseling program to improve both functional and psychological outcomes in this older population facing both medical and physical challenges.

OTHER PHYSICAL ACTIVITY STUDIES

Many other studies have also been done examining relations between SDT variables, such as autonomous causality orientations, autonomy support, autonomous self-regulation, and basic psychological need satisfaction, as they relate to exercise-related outcome variables. Teixeira, Carraça, Markland, Silva, and Ryan (2012) have done a systematic review of 66 physical activity studies guided by SDT. Methods varied, with some being experimental, some cross-sectional, and some prospective, and with varied outcomes ranging from self-reports to more objectively measured physical activity variables. The authors reported that across these studies, there was a consistent pattern of significant links from higher levels of any of the autonomy-related variables to a multitude of physical activity–related outcomes. Most of these studies were done outside of health care settings and are reviewed in the next chapter.

Motivation for Dental Care

In a very interesting application of SDT, researchers in Norway have done several studies of dental care, including two randomized clinical trials to test an SDT-based intervention for dental care and to examine a process model of the hypothesized change (Halvari & Halvari, 2006). The intervention involved an initial teeth cleaning and a checkup by a dentist (both standard for dental care) and then, 1 month later, an autonomy-supportive oral-care informational session with the dental hygienist who had done the earlier teeth cleaning. This session began with an open-ended question about any dental problems the patients had experienced. The hygienist listened carefully and acknowledged the patients' feelings. She then used an autonomy-supportive style to provide patients with personalized information about their dental condition and made recommendations for home dental care (e.g., brushing and flossing). In so doing, she gave a meaningful rationale for all oral care behaviors, demonstrated each one, and allowed patients to practice them. This seemingly cost-effective intervention was compared with a standard-care control condition in which patients received only the thorough cleaning with a checkup by the dentists.

A month before the cleaning appointment and then 6 months after it, patients' autonomous motivation for dental care was assessed, and their perceived dental competence was assessed with the Dental Coping Beliefs Scale (Wolfe, Stewart, Meader, & Hartz, 1996). Plaque, gingivitis, and caries were also assessed at those two time points by the dentist, who was not aware of which experimental condition the patients were in. In addition, at the final session, patients completed a short questionnaire about their dental health care behaviors and their degree of positive affect about caring for their own oral health.

Analyses indicated that measures of autonomous motivation, perceived competence, plaque, and gingivitis all became significantly more positive in the intervention group than in the control group, as did the dental behaviors and affect at the end of the 7-month period. The SDT process model indicated that the intervention led to increases in both perceived competence and autonomous motivation, which then predicted health behaviors and, in turn, dental health. Thus the intervention led to improvements in actual physiological indicators of dental health (i.e., less plaque and gingivitis and fewer caries) through the pathways of increased motivation and behavior.

Subsequent correlational studies elaborated the results of the first dental trial (Münster-Halvari, Halvari, Bjørnebekk, & Deci, 2010, 2012a, 2013). For example, one study showed that when patients perceived the treatment climate as more autonomy-supportive, they reported greater satisfaction of their basic psychological needs, which in turn led to less anxiety about treatment and more autonomous motivation and perceived competence regarding treatment. These motivation and emotion variables predicted better oral care behaviors, better clinic attendance, more intrinsic value of continued treatment, less intake of sugar, and greater experience of dental well-being.

The first clinical trial and the subsequent correlational studies made it very clear that greater autonomy support in a dental clinic is critical for patients' experiences, motivation, and healthy behaving. In another clinical trial, the researchers were interested in testing an expanded intervention that focused specifically on enhancing oral care competence within an autonomy-supportive context. The intervention included providing more information on plaque-related diseases; demonstrating effective brushing and flossing, with the patients practicing and getting feedback; and exploring the relations between the preventive behaviors and decreased diseases, all done with an autonomy-supportive style and climate. Because the practitioner's autonomy support had been found to be essential for effective dental care, the researchers believed it to be a moral imperative to provide the autonomy-supportive treatment to control group patients, so the control group received all of the same autonomy-supportive components as the experimental group. Hence, the test of the intervention was very stringent, as it tested only the enhanced competence-building elements. Still, the intervention led to significant improvements in the experimental group relative to the control group, including less plaque and gingivitis over a 5 ½-month period (Münster-Halvari, Halvari, Bjørnebekk, & Deci, 2012b).

Summary of Clinical Trials

Randomized clinical trials have been used to test SDT-based interventions for many health issues, including tobacco use, eating patterns, physical activity, weight loss, medication adherence, and dental self-care. Results show the interventions to have enhanced autonomous motivation and perceived competence for various behaviors, which then mediated the relation between the intervention and the behavior change or physiological outcomes. In each case, a patient-centered, autonomy-supportive counseling approach has been found effective in prompting and maintaining health-promoting behavior change and subsequent health indices. Much work remains to be done in developing and refining SDT-based interventions, yet the initial work is extremely encouraging and points the way toward the future.

Caring for the Elderly

Several studies have also examined the motivation and well-being of elderly residents in homes for the aged. The aim in doing so has been to understand whether the characteristics and interpersonal climates of the residences affect the residents' health and well-being.

In one study, O'Connor and Vallerand (1994) investigated the residents in 11 nursing homes in Canada. Trained researchers separately interviewed the head nurse and administrator in each institution about their rules and procedures. The researcher focused on the degree of choice and encouragement for self-initiation provided to residents in each setting, and they made an overall rating of the objective support for autonomy provided in each residence. In addition, each patient was asked to rate the degree to which the setting was autonomy-supportive and to provide reports of their own motivation for their various life activities (e.g., managing their health, leisure, interpersonal relations, religion), using a method based on the self-regulation questionnaire (SRQ; Ryan & Connell, 1989). Results indicated that objectively rated autonomy support significantly predicted patients' self-reported autonomous motivation, and this linkage was fully mediated by the patients' experience of autonomy support.

In a subsequent study, the research team examined the relation of the levels of the nursing home patients' autonomous motivation and controlled motivation for their life activities to their general sense of well-being. The results indicated that autonomous motivation was positively associated with self-esteem, life satisfaction, and general health, whereas controlled motivation was negatively associated with these same well-being indicators (Vallerand, O'Connor, & Hamel, 1995). Together, this and the previously reviewed study suggest that support for patients' autonomy in a residential institution for the elderly is positively predictive of their being autonomously motivated for their life activities and, in turn, of their health and well-being.

Kasser and Ryan (1999) performed another study of elderly patients in a full-care facility. These residents completed assessments of (1) the amount of autonomy support they experienced from the staff at the residence; (2) the amount of autonomy support they experienced from their family and friends; (3) their autonomous motivation for being in the nursing home and for their daily activities there; and (4) indicators of well-being, including vitality, life satisfaction, and lack of depression. In addition, patients' mortality status was recorded 13 months after these assessments. Analyses revealed that autonomy support of staff and autonomy support of family and friends both predicted less depression, more vitality, and more life satisfaction among the residents. Further, autonomous motivation predicted less depression, more vitality, and better health as indexed by whether or not they were still alive more than a year after the questionnaire data were obtained.

A related study was conducted by Custers, Westerhof, Kuin, and Riksen-Walraven (2010) in which they collected interview data on 88 patients in nursing homes. They focused on basic psychological need support in the helping relationship within their residences, need satisfaction in general, life satisfaction, and depressive symptoms. Analyses showed that the need satisfaction residents experienced in their relationships with staff members predicted their overall need satisfaction in life, and it also predicted greater life satisfaction and less depression. Further, general need satisfaction mediated the relations between need satisfaction with their caregivers and the well-being outcomes of more life satisfaction and less depression.

In sum, there is clear indication that when elderly people are living in facilities for older adults, the need satisfaction they experience has strong and important implications for their psychological well-being and physical wellness, perhaps even their longevity. Further, the amount of autonomy support and caring they experience from the staff and their own families and friends, as well as their autonomous motivation for entering the institution, affect their need satisfaction and wellness outcomes.

Aspirations and Healthy Behaving

From the beginning of SDT work on life aspirations, evidence has pointed to positive links between health outcomes and intrinsic aspirations and negative relations between health and extrinsic goals and aspirations. For example, Kasser and Ryan (1996) found that people with higher extrinsic aspirations reported more physical symptoms, such as headaches, stomach issues, and pain relative to those with intrinsic aspirations. Many of these symptoms might be reflections of the stress associated with extrinsic lifestyles. Related to this, Kasser and Ryan (2001) found that participants higher in extrinsic aspirations also engaged in more risk behaviors, such as smoking and drug use, with again possible implications for health.

Some investigators have thus begun to use the concept of aspirations or life goals to help understand health-related lifestyles and risks. In one, high school students reported on the degree to which their parents were autonomy-supportive, and they also completed the aspiration scale, which assesses the degree to which their personal long-term goals and values tend to be extrinsic relative to intrinsic (see Chapter 11 for a discussion of aspirations). The results of this study indicated that when parents were less supportive of autonomy, their adolescent children tended to place stronger value on extrinsic aspirations for wealth, fame, and image, relative to intrinsic aspirations for affiliation, growth, and community (Williams, Hedberg, Cox, & Deci, 2000). In turn, having strong extrinsic aspirations positively predicted the adolescents' engaging in high-risk behaviors, including early use of tobacco, alcohol, and marijuana.

Aspirations or life values are important for health care not only because they are associated with the onset of behaviors that tend to be health compromising but also because they can play a role in interventions intended to promote healthier behaving. Specifically, for example, in the SDT-based intervention for smoking cessation discussed earlier in the chapter, the health counselors encouraged patients to discuss their own values and to think about how behaviors such as smoking, overeating, and being sedentary tend to be consistent with or antagonistic with their valued goals. Although not researched as such, it turns out that the great majority of patients, when given this chance to reflect, focus much more on intrinsic than extrinsic goals—things such as "having the opportunity to be involved with my grandchildren"—and these goals provide an important, self-generated reason for behaving in healthier ways.

In a study of smoking cessation, Niemiec, Ryan, Deci, and Williams (2009) assessed the strength of participants' aspirations for health and fitness and found that those participants who were able to maintain a strong goal for fitness over an 18-month period were likely to be able to remain off tobacco for the longest amount of time. So the maintenance of this intrinsic life goal facilitated the healthy behavior of tobacco abstinence.

The Importance of Autonomy for Physical and Psychological Wellness

We have reviewed numerous studies, both correlational and experimental, including randomized clinical trials, in which autonomous motivation and related concepts such as autonomy support, basic need satisfaction, and intrinsic life goals have been examined in terms of their utility for facilitating health and well-being. The studies we reviewed are but a sample of the studies that have been done using the SDT variables of autonomy and need satisfaction to predict or create changes in health behaviors and health.

Ng and colleagues (2012) conducted a meta-analysis of 184 independent datasets that had examined the relations of the SDT autonomy variables and wellness outcomes. Figure 18.2 shows the categories of variables used in the meta-analysis and some of their hypothesized links. Results indicated that the relations hypothesized by the theory were significant and, further, that they provided general support for the SDT process model.

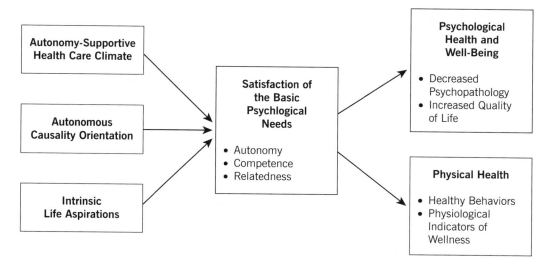

FIGURE 18.2. Relations among SDT variables used in the meta-analysis to examine healthy behaviors and medical outcomes. Adapted from Ng et al. (2012). Copyright 2012 by SAGE Publishing. Adapted by permission.

In short, it is now well confirmed that when health-care practitioners are supportive of patients' basic psychological needs and when the patients are autonomously motivated and perceive themselves to be competent, the patients are likely to display greater psychological and physical health. We also reviewed a small amount of evidence indicating that, when significant others of the patients are autonomy-supportive in relation to health behavior change, it supplemented the positive effects of the practitioners' being supportive of the patients' needs. We now consider a study examining family-member caregivers and how that role affects them.

The Benefits of Caregivers' Autonomy Support

When people become seriously ill, their family members often find themselves in the role of caregiver, which can be very challenging and stressful. In addition, caregivers themselves can be autonomy-supportive or controlling. For example, Dunbar et al. (2013) did an intervention study with partners of patients who had suffered heart failure and were in recovery that was focused on the issue of dietary restriction of salt intake. Caregivers were assigned to either usual care, an in-depth educational intervention, or the educational intervention combined with an intervention intended to foster more autonomy-supportive approaches to caregiving. This third condition, which included autonomy support, promoted earlier decrease in the patients' dietary sodium, whereas the education condition resulted in slower change. The control group appeared less likely to be adherent with dietary sodium intake than either of the intervention conditions by the end of the study.

In a study of family caregivers of persons diagnosed with dementia, Pierce, Lydon, and Yang (2001) assessed the internalization of the caregiving role (i.e., caregiver autonomy), as well as their commitment, wellness, and appraisals of problem situations.

Analyses revealed that greater identification with caregiving was associated with both greater moral commitment to and enthusiasm for the role, which in turn seems to facilitate caregiver well-being and dampen their sense of threat in problematic situations. By contrast, introjected motivations for caregiving did not predict these positive attitudes or outcomes but were associated with more sense of threat when problems arise.

The SDT perspective predicts that the motivation of family caregivers for being in that role will influence how the role affects them. A study of individuals who were caring for their spouses with cancer examined this prediction (Kim, Carver, Deci, & Kasser, 2008). Results revealed that caregiver wives who were more autonomously motivated for that role found greater benefit in the role and that caregiver husbands who were more autonomously motivated for the role were less depressed, whereas those who were more controlled experienced more depression and less life satisfaction. Further, the quality of the relatedness in the couples as experienced by the caregiver was higher if the caregiver was more autonomously motivated.

In sum, just as people's autonomous versus controlled motivation for participating in their own health care is predictive of their well-being and health outcomes, there is now preliminary evidence that autonomous versus controlled motivation for giving care to ill family members tends to affect the well-being and health outcomes of the caregivers.

Training and Supporting Medical Students and Professionals

There is now considerable evidence that when practitioners provide health care in a relatively autonomy-supportive, as opposed to controlling, way, patients experience a range of more positive health outcomes. When practitioners understand the patients' perspectives and relate to them from those perspectives, the patients tend to become more autonomously motivated for healthy behaving, feel competent at making health-promoting changes, display maintained healthy behaviors, and evidence improved health indicators. As such, helping medical trainees become autonomy-supportive practitioners of patient care would seem to be an important goal for the education of professionals in the medical fields. A number of studies have now tested the hypothesis that providing training for practitioners in an autonomy-supportive way is a crucial element in medical education to help the trainees become more autonomy-supportive in their own caregiving (Williams & Deci, 1998).

As one example, Murray et al. (2015) trained physiotherapists in communication skills intended to enhance patients' need satisfaction. This training was part of a randomized trial involving a control group of physiotherapists from other hospitals. To assess the effectiveness of the training, verbal communication between each physiotherapist and a patient was recorded and rated by an individual naïve to therapist condition using the HCCQ. The findings revealed that the training successfully increased autonomy-supportive practices. This is important because previous research suggests that adherence to physiotherapy recommendations is facilitated by autonomy-supportive communications (Chan, Lonsdale, Ho, Yung, & Chan, 2009).

Internalization of Biopsychosocial Values

One longitudinal study has examined the process of medical students' internalizing autonomy-supportive values and behaviors, which are central to the biopsychosocial approach to medicine and have meaningful implications for physicians in training (Engel, 1977; Williams & Deci, 1996). This 30-month longitudinal study of second-year medical students focused on their involvement in a medical interviewing course. Instructors teaching this course can have a range of interpersonal styles, but those with a more biopsychosocial orientation believe in the importance of both psychosocial factors in illness and health and an autonomy-supportive or patient-centered approach to practicing medicine. In this study (Williams & Deci, 1996), the students' autonomous causality orientations were assessed, as were their perceptions of the autonomy supportiveness of their instructors. These were used to predict students' internalization of the value of participation in this course, which focused on doctor–patient communications. In turn, their resulting level of autonomous motivation for learning about effective patient communications was expected to predict a variety of relevant outcomes.

Results indicated that both the students' autonomous causality orientations and the instructors' autonomy support predicted students' becoming more autonomously motivated for learning the course material. Further, the students who became more autonomously motivated for learning the material also developed stronger psychosocial beliefs, and the instructors' autonomy support positively predicted increases in psychosocial beliefs, as well as perceived competence and autonomous motivation for learning.

Six months after the interviewing course ended, students had the opportunity to interview a simulated patient who had been trained to behave in standardized ways with all interviewers. The students' interviewing behavior was rated for the degree to which it was autonomy-supportive. Analyses indicated that the students' autonomous motivation for learning about doctor–patient communication at the end of the course positively predicted their actually being more autonomy-supportive when interviewing the simulated patient 6 months later. Finally, 2 years after the course ended, the students completed a survey that assessed both their autonomous motivation for continuing to learn about medical communications and their belief in the importance of psychosocial factors in medical care. Analyses revealed that the instructors' autonomy support during the course significantly predicted the students' maintained autonomous motivation for learning and their belief in the psychosocial approach at this 30-month follow-up.

In sum, this study indicated that when medical educators were autonomy-supportive, their trainees tended to (1) become more autonomous for learning the course material, (2) develop and maintain a stronger belief in the importance of psychosocial factors in medical care, and (3) become more autonomy-supportive themselves in relating to patients. We reviewed substantial evidence earlier in the chapter indicating that when practitioners used a more autonomy-supportive style in relating to their patients, the patients evidenced improved health outcomes. We now see that this autonomy-supportive style can be most optimally taught in medical schools by instructors who themselves use an autonomy-supportive style in their teaching and who espouse a biopsychosocial approach to medicine.

Career Choice

At least two studies have examined medical students' career choices, testing the hypothesis that when preceptors on medical rotations are more autonomy-supportive, medical students will be more likely to choose that specialty as their own. In the first study (Williams, Wiener, Markakis, Reeve, & Deci, 1994), the instructors of internal medicine clerkships at various American medical schools were rated in terms of the degree to which they tended to support the trainees' autonomy rather than control the trainees' behavior, and this was used to predict whether the students selected internal medicine for their residencies. Students also completed questionnaires about their interest in and perceived competence for internal medicine. Using SEM, the researchers concluded that when instructors were more autonomy-supportive, students felt more competent at and were more interested in internal medicine, and this increased their chances of selecting internal medicine for more intensive training in their subsequent residencies.

In a second career-choice study (Williams, Saizow, Ross, & Deci, 1997), internal medicine and surgery residency choices made by students from three American medical schools were examined. At the time of data collection, fourth-year medical students had submitted their match requests but had not yet heard the results. The measure of career choice was a composite of two responses: their likelihood ratings of going into internal medicine and into surgery and whether they had requested a residency in internal medicine, surgery, or some other field. The researchers tested structural models for both medicine and surgery and found that, in both cases, autonomy support from the relevant instructor predicted students' perceived competence and interest in the corresponding field. Perceived competence also predicted interest, and interest in turn predicted increases in the likelihood of going into the corresponding field. In short, autonomy support from medical instructors was significantly related to their students' going into the same field, and the motivational variables of perceived competence and interest were the paths through which autonomy support had its effects.

Training Medical Practitioners to Do Autonomy-Supportive Counseling

As noted earlier, tobacco use is the documented cause of death for hundreds of thousand of Americans each year, yet medical practitioners spend little or no time addressing the issue with their patients. Our colleague Geoffrey Williams organized a set of 20 workshops, sponsored by the New York State Department of Health, that trained practitioners to use an autonomy-supportive style in doing tobacco-dependence counseling based on the National Institute of Health Guidelines for Treating Tobacco Use and Dependence (Fiore et al., 2000). Just before the workshops and then 3 months later, participants completed assessments of their autonomous motivation and perceived competence for doing tobacco-dependence counseling, as well as their perceptions of autonomy support from the workshop instructors and their own tobacco-counseling behaviors.

SEM, which was used to test the SDT model of change, indicated that the trainees' perceptions of their instructors' autonomy support were positively predictive of positive change over the 3 months in the trainees' autonomous motivation and perceived competence for doing the counseling, and changes in these variables, in turn, were positive predictors of the trainees' doing tobacco-dependence counseling. In short, just as autonomy support from instructors in medical schools had a positive influence on the beliefs and behaviors of medical students, autonomy support from instructors in professional development settings also was found to have positive effects on the professionals' approach to treating their patients.

Lyness, Lurie, Ward, Mooney, and Lambert (2013) reviewed these studies and other relevant SDT studies as they relate to academic medical centers and argued, in line with the findings in the preceding paragraphs, that using more need-supportive approaches to engage students and practitioners in their work would not only improve the medical care they provide but also their own well-being and thriving.

Autonomy and Medical Ethics

Within moral philosophy, the concept of autonomy has a long tradition. Kant's (1785/1964; 1788/1956) concept of the *categorical imperative* endorses the idea of treating human beings as ends in themselves rather than as means to an end. In other words, respecting people's autonomy, which means their capacity to think, decide, and act freely, is considered morally essential (Gillon, 1985). Mill (1963) argues both for the intrinsic and instrumental values of autonomy and a person's own choices and allows that only in temporary or extreme cases should autonomy be violated. Indeed, we reviewed a host of philosophical perspectives in Chapter 3 that place autonomy in the center of human values.

Autonomy as a central ethical concept exists not only in the formal philosophical literature; it has also become increasingly important in the ethical codes of medicine, health care, and human research. Beauchamp and Childress (1989) specified four central principles of biomedical ethics, one of which was autonomy. They viewed it as a universal value, as something that cuts across gender, culture, politics, socioeconomics, and religion. Currently, in medicine, autonomy is considered important as both an ethical imperative and an outcome of treatment, as reflected in the more recent National Institutes of Health's *Clinical Practice Guidelines* (e.g., Fiore et al., 2000; Fiore, 2008).

The "Belmont Report" from the U.S. National Commission for the Protection of Human Subjects of Biomedical and Behavioral Research (1979) also asserted that autonomy is one of three basic ethical principles regarding human participants. Referred to as the principle of respect for persons, it states that all individuals should be considered autonomous agents with the ability to select personal goals and act in accordance with their decisions. The report went on to say that, to the extent that people's autonomy is diminished, as can be the case with young children or individuals with neurological or mental impairments, then the individuals are entitled to protection by parents, professionals, or institutions.

This all implies that autonomy is a fundamental outcome for medical care and for research in this domain. Nonetheless, when behaviors are not reflectively endorsed—that is, are not autonomous—and could cause harm to the patient (e.g., suicide) or to others in the environment (e.g., child abuse), it is ethically mandatory, as well as in some cases legally mandatory, to do more than support autonomy—the practitioner must intervene. Still, although protecting the client and/or others may necessarily be a short-term goal, the goal for treatment with such clients would nonetheless be to promote as much autonomy and responsibility as possible. Any interventions assuming responsibility over persons thus need to be done with both serious reflection, respect, and humility (see Barilan, 2011).

Yet no matter how intrinsically or instrumentally valuable autonomy may ultimately be, in medical interventions there may be a strong tendency for professionals to push patients toward certain outcomes, based on what they see as in the patients' best interest. In other words, there can be conflicts between two ethically relevant goals—that of respecting autonomy and that of optimizing health outcomes. Kultgen (1995) describes this as a conflict between *parentalistic caring* and respect for autonomy. This conflict is often reflected in the style of interventions. For example, a central notion in all of medicine that reflects respect for autonomy is that of *informed consent*, and yet many an interventionist's communications bias the consent process by either shortchanging the process, manipulating information, or pressuring or prompting patients toward certain choices.

Based on ethical considerations, we therefore suggest that autonomy is an important outcome for medical care, rather than merely an instrument to some other outcomes, such as smoking cessation or medication adherence. This is an important point because it implies that autonomy—making true and reflective choices about whatever issue is being addressed—should be fully respected by the practitioner and is itself an appropriate goal of interventions. Patients should be considered free to make their own thoughtful choices about whether or not to make a change that the practitioner would recommend. To the extent that the decision is truly reflective and fully informed, it is the job of the practitioner to acknowledge and support that decision. This means that if a client were to make a truly reflective and informed choice after understanding and weighing tradeoffs—for example, to not exercise or to continue smoking—the choice would itself be considered a success. We simply submit that, when practitioners assume such a stance, they are actually more likely to achieve better health outcomes at a population level than they will through the more authority-based, parentalistic strategies some are too often ready to assume.

Concluding Comments

Health care is one of the life domains in which the principles of SDT are being vigorously studied. Initially, field studies suggested, in general, that practitioners' autonomy support enhances patients' autonomous motivation and perceived competence for making changes in health-compromising behaviors, resulting in eating healthier diets, exercising more regularly, stopping smoking, and taking prescribed medications. This work led to randomized clinical trials showing both the effectiveness of an SDT intervention relative to a control group and also the fit of the data to the SDT process model in both the intervention and control groups, with respect to smoking cessation and diet improvement. Not only have these various studies shown that autonomous motivation and perceived competence predict health behavior change, but they have also shown relations with physiological health indicators such as lowered LDL-C and HbA1c.

Other SDT concepts, including intrinsic aspirations and causality orientations, have also been linked to positive health outcomes, and there is varied evidence that autonomy support from practitioners facilitates each of the autonomy-related motivational concepts that in turn have positive health consequences. Finally, research shows that practitioners can learn to be more autonomy-supportive in their patient care, especially when trained by instructors who teach and practice in autonomy-supportive ways. In health-related training programs, when the faculty are autonomy-supportive in the way they teach, they will be facilitating motivational processes in the trainees that in turn lead them to be more autonomy-supportive in their patient care, which now has been strongly linked to positive health-relevant outcomes among the patients.

Autonomy is a fundamental value and a valued outcome in health care in its own right. Because health practitioners are strongly oriented toward certain behaviors or interventions as most effective and are sometimes given incentives to produce them, they can often be prone to parentalistic practices and unreflective in how they attempt to influence patient choices and behaviors. SDT practices, which are also oriented toward maximizing health outcomes per se, are nonetheless balanced by a concern for respecting autonomy and informed consent as a medical and ethical priority and thus not allowing an outcome focus to override respect for the autonomy of all persons.

CHAPTER 19

Sport, Physical Activity, and Physical Education

Physical activity is one of the most important, and yet complex, domains of motivated behaviors. People are inherently active creatures and, accordingly, they are often intrinsically motivated for physical activities. This is especially reflected in *sports,* and thus we begin by discussing sports and intrinsic motivation, applying cognitive evaluation theory (CET). We review experiments testing the effects on intrinsic motivation of external events such as rewards, athletic scholarships, feedback, and competition. The orientations of coaches and important others also have significant impact on the need satisfaction and motivation of athletes at all levels, with need satisfaction mediating the relations of coaching climates to a variety of athlete and team outcomes. *Exercise* is another form of physical activity that tends to be less intrinsically motivated than sports. Accordingly, internalization is critical to exercise maintenance, and need support from the interpersonal context is very important for promoting long-term exercise. Individual differences also matter; for instance, people who are high on the autonomous causality orientation are more motivated to exercise regularly than those low in autonomy, as are people with strong intrinsic relative to extrinsic aspirations. Finally, research in *physical education* classes shows that need support from instructors, as well as need satisfaction and autonomous motivation of students, leads to more positive physical activity outcomes.

From the time of birth, humans are, by their very nature, active, playful, and challenge-seeking organisms. They look, touch, throw, manipulate, and explore. Indeed, across the globe, anywhere that children are raised in humane conditions, active, vigorous play is a substantial part of their lives. Through self-initiated physical activity, children acquire many of the foundational competencies that allow them to adapt effectively to life: capacities not only for motor coordination and physical efficacy, but also for mental manipulation, problem solving, social interactions, and creativity. Active play is essential to healthy physical and psychological development in children, and it continues to have an important role in health and vitality throughout their lives. This is no doubt why we evolved to find it intrinsically motivating.

Our active human nature would clearly confound anyone thinking that organisms primarily seek quiescence or arousal reduction. People freely put enormous energy and effort into "leisure" activities, often in contrast to other externally rewarded life domains through which they may have to drag themselves, perhaps on a regular "nine-to-five" basis. A seemingly unmotivated woman who has difficulty finding energy for her well-compensated desk job may, for no pay at all, enthusiastically practice tennis after work. A teenager whom teachers or parents see as lazy because he doesn't like homework may persist for hours practicing his basketball jump shot. What makes such effortful activity so intriguing is precisely that it is very strongly motivated in the apparent absence of tangible rewards or external prods. In fact, sport and outdoor recreation activities are most often intrinsically motivated, supported by the inherent psychological satisfactions and vitality they yield (Frederick & Ryan, 1993; Ryan & Deci, 2007).

Of course, not all physical activities done during leisure time are intrinsically motivated. For example, whereas people usually say they are *playing* a sport, they use the term *workout* to describe vigorous exercise, reflecting that for many this may not be the most enjoyable part of their day. Yet people may nonetheless persist at such activities, perceiving them as instrumental to intrinsic (e.g., health) or extrinsic (e.g., looking attractive) goals (e.g., see Ryan, Frederick, Lepes, Rubio, & Sheldon, 1997). Other activities are done because disciplined practice and arduous training can be instrumental to enhancing sports performance. This, then, leads to the issues of when and how varied motives, whether intrinsic or extrinsic, predict persistence, performance, and vitality in physical activities.

In this chapter, we explore the motivational dynamics of sports and other physical activities, examining their intrinsic satisfactions and their potential to enhance physical and mental vitality. We highlight, however, that both sport and exercise behaviors can vary in their relative autonomy, affecting the quality of experience associated with them and long-term persistence. They can also differ in their intrinsic versus extrinsic goal focus. Yet because of their somewhat different motivational bases, we first consider motivational issues as they apply to *sports,* and subsequently we separately consider research on motivation for *exercise* and in *physical education* contexts.

Motivational Processes in Sports

Sports are a source of enormous interest and enjoyment, and for many individuals they also represent a health-promoting factor in their lives. People spend a great deal of time playing sports and watching sports. Sports are among the most popular topics in casual conversations, and incredible amounts of money and resources are spent on sports at all levels. Understanding the motivational dynamics of sports is thus no trivial matter.

Many people, both young and old, spend free time playing sports, from casual pickup games to more organized settings such as youth or amateur club leagues. This use of their natural "free choice periods" toward effortful activities suggests a high degree of intrinsic motivation. In fact, early investigations of sport motivation converged in showing that intrinsic motivation plays an especially significant role in sports. A study of physical activities in adults by Frederick and Ryan (1993) confirmed that people's engagement in sports is typically intrinsically motivated, whereas their motivation for exercise or fitness was likely to have a heavier extrinsic basis. Research on youth participation in sports (e.g., Gill, Gross, & Huddleston, 1983; Gould, Feltz, & Weiss, 1985) similarly showed that participation in sports is largely fueled by intrinsic motives such as fun, challenge, and learning. Exemplifying this, Raedeke (1997) found that adolescent swimmers who were intrinsically motivated reported lower burnout than swimmers driven by extrinsic reasons, suggesting that intrinsic motivation helps sustain involvement.

Although typically done for their inherent satisfactions, sports can, of course, be otherwise motivated. The more organized the sport settings, the more likely it is that they will generate the kinds of attention and investment from spectators, parents, and coaches that bring additional motivational dynamics into the picture. Thus, when people play for parents' or coaches' approval, for scholarships, for money, or for fame, this will change their relationship to sports in ways of interest to SDT. In addition, more advanced sport participation often requires nonintrinsically motivated activities, such as conditioning or drills, and how these extrinsic behaviors are motivated is also of interest. Accordingly, we address both intrinsic and extrinsic motivations in sports, beginning with the former.

Sporting Environments and Intrinsic Motivation

Because sports are, to an appreciable extent, intrinsically motivated, research done within the cognitive evaluation theory (CET) framework on social-contextual factors is directly relevant to sporting activities. For example, a variety of extrinsic factors, such as contingent rewards, negative feedback, competitive pressures, and controlling coaching climates, all intended to motivate athletes, are nonetheless factors that could potentially undermine sport motivation, participation, and enjoyment.

Rewards for Sports

The potential for awards and rewards to undermine intrinsic interest was first shown by Orlick and Mosher (1978). They pretested children ages 9–11 on a motor balancing task using a free-choice behavioral measure of intrinsic motivation (as described in Chapter 6). Then the children were placed in either a reward (trophy) or no-reward condition while they performed the task. Four days later, the children were given another opportunity to engage in the task, again using the free-choice assessment of intrinsic motivation. Those who had received the trophies showed a decrease in free-choice time spent on the task from the prereward to postreward sessions relative to those in the no-reward group. What such data indicate is that people are readily intrinsically motivated for even simple physical challenges and also that such intrinsic motivation can be readily undermined.

It bears noting again that, as we outlined in Chapter 6, offering trophies, prizes, or other rewards can either enhance or diminish intrinsic motivation for those who receive them, depending on factors such as the nature of the contingency and the manner in which they are delivered that influence the functional significance they foster. Further, whenever programs use rewards to recognize individuals, there are many athletes—even good athletes—who do not receive them and for whom the implicit message can be that they are not as good as the others, which is likely to diminish their ongoing motivation. The fact that so many youth drop out from sports is in part due to this functional significance; they have come to see themselves as lacking the competence to compete, often because of the salience of social comparisons.

Of course, one function of trophies and awards for many who use them is precisely that of selection or *gatekeeping*—that is, of separating the elite from the non-elite. Here the intention is not that of motivating all players but rather identifying and promoting the best athletes. This system has an important role in competitive elite athletics but may have unintended participation consequences in youth sports, where inclusiveness is an aim. Using them with young athletes or athletes who have not come into their prime runs the risk that they never will.

Supporting this idea, Matosic and Cox (2014) looked at various coaching behaviors, including the controlling use of rewards. They found, as SDT expects, that the use of rewards to motivate was associated with lower intrinsic motivation in athletes and lower basic need satisfaction. Moreover, survey research (e.g., Gill et al., 1983) with amateur athletes suggests that such extrinsic rewards play little positive role in motivating their participation and improvement in sports.

Athletic Scholarships

Relevant to the basic reward experiments are studies that have examined the relations between *athletic scholarships* and intrinsic motivation for the sports. Ryan (1977, 1980) did early field studies based on CET examining the impact of receiving scholarships on intercollegiate sports participants' desires to play their sports after college. In the first, male scholarship athletes, primarily football players, listed more extrinsic reasons for sport participation and less enjoyment of the sport than did comparable nonscholarship athletes. In the subsequent study, the researcher also explored the potential for scholarships to have informational value and enhance intrinsic motivation. He reasoned that women receiving scholarships (which at that time was rare) would interpret them as signs of competence, and thus the scholarships could have an *informational* functional significance. However, he suggested that men could be expected to experience the scholarships as more controlling because scholarships were a standard way of "buying" male collegiate athletes such as football players. He found once again that males in the common scholarship sports, such as football, displayed undermining but that neither females in general nor males in sports in which scholarships were less frequent showed evidence of the undermining effect. Such data suggested that athletes who get athletic scholarships in settings in which they are somewhat common are likely to experience them as controlling and show decrements in intrinsic motivation, but if the scholarships are less common, they may be experienced as more informational, signifying competence.

Subsequently, Amorose and Horn (2000) looked into this effect in a sample consisting largely of Division I athletes in the United States who were receiving various levels of scholarships, from none to full. They found no differences between scholarship and nonscholarship athletes on the Interest/Enjoyment subscale of the Intrinsic Motivation Inventory (IMI; Ryan, Mims, & Koestner, 1983), and they also found that scholarship athletes had higher feelings of competence and lower levels of tension than nonscholarship athletes. The same study also showed that athletes with more autocratic or controlling coaches had lower intrinsic motivation.

Further investigating the scholarship issue, Medic, Mack, Wilson, and Starkes (2007) assessed both current and anticipated future motivation in a sample of basketball players. Like Ryan (1977, 1980), they reported somewhat complex results, again with some gender effects. Men with sport scholarships had higher external regulation than both men and women nonscholarship athletes and compared with women scholarship athletes. For nonscholarship athletes, the perceived possibility of obtaining full scholarships in the future predicted increased external regulation and decreased intrinsic motivation, whereas for scholarship athletes, the possibility of removing scholarships was associated with decreased intrinsic motivation. Such results show that financial rewards for sports can have varied effects on motivation, including sometimes that of diminishing autonomous engagement, largely due to variations in their functional significance. However, further research is needed to sort out these effects and the circumstances in which scholarships will have controlling or informational significance.

Professional Sports

Few studies have examined the impact of rewards on motivation in professional contexts. However, using records from the National Basketball Association and Major League Baseball, White and Sheldon (2014) reported a provocative study on this issue. They followed players' careers in 3-year blocks that included a baseline year, a contract year, and a postcontract year. Their question was whether the salience of the players' monetary rewards highlighted during the contract year would influence their intrinsic motivation from pre- to postcontract year. The researchers found that performance in the third year was, in fact, poorer than during the first and second years, suggesting to them that the emphasis on rewards in the contract year led to a decrease in intrinsic motivation during the following year, which was lower even than baseline, as evidenced in indicators such as points scored, batting averages, and defensive performance. Understanding whether this was actually a decrease in intrinsic motivation, how general this effect would be across professional sport contexts, and what factors might potentially moderate it awaits further study.

Optimal Challenge, Feedback, and Competence

It is a basic tenet of CET that, in any context in which people experience some level of autonomy, positive feedback will likely enhance intrinsic motivation. This proposition must, however, be moderated by the concept of optimal challenge, which is essential for intrinsic motivation (Deci, 1975) and the experience of flow (Csikszentmihalyi, 1975). Optimal challenge allows people to successfully exercise and stretch their abilities, which they typically experience as enjoyable. Positive feedback is thus most motivating when it is received in an optimally challenging setting, one that requires individuals to exert themselves, do well, and feel competent but that is not so difficult that they don't have a reasonable chance of doing well. Sport and exercise activities, because they provide multiple sources of feedback, are prototypical arenas for experiencing this sense of optimal challenge so central to intrinsic motivation (Deci & Ryan, 1980a). Most sports provide varied levels of entry for any participant, from amateur pickup games to elite or professional competitions. Thus people can gravitate to their own level of optimal challenge.

The effects of feedback on intrinsic motivation were tested early on by a number of investigators. Vallerand and Reid (1984), for example, assessed the impact of positive and negative verbal feedback on participants using the stabilometer motor task. They confirmed predictions from CET that positive feedback would enhance, and negative feedback would diminish, intrinsic motivation for the task, relative to a no-feedback condition. Importantly, these investigators also assessed the participants' perceived competence for the task and found that perceived competence mediated the impact of feedback on intrinsic motivation. Weinberg and Jackson (1979) and Weinberg and Ragan (1979) found similar results in sports-related tasks, with both studies finding that positive feedback increased and negative feedback decreased intrinsic motivation. These studies represent further confirmation of the facilitating effect of positive verbal feedback concerning performance, such as the kind that coaches can provide.

As implied earlier, although providing positive feedback under most conditions except for controlling ones (e.g., Ryan, 1982) has positive effects on intrinsic motivation, people who end up getting negative feedback are likely to pay the cost of detriments to their motivation and engagement. Yet this is not inevitable. Again as CET suggests, it will depend on the functional significance of the feedback. When evaluative and controlling, it will undermine intrinsic motivation—yet when efficacy-relevant, it can enhance it.

This dynamic aspect of negative feedback was recently explored by Carpentier and Mageau (2013). They focused on what they called *change-oriented feedback,* in which constructive, effectance-relevant inputs are provided with an aim toward improvement. Based on surveys of both athletes and coaches following practice sessions, descriptive findings revealed that autonomy-supportive, change-oriented feedback is empathic, is accompanied by choices of solutions, is based on clear and attainable objectives known to athletes, avoids person-related statements, is paired with tips, and is given in a considerate tone of voice. The findings showed, more importantly, that such change-oriented feedback predicted more positive athletes' outcomes above and beyond coaches' other competence- and autonomy-supportive behaviors.

Similarly, Mouratidis, Lens, and Vansteenkiste (2010) found that when coaches gave negative feedback to their athletes in an autonomy-supportive way, the results were positive experiences and improved performance for the athletes. In other words, although negative feedback does tend to decrease people's feelings of competence and intrinsic motivation, it is possible to provide it in a way that is not so detrimental. This is an important finding, as negative feedback is very common not only in sports but in other domains of life as well. In essence, it requires reformulating negative feedback as an opportunity to support athletes', students', or employees' thinking about their own skills and about how to practice and perform more effectively. When so viewed, it provides an opportunity for growth and development rather than humiliation or despair.

Competence feedback, especially when provided in supportive rather than controlling or evaluative ways, is in fact a key element in sport motivation. One of the reasons that people in most cultures have structured their physical play into sport activities, from rugby to badminton, is that the structure of sports allows people to enhance their competencies in part by receiving meaningful competence feedback. Thus, although humans have always actively used their bodies, sport allows them to gauge improvement through the feedback provided by points, times, scores, wins, and other competitive outcomes, as well as well-crafted feedback from thoughtful coaches and instructors. Yet, as we shall shortly review, sometimes the competitive context of sports, with its inherent feedback, can undermine as well as enhance.

Ego Involvement in Sport

Thus far, much of our discussion of sport has focused on autonomous (in contrast to controlled) motivation. There is, however, another motivational concept that has been important in SDT and is highly relevant to sport, and that is *ego involvement.* We introduced the concept in Chapter 7, suggesting that it is an internal pressure resulting from people's feelings of self-worth being contingent upon outcomes, on meeting some standards or achieving some specific goals. We elaborated the concept in Chapter 8, suggesting that ego involvement is a form of introjected regulation in which people have partially internalized some value or regulation but have not fully accepted it as their own. The individuals are thus controlled by these internal contingencies in ways that are not unlike being controlled by external contingencies, except that with ego involvement the process is largely within them. Early research (Ryan, 1982) showed that when people's self-esteem was linked to proving themselves worthy—for example, doing well at a target activity that proves they are intelligent—they lost intrinsic motivation for that target activity. This suggests that ego involvement is a form of internally controlling regulation that can be detrimental to people's autonomy and sense of self.

The competitive nature of sports, along with the use of contingencies and pressures for approval, recognition, or rewards, are very likely to potentiate ego involvement in sport activities. For example, we've all seen instances of angry, aggressive, inexcusable responses to losing competitions, suggesting that the athletes' sense of worth was riding on the win. That is, these athletes may have become ego involved in competition, feeling inner pressure to win in order to feel good about themselves. Although, as we shall subsequently review, competition can be simply informational, when external pressures and contingent regard are salient, individual athletes can easily introject the standard of needing to win or to achieve specific performance outcomes in order to feel worthy. When people are ego involved and outcomes are attained, people will typically feel dominant and prideful; but when outcomes are uncertain or negative, guilt, shame, anxiety, and aggression are common experiences (Deci & Ryan, 1985b). Ego involvement is thus a motivating state; indeed, it is often very powerfully motivating, as people's self-esteem is on the line. But research has shown that there are costs, such as low need satisfaction and high negative affect, to this type of motivation (Standage, Duda, & Pensgaard, 2005).

Various studies have provided further support for these ideas. For example, Lonsdale and Hodge (2011) found that elite athletes from New Zealand who participated in their sport with a strong introjected or ego involved form of regulation were more likely to experience burnout over a 4-month period than were those with other strong regulatory styles. Sarrazin, Vallerand, Guillet, Pelletier, and Cury (2002), in a 21-month longitudinal study of adolescent handball players, found that, when there was a general coaching climate of ego involvement, the athletes reported low levels of autonomy, which were eventually detrimental to their participation in the sport. Duda and colleagues performed a series of studies related to ego involvement in sport. First, Duda (1989) found that high school students in organized sports were higher in ego involvement than those in recreational sports. Duda, Chi, Newton, Walling, and Catley (1995) later found that participants who showed greater ego involvement were less intrinsically motivated for the target activity. Seifriz, Duda, and Chi (1992) similarly found that high school basketball players who were high in dispositional ego involvement were low in intrinsic motivation.

Ego involvement and other forms of introjection are often accompanied by *self-talk* in which, for example, people may be telling themselves what to do and perhaps even threatening themselves with sanctions if they don't. However, research by Oliver, Markland, and Hardy (2010) showed that not all self-talk is necessarily controlled or ego involved. They distinguished between self-talk that is informational and typically accompanies autonomous motivation and self-talk that is controlling and accompanies forms of controlled motivation. The informational self-talk was found to be associated with positive affect, regardless of whether the person did well or poorly on the target activity, whereas controlling self-talk, which accompanies ego involvement, was found to be associated with anxiety and negative affect, especially if the person did poorly on that activity. Thus, similar to what Carpentier and Mageau (2013) suggested about coach-provided change-oriented feedback, Oliver et al. showed that people's self-coaching can involve similar dynamics.

Competition: Direct and Indirect

Sports are unique as instances of intrinsically motivated behaviors because competition is integral to many. Indeed, many people consider competition as virtually definitional for sport, and it is not unusual to hear athletes say that competition is what makes sports fun. Because competition itself has interesting motivational dynamics, we turn to a discussion of research on the impact of competition on intrinsic motivation for sport.

Ross and Van den Haag (1957) provided a classic distinction concerning competition that has informed literature since (e.g., Alderman, 1974). The term *direct competition* was defined as players struggling against one another to maximize their own success. For example, two basketball teams facing off against each other are each trying to win both by scoring points for their team and by interfering with the other teams' attempts to score; the teams would be engaged in direct competition. There is another case of competition that would also be considered direct competition, and that involves each individual or team trying to maximize success and thus beat another individual or team without the opportunity to interfere with the other team's performance, as, for example, in most track and field events or winter sports. Thibaut and Kelley (1959) added that "perfect" competition is represented by "zero-sum" situations in which the gains or wins of one side represent losses for the other. These researchers found that competition so defined tended to lead to mistrust, deceit, and aggression.

Indirect competition, in contrast, involves athletes competing against themselves in the sense of trying to perform better than they have done previously. Indirect competition is central to skill building and performance in sports and is reflected in athletes' adoption of mastery goals, which are typically, though not always, positively related to intrinsically motivated engagement (e.g., Benita, Roth, & Deci, 2014). Nonetheless, our discussion of competition focuses primarily on direct competition.

According to CET, direct competition, like so many other external events, can have both *informational* and *controlling* aspects (see Chapters 6 and 7). The informational aspect is linked to the idea that competitive environments can offer optimal challenges and competence feedback. Part of the joy in competition stems from the feedback, both immediate and in terms of scores, that one can get from performing against opponents who are also trying to do their best. On the other hand, competition can often have controlling aspects, as when a player feels that he or she "has to" win. This pressure can come from others (parents, coaches, teammates) or can result from ego involvement (Standage & Ryan, 2012). The more controlling the context, the more the game becomes only instrumental to an outcome (winning), changing one's relation to the activity. Thus competitive settings in which there is pressure to win would be expected to undermine intrinsic motivation, whereas competitive settings in which the focus is on task involvement and mastery should generally maintain or even enhance intrinsic motivation. As such, direct competition can potentially make a task either more fun or more painful as a result of these motivational dynamics.

Competition and Intrinsic Motivation

Deci, Betley, Kahle, Abrams, and Porac (1981) reported the first study examining whether competition would tend to be informational or controlling and thus would leave intrinsic motivation enhanced, undermined, or unchanged. Comparing direct competition to indirect competition, they had people complete spatial-relations puzzles as quickly as they could in an attempt either to improve their own performances (i.e., indirect competition) or to beat the other participant and win the "game" (i.e., direct competition). In both direct and indirect conditions, the target participant was allowed to solve the puzzles faster than the other player in the room, who was an experimental accomplice. Participants in the direct-competition condition, despite winning, were subsequently less intrinsically motivated for the activity than were those in the more likely mastery-motivated, indirect-competition condition.

Winning, Losing, and Pressure in Competitions

In the Deci, Betley, et al. (1981) study, the participants in the direct competition won and the participants in the indirect competition performed better than the other participant (i.e., the accomplice). What might have happened if the participants had lost or done poorly? Studies have found what is perhaps obvious to all competitors: Losing a direct competition leads to less intrinsic motivation than winning (McAuley, Duncan, & Tammen, 1989; Reeve, Olson, & Cole, 1985).

Another aspect of the Deci, Betley, et al. (1981) study was that the experimental manipulation made clear that the goal was to win, to *beat* the opponent. This raised the question of what would happen to participants' intrinsic motivation if there were a direct competition without this emphasis on winning per se. Reeve and Deci (1996) did a study of winning a competition when participants were under pressure to win compared to winning when there was no controlling pressure applied. They compared each of those two conditions to conditions of no-competition–no-feedback and of losing the competition in a nonpressuring context. Findings showed that those who won the competition (without pressure) had the highest level of intrinsic motivation, with a mean higher than that of the participants in the no-competition–no-feedback comparison group. Further, those who won in the nonpressuring context were significantly more intrinsically motivated than either those who won in the pressuring condition or those who lost the competition. First, this indicates that winning a direct competition can be positively motivating as long as the pressure to win is not what is most salient. Second, winning versus losing does make a big difference, because it conveys important information about the athletes' competence. In sum, the downsides of competition are that both the pressure to win and the losing tend to be detrimental. The upsides involve the rich competence feedback that competitive situations can entail. Finally, it is worth noting that all the effects that emerged from the Reeve and Deci study were mediated by the participants' perceptions of competence and autonomy, as SDT would predict.

Can We Ameliorate the Effects of Losing?

Losing can clearly have negative effects on intrinsic motivation, largely through diminishing feelings of competence. Vansteenkiste and Deci (2003) took interest in whether there were conditions in which, even while losing, one might feel some competence and thus maintain intrinsic motivation.

To do this, Vansteenkiste and Deci (2003) had participants compete for monetary rewards under varied conditions. The first three conditions were (1) a no-competition comparison group, (2) a win-the-reward group, and (3) a lose-the-reward group. As expected, when it came to intrinsic motivation, the win group was the highest and the lose group was very low, with a significant difference between these two conditions. Yet the more interesting part of the experiment concerns two other conditions. In both, participants lost the competition and the competitively contingent reward. Yet in one, the participants got positive feedback for doing well, even though they lost and got no reward; in the other, participants received a monetary reward for doing well even though they lost, so they lost the competitively contingent reward but received the performance-contingent reward, thus receiving the same amount of money as the group that won the competition and reward. Results revealed that when the losers received positive competence feedback, their intrinsic motivation was significantly higher than that of losers who did not get positive feedback. That is, the positive feedback had ameliorated the negative effects of losing. Finally, when losers got the performance-contingent reward for doing well, the reward had no ameliorative effect, even though the reward presumably conveyed positive feedback. Here we see that informational elements can ameliorate the effects of losing, whereas events potentially seen as controlling are less effective.

To summarize the research on competition and intrinsic motivation, competition can be either informational or controlling. When people compete and win, the winning can have an informational functional significance and enhance intrinsic motivation. However, when people win a competition in which there is pressure to win or in which there is a competitively contingent monetary reward, these pressures counteract the implicit positive feedback of winning and have an overall negative effect on intrinsic motivation. Further, when people lose a competition, their intrinsic motivation often suffers, but if there is positive feedback about things they did well in the activity, it can ameliorate the undermining effects of losing. Thus the problem with direct competition is the pressure that so often surrounds it, sometimes with great intensity, as if winning a competition were the most important thing in the world. It seems that environments that truly support the adage "it's not winning or losing, but how you play the game" are those most likely to support athletes' intrinsic motivation.

All of this research has especially important implications for youth sports, where coaches and parents may, in their zeal to see their athletes win, unwittingly undermine the participants' long-term motivation to play by bringing pressure to bear on the youth. The research also suggests that many factors beyond just competition itself can affect people's intrinsic motivation for sports because of their informational versus controlling functional significance.

Inner Experiences, Intrinsic Motivation, and Outcomes

We have now reviewed research showing that various external events such as rewards, feedback, and competition can affect intrinsic motivation for sporting activities, and we have interpreted the results in terms of these events affecting participants' experiences of autonomy and/or competence satisfactions. Some studies on the antecedents of intrinsic motivation for sports and related activities have more directly assessed participants' perceived autonomy and perceived competence or, more broadly, their experiences of autonomy, competence, and relatedness need satisfactions while doing an activity. They have then used those need-satisfaction-versus-frustration experiences to predict intrinsic motivation or related positive outcomes. For example, Smith, Ntoumanis, Duda, and Vansteenkiste (2011) found that when athletes reported autonomy for pursuing a goal at the beginning of a season, they displayed more midseason effort expenditure, which subsequently predicted their end-of-season goal attainment. Sebire, Jago, Fox, Edwards, and Thompson (2013) found that satisfactions of children's autonomy, competence, and relatedness needs were related to the children's intrinsic motivation for sport-related activities, which was associated with the children's objectively assessed physical activity. As well, in a study of Spanish adolescent soccer players, Calvo, Cervelló, Jiménez, Iglesias, and

Murcia (2010) found that those who were high in perceived autonomy were likely to persist longer at their sport, presumably reflecting greater intrinsic motivation.

Extrinsic Motivation and Sport

Although intrinsic motivation is a critical topic within sport sciences, there is much more than just intrinsic motivation at work in sports. First, people have many extrinsic reasons for engaging in sports, ranging from being accepted and approved of by friends to hopes of fame and fortune. Second, even though sporting activities have many moments of intrinsically motivated engagement and even flow (Csikszentmihalyi, 1975), these moments are often separated by long periods of hard work. In sports, practice and skill building, which are essential to high performance, can often be repetitive rather than novel and interesting. Moreover, high levels of performance typically require arduous and disciplined conditioning and exercise, from wind sprints for soccer players to weightlifting for wrestlers. Third, even when sport is highly intrinsically motivating, the social context, typically represented by parents and coaches, often involves both direct extrinsic incentives and contingencies of approval that can influence the athletes' attributions, motivations, and subjective experiences. Accordingly, any motivational psychology of sport must address the nonintrinsically motivated aspects of those pursuits.

As we explained in Chapter 8 on organismic integration theory (OIT), extrinsic motivation can vary in the degree to which it is autonomous as a function of the degree to which the target individual has internalized and integrated regulation for these instrumental behaviors. For example, for football (soccer) players, doing ball drills is certainly important, yet the activity itself may not be experienced as highly enjoyable. Instead, the motivators for this activity lie mainly in its instrumentalities, whether they be to please coaches and avoid their wrath or to become a more skilled player. All types of extrinsic motivation—external regulation, introjected regulation, identified regulation, and integrated regulation—can apply to sport behaviors. In fact, research by Chatzisarantis, Hagger, Biddle, Smith, and Wang (2003) meta-analyzed 21 published studies and reported that results supported the existence of the OIT-based continuum of autonomy for extrinsic motivation in this domain.

Optimally, athletes would be intrinsically motivated for many aspects of their sport and relatively integrated in their extrinsic motivations for the other aspects. Together, the mix of intrinsic motivation and integrated extrinsic motivation are referred to as autonomous motivation, and autonomous motivation is facilitated by satisfaction of the basic psychological needs. Much of the research on sport, particularly field research rather than laboratory experiments, has focused on autonomous motivation, sometimes predicting it from satisfaction of the basic psychological needs and sometimes using it to predict the persistence, performance, and well-being of athletes.

Lonsdale, Hodge, and Rose (2009) examined how more self-determined forms of motivation were associated with burnout in elite athletes from Canada. They found generally that the more autonomous the athlete's motivation, the fewer the symptoms of burnout he or she had (see also Hodge, Lonsdale, & Ng, 2008). Similarly, Holmberg and Sheridan (2013) examined antecedents of burnout in a large sample of U.S. college athletes from various sports. They found a strong relationship between the degree of autonomy and various indicators of burnout, such as devaluation, reduced feelings of accomplishment, and exhaustion.

Although engaging in goal-directed behavior can often be difficult, research by Ntoumanis and colleagues (2014) found that when athletes' motivation to pursue the goals was more autonomous, the athletes were more persistent, showed more positive affect, and reported more interest in future task engagement. In a study by Smith and Ntoumanis (2014) in which participants faced goals that were unattainable, those who were more autonomously motivated were slower to disengage but faster to reengage.

In an examination of need satisfaction and autonomous motivation in British athletes, Ntoumanis and Standage (2009) found that the athletes' degree of basic psychological need satisfaction predicted their autonomous motivation for the sport. In turn, their autonomous motivation predicted their behaving in more moral and sportsperson-like ways (i.e., fair play, respect for other athletes), whereas need frustration predicted controlled motivation and the display of antisocial attitudes by the athletes. In fact, growing data suggest that the more controlled, relative to autonomous, athletes' motivation is, the more they are prone to un-sportsperson-like behaviors. For example, Donahue, Miquelon, Valois, Goulet, Buist andVallerand (2006) showed that intrinsically motivated athletes had more sportsperson-like attitudes and were, in turn, less likely to use performance-enhancing drugs, as did Barkoukis, Lazuras, Tsorbatzoudis, and Rodafinos (2011), who sampled Olympic-level competitors. Hodge, Hargreaves, Gerrard, and Lonsdale (2013), in contrast, found no relationship between coaches' autonomy support and attitudes toward the use of performance-enhancing drugs, instead finding that controlling coach behaviors predicted susceptibility to such drug use, mediated by greater moral disengagement. In yet another relevant study, Hodge and Lonsdale (2011) reported that autonomy-supportive coaching styles predicted prosocial behavior toward teammates, a relation that was mediated by autonomous motivation. Athletes' controlled motivation was, in contrast, associated with greater antisocial behavior toward teammates and toward opponent players. Both of these latter relations were mediated by moral disengagement.

In sum, because sports involves extrinsic as well as intrinsic motivation, internalization is an important issue. The more that athletes and players can internalize the value of their efforts and willingly engage in the less-than-fun parts of athletics, the better will be their overall experience, persistence, and performance over time.

Coaching, Motivation, and Sport Outcomes

Although many factors can influence athletes' intrinsic motivation and internalized motivation, the coach–athlete relationship may be among the most critical (Langan, Lonsdale, Blake, & Toner, 2015). Much SDT research supports this view. Many studies have examined autonomy support provided by coaches and used it to predict the athletes' autonomous motivations, perceived competence, and need satisfactions. In turn, those important motivation variables have related to various sport and physical activity outcomes. For example, Joesaar, Hein, and Hagger (2012) did a longitudinal study in which they found that athletes in early to mid-adolescence who perceived their coaches to be more autonomy-supportive displayed higher levels of intrinsic motivation 1 year later, and Amorose and Horn (2001) found comparable results with collegiate athletes. Sheldon and Watson (2011) found that coaches' autonomy support toward varsity university athletes predicted not only the athletes' intrinsic motivation but also their autonomous extrinsic motivation, which were in turn related to the athletes' positive team experiences. Further, Smith, Ntoumanis, and Duda (2010) found coaches' autonomy-supportive behaviors to predict the athletes' autonomous motivation for sports, and this motivation predicted the athletes' well-being. Fenton, Duda, Quested, and Barrett (2014) found that autonomy support provided by coaches to adolescent football (soccer) players positively predicted autonomous motivation for sport engagement, which in turn positively predicted moderately vigorous physical activity and negatively predicted sedentary time. Mahoney, Gucciardi, Ntoumanis, and Mallett (2014) found that supportive coaching of cross-country runners yielded greater "mental toughness." As well, a longitudinal study of soccer players from Spain revealed that the degree to which coaches behaved with a supportive style predicted team cohesion and player satisfaction (García-Calvo, Leo, Gonzalez-Ponce, Sánchez-Miguel, Mouratidis, & Ntoumonis, 2014).

Unfortunately, not all coaches support the autonomy and other basic psychological needs of their athletes. Several studies have compared autonomy-supportive coaching to controlling coaching. For example, a study of adolescent athletes who perceived their coaches to be autonomy-supportive found that the athletes experienced greater sport engagement, whereas those who experienced their coaches to be controlling showed sport disaffection (Curran, Hill, Hall, & Jowett, 2014). Additionally, Healy, Ntoumanis, Veldhuijzen van Zanten, and Paine (2014), collecting data from athletes from many different sports, found that, although coaches who were autonomy-supportive promoted higher autonomous motivation and vitality and less burnout and ill-being, coaches who were controlling in their interpersonal styles prompted greater need frustration and controlled motivation among their players, which led to more burnout and physical symptoms.

Need Satisfaction in Sport

Some of our discussion of intrinsic motivation in sports focused on the importance of satisfaction of the competence and autonomy needs for promoting this type of autonomous motivation. However, satisfaction of the third basic psychological need—*relatedness*—is also considered extremely important within SDT both for intrinsic motivation in social activities (which includes many sports) and for internalization. That is, satisfaction of the autonomy, competence, and relatedness needs are all highly important for promoting autonomous motivation, and many sport studies have examined satisfaction of the basic psychological needs, often being predicted from interpersonal climates and being predictors of autonomous motivation and a range of positive sporting outcomes (Ntoumanis & Mallett, 2014). We have already mentioned a few such studies in passing, but we now discuss a few more studies of need satisfaction.

A study of handball players (Isoard-Gautheur, Guillet-Descas, & Lemyre, 2012) revealed that a perceived autonomy-supportive coaching style was associated with greater autonomy and competence need satisfaction, whereas a more controlling coaching style was associated with lower levels of autonomy and relatedness. In turn, the lower levels of fulfillment of these basic psychological needs predicted lower levels of autonomous motivation and higher levels of athlete burnout.

Using cluster analysis, Lundqvist and Raglin (2015) categorized expert athletes at the sport of *orienteering* on the basis of their well-being and stress levels. The researchers found that the athletes who showed the highest well-being and lowest stress were the ones who experienced the most need satisfaction and the least need frustration.

Sheldon, Zhaoyang, and Williams (2013) studied undergraduate basketball players to determine whether satisfaction of their basic psychological needs prior to games would predict the quality of their performance and their postgame need satisfaction. They found that the players who were high on pregame autonomy satisfaction performed very well and that performance during the game contributed to the athletes' experiencing greater postgame relatedness and competence satisfaction.

Further, Vallerand and Losier (1999) and Mageau and Vallerand (2003) both found that, when coaches were more autonomy-supportive, athletes reported greater satisfaction of the basic psychological needs, and, in a study of Mexican adolescent athletes, López-Walle, Balaguer, Castillo, and Tristán (2012) found that the youths' perceptions of more autonomy support from their coaches predicted the athletes' reporting greater need satisfaction and, in turn, higher well-being.

A study of more than 7,000 youth from soccer leagues in five European countries showed that when coaches were perceived as autonomy-supportive, the young athletes experienced more satisfaction of the basic psychological needs, which predicted lower levels of dropping out of the sport (Quested, Ntoumanis, et al. 2013). Various other investigators have found that autonomy support was associated with need satisfaction, autonomous motivation, and well-being among athletes in sports such as rugby and volleyball (e.g., Duda, Papaioannou, Appleton, Quested, & Krommidas, 2014; Felton & Jowett, 2013b; Mack, Wilson, Oster, Kowalski, Crocker, & Sylvester, 2011; Pope & Wilson, 2012).

A study by Curran, Hill, and Niemiec (2013) found that structure, which has been shown to promote competence in various domains, was related to young soccer players' behavioral engagement and that this relation was moderated by autonomy support from the coaches. In other words, autonomy-supportive structure led to need satisfaction and engagement, but structure that was not autonomy-supportive did not have these positive consequences. This finding complements a similar result in high school education (Jang, Reeve, & Deci, 2010).

In contrast, some researchers have assessed the degree to which coaches were controlling and need-thwarting (e.g., Bartholomew, Ntoumanis, & Thøgersen-Ntoumani, 2010; Bartholomew, Ntoumanis, Ryan, & Thøgersen-Ntoumani, 2011) and found that those coaching climates were associated with athletes experiencing frustration rather than satisfaction of the basic needs, with a range of negative consequences including negative affect and burnout. Bartholomew, Ntoumanis, Ryan, Bosch, & Thøgersen-Ntoumani (2011) even showed that among relatively elite athletes, a controlling coaching climate predicted increased stress entering practices, as indicated by increases in SIgA, an immunological protein that is secreted in moments of acute stress, as well as during self-reported negative experiences. In still a different setting, Sarrazin and colleagues (2002) found that when women handball players felt interpersonally controlled, or low in competence and relatedness to others in the sport, they had low levels of autonomous motivation, which led to the intention of dropping out of their sport.

PARENTS

Before we place all the responsibility for athletes' sport motivation on the coaches, we should consider that every young athlete typically faces another motivational climate at home. For example, O'Rourke, Smith, Smoll, and Cumming (2014) examined the role of both parenting climates and coaching climates as they related to young competitive swimmers' motivation, performance anxiety, and self-esteem and found that the more the parents pressured their children, the more negative influences there were on the children, in the form of less autonomous motivation, more anxiety, and lower self-esteem, over and above any influences from the coaching climates. In other words, although coaches can have a significant impact on athletes' motivation, as well as their engagement, learning, performance, and wellness, it appears that the approach taken by parents—whether it be to support or to pressure—also has an important impact on their children's motivation, quality of play, and psychological well-being in relation to sports.

Felton and Jowett (2013a) examined the degree to which athletes were securely attached to their coaches and parents and found that their degree of secure attachment to these authorities was directly related to the athletes' well-being. Importantly for our discussion, they also found that the attachment–wellness relationship was mediated by satisfaction of the three basic psychological needs.

Gagné, Ryan, and Bargmann (2003) studied the daily experiences of relatively high-level gymnasts as they practiced and performed over a 4-week period in a very competitive and sometimes grueling sport. They found that both parents' and coaches' autonomy-supportive styles facilitated the athletes' overall relative autonomy for the sport, with coaches' support being a more potent predictor of daily autonomous motivation for practice. In turn, autonomous motivation predicted positive emotions at practice and stable self-esteem. In contrast, controlling environments and the resulting controlled forms of motivation were associated with greater negative affect and unstable self-esteem. Perhaps the most unique aspect of this study was looking at variations at the within-person level in athletes' motivation for sport and the changes they experienced in well-being from pre- to postpractice. On days when practice was associated with greater experienced need supports, athletes showed more positive changes from pre- to postpractice, including vitality and positive affect.

Coaching Climates among Elite Athletes

Earlier in the chapter, when discussing the effects of awards, rewards, and athletic scholarships on athletes' intrinsic motivation, we raised the point that one function of such extrinsic factors may be gatekeeping—that is, to separate the elite from the non-elite athletes—rather than to motivate all athletes. Implicit in this view is the idea that the elite athletes are immune to negative effects of rewards and other controls; indeed, because rewards and related controls are a big part of what their athletic lives are about, they may become accustomed to them so that the rewards and controls would have little impact on these exceptional players. Or, relatedly, it may be the case that the rewards and controls are just among the myriad challenges such athletes face on a regular basis (Treasure, Lemyre, Kuczka, & Standage, 2007).

A classic study by Pelletier, Fortier, Vallerand, and Brière (2001) examined whether the elite as well as the non-elite athletes are indeed at risk for negative effects from control. Pelletier and colleagues surveyed elite, national competitor swimmers from across Canada concerning both their experiences of the coaching climate (autonomy-supportive vs. controlling) and their personal motivations for sport engagement, assessing motives specified within OIT. The swimmers were then followed over a 22-month period to track their continuing participation versus dropout. Pelletier et al. found first that controlling coaching climates were associated with the athletes' self-reported external and introjected regulation, whereas autonomy-supportive coaching was associated with more autonomous extrinsic motivation (viz., identification) and intrinsic motivation. As predicted, they also found that more autonomous forms of motivation predicted greater persistence over time, whereas both amotivation and controlled motives were associated with more rapid dropout. Indeed, attrition rates over time followed a pattern parallel to the autonomy continuum, such that the more internalized and autonomous the regulation was, the longer the swimmers were likely to persist in this competitive sport context.

Nonetheless, there is a relative dearth of investigations of coaching styles at very elite or professional levels (see Arnold & Sarkar, 2015; Lyons, Rynne, & Mallett, 2012), which is noteworthy given that at these top levels of sport there appears to be high variability in supportive versus controlling styles.

An exception in this respect is a fascinating qualitative investigation of a change in coaching styles associated with the success of the *All Blacks* national rugby team from New Zealand, which achieved consecutive world championships in 2011 and 2015. Hodge, Henry, and Smith (2014) describe the implementation of a "dual-management model" that reflected motivational principles emphasized in SDT, including an autonomy-supportive climate, and fostering basic psychological need satisfactions of autonomy, competence, and relatedness. Specifically, they saw the new coaching atmosphere as highlighting opportunities for choice, ownership, and responsibility for decision making on the part of players, encouraging athletes to take leadership initiative, and using a strength-focused feedback system that was informational rather than controlling and critical. These changes were seen as instrumental in enhancing team spirit and performance.

A rare intervention study in a highly pressured sport atmosphere was accomplished by Cheon, Reeve, Lee, and Lee (2015), who worked with coaches involved in the *London 2012 Paralympic Games*. Coaches and their respective athletes were assigned to either a control group or a group that received an intervention promoting more autonomy-supportive styles. Results revealed that athletes in the control group experienced deterioration in all indicators of motivation, engagement, and functioning over time. In contrast, the motivation, engagement, and functioning of athletes in the experimental group were generally maintained. Athletes of coaches in the experimental (autonomy-supportive coaching) group also won significantly more Olympic medals than those in the control group.

In fact, we suggest that need satisfaction, which is facilitated by autonomy-supportive coaching, is likely to be equally important at all levels of sport. Yet elite contexts can often involve more pressure toward winning, which can readily translate into more controlling styles. Focusing on process rather than outcomes may, in fact, be an effective strategy to enhance both need satisfaction and performance, even at the top of the sport world.

Support for Coaches

Studies have shown that it is possible to train coaches to be more supportive of their athletes' basic psychological needs. For example, as we reviewed above, Cheon et al. (2015) trained coaches to support their athletes by being mindful of the athletes' basic psychological needs, providing rationales when making requests, acknowledging the athletes' negative affect, using nonpressuring language, and being patient with the athletes. Intervention-group coaches became more need-supportive, and this in turn was associated with better motivational and performance outcomes.

Although it is clear that coaches' being supportive of athletes' basic psychological needs yields a range of positive outcomes for the athletes and their teams, it is important to keep in mind that the coaches themselves need to experience satisfaction of the competence, autonomy, and relatedness needs in order to be optimally engaged in coaching and to be supportive of their athletes. Research with coaches has shown that when their needs were thwarted by pressure from above (e.g., from administrators) and/or from below (e.g., from disengaged athletes), they were less autonomous in their own motivation and, predictably, they were less autonomy-supportive toward their athletes (Rocchi,

Pelletier, & Couture, 2013). In social contexts that are full of pressure to win, coaches as well as athletes pay significant costs because they fail to experience the nutrients that are so essential for effective and healthy functioning in their roles.

Coaches' satisfaction is also affected by the climate of their teams. For instance, in a study of youth soccer coaches, Curren, Hill, Hall, and Jowett (2014) assessed coaches' perceptions of social unity in their group of athletes, which could be viewed as support (and low pressure) from below. When teams were more socially unified, coaches were more autonomy-supportive of their athletes. Interestingly, the coaches' being more autonomy-supportive predicted their experiencing greater need satisfaction, suggesting that for coaches, giving autonomy support is need-satisfying. This would further suggest that the relationship between coaches being autonomy-supportive and experiencing need support is bidirectional, as studies already reviewed indicated that need satisfaction led to being autonomy-supportive.

Sports in the Contemporary World

Sporting activities provide opportunities for expressing our active nature. In sport, people engage in challenging, sometimes arduous, activities at times for the sheer delight of doing it, but at other times for some extrinsic outcomes. A merely hedonic perspective cannot adequately account for the enjoyment of sport, which at times will be accompanied by pain and discouragement, as well as joy and triumph. In our view, it can be understood in a relatively full way only by grasping the importance of the basic psychological need satisfactions—the sense of purpose, the feelings of achievement, and the satisfactions of teamwork—that sports can afford even in the moments of hardship and effort.

To a significant degree, our discussion in this chapter has been about the broad arena of youth, amateur, and recreational sports, and we have reviewed extensive research showing how such pressures in the form of rewards and recognition, ego involvements, and the intense desires to win competitions can undermine intrinsic motivation for the sports and interfere with internalization of behavioral regulations for doing the more difficult and grueling activities that contribute to honing one's skills and learning new moves. An understanding of such findings is particularly important in sports programs for youth, in which cultivating intrinsic motivation is critical for promoting maintenance of the activities over time (Cronin & Allen, 2015).

Unfortunately, all too often, coaches and parents lose sight of this, fostering atmospheres that are controlling, critical, and focused on winning (e.g., Grolnick, 2002; Mandigo & Holt, 2002; Reeve & Deci, 1996). With an intense focus on performance and the extrinsic goal of winning, adults can often drive students and youth away from sports rather than toward them, especially those children and adolescents who might benefit from participating if they had need-supportive conditions.

It is interesting that the athletes may not see the situation the same way as the coaches or parents do. For example, a study of athletic teams by Cumming, Smoll, Smith, and Grossbard (2007) found that the primary basis for young adolescent athletes' evaluating their coaches was not win–loss percentages but was, instead, the degree to which the coaches were autonomy-supportive and did *not* promote ego involvement. For most of these young athletes, winning was not the be-all and end-all. Yet to the extent that winning is an emphasis for coaches and parents, the more pressuring they are likely to be toward the athletes. That in turn was likely to increase the probability of decreasing long-term involvement in sports (see also Wang, Sproule, McNeill, Martindale & Lee, 2011).

Concerning elite and professional sports, they are much more than just games; they are an industry. And their dominance in modern cultures has no doubt added to the orientation toward pressure that seems present in university sports, high school sports, and increasingly in the recreational sports of people across the lifespan. As we saw, professional athletes, like recreational athletes, are also susceptible to having their motivation undermined by pressures, critical feedback, and rewards.

Sports are increasingly a domain in which interpersonal pressures and extrinsic rewards are used as incentives to perform well. Trophies, awards, scholarships, and other such "motivators" are frequently offered to athletes contingent upon their breaking records or defeating others. For coaches, there may be job opportunities or salary increases if they can "motivate" their athletes to perform and win, and when coaches are faced with such contingencies, they may be more prone to become more controlling and pressuring with their athletes (e.g., Rocchi et al., 2013). In short, although play and sport can serve the purpose of recreation and revitalization, when pressured and controlled, they can also drain energy and even crush the soul.

Looking across the literature on SDT and sport, it seems clear that whereas sport can be intrinsically motivated, both the disciplined aspects of practice and skill development in sports and sustained physical exercise to keep in shape for sports are optimal when a person has both (1) intrinsic motivation *and* (2) well-internalized extrinsic motivation (i.e. identified and integrated regulations). Both types of motivation facilitate what is, normatively speaking, a precarious endeavor (e.g., Matsumoto & Takenaka, 2004; Ntoumanis, 2001)—namely, adhering to disciplined sport development. The studies also show the risks entailed in attaching controlling coaching methods, evaluative pressures, or "high stakes" to sport performance, especially at the amateur level. In contrast, all aspects of the sporting endeavor that support satisfaction of the athletes' basic psychological needs for competence, autonomy, and relatedness—including parents' attitudes about their children's sporting behaviors and the interpersonal climates created by coaches—help athletes remain engaged and integrated as they act in this life domain.

Motivational Processes in Exercise

Sport represents one type of physical activity that promotes both physical and psychological health and that also happens to (on average) be intrinsically motivating. Frederick and Ryan (1993) reported that, although *exercise,* which is another health-promoting type of physical activity, is less intrinsically motivating than individual sports, adult exercisers still indicated that they have a significant degree of intrinsic motivation for exercise activities. Ongoing exercise programs such as aerobics, tae-bo, jogging, tae-kwon-do, walking, or weight training can all have aspects that are inherently satisfying. Yet there are many people who are generally sedentary and have little or no intrinsic motivation for exercise.

The literature suggests, in fact, that if exercisers do not enjoy their activity at least to some extent they are unlikely to persist at it (Ryan, Frederick, Lepes, et al., 1997; Wankel, 1993). Having some intrinsic motivation may be among the most important factors in maintaining exercise over time. Fortunately, therefore, many forms of exercise can be structured to be more interesting and intrinsically motivating (Green-Demers, Pelletier, Stewart, & Gushue, 1998; Teixeira, Silva, Mata, Palmeira, & Markland, 2012). Many exercise programs, for example, provide opportunities for optimal challenge by allowing people to start at any level of difficulty and follow the improvements in their capacities or skills. Further, the exercisers can be given choices about when and how they engage in an exercise activity and an atmosphere of relatedness can be created. Some physical activities may be more fun than others (e.g., aerobic dancing rather than jogging), so people can select the activities that seem most interesting to them. Through the opportunities individuals have to exercise at a level optimal for them and having choices about numerous factors related to the exercising, it is possible for them to experience greater perceived competence and autonomy for their activity, thus contributing to their intrinsic interest in it.

Of course, exercisers also have extrinsic reasons for engaging in physical activity, which suggests that the autonomy continuum for extrinsic motivation would also be relevant. In fact, many researchers in the exercise domain (e.g., Mullan, Markland, & Ingledew, 1997; Standage, Sebire, & Loney, 2008; Thøgersen-Ntoumani & Ntoumanis, 2006; Wilson, Rodgers, Fraser, & Murray, 2004) have successfully assessed types of regulation and found, for example, that the more autonomous types of regulation (i.e., well-internalized extrinsic motivations, as well as intrinsic motivation) were positively predictive of objectively assessed moderate to vigorous physical activity and a range of other positive behavior and wellness outcomes. For example, a study by Chang (2012) with elderly adults found that both autonomous motivation and perceived competence for physical activity contributed to self-reported health among the participants. Finally, Ha and Ng (2015) recently assessed physical activity of Hong Kong students over a 7-day period using accelerometers. They found that more moderate to vigorous activity was predicted by autonomous motivation, along with less sedentary behavior and higher reported quality of life.

A systematic review by Teixeira, Carraça, Markland, Silva, and Ryan (2012) has shown consistent positive relations between autonomous motivation and exercise persistence. Further, a meta-analytic review of 46 studies, focused on children and adolescents, found links from both autonomous and controlled motivation to physical activity. Specifically, results indicated that across the studies there was a moderate positive relation between autonomous motivation and physical activity and a small negative relation between controlled motivation and physical activity, emphasizing that facilitation of autonomous motivation but not controlled motivation among youth is important for promoting more physical activity (see also Owen, Smith, Lubans, Ng, & Lonsdale, 2014).

Ego Involvement in Exercise and Physical Activity

In the section on sport, we discussed the idea that ego involvement, which is an internally controlled type of regulation, has a range of negative consequences for athletes. However, it is not only sports that can be ego involving; so can exercise. As an example, in cultures in which increasing numbers of people have become overweight, weight is a basis for disapproval both from others and from the people themselves. People can thus become ego involved in being thinner as their self-esteem gets tied to this outcome. They may pressure themselves to exercise, thus being low in autonomy. When they fail to live up to the standards, they are likely to be self-deprecating, which may leave them discouraged and less likely to persist. For example, Markland (2009) found that when women had greater discrepancies between their actual and ideal body weights, they tended to be lower in autonomous motivation, which led them to exercise less. In sum, whereas autonomous motivation facilitates greater exercise and activity, controlled motivation, whether external or internal, tends to have negative consequences for living an active, healthy life, especially over the long term.

Supportive Contexts

Insofar as exercise is guided or led by some type of instructors, those individuals can create interpersonal contexts that support participants basic psychological need satisfaction (e.g., Mandigo & Holt, 2002; Wilson, Rodgers, Blanchard, & Gessell, 2003) and thereby promote autonomous rather than controlled motivation. As we saw with sport, when general interpersonal climates or coaches' behaviors were more autonomy-supportive and less controlling, they tended to facilitate autonomous motivation and positive physical activity outcomes, and the same has been shown to be true in exercise settings. For example, researchers using a within-person longitudinal approach found that, when dancers experienced autonomy support from their instructors, they reported more need satisfaction, less anxiety, and greater well-being (Quested, Bosch, Burns, Cumming, Ntoumanis, & Duda, 2011; Quested, Duda, Ntoumanis, & Maxwell, 2013).

Various other investigators have also found that autonomy support was associated with need satisfaction, autonomous motivation, and well-being for exercise and physical activities (e.g., Barbeau, Sweet, & Fortier, 2009; Edmunds, Ntoumanis, & Duda, 2008; Duda et al., 2014). Further, studies have shown that interpersonal contexts that supported the three basic psychological needs for autonomy, competence, and relatedness fostered need satisfaction, autonomous motivation, enhanced enjoyment, greater engagement, and sustained involvement in physical activity, whereas those that thwarted the basic needs were detrimental to motivation and engagement in physical activity (e.g., Gunnell, Crocker, Wilson, Mack, & Zumbo, 2013). The relation of basic need satisfaction to physical activity has appeared in many studies (e.g., Sylvester, Mack, Busseri, Wilson, & Beauchamp, 2012) and has held up across a variety of cultures (e.g., Vlachopoulos et al., 2013).

Another approach to examining social-contextual supports has involved various types of interventions intended to enhance autonomous motivation and yield positive outcomes. For example, in an attempt to promote greater exercise among middle-aged women, Moustaka, Vlachopoulos, Kabitsis, and Theodorakis (2012) provided some of the women with an autonomy-supportive program for promoting exercise and others with a similar program that did not have the autonomy-supportive elements. The researchers found that those in the autonomy-supportive program experienced more need satisfaction, more autonomous motivation, and greater subjective vitality than did those in the other group. Using a different approach, Duncan, Hall, Wilson, and Rodgers (2012) were able to enhance people's autonomous motivation with a verbal guided-imagery intervention for exercise participation.

Relatedness and Physical Activity

For many individuals, experiencing positive interpersonal interactions while engaged in exercising or similar kinds of physical activity is both appealing and supportive. Accordingly, Edmunds, Ntoumanis, and Duda (2006) found that people who experienced positive relatedness when engaged in exercise were more autonomously motivated and more able to sustain the exercise over time. In the context of gymnastics, Gagné et al. (2003) found that perceived relatedness predicted increases in well-being during practices. Relatedness is a basic need satisfaction that may be separable from the physical activity per se but that can help engage people in the activity by making the context more enjoyable and fostering feelings of support. That is, people may be more likely to go to their spinning classes or lift weights if they look forward to interacting with friends or believe that the instructor likes them, and the consequences of doing so are likely to be positive.

Capitalizing on this idea, Buman and colleagues (2011) did a clinical trial to test the efficacy of a peer-volunteer program for promoting physical activity among sedentary older adults over an 18-month period. Participants were assigned either to the intervention group or to usual care within the community. Results showed that at the end of 4 months both groups had become more active without being significantly different in their amount of exercise. However, at the 4-month point, the intervention group had become significantly more autonomously motivated to participate in the exercise than the control group. By the end of the 18 months, those in the intervention group had increased even more in their amount of physical activity, whereas those in the control group were less active than they had been at 4 months. In sum, for the older adults, having a peer with whom to be active led them to become more autonomous in their participation, and that led them to persist at the physical activity over the long term.

Individual Differences in Exercise

The discussion of exercise, like the discussion of sport, has focused heavily on social conditions that facilitate basic need satisfaction, autonomous motivation, and enhancement of both physical activity and well-being. Individuals themselves can, of course, affect their own autonomous motivation and exercise as a function of their personalities or individual differences, although that issue has received relatively little attention. Still, it is noteworthy that Kwan, Hooper, Mangan, and Bryan (2011) found that people high in the autonomous causality orientation were more autonomously motivated for and more engaged in exercise. Thus people's autonomous motivation and active engagement in exercise are facilitated by individual differences such as causality orientations, as well as need support from the social environment.

Goal Contents and Physical Activity

As discussed in Chapter 18, there has also been an emerging strand of SDT research that concerns the content of people's goals as it relates to health. Some theories maintain that if people have goals they value highly and attain them, the consequences will invariantly be positive, regardless of what the goals are. SDT, in contrast, suggests that the content is important when predicting outcomes. More specifically, if the contents of people's goals are consistent with satisfaction of their basic psychological needs, the consequences of pursuing and attaining the goals will be positive, whereas if the content is not consistent with need satisfaction, the consequences of holding and achieving the goals are likely to be more negative (Ryan, Sheldon, Kasser, & Deci, 1996).

Initial studies of goal content (Kasser & Ryan, 1993, 1996) found that people's aspirations or life goals tend to divide into two factors that were labeled *intrinsic aspirations* and *extrinsic aspirations*. Examples of intrinsic aspirations are personal growth, relationships, and community, whereas examples of extrinsic life goals are wealth, fame, image, and power. Further, it is noteworthy that when health or fitness values are added to the analyses, they load with intrinsic rather than extrinsic aspirations.

Various studies have examined goals or aspirations as they relate to participation in exercise. Vansteenkiste, Simons, Lens, Sheldon, and Deci (2004) studied high school students who were learning the Asian activity of tae-bo. Some were told the activity would help them lose weight and be more attractive (the extrinsic goal), and others were told the activity would help them be more physically fit and healthy (the intrinsic goal). After learning the activity, the participants demonstrated it for others, and experts rated their performance. Their engagement with the exercise was also assessed during a free-choice period. Results indicated that those who were oriented toward the intrinsic goal for doing this demanding activity were rated as having learned it better and were more persistent in their engagement with it than were those who were oriented toward the extrinsic goal. In a follow-up study, Vansteenkiste, Simons, Soenens, and Lens (2004) created similar extrinsic-goal (being attractive) and intrinsic-goal (being physically fit) conditions, as well as a no-goal comparison group. They also assessed exercise persistence up to 4 months after the training period and found that participants in the intrinsic-goal condition persisted much more than those in the no-goal or extrinsic-goal groups. The researchers also found that the persistence that occurred in the extrinsic-goal group was unrelated to enjoyment and personal commitment, whereas persistence in both the no-goal group and the intrinsic-goal group was correlated with those positive affective states.

Another study (Ingledew & Markland, 2008), this time of office workers, compared the effectiveness of weight/appearance goals versus health/fitness goals for engaging in exercise. They found that participants who were focused on fitness rather than appearance were more effective in maintaining an exercise regimen, a finding consistent with early research by Ryan, Frederick, et al. (1997) in an aerobics context.

Sebire, Standage, and Vansteenkiste (2009) surveyed working adults regarding their intrinsic and extrinsic goals for engaging in physical activity, as well as their autonomous and controlled motivations for those behaviors. Results indicated that people who had a high level of intrinsic relative to extrinsic goal contents reported higher physical self-worth, more exercise behaviors, higher well-being, and more satisfaction of the basic psychological needs. Basic need satisfaction partially mediated the relations of relative intrinsic goals to the outcomes.

In a subsequent study of adults 18–65 years of age, an accelerometer was used to provide an objective measure of moderately vigorous physical activity. After reporting on their goals and motivations, the participants wore the accelerometer for 7 days and also kept an exercise log. Participants high in relative intrinsic goal contents were more autonomously motivated for exercise, and they engaged in more daily physical activity (Sebire, Standage, & Vansteenkiste, 2011).

A study of youth in the Flemish part of Belgium applied goal contents theory (GCT) to predict levels of physical activity. Seghers, Vissers, Rutten, Decroos, and Boen (2014) measured both the goals and pedometer step counts over 7 days in more than a thousand children. Their results supported a hypothesized sequence in which intrinsic goals for leisure-time activities predicted daily step counts through autonomous motivation.

This intrinsic–extrinsic goal-content approach to studying motivation is quite different from the autonomous–controlled motives approach, and yet there are results in the two strands of SDT research that make them complementary. The fact that controlling rewards tend to undermine intrinsic motivation, impair internalization, diminish well-being, and interfere with performance is quite compatible with the findings that a focus on attaining financial goals and other external indicators of worth tends to be associated with diminished wellness, inferior learning, less satisfying relationships, and more sedentary living. What ties these two bodies of work together are their relations to satisfaction versus frustration of the basic psychological needs (Deci & Ryan, 2000).

Motivational Processes and Physical Education

In many countries around the world, children and adolescents take physical education classes, often because it is required. The reasoning for the requirements include the idea that physical activity promotes health, strength, and fitness and may also encourage participation in sports. Physical education classes thus tend to be a mix of sport and exercise. A large number of empirical studies have been done that have examined SDT concepts in physical education classes or similar settings. We review but a few of them here.

Promoting Autonomous Motivation

Early studies of physical education (PE) tended to focus on students' intrinsic motivation. For example, a study of middle school PE students found that perceived autonomy and perceived competence predicted their intrinsic motivation in the class (Goudas, Biddle, & Fox, 1994), and a study of college students studying to become PE teachers found that the students' perceived autonomy and perceived competence for a one-term Olympic gymnastics module were related to the students' intrinsic motivation for learning the module and their intentions to continue with Olympic-related learning in the future (Goudas, Biddle, & Underwood, 1995).

Other investigators focused more broadly on autonomous motivation (both intrinsic and internalized-extrinsic motivation). Taylor, Ntoumanis, Standage, and Spray (2010) used multilevel modeling with adolescent PE students and found that autonomous motivation and perceived competence predicted outcomes such as sustained physical activity outside of classes, as well as inside.

Several of the research teams who assessed autonomous motivation also examined how factors in the learning climate in PE classes influenced the students' motivation, behavior, and well-being. In one case, Mouratidis, Vansteenkiste, Sideridis, and Lens (2011) performed two field studies in PE classes for preteens that showed that, when the classes were more autonomy-supportive, the students enjoyed them more and displayed greater vitality. Further, they found that if the students were more autonomously motivated at baseline, they benefited more from the autonomy-supportive classes. In a study of PE classes in which teachers were focused on physical activities, Lonsdale, Sabiston, Raedeke, Ha, and Sum (2009) examined a particular component of autonomy support. Specifically, they found that if the teachers provided students with a free-choice period during class, their autonomous motivation showed a clear increase.

Need Support and Thwarting

Many of the studies that examined autonomy-supportive learning climates also assessed the students' need satisfaction, as well as autonomous motivation and educational outcomes. For example, Bagøien, Halvari, and Nesheim (2010) found that when PE students perceived their instructors to be more autonomy-supportive, they experienced greater need satisfaction in the classes, which generalized to their lives and resulted in greater well-being and more effort expended in physical activity. Other studies found that autonomy support from the PE teachers was associated with more student autonomous motivation (e.g., Hagger, Chatzisarantis, Barkoukis, Wang, & Baranowski, 2005; Hagger, Chatzisarantis, Culverhouse, & Biddle, 2003) and that basic need satisfaction mediated the relations from autonomy support to autonomous motivation (Standage, Duda, &

Ntoumanis, 2003). Further, Taylor and Lonsdale (2010) found that autonomy support provided by PE teachers promoted need satisfaction and, in turn, subjective vitality and effort expenditure in both British and Chinese samples, suggesting that these phenomena are cross-cultural, applying to both individualistic and collectivist cultures.

A three-wave study of secondary school students showed that their perceptions of autonomy support from their PE teachers predicted activity-related satisfaction of the basic psychological needs. In turn, relatedness need satisfaction positively predicted health-related quality of life, and competence satisfaction positively predicted both physical self-concept and autonomous motivation. Further, autonomous motivation positively predicted physical activity assessed with a pedometer, as well as health-related quality of life and physical self-concept (Standage, Gillison, Ntoumanis, & Treasure, 2012).

Additionally, Standage and colleagues (2003, 2006) found that PE students who perceived the teaching climate to be more autonomy-supportive reported greater satisfaction of the basic psychological needs and more autonomous motivation, and the teachers rated those students who were higher in autonomy as exerting more effort and being more persistent. Relatedly, a study by Parish and Treasure (2003) found that adolescent PE students whose learning climates were more need-supportive were more autonomously motivated and engaged in more physical activity, and Kalaja, Jaakkola, Watt, Liukkonen, and Ommundsen (2009), who studied seventh-grade students from Finland, found that those who were in more need-supportive interpersonal climates were higher on perceived competence, autonomous motivation, and movement in their PE classes. Another study that focused on need satisfaction in PE settings found that more need satisfaction led to more integration of motivation, which in turn was associated with greater well-being (Hagger, Chatzisarantis, & Harris, 2006).

In a study from Norway, Ulstad, Halvari, Sørebø, and Deci (2016) studied secondary PE students to test a model of PE performance that included SDT variables and learning strategies. They found that, when the teachers were perceived to be more autonomy-supportive, their students reported more satisfaction of their basic psychological needs, which predicted more autonomous motivation and perceived competence, leading to the greater use of such learning strategies as effort regulation, seeking help, and working with peers, resulting in higher grades for the students in the PE courses.

A few studies have examined motor learning, which, although not necessarily part of PE classes, is related. For example, an experiment in which participants used their nondominant hands to throw at a target found not only that autonomy support contributed to good performance—both retention and transfer—on the following day but also that having the participants focus on the target contributed in an additive fashion (Wulf, Chiviacowsky, & Drews, 2015). In other work from that group, the researchers found that providing participants with choice, even choices that were small and relatively unrelated to the target activity, had a positive effect on a motor-learning retention test (Lewthwaite, Chiviacowsky, Drews, & Wulf, 2015).

Controlling Settings

Whereas many studies reviewed herein were focused on the degree of either autonomy support or, more broadly, need support, a few studies have focused on the darker side by examining controlling or need-thwarting interpersonal environments. In a study of Belgian PE teachers, the researchers found that students' ratings of the teachers' being controlling were positively related to the ratings made by trained observers and that teachers' degree of control predicted students having controlled motivation and amotivation (De Meyer et al., 2014). Further, Papaioannou (1998) found that when there was a climate of ego involvement, which is a type of controlling context, physical education students experienced low levels of autonomy.

In sum, similar to the cases in both sport and exercise, we see that, whereas autonomy-supportive or need-supportive contexts enhance autonomous motivation and have positive consequences for physical activity, controlling or ego-involving contexts decrease autonomous motivation and promote controlled motivation or amotivation, resulting in various negative consequences.

Teachers' Need Satisfaction

The general set of findings about the consequences of autonomy-supportive versus controlling learning climates raises the interesting question of what factors might affect whether teachers are autonomy-supportive or controlling. Some researchers have investigated this question and have found results comparable to those for coaches. Simply stated, when teachers experience need satisfaction within the teaching settings, they are more likely to support the needs of their students, and when they experience need frustration, they are more likely to be need thwarting of their students. For example, Taylor and Ntoumanis (2007) found that teachers who experienced their students as being, on average, high in autonomy were more likely to provide the nutrients of autonomy support, structure, and involvement than those teachers who experienced their students as lower in autonomy. Further, this relation was found to be mediated by the teachers' own feelings of autonomy. In other words, when teachers perceived their students to be autonomous, the teachers themselves behaved more autonomously in their teaching and employed the strategies of autonomy support, structure, and involvement in relating to their students. In addition, Taylor, Ntoumanis, and Standage (2008) found that when PE teachers experienced a low level of pressure on the job, perceived their students to be high in autonomous motivation, and were themselves high in autonomous motivation, they experienced high need satisfaction, and they related to their students by gaining a better understanding of them, providing rationales for requested behaviors, and being instrumentally supportive, which previous research had shown would support students' autonomy (Deci, Eghrari, Patrick, & Leone, 1994). In short, when the PE teachers experienced support for their own needs, they in turn were more supportive of their students' needs.

In contrast, another study of PE teachers found that their perceptions of pressure on the job led to the experiences of frustration of their autonomy, competence, and relatedness needs, which in turn predicted burnout and somatic complaints. Mediation analyses confirmed the role of need frustration (Bartholomew, Ntoumanis, Cuevas, & Lonsdale, 2014), which would undoubtedly lead them to be controlling with their students (Deci, Spiegel, Ryan, Koestner, & Kauffmann, 1982).

The teachers' own personalities also made a difference to their motivation and behavior in relating to their students. For example, research with PE teachers showed that if they were high in the controlled causality orientation as an individual difference, they tended to be less autonomy-supportive and more thwarting of the students' psychological needs (Van den Berghe et al., 2013). On the other hand, PE teachers who were low on the controlled causality orientation were more likely to create autonomy-supportive teaching climates.

Interventions

Because autonomy support has been found to be so important in PE classes, researchers have begun to study interventions aimed at facilitating this attribute. For example, in one study by Perlman (2013), students were assigned to either an autonomy-supportive class, a controlling class, or a balanced class. Results indicated that those students in the autonomy-supportive class engaged in significantly more moderate to vigorous physical activity. Rosenkranz, Lubans, Peralta, Bennie, Sanders, and Lonsdale (2012) found that the use of four specific factors in class helped support students' motivation for physical activity, including standard autonomy-supportive tactics, such as providing a meaningful rationale for the activity and offering choice about activities. Research by Aelterman, Vansteenkiste, Van den Berghe, De Meyer, and Haerens (2014) found that an intervention based in SDT to facilitate PE teachers' becoming more oriented toward providing autonomy-support and structure led the teachers to value these strategies more and to behave in more autonomy-supportive ways, according to assessments by both the students and external observers. Other research testing an intervention with new PE teachers found that as the teachers improved their styles in terms of being more autonomy-supportive, structured, and interpersonally involved their students were positively responsive to these changes, experiencing more need satisfaction, more autonomy, and more engagement in the class (Tessier, Sarrazin, & Ntoumanis, 2010).

In a study illustrating practical, evidence-supported intervention, Cheon, Reeve, and Moon (2012) reported on a semester-long training program for PE teachers aimed at increasing their support for autonomy. At the beginning of the semester, they conducted a workshop focused on students' motivation and teachers' support for the students, using concepts based on SDT. They discussed concrete ways for teachers to be autonomy-supportive of the PE students, including such things as providing choice, listening and being responsive to students' ideas and questions, acknowledging mastery, providing rationales for requested behaviors, minimizing directives, not giving quick solutions to problems, reflecting students' experiences so it was clear that the teachers understood the students' perspectives, encouraging initiatives, and allowing time for independent work (e.g., Reeve, Bolt, & Cai, 1999). After 6 weeks in which the teachers were trying to put these principles into practice in their classes, there was a discussion of all the problems they had been encountering in their attempts to be autonomy-supportive. Another 6 weeks after that, there was a final discussion focused on what teachers had learned that did and didn't work for them in being autonomy-supportive. Reports from both trained observers and students in the classes indicated that teachers had become more autonomy-supportive and that the students showed improvements in their motivational and behavioral outcomes.

In a 5-month, three-wave longitudinal follow-up, Cheon and Reeve (2013) tested the stability of changes that had occurred a year earlier in the autonomy-supportive development program implemented by Cheon et al. (2012). In the follow-up study, the researchers had trained observers to rate teachers' behaviors at the middle of this 5-month period, and three times, at the beginning, middle, and end of the period, they had students report their perceptions of the teachers' autonomy support, as well as their own autonomous motivation, and various educational outcomes. Results indicated that both the trained observers and the students rated the trained teachers as more autonomy-supportive and less controlling than the teachers in the comparison group. Further, the students of teachers in the intervention group also reported more positive motivational and behavioral outcomes.

This review shows just how important and generalizable the central principles of SDT's mini-theories of CET, OIT, and basic psychological needs theory (BPNT) are to physical education. Because we see the goals of physical education as enhancing long-term interest and participation in active living and sports, especially for those already least athletically prone, the promotion of autonomy, competence, and relatedness in PE contexts is especially critical. Our hope is that this accumulating work on facilitative methods helps educators meet these goals.

Concluding Comments

People are naturally active, and physical activity is a source of great recreation and rejuvenation for many people. In this chapter, we reviewed only a fraction of the existing SDT research in three areas related to physical activity: sports, exercise, and physical education. As can be seen, interesting and parallel findings have emerged from the work in each of those three areas of inquiry. First, we saw that intrinsic motivation is important in each of these areas, albeit to different degrees. Most central is that autonomous motivation—intrinsic and well-integrated extrinsic—are extremely important for a wide range of behavioral and well-being outcomes. Further, interpersonal environments that are autonomy-supportive or, more broadly, need-supportive promote autonomous motivation and the many positive outcomes that have been shown to follow from it. Many studies have also shown that the link from environmental autonomy support or need support—for example, coaches', leaders', or teachers' supportive behaviors—to athletes', exercisers', and students' autonomous motivation are mediated by those individuals' basic psychological need satisfactions.

CHAPTER 20

Motivation and Need Satisfaction in Video Games and Virtual Environments

Humans have a remarkable capacity to imagine themselves in other places and roles, and modern technology has made such experiences ever more accessible and vivid through the creation of virtual worlds. In this chapter, we use the arena of video games to examine motivational processes in virtual worlds. Video games have become ubiquitous in part because people can readily experience satisfaction of needs for competence, relatedness, and autonomy within them. In turn these in-game need satisfactions are a function of identifiable game elements, such as the availability of choices of goals and avatar features, multiple types of competence feedback, and opportunities to cooperate with other players. Studies have further shown that the *immediacy, consistency,* and *density* of need satisfactions contribute to game-play enjoyment and immersion and are associated with variations in players' short-term well-being and future desire to play. Yet because games are designed to be both immersive and need satisfying, some gamers overplay, which SDT addresses through its *need density hypothesis,* which concerns the ratio of the player's experience of need satisfactions in game play compared to everyday life. We also review SDT research on how need frustration in games can have negative consequences, including heightened postgame aggression. Moving beyond video games, we discuss how some of the motivational features and designs of video games that make them so engaging have been, more or less adequately, imported into educational, organizational training, and behavior-change programs, a process sometimes referred to as *gamification*. We also discuss the promise and costs of augmentation devices that provide people with information that can enhance, as well as segment, their realities and wellness.

One of the unique features of being human is that we do not have to *be* where we are. Humans appear to be alone among species in their capacity to *imagine* (Leslie, 1987). Imagination is a capacity to entertain alternative possibilities and realities. It emerges early in development and is central to play, as children happily pretend to be various characters in fantasized worlds (Harris, 2000). Fortunately, imagination lives on across the lifespan. The imaginative capacity is fundamental to the ability to problem-solve, to think ahead, and to understand others' perspectives (Greene, 2000). Imagination can also be used to regulate mood and personal experience, such as by daydreaming or getting lost in novels. People can use their imaginations to escape and reenergize by allowing themselves to enter into alternative realities and, at least provisionally, accept these fabricated worlds as real.

Over the past century, technology has dramatically enhanced people's access to such alternative worlds (Bailenson & Blascovich, 2011; Rigby & Ryan, 2011, 2016). Today everyone with a computer or a smartphone and time to spare can enter into numerous software-simulated settings, or virtual worlds, in which they are able not only to watch events unfold but also to make decisions and act. We define such *virtual realities* loosely as artificial environments created through technologies within which users suspend belief and accept them as environments. Virtual realities are the media-constructed worlds that are distinct from our molecular existences, into which we can, under the right conditions, immerse ourselves. For present purposes, we contrast virtual realities with *everyday realities*, the real-time, concrete worlds that each person wakes up to in the morning.

Within SDT, we have taken virtual realities seriously because, although these worlds may be in some sense unreal, psychological experiences within them can indeed be very real. It is the ability of an alternative reality to enhance or catalyze meaningful psychological experiences, including basic psychological need satisfactions, that provide its motivational "pull" or attractiveness. Increasingly, people are finding virtual worlds engaging and even compelling, and this presents both challenges and promises with regard to human motivation and performance.

There are many varieties of virtual experiences (W. Ryan, Cornick, Blascovich, & Bailenson, in press), and many angles of research into media, imagination, and virtual worlds are relevant to SDT (e.g., see Calvo & Peters, 2014; Rigby & Ryan, 2011, 2016). Thus, in exploring the issue of alternative and virtual realities in this chapter, our approach is more illustrative than comprehensive. Our main focus is on *video games* and the virtual worlds they involve.

Video Games as an Alternative Reality

What makes the study of video games particularly intriguing from a motivational standpoint is that, unlike passive media such as movies or TV, people are actively engaged in motivated, purposive actions *within* the media. Thus one can study how motivational design and features in games specifically enhance or detract from intrinsic motivation and immersion (e.g., Peng, Lin, Pfeiffer, & Winn, 2012). Games thus provide an incredible laboratory for examining principles of human motivation at work in a controlled setting (Elson, Breuer, & Quandt, 2014). In addition, people are not only motivated *within* games; they are motivated *for* games. Research can thus explore what is energizing people's involvement with interactive entertainment media (e.g., Whitbourne, Ellenberg, & Akimoto, 2013) and what drives so many to have harmonious or obsessive passion to play (Przybylski, Weinstein, Ryan, & Rigby, 2009; Vallerand, 2015).

The new landscape of video games and other technology-inspired virtual worlds also calls out for closer examination of the boundaries between authentic and inauthentic experiences and of the psychological *reality* of need satisfactions within virtual venues. As we have studied video games, we have seen that in-game experiences affect well-being outside the game. Games can be used for either recovery or escape from what is happening outside of the games. Indeed, for a person whose everyday reality yields few satisfactions, time spent in a game world in which these psychological need satisfactions are "low-hanging fruit" may be especially attractive.

The potential for virtual worlds to be psychologically real also raises questions about people's reactions to, and involvement with, the gratifications and experiences these games offer. We thus look specifically at violent content in games and their role in motivation and aggression. Does violence in games add to intrinsic motivation? Does violence in a virtual world lead to aggression or violence in everyday reality? We also explore video game overuse and "addiction" and how these problems relate to need satisfactions and frustrations in both virtual and everyday realities. These questions all concern the boundaries between virtual and real events, which, from a psychological viewpoint, are more permeable than we might expect.

Alternative Worlds Are Not All That New; Virtual Ones Are

Since the beginning of human history, people have traveled psychologically to places beyond their natural environments to have immersive experiences. Storytelling may have been the earliest form of such imaginative transportation. Oral traditions, rituals, and myths could carry people to past worlds and heroic times. Yet hearing these would be only an occasional event, and certainly not the readily accessible portals away from the here-and-now that we possess today.

Perhaps the first popularly accessible avenue to alternative worlds opened up with the printed novel. Since Cervantes created *Don Quixote,* novels have transported people to other lands and times they might not otherwise imagine. Yet, the mass consumption of novels emerged only in the 18th century, which is recent by historical standards. Since then markets for genres, narratives, and settings of every variety have developed. Fictional "realities" from fantasy to ultrarealism are available into which any willing reader can become immersed.

Electronic mass media emerged in the 1920s with the radio, which brought narrative drama to the living rooms of millions. No one can argue that the epic storytelling exemplified by Orson Welles's *War of the Worlds* did not provide people a virtual experience. And so did the implausible detective stories so popular in the radio era. With radio also began the age of instant information, as news of the world could arrive with a speed previously unknown.

With the advent of television in the 1950s, the public's absorption with electronic media truly escalated, and in some ways the infatuation with TV has not ceased. In fact, the average U.S. adult today is exposed to more than 25 hours of TV per week (cf. Television Bureau of Advertising, 2012), suggesting that watching TV is still an activity with great motivational pull—in fact, it pulls people right onto the couch and into the virtual worlds of television events and characters.

When viewing television, people are physically sedentary and mentally passive—that is, receptive rather than active. They become immersed in the industry-scripted stories as they unfold on the screen in front of them. Whereas with novels and radio the audience must visualize events and interactions, the medium of television supplies both the story and the visuals, making it more impressive than expressive as a media form (Rigby & Ryan, 2016).

Beginning in the 1960s, a major shift in the immersive possibilities of media emerged—namely, the creation of interactive virtual environments, or video games. Video games first appeared in public arcades and moved into homes during the following decade. Early simple games such as *Pong* captured the attention of millions as, for the first time, people were provided opportunities to experience a tennis-like competence from their chairs, any time of day or night.

Since the days of *Pong*, video games have rapidly evolved. They are now available on specialized platforms (e.g., game consoles), personal computers, and, ubiquitously, on smartphones, thus further penetrating people's leisure hours. Video games have, in fact, become one of today's dominant entertainment industries. Some video games offer expansive open worlds within which there are seemingly endless places to travel and explore. Others are small games that can be played in the empty nooks and crannies of existence—on a smartphone while in line at the bank or waiting at a bus stop. Nonstop virtual engagement has become available. A 2009 Kaiser Foundation survey (see *http://kff.org/other/event/generation-m2-media-in-the-lives-of*) showed, for example, that U.S. children and teens ages 8–18 spent more than 6 hours a day with various electronic media, including games, social networking, and online programming. Norms are similar throughout East Asia and European Union countries, in fact, anyplace where technological devices have penetrated the culture.

This brief history suggests an important truth about cultural evolution. Our involvement in media-accessed alternative worlds has been massively growing, but only in very recent human history. As new mass media and technologies have made it ever more possible for people to be in mental spaces other than where they physically are, many if not most humans have been very ready to get on board. From novels to radio to TV to computer games, people have readily participated in these opportunities to experience worlds and settings separate from their molecular or everyday lived environments. Current technologies not only narrate alternative worlds but also offer alternative worlds within which people can have a role.

Video Games and Their Motivational Processes

Because video games have become ubiquitous and many people spend considerable time and effort engaged in them, often with passion and enthusiasm, games provide an excellent arena in which to study motivation and engagement. For example, researchers can examine how features of games affect in-game satisfactions and frustrations. Games can be simple and easily paced or can be complex, with steep learning curves. They can be solitary or social. They can be competitive or cooperative. Importantly, as with all human contexts, such features (and the actions and interactions they afford) can support or thwart basic psychological needs, often affecting players as strongly as "real world" interactions.

Indeed, it is clear that virtual realities, despite not being real, supply myriad opportunities for satisfying or frustrating basic psychological needs. People can, for example, feel extremely competent in a virtual game of *Tetris* or *Angry Birds*. The obtained feeling of competence may be no less real than the competence they feel in a sport match, a table game of cards, or even a school- or work-related project. It may also be a less vicarious feeling of competence than they would enjoy at the end of a movie such as *Rocky* or *Lord of the Rings*. A multiplayer game such as *World of Warcraft* (in which people typically team up with others) can also offer opportunities for relatedness that may be as psychologically satisfying for the player as any team sport or club activity. Similarly, open-world games can offer players boundless opportunities to experience autonomy, as they can personalize characters, choose goals and quests, and decide where and with whom to travel in these extensive (albeit constructed) game environments. In short, virtual realities, through their design features, narratives, feedback, and goal structures, can afford multiple and potent need satisfactions, often with more reliability than the contexts people experience in schools, workplaces, and sport fields.

When we began our initial investigations into video games (Ryan, Rigby, & Przybylski, 2006), we assumed that the gravitational pull of engaging games—the factors that make them so attractive to so many—would be the ways in which they would satisfy basic psychological needs. At that time, the literature of empirical psychology had little to say on the topic of why video games were engaging. Instead, the psychological research on video games seemed fixated on the "dark sides" of computer gaming (Przybylski, Rigby, & Ryan, 2010). Dozens of papers showed correlations between video game play and poor achievement, obesity, attention-deficit disorders, and violence. In fact, nearly every ill imaginable seemed to be correlated with video game play. As important as these relations might be, what seemed missing was any serious account of why so many people wanted to play these games and what they derived from doing so.

For many people, the answer to this question seemed perhaps too obvious: People play video games because they are "fun." Yet this seemingly self-explanatory answer is anything but. First, the word *fun* denotes an experience of amusement and enjoyment and may pertain to something whimsical or unimportant. Yet observations of people engaged in video games suggests that their involvement can look serious, as well as whimsical. Often people are concentrating, problem solving, planning, or preparing. Because there are so many facets to engagement in most games, the notion of fun is too limited to account for game motivation.

Instead of fun, our initial conception was that video gamers' engagement could be better understood using the broader concept of *intrinsic motivation*, which concerns the inherent psychological need satisfactions found in playing the games. When intrinsically motivated, people can be interested and seriously engaged. Clearly, few players receive extrinsic rewards for playing video games; indeed, most have to pay or overcome barriers in order to play. That realization led us to ask, What makes certain games so intrinsically motivating? As game developer Bartle (2004) put it, "the players must expect to get something out of their experience" (p. 128).

Ryan, Rigby, and Przybylski (2006) presented four studies that specifically looked at the relations between video games and basic psychological need satisfactions. They assumed that basic need satisfactions during play would predict changes in both motivation and short-term well-being during game play. Recall that *basic psychological need theory* (BPNT; Chapter 10) specifies that the impact of any activity on people's well-being is a function of satisfactions of the autonomy, competence, and relatedness needs. Although many might find it implausible that a nonserious activity such as playing a video game can increase well-being, these authors suggested instead that insofar as a virtual environment affords or supports experiences of volition, effectiveness, and social connection, it should yield enhancements in a player's well-being. The fact of obtaining need satisfaction from game play could thus explain in part why so many people are drawn to video games.

In the first study, participants were assigned to play a popular video game with a single-player format that offered primarily competence challenges. It was hypothesized that variations in felt competence during play would predict both liking of the game and a behavioral decision to continue playing the game during a free-choice period. The hypothesis was strongly supported. In addition, those who experienced high satisfactions of autonomy and competence in this solo game play showed a short-term enhancement in well-being, whereas those low in autonomy or competence satisfactions during play showed increased negative mood, lower subjective vitality, and lower state self-esteem.

In a second study, participants played two role-playing games on different days, in a counterbalanced order, which were known a priori to differ in popularity. The idea was to see whether need satisfaction accounted for the differential liking of these games.

Results showed that players' in-game autonomy and competence experiences accounted for their differential preference for these games, as well as differences in their rated fun and enjoyment. Expanding on this, a third study brought participants in four times to play four different games so that both between- and within-person variations in motivation and experience could be assessed. As might be expected, there were between-person differences in the overall satisfaction derived from gaming, regardless of the game played. Nonetheless, at both between- and within-person levels of analysis, experiences of autonomy and competence robustly predicted enjoyment and preferences for future play. In addition, when participants played games in which they felt more competence, they showed short-term gains in vitality, self-esteem, and positive mood. Individuals who experienced more autonomy also experienced higher self-esteem, positive mood, and expressed value for the game. These findings suggest that, like other forms of recreation, video gaming experiences can yield at least short-term positive effects on psychological wellness and mood insofar as they fulfill basic psychological needs.

Whereas the first three studies focused on autonomy and competence needs, a fourth study in this series focused on a multiplayer game, in which social interactions were possible. In this context Ryan, Rigby, and Przybylski (2006) hypothesized that relatedness satisfaction might also play a significant role, which in fact it did. Game enjoyment was a function of all three basic need satisfactions. In addition, all three need satisfactions predicted well-being outcomes and future motivation to play.

The enhancement of short-term well-being found in the Ryan, Rigby, and Przybylski (2006) studies as a function of the need satisfactions experienced in video games has since been frequently replicated. Of course, this makes sense from a general SDT perspective: Need satisfaction enhances wellness, as we argued in BPNT and have observed in studies reported across many domains and activities. Such findings have, however, unnerved those who expect only negative outcomes from video games. Although we address negative outcomes later in this chapter, for the moment we simply underscore that video games, like other forms of recreation, have, as a big part of their appeal, a capacity to yield feelings of competence, autonomy, and relatedness and the enjoyment and wellness associated with these need-satisfaction experiences.

Psychological Needs within Video Games

Because video games are to a significant degree intrinsically motivated, persistence at them necessarily depends on basic need satisfactions, as specified within CET. In what follows, we highlight some of the ways in which each of the basic psychological needs for autonomy, competence, and relatedness is satisfied in such games and some of the in-game factors that can facilitate or obstruct need satisfaction.

Competence Needs in Video Games

From the earliest video games, such as *Space Invaders,* up to more recent mobile device games, such as *Minecraft* and *Candy Crush,* perhaps the most pervasive satisfaction built into games is the feeling of *competence.* As described throughout this book, feelings of competence come about when people have opportunities to apply skills and effort to tasks that are moderately difficult, allowing them to experience efficacy and success and thus to derive feelings of mastery and competence. Most every video game builds in elements that saliently support feelings of competence. Even *Pong,* the earliest popular home-playable game in which the sole instruction was to "use the paddle to avoid missing an electronic ball," provided numeric scores that players could constantly strive to improve. Moreover, players could raise the speed of the bouncing ball to progressively find greater challenges to stretch their abilities.

Many successful games today continue with this theme of adjustable challenges. Some include a structure called *leveling,* in which players can experience competence feedback when they achieve proximal goals and move up to a higher level. Progression through levels or ranks is usually accompanied by receiving more tools or capacities (e.g., a more damaging sword or new powers). People's ranks or levels also typically dictate what type of challenges they can pursue, thereby providing more optimally scaffolding challenges for players in different spots on the learning curve. The design of most such games makes "leveling up" relatively quick and easy in the beginning but requiring increasing amounts of effort as the players' levels progress. This schedule of feedback and awards is designed to facilitate early engagement and to encourage more investment of time and effort as the players progress more deeply into the game.

Interestingly, although many people assume, based largely on flow theory (Csikszentmihalyi, 1975), that an optimal design of games would be continuously increasing challenges, this is not always the case. Intrinsic motivation is primarily predicted by feelings of mastery; thus positive feedback is particularly crucial (Rigby & Ryan, 2011; Schmierbach, Chung, Wu, & Kim, 2014). Moreover, variety matters, especially when variety is intermixed with strong success experiences. Thus challenges that move both up and down have been shown to increase immersion more than just a steady increase in difficulty (e.g., Qin, Rau, & Salvendy, 2010).

Another element in games that supports competence is the *clarity of goals.* Rarely in games is there ambiguity about what is required to get ahead. Whether it is scoring more, completing more quests, or killing more enemies, for example, it is usually spelled out clearly. Again, we can contrast this with everyday realities, in which the paths to success for many people are much less clear and along which feedback or rewards can feel quite distant or delayed.

Particularly salient in relation to competence is rich, multilevel, effectance-relevant, positive competence feedback. As specified within CET, positive feedback, assuming it is not controlling, enhances intrinsic motivation (Deci & Ryan, 1980a). Good video games are replete with positive feedback, usually offered at multiple levels and through multiple channels. Rigby and Ryan (2011) provided a prime example of rich feedback mechanisms in a former top-title game called *Guitar Hero,* a music game in which people hit notes in synchrony with music on a guitar-shaped controller. First, the game provides multiple sources of immediate *granular feedback.* When notes are hit, there are small onscreen explosions to give immediate effectance feedback. Points rise instantly, and a meter on the screen reacts to each input. Complementing granular feedback is *sustained feedback*: As successive notes are hit, an on-screen "meter" rises and becomes more green; the crowd also roars louder with each well-timed hit. Simultaneously, there are visible "point multipliers" to show that the player is "on a roll." At still another level are sources of *cumulative feedback*—both displays of point totals for a given song and statistics such as percentage of notes hit. Moreover, there is success and failure feedback for the song, with each performance adding to the band's "fame" numbers and opening up opportunities to play bigger (fantasy) venues. Throughout all of this, the players have choice about how difficult they want the tasks to be (e.g., how many "strings" must be in play), virtually guaranteeing that anyone can experience some level of success.

Many casual video games are pure competence games, with rich, dense feedback. They allow players to take on graded challenges and get positive feedback in very brief periods of time. They are loved by many people who get few affirmations of competence elsewhere in their lives. These satisfactions of casual games can effectively boost mood, as demonstrated by Russoniello, O'Brien, and Parks (2009), which also draws people back again and again to their smartphones for a fix of this pleasure.

In sum, positive feedback is ubiquitous in modern games, and it comes in many forms (Lyons, 2015). Sometimes people receive visual confirmation of success, sometimes points, sometimes achievement badges, and sometimes in-game rewards or status boosts. All these features have their motivational impact by enhancing feelings of competence (Suh, Wagner, & Liu, 2015). It is important to note, however, that often designers think badges and in-game rewards are motivating when sometimes they are not adding to the game (McKernan et al., 2015; Ronimus, Kujala, Tolvanen, & Lyytinen, 2014).

Rich feedback is only one aspect of how competence experiences are facilitated in games. Another issue concerns the smoothness of the interface through which players' actions in a game are mediated. Ryan, Rigby, and Przybylski (2006) developed a variable that they labeled *intuitive controls,* reflecting the player's sense that the mechanisms through which they control actions or avatars are easy to use and readily translate their intentions into the correct actions. The more intuitive the controls, the less the players are aware of them, and the more effectiveness and mastery they feel in their engagement. Other researchers have similarly shown the importance of controllers for feelings of competence and immersion (e.g., Skalski, Tamborini, Shelton, Buncher, & Lindmark, 2011).

Autonomy Needs in Video Games

Many games are designed almost exclusively with a focus on competence satisfaction. That is, many games are essentially elaborate puzzles or reaction-time tasks. But as the game industry has developed, in an effort to make games more compelling and engaging, it has introduced more and more elements that offer autonomy in both the game contents and game designs.

First of all, the very nature of virtual environments removes some real-world constraints and opens up choices that are often unavailable in everyday realities. Opportunities for choice are built into the basic design of many games from the start. People often begin a game by choosing an avatar—a self-representation that will enact their agency within a virtual space. Unlike the real-world facticity of having to live in the bodies they inherited, many virtual worlds allow people to select a body type, gender, race, and face (and these are not even limited to human categories). Such customization is intended to increase the personal relevance and sense of agency (Sundar & Marthe, 2010), and experimental research by Kim et al. (2015) verified that an option for customizing players' characters increased experiences of autonomy relative to a no-customization condition. Similarly, Birk, Atkins, Bowey, and Mandryk (2016) showed that identification with game avatars could enhance autonomy, immersion, effort, and game enjoyment. They further demonstrated that avatar identification predicted more free-choice time in a game.

Second, many games allow players to choose activities and roles from an increasingly large menu. In many virtual worlds, people can choose where to travel, whom to meet up with, and what missions to undertake at any time from among many options. As technology has increased capacities for information access and storage, choices over what to do in a game space, options for strategies on how to do it, and the openness of worlds in which to pursue quests, missions, and character development just keep getting greater and greater.

In Chapters 5 and 6 we discussed how primates are intrinsically motivated by opportunities simply to explore and manipulate (e.g., see Harlow, 1953a). Famous games such as *World of Warcraft* endure in popularity in part because they tap into this natural urge to explore. They provide ever-new worlds to investigate, each with its own unique landscape, cultural groups, and challenges. Part of the "fun" of these open worlds is just going around the corner to see what is there—much like a traveler in a new city of the molecular world—without the hassle of an airport security check or the expense of an airline ticket. These intrinsic satisfactions of exploration are immediate.

In fact, people who are outside of gaming experiences often miss the attractions of certain games, mistaking content for process. An excellent illustration of this is the well-publicized controversies over the *Grand Theft Auto* (GTA) series, one of the most popular and profitable games in history. As McCarthy, Curran, and Byron (2005) argued, the game's provocative antisocial content made it "easy to lose sight of why it was such a successful game in the first place. People don't play it for the violence; they play it because it affords the opportunity to do whatever they please" (p. 24). Similarly, games such as *Red Dead Redemption*, a gunslinging Wild West game, are attractive precisely because people can mount a horse and run in any direction through a rich, open landscape, finding wide-ranging adventures (from their couch).

We emphasize these open-world elements because they relate to a key factor that facilitates experiences of autonomy in virtual worlds—*opportunities for action*. These opportunities for action are not by any means limited to games of sport or war. One of the most successful games in history, *The Sims,* is played by mostly female subscribers. In *The Sims,* the players can build houses, raise families, and have careers of a "real world" sort—but in ways driven by their own whims and choices. Whether or not people approve of the cultural contents being reinforced in such games, the games clearly provide opportunities to act with agency in a virtual playground.

Relatedness in Video Games

The idea that people can satisfy the need for relatedness within games may raise some skepticism. Yet, as we reviewed in previous chapters, relatedness needs are satisfied when others recognize and support one's self and when the person feels able to connect with, feel significant with, and be helpful to others. Games can provide these satisfactions in many ways. They can even satisfy relatedness when no other players are involved.

Multiplayer Interactions and Relatedness

When massive multiplayer online games (MMOs) were introduced, they represented a new level of virtual-world experiences by allowing *player-controlled* avatars that could ambulate, gesture, and communicate with each other. People could meet, affiliate, and commune with others who might in the real world be people they would never meet. Indeed, for some people, who might, by virtue of temperament, appearance, or other obstacles, not find it easy to meet and connect with others, virtual worlds afford them previously unavailable opportunities for social interactions.

Multiplayer game designers have increasingly facilitated opportunities for player-to-player interactions through features such as guilds, chat boxes, audio capability for dialogue, and easy "grouping" mechanisms. Moreover, games are often structured so as to strongly reward cooperative play and teamwork. By design, accomplishing some tasks is made much easier by cooperation with other players (e.g., "boss fights"). In part, such designs are put in place precisely because designers expect that these cooperative experiences will foster relatedness satisfactions and add to sustained game motivation, as SDT would predict.

Video games thus offer a range of interaction options, from participating in enduring cooperatives and guilds with joint tasks and goals to momentary task-focused or competitive interactions. Multiplayer games can offer a rich and textured social world—one in which players actually have things to do together. They provide activities in which there are possibilities for cooperation, helping, and sharing, and this allows for relationship experiences that can feel deeply edifying. Indeed, even today's casual video games, often played on smartphones, allow individuals to play with or against friends or acquaintances.

Indeed, the opportunity to play with others is among the main reasons that children say they play video games, along with seeking fun and challenges and relieving stress (Ferguson & Olson, 2014). Similarly, adults say the major reason they play casual games is to connect with other people, along with gaining the feelings of competence these games supply (Whitbourne et al., 2013). Clearly, a lot of real people go to virtual worlds to connect with other real people.

NPCs and Relatedness

Early computer games were mostly a kind of solitary, pinball-like experience. People could watch you play, or, in some instances, they could compete against you, but in terms of in-game action, you (or your *Pac-man*) were mostly on your own. Yet, as technology has advanced, games have become more and more populated, both by designer-controlled characters that are called *NPCs* (non-player characters) and by other players.

NPCs were originally often little more than block figures with limited movements and a few, highly scripted words. In contrast, recent games provide NPCs that are compelling (often being performed by actors) and interactive—their words and actions can be made contingent on what the player does in the game. As this interactive nature of NPCs has become enhanced, players' experiences of relatedness to NPCs have felt ever more compelling. For example, NPCs in some current games will laud the players for specific deeds they have done in a game. Others can help a player in trouble, engendering gratitude. In a game gloomily titled *Left 4 Dead,* a player can team up with NPCs to fend off zombies. The NPCs can in turn rescue the player. Oddly, in some studies of this game (see Rigby & Ryan, 2011), some players reported more relatedness to these NPCs than to the characters controlled by their fellow human players. It seems that the players had automatic positive emotional responses to these NPCs, which had been quicker to respond to them when they were in need. Similarly, in some games (e.g., *Fallout 3*) players can acquire a companion pet that travels along with their avatars, often aiding them. Players have reported tremendous attachment to such pets and helpers. Our point is that relatedness, being in part a function of contingent responsiveness, can be experienced toward animated virtual characters who demonstrate this attribute.

Between-Genre Comparisons in Need Satisfaction

Different types or genres of video games afford distinct profiles of the psychological needs they can gratify. Solitary puzzle games such as *Solitaire* or *Candy Crush* are, for example, largely focused on competence satisfactions, as are many music (e.g., *Guitar Hero*), strategy (e.g. *Civilization*), and racing (especially early ones) games. When games offer more open worlds, with many choices for how and where to pursue adventures (e.g.,

Zelda, Halo), they also begin to enhance both competence and autonomy satisfactions, thus becoming even more compelling. This combination of autonomy and competence needs, in fact, defines the large category of games called *RPGs* (role-playing games), in which a player assumes the identity of a fictional character, typically with a heroic storyline. Many newer RPGs also afford open worlds and plenty of choices concerning quests and pursuits supporting autonomy, along with dense positive feedback concerning progress (see Rigby & Przybylski, 2009).

Games with strong features relevant to all three needs (e.g., multiplayer options in an open world with dense feedback) can become extremely engaging, often leading to tremendous persistence, even overuse, as we address shortly. In addition, just as sports teams lead to experiences of relatedness, the cooperation and coordination in the direction of group goals in video games can yield similar experiences. This is clearly the case in *M-FPS* (multiplayer first-person shooter) games such as *Call of Duty,* which require coordinated efforts and necessitate that individuals team up for success. This can lead to intense camaraderie, along with the sense of autonomy and competence that comes with complex and spontaneous "in the field" decision making, accompanied by immediate feedback, both visceral and symbolic.

Although, typically, one does not associate competitive or violent video games with relatedness, in fact, many such games engender strong team spirit and camaraderie. Fighting with others against enemies in violent video games can bring people closer. For example, Adachi, Hodson, Willoughby, and Zanette (2015) showed that playing cooperatively with outgroup members against a common enemy (viz., zombies) reduced the participants' prejudice toward that players' outgroup.

Empirical Support for Need-Satisfaction Hypotheses in Gaming Contexts

Tamborini, Bowman, Eden, Grizzard, and Organ (2010) suggested that media enjoyment was more than simple pleasure attainment and that it could be more richly described through the lens of SDT's basic psychological need satisfactions. To support their hypothesis, they examined video game enjoyment and need satisfaction in an experimental setting, while at the same time manipulating features of the game that they expected would directly impact specific need satisfactions. As they predicted, game enjoyment was indeed a function of SDT's basic need satisfactions, which accounted for more than 50% of the variance in enjoyment. Moreover, they also showed, by manipulating specific features of games, that these features influenced specific need satisfactions. For instance, offering multiplayer options increased relatedness satisfaction, whereas improved control-interface features enhanced competence.

Oliver, Bowman, Woolley, Rogers, Sherrick, and Chung (2015) critiqued the notion of fun or enjoyment as not being sufficient to understand the satisfactions that motivate video game play, or entertainment use more generally. People also seek challenges, meaning, and other satisfactions. They therefore applied SDT to study people's perceptions of both fun and meaningful games, arguing that basic psychological need satisfactions largely account for experiences of both fun and meaning. They also added that a *need for insight* could be satisfied in games and, along with basic need satisfactions, would add to meaning. Their research showed that players saw meaningful games as more story-based and more associated with the satisfaction of the relatedness need and their proposed need for insight. Moreover, regardless of whether a game was meaningful or not, autonomy and competence need satisfactions accounted for enjoyment.

Peng et al. (2012) experimentally demonstrated the strong importance of autonomy and competence need satisfactions to sustained engagement in video games. They used an exercise video game with multiple features, which they manipulated to test the effects of need satisfaction. Specifically, they created conditions in which the "exergame" was played either with or without autonomy or competence enhancements. Thus, in one condition, an autonomy enhancement was turned "on," providing players with increased choices about customizing their characters, and was compared to an "off" condition, in which no choices were offered. Similarly, in a competence-enhancement condition, the game featured a difficulty adjustment system to create more optimal challenges, whereas in the "off" condition difficulty levels remained constant. These feature changes did indeed affect players' game enjoyment, motivation for future play, game ratings, and other outcomes. Most relevantly, these enhancement features being on or off affected need satisfaction, with choice affecting autonomy satisfaction and difficulty modulation affecting competence satisfaction. Peng et al. (2012) showed that these positive effects of facilitating features on engagement-related outcomes were mediated by autonomy and competence need satisfactions, supporting the CET perspective on what makes a game intrinsically motivating (Chapters 6 and 7).

These and a growing body of studies link need satisfaction in virtual worlds to motivation, vitality, and wellness outcomes. In addition, a reciprocal point is that need frustrations in games can also have costs, as we subsequently address. Yet, before turning to these issues, we have some additional observations about the properties of virtual worlds that influence their capacity to satisfy psychological needs.

Built to Satisfy: Immediacy, Consistency, and Density

Unlike many life experiences in work, school, or even some other leisure pursuits, video games are built to provide psychological need satisfactions with an *immediacy, consistency,* and *density* unparalleled in most other contexts (Rigby & Ryan, 2011). *Immediacy* refers to the idea that people can access these opportunities for need gratification quickly and easily. With the increased mobility of games, this gratification can occur nearly anywhere. Indeed, games are increasingly being developed to conform to the needs of mobile users by providing attributes of easy access and entrance to the flow of the game, as well as having no penalty for exits. The trend is to make the satisfactions of play ever more accessible and readily at hand. Ideally, there is little delay in the feedback or outcomes derived from one's actions in these freely available virtual spaces.

Consistency conveys the idea that games will predictably and reliably deliver on their promise of engagement and need satisfaction. In contrast to non-virtual-world activities in which there are few guarantees, good video games rarely let people down. Said differently, games usually offer a "just world" in which the contingencies between actions and outcomes are clear and dependable.

Finally, *density* refers to the idea that these virtual environments are engineered to yield need satisfaction with a very high rate of frequency, often in a way that most everyday contexts cannot possibly match. Writing a book, for example, can certainly provide competence and autonomy satisfaction, yet much delay of gratification is involved, and there are likely to be times in the process when those needs may feel frustrated. In contrast, games provide goals and quests that can be rapidly completed with immediate positive feedback. Real-world altruism is need satisfying (Weinstein & Ryan, 2010), but one has to wait for a person in need. In contrast, games can provide multiple immediate situations in which players can help others and thus experience altruism and relatedness. Good games, that is, are packed with opportunities for need-satisfying actions.

These properties of immediacy, consistency, and density of satisfactions are a big part of the strong appeal of virtual realities. Satisfaction, often denied in the real world, can be had in a virtual context without delay. Yet these properties are also part of the hazards for participants. Just as we prefer sugar because in our evolutionary design this preference led us to truly safe nutrients, we prefer need-satisfying contexts because of their enhancing effects on development and wellness. Yet sugar can also be "inserted" in either nutritious or non-nutritious foods, and the same can be true in engineered virtual environments. Game designers can build need satisfactions into both healthy and unhealthy virtual activities.

Immersion: Making Experiences Psychologically Compelling

People can become so engaged in a virtual activity that they temporarily forget they are "in a game." In the same way that people gripped by a movie forget they are in the audience, immersion places the player within the virtual space and potentially amplifies in-game experiences and their impacts. Ryan, Rigby, and Przybylski (2006) referred to this absorbing engagement as *presence*, or *immersion*: people's sense that they are, psychologically speaking, *within* the game world, as opposed to experiencing themselves as agents outside the game, manipulating controls or characters. Presence involves the *illusion of nonmediation*, meaning that people perceive and respond to events within a medium as if the medium were not there (Lombard & Ditton, 1997).

Although the concept of presence applies to all media, from a good work of fiction to a TV drama, interactive virtual environments can amplify the possibilities of presence by their creation of multiple and varied cues in a world and allowing people to interact with them as they would act in the world. For example, evidence suggests that people more fully feel the rewards and failures of performance when playing a game versus watching others engage in the same actions (Kätsyri, Hari, Ravaja, & Nummenmaa, 2013).

Game designers work hard to facilitate presence by making the experience of virtual worlds feel real and authentic and by creating graphically realistic environments. Yet this investment of graphics, however aesthetically pleasing, is, interestingly, not typically the strongest predictor of whether a world can create presence for a player. The capacity for immersion is, indeed, less about graphic realism and more about a flow of psychological satisfactions that keep players fluidly and fully engaged within the game world (Rigby & Ryan, 2011). It is precisely when psychological needs are frustrated that players are apt to break into their experience and wonder "about" the game or the controls, or question why they are currently engaged. In contrast, when, within a virtual world, players feel effective, engaged in choice, and connected with others in the game, they more readily "sink in" to the virtual experience. Immersion can occur even within a highly animated physical environment, showing that it is not the graphics that primarily determine presence but, rather, ongoing opportunities for meaningful, need-satisfying activities.

Ryan, Rigby, and Przybylski (2006) described and assessed three types or aspects of presence, namely *narrative presence* (the virtual environment supplies a storyline or fantasy that players can identify with and find engaging), *emotional presence* (people have feelings and emotions that are authentic for the events and setting), and *physical presence* (the world feels compelling and practical as a field for action; movement and perception within the game are seamless). Ryan, Rigby, and Przybylski (2006) then examined the determinants of immersion in several game play contexts. For most games, the three facets of presence loaded together to form an overall presence score. Findings further showed that the overall experience of presence or immersion was stronger in games in which basic need satisfactions, especially for autonomy and competence, were more attainable.

Ryan, Rigby, and Przybylski (2006) also found that intuitive control consoles significantly contributed to presence or immersion. To the extent that players felt easy mastery over the game interface through which the character in the game was controlled, the less broken was the psychological flow of the game, so the more there was an experience of "nonmediation." In contrast, when players had to struggle to translate intentions into actions, presence was disrupted. This again bespeaks the importance of authentic agency—that is, players acting from their true experience—as an element in what makes any virtual reality psychologically compelling. Similarly, any thwarts to volition, efficacy, and connectedness can lead to feelings of disconnection, pulling players out of the game and breaking immersion (see also Skalski et al., 2011).

Problems with Video Games: Overuse, Compensation, and Aggression

The increased participation of people in video games and virtual worlds has been attended by considerable controversy about the content of games and the value of sustained play (Kirsch, 2006). Some scholars have argued that participation in computer games has a number of negative effects, including increased tendencies toward aggression and violence, lower physical and mental health, lower achievement and productivity, and more impoverished relationships (e.g., Anderson, Gentile, & Buckley, 2007; Healy, 1990; Setzer & Duckett, 2000). There is also concern that individuals can become "addicted" to games to the detriment of the rest of their lives. Yet other scholars suggest that much of the critical research on games has been heavily selective and/or biased (e.g., see Ferguson, 2007a, 2015a). Still other scholars cite psychological benefits from computer game play, including increases in player's well-being (Johnson, Jones, Scholes, & Carras, 2013) and the development of more complex cognitive and perceptual skills (Gee, 2003). SDT has a perspective on both of these issues, namely the issues of video game addiction and residual violence. We take them in turn.

Video Game Overuse and "Addiction"

A variety of surveys suggest that adolescents in developed nations are spending double-digit hours per week playing video games and related activities. Many allocate more time to gaming than they do to eating with their families, doing homework, reading, or being physically active. Yet it is not only teenagers who are so occupied. A 2005 survey conducted in the United States by the *Entertainment Software Association* (ESA) identified the prototypical gamer as a 30-year-old male who averages between 6.8 and 7.6 hours weekly playing video games. This survey further documented that 46% of regular MMO players report neglecting sleep, work, or social opportunities so they can play their games. Thus, for many players, games are crowding out important areas of their lives.

Lubans, Lonsdale, Plotnikoff, Smith, Dally, and Morgan (2013) expressed concern about the sedentary nature of screen-time activity such as video games and social networking. They were interested, therefore, in adolescents' motivation to limit or reduce the amount of time they spent on screens. They developed a *Motivation to Limit Screen-Time Questionnaire* (MLSQ), which was fashioned after the OIT motivational framework (e.g. Ryan & Connell, 1989). Limiting screen time would not typically be something that is intrinsically motivated. Instead, one would do so for extrinsic reasons. Recognizing this, Lubans et al. (2013) assessed external, introjected, and identified regulations for reducing screen time, as well as amotivation (lack of motivation) for limiting screen time. Their preliminary results suggest that more autonomous reasons (e.g., "gives me time to do other things that are important to me") for reducing screen time were associated with larger reductions. Controlled reasons (e.g., "because my parent(s) or others pressure me"; "because I feel guilty . . . ") were less negatively associated with screen time, suggesting that they are less effective than more autonomous motives for promoting reduced screen time. Finally, as expected, adolescents could be amotivated to reduce screen time, and this was positively correlated with maintaining screen time. What this suggests is that effectively facilitating self-regulation of screen time may require helping players integrate meaningful reasons for not playing. Merely attempting to externally control or induce guilt to decrease their screen time is less likely to achieve that goal, as with various other goals we have discussed in this book.

True Overusers

Embedded within the statistics are a group of outliers who play video games almost constantly during waking hours. Estimates vary, but many suggest that between 10 and 15% of gamers fall into a pattern of video game overuse or addiction. Using criteria developed by the World Health Organization (WHO), Grüsser, Thalemann, and Griffiths (2007) polled more than 7,000 U.K. gamers, finding an "addiction" rate of close to 12%. In the United States, Chak and Leung (2004) estimated that 10–15% of regular players may be overusing video games.

There have been some heated debates about whether overuse of video games can truly be labeled *addictive* and thus whether game overuse belongs diagnostically with behavioral problems such as alcohol, tobacco, drug, or gambling addictions (Ng & Wiemer-Hastings, 2005). For example, an early task force of the *American Medical Association* took up the issue of how to label excessive video game use in the official diagnostic nomenclature. They ultimately decided the word *addiction* did not apply, yet they also emphasized that this position was contentious and should remain for further research. More recently, the DSM-5 added *Internet gaming disorder* (IGD), and yet qualified it as a condition needing more research. Indeed, there are nuances to understanding what is a highly engaged player versus an "addicted" player that continue to be clarified (Lehenbauer-Baum, Klaps, Kovacovsky, Witzmann, Zahlbruckner & Stetina, 2015).

WHY SO MUCH OVERUSE?

Regardless of the label, overuse is clearly an issue for a subset of gamers. As video games have matured in variety, complexities, and budgets, they have also become ever richer in their possibilities for need satisfaction. This means that these virtual environments may sometimes be used to fulfill those psychological needs that may be harder to experience in people's "real" lives. In fact, games have advantages over real life: In games the choices, challenges, and connections that produce satisfactions may be easy to achieve, relatively speaking. That is, the draw of games, and the potential for them to become "too attractive," is a real concern.

Although games can enhance short-term well-being and positive affect (Ryan, Rigby, & Przybylski, 2006; Wang, Khoo, Liu, & Divaharan, 2008), too much gaming may crowd out opportunities to gain satisfaction outside of the world of games. To the extent that they do, people's well-being may suffer, as well as their real-world productivity, interests, and relationships. For example, in one exploratory study reported in Rigby and Ryan (2011) an online community of gamers was surveyed concerning the relations between well-being and hours per week of game play. Although the figures varied somewhat by the genre of play, in general, when playing time ranged from 0 to 18 hours per week, greater amounts of play were either unrelated to or enhancing of wellness. Yet results also suggested that when video game play exceeded 20 hours per week, well-being was significantly lower, although the causal relations are unclear. Either people with low wellness are drawn to overusing games or, as game play becomes excessive, well-being suffers, or both.

The Need Density Hypothesis

To the extent that people's actual life satisfactions cannot keep pace with the satisfactions they find within virtual worlds, then overuse may well become a problem. Of course, this is a truism that could apply to *any* activity that becomes too compelling, whether it be video games or stamp collecting. Yet unlike many other leisure activities, there are no limits to the imagination and resources that game developers will dedicate to creating in-game experiences that will be psychologically satisfying. As we discussed earlier, one of the "strengths" of video games is their capacity to deliver immediacy, consistency, and density of psychological need satisfactions (Rigby & Ryan, 2011). Yet it is these very strengths that can make video games too irresistible a siren song for some.

In fact, certain individuals may be especially vulnerable to overusing games, which Rigby and Ryan (2011) suggested in their *need density hypothesis*. They proposed that, to the degree that players experience impoverished or sparse basic psychological need satisfactions in their daily lives and at the same time are exposed to positive and densely scheduled need satisfactions within games, they will be vulnerable to overuse. Thus it will be the student who gets little competence feedback or feelings of progress at school who will most likely revel in "leveling up" on need satisfaction each evening in a virtual world. It will be the worker who feels little control or autonomy within a daytime job who may be most drawn to the freedom and, indeed, omnipotence that one can feel in some games. It will be the kids who feel left out or unpopular at school who may most anticipate connecting with their guild members in a multiplayer game. It is precisely those individuals whose daily lives are characterized by low need satisfaction and high need frustration that will find video games "too" attractive. As argued by Clark and Scott (2009), players can "get tripped up because video games provide draws that most people don't know how to balance" (p. 8).

In line with this, Przybylski, Weinstein, et al. (2009) surveyed more than 1,000 avid video game players. It was hypothesized that players reporting low levels of need satisfaction in daily life would be more prone to an obsessive passion for games—the feeling that play is something they have to do. By contrast, people who have lots of satisfaction in their nongame world might still play a lot, but it will not have the feeling of compulsion. The findings supported these conjectures. Low levels of basic need satisfaction in life constituted a risk factor for a style of game play characterized by compulsion and overuse. Interestingly, along with this compulsive style came less enjoyment and satisfaction in moment-to-moment play.

Other researchers have similarly argued that the persons most at risk for excessive gaming are those who are more socially marginalized and/or who have difficulty with real-life social interactions (e.g., Allison, von Wahlde, Shockley, & Gabbard, 2006). Such individuals may find the virtual world especially rewarding in contrast to the unrewarding experience they have outside games. A scan of websites such as gamerwidow.com will indeed uncover sad tales of gamers who are unable to control their play. One cannot read these tales without appreciating the potential of games to draw in vulnerable individuals, giving them too much of a good thing.

The need density hypothesis is not restricted to gaming but also extends to online "addictive" behaviors. For example, some people are heavily engaged in social networking. Research by Masur, Reinecke, Ziegele, and Quiring (2014) explicitly looked at social networking time in relation to SDT's basic needs. They found, as expectable, that the more people found need satisfactions in online social networking activities, the more they engaged in them. Yet in line with our need density hypothesis, the more individuals reported low need satisfaction in life, the more they were driven to social networking activities. Similarly, research by Shen, Liu, and Wang (2013) studied Chinese elementary school children's use of the Internet. First, they showed that obtaining basic need satisfactions during Internet use predicted more time spent online, as well as more positive and less negative affect during online sessions, as we would predict. Yet they also found that basic need satisfaction in daily life predicted *less* Internet usage. Those with high need satisfaction in everyday life were less likely to overuse their online Internet opportunities, as would be predicted by the need density hypothesis. A more recent study by Liu, Fang, Wan, and Zhou (2016) identified a similar pattern with respect to Internet overuse in Chinese students ages 12 to 20. Specifically, and in line with our need density hypothesis, pathological Internet use was associated with basic psychological need satisfaction while online and negatively associated with need satisfaction offline.

In addition to an enhanced density of need satisfaction, video games may also allow individuals to experience a more ideal self than the one they typically experience in their embodied existence. Przybylski, Weinstein, Murayama, Lynch, and Ryan (2011) explored this idea in a series of studies. They found that the more players experienced their avatars as representing attributes closer to their ideal than their actual selves, the more likely they were to persist in a game over time, as well as to find the game more immersive. Again, this bespeaks the idea that experiences of "self" in virtual worlds can be psychologically meaningful and that players' psychological gratifications are not bound by the usual constraints of social life. Specifically, their self-presentations are in many ways more capable of manipulation and crafting in a virtual world because they can use the mediating interface to create the character they want. Although today's games are still relatively limited in the attributes people can adopt, self-presentation choices will undoubtedly continue to expand in this area.

Those individuals who are vulnerable to overuse because of the need density issue are also likely to be vulnerable in a second, albeit related way. As we have well documented in previous chapters, persons whose basic psychological needs are not met in their daily lives are generally less able to autonomously regulate their activities and less able to make congruent decisions that match their aims and values (Di Domenico, Fournier, Ayaz, & Ruocco, 2013). Conversely, research strongly confirms that the more people receive supports for autonomy, competence, and relatedness in development, the stronger their capacities to self-regulate become (e.g., Ryan, Deci, & Vansteenkiste, 2016). When those who have been provided such supports in childhood become passionate about an avocation or activity, they will likely experience their passion in more controllable and harmonious ways (Vallerand, 2015). In contrast, those whose development entailed more frustration of basic needs are likely to be vulnerable to an obsessive focus on, and passion for, activities that do at least partially satisfy these neglected needs, so they will be less able to control that passion. In this way, those low in everyday need satisfaction will also be those less capable of autonomous self-regulation. Need density may thus combine with self-regulatory difficulties to create a perfect storm of addictive-like behaviors.

Certain genres of games are, of course, more implicated in overuse than others. Players of RPG and MMO games may spend many hours in their virtual worlds, in part because game play opportunities are nearly endless and such games can involve much preparation and planning, including activities such as "grinding" or "crafting." In addition, these genres typically provide rich gratifications of all three basic needs. As mentioned earlier, they offer autonomy because they typically have very open game worlds, with lots of choices and opportunities for action. Players design their own characters, choose professions, join guilds, and explore ever-new environments and challenges. In addition, feedback about accomplishments is both immediate and cumulative. They never lose ground, always moving ahead in levels and capabilities. Finally, these games offer multiple tools for connecting to others, from structures that support guilds and communities to dialog boxes and friend locators, all meant to facilitate both social interaction and support.

Beyond these need satisfactions, many multiplayer games offer people opportunities to simultaneously take on multiple tasks and missions. This means that there is always "unfinished business" that remains. Psychologically, this leaves players with a kind of *Zeigarnik effect*—a salience of what remains to be done that can keep them returning to the game (Zeigarnik, 1927). This sense that goals are incomplete can lead to preoccupation and tension and even intrusive thoughts about the yet-to-be-completed goals (Baumeister & Bushman, 2008).

Putting together these properties of a high density of need satisfaction, low self-regulation skills, and an ongoing lack of closure can make various games particularly potent at drawing people in. Thus it is not surprising that a game like *Everquest*, an early yet persistent MMO, has been pejoratively labeled "Evercrack" to describe its addictive nature. Although games from *Tetris* to computer poker have been described as addictive, it is these multiplayer and team-based games that present the highest risks for overuse.

Aggression and Video Games: More Complex Than It Seems

Another, even more controversial, issue concerning video games is the degree to which they may potentiate real-world aggression. Social learning theorists have raised concerns that exposure to the aggressive and violent contents of games can leave players more prone to violent acts in real life (e.g., Anderson & Bushman, 2001; Anderson et al., 2007). Yet other scholars have not accepted that viewpoint. For example, Ferguson (2007b), Sherry (2001), and others have drawn different conclusions from their reviews of the research. In addressing this topic, we first consider whether opportunities to be virtually violent have a motivational role in games, and then we turn to the ways in which game play might indeed lead to postgame aggression toward others.

Does Aggression Motivate Game Play?

Any examination of the contents of modern video games would suggest that violence and aggression must be strongly attractive and positively motivating factors in game play. From Halo to Grand Theft Auto, games are filled with violence and fighting, often accompanied by highly graphic scenes of blood and gore. The primary task in many games is simply to kill as many enemies as possible and, by doing so, to gain resources or progress toward goals. Is there a method to all that maiming, mauling, and madness?

One ready hypothesis is that for many game designers a context of war, violent crime, or battles sets up a classic set of challenges (Rigby & Ryan, 2011). Games of fighting provide an easy narrative context that gives purpose to actions and missions. War and combat also potentiate interesting competence challenges and opportunities for teamwork and strategy choices. Therefore, it may not be the violence per se that has appeal but the opportunities for action, challenge, excitement, and teamwork that such narratives and settings afford. In short, war makes for an easy script behind a game design.

Would a video game without all the blood and gore that had equal challenges, feedback, and opportunities for choice and action be just as preferred as the graphically violent game? Or do violence and gore add to player interest, motivation, and satisfaction over and above the contributions of autonomy and competence satisfactions? Indeed, this is an important question, not just about games but about human nature (see Chapter 24), because, if the latter were true, it would suggest that there may be something intrinsically motivating about aggression itself.

Przybylski, Ryan, and Rigby (2009) directly examined this question in a series of experiments and field studies. They hypothesized (with some uncertainty) that the gore, blood, and aggression are *not* why players find games of war and combat interesting. Instead, they argued that it is the opportunities for competence, autonomy, and relatedness that games of war, competition, and combat so often provide. This question concerning whether there is added value to violence was examined using multiple methods. In one study, participants played a first-person-shooter (FPS) game that typically involved shooting enemies with a gun. In this game, kills were graphically depicted, as foes vividly exploded with spurting blood at each hit (immediacy of feedback). Players were randomly assigned to play this game as originally designed or to a second condition, in which the same game was modified to be much less violent. In this condition, the game was introduced with a different storyline, as a game of "tag" in which the player's task was to target opponents with a tag device (rather than a gun). When they did so, the targets rose and drifted away, presumably to their home base. There was no blood. Otherwise, the actions, graphics, and goals of the game were exactly the same. Results showed that the violent and less violent versions did not differ with regard to players' ratings of enjoyment or desire for future play. Furthermore, in both game versions, enjoyment of the game was mediated by need satisfactions for autonomy or competence. This suggested that it is not the blood or harmdoing per se that motivates play but rather the context of challenge that games of conflict can offer.

Interestingly, participants in this study had been premeasured for trait hostility. As one might expect, individuals higher in trait hostility showed somewhat more preference for the violent and gory version of the game. Yet notably, despite these preferences, even high-hostility individuals did not rate the more violent games as more enjoyable or fun. In contrast, people low in trait hostility found the gory version of the game *less* preferable. In sum, blood, gore, and an aggressive narrative added little or nothing to player motivation and interest.

Przybylski, Ryan, and Rigby (2009) also addressed this question using other methods, including surveys of experienced players, in which sources of game satisfaction were allowed to compete for variance in predicting game enjoyment. After controlling for basic need satisfactions, violence added no meaningful variance to players' ratings of a game's enjoyment value. It seems that one reason players may like violent games is that they tend to offer considerable satisfaction of the basic needs, which are incidental to their overt, graphically violent contents.

Game Play and the Transfer of Aggression outside of Games

As we have already discussed, despite much research on the topic, there is no clear consensus regarding the ultimate effects of gaming on aggression. Some research has found support for links between violent gaming content and aggression (e.g., Anderson & Bushman, 2001; Anderson et al., 2007; Willoughby, Adachi, & Good, 2012), whereas others have failed to find meaningful links after controlling for extraneous factors (e.g., Ferguson & Kilburn, 2010; Ferguson, Rueda, Cruz, Ferguson, Fritz, & Smith, 2008).

The mainstream hypothesis regarding violence and games has come from social learning theory (SLT; e.g., Anderson & Bushman, 2001). SLT holds that people tend to engage in behaviors that they observe, and, therefore, mere exposure to violent media conduces to violence. As Anderson et al. (2003) stated it: "no one is exempt from the deleterious effects of media violence" (p. 104). Yet skeptics point out that if exposure alone were the mechanism catalyzing aggression, we would see huge increases in violence. Instead, as violent media and games have dramatically increased in distribution, violence in the population that consumes these media has decreased (Ferguson, 2015b; Markey, Markey, & French, 2014). This alone makes a direct effect hypothesis seem implausible.

Rigby and Ryan (2011) suggested that, rather than having a direct effect on everyone, the effects of violent media on propensities to behave violently reflects an interaction effect. There are individuals who are more vulnerable to transferring aggression from virtual to molecular behaviors. Underlying this vulnerability are problems in self-regulation and a backdrop of need frustration leading them to feel aggressive or hostile toward others. As we shall discuss at length in Chapter 24, according to SDT, human aggression and interpersonal violence are theorized to result largely from severe or chronic thwarting of basic psychological needs. In fact, SDT researchers have argued that people are more prone to aggression when basic needs are thwarted, either proximally, by situational threats or deprivations, or distally, by way of chronic developmental conditions.

There have been a number of experimental demonstrations of increases in violence following video game play that cannot be due to developmental factors and are more likely to be linked to proximal factors. What can SDT's model add to this complex literature? SDT would suggest that experiencing need frustrations in virtual worlds can have negative effects, sometimes comparable to those associated with need frustrations in the molecular world. It is possible that in experimental settings (and perhaps in homes across the world) need frustrations that occur within games could engender feelings of hostility that extend beyond the game. This could explain the postgame rage or violence some have reported.

NEED THWARTING IN VIDEO GAMES

Przybylski, Deci, Rigby, and Ryan (2014) applied this formulation by specifically focusing on the need for competence, something that is quite frequently frustrated in video games. Although video games can, as we have seen, readily satisfy needs for competence, when they are too challenging they can also do quite the opposite. Thus Przybylski et al. (2014) tested a range of ways that games might thwart players' competence needs to see how basic need frustration would influence postgame hostility or aggression. Their methods for frustrating competence included exposing players to games with more difficult learning curves or supplying less effective or less intuitive game controls and interfaces. The effects of these competence thwarts were then examined in relation to various measures of aggression, including short-term shifts in angry or hostile feelings, greater accessibility of aggressive thoughts, and more aggressive behaviors. The researchers also examined these relations between competence frustration and aggression while independently manipulating or controlling for the violent content of games, so they could separate the effects of violence in the content of games from the effects of competence need thwarting on aggressive outcomes. Results showed that game conditions that thwarted competence satisfaction were associated with short-term shifts in aggressive feelings, accessibility of aggressive thoughts, and aggressive behaviors. These effects were evident both with and without violent game contents being involved. Mediation analyses highlighted the central role of competence need satisfaction in accounting for postgame aggression.

COMPETITION AND EGO INVOLVEMENT IN GAMES

Such results should come as no surprise. Just as in sports, work, passionate hobbies, or any domain in which people become highly motivated and potentially ego involved, thwarting of efficacy can lead to strong need frustration and aggressive reactions. Video games are in fact an activity that is often competitive and ego involving, potentiating strong affects when competence is blocked or defeated. Such results highlight how a consideration of the dynamics of basic psychological needs holds great promise for advancing our understanding of both the good and the bad of video games.

Because games that are violent are also often games that are competitive, it is important to distinguish these attributes in understanding the causes of postgame aggression. Competitive situations can arouse their own forms of ego involvement and hostility, and this effect might be independent of any violent content or narrative in a game (see Adachi & Willoughby, 2011b). Accordingly, Adachi and Willoughby (2011a) conducted experiments to separate effects. They found that, indeed, competitiveness rather than content most reliably predicted postgame aggression. Those assigned to a competitive condition were significantly more likely to aggress (e.g., pour more hot sauce into a person's drink) than those in a noncompetitive condition.

Subsequent work by Adachi and Willoughby (2013) focused further on the links between video gaming and trajectories of aggression among adolescents. They argued that the previously detected effects of violent contents on aggression outcomes may have been due in part to the competitiveness games can arouse. In a longitudinal survey study, Adachi and Willoughby (2013) found that it was exposure to competitive video games that was associated with greater trajectories of aggression over time, whereas noncompetitive gaming was not. In addition, more aggressive youth gravitate to more competitive games, suggesting a bidirectional influence.

Serious Games, Gamification, and the Utility of Virtual Worlds

One of the reasons the focus of this chapter has been primarily on video games is that gaming studies have many implications for motivational research and theory. Games illustrate the power of motivational design because virtual environments can be engineered to be packed with, or devoid of, features that would yield psychological need satisfactions. They can also be populated with intrusive and need-thwarting features. Thus they become an important laboratory for understanding more generally how features of contexts impact basic needs, volitional motivations, and outcomes such as aggression.

This raises the question of whether technology specialists and behavioral scientists can harness the design elements seen in game-related activities to do good for the world (Calvo & Peters, 2014). It seems that many people believe they can. Games and virtual spaces are being used as models and reference points for how to engineer or construct motivating and engaging learning, health promotion, and workplace environments. This is the idea behind what has been widely called *gamification*. By using the same factors that make games engaging and need satisfying, designers could potentially increase people's engagement in "serious" pursuits. Training, education, and interventions can be most effective, perhaps, when they afford the same kinds of dense, consistent, and immediate need satisfactions found in so many nonserious games. A second application is even more direct. One creates *serious games,* which are literally video games that foster some beneficial outcome, such as enhanced skill or knowledge in some domain.

Of interest, however, is that just because something is called a game does not make it intrinsically motivating. The issue with most serious games is that, especially relative to commercial games, they have not been very need satisfying (Rigby & Ryan, 2011). Often, too, the "learning" aspect of them is too obvious making play seem like work (see, e.g., Ronimus et al., 2014). Secondly, a common feature in serious games (as in education more generally) is that they tend to be loaded with achievement badges, leader boards, rewards, and various forms of recognition to "motivate" behavior. Yet these may or may not have any meaning, significance, or value to the recipient, and sometimes can even foster undermining effects (e.g., "I spent that much time to get that?"). As we have argued, it is primarily the core need-satisfying features of game play themselves that motivate engagement, and extraneous rewards are unlikely to help, unless of course they convey informational feedback and are not experienced as controlling. In fact, a study by McKernan et al. (2015) applying SDT compared two versions of the same educational game: one with loads of rewards versus one without this feature. Findings showed that the extra rewards did not add to enjoyment or engagement. The rewards have to be intrinsic to the game play to be optimally engaging.

Research by Sørebø and Hæhre (2012) looked directly at factors that might help students find relevance and motivation for an educational game used within a business program. In this study, they applied the concept of personal interest (e.g., Boekaerts & Boscolo, 2002), as well as SDT's need-satisfaction measures, to the prediction of students' perceptions of the educational game's relevance to the discipline. They found that experiencing intrinsic motivation in the initial gaming session was clearly associated with the perception that the game had discipline relevance. In turn, intrinsic motivation was predicted by personal interest in the subject matter and, even more strongly, by need satisfaction during game play.

Educators are especially hoping to exploit the possibilities of games for promoting learning and achievement. For example, Quest to Learn is a school in New York City that announced it was putting games and interactive technology at the core of its entire curriculum. More globally, publishers of curricula are increasingly creating tablet formats with gamified lessons to engage learners. The idea is to bring the same need-satisfying elements into learning activities that sustain noneducational video game play. For example, Minnaert, Boekaerts, De Brabander, and Opdenakker (2011) examined basic psychological need satisfaction in a computer-supported collaborative learning (CSCL) project, finding that experiences of autonomy, competence, and relatedness in the CSCL activities predicted students' situational interest at various stages of engagement.

In addition to educational environments, game-like formats and feedback systems are increasingly used to facilitate positive behavior change with regards to health, safety, and other practices and to help stem the problems of obesity, diabetes, smoking, and other health-related behaviors. Commercial products such as the *Wii Fit* are also engaged in this endeavor. The Wii system offers, for example, a balance board that can be used to engage players with activities ranging from aerobics to yoga to hula hooping, providing goals and feedback meant to engage them in a more active lifestyle.

Yet, however promising the serious games and gamification movements sound, their promise has not always yielded desired results. Many educational, training-focused, and health-related games are transparently extrinsic in their focus. Moreover, when such educational and training-focused games are expected to compete for players' attention against actual games—that is, commercially developed titles—they will typically lose because the way they are designed leaves them less interesting and need satisfying. Similarly, simply adding game elements to a workplace or learning task will not typically be sufficient to enhance motivation, particularly if the activity is not already intrinsically interesting. In fact what is important and promising about gamification is not the idea of making everything look like a game, but rather the application of the principles that make games fun in the design of other activities.

That said, there are a growing number of training and learning forums that have effectively incorporated features of games. When serious games or related technology-driven venues exploit the core mechanisms that satisfy basic needs in games to support intrinsic motivation and engagement, they can promote improved outcomes in many domains. Beyond educational games, motivational designs from video games can be used for organizational training, health care interventions, physical activity promotion, simulation trainings, and even social impact and persuasion games. We should add that one can equally learn, from bad game designs, how not to motivate.

The New Augmented Realities

As technologies advance, possibilities for exploiting them to enrich or to add to our everyday realities have come of age. Games such as *Pokémon Go* are even placing virtual objects into the midst of our molecular world, changing what we perceive. *Augmented realities* represent the technological enhancement of our everyday realities. Augmentation adds events, information, structure, or regulatory guidance not otherwise available through perception, as well as also cuing and even directing attention to certain features of the environment.

A simple example of an augmented reality is a *Fitbit*-type device. In addition to the sensory experience of walking, people also have an additional input: quantitative information about steps, time, distance, and heart rate. This information can have a direct motivational impact. It may spark people's interest in competence, leading to wanting to exceed certain daily goals. The device itself provides feedback, sending out badges or praise for reaching certain daily or cumulative benchmarks. Clearly, such devices can gamify people's everyday realities, activating in them experiences and behaviors that would likely not occur without the augmentation. Nonetheless, the design of feedback and rewards from such devices has motivational consequences. As an example, Munson and Consolvo (2012) reported on an application they designed to provide prompts, feedback, and rewards focused on physical activity. Although the experiences of users were, overall, positive and appeared to enhance activity, application features varied in their effectiveness, with goal feedback and pop-up reminders generally being positive, whereas rewards did not have a positive effect, findings quite explainable through SDT principles. In fact, it appears that prompts can have mixed results on motivation, which we would suggest is a function of their functional significance to users (e.g., see Wang, Cadmus-Bertram, et al., 2015).

Of course, fitness devices are only a simple example. Augmented reality devices include, for example, eyewear that is connected to a global positioning system (GPS) and provides detailed information about locations, services, and opportunities. Various devices could give us inputs about our own or others' reactions and emotions, and, indeed, they already add reminders, tools, and enablers of supports for personal goals. The sky is the limit on the kinds of augmentation that might become available, with information telling people not only about the outer world but also about their inner reactions to it.

A formidable task awaiting attention is thus how to harness augmentation to enhance self-determined goals, rather than being deluged, detoured, or deceived by the inputs. The prospects of new and emerging technologies for positive computing will certainly expand (Calvo & Peters, 2014), and as they do, the features of augmenting devices and programs will each be either more or less conducive to need satisfaction. This will be true in terms of both the human factors aspects of augmentation (e.g., Will we like the device and its control interface?) and the content or service it provides (Does it yield satisfaction?). Thus people's engagement and persistence with augmented realities will be a function of need satisfaction, with the hope that selective pressures will lead to this technological trend improving rather than impinging on human wellness.

Into the Future: Promise and Pitfalls of Virtual Worlds and Enhanced Technologies

An important point made throughout this chapter is that the boundaries between everyday and virtual realities are less clear than one would think. Because our behaviors and experiences are largely (and always have been) driven by psychological motives and goals and are related to basic psychological need satisfactions, it is very clear that these factors are robustly in play in today's interactive technologies and virtual worlds. Humans have always been ready to enter "artificial" environments. We can now have an infinite variety of alternative realities available to us with the press of a computer key. The experiential opportunities this presents are myriad.

Beyond virtual worlds, advanced technologies bring with them both obvious efficiencies and need satisfiers, but also often hidden collateral issues (Calvo, Vella-Brodrick, Desmet, & Ryan, 2016). The introduction of home washing machines obviously brought convenience, but they also increased norms for cleanliness and for wardrobe size, adding new work and consumer burdens even as they relieved old ones. More recently, the Internet has made information and social communication across distances much more accessible, and yet it also draws many people away from nature, physical activity, and more intimate social contacts and extends their work life into all hours of the day. In the future, devices such as autonomous cars may enhance drivers' freedom from attending to the road but at the same time may deprive those who find the act of driving intrinsically motivating. The point is that SDT's analysis of motives for using, and the need satisfactions and frustrations resulting from usage, will apply to every feature of new technologies, just as it does to those features and experiences we see in video games.

Technologies are also seductive. This means that people will need to be even more effectively self-regulating so as not to become mired in wants and pleasures that ultimately distract them from what they might reflectively value most highly and find most worthy. This has always been a uniquely human problem wherever people have had surplus time and resources. It is now simply one in which people must recognize the difference between psychological gratifications that enlighten and enhance rather than distract and that move people toward, rather than away from, authentic living, whether it be within virtual or everyday realities.

CHAPTER 21

Work and Organizations
Promoting Wellness and Productivity

Work is perhaps the most dominant domain in most adults' lives, yet workers have highly varied experiences. Some find work engaging and fulfilling, others see it as a time to be endured. In this chapter, we explore motivation at work, especially within modern organizations, including both its costs and satisfactions. This discussion begins by recognizing that high-quality work engagement in today's companies is driven by both intrinsic and extrinsic motivation. Although cognitive evaluation theory (CET), which focuses on intrinsic motivation, was the first element of SDT to receive attention in organizational psychology, a fuller SDT theory of work motivation and organizational management also requires organismic integration theory (OIT), basic psychological needs theory (BPNT), causality orientations theory (COT), and goal contents theory (GCT). Applying these five mini-theories, research has shown that when managers are more autonomy-supportive, employees internalize the value of their work efforts, are more autonomously motivated, and thus perform better and display higher job satisfaction and well-being. Interventions have further shown that managers can be trained to be more autonomy-supportive, leading to such positive consequences for employees. SDT studies have also shown how important satisfaction of the three basic psychological needs is for employee outcomes. Organizations that promote intrinsic versus extrinsic values and sense of purpose further enhance employee need satisfaction and thus commitment and engagement. Among other issues, we address the issue of pay, showing that although the amount of pay does not predict either basic need satisfaction or intrinsic motivation at work, managerial autonomy support predicts both. Giving pay in a noncontrolling way and ensuring perceived equity and fairness in compensation ameliorates some of the risks associated with extrinsic motivators. We argue that because work is not only a means to survive but is itself an important arena for self and collective realization, need-supportive environments are beneficial for both workers and their organizations.

Adult life comprises many activities, but among them work is perhaps the most predominant. For most people, the time and energy expended at work exceeds that in any other domain of life, including family, leisure, and sleep, and this is true even in highly developed modern economies (e.g., American Time Use Survey data bank; U.S. Department of Labor, 2016).

For many individuals, work not only represents a source of income for survival; it is also itself a form of self-realization and personal satisfaction. People search for careers that have meaning and that provide not only money but also a sense of purpose and fulfillment. Work for many is a basis for flourishing. Yet, unfortunately for too many workers, it is a burden and a drain, a use of time from which they must recover and from which they dream of being released. In opening his classic book of interviews with workers of all types, reporter Studs Terkel (1974) described work for most people as being "by its very nature about violence—to the spirit as well as to the body . . ." (p. xi). Similarly, Shipler (2004) described the difficulties even hard-working low-wage laborers have in coping with the degradations and stresses of their jobs.

In fact, we do not have to look to impoverished nations or low-wage earners to find evidence that for most employees work exacts a toll. Ryan, Bernstein, and Brown (2010) examined how work affected experiences of well-being in a small sample of U.S. employees. Using an experience-sampling strategy, full-time workers at various jobs (e.g., construction workers, secretaries, lawyers, and nurses) were randomly assessed three times per day for 21 consecutive days. Thus the investigators were able to compare responses when the individuals were on their jobs and when they were not, and on weekdays (when most participants were working) and weekends. Ryan et al. found that employees reported lower well-being (higher negative affect, lower positive affect) during working hours than nonworking hours and lower vitality, lower positive affect, higher physical symptoms, and more negative affect on weekdays compared with weekends. Further, these results were explained by lower satisfaction of autonomy, competence, and relatedness needs during work hours and more autonomy and more relatedness satisfactions on weekends versus weekdays. It was clear that, when at work, most of these people were simply less empowered and less connected than in the rest of their lives. Although perhaps not a representative sample, such a study gives us a window into why so many people dread Mondays and are waiting for the weekends.

Autonomy and Need Satisfaction in Modern Organizations

Modern work organizations have increasingly tried to address at least some of these concerns. In part, the reason is that the very nature of work in this information and digital age requires employees who are committed, engaged, flexible, and proactive. Having workers be more self-motivated turns out to be better not just for employees but for organizational profitability and effectiveness as well (Deci, Olafsen, & Ryan, 2017). Although it is still not the norm around the world, effective modern organizations are being reshaped to foster more autonomously motivated workers.

Doshi and McGregor (2015) highlighted this trend in their review of the ingredients contributing to the success of America's most admired corporations. Central in their analysis is a concept they call *ToMo* (or total motivation), which is essentially their common-language translation of SDT's relative autonomy score. That is, ToMo scores weight intrinsic motivation and identification positively and introjection, external regulation, and amotivation negatively, resulting in a summary score for quality of motivation much like the relative autonomy index (RAI) approach (see Chapter 8). Companies such as Starbucks, Southwest Airlines, Whole Foods, and Nordstrom, all of which are well known for both employee engagement and resulting customer satisfaction, are shown to have substantially higher ToMo than their competitors, helping to explain their business success. Doshi and McGregor (2015) describe these as "magical" corporate cultures—and we agree that greater relative autonomy, and the factors that support it within organizations, are what make companies outstanding places to work. Such data suggests that the concepts of SDT are thus extremely important for the field of organizational psychology in the 21st century.

In fact, if the recent popular management literature is any indication, SDT has been a major part of a shift within the field. Motivational strategies built upon external motivators and controlling incentives are being replaced with an opposite view: By empowering workers rather than overpowering them the best motivational outcomes result. Management approaches in organizations both large and small are thus being transformed from trying to control people from the outside with carrots and sticks to actively cultivating the work conditions and supervision styles that lead to motivation from within—that is to more autonomous work motivation and job commitment (see e.g., Bock, 2015; Fowler, 2014; Friedman, 2014; Goldberg & Somerville, 2014; Pink, 2009). Around the world, organizations are finding that, by supporting autonomy rather than applying controls, they not only help employees flourish, they also benefit their own bottom line.

Let's face it: There are a lot of motivational speakers and consultants out there. Yet we believe that what has been particularly influential about SDT in that movement and in that literature is that it is more than just motivational rhetoric. Rather, SDT has specified and continuously empirically confirmed and refined its principles concerning what fosters autonomous motivation and basic psychological need satisfactions at work, as well as their positive consequences. More than just an emphasis on autonomy, SDT speaks to specific aspects of leadership styles, compensation strategies, job designs, performance evaluations, and company goals that affect the quality of employees' engagement, commitment, and well-being, as well as organizational effectiveness and profitability.

Yet despite the potential of SDT to transform organizations, its principles of autonomy support are not always embraced. Many managers and economists have trouble shaking the idea that it is only money that motivates and that top-down control is how to keep employees in line and productive. Nor do such tactics occur just because of "old school" thinking. Often it is the intense pressures faced by managers that lead them to take the short, carrot-and-stick route to prompting productivity. In turn, this often creates a self-fulfilling prophecy. Carrots and sticks, if potent enough, can create short-term behavior change. Yet the more that incentives and control become the basis of management, the more employees will themselves focus on just those issues, as these become the only motivators at work. This leads to lower quality motivation, thus requiring even more top-down monitoring and control. SDT points to pathways out of this kind of vicious organizational cycle, toward more effective and ultimately satisfying ways to manage and to work.

Not All New

Recognition of the importance of autonomy, whether or not referred to by that term, is not entirely new to the field of organizational psychology. Well before scholars in most other applied fields did so, organizational psychologists such as Argyris (1957) and McGregor (1960) recognized that concepts such as autonomous motivation or self-actualization were essential for a fuller understanding of motivation and management. McGregor (1960), who was influenced by early humanistic psychologists such as Maslow (1954), argued that when workers have lower order needs (e.g., sustenance, safety, and security) relatively satisfied, higher order needs (e.g., esteem and self-actualization) become more salient. McGregor argued that employees' needs for esteem and actualization will make accomplishment and achievement inherently satisfying to them. Although McGregor's theorizing was not empirically derived and was not formulated in terms of intrinsic motivation or autonomy, we shall see that some of the motivational principles inherent in his "Theory Y" approach to management resonate with those of SDT.

Shortly after, Vroom (1964) published his *expectancy-valence theory* of motivation, which influenced many subsequent work-motivation researchers and theorists (e.g., Mitchell, 1974; Purvis, Zagenczyk, & McCray, 2015). The central tenet of this approach was that people will be motivated to engage in behaviors that they expect will yield outcomes of high valence (i.e., psychological value). Vroom's theory was formulated with algebraic equations for calculating motivation and valence and was implicitly focused on extrinsic motivation, although others were quick to add intrinsic motivation to the formulation (e.g., Galbraith & Cummings, 1967). We note that the concept of valence is quite undifferentiated, referring to importance, attractiveness, desirability, or anticipated satisfaction of outcomes (Van Eerde & Thierry, 1996). For example, intrinsic and extrinsic satisfactions would be considered additive values in Vroom's model, in contrast to SDT's contrary assertions. In fact, where they have been differentiated, intrinsic expectancies appear to contribute more to motivational outcomes than extrinsic expectancies (see, e.g., Abadi, Jalilvand, Sharif, Salimi, & Khanzadeh, 2011; Cerasoli, Nicklin, & Ford, 2014), which would not be predicted without SDT's additional principles.

Subsequently, Porter and Lawler (1968) outlined an expectancy theory that focused on the intrinsic and extrinsic motivation of work performance, thus combining the essence of Theory Y management with the idea of using performance-contingent rewards. Specifically, Porter and Lawler proposed that work environments should be structured so that: (1) the work is made interesting and engaging through job enlargement that would therefore allow people to experience intrinsic satisfaction from doing it well, and (2) extrinsic rewards are made contingent upon performance so that doing the work well would also lead to extrinsic satisfaction. Intrinsic and extrinsic satisfactions were again considered additive, so total motivation was considered a function of the intrinsic plus extrinsic satisfaction that would result from work.

The Emergence of an SDT Approach

As discussed in Chapter 6, the original studies of intrinsic and extrinsic motivation (Deci, 1971, 1972a) showed that providing people with contingent monetary rewards for doing intrinsically satisfying activities decreased intrinsic motivation for the activities. This initial disconfirming evidence for the additivity assumption suggested that making rewards contingent upon effective performance runs the risk of diminishing the intrinsic motivation that could be facilitated by job enlargement. Although the implications of these studies were never integrated into an expectancy-valence formulation, cognitive evaluation theory (CET; see Chapters 6 and 7) did become relatively prominent within organizational psychology in the 1970s and 1980s. In fact, Ambrose and Kulik (1999) referred to it as one of the seven classic theories of work motivation.

Yet, apart from the test of the additivity assumption, which is either explicit or implicit in most psychological and economic theories of work motivation and behavior, CET was never formulated or tested as a general theory of work motivation, and in our view it is not positioned to be such a theory on its own. Only after we had developed organismic integration theory (OIT; Chapter 8) to deal with the internalization of extrinsic motivation (Ryan, Connell, & Deci, 1985) did we begin to do empirical research in work organizations and discuss SDT as a more global theory of motivation for the workplace (Deci, Connell, & Ryan, 1989). The reason is that a theory of work motivation must be able to address both extrinsic and intrinsic motivations without simply assuming (incorrectly) that they are additive. We subsequently elaborated our understanding of work motivation by applying basic psychological needs theory (BPNT; Chapter 10), which is critical for explicating issues of retention, burnout, cooperation, and workplace wellness (Gagné, Deci, & Ryan, 2017).

Together, CET, OIT, and BPNT make up the major elements of SDT's empirically based approach to work motivation and management (Deci & Ryan, 2014b). Both CET and OIT make clear that optimal motivation—that is, autonomous motivation, which comprises intrinsic motivation and well-internalized extrinsic motivation—depends on satisfaction of the basic psychological needs. Further, research on these two mini-theories indicates that there is considerable similarity in the social-contextual conditions that facilitate the two types of autonomous motivation. Opportunities for choice, voice, receiving meaningful competence feedback, and perceiving equity and inclusion are among the conditions that promote satisfaction of the basic needs for competence, relatedness, and autonomy, and thereby can enhance engagement with work, improve job performance, and (as BPNT underscores), promote greater psychological wellness and lesser ill-being at work. In what follows, we review the now large body of research supporting these ideas and present case studies in a wide variety of organizational and work contexts that show their broad utility.

Empirical Explorations of Motivation at Work

Our first large-scale SDT field study in the workplace was an organization development effort in a U.S. Fortune 500 company (Deci, Connell, & Ryan, 1989). This large company had offices all around the country, each with its own branch manger and middle-level management team overseeing the local work force. It was a difficult economic time for the company, and employee motivation was low, so the company was seeking help in changing its overall climate.

In this project, we first examined the relations between the managers' autonomy support (assessed with managers' own self-reports) and their subordinates' perceptions and satisfactions at multiple points in time. Second, we tested whether our intervention led to positive changes in managers' autonomy support for those managers who were provided it relative to those in a control group, in order to determine whether the intervention was effective in changing managers' styles. Third, to examine whether the change in managers' autonomy support would impact or radiate to their subordinates' experiences, both we and a company-administered assessment followed up to detect effects.

The intervention was focused on developing a more autonomy-supportive managerial style among the top manager and the team of managers within each branch. Three main concepts that are key to supporting autonomy were emphasized. The first is being able to *understand the others' perspectives*. Manager meetings involved both direct training in doing this and a discussion with each manager after observing him or her in a team meeting. The second concept was *informational feedback,* which seemed particularly important because it was clear from observing interactions in the branches that much of the feedback being delivered was negative and critical rather than constructive. Managers were taught how to be more supportive and positive in their use of feedback and also to "hear" the feedback they were receiving from those they supervised. The third concept was supporting subordinates' initiative, choice, and participation in work-related issues and decisions.

Analyses indicated, first, that the relations between managers' autonomy support and subordinates' positive perceptions and satisfactions grew stronger over the period of the study. Initially, there was little relation, because there was low autonomy support and little positive communications in the branches, but as time passed, the concepts became more salient and the relations stronger. It is especially noteworthy that when employees' immediate supervisors were more autonomy-supportive, the employees were not only more satisfied with these direct supervisors but also were more trusting of the top managers of the corporation, who were many levels removed from the employees in the study. Second, the results revealed that during the intervention period, experimental-group managers became more autonomy-supportive relative to the control-group managers. Third, results showed that, over the 13-month period, there were positive changes in subordinates' perceptions and satisfactions in the branches that had received the intervention. Those managers who had become most autonomy-supportive had subordinates who exhibited the most positive changes. Finally, analyses of company-developed and administered attitude surveys showed significant positive change in attitudes of the employees in the intervention branches compared with branches that did not receive the intervention.

Forest, Gilbert, Beaulieu, Le Brock, and Gagné (2014) used the results of this Deci et al (1989) study to do an economic utility analysis of the intervention. They first calculated its cost to the organization in current dollars and then calculated the mental health savings likely to accrue to the organization. Through this analysis, Forest and colleagues concluded that the return on investment to an organization of such an intervention, which yielded a meaningful impact on autonomy support and autonomous motivation, would be more than 3:1. Simply stated, not only would such an intervention improve the psychological well-being of employees, but it would also provide the organization with substantial savings.

This initial SDT foray into corporate climate change thus showed that it is possible to intervene in organizations and to train managers to be more autonomy-supportive, and it set the stage for subsequent studies examining SDT processes in the workplace. For example, Hardré and Reeve (2009) similarly applied SDT in training managers of a Fortune 500 company in autonomy support. They randomly assigned some managers to an experimental training group and others to a nonintervention control group. The autonomy support of both groups of managers was assessed before and after the training by having each manager describe a recent incident in which he or she dealt with an unmotivated employee and then having those descriptions rated for autonomy support by trained members of the research team. Results showed that, 5 weeks after the training, managers who had been trained were significantly more autonomy-supportive than managers in the control group. Further, 5 weeks after that posttraining autonomy-support assessment of the managers, their employees were assessed for their level of autonomous motivation and engagement. Analyses indicated that the employees of the trained managers were significantly more autonomous and engaged at work than those of the untrained managers.

Such field experiments show that managers can be cost-effectively trained to be more autonomy-supportive and that, when they are, there are positive motivational consequences in their employees. This is important because SDT is not just about abstract theory but about change on the ground. Yet there are many elements in what constitutes a fully functioning organization and how it can be actualized. In what follows, we turn to a consideration of these issues, including the facilitation of autonomous motivation, the impact of intrinsic goals, the effects and dynamics of compensation, and satisfaction of the basic psychological needs as they relate to workplace behavior, satisfaction, and wellness. This will allow a fuller understanding of the processes through which the motivational dynamics of SDT operate and the makings of an optimal work environment.

Autonomous Motivation at Work

SDT predicts that more autonomous forms of motivation are associated with higher quality engagement and wellness in the workplace and that more autonomously motivated employees experience less exhaustion, burnout, and ill-being. Moreover, when work requires investment of energy, care, thought, or creativity, autonomy is also expected to be associated with higher performance. Within profiles of worker motives, high autonomous motivation is predictive of performance and wellness even if some controlling motives are present, whereas the absence of high autonomy (e.g., identification with work) is problematic (e.g., Moran, Diefendorff, Kim, & Liu, 2012). In other words, although work motivation is always a complex of both internal and external motivations, having autonomous motivations in the mix is *necessary and essential* to high-quality engagement and performance. Emerging research strongly supports this formulation, and we review just a sampling of such research.

Fernet, Austin, and Vallerand (2012) found that over a 9-month period employees who were more autonomously motivated showed greater job commitment and less emotional exhaustion, whereas controlled motivation predicted great emotional exhaustion. The study also showed that those who experienced greater job resources were more likely to report increases in autonomous motivation over time. Otis and Pelletier (2005) studied French-speaking police officers in Canada. They found that the officers who perceived their immediate supervisors as highly autonomy-supportive displayed more autonomous motivation for work, and in turn they reported fewer daily hassles, a lower level of physical symptoms, and stronger intentions to remain in their jobs in the years ahead. Another study examined the motivation of teachers from the African state of Gambia (Levesque, Blais, & Hess, 2004). These researchers found that when the teachers' supervisors were more supportive of their basic psychological needs, the teachers were more autonomously motivated to do their work, and in turn they reported greater job satisfaction and, more generally, life satisfaction. Nie, Chua, Yeung, Ryan, and Chan (2015) found similar results with teachers employed in Chinese government-sponsored schools. Such research highlights that autonomy is beneficial in diverse work and cultural settings and is grounded in both managerial and practical supports for functioning.

In an opposite vein, excessive pressures and/or lack of managerial supports conduce to lower autonomy and poorer adjustment to work. For example, in a study of more than 800 public school teachers, Fernet, Guay, Senécal, and Austin (2012) showed that when the teachers experienced greater pressure on the job, they displayed diminished autonomous motivation, which led to greater emotional exhaustion. Extending this research, Trépanier, Fernet, and Austin (2013b) studied the work experiences of nurses with respect to whether or not they had endured psychological harassment on the job (e.g., being shouted at or being aggressively monitored by superiors). Those who experienced such behaviors showed less autonomous and more controlled motivation, as well as lower levels of psychological wellness and higher turnover intentions. A related study showed that bullying on the job led to greater burnout and less engagement, with need frustration as the mediator (Trépanier, Fernet, and Austin, 2013a). The importance of such findings is that they emphasize how crucial it is for managers to be supportive of employees' autonomous motivation in high-stress contexts and, of course, not to be demeaning.

Preenen, Oeij, Dhondt, Kraan, and Jansen (2016) investigated the relations between indicators of job autonomy and company-level revenue and profitability in a sample of more than 3,000 companies in the Netherlands. Employees' job autonomy was only weakly related to company revenue growth, in part because overall company performance is due to many factors—from market shifts and economic trends to competition and foreign trade. However, they found a predicted moderating effect of company maturity (young vs. older companies), such that the relation between job autonomy and company revenue growth was stronger and significant for young companies, where employee inputs may be especially important.

Coping with Change in Organizations

Promoting effective change in organizations has long been considered difficult, as people tend to resist change because of the unknowns that are associated with it. Gagné, Koestner, and Zuckerman (2000) argued that if change were introduced into an organization in a less threatening way—that is, a way that would be experienced as autonomy-supportive because the managers provided a clear and honest rationale for the change, offered some choice about how the change is implemented, and acknowledged the employees' feelings about the change (Deci, Eghrari, Patrick, & Leone, 1994)—people would be less likely to resist the change and instead would work toward carrying it out effectively.

Gagné et al. (2000) surveyed employees from a large telecommunications organization in Canada to test these hypotheses. The first set of surveys was completed prior to the implementation of a major change, which the employees were not yet aware was coming, and the second administration was done 13 months later, while the transformation was in process. The transformation was very disruptive and included some downsizing, so it is not surprising that the average for employees' ratings of the change agents' autonomy support was lower at Time 2 than at Time 1, and the same was the case for employees' acceptance of the change. Importantly, however, results of regression analyses indicated that the employees who experienced greater autonomy support from managers at Time 1 were more accepting of the change at Time 2, controlling for Time 1 acceptance of change scores. In short, although the organization was engaged in a tumultuous change, having supervisors who employed an autonomy-supportive managerial approach led subordinates to be more accepting of the organizational change.

One of the problems faced by many workplaces is keeping at the cutting edge of contemporary technology. Technology is expensive, and it is difficult to keep employees motivated to use the informational technology consistently and effectively. Research by Mitchell, Gagné, Beaudry, and Dyer (2012) addressed this issue by examining manager–employee interpersonal processes and employee motivational processes. The researchers found that when employees perceived their managers as being more responsive and supportive and perceived the rewards in the organization as being just and fair, the employees were more autonomously motivated to use the technology. Perceptions of managerial support also accounted for enjoyment and acceptance of the technology, and intrinsic motivation mediated that relation.

Lynch, Plant, and Ryan (2005) did a study of organizational change in a residential psychiatric hospital for children and adolescents. In this, as in many such hospitals, staff members were somewhat fearful for their own safety, as the patients could be aggressive toward their peers and the staff. The hospital was introducing a major change toward using less physically restrictive treatment methods and being more supportive of the youths' psychological needs. The administrators worked to introduce the changes in a way that allowed the staff to experience greater satisfaction of their basic psychological needs as they were implementing the new practices in relation to the patients. Results indicated that the more staff members experienced supports for autonomy, competence, and relatedness, the more they internalized the value and regulation of the change, thus being more autonomously motivated for implementing the new approach to treatment. Further, staff members who experienced the greater support also reported higher job satisfaction, more positive attitudes toward the new program, and higher levels of general well-being. Importantly, as the staff became less focused on restricting patients, the patients perceived the staff as being more autonomy-supportive of them, and the patients displayed more autonomous motivation for their own treatment.

Related results in a study of university professors showed that autonomous motivation affects how employees make use of new initiatives. Specifically, Fernet, Guay, and Senécal (2004) provided employees with some control over decision making in an attempt to ameliorate some of the stress of the job demands, but they found that decisional control on the job made a positive difference only for people high in autonomous motivation. In other words, those most effective in using greater decisional control on the job were the people who were autonomously motivated, and those people showed low levels of burnout. Such results again highlight the importance of autonomous motivation for successfully negotiating workplace demands.

In sum, it appears that major change can be effectively introduced into organizations, but doing so requires that managers and change agents relate to employees in ways that are responsive to the employees' needs and supportive of the employees' efforts and perspectives. As this occurs, the employees become more autonomously motivated to carry out their jobs, which is likely not only to be associated with greater well-being and thriving among them but also to have a positive effect on whomever they interact with, such as patients, customers, or clients.

Relations of Autonomous Motivation to Various Organizational Concepts

As SDT's concepts have become increasingly prevalent in research and theory on work organizations, investigators have found it interesting to examine relations between autonomous and controlled motivation and concepts from other organizational perspectives. We briefly consider a few such concepts.

Proactivity

A few organizational researchers have in recent years studied the concept of proactivity. As an empirical concept, proactive behavior is operationalized as being self-directed and innovative and taking initiative in one's job (Parker, Wall, & Jackson, 1997; Parker, Wall, & Cordery, 2001). In SDT, proactivity is one of the basic meta-theoretical assumptions, and intrinsic motivation and engagement are understood as manifestations of people's inherent proactive nature. As well, the definition of proactivity in the organizational literature—being self-directed, innovative, and initiating—is quite similar to what in SDT we refer to as autonomously motivated behavior. Further, supports for the basic needs for competence, autonomy, and relatedness have been found to maintain or enhance people's inherent proactive tendency and its manifestations in intrinsic and integrated motivations (Ryan & Deci, 2000d).

Research by Parker, Williams, and Turner (2006) has shown that the factors of autonomy, trust, and support are important antecedents of proactive work behavior, all factors that overlap significantly with SDT's basic psychological needs. It thus makes sense that Parker, Bindl, and Strauss (2010) argued that using the SDT conceptualization would be useful for studying proactivity in order to gain a better understanding of how to motivate proactive behavior in organizations. In line with this, research by Grant, Nurmohamed, Ashford, and Dekas (2011) showed that having a high level of personal initiative combined with high autonomous and low controlled work motivation fostered proactive behaviors. In two studies, they found that job applicants received more job offers and call center employees generated more revenue when they displayed these motivational characteristics. In a quite different context, White (2015) showed that customer satisfaction in a service delivery industry was substantially accounted for by employees' motivation—motives associated with high levels of autonomy were consistently strong predictors of positive emotions and quality of service, accounting for more than half the variance in these outcomes. Interactions with customers is one area in which autonomous employees, who will likely be more authentic and enthusiastic in their work, can foster greater customer loyalty.

Organizational Commitment

Much of the work on organizational commitment has used one of two conceptualizations of commitment. O'Reilly and Chatman (1986) presented the first using the work of Kelman (1958) to suggest that there are two bases for organizational commitment, namely, identification with the organization and internalization of the organization's values. Allen and Meyer (1996) formulated a second concept of affective commitment, which refers to employees' identification with, emotional attachment to, and involvement in the organization, thus representing the fullest type of commitment.

In one study of three samples from different organizations, Gagné, Chemolli, Forest, and Koestner (2008) found, as predicted, that affective commitment correlated strongly with autonomous types of motivation. Similarly, Gagné and Koestner (2002) found that the identified and internalized types of commitment correlated strongly with autonomous motivation, less strongly with introjection, and not at all with external regulation. The researchers then combined the four motivation subscales to form RAI and performed cross-lag correlations. They found that Time 1 RAI predicted Time 2 commitment (i.e., identification and internalization combined), but Time 1 commitment did not predict Time 2 RAI. It thus seems that autonomous motivation represents an important base for organizational commitment rather than the other way around.

Becker, Kernan, Clark, and Klein (2015) took a different approach to studying commitment among tenured management professors using a modified version of Allen and Meyer's (1996) commitment measure. They assessed commitment both to the participants' profession and to the organizations at which they worked. The researchers also assessed participants' intrinsic and extrinsic motivation for doing research, a key aspect of their jobs. The authors found that commitment to the profession was positively related to intrinsic motivation for research and negatively related to extrinsic motivation for research, whereas commitment to their universities was negatively related to intrinsic motivation and positively related to extrinsic motivation. In turn, intrinsic motivation for research was positively related to having high research goals and a strong commitment to those goals, which, in turn, predicted more hours spent on research and posttenure productivity.

Job Characteristics

Hackman and Oldham (1980) presented a theory of job enlargement and motivation in which they detailed a set of job characteristics, including autonomy, feedback, and task significance, that are expected to enhance what they called self-motivation and, under most circumstance, to improve performance at work. Because these are also the types of work supports that would be expected to predict more autonomous motivation, various investigators have related the job characteristics to autonomous forms of motivation and positive work outcomes. For example, Gagné, Senécal, and Koestner (1997) found that contexts with these facilitative job characteristics predicted employees' feeling empowered, which led to enhanced intrinsic motivation. Millette and Gagné (2008) examined facilitative job characteristics among volunteers in a community clinic and found that the volunteer workers who experienced high levels of these job characteristics were also high on autonomous motivation, as reflected in high scores on the RAI, which in turn related to the volunteers' job satisfaction and their work performance as rated by their supervisors.

Kuvaas (2009) found that the job characteristics of work autonomy and work interdependence both predicted work performance. Important to SDT was the finding that intrinsic motivation partially mediated these relations. This suggests that both autonomy about how one does one's job and opportunities for relatedness and cooperation with coworkers may enhance performance in part by adding to the enjoyment of work. In the same research, Kuvaas (2009) also showed that supervisors' support for autonomy, competence, and development also predicted work performance and, in this case, intrinsic motivation fully mediated these relations.

Some studies of the workplace have examined *job demands* in relations to the resources (e.g., managerial support and positive feedback) available to the employees for dealing with the job demands (Bakker & Demerouti, 2007). A study of school board employees used this approach and found that the degree of satisfaction of the three basic psychological needs for competence, autonomy, and relatedness on the job mediated the links between the resources-to-demands ratio and both personal accomplishment on the one hand and exhaustion and depersonalization on the other (Fernet, Austin, Trépanier, & Dussault, 2013). Results thus indicated that the level of basic need satisfaction that employees experienced in the workplace was the key element in determining whether the people's work would lead them to flourish or to deteriorate. Van den Broeck, Vansteenkiste, De Witte, and Lens (2008) investigated the role of basic need satisfaction in the relations between job demands, job resources, and employees' exhaustion and engagement. They assessed a large heterogeneous sample of employees in Belgium, finding that satisfaction of basic psychological needs partially explained the links from job demands to exhaustion and from job resources to engagement and fully mediated the relation between low job resources and exhaustion. Goodboy, Martin, Knight, and Long (2015) also showed how high job demands, when combined with low worker control and poor managerial need support, all conspire to foster workplace bullying.

Extrinsic and Intrinsic Values, Goals, and Aspirations

In Chapter 11 we presented goal contents theory (GCT) and reviewed many studies showing that, when people place high value on extrinsic aspirations for wealth, fame, and image, they tend to be less psychologically healthy than when they place high value on intrinsic aspirations for growth, relationships, and community. As well, when they adopt short-term extrinsic goals, they tend to learn less well and perform more poorly than when they adopt short-term intrinsic goals.

Vansteenkiste, Neyrinck, Niemiec, Soenens, De Witte, and Van den Broeck (2007) used the GCT framework as a basis to perform two studies in which they assessed the extrinsic and intrinsic work value orientations of Belgian workers—that is, values focused on pay, job security, and ample holidays versus those focused on the job being interesting and optimally challenging and allowing responsibility and initiative. The first study of nearly 900 workers established that those who held high extrinsic relative to intrinsic work values were less satisfied with their jobs and less happy with their lives. When income was taken into account, the results indicated, as would be expected, that those making higher wages were more satisfied and happy in their lives than those making lower wages, but income did not moderate the negative relations of extrinsic goals to satisfaction and happiness. In other words, people with higher salaries were somewhat more satisfied than those with lower salaries, but if those with higher salaries were strongly extrinsically oriented in their aspirations, they were less satisfied and happy than those with higher salaries who had aspirations that were more strongly intrinsic.

In a second study by Vansteenkiste, Neyrinck, et al. (2007), employees in Belgium completed questionnaires assessing a broader range of variables, including work–family conflict, emotional exhaustion, and turnover intentions. In addition, the researchers also assessed basic psychological need satisfaction at work. Analyses revealed that higher scores on extrinsic relative to intrinsic life goals related strongly to poor outcomes on each of the dependent variables. Importantly, basic psychological need satisfaction mediated each of these relations. These results confirm and extend what was shown in various studies reviewed in Chapter 11, namely, that the relations from values or goal contents to well-being indicators were mediated by satisfaction of the basic psychological needs.

Research conducted in New Zealand by Roche and Haar (2013) found that employees who were higher on intrinsic goals engaged in more organizational citizenship behaviors toward their fellow workers, and a study by Van den Broeck, Vansteenkiste, Lens, and De Witte (2010) found that holding extrinsic work goals was negatively associated with flexibility on the job, whereas holding intrinsic work goals was positively associated with flexibility.

Some studies of goal contents or value orientations in the workplace (e.g., Van den Broeck, Van Ruysseveldt, Smulders, & De Witte, 2011) have used somewhat different value indicators, although they are generally quite similar in their general meaning. For example, in the research by Van den Broeck, Van Ruysseveldt, and colleagues, the extrinsic orientation included such factors as working hours, rewards, and security, whereas the intrinsic orientation included opportunities to learn and grow, as well as autonomy and variety on the job. Van den Broeck, Van Ruysseveldt, and colleagues (2011) examined these value orientations in relation to the job demands–resource model (Bakker & Demerouti, 2007) and found, for example, that an intrinsic value orientation at work served as a resource that strengthened the negative relations both between learning opportunities and work exhaustion and between work autonomy and impaired health responses to work, thus showing positive outcomes for the intrinsic value orientation.

Other research has shown that employees' surroundings can affect their goal or value orientations and the outcomes that accordingly accrue. For example, Schreurs, van Emmerik, Van den Broeck, and Guenter (2014) used SDT-based work values similar to those employed by Vansteenkiste, Neyrinck, et al. (2007) and had workers assess their work teams' general value orientations. Schreurs and colleagues found that when employees experienced their work teams to be more intrinsically oriented in their values, the employees were more engaged in their work, and this relation was partially mediated by the employees' basic psychological need satisfactions. Along these same lines, Van den Broeck, De Cuyper, Baillien, Vanbelle, Vanhercke, and De Witte (2014) found that when a work organization endorsed the intrinsic work value of personal growth rather than the extrinsic work value of status, employees of the organization felt more employable in the organization—that is, they felt more able to change jobs there, for example, to get higher level jobs—suggesting that a general intrinsic work orientation in the organization facilitated employees' experiences of openness and flexibility in that organization.

Finally, in considering how intrinsic and extrinsic goals fit in to the workplace, we review two studies that used concepts similar to that of work value orientations. First, in Chapter 11, we discussed the concept of materialism, which is closely related to extrinsic aspirations and values. A study by Deckop, Jurkiewicz, and Giacalone (2010) showed that materialism, which is negatively related to personal well-being (see Chapter 11), was also negatively associated with a set of work-related well-being indicators such as job satisfaction. Second, Grant (2008) examined what workers felt their efforts were yielding. Some saw their efforts in their companies as producing something good for the world—helping others or creating a useful and reliable product. Others saw their companies as purely extrinsically oriented—that is, just out for the profit. Grant suggested that this has to do with the workers' experience of task significance, which is related to the idea of more intrinsic aspirations or values, especially that of contributing to the broader community. He found significance to be a strong motivator of effective performance and suggested that the reason is that task significance allows satisfaction of the needs for relatedness and competence and thus promotes identified motivation, which, we would add, is autonomous and as such also provides satisfaction for the autonomy need. Grant and colleagues found that the enhancements theorized to be associated with task significance could be facilitated by providing workers the opportunity to have direct contact with the beneficiaries of their work (Grant, 2007; Grant, Campbell, Chen, Cottone, Lapedis, & Lee, 2007).

The Role of Pay in Work Organizations

The very concept of work implies human effort being exchanged for compensation. Yet when it comes to compensation, the question is not simply whether pay will bring people to the workplace and keep them there, but whether it is an effective means of motivating high-quality performance. In addition, there are questions about how the bases by which people are paid affect psychological and physical wellness.

Regarding the first question, SDT suggests that the way in which pay is administered and the type of contingency it entails (e.g., engagement-contingent versus performance-contingent) will differentially affect worker's experiences of autonomy and competence and that perceptions of one's pay relative to the pay of others will impact feelings of equity and relatedness. That is, pay has a functional significance that affects need satisfaction in ways that will affect work quality, as well as quantity. The old idea that more pay results in more effort is simply too simplistic a model, particularly when work tasks go beyond easily accomplished and measurable outputs. Expectancy-valence theories, which have tended to focus exclusively on extrinsic sources of value, often fall into such assumptions. Similarly, many economists have endorsed *principal–agent theory,* which suggests that the principal (i.e., owner or manager) pays the agent (i.e., employee or subordinate) in accordance with his or her performance (e.g., Petersen, 1993), so it is assumed that employees will behave to attain as large an amount of incentives as they can reasonably do within the circumstances. Yet research reviewed earlier has made clear that extrinsic incentives do not always foster high-quality motivation, and they may even undermine it. Extrinsic and intrinsic motivations are often interactive rather than directly correlated or additive.

Nonetheless, most studies on the undermining phenomenon, in which extrinsic rewards undermined intrinsic motivation (see Chapter 6), have been laboratory experiments, which some have argued make them less relevant to the workplace. Recently, however, there have been several studies examining the relation of pay, awards, or incentives on need satisfaction or intrinsic motivation in the workplace whose results are highly consistent with those from the lab. For example, research by Kuvaas, Dysvik, and Buch (2014) found in varied workplaces (gas stations and financial organizations) that employees' extrinsic motivation (i.e., the external regulation of working for the money) and intrinsic motivation (i.e., working for the interest value and enjoyment) were negatively correlated, thus providing support from a field study that these motivations can be antagonistic. Further, a few behavioral economists have begun to take interest in the undermining effect (often called the "crowding out effect" by the behavioral economists who acknowledge it). Some of them have replicated the crowding-out phenomenon (e.g., Ariely, Gneezy, Loewenstein, & Mazar, 2009), and others have formulated theories that relate the phenomenon to the classic economic perspective. Frey (1993) argued, for example, that when superiors offer monetary rewards for performing a task, the rewards are likely to affect intrinsic motivation negatively if the recipients' sense of autonomy, fairness, or recognition is negatively affected. Furthermore, he suggested, if the recipients find it costly to distinguish their types of motivation across domains, the undermining that occurred in one domain may spill over into others, which would essentially mean, within SDT, that the individuals would be generalizing a more extrinsic focus, and lowered autonomy, to other work tasks.

Gubler, Larkin, and Pierce (2016) described the phenomenon of "motivational spillovers" as a function of awards within organizations. *Spillover* refers to the collateral negative effects of extrinsic rewards that are associated with the undermining of autonomous motivation for the rewarded activity and the additional negative effects this can yield (see Frey, 1997). Gubler et al. used data from an attendance award program that was applied to employees at an industrial laundry plant. As SDT expects from the application of contingent rewards, their findings were that the attendance awards had a direct, positive effect on the attendance of employees who had previously had punctuality problems. Yet the award program was also strategically gamed by workers, which we would again predict. Although the program had temporary positive effects on the behavior of eligible workers, it did not lead to internalization or more attendance in an ongoing way. Further, the extrinsic rewards associated with the award program negatively affected the internal motivation of those employees who previously had had excellent attendance, resulting in reduced punctuality during periods of ineligibility. Perhaps most relevant to SDT's position, they reported that the award program also "crowded out" workers' internal motivation and performance in tasks that were not the focus of the program. Employees who had shown above-average preprogram attendance lost efficiency in daily laundry tasks once the program began. Gubler et al. interpreted these findings as resulting from the inequity perceived by previously responsible employees whose previous good behavior had not been rewarded.

The SDT Perspective on Pay: The Functional Significance of Rewards

To understand the meaning of pay from an SDT perspective, we begin by briefly considering experiments on intrinsic motivation. The most cited finding from the experiments is that, on average, tangible rewards undermined intrinsic motivation (e.g., Deci, Koestner, & Ryan, 1999; Ryan, Mims, & Koestner, 1983). Importantly, SDT suggests that this undermining occurs largely through the impact of rewards on autonomy, which is a concept that extends beyond intrinsic motivation per se.

Yet both SDT and our meta-analytic findings also highlight that the interactions of extrinsic and intrinsic motivations are not so simple as to be captured by that one finding. Not all rewards, that is, are undermining of intrinsic motivation or interfere with autonomy. For example, when tangible rewards were noncontingent (e.g., Deci, 1972a), unexpected (Lepper, Greene, & Nisbett, 1973), or not made salient (Ross, 1975), they were not detrimental to intrinsic motivation, and when performance-contingent tangible rewards conveyed a job well done within an autonomy-supportive, interpersonal context, they tended to enhance intrinsic motivation relative to no rewards and no feedback, although if they were given controllingly they undermined intrinsic motivation (Ryan et al., 1983).

As we described in depth in Chapters 6 and 7, these findings fit with the idea of *functional significance*—that events tend to be meaningful as either informational or controlling inputs to motivation. *Informational* events are ones that are experienced as supports for basic psychological need satisfaction for autonomy and competence, and *controlling* events are ones that are experienced as pressures to think, feel, or behave in particular ways. SDT suggests that in workplace settings individuals will interpret the meaning of compensation for themselves—that is, they give a functional significance to rewards and incentives (and to other external events such as feedback)—and it is the functional significance that is the proximal antecedent of how the reward affects the quality, quantity, and persistence of their efforts. Some forms of compensation have, on average, a clear functional significance. For example, the reason that task-noncontingent, unexpected, or nonsalient rewards do not undermine intrinsic motivation is that they are not, on average, controlling. However, factors in the situation and in the person may lead to different functional significances for such rewards.

The Deci et al. (1999) meta-analysis also reflected the many experiments, both in and not in that analysis, showing that, on average, positive feedback can enhance intrinsic motivation because it is interpreted as an affirmation of the person's competence. Again feelings of competence are important to both intrinsic and internalized forms of motivation. This is interesting in relation to the findings for performance-contingent rewards mentioned above. Specifically, the performance-contingent monetary rewards that were given in an autonomy-supportive social context (e.g., Ryan et al., 1983) led to greater intrinsic motivation than the comparison condition with no rewards and no feedback, thus indicating that people tended to give such rewards an *informational* significance. In workplaces, this is common. Positive feedback implicit in well-administered rewards can signify to individuals that they are both competent and appreciated for their competence. Clearly, in workplaces, people often experience the amount of pay they receive as reflective of competence, talent, or contributions. However, when employers attempt to use pay to drive people to work harder (dangling the carrot) and make differential rewards salient in the work context, its controlling significance can be heightened, detracting from the informational value of higher compensation, as well as potentially hampering relatedness. In short, when rewards are applied in controlling ways, they tend to offset the benefits of the positive competence feedback they might otherwise convey.

Motivation and Performance

In our discussion on the SDT approach to pay, we have focused on rewards in relation to autonomous motivation, but it is noteworthy that autonomous motivation is important in organizations not only because it has long been tied to psychological well-being (Ryan & Deci, 2001) but also because it is associated with effective performance. For example, a recent meta-analysis (Cerasoli, Nicklin, & Ford, 2014) examined how both intrinsic motivation and extrinsic incentives, when considered together, would affect performance. Using many dozens of studies, the researchers found that intrinsic motivation was a moderate to strong predictor of performance, a finding that is consistent with several studies that have been reviewed throughout this book. Further, with performance-contingent rewards, there was evidence of the undermining effect with respect to performance. Finally, although intrinsic motivation was a strong predictor of performance on heuristic tasks in which quality of performance is critical, extrinsic rewards tended to be a better predictor of performance on algorithmic tasks in which it is quantity rather than quality that is the focal outcome. In fact, another meta-analysis by Weibel, Rost, and Osterloh (2010) of studies with employees in the public sector found that pay-for-performance compensation systems led to improved performance on simple tasks but impaired performance on more complex tasks.

The idea of functional significance is relevant not only to intrinsic motivation but also to internalization. Conditions that facilitate internalization include the provision of some type of structure that conveys the importance of the target activity (e.g., Deci et al., 1994; Jang, Reeve, & Deci, 2010; Koestner, Ryan, Bernieri, & Holt, 1984), and in Chapter 8 we acknowledged that the careful offer of rewards without any pressuring could convey that the organization values the activities associated with the rewards. As such, a reward could facilitate internalization of the regulation for that activity and thus the autonomous enactment of it. Yet research has shown that this is most likely to happen when the pay is not directly linked to the employees' performance (Kuvaas, Buch, Gagné, Dysvik, & Forest, 2016).

In sum, although tangible rewards (e.g., pay) can undermine intrinsic and autonomous extrinsic motivation because the rewards are often experienced as controlling, pay and rewards may also support motivation and engagement if they are structured so as not to thwart satisfaction of the autonomy and competence needs. They can do this when they are used to affirm and recognize people's competence, are administered in an autonomy-supportive way, and communicate the value of various efforts and accomplishments to the organization. Yet when used to control behavior, as is frequently the aim of performance-contingent rewards, they lead to less autonomous forms of extrinsic motivation, such as external regulation or introjection.

More generally, because autonomous extrinsic motivation depends upon volition and endorsement of a goal, SDT suggests that contingent incentives may not be the most effective method. More important is a sense of purpose and vision to which workers can commit. This was nicely illustrated by Clayton (2014), who studied senior-level managers involved in mergers and acquisitions. Clayton looked at how both incentive packages and the combination of organizational supports and shared vision would affect the outcomes of (1) self-reported in-role performance (the behaviors directly targeted by incentives and rewards) and (2) "championing behaviors," which are sometimes referred to as organizational citizenship and are the discretionary behaviors an individual exhibits that go above and beyond in-role duties to correct problems and to promote organizational improvements. Clayton found that both organizational supports and shared vision enhanced managers' autonomous motivation, which in turn was strongly associated with more championing behaviors. By contrast, individual performance incentives predicted more in-role behavior and yet were negatively predictive of the discretionary championing behaviors. As we would expect, individual-performance incentives (i.e., performance-contingent rewards) can lead managers to do the specific behaviors that result in rewards; but this does not foster autonomous motivation, and it is this latter motivation that underlies more engaged and self-initiated championing activities that are required for organizational transformation, especially during mergers and acquisitions.

Reward Choice

Over the past quarter century, increasing numbers of organizations have introduced an interesting way of making compensation more informational and effective. Specifically, rather than offering an employee a particular amount of pay, stipulated levels of specific benefits, and other clearly stated aspects of the compensation package, they have been giving the employee significant choice about these various aspects of compensation. That is, employees can choose, for example, less pay and more health insurance coverage or perhaps more vacation time. Stated differently, the compensation package for each employee is individualized, which not only gives the employees what they want but also gives them a sense of choice and control over an aspect of their work lives. From the SDT perspective, this is likely to have a range of positive consequences, and studies by Caza, McCarter, and Northcraft (2015) showed that this policy of "reward choice" enhanced employees' productivity, but only if the options from which they chose their compensation package were attractive to them.

Use of Rewards in Organizations

From the perspective of managers, the important summary point from this discussion of rewards, pay, and functional significance is that the effective use of monetary rewards to motivate performance is more nuanced than many have assumed. Although there has been an enormous amount of research on compensation in organizations, very little of it has considered the relation of pay to basic psychological need satisfaction of employees, which mediates between compensation and critical outcomes such as employees' performance, morale, citizenship, and wellness.

One recent study examined whether level of pay related to distributive and procedural justice, need satisfaction, and intrinsic motivation (Olafsen, Halvari, Forest, & Deci, 2015). As well, the study included managerial autonomy support in the analyses. Results of the study showed that level of pay related to distributive justice, but it did not relate to procedural justice, need satisfaction, and intrinsic motivation. So the more money people got, the fairer they found their pay to be, but that pay level did not relate to procedural justice, did not satisfy basic psychological needs, and did not motivate them to perform well on the job. In contrast, autonomy support was strongly related to need satisfaction and intrinsic motivation, as well as to procedural justice, as would be expected by SDT.

In other research, Kuvaas et al. (2016) examined the consequences of compensation approaches in Norwegian insurance companies. They included a base-pay plan that was not contingent upon sales performance and two pay-for-performance plans in which employees were given the incentive of a bonus either at the end of each quarter or at the end of the year, in accordance with their sales performance. Analyses of the data revealed that salaries that were not contingent on performance positively predicted autonomous motivation and were unrelated to controlled motivation, whereas the plans that gave employees incentives for sales negatively predicted autonomous motivation and positively predicted controlled motivation. In other words, as in the lab studies, performance-contingent rewards were likely to diminish autonomous motivation. Analyses of the insurance company data also showed that autonomous motivation was strongly related to the effort that employees devoted to their work, whereas controlled motivation had only a weak relation to work effort. Finally, autonomous motivation had a strong negative relation to the employees' desires to leave their jobs, whereas controlled motivation was positively related to the desire to leave their jobs. In short, the performance-contingent pay led to controlled rather than autonomous motivation, resulting in less work effort and greater turnover intentions.

Still another study, this one by Harrison, Virick, and William (1996), examined employees with sales jobs in the telecommunications industry. After a 2-month introduction to the job, these employees worked entirely on commission, so all of their pay was directly linked to their sales performance. Results of the study showed that three-quarters of the salespeople had left the company within a year and that those who received the lower pay were likely to leave sooner. In short, this strong pay-for-performance situation led to extremely high turnover for both high and low performers, although it was higher for the lower performers.

Summary of Pay and Motivation

Our interpretation of this research with respect to how to use pay to motivate high-quality performance is as follows. First, contrary to some interpretations of our work, SDT sees pay as an important element in job motivation. Although working is instrumental to pay, positive motivation to work, especially motivation to accomplish quality work, is more a function of psychological incentives than financial incentives, so pay arrangements should support rather than undermine the psychological incentives. Thus strategies of pay should be informed by an understanding of their functional significance. Perhaps most clearly, pay should not be salient as a tool of control. Making the controlling aspects of pay more salient, for example by emphasizing the contingency between employees' behavior and their pay, in an attempt to motivate people to work hard is likely to undermine autonomous motivation and to have a range of related negative consequences on engagement, performance, and wellness.

Second, compensation approaches that are performance-contingent have a high risk of fostering external motivation and of being experienced as controlling. The performance contingency in which different people received different amounts of pay for doing the same task was found to be the most detrimental reward contingency in the rewards meta-analysis (Deci et al., 1999), and a study by Kuvaas (2006) found that even performance-contingent bonuses did not improve performance. Findings such as these led Frey and Osterloh (2005) to argue for fixed pay, which studies reviewed above found more effective than performance-contingent pay. The study by Kuvaas et al. (2016) found that performance-contingent pay based on sales in insurance companies led to controlled rather than autonomous motivation and resulted in less effort on the job and a greater likelihood of leaving the organization. Such field studies also support the "nonadditivity" assumptions of SDT and confirm our view that incentive systems must consider the functional significance of how rewards and pay are awarded and delivered in order to be maximally effective.

Third, pay needs to be equitable (Adams, 1963) or perceived to be high in distributive and procedural justice (Colquitt & Greenberg, 2003). Perceptions of fairness and equity influence job satisfaction, commitment, and turnover intentions (e.g. Deconinck & Bachmann, 2007). Of course, one might think that a good way to accomplish that equity would be to use performance-contingent pay, but, as already noted, that can have a range of negative consequences, and pay has been found to relate only to distributive justice but not procedural justice. Further, performance is not the only input to an equitable ratio to determine pay. There are many things that figure into what is equitable pay for a person—education or training, amount of time working for the company, quantity and quality of performance, and being a team player, among others. Effective managers, assuming they are free to determine the level of pay for employees they supervise, would be able to take account of such factors in determining what is equitable and then communicating it in a need-supportive way. And fourth, when it comes to motivating effective performance, there is every reason to believe that managers supporting employees' basic psychological needs through being autonomy-supportive in their interactions with the employees is more important and effective in motivating performance than is trying to use pay as a motivator.

As consultants, we have observed many case studies that illustrate dynamic issues associated with compensation and its functional significance to employees. We have seen, for example, sales organizations in which the commission-based nature of incentives leads to a focus only on sales. Accordingly, sales representatives make product promises that service or manufacturing divisions cannot meet, maximizing proximal incentives for the salespeople while harming long-term customer loyalty. We have also seen performance incentives divide work forces, especially when people compete internally for bonuses or for recognition. Performance incentives to individuals or groups can also disrupt relatedness and teamwork. Finally, it can be difficult to design fair and equitable performance-contingent rewards in many contexts. For example, both sales and service workers may have different demands as a function of the territories they cover, meaning that compensation that is poorly designed can seem very unfair, leading to alienation.

These are just a few examples of why, when it comes to compensation, SDT focuses especially on its functional significance or meaning for autonomy, competence and relatedness, all of which affect the employees' efforts, focus, and commitment to the organization's goals. In the design of compensation packages, the entire ecology of a workplace and its aims must be considered. Because these need satisfactions are accessible and measurable, SDT can contribute greatly to the design of compensation packages and the understanding of their organizational impacts.

A Note on Outcome-Focused Rewards and CEO Pay

Before leaving the topic of pay, we pause to highlight a particularly noteworthy trend toward wildly escalating CEO pay and its contingency management. Traditionally, chief executive officers (CEOs) of American companies have served as principals, representing the board of directors to motivate employees (i.e., the agents) through effective administration of incentives. In recent decades, however, some economists began to view top executives more as agents to be motivated by the directors (e.g., see Jensen & Murphy, 1990; Wang, Chung & Lim, 2015). Some economists have advocated, for example, making top executives' compensation directly contingent upon the performance of the company, indexed by the price of company stock. This has been implemented by giving executives stock option bonuses so that, at some future time, when they choose to do so, they could purchase company stocks at the price of the stock on the day their options were issued. Thus, when stock values increase, top managers can buy the stock at the lower price and then sell it at the higher price, thus potentially making huge profits. This provides a performance-contingent incentive to the executives to increase (or inflate) the value of the stocks.

Using the language of SDT, such CEO incentive packages are based on *outcome-focused rewards,* with stock prices as the target outcome. As we suggested in Chapter 6, outcome-focused rewards reinforce any and all routes to the target. As a result, they often fuel motivation to take the shortest route to the end, often with considerable collateral damage, as we have discussed in previous writings (e.g., Ryan & Brown, 2005; Deci & Ryan, 2013b). In fact, in the very few studies that have tried to evaluate the impact of such pay arrangements, results have been negative or mixed (e.g., see Cooper, Gulen & Rau, 2014; Hou, Priem, & Goranova, 2014). Even more famous are cases in which the path to increased stock prices (and therefore executive profits) was not only short but also deceptive and unethical. This was the case at Enron (Ryan & Brown, 2005; Schilit & Perler, 2002), in which contingency-based rewards were abused, leading to negative financial consequences that rippled around the globe.

Of interest here is how various stakeholders have different agendas for companies and how these agendas are reflected in the aims (effective or not) of their compensation plans for senior executives. A focus only on stockholder (owner) interest leads to concern about short-term profits, a result that many presume will be maximized by CEO outcome-focused rewards. But if the interest is in the long-term health of a company or of the employees who compose it, such outcome-focused rewards may be counterproductive. There are many ways to increase profitability that undermine success over time—such as reducing employee benefits or employees themselves, halting infrastructure investment, or even hiding losses or inflating quarterly profit reports. Pay can be structured to be supportive of either short-term or long-term organizational aims, and thus it requires thinking about the whole psychology rather than the narrow "economics" of rewards. SDT first and foremost suggests that rewards and their contingencies have varied functional significance, which will predict both their motivational impact and the instrumental behaviors they drive. Careful design of compensation packages thus affects bottom lines, both for better and for worse. In our view, such outcomes are predictable on the basis of motivational principles combined with an understanding of the varied gravitational pulls of contingency structures.

The SDT Approach to Management

Both intrinsic motivation and well-internalized extrinsic motivation in organizations are facilitated when managers are autonomy-supportive, and, as already mentioned, evidence shows that it is possible to train managers within an organization to be more autonomy-supportive (e.g., Hardré & Reeve, 2009). The aims of such training include helping managers: (1) to be better able to take the employees' perspectives and understand better their feelings and beliefs without becoming controlling; (2) to provide greater choice and inputs to decision making; (3) to understand that turning to rewards and sanctions as the way to motivate employees is often maladaptive; (4) to learn how to give more informational positive feedback and support competence experiences; (5) to conceptualize "negative feedback" as a process of supporting employees to find a meaningful solution for some ineffective behaviors; (5) to encourage exploration and self-initiation; and (6) to understand how communications and communication styles can affect employees' motivation, performance, and well-being (e.g., providing meaningful rationales when requesting a behavior; minimizing, controlling language, etc.).

Managers have many responsibilities. These include decision making, goal setting, and performance evaluations, among others. Each of these functions can be carried out in a relatively autonomy-supportive way. First, that means providing informational feedback, supplying rationales, making work optimally challenging, acknowledging people's feelings and opinions, and encouraging choice and participative decision making. There are times when some of these events will be relevant and times when they will not, as has been shown by Vroom and Jago (1988) in their theory of decision making, which specifies the conditions under which participative decision making is most effective. Still, the rule of thumb is to implement the facilitative external events whenever reasonable.

Goal Setting and Performance Evaluations

Goal setting and performance evaluation can be closely related managerial activities. Although goal setting within an organizational unit may have inputs from higher levels of the organization, there is generally room for inputs from members of the target unit itself. This participation will facilitate the group's and individuals' internalizing the goals and being committed to attaining them. Then, when it is time for performance evaluations, the process becomes an easier one that can also be done in an autonomy-supportive way. Managers can encourage their subordinates to reflect on the goals that, ideally, they would have played a role in setting and then talk about things that have gone well and things that have not. For the latter category, a problem-solving approach that seriously involves a subordinate in formulating new ways of overcoming barriers to performance can be both effectance-relevant and positively motivating. In this process, the extent to which the employee had been involved in setting the goals is likely to be an important factor in the degree to which the employee accepts them as criteria. Further, the extent to which the supervisor is autonomy-supportive and responsive in the performance evaluation conversation, rather than simply imposing her or his own viewpoints on the employees, will similarly influence how effectively the performance evaluation proceeds.

Transformational Leadership

The concept of a transformational leader was originally articulated by Burns (1978) and later extended by Bass (1985). These theorists conceived of a transformational leader as one who leads through charisma, inspiration, stimulation, and problem solving and by attending to the needs of employees, whom she or he treats with individualized consideration. Transformational leaders are often contrasted with transactional leaders, who use the more standard approaches of using contingent rewards, relying on norms and regulations, and focusing on the detection of problems instead of improvement and growth. Whereas transactional leadership has clearly controlling elements, transformational leaders would in theory facilitate SDT's basic need satisfactions and inspire more autonomous work engagement (Gözükara & Şimşek, 2015a). In fact, Burns (1978) portrayed a transformational leader as one who "seeks to satisfy higher needs and engages the full potential of the follower" (p. 4).

It is thus not a surprise that the effects of transformational leadership on work engagement are mediated by autonomy satisfactions (Gözükara & Şimşek, 2015b).

Specifically, those investigators looked at the impact of transformational leadership on Turkish academic personnel. Their results showed that job autonomy fully mediated the effect of transformational leadership on work engagement. Bono and Judge (2003) similarly found that the followers of transformational leaders tended to adopt more autonomous work goals and to be more affectively committed to the organization, as well as displaying higher job satisfaction.

Research by Kovjanic, Schuh, Jonas, Van Quaquebeke, and Van Dick (2012) reported that transformational leadership was associated with greater job satisfaction and commitment. More importantly for our purposes, this linkage was mediated by SDT's basic psychological need satisfactions. Extending this, Kovjanic, Schuh, and Jonas (2013) tested the role of basic psychological needs and work engagement in the relations between transformational leadership and specific performance outcomes. In an experimental setting, participants worked on a "brainstorming" task led by either a transformational or a nontransformational leader. Performance was assessed using measures of quantity, quality, and task persistence. All three basic psychological needs were associated with more positive outcomes, although in the resultant model, needs for competence and relatedness emerged as most strongly mediating between leadership type and these performance outcomes.

Yet even transformational leaders themselves require supports to inspire and guide. Research on school principals by Trépanier, Fernet, and Austin (2012), for example, found that school principals whose styles of leadership were more transformational were also those who experienced more interpersonal support, who were more autonomously motivated, and who perceived themselves as competent in their jobs. Hetland, Hetland, Andreassen, Pallesen, and Notelaers (2011) similalrly found that transformational leader behaviors had higher satisfaction of the autonomy, competence, and relatedness needs. In short, it appears that standing behind a transformational leader is support for her or his basic psychological needs, conducing to a sense of autonomy in the role of leader.

Basic Need Supports in Organizations

Ultimately, the SDT perspective emphasizes the importance of promoting basic psychological need satisfaction in any work organization. Indeed, substantial research has indicated that highly effective organizations are those in which basic psychological needs are satisfied as workers autonomously engage in work that they value and for which they feel respected and fairly compensated. These positive effects on organizations and the positive engagement of employees are apparent across diverse types of companies and job types, and they are evident across diverse cultures (see Meyer & Gagné, 2008; Shuck, Zigarmi, & Owen, 2015). Other studies have shown that, when people experience greater satisfaction of their basic psychological needs, they are also more autonomously motivated (e.g., Grouzet, Vallerand, Thill, & Provencher, 2004). Not only has satisfaction of these three needs been found to be critical for motivation in the work domain (e.g., Van den Broeck, Vansteenkiste, De Witte, Soenens, & Lens, 2010), but it has more genenerally been found to be the basis for human flourishing across domains and lifestyles (Ryan, Huta, & Deci, 2008). We now review some additional organizational studies in quite distinct organizational contexts in which need satisfaction played a central role in order to further illustrate the generalizability of these principles.

Work in a Shoe Factory

Ilardi, Leone, Kasser, and Ryan (1993) assessed both employees' and supervisors' experiences of basic need satisfaction in a manufacturing facility that produced footwear. Regression analyses were used to predict four outcome variables from need satisfactions—general job satisfaction, satisfaction with specific work tasks, self-esteem, and general health symptoms. The results indicated that, even after controlling for level of pay and job status, need satisfaction was a significant predictor of these four outcomes. Thus, in a standard factory setting, basic psychological need satisfaction proved to be important for predicting organizational outcomes. Further, need-satisfaction assessments were done both as self-reports and as ratings by the employees' supervisors, adding to the validity of the findings.

Adults in a Sheltered Workshop

Adult psychiatric outpatients in a sheltered workshop and transitional employment program were the participants in what was in fact the first SDT study of work motivation that focused on satisfaction of the basic psychological needs for competence, autonomy, and relatedness (Kasser, Davey, & Ryan, 1992). The majority of the patients were diagnosed with schizophrenia or bipolar disorders, although other major mental illnesses were represented. In this program, the patients received training and were provided with work contracted from outside vendors. Hospital staff, as well as staff from the participating vendors, supervised the patients, whose participation in the program provided them with income, as well as rehabilitation job training. Many of them lived in group homes or other supervised residences, some of which required them to be involved in a rehabilitation program, and the majority received social security disability benefits. These factors were used as control variables in the analyses.

Both the patients and their work supervisors completed ratings focused on the patients' experience of need satisfaction on the job. The dependent variables in the study were indicators of work adjustment—specifically, hours worked and pay received—taken from the hospital records, as well as the program director's ratings of the workers' readiness for employment. Results indicated that participants' satisfaction of the needs for competence, autonomy, and relatedness on the job, whether rated by themselves or by their supervisors, significantly predicted the work adjustment indicators of hours worked, pay earned, and readiness for competitive employment. Even though this is an unusual setting and population for studies of organizational behavior, the results are wholly consistent with the results of studies that have used more conventional populations and work settings, thus indicating the generalizability of the importance of basic need satisfaction across workplaces.

Work for the United Nations

In another, quite different work setting, highly educated employees from four of the United Nations international agencies participated in an online research project concerned with their experiences regarding competence, autonomy, and relatedness while they were involved in electronic learning courses on professional and analytical skills that were offered on their jobs (Roca & Gagné, 2008). Results of the research indicated that their perceptions of competence predicted the perceived usefulness of the electronic learning and the ease of putting the learning to use and that perceived autonomy support and perceived relatedness also predicted the employees' sense of playfulness and enjoyment of the learning. Further, the usefulness and enjoyment variables positively predicted the participants' intentions to continue with electronic learning opportunities. This study shows the importance of employees' experiencing autonomy, competence, and relatedness satisfaction to be effectively involved with learning on their jobs.

Business School Alumni

A study of nearly 500 alumni from a Canadian university business program who worked in both the public and private sectors used structural equation modeling (SEM) to examine experiences of competence, autonomy, and relatedness (Richer, Blanchard, & Vallerand, 2002). These employees' reports of perceived competence and perceived relatedness were associated with perceived autonomy, and that perceived autonomy was a positive predictor of job satisfaction and a negative predictor of emotional exhaustion. Further, job satisfaction negatively predicted turnover intentions, whereas emotional exhaustion positively predicted that outcome. Data collected 1 year later indicated that turnover intentions at the time of the first data collection was a significant predictor of actual turnover during the subsequent year. The SEM of motivation that predicted job satisfaction and emotional exhaustion and that, in turn, predicted turnover intentions and, finally, turnover behavior was thus supported.

American Bankers

Many people think of employees in the banking and investment industry as very extrinsically focused on money and compensation. Yet, in research on employees from banking organizations, Baard, Deci, and Ryan (2004) found results showing that, as in other workplaces, basic need satisfaction is quite central to motivation and wellness. They tested a structural model in which the employees' autonomy orientation (see Chapter 9) and their perceptions of their managers' autonomy support were used to predict basic psychological need satisfactions, and, in turn, basic need satisfaction would be used to predict both work performance and well-being. Work performance was measured by asking employees to report their most recent performance evaluations by their managers, who had rated performance on a 1–4 scale, from below standard to excellent. Well-being was a composite of anxiety, physical symptoms, and vitality. Both the autonomy orientation and perceived autonomy support were significantly related to satisfaction of the three needs, and satisfaction of the needs was related significantly, as predicted, to work performance and well-being at work.

Baard et al. found that women in this banking sample tended to perceive their managers as less autonomy-supportive, to feel marginally less relatedness satisfaction, to receive poorer evaluations, and to display poorer adjustment. This is, sadly, not an uncommon phenomenon. As Sandberg (2014) articulated, women's voices are underrepresented in the workplace, and often their needs are not addressed or are downplayed. The rampant sexism observed in workplaces around the world represents a tremendous loss of social capital and talent, as motivation is undermined, and, as Sandberg points out, conduces to women "leaning out" rather than in. This only underscores the critical importance of autonomy support, which requires responsiveness to the perspectives of all employees, with all their diversities.

Volunteers in a Not-for-Profit Organization

Like Baard et al., Gagné (2003) used both the participants' autonomy orientation and their perceptions of managers' autonomy support to predict need satisfaction and work outcomes, although in this case it was with volunteers working in an animal shelter. The outcomes were the number of hours volunteered and self-reports of engagement with the work, which were both associated with greater perceived autonomy support. In addition, however, there was another direct path from the autonomy orientation to work engagement, suggesting that it is autonomy-oriented individuals who are most likely to be engaged in volunteer work for nonprofit organizations.

Need Satisfaction in the Eastern Bloc

A cross-cultural study in Bulgaria and the United States examined a need-satisfaction-at-work model very similar to the one used in the Baard et al. (2004) and Gagné (2003) studies. This cross-cultural study was conducted in 10 state-owned companies within a country that, at the time of data collection, was still operating with a central-planning economy (Deci, Ryan, Gagné, Leone, Usunov, & Kornazheva, 2001). Because this study is reviewed in more detail in Chapter 22, we only briefly present the results here. The model stated that perceived autonomy support from managers would predict satisfaction of the needs for competence, autonomy, and relatedness, which in turn would predict both work engagement and self-esteem positively and anxiety negatively. After using means and covariance structure analysis (Little, 1997) to determine that the structure of the model in these two very different countries was largely invariant, we also found that the model fit the data well in each country.

We could continue with additional studies of this sort in yet more diverse settings. But our intention is less to be comprehensive than to illustrate that across quite varied organizations, need support matters. Results highlight that in very different types of companies, in different cultural contexts, in different economic systems, and for different levels of employees, basic psychological need satisfaction is reliably important for work engagement and wellness.

Autonomous Unemployment? Searching or Not Searching for Work

We have focused on work within organizations, both its joys and its costs. But not everyone can find work, and some people don't want to. Although generally we assume that unemployment can be a devastating condition, largely because people need work both to survive and to feel like contributing citizens, SDT's differentiated view of motivation suggests a more complex picture.

Vansteenkiste, Lens, De Witte, and Feather (2005) studied more than 400 unemployed individuals in Belgium. They found, as expected, that the value of having a job for unemployed individuals predicted their job search intensity, but it also predicted their feeling worthless, isolated, and less satisfied with life because a centrally important aspect of life was being denied to them. At the same time, positive expectancies of finding jobs predicted greater well-being and less negative feelings because they were confident that they would get jobs. The researchers further found that when the motivation for finding a job was more autonomous, individuals showed greater job search intensity. They were more energized to find work. In contrast, controlled motivation to seek employment predicted stronger negative feelings about oneself and lower well-being.

Why Don't People Search for Jobs?

Vansteenkiste, Lens, Dewitte, De Witte, and Deci (2004) raised the possibility that some of people's seemingly passive attitudes toward job searching might be purposively amotivated. Instead of having simply lost their motivation to look for jobs, they might have some motivation for not looking. The researchers thus developed a scale assessing people's autonomous and controlled motivation for not searching. Some people, for example, may have a genuine, autonomous desire to work less and live a simpler life, so they may search for the right job in a more casual way; others might feel controlled by family obligations or other conflicts not to search, so their lack of searching may be pressured and controlled by other people or forces. In two studies, the measure of autonomous and controlled motivation for not searching was used in conjunction with a scale assessing people's autonomy, control, and amotivation for searching. The question explored was whether people's motivation for not searching would predict variance in relevant job-search outcomes over and above the variance accounted for by amotivation with regard to searching.

In both studies, results indicated that autonomous motivation for not searching was a significant *negative* predictor of commitment to having a job, expectations about finding a job, job optimism, unpleasant search experiences, and extrinsic job aspirations; it was also a positive predictor of pleasant search experiences and life satisfaction. Controlled motivation to not search was also a negative predictor of expecting to find a job and job optimism, but it was a positive predictor of unpleasant job experiences. In sum, understanding unemployed people's motivation not to search for jobs requires addressing more than just their amotivation with respect to searching; it also requires considering their motivation not to search.

In interpreting such findings, however, let us remember the context of these studies. They were done in Belgium, a wealthy country with a very high safety net relative to other nations in the world. Most people around the globe, especially those with lower socioeconomic backgrounds, experience little or no choice about whether or not to seek work and are frequently driven to take jobs they would not, unless economically pressured, undertake. We discuss the issues of choice and safety nets further in Chapter 23, arguing that without safety nets, both worker choice and employer motivation to supply attractive working conditions are undermined. Yet for now, with our focus on the individual, we simply highlight that even in unemployment, the nature of one's motivation matters.

Career Indecision

Motivation is involved not just in finding a job; it matters for identifying and developing a career. Several studies have examined career indecision among college students as an outcome of autonomy support and autonomous motivation. Guay, Senécal, Gauthier, and Fernet (2003) found that when parents and peers of participants were autonomy-supportive with respect to the participants' career choices, the participants felt more autonomous in finding information about various possible careers, and they perceived themselves to be more competent at such activities. These two motivation variables, in turn, predicted less career indecision. In two subsequent data collections, 1 and 2 years later (Guay, Ratelle, Senécal, Larose, & Deschênes, 2006), the researchers found that some of the sample had made their decisions and that the remaining fell into two groups—those who were chronically undecided and those who were undecided as part of a process that was developmentally appropriate. Using a cluster-type analytic strategy, the researchers determined that the major basis for distinguishing between the two types of indecision was that the chronically undecided students were low in autonomous motivation, whereas the developmentally appropriate undecided students were higher on autonomous motivation.

Thriving People, Thriving Workplaces

A truly motivated employee is trying every day to do his or her best on the job. In accordance with our view of human nature, most people *want* to contribute; they *want* to experience competence in what they do, and many *want* to feel like a meaningful part of a collaborative organization. Although the simple "economic" view of work is that it is merely an exchange of labor for money, our view from the perspective of SDT is that work should be much more than that. It is optimally an opportunity to express one's human capacities and to feel the inherent satisfactions of autonomy, competence, and connection that work can so deeply provide. When these specific satisfactions are supported, both higher quality performance and wellness are the result. When they are neglected or thwarted, alienation is the result, with many costs to organizations.

Indeed, our working hypothesis is that positive wellness at work, particularly the full functioning and vitality that results from satisfaction of the basic psychological needs for competence, autonomy, and relatedness, contributes to long-term organizational health and performance. Studies using SDT concepts with varied participant populations, economic systems, ages, occupations, countries, and work outcomes have consistently provided support for the relevance and importance of the interplay of SDT concepts for understanding motivation in the workplace and other organizations. The science of SDT is, however, still incomplete. We must continually refine our understanding of how elements in the work environments—from managerial inputs and job design to scheduling and compensation—affect these vitality-sustaining need satisfactions. By pinpointing these points of leverage, organizations can fine-tune their practices and policies to optimize the work climate, for the long-term welfare of both employees and the organization's stakeholders.

PART VI

Basic Psychological Needs in Pervasive Social Contexts

CHAPTER 22

Pervasive Social Influences, Part I
Cultural Contexts

The proximal social contexts that influence people's motivation and well-being are embedded within broader social contexts that include cultures, economic structures, and political systems. In this chapter, we examine culture as a pervasive influence, discussing the ways in which cultures both directly and indirectly affect the satisfaction and frustration of basic psychological needs, and thus their constituents' motivation and wellness. Cultures differ both in styles of socialization and in differentially valuing people's relatedness, interdependence, competence, and autonomy. The issue of autonomy has been particularly controversial, as some psychologists have argued that it is a concept relevant to Western, male, wealthy individuals but not to people of many other cultures and subgroups. We review research showing that when people from various cultures are more autonomous in enacting their own cultural values, they evidence greater psychological health and integrity. Other research is reviewed showing that, across cultures, autonomy support generally enhances well-being and performance, mediated by satisfaction of the basic psychological needs. Also discussed is the meaning of choice and its relevance in both collectivist and individualistic cultures. We also suggest that not all cultural contents are equally capable of integration, in large part because of their incongruence with basic needs. Finally, we discuss the importance of respecting autonomy in cultural competence, which involves appreciating the multiple ways in which people are connected in communities.

Throughout this book, we have focused primarily on the influences of *proximal social contexts*—for example, families, peer groups, schools, teams, and work organizations—on the individuals' motivation, development, and wellness. We describe these contexts as "proximal" in the sense that the individuals have direct interpersonal contacts with the people who make up these contexts. As SDT evidence has shown, proximal social contexts have a powerful impact on motivation, behavior, and experience, effects that are strongly mediated by basic psychological need satisfactions and frustrations.

Yet proximal social contexts are themselves embedded within broader or more encompassing social systems, both formal and informal, which influence need satisfaction and behavior in myriad ways. These *pervasive contexts* include the overarching cultural and religious identifications, political structures, and economic systems within which proximal social contexts are constructed and occur (Ryan & Deci, 2011). Every proximal social context, with its controlling and autonomy-affording elements and its affordances and obstacles to need satisfaction, is, in fact, strongly shaped by these more pervasive and distally organized social systems, which are themselves varied in their characteristic values, pressures, reward structures, and norms.

Pervasive contexts can at times *directly* affect people's behaviors and need satisfactions by actively regulating or even blocking their activities. For example, governments can raise barriers to education or economic mobility, and cultural or religious authorities can prohibit or even punish certain lifestyle choices. Yet the primary influence of these distal contexts is typically more indirect, as pervasive cultural norms or economic structures present "invisible" or implicit values, constraints, and affordances, which are then reflected in more proximal social conditions and conveyed by socializing agents from parents and teachers to cultural messengers such as religious leaders, politicians, and celebrities.

Indeed, pervasive contexts, be they economic, political, or cultural, set *psychological horizons* on the very possibilities that persons within them can envision, thereby affecting people's motivations, values, aspirations, and scope of social and personal awareness. Social, religious, and political contexts are never "neutral"—they are, instead, infused with certain beliefs, ideals, rituals, obligations, and practices that are ready for internalization and, at the same time, absent of certain other sensibilities and possibilities. For example, cultures of consumerism and individualism may draw attention away from issues of relational importance and focus people instead on social comparisons, status, and outward image, which, while offering a seductive set of interests and goals, may fail to satisfy basic psychological needs (see, e.g., Kasser, 2011; Vansteenkiste, Ryan, & Deci, 2008). In contrast, cultures of tradition, power, and distance (Hofstede, 2001) may compel individuals to suppress or neglect authentic aspects of self and relationships that could have brought them deep satisfactions.

The aspirations people hold and the forces of regulation they experience around them thus vary by culture, political context, and economic systems, as do the pathways through which these pervasive contexts influence individuals' motivations. As a first example, consider the frequent observation that psychological control (e.g., Barber, 1996) is higher among Chinese relative to Western parents and more accepted as normative by Chinese children (Cheng, Shu, Zhou, & Lam, 2016). Nonetheless, considerable evidence suggests that such psychological control is generally a costly parental approach for a child's well-being, regardless of culture (Helwig & McNiel, 2011; Qin, Pomerantz, & Wang, 2009; Vansteenkiste & Ryan, 2013).

Recent studies have, however, linked these cultural differences to the pervasive controlling pressures felt by Chinese parents. Thus Wuyts, Chen, Vansteenkiste, and Soenens (2015) sampled more than 400 Chinese and 400 Belgian parents of adolescents. First, parental styles varied considerably within both samples, yet they also found the expected between-country mean differences, with Chinese parents on average being more psychologically controlling. These between-country differences were, in turn, accounted for by Chinese parents' having greater child-invested contingent self-esteem, experiencing greater social pressure, and having feelings of unfulfilled dreams of their own. In addition, the Chinese parents perceived fewer pathways to their children's success, which heightened their intense focus on school achievement. Similar findings were reported by Ng, Pomerantz, and Deng (2014), who suggested that parents feel conditional social regard as a function of children's performance, leading to greater psychological control. Here we see how pervasive norms and pressures affect the proximal sphere of the family, leading to differences in motivation and basic psychological need satisfactions.

Similarly, consider the phenomenon of materialistic youth, who, across cultures, show lower well-being (Dittmar, 2007; Kasser, 2002a). We discussed the proximal causes of this negative relation between materialism and wellness in depth in Chapter 11. There, we outlined how individuals who are acquisitive regarding external symbols of worth are often compensating for experiences of basic need thwarting during development (e.g. Kasser, Ryan, Couchman, & Sheldon, 2004). Yet this need thwarting is also culturally embedded. Parents who are more extrinsically focused are potentially less supportive of their children's needs, as they direct their energies elsewhere. For example, Kushlev, Dunn, and Ashton-James (2012) showed how this focus on money or affluence can be associated with a diminished sense of finding meaning in caring for one's children. Using a daily diary method, they found that socioeconomic status (SES) was *negatively* related to the meaning that parents reported when taking care of their children. In a second study, they showed that parents exposed to a photograph of money (intended to prime the significance of wealth) reported a lower sense of meaning in life while spending time with their children at a festival. Such parental dynamics are obviously potentiated in a cultural context of economic competition and wealth inequality, which puts pressure on parents to succeed themselves and to display visible signs of worth (Kasser, Kanner, Cohn, & Ryan, 2007).

These two examples illustrate, first, how readily unrealized parental aspirations and culturally promoted compensatory dreams can become introjected by children, something that happens in diverse cultures. But, more generally, each represents an example, drawn from a plethora available to SDT analyses, of the complex pathways through which overarching cultural, political, and economic contexts can influence individuals' motivations and relationships in more proximal contexts—even the most intimate environments, such as that between parents and their children.

In short, all cultures, whether collectivistic or individualistic, hierarchical or egalitarian, contain pervasive influences that shape the dynamics of proximal environments, resulting in practices that tend to enhance or diminish the need satisfactions of their constituents. SDT, which places its values on the basic need satisfactions essential to wellness, thus considers it an important agenda to understand and empirically study this chain of influence from pervasive to proximal to individual characteristics.

Alongside these "downward" influences of pervasive contexts on individuals, we must also recognize (especially given the body of work we have been reviewing throughout this book), the powerful potential for the "upward" effects that individuals and groups can exert on their pervasive contexts, norms, and practices. People can, through intentional autonomous actions, modify their own cultures, sway the direction of politics, or influence economic systems. Indeed, it is the actions, both separately and collectively, of individuals, often acting with purpose and integrity, that have been at the heart of many of the progressive social and cultural changes we have seen across modern history—changes in which rights conducive to self-determination have been slowly and unsteadily, yet significantly, advanced (Chirkov, Sheldon, & Ryan, 2011). For example, Welzel (2013), using multicultural historical data, has compellingly documented that it is people's expression of emancipatory values that typically *precedes* the establishment of their actual political and social rights. That is, people's desire for autonomy and freedom is likely to expand into rights and behaviors when circumstances allow.

Needs as a Critical Focus

SDT claims applicability across political, cultural, or economic viewpoints, and yet, as we pointed out in Chapter 1, it does so as a *critical* theory. SDT especially aims to evaluate *all* environments with regard to how they support or thwart basic psychological need satisfactions. This critical perspective can be applied not only to proximal social contexts (e.g., parent–child, manager–employee) but also to the more distally organized, pervasive contexts of cultures, governments, and economies.

Clearly some cultural norms, political institutions, and economic systems contribute to basic need satisfaction, and thus to human flourishing, whereas others diminish or even crush opportunities for autonomy, competence development, and relatedness satisfactions of the individuals subjected to them, harming their capacities for self-realization and wellness. Indeed, evaluation of any culture, political structure, or economic system will reveal that, as complex and historically anchored systems, they entail both basic need-supportive and need-thwarting elements. We turn now to such pervasive contexts and their varied functional significance, beginning in this chapter with the construct of *culture* and turning in the following chapter to *political* and *economic* systems.

Self within Cultures: Psychological Needs and Their Universality

Culture, broadly defined, is perhaps the most pervasive influence on human behavior, as well as the most complex to conceptualize and measure. In a profound sense, culture supplies the waters within which the individual psyche swims. Individuals emerge *within* cultures, growing up not just as recipients of prescribed behaviors but as participants in a cultural community (Rogoff, 2003). From an SDT viewpoint, culture and individual are inseparable in the sense that the self develops through the ongoing internalization and integration of ambient cultural practices, values, and regulations (Ryan, 1993). Cultural internalization concerns not only major life issues, such as taking on and assimilating afforded identities, roles, and relationships, but also the routine microhabits of everyday living, from personal hygiene to dietary preferences to manners of speaking. All of these facets of life are influenced by culture, the specifics of which, ideally, not only are readily assimilated by individuals but also provide for them a scaffolding for growth and a sense of meaning and purpose. Further, as SDT highlights, as individuals internalize culture, they are also continuously transforming it, as part of the dialectics of societal change.

There are two fundamental processes through which cultural forms and styles differentially affect basic need satisfactions. First, SDT posits (and supplies abundant empirical evidence for) an inherent human tendency to *internalize and integrate* social practices, as specified in organismic integration theory (OIT; Chapter 8). SDT further assumes that *how* a culture transmits or conveys its regulations and values affects how well they are internalized. When more controlling methods are used to teach or enforce adherence to social practices and value systems, SDT predicts more impoverished and unstable forms of internalization, such as external regulation and introjection. By contrast, more autonomy-supportive socialization techniques foster more integrated internalization of cultural norms and practices. In part, the reason is that autonomy support conduces to openness or receptiveness to learning such that, under autonomy-supportive conditions, individuals can more consciously represent, assimilate, transform, and ultimately better integrate cultural regulations to the self.

Second, SDT posits that *cultural contents*—that is, the specific practices, values, rituals, and norms of a culture—vary in the degree to which they are functionally supportive versus thwarting of basic psychological need satisfactions. Cultural contents that are more conducive to the satisfaction of basic psychological needs for competence, autonomy, and relatedness are expected to be more readily and easily internalized and integrated, and, in accordance with goal content theory (GCT; Chapter 11), to foster greater wellness. In contrast, when the transmitted values or regulations inherently conflict with, or thwart, basic need satisfactions, individuals will less readily internalize them, and, when they do so, they will show more evidence of introjection, compartmentalization, defensiveness, inner conflict, and ill-being.

SDT, therefore, provides two distinct types of analyses that can be applied to both within-culture and between-culture studies. Cultural *methods of socialization* can be examined for their need-supportive versus need-thwarting characteristics, and *cultural contents* (the transmitted practices and values) can be examined for their affordance of basic need satisfactions. SDT hypothesizes that cultural features that are introduced and fostered in more autonomy-supportive ways and that are conducive to greater autonomy, competence, and relatedness satisfactions will yield greater integration and will thus foster more stable, engaged adherence. Cultural elements that are disseminated in more controlling or authoritarian ways and/or that involve need-frustrating practices or constraints will less likely be associated with flourishing, and individuals exposed to them will show less intrapersonal integration.

As plausible and as evidence-supported as these SDT positions may be, in the domain of cultural studies, they have tended to be highly controversial. In large part, this is due to the fact that some scholars, especially those from a *cultural relativism* perspective, resist any critiques of cultures based on universal conceptions of basic needs. Indeed, authors such as Illich (1978) have argued that any positing of common or basic needs threatens individual autonomy and cultural diversity. It risks imposing one cultural viewpoint on others whose cultural meanings may differ. Cultural relativism, instead, asks scholars to "suspend judgment when dealing with groups or societies different from one's own" (Hofstede, 2001, p. 15).

Although we can deeply appreciate cultural relativism's embrace of respect for cultural diversity, in its more radical forms cultural relativism can leave scholars and policy makers ill equipped to be in any way culturally comparative or critical. That is, certain forms of cultural relativism, while correctly emphasizing (1) the variability in people's cultural behaviors, values, attitudes, and goals and (2) the indigenous activity of social construction that has fostered that variability, seem to suggest that all expressed values must be accepted at face value as being equally *good for* those people participating in the culture. This implies that, as long as people are acting consistently with their ambient cultural norms and practices, all is well. Thus, even where cultural norms are clearly oppressive to the basic psychological needs of certain subgroups (e.g., women in cultures in which they have few rights; children in some cultures in which they can be exploited; minorities in some cultures in which they may face stigma and diminished advantages), the relativist perspective supplies no foundation for critiquing them—even though they may do objective harm. In fact, in their laudable attempts to be epistemologically accurate in understanding cultures, there has been a fear of subjecting them to any common wellness criteria.

Ironically, we suggest that the very resistance shown by some scholars to recognizing any human psychological universals arises from an implicit recognition of the fundamental importance of *respecting the autonomy of persons in every culture*. That is, the fear of imposing what is alien on others, of not understanding them in their own terms, presupposes the fundamental and universal need for human autonomy, not only at the individual level but also at the level of culture itself. In contrast to relativism, SDT, both in its theory and advocated practices, explicitly highlights the central importance of autonomy for human flourishing, along with relatedness and competence. Autonomy is a basic need that is not content-specific—indeed, one of the facts of human diversity is that different cultures, groups, and individuals will autonomously embrace and endorse different values and practices.

Values, Motives, and Needs within Cultures

We thus emphasize that, when approaching the sensitive area of cultural studies, SDT does not seek to impose cultural values, norms, or practices (see Craven et al., 2016). Rather, its task is to evaluate specific values, norms, and practices within cultures with respect to very specific criteria: whether they fulfill versus frustrate the basic psychological needs SDT posits to be universal (Chirkov et al., 2011; Deci & Ryan, 2012). This evaluation concerns both *why* people enact specific practices or values (e.g., their relative autonomy) and *what* specific values and behaviors they enact (e.g., their intrinsic vs. extrinsic aspirations). Thus SDT work separates the "why" and the "what" of enacted cultural norms, offering predictions in both areas based on the potential satisfaction versus frustration of people's basic psychological needs.

In examining these issues, careful applications of SDT must differentiate the too-often-confused constructs of *value, motive,* and *need.* Put simply, a *value* is a culturally or individually preferred sensibility or outcome; a *motive* is an implicit or explicit reason for behaving (with some relative degree of autonomy); and a *need* is an essential nutrient for thriving and wellness. These distinctions have import, especially because people can value or fail to value something they need. In addition, any given value may or may not be conducive to need satisfaction. Finally, autonomous or controlled motives can underpin attempts at value attainment, which accordingly affects need satisfactions. Thus each of these constructs can be understood as distinct, while also being interrelated.

Stated more technically, SDT claims that its central constructs concerning basic needs are *etic universals,* defined as characteristics or processes that can be empirically identified as cross-culturally valid. SDT does not claim, however, that its constructs are necessarily *emic universals,* in the sense that SDT acknowledges that these constructs vary in their salience and meaning within the ideologies and conceptual systems of different cultures. For example, SDT posits a universal need for autonomy, yet recognizes that autonomy is not always similarly valued or understood across cultural contexts (e.g., Cheng et al., 2016; Marbell & Grolnick, 2013). Yet, as McGregor (2007) argued, "although it may be differently manifest in different cultures, the concept of 'autonomy' remains essential to understand well-being in all" (p. 332).

Basic Need Satisfactions: Are the Effects Universal?

It is worth noting that, although the concept of universal or pan-cultural psychological needs appears explicitly in few theories, the needs for relatedness and competence are in some ways often acknowledged as basic and universal. For example, Harlow (1958) vividly demonstrated the importance of contact and care in social primates, research that had strong implications for primacy of relatedness in humans. Bowlby (1979), in his work on attachment, proposed a need for secure emotional attachments that he saw as basic to all human beings. Baumeister and Leary (1995) proposed a fundamental need for belongingness that few have contested. As such, the concept of a basic need for relatedness has been proposed within multiple theories, although not always evoking the specific concept of a basic need (Lieberman, 2013).

The more radical relativists, again, would be the exception to recognizing the universality of relatedness needs. Social-cognitive theorists (e.g., Cross, Morris, & Gore, 2002; Kitayama, Markus, Matsumoto, & Norasakkunkit, 1997) have argued that relatedness and belonging is more significant for persons from collectivist cultures, and they suggest that self-interest and self-enhancement are more characteristic of Westerners. In fact, some from this school of thought have used a quite pejorative term to characterize Western individuals, describing them as having a *disjointed* self, bounded and separate from others. In contrast, they describe Eastern individuals as having *conjoint* selves, connected, caring, and contextually sensitive. Instead of universalities, their dichotomous portrait suggests a lack of importance of relatedness in Western peoples.

In contrast to this dichotomous perspective, SDT sees relatedness as functionally important across both East and West (and North and South), rather than as a culturally specific need. Being disjointed is also not, as we see it, an appropriate cultural description. Instead, we see it as a potential condition of persons within all cultures, having everything to do with their sense of inclusion and relatedness and integration into the group. Unlike the dichotomous cultural views, we sadly see alienation and thwarted relatedness as crossing cultural boundaries. For example, consider the Japanese young adults described as *hikikomori*, who have withdrawn from the evaluations and pressures of their outside society but often suffer alone with depression and anxiety. Some Asians are also deeply connected with others but in ways that are controlled and crushing to their autonomous strivings, as in the "Tiger Mom" phenomenon (e.g., see Ng, Pomerantz, & Deng, 2014; Wuyts, Vansteenkiste, Soenens, & Assor, 2015). Our point is that we can find many portraits of alienation and protective or compensatory identities in *all* cultures, demonstrating that feelings of distance and separateness are not unique to the West. The issue is to understand the factors within *every* culture, group, and family that foster feelings of belonging and relatedness versus alienation and "disjointedness," rather than to claim that some cultures are connected and others are not.

Regarding competence, White (1959) proposed a basic need for competence, stating that people engage in competence-promoting behavior because it "satisfies an intrinsic need to deal with the environment" (p. 318). More recently, Elliot, McGregor, and Thrash (2002) postulated a basic need for competence that underlies achievement goal pursuits. In addition, the concept of competence or efficacy has become a core condition for motivated behavior within goal theories (e.g., Locke & Latham, 1990), expectancy theories (e.g., Bandura, 1996), and the theory of flow (Csikszentmihalyi, 1990). Although these latter theories do not endorse the concept of a "need for competence," they emphasize the necessity of experiencing control and competence for adaptation and health. Moreover, the idea of a basic need for competence has generated little debate or controversy, suggesting at least implicit acceptance by many. Yet it is also clear that opportunities for experiencing competence differ within and across cultures. Sen (2000), for example, has argued that some cultures do not afford women the capabilities of education that could help them flourish, to the detriment of the overall development of those cultures.

Although relatedness and competence are widely recognized as needs, the acceptance of a basic need for autonomy has been a quite different matter. Psychologists such as Iyengar and DeVoe (2003) have portrayed autonomy as largely a Western concept and concern not applicable to traditional societies, and in particular to East Asian societies.

Iyengar and Lepper (1999) suggested that the value of autonomy is contradictory to values for relatedness to groups, asserting that the latter is more central within Eastern cultures. Markus, Kitayama, and Heiman (1996), and later Markus and Kitayama (2003), articulated a cultural relativist position, suggesting that values such as autonomy and relatedness are culturally constructed and conveyed (rather than intrinsic and natural). Within Western individualist cultures, their view suggests, autonomy is highly valued and important to wellness, at least among people higher in socioeconomic status (SES; Snibbe & Markus, 2005), but within Eastern collectivist cultures it is considered to be neither valued nor particularly important.

In other words, unlike relatedness and competence needs, the issue of autonomy draws heavy fire in psychology. However, we suggest that among the major reasons that social learning theorists (e.g., Bandura, 1989) and cultural relativists (e.g., Markus et al., 1996) have rejected the universal importance of autonomy is that their definitions of autonomy are undifferentiated, typically conflating ideas of volition, choice, independence, and separateness, all constructs that SDT carefully distinguishes. Specifically, approaches such as social-cognitive theory, cognitive attribution theory, and cultural relativism have all understood autonomy as: (1) independence (nonreliance) on others (e.g., Markus et al., 1996); (2) "freedom from" all social-environmental influences (Bandura, 1989); or (3) separateness and detachment from others (Iyengar & Lepper, 1999). These definitions, in turn, lead them to equate autonomy with individualism and independence and, conversely, to (incorrectly) assume that persons acting in the interests of a collective, adhering with a tradition, or following a norm must somehow lack autonomy.

By differentiating autonomy from independence, as SDT has long explicitly done (e.g., Ryan & Lynch, 1989), important considerations concerning cultural psychologies are opened up. Specifically, SDT understands, along with cultural theorists such as Hofstede (2001) or Triandis and Gelfand (1998), that cultures vary considerably in their values for independence and for supporting group norms and traditions. These cultural contents, however, can be *further* examined within SDT as variously internalized within cultures by cultural subgroups and individuals, with corresponding variance in their relative autonomy (Soenens, Vansteenkiste & Van Petegem, 2015). In every culture, and for each practice within cultures, members experience more or less acceptance and integration and levels of controlled internalization.

When autonomy is understood as the experience of self-endorsement and congruence in one's actions and the result of deeper, more integrated internalization of norms and values, the view that autonomy is merely a Western idea is exposed as inaccurate. Indeed, an understanding of autonomy as a product of deep internalization is salient even in the writings of Confucius, whose views are typically associated with the vertical collectivism of East Asia. For example, Lo (2003) reflects that the Chinese word *ji* refers to one's inner, core self—that is, to the authentic identity of one's self—and that the word *shen* refers to the outer embodiment of the *ji*, which is the expression of one's authenticity. Lo suggests that in the philosophy of Confucius, *ji* and *shen* are integrated in a wise and cultivated person. Chong (2003) similarly draws on Confucian texts in arguing that autonomy, when it refers to self-directedness, is an ideal, adding that, as moral agents, people have "a deep seated desire for directing [their] own lives" (p. 277). Chong further stated that personal autonomy expresses "the individual's ability and freedom to realize projects that are important to his or her own identity" (p.169), projects that can include the values of family and tradition. Finally, Cheng (2004), discussing the Confucian philosophy of selfhood, highlighted that *self-cultivation,* a concept central to the Confucian worldview, entails that the individual develop both reflective and self-regulatory capacities (see also Chen, 2014).

Moving to Indian texts, Paranjpe (1987) pointed out that, within the very early *Upanishads,* critical distinctions were made between a reflective and agentic self versus one's image of oneself and one's identity, paralleling those distinctions we have made between self-as-process versus self-as-object (see Chapters 3 and 15). Paranjpe further argued that the deep intellectual traditions of India acknowledge the self as an experiential center of volition and, further, that these texts, including those drawn from both Yoga and Vedanta, tend to embed these considerations of self in analyses of personal and existential concerns, with an aim toward the development of self-realization.

Ryan and Rigby (2015) discussed and compared Buddhist conceptions of *no-self* with Western conceptions of self and autonomy. Buddhist traditions, in recognizing the impermanence of all things, reject attachments to self-as-object phenomena such as one's identities or self-concepts. In fact, for the Buddhist, esteeming one's self as an image, identity, or ideal are as problematic as not esteeming them (Ryan & Brown, 2005). Thus, clearly, any personal investment in self-as-object contradicts the no-self doctrines of Buddhist thought. Yet the relations of Buddhist doctrines to conceptions of self-as-process and to autonomy are more complex. Ryan and Rigby (2015) pointed to considerable evidence that those individuals higher in mindfulness demonstrate more autonomous functioning and, moreover, that the core concepts of integrity, responsibility, and reflectiveness that characterize healthy self-functioning within the SDT tradition are all supported by, and valued within, Buddhist philosophies. The properties of integrated self-regulation were, indeed, shown by the Buddha himself.

In citing these few examples of Eastern traditions, our claim is not that they exactingly express distinctions we make within our empirical-psychological theorizing in SDT. Rather, we are addressing the claims of scholars who imply that conceptions of autonomy and a self that can be responsible for actions are exclusively Western preoccupations, needs, or concerns. That claim is no less troublesome than the idea that relatedness and community are Eastern sensibilities that are not salient or important to Westerners (e.g., see Christopher & Hickinbottom, 2008; Joshanloo, 2014). Such portrayals are at best highly selective characterizations of both Eastern and Western thinking, but, more problematically, these dichotomization-focused models preclude more nuanced thinking about basic human psychological needs and the dynamics of their satisfaction within *any* culture.

An excellent example of the need for more nuanced views was illustrated in a study by Pan, Gauvain, and Schwartz (2013) of the value for *filial piety,* which concerns upholding honor of one's family and caring for parents. They sampled more than 300 Chinese parents and their eighth-grade children, examining how filial piety was both understood and conveyed. They found that when Chinese parents' collectivistic attitudes and values for filial piety emphasized *respecting and caring* for parents, this positively contributed to children's autonomous motivation, a relation that was mediated through parental autonomy support. In contrast, when parents' collectivistic attitudes and values focused on the children's *upholding parents' honor and reputation,* this was negatively associated with children's autonomous motivation, a relation mediated by parental psychological control. Such findings suggest that collectivistic values are not monolithic or uniformly antithetical to autonomy—indeed, they can support either autonomous or controlled practices and, in turn, differentially influence internalization and children's autonomy development.

Claims that autonomy is primarily a *male* concern are equally problematic (Jordan, 1991). As Friedman (2000) pointed out, the notion that autonomy is inherently inhospitable to women confuses autonomy with self-sufficiency. It also somehow assumes that women's autonomy would be achieved at the expense of connection and relatedness. The viewpoint that men are concerned with autonomy and women are concerned with relatedness simply fails to take stock of the idea that women, as much as men, require autonomy to resist controlling influences and constraints and that autonomy (more than heteronomy) facilitates connectedness, an idea supported within much of the SDT-based research we have already cited in Chapter 12 and elsewhere (see also Nussbaum, 2003). Moreover, as Collins (1991) argued, for many African American women caught in the throes of racism and poverty, autonomy as empowerment is critical to their liberation and well-being. Finally, as Sen (2000) has asserted, autonomy is a central capability, essential for flourishing and wellness in both the developing and wealthy nations. He pointed out that women's autonomy, in particular, is a hallmark of a flourishing economy, and, of course, we know that women's autonomy is an issue that is differentially treated around the world, with women's condition spanning from equal rights to legalized oppression.

Van Bergen and Saharso (2016) provided a particularly poignant example of the costs of denying women personal autonomy. They conducted qualitative interviews with 15 women from minority ethnicities (e.g., Turks, Moroccans, and Surinamese women) residing in the Netherlands who either had attempted or contemplated suicide. Examining the women's narratives, the researchers found that their suicidality was strongly connected with the women's frustration over the violation of their personal autonomy regarding life choices in areas of sexuality, career, relationships, and lifestyles. Some involved severe restrictions of choices and personal freedoms; some entailed subjection to abuse. The interviews made clear how the oppression of autonomy led to despair and depression and a desire to end life rather than endure.

Such narratives tell us why a differentiated concept of autonomy is critical to cross-cultural psychology. If we conceptualized it in terms of choice and volition rather than separateness or individualism, we believe there would be significantly less controversy about autonomy's universal importance for human flourishing or its role in fostering higher quality cultural and economic engagement.

Where tension is salient and goes beyond mere semantic debates, however, is among those who would put priority on group identity and cohesion *over* individual rights to identify or not identify with the group. For example, there are communitarian groups across the globe whose very ethos is built upon ideas of autonomy and willingness and whose vitality is a function of people volitionally adhering to them. Yet there are also communitarian cultures across the globe (and within nearly every nation) whose ethos includes the idea that individuals have *no right* to refuse to identify with them or the practices they purvey. There are, indeed, religious and political groups whose expressed ideology says that one should be *put to death* if she or he does not identify with the group or its practices. This extreme denial of individual rights explicitly puts the priority of the group's identity above the value for individual autonomy. Of interest is the extent to which individuals within such groups can willingly adhere to such beliefs or must instead comply through mechanisms such as compartmentalization, introjection, or simply external regulation.

As we suggest in this and the next chapter, the issue of individual autonomy in relation to the rights and privileges of groups to control or regulate their members is both important and highly controversial in cultural, ethical, and legal studies today. Yet those who are typically most alarmed and disturbed by ideas about the universal import of autonomy at the level of individuals are the power elites and their ideological supporters within groups who most benefit from controlling or constraining others. Cultural conservatives, by definition, are those who most fear ideas of choice or latitude for individuals to define their own values or to have the ability to reject particular identities, values, and practices—ideas associated with liberalism and cosmopolitanism (see Appiah, 2005). Nonetheless, historical trends of globalization and accessible technologies mean that more people in all societies are adopting multiple identities, each of which is more or less internalized by the person and is accordingly more versus less compatible with both her or his other identifications and needs (integration) and with other individuals within the person's social contexts (homonomy).

From Theory to Evidence: Cross-Cultural Research Using SDT

As previously stated, SDT takes interest in both the *process* of internalization within cultures and the relative autonomy of practices for individuals and the general *contents* of culture, in terms of their affordance of need satisfactions versus frustrations. We now turn to a discussion and review of each of these issues as they have so far been researched across cultures.

Cross-Cultural Research I: The Significance of Internalization and Relative Autonomy

Attempting to distinguish differences in cultural contents from the relative autonomy of their adoption, Chirkov, Ryan, Kim, and Kaplan (2003) empirically examined the idea that cultural values and practices, including those reflecting collectivism or individualism, will be endorsed to differing degrees *between* cultures, and yet the degree of internalization, or relative autonomy, in people's motives for practicing ambient norms will be associated with the level of positive outcomes *within* cultures.

Using Triandis and Gelfand's (1998) dimensional framework, Chirkov et al. (2003) identified four types of cultural norms and practices. *Horizontal collectivist* practices place priority on the societal collective and treat individuals as similar and equal. *Horizontal individualist* practices allow persons to follow their own personal beliefs or preferences, yet at the same time value all individuals as important and equal. *Vertical collectivist* cultures emphasize that the needs of the collective come before those of individuals, and individuals recognize their place within the hierarchical relationships of the collective. Finally, *vertical individualist* cultures endorse individuals' striving for recognition and distinction and their striving competitively to achieve a position of power and influence relative to others.

Chirkov et al. (2003) then recruited participants from universities in Russia, Turkey, South Korea, and the United States, because they were expected to vary in where they fell on these cultural dimensions. The participants were first asked to provide their perceptions of the frequency and importance that other people in their local cultures placed on each of the four types of practices. This provided information about the degree to which the participants saw these practices and values as central and meaningful within their ambient cultural contexts. Then they were asked why they would *personally* engage in each of the cultural practices, using the external, introjected, identified, and intrinsic constructs derived from OIT.

Results confirmed Chirkov et al.'s (2003) expectations that cultures would differ in their normative practices in line with Triandis and Gelfand's (1998) model. Yet, despite these differences in ambient values and practices, within all four cultures, for both genders, and for all cultural practices, the degree to which an individual was more autonomous in enacting the practices positively predicted well-being. Cultural membership did not moderate this relation. In short, autonomous behavior was found to be important for psychological health in all cultures, regardless of whether they were collectivist or individualist, horizontal or vertical. Noteworthy, too, was that in no country was the relation between autonomy and psychological well-being moderated by gender, suggesting that satisfaction of the need for autonomy is equally important for males and females.

Chirkov et al. (2003) raised an additional, exploratory question of whether people internalize and integrate all cultural values with equal readiness, reasoning that some societal orientations that are less compatible with satisfaction of basic psychological needs might be more difficult to accept and endorse. In this regard, they speculated that vertical value systems might be more difficult to integrate than horizontal, egalitarian value systems. The fact of being subordinate to more powerful others in vertical systems represents a high risk, for the autonomy need has a high likelihood of being thwarted by the controlling practices of powerful others, as does the relatedness need, because hierarchies often place limits on people with whom one can affiliate. If those speculations were true, then vertical practices should have a lower relative autonomy index than horizontal practices. Chirkov et al. indeed found a significant mean difference between internalization scores for horizontal, relative to vertical, practices, across cultures and across collectivism–individualism, suggesting that on average the hierarchical values and practices measured might be more difficult to integrate than the horizontal values.

Downie, Koestner, El Geledi, and Cree (2004) did a follow-up of the Chirkov at al. (2003) study that had examined cultural internalization of horizontal versus vertical cultural values. Participants were non-Canadian students living in Montreal. Each had a heritage culture (e.g., Chinese, Korean, Pakistani) and, given the bicultural context of Montreal, exposure to two host cultures (viz., English Canadian and French Canadian). The primary questions of interest were whether the degree of egalitarianism of the heritage culture would affect the degree to which participants had internalized the heritage cultures' practices, were competent in their heritage-cultural settings, and displayed well-being. Also of interest were the relations among internalization (i.e., relative autonomy), cultural competence, and well-being with respect to the host cultures. Internalization was assessed with self-reports, whereas cultural competence and well-being were assessed with both self-reports and ratings made by participants' peers.

The first focus was on the participants' *heritage culture*. Each heritage country was classified in terms of the degree to which it was egalitarian, based on Schwartz's (1994) rating system. Consistent with Chirkov et al.'s (2003) findings, the degree of egalitarianism of the heritage country predicted both greater internalization (relative autonomy) of heritage practices and greater cultural competence in the heritage culture. Autonomy and competence, in turn, predicted the participants' experiencing positive affect when acting in their heritage cultures.

Parallel results were present for internalization of the *host cultures*. The more participants had internalized one of their host culture's values, the greater their cultural competence in that culture was, and, further, both internalization and cultural competence were related to experiencing positive affect in the host cultures.

Sheldon, Elliot, et al. (2004) also examined the relation of autonomous motivation to subjective well-being in three Eastern cultures and the United States. Participants listed the personal strivings (Emmons, 1986) that were most important to them and then were asked to rate the degree to which they were pursuing each striving for external, introjected, identified, and intrinsic reasons, from which an overall relative autonomy score was derived. Although the mean level of autonomous motivation differed (with the U.S. and South Korean samples being high relative to those from China and Taiwan), autonomous motivation was significantly positively related to subjective well-being in all four cultures. As with Chirkov et al. (2003), neither gender nor demographic factors moderated the relations between autonomy and well-being. Using still different methods, Rudy, Sheldon, Awong, and Tan (2007) reported that individual autonomy was positively associated with psychological well-being among Canadians, Chinese Canadians, and Singaporeans alike. Such studies are consistent with a growing literature revealing that autonomy concerns are not unique to Western cultures and that greater autonomy predicts wellness in collectivist Eastern societies as well as Western ones.

Again, this becomes less surprising when one distinguishes autonomy as volition from independence and self-reliance. Chen, Vansteenkiste, Beyers, Soenens, and Van Petegem (2013) examined SDT's distinction between autonomy and independence in more than 500 adolescents from both urban and rural regions of China. Independence was operationalized as the degree of independent decision making within the family; autonomy was operationalized in terms of the degree of volition reflected in the motives underlying one's decision making. Chen et al. hypothesized, based on SDT, that autonomy would positively link to wellness, a result they expected to be mediated by basic psychological need satisfaction. Results confirmed that autonomy significantly predicted well-being indicators, with basic need satisfaction accounting for that result. In contrast, independent decision making was not significantly related with well-being or need satisfaction, echoing other SDT findings (e.g., Ryan & Lynch, 1989). Individual differences in collectivistic cultural orientations did not moderate any of these findings.

What this body of research shows is that, despite the fact that *what* people may practice or value differs as a function of culture, the issue of *why* they engage in practices or values has universal import. Internalization and integration, reflected in one's relative autonomy when enacting cultural practices, has more generalized effects. The less well integrated one's values and practices are, the lower will be one's wellness, a fact that applies across highly diverse cultural values and practices and across gender.

Cross-Cultural Research II: Autonomy Support's Impact

Given the universal import of autonomy and integrated internalization of cultures, it follows that the issue of autonomy support and control would also be important as a cross-cultural issue. In this regard, one thing is clear—parenting practices differ across cultures. Moreover, beneath surface differences in style and content, there is, from an SDT viewpoint, an important, underlying universal issue concerning how parents motivate their children and the perceived locus of causality (PLOC) for actions that follows within the children. That is, across the globe SDT expects that children can be pawns or origins, as de Charms (1968) would have described it.

Chirkov and Ryan (2001) examined parents' and teachers' autonomy support of high school students in Russia and the United States, Russia being a moderately collectivist culture and the United States being a highly individualist culture. They predicted that autonomy support from parents and teachers would predict both autonomous motivation and psychological health in both countries. Well-being was measured with a composite of self-esteem, self-actualization, life satisfaction, and the reverse of depression, whereas autonomous and controlled motivations were measured with an adapted self-regulation questionnaire (Ryan & Connell, 1989). All measures were translated into Russian and back-translated, as well as examined for comparability using means and covariance structure (MACS) analysis (Little, 1997). Results indicated that, although both parent and teacher autonomy support tended to be lower in Russia than in the United States, in both cultural settings they were related positively to more autonomous forms of motivation and more negatively to controlled motivations. Further, autonomy support from both parents and teachers were comparably positive predictors of the mental-health indicators in both countries.

Although not cross-cultural, Jang, Kim, and their colleagues published several papers specifically challenging statements by authors such as Murphy-Berman and Berman (2003) and Iyengar and DeVoe (2003), which suggest that autonomy and autonomy support would not be important in East Asian contexts. As one example, Jang, Reeve, Ryan, and Kim (2009) presented four studies focused on high school students in South Korea. In the first two, they asked the students about their most and least satisfying learning experiences and their most productive experiences, demonstrating that these were strongly predicted by basic need satisfactions for autonomy, competence, and relatedness. A third study replicated and extended these findings by showing that such results held even when controlling for cultural and parental influences, including the collectivistic value orientation. A fourth, semester-long prospective study showed that teacher support for autonomy was positively related to student need satisfactions, which in turn related to an array of well-being and performance outcomes, whereas controlling practices were negatively related to these outcomes.

Taylor and Lonsdale (2010) explored cultural differences in the relations between teacher autonomy support, basic psychological need satisfactions, subjective vitality, and effort among students ages 13–15 in physical education classes from both the United Kingdom and Hong Kong, China. Using a multilevel analysis, they found in both samples positive relations between autonomy support and students' vitality and effort in class. These relations were, in turn, mediated by students' basic psychological need satisfaction. Among the few differences in patterns, the relation between autonomy support and competence was stronger in the Chinese sample compared with the U.K. sample. Taylor and Lonsdale argued that their findings supported the view that, for both Chinese and British students, an autonomy-supportive environment facilitated more positive student engagement and experience. Indeed, many studies echo these findings, revealing that autonomy support provided by parents and teachers positively predicted Chinese and South Korean students' academic functioning and psychological well-being (D'Ailly, 2003; Jang, Kim, & Reeve, 2012; Vansteenkiste, Simons, Lens, Sheldon, & Deci, 2004; Wang et al. 2007; Zhou, Ma, & Deci, 2009).

These results are not unexpected from an SDT point of view, but they surprise many who imagine that collectivist values must be heteronomously disseminated. SDT expects, in fact, that autonomy support within collectivistic cultures facilitates more autonomous internalization of ambient collectivist values. However, it also suggests that various elements of cultures may have distinct functional significances for cultural members (e.g., Pan et al., 2013, reviewed above). There is no doubt that features of broad concepts such as collectivism or individualism that support, or alternatively thwart, people's basic needs will affect their readiness to internalize and integrate these cultural elements. This is why the critical agenda for cultural studies articulated by SDT promises to be both rich and complex.

Nor is this issue restricted to East–West comparisons. Sheldon, Abad, and Omoile (2009) examined a variety of SDT variables as predictors of wellness in both Indian and Nigerian adolescents. Consistent with research in other cultures, perceived teacher autonomy support was associated with greater basic need satisfaction in schools. The three basic needs of autonomy, competence, and relatedness also predicted students' evaluations of their classes and whether they would recommend them to friends. Basic need satisfactions also predicted greater general life satisfaction in both cultural samples. Finally, the researchers obtained ratings of perceived maternal and paternal autonomy support and found that both predicted greater life satisfaction in both samples.

Consider another study by Marbell and Grolnick (2013), who examined the perceptions of parental styles by sixth-grade Ghanaian students. They reasoned that Ghana was an interesting place to test the generalizability of SDT's constructs given its collectivist and traditional culture and concerns that autonomy support might be at odds with Ghanaian children's values of strong respect for elders. Results found support for several elements of SDT's model of parenting (see Chapter 13). Provision of structure was related to cognitive perceived competence, whereas parental control was associated with greater controlled (i.e., external/introjected) regulation around academic work and decreased school engagement. Finally, parental autonomy support was negatively related to depression and positively related to autonomous forms of motivation, engagement in school, and perhaps most important for our current discussion, children's endorsement of collectivist cultural values. It seems that in this collectivist society, children who experience autonomy support more willingly assimilate its practices. Parents' support of their offspring's autonomy was not in conflict with values of respect and communalism, but instead was positively associated with children's endorsement of these cultural values. This is consistent with SDT, which holds that children are more likely to internalize cultural values when they are presented in a way that does not force adherence but, rather, invites it with provision of rationale and support, thereby deepening their ownership and integration of their culture. Autonomy is thus not antithetical to traditional cultures; it can make them more stable.

It has been argued from a relativistic approach that psychological control carries a different meaning for individuals from more collectivistic contexts. For example, Chao and Aque (2009) reported that Asian adolescents feel less angry about parents using psychological control compared with European American adolescents. We noted above that Cheng et al. (2016) reported similar findings with Chinese students. Mason, Kosterman, Hawkins, Herrenkohl, Lengua, and McCauley (2004) found that African American adolescents experience mothers' guilt-inducing behavior as more indicative of care and love than their European American counterparts. These differences in the interpretation of parenting behaviors might suggest differing effects. However, on this point the evidence is much less clear. For example, recall Chirkov and Ryan's (2001) result that, despite parental control being more normative in Russia, its negative effects were similar to those in the United States. Cheng et al. (2016) noted moderation of some outcomes but problems with controlling practices on others. Similarly, Soenens, Park, Vansteenkiste, and Mouratidis (2012) applied well-validated measures of psychological control, autonomy support, and warmth in both European (Belgian) and South Korean samples. They found that there were similar effects on wellness outcomes in the two groups, specifically, decreased depressive symptoms. Thus, although there may indeed be a different functional significance given to the same behaviors in differing cultural contexts, we think there are limits on that idea. Some kinds of parenting strategies may be inherently controlling, whatever the cultural interpretation applied to them.

Ahmad, Vansteenkiste, and Soenens (2013) extended the consideration of the functional effects of parental autonomy support and control to a sample of Jordanian adolescents. As a cultural context, Jordan has been characterized as both vertical and collectivist, yet quite culturally divergent from Asian contexts considered above. Ahmad et al. measured Jordanian teens' perceptions of maternal psychological control and responsiveness and also obtained an independent measure of teacher-rated adjustment, so their results were not based solely on self-reports. As would be predicted by SDT, maternal psychological control was negatively related to teacher-rated adjustment, whereas maternal responsiveness was positively related to this outcome. Further, the relations of these two parenting dimensions to adjustment outcomes were mediated by satisfaction of basic psychological needs, particularly those for autonomy and competence.

Our viewpoint, as well as those of other cultural theorists, is that, although the cultural contents that parents are modeling and transmitting to their children vary greatly across the world, socialization operates more smoothly and conduces to better child outcomes when parents are autonomy-supportive. Autonomy support is not inherently antithetical to traditional or collective values, nor is its importance supplanted or strongly modified by them. At the same time, there are normative differences in the functional significance of certain practices that can (within limits) moderate effects on outcomes, as offspring in different cultures may perceive different meanings to the same parental practices, resulting in differing levels of basic need satisfaction or frustration. Such nuances are an important focus of true cross-cultural research.

Cross-Cultural Research III: Basic Need Satisfaction and Wellness

The postulate that the basic psychological needs are etic universals even though they may be manifested differently in cultures with different values, goals, or practices suggests that it is important to study need satisfaction across cultures, including cultures with very different cultural values. To do this meaningfully, however, it is necessary to take a dynamic perspective that goes deeply enough into psychological processes to find linkages that relate the basic psychological needs to the phenotypic goals and behaviors that are common in different cultures and may even appear on the surface to be contradictory to a specific need. Staying at a more superficial level of behaviors and cognitions, as many investigators have done, is inadequate for dealing with the issue of etic universality. Yet, despite the difficulties of such research, there are now many cross-cultural empirical investigations focused on the needs for autonomy, competence, and relatedness, which SDT maintains are fundamental and universal needs. We, for illustrative purposes, review only some examples from this ever-expanding literature.

Among our first forays into cross-cultural work on needs was a study that took place with Bulgarian and U.S. workers in the early 1990s. Bulgaria had been under Soviet domination until 1989, with a long-standing totalitarian government in the Stalinist tradition. Virtually all industries were owned by the state and operated by central planning principles. Cultural values were collectivist, and the country was relatively isolated from the West. After the nation was freed from Soviet domination, change was slow, as, even 5 years later, none of the important state-owned companies had passed into private hands. Payments to Bulgarian workers from the state, as owner of the companies, were often weeks or months late. In a free election, Communists had been voted back into power, as the citizens struggled with change.

It was in this context that Deci, Ryan, Gagné, Leone, Usunov, and Kornazheva (2001) began to collect data on basic psychological need satisfaction among Bulgarian working adults and U.S. comparisons. Observations of work groups in several state-owned industries suggested considerable inefficiency but also unusual possibilities for need satisfaction. Within work groups, relatedness among members frequently appeared to be very important and cultivated. Work groups also often elected their leaders, giving them some feeling of autonomy in micro-decisions, although major decisions were still made in a top-down fashion. Work in many settings we observed was neither pressured by rewards nor tightly supervised. Competence, on the other hand, was of little concern, as it had never been an important criterion for employment or reward under the communist ethic; feedback and contingencies based on performance or effort were not salient.

We collected reports from employees of 10 such state-owned companies concerning their perceptions of their work climate (i.e., autonomy support vs. control), their basic need satisfactions, their motivation for work, and their psychological well-being. The same measures were also obtained from the employees of a data management firm in the United States so as to have a comparative reference point. Analyses showed that the constructs were comparably understood and meaningful in both Bulgarian and U.S. samples. More important, results revealed that autonomy support (from both immediate supervisors and top management) was positively related to satisfaction of each of the basic needs for autonomy, competence, and relatedness and that the social-contextual support for autonomy was also strongly related to motivation and well-being in *both* cultural contexts. Additionally, findings indicated that need satisfaction was strongly related to engagement and well-being, suggesting that employees who reported greater need satisfaction on the job were more motivated and engaged in their work and, in turn, were psychologically better adjusted. Finally, structural equation modeling (SEM) indicated that, across employees of state-owned Bulgarian industries and workers in the U.S. organization, autonomy support predicted need satisfaction, and that in turn predicted both engagement and well-being. In sum, need satisfaction was important for the motivation and well-being of workers in both Bulgaria and the United States, despite the especially robust differences in terms of cultural, political, and economic circumstances at the pivotal time of this research.

As we previously reviewed, Chirkov et al. (2003) similarly demonstrated strong relations between basic need satisfactions and indicators of wellness in their cross-cultural studies. Following up on this, with special interest in moving beyond "East–West" dichotomies, Chirkov, Ryan, and Willness (2005) compared Brazilian and Canadian samples. In both nations, they found that satisfaction of basic psychological needs was a predictor not only of well-being but also of the extent to which people felt "at home" in their own cultural contexts. Put differently, whether Brazilian or Canadian, persons who reported low satisfaction of SDT's basic psychological needs were also more culturally estranged. Chirkov et al. (2005) also showed that greater relative autonomy in enacting cultural practices was associated with well-being in both countries. Finally, as in the Chirkov et al. (2003) research, here, too, the researchers found that internalization tended to be higher for horizontal relative to vertical practices.

Sheldon, Elliot, Kim, and Kasser (2001) examined the phenomenal salience of basic needs in participants from both South Korea and the United States by assessing what they experienced as having been satisfied when they had what they considered satisfying experiences. The researchers assumed that need satisfactions would represent qualities of experience that people require to thrive and thus would be salient in experiences of satisfaction. They assembled a list of 10 constructs that they considered "candidate needs" that might be the basis for people's experiencing satisfaction. These candidate needs included competence, autonomy, and relatedness (SDT's basic psychological needs), as well as a range of other desires, namely, money, security, popularity, self-esteem, physical health, pleasurable stimulation, and self-actualization, none of which is considered a basic need within SDT.

Before moving on to a further description of the research, let us first reemphasize the meaning of the concept of "need" from the SDT perspective. In this theory, a basic psychological need is a satisfaction that is essential for thriving—for growth, integrity, and wellness—and that applies to all people. In other words, the importance of need satisfactions to wellness is inherent in our human design and is universal rather than learned. Further, we maintain that, in naming needs, it is important to keep the list of needs as short as possible, to include only needs that specify the content of what the organism requires to thrive and to name the needs in such a way that they will provide the basis for integrating a large number of phenomena that have been observed in psychological research. Additionally, it is important to separate the idea of needs—the basic human universals—from desires, which may or may not promote thriving. Evidence reviewed in Chapter 11 indicates, for example, that money and popularity are common desires but not needs, for their pursuit and attainment are not invariably associated with health and wellness. Finally, we believe it is important to draw a distinction between concepts that index thriving and those that promote it. In other words, we view some of the candidate needs (viz., self-esteem, self-actualization) as indicators of psychological health and thriving rather than needs in themselves. Thus, for us, although self-actualization and self-esteem are not technically needs, they do index the results of having had the needs for autonomy, competence, and relatedness satisfied.

To return to the Sheldon et al. (2001) research, participants were asked to think about the most satisfying event they have experienced in recent times and briefly describe it. They were then provided with 30 descriptive sentences (3 relating to each of the 10 candidate needs) and asked to what degree, during their described event, they had experienced the state represented in each statement. Finally, they reported the degree to which, during the event, they had felt positive affect. Evidence from these studies indicated quite clearly that autonomy, competence, and relatedness emerged as three of the four most important candidate needs across the studies and the countries, thus providing evidence that people understand these experiences to be extremely important in life satisfaction. Again, this evidence of emic commonality is not essential to our claim that basic needs are etic universals, but such shared salience is nonetheless noteworthy. The fourth candidate need that was consistently important to people was self-esteem, which we consider to be an outcome of need satisfaction rather than a need itself.

Sheldon et al. also assessed the strength of each of the 10 "candidate needs" for all participants as individual differences. The idea was to see whether the strength or importance that people place on these needs would moderate the relations between satisfaction of the needs and the individuals' well-being. A match hypothesis (e.g., Hackman & Lawler, 1971) would suggest that when people satisfy "needs" that are important to them, the positive effect on well-being would be greater than when they satisfy less important "needs." In contrast, SDT claims that satisfaction of basic needs will be positively linked to individuals' well-being regardless of whether the individuals value the needs highly. In line with SDT's postulate, results of the Sheldon et al. (2001) analyses showed that the link from need satisfaction to well-being was not moderated by strength, again showing why needs should be distinguished from desires.

New cross-cultural research on the issue of need satisfaction continues to emerge. For example, Chen, Vansteenkiste, Beyers, Boone, et al. (2015) investigated both need satisfaction (vs. lack thereof) and need frustration (vs. lack thereof) as distinct dimensions that would predict well-being and ill-being across cultures. Collecting samples from China, Peru, Belgium, and the United States, they first provided evidence for the measurement equivalence and construct validity of the psychological need satisfaction measures, with each of the three needs relating uniquely to higher well-being. Indeed, need satisfaction and need frustration accounted for considerable variance across these diverse samples in well- and ill-being indicators. Also, underscoring BPNT's universality claim, the outcomes of need satisfaction were not moderated by cultural backdrop or by individual differences in the desire for satisfaction of the needs.

Another interesting confirmation of the universal importance of basic psychological need satisfaction can be gleaned from the results of cross-cultural research using experience-sampling techniques reported by Church, Katigbak, Ching, and colleagues (2013). This international team of investigators reported two studies in which, multiple times daily, they collected brief self-reports on well-being, Big Five self-concepts, and need satisfaction, among other variables. Their first study included samples from five countries (Venezuela, Philippines, China, Japan, and the United States). In part, Church and colleagues were examining such issues as whether people in some types of cultures (collectivist, dialectical, etc.) are indeed more contextually sensitive and variable in self-concepts, as some relativists have claimed. Among their many findings, however, were ones very pertinent to SDT. Across the five diverse cultures, Church et al. found that need satisfaction commonly predicted more openness, agreeableness, conscientiousness, and emotional stability, as well as more positive and less negative affect. In summarizing their findings, Church et al. stated that need satisfaction accounted for "a substantial portion (about 20–45%) of the within-person variability in personality traits. The latter results provide support for self-determination theory (Deci & Ryan, 2000), which predicts that people in all cultures will express their traits differently as a function of their need satisfaction in various situations" (Church et al., 2013, p. 932).

Chettiar (2015) reminded readers that we should not identify cultures with nations, as many nations have important cultural differences within themselves. This research examined subjective well-being (SWB) as a function of basic psychological needs within Tamilians and Keralites, both groups situated in the southern part of the Indian subcontinent. It was described that these groups reside in regions that differ both geographically and in terms of familial styles. Yet results in both groups showed that all three needs were significantly correlated with greater SWB, at nearly equal levels. Still, there were substantial overlapping variances, and thus regression equations led some needs to be nonpredictive when controlling for the others. Competence, in particular, was most the most predominant satisfaction predicting outcomes, rendering autonomy nonsignificant in regressions. Mean differences also appeared in how much each need was satisfied, bespeaking this idea that distinctions between subcultures can have import.

Cross-Cultural Research IV: Autonomy and Relatedness across Cultures

As we have pointed out, a number of cultural researchers, especially those in search of support for cultural dichotomies, have suggested that values for autonomy are antithetical to values for relatedness (Iyengar & Lepper, 1999; Joshanloo, 2014). This is so despite SDT's continuous findings that these are typically strongly positively related and synergistic (see Chapter 12). Yet a reasonable question is whether this positive relationship between autonomy and relatedness is itself culturally bound. In other words, is autonomy support conducive to relationship quality only in the "West?"

Work on the topic of emotional reliance within SDT illuminates some of the issues in this area. Ryan, La Guardia, Solky-Butzel, Chirkov, and Kim (2005) suggested that when people experience sadness, anger, or fear and when they experience joy, excitement, and exhilaration, they often want to turn to others to share their feelings. Doing so is likely to help them manage emotions and is likely to increase experiences of intimacy and provide satisfaction of the need for relatedness. Although this tendency to turn to others, to rely on them at emotional times, may be a universal desire, cultures clearly tend to have different norms with respect to emotional expression, emotion sharing, and relying on others. Accordingly, Ryan and colleagues (2005) examined *emotional reliance* on families and friends in samples from four countries—South Korea, Russia, Turkey, and the United States. They found that emotional reliance tended to be highest in Russia, with the United States being second, Turkey third, and Koreans reporting low reliance on families and friends when having emotional experiences. Like Chirkov and Ryan (2001), however, these investigators were less focused on mean differences between samples but on whether, despite these normative differences, the degree to which people within each country emotionally relied on families or friends when having emotional experiences was a positive predictor of well-being. Thus, although cultures have different norms about the appropriateness of expressing emotions to others (e.g., in Korea, people may tend to believe it would burden their families and friends if they focused too much on their own feelings), the degree to which people do so is associated with stronger mental health, regardless of the cultures' norms. This, we maintain, is because people will experience greater satisfaction of their relatedness need at these important times. Moreover, according to SDT, turning to others to authentically share experiences is facilitated, again universally, by autonomy-supportive others. Supporting this view, across all four samples people indicated more willingness to share their feelings with those others they felt were autonomy-supportive, a result not moderated by cultural membership.

Beyond sharing emotional experiences, based on relationship motivation theory (RMT; Chapter 12), one expects that when people are with others who support their autonomy, they can more easily be the people they aspire to be, and this means being closer to their own ideals. In a cross-cultural test of this expectation, Lynch, LaGuardia, and Ryan (2009) used multilevel modeling to examine the prediction that partners' autonomy support would be associated with smaller discrepancies between one's ideal self and one's self when with the partners. They had samples from the United States, Russia, and China rate their actual and ideal selves using Big Five trait measures (Costa & McCrea, 1992). They then were asked to rate how they view themselves when they are with each of several specific primary social partners. At a within-person level, participants' actual self-concept was closer to their ideal when with autonomy-supportive social partners. Although there was some weak moderation by country membership, associations were in the same direction for all countries. Specifically, people tended to be more open, extraverted, agreeable, and conscientious when with others who were autonomy-supportive, and this was also associated with greater subjective wellness across cultural samples.

It seems that quality in relating to others has some common elements across diverse cultures. When others are more autonomy-supportive, people are able to be more open, more authentic, closer to their ideal selves, and more engaged (e.g., Weinstein, Hodgins, & Ryan, 2010), as well as higher in the well-being that follows. This does not mean that cultural styles are equally characterized by autonomy support—indeed, evidence suggests that there are significant mean-level differences in autonomy supportiveness (e.g. Supple, Ghazarian, Peterson, & Bush, 2009; Chirkov & Ryan, 2001), even though within-culture correlates are similar. Rather, what does appear relatively invariant across cultures and contexts are the generally positive functional effects of autonomy support and the generally negative effects of controlling environments on human flourishing and wellness.

Cross-Cultural Research V: Choice, Autonomy, and Well-Being

Central to human autonomy is the experience of choice. When autonomously motivated, people feel that, all things considered, they would choose to do that which they are doing. Their experience is one of volition, endorsement, and choice—experiences that can be confirmed by reflective endorsement of their actions. As we have, perhaps, laboriously argued in previous chapters, this does not mean that individuals have to be the initiators of their goals, have multiple options, or be self-directive in their actions; it means only that they have to truly concur with undertaking an action, either for intrinsic or well-internalized motives.

SDT, because of its focus on the nuances of autonomous functioning, specifically distinguishes the issue of choice from the cognitive concept of making decisions. Decision making is the process of selecting among options that are available to a person. But not all decisions involve a sense of choice. The boss says "Work this weekend or get fired." The employee has a decision to make here, but he or she may not be choosing to engage either option in the sense of undertaking either willingly. When we examine decision making, then, we are careful within SDT not to confuse mere selections between options with the kinds of opportunities for choosing that facilitate autonomy. In addition, SDT recognizes that people can feel a sense of choice in following others' leads or mandates, again if they have reason to congruently assent to these directives or the legitimacy of the authority. So, even if the source of a goal is external, people can autonomously assent to it, finding in it either value or interest. Finally, the number of behavioral options available to people certainly does not necessarily index the amount of "choice" they have, nor guarantee any sense of autonomy. Too many options or selections are likely to represent the experience of additional cognitive load, rather than a meaningful choice. Instead, the facilitating aspect of options, whether few or many, is contingent on whether they afford pathways that, when chosen, are better matched with the person's values and volitional interests.

Distinguishing differences between choice, defined as mere decision making, as a number of options, or as assent to an available option are conceptual nuances that have often been lost with the experimental and cross-cultural literatures on choice. So, too, is the notion that one might feel a sense of choice and volition when following trusted others. Instead, the search for dichotomies has led researchers to forget that the very nature of cultural differences implies that there will be differential deployment of one's motivation as a function of varied cultural internalizations. Insofar as cultures differ, they will internalize, and assent to, different things. In this regard, some theorists have yet to appreciate that collectivism and traditionalism *can* be autonomously embraced. Because of the importance of this issue, we now look more closely at experimentation on choice in the area of cultures.

To set the stage, let's return to a classic experiment of choice and intrinsic motivation reviewed in Chapter 6. Zuckerman, Porac, Lathin, Smith, and Deci (1978) suggested that one social-contextual factor that could increase people's autonomy was the "experience of choice," which they operationalized experimentally as allowing people to decide what activities to do (selecting among different puzzles) and how long to work on each one they selected. The contrast was a "yoked" condition in which an experimenter told each participant which puzzles to work on and how much time to spend on each, using the decisions that had been made by the experimental-group participants to whom these no-choice participants had been yoked. Results indicated that participants who had been allowed to make choices were more intrinsically motivated for the activity than those simply assigned activities and times.

Since the Zuckerman et al. experiment, there have been many replications of the "choice" effect in samples from multiple contexts and developmental periods. A meta-analysis by Patall, Cooper, and Robinson (2008), for example, examined 41 studies on the effects of choice on intrinsic motivation and found overall that choice enhanced intrinsic motivation. This effect was stronger for children than adults, and a moderate number of options led to more positive motivational results. This general pattern of choice facilitating motivation has, it seems, been widely replicated, and research by Murayama et al. (2015) found, using Japanese participants, that the ventromedial prefrontal cortex (vmPFC) played a key role in this facilitation effect.

Replications of this choice effect come from research labs around the globe and are not unique to the West. Illustrative is a recent experiment from Chinese investigators Meng and Ma (2015). They had university students engage in tasks of equal difficulty, sometimes chosen and sometimes externally assigned. The effect of having choice was then examined both behaviorally and through electrophysiological methods. The researchers found that when choice was available, participants showed a greater stimulus-preceding negativity (SPN), (suggesting enhanced positive expectations), and a larger feedback-related negativity (FRN) loss–win difference wave (d-FRN), which they interpreted in terms of greater intrinsic motivation toward the task.

However, some cultural theorists dispute the importance of choice in collectivist contexts. For example, in a very widely cited study, Iyengar and Lepper (1999) argued that "personal choice" is not as important to people in the collectivist cultures of Asia and elsewhere. The investigators did two experiments with U.S. elementary school students to test their reasoning. In their studies, European American and Asian American children were assigned to one of three conditions: (1) making choices individually, (2) accepting the choices made by trusted ingroup members (e.g., their mothers, Study 1; ingroup close classmates, Study 2), and (3) having the choices made by outgroup members (an adult experimenter, Study 1; outgroup students in a lower grade from another school, Study 2). The ingroup and outgroup choices were yoked to the individuals' choices in the same way that Zuckerman et al. had done it, to allow the individual-choice participants a true choice while ensuring comparability in the task across conditions.

Results indicated, first, that, in *both* the European American and the Asian American groups, making individual choices led to significantly greater intrinsic motivation than having decisions made by the experimenter or outgroup children. Thus this experiment strongly replicated the Zuckerman et al. (1978) finding for participants of both ethnicities, a result frequently not acknowledged in reviews of this work. It appeared that personal choice did matter to both groups. Yet, in addition, within the European American sample, individual choices led to higher intrinsic motivation than did the trusted-others' choices, whereas in the Asian American group, the trusted-others' choices led to *higher* intrinsic motivation than did individual choices. Iyengar and Lepper interpreted the findings as evidence that students from collectivist backgrounds do not prefer to make their own decisions, and they implied, moreover, that collectivists do not need autonomy. Showing their confounding of ideas of independence and autonomy, they specifically stated that the results showed that "provision of individual choice seems to be more crucial to American independent selves, for whom the act of making a personal choice offers not only an opportunity to express and receive one's personal preference, but also a chance to establish one's unique self-identity" (p. 363). This interpretation seems to us far from what was studied, and further demonstrates the conflation of distinct constructs of individuality, autonomy, independence, and uniqueness. They further predicted that their results would have been even stronger had they not used Asian American subjects.

We first note that the Patall et al. (2008) meta-analysis of choice effects found the Iyengar and Lepper (1999) effect sizes to be so discrepant from others that, in keeping with meta-analytic protocol, these studies were eliminated from the analysis. We thus interpret their results with caution. Yet even given the observed pattern of findings, SDT would give a different interpretation. We maintain that to understand the results in terms of the meaning of choice and autonomy, it would be necessary to understand the degree to which the students experienced autonomy when enacting their parents' or close-others' decisions, and that would relate to internalization. If, for example, the participants had a close relationship with the trusted others, they may well have enacted their decisions autonomously. SDT would, in fact, hold that the positive motivational effects might have resulted from an experience of autonomy *and* relatedness satisfactions they experienced in following the trusted others' selection of the particular pen colors or puzzles they used. However, no measures of autonomy, relatedness, or reasons for assenting to others' choices were assessed.

We compare this with a more comprehensive series of studies on this phenomenon carried out by Bao and Lam (2008). They examined choice effects in elementary Chinese children from Hong Kong (rather than the Asian American groups in Iyengar and Lepper's experiment), and they measured a number of these relevant variables. They argued, in line with SDT, that when others, such as parents and teachers, make choices for their children or students, the youth could feel quite autonomous in performing the behaviors selected for them if they had a close relationship with that adult figure. As such, they would not have had to personally make the decision themselves in order to feel autonomous. However, if they did not feel such close support from the adult, they would be less likely to feel autonomous when the adult chose for them, showing the undermining effect.

Bao and Lam (2008) reported four studies. In the first, children reported on who (either they or their mothers) had selected an extracurricular course they were attending, how close to and supported they felt by their mothers, and how intrinsically motivated they were for the course. Results indicated that students who reported low relatedness to their mothers were more intrinsically motivated when they selected for themselves than when their mothers selected the course for them. For children with high relatedness to their mothers, there was no advantage to choosing for themselves. They were just as intrinsically motivated.

Two experimental studies were then reported, one with mothers and one with teachers, in which they manipulated choice. Participants were again Chinese children who reported on their closeness to their mothers (Study 2), or teachers (Study 3). They then worked on anagrams, with half selecting for themselves and half working on ones selected by their mothers (or teachers). Results showed that both relatedness and choice had positive main effects on intrinsic motivation for this task. Yet, as expected, there was also an interaction in which students with low relatedness to their mothers (or teachers) were more intrinsically motivated when they chose for themselves, but the intrinsic motivation for students with more supportive relationships was just as high (although not higher) as when choosing for themselves. Interestingly, however, on a measure of performance (rather than persistence), those in the self-selection group still evidenced the best outcomes.

In a final study, Bao and Lam assessed students' experiences of autonomy for doing schoolwork (based on the Ryan & Connell, 1989, approach), their closeness to their teachers, and their level of classroom engagement. Results indicated that both relative autonomy for schoolwork and closeness to the teachers positively predicted classroom engagement, two main effects expected by SDT. Further, there was not an interaction. Autonomy did not have its positive effects only in relationally supportive contexts; rather, feeling autonomous was advantageous, as was relational satisfaction.

These findings show that it is the experience of autonomy, whether it comes from making choices or accepting and internalizing other trusted people's choices, that is the important determinant of intrinsic motivation and engagement within both individualist and collectivist cultures. Here we see the importance of distinguishing in theory the difference between independence and autonomy and the more complex and nuanced view of what leads to a sense of volition.

Katz (2003) and her colleagues performed another set of studies that examined choice and decision making within an individualist and a collectivist culture within Israel: namely, secular Jews, who are relatively individualistic in their orientation, and Bedouins, who are relatively collectivistic in theirs. She examined the effects of making choices on intrinsic motivation of schoolchildren from these two cultures, comparing the intrinsic motivation of students who made their own choices to the intrinsic motivation of students whose parents were said to have made the choice for them. However, in this work, Katz noted that parents might make choices that are consistent with their children's preferences, thus allowing the children to do their preferred activity and also conveying to the children that their parents understand and acknowledge their interests. Alternatively, parents might make choices that are inconsistent with their children's preferences, which would likely feel to the children less supportive and acknowledging. Thus the interest-consistent parental choice would be more intrinsically interesting for the children and would promote internalization (i.e., identification with the activity), whereas the interest-inconsistent parental choice would not be intrinsically interesting and would be unlikely to promote internalization. Accordingly, there were three conditions in the Katz (2003) experiment: individual choice, parents' choice that was interest-*consistent,* and parents' choice that was interest-*inconsistent.*

High school students in the experiment were told that they would be spending some of their after-school time pursuing one of several possible subjects typically taught in a local college, and they were asked to rank order the subjects according to their interests. This was done so that the experimenter would have the information for later use. Then, at a later session, the experimental manipulations were performed for the three conditions. In the individual-choice condition, the students were asked to choose which subject they would pursue. Needless to say, they chose the topic they had rated as most interesting. In the parent-choice interest-*consistent* condition, the students were told their parents had made a choice for them, and the topic they were said to have chosen turned out to be the one the students had rated most interesting. In the parent-choice interest-*inconsistent* condition, the students were also told their parents had made a choice, but the topic they were said to have chosen was one the students had rated as very low in interest.

Katz (2003) reported that, for *both* the secular Jews and the Bedouins, the level of intrinsic motivation, behaviorally assessed, did not differ for the students in the individual-choice and the parent-choice interest-consistent conditions. However, for students from each background, the intrinsic motivation of those in the parent-choice interest-inconsistent condition was significantly lower than that of the students in the other two experimental conditions. Thus having parents choose for them did not undermine the intrinsic motivation of the children if the parents had been responsive to the students' interests, but having the parents choose when the students' interests were not acknowledged had a negative effect, whether they were part of an individualist or collectivist culture.

Again, results of this study stand in contrast to those of Iyengar and Lepper (1999), as do the results of the Bao and Lam (2008) study. Neither the Katz (2003) study nor the Bao and Lam (2008) study showed that parent or teacher selection of activities for their children led to significantly greater intrinsic motivation than did the children's own selection of activities for themselves. However, the parent selection led to significantly less intrinsic motivation when the selection of activities was interest-inconsistent or when there was not a close relationship, issues that were not examined by Iyengar and Lepper.

Yet another interesting result stemmed from Katz's (2003) research. She found that, although the behavioral measure of intrinsic motivation was undermined for Bedouin students in the parent-choice, interest-inconsistent condition, self-reports of interest were not lower in that condition than in the individual-choice condition. This finding for the self-report measure was therefore more consistent with the results of Iyengar and Lepper (1999). Subsequently, Katz and Assor (2006) did a follow-up study to clarify the Katz (2003) results. They hypothesized that students from the collectivist culture whose parents had selected an option for them that did not match their interests would not have *reported* their lack of interest in the option because they had learned that they should accept what their parents decide. In this follow-up study, Katz and Assor thus had three groups of students that paralleled those in the Katz (2003) study. However, in the Katz and Assor study, the participants (both secular Jews and Bedouins) were given descriptions of *another student* who had had an experience that mirrored what had happened in the corresponding condition of the Katz (2003) study. That is, one group was told that the hypothetical other student had made a choice for himself or herself; one group was told that the parents had made a choice that matched the student's interests; and one group was told that the parents had made a choice that did not match the student's interests. Then, using an interview format, the researchers asked the participants in this study to think about how they would feel in the various conditions. Invariantly, for both cultural groups, the students initially expressed negative feelings when they imagined parents having chosen the uninteresting option; however, whereas secular Jews continued over time to view that option less positively than the other two options, the Bedouin participants began to gravitate toward more positive reports of how they would feel in the situation in which parents had chosen the uninteresting option. Thus the important points from this study are (1) that the negative feelings of having been denied the opportunity to choose or to have gotten what they would have chosen were apparent independent of cultural values; but (2) cultural values do influence the extent to which members of a culture can outwardly express or are willing to report negative feelings about choices imposed by parents. Thus the Bedouin students gravitated toward saying they would feel fine if the parents chose for them a course that did not interest them (as behaviorally measured), presumably because their cultural value says that parents' decisions should be respected.

Important here is that there are clear cultural differences in where people draw personal boundaries and accept influence. Both American and Israeli children may well be less intrinsically motivated when close others choose for them than their Asian or Bedouin counterparts. In these latter cases, we see that autonomy and relatedness are by no means antithetical, as SDT has always maintained. But it is also clear that a sense of choice matters in all the studied cultures, with personal choice invariably enhancing motivation over external choices made by non-close others.

Autonomy, Choice, and Duty across Cultures

Consider a cultural value or its manifest normative standard that it is one's duty to follow the expectations of one's family, which scholars such as Katz (2003), Pan et al. (2013), and Miller (2002) have pointed out is a common value in some collectivist cultures. The fact that people enact specific cultural values does not, however, tell us *why* they do so (Chirkov et al., 2003). In SDT's view, within any culture people might have varied motives to enact norms of familial duty. Perhaps they autonomously embrace the importance of family and tradition (identification). Perhaps they appreciate the inherent satisfactions of fulfilling duties toward others, including enhanced relatedness (intrinsic). Perhaps, in contrast, they perform their familial duty primarily because others pressure, or even coerce, them to do so (external regulation) or because they would feel shame or disapproval were they not to appear dutiful (introjection). In this sense, SDT has no a priori concerns with familial duty *as a value,* but it does have something important to say about each of these motives and their relative autonomy as a basis for enacting the value.

The fact that some cultures endorse specific values such as familial duty also does not tell us what the functional costs and benefits of enacting the values might be. One might ask, for example, does adhering to this valued norm lead to enhanced relatedness, competence, and autonomy, or does it leave people feeling alienated, ineffective, or controlled? Conversely, does an absence of sense of duty or obligation to family in some cultures interfere with relatedness, competence, or autonomy? Could it leave people feeling "disjointed"? Accordingly, analyses considering both whether a value or behavior is autonomously internalized and whether its realization is supportive of basic psychological needs can be directed toward any culture with its norms and practices or its rejection or neglect of those norms.

Sheldon, Kasser, Houser-Marko, Jones, and Turban (2005) examined issues of duty in both U.S. and Singaporean samples. Their specific interest was on the relation of age to one's relative autonomy in fulfilling duties. They hypothesized that, as people age, they may more deeply understand and internalize the meaning of duties and thus be more autonomous in performing them. They reported three studies. In the first, they found that older Americans reported greater autonomous motivations for the duties of voting, paying taxes, and giving tips to service people. In a second study, they compared U.S. parents to their children, finding that parents expressed more autonomy in their roles as workers and citizens. Finally, in a third investigation, Sheldon et al. found that older Singaporeans reported greater autonomous motivation when obeying authorities, helping distant relatives, and being politically informed. Important, too, was that, in all three of these studies, greater autonomy was associated with higher subjective well-being.

Research by Miller, Das, and Chakravarthy (2011) comparing Indian and U.S. samples further underscored both the universality of autonomy effects concerning duty and the need for a nuanced approach to understanding its manifestations across cultures. Reasoning that expectations and duties are more likely to be more fully internalized in Indian culture and thus more autonomous, they showed that these were more positively associated with a sense of choice and satisfaction when compared to U.S. samples. Yet in both cultures experiencing a sense of choice predicted greater satisfaction. In addition, data suggested that, whereas in the Indian sample, duty and responsibility to help family members were most highly correlated with identified regulation, in the U.S. sample, they were not significantly related to autonomous regulations. Clearly, it is not the presence of norms, expectations, or obligations that defines autonomy versus heteronomy but, rather, the degree to which these are internalized (see also Roth et al., 2006; Gore & Cross, 2006).

Both we and other cultural theorists such as Kagitcibasi (1996, 2005) have emphasized the importance of carefully distinguishing the concepts of autonomy from those
of independence and separateness. People can be autonomous *and* dependent or interdependent. They can be closely related without losing a sense of autonomy or agency.
They can be obligated to one another and very much feel volition and choice in carrying
out societal and familial duties. The sensitivity and accuracy of comparative and critical cross-cultural work depends on making such careful distinctions. Along with them,
we think dimensional views that recognize the variations in values and internalization
within cultures for different practices are preferable to dichotomous views. Using both
carefully defined constructs and noncategorical thinking, we can much better understand
how cultures vary in their impact on people's wellness and flourishing.

Not All Cultural Norms Can Be Easily Integrated

Different cultural values and goals inevitably provide greater or lesser satisfaction of the
innate psychological needs for competence, autonomy, and relatedness, also affecting
wellness and thriving outcomes. This leads to another critical SDT focus, namely, the
idea that some cultural goals and values are far more difficult to integrate and, indeed,
may not be capable of being fully integrated and autonomous due to their inconsistency
with basic needs and intrinsic psychological processes. We suggest, for example, that a
cultural value that boys should not cry or that girls should not be educated could at best
be introjected or be identified with in a compartmentalized way by the boys and girls,
respectively, because of the seemingly inherent incompatibility of these cultural contents
with their basic psychological needs. Of course, these are empirical questions, well within
the methods of SDT to examine. Our view is, in fact, that *any* cultural content can be
examined for the degree to which members of the culture can readily or effectively integrate it.

Consider the case of *female genital mutilation* as an example of the necessity of
distinguishing between people's explicit endorsement of harmful practices and the relative integration of such practices. Female genital cutting is a practice that has existed
for as long as 6,000 years and that affects more than 100 million women today in many
African nations, parts of Asia, and less frequently in immigrant communities across the
world (United Nations Commission on the Status of Women, 2011). We focus here on
infibulation, one of its more radical forms. Supported by justifications concerning purity,
hygiene, tradition, or honor, the practice of infibulation is seen by many as a means
of controlling female sexuality and freedom (Favazza, 1987). It is also often obviously
painful and harmful, with consequences for many that include anemia, cysts and scar
formation, urinary incontinence, painful sexual intercourse, and complications during
childbirth, as well as enduring psychological effects from the trauma of the cutting and
its aftermath (e.g., see Alsibiani & Rouzi, 2010; Behrendt & Moritz, 2005; World Health
Organization, 2008; among many other reports). Women who have undergone these
procedures often have to have their vaginal openings "reopened" before sexual intercourse can take place, with some being cut open on the first night of marriage (Walker
& Parmar, 1993).

The practice of female infibulation is often vocally "endorsed" or justified as a
valued and even "virtuous" cultural ritual (Fiske & Rai, 2015). For example, Shweder
(2000), a strong cultural relativist, suggests that the medical fanfare over "FGM" is
overblown and culturally insensitive and represents an imposition of a liberal feminist

worldview. He argues that the girls endure the pain and suffering and value it as a sign of courage. We can only agree with him that one can find people advocating and defending the practice. But in contrast to Shweder, we raise infibulation as an example of a cultural internalization that is likely to be *inherently* problematic from the standpoint of true integration. Supporting the practice, whether one is an advocate or participant, requires that one minimize, deny, ignore, or nullify a great many obvious problems and harms (Abusharaf, 2013). It necessitates turning one's sensibilities away from the truth of the girl's pain, often discounting her perspective, and denying or minimizing the myriad and well-documented negative health consequences of the procedure.

Incongruence and compartmentalization is evident, for example, in the filmed interviews accompanying Walker and Parmar's (1993) work, in which the inconstancies in the testimonies of infibulation practitioners and of the mothers who allow it are often palpable. They say in one moment there is no pain, and minutes later they discuss the terrible pain. They say in some moments this is desirable, and at others express dismay for the practice. As another example, in a *New York Times* (May 11, 2011) interview by Kristof, a female infibulator vigorously defended her practice, but thusly: "A young girl herself will want to be cut. . . . If a girl is not cut, it would be hard for her to live in the community. She would be stigmatized." What the infibulator therefore describes is thus a form of external control and/or introjection, rather than an expression of autonomy. Girls who do not undergo the procedure know they may face ostracism or punishment.

Finally, whether or not its *advocates* portray it as a virtue, autonomy does not characterize the experience of its recipients, who in almost no cases can give, or have given, truly informed consent to be cut. Many will not understand what has happened to them, nor its far-reaching negative health consequences, until well after the ritual is performed. It is unlikely any young girl would find inherent value in such a practice being performed on her body.

Like all cultural practices, the relative autonomy of female infibulation is an empirical question. It is one worthy of study, precisely because understanding how such harmful practices are internalized and therefore anchored in cultures is critical to changing them (Abusharaf, 2013). Yet we suspect this is a practice that is likely, because of its inherent relation to basic needs, not typically integrated, at least when the concepts of autonomy and integration are meaningfully applied, even though some will laud it as a cultural value.

We use infibulation as an example because it seems clear that it is largely an interference with flourishing and something typically undergone without true consent. We will, in fact, look at other examples in Chapter 24 concerning conformity to culturally endorsed violence. But we can find practices, both minor and significant, within every culture about which we can inquire as to people's capacity to truly integrate them, from gender roles to hygienic practices. Again, a value of SDT is that, although it has no a priori investment in specific cultural contents, it has common criteria by which any can be evaluated in its understanding of both basic needs and relative integration.

On Cultural Competence
and Interventions for Thriving and Development

Within SDT, supporting autonomous motivation and wellness is a core value, and, as we have previously described, it begins by taking the *internal frame of reference* of participants (Deci & Ryan, 1985b). This means respecting the perspectives, values, and concerns of all participants (Craven et al., 2016; Wlodkowski & Ginsberg, 1995). This central idea thus suggests that SDT-based research and interventions, particularly those focused on different cultural groups, should be sensitive and responsive to participants' views and values.

Indeed, SDT seeks, through both clinical methods (Ryan & Deci, 2008b) and interventions (e.g., Ng et al., 2012; Su & Rèeve, 2011), to reflect the voices and choices of the individuals and groups to which it is applied. Through autonomy support, SDT supports diversity rather than hegemony. In other words, SDT supports person-centered approaches that maximize participant input and involvement in all inquiries and interventions, be they interpersonal or societal. In doing so, researchers and change agents are most likely to understand and appreciate barriers and resistances to change.

It is moreover a core assumption of SDT, reflected throughout these chapters, that, to the extent that the implementation of intervention or research programs is autonomy-supportive and participation is therefore experienced as elective and volitional rather than externally controlled, they will be more successfully internalized. Evidence for this is emerging in successful development programs (e.g. Ibrahim & Alkire, 2007; Sayanagi & Aikawa, 2016). Conversely, to the extent that programs, even those intended to support thriving and capabilities, are enacted in controlling ways, the theory suggests that they will be less likely to be internalized and integrated and therefore they will be less sustainable.

Although the contents of cultures vary widely, in every culture people generally want to experience ownership and initiative in processes of development and change, and they do not want external others imposing values and prescriptions without consent. This sensibility is of great importance to all cross-cultural projects and interventions and one fully congruent with the basic principles of SDT. As such, whereas some theorists have argued that positing needs and evaluating practices in a culture other than one's own would be imposing one's views and values on that culture and thus interfering with its autonomy, SDT emphasizes the importance of acting with and through autonomy support, especially when engaging with other cultures that are not one's own, and thus respecting the universal human need for autonomy.

Concluding Comments

Cultures vary greatly in the values, mores, and goals that are transmitted and the opportunities and affordances that are provided to the individuals who live within them. An important aspect of SDT is the recognition that cultural values and goals can be more or less well integrated by members of the cultures. A central focus of SDT is thus on the autonomy-supportive versus controlling approach to the socialization and maintenance of cultural norms. More authoritarian and controlling socialization is expected to lead to more controlling forms of self-regulation and, overall, to poorer quality internalization and wellness across cultural contexts.

Second, unlike extreme cultural relativist theories that assume that any culturally normative goal contents will yield positive outcomes if people take them in and succeed at them, SDT asks the question of whether specific cultural values or practices are consistent with the satisfaction of universal human needs for autonomy, competence, and relatedness. The enactment of need-incongruent goals, we maintain, will engender costs in terms of psychological growth, integrity, and well-being.

As stated earlier, there are group cohesions and ideologies that may depend on the denial of the basic psychological needs and rights to autonomy of individuals, and thus we will find individuals within such groups who—often in the service of relatedness to authorities or group norms—will explicitly accept practices that deny need satisfactions to themselves or to others, such as offspring or outgroup members. But merely providing surface evidence of such acceptance does not take the place of functional or dynamic analyses, and it is these analyses that are of primary interest within SDT.

A final speculation from the SDT perspective concerns the relation of needs to the stability of cultures and cultural and religious subgroups. Cultures transmit an array of values, some more compatible and some less compatible with basic needs. We suggest that the more a culture promotes integrated internalizations, both through the content of its values and through its normative style of socializing its members, the more harmony and thus stability will be evident in the culture. When cultures either use controlling forms of socialization or endorse goals and values that are very difficult or impossible to integrate, the cultures will tend to foster alienation, anomie, and perhaps rebellion. They will inspire more defectors when alternatives are available. As such, the cultures will be inherently less stable, and, through these ways, human needs will have constrained the dynamics of cultural evolution and the memes associated with it.

Cultures are pervasive influences, and they are adopted and expressed in various ways. They also yield different outcomes, some beneficial, some horrific. The lens of SDT can be focused on the micro and macro goals, activities, attitudes, and aspirations between and within cultures to determine their degrees of internalization, need satisfaction, and contributions to, or hindering of, human flourishing.

CHAPTER 23

Pervasive Social Influences, Part II
Economic and Political Systems

In this chapter, we continue our examination of pervasive contexts by considering the direct and indirect impacts of political and economic systems on motivations and need satisfactions. First, we discuss political systems, and in particular the issue of *political rights and freedoms*. Countries of the world have increasingly moved toward more democratic political systems. Although democratic systems allow for greater political freedom and even personal choice, they are dependent on the willing participation and compliance of their citizens. To foster internalization that anchors such behaviors, democracies must foster perceptions of legitimacy, fairness, and choice. Perceptions of control or corruption conversely lead to lower citizen trust, lower participation, and higher apathy. In authoritarian systems, there is greater reliance on external control and introjection to motivate citizens and thus less effective internalization of governmental authority. Moreover, because conditions for autonomous internalization are undermined, authoritarian systems must develop ever more pervasive controls and sense of external threat to remain stable. Moving to economic systems as pervasive influences, we discuss *wealth distribution and economic inequalities.* Capitalism is now globally influential, even in nations with considerable central planning. A first question is how levels of economic welfare influence capabilities for and attainment of basic need satisfactions. A second is how wealth disparities impact wellness. We also consider factors such as how the focus on extrinsic aspirations and competitive values can be prompted by economic systems and have negative consequences on people through both behavioral demands and altering psychological priorities.

In the previous chapter, we discussed *culture* as a pervasive influence on behavior and experience, suggesting that cultures comprise norms, values, and practices that are more or less well internalized by the members of the culture. These internalizations not only regulate the actions of the members, they also frame the very possibilities and meanings people can envision and pursue, shaping their goals, aspirations, and identities. Further, as SDT highlights, internalized cultural mores and practices can be more or less conducive to basic psychological need satisfaction across a society and, thus, the flourishing or ill-being of its constituents.

In this chapter, we focus on two more pervasive influences on motivation and wellness, namely *political* and *economic* systems. Much like the cultural contexts we discussed in the previous chapter, people are embedded within political and economic contexts that structure how they view the world, what they value, what they worry about, and how they conceptualize their own power and place within their communities. We use the term *political–economic cultures* here to convey the idea that individuals are socialized to invest in activities and aspirations that are congruent with their political–economic systems. The resulting internalizations are sometimes explicit and at other times invisible to those adopting them. Wilson (1992) referred to them as *compliance ideologies,* or the systems of beliefs and perceptions that explain and justify behavior within any given system, thus supporting adherence.

As pervasive contexts, political–economic cultures are typically experienced by the individuals within them as givens and the behaviors those cultures elicit as normative. They may, therefore, have little awareness of alternatives or of the subtle costs of those contexts. For example, in authoritarian regimes people may come to monitor self-expression so chronically that they don't sense its everyday depletion effects. In a capitalist consumer culture, people can lack awareness of how their spending desires are catalyzed or of the psychological and environmental costs of the overconsumption they consider normal. Political–economic cultures are pervasive in just this sense: They penetrate proximal belief structures and everyday forms of human interaction. Political–economic cultures, being the waters in which we swim, are often not comprehended as shaping our aspirations, self-concepts, and ways of being, except on the rare occasions when one comes up for air.

It is especially because of this way in which pervasive political and economic environments frame human experiences and motivations that bringing SDT's functional perspective to bear in the analysis of them is important. We emphasize two types of analyses that can be fruitfully applied to any aspect of political–economic cultures. The first concerns *internalization* and how systems lead people to adhere to (or fail to comply with) their values, regulations, and laws. That is, SDT is concerned with the processes through which political and economic forms become anchored within the selves of the individuals who live in them, in accordance with organismic integration theory (OIT; Chapter 8). Second, SDT is focused on the impact of economic and political systems on *basic psychological need satisfactions* and thus on people's well-being and full functioning, in accordance with basic psychological needs theory (BPNT; Chapter 10). We submit that political regimes and economic systems differentially facilitate or obstruct the basic psychological need satisfactions of individuals, primarily through a variety of mediating variables, with resulting effects on their prosperity and wellness.

SDT's analyses of internalization and need satisfaction can be applied to features of political and economic systems, both large and small. We can ask these questions of specific policies or laws or of broader beliefs and practices. Among the myriad attributes, policies, mechanisms, and methods of pervasive political–economic cultures to which we could thus apply these perspectives, we focus herein on two broad dimensions along which political–economic cultures clearly differ—namely, (1) the presence of *political rights and freedoms,* and (2) patterns of *wealth distribution and economic equality.*

Regarding rights and freedoms, we discuss how governments that are more oriented toward individual rights and democratic processes (vs. governments more oriented toward centralized power and constrained freedoms) can differentially affect people's capacity to exercise autonomy and attain basic need satisfactions. We also discuss how both authoritarian and democratic political climates can be reflected in and supported by differing proximal social contexts reflected in styles of parenting, education, employment, and religious engagement. For example, SDT expects that proximal climates that are controlling can lead to less active, less questioning, and less informed citizens, a situation essential to authoritarian regimes, whereas autonomy-supportive parenting and education can foster more critical thinking and active civic engagement, attributes needed within healthy democracies. In fact, civic engagement can itself enhance wellness through need satisfactions (e.g., Wray-Lake, DeHaan, Shubert, Ryan, & Curren, 2015).

Concerning economic inequality, we consider how differences in political–economic cultures with regard to opportunity and wealth distribution affect both individual and collective need satisfaction and wellness. Especially in the context of the global expansion of market economies, differential access to resources not only affects individuals' capabilities to pursue what they find worthwhile but also shapes their sense of empowerment, fairness, and connectedness to others. Additionally, just as political climates are reflected in more proximal social contexts, so, too, are economic ones—for example, consider the everyday frustrations, depletion effects, and experiences of diminishment and disempowerment associated with poverty (Green, 2012). We also discuss how the value systems that tend to pervade highly wealth-discrepant systems focus people toward more extrinsic life goals, social comparisons, self-enhancement biases, and consumerism, whereas those associated with greater economic equality are associated more with intrinsic goals and values (Kasser, Kanner, Cohn, & Ryan, 2007).

Again, our choice of these two broad topics (i.e., political freedoms and economic inequality) is hardly comprehensive. SDT perspectives on both processes of internalization and need satisfaction can be applied to any and all of the practices, laws, and norms making up a political–economic culture, both micro and macro, and they are probably most effectively applied the more specific the practices and norms under analysis are. Nonetheless, we are focusing on these more sweeping themes of freedoms and economic inequalities because they clearly bear on people's everyday basic psychological need satisfactions in ways that warrant reflection and further analysis.

Political Freedom versus Control

Aristotle, whose philosophy was centrally concerned with fostering eudaimonia, saw political structures as essential to a healthy societal life. In his view, a political system exists ideally to advance the wellness of all its citizens—that is, the system should work for the enhancement of the common good (Curren, 2000). May (2010) further argued that Aristotle saw the effective state as supplying a *legal ecology,* which, although external to the individual, is essential in promoting his or her flourishing. In May's analysis, this legal ecology includes support for the individual's freedom and competence to pursue multiple possible selves, conducing to autonomy and self-concordance.

Aristotle also viewed the role of citizens as being active rather than passive. In this conception, humans are *zoa politika,* or political animals, and ideally they are engaged participants in their society's system of laws, justice, and the general maintenance of the social order. That is, optimally, citizens are not just subjected to governments, but rather they identify with and autonomously participate in them. For its reciprocal part, governments would aim both to enhance the common good and to govern through consent rather than force (Curren, 2013).

Unfortunately, both past history and present-day realities highlight that actual governments have not often embraced these ideals. In fact, throughout most of human history, people have been ruled by dictators and tyrants, and, in many areas of the world, the idea of broad participation in governance has only recently become salient. Contemporary political systems thus still vary widely in whether people are treated as participants in, or objects of, state power. Nations also vary in whether their policies and practices enhance the common good or, instead, serve the narrower interests of a few, as in a plutocracy. In fact, differences in beneficence toward citizens are observable not only between nations but also within them, as rights and privileges can be equitably or inequitably distributed. Even in Aristotle's Athenian democracy, the affordance of freedoms was quite unevenly spread across Greek men, Greek women, and the members of the city-state's slave classes.

As pervasive influences, political systems influence individuals' behavioral regulation and psychological wellness both directly and indirectly. Governments create and enforce laws and policies that directly attempt to regulate, constrain, and/or channel human behaviors through external regulations (e.g., speed limits, jail terms, fines, tax incentives). Governments also indirectly regulate behaviors through normative messaging, information dissemination, policy justifications, media control, and other means of influence.

Both direct and indirect strategies of guidance and regulation may inspire more or less autonomous compliance. That is, the ways in which governments design, promote, and enforce mandates and regulations can all affect how well the laws are internalized and thus why people obey them (Tyler, 1990). For example, laws can be designed with principles of justice clearly met (Rawls, 2009). Processes for creating laws can be inclusive or exclusive; they can also be transparent or secretive. Finally, strategies and procedures of enforcing laws can be minimally coercive and respectful of individual rights or draconian and fear-inducing, as in many fascist regimes. Some governments, that is, maintain themselves through persuasion and attempts to cultivate autonomous public support, whereas others do so through power, prisons, and police, fostering controlled motives for compliance. These regulatory approaches obviously affect basic need satisfactions, as people experience more voice versus self-silencing and more empowerment versus fear (Deci & Ryan, 2012). As expressed by Zagajewski, a Polish poet in the Soviet era: ". . . even when I'm unable to define the essence of freedom, I know exactly what it is to be unfree" (cf. Ash, 2004, p. 240).

Corresponding to these differences in how governments obtain compliance, SDT asks: Are people motivated to accept and obey the government and its laws, and if so, why? Is compliance with policies or laws autonomous or controlled? Based on SDT, one would expect the quality of behavioral adherence and satisfaction with laws to be positively associated with a sense of voice, choice, inclusiveness, and fairness in decision making and enforcement.

An experimental study by DeCaro, Janssen, and Lee (2015) illustrates this principle. They specifically examined how participatory voting and enforcement in a task involving the harvesting of resources from a common resource pool influenced people's subsequent voluntary cooperation. Individuals were assigned to one of four conditions: (1) a *vote-and-enforce* condition, in which participants first voted on conservation rules and then were able to apply economic sanctions to enforce them; (2) an *imposed-and-enforce* condition, in which participants could neither vote nor enforce rules; (3) a *vote-and-no-enforcement* condition, in which participants could vote but had no power to sanction rule breakers; or (4) an *imposed* condition, in which there was enforcement but no vote. DeCaro et al. found that cooperation around harvesting resources was highest in the vote-and-enforce condition. Here there was participatory involvement, which would enhance a sense of legitimacy along with structure that would support a sense of fairness or justice. Moreover, the vote-and-enforce participants continued to cooperate *voluntarily*, even after enforcement was removed later in the experiment. Autonomous internalization had clearly occurred. In contrast, in the imposed-and-enforce condition, which would appear from an SDT point of view to be the most controlling, cooperation was the lowest. In this condition, when enforcement ceased, cooperation further decreased. Thus enforcement improved voluntary cooperation only when individuals had a voice or vote. In fact, DeCaro et al.'s further analyses showed that perceptions of procedural justice (legitimacy) and self-determination were highest in the vote-and-enforce circumstance, suggesting that factors of voice, legitimacy, and justice increased voluntary cooperation by promoting greater internalized motivation. Interestingly, those in groups that both voted and had enforcement capabilities also showed the highest relatedness—they felt closer to one another. Neither voting nor enforcement alone produced such effects. They suggested that simply having enforcement without a vote contributed to lower volitional reasons for cooperation.

SDT also expects some reciprocal processes to be at work. Specifically, the more totalitarian or fascist a government is—by definition, highly centralized power structures that use controlling methods to suppress opposition—the less common is autonomous internalization in the populace, and thus the more important are force, fear, and threat to regime maintenance. Among the tactics that totalitarian governments rely heavily upon to mobilize compliance in the masses are the suppression of free expression, controlling followers with privileges and rewards, and conjuring threats by external enemies. Conversely, the more democratic the society is, the more governmental stability and functioning must rely on autonomous internalization and active, informed participation. Thus it becomes more important within a democratic government to enhance more integrated forms of internalization and autonomous participation, because democracy functions best when an informed public freely exercises its rights and privileges and thus more fully follows the regulations and mandates of the system.

Laws, Internalization, and Perceived Legitimacy

Insofar as laws represent attempts by governmental authorities to regulate behavior, we must first briefly reprise the more extensive discussions from Chapters 3, 8, and 10 concerning the general relations between autonomy, internalization, and external authority. You may recall our argument that the concept of autonomy does not require that the source or impetus of an action originate from within the person. Instead, one can be fully autonomous even when fulfilling someone else's requests or following demands— providing, of course, that one concurs with the directives or with the authority's right to demand them. This issue of being able to assent to or concur with the content of a law or the legitimacy of the regulator is therefore critical to an SDT analysis of government regulations and their internalization.

What, then, is the relation between political regulation of behavior and autonomy? According to SDT, people will be more likely to autonomously comply with government regulations to the extent that there is a *perceived legitimacy* to those regulations (Deci & Ryan, 2012). Insofar as individual citizens accept the legitimacy of a government or its policies, they are internalizing and integrating its laws and then acting more volitionally in carrying them out. Legitimacy is a *psychological* rather than merely a legal concept. Indeed, what is *legal* may not be perceived as legitimate.

Accepting the legitimacy of a government involves identifying with and integrating the government's values, mores, and legality, just as wholly accepting the legitimacy of leadership within narrower collectives, such as families or school classrooms, involves the willing acceptance of the rules and values therein transmitted. When laws or regulations are backed only by external regulation, compliance will instead be dependent on external enforcement and thus be either poor or very costly (see, e.g., Mankad & Greenhill, 2014). It is therefore consistent with SDT that the stability and effectiveness of democratic governments is enhanced by the voluntary cooperation of its citizens (Tyler, 2006), which in turn reflects more autonomous internalization (Deci & Ryan, 2012).

SDT, in line with its focus on both internalization and need satisfactions, further highlights two major pathways to greater perceived legitimacy and thus more autonomous adherence to political leadership. The first pathway concerns the *process* of enacting laws, policies, and government services—specifically, whether there was fairness, inclusion, and transparency in the decision making, application, and enforcement of those guidelines and procedures. Second, legitimacy also concerns the *content* of the laws and policies and the perceived benefits, harms, and fairness of their impacts. Contents that threaten people's basic needs and their communities should be expected to inherently engender internal conflicts and thus to be associated with a lesser sense of legitimacy. To the extent that either of these pathways to legitimacy—namely, need support either in the process of governance or in the contents and consequences of laws or policies—is problematic, governments will need to exert greater efforts to ensure compliance through external control.

Governmental Regulation and Internalization

The first of these two elements, namely the focus on the process of governing, can be stated formally as follows:

> When citizens perceive empowerment, transparency, and voice in governance, they are more likely to see governmental regulations and laws as legitimate and thus more willingly assent and adhere to them. When they feel controlled, excluded, or without voice, internalizations are less likely to be autonomous and integrated, and they are more likely to be motivated through controlled motivations, passive compliance, or active defiance.

Our claim is that perceptions of fairness, transparency, and participatory power all influence perceived legitimacy, which, in turn, we expect to be positively associated with autonomous internalization of governmentally initiated regulations.

Supporting this idea, substantial psychological research discussed throughout this book has confirmed that the experience of perceived choice has a multitude of positive consequences in more proximal social contexts. Studies have, for example, shown that allowing people to make meaningful decisions facilitates their experience of choice and enhances their intrinsic motivation (Patall, Cooper, & Robinson, 2008), an effect presumably mediated by enhancing a sense of autonomy. Autonomy support and provision of choice have also been shown to facilitate internalization of extrinsic motivation (e.g., Deci, Eghrari, Patrick, & Leone, 1994; Grolnick & Ryan, 1989). Related to the experience of choice and voice is the concept of transparency. To the extent that the forces behind and processes of government regulations are open and visible, people will have less sense of being controlled and more opportunities to feel that they can react and participate.

DeCaro and Stokes (2008) reviewed the literature on conservation initiatives. Based on their review, they suggested that regulatory initiatives promoted through primarily non-autonomy-supportive tactics (such as to avoid economic fines or to secure economic rewards) are less motivating than those endorsed for autonomous reasons. They further posited that successful programs promote autonomous endorsement of conservation through an autonomy-supportive and fair administrative framework. These methods included providing for democratic participation in management, inclusiveness in decision making with local stakeholders, and respectful, noncoercive messaging (see also DeCaro & Stokes 2013; Osbaldiston & Sheldon, 2003).

Although data on the relations between autonomy support and leadership legitimacy are not extensive, a study in Portugal illustrates this general thesis. Graca, Calheiros, and Barata (2013) studied adolescents' respect for teachers' authority, using a measure that assessed the degree to which a student felt she or he should defer to such authority figures, voluntarily accept their decisions, and follow their rules. They found that the more students perceived teachers to be autonomy-supportive, the more they specifically recognized the legitimacy of the teacher's authority in the classroom. Although not a governmental context, the idea is that leaders who are seen as understanding and concerned with the people who will be impacted by the laws or rules are also seen as more legitimate authorities and are more autonomously followed.

Democracy, as a political system, bases its legitimacy on the principle that individuals have equal input into decision making, primarily by voting for political representatives or sometimes by voting directly on proposed laws. Elections are framed as opportunities for choice and empowerment and ideally confer upon decision makers greater legitimacy (Lanning, 2008). Still, structural democracy (having a vote) as a system is not sufficient to ensure autonomous participation or internalization. In many democracies, a lack of trust, voice, and transparency is apparent and is often accompanied by a related apathy or disengagement of citizens in government (Gonzalez & Tyler, 2008). In some modern democracies, only a minority of eligible citizens are motivated to vote. As Lane (2000) pointed out, there can be a gap between objective freedom to participate in government and the self-determination that people experience when they do. For example, if people do not think voting makes a difference, then they might not be autonomously motivated to become informed voters (Green, 2012).

Motivation for Democratic Political Engagement

SDT suggests that the most active, engaged citizens in democratic regimes would be those who are autonomously motivated. They would have more fully internalized the responsibilities of being citizens and therefore would want to exercise their rights.

These claims were tested in an interesting chain of studies by Koestner, Losier, and colleagues (see Koestner, Losier, Vallerand, & Carducci, 1996; Losier & Koestner, 1999). They surveyed potential Canadian voters several weeks before elections, assessing their motives for following politics using a measure based on the SDT taxonomy of regulations. They also assessed variables such as political information seeking, knowledge of political events, and emotional reactions to the issues of the day. After the elections, participants were recontacted to find out if they had actually voted and how they perceived the election outcomes.

In line with SDT, the major hypotheses were that more autonomous motivation for political engagement would be associated with more active, committed, and effective participation than more controlled motives based in introjection or external regulation. Results generally confirmed this hypothesis across the studies. First, both intrinsic and identified motivations were associated with more actively reading newspapers, watching debates, and seeking political information. Interestingly, intrinsic motivation for politics was associated with forming an accurate base of knowledge about current issues, but not necessarily with actually voting, whereas identification was related to both developing differentiated opinions about which political parties to support and actually turning out to cast a vote. Introjection was unrelated to voting behavior but was associated with vulnerability to persuasion, passively relying on authorities such as parents to make voting decisions, and to feeling more conflicted about political outcomes. Similar to introjection, those expressing amotivation for politics reported relying on important others in making decisions, denying the personal relevance of voting, and less actively seeking information about current issues. Amotivation was uncorrelated with actual voting behavior.

Such findings clearly suggest that people's motivation for engaging in politics matters. Those who participate autonomously—especially those finding value and importance in participating—are also likely to be the most informed and committed citizens. Again, this is important if the endeavor is democracy; as we discuss, the story is different if the endeavor is maintaining a dictatorship. However, to date there has not been sufficient work on the antecedents of autonomous versus controlled motivation and amotivation in relation to political engagement within democracies. That said, it seems evident from a wide variety of literatures that to the degree that governments are perceived as not transparent, fair, or trustworthy, people more easily become helpless, apathetic, or disengaged (e.g., see Lane, 2000; Lanning, 2008). As the studies above suggest, the consequences of a less autonomously engaged citizenry include more vulnerability to passivity and persuasion, with less appetite to stay informed.

Internalization of political forms is in many ways connected to the proximal environments of families and schools that underpin a political culture. Democratic societies are, for example, not just forms of government but ways of living. In a true democracy, each individual develops both a sense of his or her individual rights and responsibilities and a sentiment that his or her fellow citizens also command rights and respect as human beings. This sensibility often begins in the home, where parents model democracy and autonomy support, and in schools, where, ideally, democratic ideals would be modeled and employed (Curren, 2009). In other words, democratic societies depend on the institutions and citizens within them to be autonomously engaged and to respect others' rights, which accompanies an active rather than passive internalization.

Interestingly, two recent studies by Chua and Philippe (2015) examined relations between paternal autonomy support and children's support for, rather than resistance to, the government. Researching both Malaysians and Canadians, they found that more autonomy-supportive fathers had adult children who were more favorable toward their governments and less prone toward protesting government policies. Chua and Philippe suggested that autonomy support within family authority leads to more trust in external authorities to be benign (a belief that might or might not be adaptive!) It is also likely that more autonomy-supportive fathers better facilitate their children's internalization of ambient political norms and the rule of law.

It further seems the case that being able to participate in voting does have some direct beneficial effect, perhaps by virtue of the feelings of empowerment that voting engenders. For example, Frey and Stutzer (2005) showed that foreigners, relative to natives, living in Switzerland experienced less positive effects of living in this democratic context—perhaps because, being non-citizens, they did not experience a sense of participation and choice.

Internalization within Authoritarian Regimes

Although we have thus far focused on democracies, authoritarian political systems (governments that use centralized power and force to regulate citizens) are common. A regime is more authoritarian to the extent that its predominant style of ensuring compliance relies on external control and force. In most totalitarian systems, there is an ever-present mix of controlling and amotivating forces, some salient and direct, and others often more insidiously enforced. Irrespective of the content of policy decisions, the mere salience of controls is likely to make full internalization more difficult, thereby ensuring a need for more force and fear to maintain the social order. Insofar as citizens do internalize or identify with these external controls, their compliance will often depend upon the fragile mechanisms of compartmentalization within the individuals, as well as information restriction, surveillance, and coercive enforcement from the government. In short, SDT suggests that controlling political systems are often precariously anchored in their subjects' psyches and rarely integrated. This does not mean, however, that these systems are necessarily ineffective, or that some subjects may not become "true believers" (Hoffer, 1989), but rather that the nature of external controls in authoritarian contexts will more generally foster a lower level of internalization.

Moghaddam (2013) suggested that, within dictatorships and totalitarian governments, it is the *masses* who are largely kept compliant through external regulation. In contrast, the psychology of internalization among the *elite* is different. Whereas members of the masses need only comply, members of the political elites must at least appear to maintain an ideological adherence to the ruling powers. Moreover, because membership in the elite is often highly contingent and uncertain, self-presentation of ideological adherence becomes a pervasive personal concern, requiring self-monitoring and concealment of any contrary sentiments. Thus, motivated by fear, compliance often extends even into intimate communications, lest one be revealed as dissident. In this respect, SDT expects that elite groups that justify and crusade for the status quo are often regulated through introjects and compartmentalized identifications, allowing them to appear agentic and internally motivated. At the same time, the need for self-monitoring, concealment or suppression of dissonance, and compliance can have a variety of negative effects on them.

Because of their reliance on controlling strategies, SDT expects more shallow internalization of citizens within authoritarian regimes. Research supporting this was provided by an international study of religious freedoms (Stavrova & Siegers, 2013). These researchers analyzed data from more than 70 countries concerning whether religious practices were or were not externally regulated, socially pressured, or even government enforced. They found that, in those nations in which there was less social pressure and less control from governmental regulations to follow a religion, religious individuals were more likely to evidence *deeper* forms of religious internalization. Specifically, less external social regulation was associated with religious people showing a more intrinsic, relative to extrinsic, religious orientation; being more charitable; and finding lying in one's own interest or engaging in fraudulent behaviors to be less acceptable. Thus it appears that the positive effects of religiosity weaken substantially when there is more governmental and/or social enforcement of religious practices. In short, Stavrova and Siegers's (2013) data are consistent with SDT in showing that the way in which regulations are transmitted matters, with less choice and support for autonomy being associated with less internalization (Ryan, Rigby, & King, 1993).

Whereas in democracies the cultivation of more autonomous forms of internalization matters, within totalitarian regimes autonomy and more integrated internalization is not a necessary goal. This difference is also reflected in the proximal environments typically found within nations of each type. The external regulation of totalitarian governments, if pervasive and potent enough, can foster compliance, especially if supported by an elite that articulates and enforces ideology without open deviance. At the same time, without engendering more autonomous forms of internalization, leaders of authoritarian regimes necessarily become more and more dependent on external means of regulation such as surveillance, force, and coercion. This dynamic parallels that of classroom authorities in Chapter 14, in which we saw how the more teachers used controlling strategies, the more they engendered external regulation in students, and thus the more they needed to continue control to ensure compliance.

Nevertheless, a dictator's job is made easier when people are already prone to be responsive to external controls and to submit to, rather than question, authority. Again, family, religious, and school environments can reinforce and model this style of living by relying themselves on external regulation and control. In this way, people are "accustomed" to comply, especially when economic stress and lack of self-direction weighs in as a compounding factor (Oates, Schooler, & Mulatu, 2004; Schooler, Mulatu, & Oates, 2004). For example, Staub (1992, 2011), in the context of his analyses of conditions underlying genocide and cultural violence, argued that in more authoritarian societies, child rearing techniques often involve adults who set rules without explanations and who simply punish deviations. These techniques, which in SDT would be understood as autonomy-thwarting, often extend to educational and religious institutions in such societies. As another example, Chirkov and Ryan (2001) showed significant differences between both parental and teacher autonomy support in Russians versus Americans, with Russian adults on average being seen as more controlling by students. Although the negative effects of control on internalization were evident in both countries, there were mean-level differences in a direction consistent with the societies' respective political climates. Duriez, Vansteenkiste, Soenens, and De Witte (2007) found that parents who promoted the attainment of extrinsic goals (e.g., financial success and social status) over intrinsic goals (e.g., self-development, community contribution, and affiliation) had children who were more prone to socially dominant attitudes and, to a lesser extent, to rigid adherence to social norms. Parents who modeled and transmitted conservative goals similarly had teenagers more rigidly adhering to societal norms, more critical of norm transgressors, and more prone to insulate themselves from information incompatible with their core beliefs.

Our point here is that the forms of regulation evident at a political–cultural level are intertwined with, and often reflective of, more proximal forms of social control and social values expressed and modeled in families, schools, and religious institutions. These everyday social lessons concerning voice and empowerment can support the defensive psychological processes required to comply with regimes.

Nonetheless, the dynamics of how people acquire democratic versus social dominance ideals are not as straightforward as once assumed, for example, by Adorno, Frenkel-Brunswik, Levinson, and Sanford (1950). Instead, they more likely represent interactions between parental- and societally transmitted values and the methods of regulation used to foster compliance and allegiance. Here, we concur with Darling and Steinberg's (1993) suggestion that, in order to model parental influences, one must consider both parental styles of socialization (e.g., their controlling vs. autonomy supportive practices) and the type and content of goals and values they seek to promote (Duriez, Soenens, & Vansteenkiste (2007).

Through both direct and indirect cultural processes, a reciprocally supportive relation exists between pervasive political climates and the proximal values people ultimately embrace. For instance, Basabe and Valencia (2007), using data from a large-scale survey of world values, examined the relations between freedoms and values for autonomy. Specifically, they looked at the associations between a government's score on liberal development (which combines ratings on human rights, freedoms, and equality with economic development) and the personal values held by its citizens. As we would expect, they found that the less a nation affords rights and freedoms, the less individuals within it embrace values for autonomy, egalitarianism, and tolerance or respect for diversity (see also Welzel, 2013).

Basic Need Satisfaction and Internalization

As we previously suggested, at the level of both individuals and populations, SDT is concerned with how the laws, policies, and methods of a given political system impact people's wellness and capabilities. In other words, we consider how well specific policies or regimes support and nourish their constituents or, alternatively, thwart and hinder their flourishing. SDT suggests more specifically that policies and laws that support basic psychological need satisfactions will be more readily accepted and more fully internalized. The less policies, laws, and codes are congruent with needs, the less well they are likely to be internalized, and thus the more force and coercion will be necessary to maintain control. Stated formally:

> To the degree that the contents of governmental rules and regulations have the functional significance of supporting versus thwarting psychological needs, they will be more readily accepted and internalized, resulting in more willing adherence. In contrast, regulations that conflict with or frustrate basic needs will more likely form the basis of controlled motivations that are likely to require greater external monitoring, control, and coercion to ensure compliance.

Even in contexts in which decision making is transparent and inclusive, the content of laws that are passed will be more or less supportive versus thwarting of people's basic psychological needs. As the functional significance of this satisfying or frustrating effect of laws on needs becomes clear, individuals will be more or less willing to adhere. For example, if a majority were to pass a law that thwarted the basic needs of minorities or subgroups, SDT expects that, to the extent that the laws are "need violating," they will not be readily internalized by the violated individuals.

This principle can help explain the nature of historical change, as tensions mount when psychological needs are thwarted en masse. Examples from prohibition to women's rights show that factors perceived to impinge upon autonomy, competence, and relatedness will be resisted. Further, the less need-satisfying the policy is, the more governments must exercise direct external control to maintain power and promote compliance. For example, Fulbrook (1995) described how the East German (GDR) government was deeply unpopular and clearly fostered a society less conducive to flourishing than its West German neighbor. This unpopularity engendered the necessity of ever-tighter internal security and more controlling methods of regulating citizens' behavior, regulations which eventually broke down.

Similarly, we personally witnessed this pattern in the People's Republic of Bulgaria (PRB) under the 35-year dictatorship of Todor Zhivkov. In that regime, control over all aspects of society was maintained through a network of informers, a feared Committee for State Security, and an opaque set of contingencies for party privileges and social punishments that helped reward and enforce compliance. The costs of this control in terms of the suppression of the Bulgarian people's ideas, talents, and social energies are inestimable.

Promoting autonomy and competence means supporting individuals to effectively form and pursue their aspirations (Deci & Ryan, 1985b; Doyal & Gough, 1993; Sen, 2000). As such, to evaluate a policy or practice of governance based on whether it promotes autonomy or competence is not to endorse how people live their lives; it is merely to endorse a process within which individuals have the freedom and capability to make decisions for themselves, within the constraints of well-reasoned legal structures, about how to live. Although, historically, many forces have suppressed or restricted inclusive human autonomy and empowerment, SDT suggests that to the extent these are made possible within any regime, this will objectively lead to greater optimization of human outcomes and greater mobilization of human capital.

Promoting societal relatedness requires supporting the cohesion and fairness upon which a civil society depends. As we shall discuss, there cannot be strong relatedness within any society or group when supports for autonomy and competence apply only for some, or where internal competitiveness reigns. Freedoms are also constrained by issues of justice, fairness, and concern for the welfare of all, thus separating free democratic systems from libertarianism. Inequities in rights and privileges lead to lower societal trust, less empathy, and greater intrasocietal violence, all indicative of lower relatedness. In contrast, opportunities to form and participate in voluntary organizations enhance democratic attitudes (Sullivan & Transue, 1999). Political policies thus bear on all basic need satisfactions, sometimes directly, and at other times by structurally thwarting the autonomy, along with the opportunities for competence or relatedness, that people would pursue when provided autonomy support.

Insofar as human nature includes a proactive, integrative propensity, we should expect that it would be difficult to reconcile compartmentalization, repression, or oppression with that integrative tendency. Indeed, given how fundamental the human needs for autonomy, competence, and relatedness are, they inevitably will have their expression in political life. In this sense, SDT expects human nature to exert a *bottom-up* pressure on controlling political and cultural systems, even as human behavior is channeled and controlled by them.

Basic psychological needs present not only constraints on what can be internalized but also an active bottom-up pressure for voice, freedom of expression and identity, and care for human needs. These pressures are slow to boil up in cultural histories, and never in any smooth progression. Yet, especially over the past seven decades, increasing segments of humanity have been moving away from enslavement and toward liberation, and away from arbitrary tyrannical controls toward wider empowerments, individual rights, and participation. This process is readily evident within modern democratic societies, which have been characterized by increasing civil rights for minority racial and religious groups, women, lesbian–gay–bisexual–transgender (LGBT) individuals, and other historically oppressed or stigmatized groups.

More globally, consider the increases in democratic relative to authoritarian regimes: In 1989, of 167 countries only 69 (41%) were electoral democracies; but in 2016, that number was 125 of 195 (64%) (Freedom House, 2016). Clearly, democracies (though not always ideal in process) have been on the rise, indexing one expression of freedoms and rights.

Again, such progress is fitful and unsteady. There has, for example, been a slight decline in democracies since 2006, and even a rise of authoritarianism in some nations.

Yet, as Diamond (2015) suggests, this has in no way reduced the global desire for freedoms and democracy; instead, the recent decline has widened the gap between people's political aspirations and realities (see also Green, 2012). Clearly, this trajectory toward increased rights and freedoms is far from finished, as many remain oppressed and voiceless, some even enslaved. Yet we have seen an increasing spread of rights and freedoms, and where it has not yet occurred, there are nascent aspirations for change.

Although human propensities toward agency and autonomy might not entirely explain the tides of history, they represent a strong undercurrent with a directional influence. Evidence recently reviewed by Welzel (2013) provides considerable empirical support for this idea. Based on his *utility ladder of freedoms,* he argued that, because both natural selection and cultural adaptations favor higher levels of personal control and autonomy, there is an ever-present pressure upward (from individuals) for more freedoms whenever these are perceived to have utility. In times when the focus is on survival, expanding freedoms will be less salient and less useful, but as they become potentially useful, people will want to appropriate and exercise them. In SDT terms, people have a basic need for autonomy, which is especially expressed under favorable or nurturing conditions. As part of the nature of their self-organization, people will attempt to advance their freedoms, rights, and abilities to pursue what they value.

With increasing rights and freedoms come a number of human and societal benefits and responsibilities. Overall, increased freedoms and rights for individuals have been associated with such outcomes as increases in productivity and human capital (e.g., Woo, 1984; Sen, 2000), decreases in violence (see, e.g., Pinker, 2011), and increases in happiness (e.g., Downie, Koestner, & Chua, 2007). Fischer and Boer (2011) examined the influence of both wealth and "individualism" on a number of wellness indicators in samples drawn from 63 nations, numbering over 400,000 participants. They defined individualism in their studies as the affordance of autonomy and choice to individuals in their life decisions. Rather than any evidence that freedom is problematic, they found robust associations between more freedom and greater well-being. Indeed, these positive effects of greater freedoms and choice were more robust than indicators of wealth in predicting wellness and, when considered together, they often wiped out any positive effects of wealth on outcomes.

Greater rights and freedoms, again within bounds of concerns of relatedness and justice, can allow people the opportunities and choices to pursue the goals that matter to them (Deci & Ryan, 2012) and thus to experience more need satisfaction and fulfillment. Although there are claims that "too much" freedom leads to burdens of choice and loss of identity (e.g., Schwartz, 2000, 2010) the evidence largely points to a more-is-better position on the most prominent outcomes. That is, as SDT would predict, societies that allow for, and especially that support, the autonomy and empowerment of their citizens will develop more motivated, self-regulating, and prosocial citizens (see also Welzel, 2013). With systemic freedoms and basic securities comes greater opportunity for individuals to regulate their lives in self-determined ways, which, contrary to many worldviews, leads them to be *more* motivated, efficacious, creative, and concerned for others.

Group versus Individual Autonomy and the Support of Diversity

Individuals exist within groups, and group norms and value structures provide scaffolding for human development and a sense of belonging and purpose. Yet groups are of two kinds: those that are *elective* and those that people "fall into" by birth, nationality, or cultural assignment. It seems clear from our discussions of social, cultural, and political entities that human groups, particularly the most powerful of the nonelective varieties, often attempt to constrain human choice, diversity, and autonomy in the service of ensuring continuing group identification and cohesion (Appiah, 2005) or in the service of maintaining the status quo relations of power. Indeed, many of those who most strongly object to individual autonomy do so because they see individual autonomy as representing a threat to traditional cultural, ethnic, and religious groups and to compliance with their practices. Yet recent trends include an increased global demand for recognizing the rights and freedoms for previously oppressed or stigmatized groups of people and calls for acceptance and greater expression of human diversity (Franck, 2001; Solomon, 2012).

In considering the relations between group and individual autonomy, SDT takes interest in how diversities and identifications are regulated both within groups and within the nations housing them. There is invariantly a tension between the very natural diversification propensities inherent in human genetic and cultural evolutions and the inherent tendencies of existing groups and institutions to maintain continuity and cohesion. Groups and institutions can address this tension either by accommodating and supporting diversity or by suppressing variations and mandating conformity. When a group marginalizes or suppresses quite natural variations of humanity, basic psychological needs are likely to be thwarted.

As salient examples, consider cultural, religious, or political groups that cannot *tolerate* homosexuality. This rejection of gay and lesbians and insistence on heteronormativity may produce more cohesion for its non-homosexual members, but it will also produce fractures in the psyches of those who are divergent and do not naturally follow the group's pathway. These individuals will suffer, along with all those with whom they are connected.

Similarly, consider the contemporary cultures, often backed by their governments' legal systems, in which women can be economically and physically controlled by husbands or other male kin. Many people vocally laud this practice as a "cultural tradition." Yet women who might better thrive if afforded their natural human inclinations to be active, volitional, and engaged with the world will *inherently* suffer. So, too, do their cultures and economies, which are deprived of the enormous "human capital" that women could be offering (Sen, 2000).

Where the boundaries of natural versus merely constructed values and propensities of humanity lie has, of course, often been considered a philosophical question. But in SDT we posit that it is more clearly an *empirical* question. It will not optimally be answered simply by dueling ideologies or belief systems, but by the actual analysis of functional outcomes of basic human needs, including SDT's basic psychological needs, that are met or unmet by particular cultural practices and the consequences that follow from them.

Accordingly, if there is a foundational, nonempirical value in SDT, it lies in its central concern and focus on the well-being of *individuals* and the priority SDT puts on that concern. SDT will therefore be critical of cultural institutions and groups that are functionally harmful to the basic need satisfactions of individuals within them, including the harms done to the often hidden and silenced voices of persons for whom the constraints of a culture are most ill fitting. That is, respect for pluralisms of cultures cannot, in the end, trump concerns for the pluralisms of persons within cultures whose welfare is the ultimate aim of psychological theory.

Throughout history, pressure toward specific roles and norms has meant that individuals have often had to turn away from compelling interests, attributes, or concerns that appeared incompatible with dominating religious or cultural authorities. SDT holds that, as people are given room to find fitting identities, and as they perceive tolerance (both pervasive and proximal) for expressing them, they will move toward more congruent identities and heighted wellness (e.g., see Legate, DeHaan, Weinstein, & Ryan, 2103). This is again an empirical question, but our psychological view of social conditions suggests that humans flourish with support for diversity more than they do when they are constrained to ignore or suppress authentic aspects of their natures. Movements toward rights and freedoms at the political level are thus assumed to enhance opportunities for autonomy competence and relatedness satisfactions at a personal level.

Of course, it is one thing to have the *right* to pursue what one values, but it is quite another to have the capability and resources to do so. This brings us to another pervasive influence on basic psychological need satisfactions and frustrations, namely economic contexts.

On Economic Structures: Wealth, Inequality, and Human Needs

Around the world, the aims of economic activity are the same: the production of goods and services, their distribution to those who have a demand for them, and the allocation of the fruits of production among the populace according to certain metrics or rules. From time immemorial, this has been the logic of the form of organization to which all individuals must submit. To some degree, all economies are "planned economies," although they vary both in the amount of central planning and in who controls and benefits from the plans. Put differently, there is no such thing as a "natural" economy in the sense that human-built power structures and policies exist in all economies and that these heavily determine the rules for production, distribution, and allocation of resources. In turn, the distribution and regulation of wealth bear both directly and indirectly on psychological need satisfactions of constituents and therefore on their functioning and capacities to flourish. Economic systems and policies shape how individual wealth is acquired and how common resources are collected and allocated, in turn influencing people's experiences of control, efficacy, freedom, and community and thus ultimately their basic needs for autonomy, competence, and relatedness.

In undertaking this topic, we must first clarify our belief that examining economic systems and policies, both macro and micro, in terms of their capacities to support or undermine the satisfaction of basic psychological needs, although controversial, is fully appropriate to social science. Such analyses bear on psychological health and human capital—on both the wellness and productivity of all those comprising the workforce. Yet such analyses are surprisingly rare in the field of psychology. Indeed, Kasser et al. (2007) argued that analyses of the effects of capitalism on human wellness have largely been "taboo" within the journals of psychology, presumably out of the scholarly impulse to avoid appearing value-laden or ideological. Nonetheless, as behavioral scientists, it is hard to deny the multiple ways in which pervasive economic systems shape people's goals, allocations of behavior (e.g., labor, leisure), comfort, and wellness. Thus all economic systems can, and we think should, be evaluated for their capacities to motivate and catalyze human capital and to facilitate basic human need satisfactions and wellness (Ryan & Deci, 2000a). All too often, analyses have focused only on the concrete outputs of human capital without consideration of human wellness. An advantage of SDT in this respect is the clarity of its criteria for such critiques—namely, its bedrock concern with the satisfaction versus frustration of basic psychological needs, which have been unequivocally linked to long-term well-being and productive engagement of both collectives and their members.

Any comprehensive review of the interface between SDT and economic systems would require a volume of its own, so we instead focus illustratively on a few global characteristics of such systems that lend themselves to SDT analyses. As we suggested in Chapter 21, as a psychological theory, SDT is focused on both intrinsic and extrinsic rewards and resources and thus entails considerations that have been largely outside the scope of classical economic theories of behavior and value. Specifically, SDT identifies values and goods not classically conceptualized within standard economic theories, including intrinsic and extrinsic preferences and identities that are not easily "cashed out" or redeemable. Additionally, as will be seen across examples, whereas in standard economic theories the route to "better" is "more," SDT suggests that the path to wellness and flourishing, at both individual and collective levels of analysis, need not entail accumulation and excess. Wellness can, in fact, be crowded out by extrinsic appetites and acquisitions (e.g. Frey, 1997; Kasser, 2002a; Kasser & Ryan, 1996), which so frequently have negative consequences that are both direct and collateral. Instead, SDT focuses on basic need satisfactions as underlying wellness, and these are intertwined with whether individuals can acquire capabilities to pursue what they deem worthwhile and how economies support or thwart their intrinsic human aspirations.

Autonomy, Basic Need Satisfaction, and Human Capital

Individuals, whether they are moving from one country to another, starting off in the workforce, or changing jobs, confront an existing organizational–social form or structure in which they have to function. This structure will manifest as essentially a top-down entity, which has to be negotiated as people, with the aim of achieving adaptation and success, express their agency. In turn, these strivings and needs of individuals result in bottom-up influences, and they make room for themselves within existing structures and processes.

A central tenet of SDT (again, as applied to organizations in Chapter 21) is the following: the more autonomy, competence, and relatedness satisfactions individuals feel when participating in economic activities, the more productive, innovative, and persistent those people will be. Autonomy in particular, as a quality indicative of integrated engagement in activities, produces "human capital," including its role in generating greater efficiencies, expertise, and innovations. We reviewed a healthy stock of evidence for this claim in Chapter 21.

There can be no doubt, in this respect, that as a pervasive context, capitalism, broadly defined, has in some general sense catalyzed more agency—indeed, more human productive energy—than any other economic macro-system in history. It is therefore also responsible for tremendous wealth generation, and it even contains the potential to greatly diminish or eliminate world poverty (Hart, 2007). In part, this catalyzation of human energies has everything to do with structural supports for autonomy entailed in capitalism, relative to previous economic cultures. For example, individuals living within a market capitalist system typically have, on the surface, a wide array of choices about what work they can pursue and how they can engage in their personal lives. The options available to many have stimulated substantial entrepreneurial activity, and, to the extent that educational opportunities are available, the system of incentives and self-matching of careers can generate initiative and achievement. That is, some forms capitalism can support and enhance autonomy and diversity, allowing individuals to gravitate toward skill sets, talents, and interests, facilitating engagement and need-satisfying productivity.

Although this portrait of capitalism's promise is a reality for some, as we stressed in Chapter 21, more typically it is obtainable for only a privileged minority. For many individuals, the options afforded are severely narrowed by factors not within their control. People without adequate resources or supports for basic health, education, and training, or for cultivating the interests and skills required for entrepreneurship, have considerably delimited options and capacities to exercise their "freedoms" in the marketplace (Green, 2012).

As just a simple example of this, Schüz and colleagues (2016) studied older adults in various regions of Germany. They reasoned that older adults face many everyday challenges and limitations, many of which can compromise their experience of autonomy and competence. Yet results showed that, in regions of Germany where more resources were made available to elderly persons, their self-perceived autonomy was greater. Clearly, adequacy (rather than excess) of resources matters to need satisfaction.

Additionally, just as the political world can lack fairness, transparency, and participatory involvement, economic worlds can lack these same elements of legitimacy. Segments of people can be excluded from navigating the cultures of power and commerce on the basis of social class, gender, race, sexual orientation, or other characteristics. Players with bigger money and "legacy values" have advantages and leverage other agents cannot possibly possess (see Picketty, 2014). Such barriers to fair access and opportunity can thwart basic needs for autonomy and competence and/or lead to many compensatory adaptations that are costly to societies (Phelps, 2012).

Given that our central focus in this chapter is on elements of pervasive contexts that undermine or support human thriving, we will not reiterate many of the points discussed in Chapter 21 on agency and autonomous engagement at the proximate level of work and organizations. Instead, to exemplify SDT considerations, we turn here to some structural elements associated with macro-economics and wealth distribution that affect need satisfaction within and across nations.

Socioeconomic Status

It is well known that socioeconomic factors are significantly associated with both mental and physical health outcomes (e.g., Marmot, 2004, 2015). Every step down a socioeconomic status (SES) hierarchy is, in fact, predictive of worse outcomes. Myriad mediators have been posited concerning this relation, from general psychological factors such as stress to health-related behaviors such as smoking, poor diet, and sedentary lifestyles. Lower occupational status, poorer education, and other indicators of low status in the economic hierarchy have all been associated with a lower sense of control, greater demand, and less choice in many areas of life. Moreover, excessive income inequality also negatively affects wellness for all members of society, at all levels of SES, as it enhances feelings of difference and separateness, social comparison, feelings of threat, and a decreased sense of belonging and community (e.g., see Wilkinson & Pickett, 2010). Using international databases, DeNeve and Powdthavee (2016) showed that as inequality rises, happiness goes down at the country level, primarily due to increased negative experiences of citizens (rather than frequency of positive experiences).

Research by Cheung and Lucas (2016) with a sample of well over 1 million participants showed that, controlling for people's own household incomes, the income of the county within which the people lived was negatively associated with their life satisfaction, a finding consistent with prior research by Luttmer (2005) and others. Oishi, Kesebir, and Diener (2011) then replicated that finding at the societal level and showed that this relation was mediated by perceived unfairness and lack of trust, both variables that are likely to go hand-in-hand with thwarting of basic psychological need satisfaction. Cheung and Lucas (2016) further showed that income inequality moderated the negative relation between relative income and life satisfaction, such that those people who lived in wealthy counties had less life satisfaction than those in poorer counties. Finally, they reported that people whose personal incomes were lower had a stronger negative relation between county income and their own life satisfaction. These and related phenomena lead to the general expectation within SDT that both SES and wealth inequalities would negatively affect human wellness and flourishing by negatively affecting people's opportunities to satisfy basic needs.

Indeed, research suggests that SDT's central construct of satisfaction versus frustration of basic psychological needs could be among the most important mediators in the relations between socioeconomic conditions and both physical and mental health outcomes. For instance, González, Swanson, Lynch, and Williams (2016) examined a sample of U.S. employees to test whether basic need satisfactions mediated the relations between SES, rated on the basis of occupational indicators, and both physical and mental health while controlling for variables known to affect health, such as age, exercise levels, and smoking status. Results indicated that a substantial portion of the variance in health-related outcomes was accounted for by SDT's three basic need satisfactions. This speaks to how powerfully economic factors affect our basic psychological needs. People with lower SES have fewer intrinsic job satisfactions, higher work stress, more emotional exhaustion, and lower vitality, all reflective of low basic need satisfaction on a daily basis. In addition, and consistent with Inglehart (1997), the lower people's SES is, the more positively incremental gains in either wealth or the capabilities associated with it affect basic need satisfactions. Those living in conditions of poverty and scarcity not only often lack autonomy and control over outcomes, as we discuss, but they also face obstacles to relatedness. That said, evidence also suggests that, once above poverty levels, the relations between more wealth and more well-being become substantially weaker (Kasser, 2002a). In SDT's view, the reason is that, once basic obstacles to living are overcome, greater material wealth is not likely to directly enhance the basic needs that most robustly fuel wellness.

Di Domenico and Fournier (2014) similarly examined the relations between socioeconomic indicators and well-being and the extent to which these were connected through the pathway of SDT's basic psychological needs. They examined not only perceived SES but also household income and the degree of socioeconomic inequality in people's surroundings as predictors of self-reported health and wellness. They found all three were important—the higher people's perceived SES was, the greater their income was; and the lower the level of income inequality in their region was, the greater was their self-reported health and wellness. More importantly from an SDT perspective, basic need satisfactions mediated these relations. The positive impacts of these variables is largely accounted for by their enhancements of personal autonomy, relatedness to others, and experiences of control and competence.

Social status in these studies was both objectively and subjectively assessed. Yet evidence suggests it is particularly when people see themselves as low status and also internalize it as their own fault that it can be particularly destructive. For example, Jackson, Richman, LaBelle, Lempereur, and Twenge (2015) argued and showed experimentally that the thwarting of psychological needs was amplified when the individuals had internalized their lower social status or viewed it as reflective of their selves. Factors in society such as stigma and stereotypes play such an amplifying role.

Among the many implications of such research is that the factors that reduce people's status, limit choices about work conditions, or add to daily pressures and hassles all affect their wellness outcomes through frustrating their psychological needs. Such results support the general findings and reasoning of thinkers such as Marmot (2004) and Wilkinson and Pickett (2010) who have focused on how income disparities negatively affect well-being. Accordingly, we turn from this general formulation to just a few of the specific societal factors that affect these dynamics.

Social Safety Nets and Individuals' Need Satisfactions

Safety nets represent a core issue in societies regarding basic need satisfactions and their associations with economic supports. Most wage earners in market economies are at least in part, if not primarily, motivated for work by a form of external regulation, namely contingent monetary incentives. Persons understand their jobs as instrumental to a paycheck, either being paid for time or for productivity. Presuming external incentives are equal, people exercise autonomy by seeking work they find engaging, meaningful, interesting, fitting, or affording of opportunities. That is, to the extent that workers have choice, pay-and-benefit contingencies are not fully determinative of what work will be selected or how much effort and energy will be invested in it. Most people would prefer work that is psychologically fulfilling, and research testifies to the fact that although many people will trade off autonomy and relatedness at work for higher pay, many others work at jobs that are less lucrative so that they can pursue work they can endorse and value (e.g., Sheldon & Krieger, 2014a).

Unfortunately, for many employees, work is not a deep source of need satisfaction. Recall Ryan, Bernstein, and Brown's (2010) findings, in a heterogeneous sample of American workers, that well-being was lower on working days, primarily because of low autonomy and relatedness need satisfactions on the job. Market economies allow for many types of pay structures, work environments, and incentives; nevertheless, finding a need-supportive and wellness-fostering workplace can be a struggle for many individuals. For some, choice is simply not available. Given that work can be such a source of satisfaction or dissatisfaction, a sense of choice and options with respect to employment is therefore critical for employment's facilitation of autonomy satisfaction.

It is regarding this sense of choice that the size of the *economic safety net* has particular salience. Economic safety nets serve to protect the bottom rungs of the economic ladder from further falling. A *safety net* thus refers to both income and health benefits below which no citizen would be allowed to dip.

There are some clear ways in which safety nets affect psychological needs. Insofar as there are sufficiently large safety nets, people have more objective choice regarding work. People can resign from jobs with bad working conditions or that are need-thwarting and seek more solid or satisfying ones. If they have health care access, they can afford to take risks to shift careers. Thus, to the degree that a safety net allows people to leave their jobs without undue harm, selecting a job will likely facilitate their feeling more autonomously engaged. Employers in the context of larger safety nets will reciprocally be more motivated to make workplace conditions attractive and need-satisfying so as to retain workers, whereas, in the absence of safety nets, employers are "freer" to engage in maltreatment of workers, who would lack options to leave such negative conditions. Obviously, the potential impact on need satisfaction is significant.

To function as an effective support within capitalism, however, a safety net must be set at an optimal level—not so high as to discourage people from undertaking productive tasks that they might otherwise not be motivated to do, yet not so low as to prevent them from retreating from unfavorable circumstances so as to reengage in ways they perceive as betterment. An optimal range would have the safety net set high enough to functionally support a life, but not so high that it crowds out meaningful incentives and personal initiative for entry-level labor. It also suggests that a safety net would rise in keeping with the overall income of the society, lest it lose its function as an ever-present alternative to poor or exploitive working conditions. For example, in some nations, unemployment payments have historically been quite high relative to wages for low-paying jobs, so unemployed people may be motivated not to find employment, and those who have low-paying and unsatisfying jobs will be motivated to relinquish them (Vansteenkiste, Lens, De Witte, De Witte, & Deci, 2004).

Income Distribution and Inequality

In addition to safety nets, there is the issue of *income distribution,* which also impacts psychological need satisfactions at a population level. In a capitalist system, there will always be variability in income and wealth, so income equality would not be expected for a large portion of the workers, although that equality has been a value in socialist economies. Some level of uneven distribution is, of course, appropriate within capitalist systems, because different workers make contributions (e.g., skills, education, responsibilities) that vary considerably. However, what we are referring to as inequality shows up in two ways within capitalist systems: (1) when, in general, workers are not compensated in a way that is appropriate given their inputs to the organization; and (2) when huge disparities occur in which the difference between the lowest paid employees in a company and the highest paid ones are egregiously large, with the lowest paid living in near poverty and the highest paid amassing enormous wealth that is unreasonable and incommensurate with what they have contributed.

Considerable evidence, much of it compellingly assembled by Wilkinson and Pickett (2010), shows how the relative inequality in the distribution of income within a society strongly impacts the quality of life for all people within it. The greater the income inequality, the weaker the social glue that keeps a society cohesive. As Wilkinson and Pickett summarized: "We have seen how inequality affects trust, community life, and violence, and how—through the quality of life—it predisposes people to be more or less affiliative, empathic or aggressive" (p. 236).

In previous sections, we have detailed some of the mechanisms underlying this trend, as understood within SDT. Individuals living in relative poverty are less likely to provide autonomy-supportive and relatedness-supportive contexts. Poverty has, for example, been associated with less support for self-direction (e.g., Kohn & Slomczynski, 1990), which other research has shown is associated with both less trust in relationships and more investment in extrinsic values as a way of attempting to experience worth (e.g., see Kasser, Ryan, Zax, & Sameroff, 1995). That is, especially within well-developed capitalist contexts such as the United States, the more impoverished and need-thwarting the parent is, the less nurtured the offspring is, and the less growth-, community- and relationship-oriented these offspring are likely to become.

More unequal wealth distribution also brings out competitive, aggressive aspects of humans stemming from both comparative threat and deprivation threat. Considerable research has shown that when people are more focused on competition and attaining money, they are likely to be less autonomously motivated (e.g., Deci, Koestner, & Ryan, 1999; Reeve & Deci, 1996) and more likely to display a variety of negative social behaviors and a lower relatedness to their community. Lower relatedness is thus a cost of highly unequal, and especially *inequitably* unequal, economic distribution systems.

Policies that lead to more equitable distributions of wealth within a society typically have a positive influence on individuals who are recipients of their largesse, and cultures in general benefit from having a larger percentage of their members living with adequate food, shelter, and health care. Indeed, substantial research suggests that, in cultures where wealth is more unevenly distributed, overall cultural wellness is diminished, even controlling for overall wealth (Wilkinson & Pickett, 2010). Thus social-welfare policies, when combined with capitalism, can attenuate some of capitalism's more negative effects (Kasser et al., 2007). Still, many people criticize social welfare policies, often on the motivational thesis that they take away incentives for hard work and reward indolence.

Capitalist countries differ in the degree to which they value social welfare or caring for their citizens. For example, several Scandinavian countries are sometimes referred to as social-democratic states, for they have a more elaborate welfare program, with a heavier tax burden, as a result of which there are fewer people who have fallen out of the system into poverty and neglect. In fact, virtually all democratic countries, even with the more laissez-faire versions of capitalism that we find in the United States, do tend to have at least modest social welfare policies, suggesting that when people are free, at least a majority of them experience a tendency to care for those who have been ineffective in caring for themselves.

This was made obvious in a study of U.S. citizens (Norton & Ariely, 2011) in which participants were asked both about income distributions they thought were ideal and those they thought were current in the American economy. The results showed that the vast majority of Americans said they would prefer a distribution of income that approximated that of social democracies such as Sweden. Even more amazing is that most believed that the United States was much more equitable in wealth distribution than it actually is. In other words, many people do not really know what is going on macro-economically within their country, thus living within a system that is not what they say they would prefer.

In this sense, our economies "befall" us. Although we don't design them, economies redesign us in their image. In adapting to the rules of their ambient economic game, people learn how resources are earned, what is valued in human labor and attributes, what to consume, and how these things affect status. And for most people, their adaptation to the economy that befalls them will end up as a primary determinant of how they spend time, money, and their life's energy.

Internalizing Inequality: Extrinsic Aspirations and Consumerism

In discussing totalitarian political regimes, we suggested that, as pervasive environments, they are both anchored in and supported by specific beliefs, attitudes, and practices of individuals, each of which is variously internalized. Similarly, cultures of economic inequality, in which excessive wealth and dire poverty are accepted as companions, are supported by particular values internalized by individuals within proximal environments.

Specifically, the more unequal the culture, the more the people are likely to be insecure and untrusting and thus less empathic toward others. That is, inequality in wealth distribution is consistent with extrinsic orientations that focus on social comparisons and aspirations concerning image, wealth, and recognition. Associated evidence shows that income inequality predicts tendencies toward biased self-enhancement, or the tendency for people to see themselves as better than others (e.g., see Loughnan et al., 2011). Indeed, income inequality within nations (as indexed by the Gini coefficient) better predicted such self-enhancement biases than did indicators of individualism versus collectivism. Inequality is also less conducive to intrinsic goals of community care, relationships, and personal growth (Kasser et al., 2007).

Investments in extrinsic values in turn drive consumerism and a more self-interested focus in living, which dovetail with an ideology of individualism focused on achievement. The values and belief systems most explicitly associated with income inequality within a society happen to be those that are, empirically speaking, opposed to and potentially undermining of people's attempts to work for the welfare of others in the broader community and to develop a sense of connection and closeness to others (Kasser et al., 2007). For instance, insofar as income inequality is associated with increased consumerism and materialism, as Wilkinson and Pickett (2010) argued, it may also lead to less prosocial attitudes (McHoskey, 1999; Sheldon & Kasser, 1995; Sheldon & McGregor, 2000) and to the general lowering of psychological wellness associated with an emphasis on materialism (Dittmar, 2005; Kasser, 2002a). Again, those higher in materialism and the related extrinsic goals of image and fame, all of which are associated with resource inequalities, have lower wellness due to the lower need satisfaction such lifestyles and value orientations yield over time (Niemiec, Ryan, & Deci, 2009). Piff, Stancato, Cote, Mendoza-Denton, and Keltner (2012) showed, for example, that those advantaged by class differences—that is, those benefiting from inequality—may also tend toward less humanity. In seven studies using a variety of methods, they demonstrated that upper-class individuals were actually less generous and less ethical than their lower-class counterparts. This tendency was, in part, explained by the greater tendencies toward greed and materialism in these individuals, or what we would call their extrinsic value systems (Kasser & Ryan, 1996; Ryan, Sheldon, Kasser, & Deci, 1996).

Chirkov, Ryan, Kim, & Kaplan (2003) studied the internalization of ambient cultural beliefs from samples of U.S., South Korean, Russian, and Turkish individuals. Embedded in the findings was that people were likely to report having more controlled (i.e., less autonomous) reasons for believing that it is important "to work in situations involving competition with others" or to endorse that "without competition, it is impossible to have a good society." Such attitudes associated with ideologies of inequality are thus associated with less autonomy, which has been repeatedly shown to be conducive to diminished wellness.

In sum, there is good reason to believe that societies in which inequalities in wealth are more exaggerated are conducive to the internalization of behavioral regulations and attitudes that thwart basic psychological need satisfactions and thus yield lower wellness. This suggests again that macro-economic structures influence wellness through psychological pathways, often in ways that the people who constitute these systems are unaware.

Capabilities, Freedoms, and Wellness: Toward Eudaimonic Societies

As we have seen, social contexts, both proximal and pervasive, can be analyzed in terms of their supports for basic psychological needs of the individuals who constitute them. Societies that provide political freedoms, some basic economic and health care safety nets, and a distribution of wealth that is not highly inequitable and unjust (Rawls, 2009) appear to be more supportive of a population's basic needs and therefore to better support the flourishing of their members. Yet, from an SDT standpoint, these are empirical questions, as every structure, policy, and social benefit merits differentiated scrutiny in these regards.

It is also clear that SDT differs from economic views that focus on *happiness*, considered as a hedonic concept (e.g., Kahneman, Diener, & Schwarz, 1999). Indeed, we have long argued that hedonic outcomes such as the mere presence of positive affect and absence of negative affect are not reliable indicators of wellness (Ryan, Huta, & Deci, 2008) or of flourishing (Ryan & Deci, 2001), which has led us to also embrace eudaimonic perspectives (Ryan, Curren, & Deci, 2013). Here we specifically focus on the idea that the affordance of opportunities for autonomy, competence, and relatedness satisfactions are the conditions that foster a good life—a life capable of true flourishing—defined in terms of a person being fully functioning. We look for the indicators of flourishing across multiple indicators, which include not only affective outcomes but also an array of the positive variables that reflect human excellences, virtues, and meanings, as well as the absence of the hindrances to wellness reflected in psychopathology and ill health.

It is also important to note that, with regard to the issues of inequity, our analysis did not suggest that a good society guarantees an equality of *outcomes* but rather equality of access to opportunities to pursue what people deem worthwhile. Indeed, the very centrality of the concern for autonomy within SDT acknowledges that there are a diversity of aims within the human community, a diversity within which individuals have both rights and reasons to take different life routes. Attempts to make everyone productive or achieving along similar or narrow metrics (e.g., all students must be mathematically skilled at a college-ready level) inevitably crush the human spirit and disrespect the variety and diversity of talents and interests natural to our species.

Several prominent economists and philosophers have also, in recent years, contributed to the discussion of wellness promotion using the concept of eudaimonia. The thrust of their work has been to highlight what social conditions and resources provide sufficient room for the exercise of human capacities that can support people living a full and good life. The major works of this type are often said to make up the *capabilities approach*, credited primarily to Sen (e.g., 1985, 2000) and Nussbaum (e.g., 2000).

Sen has argued that for happiness to be attained, persons must have *capabilities*, the latter conceptualized as a reflection of the freedom to achieve valued *functionings*. That is, he argued that societies focused on the flourishing of their citizens ought to provide individuals with the affordances and opportunities that would allow them to freely and effectively pursue that which they have reason to value. This criterion, instead of the mere accumulation of wealth or the growth of the gross national product, is, in his view, a truer indicator of economic development and, indeed, the well-being of societies.

Also pursuing the issue of capabilities, Nussbaum (2000) adopted a more direct approach. She specifically defined 10 capabilities that she deemed essential for human flourishing. The affordance of these capabilities is understood as the foundation upon which a good life can be established. These include the following: (1) a reasonable life expectancy; (2) bodily health; (3) bodily integrity, including freedom of movement and freedom from fear of violence; (4) ability to use one's senses, imagination, and thought; (5) ability and freedom to experience and express emotions, including love; (6) practical reason; (7) affiliation, including the freedom to live with others, and respect for relational choices; (8) appreciation and accessibility of other species; (9) opportunities for play; and (10) control over the environment, both political and material. Nussbaum's view is that people possessing these general capabilities have a greater likelihood of flourishing, whereas the absence of these affordances compromises development and flourishing.

These 10 capabilities are essentially derived from Nussbaum's philosophical analysis and thus could be criticized as arbitrary or elitist insofar as her analysis presumes to articulate what constitutes a good life for everyone (e.g., see Kashdan, Biswas-Diener, & King, 2008). Yet some attempts have been made to operationalize these capabilities and to empirically connect them with traditional subjective measures of happiness or wellness. Anand, Hunter, Carter, Dowding, Guala, and Van Hees (2009), for example, developed a survey-based assessment of Nussbaum's list of capabilities, which they administered to a nationally representative sample of U.K. residents. Their results showed that these capabilities were, as a group, predictive of subjective well-being as measured by the widely used approach of Diener and colleagues (Diener, 1994; Diener, Emmons, Larsen, & Griffin, 1985).

DeHaan, Hirai, and Ryan (2015) also examined how this assessment of Nussbaum's capabilities predicted well-being, as well as the potential mediating role of basic psychological needs in the relations between capabilities and well-being. Surveys from two samples, one from the United States and one from India, produced results consistent with their proposed hypotheses. First, Nussbaum's 10 capabilities were clearly conducive to wellness, as indicated not only by affective happiness but also by vitality, meaning in life, absence of stress, and life satisfaction. The capabilities were also strongly associated with SDT's basic psychological needs. Most relevant here, basic psychological needs largely mediated the relations of capabilities to wellness outcomes, suggesting that capabilities have their impact on wellness by facilitating need satisfactions—that is, experiences of autonomy, competence, and relatedness—and by preventing the frustration of these needs. This small demonstration merely illustrates that at the center of a flourishing life are conditions that afford the satisfaction of the basic psychological needs that are central to all human beings.

Concluding Comments

The relations between the psychology of individuals and the characteristics of the pervasive environments within which they exist are complex and include asymmetries between the individual and the more encompassing political–economic systems. In no case is one level of analysis simply reducible to the other. That is, we cannot explain a system such as democracy or capitalism on the basis of individual needs and motives, nor can we explain individual needs and motives entirely from these pervasive contextual influences. Nonetheless, we take interest in the idea that there are not only downward influences of pervasive environments on individuals but also influences of the actions and attitudes of those individuals on pervasive structures. The bottom-up influences in societies often result, we speculate, from the tensions created by cultural, political, or economic factors that cannot be readily internalized and that represent barriers to basic need satisfactions, resulting in their being perceived as illegitimate or oppressive. In this regard, we particularly noted the stumbling but nonetheless forward progress toward increasing democracy and human rights around the globe, as people actively pursue their freedoms and capabilities.

Regarding political systems, we suggested that democracies rely on self-motivated, autonomous citizens. It is those individuals who have identified with politics and its value who are most informed, engaged, and active. In contrast, more authoritarian governments do not inspire or require such internalization but, instead, rely on controlled motivations. This also makes the legitimacy of these regimes generally less well-anchored in their constituents' psyches, as they are regulated not through integrated principles but rather by external contingencies and power structures. We also argued that all governmental regulations and programs can be evaluated with respect to their effectiveness at supporting basic psychological need satisfactions, and thus the flourishing of their constituents.

Regarding economic systems, we discussed the fact that greater economic resources at both national and individual levels contribute to basic psychological need satisfactions, especially for individuals at lower levels of the economic spectrum. At the same time excessive individual wealth contributes little incremental value to need satisfactions, and wealth discrepancies interfere with basic need satisfactions at all levels of income. We discuss the value of economic features like economic safety nets in supporting autonomy and other basic needs through enhancement of choice.

Although the criterion of basic need satisfaction provides a universal basis for evaluating the features of political and economic systems, such analyses are inherently critical and comparative. Herein, however, we did not strive to compare specific nations or policies but rather to focus on broader issues of political freedoms and economic inequality as examples of the kinds of issues that can affect basic need satisfactions. Freedoms, access to resources and capabilities, and human rights all appear to conspire to foster wellness and, as SDT suggests, these relationships are substantially mediated by the satisfaction of people's basic psychological needs.

CHAPTER 24

On Basic Needs and Human Natures

Altruism, Aggression,
and the Bright and Dark Sides of Human Motivation

As we bring this volume to a close, we consider what can be said about the nature of human beings. Vast literatures have addressed this question, with some scholars arguing that human nature is wholly malleable, and others portraying it as relatively fixed. Among the latter, there has been a tendency to view that fixed nature as being fundamentally competitive, self-interested, and aggressive. In contrast to both positions we argue that humans are equipped to deal with both nurturing and hostile environments. Under conditions of basic need support, SDT suggests that tendencies toward prosociality and altruism will be robust, whereas need-thwarting environments conduce to the darker elements of human nature, including defensiveness, prejudice, and interpersonal violence. Specifically, we suggest that intrinsically motivated prosocial behavior is likely to be promoted and maintained when people's basic psychological needs are satisfied and that the more selfish, aggressive, and malevolent sides of human nature emerge under conditions of thwarts and obstacles leading to basic psychological need frustrations. We further review how different forms of aggressive behavior are differentially internalized and why particularly malevolent acts, even when defended as "virtuous," cannot be easily integrated and thus fully autonomously enacted. Empirical support for these hypotheses is presented, and we also discuss the possible evolutionary and cultural foundations of these formulations. We close by reflecting on why people may be becoming less aggressive and the possibilities of social design to bring out the more positive aspects of our human natures.

Perhaps the most common, and yet often overlooked, attribute of humans is our *humanity*. We are normatively cooperative, social creatures, with robust capacities for kindness and benevolence. In societies across the globe, whether in cities or rural areas, whether among rich or poor, people are typically not only tolerant of others but even considerate and helpful. Spend a day in public places most anywhere, and you will see the vast majority of individuals moving with and around each other, communicating, making exchanges, smiling, and only quite rarely showing aggression or violence. In most families, in most classrooms, in most companies, in most clubs and organizations, incivility, lack of cooperation, and violence are not the norm. On the contrary, such behaviors trouble us wherever they appear. In fact, most people, most of the time, will show empathy and compassion for others, even strangers, and provide help when they are in a position to offer it.

Contrary, then, to a popular view of human nature as inherently selfish, aggressive, and wholly instrumentally oriented in relation to others, we suggest that both evolutionary and cultural developments have, instead, prepared individuals to be relationally engaged, norm assimilating, rule following, and generally benevolent. In SDT's organismic view, persons are, for example, "naturally" prone to attach to others and to internalize (and, where possible, to integrate) ambient social values and regulations. People will also, absent conditions of threat, spontaneously help others and derive intrinsic satisfactions from doing so. In this chapter, we discuss both how these prosocial and benevolent propensities can be linked to individual- and group-level models of fitness and how, given their potential selective advantages, proximal psychological mechanisms in the form of basic need satisfactions may have emerged to support such propensities, especially within a "good enough" cultural milieu.

Despite widespread evidence of humanity, it is also clear that people can be aggressive, greedy, and at times malevolent. That is, there are many dark sides to our species, and failure to recognize them would be both naïve and historically inaccurate. Although the sources of such antisocial and destructive behaviors and attitudes are complex, SDT research highlights that a meaningful part of the explanation for their expression lies in conditions that thwart basic psychological need satisfactions in both individual development and in broader cultural contexts (Ryan & Deci, 2000a). Research already presented throughout this book has shown how need-supportive contexts promote the inherent capacities for mutually supportive social relationships and integrative functioning and, thus, that people who are afforded nurturing developmental conditions are much more prone to show these positive human propensities. Evidence equally suggests, however, that people who are raised within need-thwarting familial or sociocultural contexts more frequently display the self-protective and aggressive features of human nature and the compensations and defenses associated with need frustration.

As one simple example, consider the issue of *honesty*, which is typically thought to be a human virtue. Bureau and Mageau (2014) investigated honesty in adolescents' communications with their parents, using SDT as a theoretical lens. They found that more controlling parents had adolescents who reported less value for honesty and who saw more costs in telling the truth to parents. Adolescent offspring of autonomy-supportive parents were more identified with the basic value of honesty, and they reported more value, and lower cost, to being honest with parents. More open and receptive parent–child communication decreased the perceived threat and tendency for self-protective responses, which provided more room for sharing and transparency.

Kanat-Maymon, Benjamin, Stavsky, Shoshani, and Roth (2015) examined cheating, an opposite behavior to honesty. Their first study used an experimental paradigm in which undergraduates were placed in one of three groups: a need-supportive condition, a neutral condition, and a need-thwarting condition. Those students in the condition that supported their autonomy, competence, and relatedness were the least likely to cheat in a task they were given; those in the condition that thwarted the three needs were the most likely to cheat; and those in the neutral condition fell between these other conditions. A second study with junior high students similarly revealed that students who experienced greater basic psychological need support in their classes were more autonomously motivated and, in turn, were less dishonest in their schoolwork.

Looking at another prosocial attribute, Miklikowska, Duriez, and Soenens (2011) explored how parent need support related to children's capacity for *empathy*. In a three-wave longitudinal study of middle adolescents, they examined the relative contributions of perceived maternal and paternal need-supportive parenting on changes in empathic concern and perspective taking over time. They found that paternal need support predicted positive changes in perspective taking in both sons and daughters. Perceived maternal need support predicted positive changes in empathic concern among daughters. Such data are important because, even in young children, empathy is a strong basis for prosocial behaviors (Williams, O'Driscoll, & Moore, 2014), and empathy, which follows from need support, is the opposite of selfish, aggressive behaviors that follow need thwarting.

Illustrating the less positive sides of human behavior is the growing body of SDT work on *bullying*. For example, Roth, Kanat-Maymon, and Bibi (2011) examined how autonomy-supportive teaching affected bullying and aggression in schools. They reasoned that teachers' being more autonomy supportive in school would lead to greater internalization of considerateness toward classmates and to less frequent aggression and bullying. Further, they predicted that the relations between teachers' autonomy-supportive styles and students' bullying would be mediated by students' identification with (i.e., autonomous internalization of) the value of considerateness toward others. In a large sample of junior high school students from different schools in Israel, the researchers found support for these hypotheses. They showed that a climate of autonomy support played a significant role in the prevention of bullying and promoted more civil behaviors in schools.

Kaplan and Assor (2012) presented a conceptualization and a 2-year program of autonomy-supportive "I–Thou" dialogue among teachers and students in Israel based on both SDT and Buber's (1960) dialogical philosophy. The intervention led to significant decreases in negative emotions and to decreases in classroom violence and bullying behaviors.

López, Bilbao, and Rodriguez (2010) looked at how classroom climate affected bullying in sixth- to eighth-graders in Chile. Even after controlling for factors such as socioeconomic status and victimization, classroom autonomy support (versus control) accounted for substantial variance in bullying. In more supportive classrooms, students felt more satisfaction, less friction, and less competitiveness, which were all associated with fewer reports of bullying. The authors suggested that the social ecologies of organizations accounts for much of the negative behavior that occurs within them.

In Estonian schools, Hein, Koka, and Hagger (2015) examined the controlling behaviors of physical education teachers, the need satisfaction of students, and reports of anger and bullying. They found that teachers' controlling behaviors, such as conditional regard or intimidation, were associated with greater student anger, relations that were mediated by (lower) perceived need satisfaction. Anger, in turn, was associated with increased bullying. They reasoned, in accord with Hawley, Little, and Pasupathi (2002) that frustration of autonomy needs in students would lead to compensatory attempts to control peers in a direct or hostile way.

Parental thwarting of autonomy also conduces to bullying and aggression. For example, Fousiani, Dimitropoulou, Michaelides, and Van Petegem (2016) investigated the relations between parent autonomy support and psychological control and cyberbullying in adolescents from Cyprus. Findings revealed both direct and indirect relations between cyberbullying and parental styles. Parental psychological control was directly related to cyberbullying. In contrast, parental autonomy support was related to lower cyberbullying through indirect pathways. Specifically, autonomy support was associated with adolescents' sense of autonomy, which predicted more empathic concern toward others, which in turn differentially related to greater recognition of humanness of victims and bullies. It thus seemed that the more the adolescents felt that their autonomy was respected, the more prone they were to respect that of others.

These multiple examples from around the world show that the more environments are supportive of autonomy and basic psychological needs more generally, the less the people within them have a need to assert power through physical or psychological bullying. The findings suggest that the more need-supportive the family and school environments are, the less students engage in bullying, and the more they are likely to identify with and internalize positive values toward others (Dillon, 2015). We posit that such humanizing effects of need support are not limited to classroom environments (e.g., see the workplace bullying research reviewed in Chapter 21) but can be seen across both micro and macro social contexts.

The darker sides of human behavior, of which dishonesty, lack of empathy, and bullying are but handy examples, are systematically related to the pattern and intensity of basic psychological need thwarting. Negative social behaviors are very often (though obviously not in all cases) responses to non-nurturing or invasive conditions, both developmental and situational. Thus people are prepared to develop and express defensive and antisocial tendencies, particularly where social contexts affording psychological need supports are missing. This observation connects with SDT's extensive experimental and field evidence that controlling, evaluative, and need-thwarting conditions focus people on more egoistic and selfish aims and lead to distrust and objectification of others. We continue with such evidence on the bright and dark sides of human nature in the current chapter. Our ultimate claim is that the more need-thwarting the social conditions are, the more damaged is our capacity for humanity.

Social Conditions and Human Malleability

There is no doubt that social conditions affect human functioning. Contexts (either situational or pervasive) that support basic psychological need satisfactions conduce to higher quality motivation, better performance, and more positive experience. Need-supportive contexts in development facilitate more coherent and effective self-regulatory capacities (e.g., Bindman, Pomerantz, & Roisman, 2015) and enhance propensities for empathy and compassion (e.g., Miklikowska et al., 2011). In contrast, need-thwarting developmental conditions impair autonomous self-regulation and emotional access, with cascading negative effects on development, often manifested as social dysfunction and psychopathology (see Ryan, Deci, & Vansteenkiste, 2016). SDT's thesis extends to pervasive cultural, political, and economic contexts, features of which both directly and indirectly impact the psychological need satisfactions of those who make up the cultures or nation states.

One might infer from this body of evidence on the powerful effects of contexts that human nature is highly malleable, if not fully shaped by social conditions. In other words, SDT's strong emphasis on social-contextual influences might imply this environmentalist view. Yet, without in any way diminishing the role of the social environment, we look at this issue somewhat differently. In the organismic view of SDT, we see the individual and the social environment as linked in more intricate ways, both within situations and in interactions with pervasive cultural and economic circumstances. The systematic impact of basic psychological need satisfactions and frustrations on self-functioning suggests to us highly patterned behavioral and psychological responses that are both natural and contingent upon ambient or anticipated supports or threats. Stated differently, distinct human "natures" are manifested as a function of whether individuals are afforded need-supportive conditions or, alternatively, face significant need threats or obstacles to need satisfaction. Moreover, these predictable and contingent patterns of behavior, within which there is great phenotypic variability, can be linked with the evolutionary foundations of human beings and with both the brighter and darker attributes and capabilities residing therein.

In this regard, SDT's assumptions concerning human nature differ from two alternative views, each of which remains actively embraced (albeit often implicitly) by some contemporary social scientists. The first is a view of a highly *malleable nature,* with few innate or universal psychological characteristics, and therefore a nature that is largely imprinted or sculpted by culture (e.g., Markus & Kitayama, 1991a; Iyengar & DeVoe, 2003). This relatively "empty organism" view is intellectually traceable to empirical psychology's behaviorist roots, in which environments were seen as controlling and shaping all behaviors. Described by Tooby and Cosmides (1992) as the *standard social science model (SSSM),* these assumptions of malleability and environmentalism still underlie many current social-cognitive and social-learning theories and more radical forms of cultural relativism. Although these frameworks correctly emphasize how external social factors can foster varying behaviors and sensibilities, by minimizing any intrinsic human needs or propensities, they attribute the action to environments, with their rewarding and punishing aspects, to determine what behaviors and values will ultimately be manifested. They also tend to imply, in accordance with expectancy-valence perspectives, that most anything could be both satisfying and wellness enhancing as long as it is culturally reinforced and valued.

In contrast to the malleability position is the viewpoint that humans have a clearly delineated *fixed nature.* Although a fixed-nature perspective need not be allied with any particular contents, many who embrace a fixed-nature view present a fairly negative view of our natural human attributes. Reasoning that humans evolved in a competitive, hostile environment, in which selfish individuals more likely survived, some theorists have argued that human nature has selected for aggressive, greedy, and dominance-oriented traits. In fact, many classic motivation theories in social psychology are founded upon assumptions of an underlying selfishness or an exchange-oriented calculus to human motivation (e.g., Homans, 1958; Thibaut & Kelley, 1959). In short, some scholars who rightly grasp that people are not "empty organisms" are nonetheless focused on the more negative and yet plausibly "adaptive" contents of human nature, as if one could functionally link the selfish gene (Dawkins, 1989) with a predominance of selfish behavioral propensities and traits.

Yet, as de Waal (2009) cogently argued, scholars who invoke evolutionary perspectives to reconstruct human nature as competitive, anxious, greedy, or inherently aggressive ignore a wealth of data from anthropology and comparative biology showing "that we are group animals, highly cooperative, sensitive to injustice, sometimes warmongering but mostly peace loving. There is thus both a social and a selfish side to our species" (p. 5).

Concluding that behaviors that are, in an evolutionary sense, selfish (i.e., that benefit reproductive success) must also be *psychologically* selfish is a dubious endeavor and cannot be derived or defended from an understanding of evolutionary mechanisms (see Hawley, 2014). *Ultimate causes* can and should be distinguished from more *proximal causes* of behavior, and they need not share the same surface "character." In fact, as we shall see, unselfish predispositions among individuals can yield beneficial effects on reproductive success, as well as personal thriving, without any contradiction in theory.

A third viewpoint, one that could be characterized as a subtype of the fixed-nature position, is the idea of a fixed nature that is made up of modular mechanisms, reflecting highly specialized adaptations, each activated under specific conditions (Fodor, 1983; Sperber, 1994). The *modular view* suggests that human nature is (more or less) composed of a collection of specialized functions or behavioral patterns that each yielded advantage for individual or group fitness during the era of evolutionary adaptation, and it is a view that matches with social-cognitive approaches such as that of Mischel and Shoda (1995). These modular units (either biological or functional) are said to operate automatically and, indeed, can represent both organizers and motivators of everyday actions, typically without requiring any representation in consciousness. Although there is plenty of support for the existence of some modular mechanisms, the denial in many modular views of any broad purpose or "domain general" adaptions or functions is more controversial. Equally controversial is the idea that modularity is associated with a general automaticity of human behavior, which is assumed in such views to be (more or less) driven by highly specific conditional reactions of modular units that have accumulated over evolutionary development.

Because some of the more extreme modularist claims have faced conceptual difficulties, the modular view itself has evolved through debate (Decety & Jackson, 2004). For example, Barrett and Kurzban (2006) reformulated a number of modularist premises, rejecting arguments that processes supporting information integration are inconsistent with modularity. In their view, such processes do not undermine more functional and flexible views of modularity, but rather only challenge the early Fodorian emphasis on narrow encapsulation and automaticity, among other criteria. In fact, Barrett and Kurzban admitted: "It might turn out that many aspects of the cognitive architecture of humans will consist in devices that are more general purpose than those proposed so far by evolutionary psychologists" (p. 644).

SDT and Our Human Natures

SDT's basic premise with respect to human nature contrasts with both the "empty and malleable" and the "fixed but competitive" views. In addition, while acknowledging the specialized and encapsulated adaptations evident in all living forms, SDT's assumptions contrast with some modular approaches, especially with respect to their assumptions concerning biological organization and adaptations related to certain domain-general functions.

In the early days of evolutionary psychology, many scholars were fixedly searching for self- and kin-selective advantages and for behavioral adaptations that could be concretely connected to individuals' genetic survival and propagation. There was thus tremendous focus on, for example, mating preferences, reactions to aggression, and other issues seemingly directly tied to sex and survival. This important focus, however, neglected to address the adaptive nature of the psychological attributes we consider most essential to thriving in, and contributing to, adaptation within small groups. For example, Buss (1991), in characterizing evolutionary struggles, suggested that other humans are our primary "hostile force of nature" (p. 472). He argued against a general need for relatedness (as posited by Epstein, 1990) because, in his view, evolutionary psychology suggests individuals only strive to maintain relatedness to those who will make good reciprocal allies—that is, those who have high status or reproductive value and those who could help us in competition or are kin. In this conception, there is a search for relatively *direct* translations of ultimate causes to psychological motives. Under such assumptions, the idea that humans might quite naturally want to help others from whom they would never expect a "return" would appear implausible.

Yet SDT research suggests otherwise. Our research on helping and benevolence demonstrates that even when *no reciprocal benefits* can be expected from the prosocial actions, people can find such acts satisfying of their basic psychological needs. Recently, for example, Martela and Ryan (2016) reported an experimental study in which participants were asked to play a word-based computer game. In one condition, they were informed that for every correct answer they provided, the game would donate rice to the United Nations World Food Program for beneficiaries they would not meet or know (benevolence condition). In the other condition, participants simply played the game for fun and were not made aware of the donations (control condition). When compared to the control condition, the group that knew their actions were benefiting others experienced more positive affect, interest, and meaningfulness and less negative affect. Results also supported the hypothesis that the positive effects of prosocial behavior on these indicators of psychological wellness were mediated by autonomy, competence, and relatedness need satisfactions. Going beyond self-reported outcomes, Martela and Ryan further demonstrated that those experiencing beneficence showed greater postgame energy, as evidenced by their enhanced performance on a subsequent Stroop task, on which diminished performance is often used as a behavioral indicator of ego depletion (e.g., Kazén, Kuhl, & Leicht, 2015).

We review more such evidence later, but our point here is that, by focusing on sex, aggression, and within-group competition, early evolutionary psychologists at times neglected what are among the most important supports for human fitness—namely, cohesive, willingly cooperative, innovative, and trustworthy interpersonal and group functioning. Since those days, the field has changed. Internalization, in fact, is now understood by many to be a quite general and yet critical aspect of both individual and group-level fitness (e.g., see Boehm, 2012). Similarly, autonomy support can facilitate diversification of traits and skills, further enhancing individual fitness and group resources (Waller, 1998; Appiah, 2005). Finally, cooperativeness and generalized caring would aid both group functioning and cohesion (Decety & Jackson, 2004).

Of late, a host of authors have discussed the potential evolutionary foundations of human helpfulness and altruism (Bloom, 2013; Tomasello, 2009; Wilson, 2015). For example, Bloom (2013) and Wilson (2015) have both reviewed evidence from evolutionary biology, cultural anthropology, and developmental psychology, concluding that humans are endowed with a variety of tools for caring about others, including abilities for empathy, judgments of fairness, and distinguishing between kindness and cruelty. Evidence from both early developmental (e.g., Warneken & Tomasello, 2008) and comparative (primate) studies (e.g., de Waal, 2009) also makes clear that the human species possesses robust propensities to resonate with others' feelings, to be helpful, and to feel vicarious pain, among other prosocial attributes. There are likely a host of such mechanisms and specific capacities that serve the maintenance and enhancement of relationships and belonging and the avoidance of ostracism and rejection.

The model of basic psychological needs outlined by SDT specifies the proximal satisfactions that individuals experience not only when acting in accordance with their intrinsic prosocial tendencies but also when assimilating group norms and values. Both of these propensities can enhance individuals' effectiveness and cohesive functioning at the group level. That is, SDT's model of basic psychological needs specifies the common internal processes supporting both natural helping of others and the internalization of regulations that inhibit or redirect antisocial deviances that would weaken group functioning and cohesion. Psychological need satisfactions subserve the acquisition of skills, information, and interests that aid the management of people's behavior when they are alone or within groups. As we have seen already, the relations of basic need satisfaction to higher quality internalization, social integration, and resulting wellness appear to be universal (see Chapter 22).

Yet capacities for internalization and thus more autonomous self-regulation and integration of identities represent the very kind of general-purpose propensities that function by recruiting multiple cortical and subcortical resources and that can be applied across varied domains. Some (though not all) modularists might deny such general-purpose capacities, but we submit that it is this very general nature that allows humans to adapt to and internalize such a wide range of cultures and practices. Because of their functional value, these generalized propensities to internalize and integrate social regulations directly afford selective advantages of group inclusion and social competence. In turn, these general propensities themselves can be served by and draw upon various modular mechanisms. In other words, general organismic propensities can often be supported by highly modular adaptations, embedded within a hierarchy of structures and functioning, rather than as an arbitrary collection of evolutionary "add-ons." In contrast, the idea that all adaptations are both modular and narrow in nature and are simply additively acquired suggests a "pile of stones" metaphor as the model of evolution, as if organisms could be built by accumulating multiple mechanisms without organization or hierarchy. Such an overarching accretive model is inconsistent with an organismic view (Ryan, 1995). We would maintain instead that new adaptations and functions would always have to operate in relation to existing needs, functions, and structures (see Jacob, 1982; Panksepp & Northoff, 2009).

In short, SDT maintains that supports and threats to basic needs deeply affect the human psychological architecture and are strong inputs to our manifest propensities and sensibilities. Our tendencies toward satisfying the basic psychological needs and defending against threats to them have emerged and persisted because satisfaction of these basic needs has allowed humans, individually and collectively, to negotiate more successfully their complex social and physical circumstances (see also Slavin & Kriegman, 1992). Being sensitive to impingements on autonomy (Waller, 1998), deficits in competence (White, 1959), and potential ostracism or rejection (de Waal, 2009), and, conversely, taking pleasure in self-regulation, effectance, and belonging (Deci & Ryan, 2000) have yielded multiple and layered benefits for individuals and groups. Each of these need satisfactions, being essential to growth, integrity, and wellness, is supported by specific adaptations and is no doubt additionally associated with multiple exaptations and spandrels that have been advantageous in interactions within the dynamic forces of cultural evolution. In turn, many cultural forms and structures have been shaped by the contours of basic human needs, including psychological ones—a dynamic history of movement toward greater global well-being and enhanced human freedom that continues to unsteadily unfold (Damasio, 2006; Welzel, 2013).

Basic psychological need satisfactions facilitate individual growth and social functioning, but these processes do not by any means encompass all of humans' evolved drives, motives, tendencies, or proclivities. Both evolutionary and cultural processes select for many tools of adaptation and for coping, most of which are to varying extents context-contingent for their expression. For example, sexual interest, although not a basic psychological need in SDT, is, of course, a natural drive and a basis of many motives, fueling behaviors such as displaying oneself and being competitive in specific contexts.

Yet unlike this and other natural inclinations, support for SDT's basic psychological need satisfactions facilitates a *superordinate* capacity for self-regulation, which can both oversee and monitor such evolved inclinations, be they toward dominance, sexual activity, acquisitiveness, or other aims, so that their expression does not lead to social rejection or harm and so the person can, in finding these gratifications, still maintain integrity and experience belonging. Especially given the variability of human social contexts, a strong case can be made for having an integrative, self-as-process system that can appropriately internalize and assimilate social practices and values and can regulate behaviors, including sexual desires, dominance, ingroup favoritism, and many other behaviors and motives that may have evolved to provide advantage when employed in specific contexts and circumstances. These self-regulatory capacities, including those functions localized to medial prefrontal cortical areas of the brain that are heavily implicated in processing self-related information and autonomous functioning (Di Domenico, Fournier, Ayaz, & Ruocco, 2013; Quirin et al., 2016) appear to be heavily influenced by social conditions of nurturance. Thus we expect need satisfactions and frustrations, especially intense or chronic ones, to have cascading effects on how people function, especially with respect to issues of self-regulation, tendencies toward aggression, and prosociality, among others. In fact, we reviewed substantial evidence for these patterns and outcomes in previous chapters, most notably Chapters 13 and 16, on parenting and developmental psychopathology, respectively.

In short, debates about human nature vary between those who deny that humans have one and those who think humans do but see its character as fixed (and typically selfish and drive-oriented). Yet SDT, itself grounded in organismic thinking (see Chapter 2), offers a somewhat different set of assumptions. Rather than being infinitely malleable, we argue that humans are equipped, and indeed adaptively designed, to develop their intrinsic, integrative, and social capacities, especially under specific conditions of nurturance (viz., need support). They are equipped to develop capacities that aid in social integration, as well as autonomous self-regulation. People's "natures" thus lead them to feel more vital and well within basic-need-supportive contexts where they can thrive. This helps also to explain why healthy people often resist controlling contexts and, at times, even despite the risks, rebel against oppressive or need-depriving social conditions.

Alternatively, when basic needs are chronically thwarted in sustained or intense ways, other potentialities and propensities emerge. These range from defensiveness and compensation, sometimes manifested as psychopathology, to aggression, selfishness, antisocial actions, and even malevolent destructiveness. In our view, the occurrences of these "dark sides" to human nature are both systematic and predictable, catalyzed by conditions that undermine or thwart people's basic psychological need satisfactions, and particularly so if the conditions threaten their identities or collectives (e.g., families, cultures) in significant ways. Stated differently, there are objectively identifiable features of environments associated with organismic thriving and sociality, the violation of which brings out characteristic patterns of behavior as well, including those often seen as the more pernicious aspects of human nature (Ryan & Deci, 2000a). These include capacities for defensive, and most often poorly integrated, reactions that frequently have negative collateral consequences. This was, of course, a deeply discussed aspect of specific psychopathologies (Chapter 16), especially as regards conduct disorders and antisocial behavior, but in the current chapter we focus on more general issues, especially those concerning reactive or malevolent aggression versus altruism and selfish versus prosocial inclinations.

Evidence Regarding Prosociality and Need Satisfactions

In a series of studies, Weinstein and Ryan (2010) examined the idea that people find inherent satisfaction in helping non-kin others. They specifically hypothesized that helping and prosocial behaviors would satisfy all three basic psychological needs, which would mediate the relations between helping behavior and outcomes such as positive mood and vitality. First, people are able to experience *competence* as they effectively help others. Second, people can experience *relatedness* while helping others, through a sense of empathy and interest in others, and their active involvement on the others' behalf. Finally, insofar as it is unforced and has an internal perceived locus of causality (I-PLOC), helping engages people's *autonomy*. Precisely because most helping and prosocial activity is *not* driven by salient external rewards or compulsions, instead reflecting people's stock and flow of personal values, it is accompanied by a sense of autonomy and choice. In sum, volitional helping was expected by Weinstein and Ryan not only to benefit the recipients but also to engender enhancements of well-being in the helpers, and these helper effects would be accounted for by satisfactions of the helpers' basic psychological needs.

Weinstein and Ryan (2010) also argued that the motivation to help others can come from different sources. Helping could be controlled, coming from a hoped-for reciprocity or sense of pressure or guilt, and other times is autonomous and volitional, coming from an interest in or value for helping, such as an authentic caring for the other. They hypothesized that when individuals autonomously helped others, they would experience greater need satisfactions and well-being enhancements, whereas, when their helping was controlled or done for instrumental or external reasons, they would not experience such satisfactions and the associated enhancement of well-being. Testing these formulations, Weinstein and Ryan (2010) reported four studies that employed varied methods.

The first of these studies used an event sampling strategy to examine the effects of both autonomous and controlled incidents of helping on the helpers' psychological need satisfaction, subjective well-being (SWB), vitality, and self-esteem, all at a daily level. As expected, helping per se had at most a weak positive effect on well-being outcomes. Yet, this effect was moderated by the relative autonomy of helping. When the helping was more autonomous, these effects were substantially stronger, having a robust impact on the outcomes.

Experimental studies in the Weinstein and Ryan (2010) paper extended this evidence. In the first, participants were given money that they were able to donate or not donate to another participant without the other knowing about the choices available to the donor. Half the participants were in a choice condition in which they decided how much to give; the other half were in a "yoked" condition and told to donate specified amounts (corresponding to donation amounts of the previous same-sex participant in the choice condition). As predicted, in the choice condition, greater giving was associated with enhanced need satisfaction and well-being, whereas in the no-choice condition, greater giving did not yield these more positive consequences.

Two additional experimental studies examined these hypotheses in reference to behavioral helping, contrasting conditions in which participants helped by choice or because of pressures to help (e.g., an experimenter suggesting one "should" help). Results confirmed, consistent with theory, that well-being was significantly enhanced in the volitional helping conditions. These helper effects were fully mediated by SDT's basic need satisfactions. Further, in these two studies, the impact of volitional helping on the *recipients* of the help was also examined. Both studies showed that not only did autonomous helping enhance the wellness of the helper (whereas controlled helping did not), but, further, that the recipients of the helping showed increased well-being (increased positive affect, vitality, and self-esteem) *only* when the helpers' motivation was autonomous. This effect was obtained even though the recipients of the help in the experiment were naïve to condition—they were not told about the helpers' motivation.

As mentioned, these studies by Weinstein and Ryan (2010) demonstrated that basic need satisfactions of competence, relatedness, and autonomy mediated the relations between prosocial actions and the enhanced wellness outcomes that followed from it. Other studies have also explained this increase in well-being by increases in feelings of autonomy (Gebauer, Riketta, Broemer, & Maio, 2008), competence (Aknin, Barrington-Leigh, et al., 2013), and relatedness (Aknin, Dunn, Sandstrom, & Norton, 2013; Aknin, Sandstrom, Dunn, & Norton, 2011). Together, such studies indicate that helping others volitionally can foster increased wellness in the helper, a result that is substantially mediated by satisfaction of the basic psychological needs. Further, being helped by another person who provides the help voluntarily can be need-gratifying for the recipient, while not demeaning people's dependency. These results thus dovetail with our studies of *emotional reliance*, reviewed in Chapter 12, in which people who were emotionally in need were most prone to turn to, and benefit from, others who were autonomy-supportive (e.g., Ryan, La Guardia, Solky-Butzel, Chirkov, & Kim, 2005). They also converge with SDT research on friendships, which show that providing autonomy support to a close friend not only benefits the recipient of the autonomy support but also enhances the well-being of the provider (e.g., Deci, La Guardia, Moller, Scheiner, & Ryan, 2006). Such results also show the importance for recipients of experiencing helpers as having an internal perceived locus of causality.

Within the developmental literature, several studies have illustrated the intrinsic and spontaneous propensities of humans to help other humans. In one highly cited study, Warneken and Tomasello (2008) examined helping behavior in 20-month-old toddlers. Their observations showed that toddlers spontaneously helped others at a very high rate, for instance, by picking up dropped objects or obtaining something out of reach. Nearly 90% of the time, toddlers spontaneously helped. But was such helping intrinsically motivated?

To answer that question, Warneken and Tomasello created three conditions. In one condition, when children helped, nothing occurred. In another condition, when they helped, they were praised in a noncontrolling way ("thank you, that's really nice"). In a third condition, they were given a desired reward (a cube needed to operate a jingle toy) for helping ("for this, you get a cube"). This condition specifically represented a reward contingency that SDT would expect to undermine motivation if it were intrinsic. Findings confirmed that the toddlers who were given rewards for helping were subsequently *less* likely to engage in these otherwise spontaneous altruistic behaviors than those in the control or noncontrolling praise condition. Helping for rewards undermined the intrinsic motivation that would otherwise *naturally* underlie such behaviors by shifting the children's perceived locus of causality.

In subsequent research on the intrinsic motivation of prosocial behaviors among young children, Warneken and Tomasello (2013) used a similar design in which an adult needed help and the 24-month-old participants were in the room with that adult. In one condition, the participants' mothers were not in the room, and in four other conditions the mothers were in the room, either being passive, highlighting the problem to the children, encouraging the children to help, or telling the children to help. Analyses revealed that in none of the four conditions with the mothers present did the children help more than when the mothers were not present. In short, the inclination to help was intrinsically motivated, and mothers' presence did not increase helping behavior in that situation or in a subsequent free-choice situation.

Subsequent research is extending such findings. For example, Chernyak and Kushnir (2013) found that providing choice to 3- and 4-year-old children increased their intrinsic motivation for helping, which the authors interpreted in terms of the autonomous choice being the critical mechanism for enhancement. Hepach, Vaish, and Tomasello (2013) also supported the view that young children's helping was motivated intrinsically rather than by extrinsic contingencies, and, using physiological data (e.g., sympathetic arousal, pupil dilation), they found that the children also experienced satisfaction if others, rather than they themselves, helped the person in need.

Although cognitive theories would describe the undermining of intrinsic motivation by extrinsic rewards or other pressures as an "overjustification" effect (e.g. Lepper, Greene, & Nisbett, 1973), it would be incorrect to ascribe it to that cognitive attribution mechanism. Overjustification is theoretically dependent on a cognitive capacity for discounting, which does not appear until children are several years older (e.g., see Morgan, 1981, 1983; Reynolds & Schiffbauer, 2004). In contrast, SDT has argued that the undermining effect is not simply cognitive but motivational—an experienced decrease in feelings of autonomy, which can be detected much earlier, even in infancy (e.g., Stern, 1985). In fact, several studies have supported the view that the undermining effects of rewards on intrinsic motivation can be observed well before cognitive discounting capacities have emerged. In addition, moral motivations emerge early in development and do not require mental calculations of such tradeoffs. These results thus speak to the intrinsic nature of the helping behavior of toddlers described in the preceding paragraphs and to the importance of perceived autonomy for the intrinsic motivation to be maintained.

The fact that receiving extrinsic rewards undermines the intrinsic motivation and the need satisfactions people experience in helping has also been shown in several other ways. For example, Newman and Shen (2012) reported six experiments that examined the effects of "thank-you" gifts on charitable giving. Thank-you gifts are the "rewards" given by some organizations to recognize and thank donors. Their results showed that although most people expect (in line with a naïve behaviorist view) that the offer of thank-you gifts will increase donations, such offers in actuality reduced charitable donations. These undermining effects of thank-you gifts were evident across a variety of charities and types of thank-you gifts and after controlling for varied potential confounds. Here again, the evidence suggests that rewarding charitable acts runs the risk of undermining the inherent satisfactions of giving.

This pattern of effects is evident even at the level of national groups, as shown by Oarga, Stavrova, and Fetchenhauer (2015). Using data from 23 countries, they found that informal helping behaviors were more positively associated with well-being outcomes when reciprocity was *not* the expectation. In addition, they found that in nations where helping each other was a normative standard, helping others more strongly predicted life satisfaction.

The idea that consciously expecting rewards or desiring reciprocity for helping others or for "doing good" detracts from the well-being enhancements and positive affects associated with such behaviors may confuse traditional economists, but makes good sense for effective group functioning. Such a mechanism makes it more likely that group members would respond freely and volitionally with aid to other group members, whereas, if they responded for instrumental motives, or only when reciprocity or exchange was anticipated, the deployment of resources would be more calculative and competitive and thus would not represent a truly cooperative group. Related to this is evidence from both primate and human studies suggesting that the more hierarchical the power structure of a group is, the *less* prone are lower ranked members to cooperate (Cronin, Acheson, Hernández, & Sánchez, 2015). Clearly, feeling controlled or unempowered detracts from this positive attribute, as individuals become more resource-defensive and exchange-oriented.

Martela and Ryan (2015) recently presented a series of studies planned to extend prior research showing that voluntary acts of benevolence enhance well-being. They developed a brief scale to assess *beneficence satisfaction,* or the feeling that one has been benevolent and helpful to others. This scale was intended to capture what has been called the immediate "warm glow" attending acts of kindness (Andreoni, 1990). In their first two studies, Martela and Ryan demonstrated that this sense of beneficence fully mediated the relations between prosocial behavior and well-being. That is, only to the extent that people felt they were being benevolent did helping or giving behaviors enhance their well-being. A second general hypothesis was that positive well-being benefits of prosocial behavior would be substantially mediated by feelings of autonomy, competence, and relatedness. Several studies in this series showed that the links between beneficence and well-being were indeed a function of autonomy, competence, and relatedness satisfactions. These results were thus complementary to those of Weinstein and Ryan (2010).

Various analytical models suggest that these effects of beneficence satisfaction on well-being are strongly mediated by autonomy, competence, and relatedness. Nonetheless, when satisfaction of the three basic needs and benevolence were simultaneously regressed on SWB, all four had significant and independent effects, together explaining substantial variance (61%) in this outcome. The fact that beneficence satisfaction remained an independent and statistically significant predictor of well-being even when controlling for autonomy, competence, and relatedness lent support to the hypothesis that there would be immediate and direct well-being benefits from acting out of beneficence.

In a third study, Martela and Ryan asked participants to recall a recent "particularly happy moment." Of course, we have seen throughout this book that SDT's basic needs predict SWB, and here we saw that a sense of beneficence also did. Yet results of this third study also tell the story that many of people's particularly happy moments entail giving or helping others. In fact, whereas the typical portrayal of personal happiness is one of selfish gratification, people's peak happiness experiences are much more frequently about giving to others, a finding that is also consistent with relationships motivation theory (RMT) propositions (Chapter 12). Extending this point, yet a fourth study in this series used a multilevel modeling approach to assess what predicts daily fluctuations in positive affect and subjective vitality. Again, results showed that autonomy, competence, relatedness, and beneficence all emerged as significant independent predictors, even when controlling for each other, for trait-level need satisfaction, gender, and day of the week effects.

This research thus shows that engaging in prosocial behavior enhances people's well-being. Across all the studies, the three psychological needs proposed by SDT play a key role in explaining the well-being benefits of feeling prosocial. These results therefore support the arguments of Dunn, Aknin, and Norton (2014, p. 43) that prosocial behavior is "most likely to produce happiness" under conditions that satisfy these three needs. At the same time, the research suggests that beneficence satisfaction per se can predict unique variance in well-being beyond the three psychological needs, both in specific prosocial situations and in day-to-day well-being. This is an important result from the point of view of research on prosocial behavior and well-being. Although not necessarily a basic psychological need, beneficence is clearly a wellness-enhancing element in human motivation in its own right.

The basic need satisfactions experienced in helping others thus clearly apply not only to kin and potential strategic allies, but also to non-kin and even strangers (e.g., Aknin, Barrington-Leigh, et al., 2013). These benefits can even extend beyond acts of giving to humans. Research on volunteer behavior by Gagné (2003) demonstrated that autonomous volunteer work in an animal shelter positively affected the volunteers' well-being though satisfaction of the basic psychological needs. These positive benefits were less in evidence for those who were instrumentally motivated to volunteer. At least in a proximal sense, altruistic behavior need not be selfish or exchange-focused; in fact, it is more satisfying and vitalizing when it is not.

Such findings return us to the more general eudaimonic stance of SDT (see, e.g., Ryan, Curren, & Deci, 2013; Ryan & Huta, 2009), in which, as Aristotle argued, it is primarily the pursuit of human virtues and excellence that fosters sustained and authentic happiness. It is not the *aim* of altruistic or helping behaviors to get more happiness; rather, happiness happens to be the result of autonomously pursuing such ends. Aristotle expected this because his views of eudaimonic living were those in most accord with human nature and thus represent the most fulfilling way of living. One might add, however, that such experiential benefits yielded by helping others make good evolutionary sense, perhaps explaining why Aristotle understood eudaimonia as the highest expression of our human natures.

This same set of ideas also helps explain how the literature discussed in *goal contents theory* (GCT; Chapter 11) connects to well-being outcomes. In the GCT literature, it is clear that intrinsic aspirations, strivings, and goals tended to be experienced as more autonomously pursued than extrinsic ones (e.g., Sheldon, Ryan, Deci, & Kasser, 2004) and to have more positive relations to well-being outcomes (Kasser, 2002a; Kasser & Ryan, 1996, 2001). Goals and aspirations that are more associated with prosocial behaviors (giving to one's community, caring about others) yield more positive personal and interpersonal outcomes, including happiness and relationship satisfaction—results that are mediated by basic psychological need satisfactions (Niemiec, Ryan, & Deci, 2009).

There is, therefore, solid empirical evidence using varied methods and measures showing that, when persons willingly behave benevolently (e.g., giving to others, contributing to their group, being generative), it is self-enhancing, even though such self-enhancements are not the goal of such activities. Yet just as with other manifestations of intrinsic motivation and autonomous extrinsic motivation, the fact that prosocial behaviors can be experienced as inherently need-satisfying does not preclude the idea that such activities can also yield additional functional benefits and perhaps even selective advantages. It may well be part of our adaptive design to be prosocial, at least under typical conditions of community, although exactly when and how these generalized propensities emerged (e.g., whether this is a Pleistocene adaptation or a later development) remains only speculative.

In either case, as primatologist de Waal (2009) argued, scholars and laypeople alike often use evolution as a basis for portraying people as selfish, aggressive, and dominance-oriented, yet in doing so they seem to ignore abundant data from multiple disciplines showing that people are also group animals who cooperate and who are typically distressed by injustices and violence. In fact, there is ample evidence that humans are quite social as living beings, often spontaneously empathic and giving, even though adverse conditions can interfere with that. SDT recognizes these features of human behavior as being common and also as being supported and sustained by proximal psychological need satisfactions.

Are Prosocial Propensities Grounded in Evolution?

Our evidence that under nurturing conditions, prosociality comes naturally to most of us is not simply Pollyannaish. It appears to be both descriptive and readily testable. In fact, our model fits well with recent trends in both motivational and evolutionary psychologies, in which there has been a growing recognition of primate and human prosocial propensities. Whereas early models of evolutionary psychology tended to highlight the intragroup competitive nature of natural selection, reflecting a "struggle for existence," the pervasive phenomenon of helping others, often referred to as "the altruism question," was a puzzle for decades. Why do individuals come to the aid of others if existence is a struggle among individuals? Evolutionary thinkers have suggested a variety of answers.

Inclusive fitness theory (Hamilton, 1964), also known as *kin selection theory,* provided an early breakthrough in explanation, suggesting that we have a selective mechanism for aiding genetic relatives. The argument is that, if a person is concerned about the welfare of a kin, that concern can be thought of as being part of the person's self-interest because "If a sister is concerned for the welfare of her brother, the sister's self-interest can be thought of as including . . . this concern for the welfare of her brother" (Axelrod & Hamilton, 1981, p. 7). Aid, one would thus predict, will be disproportionately directed toward those sharing genetic material, with those sharing more genes getting more aid, such that the cost of the helping is directly proportional to how related the individuals are.

Trivers (1971), in his work on *reciprocal altruism,* provided an additional "gene-centered" view. He proposed a natural selection mechanism among non-kin: the expectation that the favor would be returned such that benefits would be bestowed on the actor over the long term. Because the notion is that resources expended will be returned, the term *altruism* in reciprocal altruism is somewhat of a misnomer, at least biologically speaking. Typically, a biological definition of altruism would require a fitness cost on the part of the actor, but in Trivers's work no fitness cost is proposed; in fact, all costs are assumed to be recuperated over time by returned favors. Nonetheless, his reciprocal altruism model suggests one way a propensity toward benevolence might have emerged, and later potentially generalized.

An additional evolutionary mechanism that has been proposed to account for propensities to aid unrelated others is called either *multilevel selection* or *group selection* (see Nowak, Tarnita, & Wilson, 2010; Wilson, 2003, 2015). This concept refers to a potential mechanism of evolution that confers benefit to an individual (or an individual's genes) indirectly through the advancement of the social group to which the individual belongs (Wilson, 2012). One can engage in a behavior that is phenomenally or behaviorally altruistic, but the fitness costs incurred are mitigated by the benefit enjoyed by the group, which includes the person and, presumably, his or her genetic relatives. In short, what is proposed is that groups whose constituents more readily cooperated and altruistically aided each other would out reproduce those groups that did not.

Discussion and disagreements about the relative merits of these three proposed mechanisms (i.e., inclusive fitness, reciprocal altruism, and group selection) underlying the origins of altruism persist. Yet for our purposes we need not take a strong stand as to which of these three mechanisms best accounts for the emergence of psychological altruism and the concomitant need satisfactions we have highlighted. The fact is that these mechanisms can all be recruited to support claims that prosocial behavior and psychological altruism have been evolutionarily instrumental and thus are deeply embedded in the human psychological and behavioral architecture. That is, all three models highlight potential selective advantages in people's general proneness toward enacting social values and volitionally helping others. We simply add that proximal psychological satisfactions undoubtedly would increase the likelihood that such mechanisms would function reliably.

These theories suggest various mechanisms through which behavioral tendencies could have generalized as prosocial behavior toward non-kin. Yet, however *genetically* "selfish" the foundation of these mechanisms, the term *altruism* may nonetheless be appropriate to describe people's proximal *psychological* motives, as in many circumstances people are phenomenally moved to aid others (both kin and non-kin) out of concern or empathy, leading in turn to basic need satisfactions. Thus genetic selfishness need not entail psychological selfishness; nor does psychological selfishness necessarily confer genetic advantage. Stated differently, there need not be a *direct* parallelism between ultimate causes and proximal motives (Hawley, 2014; Ryan & Hawley, 2016).

This idea is analogous to our earlier differentiation of the phenomenology of intrinsic motivation and its adaptive significance (Chapters 5–7). Children (e.g. 2-year-olds) are intrinsically motivated to manipulate novel objects because of the proximal satisfaction that lies in the interest and enjoyment they experience while doing it and not because they are "aiming" to acquire skills that will aid in adaptation. Their enjoyment of and persistence at such behaviors is mediated by autonomy and competence satisfactions. These need satisfactions supply the *proximal* gratifications for manipulative and exploratory play, even as the play also provides opportunities for learning that no doubt have conveyed selective advantages. These psychological need satisfactions thus support the adaptive functioning.

Returning to prosocial behaviors, people's general proneness toward helping others has often been observed in other species (e.g., de Waal, 2008; Langford et al., 2006), as well as anthropological data from hunter–gatherer societies, with such data suggesting deep roots in our natures (Boehm, 2012; Diamond, 2012). Clearly, such positive prosocial attitudes and behaviors can be as effective as the competitive and aggressive styles so often characterized in early evolutionary psychology as examples of "fitness." In fact, they likely exist alongside other adaptive mechanisms, which, as we shall see, are called forth by different individual and group conditions. As Hawley (2014) suggested, fitness is enhanced by garnering social resources, and, in many social contexts, that will be better accomplished through positive social behaviors rather than directly competitive strategies. In nonsupportive group contexts, however, garnering resources may be better achieved by aggression and a focus on exchange relationships, rather than via proximal feelings of altruism. Indeed, in competitive or threatening settings, the giver should beware. Because individuals have access to attributes and skills associated with both of these strategies, we maintain that their differential expression will be moderated by contextual cues and conditions.

Such sensitivity to contexts and cues can be readily demonstrated. For example, Weinstein, Hodgins, and Ryan (2010) had individuals participate in an experiment in which they would play a game of "charades" with a stranger, a game that requires communication and cooperation. Before playing, participants were primed using a semantic priming technique, in one condition with words associated with being autonomous, in another with words associated with being controlled. Cameras then recorded the performance of the players for behavioral evidence of cohesiveness and connection. Those primed with autonomy words stood closer to each other, were more verbally encouraging and mirroring, and reported more liking of the partner. Pairs primed with autonomy words also performed better at this communicative game. Priming with control, in contrast, dampened participants' cooperative social natures and reduced their sensitivity to interpersonal signals. They were both less close and less effective.

In presenting these arguments, we should also explicitly note that we are not claiming that psychological flourishing, well-being, intrinsic motivation, and the like are in any way strongly correlated with reproductive success *in the modern era*. Rather, some of these factors that enhance psychological flourishing today may well represent psychological satisfactions that supported behaviors and processes that were adaptive in earlier human epochs, especially in the context of small groups and communities who were largely cooperative (Decety & Wheatley, 2015). Yet even if they are no longer associated with adaptation, strictly speaking, we still appear to be built to enjoy them!

So Why (and When) Are Humans Destructively Aggressive?

Acting in humane and benevolent ways can be intrinsically satisfying and sometimes can even be adaptive (i.e., afford reproductive advantages), but these attributes and outcomes are not reliably manifest in societies. Humans can be uncooperative, greedy, prejudiced, selfish, and even malevolent—these darker attributes are also salient aspects of our "natures."

We have focused to some extent on selfishness and greed in earlier chapters, especially in Chapter 11 on aspirations and life goals. There we saw that the more children are supported in autonomy and relatedness, the less selfish and materialistic they are likely to become. In this chapter, our focus is more specifically on aggression and malevolence. Our question is whether these attributes can, as we saw that caring and benevolence do, satisfy basic psychological needs and reflect integrated self-regulation—or whether they might instead represent reactive responses to actual or perceived threats to physical or psychological needs and/or be driven more by controlled regulations than by autonomy and integration.

We began to address the roots of human aggression in Chapter 16 on developmental psychopathology, and in our discussion of bullying earlier in this chapter. In Chapter 16, our review suggested that children who grew up in controlling or cold and rejecting environments were more likely to manifest various forms of maladjustment, including conduct disorders, aggressive tendencies, failures of social internalization, and deficiencies in self-regulation, relatedness, and empathy (Vansteenkiste & Ryan, 2013; Ryan, Deci, & Vansteenkiste, 2016). In our discussion of *bullying* earlier in this chapter, we similarly saw that this type of aggressive behavior is to a significant degree potentiated by controlling school and parental contexts. These data provide our first hint of an answer to this question of human aggression, suggesting that propensities to aggression are connected with the thwarting of basic psychological needs and rarely reflect integrated, autonomous motivations. Furthermore, the development and the exercise of people's positive human capacities—those such as restraint, compassion, empathy, and caring—depend on conditions of nurturance and a relative absence of intense or chronic threats to basic needs.

We propose, in fact, that unlike propensities toward altruism and benevolence, which we have shown can be, and often are, intrinsically satisfying of basic needs, aggression is *not* typically intrinsically motivated. In fact, it need not depend on such proximal satisfactions. The desire to aggress on others appears instead to be more reliably related to proximal need threats or, if more generalized in nature, to serious distal and chronic need thwarting over time, often beginning at quite early ages. Further, when purely destructive or malevolent aggression occurs, it is typically either a result of motivational dysregulation, defense, or poorly integrated identities and pressured introjects, rather than being autonomously motivated. As we further review, people prone to such aggressive acts will frequently be driven by ego involvements, defenses, and compensatory motives as perpetrating factors. In other cases, destructive aggression reflects impairments in the internalization of emotional and behavioral regulation, again due to conditions of need thwarting. In fact, in more extreme cases, violent offenders are statistically much more likely to have suffered severe need thwarting, such as that represented by physical and sexual abuse (e.g., see Mitchell & Aamodt, 2005).

Finally, we argue that, because violence is not inherently palatable or readily capable of integration, when people do aggress on, intentionally harm, or kill other humans, they must in some way defensively rationalize and/or compartmentalize it in order not to experience great distress and dissonance (see Grossman, 1995; Marlantes, 2011). For example, engaging in harm requires people to *dehumanize* the victim (and thus suppress awareness and empathy), which tells us much about human nature (Moller & Deci, 2010). Dehumanization facilitates harmdoing, largely because people cannot readily harm other humans without first changing them into objects. If harm to others were easily integrated, we would not require such mechanisms. We shall claim that there is a psychological link between feeling controlled or thwarted and a propensity (and defensive inclination) to objectify or dehumanize others. Finally, we consider cases in which people malevolently harming others could be conceptualized as virtuous, right, or moral. There we argue that, to the degree that moral systems support malevolence and harm to innocent others, they are themselves less fully capable of integration, and they typically emerge in troubled or threatened individuals, groups, and societies that are narrow and constricted in their humanity.

Doing Harm and Experiencing Need Thwarting

Given that doing "good" for people, even when one has no expectations of gain, satisfies basic psychological needs and adds to subjective wellness, one might ask whether doing harm to others who have done one no harm would thwart basic psychological need satisfaction and detract from SWB. Although many have noted that people have an inherent unease with harming others (e.g., Baumeister, 1997), the question is what factors explain this distress.

Legate, DeHaan, Weinstein, and Ryan (2013) reported the results of experiments meant to answer this question, which is essentially the converse of what was investigated by Weinstein and Ryan's (2010) research on helping behaviors. In the tradition of Milgram (1963), who directed participants to cause significant *physical pain* to others and found that most of them believed that they had, Legate and colleagues asked participants in an experimental setting to inflict *social pain* on strangers by excluding them from an activity. To do so, they used the now classic *cyberball* paradigm (Williams, Yeager, Cheung, & Choi, 2012). In this paradigm, people engage in a computerized ball toss game involving three avatars, each presumably controlled by an actual participant. As the game proceeds, participants in the ostracism conditions are excluded as they observe the other two participants' avatars throw the ball only to each other. Studies have shown that even this virtual exclusion from a small group can cause significant social pain (Williams, 2001), which in SDT we see as strong evidence of our basic psychological need for relatedness. Harnessing this paradigm, Legate et al. (2013) reversed the usual design in the following way: Instead of ostracizing the participant, in this study participants were asked to be an *ostracizer*—to exclude or ostracize one of the other apparent participants (who was actually an experimental accomplice). These naïve participants were thus being asked to cause social harm to others whom they had not previously met.

Like Milgram (1963), Legate and colleagues found that, although most people did follow instructions to inflict harm, they experienced their compliance with these instructions as distressing. Specifically, the participants in Legate et al.'s experiment who excluded others (with whom they had no face-to-face contact) reported significantly more negative affect. In fact, people who excluded others showed levels of distress comparable to that of excluded or ostracized participants in these studies, although there were different patterns of negative affect. Ostracized people reported feeling anger, whereas ostracizers reported guilt and shame. These negative affective outcomes were, in turn, fully mediated by basic psychological need frustrations. Excluders especially reported lowered autonomy and relatedness. People thus did not derive satisfaction from complying with potentially hurtful acts, even against faceless or virtual strangers, whereas we earlier saw how they are strongly satisfied by aiding others, even those they had not previously known or would not meet (e.g., Martela & Ryan, 2015; Weinstein & Ryan, 2010).

Legate, DeHaan, and Ryan (2015) followed up on this "going-along-with-social-exclusion" study by employing a face-to-face interaction paradigm. Specifically, they asked participants not to talk to one of the other participants (who was actually a confederate) during a social interaction task. Results showed that, compared with participants in a neutral condition in which they could talk freely to all, compliant ostracizers suffered when excluding another participant. Their self-reported distress from excluding another person was, as in previous studies, accounted for (i.e., mediated) by frustration of basic psychological needs for autonomy and relatedness. Extending the research, in this study excluders were additionally also given a chance to again interact with the excluded person in a subsequent cyberball session. Results showed that ostracizers were more inclusive of the person they had previously excluded, throwing the ball to them more frequently than participants in a control condition. These data suggested a spontaneous desire to redress the harm they felt they had done.

Clearly, in these experiments people were essentially asked to exclude an "innocent" other, someone they had no reason to harm. In fact, in complying, these participants were trying to "do good" by cooperating with an experimenter rather than trying to be antisocial. Yet, in carrying out this act of exclusion, participants who believed that they had done harm to another person suffered distress, paralleling, albeit at a much less intense level, the apparent suffering incurred by the compliant participants in Milgram's (1963) classic but more extreme experiments (see Fromm, 1973).

Even when people discriminate against an outgroup member, they may often do so with little autonomy. Amiot, Sansfaçon, Louis, and Yelle (2012) applied SDT to intergroup behaviors, and specifically to group norms toward discrimination versus respect and parity. They reported two studies that examined how group norms that were oriented more toward discrimination than parity would be associated with less autonomous behaviors. Specifically, Amiot et al. manipulated ingroup norms in favor of parity rather than discrimination, and they assessed the behaviors that group members displayed (consistent or inconsistent with the norms), as well as their motivations for engaging in the behaviors. Results showed that when the salient ingroup norm was parity and fairness, members whose behaviors were congruent with the norm reported more self-determination. Yet, when the ingroup norm was discrimination, group members who behaved in accordance with the norm were less autonomous. This suggests to us that internalizing discrimination and exclusion is harder than internalizing equality and inclusion.

The Relative Autonomy of Varied Types of Aggression

Although the preceding experiments suggest that doing harm to others without provocation is distressing and need thwarting, clearly there are aggressive acts for which people are strongly motivated and even feel that they have good reason to commit. To proceed more deeply with our analysis of aggression thus requires looking at different types of aggression and the forms of self-regulation (or nonregulation) underlying them.

Relatively Autonomous Forms of Aggression

First, there are certain forms of behavior often labeled as "aggressive" that are not oriented toward harming others. These include certain forms of play, such as rough and tumble play (see Chapter 5), contact sports such as rugby and American football (Chapter 19), and competitive, "violent" video games (Chapter 20), in which harm to others is typically not a focal intent, nor central to the satisfactions of the activities. The gratifications these aggressive activities yield stem not from an enjoyment of violence or desire to harm the others but instead lie in the experiences of autonomy and competence inherent in them. Indeed, it is precisely these intrinsic satisfactions that support individuals' motivation for engaging in these play activities, whereas effecting violence per se does not provide those satisfactions.

Many sports involve aggressive physical play, but nonetheless causing harm to others is not typically the intent of most players. Yet sometimes players in sports or in gaming contexts do intend to harm their opponents. For example, Vansteenkiste, Mouratidis, and Lens (2010) investigated athletes' willingness to foul or harm opponents. Assessing soccer players from Belgium from a range of club levels, they found that *performance-approach goals*—wanting to outperform others—were unrelated to moral attitudes or sportspersonship in play. However, in a second study, they looked at the athletes' controlled and autonomous motivations underlying this desire to outperform others. When the motivation for performance approach goals was controlled (e.g., driven by introjects, pressures, and ego involvements), players showed a greater tendency to depersonalize their opponents and to view them as merely "objects in the way." Such objectification was, in turn, positively associated with a willingness to foul or injure opponents to achieve their goals, as evidenced by more sport-related antisocial attitudes, greater willingness to aggress on other players, and, marginally, receiving more "yellow cards" during officiated games.

Regarding aggression in many video games, we similarly suggest that the fun of these games lies not in the experience of virtual violence itself but in the challenges that games with violent scenarios provide (see Rigby & Ryan, 2011). As described in Chapter 20, Przybylski, Ryan, and Rigby (2009) did a series of experiments and field studies testing this idea. They showed that the enjoyment and draw of violent video games is accounted for not by their violent contents but rather by the opportunities for competence, relatedness, and autonomy that such games so often afford. As these experiments revealed, raising the violent content of the games added no intrinsic motivation, even for male adolescent players, who are a prime audience. What was clear instead is that the game contents and narratives of war, crime, and zombie killing provided ready scenarios for challenges, choices, and teamwork, yielding salient experiences of competence, autonomy, and relatedness. It was these need satisfactions, rather than the violent contents per se, that accounted for the "fun" of these games. The importance of this research for our current discussion is in showing that players are not intrinsically motivated by the violence or gore itself. In contrast to research findings pointing to the intrinsic satisfactions of benevolence (e.g., Martela & Ryan, 2015; Weinstein & Ryan, 2010), we have not found such evidence for intrinsic satisfactions being derived from the opposing concept of malevolence.

Still, experiences in video games can sometimes potentiate aggression once players exit the virtual experience. Here again, the concept of need thwarting is relevant. Przybylski, Deci, Rigby, and Ryan (2014) specifically examined the role of competence frustrations in engendering aggressive postgame affects and reactions. In six studies, they tested the hypothesis that, independent of violent game contents, video game engagement would increase postgame aggression to the degree that complexity of game controls or other comparable factors thwarted players' satisfaction of the need for competence. Using a variety of methods and outcomes, their results indicated that thwarting competence (e.g., by complicating or degrading game devices, increasing game complexity, or limiting the players' opportunity to practice with the controls) predicted higher postgame aggression, as well as lower short-term well-being.

A second type of relatively autonomous aggression, beyond that contained in game play, involves violence that is clearly motivated by truly self-and-other-protective motives—that is, when aggressive acts are committed *in the service of life or safety*. Here, if our theory is correct, individuals may act with violence because it seems necessary, not because it is something they would enjoy or volitionally emit in its own right. Violence that is truly in defense of life—for example, fending off an attack on oneself, one's children, or one's community—can be internalized and committed through identified regulation, as in some kinds of military service in which soldiers understand the value and importance of their missions. Yet even when the cause is just and the motivation autonomous, such violence to others is still not easily integrated (see Grossman, 1995; Marlantes, 2011). Symptoms of posttraumatic stress disorder (PTSD) in returning soldiers attest to the difficulties of assimilating acts of violence. PTSD is not only associated with being a victim of violence but is also frequent among those who must commit violence toward others (e.g., see MacNair, 2002). Thus aggressive acts with the goal of self- or group protection may range in their relative autonomy, but even when belief in the necessity of the cause engenders willing engagement, such acts often remain difficult to integrate.

Related to the aggression that is protective of others is aggression focused on maintaining group cooperation and social fairness and equity. Considerable data, both developmental and societal, suggest that humans are sensitive to cheaters and people who would violate principles of fairness and reciprocity (Stevens & Hauser, 2004; Tomasello, 2009). In fact, the evidence suggests that such costly actions will even be undertaken by third parties who are not biologically related to the individuals being unfairly treated (Fehr & Fischbacher, 2004). This propensity is thus sometimes referred to as *altruistic punishment*. Here we see aggression in the service of prosocial aims, and it occurs even when transgressions are not directed at the self or kin (e.g., Corradi-Dell'Acqua, Civai, Rumiati, & Fink, 2013; Fowler, 2005). What is interesting from a motivational point of view is that punishing transgressors can even be experienced as rewarding (e.g., Strobel et al., 2011), perhaps especially when the transgressor is a stranger (e.g., Campanhã,

Minati, Fregni, & Boggio, 2011). Thus, whereas we showed in our own experiments using similar paradigms that people find intrinsic satisfaction in giving (Weinstein & Ryan, 2010), studies show that punishing "takers" and "cheaters" can also feel good (e.g., Fowler, Johnson, & Smirnov, 2005), although we have not yet seen data on how this impacts basic need satisfactions per se. In any case, all these studies join an emerging set of findings helping to explain how humans have become generally cooperative, as we have claimed, and why transgression is rarer and typically less psychologically satisfying than contributing to others and acting fairly. They also point to situations in which aggression itself can be supported by autonomous motivation and perhaps even integrated regulations, although more research on that issue is still needed.

Reactive Aggression and Need Thwarting

As we saw in the literature of developmental psychology, many researchers have suggested that children who develop aggressive tendencies and other externalizing behavior problems come from backgrounds associated with low-responsive, controlling, and coercive parenting (e.g., see Rothbaum & Weisz, 1994). When we place these ideas within the SDT framework, it suggests that, to the extent that children grow up in, or find themselves within, controlling and need-thwarting contexts, they are likely to exhibit more destructive and/or problematic aggression (Ryan, Deci, & Vansteenkiste, 2016). That is, when psychological needs, including autonomy, are frustrated or go unmet, children become more aggressive, both because of the negative impact that lack of need support has on the development of self-regulation and internalization and, sometimes more directly, because of the proximal experience of frustration in need-thwarting contexts.

Ryan and Grolnick (1986) reported early findings supporting this idea in a study of elementary schoolchildren. The children were surveyed concerning the *classroom climate* they were experiencing—specifically, whether the climate had them feeling more like origins (autonomous) or pawns (controlled), using a measure adapted from de Charms (1976). Separately, the researchers also gave these children a projective assessment in which they wrote stories about a neutral scene depicting a teacher standing before a classroom. Among the variables rated from the projective stories was aggression—depictions of acting out or violence. Children in classrooms that were characterized by a more controlling climate evidenced more aggression in their stories (as well as less protagonist autonomy).

Shields, Ryan, and Cicchetti (2001) examined narratives of a sample of both maltreated and nonmaltreated boys and girls, ages from 8 to 12, specifically coding for their representations of parents. Narratives that were more negative or constricted (e.g., those containing more instances of coercion) and those containing less positive features (e.g., lower autonomy support) were associated with children being both more prone to aggression (e.g., starting more fights, more disruptive behavior) and to rejecting their peers.

In a comprehensive longitudinal study (discussed in Chapter 16), Joussemet and her colleagues (2008) reported on a large-scale, multischool sample, in which trajectories of aggressive behavior were measured over several years of development. They noted that, generally, overt aggressive behavior decreased over development as children internalized values and developed self-regulatory skills. Although many preschool children moved away from strong and problematic aggressive tendencies or developed the capacity to regulate such behaviors, approximately 5% showed strongly aggressive behaviors, and others retained or escalated in aggressive tendencies. By examining the trajectories of more than 1,000 children to detect such trends, Joussemet et al. identified a number of risk factors for being aggressive. Some of these are well known and include being male, having a reactive temperament, or having parents who are separated or divorced. Yet even after accounting for these factors, maternal controllingness (vs. autonomy support) was a robust predictor of the children's remaining more aggressive. Especially where maternal control was high, tendencies toward aggression were also high.

Another body of evidence concerning risk factors for aggressive behaviors grows out of the literature on *causality orientations*. For example, Knee, Neighbors, and Vietor (2001) were interested in factors predicting road rage and aggressive driving behaviors. They surveyed college students and found that those with high controlled orientations reported more anger at other drivers, more aggressive driving behaviors, and more driving tickets or citations. These findings held up even when controlling for factors such as self-esteem. Goldstein and Iso-Ahola (2008) similarly took interest in the spectator aggression so often seen in parents on the sidelines at youth sporting events. Like Knee et al., they found that more parental anger and aggression was associated with stronger controlled causality orientations. These more aggressive parents also evidenced more ego defensiveness and feelings of pressure, which are symptomatic of vicarious ego involved participation. McHoskey (1999) used the causality orientations measure to examine another related phenomenon, namely Machiavellianism. He found that persons high on the controlled orientation who were also high in the extrinsic goal-content orientation also scored higher on measures of Machiavellian attitudes—including a willingness to manipulate others or to use the others to accomplish their own ends. Those high in controlled orientation also reported more antisocial behavior and nihilism. Autonomy orientations were inversely associated with the outcomes.

We have suggested that doing violence to others is not easily integrated (e.g., Marlantes, 2011), so treating others with aggression or cruelty typically requires that the others be seen as not really being human, lest sensibilities for empathy or compassion be awakened. Moller and Deci (2010) argued, in line with SDT, that when people are controlled, they themselves feel less human and more like objects. Extrapolating from this idea, the authors reasoned that, when people are high on the controlled orientation, they may perceive others in more object-like, mechanistic terms. They verified this using a measure in which control-oriented persons were more likely to associate others with machines. Moreover, higher control orientations were associated with higher endorsement of physical aggression, more hostility and anger, and greater acceptance of violence. These relations between control orientations and aggression-relevant outcomes were, in part, mediated by the dehumanizing, object-oriented associations. In contrast, autonomy orientations were inversely related to anger, hostility, physical aggression, and acceptance of violence.

Aggression has also been related to more extrinsic goal orientations. For example, Duriez, Soenens, and Vansteenkiste (2007) found that those endorsing extrinsic aspirations and goals were higher in right-wing authoritarian attitudes, desires for social dominance over others, and racial prejudice. Subsequently, Duriez, Meeus, and Vansteenkiste (2012) did a scenario study with high-school students that showed that only those who attached greater relative importance to extrinsic values reacted with a negative attitude toward an outgroup that was portrayed as threatening. They then reported results from a longitudinal study with university students that further showed that people with relatively greater extrinsic aspirations were not only more likely to react to threat but also to perceive threat from outgroups. Their cross-lagged analyses showed that a relatively greater extrinsic value orientation predicted increases in threat perceptions over time.

All of these studies suggest that blocks or thwarts to autonomy, either represented by controlling environments or as assessed through controlled or extrinsic value orientations, are associated with more aggression and aggression-related outcomes. Again, we suggest that this occurs because, at a developmental level, lack of autonomy support leads to poorer regulation of aggressive impulses and/or lower internalization of values that would support more empathic and compassionate behaviors. At a more proximal level, people are also reactive when autonomy is constrained and show fewer prosocial and more defensive tendencies.

The relations between aggression and basic psychological need thwarting are just beginning to be investigated. Although the studies just reviewed largely concerned autonomy, SDT suggests that thwarting of any of the basic psychological needs could be a source of reactive aggression. Thus Weinstein (2010) examined whether people experiencing rejection, which of course is a thwarting of relatedness, might transfer hostility to an innocent participant who was not party to the rejection, especially under conditions in which they were less reflective regarding the event. Participants were led to believe that a peer had rejected them and then were asked to write for several minutes under one of three conditions. In a *suppression* condition, they were asked to suppress their feelings and write about something else. In an *expression* condition, participants were asked to express thoughts and feelings but were given no more instructions on how to do so. In an *interest-taking* condition, participants were asked not only to express but also to "take an interest in and be curious about" their emotional experiences related to having been rejected. Participants' emotions were measured immediately after writing and at the end of the study. Additionally, participants rated audiotaped speeches: first, of the individual who had rejected them, and, second, of an unrelated individual who also made a speech. Each spoke about topics that involved moderate self-disclosure. Self-reported affect of the participants who had been rejected did not differ by condition, although individuals in the interest-taking condition showed lower implicit aggression immediately after writing. Then, assessments at the end of study showed that individuals in the interest-taking condition reported less anger and more prosocial affect. Most importantly, results further showed that although individuals in all conditions judged the rejecting target similarly negatively, interest-taking individuals were kinder to the *unrelated* targets—that is, their anger was not displaced onto individuals who were not involved in the original rejection, although participants in the other condition did tend to displace their anger onto the innocent speaker.

Need Thwarting and Malevolent Aggression

An important focus of this discussion of human nature concerns violence toward persons who have neither threatened nor done harm to the actor and acts in which one causes harm or pain beyond that which is instrumentally necessary. These are acts that we shall for convenience term *malevolent aggression*. We suggest that engaging in malevolent aggression is either a product of strong and often dissonant social pressures or a result of compensatory and defensive responses to serious frustration of the individual's basic psychological needs. We now proceed to further clinical and experimental evidence regarding this formulation.

Since early studies on aggression, most research has, for obvious practical reasons, focused on mild instances of aggression or indicators of aggression, such as anger or willingness to punish others. Thus the SDT research on aggression reviewed above does not speak strongly to serious forms of aggression, such as ongoing physical abusers or serial murderers. Nonetheless, there is a large body of literature on both of these topics that is suggestive of the role of need thwarting in development as an underlying factor, a theme that is echoed in our chapter on psychopathology (Chapter 16).

It is clear, for example, that there are individuals who are biologically vulnerable to becoming aggressive (Raine, 2013), and a very few are violent even without strong evidence of need thwarting or maltreatment. Although there are both evolutionary and biological reasons for these exceptions, this is not the usual background of violence, which is much more likely to be related to serious psychological need thwarting, sometimes in interaction with biological vulnerabilities. In fact, as Raine reviewed, because the predictive value of psychologically adverse conditions tends to swamp evidence for biological contributions to violence, the biological vulnerabilities become most detectable in those (statistically rarer) instances in which violence is unrelated to background factors. Anderson (2006), in reviewing research on biological influences on crime, similarly concluded that, although there is some genetic predisposition toward crime, especially property crimes, this is not appreciable for violent crimes such as homicide. As Moffatt (2002) stated: "Even though there are a few rare exceptions, violent individuals are not born that way" (p. 19).

Many if not most heinous crimes involve a perpetrator who had endured odious developmental conditions (Mitchell & Aamodt, 2005). Rampage killers and terrorists, for example, typically have histories of struggle with personal problems and experiences of marginalization, frustration, and family problems (Lankford, 2014). Goldberg (1996, 2000) has written extensively on the topic of serial killers based upon interviews and clinical work. He highlights how most of these killers, whatever their biological vulnerabilities, had themselves been victims of humiliation and excessive control in childhood, often combined with father absence or neglect, which interferes with internalization of important self- and social regulations. Goldberg further argued that the extreme frustration and anger resulting from experiences of humiliation and control later become transformed into fantasies of controlling others—attempts seemingly to compensate for the feelings of having been without any control over themselves or desired outcomes in their early developmental experiences. Even though many serial killings have a sexual-abuse component, the real fantasy is more about controlling the victim, showing this to be a basic need-frustration precipitate, in an extreme form.

On So-Called "Virtuous" Violence

Fiske and Rai (2015) argued quite provocatively, in seeming contrast to the evidence above, that violence to innocent others is typically "moral" or "virtuous" from the perpetrators' point of view. Specifically, they stated: "when people kill, rape, or drive out a whole category of persons the perpetrators' motives are usually moral" (p. 208). In some of the cases they present of self- and group protection, we agree that it may be so conceived by the aggressor, and, as we argued above, might even be autonomously enacted, although likely not integrated. Yet Fisk and Rai's expansive definition of being virtuous or moral encompasses nearly any emotionally or ideologically driven reactions to perceived rejections or injustices, including acts of malevolent aggression. In doing so, they do not distinguish unregulated, controlled, ego-involved, or pathological motives from authentic moral sensibilities and experiences of virtue.

Rape

For instance, Fiske and Rai (2015) describe some behaviors as virtuous or moral that are clearly neither and that, on deeper clinical and phenomenological inquiry, would be shown to be anchored in neither autonomous nor integrated motives, but rather introjections, compartmentalized identifications, and/or serious disturbances in self-regulation (e.g., dissociation, impulsivity). Among these is their inclusion of *rape*. For example, they suggest that a man who has little control in his life or has felt humiliated when rejected by women may find gratification in raping women because he can "feel in total control." He may even say to himself, "she deserved it" or "she asked for it," which Fiske and Rai categorize as moral motives because the man is attempting to "regulate" his sense of unjust relationships or regain what he feels "entitled" to.

In labeling such rationalizations for rape (or serial killing, mass killings, or spousal abuse) moral or virtuous, Fiske and Rai admitted that their definitions of morality and virtue are not consistent with common English usage, philosophical discourse, or past research, and they emphasized that they are not personally endorsing these repugnant behaviors. Instead, they are suggesting that perpetrators often self-justify, rationalize, compartmentalize, or defend their actions to themselves or others. Yet, in our view, these justifications and reasons, even when considered from the perpetrator's perspective, fail to meet any critical criteria for being virtuous. Calling them so loses sight of needed definitional boundaries and represents a quite radical cultural and personal relativism in moral reasoning. Furthermore, rapists and serial killers are not, within typical civil societies, behaving in accordance with a larger moral system internalized from their culture.

In defining morality and virtue, Fiske and Rai (2015) are overly expansive by including any and all reactions to rejection, psychological hurt, or ego blows. This then compromises their further claim that *most* malevolent violence is based in morality and virtue. We can agree with them that *some* violent acts, including some malevolent ones, are supported by internalized conceptions of morality and virtue, as we reviewed above. But others are justified by virulent ideologies adopted by perpetrators of violence (e.g., see Goldhagen, 1996; Staub, 1989). As we have noted, especially in Chapters 4, 10, 12, and 22, not all internalized practices, even ones strongly endorsed as moral or righteous, are congruent with people's basic psychological needs and sensibilities, and therefore they are not likely to be truly autonomously motivated or integrated. SDT suggests that malevolent crimes and social practices that harm innocent parties are, in fact, not typically autonomously motivated or motivated through integrated regulations, as would be required definitionally for acting with virtue or morality. To advance this latter claim, we proceed with another salient example from Fiske and Rai's list of "virtuously violent" acts, namely genocide.

Genocide

When we think of violent genocidal cultures, the image of Nazi Germany in the 1930s and '40s comes readily to the fore. Yet this is too convenient. Few cultures, ethnic groups, or parts of the globe can be easily excluded from such activities (see Diamond, 1997). White settlers in America slaughtered indigenous tribes; Japanese soldiers engaged in horrific acts in Nanking and other Chinese cities; the Khmer Rouge killed millions of their own Cambodian countrymen; Turks exterminated Armenians; the Spanish wiped out whole civilizations in Central America; Australian settlers systematically eliminated Aboriginal persons from their homelands; and genocide by the Hutu tribe of Rwanda more recently shocked the world. No part of the globe has been exempt from such crimes, and genocide has not been limited to East or West, North or South, and has been displayed by individualist and collectivist cultures alike.

Many analyses of genocidal behaviors have been offered, and collectively they suggest that many motives can operate in driving such mass killings. Clearly, many individuals may have participated in genocide based on externally regulated obedience (Kelman & Hamilton, 1989; Milgram, 1963) or introjection (Arendt, 1970; Browning, 1998a). Yet most relevant to our current discussion are genocidal acts that appear to be committed willingly and enthusiastically, and even as righteous, with perpetrators seemingly being "autonomous executioners" (Goldhagen, 1996).

From the SDT perspective, when people identify with the extermination of others, as graphically depicted by Goldhagen's (1996) and Browning's (1998a) examinations of German soldiers who killed innocent Jewish persons, these identifications are of necessity nearly always compartmentalized. The German soldiers kept their identification with killing civilians separate from their other identifications—for example, those of being good Christians, or of being caring family men (Browning, 1998a). They also needed to numb or distance themselves from the natural empathic sensibilities associated with civility and humanity (Smith, 2011). Doing so allowed them to enact an internalized, "semi-autonomous" value to exterminate humans, while minimizing the conflict and the significant inner strain and inherent clash of emotions that would have occurred if the meaning of these acts came into contact with these other identifications, values, and sensibilities. As Browning (1998a) showed, many found the killing repugnant and yet performed it in solidarity with their comrades. Thus, from the perspective of SDT, the motives would be a mix of external regulation, introjection, and compartmentalized identifications rather than true autonomy, and they would entail a psychological resistance to reflective integration with the person's other self-endorsed values. This is also highly evident after the fact, as perpetrators so often deny or externalize responsibility for their acts, rather than owning or embracing them (see Zillmer, Harrower, Ritzler, & Archer, 2013). A person acting with moral integrity would not need to do so.

This idea that genocide cannot be integrated does not deny that people can be zealous in pursuit of their compartmentalized values, whether the identifications are based in religious beliefs, chauvinism, racism, or politics, but it does mean that the zealousness is itself often symptomatic of the closed character of the underlying motivations, as we saw in research reviewed earlier on homophobic aggression (Weinstein, Ryan, DeHaan, Przybylski, Legate, & Ryan, 2012). Closed identifications differ from introjects in being characterized by less outward ambivalence: People can enact closed identifications with a reasonable feeling of certainty and volition, but this is dependent on keeping these identifications separate from important other values. Indeed, closed identifications may gain their power in part by precluding access to the individuals' conflicting holistic self-representations and by selectively numbing sensibilities or considerations that might be contradictory (Lamm et al., 2007). Presumably, closed identifications help in the immediate to reduce anxiety and tension, although it is likely the case that they also exact a toll on the vitality and integrated functioning of the individual. In fact, perpetrators of terrorism and genocide frequently suffer later, experiencing ongoing regret, inner conflict, and various symptoms of stress and bad conscience (Horgan, 2009), symptoms that betray the difficulties of assimilating malevolence. There are typically no such negative sequelae for truly integrated behaviors.

Also as we suggested earlier, the cognitive and emotional constrictions and distortions required to perpetrate genocidal acts entails the victims being treated as mere objects or "vermin-like" organisms rather than as human persons (Smith, 2011). Fiske and Rai (2015) describe the perpetrator as having a *null relationship* with the other (p. 213). What we submit is that even a null relationship requires a compartmentalization of mind (e.g., Lamm et al., 2007) and/or what Bandura (1999) has described as *moral disengagement*. It is not simply a non-act, but an act of suppression or repression of empathic and humane sensibilities. Fiske and Rai argued, in contrast, that if there is no relationship with the targets of genocide, then moral disengagement is a false concept. Yet, claiming that Germans who listened to Jewish composers, who shopped in their stores, who passed their children on the streets, had "no relationship" with these other humans is simply not credible. More generally, to dehumanize others for economic, political, or ideological purposes, no matter how "rational" it might be, is not a specific form of integration; it instead necessitates a withdrawal from the integrative experience. That people engage in such compartmentalization and justify harming of innocents as moral is, as Fiske and Rai document, quite evident—but it still entails a shrinkage from full humanness, and it requires a suppression of one's emotional responsiveness and reflective capacities.

In some cases of genocide, heinous behaviors are at least temporarily culturally endorsed. Yet even where local cultures have seemingly supported such practices (e.g., ISIS's justifications of child rape and female enslavement as "holy acts"; Khmer Rouge's slaughter of millions as "societal cleansing"; and German society's accepting the Jewish extermination as a "solution"), this still does not qualify them as moral or virtuous; rather, it defines the culture and those local norms as pathological and immoral. We do not look back on Nazi, Hutu, Pol Pot, or Stalin-period genocides as moral moments of history. Nor, informatively, do those societies today see them that way. Instead, we see that people did horrible things and rationalized them, and we understand that their motives were usually malevolent rather than benevolent or virtuous.

In sum, we concur with scholars Fiske and Rai (2015), Goldhagen (1996), Staub (1989), and others that people will engage in heinous acts through internalized motivations and ideologies, but we further suggest these are rarely if ever fully integrated. Sometimes perpetrators justify malevolent actions with labels of morality or righteousness, but such conceptions of morality are not equal in credibility, congruence, or integrative span. Heinous acts, even in the name of virtue or cultural tradition, still require a severe contraction both of mindfulness and of one's sphere of identifications—they require people to exclude, objectify, and nullify other living things in order to act without compassion and to justify the cruelty. They require, that is, a *radical constriction in one's humanity*. The more constricted, controlled, and compartmentalized one's moral conceptions, the more malevolence one can commit.

The Bright and Dark Sides of Internalization

In sum, we have seen that humans are well equipped to experience intrinsic satisfactions for prosocial and benevolent behaviors toward others. Helping others, even without reciprocation, is accompanied by inherent satisfactions of basic psychological needs. In contrast, hurting others who have not caused harm is distressing, a result mediated by psychological need frustrations. People are also readily equipped to internalize and fully integrate true morality and virtue and to accept or even commit aggression in the service of prosocial outcomes, as in altruistic punishment scenarios. SDT thus suggests that the more compassionate and humane one's practices, ideals, and virtues are—that is, the more they are in the service of human welfare—the more easily they can be integrated and autonomously regulated, and the more likely it is that people will experience basic need satisfactions in enacting them. This tells us much about the positive features of human nature.

Yet our human capacities for internalization are not all positive. People can also internalize inhumane attitudes and behaviors, and this is especially likely when they have been exposed to environments that have thwarted their basic psychological needs.

Reactive and malevolent forms of aggression are, however, not typically autonomously regulated; instead, these are much more likely to be regulated through external motivations, introjections, or at best highly compartmentalized identifications. The more these internalized "moralities" are malevolent and harmful to others, the more SDT would expect them both to be incapable of full integration and to have more rigid and compartmentalized psychological anchoring. People so disposed may call their intolerant, chauvinistic, or coercive beliefs "moral" or "virtuous," but, when used to support malevolent acts, such labeling neither fits well with philosophical definitions of those concepts nor is likely to be supported through fully autonomous or integrated regulation. Autonomy and integration come about through actual rather than forced congruence. As such, so-called virtuous violence (that is actually malevolent) is made more likely when parents, societies, and deities are highly controlling. These latter conditions conduce to regulatory spans that are narrow and ultimately less supportive of truly autonomous, integrated functioning.

Our Better Natures: Why People Are Becoming Less Aggressive

Having discussed various forms of aggression, their relative autonomy, and their relations to need frustration, it is good to emphasize once again that unprovoked aggression and, more extremely, violence and murder are by no means normative; the vast majority of individuals in society have never violently attacked anyone. To find a single murderer in the United States (which stands at about the midpoint of the world in murder rates), one would have to comb through more than 25,000 people. And only a small number of those who do kill do so without strong need threats or thwarts. These very low odds strongly suggest that humans are by no means "naturally" born killers. Pinker (2011), who documents that there were historical epochs in which murder and torture were much more common, noted that, even in such periods, killing and torture were activities in which only a few out of thousands engaged. Moreover, during the course of recent human history, as civilizations have developed, the incidence of violence has continually and dramatically decreased (Pinker, 2011; Wenar, 2015). This factual point (which often clashes with popular perceptions of violence based on media accessibility) converges with our thesis that the more nurturing and nonthreatening our social conditions are, the less "inhuman" we are likely to be.

   Such trends toward decreasing violence also certainly call into question the empty-organism view that is essentially held by social learning theory and the *script theory* stemming from it (e.g., Anderson & Bushman, 2001). These theorists have argued that people tend to do what they see. Violence has been increasingly modeled in television media and video games, and script theory researchers have argued that the mere exposure to such models of violence *directly* leads to increased violence in the real world. And yet, even in countries where media exposure to murder and violence has dramatically trended upward, murder rates have been generally decreasing (see Ferguson & Kilburn, 2010). Clearly, the sources of human aggression are not as simple as "we do what we see." Instead, to explain aggression requires a theory of what engenders aggressive reactions and the hostility, frustration, and anger associated with them.

   At the same time, families and societies that do not meet the basic psychological needs of their members foster individuals who will more likely exhibit destructive aggression and antisocial behaviors. Need frustrations in development can interact with biological vulnerabilities (see Raine, 2013) and with exposure to and modeling of violence

(Bandura, 1999), making some individuals especially at risk for antisocial and aggressive behaviors. In people with extreme vulnerabilities, need thwarting is, in fact, often a proximal catalyzing factor in their aggressive behaviors. No model will ever explain all human violence, and there can indeed be "broken" organisms, but basic psychological need supports and thwarts can account for a substantial amount of the variance in human kindness versus aggression.

As already noted, Pinker (2011) documented a general trend away from violence and aggression within human societies. He also explained the civilizing of humans largely in terms of increasing self-control and empathy toward others and increasing external regulation of behavior through civil controls and regulations. In fact, both of these factors seem to contribute to this trend, yet with some caveats.

First, as we have emphasized throughout this book, we differentiate self-control from self-regulation. We characterize self-control as a form of motivation that is controlled rather than autonomous and that thus more easily breaks down and is less reliable. In the situations that call forth aggression, self-control is especially vulnerable to being overridden by impulse and emotion, whereas more integrated self-regulation is less susceptible to akrasia (Ryan, Kuhl & Deci, 1997). In contrast, true self-regulation, which is characterized by autonomy and integration, is more stable and effective, especially under conditions of challenges and threat.

Second, although the rule of law is indeed a civilizing influence, it is especially well-internalized law that creates truly civil societies. In fact, SDT suggests that the more controlling and draconian the external regulation is, typically the less effective is the type of internalization upon which the curtailment of aggression most fundamentally depends. It is, instead, greater support for basic psychological needs, including autonomy, which facilitates greater self-regulation and true morality, whereas regulation through merely external controls tends to thwart autonomy and thus the processes of internalization and integration.

Societies with harsher parenting, more brutal retaliation for crimes, and more "eye-for-eye" mentalities conduce to more rather than less aggression. Staub (1992, 2011) in his analyses of genocide and intercultural violence, argued that such malevolence is more likely to emerge in authoritarian societies, especially those in which parenting and socialization strategies are punitive and deviations from norms are met with intolerance. He has further argued that in societies in which basic human needs are met, more caring and less aggressive citizens are the result (Staub, 1992; 2005), a thesis that strongly concurs with our SDT formulation. In fact, evidence supports the view that people are less prosocial and more violent when they exist in harsh, need-thwarting, non-nurturing conditions (e.g., Biglan, Flay, Embry, & Sandler, 2012; Ryan, Deci, Grolnick, & La Guardia, 2006). Conversely, research highlights that parenting strategies in some of the least violent societies have been moving over time toward less rather than more authoritarian tactics (e.g., Trifan, Stattin, & Tilton-Weaver, 2014). In families that are less punitive and controlling, children grow up to be less antisocial and less aggressive (e.g., Kasser, Ryan, Zax, & Sameroff, 1995; Joussemet et al., 2008; Ryan, Deci, & Vansteenkiste, 2016).

Similarly, some evidence suggests that, as societies move toward more human rights, freedoms, and supports for basic needs, there is typically greater human thriving and usually lower violence (Biglan et al., 2012; Rummel, 2002). As summarized by Nelson Mandela, "Violence thrives in the absence of democracy, respect for human rights, and good governance" (as cited in Krug, Mercy, Dahlberg, & Zwi, 2002, p. ix). Advances toward fairness, transparency, participatory involvement, and equitable distribution of wealth, as discussed in Chapter 23, also decrease tendencies toward corruption and violence (e.g., Brunetti & Weder, 2003; Elbadawi & Sambanis, 2000; Staub, 2001; Wilkinson & Pickett, 2007; and others), and greater acceptance of human diversities (Appiah, 2005), albeit with caveats and moderators of these effects. In turn, these more positive pervasive conditions are likely to be connected with better proximal supports for human development—for example, families and caregivers who are more available to support the psychological needs of children (e.g., Landry et al., 2008). By supplying nurturing grounds for psychological growth, both vitality and wellness can be increased and more caring communities promoted. In contrast, if we depended primarily on external controls rather than internalization to increase civility and reduce violence, we would likely see less rather than more humanity.

Whereas theories of control assume a human nature that is inherently aggressive and selfish and that therefore must be constrained by strong external forces, SDT suggests that it is increases in need-supportive (e.g., high support for autonomy and adequate scaffolding) rather than controlling or coercive conditions that best account for the human trajectories away from aggression and violence. The benefits of policies aimed at supporting basic physical and psychological need satisfactions are clear—from greater responsibility and productivity to lower mental illness and less interpersonal violence. Obviously, we still have a long way to go. Yet, by deciding to focus on the processes that result in positive development rather than trying to directly control, pressure, or extrinsically incentivize desired outcomes, more truly eudaimonic cultures will emerge, cultures within which human beings flourish as they regulate themselves.

A Very Brief Epilogue

Throughout this book, we have focused much of our attention on specifying how social environments, both proximal and pervasive, affect people's motivation, learning, performance, creativity, health, and humanity by supporting or thwarting their basic psychological needs. We have taken this strong social-psychological focus for two main reasons. First, it allows us to make recommendations about how to optimally structure schools, clinics, workplaces, and other proximal social contexts to support engagement, vitality, thriving, and ascendant human functioning, as well as to make policy recommendations about more pervasive social contexts. Second, by specifying the environmental and interpersonal factors that affect people's motivation, well-being, and performance, we hope that the work will promote greater awareness of processes that affect everyone and, accordingly, allow them to make the choices and engage in the actions that constitute a more eudaimonic life.

It is this second reason to which we now turn, for we cannot conclude a treatise on *self-determination* by looking wholly to environments to improve the human condition. It is true that humans are social organisms, embedded in and influenced to a significant degree by their cultures and families on the one hand and their biological foundations on the other. Yet what is unique and critically important about humans, and what makes our capability for autonomy all the more powerful, is our capacity for reflective awareness, through which we have the possibility of making choices that allow us to better satisfy basic needs, to care for others, and to have fuller and more meaningful existences.

People's choices are not limited to what has been reinforced in the past, to what others are demanding, or to incentivized behaviors, nor are they inevitably driven by emotional reactions or by nonconscious processes. Although all these influences *can* control behavior, people's possibilities remain prolific. Under average expectable conditions, humans have capacities to effectively regulate their own behaviors, including those associated with inherited temperaments, drives, emotions, and biological vulnerabilities. They can be guided by their natural propensities to detect inner conflict and to produce integrative solutions to decisional and regulatory challenges and to social issues, small and large.

What are these capacities? We have been describing them throughout this work, but they are worth revisiting. They begin with *awareness*. Open and receptive attention to what is occurring, as in *mindfulness*, allows people to better contact both the internal and external stimuli that are influencing them. Awareness allows people to take stock of events and forces in their environments, as well as those arising from impulses and affective reactions, to identify conflicts both inner and outer, and to interpret events as being informational rather than controlling. *Taking interest* in experience allows people to more closely and curiously inspect and reflectively deliberate upon their motives and reactions. Exercising such reflective capacities allows people *choice*—the placing of value and effort on some possibilities over others.

We also have the capacity to connect with, and learn from, others. *Emotional reliance* on others allows people to share their experiences and thus to understand multiple views on what can occur, especially when the relationships involve mutuality and autonomy support. *Internalization* and *integration* are, in fact, dependent on the social processing of events and experiences, and it is through communication that people come to appreciate what behaviors have more value and meaning than others and why. *Reason*, too, plays a role here, because endorsing some behaviors and values over others is supported by understanding and coherent rationales. In this regard, *education* and *learning* enhance our capabilities for growth, integration, and autonomous functioning.

Yet perhaps most important of all is *relatedness*, which is what brings people into dispositions of caring. The larger their spheres of relatedness, the more people identify with and are mindful of concerns that are less self-focused and defensive. The more they identify with others and with concerns beyond themselves, the more *intrinsic aspirations* become salient, which, as we have seen, conduces toward greater need satisfaction and wellness both for others and for themselves. Through all these processes, each an inherent capacity afforded by our human natures, people can become more *authentic*, taking responsibility for getting their own needs satisfied, acting more volitionally, and at the same time becoming more humane and transcendent.

These capacities involved in becoming proactive and living a eudaimonic life are clearly manifold and complex. Yet these complexities are part of what makes the pursuit of knowledge about self-determination both challenging and rewarding. SDT, when well applied, has had observable and empirically supported positive results on both individuals and groups. With greater understanding of these capacities, their causes, the mechanisms through which they operate, and the factors that support or thwart them, individuals may thus be ever better enabled to find pathways to wellness both in their own lives and in their societies. They can become more fully human, acting autonomously to select or create goals and activities that improve the world and creating more facilitating conditions for those in their sphere of influence.

Self-determination, as it turns out, *is ultimately a problem of integration*. The more one's actions are regulated through integration, the more autonomous they are. However, integration is not simply an open matter. It is constrained by our human nature and the basic needs it entails. People have often feared autonomy because they have equated it with individualism. But because humans are not just individuals, but rather social creatures who seek competence and relatedness, their nature is not, in its most integrated forms, selfish. It is a synthesis of self with others. Thus, ultimately, the most integrated persons are not those who act only on their own behalf but also with others in mind. We are, at our best, a synthesis of autonomy and relatedness.

Being "our best," represented in eudaimonic living, leads us to a notion of values and a conception of human morality. Whereas nihilists (and positivists) have argued that morality has no objective meaning, and ideologues have said that morality is some particular subjective meaning, SDT points to another idea of morality—that of acting with integrity. It thus means acting, with as much receptive and nondefensive awareness as possible, in ways that maximize competence, relatedness, and autonomy. And the more open and nondefensive we are, the less parochial our integrative span, and the more of the living world we see ourselves relating to. This is an active process, and one to which self-cultivation and personal growth contribute.

In our analysis we have seen that the more integrated one's considerations are, the harder it becomes to justify greed, cruelty, and oppression. Even more difficult is, in an integrated manner, to engage in violence against innocents, such as rape or genocide. Indeed, these acts are nearly invariably betrayed by their lack of integration. They stem from psychological injuries, defensiveness and reactivity, and they require distorting or restraining one's awareness and humanity. In this sense, morality is neither a meaningless issue nor merely a subjective or culturally relative question. It is a *naturalistic* one. The more we act in accordance with our basic psychological needs, the more moral we become. Yet the more we act in compartmentalized, defensive, introjected, or otherwise controlled ways, they more we are susceptible to the "non-good."

We also saw that social conditions affect people's capacities for integration. The more controlling, rejecting, and competence-limiting people's environments are, the more they are hampered in developing and exercising their inherent integrative capacities. Oppositely, the more need supports are provided, the more individuals grow in more humane directions. This, then, provides us at least a tentative way to support a "true north" for people's moral compasses—the creation of more basic need-supportive human conditions, which in turn leads to more compassionate and caring societies. The body of knowledge represented by SDT is hopefully contributing to this.

In our preface, we confessed that this book is unfinished, and now, we must admit, so, too, is the theory itself. As an empirically based framework, SDT has always been open to challenges, to revisions, and to disconfirmations of any of its tenets. This openness is not a weakness of the framework but its strength, as it engages researchers and practitioners alike to question, expand, and refine the theory.

We have many times thought that the work in SDT was consolidating and coming to closure, only to have new questions arise and extensions emerge. We began, in fact, by only exploring *intrinsic motivation* and what undermines or facilitates it, as described in *cognitive evaluation theory* (CET). Yet this work led us to take a closer look at *extrinsic motivation* and then to differentiate it into various forms described by a continuum of autonomy and *internalization,* an approach that developed into *organismic integration theory* (OIT). We also saw how individual differences in vulnerabilities and strengths made the process of acting with autonomy and integrity more or less difficult, which we researched within *causality orientations theory* (COT). Exploring what supported intrinsic motivation, more integrated forms of extrinsic motivation, and more autonomous causality orientations, we saw again and again how three fundamental psychological need satisfactions, those for *autonomy, competence,* and *relatedness,* underpinned all these processes and explained much of the variance in human wellness and flourishing, which we then described in *basic psychological needs theory* (BPNT). In researching human flourishing, it became evident that some life goals, especially those we characterized as *intrinsic aspirations,* conduced to greater basic need satisfactions and yielded greater wellness, whereas others, described as *extrinsic aspirations,* generally led to lower thriving and wellness, findings summarized in *goal contents theory* (GCT). Understanding wellness also inspired specific studies of *subjective vitality* and its connections with basic need satisfactions and exposure to living nature. Wellness studies also led to SDT's conceptions of *eudaimonia* and full functioning, along with their enhancement by *mindfulness*. Finally, across studies we became clearer about how *relatedness*, as a fundamental human need, was deeply intertwined with *autonomy support*, a dynamic process that was outlined in *relationships motivation theory* (RMT).

Each of these extensions in the journey of SDT has been accompanied by both mechanistic and social-psychological explorations, expanding the science in both directions. In fact, although SDT is primarily a psychological perspective, it has always aimed at consilience and thus has been open to inputs from other disciplines, from biology to sociology. And although SDT is thoroughly empirically based, it has remained receptive to both clinical perspectives and philosophical critique.

In some areas, the theory has yet to make deep inroads. Perhaps most incomplete is research on just these issues of personal change and responsibility that we have emphasized in this epilogue—the capacities, experiences, mechanisms, and conditions by and through which individuals become more self-aware and activated to create change in the direction of human betterment. This topic is, in fact, currently an active and explicit agenda within the community of SDT researchers, as teams of researchers are working to advance our understanding of the *self-as-process* and how people develop and maintain a healthy, integrative, inner compass. Also insufficient is our understanding of macroprocesses and the impact of pervasive environments (i.e., cultures, political systems, and economic structures) on human thriving, which our final chapters have only begun to outline. Finally, we are just beginning to develop a neuropsychology of autonomy and self-regulation, as emerging studies are building toward a better picture of the connectivities involved.

Awareness and knowledge do indeed matter, and choices do exist. Autonomy is, as we have argued, no illusion. It is instead a way of functioning that we can exercise or not. In fact, it is only through its exercise that we can be reliably moving toward ever-greater humanity and community. Yet acting with autonomy, no matter how natural or strong its organismic underpinnings, does not happen automatically, as existentialist writers have so clearly understood. Being authentic and benevolent—living a eudaimonic life—involves effort and commitment; it entails taking responsibility for oneself. Doing so is not always easy, and, in fact, requires everyday acts of courage. Engaging our capacities for autonomy often means resisting or redirecting temptations, cultural seductions and pressures, and strong controlling forces, both external and internal to the person. Yet those of you who have read this far have seen the ample evidence that such courage can be mustered. Even further, you have seen that such courage is most effectively mobilized with the support and cooperation of others. Thus, acting with an understanding of determinants and obstacles, we as individuals can join with others to make a meaningful difference in creating conditions that facilitate basic human need satisfactions in our homes, schools, places of work, and natural environments, as well as in our wider cultures and political systems. It is in this regard that we hope the broad and yet integrated philosophical and scientific framework of SDT advances the cause of humanity and the preservation and flourishing of humanity's only home—this living earth.

References

Aarts, H., & Custers, R. (2012). Unconscious goal pursuit: Nonconscious goal regulation and motivation. In R. M. Ryan (Ed.), *The Oxford handbook of human motivation* (pp. 232–247). Oxford, UK: Oxford University Press.

Abadi, F. E., Jalilvand, M. R., Sharif, M., Salimi, G. A., & Khanzadeh, S. A. (2011). A study of influential factors on employees' motivation for participating in the in-service training courses based on modified expectancy theory. *International Business and Management, 2*(1), 157–169.

Abelson, R. P., Aronson, E., McGuire, W. J., Newcomb, T. M., Rosenberg, M. J., & Tannenbaum, P. H. (1968). *Theories of cognitive consistency: A sourcebook*. Chicago: Rand McNally.

Abramson, L. Y., Seligman, M. E., & Teasdale, J. D. (1978). Learned helplessness in humans: Critique and reformulation. *Journal of Abnormal Psychology, 87*(1), 49–74.

Abusharaf, R. M. (Ed.). (2013). Introduction: The custom in question. In R. M. Abusharaf (Ed.), *Female circumcision: Multicultural perspectives* (pp. 1–25). Philadelphia: University of Pennsylvania Press.

Adachi, P. J. C., Hodson, G., Willoughby, T., & Zanette, S. (2015). Brothers and sisters in arms: Intergroup cooperation in a violent shooter game can reduce intergroup bias. *Psychology of Violence, 5*(4), 455–462.

Adachi, P. J. C., & Willoughby, T. (2011a). The effect of video game competition and violence on aggressive behavior: Which characteristic has the greatest influence? *Psychology of Violence, 1*(4), 259–274.

Adachi, P. J. C., & Willoughby, T. (2011b). The effect of violent video games on aggression: Is it more than just the violence? *Aggression and Violent Behavior, 16*(1), 55–62.

Adachi, P. J. C., & Willoughby, T. (2013). Demolishing the competition: The longitudinal link between competitive video games, competitive gambling, and aggression. *Journal of Youth and Adolescence, 42*(7), 1090–1104.

Adams, G. R., & Marshall, S. K. (1996). A developmental social psychology of identity: Understanding the person-in-context. *Journal of Adolescence, 19*(5), 429–442.

Adams, J. S. (1963). Toward an understanding of inequity. *Journal of Abnormal and Social Psychology, 67*(5), 422–436.

Adorno, T. W., Frenkel-Brunswik, E., Levinson, D. J., & Sanford, R. N. (1950). *The authoritarian personality*. New York: Harper & Row.

Aelterman, N., Vansteenkiste, M., Van den Berghe, L., De Meyer, J., & Haerens, L. (2014). Fostering a need-supportive teaching style: Intervention effects on physical education teachers' beliefs and teaching behaviors. *Journal of Sport and Exercise Psychology, 36*(6), 595–609.

Ahmad, I., Vansteenkiste, M., & Soenens, B. (2013). The relations of Arab Jordanian adolescents' perceived maternal parenting to teacher-rated adjustment and problems: The intervening role of perceived need satisfaction. *Developmental Psychology, 49*(1), 177–183.

Ainsworth, M. D. S., Blehar, M. C., Waters, E., & Wall, S. N. (1978). *Patterns of attachment: A psychological study of the Strange Situation*. Hillsdale, NJ: Erlbaum.

Aknin, L. B., Barrington-Leigh, C. P., Dunn, E. W.,

Helliwell, J. F., Burns, J., Biswas-Diener, R., et al. (2013). Prosocial spending and well-being: Cross-cultural evidence for a psychological universal. *Journal of Personality and Social Psychology, 104*(4), 635–652.

Aknin, L. B., Dunn, E. W., Sandstrom, G. M., & Norton, M. I. (2013). Does social connection turn good deeds into good feelings? On the value of putting the "social" in prosocial spending. *International Journal of Happiness and Development, 1*(2), 155.

Aknin, L. B., Sandstrom, G. M., Dunn, E. W., & Norton, M. I. (2011). It's the recipient that counts: Spending money on strong social ties leads to greater happiness than spending on weak social ties. *PLoS ONE, 6*(2), e17018.

Alderfer, C. P. (1972). Conflict resolution among behavioral scientists. *Professional Psychology, 3*(1), 41–47.

Alderman, R. B. (1974). *Psychological behavior in sport.* Philadelphia: Saunders.

Alkire, S. (2007). Measuring freedoms alongside wellbeing. In I. Gough & J. A. McGregor (Eds.), *Wellbeing in developing countries: From theory to research* (pp. 93–108). Cambridge, UK: Cambridge University Press.

Allen, N. J., & Meyer, J. P. (1996). Affective, continuance, and normative commitment to the organization: An examination of construct validity. *Journal of Vocational Behavior, 49*(3), 252–276.

Allison, S. E., von Wahlde, L., Shockley, T., & Gabbard, G. O. (2006). The development of the self in the era of the Internet and role-playing fantasy games. *American Journal of Psychiatry, 163*(3), 381–385.

Allport, G. W. (1937). The functional autonomy of motives. In S. Chalmers & D. Manfred (Eds.), *Understanding human motivation* (pp. 69–81). Cleveland, OH: Howard Allen.

Alsibiani, S. A., & Rouzi, A. A. (2010). Sexual function in women with female genital mutilation. *Fertility and Sterility, 93*(3), 722–724.

Amabile, T. M. (1979). Effects of external evaluation on artistic creativity. *Journal of Personality and Social Psychology, 37*(2), 221–233.

Amabile, T. M. (1982). Children's artistic creativity: Detrimental effects of competition in a field setting. *Personality and Social Psychology Bulletin, 8*(3), 573–578.

Amabile, T. M. (1983). The social psychology of creativity: A componential conceptualization. *Journal of Personality and Social Psychology, 45*(2), 357–376.

Amabile, T. M. (1996). *Creativity in context.* Boulder, CO: Westview Press.

Amabile, T. M., DeJong, W., & Lepper, M. R. (1976). Effects of externally imposed deadlines on subsequent intrinsic motivation. *Journal of Personality and Social Psychology, 34*(1), 92–98.

Amabile, T. M., & Gitomer, J. (1984). Children's artistic creativity: Effects of choice in task materials. *Personality and Social Psychology Bulletin, 10*(2), 209–215.

Amabile, T. M., Hennessey, B. A., & Grossman, B. S. (1986). Social influences on creativity: The effects of contracted-for reward. *Journal of Personality and Social Psychology, 50*(1), 14–23.

Amabile, T. M., Hill, K. G., Hennessey, B. A., & Tighe, E. M. (1994). The work preference inventory: Assessing intrinsic and extrinsic motivational orientations. *Journal of Personality and Social Psychology, 66*(5), 950–967.

Ambrose, M. L., & Kulik, C. T. (1999). Old friends, new faces: Motivation research in the 1990s. *Journal of Management, 25*(3), 231–292.

Amiot, C. E., Sansfacon, S., Louis, W. R., & Yelle, M. (2012). Can intergroup behaviors be emitted out of self-determined reasons?: Testing the role of group norms and behavioral congruence in the internalization of discrimination and parity behaviors. *Personality and Social Psychology Bulletin, 38*(1), 63–76.

Amorose, A. J., & Horn, T. S. (2000). Intrinsic motivation: Relationships with collegiate athletes' gender, scholarship status, and perceptions of their coaches' behavior. *Journal of Sport and Exercise Psychology, 22*, 63–84.

Amorose, A. J., & Horn, T. S. (2001). Pre- to post-season changes in the intrinsic motivation of first year college athletes: Relationships with coaching behavior and scholarship status. *Journal of Applied Sport Psychology, 13*(4), 355–373.

Amrein, A., & Berliner, D. (2002). *An analysis of some unintended and negative consequences of high-stakes testing.* Tempe: Arizona State University Education Policy Studies Laboratory. Retrieved from *http://nepc.colorado.edu/files/EPSL-0211–125-EPRU.pdf*.

Anand, P., Hunter, G., Carter, I., Dowding, K., Guala, F., & Van Hees, M. (2009). The development of capability indicators. *Journal of Human Development and Capabilities, 10*(1), 125–152.

Anderluh, M. B., Tchanturia, K., Rabe-Hesketh, S., & Treasure, J. (2003). Childhood obsessive-compulsive personality traits in adult women with eating disorders: Defining a broader eating disorder phenotype. *American Journal of Psychiatry, 160*(2), 242–247.

Andersen, S. M., & Chen, S. (2002). The relational self: An interpersonal social-cognitive theory. *Psychological Review, 109*(4), 619–645.

Andersen, S. M., Chen, S., & Carter, C. (2000). Fundamental human needs: Making social cognition relevant. *Psychological Inquiry, 11*(4), 269–318.

Anderson, C. A., Berkowitz, L., Donnerstein, E., Huesmann, L. R., Johnson, J. D., Linz, D., et al. (2003). The influence of media violence on youth. *Psychological Science in the Public Interest, 4*(3), 81–110.

Anderson, C. A., & Bushman, B. J. (2001). Effects of violent video games on aggressive behavior, aggressive cognition, aggressive affect, physiological arousal, and prosocial behavior: A meta-analytic review of the scientific literature. *Psychological Science, 12*(5), 353–359.

Anderson, C. A., Gentile, D. A., & Buckley, K. E. (2007). *Violent video game effects on children and adolescents: Theory, research, and public policy.* New York: Oxford University Press.

Anderson, G. S. (2006). *Biological influences on criminal behavior.* Boca Raton, FL: CRC Press.

Anderson, R., Manoogian, S. T., & Reznick, S. J. (1976). The undermining and enhancing of intrinsic motivation in preschool children. *Journal of Personality and Social Psychology, 34*(5), 915–922.

Anderson, S., & Rodin, J. (1989). Is bad news always bad?: Cue and feedback effects on intrinsic motivation. *Journal of Applied Social Psychology, 19*(6), 449–467.

Andreoni, J. (1990). Impure altruism and donations to public goods: A theory of warm-glow giving. *Economic Journal, 100*(401), 464–477.

Angyal, A. (1941). *Foundations for a science of personality.* New York: Commonwealth Fund.

Angyal, A. (1965). *Neurosis and treatment: A holistic theory.* Hoboken, NJ: Wiley.

Antony, M. M., & Roemer, L. (2003). Behavior therapy. In A. S. Gurman & S. Messer (Eds.), *Essential psychotherapies* (pp. 182–223). New York: Guilford Press.

Antony, M. M., & Roemer, L. (2014). Behavior therapy. In G. R. Vandenbos, E. Meidenbauer, & J. Frank-McNeil (Eds.), *Psychotherapy theories and techniques: A reader* (pp. 29–34). Washington, DC: American Psychological Association.

Appiah, K. A. (2005). *The ethics of identity.* Princeton, NJ: Princeton University Press.

Arch, J. J., & Craske, M. G. (2009). Mechanisms of mindfulness: Emotion regulation following a focused breathing induction. *Behaviour Research and Therapy, 44*(12), 1849–1858.

Arend, R., Gove, F. L., & Sroufe, L. A. (1979). Continuity of individual adaptation from infancy to kindergarten: A predictive study of ego-resiliency and curiosity in preschoolers. *Child Development, 50*(4), 950–959.

Arendt, H. (1970). *On violence.* New York: Houghton Mifflin Harcourt.

Argyris, C. (1957). *Personality and organization.* New York: Harper.

Ariely, D., Gneezy, U., Loewenstein, G., & Mazar, N. (2009). Large stakes and big mistakes. *Review of Economic Studies, 76*(2), 451–469.

Aristotle. (1869). *The nichomachean ethics of Aristotle* (R. Williams, Trans.). London: Longmans Green.

Arnold, R., & Sarkar, M. (2015). Preparing athletes and teams for the Olympic Games: Experiences and lessons learned from the world's best sport psychologists. *International Journal of Sport and Exercise Psychology, 13*(1), 4–20.

Aronfreed, J. M. (1968). *Conduct and conscience: The socialization of internalized control over behavior.* New York: Academic Press.

Aronson, E. (1969). A theory of cognitive dissonance: A current perspective. In L. Berkowitz (Ed.), *Advances in experimental social psychology* (Vol. 4, pp. 1–34). New York: Academic Press.

Ash, T. G. (2004). *Free world.* London: Penguin.

Assagioli, R. (1965). *Psychosynthesis: A manual of principles and techniques.* New York: Hobbs Dorman.

Assor, A. (2011). Autonomous moral motivation: Consequences, socializing antecedents and the unique role of integrated moral principles. In M. Mikulincer & P. R. Shaver (Eds.), *Social psychology of morality: Exploring the causes of good and evil* (pp. 239–255). Washington, DC: American Psychological Association.

Assor, A., Kaplan, H., Feinberg, O., & Tal, K. (2009). Combining vision with voice: A learning and implementation structure promoting teachers' internalization of practices based on self-determination theory. *Theory and Research in Education, 7*(2), 234–243.

Assor, A., Kaplan, H., Kanat-Maymon, Y., & Roth, G. (2005). Directly controlling teacher behaviors as predictors of poor motivation and engagement in girls and boys: The role of anger and anxiety. *Learning and Instruction, 15*(5), 397–413.

Assor, A., Roth, G., & Deci, E. L. (2004). The emotional costs of parents' conditional regard: A self-determination theory analysis. *Journal of Personality, 72*(1), 47–88.

Assor, A., & Tal, K. (2012). When parents' affection depends on child's achievement: Parental conditional positive regard, self-aggrandizement, shame and coping in adolescents. *Journal of Adolescence, 35*(2), 249–260.

Augros, R., & Stanciu, G. (1987). *The new biology: Discovering the wisdom of nature.* Boulder, CO: Shambhala.

Austin, S., Guay, F., Senécal, C., Fernet, C., & Nouwen, A. (2013). Longitudinal testing of a dietary self-care motivational model in adolescents with diabetes. *Journal of Pyschosomatic Research, 75*(2), 153–159.

Austin, S., Senécal, C., Guay, F., & Nouwen, A. (2011). Effects of gender, age, and diabetes duration on dietary self-care in adolescents with Type 1 diabetes: A self-determination theory perspective. *Journal of Health Psychology, 16*(6), 917–928.

Axelrod, R., & Hamilton, W. D. (1981). The evolution of cooperation. *Science, 211*, 1390–1396.

Baard, P. P., Deci, E. L., & Ryan, R. M. (2004).

Intrinsic need satisfaction: A motivational basis of performance and well-being in two work settings. *Journal of Applied Social Psychology, 34*(10), 2045–2068.

Bagøien, T. E., Halvari, H., & Nesheim, H. (2010). Self-determined motivation in physical education and its links to motivation for leisure-time physical activity, physical activity, and well-being in general. *Perceptual and Motor Skills, 111*(2), 407–432.

Bailenson, J. N., & Blascovich, J. (2011). This is your mind online. *IEEE Spectrum, 48*(6), 78–83.

Bakker, A. B., & Demerouti, E. (2007). The job demands-resources model: State of the art. *Journal of Managerial Psychology, 22*(3), 309–328.

Baldwin, A. L. (1955). *Behavior and development in childhood*. New York: Dryden.

Baldwin, A. L., Kalhorn, J., & Breese, F. H. (1945). Patterns of parent behavior. *Psychological Monographs, 58*(3), 1–75.

Bandura, A. (1977). Self-efficacy: Toward a unifying theory of behavioral change. *Psychological Review, 84*(2), 191–215.

Bandura, A. (1989). Human agency in social cognitive theory. *American Psychologist, 44*(9), 1175–1184.

Bandura, A. (1995). *Self-efficacy in changing societies*. Cambridge, UK: Cambridge University Press.

Bandura, A. (1996). Regulation of cognitive processes through perceived self-efficacy. In G. H. Jennings & D. Belanger (Eds.), *Passages beyond the gate: A Jungian approach to understanding the nature of American psychology at the dawn of the new millennium* (pp. 96–107). Needham Heights, MA: Simon & Schuster.

Bandura, A. (1997). *Self-efficacy: The exercise of control*. New York: Freeman.

Bandura, A. (1999). Moral disengagement in the perpetration of inhumanities. *Personality and Social Psychology Review, 3*(3), 193–209.

Bandura, A., & Walters, R. H. (1963). *Social learning and personality development*. New York: Holt, Rinehart & Winston.

Bao, X.-H., & Lam, S.-F. (2008). Who makes the choice?: Rethinking the role of autonomy and relatedness in Chinese children's motivation. *Child Development, 79*(2), 269–283.

Baranes, A. F., Oudeyer, P.-Y., & Gottlieb, J. (2014). The effects of task difficulty, novelty and the size of the search space on intrinsically motivated exploration. *Frontiers in Neuroscience, 8*(317), 1–9.

Barbeau, A., Sweet, S. N., & Fortier, M. (2009). A path-analytic model of self-determination theory in a physical activity context. *Journal of Applied Biobehavioral Research, 14*(3), 103–118.

Barber, B. K. (1996). Parental psychological control: Revisiting a neglected construct. *Child Development, 67*(6), 3296–3319.

Barber, B. K., Olsen, J. E., & Shagle, S. C. (1994). Associations between parental psychological and behavioral control and youth internalized and externalized behaviors. *Child Development, 65*(4), 1120–1136.

Barber, B. K., Stolz, H. E., & Olsen, J. A. (2005). Parental support, psychological control, and behavioral control: Assessing relevance across time, culture, and method. *Monographs of the Society for Research in Child Development, 70*(4), 1–147.

Barclay, L. (2000) Autonomy and the social self. In C. Mackenzie & N. Stoljar (Eds.), *Relational autonomy: Feminist perspectives on autonomy, agency, and the social self* (pp. 52–71). Oxford, UK: Oxford University Press.

Bargh, J. A. (1997). The automaticity of everyday life. In R. S. Wyer, Jr. (Ed.), *The automaticity of everyday life: Advances in social cognition* (pp. 1–61). Mahwah, NJ: Erlbaum.

Bargh, J. A. (2007). Social psychological approaches to consciousness. In P. D. Zelazo, M. Moscovitch, & E. Thompson (Eds.), *The Cambridge handbook of consciousness* (pp. 555–570). New York: Cambridge University Press.

Bargh, J. A. (2008). Free will is un-natural. In J. Baer, J. Kaufman, & R. F. Baumeister (Eds.), *Are we free?: Psychology and free will* (pp. 128–154). New York: Oxford University Press.

Bargh, J. A., Chen, M., & Burrows, L. (1996). Automaticity of social behavior: Direct effects of trait construct and stereotype activation on action. *Journal of Personality and Social Psychology, 71*(2), 230–244.

Bargh, J. A., & Ferguson, M. J. (2000). Beyond behaviorism: On the automaticity of higher mental processes. *Psychological Bulletin, 126*(6), 925–945.

Barilan, M. Y. (2011). Respect for personal autonomy, human dignity, and the problems of self-directedness and botched autonomy. *Journal of Medicine and Philosophy, 36*(5), 496–515.

Barkoukis, V., Lazuras, L., Tsorbatzoudis, H., & Rodafinos, A. (2011). Motivational and sportspersonship profiles of elite athletes in relation to doping behavior. *Psychology of Sport and Exercise, 12*(3), 205–212.

Barnes, S., Brown, K. W., Krusemark, E., Campbell, W. K., & Rogge, R. D. (2007). The role of mindfulness in romantic relationship satisfaction and responses to relationship stress. *Journal of Marital and Family Therapy, 33*(4), 482–500.

Barrett, H. C., & Kurzban, R. (2006). Modularity in cognition: Framing the debate. *Psychological Review, 113*(3), 628–647.

Barrett, J., Della-Maggiore, V., Chouinard, P. A., & Paus, T. (2004). Mechanisms of action underlying the effect of repetitive transcranial magnetic stimulation on mood: Behavioral and brain imaging studies. *Neuropsychopharmacology, 29,* 1172–1189.

Bartholomew, K. J., Ntoumanis, N., Cuevas, R., & Lonsdale, C. (2014). Job pressure and ill-health in physical education teachers: The mediating role of psychological need thwarting. *Teaching and Teacher Education, 37,* 101–107.

Bartholomew, K. J., Ntoumanis, N., Ryan, R. M., Bosch, J. A., & Thøgersen-Ntoumani, C. (2011). Self-determination theory and diminished functioning: The role of interpersonal control and psychological need thwarting. *Personality and Social Psychology Bulletin, 37*(11), 1459–1473.

Bartholomew, K. J., Ntoumanis, N., Ryan, R. M., & Thøgersen-Ntoumani, C. (2011). Psychological need thwarting in the sport context: Assessing the darker side of athletic experience. *Journal of Sport and Exercise Psychology, 33*(1), 75–102.

Bartholomew, K. J., Ntoumanis, N., & Thøgersen-Ntoumani, C. (2010). The controlling interpersonal style in a coaching context: Development and initial validation of a psychometric scale. *Journal of Sport and Exercise Psychology, 32*(2), 193–216.

Bartle, R. A. (2004). *Designing virtual worlds.* San Francisco: NewRiders.

Bartley, W. W. (1987). Philosophy of biology versus philosophy of physics. In G. Radnitzky & W. W. Bartley (Eds.), *Evolutionary epistemology, rationality, and the sociology of knowledge* (pp. 7–45). La Salle, IL: Open Court.

Basabe, N., & Valencia, J. (2007). Culture of peace: Sociostructural dimensions, cultural values, and emotional climate. *Journal of Social Issues, 63*(2), 405–419.

Bass, B. M. (1985). *Leadership and performance beyond expectations.* New York: Free Press.

Bauer, J. J., & McAdams, D. P. (2004). Personal growth in adults' stories of life transitions. *Journal of Personality, 72*(3), 573–602.

Bauer, J. J., McAdams, D. P., & Sakaeda, A. R. (2005). Interpreting the good life: Growth memories in the lives of mature, happy people. *Journal of Personality and Social Psychology, 88*(1), 203–217.

Bauman, N., Kuhl, J., & Kazén, M. (2005). Left-hemispheric activation and self-infiltration: Testing a neuropsychological model of internalization. *Motivation and Emotion, 29*(3), 135–163.

Baumeister, R. F. (1991). *Escaping the self: Alcoholism, spirituality, masochism, and other flights from the burden of selfhood.* New York: Basic Books.

Baumeister, R. F. (1997). *Evil: Inside human violence and cruelty.* New York: Holt.

Baumeister, R. F., Bratslavsky, E., Muraven, M., & Tice, D. M. (1998). Ego depletion: Is the active self a limited resource? *Journal of Personality and Social Psychology, 74*(5), 1252–1265.

Baumeister, R. F., & Bushman, B. J. (2008). *Social psychology and human nature.* Toronto, Ontario, Canada: Thomson Higher Education.

Baumeister, R. F., Heatherton, T. F., & Tice, D. M. (1993). When ego threats lead to self-regulation failure: Negative consequences of high self-esteem. *Journal of Personality and Social Psychology, 64*(1), 141–156.

Baumeister, R. F., & Leary, M. R. (1995). The need to belong: Desire for interpersonal attachments as a fundamental human motivation. *Psychological Bulletin, 117*(3), 497–529.

Baumeister, R. F., Muraven, M., & Tice, D. M. (2000). Ego depletion: A resource model of volition, self-regulation, and controlled processing. *Social Cognition, 18*(2), 130–150.

Baumeister, R. F., & Tice, D. M. (1985). Self-esteem and responses to success and failure: Subsequent performance and intrinsic motivation. *Journal of Personality, 53*(3), 450–467.

Baumeister, R. F., & Vohs, K. D. (2007). Self-regulation, ego depletion, and motivation. *Social and Personality Psychology Compass, 1*(1), 115–128.

Baumrind, D. (1967). Child care practices anteceding three patterns of preschool behavior. *Genetic Psychology Monographs, 75*(1), 43–88.

Baumrind, D. (1971). Current patterns of parental authority. *Developmental Psychology, 4*(1), 1–103.

Baumrind, D. (1996). The discipline controversy revisited. *Family Relations: An Interdisciplinary Journal of Applied Family Studies, 45*(4), 405–414.

Baumrind, D., Larzelere, R. E., & Cowan, P. A. (2002). Ordinary physical punishment: Is it harmful? Comment on Gershoff (2002). *Psychological Bulletin, 128*(4), 580–589.

Beauchaine, T. P., & Gatzke-Kopp, L. M. (2012). Instantiating the multiple levels of analysis perspective in a program of study on externalizing behavior. *Development and Psychopathology, 24*(3), 1003–1018.

Beauchamp, T. L., & Childress, J. F. (1989). *Principles of biomedical ethics.* Oxford, UK: Oxford University Press.

Beck, A. T. (1972). *Depression: Causes and treatment.* Philadelphia: University of Pennsylvania Press.

Beck, A. T., Emery, G., & Greenberg, R. (1985). *Anxiety disorders and phobias: A cognitive perspective.* New York: Basic Books.

Beck, A. T., Freeman, A., & Davis, D. D. (1990). *Cognitive therapy of personality disorders.* New York: Guilford Press.

Beck, A. T., Rush, A. J., Shaw, B. F., & Emery, G. (1979). *Cognitive therapy of depression.* New York: Guilford Press.

Beck, A. T., & Weishaar, M. E. (2008). Cognitive

therapy. In R. J. Corsini & D. Wedding (Eds.), *Current psychotherapies* (pp. 263–294). Belmont, CA: Thomson Brooks/Cole.

Becker, T. E., Kernan, M. C., Clark, K. D., & Klein, H. J. (2015). Dual commitments to organizations and professions: Different motivational pathways to productivity. *Journal of Management.* Advance online publication.

Bedau, M. (2002). Downward causation and the autonomy of weak emergence. *Principia, 6*(1), 5–50.

Behrendt, A., & Moritz, S. (2005). Posttraumatic stress disorder and memory problems after female genital mutilation. *American Journal of Psychiatry, 162*(5), 1000–1002.

Beitel, M., Ferrer, E., & Cecero, J. J. (2005). Psychological mindedness and awareness of self and others. *Journal of Clinical Psychology, 61*(6), 739–750.

Bell, R. Q., & Chapman, M. (1986). Child effects in studies using experimental or brief longitudinal approaches to socialization. *Developmental Psychology, 22*(5), 595–603.

Bem, D. J. (1967). Self-perception: An alternative interpretation of cognitive dissonance phenomena. *Psychological Review, 74*(3), 183–200.

Bem, D. J. (1972). Self-perception theory. In L. Berkowitz (Ed.), *Advances in experimental social psychology* (Vol. 6, pp. 1–62). New York: Academic Press.

Bemporad, J. R., Smith, H. F., Hanson, G., & Cicchetti, D. (1982). Borderline syndromes in childhood: Criteria for diagnosis. *American Journal of Psychiatry, 139*(5), 596–602.

Benita, M., Roth, G., & Deci, E. L. (2014). When are mastery goals more adaptive?: It depends on experiences of autonomy support and autonomy. *Journal of Educational Psychology, 106*(1), 258–267.

Benjamin, L. S. (2002). *Interpersonal diagnosis and treatment of personality disorders.* New York: Guilford Press.

Benware, C. A., & Deci, E. L. (1984). Quality of learning with an active versus passive motivational set. *American Educational Research Journal, 21*(4), 755–765.

Benyamini, Y., Idler, E. L., Leventhal, H., & Leventhal, E. A. (2000). Positive affect and function as influences on self-assessments of health: Expanding our view beyond illness and disability. *Journals of Gerontology, Series B: Psychological Sciences and Social Sciences, 55*(2), 107–116.

Berenson, K. R., & Andersen, S. M. (2006). Childhood physical and emotional abuse by a parent: Transference effects in adult interpersonal relations. *Personality and Social Psychology Bulletin, 33*(11), 1509–1522.

Bergson, H. (1911). *Creative evolution* (A. Mitchell, Trans.). New York: Holt.

Berlyne, D. E. (1967). Arousal and reinforcement. In D. Levine (Ed.), *Nebraska Symposium on Motivation* (Vol. 15, pp. 1–110). Lincoln: University of Nebraska Press.

Berlyne, D. E. (1971). *Aesthetics and psychobiology.* New York: Appleton Century Crofts.

Berlyne, D. E. (1973). The vicissitudes of aplopathematic and thelematoscopic pneumatology (or the hydrography of hedonism). In D. E. Berlyne & K. B. Madsen (Eds.), *Pleasure, reward, preference* (pp. 1–33). New York: Academic Press.

Bernheim, K. F., Rescorla, L., & Rocissano, L. (1999). *The Lanahan cases in developmental psychopathology.* Baltimore: Lanahan.

Bernier, A., Carlson, S. M., & Whipple, N. (2010). From external regulation to self-regulation: Early parenting precursors of young children's executive functioning. *Child Development, 81*(1), 326–339.

Bernier, A., Matte-Gagné, C., Bélanger, M.-È., & Whipple, N. (2014). Taking stock of two decades of attachment transmission gap: Broadening the assessment of maternal behavior. *Child Development, 85*(5), 1852–1865.

Bertalanffy, L. von. (1950). The theory of open systems in physics and biology. *Science, 111*(2872), 23–29.

Bertalanffy, L. von. (1968). *General system theory: Foundations, development, applications.* New York: Braziller.

Berzonsky, M. D. (1990). Self-construction over the life-span: A process perspective on identity formation. In G. J. Neimeyer & R. A. Neimeyer (Eds.), *Advances in personal construct psychology* (Vol. 1, pp. 155–186). Greenwich, CT: JAI.

Berzonsky, M. D. (2004). Identity style, parental authority, and identity commitment. *Journal of Youth and Adolescence, 33*(3), 213–220.

Bettelheim, B. (1982). *Freud and man's soul: An important re-interpretation of Freudian theory.* New York: Knopf.

Beyers, W., Goossens, L., Vansant, I., & Moors, E. (2003). A structural model of autonomy in middle and late adolescence: Connectedness, separation, detachment, and agency. *Journal of Youth and Adolescence, 32*(5), 351–365.

Bichat, X. (1822). *General anatomy, applied to physiology and medicine.* Boston: Richardson and Lord.

Biddle, S. J. H. (1999). Motivation and perceptions of control: Tracing its development and plotting its future in exercise and sport psychology. *Journal of Sport and Exercise Psychology, 21*(1), 1–23.

Biglan, A., Flay, B. R., Embry, D. D., & Sandler, I. N. (2012). The critical role of nurturing environments for promoting human well-being. *American Psychologist, 67*(4), 257–271.

Bindman, S. W., Pomerantz, E. M., & Roisman, G. I. (2015). Do children's executive functions account for associations between early autonomy-supportive parenting and achievement through high school? *Journal of Educational Psychology, 107*(3), 756–770.

Birk, M. V., Atkins, C., Bowey, J. T., & Mandryk, R. L. (2016). Fostering intrinsic motivation through avatar identification in digital games. *Proceedings of the SIGCHI Conference on Human Factors in Computing Systems, San Jose, CA.*

Bjelland, M., Soenens, B., Bere, E., Kovács, E., Lien, N., Maes, L., et al. (2015, October 1). Associations between parental rules, style of communication and children's screen time. *BMC Public Health, 15*(1002).

Black, A. E., & Deci, E. L. (2000). The effects of student self-regulation and instructor autonomy support on learning in a college-level natural science course: A self-determination theory perspective. *Science Education, 84*(6), 740–756.

Blais, M. R., Sabourin, S., Boucher, C., & Vallerand, R. J. (1990). Toward a motivational model of couple happiness. *Journal of Personality and Social Psychology, 59*(5), 1021–1031.

Blascovich, J., & Bailenson, J. (2011). *Infinite reality: Avatars, eternal life, new worlds, and the dawn of the virtual revolution.* New York: Morrow.

Blatt, S. J. (2004). *Experiences of depression: Theoretical, clinical, and research perspectives.* Washington, DC: American Psychological Association.

Blatt, S. J., Schaffer, C. E., Bers, S. A., & Quinlan, D. M. (1992). Psychometric properties of the Depressive Experiences Questionnaire for Adolescents. *Journal of Personality Assessment, 59*(1), 82–98.

Bleiberg, E. (2004). *Treating personality disorders in children and adolescents: A relational approach.* New York: Guilford Press.

Bloom, P. (2013). *Just babies: The origins of good and evil.* New York: Crown Random House.

Blos, P. (1979). *The adolescent passage: Developmental issues.* New York: International Universities Press.

Blustein, D. L. (1989). The role of goal instability and career self-efficacy in the career exploration process. *Journal of Vocational Behavior, 35*(2), 194–203.

Bober, S., & Grolnick, W. S. (1995). Motivational factors related to differences in self-schemas. *Motivation and Emotion, 19*(4), 307–327.

Bock, L. (2015). *Work rules!: Insights from inside Google that will transform how you live and lead.* New York: Grand Central.

Boehm, C. (2012). *Moral origins: The evolution of virtue, altruism, and shame.* New York: Basic Books.

Boekaerts, M., & Boscolo, P. (2002). Interest in learning, learning to be interested. *Learning and Instruction, 12*(4), 375–382.

Boggiano, A. K., & Ruble, D. N. (1979). Competence and the overjustification effect: A developmental study. *Journal of Personality and Social Psychology, 37*(9), 1462–1468.

Bono, J. E., & Judge, T. A. (2003). Self-concordance at work: Toward understanding the motivational effects of transformational leaders. *Academy of Management Journal, 46*(5), 554–571.

Boone, L., Vansteenkiste, M., Soenens, B., Van der Kaap-Deeder, J., & Verstuyf, J. (2014). Self-critical perfectionism and binge eating symptoms: A longitudinal test of the intervening role of psychological need frustration. *Journal of Counseling Psychology, 61*(3), 363–373.

Bordin, E. S. (1979). The generalizability of the psychoanalytic concept of the working alliance. *Psychotherapy: Theory, Research and Practice, 16*(3), 252–260.

Bouchard, G., Lee, C. M., Asgary, V., & Pelletier, L. (2007). Fathers' motivation for involvement with their children: A self-determination theory perspective. *Fathering: A Journal of Theory, Research, and Practice about Men as Fathers, 5*(1), 25–41.

Bowlby, J. (1969). *Attachment and loss.* New York: Pimlico.

Bowlby, J. (1973). Self-reliance and some conditions that promote it. In R. Gosling (Eds.), *Support, innovation, and autonomy* (pp. 23–48). London: Tavistock.

Bowlby, J. (1979). *The making and breaking of affectional bonds.* London: Tavistock.

Bowlby, J. (1988). *A secure base: Clinical applications of attachment theory.* Oxford, UK: Psychology Press.

Brambilla, M., Assor, A., Manzi, C., & Regalia, C. (2015). Autonomous versus controlled religiosity: Family and group antecedents. *International Journal for the Psychology of Religion, 25*(3), 193–210.

Braybrooke, D. (1987). *Meeting needs.* Princeton, NJ: Princeton University Press.

Breitborde, N. J. K., Kleinlein, P., & Srihari, V. H. (2012). Self-determination and first-episode psychosis: Associations with symptomatology, social and vocational functioning, and quality of life. *Schizophrenia Research, 137*(1), 132–136.

Breland, K., & Breland, M. (1961). The misbehavior of organisms. *American Psychologist, 16*(11), 681–684.

Brenman, L., Walkley, J., Fraser, S., Greenway, K., & Wilks, R. (2008). Motivational interviewing and cognitive behaviour therapy in the treatment of adolescent overweight and obesity: Study design and methodology. *Contemporary Clinical Trials, 29*(3), 359–375.

Brentano, F. (1973). *Psychology from an empirical standpoint* (L. L. MacAlister, Trans.). New York: Routledge.

Bretherton, I. (1987). New perspectives on attachment relations: Security, communication and internal working models. In J. Osofsky (Ed.),

Handbook of infant development (pp. 1061–1100). New York: Wiley.

Bretherton, I., & Munholland, K. A. (1999). Internal working models in attachment relationships: A construct revisited. In J. Cassidy & P. Shaver (Eds.), *Handbook of attachment: Theory, research, and clinical applications* (pp. 89–111). New York: Guilford Press.

Breuer, J., & Freud, S. (1955). Studies on hysteria. In J. Strachey (Ed. & Trans.), *The standard edition of the complete psychological works of Sigmund Freud* (Vol. 2, pp. 1–311). London: Hogarth Press. (Original work published 1893–1895)

Bridges, L., Frodi, A., Grolnick, W. S., & Spiegel, N. H. (1983). *Mothers' styles and mother–infant attachment patterns.* Unpublished manuscript, University of Rochester, Rochester, NY.

Britton, P. C., Van Orden, K. A., Hirsch, J. K., & Williams, G. C. (2014). Basic psychological needs, suicidal ideation, and risk for suicidal behavior in young adults. *Suicide and Life-Threatening Behavior, 44*(4), 362–371.

Brody, S. (1956). *Patterns of mothering: Maternal influence during infancy.* New York: International Universities Press.

Bronson, M. B. (2000). *Self-regulation in early childhood: Nature and nurture.* New York: Guilford Press.

Brooks, C. V. W. (1974). *Sensory awareness: The rediscovery of experiencing.* New York: Viking Press.

Brown, J. S. (1961). *The motivation of behavior.* New York: McGraw-Hill.

Brown, K. W., & Kasser, T. (2005). Are psychological and ecological well-being compatible?: The role of values, mindfulness, and lifestyle. *Social Indicators Research, 74*(2), 349–368.

Brown, K. W., Kasser, T., Ryan, R. M., Linley, A. P., & Orzech, K. (2009). When what one has is enough: Mindfulness, financial desire discrepancy, and subjective well-being. *Journal of Research in Personality, 43*(5), 727–736.

Brown, K. W., & Ryan, R. M. (2003). The benefits of being present: Mindfulness and its role in psychological well-being. *Journal of Personality and Social Psychology, 84*(4), 822–848.

Brown, K. W., & Ryan, R. M. (2004). Fostering healthy self-regulation from within and without: A self-determination theory perspective. In A. P. Linley & S. Joseph (Eds.), *Positive psychology in practice* (pp. 105–124). Hoboken, NJ: Wiley.

Brown, K. W., Ryan, R. M., & Creswell, J. D. (2007). Mindfulness: Theoretical foundations and evidence for its salutary effects. *Psychological Inquiry, 18*(4), 211–237.

Brown, K. W., Ryan, R. M., Creswell, J. D., & Niemiec, C. P. (2008). Beyond me: Mindful responses to social threat. In H. A. Wayment & J. J. Bauer (Eds.), *Transcending self-interest: Psychological explorations of the quiet ego* (pp. 75–84). Washington, DC: American Psychological Association.

Brown, S. (2009). *Play: How it shapes the brain, opens the imagination, and invigorates the soul.* New York: Penguin.

Browning, C. R. (1998a). *Ordinary men: Reserve Police Battalion 101 and the final solution in Poland.* New York: HarperCollins.

Browning, C. R. (1998b). Ordinary Germans or ordinary men?: A reply to the critics. In M. Berenbaum & A. J. Peck (Eds.), *The Holocaust and history: The known, the unknown, the disputed, and the reexamined* (pp. 252–265). Bloomington: Indiana University Press.

Bruch, H. (1973). *Eating disorders: Obesity, anorexia nervosa, and the person within.* New York: Basic Books.

Bruch, H. (1978). *The golden cage: The enigma of anorexia nervosa.* Cambridge, MA: Harvard University Press.

Brunet, J., Gunnell, K. E., Gaudreau, P., & Sabiston, C. M. (2015). An integrative analytical framework for understanding the effects of autonomous and controlled motivation. *Personality and Individual Differences, 84*, 2–15.

Brunetti, A., & Weder, B. (2003). A free press is bad news for corruption. *Journal of Public Economics, 87*(7), 1801–1824.

Buber, M. (1970). *I and thou* (2nd ed.) (R. G. Smith, Trans.). New York: Scribner.

Buckner, J. D., & Schmidt, N. B. (2009). A randomized pilot study of motivation enhancement therapy to increase utilization of cognitive-behavioral therapy for social anxiety. *Behaviour Research and Therapy, 47*(8), 710–715.

Buman, M., Giacobbi, P., Dzierzewski, J., Morgan, A., McCrae, C., Roberts, B., et al. (2011). Peer volunteers improve long-term maintenance of physical activity with older adults: A randomized controlled trial. *Journal of Physical Activity and Health, 8*, S257–S266.

Bureau, J., & Mageau, G. A. (2014). Parental autonomy support and honesty: The mediating role of identification with the honesty value and perceived costs and benefits of honesty. *Journal of Adolescence, 37*, 225–236.

Burgers, C., Eden, A., Van Engelenburg, M. D., & Buningh, S. (2015). How feedback boosts motivation and play in a brain-training game. *Computers in Human Behavior, 48*, 94–103.

Burnette, M. L., & Cicchetti, D. (2012). Multilevel approaches toward understanding antisocial behavior: Current research and future directions. *Development and Psychopathology, 24*(3), 703–704.

Burns, J. M. (1978). *Leadership.* New York: Harper & Row.

Burton, K. D., Lydon, J. E., D'Alessandro, D. U., & Koestner, R. (2006). The differential effects of intrinsic and identified motivation on well-being and performance: Prospective, experimental, and implicit approaches to self-determination theory. *Journal of Personality and Social Psychology, 91*(4), 750–762.

Busch, F. (1995). *The ego at the center of clinical technique.* Lanham, MD: Aronson.

Buss, D. M. (1991). Evolutionary personality psychology. *Annual Review of Psychology, 42,* 459–491.

Butler, R. (1987). Task-involving and ego-involving properties of evaluation: Effects of different feedback conditions on motivational perceptions, interest, and performance. *Journal of Educational Psychology, 79*(4), 474–482.

Butler, R. A. (1953). Discrimination learning by rhesus monkeys to visual-exploration motivation. *Journal of Comparative and Physiological Psychology, 46*(2), 95–98.

Byrne, B. M. (2001). Structural equation modeling with AMOS, EQS, and LISREL: Comparative approaches to testing for the factorial validity of a measuring instrument. *International Journal of Testing, 1*(1), 55–87.

Calder, B. J., & Staw, B. M. (1975). Self-perception of intrinsic and extrinsic motivation. *Journal of Personality and Social Psychology, 31*(4), 599–605.

Calvo, R. A., & Peters, D. (2014). *Positive computing: Technology for wellbeing and human potential.* Cambridge, MA: MIT Press.

Calvo, R. A., Vella-Brodrick, D., Desmet, P., & Ryan, R. M. (2016). Editorial for "Positive computing: A new partnership between psychology, social sciences and technologists." *Psychology of Well-Being, 6,* 10.

Calvo, T. G., Cervelló, E., Jiménez, R., Iglesias, D., & Murcia, J. A. M. (2010). Using self-determination theory to explain sport persistence and dropout in adolescent athletes. *Spanish Journal of Psychology, 13*(2), 677–684.

Cameron, J., & Pierce, W. D. (1994). Reinforcement, reward, and intrinsic motivation: A meta-analysis. *Review of Educational Research, 64*(3), 363–423.

Campanhã, C., Minati, L., Fregni, F., & Boggio, P. S. (2011). Responding to unfair offers made by a friend: Neuroelectrical activity changes in the anterior medial prefrontal cortex. *Journal of Neuroscience, 31*(43), 15569–15574.

Carcone, A. I., Naar-King, S., Brogan, K., Albrecht, T., Barton, E., Foster, T., et al. (2013). Provider communication behaviors that predict motivation to change in black adolescents with obesity. *Journal of Developmental and Behavioral Pediatrics, 34,* 599–608.

Carpentier, J., & Mageau, G. A. (2013). When change-oriented feedback enhances motivation, well-being and performance: A look at autonomy-supportive feedback in sport. *Psychology of Sport and Exercise, 14*(3), 423–435.

Carroll, P. J., Arkin, R. M., Seidel, S. D., & Morris, J. (2009). The relative importance of needs among traumatized and non-traumatized samples. *Motivation and Emotion, 33*(4), 373–386.

Carter, E. C., Kofler, L. M., Forster, D. E., & McCullough, M. E. (2015). A series of meta-analytic tests of the depletion effect: Self-control does not seem to rely on a limited resource. *Journal of Experimental Psychology, 144*(4), 796–815.

Carter, J. C., & Kelly, A. C. (2015). Autonomous and controlled motivation for eating disorders treatment: Baseline predictors and relationship to treatment outcome. *British Journal of Clinical Psychology, 54*(1), 76–90.

Carter, T. J., & Gilovich, T. (2012). I am what I do, not what I have: The differential centrality of experiential and material purchases to the self. *Journal of Personality and Social Psychology, 102*(6), 1304–1317.

Carton, J. S. (1996). The differential effects of tangible rewards and praise on intrinsic motivation: A comparison of cognitive evaluation theory and operant theory. *Behavior Analyst, 19*(2), 237–255.

Carver, C. S., & Baird, E. (1998). The American dream revisited: Is it what you want or why you want it that matters? *Psychological Science, 9*(4), 289–292.

Carver, C. S., & Scheier, M. F. (1981). *Attention and self-regulation: A control-theory approach to human behavior.* New York: Springer-Verlag.

Case, R., & Okamoto, Y. (1996). *The role of central conceptual structures in the development of children's thought.* Hoboken, NJ: Wiley Blackwell.

Catania, A. C. (2013). A natural science of behavior. *Review of General Psychology, 17*(2), 133–139.

Caza, A., McCarter, M. W., & Northcraft, G. B. (2015). Performance benefits of reward choice: A procedural justice perspective. *Human Resource Management Journal, 25*(2), 184–199.

Cerasoli, C. P., Nicklin, J. M., & Ford, M. T. (2014). Intrinsic motivation and extrinsic incentives jointly predict performance: A 40-year meta-analysis. *Psychological Bulletin, 140*(4), 980–1008.

Chak, K., & Leung, L. (2004). Shyness and locus of control as predictors of Internet addiction and Internet use. *Cyberpsychology and Behavior, 7*(5), 559–570.

Chan, D. K., Lonsdale, C., Ho, P. Y., Yung, P. S., & Chan, K. M. (2009). Patient motivation and adherence to postsurgery rehabilitation exercise recommendations: The influence of physiotherapists' autonomy-supportive behaviors. *Archives of Physical Medicine and Rehabilitation, 90*(12), 1977–1982.

Chandler, C. L., & Connell, J. P. (1987). Children's intrinsic, extrinsic and internalized motivation:

A developmental study of children's reasons for liked and disliked behaviours. *British Journal of Developmental Psychology, 5*(4), 357–365.

Chandler, M. J., & Chapman, M. (1991). *Criteria for competence: Controversies in the conceptualization and assessment of children's abilities.* Hillsdale, NJ: Erlbaum.

Chang, L.-C. (2012). An interaction effect of leisure self-determination and leisure competence on older adults' self-rated health. *Journal of Health Psychology, 17*(3), 324–332.

Chao, R. K., & Aque, C. (2009). Interpretations of parental control by Asian immigrant and European American youth. *Journal of Family Psychology, 23*(3), 342–354.

Chatzisarantis, N. L. D., Biddle, S. J. H., & Meek, G. A. (1997). A self-determination theory approach to the study of intentions and the intention–behaviour relationship in children's physical activity. *British Journal of Health Psychology, 2*(4), 343–360.

Chatzisarantis, N. L. D., Hagger, M. S., Biddle, S. J. H., Smith, B., & Wang, J. C. K. (2003). A meta-analysis of perceived locus of causality in exercise, sport, and physical education contexts. *Journal of Sport and Exercise Psychology, 25*(3), 284–306.

Chemolli, E., & Gagné, M. (2014). Evidence against the continuum structure underlying motivation measures derived from self-determination theory. *Psychological Assessment, 26*(2), 575–585.

Chen, B., Van Assche, J., Vansteenkiste, M., Soenens, B., & Beyers, W. (2015). Does psychological need satisfaction matter when environmental or financial safety are at risk? *Journal of Happiness Studies, 16*(3), 745–766.

Chen, B., Vansteenkiste, M., Beyers, W., Boone, L., Deci, E. L., Van der Kaap-Deeder, J., et al. (2015). Basic psychological need satisfaction, need frustration, and need strength across four cultures. *Motivation and Emotion, 39*(2), 216–236.

Chen, B., Vansteenkiste, M., Beyers, W., Soenens, B., & Van Petegem, S. (2013). Autonomy in family decision making for Chinese adolescents: Disentangling the dual meaning of autonomy. *Journal of Cross-Cultural Psychology, 44*(7), 1184–1209.

Chen, X. (2014). The ethics of self: Another version of Confucian ethics. *Asian Philosophy, 24*(1), 67–81.

Cheng, C.-Y. (2004). A theory of Confucian selfhood: Self-cultivation and free will in Confucian philosophy. In K.-L. Shun & D. B. Wong (Eds.), *Confucian ethics: A comparative study of self, autonomy, and community* (pp. 124–147). Cambridge, UK: Cambridge University Press.

Cheng, R. W. Y., Shu, T. M., Zhou, N., & Lam, S. F. (2016). Motivation of Chinese learners: An integration of etic and emic approaches. In R. B. King & A. B. I. Bernardo (Eds.), *The psychology of Asian learners* (pp. 355–368). Singapore: Springer.

Cheon, S. H., & Reeve, J. (2013). Do the benefits from autonomy-supportive PE teacher training programs endure?: A one-year follow-up investigation. *Psychology of Sport and Exercise, 14*(4), 508–518.

Cheon, S. H., Reeve, J., Lee, J. W., & Lee, Y. S. (2015). Giving and receiving autonomy support in a high-stakes sport context: A field-based experiment during the 2012 London Paralympic Games. *Psychology of Sport and Exercise, 19*, 59–69.

Cheon, S. H., Reeve, J., & Moon, I. S. (2012). Experimentally based, longitudinally designed, teacher-focused intervention to help physical education teachers be more autonomy supportive toward their students. *Journal of Sport and Exercise Psychology, 34*(3), 365–396.

Chernyak, N., & Kushnir, T. (2013). Giving preschoolers choice increases sharing behavior. *Psychological Science, 24*(10), 1971–1979.

Chettiar, C. (2015). A study on need satisfactions, causality, orientations and subjective well-being. *Indian Journal of Mental Health, 2*(1), 48–55.

Cheung, C. S.-S., & Pomerantz, E. M. (2011). Parents' involvement in children's learning in the United States and China: Implications for children's academic and emotional adjustment. *Child Development, 82*(3), 932–950.

Cheung, F., & Lucas, R. E. (2016). Income inequality is associated with stronger social comparison effects: The effect of relative income on life satisfaction. *Journal of Personality and Social Psychology, 110*(2), 332–341.

Chirkov, V. I., & Ryan, R. M. (2001). Parent and teacher autonomy-support in Russian and U.S. adolescents: Common effects on well-being and academic motivation. *Journal of Cross-Cultural Psychology, 32*(5), 618–635.

Chirkov, V. I., Ryan, R. M., Kim, Y., & Kaplan, U. (2003). Differentiating autonomy from individualism and independence: A self-determination theory perspective on internalization of cultural orientations and well-being. *Journal of Personality and Social Psychology, 84*(1), 97–110.

Chirkov, V. I., Ryan, R. M., & Willness, C. (2005). Cultural context and psychological needs in Canada and Brazil: Testing a self-determination approach to the internalization of cultural practices, identity, and well-being. *Journal of Cross-Cultural Psychology, 36*(4), 423–443.

Chirkov, V. I., Sheldon, K. M., & Ryan, R. M. (2011). Introduction: The struggle for happiness and autonomy in cultural and personal contexts: An overview. In V. I. Chirkov, R. M. Ryan, & K. M. Sheldon (Eds.), *Human autonomy in cross-cultural context: Perspectives on the psychology* of agency, freedom, and well-being (pp. 1–32). New York: Springer.

Chong, K.-C. (2003). Autonomy in the Analects. In K.-C. Chong, S.-H. Tan, & C. L. Ten (Eds.), *The moral circle and the self: Chinese and western approaches* (pp. 269–282). Chicago: Open Court.

Christie, R., & Geis, F. L. (1970). *Studies in Machiavellianism.* Cambridge, MA: Academic Press.

Christopher, J. C., & Hickinbottom, S. (2008). Positive psychology, ethnocentrism, and the disguised ideology of individualism. *Theory and Psychology, 18*(5), 563–589.

Chua, A. (2011). *Battle hymn of the tiger mother.* New York: Penguin Press.

Chua, S. N., & Philippe, F. L. (2015). Autonomy supportive fathers beget system-supporting children: The role of autonomy support on protesting behavior. *Personality and Individual Differences, 86,* 348–353.

Church, A. T., Katigbak, M. S., Ching, C. M., Zhang, H., Shen, J., Arias, R. M., et al. (2013). Within-individual variability in self-concepts and personality states: Applying density distribution and situation-behavior approaches across cultures. *Journal of Research in Personality, 47*(6), 922–935.

Church, A. T., Katigbak, M. S., Locke, K. D., Zhang, H., Shen, J., de Jesus Vargas-Flores, J., et al. (2013). Need satisfaction and well-being: Testing self-determination theory in eight cultures. *Journal of Cross-Cultural Psychology, 44*(4), 507–534.

Cicchetti, D. (2006). Development and psychopathology. In D. Cicchetti & D. J. Cohen (Eds.), *Developmental psychopathology: Theory and method* (2nd ed., pp. 1–24). New York: Wiley.

Cicchetti, D. (2016). Socioemotional, personality, and biological development: Illustrations from a multilevel developmental psychopathology perspective on child maltreatment. *Annual Review of Psychology, 67,* 187–211.

Cicchetti, D., & Rogosch, F. A. (1996). Equifinality and multifinality in developmental psychopathology. *Development and Psychopathology, 8*(4), 597–600.

Cicchetti, D., & Toth, S. L. (2007). Developmental psychopathology and preventive intervention: Child psychology in practice. In W. Dahom & R. M. Lerner (Eds.), *Handbook of child psychology* (pp. 497–547). Hoboken, NJ: Wiley.

Cicchetti, D., & Toth, S. L. (2009). The past achievements and future promises of developmental psychopathology: The coming of age of a discipline. *Journal of Child Psychology and Psychiatry, 50*(1–2), 16–25.

Clark, M. S., & Mills, J. R. (2011). A theory of communal (and exchange) relationships. In P. A. M. Van Lange, A. W. Kruglanski, & E. T. Higgins (Eds.), *Handbook of theories of social psychology* (pp. 232–250). Thousands Oaks, CA: Sage.

Clark, N., & Scott, P. S. (2009). *Game addiction: The experience and the effects.* Jefferson, NC: McFarland.

Clayton, B. C. (2014). Shared vision and autonomous motivation vs. financial incentives driving success in corporate acquisitions. *Frontiers in Psychology, 5,* 77–96.

Code, L. (1991). *What can she know?: Feminist theory and the construction of knowledge.* Ithaca, NY: Cornell University Press.

Cohen, S., Alper, C. M., Doyle, W. J., Treanor, J. J., & Turner, R. B. (2006). Positive emotional style predicts resistance to illness after experimental exposure to Rhinovirus or Influenza A Virus. *Psychosomatic Medicine, 68*(6), 809–815.

Coie, J. D., & Jacobs, M. R. (1993). The role of social context in the prevention of conduct disorder. *Development and Psychopathology, 5*(1–2), 263–275.

Collins, P. H. (1991). *Black feminist thought: Knowledge, consciousness, and the politics of empowerment.* New York: Routledge.

Colquitt, J. A., & Greenberg, J. (2003). Organizational justice: A fair assessment of the state of the literature. In J. Greenberg (Ed.), *Organizational behavior: The state of the science* (pp. 165–210). Mahwah, NJ: Erlbaum.

Conger, R. D., Patterson, G. R., & Ge, X. (1995). It takes two to replicate: A meditational model for the impact of parents' stress on adolescent adjustment. *Child Development, 66*(1), 80–97.

Cooley, C. H. (1902). *Human nature and the social order.* New York: Scribner.

Cooper, M. J., Gulen, H., & Rau, P. R. (2014). Performance for pay? The relation between CEO incentive compensation and future stock price performance. *Social Science Research Network.* Available at *http://papers.ssrn.com/sol3/papers.cfm?abstract_id=1572085.*

Cooper, S., Lavaysse, L. M., & Gard, D. E. (2015). Assessing motivation orientations in schizophrenia: Scale development and validation. *Psychiatry Research, 225*(1), 70–78.

Cordeiro, P., Paixão, P., Lens, W., Lacante, M., & Sheldon, K. (2016). Factor structure and dimensionality of the balanced measure of psychological needs among Portuguese high school students: Relations to well-being and ill-being. *Learning and Individual Differences, 47,* 51–60.

Cordova, D. I., & Lepper, M. R. (1996). Intrinsic motivation and the process of learning: Beneficial effects of contextualization, personalization, and choice. *Journal of Educational Psychology, 88*(4), 715–730.

Corradi-Dell'Acqua, C., Civai, C., Rumiati, R. I., & Fink, G. R. (2013). Disentangling self-and fairness-related neural mechanisms involved in the ultimatum game: An fMRI study. *Social Cognitive and Affective Neuroscience, 8*(4), 424–431.

Costa, P. T., & McCrae, R. R. (1985). *The NEO Personality Inventory manual.* Lutz, FL: Psychological Assessment Resources.

Costa, P. T., & McCrae, R. R. (1992). The five-factor model of personality and its relevance to personality disorders. *Journal of Personality Disorders, 6*(4), 343–359.

Costa, S., Ntoumanis, N., & Bartholomew, K. J. (2015). Predicting the brighter and darker sides of interpersonal relationships: Does psychological need thwarting matter? *Motivation and Emotion, 39*(1), 11–24.

Costa, S., Soenens, B., Gugliandolo, M. C., Cuzzocrea, F., & Larcan, R. (2015). The mediating role of experiences of need satisfaction in associations between parental psychological control and internalizing problems: A study among Italian college students. *Journal of Child and Family Studies, 24*(4), 1106–1116.

Cozzolino, P. J., Staples, A. D., Meyers, L. S., & Samboceti, J. (2004). Greed, death, and values: From terror management to transcendence management theory. *Personality and Social Psychology Bulletin, 30*(3), 278–292.

Craven, R. G., Ryan, R. M, Mooney, J., Vallerand, R. J., Dillon, A., Blacklock, F., et al. (2016). Toward a positive psychology of indigenous thriving and reciprocal research partnership model. *Contemporary Educational Psychology.* Advance online publication.

Creswell, J. D., Way, B. M., Eisenberger, N. I., & Liberman, M. D. (2007). Neural correlates of dispositional mindfulness during affect labeling. *Psychosomatic Medicine, 69*(6), 560–565.

Crocker, J. (2008). From egosystem to ecosystem: Implications for relationships, learning, and well-being. In H. A. Wayment & J. J. Bauer (Eds.), *Transcending self-interest: Psychological explorations of the quiet ego* (pp. 63–72). Washington, DC: American Psychological Association.

Cronin, D. L., & Allen, J. B. (2015). Developmental experiences and well-being in sport: The importance of the coaching climate. *Sport Psychologist, 29*(1), 62–71.

Cronin, K. A., Acheson, D. J., Hernández, P., & Sánchez, A. (2015). Hierarchy is detrimental for human cooperation. *Scientific Reports, 5.* Available at *www.nature.com/articles/srep18634.*

Cross, S. E., Gore, J. S., & Morris, M. L. (2003). The relational-interdependent self-construal, self-concept consistency, and well-being. *Journal of Personality and Social Psychology, 85*(5), 933–944.

Cross, S. E., Morris, M. L., & Gore, J. S. (2002). Thinking about oneself and others: The relational-interdependent self-construal and social cognition. *Journal of Personality and Social Psychology, 82*(3), 399–418.

Csikszentmihalyi, M. (1975). *Beyond boredom and anxiety.* San Francisco: Jossey-Bass.

Csikszentmihalyi, M. (1990). *Flow: The psychology of optimal experience.* New York: Harper & Row.

Csikszentmihalyi, M., Abuhamdeh, S., & Nakamura, J. (2005). Flow. In A. J. Elliot & C. S. Dweck (Eds.), *Handbook of competence* (pp. 598–608). New York: Guilford Press.

Cumming, S. P., Smoll, F. L., Smith, R. E., & Grossbard, J. R. (2007). Is winning everything? The relative contributions of motivational climate and won–lost percentage in youth sports. *Journal of Applied Sport Psychology, 19*(3), 322–336.

Curran, T., Hill, A. P., Hall, H. K., & Jowett, G. E. (2014). Perceived coach behaviors and athletes' engagement and disaffection in youth sport: The mediating role of the psychological needs. *International Journal of Sport Psychology, 45*(6), 559–580.

Curran, T., Hill, A. P., & Niemiec, C. P. (2013). A conditional process model of children's behavioral engagement and behavioral disaffection in sport based on self-determination theory. *Journal of Sport and Exercise Psychology, 35*(1), 30–43.

Curren, R. R. (2000). *Aristotle on the necessity of public education.* Lanham, MD: Rowman & Littlefield.

Curren, R. R. (2009). Education as a social right in a diverse society. *Journal of Philosophy of Education, 43*(1), 45–56.

Curren, R. R. (2013). Aristotelian necessities. *The Good Society, 22*(2), 247–263.

Curry, S. J., Wagner, E. H., & Grothaus, L. C. (1991). Evaluation of intrinsic and extrinsic motivation interventions with a self-help smoking cessation program. *Journal of Consulting and Clinical Psychology, 59*(2), 318–324.

Custers, A. F., Westerhof, G. J., Kuin, Y., & Riksen-Walraven, M. (2010). Need fulfillment in caring relationships: Its relation with well-being of residents in somatic nursing homes. *Aging and Mental Health, 14*(6), 731–739.

D'Ailly, H. (2003). Children's autonomy and perceived control in learning: A model of motivation and achievement in Taiwan. *Journal of Educational Psychology, 95*(1), 84–96.

D'Angelo, M., Reid, R. D., & Pelletier, L. G. (2007). A model for exercise behavior change regulation in patients with heart disease. *Journal of Sport and Exercise Psychology, 29*(2), 208–224.

Damasio, A. (2006). Feelings of emotion and the self. *Annals of the New York Academy of Sciences, 1001,* 253–261.

Daniel, T. L., & Esser, J. K. (1980). Intrinsic motivation as influenced by rewards, task interest, and task structure. *Journal of Applied Psychology, 65*(5), 566–573.

Danner, F. W., & Lonky, E. (1981). A cognitive-developmental approach to the effects of rewards on intrinsic motivation. *Child Development, 52*(3), 1043–1052.

Darling, N., & Steinberg, L. (1993). Parenting style as context: An integrative model. *Psychological Bulletin, 113*(3), 487–496.

Davies, P. T., & Sturge-Apple, M. L. (2007). Advances in the formulation of emotional security theory: An ethologically based perspective. *Advances in Child Development and Behavior, 35,* 87–137.

Davis, W. E., Kelley, N. J., Kim, J., Tang, D., & Hicks, J. A. (2016). Motivating the academic mind: High-level construal of academic goals enhances goal meaningfulness, motivation, and self-concordance. *Motivation and Emotion, 40*(2), 193–202.

Dawkins, R. (1989). *The selfish gene.* New York: Oxford University Press.

Dean, A. L., & Youniss, J. (1991). The transformation of Piagetian theory by American psychology: The early competence issue. In M. Chapman & M. Chandler (Eds.), *Criteria for competence: Controversies in the conceptualization and assessment of children's abilities* (pp. 93–109). Hillsdale, NJ: Erlbaum.

DeCaro, D. A., Janssen, M. A., & Lee, A. (2015). Synergistic effects of voting and enforcement on internalized motivation to cooperate in a resource dilemma. *Judgment and Decision Making, 10*(6), 511–537.

DeCaro, D. A., & Stokes, M. K. (2008). Social–psychological principles of community-based conservation and conservancy motivation: Attaining goals within an autonomy-supportive environment. *Conservation Biology, 22*(6), 1443–1451.

DeCaro, D. A., & Stokes, M. K. (2013). Public participation and institutional fit: A social-psychological perspective. *Ecology and Society, 18*(4), 40.

Decety, J., & Jackson, P. L. (2004). The functional architecture of human empathy. *Behavioral and Cognitive Neuroscience Reviews, 3*(2), 71–100.

Decety, J., & Wheatley, T. (2015). *The moral brain: A multidisciplinary perspective.* Cambridge, MA: MIT Press.

de Charms, R. (1968). *Personal causation: The internal affective determinants of behavior.* New York: Academic Press.

de Charms, R. (1976). *Enhancing motivation: Change in the classroom.* New York: Irvington.

Deci, E. L. (1971). Effects of externally mediated rewards on intrinsic motivation. *Journal of Personality and Social Psychology, 18*(1), 105–115.

Deci, E. L. (1972a). The effects of contingent and non-contingent rewards and controls on intrinsic motivation. *Organizational Behavior and Human Performance, 8*(2), 217–229.

Deci, E. L. (1972b). Intrinsic motivation, extrinsic reinforcement, and inequity. *Journal of Personality and Social Psychology, 22*(1), 113–120.

Deci, E. L. (1975). *Intrinsic motivation.* New York: Plenum Press.

Deci, E. L. (1980). *The psychology of self-determination.* Lanham, MD: Lexington Books.

Deci, E. L. (1992). The relation of interest to the motivation of behavior: A self-determination theory perspective. In K. A. Renninger, S. Hidi, & A. Krapp (Eds.), *The role of interest in learning and development* (pp. 43–70). Hillsdale, NJ: Erlbaum.

Deci, E. L. (2009). Large-scale school reform as viewed from the self-determination theory perspective. *Theory and Research in Education, 7*(2), 244–253.

Deci, E. L., Betley, G., Kahle, J., Abrams, L., & Porac, J. (1981). When trying to win: Competition and intrinsic motivation. *Personality and Social Psychology Bulletin, 7*(1), 79–83.

Deci, E. L., & Cascio, W. F. (1972, June). *Changes in intrinsic motivation as a function of negative feedback and threats.* Paper presented at the meeting of the Eastern Psychological Association, Boston, MA.

Deci, E. L., Cascio, W. F., & Krusell, J. (1975). Cognitive evaluation theory and some comments on the Calder and Staw critique. *Journal of Personality and Social Psychology, 31*(1), 81–85.

Deci, E. L., Connell, J. P., & Ryan, R. M. (1989). Self-determination in a work organization. *Journal of Applied Psychology, 74*(4), 580–590.

Deci, E. L., Driver, R. E., Hotchkiss, L., Robbins, R. J., & Wilson, I. M. (1993). The relation of mothers' controlling vocalizations to children's intrinsic motivation. *Journal of Experimental Child Psychology, 55*(2), 151–162.

Deci, E. L., Eghrari, H., Patrick, B. C., & Leone, D. R. (1994). Facilitating internalization: The self-determination theory perspective. *Journal of Personality, 62*(1), 119–142.

Deci, E. L., Hodges, R., Pierson, L., & Tomassone, J. (1992). Autonomy and competence as motivational factors in students with learning disabilities and emotional handicaps. *Journal of Learning Disabilities, 25*(7), 457–471.

Deci, E. L., Koestner, R., & Ryan, R. M. (1999). A meta-analytic review of experiments examining the effects of extrinsic rewards on intrinsic motivation. *Psychological Bulletin, 125*(6), 627–668.

Deci, E. L., Koestner, R., & Ryan, R. M. (2001). Extrinsic rewards and intrinsic motivation in education: Reconsidered once again. *Review of Educational Research, 71*(1), 1–27.

Deci, E. L., La Guardia, J. G., Moller, A. C., Scheiner, M. J., & Ryan, R. M. (2006). On the benefits of giving as well as receiving autonomy support: Mutuality in close friendships. *Personality and Social Psychology Bulletin, 32*(3), 313–327.

Deci, E. L., & Moller, A. C. (2005). The concept of competence: A starting place for understanding intrinsic motivation and self-determined extrinsic motivation. In A. J. Elliot & C. S. Dweck (Eds.), *Handbook of competence and motivation* (pp. 579–597). New York: Guilford Press.

Deci, E. L., Nezlek, J., & Sheinman, L. (1981). Characteristics of the rewarder and intrinsic motivation of the rewardee. *Journal of Personality and Social Psychology, 40*(1), 1–10.

Deci, E. L., Olafsen, A. H., & Ryan, R. M. (2017). Self-Determination Theory in work organizations: The state of a science. *Annual Review of Organizational Psychology and Organizational Behavior.* Advance online publication.

Deci, E. L., & Ryan, R. M. (1980a). The empirical exploration of intrinsic motivational processes. In L. Berkowitz (Ed.), *Advances in experimental social psychology* (Vol. 13, pp. 39–80). New York: Academic Press.

Deci, E. L., & Ryan, R. M. (1980b). Self-determination theory: When mind mediates behavior. *Journal of Mind and Behavior, 1*(1), 33–43.

Deci, E. L., & Ryan, R. M. (1985a). The general causality orientations scale: Self-determination in personality. *Journal of Research in Personality, 19*(2), 109–134.

Deci, E. L., & Ryan, R. M. (1985b). *Intrinsic motivation and self-determination in human behavior.* New York: Plenum Press.

Deci, E. L., & Ryan, R. M. (1987). The support of autonomy and the control of behavior. *Journal of Personality and Social Psychology, 53*(6), 1024–1037.

Deci, E. L., & Ryan, R. M. (1991). A motivational approach to self: Integration in personality. In R. Dienstbier (Ed.), *Nebraska Symposium on Motivation: Vol. 38. Perspectives on motivation* (pp. 237–288). Lincoln: University of Nebraska Press.

Deci, E. L., & Ryan, R. M. (1995). Human autonomy: The basis for true self-esteem. In M. H. Kernis (Ed.), *Efficacy, agency, and self-esteem* (pp. 31–49). New York: Plenum.

Deci, E. L., & Ryan, R. M. (2000). The "what" and "why" of goal pursuits: Human needs and the self-determination of behavior. *Psychological Inquiry, 11*(4), 227–268.

Deci, E. L., & Ryan, R. M. (2008). Facilitating optimal motivation and psychological well-being across life's domains. *Canadian Psychology/Psychologie Canadienne, 49*(1), 14–23.

Deci, E. L., & Ryan, R. M. (2012). Motivation, personality, and development within embedded social contexts: An overview of self-determination theory. In R. M. Ryan (Ed.), *The Oxford handbook of human motivation* (pp. 85–107). Oxford, UK: Oxford University Press.

Deci, E. L., & Ryan, R. M. (2013a). The importance of autonomy for development and well-being. In B. W. Sokol, F. M. E. Grouzet, & U. Muller (Eds.), *Self-regulation and autonomy: Social and developmental dimensions of human conduct* (pp. 19–46). New York: Cambridge University Press.

Deci, E. L., & Ryan, R. M. (2013b). The ombudsman: Do CEOs' aspirations for wealth harm stockholders? *Interfaces, 43*(6), 593–595.

Deci, E. L., & Ryan, R. M. (2014a). Autonomy and need satisfaction in close relationships: Relationships motivation theory. In N. Weinstein (Ed.), *Human motivation and interpersonal relationships: Theory, research and applications* (pp. 53–73). Dordrecht, Netherlands: Springer.

Deci, E. L., & Ryan, R. M. (2014b). The importance of universal psychological needs for understanding motivation in the workplace. In M. Gagné (Ed.), *Oxford handbook of work engagement, motivation, and self-determination theory* (pp. 13–32). New York: Oxford University Press.

Deci, E. L., & Ryan, R. M. (2016). Optimizing students' motivation in the era of testing and pressure: A self-determination theory perspective. In W. C. Liu, J. C. K. Wang, & R. M. Ryan (Eds.), *Building autonomous learners: Perspectives from research and practice using self-determination theory* (pp. 9–29). New York: Springer.

Deci, E. L., Ryan, R. M., Gagné, M., Leone, D. R., Usunov, J., & Kornazheva, B. P. (2001). Need satisfaction, motivation, and well-being in the work organizations of a former Eastern Bloc country: A cross-cultural study of self-determination. *Personality and Social Psychology Bulletin, 27*(8), 930–942.

Deci, E. L., Ryan, R. M., Schultz, P. P., & Niemiec, C. P. (2015). Being aware and functioning fully: Mindfulness and interest-taking within self-determination theory. In K. W. Brown, J. D. Creswell, & R. M. Ryan (Eds.), *Handbook of mindfulness* (pp. 112–129). New York: Guilford Press.

Deci, E. L., Ryan, R. M., & Williams, G. C. (1996). Need satisfaction and the self-regulation of learning. *Learning and Individual Differences, 8*(3), 165–183.

Deci, E. L., Schwartz, A. J., Sheinman, L., & Ryan, R. M. (1981). An instrument to assess adults' orientations toward control versus autonomy with children: Reflections on intrinsic motivation and perceived competence. *Journal of Educational Psychology, 73*(5), 642–650.

Deci, E. L., Spiegel, N. H., Ryan, R. M., Koestner, R., & Kauffman, M. (1982). Effects of performance standards on teaching styles: Behavior of controlling teachers. *Journal of Educational Psychology, 74*(6), 852–859.

Deci, E. L., Weinstein, N., & Ryan, R. M. (2006, January). *Is meaning a basic need: Viewing it from the self-determination theory perspective.* Paper presented at the annual conference of the Society for Personality and Social Psychology, Palm Springs, CA.

Deckop, J. R., Jurkiewicz, C. L., & Giacalone, R. A. (2010). Effects of materialism on work-related personal well-being. *Human Relations, 63*(7), 1007–1030.

Deconinck, J., & Bachmann, D. (2007). The impact of equity sensitivity and pay fairness on marketing managers' job satisfaction, organizational commitment and turnover intentions. *Marketing Management Journal, 17*(2), 134–141.

DeHaan, C. R., Hirai, T., & Ryan, R. M. (2015, October). Nussbaum's capabilities and self-determination theory's basic psychological needs: Relating some fundamentals of human wellness. *Journal of Happiness Studies*, 1–13. Available at *http://link.springer.com/article/10.1007%2Fs10902-015-9684-y.*

Delle Fave, A. (2009). Optimal experience and meaning: Which relationship? *Psychological Topics, 18*(2), 285–302.

Demetriou, A., Efklides, A., & Platsidou, M. (1993). The architecture and dynamics of developing mind: Experiential structuralism as a frame for unifying cognitive developmental theories. *Monographs of the Society for Research in Child Development, 58*(5/6), 1–205.

De Meyer, J., Tallir, I. B., Soenens, B., Vansteenkiste, M., Aelterman, N., Van den Berghe, L., et al. (2014). Does observed controlling teaching behavior relate to students' motivation in physical education? *Journal of Educational Psychology, 106*(2), 541–554.

DeNeve, J.-E., & Powdthavee, N. (2016). Income inequality makes whole countries less happy. *Harvard Business Review*. Available at *https://hbr.org/2016/01/income-inequality-makes-whole-countries-less-happy.*

Dennett, D. C. (1991). *Consciousness explained.* Boston: Little, Brown.

DePasque, S., & Tricomi, E. (2015). Effects of intrinsic motivation on feedback processing during learning. *NeuroImage, 119*, 175–186.

Depue, R. A., & Lenzenweger, M. F. (2001). A neurobehavioral dimensional model. *Handbook of personality disorders* (pp. 136–176). New York: Guilford Press.

de Waal, F. (2008). Putting the altruism back into altruism: The evolution of empathy. *Annual Review of Psychology, 59*, 279–300.

de Waal, F. (2009). *The age of empathy: Nature's lessons for a kinder society.* New York: Crown Archetype.

Dewey, J. (1922). *Human nature and conduct: An introduction to social psychology.* New York: Henry Holt.

Dewey, J. (1938). *Experience and education.* New York: Macmillan.

De Young, R. (1996). Some psychological aspects of reduced consumption behavior: The role of intrinsic satisfaction and competence motivation. *Environment and Behavior, 28*(3), 358–409.

De Young, R. (2000). Expanding and evaluating motives for environmentally responsible behavior. *Journal of Social Issues, 56*(3), 509–526.

Diamond, J. (1997). *Guns, germs and steel: The fates of human societies.* New York: Vintage Press.

Diamond, J. (2012). *The world until yesterday: What can we learn from traditional societies?* New York: Penguin.

Diamond, L. (2015). Facing up to the democratic recession. *Journal of Democracy, 26*(1), 141–155.

Dickinson, A. M. (1989). The detrimental effects of extrinsic reinforcement on "intrinsic motivation." *Behavior Analyst, 12*(1), 1–15.

Di Domenico, S. I., & Fournier, M. A. (2014). Socioeconomic status, income inequality, and health complaints: A basic psychological needs perspective. *Social Indicators Research, 119*(3), 1679–1697.

Di Domenico, S. I., Fournier, M. A., Ayaz, H., & Ruocco, A. C. (2013). In search of integrative processes: Basic psychological need satisfaction predicts medial prefrontal activation during decisional conflict. *Journal of Experimental Psychology: General, 142*(3), 967–978.

Di Domenico, S. I., Le, A., Liu, Y., Ayaz, H., & Fournier, M. A. (2016). Basic psychological needs and neurophysiological responsiveness to decisional conflict: An event-related-potential study of integrative self processes. *Cognitive, Affective and Behavioral Neuroscience.* Advance online publication.

Di Domenico, S. I., & Ryan, R. M. (in press). Growth needs. In V. Zeigler-Hill & T. K. Shackelford (Eds.), *The encyclopedia of personality and individual differences.* New York: Springer.

Diener, E. (1994). Assessing subjective well-being: Progress and opportunities. *Social Indicators Research, 31*(2), 103–157.

Diener, E. (2000). Subjective well-being: The science of happiness and a proposal for a national index. *American Psychologist, 55*(1), 34–43.

Diener, E., Emmons, R. A., Larsen, R. J., & Griffin, S. (1985). The Satisfaction with Life Scale. *Journal of Personality Assessment, 49*(1), 71–75.

Diener, E., Inglehart, R., & Tay, L. (2012). Theory and validity of life satisfaction scales. *Social Indicators Research, 112*(3), 497–527.

Dietrich, E., & Markman, A. B. (2000). Cognitive dynamics: Computation and representation regained. In E. Dietrich & A. B. Markman (Eds.), *Cognitive dynamics* (pp. 5–29). Mahwah, NJ: Erlbaum.

Dillon, J. (2015). *Reframing bullying prevention to build stronger school communities.* Thousand Oaks, CA: Corwin Press.

Di Pietro, G., Valoroso, L., Fichele, M., Bruno, C., & Sorge, F. (2002). What happens to eating disorder outpatients who withdrew from therapy? *Eating and Weight Disorders: Studies on Anorexia, Bulimia and Obesity, 7*(4), 298–303.

Dittmar, H. (2005). Compulsive buying: A growing concern? An examination of gender, age, and endorsement of materialistic values as predictors. *British Journal of Psychology, 96*(4), 467–491.

Dittmar, H. (2007). The costs of consumer culture and the "cage within": The impact of the material "good life" and "body perfect" ideals on individuals' identity and well-being. *Psychological Inquiry, 18*(1), 23–31.

Dittmar, H. (2008). What is the price of consumer culture: Consequences, implications and the cage within. In H. Dittmar (Ed.) *Consumer culture, identity and well-being: The search for the "good life" and the "body perfect"* (pp. 199–222). New York: Psychology Press.

Dittmar, H., Bond, R., Hurst, M., & Kasser, T. (2014). The relationship between materialism and personal well-being: A meta-analysis. *Journal of Personality and Social Psychology, 107*(5), 879–924.

Dodge, K. A., Pettit, G. S., & Bates, J. E. (1994). Socialization mediators of the relation between socioeconomic status and child conduct problems. *Child Development, 65*(2), 649–665.

Doi, T. (1973). *The anatomy of dependence* (Vol. 101). Tokyo: Kodansha International.

Dollinger, S. J., & Thelen, M. H. (1978). Overjustification and children's intrinsic motivation: Comparative effects of four rewards. *Journal of Personality and Social Psychology, 36*(11), 1259–1269.

Dollinger, S. M. C. (1995). Identity styles and the five-factor model of personality. *Journal of Research in Personality, 29*(4), 475–479.

Dominguez, P. R., Gámiz, F., Gil, M., Moreno, H., Zanmora, R. M., Gallo, M., et al. (2013). Providing choice increases children's vegetable intake. *Food Quality and Preference, 30*(2), 108–113.

Donahue, E. G., Miquelon, P., Valois, P., Goulet, C., Buist, A., & Vallerand, R. J. (2006). A motivational model of performance-enhancing substance use in elite athletes. *Journal of Sport and Exercise Psychology, 28*(4), 511–520.

Doshi, N., & McGregor, L. (2015). *Primed to perform: How to build the highest performing cultures through the science of total motivation.* New York: HarperCollins.

Douvan, E., & Adelson, J. (1966). *The adolescent experience.* New York: Wiley.

Dover, M. A. (2016). Human needs: Overview. In C. Franklin (Ed.), *Encyclopedia of social work* (Electronic ed.). New York: Oxford University Press and National Association of Social Workers. Retrieved from *http://socialwork.oxfordre.com*.

Downie, M., Chua, S. N., Koestner, R., Barrios, M.-F., Rip, B., & M'Birkou, S. (2007). The relations of parental autonomy support to cultural internalization and well-being of immigrants and sojourners. *Cultural Diversity and Ethnic Minority Psychology, 13*(3), 241–249.

Downie, M., Koestner, R., & Chua, S. N. (2007). Political support for self-determination, wealth, and national subjective well-being. *Motivation and Emotion, 31*(3), 174–181.

Downie, M., Koestner, R., El Geledi, S., & Cree, K. (2004). The impact of cultural internalization and integration on well-being among tricultural individuals. *Personality and Social Psychology Bulletin, 30*(3), 305–314.

Downie, M., Mageau, G. A., & Koestner, R. (2008). What makes for a pleasant social interaction?: Motivational dynamics of interpersonal relations. *Journal of Social Psychology, 148*(5), 523–534.

Doyal, L., & Gough, I. (1991). *A theory of human need.* New York: Guilford Press.

Doyal, L., & Gough, I. (1993). Need satisfaction as a measure of human welfare. In W. Blaas & J. Foster (Eds.), *Mixed Economies in Europe: An evolutionary perspective on their emergence, transition and regulation* (pp. 178–199). Northampton, MA: Elgar.

Driesch, H. (1908). *The science and philosophy of the organism: The Gifford lectures delivered before the University of Aberdeen in the year 1907.* London: Black.

Dryden, W., & Branch, R. (2008). *Fundamentals of rational emotive behaviour therapy: A training handbook.* New York: Wiley.

Ducat, W., & Zimmer-Gembeck, M. (2007, May). *A model of romantic relationship quality, psychological need fulfillment, and well-being in emerging adulthood.* Poster presented at the third International Conference on Self-Determination Theory, Toronto, Ontario, Canada.

Duda, J. L. (1989). Goal perspectives, participation and persistence in sport. *International Journal of Sport Psychology, 20*(1), 42–56.

Duda, J. L., Chi, L., Newton, M. L., Walling, M. D., & Catley, D. (1995). Task and ego orientation and intrinsic motivation in sport. *International Journal of Sport Psychology, 26*(1), 40–63.

Duda, J. L., Papaioannou, A. G., Appleton, P. R., Quested, E. J., & Krommidas, C. (2014). Creating adaptive motivational climates in sport and physical activity. In A. G. Papaioannou & D. Hackfort (Eds.), *Routledge companion to sport and exercise psychology: Global perspectives and fundamental concepts* (pp. 544–558). New York: Routledge.

Dunbar, S. B., Clark, P. C., Reilly, C. M., Gary, R. A., Smith, A., McCarty, F., et al. (2013). A trial of family partnership and education interventions in heart failure. *Journal of Cardiac Failure, 19*(12), 829–841.

Duncan, L. R., Hall, C. R., Wilson, P. M., & Rodgers, W. M. (2012). The use of a mental imagery intervention to enhance integrated regulation for exercise among women commencing an exercise program. *Motivation and Emotion, 36*(4), 452–464.

Dunn, E. W., Aknin, L. B., & Norton, M. I. (2014). Prosocial spending and happiness: Using money to benefit others pays off. *Current Directions in Psychological Science, 23*(1), 41–47.

Duriez, B., Meeus, J., & Vansteenkiste, M. (2012). Why are some people more susceptible to ingroup threat than others? The importance of a relative extrinsic to intrinsic value orientation. *Journal of Research in Personality, 46*(2), 164–172.

Duriez, B., Soenens, B., & Beyers, W. (2004). Personality, identity styles, and religiosity: An integrative study among late adolescents in Flanders (Belgium). *Journal of Personality, 72*(5), 877–910.

Duriez, B., Soenens, B., & Vansteenkiste, M. (2007). In search of the antecedents of adolescent authoritarianism: The relative contribution of parental goal promotion and parenting style dimensions. *European Journal of Personality, 21*(4), 507–527.

Duriez, B., Vansteenkiste, M., Soenens, B., & De Witte, H. (2007). The social costs of extrinsic relative to intrinsic goal pursuits: Their relation with social dominance and racial and ethnic prejudice. *Journal of Personality, 75*(4), 757–782.

Duval, S., & Wicklund, R. A. (1972). *A theory of objective self awareness.* New York: Academic Press.

Dweck, C. S. (1986). Motivational processes affecting learning. *American Psychologist, 41*(10), 1040–1048.

Dweck, C. S. (2000). *Self theories: Their role in motivation, personality, and development.* Philadelphia: Psychology Press.

Dweck, C. S., & Leggett, E. L. (1988). A social-cognitive approach to motivation and personality. *Psychological Review, 95*(2), 256–273.

Dworkin, G. B. (1988). *The theory and practice of autonomy.* Cambridge, UK: Cambridge University Press.

Dwyer, L. A., Hornsey, M. J., Smith, L. G. E., Oei, T. P. S., & Dingle, G. A. (2011). Participant autonomy in cognitive-behavioral group therapy: An integration of self-determination and cognitive-behavioral theories. *Journal of Social and Clinical Psychology, 30*(1), 24–46.

Eagle, M. (1991). *Psychoanalytic conceptions of the self.* New York: Springer Verlag.

Early, D. M., Berg, J. K., Alicea, S., Si, Y., Aber, J. L., Ryan, R. M., et al. (2016). The impact of every classroom, every day on high school student achievement: Results from a school-randomized trial. *Journal of Research on Educational Effectiveness, 9*(1), 3–29.

Early, D. M., Rogge, R. D., & Deci, E. L. (2014). Engagement, alignment, and rigor as vital signs of high-quality instruction: A classroom visit protocol for instructional improvement and research. *High School Journal, 97*, 219–239.

Easterbrook, M. J., Wright, M. L., Dittmar, H., & Banerjee, R. (2014). Consumer culture ideals, extrinsic motivations, and well-being in children. *European Journal of Social Psychology, 44*(4), 349–359.

Edelman, G. M. (1992). *Bright air, brilliant fire: On the matter of the mind.* New York: Basic Books.

Edmunds, J., Ntoumanis, N., & Duda, J. L. (2006). A test of self-determination theory in the exercise domain. *Journal of Applied Social Psychology, 36*(9), 2240–2265.

Edmunds, J., Ntoumanis, N., & Duda, J. L. (2008). Testing a self-determination-theory-based teaching style in the exercise domain. *European Journal of Social Psychology, 38*(2), 375–388.

Ehrlich, P. R. (2000). *Human natures: Genes, cultures, and the human prospect.* Washington, DC: Island Press.

Eisenberger, N. I., Lieberman, M. D., & Williams, K. D. (2003). Does rejection hurt?: An fMRI study of social exclusion. *Science, 302,* 290–292.

Eisenberger, R., & Cameron, J. (1996). Detrimental effects of reward: Reality or myth? *American Psychologist, 51*(11), 1153–1166.

Eisenberger, R., Pierce, W. D., & Cameron, J. (1999). Effects of reward on intrinsic motivation—negative, neutral, and positive: Comment on Deci, Koestner, and Ryan. *Psychological Bulletin, 125*(6), 677–691.

Elbadawi, E., & Sambanis, N. (2000). Why are there so many civil wars in Africa? Understanding and preventing violent conflict. *Journal of African Economies, 9*(3), 244–269.

Elkind, D. (1971). Cognitive growth cycles in mental development. In J. K. Cole (Ed.), *Nebraska Symposium on Motivation* (pp. 1–31). Lincoln: University of Nebraska.

Elkind, D. (1985). Egocentrism redux. *Developmental Review, 5*(3), 218–226.

Elliot, A. J. (1999). Approach and avoidance motivation and achievement goals. *Educational Psychologist, 34*(3), 169–189.

Elliot, A. J. (2005). A conceptual history of the achievement goal construct. In A. Elliot & C. Dweck (Eds.), *Handbook of competence and motivation* (pp. 52–72). New York: Guilford Press.

Elliot, A. J., & McGregor, H. A. (2001). A 2 X 2 achievement goal framework. *Journal of Personality and Social Psychology, 80*(3), 501–519.

Elliot, A. J., McGregor, H. A., & Thrash, T. M. (2002). The need for competence. In E. L. Deci & R. M. Ryan (Eds.), *Handbook of self-determination research* (pp. 361–387). Rochester, NY: University of Rochester Press.

Elliott, R., Greenberg, L. S., & Lietaer, G. (2004). Research on experiential psychotherapies. In M. J. Lambert (Ed.), *Bergin and Garfield's handbook of psychotherapy and behavior change* (pp. 493–539). New York: Wiley.

Ellis, G. F. R. (2009). Top-down causation and the human brain. In N. Murphy, G. Ellis, & T. O'Connor (Eds.), *Downward causation and the neurobiology of free will* (pp. 63–81). Berlin: Springer Science & Business Media.

Elson, M., Breuer, J., & Quandt, T. (2014). Know thy player: An integrated model of player experience for digital games research. In M. C. Angelides & H. Agius (Eds.), *Handbook of digital games* (pp. 362–387). Hoboken, NJ: Wiley.

Elvins, R., & Green, J. (2008). The conceptualization and measurement of therapeutic alliance: An empirical review. *Clinical Psychology Review, 28*(7), 1167–1187.

Emery, A. A., Heath, N. L., & Mills, D. J. (2016). Basic psychological need satisfaction, emotion dysregulation, and non-suicidal self-injury engagement in young adults: An application of self-determination theory. *Journal of Youth and Adolescence, 45*(3), 612–623.

Emmons, R. A. (1986). Personal strivings: An approach to personality and subjective well-being. *Journal of Personality and Social Psychology, 51*(5), 1058–1068.

Engel, G. (1977). The need for a new medical model: A challenge for biomedicine. *Science, 196*(4286), 129–136.

Enns, M. W., Cox, B. J., & Clara, I. (2002). Adaptive and maladaptive perfectionism: Developmental origins and association with depression proneness. *Personality and Individual Differences, 33*(6), 921–935.

Enzle, M. E., & Anderson, S. C. (1993). Surveillant intentions and intrinsic motivation. *Journal of Personality and Social Psychology, 64*(2), 257–266.

Epstein, S. (1990). Cognitive–experiential self-theory. In L. Pervin (Ed.), *Handbook of personality: Theory and research* (pp. 165–192). New York: Guilford Press.

Erikson, E. H. (1950). *Childhood and society.* New York: Norton.

Erikson, E. H. (1959). *Identity and the life cycle: Selected papers.* New York: International Universities Press.

Erikson, E. H. (1994). *Identity and the life cycle.* New York: Norton.

Evans, P., & Bonneville-Roussy, A. (2015). Self-determined motivation for practice in university music students. *Psychology of Music.* Advance online publication.

Fabes, R. A., Moran, J. D., & McCullers, J. C. (1981). The hidden costs of reward and WAIS subscale performance. *American Journal of Psychology, 94*(3), 387–398.

Fairbairn, W. R. D. (1952). *Psychoanalytic studies of the personality.* London: Routledge.

Fairbairn, W. R. D. (1954). *An object relations theory of the personality.* New York: Basic Books.

Farkas, M. S., & Grolnick, W. S. (2010). Examining the components and concomitants of parental structure in the academic domain. *Motivation and Emotion, 34*(3), 266–279.

Farmer, R., & Sundberg, N. D. (1986). Boredom proneness: The development and correlates of a new scale. *Journal of Personality Assessment, 50*(1), 4–17.

Favazza, A. (1987). *Bodies under siege: Self-mutilation in culture and psychiatry.* Baltimore: Johns Hopkins University Press.

Feather, N. T. (1990) Bridging the gap between values and actions: Recent applications of the expectancy-value model. In E. T. Higgins, & R. M. Sorrentino (Eds.), *Handbook of motivation and cognition: Foundations of social behavior* (Vol. 2, pp. 151–192). New York: Guilford Press.

Fehr, E., & Fischbacher, U. (2004). Third-party punishment and social norms. *Evolution and Human Behavior, 25,* 63–87.

Feinberg, O., Kaplan, H., Assor, A., & Kanat-Maymon, Y. (2007, May). *The concept of "internalization" (based on SDT) as a guide for a school reform program.* Paper presented at the third International Conference on Self-Determination Theory, Toronto, Ontario, Canada.

Feldman Barrett, L., Cleveland, J., Conner, T., & Williams, N. L. (2000). *Manual for the Defensive Verbal Behavior Rating Scale (Version 3.0).* Unpublished manuscript, Boston College, Chestnut Hill, MA.

Felton, L., & Jowett, S. (2013a). Attachment and well-being: The mediating effects of psychological needs satisfaction within the coach–athlete and parent–athlete relational contexts. *Psychology of Sport and Exercise, 14,* 57–65.

Felton, L., & Jowett, S. (2013b). "What do coaches do" and "how do they relate": Their effects on athletes' psychological needs and functioning. *Scandinavian Journal of Medicine and Science in Sports, 23*(2), e130–e139.

Fenichel, O. (1945). *The psychoanalytic theory of neurosis.* New York: Norton.

Fenigstein, A., Scheier, M. F., & Buss, A. H. (1975). Public and private self-consciousness: Assessment and theory. *Journal of Consulting and Clinical Psychology, 43,* 522–527.

Fenton, S. A. M., Duda, J. L., Quested, E., & Barrett, T. (2014). Coach autonomy support predicts autonomous motivation and daily moderate-to-vigorous physical activity and sedentary time in youth sport participants. *Psychology of Sport and Exercise, 15*(5), 453–463.

Ferguson, C. J. (2007a). Evidence for publication bias in video game violence effects literature: A meta-analytic review. *Aggression and Violent Behavior, 12*(4), 470–482.

Ferguson, C. J. (2007b). The good, the bad and the ugly: A meta-analytic review of positive and negative effects of violent video games. *Psychiatric Quarterly, 78*(4), 309–316.

Ferguson, C. J. (2015a). Do angry birds make for angry children?: A meta-analysis of video game influences on children's and adolescents' aggression, mental health, prosocial behaviour, and academic performance. *Perspectives on Psychological Science, 10(5),* 646–666.

Ferguson, C. J. (2015b). Does movie or video game violence predict societal violence?: It depends on what you look at and when. *Journal of Communication, 65,* 193–212.

Ferguson, C. J., & Kilburn, J. (2010). Much ado about nothing: The misestimation and overinterpretation of violent video game effects in Eastern and Western nations: Comment on Anderson et al. (2010). *Psychological Bulletin, 136(2),* 174–178.

Ferguson, C. J., & Olson, C. K. (2014). Video game violence use among "vulnerable" populations: The impact of violent games on delinquency and bullying among children with clinically elevated depression or attention deficit symptoms. *Journal of Youth and Adolescence, 43(1),* 127–136.

Ferguson, C. J., Rueda, S. M., Cruz, A. M., Ferguson, D. E., Fritz, S., & Smith, S. M. (2008). Violent video games and aggression: Causal relationship or byproduct of family violence and intrinsic violence motivation? *Criminal Justice and Behavior, 35(3),* 311–332.

Fernet, C., Austin, S., Trépanier, S.-G., & Dussault, M. (2013). How do job characteristics contribute to burnout?: Exploring the distinct mediating roles of perceived autonomy, competence, and relatedness. *European Journal of Work and Organizational Psychology, 22(2),* 123–137.

Fernet, C., Austin, S., & Vallerand, R. J. (2012). The effects of work motivation on employee exhaustion and commitment: An extension of the JD-R model. *Work and Stress: An International Journal of Work, Health, and Organizations, 26(3),* 213–229.

Fernet, C., Guay, F., & Senécal, C. (2004). Adjusting to job demands: The role of work self-determination and job control in predicting burnout. *Journal of Vocational Behavior, 65(1),* 39–56.

Fernet, C., Guay, F., Senécal, C., & Austin, S. (2012). Predicting intraindividual changes in teacher burnout: The role of perceived school environment and motivational factors. *Teaching and Teacher Education, 28(4),* 514–525.

Festinger, L. (1957). *A theory of cognitive dissonance.* Evanston, IL: Peterson.

Fiore, M. C. (2008). *Treating tobacco use and dependence: 2008 update: Clinical practice guideline.* Collingdale, PA: Diane Publishing.

Fiore, M. C., Bailey, W. C., Cohen, S. J., Dorfman, S. F., Goldstein, M. G., Gritz, E. R., et al. (2000). *Treating tobacco use and dependence. Clinical practice guideline.* Rockville, MD: U.S. Department of Health and Human Services, Public Health Service.

Fischer, K., Knight, C. C., & Van Parys, M. (1993). Analyzing diversity in developmental pathways. In R. Case & W. Edelstein (Eds.), *The new structuralism in cognitive development: Theory and research on individual pathways* (pp. 33–56). Basel, Switzerland: Karger Verlag.

Fischer, M. A., Stedman, M. R., Lii, J., Vogeli, C., Shrank, W. H., Brookhart, M. A., et al. (2010). Primary medication non-adherence: Analysis of 195,930 electronic prescriptions. *Journal of General Internal Medicine, 25(4),* 284–290.

Fischer, R., & Boer, D. (2011). What is more important for national well-being: Money or autonomy? A meta-analysis of well-being, burnout, and anxiety across 63 societies. *Journal of Personality and Social Psychology, 101(1),* 164–184.

Fisher, C. D. (1978). The effects of personal control, competence, and extrinsic reward systems on intrinsic motivation. *Organizational Behavior and Human Performance, 21(3),* 273–288.

Fiske, A. P., & Rai, T. S. (2015). *Virtuous violence.* Cambridge, UK: Cambridge University Press.

Fiske, S. T. (2004). Intent and ordinary bias: Unintended thought and social motivation create casual prejudice. *Social Justice Research, 17(2),* 117–127.

Flanagan, O. (2002). *The problem of the soul: Two visions of mind and how to reconcile them.* New York: Basic Books.

Flavell, J. H. (1977). *Cognitive development.* Upper Saddle River, NJ: Prentice Hall.

Flavell, J. H., Miller, P. H., & Miller, S. A. (2002). *Cognitive development.* New York: Pearson.

Flavell, J. H., & Wohlwill, J. F. (1969). Formal and functional aspects of cognitive development. In D. Elkind & J. H. Flavell (Eds.), *Studies in cognitive development: Essays in honor of Jean Piaget* (pp. 67–120). New York: Oxford University Press.

Flegal, K. M., Kit, B. K., Orpana, H., & Graubard, B. I. (2013). Association of all-cause mortality with overweight and obesity using standard body mass index categories: A systematic review and meta-analysis. *Journal of the American Medical Association, 309(1),* 71–82.

Flett, G. L., Hewitt, P. L., & Singer, A. (1995). Perfectionism and parental authority styles. *Individual Psychology: Journal of Adlerian Theory, Research and Practice, 51(1),* 50–60.

Flink, C., Boggiano, A. K., & Barrett, M. (1990). Controlling teaching strategies: Undermining children's self-determination and performance. *Journal of Personality and Social Psychology, 59(5),* 916–924.

Flock, E. (2011, July 11). APS (Atlanta Public Schools) embroiled in cheating scandal. *The Washington Post.* Retrieved August 12, 2015, from *www.washingtonpost.com/blogs/blogpost/post/aps-atlanta-public-schools-embroiled-in-cheating-scandal/2011/07/11/gIQAJl9m8H_blog.html.*

Flora, S. R. (1990). Undermining intrinsic interest

from the standpoint of a behaviorist. *Psychological Record, 40,* 323–346.

Fodor, J. A. (1983). *The modularity of mind.* Cambridge, MA: MIT Press.

Fogarty, F. A., Lu, L. M., Sollers, J. J., III, Krivoschekov, S. G., Booth, R. J., & Consedine, N. S. (2015). Why it pays to be mindful: Trait mindfulness predicts physiological recovery from emotional stress and greater differentiation among negative emotions. *Mindfulness, 6*(2), 175–185.

Fonagy, P., & Target, M. (1997). Attachment and reflective function: Their role in self-organization. *Development and Psychopathology, 9*(4), 679–700.

Foote, J., DeLuca, A., Magura, S., Warner, A., Grand, A., Rosenblum, A., et al. (1999). A group motivational treatment for chemical dependency. *Journal of Substance Abuse, 17*(3), 181–192.

Ford, M. E. (1992). *Motivating humans: Goals, emotions, and personal agency beliefs.* Newbury Park, CA: Sage.

Forest, J., Gilbert, M.-H., Beaulieu, G., Le Brock, P., & Gagné, M. (2014). Translating research results in economic terms: An application of economic utility analysis using SDT-based interventions. In M. Gagné (Ed.), *Oxford handbook of work engagement, motivation, and self-determination theory* (pp. 335–346). New York: Oxford University Press.

Fortier, M. S., Hogg, W., O'Sullivan, T. L., Blanchard, C., Reid, R. D., Sigal, R. J., et al. (2007). The physical activity counselling (PAC) randomized controlled trial: Rationale, methods, and interventions. *Applied Physiology, Nutrition, and Metabolism, 32*(6), 1170–1185.

Fortier, M. S., Sweet, S. N., O'Sullivan, T. L., & Williams, G. C. (2007). A self-determination process model of physical activity adoption in the context of a randomized controlled trial. *Psychology of Sport and Exercise, 8*(5), 741–757.

Fortier, M. S., Wiseman, E., Sweet, S. N., O'Sullivan, T. L., Blanchard, C. M., Sigal, R. J., et al. (2011). A moderated mediation of motivation on physical activity in the context of the physical activity counseling randomized control trial. *Psychology of Sport and Exercise, 12*(2), 71–78.

Fousiani, K., Dimitropoulou, P., Michaelides, M. P., & Van Petegem, S. (2016). Perceived parenting and adolescent cyber-bullying: Examining the intervening role of autonomy and relatedness need satisfaction, empathic concern and recognition of humanness. *Journal of Child and Family Studies, 25*(7), 2120–2129.

Fowler, J. H. (2005). Altruistic punishment and the origin of cooperation. *Proceedings of the National Academy of Sciences of the USA, 102*(19), 7047–7049.

Fowler, J. H., Johnson, T., & Smirnov, O. (2005). Egalitarian motive and altruistic punishment. *Nature, 433.* Available at *http://fowler.ucsd.edu/egalitarian_motive_and_altruistic_punishment.pdf.*

Fowler, S. (2014). *Why motivating people doesn't work . . . and what does: The new science of leading, energizing, and engaging.* Oakland, CA: Berrett-Koehler.

Franck, T. (2001). *The empowered self: Law and society in the age of individualism.* Oxford, UK: Oxford University Press.

Frank, J. D. (1961) *Persuasion and healing: A comparative study of psychotherapy.* Baltimore: John Hopkins Press.

Frank, J. D. (1988). What is psychotherapy? In S. Bloch (Ed.), *Introduction to the psychotherapies* (pp. 1–2). Oxford, UK: Oxford University Press.

Frankfurt, H. G. (1971) Freedom of the will and the concept of a person. *Journal of Philosophy, 68*(1), 5–20.

Frankfurt, H. G. (2004). *The reasons of love.* Princeton, NJ: Princeton University Press.

Frankl, V. E. (1959). *Man's search for meaning: An introduction to logotherapy.* Boston: Beacon Press.

Frankl, V. E. (1978). *The unheard cry for meaning.* New York: Simon & Schuster.

Frederick, C. M., & Ryan, R. M. (1993). Differences in motivation for sport and exercise and their relations with participation and mental health. *Journal of Sport Behavior, 16*(3), 124–146.

Frederick, C. M., & Ryan, R. M. (1995). Self-determination in sport: A review using cognitive evaluation theory. *International Journal of Sport Psychology, 26*(1), 5–23.

Freedom House. (2016). *Electorial democracy data: Number and percentages of electorial democracies, FIW 1989–2016.* Washington, DC. Retrieved from *https://freedomhouse.org/report-types/freedom-world.*

French, T. M. (1958). The art and science of psychoanalysis. *Journal of the American Psychoanalytic Association, 6*(2), 197–214.

Freud, A. (1937). *The ego and the mechanisms of defence* (C. Baines, Trans.). London: Karnac Books.

Freud, A. (1958). Adolescence. *Psychoanalytic Study of the Child, 13,* 255–278.

Freud, S. (1920). *A general introduction of psychoanalysis* (G. S. Hall, Trans.). New York: Boni & Liveright.

Freud, S. (1923). *The ego and the id.* New York: Norton.

Freud, S. (1925). The instincts and their vicissitudes. In J. Riviere (Ed. & Trans.), *Collected papers* (Vol. 4. pp. 60–83). London: Hogarth Press.

Freud, S. (1953). The interpretation of dreams. In J. Strachey (Ed. & Trans.), *The standard edition of the complete psychological works of Sigmund*

Freud (Vols. 4–5, pp. 1–627). London: Hogarth Press. (Original work published 1900)

Freud, S. (1961). Beyond the pleasure principle. In J. Strachey (Ed. & Trans.), *The standard edition of the complete psychological works of Sigmund Freud* (Vol. 18, pp. 1–64). London: Hogarth Press. (Original work published 1920)

Frey, B. S. (1993). Motivation as a limit to pricing. *Journal of Economic Psychology, 14*(4), 635–664.

Frey, B. S. (1997). *Not just for the money: An economic theory of personal motivation.* Northampton, MA: Elgar.

Frey, B. S., & Osterloh, M. (2005). Yes, managers should be paid like bureaucrats. *Journal of Management Inquiry, 14*(1), 96–111.

Frey, B. S., & Stutzer, A. (2005). Testing theories of happiness. In L. Bruni & P. L. Porta (Eds.). *Economics and happiness: Framing the analysis* (pp. 116–146). New York: Oxford University Press.

Friedman, M. (2000). Educating for world citizenship. *Ethics, 110*(3), 586–601.

Friedman, M. (2003). *Autonomy, gender, politics.* New York: Oxford University Press.

Friedman, R. (2014). *The best place to work: The art and science of creating an extraordinary workplace.* New York: Penguin.

Frodi, A., Bridges, L., & Grolnick, W. (1985). Correlates of mastery-related behavior: A short-term longitudinal study of infants in their second year. *Child Development, 56*(5), 1291–1298.

Froiland, J. M., & Worrell, F. C. (2016). Intrinsic motivation, learning goals, engagement, and achievement in a diverse high school. *Psychology in the Schools, 53*(3), 321–336.

Fromm, E. (1955). *The sane society.* New York: Rinehart.

Fromm, E. (1973). *The anatomy of human destructiveness.* New York: Holt, Rinehart & Winston.

Fromm, E. (1976). *To have or to be.* New York: Bloomsbury.

Frost, K. M., & Frost, C. J. (2000). Romanian and American life aspirations in relation to psychological well-being. *Journal of Cross-Cultural Psychology, 31*(6), 726–751.

Frost, R. O., Novara, C., & Rhéaume, J. (2002). Perfectionism in obsessive compulsive disorder. In R. O. Frost & G. Steketee (Eds.), *Cognitive approaches to obsessions and compulsions* (pp. 91–105). New York: Pergamon.

Fryer, L. K., Ginns, P., & Walker, R. (2014). Between students' instrumental goals and how they learn: Goal content is the gap to mind. *British Journal of Educational Psychology, 84*(4), 612–630.

Fryer, R. G. (2011). Financial incentives and student achievement: Evidence from randomized trials. *Quarterly Journal of Economics, 126*(4), 1755–1798.

Fujita, K. (2011). On conceptualizing self-control as more than the effortful inhibition of impulses. *Personality and Social Psychology Review, 15*(4) 352–366.

Fulbrook, M. (1995). *Anatomy of a dictatorship: Inside the GDR, 1949–1989.* New York: Oxford University Press.

Gabbard, G. O. (2000). A neurobiologically informed perspective on psychotherapy. *British Journal of Psychiatry, 177*(2), 117–122.

Gabbard, G. O. (2005). *Psychodynamic psychiatry in clinical practice.* Washington, DC: American Psychiatric Publishing.

Gagné, M. (2003). The role of autonomy support and autonomy orientation in prosocial behavior engagement. *Motivation and Emotion, 27*(3), 199–223.

Gagné, M., Chemolli, E., Forest, J., & Koestner, R. (2008). The temporal relations between work motivation and organizational commitment. *Psychologica Belgica, 48*(2–3), 219–241.

Gagné, M., Deci, E. L., & Ryan, R. M. (2017). Self-determination theory applied to work motivation and organizational behavior. In D. S. Ones, N. Anderson, H. K. Sinangil, & C. Viswesvaran (Eds.), *The SAGE handbook of industrial, work, and organizational psychology* (2nd ed.). Thousand Oaks, CA: Sage.

Gagné, M., & Koestner, R. (2002, April). *Self-determination theory as a framework for understanding organizational commitment.* Paper presented at the annual meeting of the Society for Industrial and Organizational Psychology, Toronto, Ontario, Canada.

Gagné, M., Koestner, R., & Zuckerman, M. (2000). Facilitating acceptance of organizational change: The importance of self-determination. *Journal of Applied Social Psychology, 30*(9), 1843–1852.

Gagné, M., Ryan, R. M., & Bargmann, K. (2003). The effects of parent and coach autonomy support on need satisfaction and well-being of gymnasts. *Journal of Applied Sport Psychology, 15,* 372–390.

Gagné, M., Senécal, C., & Koestner, R. (1997). Proximal job characteristics, feelings of empowerment, and intrinsic motivation: A multidimensional model. *Journal of Applied Social Psychology, 27*(14), 1222–1240.

Gaine, G. S., & La Guardia, J. G. (2009). The unique contributions of motivations to maintain a relationship and motivations toward relational activities to relationship well-being. *Motivation and Emotion, 33*(2), 184–202.

Galbraith, J., & Cummings, L. L. (1967). An empirical investigation of task performance: Interactive effects between instrumentality-valence and motivation-ability. *Organizational Behavior and Human Performance, 2*(3), 237–257.

Garcia, J., & Koelling, R. A. (1966). The relation of cue to consequence in avoidance learning. *Psychonomic Science, 4*(1), 123–124.

García-Calvo, T., Leo, F. M., Gonzalez-Ponce, I., Sánchez-Miguel, P. A., Mouratidis, A., & Ntoumanis, N. (2014). Perceived coach-created and peer-created motivational climates and their associations with team cohesion and athlete satisfaction: Evidence from a longitudinal study. *Journal of Sports Sciences, 32*(18), 1738–1750.

Garn, A. C., & Jolly, J. L. (2015). A model of parental achievement-oriented psychological control in academically gifted students. *High Ability Studies, 26*(1), 105–116.

Gaspar, D. (2007). Conceptualising human needs and wellbeing. In I. Gough & J. A. McGregor (Eds.), *Wellbeing in developing countries: From theory to research* (pp. 47–70). Cambridge, UK: Cambridge University Press.

Gaston, L., & Marmar, C. (1994). California psychotherapy alliance scale. In H. O. Horvarth & L. S. Greenberg (Eds.), *The working alliance: Theory, research, and practice* (pp. 85–108). New York: Wiley.

Gately, M. J. (1950). *Manipulation drive in experimentally naive rhesus monkeys.* Unpublished manuscript, University of Wisconsin, Madison, WI.

Gebauer, J. E., Riketta, M., Broemer, P., & Maio, G. R. (2008). Pleasure and pressure based prosocial motivation: Divergent relations to subjective well-being. *Journal of Research in Personality, 42*(2), 399–420.

Gee, J. P. (2003). *What video games have to teach us about learning and literacy.* New York: Palgrave/Macmillan.

Gendolla, G. H. E., & Richter, M. (2013). Opportunity-cost calculations only determine justified effort: Or, what happened to the resource conservation principle? (Commentary). *Behavioral and Brain Sciences, 36*, 686–687.

Gergen, K. J. (1991). *The saturated self: Dilemmas of identity in contemporary life.* New York: Basic Books.

Gewirtz, J. L., & Pelaez-Nogueras, M. (1991). Proximal mechanisms underlying the acquisition of moral behavior patterns. In W. M. Kurtines & J. L. Gewirtz (Eds.), *Handbook of moral behavior and development* (pp. 153–182). Hillsdale, NJ: Erlbaum.

Ghane, A., Huynh, H. P., Andrews, S. E., Legg, A. M., Tabuenca, A., & Sweeny, K. (2014). The relative importance of patients' decisional control preferences and experiences. *Psychology and Health, 29*(10), 1105–1118.

Gibson, E. J. (1969). *Principles of perceptual learning and development.* New York: Appleton-Century-Crofts.

Gill, D. L., Gross, J. B., & Huddleston, S. (1983). Participation motives in youth sports. *International Journal of Sport Psychology, 14*, 1–14.

Gill, M. M. (1982). *The analysis of transference: Vol. I. Theory and technique.* Madison, CT: International Universities Press.

Gillet, N., Lafrenière, M.-A., Huyghebaert, T., & Fouquereau, E. (2015). Autonomous and controlled reasons underlying achievement goals: Implications for the 3 × 2 achievement goal model in educational and work settings. *Motivation and Emotion, 39*(6), 858–875.

Gillet, N., Vallerand, R. J., & Lafreniere, M. K. (2012) Intrinsic and extrinsic school motivation as a function of age: The mediating role of autonomy support. *Social Psychology of Education, 15*, 77–95.

Gilligan, C. (1982). *In a different voice.* Cambridge, MA: Harvard University Press.

Gillon, R. (1985). Philosophical medical ethics. Rights. *British Medical Journal (Clinical Research Edition), 290*(6485), 1890–1891.

Gino, F., & Mogilner, C. (2014). Time, money, and morality. *Psychological Science, 25*(2), 414–421.

Gnambs, T., & Hanfsting, B. (2015). The decline of academic motivation during adolescence: An accelerated longitudinal cohort analysis on the effect of psychological need satisfaction. *Educational Psychology.* Advance online publication.

Goldberg, C. (1996). *Speaking with the devil: A dialogue with evil.* New York: Viking Press.

Goldberg, C. (2000). *The evil we do: The psychoanalysis of destructive people.* Amherst, NY: Prometheus Books.

Goldberg, D. E., & Somerville, M. (2014*). A whole new engineer.* Doulas, MI: Threejoy Associates.

Goldhagen, D. J. (1996). *Hitler's willing executioners.* New York: Knopf.

Goldman, S. J., D'Angelo, E. J., & DeMaso, D. R. (1993). Psychopathology in the families of children and adolescence with borderline personality disorder. *American Journal of Psychiatry, 150*(12), 1832–1835.

Goldsmith, L. P., Lewis, S. W., Dunn, G., & Bentall, R. P. (2015). Psychological treatments for early psychosis can be beneficial or harmful, depending on the therapeutic alliance: An instrumental variable analysis. *Psychological Medicine, 45*(11), 2365–2373.

Goldstein, A. P., Lopez, M., & Greenleaf, D. O. (1979). Introduction. In A. P. Goldstein & F. H. Kanfer (Eds.), *Maximizing treatment gains: Transfer enhancement in psychotherapy* (pp. 1–22). New York: Academic Press.

Goldstein, J. D., & Iso-Ahola, S. E. (2008). Determinants of parents' sideline-rage emotions and behaviors at youth soccer games. *Journal of Applied Social Psychology, 38*(6), 1442–1462.

Goldstein, J. D., & Kornfield, J. (1987). *Seeking the heart of wisdom: The path of insight meditation.* Boulder, CO: Shambhala.

Goldstein, K. (1939). *The organism: A holistic*

approach to biology derived from pathological data in man. New York: American Book Company.

Gollwitzer, P. M. (1999). Implementation intentions: Strong effects of simple plans. *American Psychologist, 54*(7), 493–503.

Gollwitzer, P. M., & Brandstätter, V. (1997). Implementation intentions and effective goal pursuit. *Journal of Personality and Social Psychology, 73*(1), 186–199.

Gonzalez, C. M., & Tyler, T. R. (2008). The psychology of enfranchisement: Engaging and fostering inclusion of members through voting and decision-making procedures. *Journal of Social Issues, 64*(3), 447–466.

González, M. G., Swanson, D. P., Lynch, M., & Williams, G. C. (2016). Testing satisfaction of basic psychological needs as a mediator of the relationship between socioeconomic status and physical and mental health. *Journal of Health Psychology, 21*(6), 972–982.

Goodboy, A. K., Martin, M. M., Knight, J. M., & Long, Z. (2015). Creating the boiler room environment: The job demand–control–support model as an explanation for workplace bullying. *Communication Research.* Advance online publication.

Goodman, P. (1960). *Growing up absurd: Problems of youth in the organized system.* New York: Random House.

Gore, J. S., & Cross, S. E. (2006). Pursuing goals for us: Relationally autonomous reasons in long-term goal pursuit. *Journal of Personality and Social Psychology, 90*(5), 848.

Gore, J. S., Cross, S. E., & Kanagawa, C. (2009). Acting in our interests: Relational self-construal and goal motivation across cultures. *Motivation and Emotion, 33*(1), 75–87.

Gorin, A. A., Powers, T. A., Koestner, R., Wing, R. R., & Raynor, H. A. (2013). Autonomy support, self-regulation, and weight loss. *Health Psychology, 33*(4), 332–339.

Gottfried, A. E., Gottfried, A. W., Morris, P. E., & Cook, C. R. (2008) Low academic intrinsic motivation as a risk factor for adverse educational outcomes: A longitudinal study from early childhood through early adulthood. In C. Hudley & A. E. Gottfried (Eds.), *Academic motivation and the culture of school in childhood and adolescence* (pp. 36–69). Oxford, UK: Oxford.

Gottfried, A. E., Marcoulides, G. A., Gottfried, A. W., & Oliver, P. H. (2009). A latent curve model of parental motivational practices and developmental decline in math and science academic intrinsic motivation. *Journal of Educational Psychology, 101*(3), 729–739.

Gottlieb, G. (1992). *Individual development and evolution: The genesis of novel behavior.* Oxford, UK: Oxford University Press.

Goudas, M., Biddle, S., & Fox, K. (1994). Perceived locus of causality, goal orientations, and perceived competence in school physical-education classes. *British Journal of Educational Psychology, 64*(3), 453–463.

Goudas, M., Biddle, S., & Underwood, M. (1995). A prospective study of the relationships between motivational orientations and perceived competence with intrinsic motivation and achievement in a teacher education course. *Educational Psychology, 15*(1), 89–96.

Gough, H. G., & Heilbrun, A. B. (1983). *The Revised Adjective Checklist manual.* Palo Alto, CA: Consulting Psychologists Press.

Gould, D., Feltz, D., & Weiss, M. R. (1985). Motives for participating in competitive youth swimming. *International Journal of Sport Psychology, 16*(2), 126–140.

Gould, S. J. (2002). *The structure of evolutionary theory.* Cambridge, MA: Harvard University Press.

Gözükara, İ., & Şimşek, Ö. F. (2015a). Work engagement as mediator in the relationship between transformational leadership and job satisfaction. *International Scientific Publications: Economy and Business, 9*(1), 195–202.

Gözükara, İ., & Şimşek, Ö. F. (2015b). Linking transformational leadership to work engagement and the mediator effect of job autonomy: A study in a Turkish private non-profit university. *Procedia: Social and Behavioral Sciences 195*(3), 963–971.

Graca, J., Calheiros, M. M., & Barata, M. C. (2013). Authority in the classroom: Adolescent autonomy, autonomy support, and teachers' legitimacy. *European Journal of Psychology of Education, 28*(3), 1065–1076.

Grant, A. M. (2007). Relational job design and the motivation to make a prosocial difference. *Academy of Management Review, 32*(2), 393–417.

Grant, A. M. (2008). Does intrinsic motivation fuel the prosocial fire?: Motivational synergy in predicting persistence, performance, and productivity. *Journal of Applied Psychology, 93*(1), 48–58.

Grant, A. M., Campbell, E. M., Chen, G., Cottone, K., Lapedis, D., & Lee, K. (2007). Impact and the art of motivation maintenance: The effects of contact with beneficiaries on persistence behavior. *Organizational Behavior and Human Decision Processes, 103*(1), 53–67.

Grant, A. M., Nurmohamed, S., Ashford, S. J., & Dekas, K. (2011). The performance implications of ambivalent initiative: The interplay of autonomous and controlled motivations. *Organizational Behavior and Human Decision Processes, 116*(2), 241–251.

Graves, M. F., Juel, C., Graves, B. B. (2007). *Teaching reading in the 21st century* (4th ed.). Boston: Allyn & Bacon.

Green, D. (2012). *From poverty to power: How active citizens and effective states can change the world.* Oxford, UK: Oxfam and Practical Action Publishing.

Greenberg, J. R., Pyszczynski, T., & Solomon, S. (1995). Toward a dual-motive depth psychology of self and social behavior. In M. H. Kernis (Ed.), *Efficacy, agency, and self-esteem* (pp. 73–99). New York: Springer.

Greenberg, J. R., Solomon, S., & Pyszczynski, T. (1997). Terror management theory of self-esteem and social behavior: Empirical assessments and conceptual refinements. In M. P. Zanna (Ed.), *Advances in experimental social psychology* (pp. 61–139). New York: Academic Press.

Greenberg, M. T., Speltz, M. L., & DeKlyen, M. (1993). The role of attachment in the early development of disruptive behavior problems. *Development and Psychopathology, 5*(1–2), 191–213.

Green-Demers, I., Pelletier, L. G., & Menard, S. (1997). The impact of behavioural difficulty on the saliency of the association between self-determined motivation and environmental behaviours. *Canadian Journal of Behavioural Science/Revue Canadienne des Sciences du Comportement, 29*(3), 157–166.

Green-Demers, I., Pelletier, L. G., Stewart, D. G., & Gushue, N. R. (1998). Coping with the less interesting aspects of training: Toward a model of interest and motivation enhancement in individual sports. *Basic and Applied Social Psychology, 20*(4), 251–261.

Greene, D., & Lepper, M. R. (1974). Effects of extrinsic rewards on children's subsequent intrinsic interest. *Child Development, 45*(4), 1141–1145.

Greene, J. P., & Winters, M. A. (2005). *Public high school graduation and college-readiness rates, 1991–2002.* New York: Center for Civic Innovation at the Manhattan Institute.

Greene, M. (2000). *Releasing the imagination: Essays on education, the arts, and social change.* San Francisco: Jossey-Bass.

Greenspan, S. I. (1979). *Intelligence and adaptation: An integration of psychoanalytic and Piagetian developmental psychology.* Madison, CT: International Universities Press.

Greenstein, A., & Koestner, R. (1996, August). *Success in maintaining New Year's resolutions: The value of self-determined reasons.* Paper presented at the International Congress of Psychology, Montreal, Quebec, Canada.

Greenwald, A. G. (1982). Ego task analysis: An integration of research on ego-involvement and self-awareness. In A. Hastorf & A. M. Isen (Eds.), *Cognitive social psychology* (pp. 109–147). New York: Elsevier.

Greenwald, A. G., McGhee, D. E., & Schwartz, J. L. K. (1998). Measuring individual differences in implicit cognition: The Implicit Association Test. *Journal of Personality and Social Psychology, 74*(6), 1464–1480.

Greenway, R. (1995). The wilderness effect and ecopsychology. In T. Roszak, M. E. Gomes, & A. D. Kanner (Eds.), *Ecopsychology: Restoring the earth, healing the mind* (pp. 122–135). San Francisco: Sierra Club Books.

Griffin, D., & Gonzalez, R. (1995). Correlational analysis of dyad-level data in the exchangeable case. *Psychological Bulletin, 118*(3), 430–439.

Griffin, S. (1995). A cognitive-developmental analysis of pride, shame, and embarrassment in middle childhood. In J. P. Tangney & K. W. Fischer (Eds.), *Self-conscious emotions: The psychology of shame, guilt, embarrassment, and pride* (pp. 219–236). New York: Guilford Press.

Grolnick, W. S. (2002). *The psychology of parental control: How well-meant parenting backfires.* Mahwah, NJ: Erlbaum.

Grolnick, W. S. (2009). The role of parents in facilitating autonomous self-regulation for education. *Theory and Research in Education, 7*(2), 164–173.

Grolnick, W. S. (2015). Mothers' motivation for involvement in their children's schooling: Mechanisms and outcomes. *Motivation and Emotion, 39*(1), 63–73.

Grolnick, W. S., Deci, E. L., & Ryan, R. M. (1997). Internalization within the family: The self-determination theory perspective. In J. E. Grusec & L. Kuczynski (Eds.), *Parenting and children's internalization of values: A handbook of contemporary theory* (pp. 135–161). New York: Wiley.

Grolnick, W. S., Frodi, A., & Bridges, L. (1984). Maternal control style and the mastery motivation of one-year-olds. *Infant Mental Health Journal, 5*(2), 72–82.

Grolnick, W. S., Gurland, S. T., DeCourcey, W., & Jacob, K. (2002). Antecedents and consequences of mothers' autonomy support: An experimental investigation. *Developmental Psychology, 38*(1), 143–155.

Grolnick, W. S., Gurland, S. T., Jacob, K. F., & DeCourcey, W. (2002). The development of self-determination in middle childhood and adolescence. In A. Wigfield & J. S. Eccles (Eds.), *Development of achievement motivation* (pp. 147–171). San Diego, CA: Academic Press.

Grolnick, W. S., Kurowski, C. O., & Gurland, S. T. (1999). Family processes and the development of children's self-regulation. *Educational Psychologist, 34*(1), 3–14.

Grolnick, W. S., Kurowski, C. O., McMenamy, J. M., Rivkin, I., & Bridges, L. J. (1998). Mothers' strategies for regulating their toddlers' distress. *Infant Behavior and Development, 21*(3), 437–450.

Grolnick, W. S., & Pomerantz, E. M. (2009). Issues

and challenges in studying parental control: Toward a new conceptualization. *Child Development Perspectives, 3*(3), 165–170.

Grolnick, W. S., Price, C. E., Beiswenger, K. L., & Sauck, C. C. (2007). Evaluative pressure in mothers: Effects of situation, maternal, and child characteristics on autonomy supportive versus controlling behavior. *Developmental Psychology, 43*(4), 991–1002.

Grolnick, W. S., Raftery-Helmer, J. N., Marbell, K. N., Flamm, E. S., Cardemil, E. V., & Sanchez, M. (2014). Parental provision of structure: Implementation and correlates and outcomes in three domains. *Merrill–Palmer Quarterly, 60*(3), 355–384.

Grolnick, W. S., & Ryan, R. M. (1987). Autonomy in children's learning: An experimental and individual difference investigation. *Journal of Personality and Social Psychology, 52*(5), 890–898.

Grolnick, W. S., & Ryan, R. M. (1989). Parent styles associated with children's self-regulation and competence in school. *Journal of Educational Psychology, 81*(2), 143–154.

Grolnick, W. S., & Ryan, R. M. (1990). Self-perceptions, motivation, and adjustment in children with learning disabilities: A multiple group comparison study. *Journal of Learning Disabilities, 23*(3), 177–184.

Grolnick, W. S., Ryan, R. M., & Deci, E. L. (1991). Inner resources for school achievement: Motivational mediators of children's perceptions of their parents. *Journal of Educational Psychology, 83*(4), 508–517.

Grolnick, W. S., & Seal, K. (2008). *Pressured parents, stressed-out kids: Dealing with competition while raising a successful child.* Amherst, NY: Prometheus Books.

Grolnick, W. S., & Slowiaczek, M. L. (1994). Parents' involvement in children's schooling: A multidimensional conceptualization and motivational model. *Child Development, 65*(1), 237–252.

Grolnick, W. S., Weiss, L., McKenzie, L., & Wrightmen, J. (1996). Contextual, cognitive and adolescent factors associated with parenting in adolescence. *Journal of Youth and Adolescence, 25*(1), 33–54.

Grolnick, W. S., & Wellborn, J. (1988). *Parent influences on children's school-related self-system processes.* Paper presented at the annual meeting of the American Education Research Association, New Orleans, LA.

Groos, K. (1898). *The play of animals.* New York: Appleton.

Groos, K. (1901). *The play of man.* New York: Appleton.

Gross, J. J., & Muñoz, R. F. (1995). Emotion regulation and mental health. *Clinical Psychology: Science and Practice, 2*(2), 151–164.

Grossman, D. A. (1995). *On killing: The psychological cost of learning to kill in war and society.* New York: Back Bay Books

Grouzet, F. M. E., Kasser, T., Ahuvia, A., Dols, J. M. F., Kim, Y., Lau, S., et al. (2005). The structure of goal contents across 15 cultures. *Journal of Personality and Social Psychology, 89*(5), 800–816.

Grouzet, F. M. E., Vallerand, R. J., Thill, E. E., & Provencher, P. J. (2004). From environmental factors to outcomes: A test of an integrated motivational sequence. *Motivation and Emotion, 28*(4), 331–346.

Grusec, J. E. (2011). Domains of social knowledge and socialization theory. *Human Development, 54*(5), 343–347.

Grusec, J. E., & Goodnow, J. J. (1994). Summing up and looking to the future. *Developmental Psychology, 30*(1), 29–31.

Grüsser, S. M., Thalemann, R., & Griffiths, M. D. (2007). Excessive computer game playing: Evidence for addiction and aggression? *CyberPsychology and Behavior, 10*(2), 290–292.

Guay, F., Delisle, M.-N., Fernet, C., Julien, É., & Senécal, C. (2008). Does task-related identified regulation moderate the sociometer effect?: A study of performance feedback, perceived inclusion, and state self-esteem. *Social Behavior and Personality: An International Journal, 36*(2), 239–254.

Guay, F., Ratelle, C. F., Roy, A., & Litalien, D. (2010). Academic self-concept, autonomous academic motivation, and academic achievement: Mediating and additive effects. *Learning and Individual Differences, 20*(6), 644–653.

Guay, F., Ratelle, C. F., Senécal, C., Larose, S., & Deschênes, A. (2006). Distinguishing developmental from chronic career indecision: Self-efficacy, autonomy, and social support. *Journal of Career Assessment, 14*(2), 235–251.

Guay, F., Senécal, C., Gauthier, L., & Fernet, C. (2003). Predicting career indecision: A self-determination theory perspective. *Journal of Counseling Psychology, 50*(2), 165–177.

Guay, F., & Vallerand, R. J. (1997). Social context, student's motivation, and academic achievement: Toward a process model. *Social Psychology of Education, 1*(3), 211–233.

Gubler, T., Larkin, I., & Pierce, L. (2016). Motivational spillovers from awards: Crowding out in a multi-tasking environment. *Organization Science, 27*(2), 286–303.

Guertin, C., Rocchi, M., Pelletier, L. G., Edmond, C., & Lalande, G. (2015). The role of motivation and the regulation of eating on the physical and psychological health of patients with cardiovascular disease. *Journal of Health Psychology, 20*(5), 543–555.

Guiffrida, D. A. (2014). *Constructive clinical supervision in counseling and psychotherapy*. New York: Routledge.

Gunnell, K. E., Crocker, P. R. E., Wilson, P. M., Mack, D. E., & Zumbo, B. D. (2013). Psychological need satisfaction and thwarting: A test of basic psychological needs theory in physical activity contexts. *Psychology of Sport and Exercise, 14*(5), 599–607.

Gurland, S. T., & Grolnick, W. S. (2003). Children's expectancies and perceptions of adults: Effects of rapport. *Child Development, 74*(4), 1212–1224.

Gurland, S. T., & Grolnick, W. S. (2005). Perceived threat, controlling parenting, and children's achievement orientations. *Motivation and Emotion, 29*(2), 103–121.

Gurley, J. (2011). Behavior assessment system for children: Second edition (BASC-2). In S. Goldstein & J. A. Naglieri (Eds.), *Encyclopedia of child behavior and development* (pp. 222–223). New York: Springer.

Guttman, L. (1954). A new approach to factor analysis: The radex. In P. Lazarfeld (Ed.), *Mathematical thinking in the social sciences* (pp. 258–348). Glencoe, IL: Free Press.

Ha, A. S., & Ng, J. Y. Y. (2015). Autonomous motivation predicts 7-day physical activity in Hong Kong students. *Applied Psychology Health and Well-Being, 7*(2), 214–229.

Hackman, J. R., & Lawler, E. E. (1971). Employee reactions to job characteristics. *Journal of Applied Psychology, 55*(3), 259–286.

Hackman, J. R., & Oldham, G. R. (1980). *Work redesign*. Boston: Addison-Wesley.

Hadden, B. W., Rodriguez, L. M., Knee, C. R., & Porter, B. (2015). Relationship autonomy and support provision in romantic relationships. *Motivation and Emotion, 39*, 359–373.

Haerens, L., Aelterman, N., Van den Berghe, L., De Meyer, J., Soenens, B., & Vansteenkiste, M. (2013). Observing physical education teachers' need-supportive interactions in classroom settings. *Journal of Sport and Exercise Psychology, 35*(1), 3–17.

Hagger, M. S., & Chatzisarantis, N. L. D. (Eds.). (2007). *Intrinsic motivation and self-determination in exercise and sport*. Champaign, IL: Human Kinetics.

Hagger, M. S., & Chatzisarantis, N. L. D. (2011). Causality orientations moderate the undermining effect of rewards on intrinsic motivation. *Journal of Experimental Social Psychology, 47*(2), 485–489.

Hagger, M. S., Chatzisarantis, N. L. D., Barkoukis, V., Wang, C. K. J., & Baranowski, J. (2005). Perceived autonomy support in physical education and leisure-time physical activity: A cross-cultural evaluation of the trans-contextual model. *Journal of Educational Psychology, 97*(3), 376–390.

Hagger, M. S., Chatzisarantis, N. L. D., Culverhouse, T., & Biddle, S. J. H. (2003). The processes by which perceived autonomy support in physical education promotes leisure-time physical activity intentions and behavior: A trans-contextual model. *Journal of Educational Psychology, 95*(4), 784–795.

Hagger, M. S., Chatzisarantis, N. L. D., & Harris, J. (2006). The process by which relative autonomous motivation affects intentional behavior: Comparing effects across dieting and exercise behaviors. *Motivation and Emotion, 30*(4), 307–321.

Hagger, M. S., Chatzisarantis, N. L. D., Hein, V., Pihu, M., Soos, I., & Karsai, I. (2007). The Perceived Autonomy Support Scale for Exercise Settings (PASSES): Development, validity, and cross-cultural invariance in young people. *Psychology of Sport and Exercise, 8*(5), 632–653.

Hagger, M. S., Koch, S., & Chatzisarantis, N. L. (2015). The effect of causality orientations and positive competence-enhancing feedback on intrinsic motivation: A test of additive and interactive effects. *Personality and Individual Differences 72*, 107–111.

Hall, T. S. (1969). *Ideas of life and matter* (Vol. 2). Chicago: University of Chicago Press.

Halvari, A. E. M., & Halvari, H. (2006). Motivational predictors of change in oral health: An experimental test of self-determination theory. *Motivation and Emotion, 30*(4), 294–306.

Hamilton, L. A. (2003). *The political philosophy of needs*. Cambridge, UK: Cambridge University Press.

Hamilton, W. D. (1964). The genetical evolution of social behavior. *Journal of Theoretical Biology, 7*, 1–16.

Hampton-Robb, S., Qualls, R. C., & Compton, W. C. (2003). Predicting first-session attendance: The influence of referral source and client income. *Psychotherapy Research, 13*(2), 223–233.

Hanh, T. N. (1976). *The miracle of mindfulness*. Boston: Beacon Press.

Hanh, T. N. (1998). *The heart of the Buddha's teaching: Transforming suffering into peace, joy, and liberation: The four noble truths, the noble eightfold path, and other basic Buddhist teachings*. New York: Broadway Books.

Harackiewicz, J. M. (1979). The effects of reward contingency and performance feedback on intrinsic motivation. *Journal of Personality and Social Psychology, 37*(8), 1352–1363.

Harackiewicz, J. M., Abrahams, S., & Wageman, R. (1987). Performance evaluation and intrinsic motivation: The effects of evaluative focus, rewards, and achievement orientation. *Journal of Personality and Social Psychology, 53*(6), 1015–1023.

Harackiewicz, J. M., & Elliot, A. J. (1998). The joint effects of target and purpose goals on intrinsic motivation: A mediational analysis. *Personality and Social Psychology Bulletin, 24*(7), 675–689.

Hardré, P. L., & Reeve, J. (2003). A motivational model of rural students' intentions to persist in, versus drop out of, high school. *Journal of Educational Psychology, 95*(2), 347–356.

Hardré, P. L., & Reeve, J. (2009). Training corporate managers to adopt a more autonomy-supportive motivating style toward employees: An intervention study. *International Journal of Training and Development, 13*(3), 165–184.

Harlow, H. F. (1950). Learning and satiation of response in intrinsically motivated complex puzzle performance by monkeys. *Journal of Comparative and Physiological Psychology, 43*(4), 289–294.

Harlow, H. F. (1953a). Mice, monkeys, men, and motives. *Psychological Review, 60*(1), 23–32.

Harlow, H. F. (1953b). Motivation as a factor in the acquisition of new responses. In J. S. Brown, H. F. Harlow, L. J. Postman, V. N. T. M. Nowlis, & O. H. Mowrer (Eds.), *Current theory and research on motivation* (pp. 24–49). Lincoln: University of Nebraska Press.

Harlow, H. F. (1958). The nature of love. *American Psychologist, 13*(12), 673–685.

Harlow, H. F., Harlow, M. K., & Meyer, D. R. (1950). Learning motivated by a manipulation drive. *Journal of Experimental Psychology, 40*(2), 228–234.

Harris, P. L. (2000). *Understanding children's worlds: The work of the imagination.* New York: Wiley Blackwell.

Harrison, D. A., Virick, M., & William, S. (1996). Working without a net: Time, performance, and turnover under maximally contingent rewards. *Journal of Applied Psychology, 81*(4), 331–345.

Hart, S. L. (2007). *Capitalism at the crossroads: Aligning business, earth, and humanity.* Upper Saddle River, NJ: Pearson Prentice Hall.

Harter, S. (1974). Pleasure derived by children from cognitive challenge and mastery. *Child Development, 45*(3), 661–669.

Harter, S. (1978a). Effectance motivation reconsidered: Toward a developmental model. *Human Development, 21*(1), 34–64.

Harter, S. (1978b). Pleasure derived from optimal challenge and the effects of extrinsic rewards on children's difficulty level choices. *Child Development, 49*, 788–799.

Harter, S. (1981). A new self-report scale of intrinsic versus extrinsic orientation in the classroom: Motivational and informational components. *Developmental Psychology, 17*(3), 300–312.

Harter, S. (1999). *The construction of the self: A developmental perspective.* New York: Guilford Press.

Harter, S. (2012). *The construction of the self: Developmental and sociocultural foundations* (2nd ed.). New York: Guilford Press.

Hartmann, H. (1958). *Ego psychology and the problem of adaptation* (D. Rapaport, Trans.). Madison, CT: International Universities Press.

Hass, H. (1970). *The human animal: The mystery of man's behavior.* New York: Putnam.

Hatfield, E., & Rapson, R. L. (2011). Equity theory in close relationships. In P. A. M. Van Lange, A. W. Kruglanski, & E. T. Higgins (Eds.), *Handbook of theories of social psychology* (pp. 200–217). London: Glyph International.

Hatfield, J. S., Ferguson, L. R., & Alpert, R. (1967). Mother–child interaction and the socialization process. *Child Development, 38*(2), 365–414.

Hawley, P. H. (2014). The duality of human nature: Coercion and prosociality in youths' hierarchy ascension and social success. *Current Directions in Psychological Science, 23*(6), 433–438.

Hawley, P. H., Little, T. D., & Pasupathi, M. (2002). Winning friends and influencing peers: Strategies of peer influence in late childhood. *International Journal of Behavioral Development, 26*(5), 466–474.

Hayes, L., & Ciarrochi, J. (2015). Using acceptance and commitment therapy to help young people develop and grow to their full potential. In B. Kirkcaldy (Ed.), *Promoting psychological wellbeing in children and families* (pp. 102–122). Basingstoke, UK: Palgrave Macmillan.

Hayes, S. C., Luoma, J. B., Bond, F. W., Masuda, A., & Lillis, J. (2006). Acceptance and commitment therapy: Model, processes, and outcomes. *Behaviour Research and Therapy, 44*(1), 1–25.

Healy, J. M. (1990). *Endangered minds: Why children don't think and what we can do about it.* New York: Simon & Schuster.

Healy, L. C., Ntoumanis, N., Veldhuijzen van Zanten, J. J., & Paine, N. (2014). Goal striving and well-being in sport: The role of contextual and personal motivation. *Journal of Sport and Exercise Psychology, 36*(5), 446–459.

Hebb, D. O. (1955). Drives and the CNS (conceptual nervous system). *Psychological Review, 62*(4), 243–254.

Hebb, D. O. (1961). *The organization of behavior: A neuropsychological approach.* New York: Wiley.

Heidegger, M. (1962). *Being and time.* New York: Harper Collins. (Original work published 1927)

Heider, F. (1958). *The psychology of interpersonal relations.* New York: Wiley.

Heider, F. (1960). The gestalt theory of motivation. In M. R. Jones (Ed.), *Nebraska Symposium on Motivation* (pp. 145–172). Lincoln: University of Nebraska Press.

Heider, F., & Simmel, M. (1944). An experimental study of apparent behavior. *American Journal of Psychology, 57*(2), 243–259.

Heilbrun, A. B. (1965). The measurement of identification. *Child Development, 36*(1), 111–127.

Hein, V., Koka, A., & Hagger, M. S. (2015). Relationships between perceived teachers' controlling behaviour, psychological need thwarting, anger and bullying behaviour in high-school students. *Journal of Adolescence, 42,* 103–114.

Heine, S. J., Proulx, T., & Vohs, K. D. (2006). The meaning maintenance model: On the coherence of social motivations. *Personality and Social Psychology Review, 10*(2), 88–110.

Helmholtz, H. (1873). *Popular lectures on scientific subjects* (E. Atkinson, Trans.). New York: Appleton.

Helwig, C. C., & McNiel, J. (2011). The development of conceptions of personal autonomy, rights, and democracy and their relation to psychological well-being. In V. I. Chirkov, R. M. Ryan, & K. M. Sheldon (Eds.), *Human autonomy in cross-cultural context* (pp. 241–256). New York: Springer.

Helwig, C. C., To, S., Wang, Q., Liu, C., & Yang, S. (2014). Judgments and reasoning about parental discipline involving induction and psychological control in China and Canada. *Child Development, 85*(3), 1150–1167.

Henderlong, J., & Lepper, M. R. (2002). The effects of praise on children's intrinsic motivation: A review and synthesis. *Psychological Bulletin, 128*(5), 774–795.

Hendrick, I. (1942). Instinct and the ego during infancy. *Psychoanalytic Quarterly, 11,* 33–58.

Hepach, R., Vaish, A., & Tomasello, M. (2013). A new look at children's prosocial motivation. *Infancy, 18*(1), 67–90.

Herman, J. L., Perry, J. C., & van der Kolk, B. A. (1989). Childhood trauma in borderline personality disorder. *American Journal of Psychiatry, 146,* 490–495.

Hermans, H. J. (2002). The dialogical self as a society of mind: Introduction. *Theory and Psychology, 12*(2), 147–160.

Hesse, H. (1965). *Demian* (M. Roloff & M. Lebeck, Trans.). New York: Harper & Row.

Hetland, H., Hetland, J., Andreassen, C. S., Pallesen, S., & Notelaers, G. (2011). Leadership and fulfillment of the three basic psychological needs at work. *Career Development International, 16*(5), 507–523.

Hewett, R., & Conway, N. (2015). The undermining effect revisited: The salience of everyday verbal rewards and self-determined motivation. *Journal of Organizational Behavior, 37*(3), 436–455.

Hidi, S., & Harackiewicz, J. M. (2000). Motivating the academically unmotivated: A critical issue for the 21st century. *Review of Educational Research, 70*(2), 151–179.

Higgins, S. T., Wong, C. J., Badger, G. J., Haug-Ogden, D. E. H., & Dantona, R. L. (2000). Contingent reinforcement increases cocaine abstinence during outpatient treatment and 1 year of follow-up. *Journal of Consulting and Clinical Psychology, 68*(1), 64–72.

Hilgard, E. R. (1987). Perspectives on educational psychology. In J. A. Glover & R. R. Ronning (Eds.), *Historical foundations of educational psychology* (pp. 415–423). New York: Springer.

Hirschfeld, R. M. A., Klerman, G. L., Gough, H. G., Barrett, J., Korchin, S. J., & Chodoff, P. (1977). A measure of interpersonal dependency. *Journal of Personality Assessment, 41*(6), 610–618.

Hmel, B. A., & Pincus, A. L. (2002). The meaning of autonomy: On and beyond the interpersonal circumplex. *Journal of Personality, 70*(3), 277–310.

Hodge, K., Hargreaves, E. A., Gerrard, D., & Lonsdale, C. (2013). Psychological mechanisms underlying doping attitudes in sport: Motivation and moral disengagement. *Journal of Sport and Exercise Psychology, 35*(4), 419–432.

Hodge, K., Henry, G., & Smith, W. (2014). A case study of excellence in elite sport: Motivational climate in a world champion team. *Sport Psychologist, 28,* 60–74.

Hodge, K., & Lonsdale, C. (2011). Prosocial and antisocial behavior in sport: The role of coaching style, autonomous vs. controlled motivation, and moral disengagement. *Journal of Sport and Exercise Psychology, 33,* 527–547.

Hodge, K., Lonsdale, C., & Jackson, S. (2009). Athlete engagement in elite sport: An exploratory investigation of antecedents and consequences. *Sport Psychologist, 23*(2), 186–202.

Hodge, K., Lonsdale, C., & Ng, J. Y. Y. (2008). Burnout in elite rugby: Relationships with basic psychological needs fulfillment. *Journal of Sports Sciences, 26,* 835–844.

Hodgins, H. S. (2008). Motivation, threshold for threat, and quieting the ego. In H. A. Wayment & J. J. Bauer (Eds.), *Transcending self-interest: Psychological explorations of the quiet ego* (pp. 117–124). Washington, DC: American Psychological Association.

Hodgins, H. S., Brown, A. B., & Carver, B. (2007). Autonomy and control motivation and self-esteem. *Self and Identity, 6*(2–3), 189–208.

Hodgins, H. S., & Knee, C. R. (2002). The integrating self and conscious experience. In E. L. Deci & R. M. Ryan (Eds.), *Handbook of self-determination research* (pp. 87–100). Rochester, NY: University of Rochester Press.

Hodgins, H. S., Koestner, R., & Duncan, N. (1996). On the compatibility of autonomy and relatedness. *Personality and Social Psychology Bulletin, 22*(3), 227–237.

Hodgins, H. S., & Liebeskind, E. (2003). Apology versus defense: Antecedents and consequences. *Journal of Experimental Social Psychology, 39*(4), 297–316.

Hodgins, H. S., Liebeskind, E., & Schwartz, W.

(1996). Getting out of hot water: Facework in social predicaments. *Journal of Personality and Social Psychology, 71*(2), 300–314.

Hodgins, H. S., Weibust, K. S., Weinstein, N., Shiffman, S., Miller, A., Coombs, G., et al. (2010). The cost of self-protection: Threat response and performance as a function of autonomous and controlled motivations. *Personality and Social Psychology Bulletin, 36*(8), 1101–1114.

Hodgins, H. S., Yacko, H. A., & Gottlieb, E. (2006). Autonomy and nondefensiveness. *Motivation and Emotion, 30*(4), 283–293.

Hoff, D. J. (2000). As stakes rise, definition of cheating blurs. *Education Week, 19*(41), 14–16.

Hoffer, E. (1989). *The true believer: Thoughts on the nature of man.* New York: Harper Collins.

Hoffman, M. L. (1960). Power assertion by the parent and its impact on the child. *Child Development, 31,* 129–143.

Hofstadter, D. R., & Dennett, D. C. (1981). *The mind's I: Fantasies and reflections on self and soul.* New York: Basic Books.

Hofstede, G. (2001). *Culture's consequences: Comparing values, behaviors, institutions, and organizations across nations.* New York: Sage.

Holmberg, P. M., & Sheridan, D. A. (2013). Self-determined motivation as a predictor of burnout among college athletes. *Sport Psychologist, 27*(2), 177–187.

Homans, G. C. (1958). Social behavior as exchange. *American Journal of Sociology, 63*(6), 597–606.

Hood, B. (2012). *The self-illusion: How the social brain creates identity.* Oxford, UK: Oxford University Press.

Hoover, C. F., & Insel, T. R. (1984). Families of origin in obsessive–compulsive disorder. *Journal of Nervous and Mental Disease, 172*(4), 207–215.

Horgan, J. (2009). *Walking away from terrorism: Accounts of disengagement from radical and extremist movements.* Abingdon, Oxon: Routledge.

Horney, K. (1950). *Neurosis and human growth.* New York: Norton.

Horvath, A. O., & Symonds, B. D. (1991). Relation between working alliance and outcome in psychotherapy: A meta-analysis. *Journal of Consulting and Clinical Psychology, 38*(2), 139–149.

Hou, W., Priem, R. L., & Goranova, M. (2014). Does one size fit all?: Investigating pay–future performance relationships over the "seasons" of CEO tenure. *Journal of Management.* Advance online publication.

Houlfort, N., Koestner, R., Joussemet, M., Nantel-Vivier, A., & Lekes, N. (2002). The impact of performance-contingent rewards on perceived autonomy and competence. *Motivation and Emotion, 26*(4), 279–295.

Hout, M., & Elliott, S. W. (2011). *Incentives and test-based accountability in education.* Washington, DC: National Academy Press.

Howard, J. L., Gagné, M., Morin, A. J. S., Wang, Z. N., & Forest, J. (2016). Using bifactor exploratory structural equation modeling to test for a continuum structure of motivation. *Journal of Management.* Advance online publication.

Howell, R. T., Chenot, D., Hill, G., & Howell, C. J. (2011). Momentary happiness: The role of psychological need satisfaction. *Journal of Happiness Studies, 12*(1), 1–15.

Howell, R. T., & Hill, G. (2009). The mediators of experiential purchases: Determining the impact of psychological needs satisfaction and social comparison. *Journal of Positive Psychology, 4*(6), 511–522.

Hull, C. L. (1943). *Principles of behavior: An introduction to behavior theory.* Oxford, UK: Appleton-Century.

Hunt, J. M. (1965). Intrinsic motivation and its role in psychological development. In D. Levine (Ed.), *Nebraska Symposium on Motivation* (Vol. 13, pp. 189–282). Lincoln: University of Nebraska Press.

Huppert, F. A., & So, T. T. C. (2013). Flourishing across Europe: Application of a new conceptual framework for defining well-being. *Social Indicators Research, 110*(3), 837–861.

Hurst, M., Dittmar, H., Bond, R., & Kasser, T. (2013). The relationship between materialistic values and environmental attitudes and behaviors: A meta-analysis. *Journal of Environmental Psychology, 36,* 257–269.

Husserl, E. (1980). *Phenomenology and the foundations of the sciences.* New York: Springer.

Ibrahim, S., & Alkire, S. (2007). Agency and empowerment: A proposal for internationally comparable indicators *Oxford Development Studies, 35*(4), 379–403.

Ilardi, B. C., Leone, D., Kasser, T., & Ryan, R. M. (1993). Employee and supervisor ratings of motivation: Main effects and discrepancies associated with job satisfaction and adjustment in a factory setting. *Journal of Applied Social Psychology, 23*(21), 1789–1805.

Illich, I. (1978). *Toward a history of needs.* New York: Pantheon.

Ingledew, D. K., & Markland, D. (2008). The role of motives in exercise participation. *Psychology and Health, 23*(7), 807–828.

Inglehart, R. (1981). Post-materialism in an environment of insecurity. *American Political Science Review, 75*(4), 880–900.

Inglehart, R. (1997). *Modernization and postmodernization: Cultural, economic, and political change in 43 societies* (Vol. 19). Princeton, NJ: Princeton University Press.

Inguglia, C., Ingoglia, S., Liga, F., Lo Coco, A., &

Lo Cricchio, M. G. (2015). Autonomy and relatedness in adolescence and emerging adulthood: Relationships with parental support and psychological distress. *Journal of Adult Development, 22*(1), 1–13.

Isaac, W. (1962). Evidence for a sensory drive in monkeys. *Psychological Reports, 11*(5), 175–181.

Isoard-Gautheur, S., Guillet-Descas, E., & Lemyre, P.-N. (2012). A prospective study of the influence of perceived coaching style on burnout propensity in high level young athletes: Using a self-determination theory perspective. *Sport Psychologist, 26*(2), 282–298.

Israeli-Halevi, M., Assor, A., & Roth, G. (2015). Using maternal conditional positive regard to promote anxiety suppression in adolescents: A benign strategy? *Parenting: Science and Practice, 15*(3), 187–206.

Iyengar, S. S., & DeVoe, S. E. (2003). Rethinking the value of choice: Considering cultural mediators of intrinsic motivation. In V. Murphy-Berman & J. J. Berman (Eds.), *Nebraska Symposium on Motivation: Cross-cultural differences in perspectives on self* (pp. 129–174). Lincoln: University of Nebraska Press.

Iyengar, S. S., & Lepper, M. R. (1999). Rethinking the value of choice: A cultural perspective on intrinsic motivation. *Journal of Personality and Social Psychology, 76*(3), 349–366.

Iyengar, S. S., & Lepper, M. R. (2000). When choice is demotivating: Can one desire too much of a good thing? *Journal of Personality and Social Psychology, 79*(6), 995–1006.

Izuma, K., Akula, S., Murayama, K., Wu, D.-A., Lacoboni, M., & Adolphs, R. (2015). A causal role for posterior medial frontal cortex in choice-induced preference change. *Journal of Neuroscience, 35*(8), 3598–3606.

Jackson, B., Richman, L., LaBelle, O., Lempereur, M., & Twenge, J. (2015). Experimental evidence that low social status is most toxic to well-being when internalized. *Self and Identity, 14*(2), 157–172.

Jacob, F. (1973). *The logic of life: A history of heredity*. New York: Pantheon Books.

Jacob, F. (1982). *The possible and the actual*. New York: Pantheon Books.

Jahoda, M. (1958). *Current concepts of positive mental health*. New York: Basic Books.

Janet, P. (1937). Psychological strength and weakness in mental diseases. In R. K. Merton (Ed.), *Factors determining human behavior* (pp. 64–106). Cambridge, MA: Harvard University Press.

Jang, H. (2008). Supporting students' motivation, engagement, and learning during an uninteresting activity. *Journal of Educational Psychology, 100*(4), 798–811.

Jang, H., Kim, E. J., & Reeve, J. (2012). Longitudinal test of self-determination theory's motivation mediation model in a naturally occurring classroom context. *Journal of Educational Psychology, 104*(4), 1175–1188.

Jang, H., Reeve, J., & Deci, E. L. (2010). Engaging students in learning activities: It is not autonomy support or structure, but autonomy support and structure. *Journal of Educational Psychology, 102*(3), 588–600.

Jang, H., Reeve, J., Ryan, R. M., & Kim, A. (2009). Can self-determination theory explain what underlies the productive, satisfying learning experiences of collectivistically oriented Korean students? *Journal of Educational Psychology, 101*(3), 644–661.

Jenike, M. A. (1991). Obsessive–compulsive disorder. In B. D. Beitman & G. L. Klerman (Eds.), *Integrating pharmacotherapy and psychotherapy* (pp. 183–210). Washington, DC: American Psychiatric Association.

Jenkins, D. C., Rosenman, R. H., & Friedman, M. (1967). Development of an objective psychological test for the determination of the coronary-prone behavior pattern in employed men. *Journal of Clinical Epidemiology, 20*(6), 371–379.

Jenkins, O. (2011). *The intrinsic and extrinsic motivation factors of scholarship and non-scholarship athletes at a historically black college*. Unpublished master's thesis, Michigan State University, East Lansing, MI.

Jensen, M. C., & Murphy, K. J. (1990). Performance pay and top-management incentives. *Journal of Political Economy, 98*(2), 225–264.

Jha, P., Ramasundarahettige, C., Landsman, V., Rostron, B., Thun, M., Anderson, R. N., et al. (2013). 21st-century hazards of smoking and benefits of cessation in the United States. *New England Journal of Medicine, 368*, 341–350.

Joesaar, H., Hein, V., & Hagger, M. (2012). Youth athletes' perception of autonomy support from the coach, peer motivational climate and intrinsic motivation in sport setting: One-year effects. *Psychology of Sport and Exercise, 13*(3), 257–262.

Johnson, D., Jones, C., Scholes, L., & Carras, M. C. (2013). *Videogames and wellbeing: A comprehensive review*. Melbourne, Australia: Young and Well Cooperative Research Centre.

Johnson, F. A. (1993). *Dependency and Japanese socialization: Psychoanalytic and anthropological investigations in amae*. New York: New York University Press.

Johnston, R. C. (1999). Texas presses districts in alleged test-tampering cases. *Education Week, 18*(27), 22–28.

Jones, G. (2002). *Killing monsters: Why children need fantasy, super heroes, and make-believe violence*. New York: Basic Books.

Jordan, J. V. (1991). The relational self: A new perspective for understanding women's development. In J. Strauss & G. R. Goethals (Eds.), *The self:*

Interdisciplinary approaches (pp. 136–149). New York: Springer.

Joshanloo, M. (2014). Eastern conceptualizations of happiness: Fundamental differences with Western views. *Journal of Happiness Studies, 15*(2), 475–493.

Jourard, S. M. (1968). *Disclosing man to himself.* Princeton, NJ: Van Nostrand.

Joussemet, M., & Koestner, R. (1999). Effect of expected rewards on children's creativity. *Creativity Research Journal, 12*(4), 231–239.

Joussemet, M., Koestner, R., Lekes, N., & Landry, R. (2005). A longitudinal study of the relationship of maternal autonomy support to children's adjustment and achievement in school. *Journal of Personality, 73*(5), 1215–1236.

Joussemet, M., Mageau, G. A., & Koestner, R. (2014). Promoting optimal parenting and children's mental health: A preliminary evaluation of the how-to parenting program. *Journal of Child and Family Studies, 23*(6), 949–964.

Joussemet, M., Vitaro, F., Barker, E. D., Cote, S., Nagin, D. S., Zoccolillo, M., et al. (2008). Controlling parenting and physical aggression during elementary school. *Child Development, 79*(2), 411–425.

Julien, E., Senécal, C., & Guay, F. (2009). Longitudinal relations among perceived autonomy support from health care practitioners, motivation, coping strategies, and dietary compliance in a sample of adults with type 2 diabetes. *Journal of Health Psychology, 14*(3), 457–470.

Jung, C. G. (1951). The structure and dynamics of the self. In *Collected works: Aion* (Vol. 9). Princeton, NJ: Princeton University Press.

Jung, C. G. (1951/1959). *The collected works of C. G. Jung: Aion* (R. F. C. Hull, Trans.). Princeton, NJ: Princeton University Press.

Kaap-Deeder, J., Vansteenkiste, M., Soenens, B., Loeys, T., Mabbel, E., & Gargurevich, R. (2015). Autonomy-supportive parenting and autonomy-supportive sibling interactions: The role of mothers' and siblings' psychological need satisfaction. *Personality and Social Psychology Bulletin, 41*(11), 1590–1604.

Kaap-Deeder, J., Vansteenkiste, M., Soenens, B., Verstuyf, J., Boone, L., & Smets, J. (2014). Fostering self-endorsed motivation to change in patients with an eating disorder: The role of perceived autonomy support and psychological need satisfaction. *International Journal of Eating Disorders, 47*(6), 585–600.

Kabat-Zinn, J. (2003). Mindfulness-based interventions in context: Past, present, and future. *Clinical Psychology Science and Practice, 10*(2), 144–156.

Kage, M., & Namiki, H. (1990). The effects of evaluation structure on children's intrinsic motivation and learning. *Japanese Journal of Educational Psychology, 38*, 36–45.

Kahneman, D., Diener, E., & Schwarz, N. (1999). *Well-being: The foundations of hedonic psychology.* New York: Russell Sage Foundation.

Kahneman, D., Krueger, A. B., Schkade, D., Schwarz, N., & Stone, A. A. (2006). Would you be happier if you were richer?: A focusing illusion. *Science, 312*(5782), 1908–1910.

Kagitcibasi, C. (1996). The autonomous–relational self. *European Psychologist, 1*(3), 180–186.

Kagitcibasi, C. (2005). Autonomy and relatedness in cultural context: Implications for self and family. *Journal of Cross-Cultural Psychology, 36*, 403–422.

Kalaja, S., Jaakkola, T., Watt, A., Liukkonen, J., & Ommundsen, Y. (2009). The associations between seventh-grade Finnish students' motivational climate, perceived competence, self-determined motivation, and fundamental movement skills. *European Physical Education Review, 15*(3), 315–335.

Kanat-Maymon, Y., Benjamin, M., Stavsky, A., Shoshani, A., & Roth, G. (2015). The role of basic need fulfillment in academic dishonesty: A self-determination theory perspective. *Contemporary Educational Psychology, 43*, 1–9.

Kanat-Maymon, Y., Roth, G., Assor, A., & Raizer, A. (2016). Controlled by love: The harmful consequences of perceived conditional regard. *Journal of Personality, 84*(4), 446–460.

Kaner, A., & Prelinger, E. (2005). *The craft of psychodynamic psychotherapy.* Lanham, MD: Aronson.

Kanfer, F. H., & Gaelick-Buys, L. (1991). Self-management methods. In F. H. Kanfer & A. P. Goldstein (Eds.), *Helping people change* (pp. 305–360). New York: Pergamon.

Kant, I. (1899). *The critique of pure reason* (J. M. D. Meiklejohn, Trans.). Miami, FL: Colonial Press.

Kant, I. (1956). *Critique of practical reason* (L. White Beck, Trans.). Indianapolis, IN: Bobbs-Merrill. (Original work published 1788)

Kant, I. (1964). *Groundwork of the metaphysic of morals* (H. J. Paton, Trans.). New York: Harper & Row. (Original work published 1785)

Kaplan, H., & Assor, A. (2012). Enhancing autonomy-supportive I–Thou dialogue in schools: Conceptualization and socio-emotional effects of an intervention program. *Social Psychology of Education, 15*(2), 251–269.

Kaplan, R., & Kaplan, S. (1989). *The experience of nature: A psychological perspective.* Cambridge, UK: Cambridge University Press.

Karlamangla, A. S., Singer, B. H., McEwen, B. S., Rowe, J. W., & Seeman, T. E. (2002). Allostatic load as a predictor of functional decline: MacArthur studies of successful aging. *Journal of Clinical Epidemiology, 55*(7), 696–710.

Karniol, R., & Ross, M. (1977). The effect of performance-relevant and performance-irrelevant rewards on children's intrinsic motivation. *Child Development, 48*(2), 482–487.

Kashdan, T. B., Biswas-Diener, R., & King, L. A. (2008). Reconsidering happiness: The costs of distinguishing between hedonics and eudaimonia. *Journal of Positive Psychology, 3*(4), 219–233.

Kashdan, T. B., Rose, P., & Fincham, F. D. (2004). Curiosity and exploration: Facilitating positive subjective experiences and personal growth opportunities. *Journal of Personality Assessment, 82*(3), 291–305.

Kasser, T. (1996). Aspirations and well-being in a prison setting. *Journal of Applied Social Psychology, 26,* 1367–1377.

Kasser, T. (2002a). *The high price of materialism.* Cambridge, MA: MIT Press.

Kasser, T. (2002b). Sketches for a self-determination theory of values. In E. L. Deci & R. M. Ryan (Eds.), *Handbook of self-determination research* (pp. 123–140). Rochester, NY: University of Rochester Press.

Kasser, T. (2011). Cultural values and the well-being of future generations: A cross-national study. *Journal of Cross-Cultural Psychology, 42*(2), 206–215.

Kasser, T., & Ahuvia, A. (2002). Materialistic values and well-being in business students. *European Journal of Social Psychology, 32*(1), 137–146.

Kasser, T., Davey, J., & Ryan, R. M. (1992). Motivation and employee–supervisor discrepancies in a psychiatric vocational rehabilitation setting. *Rehabilitation Psychology, 37*(3), 175–188.

Kasser, T., & Kanner, A. D. (Eds.). (2004). *Psychology and consumer culture: The struggle for a good life in a materialistic world.* New York: American Psychological Association.

Kasser, T., Kanner, A. D., Cohn, S., & Ryan, R. M. (2007). Psychology and American corporate capitalism: Further reflections and future directions. *Psychological Inquiry, 18*(1), 60–71.

Kasser, T., Rosenblum, K. L., Sameroff, A. J., Deci, E. L., Niemiec, C. P., Ryan, R. M., et al. (2013). Changes in materialism, changes in psychological well-being: Evidence from three longitudinal studies and an intervention experiment. *Motivation and Emotion, 38*(1), 1–22.

Kasser, T., & Ryan, R. M. (1993). A dark side of the American dream: Correlates of financial success as a central life aspiration. *Journal of Personality and Social Psychology, 65*(2), 410–422.

Kasser, T., & Ryan, R. M. (1996). Further examining the American dream: Differential correlates of intrinsic and extrinsic goals. *Personality and Social Psychology Bulletin, 22*(3), 280–287.

Kasser, T., & Ryan, R. M. (2001). Be careful what you wish for: Optimal functioning and the relative attainment of intrinsic and extrinsic goals. In P. Schmuck & K. M. Sheldon (Eds.), *Life goals*

and well-being: Towards a positive psychology of human striving (pp. 116–131). Ashland, OH: Hogrefe & Huber.

Kasser, T., Ryan, R. M., Couchman, C. E., & Sheldon, K. M. (2004). Materialistic values: Their causes and consequences. In T. Kasser & A. D. Kanner (Eds.), *Psychology and consumer culture: The struggle for a good life in a materialistic world* (pp. 11–28). Washington, DC: American Psychological Association.

Kasser, T., Ryan, R. M., Zax, M., & Sameroff, A. J. (1995). The relations of maternal and social environments to late adolescents' materialistic and prosocial values. *Developmental Psychology, 31*(6), 907–914.

Kasser, V. G., & Ryan, R. M. (1999). The relation of psychological needs for autonomy and relatedness to vitality, well-being, and mortality in a nursing home. *Journal of Applied Social Psychology, 29*(5), 935–954.

Kast, A., & Connor, K. (1988). Sex and age differences in response to informational and controlling feedback. *Personality and Social Psychology Bulletin, 14*(3), 514–523.

Kätsyri, J., Hari, R., Ravaja, N., & Nummenmaa, L. (2013). Just watching the game ain't enough: Striatal fMRI reward responses to successes and failures in a video game during active and vicarious playing. *Frontiers in Human Neuroscience,* 20–32. Available at *http://journal.frontiersin.org/article/10.3389/fnhum.2013.00278/full.*

Katz, I. (2003). *The effect of autonomy support on intrinsic motivation in children from diverse cultural backgrounds.* Unpublished manuscript, Ben-Gurion University of the Negev, Israel.

Katz, I., & Assor, A. (2006). *Choice and the need for autonomy: A cross cultural investigation of various aspects of autonomy support.* Unpublished manuscript, Ben-Gurion University of the Negev, Israel.

Katz, I., Kaplan, A., & Buzukashvily, T. (2009). The role of parents' motivation in students' autonomous motivation for doing homework. *Learning and Individual Differences, 21*(4), 376–386.

Kauffman, S. A. (2000). *Investigations.* Oxford, UK: Oxford University Press.

Kawamura, K. Y., Frost, R. O., & Harmatz, M. G. (2002). The relationship of perceived parenting styles to perfectionism. *Personality and Individual Differences, 32*(2), 317–327.

Kazdin, A. E. (1977). *The token economy: A review and evaluation.* New York: Plenum Press.

Kazén, M., Baumann, N., & Kuhl, J. (2003). Self-infiltration vs. self-compatibility checking in dealing with unattractive tasks: The moderating influence of state vs. action orientation. *Motivation and Emotion, 27*(3), 157–197.

Kazén, M., Kuhl, J., & Leicht, E. M. (2015). When

the going gets tough . . . Self-motivation is associated with invigoration and fun. *Psychological Research, 79*(6), 1064–1076.

Keijsers, G. P. J., Kampman, M., & Hoogduin, C. A. L. (2001). Dropout prediction in cognitive behavior therapy for panic disorder. *Behavior Therapy, 32*(4), 739–749.

Kelley, H. H. (1967). Attribution theory in social psychology. In D. Levine (Ed.), *Nebraska Symposium on Motivation* (Vol. 15, pp. 192–240). Lincoln: University of Nebraska Press.

Kelley, H. H., & Thibaut, J. W. (1978). *Interpersonal relations: A theory of interdependence.* New York: Wiley-Interscience.

Kelman, H. C. (1958). Compliance, identification, and internalization: Three processes of attitude change. *Journal of Conflict Resolution, 2*(1), 51–60.

Kelman, H. C., & Hamilton, V. L. (1989). *Crimes of obedience: Toward a social psychology of authority and responsibility.* New Haven, CT: Yale University Press.

Kennedy, S., Goggin, K., & Nollen, N. (2004). Adherence to HIV medications: Utility of the theory of self-determination. *Cognitive Therapy and Research, 28*(5), 611–628.

Kenney-Benson, G., & Pomerantz, E. (2005). The role of mothers' use of control in children's perfectionism: Implications for the development of children's depressive symptoms. *Journal of Personality, 73*(1), 23–46.

Kernberg, O. (1967). Borderline personality organization. *Journal of the American Psychoanalytic Association, 15*(3), 641–685.

Kernis, M. H. (1993). The role of stability and level of self-esteem in psychological functioning. In R. F. Baumeister (Ed.), *Self-esteem: The puzzle of low self-regard* (pp. 167–182). New York: Plenum Press.

Kernis, M. H. (2000). Substitute needs and the distinction between fragile and secure high self-esteem. *Psychological Inquiry, 11*(4), 298–300.

Kernis, M. H. (2003). Optimal self-esteem and authenticity: Separating fantasy from reality. *Psychological Inquiry, 14*(1), 83–89.

Kernis, M. H., & Goldman, B. M. (2003). Stability and variability in self-concept and self-esteem. In M. R. Leary & J. P. Tangney (Eds.), *Handbook of self and identity* (pp. 106–127). New York: Guilford Press.

Kernis, M. H., & Goldman, B. M. (2006). A multicomponent conceptualization of authenticity: Theory and research. In M. Zanna (Ed.), *Advances in experimental social psychology* (Vol. 38, pp. 284–357). New York: Academic Press.

Kernis, M. H., & Paradise, A. W. (2002). Distinguishing between secure and fragile forms of high self-esteem. In E. L. Deci & R. M. Ryan (Eds.), *Handbook of self-determination research* (pp. 339–360). Rochester, NY: University of Rochester Press.

Kernis, M. H., Paradise, A. W., Whitaker, D. J., Wheatman, S. R., & Goldman, B. N. (2000). Master of one's psychological domain?: Not likely if one's self-esteem is unstable. *Personality and Social Psychology Bulletin, 26*(10), 1297–1305.

Kerr, D. (2002). Devoid of community: Examining conceptions of autonomy in education. *Educational Theory, 52*(1), 13–25.?

Khanna, S., & Kasser, T. (1999). *Materialism and objectification in relationships.* Unpublished manuscript, Knox College, Galesburg, IL.

Khema, S. (1983). *Meditating on no-self: A Dhamma talk.* Kandy, Sri Lanka: Buddhist Publication Society.

Kierkegaard, S. (1987). *Fear and trembling, and the sickness unto death* (R. L. Perkins, Trans.). Macon, GA: Mercer University Press.

Kim, K., Schmierbach, M. G., Bellur, S. S., Chung, M.-Y., Fraustino, J. D., Dardis, F., et al. (2015). Is it a sense of autonomy, control, or attachment? Exploring the effects of in-game customization on game enjoyment. *Computers in Human Behavior, 48*(C), 695–705.

Kim, S. Y., Wang, Y., Orozco-Lapray, D., Shen, Y., & Murtuza, M. (2013). Does "tiger parenting" exist? Parenting profiles of Chinese Americans and adolescent developmental outcomes. *Asian American Journal of Psychology, 4*(1), 7–18.

Kim, Y., Carver, C. S., Deci, E. L., & Kasser, T. (2008). Adult attachment and psychological well-being in cancer caregivers: The mediational role of spouses' motives for caregiving. *Health Psychology, 27*(2S), S144–S154.

Kim, Y., Kasser, T., & Lee, H. (2003). Self-concept, aspirations, and well-being in South Korea and the United States. *Journal of Social Psychology, 143*(3), 277–290.

Kindt, S., Vansteenkiste, M., Loeys, T., Cano, A., Lauwerier, E., Verhofstadt, L., et al. (2015). When is helping your partner with chronic pain a burden?: The relation between helping motivation and personal and relational functioning. *Pain Medicine, 16*, 1732–1744.

King, K. B. (1984). *Coping with cardiac surgery.* Unpublished doctoral dissertation, University of Rochester, Rochester, NY.

Kins, E., Beyers, W., Soenens, B., & Vansteenkiste, M. (2009). Patterns of home leaving and subjective well-being in emerging adulthood: The role of motivational processes and parental autonomy support. *Developmental Psychology, 45*(5), 1416–1429.

Kirsch, S. J. (2006). *Children, adolescents, and media violence: A critical look at the research.* Thousand Oaks, CA: Sage.

Kirschenbaum, H., & Jourdan, A. (2005). The current status of Carl Rogers and the person-centered approach. *Psychotherapy: Theory, Research, Practice, Training, 42*(1), 37–51.

Kitayama, S., Markus, H. R., Matsumoto, H., & Norasakkunkit, V. (1997). Individual and collective processes in the construction of the self: Self-enhancement in the United States and self-criticism in Japan. *Journal of Personality and Social Psychology, 72*(6), 1245–1267.

Klapp, A. (2015) Does grading affect educational attainment?: A longitudinal study. *Assessment in Education: Principles, Policy and Practice, 22*(3), 302–323.

Klerman, G. L., Weissman, M. M., Rounsaville, B. J., & Chevron, E. S. (1984). *Interpersonal psychotherapy of depression.* New York: Basic Books.

Knafo, A., & Assor, A. (2007). Motivation for agreement with parental values: Desirable when autonomous, problematic when controlled. *Motivation and Emotion, 31*(3), 232–245.

Knee, C. R., Canevello, A., Bush, A. L., & Cook, A. (2008). Relationship-contingent self-esteem and the ups and downs of romantic relationships. *Journal of Personality and Social Psychology, 95*(3), 608–627.

Knee, C. R., Lonsbary, C., Canevello, A., & Patrick, H. (2005). Self-determination and conflict in romantic relationships. *Journal of Personality and Social Psychology, 89*(6), 997–1009.

Knee, C. R., Neighbors, C., & Vfetor, N. A. (2001). Self-determination theory as a framework for understanding road rage. *Journal of Applied Social Psychology, 31*(5), 889–904.

Knee, C. R., Patrick, H., Vietor, N. A., Nanayakkara, A., & Neighbors, C. (2002). Self-determination as growth motivation in romantic relationships. *Personality and Social Psychology Bulletin, 28*(5), 609–619.

Knee, C. R., & Zuckerman, M. (1996). Causality orientations and the disappearance of the self-serving bias. *Journal of Research in Personality, 30*(1), 76–87.

Knee, C. R., & Zuckerman, M. (1998). A nondefensive personality: Autonomy and control as moderators of defensive coping and self-handicapping. *Journal of Research in Personality, 32*(2), 115–130.

Kobak, R., Cassidy, J., & Ziv, Y. (2004). Attachment related trauma and posttraumatic stress disorder: Implications for adult adaptation. In S. W. Rholes & J. A. Simpson (Eds.), *Adult attachment: Theory, research, and clinical implications* (pp. 388–407). New York: Guilford Press.

Koestner, R., Bernieri, F., & Zuckerman, M. (1992). Self-regulation and consistency between attitudes, traits, and behaviors. *Personality and Social Psychology Bulletin, 18*(1), 52–59.

Koestner, R., Gingras, I., Abutaa, R., Losier, G. F., DiDio, L., & Gagné, M. (1999). To follow expert advice when making a decision: An examination of reactive versus reflective autonomy. *Journal of Personality, 67*(5), 851–872.

Koestner, R., Houlfort, N., Paquet, S., & Knight, C. (2001). On the risks of recycling because of guilt: An examination of the consequences of introjection. *Journal of Applied Social Psychology, 31*(12), 2545–2560.

Koestner, R., Lekes, N., Powers, T. A., & Chicoine, E. (2002). Attaining personal goals: Self-concordance plus implementation intentions equals success. *Journal of Personality and Social Psychology, 83*, 231–244.

Koestner, R., & Losier, G. F. (1996). Distinguishing reactive versus reflective autonomy. *Journal of Personality, 64*(2), 465–494.

Koestner, R., Losier, G. F., Vallerand, R. J., & Carducci, D. (1996). Identified and introjected forms of political internalization: Extending self-determination theory. *Journal of Personality and Social Psychology, 70*(5), 1025–1036.

Koestner, R., & McClelland, D. C. (1990). Perspectives on competence motivation. In L. Pervin (Ed.), *Handbook of personality: Theory and research* (pp. 527–548). New York: Guilford Press.

Koestner, R., Otis, N., Powers, T. A., Pelletier, L., & Gagnon, H. (2008). Autonomous motivation, controlled motivation, and goal progress. *Journal of Personality, 76*(5), 1201–1230.

Koestner, R., Powers, T. A., Carbonneau, N., Milyavskaya, M., & Chua, S. N. (2012). Distinguishing autonomous and directive forms of goal support: Their effects on goal progress, relationship quality, and subjective well-being. *Personality and Social Psychology Bulletin, 38*(12), 1609–1620.

Koestner, R., Ryan, R. M., Bernieri, F., & Holt, K. (1984). Setting limits on children's behavior: The differential effects of controlling versus informational styles on intrinsic motivation and creativity. *Journal of Personality, 52*(3), 233–248.

Koestner, R., & Zuckerman, M. (1994). Causality orientations, failure, and achievement. *Journal of Personality, 62*(3), 321–346.

Koestner, R., Zuckerman, M., & Koestner, J. (1987). Praise, involvement, and intrinsic motivation. *Journal of Personality and Social Psychology, 53*(2), 383–390.

Kohlberg, L. (1969). Stages and sequence: The cognitive-developmental approach to socialization. In D. A. Goslin (Ed.), *Handbook of socialization theory and research* (pp. 347–380). Chicago: Rand McNally.

Kohn, M. L., & Slomczynski, K. M. (1990). *Social structure and self-direction: A comparative analysis of the United States and Poland.* Oxford, UK: Blackwell.

Kohut, H. (1971). *The analysis of the self: A systematic approach to the psychoanalytic treatment of narcissistic personality disorders*. New York: International Universities Press.

Koka, A., & Hein, V. (2003). Perceptions of teacher's feedback and learning environment as predictors of intrinsic motivation in physical education. *Psychology of Sport and Exercise, 4,* 333–346.

Koole, S. L., & Kuhl, J. (2003). In search of the real self: A functional perspective on optimal self-esteem and authenticity. *Psychological Inquiry, 14*(1), 43–48.

Korsgaard, C. (2009). *Self-constitution: Agency, identity, and integrity*. Oxford, UK: Oxford University Press.

Kovjanic, S., Schuh, S. C., & Jonas, K. (2013). Transformational leadership and performance: An experimental investigation of the mediating effects of basic needs satisfaction and work engagement. *Journal of Occupational and Organizational Psychology, 86*(4), 543–555.

Kovjanic, S., Schuh, S. C., Jonas, K., Van Quaquebeke, N. V., & Van Dick, R. (2012). How do transformational leaders foster positive employee outcomes?: A self-determination-based analysis of employees' needs as mediating links. *Journal of Organizational Behavior, 33*(8), 1031–1052.

Krapp, A. (2002). An educational-psychological theory of interest and its relation to SDT. In E. L. Deci & R. M. Ryan (Eds.), *Handbook of self-determination research* (pp. 405–427). Rochester, NY: University of Rochester Press.

Kristof, N. (2011, May 11). A rite of torture for girls. *The New York Times*. Retrieved from *www.nytimes.com*.

Krug, E. G., Mercy, J. A., Dahlberg, L. L., & Zwi, A. B. (2002). The world report on violence and health. *The Lancet, 360*(9339), 1083–1088.

Kruglanski, A. W., Riter, A., Amitai, A., Margolin, B.-S., Shabtai, L., & Zaksh, D. (1975). Can money enhance intrinsic motivation?: A test of the content–consequence hypothesis. *Journal of Personality and Social Psychology, 31*(4), 744–750.

Ku, L., Dittmar, H., & Banerjee, R. (2014). To have or to learn?: The effects of materialism on British and Chinese children's learning. *Journal of Personality and Social Psychology, 106*(5), 803–821.

Kuhl, J. (1996). Who controls whom when "I control myself"? *Psychological Inquiry, 7*(1), 61–68.

Kuhl, J. (2000). The volitional basis of personality systems interaction theory: Applications in learning and treatment contexts. *International Journal of Educational Research, 33*(7), 665–703.

Kuhl, J., & Kazén, M. (1994). Self-discrimination and memory: State orientation and false self-ascription of assigned activities. *Journal of Personality and Social Psychology, 66*(6), 1103–1115.

Kuhl, J., Quirin, M., & Koole, S. L. (2015). Being someone: The integrated self as a neuropsychological system. *Social and Personality Psychology Compass, 9*(3), 115–132.

Kultgen, J. (1995). *Autonomy and intervention: Parentalism in the caring life*. Oxford, UK: Oxford University Press.

Kumagai, H. A. (1988). Ki: The "fervor of vitality" and the subjective self. *Symbolic Interaction, 11*(2), 175–190.

Kurdek, L. A., & Schnopp-Wyatt, D. (1997). Predicting relationship commitment and relationship stability from both partners' relationship values: Evidence from heterosexual dating couples. *Personality and Social Psychology Bulletin, 23*(10), 1111–1119.

Kushlev, K., Dunn, E. W., & Ashton-James, C. E. (2012). Does affluence impoverish the experience of parenting? *Journal of Experimental Social Psychology, 48,* 1381–1384.

Kuvaas, B. (2006). Work performance, affective commitment, and work motivation: The roles of pay administration and pay level. *Journal of Organizational Behavior, 27*(3), 365–385.

Kuvaas, B. (2009). A test of hypotheses derived from self-determination theory among public sector employees. *Employee Relations, 31*(1), 39–56.

Kuvaas, B., Buch, R., Gagné, M., Dysvik, A., & Forest, J. (2016). Do you get what you pay for? Sales incentives and implications for motivation and changes in turnover intention and work effort. *Motivation and Emotion, 40,* 667–680.

Kuvaas, B., Dysvik, A., & Buch, R. (2014, August). *The relative impact of extrinsic and intrinsic motivation on employee outcomes*. Paper presented at the annual meeting of the Academy of Management, Philadelphia, PA.

Kwan, B. M., Hooper, A., Magnan, R. E., & Bryan, A. D. (2011). A longitudinal diary study of the effects of causality orientations on exercise-related affect. *Self and Identity, 10*(3), 363–374.

La Guardia, J. G. (2006, January). *Emotional engagement within couples: Impact on personal and relationship functioning*. Paper presented at the annual meeting of the Society for Personality and Social Psychology, Palm Springs, CA.

La Guardia, J. G., & Patrick, H. (2008). Self-determination theory as a fundamental theory of close relationships. *Canadian Psychology/Psychologie Canadienne, 49*(3), 201–209.

La Guardia, J. G., Ryan, R. M., Couchman, C. E., & Deci, E. L. (2000). Within-person variation in security of attachment: A self-determination theory perspective on attachment, need fulfillment, and well-being. *Journal of Personality and Social Psychology, 79*(3), 367–384.

Laing, R. D. (1960). *The divided self: An existential study in sanity and madness*. Middlesex, UK: Penguin Books.

Lalande, D., Vallerand, R. J., Lafrenière, M.-A. K., Verner-Filion, J., Laurent, F.-A., Forest, J., et al. (2016). Obsessive passion: A compensatory response to unsatisfied needs. *Journal of Personality*. Advance online publication.

Lam, C. F., & Gurland, S. T. (2008). Self-determined work motivation predicts job outcomes, but what predicts self-determined work motivation? *Journal of Research in Personality, 42*, 1109–1115.

Lamm, C., Batson, C. D., & Decety, J. (2007). The neural substrate of human empathy: Effects of perspective-taking and cognitive appraisal. *Journal of Cognitive Neuroscience, 19*(1), 42–58.

Lammers, J., Stoker, J. I., Rink, F., & Galinsky, A. D. (2016). To have control over or to be free from others? The desire for power reflects a need for autonomy. *Personality and Social Psychology Bulletin, 42*(4), 498.

Landry, A. T., Kindlein, J., Trépanier, S.-G., Forest, J., Zigarmi, D., Houson, D., et al. (2016). Why individuals want money is what matters: Using self-determination theory to explain the differential relationship between motives for making money and employee psychological health. *Motivation and Emotion, 40*(2), 226–242.

Landry, R., Whipple, N., Mageau, G., Joussemet, M., Koestner, R., Di Dio, L., et al. (2008). Trust in organismic development, autonomy support, and adaptation among mothers and their children. *Motivation and Emotion, 32*(3), 173–188.

Lane, R. E. (2000). *The loss of happiness in market democracies.* New Haven, CT: Yale University Press.

Langan, E., Lonsdale, C., Blake, C., & Toner, J. (2015). Testing the effects of a self-determination theory-based intervention with youth Gaelic football coaches on athlete motivation and burnout. *Sport Psychologist, 29*(4), 293–301.

Langer, E. J. (1989). *Mindfulness.* Boston: Addison-Wesley.

Langford, D., Crager, S., Shehzad, Z., Smith, S., Sotocinal, S., Levenstadt, J., et al. (2006). Social modulation of pain as evidence for empathy in mice. *Science, 312*, 1967–1970.

Lankford, A. (2014). Précis of the myth of martyrdom: What really drives suicide bombers, rampage shooters, and other self-destructive killers. *Behavioral and Brain Sciences, 37*(4), 351–362.

Lanning, K. (2008). Democracy, voting, and disenfranchisement in the United States: A social psychological perspective. *Journal of Social Issues, 64*(3), 431–446.

Lasch, C. (1991). *The culture of narcissism: American life in an age of diminishing expectations.* New York: Norton.

Laszlo, E. (1987). *Evolution: The grand synthesis.* Boulder, CO: Shambhala.

Lawson, T. (2013). Emergence and morphogenesis: Causal reduction and downward causa-

tion? In M. S. Archer (Ed.), *Social morphogenesis* (pp. 61–84). Dordrecht, The Netherlands: Springer.

Leak, G. K., & Cooney, R. R. (2001). Self-determination, attachment styles, and well-being in adult romantic relationships. *Representative Research in Social Psychology, 25*, 55–62.

Leary, M. R. (2004). The sociometer, self-esteem, and the regulation of interpersonal behavior. In R. F. Baumeister & K. Vohs (Eds.), *Handbook of self-regulation* (2nd ed., pp. 373–391). New York: Guilford Press.

Leary, M. R., & Baumeister, R. F. (2000). The nature and function of self-esteem: Sociometer theory. In M. P. Zanna (Ed.), *Advances in experimental social psychology* (pp. 1–62). San Diego, CA: Academic Press.

Leary, M. R., & Tate, E. B. (2007). The multi-faceted nature of mindfulness. *Psychological Inquiry, 18*(4), 251–255.

Lee, W., & Reeve, J. (2013). Self-determined, but not non-self-determined, motivation predicts activations in the anterior insular cortex: An fMRI study of personal agency. *Social Cognitive and Affective Neuroscience, 8*(5), 538–545.

Lee, W., Reeve, J., Xue, Y., & Xiong, J. (2012). Neural differences between intrinsic reasons for doing versus extrinsic reasons for doing: An fMRI study. *Neuroscience Research, 73*(1), 68–72.

Legate, N., DeHaan, C., & Ryan, R. (2015) Righting the wrong: Reparative coping after going along with ostracism. *Journal of Social Psychology, 155*(5), 471–482.

Legate, N., DeHaan, C. R., Weinstein, N., & Ryan, R. M. (2013). Hurting you hurts me too: The psychological costs of complying with ostracism. *Psychological Science, 24*(4), 583–588.

Legate, N., Ryan, R. M., & Weinstein, N. (2012). Is coming out always a "good thing"? Exploring the relations of autonomy support, outness, and wellness for lesbian, gay, and bisexual individuals. *Social Psychological and Personality Science, 3*(2), 145–152.

Legault, L., Green-Demers, I., Grant, P., & Chung, J. (2007). On the self-regulation of implicit and explicit prejudice: A self-determination theory perspective. *Personality and Social Psychology Bulletin, 33*(5), 732–749.

Legault, L., Green-Demers, I., & Pelletier, L. (2006). Why do high school students lack motivation in the classroom?: Toward an understanding of academic amotivation and the role of social support. *Journal of Educational Psychology, 98*(3), 567–582.

Legault, L., Gutsell, J. N., & Inzlicht, M. (2011). Ironic effects of antiprejudice messages: How motivational interventions can reduce (but also increase) prejudice. *Psychological Science, 22*(12), 1472–1477.

Legault, L., & Inzlicht, M. (2013). Self-determination, self-regulation, and the brain: Autonomy improves performance by enhancing neuroaffective responsiveness to self-regulation failure. *Journal of Personality and Social Psychology*, 105(1), 123–138.

Lehenbauer-Baum, M., Klaps, A., Kovacovsky, Z., Witzmann, K., Zahlbruckner, R., & Stetina, B. U. (2015). Addiction and engagement: An explorative study toward classification criteria for Internet gaming disorder. *Cyberpsychology, Behavior, and Social Networking*, 18(6), 343–349.

Lekes, N., Hope, N. H., Gouveia, L., Koestner, R., & Philippe, F. L. (2012). Influencing value priorities and increasing well-being: The effects of reflecting on intrinsic values. *Journal of Positive Psychology*, 7(3), 249–261.

Leotti, L. A., & Delgado, M. R. (2011). Processing social and nonsocial rewards in the human brain. In J. Decety & J. Cacioppo (Eds.), *Oxford handbook of social neuroscience* (pp. 178–194). New York: Oxford University Press.

Lepper, M. R., Corpus, J. H., & Iyengar, S. S. (2005). Intrinsic and extrinsic motivational orientations in the classroom: Age differences and academic correlates. *Journal of Educational Psychology*, 97(2), 184–196.

Lepper, M. R., & Greene, D. (1975). Turning play into work: Effects of adult surveillance and extrinsic rewards on children's intrinsic motivation. *Journal of Personality and Social Psychology*, 31(3), 479–486.

Lepper, M. R., & Greene, D. (1978). *The hidden costs of reward* (pp. 193–203). Hillsdale, NJ: Erlbaum.

Lepper, M. R., Greene, D., & Nisbett, R. E. (1973). Undermining children's intrinsic interest with extrinsic reward: A test of the "overjustification" hypothesis. *Journal of Personality and Social Psychology*, 28(1), 129–137.

Lepper, M. R., Sagotsky, G., Dafoe, J. L., & Greene, D. (1982). Consequences of superfluous social constraints: Effects on young children's social inferences and subsequent intrinsic interest. *Journal of Personality and Social Psychology*, 42(1), 51–65.

Lerner, H. G. (1988). *Women in therapy: Devaluation, anger, aggression, depression, self-sacrifice, mothering, mother blaming, self-betrayal, sex-role stereotypes, dependency, work and success inhibitions.* Lanham, MD: Aronson.

Leslie, A. M. (1987). Pretense and representation: The origins of "theory of mind." *Psychological Review*, 94(4), 412–426.

Lettieri, R. (2005). The ego revisited. *Psychoanalytic Psychology*, 22(3), 370–381.

Levesque, C., & Brown, K. W. (2003). *The emotional consequences of implicit–explicit autonomy motive incongruence.* Paper presented at the fourth annual meeting of the Society for Personality and Social Psychology, Los Angeles, CA.

Levesque, C., & Brown, K. W. (2007). Mindfulness as a moderator of the effect of implicit motivational self-concept on day-to-day behavioral motivation. *Motivation and Emotion*, 31(4), 284–299.

Levesque, C., & Pelletier, L. G. (2003). On the investigation of primed and chronic autonomous and heteronomous motivational orientations. *Personality and Social Psychology Bulletin*, 29(12), 1570–1584.

Levesque, C., Zuehlke, A. N., Stanek, L. R., & Ryan, R. M. (2004). Autonomy and competence in German and American university students: A comparative study based on self-determination theory. *Journal of Educational Psychology*, 96(1), 68–84.

Levesque, C. S., Williams, G. C., Elliot, D., Pickering, M. A., Bodenhamer, B., & Finley, P. J. (2007). Validating the theoretical structure of the Treatment Self-Regulation Questionnaire (TSRQ) across three different health behaviors. *Health Education Research*, 22(5), 691–702.

Levesque, M., Blais, M. R., & Hess, U. (2004). Motivation, discretionary organisational attitudes and well-being in an African environment: When does duty call? *Canadian Journal of Behavioural Science/Revue Canadienne des Sciences du Comportement*, 36(4), 321–332.

Lewin, K. (1951). Intention, will, and need. In D. Rapaport (Ed.), *Organization and pathology of thought* (pp. 95–153). New York: Columbia University Press.

Lewis, C. C., Simons, A. D., Silva, S. G., Rohde, P., Small, D. M., Murakami, J. L., et al. (2009). The role of readiness to change in response to treatment of adolescent depression. *Journal of Consulting and Clinical Psychology*, 77(3), 422–428.

Lewis, M. A., & Neighbors, C. (2005). Self-determination and the use of self-presentation strategies. *Journal of Social Psychology*, 145(4), 469–490.

Lewis, M. D. (1994). Reconciling stage and specificity in neo-Piagetian theory: Self-organizing conceptual structures. *Human Development*, 37(3), 143–169.

Lewthwaite, R., Chiviacowsky, S., Drews, R., & Wulf, G. (2015). Choose to move: The motivational impact of autonomy support on motor learning. *Psychonomic Bulletin and Review*, 22(5), 1383–1388.

Li, F., Harmer, P., Duncan, T. E., Duncan, S. C., Acock, A., & Boles, S. (1998). Approaches to testing interaction effects using structural equation modeling methodology. *Multivariate Behavioral Research*, 33(1), 1–39.

Libet, B. (1999). How does conscious experience arise?: The neural time factor. *Brain Research Bulletin*, 50(5/6), 339–340.

Lieberman, M. D. (2013). *Social: Why our brains are wired to connect*. New York: Crown.

Linehan, M. M. (1987). Dialectical behavior therapy for borderline personality disorder: Theory and method. *Bulletin of the Menninger Clinic, 51*(3), 261–276.

Linehan, M. M. (1993). *Cognitive-behavioral treatment of borderline personality disorder*. New York: Guilford Press.

Linville, P. W. (1985). Self-complexity and affective extremity: Don't put all of your eggs in one cognitive basket. *Social Cognition, 3*(1), 94–120.

Linville, P. W. (1987). Self-complexity as a cognitive buffer against stress-related illness and depression. *Journal of Personality and Social Psychology, 52*(4), 663–676.

Litalien, D., Lüdtke, O., Parker, P., & Trautwein, U. (2013). Different pathways, same effects: Autonomous goal regulation is associated with subjective well-being during the post-school transition. *Motivation and Emotion, 37*(3), 444–456.

Litalien, D., Morin, A. J. S., Gagné, M., Vallerand, R. J., Losier, G., & Ryan, R. M. (2016). *Evidence of a continuum structure of academic self-determination: A two-study test using a Bifactor-ESEM representation of academic motivation.* Manuscript submitted for publication.

Little, B. R. (1998). Personal project pursuit: Dimensions and dynamics of personal meaning. In P. T. P. Wong & P. S. Fry (Eds.), *The human quest for meaning: A handbook of psychological research and clinical applications* (pp. 193–212). Mahwah, NJ: Erlbaum.

Little, T. D. (1997). Mean and covariance structures (MACS) analyses of cross-cultural data: Practical and theoretical issues. *Multivariate Behavioral Research, 32*(1), 53–76.

Liu, Q., Fang, X., Wan, J., & Zhou, Z. (2016). Need satisfaction and adolescent pathological internet use: Comparison of satisfaction perceived online and offline. *Computers in Human Behavior, 55*, 695–700.

Lo, Y. K. (2003). Finding the self in the *Analects*: A philosophical approach. In K. C. Chong, S. H. Tan, & C. L. Ten (Eds.), *The moral circle of the self: Chinese and Western approaches* (pp. 249–267). Chicago: Open Court.

Locke, E. A., & Latham, G. P. (1990). *A theory of goal setting and task performance*. Upper Saddle River, NJ: Prentice Hall.

Loeb, J. (1906). *The dynamics of living matter*. London: Columbia University Press.

Loevinger, J. (1957). Objective tests as instruments of psychological theory. *Psychological Reports, 3*(3), 635–694.

Loevinger, J. (1959). Theory and techniques of assessment. *Annual Review of Psychology, 10*(1), 287–316.

Loevinger, J. (1976). *Ego development*. San Francisco: Jossey-Bass.

Loevinger, J., & Blasi, A. (1991). Development of the self as subject. In J. Strauss, & G. R. Goethals (Eds.), *The self: Interdisciplinary approaches* (pp. 150–167). New York: Springer-Verlag.

Lombard, M., & Ditton, T. (1997). At the heart of it all: The concept of presence. *Journal of Computer-Mediated Communication, 3*(2).

Lonky, E., & Reihman, J. M. (1990). *Self-regulation and moral reasoning as mediators of moral behavior*. Unpublished manuscript, State University of New York, Oswego, NY.

Lonsdale, C., & Hodge, K. (2011). Temporal ordering of motivational quality and athlete burnout in elite sport. *Medicine and Science in Sports and Exercise, 43*(5), 913–921.

Lonsdale, C., Hodge, K., Hargreaves, E., & Ng, J. Y. Y. (2014). Comparing sport motivation scales: A response to Pelletier et al. *Psychology of Sport and Exercise, 15*, 446–452.

Lonsdale, C., Hodge, K., & Rose, E. (2009) Athlete burnout in elite sport: A self-determination perspective. *Journal of Sports Sciences, 27*(8), 785–795.

Lonsdale, C., Sabiston, C. M., Raedeke, T. D., Ha, A. S., & Sum, R. K. (2009). Self-determined motivation and students' physical activity during structured physical education lessons and free choice periods. *Preventive Medicine, 48*(1), 69–73.

López, V., Bilbao, M. D. L. A., & Rodriguez, J. I. (2011). La sala de clases sí importa: incidencia del clima de aula sobre la percepción de intimidación y victimización entre escolares [The classroom does matter: Incidence of classroom climate on the perception of bullying and victimization among schoolchildren]. *Universitas Psychologica, 11*(1), 91–101.

López-Walle, J., Balaguer, I., Castillo, I., & Tristán, J. (2012). Autonomy support, basic psychological needs and well-being in Mexican athletes. *Spanish Journal of Psychology, 15*(3), 1283–1292.

Lorenz, K. (1950). Ganzheit und teil in der tierischen und menschlichen gemeinscha: Eine methodolgische erörterung [Part and parcel in animal and human societies: A methodological discussion], *Stadium Generale, 3*(9), 455–499.

Losier, G. F., & Koestner, R. (1999). Intrinsic versus identified regulation in distinct political campaigns: The consequences of following politics for pleasure versus personal meaningfulness. *Personality and Social Psychology Bulletin, 25*(3), 287–298.

Losier, G. F., Perreault, S., Koestner, R., & Vallerand, R. J. (2001). Examining individual differences in the internalization of political values: Validation of the self-determination scale of political motivation. *Journal of Research in Personality, 35*, 41–61.

Loughnan, S., Kuppens, P., Allik, J., Balazs, K., De Lemus, S., Dumont, K., et al. (2011). Economic inequality is linked to biased self-perception. *Psychological Science, 22*(10), 1254–1258.

Lubans, D. R., Lonsdale, C., Plotnikoff, R. C., Smith, J., Dally, K., & Morgan, P. J. (2013). Development and evaluation of the Motivation to Limit Screen-Time Questionnaire (MLSQ) for adolescents. *Preventive Medicine, 57*(5), 561–566.

Lundqvist, C., & Raglin, J. S. (2015). The relationship of basic need satisfaction, motivational climate and personality to well-being and stress patterns among elite athletes: An explorative study. *Motivation and Emotion, 39*(2), 237–246.

Lussier, J. P., Heil, S. H., Mongeon, J. A., Badger, G. J., & Higgins, S. T. (2006). A meta-analysis of voucher-based reinforcement therapy for substance use disorders. *Addiction, 101*(2), 192–203.

Luttmer, E. F. (2005). Neighbors as negatives: Relative earnings and well-being. *Quarterly Journal of Economics, 120*(3), 963–1002.

Luyckx, K., Vansteenkiste, M., Goossens, L., & Duriez, B. (2009). Basic need satisfaction and identity formation: Bridging self-determination theory and process-oriented identity research. *Journal of Counseling Psychology, 56*(2), 276–288.

Lynch, M. F., La Guardia, J. G., & Ryan, R. M. (2009). On being yourself in different cultures: Ideal and actual self-concept, autonomy support, and well-being in China, Russia, and the United States. *Journal of Positive Psychology, 4*(4), 290–304.

Lynch, M. F., Plant, R. W., & Ryan, R. M. (2005). Psychological needs and threat to safety: Implications for staff and patients in a psychiatric hospital for youth. *Professional Psychology: Research and Practice, 36*(4), 415–425.

Lyness, J. M., Lurie, S. J., Ward, D. S., Mooney, C. J., & Lambert, D. R. (2013). Engaging students and faculty: Implications of self-determination theory for teachers and leaders in academic medicine. *BMC Medical Education, 13*, 151.

Lyons, E. J. (2015). Cultivating engagement and enjoyment in exergames using feedback, challenge, and rewards. *Games for Health Journal, 4*(1), 12–18.

Lyons, M., Rynne, S. B., & Mallett, C. J. (2012). Reflection and the art of coaching: Fostering high-performance in Olympic Ski Cross. *Reflective Practice, 13*(3), 359–372.

Ma, Q., Jin, J., Meng, L., & Shen, Q. (2014). The dark side of monetary incentive: How does extrinsic reward crowd out intrinsic motivation. *NeuroReport, 25*(3), 194–198.

Maccoby, E. E. (1980). *Social development: Psychological growth and the parent–child relationship.* New York: Harcourt Brace Jovanovich.

Mack, D. E., Wilson, P. M., Oster, K. G., Kowalski, K. C., Crocker, P. R. E., & Sylvester, B. D. (2011). Well-being in volleyball players: Examining the contributions of independent and balanced psychological need satisfaction. *Psychology of Sport and Exercise, 12*(5), 533–539.

Mackenzie, C., & Stoljar, N. (2000). Introduction: Autonomy refigured. In C. Mackenzie & N. Stoljar (Eds.), *Relational autonomy: Feminist perspectives on autonomy, agency and the social self* (pp. 3–31). New York: Oxford University Press.

MacKinnon, R. A., Michels, R., & Buckley, P. J. (2015). *The psychiatric interview in clinical practice* (3rd ed.). Washington, DC: American Psychiatric.

MacNair, R. M. (2002). Perpetration-induced atic stress in combat veterans. *Peace and Conflict: Journal of Peace Psychology, 8*(1), 63–72.

Madjar, N., & Cohen-Malayev, M. (2013). Youth movements as educational settings promoting personal development: Comparing motivation and identity formation in formal and non-formal education contexts. *International Journal of Educational Research, 62*, 162–174.

Maehr, M. L., & Stallings, W. M. (1972). Freedom from external evaluation. *Child Development, 43*(1), 177–185.

Mageau, G., & Vallerand, R. J. (2003). The coach–athlete relationship: A motivational model. *Journal of Sports Sciences, 21*(11), 883–904.

Magid, K., & McKelvey, C. A. (1987). *High risk.* New York: Bantam Books.

Mahoney, J. W., Gucciardi, D. F., Ntoumanis, N., & Mallett, C. J. (2014). Mental toughness in sport: Motivational antecedents and associations with performance and psychological health. *Journal of Sport and Exercise Psychology, 36*(3), 281–292.

Majolo, B., Ames, K., Garratt, R., Hall, K., & Wilson, N. (2006). Human friendship favours cooperation in the iterated prisoner's dilemma. *Behaviour, 143*(11), 1383–1395.

Mandigo, J. L., & Holt, N. L. (2002). Putting theory into practice: Enhancing motivation through OPTIMAL strategies. *Avante, 8*(3), 21–29.

Mankad, A., & Greenhill, M. (2014). Motivational indictors predicting the engagement, frequency and adequacy of rainwater tank maintenance. *Water Resources Research, 50*, 29–38.

Marbell, K. N., & Grolnick, W. S. (2013). Correlates of parental control and autonomy support in an interdependent culture: A look at Ghana. *Motivation and Emotion, 37*(1), 79–92.

Marinak, B. A., & Gambrell, L. B. (2008). Intrinsic motivation and rewards: What sustains young children's engagement with text? *Literacy Research and Instruction, 47*(1), 9–26.

Markey, P. M., Markey, C. N., & French, J. E. (2014). Violent video games and real-world violence: Rhetoric versus data. *Psychology of Popular Media Culture, 4*(4), 277–295.

Markland, D. A. (2009). The mediating role of behavioural regulations in the relationship between perceived body size discrepancies and physical activity among adult women. *Hellenic Journal of Psychology, 6,* 169–182.

Markland, D. A., Ryan, R. M., Tobin, V. J., & Rollnick, S. (2005). Motivational interviewing and self-determination theory. *Journal of Social and Clinical Psychology, 24*(6), 811–831.

Markus, H. R., & Kitayama, S. (1991a). Culture and the self: Implications for cognition, emotion, and motivation. *Psychological Review, 98*(2), 224–253.

Markus, H. R., & Kitayama, S. (1991b). Cultural variation in the self-concept. In J. Strauss & G. R. Goethals (Eds.), *The self: Interdisciplinary approaches* (pp. 18–48). New York: Springer-Verlag.

Markus, H. R., & Kitayama, S. (2003). Models of agency: Sociocultural diversity in the construction of action. In V. Murphy-Berman & J. J. Berman (Eds.), *Nebraska Symposium on Motivation* (pp. 18–74). Lincoln: University of Nebraska Press.

Markus, H. R., Kitayama, S., & Heiman, R. J. (1996). Culture and basic psychological principles. In E. T. Higgins & A. W. Kruglanski (Eds.), *Social psychology: Handbook of basic principles* (pp. 857–913). New York: Guilford Press.

Markus, H. R., & Nurius, P. S. (1986). Possible selves. *American Psychologist, 41*(9), 954–969.

Marlantes, K. (2011). *What it is like to go to war.* New York: Grove/Atlantic.

Marmot, M. (2004). Status syndrome. *Significance, 1*(4), 150–154.

Marmot, M. (2015). *The health gap.* London, UK: Bloomsbury.

Marsden, K. E., Ma, W. J., Deci, E. L., Ryan, R. M., & Chiu, P. (2015). Diminished neural responses predict enhanced intrinsic motivation and sensitivity to external incentive. *Cognitive, Affective, and Behavioral Neuroscience, 15*(2), 276–286.

Martela, F., DeHaan, C. R., & Ryan, R. M. (2016). On enhancing and diminishing energy through psychological means: Research on vitality and depletion from self-determination theory. In E. Hirt (Ed.), *Self-regulation and ego control.* New York: Elsevier.

Martela, F., & Ryan, R. M. (2015). The benefits of benevolence: Basic psychological needs, beneficence, and the enhancement of well-being. *Journal of Personality.*

Martela, F., & Ryan, R. M. (2016). Prosocial behavior increases well-being and vitality even without contact with the beneficiary: Causal and behavioral evidence. *Motivation and Emotion, 40*(3), 351–357

Martela, F., Steger, M., & Ryan, R. M. (2016). *Meaning in life is more than happiness: Autonomy, competence, relatedness, and benevolence as consistent predictors of meaning.* Manuscript submitted for publication.

Martin, D. J., Garske, J. P., & Davis, M. K. (2000). Relation of the therapeutic alliance with outcome and other variables: A meta-analytic review. *Journal of Consulting and Clinical Psychology, 68*(3), 438–450.

Martos, T., & Kopp, M. (2014). Life goals and well-being in Hungary. In A. C. Michalos (Ed.), *Encyclopedia of quality of life and well-being research* (pp. 3571–3576). Dordrecht, The Netherlands: Springer.

Maslow, A. (1971). *The farther reaches of human nature.* New York: Viking Press.

Maslow, A. H. (1943). A theory of human motivation. *Psychological Review, 50*(4), 370–396.

Maslow, A. H. (1954). *Motivation and personality.* New York: Harper.

Mason, W. A., Kosterman, R., Hawkins, J. D., Herrenkohl, T. I., Lengua, L. J., & McCauley, E. (2004). Predicting depression, social phobia, and violence in early adulthood from childhood behavior problems. *Journal of the American Academy of Child and Adolescent Psychiatry, 43*(3), 307–315.

Masterson, J. F. (1985). *Treatment of the borderline adolescent: A developmental approach.* New York: Brunner/Mazel.

Masur, P. K., Reinecke, L., Ziegele, M., & Quiring, O. (2014). The interplay of intrinsic need satisfaction and Facebook-specific motives in explaining addictive behavior on Facebook. *Computers in Human Behavior, 39,* 376–386.

Matosic, D., & Cox, A. E. (2014). Athletes' motivation regulations and need satisfaction across combinations of perceived coaching behaviors. *Journal of Applied Sport Psychology, 26*(3), 302–317.

Matsumoto, H., & Takenaka, K. (2004). Motivational profiles and stages of exercise behavior change. *International Journal of Sport and Health Science, 2,* 89–96.

Maturana, H. R., & Varela, F. J. (1992). *The tree of knowledge: The biological roots of human understanding.* Boston: Shambhala.

May, H. (2010). *Aristotle's ethics: Moral development and human nature.* London: Bloomsbury.

May, R. (1969). *Love and will.* New York: Norton.

May, R. (1983). *The discovery of being.* New York: Norton.

Mayr, E. (1982). *The growth of biological thought: Diversity, evolution, and inheritance.* Cambridge, MA: Belknap Press.

McAdams, D. P. (1990). *The person: An introduction to personality psychology.* San Diego, CA: Harcourt Brace Jovanovich.

McAdams, D. P. (1993). *The stories we live by: Personal myths and the making of the self.* New York: Morrow.

McAdams, D. P. (2001). The psychology of life stories. *Review of General Psychology, 5*(2), 100–122.

McAdams, D. P., & Pals, J. L. (2006). A new big five: Fundamental principles for an integrative science of personality. *American Psychologist, 61*(3), 204–217.

McAuley, E., Duncan, T., & Tammen, V. V. (1989). Psychometric properties of the intrinsic motivation inventory in a competitive sport setting: A confirmatory factor analysis. *Research Quarterly for Exercise and Sport, 60*(1), 48–58.

McBride, C., Zuroff, D. C., Ravitz, P., Koestner, R., Moskowitz, D. S., Quilty, L., et al. (2010). Autonomous and controlled motivation and interpersonal therapy for depression: Moderating role of recurrent depression. *British Journal of Clinical Psychology, 49*(4), 529–545.

McBride-Chang, C., & Chang, L. (1998). Adolescent–parent relations in Hong Kong: Parenting styles, emotional autonomy, and school achievement. *Journal of Genetic Psychology: Research and Theory on Human Development, 159*(4), 421–436.

McCall, R. B. (1977). Challenges to a science of developmental psychology. *Child Development, 48*(2), 333–344.

McCarthy, D., Curran, S., & Byron, S. (2005). *The art of producing games*. Boston: Thomson.

McClelland, D. C. (1985). *Human motivation*. Glenview, IL: Scott Foresman.

McClelland, D. C., Atkinson, J. W., Clark, R. A., & Lowell, E. L. (1953). *The achievement motive*. New York: Appleton-Century Crofts.

McCord, W., & McCord, J. (1964). *The psychopath: An essay on the criminal mind*. Oxford, UK: Van Nostrand.

McCrae, R. R., & Costa, P. T. (2003). *Personality in adulthood: A five-factor theory perspective*. New York: Guilford Press.

McCranie, E. W., & Bass, J. D. (1984). Childhood family antecedents of dependency and self-criticism: Implications for depression. *Journal of Abnormal Psychology, 93*(1), 3–8.

McGraw, K. O. (1978). The detrimental effects of reward on performance: A literature review and a prediction model. In M. R. Lepper & D. Greene (Eds.), *The hidden costs of reward: New perspectives on the psychology of human motiation* (pp. 33–60). Hillsdale, NJ: Erlbaum.

McGraw, K. O., & McCullers, J. C. (1979). Evidence of a detrimental effect of extrinsic incentives on breaking a mental set. *Journal of Experimental Social Psychology, 15*(3), 285–294.

McGregor, D. (1960). *The human side of enterprise*. New York: McGraw-Hill.

McGregor, J. A. (2007). Researching wellbeing: From concepts to methodology. In I. Gough & J. A. McGregor (Eds.), *Wellbeing in developing countries: from theory to research*. Cambridge, UK: Cambridge University Press.

McHoskey, J. W. (1999). Machiavellianism, intrinsic versus extrinsic goals, and social interest: A self-determination theory analysis. *Motivation and Emotion, 23*(4), 267–283.

McKernan, B., Martey, R. M., Stromer-Galley, J., Kenski, K., Clegg, B. A., Folkestad, J. E., et al. (2015). We don't need no stinkin' badges: The impact of reward features and feeling rewarded in educational games. *Computers in Human Behavior, 45*, 299–306.

McLeod, J. (2001). *Qualitative research in counseling and psychotherapy*. Thousand Oaks, CA: Sage.

McNair, D. M., Lorr, M., & Doppleman, L. F. (1971). *EITS manual for the Profile of Mood States*. San Diego, CA: Educational and Industrial Testing Service.

McSpadden, K. E., Patrick, H., Oh, A., Yaroch, A. L., Dwyer, L. A., & Nebeling, L. C. (2016). The association between motivation and fruit and vegetable intake: The moderating role of social support. *Appetite, 1*(96), 87–94.

Mead, G. H. (1934). *Mind, self, and society*. Chicago: University of Chicago Press.

Medawar, P. B. (1961). *The uniqueness of the individual*. New York: Basic Books.

Medic, N., Mack, D. E., Wilson, P. M., & Starkes, J. L. (2007). The effects of athletic scholarships on motivation in sport. *Journal of Sport Behavior, 30*(3), 292–305.

Meglino, B. M., Ravlin, E. C., & Adkins, C. L. (1989). A work values approach to corporate culture: A field test of the value congruence process and its relationship to individual outcomes. *Journal of Applied Psychology, 74*(3), 424–432.

Meichenbaum, D. (1986). Cognitive behavior modification. In F. H. Kanfer & A. P. Goldstein (Eds.), *Helping people change: A textbook of methods* (pp. 346–380). New York: Pergamon Press.

Meissner, W. W. (1981). *Internalization in psychoanalysis*. Madison, CT: International Universities Press.

Meissner, W. W. (1988). *Treatment of patients in the borderline spectrum*. New York: Aronson.

Meissner, W. W. (1996). *The therapeutic alliance*. New Haven, CT: Yale University Press.

Mendes, W. B., Blascovich, J., Hunter, S. B., Lickel, B., & Jost, J. T. (2007). Threatened by the unexpected: Physiological responses during social interactions with expectancy-violating partners. *Journal of Personality and Social Psychology, 92*(4), 698–716.

Meng, L., & Ma, Q. (2015). Live as we choose: The role of autonomy support in facilitating intrinsic motivation. *International Journal of Psychophysiology, 98*(3), 441–447.

Merker, B. (2007). Consciousness without a cerebral cortex: A challenge for neuroscience and medicine. *Behavioral and Brain Sciences, 30*(1), 63–81.

Merleau-Ponty, M. (1962). *Phenomenology of perception* (C. Smith, Trans.). New York: Routledge.

Meyer, J. P., & Gagné, M. (2008). Employee engagement from a self-determination theory perspective. *Industrial and Organizational Psychology, 1*(1), 60–62.

Michalak, J., Klappheck, M. A., & Kosfelder, J. (2004). Personal goals of psychotherapy patients: The intensity and the "why" of goal-motivated behavior and their implications for the therapeutic process. *Psychotherapy Research, 14*(2), 193–209.

Michotte, A. E. (1950). The emotions regarded as functional connections. In M. I. Reymert (Ed.), *Feelings and emotions; The Mooseheart symposium* (pp. 114–126). New York: McGraw-Hill.

Miklikowska, M., Duriez, B., & Soenens, B. (2011). Family roots of empathy-related characteristics: The role of perceived maternal and paternal need support in adolescence. *Developmental Psychology, 47*(5), 1342–1352.

Mikulincer, M., & Shaver, P. R. (2007). *Attachment in adulthood: Structure, dynamics, and change.* New York: Guilford Press.

Milgram, S. (1963). Behavioral study of obedience. *Journal of Abnormal and Social Psychology, 67*(4), 371–378.

Mill, J. S. (1963) *On liberty: Collected works.* Toronto, Ontario, Canada: University of Toronto Press.

Miller, A. (1981). *The drama of the gifted child* (R. Ward, Trans.). New York: Basic Books.

Miller, G. A., Galanter, E., & Pribram, K. H. (1960). *Plans and the structure of behavior.* New York: Henry Holt.

Miller, J. G. (2002). Bringing culture to basic psychological theory—beyond individualism and collectivism: Comment on Oyserman et al.(2002). *Psychological Bulletin, 128*(1), 97–109.

Miller, J. G., Das, R., & Chakravarthy, S. (2011). Culture and the role of choice in agency. *Journal of Personality and Social Psychology, 101*(1), 46–61.

Miller, J. J., Fletcher, K., & Kabat-Zinn, J. (1995). Three-year follow-up and clinical implications of a mindfulness meditation-based stress reduction intervention in the treatment of anxiety disorders. *General Hospital Psychiatry, 17*(3), 192–200.

Miller, S. M., Birnbaum, A., & Durbin, D. (1990). Etiologic perspectives on depression in childhood. In M. Lewis & S. M. Miller (Eds.), *Handbook of developmental psychopathology* (pp. 311–325). New York: Plenum Press.

Miller, W. R., & Rollnick, S. (2002). *Motivational interviewing: Preparing people for change.* New York: Guilford Press.

Miller, W. R., & Rose, G. S. (2009). Toward a theory of motivational interviewing. *American Psychologist, 64*(6), 527–537.

Miller, W. R., Zweben, A., DiClimente, C. C., &

Rychtarik, R. G. (1995). *Motivational enhancement therapy manual: A clinical research guide for therapists treating individuals with alcohol abuse and dependence.* Rockville, MD: National Institute on Alcohol Abuse and Alcoholism.

Millette, V., & Gagné, M. (2008). Designing volunteers' tasks to maximize motivation, satisfaction and performance: The impact of job characteristics on volunteer engagement. *Motivation and Emotion, 32*(1), 11–22.

Milyavskaya, M., Gingras, I., Mageau, G. A., Koestner, R., Gagnon, H., Fang, J., et al. (2009). Balance across contexts: Importance of balanced need satisfaction across various life domains. *Personality and Social Psychology Bulletin, 35*(8), 1031–1045.

Milyavskaya, M., Philippe, F., & Koestner, R. (2013). Psychological need satisfaction across levels of experience: The contribution of specific-level need satisfaction to general well-being. *Journal of Research in Personality, 47*(1), 41–51.

Minnaert, A., Boekaerts, M., De Brabander, C., & Opdenakker, M. C. (2011). Students' experiences of autonomy, competence, social relatedness and interest within a CSCL environment in vocational education: The case of commerce and business administration. *Vocations and Learning, 4*(3), 175–190.

Minuchin, S., Rosman, B. L., & Baker, L. (1978). *Psychosomatic families: Anorexia nervosa in context.* Cambridge, MA: Harvard University Press.

Miquelon, P., Vallerand, R. J., Grouzet, F. M. E., & Cardinal, G. (2005). Perfectionism, academic motivation, and psychological adjustment: An integrative model. *Personality and Social Psychology Bulletin, 31*(7), 913–924.

Mischel, W., & Shoda, Y. (1995). A cognitive–affective system theory of personality: Reconceptualizing situations, dispositions, dynamics, and invariance in personality structure. *Psychological Review, 102*(2), 246–268.

Miserandino, M. (1996). Children who do well in school: Individual differences in perceived competence and autonomy in above-average children. *Journal of Educational Psychology, 88*(2), 203–214.

Mitchell, H., & Aamodt, M. G. (2005). The incidence of child abuse in serial killers. *Journal of Police and Criminal Psychology, 20*(1), 40–47.

Mitchell, J. I. (2003). *Siblings: Sex and violence.* Cambridge, UK: Polity Press.

Mitchell, J. I., Gagné, M., Beaudry, A., & Dyer, L. (2012). The role of perceived organizational support, distributive justice and motivation in reactions to new information technology. *Computers in Human Behavior, 28*(2), 729–738.

Mitchell, S. A., & Black, M. J. (1995). *Freud and beyond: A history of modern psychoanalytic thought.* New York: Basic Books.

Mitchell, T. R. (1974). Expectancy models of job satisfaction, occupational preference and effort: A theoretical, methodological, and empirical appraisal. *Psychological Bulletin, 81*(12), 1053–1077.

Moffatt, G. K. (2002). *A violent heart: Understanding aggressive individuals.* Westport, CT: Praeger.

Moghaddam, F. M. (2013). *The psychology of dictatorship.* Washington, DC: American Psychological Association.

Moller, A. C., Buscemi, J., McFadden, H. G., Hedeker, D., & Spring, B. (2014). Financial motivation undermines potential enjoyment in an intensive diet and activity intervention. *Journal of Behavioral Medicine, 37*(5), 819–827.

Moller, A. C., & Deci, E. L. (2010). Interpersonal control, dehumanization, and violence: A self-determination theory perspective. *Group Processes and Intergroup Relations, 13*(1), 41–53.

Moller, A. C., Deci, E. L., & Ryan, R. M. (2006). Choice and ego-depletion: The moderating role of autonomy. *Personality and Social Psychology Bulletin, 32*(8), 1024–1036.

Moller, A. C., Friedman, R., & Deci, E. L. (2006). A self-determination theory perspective on the interpersonal and intrapersonal aspects of self-esteem. In M. H. Kernis (Ed.), *Self-esteem: Issues and answers* (pp. 188–194). New York: Psychology Press.

Moller, A. C., McFadden, H. G., Hedeker, D., & Spring, B. (2012). Financial motivation undermines maintenance in an intensive diet and activity intervention. *Journal of Obesity.* Available at *www.hindawi.com/journals/jobe/2012/740519.*

Moller, A. C., Roth, G., Niemiec, C. P., Kanat-Maymon, Y., & Deci, E. L. (2016). *Selecting and projecting: Relations of parents' conditional regard to children's peer-relationship quality.* Manuscript submitted for publication.

Montasem, A., Brown, S. L., & Harris, R. (2013). Subjective well-being in dentists: The role of intrinsic aspirations. *Community Dental Oral Epidemiology, 42*(3), 279–288.

Montessori, M. (1967). *The discovery of the child.* Notre Dame, IN: Fides.

Montgomery, K. C. (1952). A test of two explanations of spontaneous alternation. *Journal of Comparative and Physiological Psychology, 45*(3), 287–293.

Montgomery, K. C. (1955). The relation between fear induced by novel stimulation and exploratory drive. *Journal of Comparative and Physiological Psychology, 48*(4), 254–260.

Moore, J. (2008). *Conceptual foundations of radical behaviorism.* Cornwall-on-Hudson, NY: Sloan.

Moran, C. M., Diefendorff, J. M., Kim, T.-Y., & Liu, Z.-Q. (2012). A profile approach to self-determination theory motivations at work. *Journal of Vocational Behavior, 81*(3), 354–363.

Moran, D. (2000). *Introduction to phenomenology.* London: Routledge.

Morgan, C. D., & Murray, H. A. (1935). A method for investigating fantasies: The Thematic Apperception Test. *Archives of Neurological Psychology, 34*(2), 289–306.

Morgan, M. (1981). The overjustification effect: A developmental test of self-perception interpretations. *Journal of Personality and Social Psychology, 40*(5), 809–821.

Morgan, M. (1983). Decrements in intrinsic interest among rewarded and observer subjects. *Child Development, 54*(3), 636–644.

Morin, A. J., Arens, A. K., & Marsh, H. W. (2016). A bifactor exploratory structural equation modeling framework for the identification of distinct sources of construct-relevant psychometric multidimensionality. *Structural Equation Modeling: A Multidisciplinary Journal, 23*(1), 116–139.

Mossholder, K. W. (1980). Effects of externally mediated goal setting on intrinsic motivation: A laboratory experiment. *Journal of Applied Psychology, 65*(2), 202–210.

Mouratidis, A., Lens, W., & Vansteenkiste, M. (2010). How you provide corrective feedback makes a difference: The motivating role of communicating in an autonomy-supporting way. *Journal of Sport and Exercise Psychology, 32,* 619–637.

Mouratidis, A., Vansteenkiste, M., Lens, W., & Sideridis, G. D. (2008). The motivating role of positive feedback in sport and physical education: Evidence for a motivational model. *Journal of Sport and Exercise Psychology, 30*(2), 240–268.

Mouratidis, A., Vansteenkiste, M., Michou, A., & Lens, W. (2013). Perceived structure and achievement goals as predictors of students' self-regulated learning and affect and the mediating role of competence need satisfaction. *Learning and Individual Differences, 23,* 179–186.

Mouratidis, A. A., Vansteenkiste, M., Sideridis, G., & Lens, W. (2011). Vitality and interest-enjoyment as a function of class-to-class variation in need-supportive teaching and pupils' autonomous motivation. *Journal of Educational Psychology, 103*(2), 353–366.

Moustaka, F. C., Vlachopoulos, S. P., Kabitsis, C., & Theodorakis, Y. (2012). Effects of an autonomy-supportive exercise instructing style on exercise motivation, psychological well-being, and exercise attendance in middle-age women. *Journal of Physical Activity and Health, 9*(1), 138–150.

Muhtadie, L., Zhou, Q., Eisenberg, N., & Wang, Y. (2013). Predicting internalizing problems in Chinese children: The unique and interactive effects of parenting and child temperament. *Development and Psychopathology, 25*(3), 653–667.

Mullan, E., Markland, D., & Ingledew, D. K. (1997). A graded conceptualisation of self-determination in the regulation of exercise behaviour: Development of a measure using confirmatory factor analytic procedures. *Personality and Individual Differences, 23*(5), 745–752.

Mullen, J. D. (1981). *Kierkegaard's philosophy: Self deception and cowardice in the present age.* New York: New American Library.

Munson, S. A., & Consolvo, S. (2012, May). Exploring goal-setting, rewards, self-monitoring, and sharing to motivate physical activity. In *6th International Conference on Pervasive Computing Technologies for Healthcare (PervasiveHealth),* (pp. 25–32). Piscataway, NJ: Institute of Electrical and Electronics Engineers.

Münster-Halvari, A. E., Halvari, H., Bjørnebekk, G., & Deci, E. L. (2010). Motivation and anxiety for dental treatment: Testing a self-determination theory model of oral self-care behaviour and dental clinic attendance. *Motivation and Emotion, 34*(1), 15–33.

Münster-Halvari, A. E., Halvari, H., Bjørnebekk, G., & Deci, E. L. (2012a). Motivation for dental home care: Testing a self-determination theory model. *Journal of Applied Social Psychology, 42*(1), 1–39.

Münster-Halvari, A. E., Halvari, H., Bjørnebekk, G., & Deci, E. L. (2012b). Self-determined motivational predictors of increases in dental behaviors, decreases in dental plaque, and improvement in oral health: A randomized clinical trial. *Health Psychology, 31*(6), 777–788.

Münster-Halvari, A. E., Halvari, H., Bjørnebekk, G., & Deci, E. L. (2013). Oral health and dental well-being: Testing a self-determination theory model. *Journal of Applied Social Psychology, 43*(2), 275–292.

Muraven, M. (2008). Autonomous self-control is less depleting. *Journal of Research in Personality, 42*(3), 763–770.

Muraven, M. (2012). Ego depletion: Theory and evidence. In R. M. Ryan (Ed.), *The Oxford handbook of human motivation* (pp. 111–126). Oxford, UK: Oxford University Press.

Muraven, M., & Baumeister, R. F. (2000). Self-regulation and depletion of limited resources: Does self-control resemble a muscle? *Psychological Bulletin, 126*(2), 247–259.

Muraven, M., Gagné, M., & Rosman, H. (2008). Helpful self-control: Autonomy support, vitality, and depletion. *Journal of Experimental Social Psychology, 44*(3), 573–585.

Muraven, M., Rosman, H., & Gagné, M. (2007). Lack of autonomy and self-control: Performance-contingent rewards lead to greater depletion. *Motivation and Emotion, 31*(4), 322–330.

Muraven, M., Tice, D. M., & Baumeister, R. F. (1998). Self-control as a limited resource: Regulatory depletion patterns. *Journal of Personality and Social Psychology, 74*(3), 774–789.

Murayama, K., Elliot, A. J., & Friedman, R. (2012). Achievement goals and approach–avoidance motivation. In R. M. Ryan (Ed.), *The Oxford handbook of human motivation* (pp. 191–207). Oxford, UK: Oxford University Press.

Murayama, K., Matsumoto, M., Izuma, K., & Matsumoto, K. (2010). Neural basis of the undermining effect of monetary reward on intrinsic motivation. *Proceedings of the National Academy of Sciences, 107*(49), 20911–20916.

Murayama, K., Matsumoto, M., Izuma, K., Sugiura, A., Ryan, R. M., Deci, E. L., et al. (2015). How self-determined choice facilitates performance: A key role of the ventromedial prefrontal cortex. *Cerebral Cortex, 25*(5), 1241–1251.

Murphy-Berman, V., & Berman. J. J. (2003). Introduction. In V. Murphy-Berman & J. J. Berman (Eds.), *Nebraska Symposium on Motivation: Vol. 49. Cross-cultural differences in perspectives on the self* (pp. ix–xv). Lincoln: University of Nebraska Press.

Murray, A., Hall, A. M., Williams, G. C., McDonough, S. M., Ntoumanis, N., Taylor, I. M., et al. (2015). Effect of a self-determination-theory-based communication skills training program on physiotherapists' psychological support for their patients with chronic low back pain: A randomized controlled trial. *Archives of Physical Medicine and Rehabilitation, 96*(5), 809–816.

Murray, H. A. (1938). *Explorations in personality.* New York: Oxford University Press.

Nagy, M. (1991). *Philosophical issues in the psychology of C. G. Jung.* Albany: State University of New York Press.

Nakao, T., Osumi, T., Ohira, H., Kasuya, Y., Shinoda, J., & Yamada, J. (2009). Neural bases of behavior selection without an objective correct answer. *Neuroscience Letters, 459*(1), 30–34.

Nakao, T., Osumi, T., Ohira, H., Kasuya, Y., Shinoda, J., Yamada, J., & Northoff, G. (2010). Medial prefrontal cortex–dorsal anterior cingulate cortex connectivity during behavior selection without an objective correct answer. *Neuroscience Letters, 482*(3), 220–224.

National Community Pharmacists Association. (2013). Medication adherence in America: A report card. Available at *www.ncpanet.org/solutions/adherence-simplify-my-meds/simplify-my-meds/preview-of-simplify-my-meds-/medication-adherence-in-america-a-national-report-card.*

Neighbors, C., & Knee, C. R. (2003). Self-determination and the consequences of social comparison. *Journal of Research in Personality, 37*(6), 529–546.

Neighbors, C., & Larimer, M. E. (2004). Self-determination and problem gambling among college students. *Journal of Social and Clinical Psychology, 23*(4), 565–583.

Neighbors, C., Larimer, M. E., Geisner, I. M., & Knee, C. R. (2004). Feeling controlled and drinking motives among college students: Contingent self-esteem as a mediator. *Self and Identity, 3*(3), 207–224.

Neighbors, C., Vietor, N. A., & Knee, C. R. (2002). A motivational model of driving anger and aggression. *Personality and Social Psychology Bulletin, 28*(3), 324–335.

Nemeth, C. J. (1986). Differential contributions of majority and minority influence. *Psychological Review, 93*(1), 23–32.

Newman, G. E., & Shen, Y. J. (2012). The counterintuitive effects of thank-you gifts on charitable giving. *Journal of Economic Psychology, 33*(5), 973–983.

Neyrinck, B., Vansteenkiste, M., Lens, W., Duriez, B., & Hutsebaut, D. (2006). Cognitive, affective and behavioral correlates of internalization of regulations for religious activities. *Motivation and Emotion, 30*(4), 323–334.

Ng, B. D., & Wiemer-Hastings, P. (2005). Addiction to the Internet and online gaming. *CyberPsychology and Behavior, 8*(2), 110–113.

Ng, F. F. Y., Pomerantz, E. M., & Deng, C. (2014). Why are Chinese mothers more controlling than American mothers?: "My child is my report card." *Child Development, 85*(1), 355–369.

Ng, J. Y. Y., Ntoumanis, N., & Thøgersen-Ntoumani, C. (2013). Autonomy support and control in weight management: What important others do and say matters. *British Journal of Health Psychology, 19*(3), 540–552.

Ng, J. Y. Y., Ntoumanis, N., Thøgersen-Ntoumani, C., Deci, E. L., Ryan, R. M., Duda, J. L., et al. (2012). Self-determination theory applied to health contexts: A meta-analysis. *Perspectives on Psychological Science, 7*(4), 325–340.

Ng, J. Y. Y., Ntoumanis, N., Thøgersen-Ntoumani, C., Stott, K., & Hindle, L. (2013). Predicting psychological needs and well-being of individuals engaging in weight management: The role of important others. *Applied Psychology: Health and Well-Being, 5*(3), 291–310.

Nicholls, J. G. (1984). Achievement motivation: Conceptions of ability, subjective experience, task choice, and performance. *Psychological Review, 91*(3), 328–346.

Nichols, S. L., & Berliner, D. C. (2007). *Collateral damage: How high-stakes testing corrupts America's schools.* Cambridge, MA: Harvard Education Press.

Nie, Y., Chua, B. L., Yeung, A. S., Ryan, R. M., & Chan, W. Y. (2015). The importance of autonomy support and the mediating role of work motivation for well-being: Self-determination theory in a Chinese work organization. *International Journal of Psychology, 50*(4), 245–255.

Niemiec, C. P. (2010). *Contextual supports for autonomy and the development of high-quality relationships following mutual self-disclosure.* Unpublished doctoral dissertation, University of Rochester, Rochester, NY.

Niemiec, C. P., Brown, K. W., Kashdan, T. B., Cozzolino, P. J., Breen, W. E., Levesque-Bristol, C., et al. (2010). Being present in the face of existential threat: The role of trait mindfulness in reducing defensive responses to mortality salience. *Journal of Personality and Social Psychology, 99*(2), 344–365.

Niemiec, C. P., Lynch, M. F., Vansteenkiste, M., Bernstein, J., Deci, E. L., & Ryan, R. M. (2006). The antecedents and consequences of autonomous self-regulation for college: A self-determination theory perspective on socialization. *Journal of Adolescence, 29*(5), 761–775.

Niemiec, C. P., & Ryan, R. M. (2009). Autonomy, competence, and relatedness in the classroom: Applying self-determination theory to educational practice. *Theory and Research in Education, 7*(2), 133–144.

Niemiec, C. P., & Ryan, R. M. (2013). What makes for a life well lived? Autonomy and its relation to full functioning and organismic wellness. In I. Boniwell, S. A. David, & A. Conley Ayers (Eds.), *Oxford handbook of happiness* (pp. 214–226). Oxford, UK: Oxford University Press.

Niemiec, C. P., Ryan, R. M., & Brown, K. W. (2008). The role of awareness and autonomy in quieting the ego: A self-determination theory perspective. In H. A. Wayment & J. J. Bauer (Eds.), *Transcending self-interest: Psychological explorations of the quiet ego* (pp. 107–115). Washington, DC: American Psychological Association.

Niemiec, C. P., Ryan, R. M., & Deci, E. L. (2009). The path taken: Consequences of attaining intrinsic and extrinsic aspirations in post-college life. *Journal of Research in Personality, 73*(3), 291–306.

Niemiec, C. P., Ryan, R. M., Deci, E. L., & Williams, G. C. (2009). Aspiring to physical health: The role of aspirations for physical health in facilitating long-term tobacco abstinence. *Patient Education and Counseling, 74*(2), 250–257.

Niemiec, C. P., Ryan, R. M., Patrick, H., Deci, E. L., & Williams, G. C. (2010). The energization of health-behavior change: Examining the associations among autonomous self-regulation, subjective vitality, depressive symptoms, and tobacco abstinence. *Journal of Positive Psychology, 5*(2), 122–138.

Nissen, H. W. (1930). A study of exploratory behavior in the white rat by means of the obstruction method. *Pedagogical Seminary and Journal of Genetic Psychology, 37*(3), 361–376.

Nix, G. A., Ryan, R. M., Manly, J. B., & Deci, E. L. (1999). Revitalization through self-regulation: The effects of autonomous and controlled motivation on happiness and vitality. *Journal of Experimental Social Psychology, 35*(3), 266–284.

Noom, M. J., Deković, M., & Meeus, W. H. J. (1999). Autonomy, attachment, and psychosocial adjustment during adolescence: A double-edged sword? *Journal of Adolescence, 22*(6), 771–783.

Norton, M. I., & Ariely, D. (2011). Building a better America: One wealth quintile at a time. *Perspectives on Psychological Science, 6*(1), 9–12.

Nowak, M. A., Tarnita, C. E., & Wilson, E. O. (2010). The evolution of eusociality. *Nature, 466*(7310), 1057–1062.

Ntoumanis, N. (2001). A self-determination approach to the understanding of motivation in physical education. *British Journal of Educational Psychology, 71*(2), 225–242.

Ntoumanis, N. (2002). Motivational clusters in a sample of British physical education classes. *Psychology of Sport and Exercise, 3*(3), 177–194.

Ntoumanis, N., Healy, L. C., Sedikides, C., Duda, J., Stewart, B., Smith, A., et al. (2014). When the going gets tough: The "why" of goal striving matters. *Journal of Personality, 82*(3), 225–236.

Ntoumanis, N., & Mallett, C. J. (2014). Motivation in sport: A self-determination theory perspective. In A. G. Papaioannou & D. Hackfort (Eds.), *Routledge companion to sport and exercise psychology: Global perspectives and fundamental concepts* (pp. 67–82). New York: Routledge.

Ntoumanis, N., & Standage, M. (2009). Morality in sport: A self-determination theory perspective. *Journal of Applied Sport Psychology, 21*(4), 365–380.

Nunberg, H. (1931). The synthetic function of the ego. *International Journal of Psychoanalysis, 12*, 123–140.

Nussbaum, M. C. (2000). *Women and human development: The capabilities approach.* Cambridge, UK: Cambridge University Press.

Nussbaum, M. C. (2003). *Upheavals of thought: The intelligence of emotions.* Cambridge, UK: Cambridge University Press.

Nuttin, J. (1984) *Motivation, planning, and action: A relational theory of behavior dynamics.* Mahwah, NJ: Erlbaum.

Nyanaponika, T. (1972). *The power of mindfulness.* Oklahoma City, OK: Unity Press.

Oarga, C., Stavrova, O., & Fetchenhauer, D. (2015). When and why is helping others good for well-being?: The role of belief in reciprocity and conformity to society's expectations. *European Journal of Social Psychology, 45*(2), 242–254.

Oates, G., Schooler, C., & Mulatu, M. S. (2004). Occupational self-direction, intellectual functioning, and self-directed orientation in older workers: Findings and implications for individuals and societies. *Sociology Faculty Publications, 110*(1), 161–197.

Ockene, J. K., Kristeller, J., Goldberg, R., Amick, T. L., Pekow, P. S., Hosmer, D., et al. (1991). Increasing the efficacy of physician-delivered smoking interventions: A randomized clinical trial. *Journal of General Internal Medicine, 6*(1), 1–8.

O'Connor, B. P., & Vallerand, R. J. (1990). Religious motivation in the elderly: A French-Canadian replication and an extension. *Journal of Social Psychology, 130*(1), 53–59.

O'Connor, B. P., & Vallerand, R. J. (1994). The relative effects of actual and experienced autonomy on motivation in nursing-home residents. *Canadian Journal on Aging/La Revue Canadienne du Vieillissement, 13*(4), 528–538.

Odgers, C. L., Caspi, A., Russell, M. A., Sampson, R. J., Arseneault, L., & Moffitt, T. E. (2012). Supportive parenting mediates neighborhood socioeconomic disparities in children's anti-social behavior from ages 5 to 12. *Development and Psychopathology, 24*(3), 705–721.

Ogrodniczuk, J. S., Joyce, A. S., & Piper, W. E. (2007). Effect of patient dissatisfaction with the therapist on group therapy outcome. *Clinical Psychology and Psychotherapy, 14*(2), 126–134.

Oishi, S., Kesebir, S., & Diener, E. (2011). Income inequality and happiness. *Psychological Science, 22*(9), 1095–1100.

Olafsen, A. H., Halvari, H., Forest, J., & Deci, E. L. (2015). Show them the money?: The role of pay, managerial need support, and justice in a self-determination theory model of intrinsic work motivation. *Scandinavian Journal of Psychology, 56*(4), 447–457.

Olafson, F. A. (1967). *Principles and persons.* Baltimore: Johns Hopkins Press.

Olesen, M. H. (2011). General causality orientations are distinct from but related to dispositional traits. *Personality and Individual Differences, 51*(4), 460–465.

Olesen, M. H., Thomsen, D. K., Schnieber, A., & Tønnesvang, J. (2010). Distinguishing general causality orientations from personality traits. *Personality and Individual Differences, 48*(5), 538–543.

Oliver, E. J., Markland, D., & Hardy, J. (2010). Interpretation of self-talk and post-lecture affective states of higher education students: A self-determination theory perspective. *British Journal of Educational Psychology, 80*(2), 307–323.

Oliver, M. B., Bowman, N. D., Woolley, J. K., Rogers, R., Sherrick, B. I., & Chung, M.-Y. (2015, April 6). Video games as meaningful entertainment experiences. *Psychology of Popular Media Culture.*

Olmstead, F. L. (1865). *Yosemite and the Maiposa Grove: A preliminary report, 1865.* Retrieved from Yosemite National Park Website *http://www.yosemite.ca.us/library/Olmstead/report.html.*

O'Neill, J. (2011). The overshadowing of needs. In F. Rauschmayer, I. Omann, & J. Fruhmann (Eds.),

Sustainable development: Capabilities, needs and well-being (pp. 25–42). New York: Routledge.

O'Reilly, C. A., III, & Chatman, J. (1986). Organizational commitment and psychological attachment: The effects of compliance, identification, and internalization on prosocial behavior. *Journal of Applied Psychology, 71*(3), 492–499.

O'Reilly, C. A., III, Chatman, J., & Caldwell, D. F. (1991). People and organizational culture: A profile comparison approach to assessing person–organization fit. *Academy of Management Journal, 34*(3), 487–516.

Orlick, T. D., & Mosher, R. (1978). Extrinsic awards and participant motivation in a sport-related task. *International Journal of Sport Psychology, 9,* 27–39.

O'Rourke, D., Smith, R. E., Smoll, F. L., & Cumming, S. P. (2014). Relations of parent- and coach-initiated motivational climates to young athletes' self-esteem, performance anxiety, and autonomous motivation: Who is more influential? *Journal of Applied Sport Psychology, 26*(4), 395–408.

Osbaldiston, R., & Sheldon, K. M. (2003). Promoting internalized motivation for environmentally responsible behavior: A prospective study of environmental goals. *Journal of Environmental Psychology, 23*(4), 349–357.

Osterberg, L., & Blaschke, T. (2005). Adherence to medication. *New England Journal of Medicine, 353*(5), 487–497.

Otero-López, J. M., & Villardefrancos, E. (2015). Compulsive buying and life aspirations: An analysis of intrinsic and extrinsic goals. *Personality and Individual Differences, 76,* 166–170.

Othmer, E., & Othmer, S. C. (2002). *The clinical interview using DSM-IV-TR* (Vols. 1 & 2). Washington, DC: American Psychiatric Publishing.

Otis, N., Grouzet, F. M. E., & Pelletier, L. G. (2005). Latent motivational change in an academic setting: A 3-year longitudinal study. *Journal of Educational Psychology, 97*(2), 170–183.

Otis, N., & Pelletier, L. G. (2005). A motivational model of daily hassles, physical symptoms, and future work intentions among police officers. *Journal of Applied Social Psychology, 35*(10), 2193–2214.

Overton, W. F. (1991). The structure of developmental theory. In H. W. Reese (Ed.), *Advances in child development and behavior* (pp. 1–37). New York: Academic Press.

Owen, K., Smith, J., Lubans, D., Ng, J., & Lonsdale, C. (2014). Self-determined motivation and physical activity in children and adolescents: A systematic review and meta-analysis. *Preventive Medicine, 67,* 270–279.

Oyserman, D., Elmore, K., & Smith, G. (2012). Self, self-concept, and identity. In M. R. Leary & J. P. Tangney (Eds.), *Handbook of self and identity,* (pp. 69–104). New York: Guilford Press.

Pan, Y., Gauvain, M., & Schwartz, S. J. (2013). Do parents' collectivistic tendency and attitudes toward filial piety facilitate autonomous motivation among young Chinese adolescents? *Motivation and Emotion, 37*(4), 701–711.

Panksepp, J., Moskal, J., Panksepp, J. B., & Kroes, R. (2002). Comparative approaches in evolutionary psychology: Molecular neuroscience meets the mind. *Neuroendocrinology Letters, 23*(Suppl. 4), 105–115.

Panksepp, J., & Northoff, G. (2009). The transspecies core SELF: The emergence of active cultural and neuro-ecological agents through self-related processing within subcortical–cortical midline networks. *Consciousness and Cognition, 18*(1), 193–215.

Papaioannou, A. (1998). Goal perspectives, reasons for being disciplined, and self-reported discipline in physical education lessons. *Journal of Teaching in Physical Education, 17,* 421–441.

Paranjpe, A. C. (1987). The self beyond cognition, action, pain and pleasure: An Eastern perspective. In K. Yardley & T. Honess (Eds.), *Self and identity: Psychosocial perspectives* (pp. 27–40). Hoboken, NJ: Wiley.

Parish, L. E., & Treasure, D. C. (2003). Physical activity and situational motivation in physical education: Influence of the motivational climate and perceived ability. *Research Quarterly for Exercise and Sport, 74*(2), 173–182.

Parker, S. K., Bindl, U. K., & Strauss, K. (2010). Making things happen: A model of proactive motivation. *Journal of Management, 36*(4), 827–856.

Parker, S. K., Wall, T. D., & Cordery, J. L. (2001). Future work design research and practice: Towards an elaborated model of work design. *Journal of Occupational and Organizational Psychology, 74*(4), 413–440.

Parker, S. K., Wall, T. D., & Jackson, P. R. (1997). "That's not my job": Developing flexible employee work orientations. *Academy of Management Journal, 40*(4), 899–929.

Parker, S. K., Williams, H. M., & Turner, N. (2006). Modeling the antecedents of proactive behavior at work. *Journal of Applied Psychology, 91*(3), 636–652.

Parra, A., Oliva, A., & Sanchez-Queija, I. (2015). Development of emotional autonomy from adolescence to young adulthood in Spain. *Journal of Adolescence 38,* 57–67.

Patall, E. A., Cooper, H., & Robinson, J. C. (2008). The effects of choice on intrinsic motivation and related outcomes: A meta-analysis of research findings. *Psychological Bulletin, 134*(2), 270–300.

Patall, E. A., Cooper, H., & Wynn, S. R. (2010). The effectiveness and relative importance of choice in the classroom. *Journal of Educational Psychology, 102*(4), 896–915.

Patall, E. A., Dent, A. L., Oyer, M., & Wynn, S. R. (2012). Student autonomy and course value: The unique and cumulative roles of various teacher practices. *Motivation and Emotion, 37*(1), 14–32.

Patrick, H. (2007). *Pro-relationship behaviors and self-determination: Why you do it matters as much as doing it at all.* Paper presented at the Third International Conference on Self-Determination Theory, Toronto, Ontario, Canada.

Patrick, H., Knee, C. R., Canevello, A., & Lonsbary, C. (2007). The role of need fulfillment in relationship functioning and well-being: A self-determination theory perspective. *Journal of Personality and Social Psychology, 92*(3), 434–457.

Pattee, H. H. (1973). *Hierarchy theory: The challenge of complex systems.* New York: Braziller.

Patterson, G. R. (1976). The aggressive child: Victim and architect of a coercive system. In E. J. Mash, L. A. Hamerlynck, & L. C. Handy (Eds.), *Behavior modification and families* (pp. 267–316). New York: Brunner/Mazel.

Patterson, T. G., & Joseph, S. (2007). Person-centered personality theory: Support from self-determination theory and positive psychology. *Journal of Humanistic Psychology, 47*(1), 117–139.

Paulhus, D. L. (2002). Socially desirable responding: The evolution of a construct. In H. I. Braun, D. N. Jackson, & D. E. Wiley (Eds.), *The role of constructs in psychological and educational measurement* (pp. 49–69). Mahwah, NJ: Erlbaum.

Pavey, L. J., & Sparks, P. (2012). Autonomy and defensiveness: Experimentally increasing adaptive responses to health-risk information via priming and self-affirmation. *Psychology and Health, 27*(3), 259–276.

Pavlov, I. P. (1927). *Conditioned reflexes.* New York: Dover.

Pederson, D. R., & Moran, G. (1995). A categorical description of infant–mother relationships in the home and its relation to Q-sort measures of infant–mother interaction. In I. Bretherton & E. Waters (Eds.), *Monographs of the Society for Research in Child Development: Caregiving, cultural, and cognitive perspectives on secure-base behavior and working models: New growing points of attachment theory and research* (Vol. 60, No. 2/3, pp. 111–132).

Pellegrini, A. D., & Smith, P. K. (1998). Physical activity play: The nature and function of a neglected aspect of play. *Child Development, 69*(3), 577–598.

Pelletier, L. G., Dion, S. C., Slovinec-D'Angelo, M., & Reid, R. (2004). Why do you regulate what you eat?: Relationships between forms of regulation, eating behaviors, sustained dietary behavior change, and psychological adjustment. *Motivation and Emotion, 28*(3), 245–277.

Pelletier, L. G., Dion, S. C., Tuson, K., & Green-Demers, I. (1999). Why do people fail to adopt environmental protective behaviors?: Toward a taxonomy of environmental amotivation. *Journal of Applied Social Psychology, 29*(12), 2481–2504.

Pelletier, L. G., Fortier, M. S., Vallerand, R. J., & Brière, N. M. (2001). Associations among perceived autonomy support, forms of self-regulation, and persistence: A prospective study. *Motivation and Emotion, 25*(4), 279–306.

Pelletier, L. G., Fortier, M. S., Vallerand, R. J., Tuson, K. M., Brière, N. M., & Blais, M. R. (1995). Toward a new measure of intrinsic motivation, extrinsic motivation, and amotivation in sports: The Sport Motivation Scale (SMS). *Journal of Sport and Exercise Psychology, 17,* 35–53.

Pelletier, L. G., Rocchi, M. A., Vallerand, R. J., Deci, E. L., & Ryan, R. M. (2013). Validation of the revised Sport Motivation Scale (SMS-II). *Psychology of Sport and Exercise, 14,* 329–341.

Pelletier, L. G., Séguin-Lévesque, C., & Legault, L. (2002). Pressure from above and pressure from below as determinants of teachers' motivation and teaching behaviors. *Journal of Educational Psychology, 94*(1), 186–196.

Pelletier, L. G., Tuson, K. M., Green-Demers, I., Noels, K., & Beaton, A. M. (1998). Why are you doing things for the environment?: The Motivation Toward the Environment Scale (MTES). *Journal of Applied Social Psychology, 28*(5), 437–468.

Pelletier, L. G., Tuson, K. M., & Haddad, N. K. (1997). Client motivation for therapy scale: A measure of intrinsic motivation, extrinsic motivation, and amotivation for therapy. *Journal of Personality Assessment, 68*(2), 414–435.

Peng, W., Lin, J.-H., Pfeiffer, K. A., & Winn, B. (2012). Need satisfaction supportive game features as motivational determinants: An experimental study of a self-determination-theory-guided exergame. *Media Psychology, 15*(2), 175–196.

Penninx, B. W. J. H., Deeg, D. J. H., Van Eijk, J. T. M., Beekman, A. T. F., & Guralnik, J. M. (2000). Changes in depression and physical decline in older adults: A longitudinal perspective. *Journal of Affective Disorders, 61*(1–2), 1–12.

Pepper, J. W., & Herron, M. D. (2008). Does biology need an organism concept? *Biological Reviews, 83*(4), 621–627.

Perlman, D. J. (2013). The influence of the social context on students' in-class physical activity. *Journal of Teaching in Physical Education, 32*(1), 46–60.

Perls, F. (1973). *The gestalt approach and eyewitness to therapy.* Palo Alto, CA: Science & Behavior Books.

Perls, F. S., Hefferline, R., & Goodman, P. (1951). *Gestalt therapy.* New York: Julian Press.

Perry, J. C., Herman, J. L., van der Kolk, B. A., & Hoke, L. A. (1990). Psychotherapy and psychological trauma in borderline personality disorder. *Psychiatric Annals, 20*(1), 33–43.

Persons, J. B., Burns, D. D., & Perloff, J. M. (1988). Predictors of dropout and outcome in cognitive therapy for depression in a private practice setting. *Cognitive Therapy and Research, 12*(6), 557–575.

Petersen, T. (1993). The economics of organization: The principal–agent relationship. *Acta Sociologica, 36*(3), 277–293.

Petrou, P., & Bakker, A. B. (2016). Crafting one's leisure time in response to high job strain. *Human Relations, 69*(2), 507–529.

Petry, N. M., Alessi, S. M., Hanson, T., & Sierra, S. (2007). Randomized trial of contingent prizes versus vouchers in cocaine-using methadone patients. *Journal of Consulting and Clinical Psychology, 75*(6), 983–991.

Pfander, A. (1967). Motives and motivation (H. Spiegelberg, Trans.). In A. Pfander (Ed.), *Munchener philosophische abhandlungen (festschrift fur Theodor Lipps)* [Phenomenology of willing and motivation: And other phaenomenlogica] (pp. 163–195). Evanston, IL: Northwestern University Press.

Phelps, E. S. (2012). *Refounding capitalism.* Oxford, UK: Oxford Handbooks Online.

Philippe, F. L., Koestner, R., Beaulieu-Pelletier, G., Lecours, S., & Lekes, N. (2012). The role of episodic memories in current and future well-being. *Personality and Social Psychology Bulletin, 38*(4), 505–519.

Phillips, D. C. (1995). The good, the bad, and the ugly: The many faces of constructivism. *Educational Researcher, 24*(7), 5–12.

Piaget, J. (1952). *The origins of intelligence in children.* New York: International Universities Press.

Piaget, J. (1971). *Biology and knowledge: An essay on the relations between organic regulations and cognitive processes.* Chicago: University of Chicago Press.

Piaget, J. (1981). *Intelligence and affectivity: Their relation during child development* (T. A. Brown & C. E. Kaegi, Trans.). Palo Alto, CA: Annual Reviews.

Picketty, T. (2014). *Capital in the 21st century.* Cambridge, MA: Harvard University Press.

Pierce, W. D., & Cameron, J. (2002). A summary of the effects of reward contingencies on interest and performance. *Behavior Analyst Today, 3*(2), 221–228.

Pierce, T., Lydon, J. E., & Yang, S. (2001). Enthusiasm and moral commitment: What sustains family caregivers of those with dementia. *Basic and Applied Social Psychology, 23*(1), 29–41.

Pieters, R. (2013). Bidirectional dynamics of materialism and loneliness: Not just a vicious cycle. *Journal of Consumer Research, 40*(4), 615–631.

Piff, P. K., Stancato, D. M., Cote, S., Mendoza-Denton, R., & Keltner, D. (2012). Higher social class predicts increased unethical behavior. *Proceedings of the National Academy of Sciences, 109*(11), 4086–4091.

Pines, A. M. (2004). Why are Israelis less burned out? *European Psychologist, 9*(2), 69–77.

Pink, D. H. (2009). *Drive.* New York: Riverhead Books.

Pinker, S. (2002). *The blank slate: The modern denial of human nature.* New York: Viking.

Pinker, S. (2011). *The better angels of our nature.* New York: Viking.

Pinto, R. Z., Ferreira, M. L., Oliveira, V. C., Franco, M. R., Adams, R., Maher, C. G., et al. (2012). Patient-centred communication is associated with positive therapeutic alliance: A systematic review. *Journal of Physiotherapy, 58*(2), 77–87.

Piotrowski, J. T., Lapierre, M. A., & Linebarger, D. L. (2013). Investigating correlates of self-regulation in early childhood with a representative sample of English-speaking American families. *Journal of Child and Family Studies, 22*(3), 423–436.

Pittman, T. S., Cooper, E. E., & Smith, T. W. (1977). Attribution of causality and the overjustification effect. *Personality and Social Psychology Bulletin, 3*(2), 280–283.

Pittman, T. S., Davey, M. E., Alafat, K. A., Wetherill, K. V., & Kramer, N. A. (1980). Informational versus controlling verbal rewards. *Personality and Social Psychology Bulletin, 6*(2), 228–233.

Pittman, T. S., & Zeigler, K. R. (2007). Basic human needs. In A. W. Kruglanski & E. T. Higgins (Eds.), *Social psychology: Handbook of basic principles* (2nd ed., pp. 473–489). New York: Guilford Press.

Plant, R., Lesser, H., & Taylor-Gooby, P. (1980). *Political philosophy and social welfare: Essays on the normative basis of welfare provision.* London: Routledge & Kegan Paul.

Plant, R. W., & Ryan, R. M. (1985). Intrinsic motivation and the effects of self-consciousness, self-awareness, and ego-involvement: An investigation of internally controlling styles. *Journal of Personality, 53*(3), 435–449.

Platt, J. J. (1975). "Addiction proneness" and personality in heroin addicts. *Journal of Abnormal Psychology, 84*(3), 303–306.

Polanyi, M. (1958). *Personal knowledge: Towards a post-critical philosophy.* Chicago: University of Chicago Press.

Polk, D. E., Cohen, S., Doyle, W. J., Skoner, D. P., & Kirschbaum, C. (2005). State and trait affect as predictors of salivary cortisol in healthy adults. *Psychoneuroendocrinology, 30*(3), 261–272.

Pomerantz, E. M., & Eaton, M. M. (2001). Maternal intrusive support in the academic context: Transactional socialization processes. *Developmental Psychology, 37*(2), 174–186.

Pomerantz, E. M., Ng, F. F.-Y., & Wang, Q. (2008). Culture, parenting, and motivation: The case of

East Asia and the United States. In M. L. Maehr, S. A. Karabenick, & T. C. Urdan (Eds.), *Advances in motivation and achievement: Social psychological perspectives* (Vol. 15, pp. 209–240). Bingley, UK: JAI Press.

Pope, J., & Wilson, P. (2012). Understanding motivational processes in university rugby players: A preliminary test of the hierarchical model of intrinsic and extrinsic motivation at the contextual level. *International Journal of Sports Science and Coaching, 7*(1), 89–107.

Porter, L. W., & Lawler, E. E. (1968). *Managerial attitudes and performance*. Homewood, IL: Irwin.

Powers, T. A., Koestner, R., & Gorin, A. A. (2008). Autonomy support from family and friends and weight loss in college women. *Families, Systems, and Health, 26*(4), 404–416.

Powers, T. A., Koestner, R., & Zuroff, D. C. (2007). Self–criticism, goal motivation, and goal progress. *Journal of Social and Clinical Psychology, 26*(7), 826–840.

Preenen, P. T. Y., Oeij, P. R. A., Dhondt, S., Kraan, K. O., & Jansen, E. (2016). Why job autonomy matters for young companies' performance: Company maturity as a moderator between job autonomy and company performance. *World Review of Entrepeneurship, Management and Sustainable Development, 12*(1), 74–100.

Prendergast, M., Podus, D., Finney, J., Greenwell, L., & Roll, J. (2006). Contingency management for treatment of substance use disorders: A meta-analysis. *Addiction, 101*(11), 1546–1560.

Prigogine, I., & Stengers, I. (1984). *Order out of chaos: Man's new dialogue with nature*. New York: Bantam Books.

Pritchard, R. D., Campbell, K. M., & Campbell, D. J. (1977). Effects of extrinsic financial rewards on intrinsic motivation. *Journal of Applied Psychology, 62*(1), 9–15.

Przybylski, A. K., Deci, E. L., Rigby, C. S., & Ryan, R. M. (2014). Competence-impeding electronic games and players' aggressive feelings, thoughts, and behaviors. *Journal of Personality and Social Psychology, 106*(3), 441–457.

Przybylski, A. K., Rigby, C. S., & Ryan, R. M. (2010). A motivational model of video game engagement. *Review of General Psychology, 14*(2), 154–166.

Przybylski, A. K., Ryan, R. M., & Rigby, C. S. (2009). The motivating role of violence in video games. *Personality and Social Psychology Bulletin, 35*(2), 243–259.

Przybylski, A. K., Weinstein, N., Murayama, K., Lynch, M. F., & Ryan, R. M. (2011). The ideal self at play: The appeal of video games that let you be all you can be. *Psychological Science, 23*(1), 69–76.

Przybylski, A. K., Weinstein, N., Ryan, R. M., &

Rigby, C. S. (2009). Having to versus wanting to play: Background and consequences of harmonious versus obsessive engagement in video games. *CyberPsychology and Behavior, 12*(5), 485–492.

Pulfrey, C., Buchs, C., & Butera, F. (2011). Why grades engender performance-avoidance goals: The mediating role of autonomous motivation. *Journal of Educational Psychology, 103*(3), 683–700.

Purvis, R. L., Zagenczyk, T. J., & McCray, G. E. (2015). What's in it for me?: Using expectancy theory and climate to explain stakeholder participation, its direction and intensity. *International Journal of Project Management, 33*(1), 3–14.

Pyszczynski, T., Greenberg, J., & Solomon, S. (1997). Why do we need what we need?: A terror management perspective on the roots of human social motivation. *Psychological Inquiry, 8*(1), 1–20.

Pyszczynski, T., Greenberg, J., Solomon, S., Arndt, J., & Schimel, J. (2004). Why do people need self-esteem? A theoretical and empirical review. *Psychological Bulletin, 130*(3), 435–468.

Qin, H., Rau, P.-L. P., & Salvendy, G. (2010). Effects of different scenarios of game difficulty on player immersion. *Interacting with Computers, 22*(3), 230–239.

Qin, L., Pomerantz, E. M., & Wang, Q. (2009). Are gains in decision-making autonomy during early adolescence beneficial for emotional functioning?: The case of the United States and China. *Child Development, 80*, 1705–1721.

Quested, E., Bosch, J. A., Burns, V. E., Cumming, J., Ntoumanis, N., & Duda, J. L. (2011). Basic psychological need satisfaction, stress-related appraisals, and dancers' cortisol and anxiety responses. *Journal of Sport and Exercise Psychology, 33*(6), 828–846.

Quested, E., & Duda, J. L. (2009). Perceptions of the motivational climate, need satisfaction, and indices of well- and ill-being among hip hop dancers. *Journal of Dance Medicine and Science, 13*(1), 10–19.

Quested, E., Duda, J., Ntoumanis, N., & Maxwell, J. (2013). Daily fluctuations in the affective states of dancers: A cross-situational test of basic needs theory. *Psychology of Sport and Exercise, 14*(4), 586–595.

Quested, E., Ntoumanis, N., Viladrich, C., Haug, E., Ommundsen, Y., Van Hoye, A., et al. (2013). Intentions to drop out of youth soccer: A test of the basic needs theory among European youth from five countries. *International Journal of Sport and Exercise Psychology, 11*(4), 395–407.

Quinn, D. M., Williams, M. K., Quintana, F., Gaskins, J. L., Overstreet, N. M., Pishori, A., et al. (2014). Examining effects of anticipated stigma, centrality, salience, internalization, and outness on psychological distress for people with concealable stigmatized identities. *PLoS ONE, 9*(5). Retrieved from *http://journals.plos.org/plosone/article?id=10.1371%2Fjournal.pone.0096977.*

Quirin, M., Kerber, A., Kustermann, E., Kazen, M., Radtke, E., Ryan, R. M., Konrad, C., & Kuhl, J. (2016). *Distinguishing mine from yours: Brain correlates of own, imposed and introjected goals.* Manuscript under review.

Quirin, M., & Kuhl, J. (2008). Positive affect, self-access, and health. *Zeitschrift für Gesundheitspsychologie, 16*(3), 139–142.

Radel, R., Sarrazin, P., Legrain, P., & Wild, T. C. (2010). Social contagion of motivation between teacher and student: Analyzing underlying processes. *Journal of Educational Psychology, 102*(3), 577–587.

Radloff, L. S. (1977). The CES-D scale: A self-report depression scale for research in the general population. *Applied Psychological Measurement, 1*(50), 385–401.

Raedeke, T. D. (1997). Is athlete burnout more than just stress?: A sport commitment perspective. *Journal of Sport and Exercise Psychology, 19,* 396–417.

Raff, M. C., Barres, B. A., Burne, J. F., Coles, H. S., Ishizaki, Y., & Jacobson, M. D. (1993). Programmed cell death and the control of cell survival: Lessons from the nervous system. *Science, 262*(5134), 695–700.

Ragins, B. R. (2008). Disclosure disconnects: Antecedents and consequences of disclosing invisible stigmas across life domains. *Academy of Management Review, 33*(1), 194–215.

Raine, A. (2013). *Anatomy of violence: The biological roots of crime.* New York: Random House.

Rank, O. (1932). *Art and artist: Creative urge and personality development.* New York: Knopf.

Rasmussen, S. A., & Tsuang, M. T. (1986). Clinical characteristics and family history in DSM-III obsessive–compulsive disorder. *American Journal of Psychiatry, 143*(3), 317–322.

Rasskazova, E., Ivanova, T., & Sheldon, K. M. (2016). Comparing the effects of low-level and high-level worker need-satisfaction: A synthesis of the self-determination and Maslow need theories. *Motivation and Emotion, 40*(4), 541–555.

Ratelle, C. F., Larose, S., Guay, F., & Senécal, C. (2005). Perceptions of parental involvement and support as predictors of college students' persistence in a science curriculum. *Journal of Family Psychology, 19*(2), 286–293.

Rawls, J. (2009). *A theory of justice.* Cambridge, MA: Harvard University Press.

Rawsthorne, L. J., & Elliot, A. J. (1999). Achievement goals and intrinsic motivation: A meta-analytic review. *Personality and Social Psychology Review, 3*(4), 326–344.

Reader, M. J., & Dollinger, S. J. (1982). Deadlines, self-perceptions, and intrinsic motivation. *Personality and Social Psychology Bulletin, 8*(4), 742–747.

Reader, S. (2005). Aristotle on necessities and needs. *Royal Institute of Philosophy Supplement, 57,* 113–136.

Reeve, J. (2002). Self-determination theory applied to educational settings. In E. L. Deci & R. M. Ryan (Eds.), *Handbook of self-determination research* (pp. 183–203). Rochester, NY: University of Rochester Press.

Reeve, J., Bolt, E., & Cai, Y. (1999). Autonomy-supportive teachers: How they teach and motivate students. *Journal of Educational Psychology, 91*(3), 537–548.

Reeve, J., & Deci, E. L. (1996). Elements of the competitive situation that affect intrinsic motivation. *Personality and Social Psychology Bulletin, 22*(1), 24–33.

Reeve, J., Deci, E. L., & Ryan, R. M. (2004). Self-determination theory: A dialectical framework for understanding socio-cultural influences on student motivation. In D. M. McInerney & S. Van Etten (Eds.), *Big theories revisited* (pp. 31–60). Scottsdale, AZ: Information Age.

Reeve, J., & Halusic, M. (2009). How K–12 teachers can put self-determination theory principles into practice. *Theory and Research in Education, 7*(2), 145–154.

Reeve, J., & Jang, H. (2006). What teachers say and do to support students' autonomy during a learning activity. *Journal of Educational Psychology, 98*(1), 209–218.

Reeve, J., Jang, H., Carrell, D., Barch, J., & Jeon, S. (2004). Enhancing high school students' engagement by increasing their teachers' autonomy support. *Motivation and Emotion, 28*(2), 147–169.

Reeve, J., Jang, H., Hardre, P., & Omura, M. (2002). Providing a rationale in an autonomy-supportive way as a strategy to motivate others during an uninteresting activity. *Motivation and Emotion, 26*(3), 183–207.

Reeve, J., & Lee, W. (2012). Neuroscience and human motivation. In R. M. Ryan (Ed.), *The Oxford handbook of human motivation* (pp. 365–380). Oxford, UK: Oxford University Press.

Reeve, J., & Lee, W. (2014). Students' classroom engagement produces longitudinal changes in classroom motivation. *Journal of Educational Psychology, 106*(2), 527–540.

Reeve, J., Nix, G., & Hamm, D. (2003). Testing models of the experience of self-determination in intrinsic motivation and the conundrum of choice. *Journal of Educational Psychology, 95*(2), 375–392.

Reeve, J., Olson, B. C., & Cole, S. G. (1985). Motivation and performance: Two consequences of winning and losing in competition. *Motivation and Emotion, 9*(3), 291–298.

Reeve, J., Ryan, R. M., Deci, E. L., & Jang, H. (2007). Understanding and promoting autonomous self-regulation: A self-determination theory perspective. In D. Schunk & B. Zimmerman (Eds.), *Motivation and self-regulated learning: Theory, research, and application* (pp. 223–244). Mahwah, NJ: Erlbaum.

Reeve, J., & Tseng, C.-M. (2011). Cortisol reactivity to a teacher's motivating style: The biology of being controlled versus supporting autonomy. *Motivation and Emotion, 35*(1), 63–74.

Reis, H. T. (1994). Domains of experience: Investigating relationship processes from three perspectives. In R. Erber & R. Gilmour (Eds.), *Theoretical frameworks for personal relationships* (pp. 87–110). Hilsdale, NJ: Erlbaum.

Reis, H. T., & Shaver, P. (1988). Intimacy as an interpersonal process. In S. Duck, D. F. Hay, S. E. Hobfoll, W. Ickes, & B. M. Montgomery (Eds.), *Handbook of personal relationships: Theory, research, and interventions* (pp. 367–389). Oxford, UK: Wiley.

Reis, H. T., Sheldon, K. M., Gable, S. L., Roscoe, J., & Ryan, R. M. (2000). Daily well-being: The role of autonomy, competence, and relatedness. *Personality and Social Psychology Bulletin, 26*(4), 419–435.

Reiss, J. (2013). Contextualising causation: Part II. *Philosophy Compass, 8*(11), 1076–1090.

Rempel, J. K., Holmes, J. G., & Zanna, M. P. (1985). Trust in close relationships. *Journal of Personality and Social Psychology, 49*(1), 95–112.

Reynolds, B., & Schiffbauer, R. (2004). Measuring state changes in human delay discounting: An experiential discounting task. *Behavioural Processes, 67*(3), 343–356.

Richer, S. F., Blanchard, C., & Vallerand, R. J. (2002). A motivational model of work turnover. *Journal of Applied Social Psychology, 32*(10), 2089–2113.

Richins, M. L., & Dawson, S. (1992). A consumer values orientation for materialism and its measurement: Scale development and validation. *Journal of Consumer Research, 19*(3), 303–316.

Ricoeur, P. (1966). *Freedom and nature: The voluntary and the involuntary*. Evanston, IL: Northwestern University Press.

Rigby, C. S., & Przybylski, A. K. (2009). Virtual worlds and the learner hero: How today's video games can inform tomorrow's digital learning environments. *Theory and Research in Education, 7*(2), 214–233.

Rigby, C. S., & Ryan, R. (2011). *Glued to games: How video games draw us in and hold us spellbound*. Santa Barbara, CA: Praeger.

Rigby, C. S., & Ryan, R. M. (2016). Time well-spent?: Motivation for entertainment media and its eudaimonic aspects through the lens of self-determination theory. In L. Reinecke & M. B. Oliver (Eds.), *Handbook of media use and well-being: International perspectives on theory and research on positive media effects* (pp. 34–48). New York: Routledge.

Roberts, B. W., & Donahue, E. M. (1994). One personality, multiple selves: Integrating personality and social roles. *Journal of Personality, 62*(2), 199–218.

Roberts, T.-A., & Waters, P. L. (2012). The gendered body project: Motivational components of objectification theory. In R. M. Ryan (Ed.), *The Oxford handbook of human motivation* (pp. 323–334). Oxford, UK: Oxford University Press.

Roca, J. C., & Gagné, M. (2008). Understanding e-learning continuance intention in the workplace: A self-determination theory perspective. *Computers in Human Behavior, 24*(4), 1585–1604.

Rocchi, M. A., Pelletier, L. G., & Couture, A. L. (2013). Determinants of coach motivation and autonomy supportive coaching behaviours. *Psychology of Sport and Exercise, 14*(6), 852–859.

Roche, M., & Haar, J. M. (2013). A metamodel approach towards self-determination theory: A study of New Zealand managers' organisational citizenship behaviours. *International Journal of Human Resource Management, 24*(18), 3397–3417.

Rodriguez, L. M., Hadden, B. W., & Knee, C. R. (2015). Not all ideals are equal: Intrinsic and extrinsic ideals in relationships. *Personal Relationships, 22*(1), 138–152.

Rogat, T. K., Witham, S. A., & Chinn, C. A. (2014). Teachers' autonomy relevant practices within an inquiry-based science curricular context: Extending the range of academically significant autonomy supportive practices. *Teachers College Record, 116*(7), 1–46.

Rogers, C. R. (1951). *Client-centered therapy: Its current practice, implications and theory*. London: Constable & Robinson.

Rogers, C. R. (1957). The necessary and sufficient conditions of therapeutic change. *Journal of Consulting and Clinical Psychology, 21*(2), 95–103.

Rogers, C. R. (1961). *On becoming a person: A therapist's view of psychotherapy*. Boston: Houghton Mifflin.

Rogers, C. R. (1963). The actualizing tendency in relation to "motives" and to consciousness. In M. R. Jones (Ed.), *Nebraska Symposium on Motivation* (Vol. 11, pp. 1–24). Lincoln: University of Nebraska Press.

Rogers, C. R. (1969). *Freedom to learn: A view of what education might become*. Columbus, OH: Merrill.

Rogoff, B. (2003). *The cultural nature of human development*. Oxford, UK: Oxford University Press.

Rollins, B. C., & Thomas, D. L. (1979). Parental support, power, and control techniques in the socialization of children. In W. R. Burr, R. Hill, F. I. Nye, & I. L. Reiss (Eds.), *Contemporary theories about the family: Research based theories* (pp. 317–364). New York: Free Press.

Ronimus, M., Kujala, J., Tolvanen, A., & Lyytinen, H. (2014). Children's engagement during digital game-based learning of reading: The effects of time, rewards, and challenge. *Computers and Education, 71,* 237–246.

Rose, E. A., Markland, D., & Parfitt, G. (2001). The development and initial validation of the Exercise Orientations Scale. *Journal of Sports Sciences, 19,* 445–462.

Rosenberg, A. (1985). *The structure of biological science.* Cambridge, UK: Cambridge University Press.

Rosenfield, D., Folger, R., & Adelman, H. F. (1980). When rewards reflect competence: A qualification of the overjustification effect. *Journal of Personality and Social Psychology, 39*(3), 368–376.

Rosenkranz, R. R., Lubans, D. R., Peralta, L. R., Bennie, A., Sanders, T., & Lonsdale, C. (2012). A cluster-randomized controlled trial of strategies to increase adolescents' physical activity and motivation during physical education lessons: The Motivating Active Learning in Physical Education (MALP) trial. *BMC Public Health, 12*(1), 834.

Ross, M. (1975). Salience of reward and intrinsic motivation. *Journal of Personality and Social Psychology, 32*(2), 245–254.

Ross, R. G., & Van den Haag, E. (1957). *The fabric of society: An introduction to the social sciences.* San Diego, CA: Harcourt.

Roth, G. (2008). Perceived parental conditional regard and autonomy support as predictors of young adults' self- versus other-oriented prosocial tendencies. *Journal of Personality, 76*(3), 513–534.

Roth, G., & Assor, A. (1999, August). *The effect of conditional parental regard and intrinsic value demonstration on academic and pro-social motivation.* Paper presented at the conference of the European Association for Learning and Instruction (EARLI), Malmoe, Sweden.

Roth, G., & Assor, A. (2010). Parental conditional regard as a predictor of deficiencies in young children's capacities to respond to sad feelings. *Infant and Child Development, 19*(5), 465–477.

Roth, G., & Assor, A. (2012). The cost of parental pressure to express emotions: Conditional regard and autonomy support as predictors of emotion regulation and intimacy. *Journal of Adolescence, 35*(4), 799–808.

Roth, G., Assor, A., Kanat-Maymon, Y., & Kaplan, H. (2006). Assessing the experience of autonomy in new cultures and contexts. *Motivation and Emotion, 30*(4), 365–376.

Roth, G., Assor, A., Niemiec, C. P., Ryan, R. M., & Deci, E. L. (2009). The emotional and academic consequences of parental conditional regard: Comparing conditional positive regard, conditional negative regard, and autonomy support as parenting practices. *Developmental Psychology, 45*(4), 1119–1142.

Roth, G., Benita, M., Amrani, C., Shachar, B. H., Asoulin, H., Moed, A., Bibi, U., & Kanat-Maymon, Y. (2014). Integration of negative emotional experience versus suppression: Addressing the question of adaptive functioning. *Emotion, 14*(5), 908–919.

Roth, G., Kanat-Maymon, Y., & Assor, A. (2015). The role of unconditional parental regard in autonomy-supportive parenting. *Journal of Personality.* Advance online publication.

Roth, G., Kanat-Maymon, Y., & Bibi, U. (2011). Prevention of school bullying: The important role of autonomy-supportive teaching and internalization of pro-social values. *British Journal of Educational Psychology, 81*(4), 654–666.

Roth, G., Shachar, B., Benita, M., Zohar-Shefer, Y., Moed, A., & Ryan, R. M. (2016). *Benefits of emotional integration and costs of emotional avoidance.* Manuscript submitted for publication.

Rothbaum, F., & Weisz, J. R. (1994). Parental caregiving and child externalizing behavior in nonclinical samples: A meta-analysis. *Psychological Bulletin, 116*(1), 55–74.

Rotter, J. B. (1954). *Social learning and clinical psychology.* New York: Prentice-Hall.

Rotter, J. B. (1966). Generalized expectancies for internal versus external control of reinforcement. *Psychological Monographs: General and Applied, 80*(1), 1–28.

Rozanski, A., Blumenthal, J. A., Davidson, K. W., Saab, P. G., & Kubzansky, L. (2005). The epidemiology, pathophysiology, and management of psychosocial risk factors in cardiac practice: The emerging field of behavioral cardiology. *Journal of the American College of Cardiology, 45*(5), 637–651.

Rudy, D., Sheldon, K. M., Awong, T., & Tan, H. H. (2007). Autonomy, culture, and well-being: The benefits of inclusive autonomy. *Journal of Research in Personality, 41*(5), 983–1007.

Ruiz-Gallardo, J. R., Verde, A., & Valdés, A. (2013). Garden-based learning: An experience with "at risk" secondary education students. *Journal of Environmental Education, 44*(4), 252–270.

Ruiz-Mirazo, K., Etxeberria, A., Moreno, A., & Ibáñez, J. (2000). Organisms and their place in biology. *Theory in Biosciences, 119*(3–4), 209–233.

Rummel, A., & Feinberg, R. (1988). Cognitive evaluation theory: A meta-analytic review of the literature. *Social Behavior and Personality: An International Journal, 16*(2), 147–164.

Rummel, R. J. (2002). *Power kills: Democracy as a method of nonviolence.* New Brunswick, NJ: Transaction Publishers.

Russoniello, C. V., O'Brien, K., & Parks, J. M. (2009). The effectiveness of casual video games in improving mood and decreasing stress. *Journal of CyberTherapy and Rehabilitation, 2*(1), 53–66.

Rutter, M., & Sroufe, L. A. (2000). Developmental psychopathology: Concepts and challenges. *Development and Psychopathology, 12*(3), 265–296.

Ryan, E. D. (1977). Attribution, intrinsic motivation, and athletics. *Proceedings of the National College Physical Education Association for Men/ National Association for Physical Education of College Women, National Conference.* Chicago: University of Illinois, Chicago, Office of Publications Services.

Ryan, E. D. (1980). Attribution, intrinsic motivation, and athletes: A replication and extension. In C. H. Nadeau, W. R. Halliwell, K. M. Newell, & G. C. Roberts (Eds.), *Psychology of motor behavior and sport—1979* (pp. 19–26). Champaign, IL: Human Kinetics Press.

Ryan, R. M. (1982). Control and information in the intrapersonal sphere: An extension of cognitive evaluation theory. *Journal of Personality and Social Psychology, 43*(3), 450–461.

Ryan, R. M. (1989). Social ontology and its relevance for psychological theory. *New Ideas in Psychology, 7,* 115–124.

Ryan, R. M. (1993). Agency and organization: Intrinsic motivation, autonomy and the self in psychological development. In J. Jacobs (Ed.), *Nebraska Symposium on Motivation: Vol. 40. Developmental perspectives on motivation* (pp. 1–56). Lincoln: University of Nebraska Press.

Ryan, R. M. (1995). Psychological needs and the facilitation of integrative processes. *Journal of Personality, 63*(3), 397–427.

Ryan, R. M. (2005). The developmental line of autonomy in the etiology, dynamics, and treatment of borderline personality disorders. *Development and Psychopathology, 17*(4), 987–1006.

Ryan, R. M., Bernstein, J. H., & Brown, K. W. (2010). Weekends, work, and well-being: Psychological need satisfactions and day of the week effects on mood, vitality, and physical symptoms. *Journal of Social and Clinical Psychology, 29*(1), 95–122.

Ryan, R. M., & Brown, K. W. (2003). Why we don't need self-esteem: Basic needs, mindfulness, and the authentic self. *Psychological Inquiry, 14,* 71–76.

Ryan, R. M., & Brown, K. W. (2005). Legislating competence: The motivational impact of high stakes testing as an educational reform. In A. J. Elliot & C. S. Dweck (Eds.), *Handbook of competence* (pp. 354–374). New York: Guilford Press.

Ryan, R. M., & Brown, K. W. (2006). What is optimal self-esteem?: The cultivation and consequences of contingent vs. true self-esteem as viewed from the self-determination theory perspective. In M. H. Kernis (Ed.), *Self-esteem issues and answers: A sourcebook on current perspectives* (pp. 125–131). New York: Psychology Press.

Ryan, R. M., Brown, K. W., & Creswell, J. D. (2007). How integrative is attachment theory?: Unpacking the meaning and significance of felt security. *Psychological Inquiry, 18*(3), 177–182.

Ryan, R. M., Chirkov, V. I., Little, T. D., Sheldon, K. M., Timoshina, E., & Deci, E. L. (1999). The American dream in Russia: Extrinsic aspirations and well-being in two cultures. *Personality and Social Psychology Bulletin, 25*(12), 1509–1524.

Ryan, R. M., & Connell, J. P. (1989). Perceived locus of causality and internalization: Examining reasons for acting in two domains. *Journal of Personality and Social Psychology, 57*(5), 749–761.

Ryan, R. M., Connell, J. P., & Deci, E. L. (1985). A motivational analysis of self-determination and self-regulation in education. In C. Ames & R. E. Ames (Eds.), *Research on motivation in education: The classroom milieu* (pp. 13–51). Waltham, MA: Academic Press.

Ryan, R. M., Connell, J. P., & Plant, R. W. (1990). Emotions in nondirected text learning. *Learning and Individual Differences, 2*(1), 1–17.

Ryan, R. M., Curren, R. R., & Deci, E. L. (2013). What humans need: Flourishing in Aristotelian philosophy and self-determination theory. In A. S. Waterman (Eds.), *The best within us: Positive psychology perspectives on eudaimonia* (pp. 57–75). Washington, DC: American Psychological Association.

Ryan, R. M., & Deci, E. L. (1996). When paradigms clash: Comments on Cameron and Pierce's (1994) claim that rewards don't affect intrinsic motivation. *Review of Educational Research, 66,* 33–38.

Ryan, R. M., & Deci, E. L. (2000a). Darker and brighter sides of human existence: Basic psychological needs as a unifying concept. *Psychological Inquiry, 11*(4), 319–338.

Ryan, R. M., & Deci, E. L. (2000b). Intrinsic and extrinsic motivations: Classic definitions and new directions. *Contemporary Educational Psychology, 25*(1), 54–67.

Ryan, R. M., & Deci, E. L. (2000c). Self-determination theory and the facilitation of intrinsic motivation, social development, and well-being. *American Psychologist, 55*(1), 68–78.

Ryan, R. M., & Deci, E. L. (2000d). When rewards compete with nature: The undermining of intrinsic motivation and self-regulation. In C. Sansone & J. M. Harackiewicz (Eds.), *Intrinsic motivation: The search for optimal motivation and performance* (pp. 13–54). San Diego, CA: Academic Press.

Ryan, R. M., & Deci, E. L. (2001). On happiness and human potentials: A review of research on hedonic and eudaimonic well-being. *Annual Review of Psychology, 52,* 141–166.

Ryan, R. M., & Deci, E. L. (2004a). Autonomy is no illusion: Self-determination theory and the empirical study of authenticity, awareness, and will. In J. Greenberg, S. L. Koole, & T. Pyszczynski (Eds.), *Handbook of experimental existential psychology* (pp. 449–479). New York: Guilford Press.

Ryan, R. M., & Deci, E. L. (2004b). Avoiding death and engaging life as accounts of meaning and culture: A Comment on Pyszczynski, Greenberg, Solomon, Arndt, and Schimel (2004). *Psychological Bulletin, 130*(3), 473–477.

Ryan, R. M., & Deci, E. L. (2006). Self-regulation and the problem of human autonomy: Does psychology need choice, self-determination, and will? *Journal of Personality, 74*(6), 1557–1586.

Ryan, R. M., & Deci, E. L. (2007). Active human nature: Self-determination theory and the promotion and maintenance of sport, exercise, and health. In M. S. Haggar & N. L. Chatzisarantis (Eds.), *Intrinsic motivation and self-determination in exercise and sport* (pp. 1–19). Champaign, IL: Human Kinetics.

Ryan, R. M., & Deci, E. L. (2008a). From ego depletion to vitality: Theory and findings concerning the facilitation of energy available to the self. *Social and Personality Psychology Compass, 2*(2), 702–717.

Ryan, R. M., & Deci, E. L. (2008b). A self-determination theory approach to psychotherapy: The motivational basis for effective change. *Canadian Psychology, 49*(3), 186–193.

Ryan, R. M., & Deci, E. L. (2011). A self-determination theory perspective on social, institutional, cultural, and economic supports for autonomy and their importance for well-being. In V. I. Chirkov, R. M. Ryan, & K. M. Sheldon (Eds.), *Human autonomy in cross-cultural context: Perspectives on the psychology of agency, freedom, and well-being* (pp. 45–64). New York: Springer.

Ryan, R. M., & Deci, E. L. (2012). Multiple identities within a single self: A self-determination theory perspective on internalization within contexts and cultures. In M. R. Leary & J. P. Tangney (Eds.), *Handbook of self and identity* (2nd ed., pp. 225–246). New York: Guilford Press.

Ryan, R. M., & Deci, E. L. (2013). Toward a social psychology of assimilation: Self-determination theory in cognitive development and education. In B. W. Sokol, F. M. E. Grouzet, & U. Muller (Eds.), *Self-regulation and autonomy: Social and developmental dimensions of human conduct* (pp. 191–207). New York: Cambridge University Press.

Ryan, R. M., & Deci, E. L. (2016). Facilitating and hindering motivation, learning, and well-being in schools: Research and observations from self-determination theory. In K. R. Wentzel & D. B. Miele (Eds.), *Handbook of motivation at school* (pp. 96–119). New York: Routledge.

Ryan, R. M., Deci, E. L., Grolnick, W. S., & La Guardia, J. G. (2006). The significance of autonomy and autonomy support in psychological development and psychopathology. In D. Cicchetti & D. Cohen (Eds.), *Developmental psychopathology: Theory and methods* (pp. 795–849). Hoboken, NJ: Wiley.

Ryan, R. M., Deci, E. L., & Vansteenkiste, M. (2016). Autonomy and autonomy disturbances in self-development and psychopathology: Research on motivation, attachment, and clinical process. In D. Cicchetti (Ed.), *Developmental psychopathology: Vol. 1. Theory and method* (3rd ed., pp. 385–438). New York: Wiley.

Ryan, R. M., & Di Domenico, S. I. (2016). Distinct motivations and their differentiated mechanisms: Reflections on the emerging neuroscience of human motivation. In S. Kim, J. Reeve, & M. Bong (Eds.), *Advances in motivation and achievement, Vol. 19: Recent developments in neuroscience research on human motivation.* Bingley, UK: Emerald.

Ryan, R. M., & Frederick, C. (1997). On energy, personality, and health: Subjective vitality as a dynamic reflection of well-being. *Journal of Personality, 65*(3), 529–565.

Ryan, R. M., Frederick, C., Lepes, D., Rubio, N., & Sheldon, K. (1997). Intrinsic motivation and exercise adherence. *International Journal of Sport Psychology, 28*(4), 335–354.

Ryan, R. M., & Grolnick, W. S. (1986). Origins and pawns in the classroom: Self-report and projective assessments of individual differences in children's perceptions. *Journal of Personality and Social Psychology, 50*(3), 550–558.

Ryan, R. M., & Hawley, P. (2016). Naturally good?: Basic psychological needs and the proximal and evolutionary bases of human benevolence. In K. W. Brown & M. Leary (Eds.), *The Oxford handbook of hypo-egoic phenomena* (pp. 205–222). New York: Oxford University Press.

Ryan, R. M., & Huta, V. (2009). Wellness as healthy functioning or wellness as happiness: The importance of eudaimonic thinking (response to the Kashdan et al. and Waterman discussion). *Journal of Positive Psychology, 4*(3), 202–204.

Ryan, R. M., Huta, V., & Deci, E. L. (2008). Living well: A self-determination theory perspective on eudaimonia. *Journal of Happiness Studies, 9*(1), 139–170.

Ryan, R. M., Koestner, R., & Deci, E. L. (1991). Ego-involved persistence: When free-choice behavior is not intrinsically motivated. *Motivation and Emotion, 15*(3), 185–205.

Ryan, R. M., & Kuczkowski, R. (1994). The imaginary audience, self-consciousness, and public individuation in adolescence. *Journal of Personality, 62*(2), 219–238.

Ryan, R. M., Kuhl, J., & Deci, E. L. (1997). Nature and autonomy: An organizational view of social and neurobiological aspects of self-regulation in behavior and development. *Development and Psychopathology, 9*(4), 701–728.

Ryan, R. M., & La Guardia, J. G. (1999). Achievement motivation within a pressured society: Intrinsic and extrinsic motivations to learn and the politics of school reform. In T. Urdan (Ed.), *Advances in motivation and achievement* (Vol. 11 pp. 45–85). Greenwich, CT: JAI Press.

Ryan, R. M., La Guardia, J. G., & Rawsthorne, L. J. (2005). Self-complexity and the authenticity of self-aspects: Effects on well being and resilience to stressful events. *North American Journal of Psychology, 7*(3), 431–448.

Ryan, R. M., La Guardia, J. G., Solky-Butzel, J., Chirkov, V., & Kim, Y. (2005). On the interpersonal regulation of emotions: Emotional reliance across gender, relationships, and cultures. *Personal Relationships, 12*(1), 145–163.

Ryan, R. M., Legate, N., Niemiec, C. P., & Deci, E. L. (2012). Beyond illusions and defense: Exploring the possibilities and limits of human autonomy and responsibility through self-determination theory. In P. R. Shaver & M. Mikulincer (Eds.), *Meaning, morality, and choice: The social psychology of existential concerns* (pp. 215–233). Washington, DC: American Psychological Association.

Ryan, R. M., & Lynch, J. H. (1989). Emotional autonomy versus detachment: Revisiting the vicissitudes of adolescence and young adulthood. *Child Development, 60*(2), 340–356.

Ryan, R. M., & Lynch, M. F. (2003). Motivation and classroom management. In R. Curren (Ed.), *Blackwell companions to philosophy: A companion to the philosophy of education* (pp. 260–271). Hoboken, NJ: Blackwell.

Ryan, R. M., Lynch, M. F., Vansteenkiste, M., & Deci, E. L. (2011). Motivation and autonomy in counseling, psychotherapy, and behavior change: A look at theory and practice. *Counseling Psychologist, 39*(2), 193–260.

Ryan, R. M., & Manly, J. B. (2005). Thematic Apperception Test. In D. J. Keyser (Ed.), *Test critiques* (Vol. 11, pp. 487–504). Kansas City, MO: Test Corporation of America.

Ryan, R. M., Mims, V., & Koestner, R. (1983). Relation of reward contingency and interpersonal context to intrinsic motivation: A review and test using cognitive evaluation theory. *Journal of Personality and Social Psychology, 45*(4), 736–750.

Ryan, R. M., & Moller, A. C. (2016). Competence as a necessary but not sufficient condition for high quality motivation: A self-determination theory perspective. In A. Elliot, C. Dweck, & D. Yeager, *Handbook of competence and motivation* (2nd ed.). New York: Guilford Press.

Ryan, R. M., & Niemiec, C. P. (2009). Self-determination theory in schools of education: Can an empirically supported framework also be critical and liberating? *Theory and Research in Education, 7*(2), 263–272.

Ryan, R. M., Patrick, H., Deci, E. L., & Williams, G. C. (2008). Facilitating health behaviour change and its maintenance: Interventions based on self-determination theory. *European Health Psychologist, 10*, 2–5.

Ryan, R. M., Plant, R. W., & O'Malley, S. (1995). Initial motivations for alcohol treatment: Relations with patient characteristics, treatment involvement, and dropout. *Addictive Behaviors, 20*(3), 279–297.

Ryan, R. M., & Powelson, C. L. (1991). Autonomy and relatedness as fundamental to motivation and education. *Journal of Experimental Education, 60*(1), 49–66.

Ryan, R. M., & Rigby, C. S. (2015). Did the Buddha have a self?: No-self, self, and mindfulness in Buddhist thought and Western psychologies. In K. W. Brown, J. D. Creswell, & R. M. Ryan (Eds.), *Handbook of mindfulness: Theory, research, and practice* (pp. 245–265). New York: Guilford Press.

Ryan, R. M., Rigby, C. S., & King, K. (1993). Two types of religious internalization and their relations to religious orientations and mental health. *Journal of Personality and Social Psychology, 65*(3), 586–596.

Ryan, R. M., Rigby, C. S., & Przybylski, A. K. (2006). The motivational pull of video games: A self-determination theory approach. *Motivation and Emotion, 30*(4), 344–360.

Ryan, R. M., Sheldon, K. M., Kasser, T., & Deci, E. L. (1996). All goals are not created equal: An organismic perspective on the nature of goals and their regulation. In P. M. Gollwitzer & J. A. Bargh (Eds.), *The psychology of action: Linking cognition and motivation to behavior* (pp. 7–26). New York: Guilford Press.

Ryan, R. M., & Solky, J. A. (1996). What is supportive about social support?: On the psychological needs for autonomy and relatedness. In G. R. Pierce, B. K. Sarason, & I. G. Sarason (Eds.), *Handbook of social support and the family* (pp. 249–268). New York: Plenum Press.

Ryan, R. M., Stiller, J. D., & Lynch, J. H. (1994). Representations of relationships to teachers, parents, and friends as predictors of academic motivation and self-esteem. *Journal of Early Adolescence, 14*(2), 226–249.

Ryan, R. M., & Weinstein, N. (2009). Undermining quality teaching and learning: A self-determination theory perspective on high-stakes testing. *Theory and Research in Education, 7*(2), 224–233.

Ryan, R. M., Weinstein, N., Bernstein, J., Brown, K. W., Mistretta, L., & Gagné, M. (2010). Vitalizing effects of being outdoors and in nature. *Journal of Environmental Psychology, 30*(2), 159–168.

Ryan, R. M., Williams, G. C., Patrick, H., & Deci, E. L. (2009). Self-determination theory and physical activity: The dynamics of motivation in development and wellness. *Hellenic Journal of Psychology, 6*, 107–124.

Ryan, W. S., Cornick, J., Blascovich, J., & Bailenson, J. N. (in press). Virtual reality: Whence, how and what for? In S. Bouchard & P. Sharkey (Eds.), *Virtual reality technologies for health and clinical applications: Psychological and neurocognitive interventions* (Vol. 2). New York: Springer.

Ryan, W. S., Legate, N., & Weinstein, N. (2015) Coming out as lesbian, gay, or bisexual: The lasting impact of initial disclosure experiences. *Self and Identity, 14*(5), 549–569.

Ryff, C. D. (1989). Happiness is everything, or is it?: Explorations on the meaning of psychological well-being. *Journal of Personality and Social Psychology, 57*(6), 1069–1081.

Ryff, C. D. (1995). Psychological well-being in adult life. *Current Directions in Psychological Science, 4*(4), 99–104.

Safran, J. D., & Muran, J. C. (2006). Has the concept of the therapeutic alliance outlived its usefulness? *Psychotherapy, 43*(3), 286–291.

Sagiv, L., & Schwartz, S. H. (2000). Value priorities and subjective well-being: Direct relations and congruity effects. *European Journal of Social Psychology, 30*(2), 177–198.

Salovey, P., Mayer, J. D., Goldman, S. L., Turvey, C., & Palfai, T. P. (1995). Emotional attention, clarity, and repair: Exploring emotional intelligence using the Trait Meta-Mood Scale. In J. W. Pennebaker (Ed.), *Emotion, disclosure, and health* (pp. 125–154). Washington, DC: American Psychological Association.

Samuels, F. (1984). *Human needs and behavior.* Rochester, VT: Schenkman Books.

Sandberg, S. (2014). *Lean in: Women, work, and the will to lead.* New York: Knopf Doubleday.

Sansone, C. (1986). A question of competence: The effects of competence and task feedback on intrinsic interest. *Journal of Personality and Social Psychology, 51*(5), 918–931.

Santelices, B. (1999). How many kinds of individual are there? *Trends in Ecology and Evolution, 14*(4), 152–155.

Sarrazin, P., Vallerand, R., Guillet, E., Pelletier, L., & Cury, F. (2002). Motivation and dropout in female handballers: A 21-month prospective study. *European Journal of Social Psychology, 32*(3), 395–418.

Sartre, J.-P. (1956). *Being and nothingness.* New York: Philosophical Library.

Savard, A., Joussemet, M., Pelletier, J. E., & Mageau, G. A. (2013). The benefits of autonomy support for adolescents with severe emotional and behavioral problems. *Motivation and Emotion, 37*(4), 688–700.

Sayanagi, N. R., & Aikawa, J. (2016). *The motivation of participants in successful development aid projects: A self-determination theory analysis of reasons for participating.* (Working Paper No. 121). Tokyo: Japan International Cooperation Agency

Schaefer, E. S. (1965). Children's reports of parental behavior: An inventory. *Child Development, 36*(2), 413–424.

Schafer, R. (1968). *Aspects of internalization.* New York: International Universities Press.

Schafer, R. (1983). *The analytic attitude.* New York: Basic Books.

Schattke, K., Koestner, R., & Kehr, H. M. (2011). Childhood correlates of adult levels of incongruence between implicit and explicit motives. *Motivation and Emotion, 35*(3), 306–316.

Scheel, M. J. (2011). Client common factors represented by client motivation and autonomy. *Counseling Psychologist, 39*(2), 276–285.

Schilit, H., & Perler, J. (2002). *Financial shenanigans: How to detect accounting gimmicks and fraud in financial reports.* New York: McGraw Hill.

Schmierbach, M., Chung, M.-Y., Wu, M., & Kim, K. (2014). No one likes to lose: The effect of game difficulty on competency, flow, and enjoyment. *Journal of Media Psychology: Theories, Methods, and Applications, 26*(3), 105–110.

Schmuck, P., Kasser, T., & Ryan, R. M. (2000). Intrinsic and extrinsic goals: Their structure and relationship to well-being in German and U.S. college students. *Social Indicators, 50*(2), 225–241.

Schooler, C., Mulatu, M. S., & Oates, G. (2004). Occupational self-direction, intellectual functioning, and self-directed orientation in older workers: Findings and implications for individuals and societies. *American Journal of Sociology, 110*(1), 161–197.

Schreurs, B., Van Emmerik, I. H., Van den Broeck, A., & Guenter, H. (2014). Work values and work engagement within teams: The Mediating role of need satisfaction. *Group Dynamics: Theory, Research, and Practice, 18*(4), 267–281.

Schröder, E., & Edelstein, W. (1991). Intrinsic and external constraints on the development of cognitive competence. In M. Chandler & M. Chapman (Eds.), *Criteria for competence: Controversies in the conceptualization and assessment of children's abilities* (pp. 131–152). Hillsdale, NJ: Erlbaum.

Schrödinger, E. (1944). *What is life?: The physical*

aspect of the living cell. Cambridge, UK: Cambridge University Press.

Schüler, J., Brandstätter, V., & Sheldon, K. M. (2013). Do implicit motives and basic psychological needs interact to predict well-being and flow?: Testing a universal hypothesis and a matching hypothesis. *Motivation and Emotion, 37*(3), 480–495.

Schultheiss, O. C. (2008). Implicit motives. In O. P. John, R. W. Robins, & L. A. Pervin (Eds.), *Handbook of personality: Theory and research* (3rd ed., pp. 603–633). New York: Guilford Press.

Schultz, P. P., & Ryan, R. M. (2015). The "why," "what," and "how" of healthy self-regulation: Mindfulness and well being from a self-determination theory perspective. In B. Ostafin (Ed.), *Handbook of mindfulness and self-regulation* (pp. 81–94). New York: Springer.

Schultz, P., Ryan, R. M., Niemeic, C., Legate, N., & Williams, G. C. (2015). Mindfulness, work climate, and psychological need satisfaction in employee well-being. *Mindfulness, 6*(5), 971–985.

Schüz, B., Westland, J. N., Wurm, S., Tesch-Römer, C., Wolff, J. K., Warner, L. M., et al. (2016). Regional resources buffer the impact of functional limitations on perceived autonomy in older adults with multiple illnesses. *Psychology and Aging, 2,* 139–148.

Schwartz, B. (1994). *The costs of living: How market freedom erodes the best things in life*. New York: Norton.

Schwartz, B. (2000). Self-determination: The tyranny of freedom. *American Psychologist, 55*(1), 79–88.

Schwartz, B. (2010). Be careful what you wish for: The dark side of freedom. In R. M. Arkin, K. C. Oleson, & P. J. Carroll (Eds.), *Handbook of the uncertain self* (pp. 62–77). New York: Psychology Press.

Schwartz, B., & Lacey, H. (1982). *Behaviorism, science, and human nature*. New York: Norton.

Schwartz, S. J. (2001). The evolution of Eriksonian and neo-Eriksonian identity theory and research: A review and integration. *Identity: An International Journal of Theory and Research, 1*(1), 7–58.

Schwartz, S. J., Beyers, W., Luyckx, K., Soenens, B., Zamboanga, B. L., Forthun, L. F., et al. (2011). Examining the light and dark sides of emerging adults' identity: A study of identity status differences in positive and negative psychosocial functioning. *Journal of Youth and Adolescence, 40*(7), 839–859.

Scott, W. E. (1976). The effects of extrinsic rewards on "intrinsic motivation": A critique. *Organizational Behavior and Human Performance, 15,* 117–129.

Sears, R. R., Maccoby, E. E., & Levin, H. (1957). *Patterns of childrearing*. Evanston, IL: Row Peterson.

Sebire, S. J., Jago, R., Fox, K. R., Edwards, M. J., & Thompson, J. L. (2013). Testing a self-determination theory model of children's physical activity motivation: A cross-sectional study. *International Journal of Behavioral Nutrition and Physical Activity, 10*(111). Retrieved from *https://ijbnpa.biomedcentral.com/articles/10.1186/1479-5868-10-111.*

Sebire, S. J., Standage, M., & Vansteenkiste, M. (2009). Examining intrinsic versus extrinsic exercise goals: Cognitive, affective, and behavioural outcomes and psychological need satisfaction. *Journal of Sport and Exercise Psychology, 31,* 189–210.

Sebire, S. J., Standage, M., & Vansteenkiste, M. (2011). Predicting objectively assessed physical activity from the content and regulation of exercise goals: Evidence for a mediational model. *Journal of Sport and Exercise Psychology, 33*(2), 175–197.

Sedikides, C., & Gaertner, L. (2001). A homecoming to the individual self: Emotional and motivational primacy. In C. Sedikides & M. B. Brewer (Eds.), *Individual self, relational self, collective self* (pp. 7–23). Hove, UK: Psychology Press.

Sedikides, C., & Skowronski, J. J. (2000). On the evolutionary functions of the symbolic self: The emergence of self-evaluation motives. In A. Tesser, R. B. Felson, & J. M. Suls (Eds.), *Psychological perspectives on self and identity* (pp. 91–117). Washington, DC: American Psychological Association.

Seeman, M. (1991). Alienation and anomie. In J. P. Robinson, P. R. Shaver, & L. S. Wrightsman (Eds.), *Measures of personality and social psychological attitudes* (pp. 291–371). New York: Academic Press.

Seery, M. D., Blascovich, J., Weisbuch, M., & Vick, S. B. (2004). Relationship between self-esteem level, self-esteem stability, and cardiovascular reactions to performance feedback. *Journal of Personality and Social Psychology, 87*(1), 133–145.

Segatto, B. L., Sabiston, C. M., Harvey, W. J., & Bloom, G. A. (2013). Exploring relationships among distress, psychological growth, motivation, and physical activity among transplant recipients. *Disability and Rehabilitation, 35*(24), 2097–2103.

Seghers, J., Vissers, N., Rutten, C., Decroos, S., & Boen, F. (2014). Intrinsic goals for leisure-time physical activity predict children's daily step counts through autonomous motivation. *Psychology of Sport and Exercise, 15*(3), 247–254.

Séguin, C., Pelletier, L. G., & Hunsley, J. (1999). Predicting environmental behaviors: The influence of self-determined motivation and information about perceived environmental health risks. *Journal of Applied Social Psychology, 29*(8), 1582–1604.

Seifriz, J. J., Duda, J. L., & Chi, L. (1992). The relationship of perceived motivational climate to intrinsic motivation and beliefs about success in basketball. *Journal of Sport and Exercise Psychology, 14*(4), 375–391.

Selhub, E. M., & Logan, A. C. (2012). *Your brain on nature: The science of nature's influence on your health, happiness, and vitality.* New York: Wiley.

Seligman, M. E. P. (1975). *Helplessness: On depression, development, and death.* San Francisco: Freeman.

Sen, A. (1985). *Commodities and capabilities.* Oxford, UK: Oxford University Press.

Sen, A. (2000). *Development as freedom.* New York: Anchor Books.

Senécal, C., Nouwen, A., & White, D. (2000). Motivation and dietary self-care in adults with diabetes: Are self-efficacy and autonomous self-regulation complementary or competing constructs? *Health Psychology, 19*(5), 452–457.

Setzer, V. W., & Duckett, G. E. (2000). *The risks to children using electronic games.* Retrieved from *www.ime.usp.br/~vwsetzer/video-g-risks.html.*

Seyfarth, R. M., & Cheney, D. L. (2012). The evolutionary origins of friendship. *Annual Review of Psychology, 63,* 153–177.

Shah, K. N., Majeed, Z., Yoruk, Y. B., Yang, H., Hilton, T. N., McMahon, J. M., et al. (2016). Enhancing physical function in HIV-infected older adults: A randomized controlled clinical trial. *Health Psychology, 35*(6), 563–573.

Shahar, G., Henrich, C. C., Blatt, S. J., Ryan, R. M., & Little, T. D. (2003). Interpersonal relatedness, self-definition, and their motivational orientation during adolescence: A theoretical and empirical integration. *Developmental Psychology, 39*(3), 470–483.

Shaikh, A. R., Vinokur, A. D., Yaroch, A. L., Williams, G. C., & Resnicow, K. (2011). Direct and mediated effects of two theoretically based interventions to increase consumption of fruits and vegetables in the Healthy Body Healthy Spirit trial. *Health Education and Behavior, 38*(5), 492–501.

Shalev, I. (2016). Pictorial and mental arid landscape images reduce the motivation to change negative habits. *Journal of Environmental Psychology, 45,* 30–39.

Shapira, Z. (1976). Expectancy determinants of intrinsically motivated behavior. *Journal of Personality and Social Psychology, 34*(6), 1235–1244.

Shapiro, D. (1965). *Neurotic styles.* New York: Basic Books.

Shapiro, D. (1981). *Autonomy and rigid character.* New York: Basic Books.

Shaver, P. R., & Mikulincer, M. (2011). Attachment theory. In P. A. Van Lange, A. W. Kruglanski, & E. T. Higgins (Eds.), *Handbook of theories of social psychology* (pp. 160–179). Thousand Oaks, CA: Sage.

Shea, N. M., Millea, M. A., & Diehl, J. J. (2013). Perceived autonomy support in children with autism spectrum disorder. *Autism: Open Access.* Available at *www.omicsgroup.org/journals/perceived-autonomy-support-in-children-with-autism-spectrum-disorder-2165-7890.1000114.php?aid=11537.*

Shedler, J. (2010). The efficacy of psychodynamic psychotherapy. In R. A. Levy, J. S. Ablon, & H. Kächele (Eds.), *Psychodynamic psychotherapy research: Evidence-based practice and practice-based evidence* (pp. 9–25). New York: Humana Press.

Sheeran, P., Aubrey, R., & Kellett, S. (2007). Increasing attendance for psychotherapy: Implementation intentions and the self-regulation of attendance-related negative affect. *Journal of Consulting and Clinical Psychology, 75*(6), 853–863.

Sheldon, K. M. (2005). Positive value change during college: Normative trends and individual differences. *Journal of Research in Personality, 39*(2), 209–223.

Sheldon, K. M. (2011). Integrating behavioral-motive and experiential-requirement perspectives on psychological needs: A two process model. *Psychological Review, 118*(4), 552–569.

Sheldon, K. M. (2014). Becoming oneself: The central role of self-concordant goal selection. *Personality and Social Psychology Review, 18,* 349–365.

Sheldon, K. M., Abad, N., Ferguson, Y., Gunz, A., Houser-Marko, L., Nichols, C. P., et al. (2009). Persistent pursuit of need-satisfying goals leads to increased happiness: A 6-month experimental longitudinal study. *Motivation and Emotion, 34*(1), 39–48.

Sheldon, K. M., Abad, N., & Omoile, J. (2009). Testing self-determination theory via Nigerian and Indian adolescents. *International Journal of Behavioral Development, 33*(5), 451–459.

Sheldon, K. M., Arndt, J., & Houser-Marko, L. (2003). In search of the organismic valuing process: The human tendency to move towards beneficial goal choices. *Journal of Personality, 71*(5), 835–869.

Sheldon, K. M., & Elliot, A. J. (1999). Goal striving, need satisfaction, and longitudinal well-being: The self-concordance model. *Journal of Personality and Social Psychology, 76*(3), 482–497.

Sheldon, K. M., Elliot, A. J., Kim, Y., & Kasser, T. (2001). What is satisfying about satisfying events? Testing 10 candidate psychological needs. *Journal of Personality and Social Psychology, 80*(2), 325–339.

Sheldon, K. M., Elliot, A. J., Ryan, R. M., Chirkov, V., Kim, Y., Wu, C., et al. (2004). Self-concordance and subjective well-being in four cultures. *Journal of Cross-Cultural Psychology, 35*(2), 209–223.

Sheldon, K. M., & Gunz, A. (2009). Psychological needs as basic motives, not just experiential requirements. *Journal of Personality, 77*(5), 1467–1492.

Sheldon, K. M., & Houser-Marko, L. (2001). Self-concordance, goal attainment, and the pursuit of happiness: Can there be an upward spiral? *Journal of Personality and Social Psychology, 80*(1), 152–165.

Sheldon, K. M., & Kasser, T. (1995). Coherence and congruence: Two aspects of personality integration. *Journal of Personality and Social Psychology, 68*(3), 531–543.

Sheldon, K. M., & Kasser, T. (1998). Pursuing personal goals: Skills enable progress, but not all progress is beneficial. *Personality and Social Psychology Bulletin, 24*(12), 1319–1331.

Sheldon, K. M., Kasser, T., Houser-Marko, L., Jones, T., & Turban, D. (2005). Doing one's duty: Chronological age, felt autonomy, and subjective well-being. *European Journal of Personality, 19*(2), 97–115.

Sheldon, K. M., & Krieger, L. S. (2007). Understanding the negative effects of legal education on law students: A longitudinal test of self-determination theory. *Personality and Social Psychology Bulletin, 33*(6), 883–897.

Sheldon, K. M., & Krieger, L. S. (2014a). Service job lawyers are happier than money job lawyers, despite their lower income. *Journal of Positive Psychology, 90*(3), 219–226.

Sheldon, K. M., & Krieger, L. S. (2014b). Walking the talk: Value importance, value enactment, and well-being. *Motivation and Emotion, 38*(5), 609–619.

Sheldon, K. M., & McGregor, H. A. (2000). Extrinsic value orientation and "the tragedy of the commons." *Journal of Personality, 68*(2), 383–411.

Sheldon, K. M., & Niemiec, C. P. (2006). It's not just the amount that counts: Balanced need satisfaction also affects well-being. *Journal of Personality and Social Psychology, 91*(2), 331–341.

Sheldon, K. M., Osin, E. N., Gordeeva, T. O., Suchkov, D. D., & Sychev, O. A. (2016). *Evaluating the dimensionality of the relative autonomy continuum: A theoretical confirmation, and a standardized assessment tool.* Manuscript submitted for publication.

Sheldon, K. M., Ryan, R. M., Deci, E. L., & Kasser, T. (2004). The independent effects of goal contents and motives on well-being: It's both what you pursue and why you pursue it. *Personality and Social Psychology Bulletin, 30*(4), 475–486.

Sheldon, K. M., Ryan, R. M., Rawsthorne, L. J., & Ilardi, B. (1997). Trait self and true self: Cross-role variation in the big-five personality traits and its relations with psychological authenticity and subjective well-being. *Journal of Personality and Social Psychology, 73*(6), 1380–1393.

Sheldon, K. M., Ryan, R. M., & Reis, H. T. (1996). What makes for a good day?: Competence and autonomy in the day and in the person. *Personality and Social Psychology Bulletin, 22*(12), 1270–1279.

Sheldon, K. M., Sheldon, M. S., & Osbaldiston, R. (2000). Prosocial values and group assortation: Within an N-person prisoner's dilemma game. *Human Nature, 11*(4), 387–404.

Sheldon, K. M., & Watson, A. (2011). Coach's autonomy support is especially important for varsity compared to club and recreational athletes. *International Journal of Sports Science and Coaching, 6*(1), 109–123.

Sheldon, K. M., Zhaoyang, R., & Williams, M. J. (2013). Psychological need-satisfaction and basketball performance. *Psychology of Sport and Exercise, 14*(5), 675–681.

Shen, C.-X., Liu, R.-D., & Wang, D. (2013). Why are children attracted to the Internet?: The role of need satisfaction perceived online and perceived in daily real life. *Computers in Human Behavior, 29*(1), 185–192.

Sherif, M., & Cantril, H. (1947). *The psychology of ego-involvements, social attitudes and identifications.* New York: Wiley.

Sherif, M., Harvey, O. J., White, B. J., Hood, W. R., & Sherif, C. (1961). *The robbers cave experiment: Intergroup conflict and cooperation,* Norman: University of Oklahoma Press.

Sherry, J. L. (2001). The effects of violent video games on aggression. *Human Communication Research, 27*(3), 409–431.

Shields, A., Cicchetti, D., & Ryan, R. M. (1994). The development of emotional and behavioral self-regulation and social competence among maltreated school-age children. *Development and Psychopathology, 6*(1), 57–75.

Shields, A., Ryan, R. M., & Cicchetti, D. (2001). Narrative representations of caregivers and emotion dysregulation as predictors of maltreated children's rejection by peers. *Developmental Psychology, 37*(3), 321–337.

Shipler, D. K. (2004). *The working poor: Invisible in America.* New York: Knopf.

Shogren, K. A., & Shaw, L. A. (2016). The role of autonomy, self-realization, and psychological empowerment in predicting outcomes for youth with disabilities. *Remedial and Special Education, 37,* 55–62.

Shostrom, E. L. (1964). A test for the measurement of self-actualization. *Educational and Psychological Measurement, 24*(2), 207–218.

Shuck, B., Zigarmi, D., & Owen, J. (2015). Psychological needs, engagement, and work intentions: A Bayesian multi-measurement mediation approach and implications for HRD. *European Journal of Training and Development, 39*(1), 2–21.

Shweder, R. A. (2000). What about "female genital

mutilation"?: And why understanding culture matters in the first place. *Daedalus, 129*(4), 209–232.

Shweder, R. A., & Sullivan, M. (1993). Cultural psychology: Who needs it? *Annual Review of Psychology, 44,* 497–523.

Sierens, E., Vansteenkiste, M., Goossens, L., Soenens, B., & Dochy, F. (2009). The synergistic relationship of perceived autonomy support and structure in the prediction of self-regulated learning. *British Journal of Educational Psychology, 79*(1), 57–68.

Siff, J. (2014). *Thoughts are not the enemy: An innovative approach to meditation practice.* Boston: Shambhala.

Silk, J. S., Morris, A. S., Kanaya, T., & Steinberg, L. (2003). Psychological control and autonomy granting: Opposite ends of a continuum or distinct constructs? *Journal of Research on Adolescence, 13*(1), 113–128.

Silva, M. N., Markland, D., Carraça, E. V., Vieira, P. N., Coutinho, S. R., Minderico, C. S., et al. (2011). Exercise autonomous motivation predicts 3-year weight loss in women. *Medicine and Science in Sports and Exercise, 43*(4), 728–737.

Silva, M. N., Vieira, P. N., Coutinho, S. R., Minderico, C. S., Matos, M. G., Sardinha, L. B., et al. (2010). Using self-determination theory to promote physical activity and weight control: A randomized controlled trial in women. *Journal of Behavioral Medicine, 33*(2), 110–122.

Silvia, P. J. (2006). *Exploring the psychology of interest.* New York: Oxford University Press.

Simon, M. A. (1971). *The matter of life: Philosophical problems of biology.* New Haven, CT: Yale University Press.

Singelis, T. M. (1994). The measurement of independent and interdependent self-construals. *Personality and Social Psychology Bulletin, 20*(5), 580–591.

Skalski, P., Tamborini, R., Shelton, A., Buncher, M., & Lindmark, P. (2011). Mapping the road to fun: Natural video game controllers, presence, and game enjoyment. *New Media and Society, 13*(2), 224–242.

Skinner, B. F. (1938). *The behavior of organisms: An experimental analysis.* Oxford, UK: Appleton-Century.

Skinner, B. F. (1953). *Science and human behavior.* New York: Macmillan.

Skinner, B. F. (1971). *Beyond freedom and dignity.* New York: Knopf.

Skinner, B. F. (1974). *About behaviorism.* New York: Knopf.

Skinner, E. A. (1995). *Perceived control, motivation, and coping.* Thousand Oaks, CA: Sage.

Skinner, E. A., & Belmont, M. J. (1993). Motivation in the classroom: Reciprocal effects of teacher behavior and student engagement across the school year. *Journal of Educational Psychology, 85*(4), 571–581.

Skinner, E. A., Chi, U., & the Learning-Gardens Educational Association. (2012). Intrinsic motivation and engagement as "active ingredients" in garden-based education: Examining models and measures derived from self-determination theory. *Journal of Environmental Education, 43*(1), 16–36.

Skinner, E. A., Johnson, S., & Snyder, T. (2005). Six dimensions of parenting: A motivational model. *Parenting: Science and Practice, 5*(2), 175–235.

Skinner, E. A., Zimmer-Gembeck, M. J., Connell, J. P., Eccles, J. S., & Wellborn, J. G. (1998). Individual differences and the development of perceived control. *Monographs of the Society for Research in Child Development, 63*(2–3), 1–231.

Slavin, M. O., & Kriegman, D. (1992). *The adaptive design of the human psyche: Psychoanalysis, evolutionary biology, and the therapeutic process.* New York: Guilford Press.

Smith, A. L., & Ntoumanis, N. (2014). An examination of goal motives and athletes' self-regulatory responses to unattainable goals. *International Journal of Sport Psychology, 45*(6), 538–558.

Smith, A. L., Ntoumanis, N., & Duda, J. L. (2010). An investigation of coach behaviors, goal motives, and implementation intentions as predictors of well-being in sport. *Journal of Applied Sport Psychology, 22*(1), 17–33.

Smith, A. L., Ntoumanis, N., Duda, J. L., & Vansteenkiste, M. (2011). Goal striving, coping, and well-being: A prospective investigation of the self-concordance model in sport. *Journal of Sport and Exercise Psychology, 33*(1), 124–145.

Smith, D. L. (2011). *Less than human: Why we demean, enslave, and exterminate others.* New York: Macmillan.

Smith, W. E. (1975). *The effect of anticipated vs. unanticipated social reward on subsequent intrinsic motivation.* Unpublished doctoral dissertation, Cornell University, Ithaca, NY.

Smits, I., Soenens, B., Vansteenkiste, M., Luyckx, K., & Goossens, L. (2010). Why do adolescents gather information or stick to parental norms?: Examining autonomous and controlled motives behind adolescents' identity style. *Journal of Youth and Adolescence, 39*(11), 1343–1356.

Smolders, K. C. H. J., De Kort, Y. A. W., & Van den Berg, S. M. (2013). Daytime light exposure and feelings of vitality: Results of a field study during regular weekdays. *Journal of Environmental Psychology, 36,* 270–279.

Snibbe, A. C., & Markus, H. R. (2005). You can't always get what you want: Educational attainment, agency, and choice. *Journal of Personality and Social Psychology, 88*(4), 703–720.

Soenens, B., Berzonsky, M. D., Dunkel, C. S., Papini, D. R., & Vansteenkiste, M. (2011). Are all identity commitments created equally?: The importance of motives for commitment for late adolescents' personal adjustment. *International Journal of Behavioral Development, 35*(4), 358–369.

Soenens, B., Berzonsky, M. D., Vansteenkiste, M., Beyers, W., & Goossens, L. (2005). Identity styles and causality orientations: In search of the motivational underpinnings of the identity exploration process. *European Journal of Personality, 19*(5), 427–442.

Soenens, B., Elliot, A. J., Goossens, L., Vansteenkiste, M., Luyten, P., & Duriez, B. (2005). The intergenerational transmission of perfectionism: Parents' psychological control as an intervening variable. *Journal of Family Psychology, 19*(3), 358–366.

Soenens, B., Luyckx, K., Vansteenkiste, M., Luyten, P., Duriez, B., & Goossens, L. (2008). Maladaptive perfectionism as an intervening variable between psychological control and adolescent depressive symptoms: A three-wave longitudinal study. *Journal of Family Psychology, 22*(3), 465–474.

Soenens, B., Park, S. Y., Vansteenkiste, M., & Mouratidis, A. (2012). Perceived parental psychological control and adolescent depressive experiences: A cross-cultural study with Belgian and South Korean adolescents. *Journal of Adolescence, 35*(2), 261–272.

Soenens, B., Sierens, E., Vansteenkiste, M., Dochy, F., & Goossens, L. (2012). Psychologically controlling teaching: Examining outcomes, antecedents, and mediators. *Journal of Educational Psychology, 104*(1), 108–120.

Soenens, B., & Vansteenkiste, M. (2005). Antecedents and outcomes of self-determination in three life domains: The role of parents' and teachers' autonomy support. *Journal of Youth and Adolescence, 34*(6), 589–604.

Soenens, B., & Vansteenkiste, M. (2010). A theoretical upgrade of the concept of parental psychological control: Proposing new insights on the basis of self-determination theory. *Developmental Review, 30*(1), 74–99.

Soenens, B., & Vansteenkiste, M. (2011). When is identity congruent with the self?: A self-determination theory perspective. In S. J. Schwartz, K. Luyckx, & V. L. Vignoles (Eds.), *Handbook of identity theory and research* (pp. 381–402). New York: Springer.

Soenens, B., Vansteenkiste, M., Duriez, B., & Goossens, L. (2006). In search of the sources of psychologically controlling parenting: The role of parental separation anxiety and parental maladaptive perfectionism. *Journal of Research on Adolescence, 16*(4), 539–559.

Soenens, B., Vansteenkiste, M., Goossens, L., Duriez, B., & Niemiec, C. P. (2008). The intervening role of relational aggression between psychological control and friendship quality. *Social Development, 17*(3), 661–681.

Soenens, B., Vansteenkiste, M., Lens, W., Luyckx, K., Goossens, L., Beyers, W., et al. (2007). Conceptualizing parental autonomy support: Adolescent perceptions of promotion of independence versus promotion of volitional functioning. *Developmental Psychology, 43*(3), 633–646.

Soenens, B., Vansteenkiste, M., & Luyten, P. (2010). Toward a domain-specific approach to the study of parental psychological control: Distinguishing between dependency-oriented and achievement-oriented psychological control. *Journal of Personality, 78*(1), 217–256.

Soenens, B., Vansteenkiste, M., Luyten, P., Duriez, B., & Goossens, L. (2005). Maladaptive perfectionistic self-representations: The mediational link between psychological control and adjustment. *Personality and Individual Differences, 38*(2), 487–498.

Soenens, B., Vansteenkiste, M., & Niemiec, C. P. (2009). Should parental prohibition of adolescents' peer relationships be prohibited? *Personal Relationships, 16*(4), 507–530.

Soenens, B., Vansteenkiste, M., & Sierens, E. (2009). How are parental psychological control and autonomy support related?: A cluster-analytic approach. *Journal of Marriage and Family, 71*(1), 187–202.

Soenens, B., Vansteenkiste, M., & Van Petegem, S. (2015). Let us not throw out the baby with the bathwater: Applying the principle of universalism without uniformity to autonomy-supportive and controlling parenting. *Child Development Perspectives, 9*(1), 44–49.

Soenens, B., Vansteenkiste, M., Vandereycken, W., Luyten, P., Sierens, E., & Goossens, L. (2008). Perceived parental psychological control and eating-disordered symptoms: Maladaptive perfectionism as a possible intervening variable. *Journal of Nervous and Mental Disease, 196*(2), 144–152.

Sokol, B., Grouzet, F. M. E., & Müller, U. (2013). *Self-regulation and autonomy: Social, developmental, educational, and neurological dimensions of human contact.* New York: Cambridge University Press.

Solomon, A. (2012). *Far from the tree: Parents, children and the search for identity.* New York: Scribner.

Sørebø, O., & Hæhre, R. (2012). Investigating students' perceived discipline relevance subsequent to playing educational computer games: A personal-interest and self-determination theory approach. *Scandinavian Journal of Educational Research, 56*(4), 345–362.

Spence, K. W. (1958). A theory of emotionally based drive (D) and its relation to performance in simple learning situations. *American Psychologist, 13*(4), 131–141

Sperber, D. (1994). *The modularity of thought and the epidemiology of representations.* New York: Cambridge University Press.

Sperry, L. (2003). *Handbook of diagnosis and treatment of DSM-IV-TR personality disorders.* New York: Brunner-Routledge.

Sperry, R. W. (1976). Changing concepts of consciousness and free will. *Perspectives in Biology and Medicine, 20*(1), 9–19.

Spitz, R. A. (1965). *The first year of life: A psychoanalytic study of normal and deviant development of object relations.* New York: International Universities Press.

Springer, M. G., Ballou, D., Hamilton, L., Le, V., Lockwood, J. R., McCaffrey, D. F., et al. (2010). *Teacher pay for performance: Experimental evidence from the project on incentives in teaching.* Nashville, TN: Vanderbilt University National Center on Performance Incentives.

Srivastava, A., Locke, E. A., & Bartol, K. M. (2001). Money and subjective well-being: It's not the money, it's the motives. *Journal of Personality and Social Psychology, 80*(6), 959–971.

Sroufe, L. A. (1990). An organizational perspective on the self. In D. Cicchetti & M. Beeghly (Eds.), *The self in transition: Infancy to childhood* (pp. 281–307). Chicago: University of Chicago Press.

Sroufe, L. A., & Waters, E. (1977). Attachment as an organizational construct. *Child Development, 48*(4), 1184–1199.

Standage, M., Duda, J. L., & Ntoumanis, N. (2003). A model of contextual motivation in physical education: Using constructs from self-determination and achievement goal theories to predict physical activity intentions. *Journal of Educational Psychology, 95*(1), 97–110.

Standage, M., Duda, J. L., & Ntoumanis, N. (2006). Students' motivational processes and their relationship to teacher ratings in school physical education: A self-determination theory approach. *Research Quarterly for Exercise and Sport, 77*(1), 100–110.

Standage, M., Duda, J. L., & Pensgaard, A. M. (2005). The effect of competitive outcome and task-involving, ego-involving, and cooperative structures on the psychological well-being of individuals engaged in a co-ordination task: A self-determination approach. *Motivation and Emotion, 29*(1), 41–68.

Standage, M., Gillison, F. B., Ntoumanis, N., & Treasure, D. C. (2012). Predicting students' physical activity and health-related well-being: A prospective cross-domain investigation of motivation across school physical education and exercise settings. *Journal of Sport and Exercise Psychology, 34*(1), 37–60.

Standage, M., & Ryan, R. M. (2012). Self-determination theory and exercise motivation: Facilitating self-regulatory processes to support and maintain health and well-being. In G. C. Roberts & D. C. Treasure (Eds.), *Advances in motivation in sport and exercise* (pp. 233–270). Champaign, IL: Human Kinetics.

Standage, M., Sebire, S. J., & Loney, T. (2008). Does exercise motivation predict engagement in objectively assessed bouts of moderate-intensity exercise?: A self-determination theory perspective. *Journal of Sport and Exercise Psychology, 30*(4), 337–352.

Standage, M., Treasure, D. C., Hooper, K., & Kuczka, K. (2007). Self-handicapping in school physical education: The influence of the motivational climate. *British Journal of Educational Psychology, 77*(1), 81–99.

Stansbury, K., & Gunnar, M. R. (1994). Adrenocortical activity and emotion regulation. *Monographs of the Society for Research in Child Development, 59*(2–3), 108–134.

Staub, E. (1989). *The roots of evil: The origins of genocide and other group violence.* New York: Cambridge University Press.

Staub, E. (1992). The origins of caring, helping, and nonaggression: Parental socialization, the family system, schools, and cultural influences. In P. M. Oliner, S. P. Oliner, L. Baron, L. A. Blum, D. L. Krebs, & M. Z. Smolenska (Eds.), *Embracing the other: Philosophical, psychological, and historical perspectives on altruism* (pp. 390–409). New York: New York University Press.

Staub, E. (2001). Genocide and mass killing: Their roots and prevention. In D. Christie, R. Wagner, & D. Winter (Eds.), *Peace, conflict, and violence: Peace psychology for the 21st century* (pp. 76–86). Englewood Cliffs, NJ: Prentice-Hall.

Staub, E. (2005). The roots of goodness: The fulfillment of basic human needs and the development of caring, helping and nonaggression, inclusive caring, moral courage, active bystandership, and altruism born of suffering. In G. Carlo & C. P. Edwards, (Eds). *Moral motivation through the life span* (pp. 33–72). Lincoln: University of Nebraska Press.

Staub, E. (2011). *Overcoming evil: Genocide, violent conflict and terrorism.* New York: Oxford University Press.

Stavrova, O., & Siegers, P. (2013). Religious prosociality and morality across cultures: How social enforcement of religion shapes the effects of personal religiosity on prosocial and moral attitudes and behaviors. *Personality and Social Psychology Bulletin, 40*(3), 315–333.

Steel, Z., Jones, J., Adcock, S., Clancy, R., Bridgford-West, L., & Austin, J. (2000). Why the high rate of dropout from individualized cognitive-behavior therapy for bulimia nervosa? *International Journal of Eating Disorders, 28*(2), 209–214.

Steger, M. F., Frazier, P., Oishi, S., & Kaler, M. (2006). The Meaning In Life Questionnaire: Assessing the presence of and search for meaning in life. *Journal of Counseling Psychology, 53*(1), 80–93.

Steinberg, L. (1990). Autonomy, conflict, and harmony in the family relationship. In S. S. Feldman & G. R. Elliot (Eds.), *At the threshold: The developing adolescent* (pp. 255–276). Cambridge, MA: Harvard University Press.

Steinberg, L. (2005). Psychological control: Style or substance? *New Directions for Child and Adolescent Development, 108,* 71–78.

Steinberg, L., & Silk, J. S. (2002). Parenting adolescents. In M. H. Bornstein (Ed.), *Handbook of parenting: Children and parenting* (pp. 103–133). Mahwah, NJ: Erlbaum.

Steinberg, L., & Silverberg, S. B. (1986). The vicissitudes of autonomy in early adolescence. *Child Development, 57*(4), 841–851.

Steinberg, M., & Schnall, M. (2001). *The stranger in the mirror.* New York: Cliff Street Books.

Stern, D. N. (1985). *The interpersonal world of the infant: A view from psychoanalysis and developmental psychology.* New York: Basic Books.

Stevens, J. R., & Hauser, M. D. (2004). Why be nice?: Psychological constraints on the evolution of cooperation. *Trends in Cognitive Sciences, 8*(2), 60–65.

Stevenson, M. B., & Lamb, M. E. (1981). The effects of social experience and social style on cognitive competence and performance. In M. E. Lamb & L. R. Sherrod (Eds.), *Infant social cognition: Empirical and theoretical considerations* (pp. 375–394). Hillsdale, NJ: Erlbaum.

Stolz, H. E., Barber, B. K., & Olsen, J. A. (2005). Toward disentangling fathering and mothering: An assessment of relative importance. *Journal of Marriage and Family, 67*(4), 1076–1092.

Strauss, J., & Ryan, R. M. (1987). Autonomy disturbances in subtypes of anorexia nervosa. *Journal of Abnormal Psychology, 96*(3), 254–258.

Strauss, J., & Ryan, R. M. (1988). Cognitive dysfunction in eating disorders. *International Journal of Eating Disorders, 7*(1), 19–27.

Streb, J., Keis, O., Lau, K., Hille, L., Spitzer, M., & Sosic-Vasic, Z. (2015). Emotional engagement in kindergarten and school children: A self-determination theory perspective. *Trends in Neuroscience and Education, 4*(4), 102–107.

Strobel, A., Zimmermann, J., Schmitz, A., Reuter, M., Lis, S., Windmann, S., et al. (2011). Beyond revenge: Neural and genetic bases of altruistic punishment. *NeuroImage, 54*(1), 671–680.

Strober, M., & Humphrey, L. L. (1987). Familial contributions to the etiology and course of anorexia nervosa and bulimia. *Journal of Consulting and Clinical Psychology, 55*(5), 654–659.

Stuart, S. (2004). Brief interpersonal psychotherapy. In M. J. Dewan, B. N. Steenbarger, & R. P. Greenberg (Eds.), *The art and science of brief psychotherapies: A practitioner's guide* (pp. 119–156). Arlington, VA: American Psychiatric Publishing.

Stump, K. N., Ratliff, J. M., Wu, Y. P., & Hawley,

P. H. (2009). Theories of social competence from the top-down to the bottom-up: A case for considering foundational human needs. In J. L. Matson (Ed.), *Social behavior and skills in children* (pp. 23–37.) New York: Springer Science & Business Media.

Su, Y.-L., & Reeve, J. (2011). A meta-analysis of the effectiveness of intervention programs designed to support autonomy. *Educational Psychology Review, 23*(1), 159–188.

Sue, D. W., & Sue, D. (2008). *Counseling the culturally diverse.* New York: Wiley.

Suh, A., Wagner, C., & Liu, L. (2015). *The effects of game dynamics on user engagement in gamified systems.* Paper presented at the 48th Hawaii International Conference on System Sciences. Available at *http://ieeexplore.ieee.org/xpl/login.jsp?tp=& arnumber=7069736&url=http%3A%2F%2Fiee explore.ieee.org%2Fstamp%2Fstamp.jsp%3Ftp %3D%26arnumber%3D7069736.*

Sullivan, J. L., & Transue, J. E. (1999). The psychological underpinnings of democracy: A selective review of research on political tolerance, interpersonal trust, and social capital. *Annual Review of Psychology, 50,* 625–650.

Sulloway, F. J. (1979). *Freud, biologist of the mind: Beyond the psychoanalytic legend.* New York: Basic Books.

Sun, J., Dunne, M. P., Hou, X.-Y., & Xu, A.-Q. (2013) Educational stress among Chinese adolescents: Individual, family, school and peer influences. *Educational Review, 65*(3), 284–302.

Sundar, S. S., & Marthe, S. S. (2010). Personalization versus customization: The importance of agency, privacy, and power usage. *Human Communication Research, 36*(3), 261–467.

Supple, A. J., Ghazarian, S. R., Peterson, G. W., & Bush, K. R. (2009). Assessing the cross-cultural validity of a parental autonomy granting measure comparing adolescents in the United States, China, Mexico, and India. *Journal of Cross-Cultural Psychology, 40*(5), 816–833.

Susman, E. J. (2006). Psychobiology of persistent antisocial behavior: Stress, early vulnerabilities, and the attenuation hypothesis. *Neuroscience and Biobehavioral Reviews, 30*(3), 376–389.

Suzuki, S. (1970). *Zen mind, beginner's mind.* Boston: Shambhala Publications.

Svancara, L. K., Scott, M., Groves, C. R., Noss, R. F., & Pressey, R. L. (2005). Policy-driven versus evidence-based conservation: A review of political targets and biological needs. *BioScience, 55*(11), 989–995.

Swallow, S. R., & Kuiper, N. A. (1988). Social comparison and negative self-evaluations: An application to depression. *Clinical Psychology Review, 8*(1), 55–76.

Swann, W. B. (1983). Self-verification: Bringing social reality into harmony with the self. In J. Suls

& A. G. Greenwald (Eds.), *Psychological perspectives on the self* (pp. 33–66). Hillsdale, NJ: Erlbaum.

Swanson, S. D., & Tricomi, E. (2014). Goals and task difficulty expectations modulate striatal responses to feedback. *Cognitive, Affective, and Behavioral Neuroscience, 14*(2), 610–620.

Swedo, S. E., & Rapoport, J. L. (1990). Obsessive–compulsive disorder in childhood. In M. Hersen & C. G. Last (Eds.), *Handbook of child and adult psychopathology: A longitudinal perspective* (pp. 211–219). Elmsford, NY: Pergamon Press.

Sylvester, B. D., Mack, D. E., Busseri, M. A., Wilson, P. M., & Beauchamp, M. R. (2012). Health-enhancing physical activity, psychological need satisfaction, and well-being: Is it how often, how long, or how much effort that matters? *Mental Health and Physical Activity, 5*(2), 141–147.

Szadejko, K. (2007, May). *Meaningful life and intrinsic motivation.* Paper presented at the Third International Conference on Self-Determination Theory, Toronto, Ontario, Canada.

Tamborini, R., Bowman, N. D., Eden, A., Grizzard, M., & Organ, A. (2010). Defining media enjoyment as the satisfaction of intrinsic needs. *Journal of Communication, 60*(4), 758–777.

Tang, H., Kuang, C., & Yao, S. (2008). The Chinese version of Aspiration Index: Reliability and validity. *Chinese Journal of Clinical Psychology, 16*(1), 15–17.

Tang, S.-H., & Hall, V. C. (1995). The overjustification effect: A meta-analysis. *Applied Cognitive Psychology, 9*(5), 365–404.

Taylor, C. (1991). Responsibility for self. In P. French (Ed.), *The spectrum of responsibility* (pp. 214–224). London: St. Martin's Press.

Taylor, G., Jungert, T., Mageau, G. A., Schattke, K., Dedic, H., Rosenfield, S., et al. (2014). A self-determination theory approach to predicting school achievement over time: The unique role of intrinsic motivation. *Contemporary Educational Psychology, 39*(4), 342–358.

Taylor, I. M., & Lonsdale, C. (2010). Cultural differences in the relationships among autonomy support, psychological need satisfaction, subjective vitality, and effort in British and Chinese physical education. *Journal of Sport and Exercise Psychology, 32,* 655–673.

Taylor, I. M., & Ntoumanis. N. (2007). Teacher motivational strategies and student self-determination in physical education. *Journal of Educational Psychology, 99*(4), 747–760.

Taylor, I. M., Ntoumanis, N., & Standage, M. (2008). A self-determination theory approach to understanding the antecedents of teachers' motivational strategies in physical education. *Journal of Sport and Exercise Psychology, 30*(1), 75–94.

Taylor, I. M., Ntoumanis, N., Standage, M., & Spray, C. M. (2010). Motivational predictors of physical education students' effort, exercise intentions, and leisure-time physical activity: A multilevel linear growth analysis. *Journal of Sport and Exercise Psychology, 32*(1), 99–120.

Taylor, S. E. (1989). *Positive illusions: Creative self-deception and the healthy mind.* New York: Basic Books.

Taylor, S. E. (2002). *The tending instinct: How nurturing is essential to who we are and how we live.* New York: Henry Holt.

Teixeira, P. J., Carraça, E., Markland, D., Silva, M. N., & Ryan, R. M. (2012). Exercise, physical activity, and self-determination theory: A systematic review. *International Journal of Behavioral Nutrition and Physical Activity, 9*(1), 78–107.

Teixeira, P. J., Patrick, H., & Mata, J. (2011). Why we eat what we eat: The role of autonomous motivation in eating behaviour regulation. *Nutrition Bulletin, 36*(1), 102–107.

Teixeira, P. J., Silva, M. N., Mata, J., Palmeira, A. L., & Markland, D. (2012). Motivation, self-determination, and long-term weight control. *International Journal of Behavioral Nutrition and Physical Activity, 9*(22). Retrieved from *https://ijbnpa.biomedcentral.com/articles/10.1186/1479-5868-9-22.*

Television Bureau of Advertising. (2012). *TVB media comparisons 2010/2012.* Retrieved from *http://studylib.net/doc/5667034/media-comparisons-2010---television-bureau-of-advertising.*

Terkel, S. (1974). *Working: People talk about what they do all day and how they feel about what they do.* New York: New Press.

Tessier, D., Sarrazin, P., & Ntoumanis, N. (2010). The effect of an intervention to improve newly qualified teachers' interpersonal style, students' motivation and psychological need satisfaction in sport-based physical education. *Contemporary Educational Psychology, 35*(4), 242–253.

Thayer, R. E. (1987). Energy, tiredness, and tension effects of a sugar snack versus moderate exercise. *Journal of Personality and Social Psychology, 52*(1), 119–125.

Thayer, R. E. (1996). *The origin of everyday moods.* New York: Oxford University Press.

Thayer, R. E. (2003). *Calm energy: How people regulate mood with food and exercise.* New York: Oxford University Press.

Thibaut, J. W., & Kelley, H. H. (1959). *The social psychology of groups.* New York: Wiley.

Thøgersen-Ntoumani, C., & Ntoumanis, N. (2006). The role of self-determined motivation in the understanding of exercise-related behaviours, cognitions and physical self-evaluations. *Journal of Sports Sciences, 24*(4), 393–404.

Thompson, R. A. (2006). The development of the person: Social understanding, relationships, self, conscience. In W. Damon & R. M. Lerner (Eds.), *Handbook of child psychology: Vol. 3. Social, emotional, and personality development* (6th ed., pp. 226–299). New York: Wiley.

Thorndike, E. L. (1913). *The psychology of learning.* New York: Columbia University, Teachers College.

Tian, L., Chen, H., & Huebner, E. S. (2014). The longitudinal relationships between basic psychological needs satisfaction at school and school-related subjective well-being in adolescents. *Social Indicators Research, 119*(1), 353–372.

Tienken, C. (2008). Rankings of International Achievement Test Performance and Economic Strength:Correlation or Conjecture? *International Journal of Educatiuon Poicy and Leadership, 3*(4). Retrieved April 25, 2008, from *http://www.ijepl.org.*

Titmuss, R. (1971). The gift of blood. *Society, 8*(3), 18–26.

Tolman, E. C. (1959). Principles of purposive behavior. In S. Koch (Ed.), *Psychology: A study of a science* (pp. 92–157). New York: McGraw-Hill.

Tomaka, J., Blascovich, J., Kelsey, R. M., & Leitten, C. L. (1993). Subjective, physiological, and behavioral effects of threat and challenge appraisal. *Journal of Personality and Social Psychology, 65*(2), 248–260.

Tomasello, M. (2009). *Why we cooperate.* Boston: MIT Press.

Toobert, D. J., & Glasgow, R. E. (1994). Assessing diabetes self-management: The summary of diabetes self-care activities questionnaire. In C. Bradley (Ed.), *Handbook of psychology and diabetes* (pp. 351–378). Hove, UK: Psychology Press.

Tooby, J., & Cosmides, L. (1992). The psychological foundations of culture. In J. Barkow, L. Cosmides, & J. Tooby (Eds.), *The adapted mind: Evolutionary psychology and the generation of culture* (pp. 19–136). New York: Oxford University Press.

Treasure, D. C., Lemyre, P., Kuczka, K. K., & Standage, M. (2007). Motivation in elite-level sport: A self-determination theory perspective. In M. S. Hagger & N. L. Chatzisarantis (Eds.), *Intrinsic motivation and self-determination in exercise and sport* (pp. 153–166). Champaign, IL: Human Kinetics.

Treasure, J. L., Katzman, M., Schmidt, U., Troop, N., Todd, G., & De Silva, P. (1999). Engagement and outcome in the treatment of bulimia nervosa: First phase of a sequential design comparing motivation enhancement therapy and cognitive behavioural therapy. *Behaviour Research and Therapy, 37*(5), 405–418.

Treasure, J. L., & Ward, A. (1997). A practical guide to the use of motivational interviewing in anorexia nervosa. *European Eating Disorder Review, 5*(2), 102–114.

Trépanier, S. G., Fernet, C., & Austin, S. (2012). Social and motivational antecedents of perceptions of transformational leadership: A self-

determination theory perspective. *Canadian Journal of Behavioural Science/Revue Canadienne des Sciences du Comportement, 44*(4), 272.

Trépanier, S. G., Fernet, C., & Austin, S. (2013a). Workplace bullying and psychological health at work: The mediating role of satisfaction of needs for autonomy, competence and relatedness. *Work and Stress: An International Journal of Work, Health, and Organizations, 27*(2), 123–140.

Trépanier, S. G., Fernet, C., & Austin, S. (2013b). Workplace psychological harassment among Canadian nurses: A descriptive study. *Journal of Health Psychology, 18,* 383–396.

Triandis, H. C., & Gelfand, M. J. (1998). Converging measurement of horizontal and vertical individualism and collectivism. *Journal of Personality and Social Psychology, 74*(1), 118–128.

Trifan, T. A., Stattin, H., & Tilton-Weaver, L. (2014). Have authoritarian parenting practices and roles changed in the last 50 years? *Journal of Marriage and Family, 76*(4), 744–761.

Trivers, R. L. (1971). The evolution of reciprocal altruism. *Quarterly Review of Biology, 46*(1), 35–57.

Tsai, Y.-M., Kunter, M., Lüdtke, O., Trautwein, U., & Ryan, R. M. (2008). What makes lessons interesting?: The role of situational and individual factors in three school subjects. *Journal of Educational Psychology, 100*(2), 460–472.

Turkle, S. (1995). *Life on the screen: Identity in the age of the Internet.* New York: Simon & Schuster.

Twenge, J. M., Campbell, W. K., & Freeman, E. C. (2012). Generational differences in young adults' life goals, concern for others, and civic orientation, 1966–2009. *Journal of Personality and Social Psychology, 102*(5), 1045–1062.

Tyler, T. R. (1990). *Why people obey the law: Procedural justice, legitimacy, and compliance.* New Haven, CT: Yale University Press.

Tyler, T. R. (2006). Psychological perspectives on legitimacy and legitimation. *Annual Review of Psychology, 57,* 375–400.

Ulstad, S. O., Halvari, H., Sørebø, O., & Deci, E. L. (2016). Motivation, learning strategies, and performance in physical education at secondary school. *Advances in Physical Education, 6*(1), 27–41.

Unanue, W., Dittmar, H., Vignoles, V. L., & Vansteenkiste, M. (2014). Materialism and well-being in the UK and Chile: Basic need satisfaction and basic need frustration as underlying psychological processes. *European Journal of Personality, 28*(6), 569–585.

Unanue, W., Vignoles, V. L., Dittmar, H., & Vansteenkiste, M. (2016). Life goals predict environmental behaviour: Cross-cultural and longitudinal evidence. *Journal of Environmental Psychology, 46,* 10–22.

United Nations Commission on the Status of Women.

(2011). *Ending female genital mutilation: Report of the Secretary-General* (E/CN.6/2012/8). New York: United Nations Economic and Social Council.

U.S. Department of Education. (2006). NAEP data explorer. Retrieved from *http://nces.ed.gov/ nationsreportcard/nde*.

U.S. Department of Labor, Bureau of Labor Statistics. (2016, March). American time use survey. Retrieved from *www.bls.gov/tus*.

U.S. National Commission for the Protection of Human Subjects of Biomedical and Behavioral Research. (1979). *The Belmont report: Ethical guidelines for the protection of human subjects of research*. Washington, DC: U.S. Government Printing Office.

Utman, C. H. (1997). Performance effects of motivational state: A meta-analysis. *Personality and Social Psychology Review, 1*(2), 170–182.

Utvær, B. K. S., Hammervold, R., & Haugan, G. (2014). Aspiration Index in vocational students: Dimensionality, reliability, and construct validity. *Education Inquiry, 5*(3), 359–383.

Uysal, A., Lin, H. L., & Knee, C. R. (2010). The role of need satisfaction in self-concealment and well-being. *Personality and Social Psychology Bulletin, 36*(2), 187–199.

Uysal, A., Lin, H. L., Knee, C. R., & Bush, A. L. (2012). The association between self-concealment from one's partner and relationship well-being. *Personality and Social Psychology Bulletin, 38*(1), 39–51.

Vallerand, R. J. (1997). Toward a hierarchical model of intrinsic and extrinsic motivation. *Advances in Experimental Social Psychology, 29,* 271–360.

Vallerand, R. J. (2010). On passion for life activities: The dualistic model of passion. In M. Zanna (Ed.), *Advances in experimental social psychology* (pp. 97–193). Atlanta, GA: Elsevier.

Vallerand, R. J. (2015). *The psychology of passion: A dualistic model*. Oxford, UK: Oxford University Press.

Vallerand, R. J., & Bissonnette, R. (1992). Intrinsic, extrinsic, and amotivational styles as predictors of behavior: A prospective study. *Journal of Personality, 60*(3), 599–620.

Vallerand, R. J., Blais, M. R., Lacouture, Y., & Deci, E. L. (1987). L'échelle des Orientations Générales á la Causalité: Validation canadienne française du General Causality Orientations scale. *Canadian Journal of Behavioral Science, 19*(1), 1–15.

Vallerand, R. J., Fortier, M. S., & Guay, F. (1997). Self-determination and persistence in a real-life setting: Toward a motivational model of high school dropout. *Journal of Personality and Social Psychology, 72*(5), 1161–1176.

Vallerand, R. J., Gagné, F., Senécal, C., & Pelletier, L. G. (1994). A comparison of the school intrinsic motivation and perceived competence of gifted and regular students. *Gifted Child Quarterly, 38*(4), 172–175.

Vallerand, R. J., & Houlfort, N. (2003). Passion at work: Toward a new conceptualization. In S. W. Gilliland, D. D. Steiner, & D. P. Skarlicki (Eds.), *Emerging perspectives on values in organizations* (pp. 175–204). Greenwich, CT: Information Age.

Vallerand, R. J., & Losier, G. F. (1994). Self-determined motivation and sportsmanship orientations: An assessment of their temporal relationship. *Journal of Sport and Exercise Psychology, 16*(3), 229–245.

Vallerand, R. J., & Losier, G. F. (1999). An integrative analysis of intrinsic and extrinsic motivation in sport. *Journal of Applied Sport Psychology, 11*(1), 142–169.

Vallerand, R. J., & O'Connor, B. P. (1989). Motivation in the elderly: A theoretical framework and some promising findings. *Canadian Psychology/ Psychologie Canadienne, 30*(3), 538–550.

Vallerand, R. J., O'Connor, B. P., & Hamel, M. (1995). Motivation in later life: Theory and assessment. *International Journal of Aging and Human Development, 41*(3), 221–238.

Vallerand, R. J., Pelletier, L. G., Blais, M. R., Briere, N. M., Senécal, C., & Vallieres, E. F. (1993). On the assessment of intrinsic, extrinsic, and amotivation in education: Evidence on the concurrent and construct validity of the Academic Motivation Scale. *Educational and Psychological Measurement, 53*(1), 159–172.

Vallerand, R. J., & Ratelle, C. F. (2002). Intrinsic and extrinsic motivation: A hierarchical model. In E. L. Deci & R. M. Ryan (Eds.), *Handbook of self-determination research* (pp. 37–64). Rochester, NY: University of Rochester Press.

Vallerand, R. J., & Reid, G. (1984). On the causal effects of perceived competence on intrinsic motivation: A test of cognitive evaluation theory. *Journal of Sport Psychology, 6*(1), 94–102.

Vallerand, R. J., Rousseau, F. L., Grouzet, F. M. E., Dumais, A., Grenier, S., & Blanchard, C. M. (2006). Passion in sport: A look at determinants and affective experiences. *Journal of Sport and Exercise Psychology, 28*(4), 454–478.

Van Bergen, D. D., & Saharso, S. (2016). Suicidality of young ethnic minority women with an immigrant background: The role of autonomy. *European Journal of Women's Studies, 23*(3), 297–311.

Vancampfort, D., De Hert, M., Vansteenkiste, M., De Herdt, A., Scheewe, T. W., Soundy, A., et al. (2013). The importance of self-determined motivation towards physical activity in patients with schizophrenia. *Psychiatry Research, 210*(3), 812–818.

Van den Berghe, L., Soenens, B., Vansteenkiste, M., Aelterman, N., Cardon, G., Tallir, I. B., et al. (2013). Observed need-supportive and need-thwarting teaching behavior in physical education: Do teachers' motivational orientations matter? *Psychology of Sport and Exercise, 14*(5), 650–661.

Van den Broeck, A., De Cuyper, N., Baillien, E., Vanbelle, E., Vanhercke, D., & De Witte, H. (2014). Perception of organization's value support and perceived employability: Insights from self-determination theory. *International Journal of Human Resource Management, 25*(13), 1904–1918.

Van den Broeck, A., Van Ruysseveldt, J., Smulders, P., & De Witte, H. (2011). Does an intrinsic work value orientation strengthen the impact of job resources? A perspective from the job demands-resources model. *European Journal of Work and Organizational Psychology, 20*(5), 581–609.

Van den Broeck, A., Vansteenkiste, M., De Witte, H., & Lens, W. (2008). Explaining the relationships between job characteristics, burnout, and engagement: The role of basic psychological need satisfaction. *Work and Stress: An International Journal of Work, Health, and Organizations, 22*(3), 277–294.

Van den Broeck, A., Vansteenkiste, M., De Witte, H., Soenens, B., & Lens, W. (2010). Capturing autonomy, competence, and relatedness at work: Construction and initial validation of the work-related basic need satisfaction scale. *Journal of Occupational and Organizational Psychology, 83*(4), 981–1002.

Van den Broeck, A., Vansteenkiste, M., Lens, W., & De Witte, H. (2010). Unemployed individuals' work values and job flexibility: An explanation from expectancy-value theory and self-determination theory. *Applied Psychology, 59*(2), 296–317.

Van der Giessen, D., Branje, S., & Meeus, W. (2014). Perceived autonomy support from parents and best friends: Longitudinal associations with adolescents' depressive symptoms. *Social Development, 23*(3), 537–555.

van der Hart, O., Nijenhuis, E. R. S., & Steele, K. (2006). *The haunted self: Structural dissociation and the treatment of chronic traumatization.* New York: Norton.

Van Deurzen-Smith, E. (1997). *Everyday mysteries: Existential dimensions of psychotherapy.* London: Sage.

Van Eerde, W., & Thierry, H. (1996). Vroom's expectancy models and work-related criteria: A meta-analysis. *Journal of Applied Psychology, 81*(5), 575–886.

Van Hiel, A., & Vansteenkiste, M. (2009). Ambitions fulfilled?: The effects of intrinsic and extrinsic goal attainment on older adults' ego-integrity and death attitudes. *International Journal of Aging and Human Development, 68*(1), 27–51.

Van Petegem, S., Beyers, W., Vansteenkiste, M., & Soenens, B. (2012). On the association between adolescent autonomy and psychosocial functioning: Examining decisional independence from a self-determination theory perspective. *Developmental Psychology, 48*(1), 76–88.

Van Petegem, S., Soenens, B., Vansteenkiste, M., & Beyers, W. (2015). Rebels with a cause?: Adolescent defiance from the perspective of reactance theory and self-determination theory. *Child Development, 86*(3), 903–918.

Van Petegem, S., Vansteenkiste, M., & Beyers, W. (2013). The jingle-jangle fallacy in adolescent autonomy in the family: In search of an underlying structure. *Journal of Youth and Adolescence, 42*(7), 994–1014.

Van Petegem, S., Vansteenkiste, M., Soenens, B., Beyers, W., & Aelterman, N. (2015). Examining the longitudinal association between oppositional defiance and autonomy in adolescence. *Developmental Psychology, 51*(1), 67–74.

Vansteenkiste, M., & Deci, E. L. (2003). Competitively contingent rewards and intrinsic motivation: Can losers remain motivated? *Motivation and Emotion, 27*(4), 273–299.

Vansteenkiste, M., Duriez, B., Simons, J., & Soenens, B. (2006). Materialistic values and well-being among business students: Further evidence of their detrimental effect. *Journal of Applied Social Psychology, 36*(12), 2892–2908.

Vansteenkiste, M., Lens, W., & Deci, E. L. (2006). Intrinsic versus extrinsic goal contents in self-determination theory: Another look at the quality of academic motivation. *Educational Psychologist, 41*(1), 19–31.

Vansteenkiste, M., Lens, W., De Witte, H., & Feather, N. T. (2005). Understanding unemployed people's job search behaviour, unemployment experience and well-being: A comparison of expectancy-value theory and self-determination theory. *British Journal of Social Psychology, 44*(2), 269–287.

Vansteenkiste, M., Lens, W., Dewitte, S., De Witte, H., & Deci, E. L. (2004). The "why" and "why not" of job search behaviour: Their relation to searching, unemployment experience, and well-being. *European Journal of Social Psychology, 34*(3), 345–363.

Vansteenkiste, M., Lens, W., Elliot, A. J., Soenens, B., & Mouratidis, A. (2014). Moving the achievement goal approach one step forward: Toward a systematic examination of the autonomous and controlled reasons underlying achievement goals. *Educational Psychologist, 49*(3), 153–174.

Vansteenkiste, M., Mouratidis, A., & Lens, W. (2010). Detaching reasons from aims: Fair play and well-being in soccer as a function of pursuing performance-approach goals for autonomous or controlling reasons. *Journal of Sport and Exercise Psychology, 32*(2), 217–242.

Vansteenkiste, M., Neyrinck, B., Niemiec, C. P.,

Soenens, B., De Witte, H., & Van den Broeck, A. (2007). On the relations among work value orientations, psychological need satisfaction and job outcomes: A self-determination theory approach. *Journal of Occupational and Organizational Psychology, 80*(2), 251–277.

Vansteenkiste, M., & Ryan, R. M. (2013). On psychological growth and vulnerability: Basic psychological need satisfaction and need frustration as a unifying principle. *Journal of Psychotherapy Integration, 23*(3), 263–280.

Vansteenkiste, M., Ryan, R. M., & Deci, E. L. (2008). Self-determination theory and the explanatory role of psychological needs in human well-being. In L. Bruni, F. Comim, & M. Pugno (Eds.), *Capabilities and happiness* (pp. 187–223). Oxford, UK: Oxford University Press.

Vansteenkiste, M., Sierens, E., Goossens, L., Soenens, B., Dochy, F., Mouratidis, A., et al. (2012). Identifying configurations of perceived teacher autonomy support and structure: Associations with self-regulated learning, motivation and problem behavior. *Learning and Instruction, 22*(6), 431–439.

Vansteenkiste, M., Sierens, E., Soenens, B., Luyckx, K., & Lens, W. (2009). Motivational profiles from a self-determination perspective: The quality of motivation matters. *Journal of Educational Psychology, 101*(3), 671–688.

Vansteenkiste, M., Simons, J., Lens, W., Sheldon, K. M., & Deci, E. L. (2004). Motivating learning, performance, and persistence: The synergistic effects of intrinsic goal contents and autonomy-supportive contexts. *Journal of Personality and Social Psychology, 87*(2), 246–260.

Vansteenkiste, M., Simons, J., Lens, W., Soenens, B., Matos, L., & Lacante, M. (2004). Less is sometimes more: Goal content matters. *Journal of Educational Psychology, 96*(4), 755–764.

Vansteenkiste, M., Simons, J., Soenens, B., & Lens, W. (2004). How to become a persevering exerciser? Providing a clear, future intrinsic goal in an autonomy-supportive way. *Journal of Sport and Exercise Psychology, 26*(2), 232–249.

Vansteenkiste, M., Smeets, S., Soenens, B., Lens, W., Matos, L., & Deci, E. L. (2010). Autonomous and controlled regulation of performance-approach goals: Their relations to perfectionism and educational outcomes. *Motivation and Emotion, 34*(4), 333–353.

Vansteenkiste, M., Soenens, B., & Vandereycken, W. (2005). Motivation to change in eating disorder patients: A conceptual clarification on the basis of self-determination theory. *International Journal of Eating Disorders, 37*(3), 207–219.

Vansteenkiste, M., Soenens, B., Van Petegem, S., & Duriez, B. (2014). Longitudinal associations between adolescent perceived degree and style of parental prohibition and internalization and defiance. *Developmental Psychology, 50*(1), 229–236.

Varela, F. J., Thompson, E., & Rosch, E. (1991). *The embodied mind: Cognitive science and human experience.* Cambridge, MA: MIT Press.

Vasquez, A. C., Patall, E. A., Fong, C. J., Corrigan, A. S., & Pine, L. (2015). Parent autonomy support, academic achievement, and psychosocial functioning: A meta-analysis of research. *Educational Psychology Review.* Available at *http://link.springer.com/article/10.1007%2Fs10648-015-9329-z#/page-1.*

Vlachopoulos, S. P., Asci, F. H., Cid, L., Ersoz, G., González-Cutre, D., Moreno-Murcia, J. A., et al. (2013). Cross-cultural invariance of the Basic Psychological needs in Exercise Scale and need satisfaction latent mean differences among Greek, Spanish, Portuguese and Turkish samples. *Psychology of Sport and Exercise, 14*(5), 622–631.

Vlachopoulos, S. P., & Karavani, E. (2009). Psychological needs and subjective vitality in exercise: A cross-gender situational test of the needs universality hypothesis. *Hellenic Journal of Psychology, 6,* 207–222.

Vohs, K. D., & Heatherton, T. F. (2000). Self-regulatory failure: A resource-depletion approach. *Psychological Science, 11*(3), 249–254.

Volpp, K. G., John, L. K., Troxel, A. B., Norton, L., Fassbender, J., & Loewenstein, G. (2008). Financial incentive–based approaches for weight loss. *Journal of the American Medical Association, 300*(22), 2631–2637.

Vroom, V. H. (1964). *Work and motivation.* Hoboken, NJ: Wiley.

Vroom, V. H., & Jago, A. G. (1988). *The new leadership: Managing participation in organizations.* Englewood Cliffs, NJ: Prentice Hall.

Walker, A., & Parmar, P. (1993). *Warrior marks: Female genital mutilation and the sexual blinding of women.* New York: Harcourt Brace

Wallace, T. L. B., Sung, H. C., & Williams, J. D. (2014). The defining features of teacher talk within autonomy-supportive classroom management. *Teaching and Teacher Education, 42,* 34–46.

Waller, B. N. (1998). *The natural selection of autonomy.* Albany: State University of New York Press.

Wallis, K. C., & Poulton, J. L. (2001). *Internalization: The origins and construction of internal reality.* Maidenhead, UK: Open University.

Wallston, K. A. (1988). *Manual for administration of Form C of the Multidimensional Health Locus of Control Scales.* Nashville, TN: Vanderbilt University.

Wallston, K. A., Wallston, B. S., & DeVellis, R. (1978). Development of the Multidimensional Health Locus of Control (MHLC) scales. *Health Education Monographs, 6*(2), 160–170.

Wang, C. K. J., Khoo, A., Liu, W. C., & Divaharan,

S. (2008). Passion and intrinsic motivation in digital gaming. *CyberPsychology and Behavior, 11*(1), 39–45.

Wang, C. K. J., Sproule, J., McNeill, M., Martindale, R. J. J., & Lee, K. S. (2011). Impact of the talent development environment on achievement goals and life aspirations in Singapore. *Journal of Applied Sport Psychology, 23*(3), 263–276.

Wang, J. B., Cadmus-Bertram, L. A., Natarajan, L., White, M. M., Madanat, H., Nichols, J. F., et al. (2015). Wearable sensor/device (Fitbit One) and SMS text-messaging prompts to increase physical activity in overweight and obese adults: A randomized controlled trial. *Telemedicine and e-Health, 21*(10), 782–792.

Wang, J. C. K., Morin, A. J. S., Ryan, R. M., & Liu, W. C. (2016). *Students' motivational profiles in the physical education context.* Manuscript submitted for publication.

Wang, Q., Pomerantz, E. M., & Chen, H. (2007). The role of parents' control in early adolescents' psychological functioning: A longitudinal investigation in the United States and China. *Child Development, 78*(5), 1592–1610.

Wang, Y. K. M., Chung, C. C., & Lim, D. S. (2015). The drivers of international corporate entrepreneurship: CEO incentive and CEO monitoring mechanisms. *Journal of World Business, 50*(4), 742–753.

Wankel, L. (1993). The importance of enjoyment to adherence and psychological benefits from physical activity. *International Journal of Sport Psychology, 24*(2), 151–169.

Warneken, F., & Tomasello, M. (2008). Extrinsic rewards undermine altruistic tendencies in 20-month-olds. *Developmental Psychology, 44*(6), 1785–1788.

Warneken, F., & Tomasello, M. (2013). Parental presence and encouragement do not influence helping in young children. *Infancy, 18*(3), 345–368.

Waterman, A. S. (1993). Two conceptions of happiness: Contrasts of personal expressiveness (eudaimonia) and hedonic enjoyment. *Journal of Personality and Social Psychology, 64*(4), 678–691.

Waters, E., Wippman, J., & Sroufe, L. A. (1979). Attachment, positive affect, and competence in the peer group: Two studies in construct validation. *Child Development, 50*(3), 821–829.

Watkins, R., & Kavale, J. (2014). Needs: Defining what you are assessing. In J. W. Altschuld & R. Watkins (Eds.), *Needs Assessment: Trends and a View toward the Future* [Special issue]. *New Directions for Evaluation, 144*, 19–31.

Watson, J. B. (1913). Psychology as the behaviorist views it. *Psychological Review, 20*(2), 158–177.

Watson, J. S. (1966). The development and generalization of "contingency awareness" in early infancy: Some hypotheses. *Merrill–Palmer Quarterly of Behavior and Development, 12*(2), 123–135.

Wegner, D. M. (2002). *The illusion of conscious will.* Cambridge, MA: MIT Press.

Wegner, D. M. (2007). Dangers of brain-o-vision. *Science, 315*, 1078.

Wegner, D. M., & Wheatley, T. (1999). Apparent mental causation: Sources of the experience of will. *American Psychologist, 54*(7) 480–492.

Wehmeyer, M. L. (Ed.). (2011). *Oxford handbook of positive psychology and disability.* New York: Oxford University Press.

Wehmeyer, M. L., & Little, T. D. (2011). Self-determination. In M. L. Wehmeyer (Ed.), *Oxford handbook of positive psychology and disability* (pp. 116–136). New York: Oxford University Press.

Wehmeyer, M. L., Shogren, K. A., Little, T. D., & Lopez, S. J. (Eds.). (2016). *Handbook of the development of self-determination.* New York: Springer.

Wei, M., Shaffer, P. A., Young, S. K., & Zakalik, R. A. (2005). Adult attachment, shame, depression, and loneliness: The mediation role of basic psychological needs satisfaction. *Journal of Counseling Psychology, 52*(4), 591–601.

Weibel, A., Rost, K., & Osterloh, M. (2010). Pay for performance in the public sector—benefits and (hidden) costs. *Journal of Public Administration Research and Theory, 20*(2), 387–412.

Weinberg, R. S., & Jackson, A. (1979). Competition and extrinsic rewards: Effect on intrinsic motivation and attribution. *Research Quarterly: American Alliance for Health, Physical Education, Recreation and Dance, 50*(3), 494–502.

Weinberg, R. S., & Ragan, J. (1979). Effects of competition, success/failure, and sex on intrinsic motivation. *Research Quarterly: American Alliance for Health, Physical Education, Recreation and Dance, 50*(3), 503–510.

Weinstein, N. (2010). *Interest-taking and carry-over effects of incidental rejection emotions.* Unpublished doctoral dissertation, University of Rochester, Rochester, New York.

Weinstein, N., Balmford, A., DeHaan, C. R., Gladwell, V., Bradbury, R. B., & Amano, T. (2015). Seeing community for the trees: The links among contact with natural environments, community cohesion, and crime. *BioScience, 65*(12), 1141–1153.

Weinstein, N., Brown, K. W., & Ryan, R. M. (2009). A multi-method examination of the effects of mindfulness on stress attribution, coping, and emotional well-being. *Journal of Research in Personality, 43*(3), 374–385.

Weinstein, N., Deci, E. L., & Ryan, R. M. (2011). Motivational determinants of integrating positive and negative past identities. *Journal of Personality and Social Psychology, 100*(3), 527–544.

Weinstein, N., DeHaan, C. R., & Ryan, R. M. (2010). Attributing autonomous versus introjected motivation to helpers and the recipient experience: Effects on gratitude, attitudes, and well-being. *Motivation and Emotion, 34*(4), 418–431.

Weinstein, N., & Hodgins, H. S. (2009). The moderating role of autonomy and control on the benefits of written emotion expression. *Personality and Social Psychology Bulletin, 35*(3), 351–364.

Weinstein, N., Hodgins, H. S., & Ryan, R. M. (2010). Autonomy and control in dyads: Effects on interaction quality and joint creative performance. *Personality and Social Psychology Bulletin, 36*(12), 1603–1617.

Weinstein, N., Przybylski, A. K., & Ryan, R. M. (2009). Can nature make us more caring? Effects of immersion in nature on intrinsic aspirations and generosity. *Personality and Social Psychology Bulletin, 35*(10), 1315–1329.

Weinstein, N., & Ryan, R. M. (2010). When helping helps: Autonomous motivation for prosocial behavior and its influence on well-being for the helper and recipient. *Journal of Personality and Social Psychology, 98*(2), 222–244.

Weinstein, N., & Ryan, R. M. (2011). A self-determination theory approach to understanding stress incursion and responses. *Stress and Health, 27*(1), 4–17.

Weinstein, N., Ryan, R. M., & Deci, E. L. (2012). Motivation, meaning and wellness: A self-determination perspective on the creation and internalization of personal meanings and life goals. In P. T. Wang (Ed.), *The human quest for meaning* (pp. 81–106). New York: Routledge.

Weinstein, N., Ryan, W. S., DeHaan, C. R., Przybylski, A. K., Legate, N., & Ryan, R. M. (2012). Parental autonomy support and discrepancies between implicit and explicit sexual identities: Dynamics of self-acceptance and defense. *Journal of Personality and Social Psychology, 102*(4), 815–832.

Weiss, L. A., & Grolnick, W. S. (1991, April). *The roles of parental involvement and support for autonomy in adolescent symptomatology.* Paper presented at the biennial meeting of the Society for Research in Child Development, Seattle, WA.

Weiss, P. A. (1969). Living systems: Determinism stratified. In A. Koestler & J. R. Smythies (Eds.), *Beyond reductionism: New perspectives in the life sciences* (pp. 3–55). London: Hutchinson.

Welzel, C. (2013). *Freedom rising: Human empowerment and the quest for emancipation.* Cambridge, UK: Cambridge University Press.

Wenar, L. (2015). *Blood oil: Tyrants, violence, and the rules that run the world.* New York: Oxford University Press.

Werner, H. (1948). *Comparative psychology of mental development.* Chicago: Follett.

Westen, D. (1991). Cognitive-behavioral interventions in the psychoanalytic psychotherapy of borderline personality disorders. *Clinical Psychology Review, 11*(3), 211–230.

Westen, D., Ludolph, P., Misle, B., Ruffins, S., & Block, J. (1990). Physical and sexual abuse in adolescent girls with borderline personality disorder. *American Journal of Orthopsychiatry, 60*(1), 55–66.

Westen, D., & Morrison, K. (2001). A multidimensional meta-analysis of treatments for depression, panic, and generalized anxiety disorder: An empirical examination of the status of empirically supported therapies. *Journal of Consulting and Clinical Psychology, 69*(6), 875–899.

Westen, D., Novotny, C. M., & Thompson-Brenner, H. (2004). The empirical status of empirically supported psychotherapies: Assumptions, findings, and reporting in controlled clinical trials. *Psychological Bulletin, 130*(4), 631–663.

Whiffen, V. E., & Sasseville, T. M. (1991). Dependency, self-criticism, and recollections of parenting: Sex differences and the role of depressive affect. *Journal of Social and Clinical Psychology, 10*(2), 121–133.

Whitbourne, S. K., Ellenberg, S., & Akimoto, K. (2013). Reasons for playing casual video games and perceived benefits among adults 18–80 years old. *Cyberpsychology, Behavior and Social Networking, 16*(12), 892–897.

White, C. (2015). The impact of motivation on customer satisfaction formation: A self-determination perspective. *European Journal of Marketing, 49*(11/12), 1923–1940.

White, M. H., II, & Sheldon, K. M. (2014). The contract year syndrome in the NBA and MLB: A classic undermining pattern. *Motivation and Emotion, 38*(2), 196–205.

White, R. W. (1959). Motivation reconsidered: The concept of competence. *Psychological Review, 66*(5), 297–333.

White, R. W. (1963). *Ego and reality in psychoanalytic theory: A proposal regarding independent ego energies.* Madison, CT: International Universities Press.

Whiting, J. W. M., & Mowrer, O. H. (1943). Habit progression and regression: A laboratory study of some factors relevant to human socialization. *Journal of Comparative Psychology, 36*(3), 229–253.

Wiersma, U. J. (1992). The effects of extrinsic rewards in intrinsic motivation: A meta-analysis. *Journal of Occupational and Organizational Psychology, 65*(2), 101–114.

Wiggins, D. (2005). An idea we cannot do without: What difference will it make (e.g. to moral, political and environmental philosophy) to recognize and put to use a substantial conception of need? *Royal Institute of Philosophy Supplement, 57,* 25–50.

Wild, J. (1965). Authentic existence: A new approach to "value theory." In J. M. Edie (Ed.), *An invitation to phenomenology: Studies in the philosophy of experience* (pp. 59–78). Chicago: Quadrangle.

Wild, T. C., Cunningham, J. A., & Ryan, R. M. (2006). Social pressure, coercion, and client engagement at treatment entry: A self-determination theory perspective. *Addictive Behaviors, 31,* 1858–1872.

Wild, T. C., Enzle, M. E., & Hawkins, W. L. (1992). Effects of perceived extrinsic versus intrinsic teacher motivation on student reactions to skill acquisition. *Personality and Social Psychology Bulletin, 18*(2), 245–251.

Wild, T. C., Enzle, M. E., Nix, G., & Deci, E. L. (1997). Perceiving others as intrinsically or extrinsically motivated: Effects on expectancy formation and task engagement. *Personality and Social Psychology Bulletin, 23*(8), 837–848.

Wilkinson, R. G., & Pickett, K. E. (2007). The problems of relative deprivation: Why some societies do better than others. *Social Science and Medicine, 65*(9), 1965–1978.

Wilkinson, R. G., & Pickett, K. E. (2010). *The spirit level: Why equality is better for everyone.* London: Penguin.

Williams, A., O'Driscoll, K., & Moore, C. (2014). The influence of empathic concern on prosocial behavior in children. *Frontiers in Psychology, 5,* 425.

Williams, G. C., Cox, E. M., Kouides, R., & Deci, E. L. (1999). Presenting the facts about smoking to adolescents: Effects of an autonomy-supportive style. *Archives of Pediatrics and Adolescent Medicine, 153*(9), 959–964.

Williams, G. C., & Deci, E. L. (1996). Internalization of biopsychosocial values by medical students: A test of self-determination theory. *Journal of Personality and Social Psychology, 70*(4), 767–779.

Williams, G. C., & Deci, E. L. (1998). The importance of supporting autonomy in medical education. *Annals of Internal Medicine, 129*(4), 303–308.

Williams, G. C., & Deci, E. L. (2001). Activating patients for smoking cessation through physician autonomy support. *Medical Care, 39*(8), 813–823.

Williams, G. C., Deci, E. L., & Ryan, R. M. (1998). Building health-care partnerships by supporting autonomy: Promoting maintained behavior change and positive health outcomes. In A. L. Suchman, P. Hinton-Walker, & R. Botelho (Eds.), *Partnerships in healthcare: Transforming relational process* (pp. 67–87). Rochester, NY: University of Rochester Press.

Williams, G. C., Freedman, Z. R., & Deci, E. L. (1998). Supporting autonomy to motivate patients with diabetes for glucose control. *Diabetes Care, 21*(10), 1644–1651.

Williams, G. C., Gagné, M., Mushlin, A. I., & Deci, E. L. (2005). Motivation for behavior change in patients with chest pain. *Health Education, 105*(4), 304–321.

Williams, G. C., Gagné, M., Ryan, R. M., & Deci, E. L. (2002). Facilitating autonomous motivation for smoking cessation. *Health Psychology, 21*(1), 40–50.

Williams, G. C., Grow, V. M., Freedman, Z. R., Ryan, R. M., & Deci, E. L. (1996). Motivational predictors of weight loss and weight-loss maintenance. *Journal of Personality and Social Psychology, 70*(1), 115–126.

Williams, G. C., Hedberg, V. A., Cox, E. M., & Deci, E. L. (2000). Extrinsic life goals and health-risk behaviors in adolescents. *Journal of Applied Social Psychology, 30*(8), 1756–1771.

Williams, G. C., McGregor, H., Sharp, D., Kouides, R. W., Lévesque, C. S., Ryan, R. M., et al. (2006). A self-determination multiple risk intervention trial to improve smokers' health. *Journal of General Internal Medicine, 21*(12), 1288–1294.

Williams, G. C., McGregor, H. A., Sharp, D., Lévesque, C., Kouides, R. W., Ryan, R. M., et al. (2006). Testing a self-determination theory intervention for motivating tobacco cessation: Supporting autonomy and competence in a clinical trial. *Health Psychology, 25*(1), 91–101.

Williams, G. C., McGregor, H. A., Zeldman, A., Freedman, Z. R., & Deci, E. L. (2004). Testing a self-determination theory process model for promoting glycemic control through diabetes self-management. *Health Psychology, 23*(1), 58–66.

Williams, G. C., McGregor, H. A., Zeldman, A., Freedman, Z. R., Deci, E. L., & Elder, D. (2005). Promoting glycemic control through diabetes self-management: Evaluating a patient activation intervention. *Patient Education and Counseling, 56*(1), 28–34.

Williams, G. C., Minicucci, D. S., Kouides, R. W., Levesque, C. S., Chirkov, V. I., Ryan, R. M., et al. (2002). Self-determination, smoking, diet and health. *Health Education Research, 17*(5), 512–521.

Williams, G. C., Niemiec, C. P., Patrick, H., Ryan, R. M, & Deci, E. L. (2009). The importance of supporting autonomy and perceived competence in facilitating long-term tobacco abstinence. *Annals of Behavioral Medicine, 37*(3), 315–324.

Williams, G. C., Patrick, H., Niemiec, C. P., Williams, L. K., Divine, G., Lafata, J. E., et al. (2009). Reducing the health risks of diabetes: How self-determination theory may help improve medication adherence and quality of life. *Diabetes Educator, 35*(3), 484–492.

Williams, G. C., Rodin, G. C., Ryan, R. M., Grolnick, W. S., & Deci, E. L. (1998). Autonomous regulation and long-term medication adherence in adult outpatients. *Health Psychology, 17*(3), 269–276.

Williams, G. C., Saizow, R., Ross, L., & Deci, E. L. (1997). Motivation underlying career choice for internal medicine and surgery. *Social Science and Medicine, 45*(11), 1705–1713.

Williams, G. C., Wiener, M. W., Markakis, K. M., Reeve, J., & Deci, E. L. (1994). Medical students' motivation for internal medicine. *Journal of General Internal Medicine, 9*(6), 327–333.

Williams, K. D. (2001). *Ostracism: The power of silence.* New York: Guilford Press.

Williams, K. D. (2009). Ostracism: Effects of being excluded and ignored. In M. P. Zanna (Ed.), *Advances in experimental social psychology* (pp. 275–314). New York: Academic Press.

Williams, K. D., Yeager, D. S., Cheung, C. K. T., & Choi, W. (2012). *User manual for Cyberball 4.0.* West Lafayette, IN: Purdue University, Department of Psychological Sciences.

Willoughby, T., Adachi, P. J. C., & Good, M. (2012). A longitudinal study of the association between violent video game play and aggression among adolescents. *Developmental Psychology, 48*(4), 1044–1057.

Wilson, D. S. (2003). Evolution, morality and human potential. In S. J. Scher & F. Rauscher (Eds.), *Evolutionary psychology: Alternative approaches* (pp. 55–70). New York: Springer.

Wilson, D. S. (2015). *Does altruism exist?: Culture genes and the welfare of others.* New Haven, CT: Yale University Press.

Wilson, E. O. (1982). *Sociobiology: The new synthesis.* Cambridge, MA: Harvard University Press.

Wilson, E. O. (2012). *The social conquest of earth.* New York: Norton.

Wilson, P. M., Rodgers, W. M., Blanchard, C. M., & Gessell, J. (2003). The relationship between psychological needs, self-determined motivation, exercise attitudes, and physical fitness. *Journal of Applied Social Psychology, 33*(11), 2373–2392.

Wilson, P. M., Rodgers, W. M., & Fraser, S. N. (2002). Cross-validation of the Revised Motivation for Physical Activity measure in active women. *Research Quarterly for Exercise and Sport, 73*(4), 471–477.

Wilson, P. M., Rodgers, W. M., Fraser, S. N., & Murray, T. C. (2004). Relationships between exercise regulations and motivational consequences in university students. *Research Quarterly for Exercise and Sport, 75*(1), 81–91.

Wilson, R. W. (1992). *Compliance ideologies: Rethinking political culture.* Cambridge, UK: Cambridge University Press.

Winnicott, D. W. (1965). *The maturational processes and the facilitating environment: Studies in the theory of emotional development.* Madison, CT: International Universities Press.

Winnicott, D. W. (1971). *Playing and reality.* New York: Basic Books.

Witherington, D. C. (2014). Self-organization and explanatory pluralism: Avoiding the snares of reductionism in developmental science. *Research in Human Development, 11*(1), 22–36.

Wlodkowski, R. J., & Ginsberg, M. B. (1995). *Diversity and motivation: Culturally responsive teaching.* San Francisco: Jossey-Bass.

Wolf, S. (1990). *Freedom within reason.* New York: Oxford University Press.

Wolfe, G. R., Stewart, J. E., Maeder, L. A., & Hartz, G. W. (1996). Use of Dental Coping Beliefs Scale to measure cognitive changes following oral hygiene interventions. *Community Dentistry and Oral Epidemiology, 24*(1), 37–41.

Wolff, P. H. (1960). *The developmental psychologies of Jean Piaget and psychoanalysis.* New York: International Universities Press.

Wolpe, J. (1982). *The practice of behavior therapy.* Oxford, UK: Pergamon Press.

Wong, P. T. (2012). Toward a dual-systems model of what makes life worth living. In P. T. Wong (Ed.), *The human quest for meaning: Theories, research, and applications* (pp. 3–22). New York: Routledge.

Woo, H. K. H. (1984). *Unseen dimensions of wealth: Towards a generalized economic theory.* London: Victoria Press.

Woodworth, R. S. (1918). *Dynamic psychology.* New York: Columbia University Press.

Woodworth, R. S. (1958). *Dynamics of behavior.* New York: Holt.

World Health Organization. (2008). *Eliminating female genital mutilation: An interagency statement.* Geneva: Author. Retrieved from *http://whqlibdoc.who.int/publications/2008/9789241596442_eng.pdf.*

Wouters, S., Duriez, B., Luyckx, K., Colpin, H., Bijttebier, P., & Verschueren, K. (2014). *Parental goal promotion and late adolescents' self-esteem level and fragility: The mediating role of parental psychological control.* Paper presented at the Joint SELF Biennial International Conference and Educational Research Association of Singapore (ERAS) Conference, Singapore.

Wray-Lake, L., DeHaan, C. R., Shubert, J., Ryan, R. M., & Curren, R. (2015, May). *Does civic engagement enhance well-being?: A daily diary study with college students.* Poster presented at the annual meeting of the Association for Psychological Science, New York.

Wulf, G., Chiviacowsky, S., & Drews, R. (2015). External focus and autonomy support: Two important factors in motor learning have additive benefits. *Human Movement Science, 40,* 176–184.

Wuyts, D., Chen, B., Vansteenkiste, M., & Soenens, B. (2015). Social pressure and unfulfilled dreams among Chinese and Belgian parents. *Journal of Cross-Cultural Psychology, 46*(9), 1150–1168.

Wuyts, D., Vansteenkiste, M., Soenens, B., & Assor, A. (2015). An examination of the dynamics involved in parental child-invested contingent self-esteem. *Parenting, 15*(2), 55–74.

Yalom, I. D. (1980). *Existential psychotherapy*. New York: Basic Books.

Yalom, I. D. (2002). *The gift of therapy*. New York: Harper Collins.

Yamauchi, H., & Tanaka, K. (1998). Relations of autonomy, self-referenced beliefs, and self-regulated learning among Japanese children. *Psychological Reports, 82*(3), 803–816.

Yu, S., Assor, A., & Liu, X. (2015). Perception of parents as demonstrating the inherent merit of their values: Relations with self-congruence and subjective well-being. *International Journal of Psychology, 50*(1), 70–74.

Zajonc, R. B. (1965). Social facilitation. *Science, 149*(3681), 269–274.

Zanarini, M. C. (1997). *Role of sexual abuse in the etiology of borderline personality disorder*. Washington, DC: American Psychiatric Press.

Zeigarnik, B. (1927). Das behalten erledigter und unerledigter handlungen [The rentention of completed and uncompleted activities]. *Psychologische Forschung, 9,* 1–85.

Zeldman, A., Ryan, R. M., & Fiscella, K. (2004). Motivation, autonomy support, and entity beliefs: Their role in methadone maintenance treatment. *Journal of Social and Clinical Psychology, 23*(5), 675–696.

Zhou, M., Ma, W. J., & Deci, E. L. (2009). The importance of autonomy for rural Chinese children's motivation for learning. *Learning and Individual Differences, 19*(4), 492–498.

Zillmer, E. A., Harrower, M., Ritzler, B. A., & Archer, R. P. (2013). *The quest for the Nazi personality: A psychological investigation of Nazi war criminals*. London: Routledge.

Ziviani, J., & Poulsen, A. A. (2015). Autonomy in the process of goal setting. In A. A. Poulsen, J. Ziviani, & M. Cuskelly (Eds.), *Goal setting and motivation in therapy: Engaging children and parents* (pp. 40–50). London: Jessica Kingsley.

Ziviani, J., Poulsen, A. A., & Cuskelly, M. (2013). *The art and science of motivation: A therapist's guide to working with children*. London: Jessica Kingsley.

Zuckerman, M., Gioioso, C., & Tellini, S. (1988). Control orientation, self-monitoring, and preference for image versus quality approach to advertising. *Journal of Research in Personality, 22*(1), 89–100.

Zuckerman, M., Porac, J., Lathin, D., Smith, R., & Deci, E. L. (1978). On the importance of self-determination for intrinsically motivated behavior. *Personality and Social Psychology Bulletin, 4*(3), 443–446.

Zuroff, D. C., Koestner, R., Moskowitz, D. S., McBride, C., & Bagby, R. M. (2012). Therapist's autonomy support and patient's self-criticism predict motivation during brief treatments for depression. *Journal of Social and Clinical Psychology, 31*(9), 903–932.

Zuroff, D. C., Koestner, R., Moskowitz, D. S., McBride, C., Marshall, M., & Bagby, M. R. (2007). Autonomous motivation for therapy: A new common factor in brief treatments for depression. *Psychotherapy Research, 17*(2), 137–147.

Zuroff, D. C., Mongrain, M., & Santor, D. A. (2004). Conceptualizing and measuring personality vulnerability to depression: Comment on Coyne and Whiffen (1995). *Psychological Bulletin, 130*(3), 489–511.

Zussman, J. U. (1980). Situational determinants of parental behavior: Effects of competing cognitive activity. *Child Development, 51*(3), 792–800.

Author Index

Subject Index

Note. f or t following a page number indicates a figure or a table.